NPV	Net present value
P	(1) Price of a share of stock in Period t; P_0 = price of the stock today
	(2) Sales price per unit of product sold
P_c	Conversion price
P_f	Price of good in foreign country
P_h	Price of good in home country
P_N	A stock's horizon, or terminal, value
P/E	Price/earnings ratio
PMT	Payment of an annuity
PPP	Purchasing power parity
PV	Present value
PVA_N	Present value of an annuity for N years
Q	Quantity produced or sold
Q_{BE}	Break-even quantity
r	(1) A percentage discount rate, or cost of capital; also referred to as I
	(2) Nominal risk-adjusted required rate of return
$\bar{r}$	"r bar," historic, or realized, rate of return
$\hat{r}$	"r hat," an expected rate of return
r^*	Real risk-free rate of return
r_d	Before-tax cost of debt
r_e	Cost of new common stock (outside equity)
r_f	Interest rate in foreign country
r_h	Interest rate in home country
r_i	Required return for an individual firm or security
r_M	Return for "the market," or an "average" stock
r_{NOM}	Nominal rate of interest; also referred to as I_{NOM}
r_p	Portfolio's return
r_{ps}	Cost of preferred stock
r_{PER}	Periodic rate of return
r_{RF}	Rate of return on a risk-free security
r_s	(1) Required return on common stock
	(2) Cost of old common stock (inside equity)
ρ	Correlation coefficient; also denoted as R when using historical data
ROA	Return on assets
ROE	Return on equity
RP	Risk premium
RP_M	Market risk premium
RR	Retention rate
S	(1) Sales
	(2) Estimated standard deviation for sample data
SML	Security Market Line
Σ	Summation sign (capital sigma)
σ	Standard deviation (lowercase sigma)
σ^2	Variance
t	Time period
T	Marginal income tax rate
TV_N	A stock's horizon, or terminal, value
TIE	Times-interest-earned
V	Variable cost per unit
V_B	Bond value
V_L	Total market value of a levered firm
V_{ps}	Value of preferred stock
V_U	Total market value of an unlevered firm
VC	Total variable costs
w	Proportion or weight
w_d	Weight of debt
w_{ps}	Weight of preferred stock
w_{ce}	Weight of common equity
WACC	Weighted averaged cost of capital
X	Strike (or exercise) price of option
YTC	Yield to call
YTM	Yield to maturity

DON'T THROW THIS CARD AWAY!
THIS MAY BE REQUIRED FOR YOUR COURSE!

1 YEAR ACCESS FREE WITH THIS TEXT!

THOMSON ONE | Business School Edition

Congratulations!

Your purchase of this NEW textbook includes complimentary access to Thomson ONE – Business School Edition for Finance. Thomson ONE – Business School Edition is a Web-based portal product that provides integrated access to Thomson Financial content for the purpose of financial analysis. This is an educational version of the same financial resources used by Wall Street analysts on a daily basis!

For hundreds of companies, this online resource provides seamless access to:

- **Current and Past Company Data:** Worldscope which includes company profiles, financials and accounting results, market per-share data, annual information, and monthly prices going back to 1980.

- **Financial Analyst Data and Forecasts:** I/B/E/S Consensus Estimates which provides consensus estimates, analyst-by-analyst earnings coverage, and analysts' forecasts.

- **SEC Disclosure Statements:** Disclosure SEC Database which includes company profiles, annual and quarterly company financials, pricing information, and earnings.

- **And More!**

Copyright ©2005 South-Western, a part of Cengage Learning.
ISBN-13: 978-0-324-23597-5
ISBN-10: 0-324-23597-6

SOUTH-WESTERN
CENGAGE Learning

THOMSON ONE | Business School Edition

SERIAL NUMBER

PGBGMRMPP4Q417

HOW TO REGISTER YOUR SERIAL NUMBER

1. Launch a web browser and go to **http://tobsefin1.swlearning.com**

2. Click the "Register" button to enter your serial number.

3. Enter your serial number **exactly** as it appears here and create a unique User ID, or enter an existing User ID if you have previously registered for a different South-Western product via a serial number.

4. When prompted, create a password (or enter an existing password, if you have previously registered for a different product via a serial number). Submit the necessary information when prompted. **Record your User ID and password in a secure location.**

5. Once registered, return to the URL above and select the "Enter" button; have your User ID and password handy.

Note: The duration of your access to the product begins when registration is complete.

For technical support, contact 1-800-423-0563 or email **support@cengage.com**

Financial Management

12e

Financial Management

Theory and Practice

Eugene F. Brigham
University of Florida

Michael C. Ehrhardt
University of Tennessee

SOUTH-WESTERN
CENGAGE Learning™

Australia • Brazil • Japan • Korea • Mexico • Singapore • Spain • United Kingdom • United States

SOUTH-WESTERN
CENGAGE Learning

Financial Management: Theory and Practice
Twelfth Edition
Eugene F. Brigham and Michael C. Ehrhardt

VP/Editorial Director:
Jack W. Calhoun

Editor-in-Chief:
Alex von Rosenberg

Executive Editor:
Mike Reynolds

Sr. Developmental Editor:
Elizabeth Thomson

Editorial Assistant:
Adele Scholtz

Sr. Content Project Manager:
Cliff Kallemeyn

Marketing Manager:
Jason Krall

**Sr. Marketing
Communications Manager:**
Jim Overly

Technology Project Manager:
Matt McKinney

Art Director:
Bethany Casey

Sr. First Print Buyer:
Sandee Milewski

Printer:
RR Donnelley & Sons,
Willard OH

Library of Congress Control
Number: 2007921348

For more information about
our products, contact us at:

Cengage Learning
Customer & Sales Support
1-800-354-9706

**South-Western Cengage
Learning**
5191 Natorp Boulevard
Mason, OH 45040
USA

preface

When we wrote the first edition of *Financial Management: Theory and Practice*, we had four goals: (1) to create a text that would help students make better financial decisions; (2) to provide a book that could be used in the introductory MBA course, but one that was complete enough for use as a reference text in follow-on case courses and after graduation; (3) to motivate students by demonstrating that finance is both interesting and relevant; and (4) to make the book clear enough so that students could go through the material without wasting either their time or their professor's time trying to figure out what we were saying.

FM
e-resource

Be sure to visit the *Financial Management: Theory and Practice* (12th Edition) Web site at **academic.cengage.com/ finance/brigham.** This site provides access for instructors and students.

Valuation as a Unifying Theme

Our emphasis throughout the book is on the actions that a manager can and should take to increase the value of the firm. Structuring the book around valuation enhances continuity and helps students see how various topics are related to one another.

As its title indicates, this book combines theory and practical applications. An understanding of finance theory is absolutely essential for anyone developing and/or implementing effective financial strategies. But theory alone isn't sufficient, so we provide numerous examples in the book and the accompanying *Excel* spreadsheets to illustrate how theory is applied in practice. Indeed, we believe that the ability to analyze financial problems using *Excel* is absolutely essential for a student's successful job search and subsequent career. Therefore, many exhibits in the book come directly from the accompanying *Excel* spreadsheets. Many of the spreadsheets also provide brief "tutorials" by way of detailed comments on *Excel* features that we have found to be especially useful, such as Goal Seek, Tables, and many financial functions.

The book begins with fundamental concepts, including background on the economic and financial environment, the time value of money, financial statements (with an emphasis on cash flows), bond valuation, risk analysis, and stock valuation. With this background, we go on to discuss how specific techniques and decision rules can be used to help maximize the value of the firm. This organization provides four important advantages:

1. Covering time value of money early helps students see how and why expected future cash flows determine the value of the firm. Also, it takes time for students to digest TVM concepts and to learn how to do the required calculations, so it is good to cover TVM concepts early and often.
2. Managers should try to maximize the fundamental value of a firm, which is determined by cash flows as revealed in financial statements. Our early coverage of financial statements thus helps students see how particular financial decisions affect the various parts of the firm and the resulting cash flow. Also, financial statement analysis provides an excellent vehicle for illustrating the usefulness of spreadsheets.

3. Most students—even those who do not plan to major in finance—are interested in stock and bond values, rates of return on investments, and the like. The ability to learn is a function of individual interest and motivation, so *Financial Management's* early coverage of securities and security markets is pedagogically sound.

4. Once basic concepts have been established, it is easier for students to understand both how and why corporations make specific decisions in the areas of capital budgeting, raising capital, working capital management, mergers, and the like.

Intended Market and Use

Financial Management is designed primarily for use in the introductory MBA finance course and as a reference text in follow-on case courses and after graduation. There is enough material for two terms, especially if the book is supplemented with cases and/or selected readings. The book can also be used as an undergraduate introductory text with exceptionally good students, or where the introductory course is taught over two terms.

Improvements in the 12th Edition

As in every revision, we updated and clarified materials throughout the text, reviewing the entire book for completeness, ease of exposition, and currency. We made hundreds of small changes to keep the text up-to-date, with particular emphasis on updating the real world examples and including the latest changes in the financial environment and financial theory. In addition, we made a number of larger changes. Some affect all chapters, some involve reorganizing sections among chapters, and some modify material covered within specific chapters.

Changes That Affect All Chapters

Better integration of the textbook and the accompanying *Excel Tool Kit* spreadsheet models for each chapter.
We assigned a section number to each major section in each chapter and used the section numbers to identify the corresponding material in the *Excel* spreadsheets that accompany the chapters. In addition, many tables within the text involve examples of financial analysis that were worked out in the accompanying spreadsheets. For many such Tables, we now show the *Excel* row and column headings so that students can easily understand the spreadsheet analysis that underlies the Table.

End-of-section Self-Test problems.
Students learn specific concepts and understand particular numerical examples best if they work with illustrative problems immediately after they read the section that explains that particular material. Therefore, we now provide an opportunity for immediate reinforcement by having numerical problems at the end of each major section. The answers to the problems are shown in the text, and the worked out solutions are provided in the *Excel Tool Kit* spreadsheet model for the chapter.

End-of-chapter problems ranked by difficulty.
In past editions we arranged the end-of-chapter problems by topic, not by difficulty level. Students would often start working the problems, hit a difficult one relatively quickly, become frustrated, and give up. In this edition we arranged the problems by difficulty. The first set of problems is designated "Easy," and most

students should be able to work them without much trouble. Then come "Intermediate" problems, which are a bit harder, and then "Challenging," which are still longer and more complex. This ranking procedure reduces students' stress and frustration because they can clearly identify the problems that are going to require more effort.

Improved *Test Bank*.
We made substantial improvements to the *Test Bank*, including the addition of numerous problems that are similar to the "Easy," "Intermediate," and "Challenging" problems at the end of each chapter. Different instructors have different views on how students should be tested, but the new *Test Bank* can be used to provide a set of relatively straightforward problems ("Easy" and "Intermediate") that deal with all aspects of financial management. Most instructors also use a few "Challenging" exam problems, where students must figure out how to apply finance concepts to deal with new and different situations they haven't seen before. The problems can also be changed algorithmically, as discussed below.

The CengageNOW Web-based course platform.
We discuss the new CengageNOW Web-based course delivery system in more detail later in the preface, but one very important feature of CengageNOW is the availability of algorithmic versions of the end-of-chapter problems and the *Test Bank* problems. This allows an instructor to easily create Web-based homework assignments with problem inputs and answers that are unique to each student. The assignments are automatically graded, and the scores are posted to a gradesheet that can be exported into *Excel*. Because the assignments are unique to each student and are automatically graded, it is feasible for a busy instructor (Is there any other kind?!) to assign homework frequently. In our own classes, we typically assign a short Web-based homework "quiz" for every 1-2 class sessions. Our students have told us that they appreciate having such frequent assignments because it helps them keep up in the course. Moreover, we have noticed an improvement in our students' ability to work problems in subsequent in-class tests and exams.

More focused Web Extensions in the e-Library.
New material must be added with each edition to keep students on the cutting edge. To make room for the new material, we identified specialized topics that are important but not essential in every introductory finance course. We then made this material accessible as a chapter Web Extension, provided as an Adobe PDF file on the textbook's Web site. In the previous edition, there was only one Web Extension for a chapter, with some chapters' Web Extensions covering multiple topics. We now have multiple Web Extensions for those chapters, with each Extension focused on a particular topic. This makes it easier for an instructor to "pick and choose" any additional individual topics he or she wishes to cover.

Improved *PowerPoint* Shows.
We carefully reviewed and revised each *PowerPoint* show for clarity and effectiveness. In addition, the shows are now in a standard Microsoft template and thus can be easily customized by instructors.

Significant Reorganization of Some Chapters

Reorganized the discussion of financial markets.
In the previous edition, the coverage of financial markets was somewhat fragmented, with related topics being covered in the introductory chapter, the bond valuation chapter, and the stock valuation chapter. We have now consolidated this material, discussing financial securities, institutions, and markets in Chapter 1.

This consolidation allowed us to eliminate some redundancies and provide a more integrated discussion of the material. As it now stands, Chapter 1 includes a detailed discussion of financial securities, hedge funds, global stock markets, and IPOs. This new structure provides two important advantages. First, an instructor can hit the ground running and cover financial markets during the first class. Because this material is descriptive rather than problem-oriented, it is not absolutely critical for students to have read the material before the first class; instead, they can go back and read it after the first class. Second, students are typically interested in financial markets, and comprehensive coverage in the first class stimulates student interest and enthusiasm.

Financial statement analysis moved up to immediately follow financial statements and cash flows.
Chapter 4, Analysis of Financial Statements, now immediately follows financial statements and cash flows. This early coverage of financial statement analysis helps provide vocabulary and concepts that are important for the remainder of the book.

Reorganized the discussion of the determinants of interest rates.
In the previous edition, our discussion of the determinants and implications of interest rates was fragmented, with coverage in both the introductory and the bond valuation chapters. We have now consolidated this material in Chapter 5 (Bonds, Bond Valuation, and Interest Rates) in a section that immediately follows our discussion of bond pricing. This new structure is pedagogically better because students who understand the basics of bond pricing are in a better position to benefit from a discussion of why different fixed-income securities have different yields.

Better link between risk, return, and stock pricing.
We now cover the chapters on risk and return (Chapters 6 and 7) immediately before the chapter on stock pricing (Chapter 8). This permits students to apply the concepts they learned about the risk/return tradeoff to stock pricing.

Notable Changes within Selected Chapters

We made too many small improvements within each chapter to mention them all, but some of the more notable ones are discussed below.

Chapter 1: An Overview of Financial Management and the Financial Environment.
The opening vignette now has a global scope, and there is a new box on ethics, "Ethics for Individuals and Businesses." As noted earlier, we consolidated and improved our discussion of securities, institutions, and markets. Because many MBA students will not take a separate Investments course, many instructors like to cover or at least recommend additional material on securities and financial markets. With that in mind, we added three new Web Extensions that (1) describe securitization, (2) provide an overview of derivatives, and (3) cover stock markets in more detail, including discussions of market indexes and the costs of trading. Each of these new Web Extensions now has its own separate *PowerPoint* show.

Chapter 2: Time Value of Money.
We added a new opening vignette on the role played by TVM concepts in the current pension fund crisis. We also improved the coverage of annuities, with the annuity formula now based on the differences between time lines of different perpetuities, which makes the formula a bit more intuitive. We added three new Web Extensions, one on the derivation of annuity formulas, another on continuous compounding, and a third on the tabular approach.

We also improved our calculator tutorials for the most popular TI and HP calculators, using illustrations that are identical to the text examples. Therefore, when a student reads about, say, the future values in the text, he or she can simultaneously learn from the tutorial how to find the specific FV with a calculator. Students tell us that learning how to use their calculators as they learn TVM concepts is much more efficient than studying the two separately.

Chapter 3: Financial Statements, Cash Flow, and Taxes.
We added a new box on Sarbanes-Oxley and financial fraud.

Chapter 4: Analysis of Financial Statements.
We added a new opening vignette on how firms guide analysts' earnings estimates. The analyses of common sized and percent change statements are now better integrated with the *Excel Tool Kit*, which shows students how easy it is to do all the calculations involved in financial analysis using a spreadsheet.

Chapter 5: Bonds, Bond Valuation, and Interest Rates.
The chapter on bond pricing now comes earlier in the book, closer to the chapter on time value of money. This permits students to apply their financial calculator and *Excel* skills to bond analysis while time value of money concepts are still fresh in their minds. Also, the section on calculating bond yields now follows immediately the section on calculating bond prices, since these topics are so closely related. We also improved our coverage of *Excel's* PRICE and YIELD functions, providing detailed examples in the *Tool Kit*. We consolidate and better integrated coverage of interest rate determinants with our discussion of default and interest rate price risk. We improved the discussion of TIPS, and we show how to use them in estimating the real risk-free rate and the inflation premium. Finally, we now have separate Web Extensions for (1) zero coupon bonds and their taxation, (2) a more detailed explanation of TIPS, (3) duration analysis, and (4) the pure expectations theory of the term structure (using geometric averages).

Chapter 6: Risk, Return, and the Capital Asset Pricing Model.
We improved the explanation of correlation and covariance, including a better explanation for how *Excel* can be used in estimating correlation and covariance from historic data. We also improved the discussion of beta and how to estimate beta.

Chapter 7: Portfolio Theory and Other Asset Pricing Models.
We eliminated the opening section on measuring portfolio risk (because this is now covered in Chapter 6), so the chapter begins with a discussion of efficient portfolios. We added a new section on the standard deviation of an N-asset portfolio, including an easy approach for calculating the portfolio standard deviation. In the section on the Fama-French model we now provide the URL for Kenneth French's Web site, which has data for use in estimating parameters of the Fama-French model. We also beefed up our discussion of behavioral finance.

Chapter 8: Stocks, Stock Valuation, and Stock Market Equilibrium.
We now discuss stock market data as reported in *The Wall Street Journal* and other sources early in the chapter so students will be familiar with stock quotations and price ranges before we cover stock valuation. We also added a brief discussion of the FCF model for stock valuation (which is covered in more detail in Chapter 15). The section on preferred stock pricing now immediately follows common stock valuation, and the chapter ends with an improved discussion of efficient markets.

Chapter 9: Financial Options and Applications in Corporate Finance.
To be consistent with the nomenclature used by options traders, we changed some of the chapter's terms. We also improved the explanation of the binomial model,

including the formula for the number of shares in the hedge portfolio. Moreover, we added new boxes on "Financial Reporting and Employee Stock Options" and "Taxes and Stock Options," and we added a new section entitled "Applications of Option Pricing in Corporate Finance."

Chapter 10: The Cost of Capital.

Flotation costs are no longer in a separate section but are covered with each component cost of capital, e.g., flotation costs of debt are covered with the cost of debt. We improved and streamlined the discussion of the divisional cost of capital and the project cost of capital, and we added a new section on the cost of capital for privately held or small firms.

Chapter 11: The Basics of Capital Budgeting: Evaluating Cash Flows.

Because many students have trouble understanding the relative merits of different ranking criteria, we now cover NPV first, and we present it as the primary criterion because it is directly related to the maximization of shareholder wealth. We then cover the IRR and other methods and present them as supplements to NPV. In addition, we moved the equivalent annual annuity (EAA) approach out of the last edition's Web Extension and into this edition's textbook section that covers replacement chains.

Chapter 12: Cash Flow Estimation and Risk Analysis.

We more clearly show the link between FCF as applied to financial statements and FCF as applied to a project. We moved the numerical example to the beginning of the chapter so that students can see a concrete application before we discuss such concepts as sunk costs, opportunity costs, etc. We also added an explanation of NPV breakeven analysis.

Chapter 13: Real Options.

We added discussion and a numerical example for the valuation of a growth option.

Chapter 14: Financial Planning and Forecasting Financial Statements.

We added a new opening vignette on how companies do financial planning based on a recent survey of corporate executives. We also moved the section on AFN so that it now precedes the projected financial statement approach. With this arrangement, students can get an understanding of the basic logic of financial forecasting from the simple AFN approach, and this helps follow the logic of the more complex projected financial statement approach.

Chapter 15: Corporate Valuation, Value-Based Management, and Corporate Governance.

We rewrote and expanded our coverage of corporate governance. In addition, we added a new box on "The Sarbanes-Oxley Act of 2002 and Corporate Governance."

Chapter 16: Capital Structure Decisions: The Basics.

We use the corporate valuation model to develop a new explanation of recapitalization that gives students a better understanding of stock repurchases and other capital structure changes. We also added a discussion of the "windows of opportunity" theory, and we added a section that discusses and synthesizes the results of recent empirical studies on capital structure.

Chapter 18: Distributions to Shareholders: Dividends and Repurchases.

We added a new opening vignette discussing Microsoft's recent cash distributions. We also added a discussion of the "life-cycle" hypothesis.

Chapter 20: Lease Financing.

We added a new box on hidden dangers in leasing, "What You Don't Know *Can* Hurt You!"

Chapter 22: Working Capital Management.
We added a new opening vignette based upon *CFO* magazine's annual survey on working capital management. We added a new box based on the annual *CFO* cash management scorecard and we discuss the provisions and implications of "Check 21."

Chapter 25: Mergers, LBOs, Divestitures, and Holding Companies.
We added a new opening vignette on the P&G/Gillette merger, we improved the discussion of the adjusted present value approach, and we added a section covering the free-cash-flow-to-equity approach.

Chapter 26: Multinational Financial Management.
We completely re-wrote the discussion of international monetary systems and the links between exchange rate regimes, international trade, and inflation. We also added a new section that provides a detailed discussion and illustration of capital budgeting for international projects.

CengageNOW: A New Web-Based Course Management Platform

CengageNOW is Cengage Learning's new Web-based course management system, and it can be seamlessly integrated into Blackboard and WebCT for those instructors already using those Web-based course management systems. CengageNOW includes the following features, with more to be added over time.

The Courseware Individualized Learning Plan

For each chapter, a student can take a "pre-test" in the Courseware section of CengageNOW. This pre-test is automatically scored, and the student is given a learning plan that identifies the chapter's sections on which the student needs to improve. This learning plan has links to an e-book for each chapter, so a student can also read and study the material without leaving the computer. In addition, a "post-test" helps the student determine if he or she has mastered the material.

Algorithmic Homework Assignments with Automatic Grading

As previously noted, CengageNOW can create algorithmic versions of select end-of-chapter and *Test Bank* problems. With just a few clicks, an instructor can create a Web-based homework assignment that contains unique problems and answers for each student. The assignment is automatically graded, and the scores are posted to a gradesheet that can be exported into *Excel* or into the gradesheets of Blackboard and WebCT. Similarly, an instructor can create sets of practice problems (based on algorithmic versions of the end-of-chapter problems and *Test Bank* problems). In Finance, practice makes perfect, so CengageNOW's ability to quickly and easily create practice problems and grade homework assignments can have a dramatic impact on a student's progress and knowledge.

e-book

CengageNOW also contains an e-book, which is very helpful to students who use the Individualized Learning Plan in CengageNOW's Courseware—they can read the e-book and work practice problems without ever leaving the computer.

FM
e-resource

To enter the CengageNOW Web site, go to **academic. cengage.com/cengagenow.** For new users, select "Create an Account" and follow the directions for either an instructor or a student.

Thomson One—Business School Edition

Thomson ONE—Business School Edition is an online database that draws from the world acclaimed Thomson Financial data sources, including the SEC Disclosure, Datastream, First Call, and Worldscope databases. Now you can give your students the opportunity to practice with a business school version of the same Internet-based database that brokers and analysts around the world use every day. Thomson ONE—BSE provides (1) one-click download of financial statements to *Excel*, (2) data from domestic *and* international companies, (3) 10 years of financial data; and (4) one-click Peer Set analyses.

We also have available problems that rely on data from Thomson ONE—BSE. Due to the ever-changing nature of the Web, these problems are updated frequently, and they can be found on the textbook's Web site, **academic. cengage.com/finance/brigham.**

Here is some of the data provided by Thomson ONE—BSE:

I/B/E/S Consensus Estimates.
Includes consensus estimates—averages, means, and medians; analyst-by-analyst earnings coverage; analysts' forecasts based on 15 industry standard measures; current and historic coverage for the selected 500 companies. Current coverage is 5 years forward plus historic data from 1976 for U.S. companies and from 1987 for international companies, with current data updated daily and historic data updated monthly.

Worldscope.
Includes company profiles, financials, accounting results, and market per-share data for the selected 500 companies going back to 1980, all updated daily.

Disclosure SEC Database.
Includes company profiles, annual and quarterly company financials, pricing information, and earnings estimates for selected U.S. and Canadian companies, annually from 1987, quarterly for the last 10 years, and monthly for prices, all updated weekly.

DataStream Pricing.
Daily international pricing, including share price information (open, high, low, close, P/E) plus index and exchange rate data, for the last 10 years.

ILX Systems Delayed Quotes.
Includes 20-minute delayed quotes of equities and indices from U.S. and global tickers covering 130 exchanges in 25 developed countries.

Comtex Real-Time News.
Includes current news releases.

SEC Edgar Filings and Global Image Source Filings.
Includes regulatory and nonregulatory filings for both corporate and individual entities. Edgar filings are real-time and go back 10 years; image filings are updated daily and go back 7 years.

The Instructional Package: An Integrated Learning System

Financial Management includes a broad range of ancillary materials designed to enhance students' learning and to make it easier for instructors to prepare for and conduct classes. All resources available to students are of course also available to instructors, and instructors also have access to the course management tools.

Learning Tools Available for Students and Instructors

Study Guide.
This supplement outlines the key sections of each chapter, and it provides students with a set of questions and problems similar to those in the text and in the *Test Bank*, along with worked-out solutions. Instructors seldom use the *Study Guide* themselves, but students often find it useful, so we recommend that instructors ask their bookstores to have copies available. Our bookstores generally have to reorder it, which attests to its popularity with students.

Technology Supplement.
The *Technology Supplement* on CengageNOW contains tutorials for four commonly used financial calculators, for *Excel*, and for *PowerPoint*. The calculator tutorials cover those features students need to work the problems in the text.

Effective Use of a Financial Calculator.
Written by Pamela Hall, this handbook is designed to help increase students' understanding of both finance and financial calculators, enabling them to work problems more quickly and effectively.

In addition to these printed resources and the items noted above, many other resources are available on the Web at *Financial Management's* Web site, **academic.cengage.com/finance/brigham.** These ancillaries are also available at both the Instructor's Web site and the CengageNOW site. These ancillaries include:

Excel Tool Kits.
Proficiency with spreadsheets is an absolute necessity for all MBA students. With this in mind, we created *Excel* spreadsheets, called *"Tool Kits,"* for each chapter to show how the calculations used in the chapter were actually done. The *Tool Kit* models include explanations and screen shots that show students how to use many of the features and functions of *Excel*, enabling the *Tool Kits* to serve as self-taught tutorials.

An e-Library: Web Extensions and Web Chapters.
Many chapters have Adobe PDF "appendices" that provide more detailed coverage of topics that were addressed in the chapter. In addition, these four specialized topics are covered in PDF Web chapters: Banking Relationships, Working Capital Management Extensions, Pension Plan Management, and Financial Management in Not-for-Profit Businesses.

NewsEdge.
NewsEdge is a "push" service of daily news, offering coverage of breaking stories. It is timely, authoritative, and advertising-free.

NewsWire: Finance in the News.
NewsWire provides summaries of recent finance news stories, indexed by topic. A headline, subject category, key words, summary of the news article, article source line, and questions to spur further thought and discussion are included. The summaries are carefully selected and prepared by Paul Bolster and Emery Trahan of Northeastern University, and they facilitate the incorporation of late-breaking news into the classroom.

End-of-Chapter Spreadsheet Problems.
Each chapter has a *"Build a Model"* problem, where students start with a spreadsheet that contains financial data plus general instructions relating to solving a specific problem. The model is partially completed, with headings but no formulas, so the student must literally build a model. This structure guides the student

through the problem, minimizes unnecessary typing and data entry, and also makes it easy to grade the work, since all students' answers are in the same locations on the spreadsheet. The partial spreadsheets for the *"Build a Model"* problems are available to students on the book's Web site, while the completed models are in files on the Instructor's portion of the Web site.

Thomson ONE—BSE Problem Sets.

The book's Web site has a set of problems that require accessing the Thomson ONE—Business School Edition Web data. Using real world data, students are better able to develop the skills they will need in the real world.

Cyberproblems.

The Web site also contains "Cyberproblems," which require students to go to specific Web sites and answer a series of questions. Answers are available on the Instructors' Web site.

Interactive Study Center.

The textbook's Web site contains links to all Web sites that are cited in each chapter.

Course Management Tools Available Only to Instructors

Instructors have access to all of the materials listed above, plus additional course management tools. These are available at: (1) *Financial Management's* Instructor companion Web site, **academic.cengage.com/finance/brigham**, or on the Instructor's Resource CD, or on the Instructor's portion of the CengageNOW Web site. These materials include:

Solutions Manual.

This comprehensive manual contains worked-out solutions to all end-of-chapter materials. It is available in both print and electronic forms at the Instructor's Web site.

PowerPoint Slides.

There is a Mini Case at the end of each chapter. These cases cover all the essential issues presented in the chapter, and they provide the structure for our class lectures. For each Mini Case, we developed a set of *PowerPoint* slides that present graphs, tables, lists, and calculations for use in lectures. Although based on the Mini Cases, the slides are completely self-contained in the sense that they can be used for lectures regardless of whether students are required to read the mini cases. Also, instructors can easily customize the slides, and they can be converted quickly into any *PowerPoint* Design Template.[1] Copies of these files are on the Instructor's Web site and the CengageNOW site. If instructors want students to have copies of the *PowerPoint* shows before class to facilitate note taking, they can give students access to these files through the CengageNOW site.

Mini Case Spreadsheets.

In addition to the *PowerPoint* slides, we also provide *Excel* spreadsheets that do the calculations required in the Mini Cases. These spreadsheets are similar to the *Tool Kits* except (a) the numbers correspond to the Mini Cases rather than the chapter examples, and (b) we added some features that make it possible to do what-if analysis on a real-time basis in class. We usually begin our lectures with the *PowerPoint* presentation, but after we have explained a basic concept we "toggle"

---

[1]To convert into *PowerPoint*, select Format, Apply Design Template, and then pick any template. Always double-check the conversion, since some templates use differently sized fonts, which can cause some slide titles to run over their allotted space.

to the mini case *Excel* file and show how the analysis can be done in *Excel*.[2] For example, when teaching bond pricing, we begin with the *PowerPoint* show and cover the basic concepts and calculations. Then we toggle to *Excel* and use a sensitivity-based graph to show how bond prices change as interest rates and time to maturity vary. More and more students are bringing their laptops to class, and they can follow along, doing the what-if analysis for themselves. Instructors can give students access to these files through the CengageNOW Web site.

Solutions to End-of-Chapter Spreadsheet Problems.
The partial spreadsheets for the *"Build a Model"* problems are available to students, while the completed models are in files on the Instructor's Web site.

Solutions to Thomson ONE—BSE Problem Sets.
The Thomson ONE—BSE problems set require students to use real world data. Although the solutions change daily as the data change, we provide instructors with "representative" answers.

Solutions to Cyberproblems.
The "Cyberproblems" require students to go to specific Web sites and answer a series of questions. Although the solutions change frequently as the data change, we provide "representative" answers on the Instructor's Web site.

Test Bank.
The *Test Bank* contains more than 1,200 class-tested questions and problems. Information regarding the topic and degree of difficulty, along with the complete solution for all numerical problems, is provided with each question. The *Test Bank* is available in four forms: (1) in a printed book; (2) in Microsoft Word files; (3) in a computerized test bank software package, Exam View, which has many features that make test preparation, scoring, and grade recording easy; and (4) on CengageNOW, which features the ability to create algorithmic assignments on the Web that are unique to each student and that are automatically scored and put in gradesheets that can be exported into *Excel* or integrated with the gradesheets of Blackboard and WebCT.

Textchoice, **the Cengage Learning Online Case Library.**
More than 100 cases written by Eugene F. Brigham, Linda Klein, and Chris Buzzard are now available via the Internet, and new cases are added every year. These cases are in a database that allows instructors to select cases and create their own customized casebooks. Most of the cases have accompanying spreadsheet models that, while not essential for working the case, do reduce number crunching and thus leave more time for students to consider conceptual issues. The models also illustrate how computers can be used to make better financial decisions. Cases that we have found particularly useful for the different chapters are listed in the end-of-chapter references. The cases, case solutions, and spreadsheet models can be previewed and ordered by instructors at **http://www.textchoice2.com.**

South-Western will provide complimentary supplements or supplement packages to those adopters qualified under Cengage Learning's adoption policy. Please contact your sales representative to learn how you may qualify. If, as an adopter or potential user, you receive supplements you do not need, please return them to your sales representative.

---

[2]Note: To toggle between two open programs, such as *Excel* and *PowerPoint*, hold the Alt key down and hit the Tab key until you have selected the program you want to show.

Acknowledgments

This book reflects the efforts of a great many people over a number of years. First, we would like to thank the following people who helped with the Twelfth Edition:

Steve Johnson – University of Northern Iowa
Patty Hatfield – Bradley University
Alex Tang – Morgan State University
Eric Blazer – Millersville University
Partha Gangopadhyay – St. Cloud State University
John Stansfield – University of Missouri
Stuart Gillan – Arizona State University

Second, professors and professionals who are experts on specific topics reviewed earlier versions of individual chapters or groups of chapters. We are grateful for the insights provided by: Edward I. Altman, New York University; Mary Schary Amram, Analysis Group Economics; Nasser Arshadi, University of Missouri; Abdul Aziz, Humboldt State University; William Beranek, University of Georgia; Gordon R. Bonner, University of Delaware; Ben S. Branch, Bank of New England and University of Massachusetts; David T. Brown, University of Florida; Mark Flannery, University of Florida; E. Bruce Frederickson, Syracuse University; Myron Gordon, University of Toronto; Hal Heaton, Brigham Young University; John Helmuth, Rochester Institute of Technology; Hugh Hunter, Eastern Washington University; James E. Jackson, Oklahoma State University; Vahan Janjigian, Northeastern University; Keith H. Johnson, University of Kentucky; Robert Kieschnick, George Mason University; Richard LeCompte, Wichita State University; Ilene Levin, University of Minnesota-Duluth; James T. Lindley, University of South Mississippi; R. Daniel Pace, Valparaiso University; Ralph A. Pope, California State University-Sacramento; Jay Ritter, University of Florida; Allen Rappaport, University of Northern Iowa; Michael Ryngaert, University of Florida; Fiona Robertson, Seattle University; James Schallheim, University of Utah; G. Bennett Stewart, Stern Stewart & Co.; Robert Strong, University of Maine at Orono; Eugene Swinnerton, University of Detroit-Mercy; Robert Taggart, Boston College; Jonathan Tiemann, Wells Fargo Nikko Investment Advisors; Sheridan Titman, University of Texas at Austin; Alan L. Tucker, Temple University; David Vang, University of St. Thomas; Gary R. Wells, Idaho State University; and David Ziebart, University of Illinois at Urbana.

In addition, we would like to thank the following people, whose reviews and comments on earlier editions and companion books have contributed to this edition: Mike Adler, Syed Ahmad, Sadhana M. Alangar, Ed Altman, Bruce Anderson, Ron Anderson, Bob Angell, Vince Apilado, Henry Arnold, Bob Aubey, Gil Babcock, Peter Bacon, Kent Baker, Tom Bankston, Les Barenbaum, Charles Barngrover, Michael Barry, Bill Beedles, Moshe Ben-Horim, Bill Beranek, Tom Berry, Bill Bertin, Roger Bey, Dalton Bigbee, John Bildersee, Russ Boisjoly, Keith Boles, Geof Booth, Kenneth Boudreaux, Helen Bowers, Oswald Bowlin, Don Boyd, G. Michael Boyd, Pat Boyer, Joe Brandt, Elizabeth Brannigan, Greg Brauer, Mary Broske, Dave Brown, Kate Brown, Bill Brueggeman, Kirt Butler, Robert Button, Bill Campsey, Bob Carleson, Severin Carlson, David Cary, Steve Celec, Don Chance, Antony Chang, Susan Chaplinsky, Jay Choi, S. K. Choudhury, Lal Chugh, Maclyn Clouse, Margaret Considine, Phil Cooley, Joe Copeland, David Cordell, John Cotner, Charles Cox, David Crary, John Crockett, Roy Crum, Brent Dalrymple, Bill Damon, Joel Dauten, Steve Dawson, Sankar De, Miles Delano, Fred Dellva, Anand Desai,

Bernard Dill, Greg Dimkoff, Les Dlabay, Mark Dorfman, Gene Drycimski, Dean Dudley, David Durst, Ed Dyl, Dick Edelman, Charles Edwards, John Ellis, Dave Ewert, John Ezzell, Richard Fendler, Michael Ferri, Jim Filkins, John Finnerty, Susan Fischer, Steven Flint, Russ Fogler, Dan French, Tina Galloway, Phil Gardial, Michael Garlington, Jim Garvin, Adam Gehr, Jim Gentry, Philip Glasgo, Rudyard Goode, Walt Goulet, Bernie Grablowsky, Theoharry Grammatikos, Ed Grossnickle, John Groth, Alan Grunewald, Manak Gupta, Sam Hadaway, Don Hakala, Janet Hamilton, Sally Hamilton, Gerald Hamsmith, William Hardin, John Harris, Paul Hastings, Bob Haugen, Steve Hawke, Del Hawley, Robert Hehre, George Hettenhouse, Hans Heymann, Kendall Hill, Roger Hill, Tom Hindelang, Linda Hittle, Ralph Hocking, J. Ronald Hoffmeister, Jim Horrigan, John Houston, John Howe, Keith Howe, Steve Isberg, Jim Jackson, Kurt Jesswein, Kose John, Craig Johnson, Keith Johnson, Ramon Johnson, Ray Jones, Manuel Jose, Gus Kalogeras, Mike Keenan, Bill Kennedy, Joe Kiernan, Rick Kish, Linda Klein, Don Knight, Dorothy Koehl, Theodor Kohers, Jaroslaw Komarynsky, Duncan Kretovich, Harold Krogh, Charles Kroncke, Lynn Phillips Kugele, Joan Lamm, P. Lange, Howard Lanser, Martin Laurence, Ed Lawrence, Wayne Lee, Jim LePage, Jules Levine, John Lewis, Chuck Linke, Bill Lloyd, Susan Long, Judy Maese, Bob Magee, Ileen Malitz, Phil Malone, Terry Maness, Chris Manning, Terry Martell, D. J. Masson, John Mathys, John McAlhany, Andy McCollough, Bill McDaniel, Robin McLaughlin, Tom McCue, Jamshid Mehran, Ilhan Meric, Larry Merville, Rick Meyer, Stuart E. Michelson, Jim Millar, Ed Miller, John Mitchell, Carol Moerdyk, Bob Moore, Barry Morris, Gene Morris, Fred Morrissey, Chris Muscarella, Stu Myers, David Nachman, Tim Nantell, Don Nast, Bill Nelson, Bob Nelson, Bob Niendorf, Tom O'Brien, Dennis O'Connor, John O'Donnell, Jim Olsen, Robert Olsen, Frank O'Meara, David Overbye, Coleen Pantalone, Jim Pappas, Stephen Parrish, Pam Peterson, Glenn Petry, Jim Pettijohn, Rich Pettit, Dick Pettway, Hugo Phillips, John Pinkerton, Gerald Pogue, R. Potter, Franklin Potts, R. Powell, Chris Prestopino, Jerry Prock, Howard Puckett, Herbert Quigley, George Racette, Bob Radcliffe, Bill Rentz, Ken Riener, Charles Rini, John Ritchie, Pietra Rivoli, Antonio Rodriguez, E. M. Roussakis, Dexter Rowell, Mike Ryngaert, Jim Sachlis, Abdul Sadik, Thomas Scampini, Kevin Scanlon, Frederick Schadler, Mary Jane Scheuer, Carl Schweser, John Settle, Alan Severn, Sol Shalit, Elizabeth Shields, Frederic Shipley, Dilip Shome, Ron Shrieves, Neil Sicherman, J. B. Silvers, Clay Singleton, Joe Sinkey, Stacy Sirmans, Jaye Smith, Steve Smith, Don Sorenson, David Speairs, Ken Stanly, Ed Stendardi, Alan Stephens, Don Stevens, Jerry Stevens, Mark Stohs, Glen Strasburg, Philip Swensen, Ernie Swift, Paul Swink, Gary Tallman, Dennis Tanner, Craig Tapley, Russ Taussig, Richard Teweles, Ted Teweles, Andrew Thompson, George Trivoli, George Tsetsekos, Mel Tysseland, David Upton, Howard Van Auken, Pretorious Van den Dool, Pieter Vanderburg, Paul Vanderheiden, Jim Verbrugge, Patrick Vincent, Steve Vinson, Susan Visscher, John Wachowicz, Mark D. Walker, Mike Walker, Sam Weaver, Kuo Chiang Wei, Bill Welch, Fred Weston, Norm Williams, Tony Wingler, Ed Wolfe, Larry Wolken, Don Woods, Thomas Wright, Michael Yonan, Zhong-guo Zhou, Dennis Zocco, and Kent Zumwalt.

Special thanks are due to Fred Weston, Myron Gordon, Merton Miller, and Franco Modigliani, who have done much to help develop the field of financial management and who provided us with instruction and inspiration; to Roy Crum, who contributed to the multinational finance chapter; to Larry Wolken, who offered his hard work and advice for the development of the *PowerPoint* shows; to Dana Clark and Chris Buzzard, who helped us develop the spreadsheet models; to Amelia Bell, Stephanie Hodge, Matt Brock, Susan Whitman, and Andrea Booher, who provided editorial support; and to Joel Houston and Phillip Daves, whose work with us on other books is reflected in this text. We owe special thanks to Lou Gapenski, our past coauthor, for his many contributions.

Our colleagues and our students at the Universities of Florida and Tennessee gave us many useful suggestions, and the South-Western staff—especially Elizabeth Thomson, Matt McKinney, Jason Krall, Cliff Kallemeyn, and Mike Reynolds—helped greatly with all phases of text development, production, and marketing.

Errors in the Text

At this point, authors generally say something like this: "We appreciate all the help we received from the people listed above, but any remaining errors are, of course, our own responsibility." And in many books, there are plenty of remaining errors. Having experienced difficulties with errors ourselves, both as students and as instructors, we resolved to avoid this problem in *Financial Management*. As a result of our error detection procedures, we are convinced that the book is relatively free of mistakes.

Partly because of our confidence that few such errors remain, but primarily because we want to detect any errors in the textbook that may have slipped by so we can correct them in subsequent printings, we decided to offer a reward of $10 per error to the first person who reports a textbook error to us. For purposes of this reward, errors in the textbook are defined as misspelled words, nonrounding numerical errors, incorrect statements, and any other error that inhibits comprehension. Typesetting problems such as irregular spacing and differences in opinion regarding grammatical or punctuation conventions do not qualify for this reward. Also, given the ever-changing nature of the Internet, changes in Web addresses do not qualify as errors, although we would appreciate reports of changed Web addresses. Finally, any qualifying error that has follow-through effects is counted as two errors only. **Please report any errors to Michael C. Ehrhardt at the e-mail address given below.**

Conclusion

Finance is, in a real sense, the cornerstone of the free enterprise system. Good financial management is therefore vitally important to the economic health of business firms, hence to the nation and the world. Because of its importance, corporate finance should be thoroughly understood. However, this is easier said than done—the field is relatively complex, and it is undergoing constant change in response to shifts in economic conditions. All of this makes corporate finance stimulating and exciting, but also challenging and sometimes perplexing. We sincerely hope that *Financial Management: Theory and Practice* will help readers understand and solve the financial problems faced by businesses today.

Michael C. Ehrhardt	**Eugene F. Brigham**
University of Tennessee	University of Florida
Ehrhardt@utk.edu	Gene.Brigham@cba.ufl.edu

January 2007

brief contents

contents

Part 2
Securities and Their Valuation 155

Chapter 5
Bonds, Bond Valuation, and Interest Rates 156

Web Extensions

Chapter 6
Risk, Return, and the Capital Asset Pricing Model 200

Appendixes

Web Chapters

part 1

Fundamental Concepts of Financial Management

chapter 1

An Overview of Financial Management and the Financial Environment

See **http:// money.cnn.com /magazines/ fortune/**for updates on the ranking.

In a global beauty contest for companies, the winner is . . . General Electric. Or at least General Electric is the most admired company in the world, according to *Fortune* magazine's annual survey. The other top ten global finalists are FedEx, Southwest Airlines, Procter & Gamble, Starbucks, Johnson & Johnson, Berkshire Hathaway, Dell Computers, Toyota Motor, and Microsoft. What do these companies have that separates them from the rest of the pack?

According to more than 10,000 executives, directors, and security analysts, these companies have the highest average scores across nine attributes: (1) innovativeness, (2) quality of management, (3) long-term investment value, (4) social responsibility, (5) employee talent, (6) quality of products and services, (7) financial soundness, (8) use of corporate assets, and (9) effectiveness in doing business globally.

Many of these companies compete in commodity industries in which it is very difficult to differentiate their products from those of their competitors. How do they survive and thrive in such an environment? First, they have an incredible focus on using technology to understand their customers, reduce costs, reduce inventory, and speed up product delivery. Second, they continually innovate and invest in ways to differentiate their products. For example, GE is investing in new technologies, such as nanometals, hydrogen power, and photovoltaics. CEO Jeff Immelt says that these are areas in which "very few can follow."

Many companies have a difficult time attracting employees. Not so for the most admired companies, which have many more applicants than job openings. In addition to their acumen with technology and customers, they are also on the leading edge when it comes to training employees and providing a workplace in which people can thrive.

In a nutshell, these companies reduce costs by having innovative production processes, they create value for customers by providing high-quality products and services, and they create value for employees through training and fostering an environment that allows employees to utilize all of their skills and talents.

Do investors benefit from this focus on processes, customers, and employees? During the most recent 5-year period, these ten companies posted an average annual stock return of 7.6%, which is quite impressive when compared with the 1.1% average annual decline in the S&P 500. These superior returns are due to superior cash flow generation. But, as you will see throughout this book, a company can generate cash flow only if it also creates value for its customers, employees, and suppliers.

This chapter should give you an idea of what financial management is all about, including an overview of the financial markets in which corporations operate. Before getting into details, let's look at the big picture. You're probably back in school because you want an interesting, challenging, and rewarding career. To see where finance fits in, here's a five-minute MBA.

1.1 The Five-Minute MBA

Okay, we realize you can't get an MBA in five minutes. But just as an artist quickly sketches the outline of a picture before filling in the details, we can sketch the key elements of an MBA education. In a nutshell, the objective of an MBA is to provide managers with the knowledge and skills they need to run successful companies, so we start our sketch with some common characteristics of successful companies. In particular, all successful companies are able to accomplish two main goals:

1. They identify, create, and deliver products or services that are highly valued by customers—so highly valued that customers choose to purchase them from the company rather than from its competitors.
2. All successful companies sell their products/services at prices that are high enough to cover costs and to compensate owners and creditors for their exposure to risk.

It's easy to talk about satisfying customers and investors, but it's not so easy to accomplish these goals. If it were, then all companies would be successful, and you wouldn't need an MBA!

FM

e-resource

Visit the textbook's Web site. This ever-evolving site, for students and instructors, is a tool for teaching, learning, financial research, and job searches.

The Key Attributes of Successful Companies

First, *successful companies have skilled people* at all levels inside the company, including leaders, managers, and a capable workforce.

Second, *successful companies have strong relationships* with groups outside the company. For example, successful companies develop win–win relationships with suppliers and excel in customer relationship management.

Third, *successful companies have enough funding* to execute their plans and support their operations. Most companies need cash to purchase land, buildings, equipment, and materials. Companies can reinvest a portion of their earnings, but most growing companies must also raise additional funds externally, by some combination of selling stock and/or borrowing in the financial markets.

Just as a stool needs all three legs to stand, a successful company must have all three attributes: skilled people, strong external relationships, and sufficient capital.

Consult **http://www .careers-in-finance.com** for an excellent site containing information on a variety of business career areas, listings of current jobs, and other reference materials.

The MBA, Finance, and Your Career

To be successful, a company must meet its first main goal: identifying, creating, and delivering highly valued products and services to its customers. This requires that it possess all three of the key attributes mentioned above. Therefore, it's not surprising that most of your MBA courses are directly related to these attributes. For example, courses in economics, communication, strategy, organizational behavior, and human resources should prepare you for a leadership role and enable you to effectively manage your company's workforce. Other courses, such as marketing, operations management, and information technology, increase your knowledge of specific disciplines, enabling you to develop the efficient business processes and strong external relationships your company needs. Portions of *this* finance course will address raising the capital your company needs to implement its plans. In short, your MBA courses will give you the skills you need to help a company achieve its first goal: producing goods and services that customers want.

Recall, though, that it's not enough just to have highly valued products and satisfied customers. Successful companies must also meet their second main goal, which is generating enough cash to compensate the investors who provided the necessary capital. To help your company accomplish this second goal, you must be able to evaluate any proposal, whether it relates to marketing, production, strategy, or any other area, and implement only the projects that add value for your investors. For this, you must have expertise in finance, no matter your major. Thus, finance is a critical part of an MBA education, and it will help you throughout your career.

SELF-TEST

What are the goals of successful companies?

What are the three key attributes common to all successful companies?

How does expertise in finance help a company become successful?

1.2   The Corporate Life Cycle

Many major corporations had humble origins, perhaps even in a garage or basement, including Apple Computer and Hewlett-Packard. How is it possible for such companies to grow into the giants we see today? No two companies develop in exactly the same way, but the following sections describe some typical stages in the corporate life cycle.

Starting Up as a Proprietorship

Many companies begin as a **proprietorship,** which is an unincorporated business owned by one individual. Starting a business as a proprietor is easy—one merely begins business operations after obtaining any required city or state business licenses. The proprietorship has three important advantages: (1) It is easily and inexpensively formed, (2) it is subject to few government regulations, and (3) its income is not subject to corporate taxation but is taxed only as a part of the proprietor's personal income.

However, the proprietorship also has three important limitations: (1) It is difficult for a proprietorship to obtain the capital needed for growth; (2) the proprietor has unlimited personal liability for the business's debts, which can result in losses that exceed the money he or she invested in the company (creditors may even be able to seize a proprietor's house or other personal property!); and (3) the life of a proprietorship is limited to the life of its founder. For these three reasons, sole proprietorships are used primarily for small businesses. In fact, proprietorships account for only about 13% of all sales, based on dollar values, even though about 80% of all companies are proprietorships.

More Than One Owner: A Partnership

Some companies start with more than one owner, and some proprietors decide to add a partner as the business grows. A **partnership** exists whenever two or more persons or entities associate to conduct a noncorporate business for profit. Partnerships may operate under different degrees of formality, ranging from informal, oral understandings to formal agreements filed with the secretary of the state in which the partnership was formed. Partnership agreements define the ways any profits and losses are shared between partners. A partnership's advantages and disadvantages are similar to those of a proprietorship.

Regarding liability, the partners can potentially lose all of their personal assets, even assets not invested in the business, because under partnership law, each partner is liable for the business's debts. Therefore, in the event the partnership goes bankrupt, if any partner is unable to meet his or her pro rata liability, the remaining partners must make good on the unsatisfied claims, drawing on their personal assets to the extent necessary. To avoid this, it is possible to limit the liabilities of some of the partners by establishing a **limited partnership,** wherein certain partners are designated **general partners** and others **limited partners.** In a limited partnership, the limited partners are liable only for the amount of their investment in the partnership, while the general partners have unlimited liability. However, the limited partners typically have no control—it rests solely with the general partners—and their returns are likewise limited. Limited partnerships are common in real estate, oil, equipment leasing ventures, and venture capital. However, they are not widely used in general business situations because no one partner is usually willing to be the general partner and thus accept the majority of the business's risk, and none of the others are willing to be limited partners and give up all control.

In both regular and limited partnerships at least one partner is liable for the debts of the partnership. However, in a **limited liability partnership (LLP),** sometimes called a **limited liability company (LLC),** all partners enjoy limited liability with regard to the business's liabilities, and their potential losses are limited to their investment in the LLP. Of course, this arrangement increases the risk faced by an LLP's lenders, customers, and suppliers.

Many Owners: A Corporation

Most partnerships have difficulty attracting substantial amounts of capital. This is generally not a problem for a slow-growing business, but if a business's products or services really catch on, and if it needs to raise large sums of money to capitalize on its opportunities, the difficulty in attracting capital becomes a real drawback. Thus, many growth companies, such as Hewlett-Packard and Microsoft, began life as a proprietorship or partnership, but at some point their founders found it necessary to convert to a corporation. Some companies, in anticipation of growth, actually begin as corporations. A **corporation** is a legal entity created by state laws, and it is separate and distinct from its owners and managers. This separation gives the corporation three major advantages: (1) *unlimited* life—a corporation can continue after its original owners and managers are deceased; (2) *easy transferability of ownership interest*—ownership interests can be divided into shares of stock, which can be transferred far more easily than can proprietorship or partnership interests; and (3) *limited liability*—losses are limited to the actual funds invested.

To illustrate limited liability, suppose you invested $10,000 in a partnership that then went bankrupt and owed $1 million. Because the owners are liable for the debts of a partnership, you could be assessed for a share of the company's debt, and you could be held liable for the entire $1 million if your partners could not pay their shares. On the other hand, if you invested $10,000 in the stock of a corporation that then went bankrupt, your potential loss on the investment would be limited to your $10,000 investment.[1] Unlimited life, easy transferability of ownership interest, and limited liability make it much easier for corporations than for proprietorships or partnerships to raise money in the financial markets and grow into large companies.

The corporate form offers significant advantages over proprietorships and partnerships, but it also has two disadvantages: (1) Corporate earnings may be subject to double taxation—the earnings of the corporation are taxed at the corporate level, and then earnings paid out as dividends are taxed again as income to the stockholders.[2] (2) Setting up a corporation involves preparing a charter, writing a set of bylaws, and filing the many required state and federal reports, which is more complex and time-consuming than creating a proprietorship or a partnership.

The **charter** includes the following information: (1) name of the proposed corporation, (2) types of activities it will pursue, (3) amount of capital stock, (4) number of directors, and (5) names and addresses of directors. The charter is filed with the secretary of the state in which the firm will be incorporated, and when it is approved, the corporation is officially in existence.[3] After the corporation begins operating, quarterly and annual employment, financial, and tax reports must be filed with state and federal authorities.

The **bylaws** are a set of rules drawn up by the founders of the corporation. Included are such points as (1) how directors are to be elected (all elected each year, or perhaps one-third each year for 3-year terms); (2) whether the existing stockholders will have the first right to buy any new shares the firm issues; and (3) procedures for changing the bylaws themselves, should conditions require it.

There are actually several different types of corporations. Professionals such as doctors, lawyers, and accountants often form a **professional corporation (PC)** or a **professional association (PA).** These types of corporations do not relieve the participants of professional (malpractice) liability. Indeed, the primary motivation behind the professional corporation was to provide a way for groups of professionals to incorporate and thus avoid certain types of unlimited liability, yet still be held responsible for professional liability.

Finally, if requirements are met, particularly with regard to size and number of stockholders, owners can establish a corporation but elect to be taxed as if the busi-

---

[1] In the case of very small corporations, the limited liability may be fiction because lenders frequently require personal guarantees from the stockholders.
[2] The 2003 tax act reduced, but did not eliminate, the taxation of dividends received by investors.
[3] More than 60% of major U.S. corporations are chartered in Delaware, which has, over the years, provided a favorable legal environment for corporations. It is not necessary for a firm to be headquartered, or even to conduct operations, in its state of incorporation, or even in its country of incorporation.

ness were a proprietorship or partnership. Such firms, which differ not in organizational form but only in how their owners are taxed, are called **S corporations.**

Growing and Managing a Corporation

Once a corporation has been established, how does it evolve? When entrepreneurs start a company, they usually provide all the financing from their personal resources, which may include savings, second mortgages, or even credit cards. As the corporation grows, it needs factories, equipment, inventory, and other resources to support its growth. In time, the entrepreneurs usually deplete their own resources and must turn to external financing. Many young companies are too risky for banks, so the founders must sell stock to outsiders, such as friends, family, private investors (often called angels), or venture capitalists. If the corporation continues to grow, it may become successful enough to attract lending from banks, or it may even raise additional funds through an **initial public offering (IPO)** by selling stock to the public at large. After an IPO, corporations support their growth by borrowing from banks, issuing debt, or selling additional shares of stock. In short, a corporation's ability to grow depends on its interactions with the financial markets, which we describe in much more detail later in this chapter.

For proprietorships, partnerships, and small corporations, the firm's owners are also its managers. This is usually not true for a large corporation, which means that large firms' stockholders, who are its owners, face a very serious problem. What is to prevent managers from acting in their own best interests, rather than in the best interests of the owners? This is called an **agency problem** because managers are hired as agents to act on behalf of the owners. Agency problems can be addressed by a company's **corporate governance,** which is the set of rules that control a company's behavior towards its directors, managers, employees, shareholders, creditors, customers, competitors, and community. We will have much more to say about agency problems and corporate governance throughout the book, especially in Chapters 15, 16, 21, and 25.[4]

SELF-TEST What are the key differences between proprietorships, partnerships, and corporations?

Describe some special types of partnerships and corporations, and explain the differences among them.

1.3 The Primary Objective of the Corporation: Value Maximization

Shareholders are the owners of a corporation, and they purchase stocks because they want to earn a good return on their investment without undue risk exposure. In most cases, shareholders elect directors, who then hire managers to run the corporation on a day-to-day basis. Because managers are supposed to be working on

---

[4]The classic work on agency theory is Michael C. Jensen and William H. Meckling, "Theory of the Firm, Managerial Behavior, Agency Costs, and Ownership Structure," *Journal of Financial Economics*, October 1976, 305–360. Another article by Jensen specifically addresses these issues; see "Value Maximization, Stakeholder Theory, and the Corporate Objective Function," *Journal of Applied Corporate Finance*, Fall 2001, 8–21. For an overview of corporate governance, see Stuart Gillan, "Recent Developments in Corporate Governance: An Overview," *Journal of Corporate Finance*, June 2006, 381–402.

behalf of shareholders, they should pursue policies that enhance shareholder value. Consequently, throughout this book we operate on the assumption that management's primary objective should be **stockholder wealth maximization.**

The **market price** is the stock price that we observe in the financial markets. We later explain in detail how stock prices are determined, but for now it is enough to say that a company's market price incorporates the information available to investors. If the market price reflects all *relevant* information, then the observed price is also the **fundamental, or intrinsic, price.** However, investors rarely have all relevant information. For example, companies report most major decisions, but they sometimes withhold critical information to prevent competitors from gaining strategic advantages.

Unfortunately, some managers deliberately mislead investors by taking actions to make their companies appear more valuable than they truly are. Sometimes these actions are illegal, such as those taken by the senior managers at Enron. Sometimes the actions are legal, but they are taken to push the current market price above its fundamental price in the short term. For example, suppose a utility's stock price is equal to its fundamental price of $50 per share. What would happen if the utility substantially reduced its tree-trimming program, but didn't tell investors? This would lower current costs and thus boost current earnings and current cash flow, but it would also lead to major expenditures in the future when breaking limbs damage the lines. If investors were told about the major repair costs facing the company, the market price would immediately drop to a new fundamental value of $45. But if investors were kept in the dark, they might misinterpret the higher-than-expected current earnings, and the market price might go up to $52. Investors would eventually understand the situation when the company later incurred large costs to repair the damaged lines; when that happened, the price would fall to its fundamental value of $45.

Consider the hypothetical sequence of events. The company's managers deceived investors, and the price rose to $52 when it would have fallen to $45 if not for the deception. Of course, this benefited those who owned the stock at the time of the deception, including managers with stock options. But when the deception came to light, those stockholders who still owned the stock suffered a significant loss, ending up with stock worth less than its original fundamental value. If the managers cashed in their stock options prior to this, then only the stockholders were hurt by the deception. Because the managers were hired to act in the interests of stockholders, their deception was a breach of their fiduciary responsibility. In addition, the managers' deception damaged the company's credibility, making it harder to raise capital in the future.

Therefore, when we say management's objective should be to maximize stockholder wealth, we really mean it is to *maximize the fundamental price of the firm's common stock*, not just the current market price. Firms do, of course, have other objectives; in particular, the managers who make the actual decisions are interested in their own personal satisfaction, in their employees' welfare, and in the good of the community and of society at large. Still, for the reasons set forth in the following sections, *maximizing the fundamental stock price is the most important objective for most corporations.*

Stock Price Maximization and Social Welfare

If a firm attempts to maximize its fundamental stock price, is this good or bad for society? In general, it is good. Aside from such illegal actions as fraudulent

Ethics for Individuals and Businesses

Business ethics are a company's attitude and conduct toward its employees, customers, community, and stockholders. A firm's commitment to business ethics can be measured by the tendency of its employees, from the top down, to adhere to laws, regulations, and moral standards relating to product safety and quality, fair employment practices, fair marketing and selling practices, the use of confidential information for personal gain, community involvement, and illegal payments to obtain business.

Ethical Dilemmas

When conflicts arise between profits and ethics, sometimes legal and ethical considerations make the choice obvious. At other times the right choice isn't clear. For example, suppose Norfolk Southern's managers know that its coal trains are polluting the air, but the amount of pollution is within legal limits and further reduction would be costly, causing harm to their shareholders. Are the managers ethically bound to reduce pollution? Aren't they also ethically bound to act in their shareholders' best interests?

Merck's own research indicated that its Vioxx pain medicine might be causing heart attacks, but the evidence was not overwhelmingly strong and the product was clearly helping some patients. If the company released negative but still questionable information, this would hurt sales, possibly preventing its beneficial use by some patients. If it delayed release, more and more patients might suffer irreversible harm. At what point should Merck make the potential problem known to the public? There are no obvious answers to questions such as these, but companies must deal with them, and a failure to handle them properly can lead to severe consequences.

Ethical Responsibility

Over the past few years ethical lapses have led to a number of bankruptcies, which have rasied the question: Were the *companies* unethical, or was it just some of their employees? That issue came up in the case of Arthur Andersen, the accounting firm that audited Enron, WorldCom, and several other companies that committed accounting fraud. Evidence showed that some Andersen accountants helped perpetrate the frauds, but its top managers argued that while some rogue employees behaved unethically, the firm's 85,000 other employees, and the firm itself, were innocent. The U.S. Justice Department disagreed, concluding that the firm itself was guilty because it fostered a climate where unethical behavior was permitted, and it built an incentive system that made such behavior profitable to both the perpetrators and the firm itself. As a result, Andersen was put out of business, its partners lost millions of dollars, and its 85,000 employees lost their jobs. In most other cases, individuals rather than firms were tried, and while the firms survived, they suffered reputational damage that greatly lowered their future profit potential and value.

Protecting Ethical Employees

If employees discover questionable activities or are given questionable orders, should they obey their bosses' orders, refuse to obey those orders, or report the situation to a higher authority, such as the company's board of directors, its auditors, or a federal prosecutor? Employees who report improper actions are often fired or otherwise penalized, and this keeps many people from reporting situations that should be investigated. To help alleviate this problem, Congress in 2002 passed the Sarbanes-Oxley Act, with a provision designed to protect "whistle-blowers." If an employee reports corporate wrongdoing and is later penalized, he or she can ask the Occupational Safety and Health Administration to investigate the situation, and if the employee was improperly penalized, the company can be required to reinstate the person, along with back pay and a sizable penalty award. Several big awards have been handed out since the act was passed, and a National Whistle-blower Center has been established.

accounting, exploiting monopoly power, violating safety codes, and failing to meet environmental standards, *the same actions that maximize fundamental stock prices also benefit society.* Here are some of the reasons:

1. **To a large extent, the owners of stock *are* society.** Seventy-five years ago this was not true, because most stock ownership was concentrated in the hands of

The Security Industry Association's Web site, **http://www.sia.com**, is a great source of information. To find data on stock ownership, go to their Web page, click on Research/Statistics/Surveys, click on Securities Industry Fact Book, choose Surveys, then Equity Ownership in America. You can purchase the most recent data, or look at the prior year for free.

a relatively small segment of society, comprised of the wealthiest individuals. Since then, there has been explosive growth in pension funds, life insurance companies, and mutual funds. These institutions now own more than 61% of all stock, which means that most individuals have an indirect stake in the stock market. In addition, more than 50% of all U.S. households now own stock directly, as compared with only 32.5% in 1989. Thus, most members of society now have an important stake in the stock market, either directly or indirectly. Therefore, when a manager takes actions to maximize the stock price, this improves the quality of life for millions of ordinary citizens.

2. **Consumers benefit.** Stock price maximization requires efficient, low-cost businesses that produce high-quality goods and services at the lowest possible cost. This means that companies must develop products and services that consumers want and need, which leads to new technology and new products. Also, companies that maximize their stock price must generate growth in sales by creating value for customers in the form of efficient and courteous service, adequate stocks of merchandise, and well-located business establishments.

   People sometimes argue that firms, in their efforts to raise profits and stock prices, increase product prices and gouge the public. In a reasonably competitive economy, which we have, prices are constrained by competition and consumer resistance. If a firm raises its prices beyond reasonable levels, it will simply lose its market share. Even giant firms such as General Motors lose business to Japanese and German firms, as well as to Ford and Chrysler, if they set prices above the level necessary to cover production costs plus a "normal" profit. Of course, firms *want* to earn more, and they constantly try to cut costs, develop new products, and so on, and thereby earn above-normal profits. Note, though, that if they are indeed successful and do earn above-normal profits, those very profits will attract competition, which will eventually drive prices down. So again, the main long-term beneficiary is the consumer.

3. **Employees benefit.** There are cases in which a stock increases when a company announces a plan to lay off employees, but viewed over time this is the exception rather than the rule. In general, companies that successfully increase stock prices also grow and add more employees, thus benefiting society. Note too that many governments across the world, including U.S. federal and state governments, are privatizing some of their state-owned activities by selling these operations to investors. Perhaps not surprisingly, the sales and cash flows of recently privatized companies generally improve. Moreover, studies show that these newly privatized companies tend to grow and thus require more employees when they are managed with the goal of stock price maximization.

One of *Fortune* magazine's key criteria in determining their list of most admired companies is a company's ability to attract, develop, and retain talented people. Their results consistently show high correlations among admiration for a company, its ability to satisfy employees, and its creation of value for shareholders. Employees find that it is both fun and financially rewarding to work for successful companies. Thus, successful companies get the cream of the employee crop, and skilled, motivated employees are one of the keys to corporate success.

Corporate Scandals and Maximizing Stock Price

The list of corporate scandals seems to go on forever: Sunbeam, Enron, ImClone, WorldCom, Tyco, Adelphia . . . . At first glance, it's tempting to say, "Look what happens when managers care only about maximizing stock price." But a closer look reveals a much different story. In fact, if these managers were trying to maximize stock price, given the resulting values of these companies, they failed dismally.

Although details vary from company to company, a few common themes emerge. First, managerial compensation was linked to the short-term performance of the stock price via poorly designed stock option and stock grant programs. This provided managers with a powerful incentive to drive up the stock price at the option vesting date without worrying about the future. Second, it is virtually impossible to take *legal* actions that drive up the stock price in the short term but harm it in the long term because the value of a company is based on all of its future free cash flows and not just cash flows in the immediate future. Because legal actions to quickly drive up the stock price didn't exist (other than the old-fashioned

ones, such as increasing sales, cutting costs, or reducing capital requirements), these managers began bending a few rules. Third, as they initially got away with bending rules, their egos and hubris grew to such an extent that they felt they were above all rules, and so they began breaking even more rules.

Stock prices did go up, at least temporarily, but as Abraham Lincoln said, "You can't fool all of the people all of the time." As the scandals became public, the stocks' prices plummeted, and in some cases the companies were ruined.

There are several important lessons to be learned from these examples. First, people respond to incentives, and poorly designed incentives can cause disastrous results. Second, ethical violations usually begin with small steps; if stockholders want managers to avoid large ethical violations, then they shouldn't let them make the small ones. Third, there is no shortcut to creating lasting value. It takes hard work to increase sales, cut costs, and reduce capital requirements, but this is the formula for success.

Managerial Actions to Maximize Shareholder Wealth

What types of actions can managers take to maximize shareholder wealth? To answer this question, we first need to ask, "What determines a firm's value?" In a nutshell, it is *a company's ability to generate cash flows now and in the future.*

We address different aspects of this in detail throughout the book, but we can lay out three basic facts now: (1) Any financial asset, including a company's stock, is valuable only to the extent that it generates cash flows; (2) the timing of cash flows matters—cash received sooner is better; and (3) investors are averse to risk, so all else equal, they will pay more for a stock whose cash flows are relatively certain than for one whose cash flows are more risky. Because of these three facts, managers can enhance their firm's value by increasing the size of the expected cash flows, by speeding up their receipt, and by reducing their risk.

The cash flows that matter are called **free cash flows (FCFs),** not because they are free, but because they are available (or free) for distribution to all of the company's investors, including creditors and stockholders. You will learn how to calculate free cash flows in Chapter 3, but for now you should know that free cash flows depend on three factors: (1) sales revenues, (2) operating costs and taxes, and (3) required investments in operating capital. In particular, free cash flow is equal to

$$\text{FCF} = \text{Sales revenues} - \text{Operating costs} - \text{Operating taxes}$$
$$- \text{Required investments in operating capital.}$$

Brand managers and marketing managers can increase sales (and prices) by truly understanding their customers and then designing goods and services that customers want. Human resource managers can improve productivity through training and employee retention. Production and logistics managers can improve profit margins, reduce inventory, and improve throughput at factories by implementing supply chain management, just-in-time inventory management, and lean manufacturing. In fact, all managers make decisions that can increase free cash flows.

One of the financial manager's roles is to help others see how their actions affect the company's ability to generate cash flow and, hence, its fundamental value. Financial managers also must decide *how to finance the firm*. In particular, they must choose what mix of debt and equity should be used, and what specific types of debt and equity securities should be issued. They must also decide what percentage of current earnings should be retained and reinvested rather than paid out as dividends. Along with these financing decisions, the general level of interest rates in the economy, the risk of the firm's operations, and stock market investors' overall attitude toward risk determine the rate of return that is required to satisfy a firm's investors. This rate of return from investors' perspectives is a cost from the company's point of view. Therefore, the rate of return required by investors is called the **weighted average cost of capital (WACC)**.

The relationship between a firm's fundamental value, its free cash flows, and its cost of capital is defined by the following equation:

$$\text{Value} = \frac{\text{FCF}_1}{(1 + \text{WACC})^1} + \frac{\text{FCF}_2}{(1 + \text{WACC})^2}$$

$$+ \frac{\text{FCF}_3}{(1 + \text{WACC})^3} + \cdots + \frac{\text{FCF}_\infty}{(1 + \text{WACC})^\infty}.$$

(1-1)

We will explain this equation and how to use it in detail later, beginning with Chapter 2. But for now, recall that growing firms often need to raise external funds, so the rest of this chapter focuses upon financial markets.

SELF-TEST

What should be management's primary objective?

How does maximizing the fundamental stock price benefit society?

What are the three primary determinants of free cash flows?

How is a firm's fundamental value related to its free cash flows and its cost of capital?

1.4 An Overview of the Capital Allocation Process

Businesses often need capital to implement growth plans; governments require funds to finance building projects; and individuals frequently want loans to purchase cars, homes, and education. Where can they get this money? Fortunately, there are other individuals and firms with incomes greater than their expenditures. In contrast to William Shakespeare's advice, most individuals and firms are both borrowers and lenders. For example, an individual might borrow money with a car loan or a home mortgage, but might also lend money through a bank savings account. In aggregate, individual households are net savers and provide most of the funds ultimately used by nonfinancial corporations. Although most

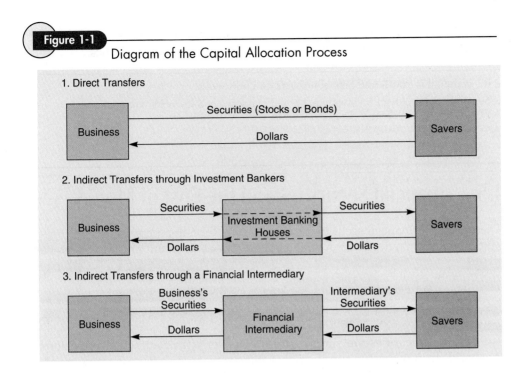

Figure 1-1

Diagram of the Capital Allocation Process

1. Direct Transfers

| Business | Securities (Stocks or Bonds) → | Savers |
| Business | ← Dollars | Savers |

2. Indirect Transfers through Investment Bankers

Business — Securities → Investment Banking Houses — Securities → Savers

Business ← Dollars — Investment Banking Houses ← Dollars — Savers

3. Indirect Transfers through a Financial Intermediary

Business — Business's Securities → Financial Intermediary — Intermediary's Securities → Savers

Business ← Dollars — Financial Intermediary ← Dollars — Savers

nonfinancial corporations own some financial securities, such as short-term Treasury bills, nonfinancial corporations are net borrowers in aggregate. It should be no surprise to you that federal, state, and local governments are also net borrowers in aggregate. Banks and other financial corporations raise money with one hand and invest it with the other. For example, a bank might raise money from individuals in the form of a savings account, but then lend most of that money to a business customer. In aggregate, financial corporations borrow slightly more than they lend.

Transfers of capital between savers and those who need capital take place in the three different ways. Direct transfers of money and securities, as shown in the top section of Figure 1-1, occur when a business sells its stocks or bonds directly to savers, without going through any type of financial institution. The business delivers its securities to savers, who in turn give the firm the money it needs.

As shown in the middle section, indirect transfers may go through an **investment banking house** such as Merrill Lynch, which *underwrites* the issue. An underwriter serves as a middleman and facilitates the issuance of securities. The company sells its stocks or bonds to the investment bank, which in turn sells these same securities to savers. Because new securities are involved and the corporation receives the proceeds of the sale, this is a primary market transaction.

Transfers can also be made through a **financial intermediary** such as a bank or mutual fund. Here the intermediary obtains funds from savers in exchange for its own securities. The intermediary then uses this money to purchase and then hold businesses' securities. For example, a saver might give dollars to a bank, receiving from it a certificate of deposit, and then the bank might lend the money to a small business in the form of a mortgage loan. Thus, intermediaries literally create new forms of capital.

There are three important characteristics of the capital allocation process. First, new financial securities are created. Second, financial institutions are often

e-resource

See *Web Extension 1A* at the textbook's Web site for more discussion of the ways that financial intermediaries in the home mortgage industry create new financial securities.

involved. Third, allocation between providers and users of funds occurs in financial markets. The following sections discuss each of these characteristics.

1.5   Financial Securities and the Cost of Money

You can access current and historical interest rates and economic data as well as regional economic data for the states of Arkansas, Illinois, Indiana, Kentucky, Mississippi, Missouri, and Tennessee from the Federal Reserve Economic Data (FRED) site at **http://www.stls .frb.org/fred/**.

The variety of financial securities is limited only by human creativity and ingenuity, which isn't much of a limit. At the risk of oversimplification, we can classify most financial securities along two dimensions: (1) time until maturity and (2) debt, equity, or derivatives.

In general, short-term securities are those that mature in less than a year; these are called money market securities. Those that mature in more than a year are called capital market securities.

Financial securities are simply pieces of paper with contractual provisions that entitle their owners to specific rights and claims on specific cash flows or values. Debt instruments typically have specified payments and a specified maturity. For example, an IBM bond might promise to pay 10% interest for 30 years, at which time it makes a $1,000 principal payment. Equity instruments are a claim upon a residual value. For example, IBM's stockholders are entitled to IBM's cash flows after its bondholders, creditors, and other claimants have been satisfied. Notice that debt and equity represent claims upon the cash flows generated by real assets, such as the cash flows generated by IBM. In contrast, **derivatives** are securities whose values depend on, or are *derived* from, the values of some other traded assets. For example, futures and options are two important types of derivatives, and their values depend on the prices of other assets, such as IBM stock, Japanese yen, or pork bellies.

Most conventional securities are forms of debt or equity, and most derivatives are forms of options, futures, forward contracts, or swaps. However, there are hybrid securities for which these distinctions blur. For example, preferred stock has some features like debt and some like equity, while convertible debt has debt-like features and option-like features. We discuss many financial securities in detail later in the book, but Table 1-1 (on pages 16 and 17) provides a summary of the most important conventional financial securities. See *Web Extension 1B* for an overview of derivatives and see Chapter 23 for a more detailed discussion within the context of risk management.

e-resource

For an overview of derivatives, see **Web Extension 1B** at the textbook's Web site.

In a free economy, capital from providers with available funds is allocated through the price system to users that have a demand for funds. The interaction of the providers' supply and the users' demand determines the cost (or price) of money, which is the rate users pay to providers. For debt, we call this price the **interest rate.** For equity, we call this price the **cost of equity,** and it consists of the dividends and capital gains stockholders expect. Keep in mind that the cost of money from a user's perspective is a return from the provider's point of view, so we often use those terms interchangeably.

Notice in Table 1-1 that a financial security's rate of return generally increases as its maturity and risk increase. We will have much more to say about the relationships among an individual security's features, risk, and return later in the book, but there are some fundamental factors and economic conditions that affect all securities.

Fundamental Factors That Affect the Cost of Money

The four most fundamental factors affecting the cost of money are (1) **production opportunities,** (2) **time preferences for consumption,** (3) **risk,** and (4) **inflation.** By production opportunities, we mean the ability to turn capital into benefits. If a business raises capital, the benefits are determined by the expected rates of return on its production opportunities. If a student borrows to finance education, the benefits are higher expected future salaries (and, of course, the sheer joy of learning!). If a homeowner borrows, the benefits are the pleasure from living in his or her own home, plus any expected appreciation in the value of the home. Notice that the expected rates of return on these "production opportunities" put an upper limit on how much users can pay to providers.

Providers can use their current funds for consumption or saving. By saving, they give up consumption now in the expectation of having more consumption in the future. If providers have a strong preference for consumption now, then it takes high interest rates to induce them to trade current consumption for future consumption. Therefore, the time preference for consumption has a major impact on the cost of money. Notice that the time preference for consumption varies for different individuals, for different age groups, and for different cultures. For example, people in Japan have a lower time preference for consumption than those in the United States, which partially explains why Japanese families tend to save more than U.S. families even though interest rates are lower in Japan.

If the expected rate of return on an investment is risky, then providers require a higher expected return to induce them to take the extra risk, which drives up the cost of money. As you will see later in this book, the risk of a security is determined by market conditions and the security's particular features.

Inflation also leads to a higher cost of money. For example, suppose you earned 10% one year on your investment, but inflation caused prices to increase by 20%. This means you can't consume as much at the end of the year as when you originally invested your money. Obviously, if you had expected 20% inflation, you would have required a higher rate of return than 10%.

Economic Conditions and Policies That Affect the Cost of Money

Economic conditions and policies also affect the cost of money. These include: (1) Federal Reserve policy; (2) the federal budget deficit or surplus; (3) the level of business activity; and (4) international factors, including the foreign trade balance, the international business climate, and exchange rates.

The home page for the Board of Governors of the Federal Reserve System can be found at **http://www .federalreserve.gov.** You can access general information about the Federal Reserve, including press releases, speeches, and monetary policy.

Federal Reserve Policy As you probably learned in your economics courses, (1) the money supply has a major effect on both the level of economic activity and the inflation rate, and (2) in the United States, the Federal Reserve Board controls the money supply. If the Fed wants to stimulate the economy, it increases growth in the money supply. The initial effect would be to cause interest rates to decline. However, a larger money supply may also lead to an increase in expected inflation, which would push interest rates up. The reverse holds if the Fed tightens the money supply.

Table 1-1

Summary of Major Financial Securities

Instrument	Major Participants	Risk	Original Maturity	Rates of return on 4/25/06[a]
U.S. Treasury bills	Sold by U.S. Treasury	Default-free	91 days to 1 year	4.79%
Banker's acceptances	A firm's promise to pay, guaranteed by a bank	Low if strong bank guarantees	Up to 180 days	5.11%
Commercial paper	Issued by financially secure firms to large investors	Low default risk	Up to 270 days	4.97%
Negotiable certificates of deposit (CDs)	Issued by major banks to large investors	Depends on strength of issuer	Up to 1 year	5.07%
Money market mutual funds	Invest in short-term debt; held by individuals and businesses	Low degree of risk	No specific maturity (instant liquidity)	4.09%
Eurodollar market time deposits	Issued by banks outside United States	Depends on strength of issuer	Up to 1 year	5.10%
Consumer credit loans	Loans by banks/credit unions/finance companies	Risk is variable	Variable	Variable
Commercial loans	Loans by banks to corporations	Depends on borrower	Up to 7 years	Tied to prime rate (7.75%) or LIBOR (5.13%)[b]

[a]Data are from *The Wall Street Journal* (**http://online.wsj.com**) or the *Federal Reserve Statistical Release* (**http://www.federalreserve.gov/releases/H15/update**). Banker's acceptances assume a 3-month maturity. Money market rates are for the Merrill Lynch Ready Assets Trust. The corporate bond rate is for AAA-rated bonds.
[b]The prime rate is the rate U.S. banks charge to good customers. LIBOR (London Interbank Offered Rate) is the rate that U.K. banks charge one another.

Budget Deficits or Surpluses If the federal government spends more than it takes in from tax revenues, it runs a deficit, and that deficit must be covered either by borrowing or by printing money (increasing the money supply). If the government borrows, this added demand for funds pushes up interest rates. If it prints money, this increases expectations for future inflation, which also drives up interest rates. Thus, the larger the federal deficit, other things held constant, the higher the level of interest rates.

Business Activity Figure 1-2 shows business conditions, interest rates, and inflation. The shaded areas in the graph represent recessions. Consumer demand slows during a recession, keeping companies from increasing prices, which reduces price inflation. Companies also cut back on hiring, which reduces wage inflation. Less disposable income causes consumers to reduce their purchases of homes and automobiles, reducing consumer demand for loans. Companies reduce investments in new operations, which reduces their demand for funds. The cumulative effect is downward pressure on inflation and interest rates. The Federal Reserve is also active during recessions, trying to stimulate the economy.

> **Table 1-1**
>
> Summary of Major Financial Securities—*Continued*

Instrument	Major Participants	Risk	Original Maturity	Rates of return on 4/25/06[a]
U.S. Treasury notes and bonds	Issued by U.S. government	No default risk, but price falls if interest rates rise	2 to 30 years	5.04%
Mortgages	Loans secured by property	Risk is variable	Up to 30 years	6.15%
Municipal bonds	Issued by state and local governments to individuals and institutions	Riskier than U.S. government bonds, but exempt from most taxes	Up to 30 years	4.66%
Corporate bonds	Issued by corporations to individuals and institutions	Riskier than U.S. government debt; depends on strength of issuer	Up to 40 years[c]	5.93%
Leases	Similar to debt; firms lease assets rather than borrow	Risk similar to corporate bonds	Generally 3 to 20 years	Similar to bond yields
Preferred stocks	Issued by corporations to individuals and institutions	Riskier than corporate bonds	Unlimited	6% to 9%
Common stocks[d]	Issued by corporations to individuals and institutions	Riskier than preferred stocks	Unlimited	9% to 15%

[c]A few corporations have issued 100-year bonds; however, most have issued bonds with maturities less than 40 years.
[d]Common stocks are expected to provide a "return" in the form of dividends and capital gains rather than interest. Of course, if you buy a stock, your *actual* return may be considerably higher or lower than your *expected* return.

One way it does this is by purchasing Treasury bonds that are held by banks. This has two effects. Because they sell some of their bonds, the banks have more cash, which increases their supply of loanable funds, which in turn makes them willing to lend at lower interest rates. Also, the Fed's bond purchases drive up bond prices, which drives down bond interest rates. The combined effect of the Fed's activities is to reduce interest rates.

International Trade Deficits or Surpluses Businesses and individuals in the United States buy from and sell to people and firms in other countries. If we buy more than we sell (that is, if we import more than we export), we are said to be running a *foreign trade deficit*. When trade deficits occur, they must be financed, and the main source of financing is debt. In other words, if we import $200 billion of goods but export only $90 billion, we run a trade deficit of $110 billion, and we will probably borrow the $110 billion.[5] Therefore, the larger our trade deficit, the more we

---

[5]The deficit could also be financed by selling assets, including gold, corporate stocks, entire companies, and real estate. The United States has financed its massive trade deficits by all of these means in recent years, but the primary method has been by borrowing from foreigners.

Figure 1-2

Business Activity, Interest Rates, and Inflation

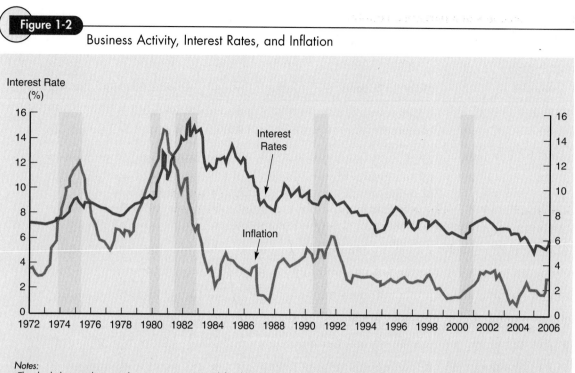

Notes:
[a]The shaded areas designate business recessions as defined by the National Bureau of Economic Research; see **http://www.nber.org/cycles.** Tick marks represent the beginning of the year.
[b]Interest rates are for AAA corporate bonds; see the St. Louis Federal Reserve Web site known as FRED: **http://research.stlouisfed.org /fred/.**
[c]Inflation is measured by the annual rate of change for the Consumer Price Index (CPI); see **http://research.stlouisfed.org/fred/.**

must borrow, and as we increase our borrowing, this drives up interest rates. Also, international investors are willing to hold U.S. debt if and only if the rate paid on this debt is competitive with interest rates in other countries. Therefore, if the Federal Reserve attempts to lower interest rates in the United States, causing our rates to fall below rates abroad (after adjustments for expected changes in the exchange rate), then international investors will sell U.S. bonds, which will depress bond prices and result in higher U.S. rates. Thus, if the trade deficit is large relative to the size of the overall economy, it will hinder the Fed's ability to combat a recession by lowering interest rates.

The United States has been running annual trade deficits since the mid-1970s, and the cumulative effect of these deficits is that the United States has become the largest debtor nation of all time. As a result, our interest rates are very much influenced by interest rates in other countries around the world: Higher rates abroad lead to higher U.S. rates, and vice versa. Because of all this, U.S. corporate treasurers—and anyone else who is affected by interest rates—must keep up with developments in the world economy.

International Country Risk International risk factors may increase the cost of money that is invested abroad. **Country risk** is the risk that arises from investing or doing business in a particular country. This risk depends on the country's economic, political, and social environment. Countries with stable economic, social, political, and regulatory systems provide a safer climate for investment, and therefore have less country risk than less stable nations. Examples of country risk include the risk associated with changes in tax rates, regulations, currency conversion, and exchange rates. Country risk also includes the risk that property will be expropriated without adequate compensation, as well as new host country stipulations about local production, sourcing or hiring practices, and damage or destruction of facilities due to internal strife.

Transparency International provides a ranking of countries based on their levels of perceived corruption. See **http://www .transparency.org/ policy_research/surveys_ indices/cpi/2005.** The U.S. Department of State provides thorough descriptions of countries' business climates at **http://www.state.gov/ e/eb/ifd/2005/.**

International Exchange Rate Risk International securities usually are denominated in a currency other than the dollar, which means that the value of your investment depends on what happens to exchange rates. This is known as **exchange rate risk**. For example, if a U.S. investor purchases a Japanese bond, interest will probably be paid in Japanese yen, which must then be converted into dollars if the investor wants to spend his or her money in the United States. If the yen weakens relative to the dollar, then it will buy fewer dollars; hence the investor will receive fewer dollars when it comes time to convert. Alternatively, if the yen strengthens relative to the dollar, the investor will earn higher dollar returns. It therefore follows that the effective rate of return on a foreign investment will depend on both the performance of the foreign security and on what happens to exchange rates over the life of the investment. We will discuss exchange rates in detail in Chapter 26.

SELF-TEST

What four fundamental factors affect the cost of money?

Name some economic conditions that influence interest rates, and explain their effects.

1.6 Financial Institutions

Direct funds transfers are more common among individuals and small businesses, and in economies where financial markets and institutions are less developed. While businesses in more developed economies do occasionally rely on direct transfers, they generally find it more efficient to enlist the services of one or more financial institutions when it comes time to raise capital. Here are the major categories of financial institutions:

1. **Investment banking houses** such as Merrill Lynch, Morgan Stanley, Goldman Sachs, or Credit Suisse Group provide a number of services to both investors and companies planning to raise capital. Such organizations (1) help corporations design securities with features that are currently attractive to investors, (2) then buy these securities from the corporation, and (3) resell them to savers. Although the securities are sold twice, this process is really one primary market transaction, with the investment banker acting as a facilitator to help transfer capital from savers to businesses.

2. **Commercial banks,** such as Bank of America, Wells Fargo, Wachovia, and JPMorgan Chase, are the traditional "department stores of finance" because

they serve a variety of savers and borrowers. Historically, commercial banks were the major institutions that handled checking accounts and through which the Federal Reserve System expanded or contracted the money supply. Today, however, several other institutions also provide checking services and significantly influence the money supply. Conversely, commercial banks are providing an ever-widening range of services, including stock brokerage services and insurance.

3. **Financial services corporations** are large conglomerates that combine many different financial institutions within a single corporation. Examples of financial services corporations, most of which started in one area but have now diversified to cover most of the financial spectrum, include Citigroup, American Express, Fidelity, and Prudential.

4. **Savings and loan associations (S&Ls),** which have traditionally served individual savers and residential and commercial mortgage borrowers, take the funds of many small savers and then lend this money to home buyers and other types of borrowers. Because the savers obtain a degree of liquidity that would be absent if they made the mortgage loans directly, perhaps the most significant economic function of the S&Ls is to "create liquidity" that would otherwise be lacking. Also, the S&Ls have more expertise in analyzing credit, setting up loans, and making collections than individual savers, so S&Ls can reduce the costs of processing loans, thereby increasing the availability of real estate loans. Finally, the S&Ls hold large, diversified portfolios of loans and other assets and thus spread risks in a manner that would be impossible if small savers were making mortgage loans directly. Because of these factors, savers benefit by being able to invest in more liquid, better managed, and less risky assets, whereas borrowers benefit by being able to obtain more capital, and at a lower cost, than would otherwise be possible.

5. **Mutual savings banks** are similar to S&Ls, but they operate primarily in the northeastern states.

6. **Credit unions** are cooperative associations whose members are supposed to have a common bond, such as being employees of the same firm. Members' savings are loaned only to other members, generally for auto purchases, home improvement loans, and home mortgages. Credit unions are often the cheapest source of funds available to individual borrowers.

7. **Life insurance companies** take savings in the form of premiums; invest these funds in stocks, bonds, real estate, and mortgages; and make payments to beneficiaries. Life insurance companies also offer a variety of tax-deferred savings plans designed to provide retirement benefits.

8. **Mutual funds** are corporations that accept money from savers and then use these funds to buy financial instruments. These organizations pool funds and thus reduce risks by diversification. They also achieve economies of scale in analyzing securities, managing portfolios, and buying and selling securities. Different funds are designed to meet the objectives of different types of savers. Hence, there are bond funds for those who desire safety, stock funds for savers who are willing to accept significant risks in the hope of higher returns, and still other funds that are used as interest-bearing checking accounts (the **money market funds**). There are literally thousands of different mutual funds with dozens of different goals and purposes. Some funds are actively managed, with their managers trying to find undervalued securities, while other funds are passively managed and simply try to minimize expenses by replicating a particular market index. Most traditional mutual funds allow investors to redeem their share of the fund only at the close of business. A new

type of mutual fund, the **exchange traded fund (ETF)**, allows investors to sell their share at any time during normal trading hours. ETFs usually have very low management expenses and are rapidly gaining in popularity.

9. Traditional **pension funds** are retirement plans funded by corporations or government agencies for their workers and usually administered by the trust departments of commercial banks or by life insurance companies. Pension funds invest primarily in bonds, stocks, mortgages, and real estate. Many companies now offer self-directed retirement plans, such as 401(k) plans, as an addition to or substitute for traditional pension plans. In traditional plans, the plan administrators determine how to invest the funds; in self-directed plans, all individual participants must decide how to invest their own funds.

10. **Hedge funds** raise money from investors and engage in a variety of investment activities. Unlike typical mutual funds, which can have thousands of investors, hedge funds are limited to a relatively small number of high-wealth individuals or institutional investors. As such, hedge funds are much less regulated than mutual funds. The first hedge funds literally tried to hedge their bets by forming portfolios of conventional securities and derivatives in such a way that they limited their potential losses without sacrificing too much of their potential gains. Most hedge funds also levered their positions by borrowing heavily. During the early and mid-1990s many hedge funds had spectacular rates of return. This success attracted more investors and more hedge funds were created. Much of the low-hanging fruit had already been picked, so many hedge funds began pursuing much riskier (and unhedged) strategies. Perhaps not surprisingly (at least in retrospect!), some funds have produced spectacular losses. For example, many hedge fund investors suffered large losses in 1998 when the Russian economy collapsed. That same year, the Federal Reserve had to step in to help rescue Long Term Capital Management, a high-profile hedge fund whose managers included several well-respected practitioners as well as two Nobel Prize–winning professors who were experts in investment theory.[6]

With the notable exception of hedge funds, financial institutions have been heavily regulated to ensure the safety of these institutions and thus to protect investors. Historically, many of these regulations—which have included a prohibition on nationwide branch banking, restrictions on the types of assets the institutions could buy, ceilings on the interest rates they could pay, and limitations on the types of services they could provide—tended to impede the free flow of capital and thus hurt the efficiency of our capital markets. Recognizing this fact, policymakers took several steps during the 1980s and 1990s to deregulate financial services companies. For example, the barriers that restricted banks from expanding nationwide were eliminated. Likewise, regulations that once forced a strict separation of commercial and investment banking have been relaxed.

The result of the ongoing regulatory changes has been a blurring of the distinctions between the different types of institutions. Indeed, the trend in the United States today is toward huge financial services corporations, which own banks, S&Ls, investment banking houses, insurance companies, pension plan operations, and mutual funds, and which have branches across the country and around the world. For example, Citigroup combines one of the world's largest

---

[6]See Franklin Edwards, "Hedge Funds and the Collapse of Long Term Capital Management," *Journal of Economic Perspectives*, Spring 1999, 189–210 for a thoughtful review of the implications of Long Term Capital Management's collapse.

commercial banks (Citibank), a huge insurance company (Travelers), and a major investment bank (Smith Barney), along with numerous other subsidiaries that operate throughout the world. Citigroup's structure is similar to that of major institutions in Europe, Japan, and elsewhere around the globe.

Among the world's largest world banking companies, only one (Citigroup) is based in the United States. While U.S. banks have grown dramatically as a result of recent mergers, they are still relatively small by global standards.

SELF-TEST

What is the difference between a pure commercial bank and a pure investment bank?

List the major types of financial institutions and briefly describe the primary function of each.

What are some important differences between mutual and hedge funds? How are they similar?

1.7 Types of Financial Markets

Financial markets bring together people and organizations needing money with those having surplus funds. There are many different financial markets in a developed economy. Each market deals with a somewhat different type of instrument, customer, or geographic location. Here are some of the major types of markets:

1. **Physical asset markets** (also called "tangible" or "real" asset markets) are those for such products as wheat, autos, real estate, computers, and machinery. **Financial asset markets**, on the other hand, deal with stocks, bonds, notes, mortgages, and other **financial instruments.**

2. **Spot markets** and **futures markets** are markets where assets are being bought or sold for "on-the-spot" delivery (literally, within a few days) or for delivery at some future date, such as 6 months or a year into the future.

3. **Money markets** are the markets for short-term, highly liquid debt securities. **Capital markets** are the markets for intermediate- or long-term debt and corporate stocks. The New York Stock Exchange is an example of a capital market. When describing debt markets, "short term" generally means less than 1 year, "intermediate term" means 1 to 5 years, and "long term" means more than 5 years.

4. **Mortgage markets** deal with loans on residential, agricultural, commercial, and industrial real estate, while **consumer credit markets** involve loans for autos, appliances, education, vacations, and so on.

5. **World, national, regional**, and **local markets** also exist. Thus, depending on an organization's size and scope of operations, it may be able to borrow all around the world, or it may be confined to a strictly local, even neighborhood, market.

6. **Primary markets** are the markets in which corporations raise new capital. If Microsoft were to sell a new issue of common stock to raise capital, this would be a primary market transaction. The corporation selling the newly created stock receives the proceeds from the sale in a primary market transaction. The **initial public offering (IPO) market** is a subset of the primary market. Here firms "go public" by offering shares to the public for the first time. Microsoft had its IPO in 1986. Previously, Bill Gates and other insiders owned all the shares. In many IPOs, the insiders sell some of their shares plus the company sells newly created shares to raise additional capital. **Secondary markets** are markets in which existing, already outstanding securities are traded among

investors. Thus, if you decided to buy 1,000 shares of AT&T stock, the purchase would occur in the secondary market. The New York Stock Exchange is a secondary market, since it deals in outstanding, as opposed to newly issued, stocks. Secondary markets also exist for bonds, mortgages, and other financial assets. The corporation whose securities are being traded is not involved in a secondary market transaction and, thus, does not receive any funds from such a sale.

7. **Private markets,** where transactions are worked out directly between two parties, are differentiated from **public markets,** where standardized contracts are traded on organized exchanges. Bank loans and private placements of debt with insurance companies are examples of private market transactions. Since these transactions are private, they may be structured in any manner that appeals to the two parties. By contrast, securities that are issued in public markets (for example, common stock and corporate bonds) are ultimately held by a large number of individuals. Public securities must have fairly standardized contractual features, to appeal to a broad range of investors and also because public investors cannot afford the time to study unique, nonstandardized contracts. Private market securities are, therefore, more tailor-made but less liquid, whereas public market securities are more liquid but subject to greater standardization.

The distinctions among markets are often blurred. For example, it makes little difference if a firm borrows for 11, 12, or 13 months, hence, whether such a transaction is a "money" or "capital" market transaction. You should recognize the big differences among types of markets, but don't get hung up trying to distinguish them at the boundaries.

SELF-TEST —————————————————————————————————————
Distinguish between (1) physical asset markets and financial asset markets, (2) spot and futures markets, (3) money and capital markets, (4) primary and secondary markets, and (5) private and public markets.

1.8 Trading Procedures in Financial Markets

The vast majority of trading occurs in the secondary markets. Although there are many secondary markets for a wide variety of securities, we can classify their trading procedures along two dimensions: location and method of matching orders.

A secondary market can be either a **physical location exchange** or a **computer/telephone network.** For example, the New York Stock Exchange, the American Stock Exchange (AMEX), the Chicago Board of Trade (the CBOT trades futures and options), and the Tokyo Stock Exchange are all physical location exchanges. In other words, the traders actually meet and trade in a specific part of a specific building. In contrast, Nasdaq, which trades U.S. stocks, is a network of linked computers. Other examples are the markets for U.S. Treasury bonds and foreign exchange, which are conducted via telephone and/or computer networks. In these electronic markets, the traders never see one another.

The second dimension is the way orders from sellers and buyers are matched. This can occur through an open outcry **auction** system, through dealers, or by automated order matching. An example of an outcry auction is the CBOT, where traders actually meet in a pit and sellers and buyers communicate with one another through shouts and hand signals.

In a **dealer market,** there are "market makers" who keep an inventory of the stock (or other financial instrument) in much the same way that any merchant keeps an inventory. These dealers list bid and asked quotes, which are the prices at which they are willing to buy or sell. Computerized quotation systems keep track of all bid and asked prices, but they don't actually match buyers and sellers. Instead, traders must contact a specific dealer to complete the transaction. Nasdaq (U.S. stocks) is one such market, as are the London SEAQ (U.K. stocks) and the Neuer Market (stocks of small German companies).

The third method of matching orders is through an **electronic communications network (ECN).** Participants in an ECN post their orders to buy and sell, and the ECN automatically matches orders. For example, someone might place an order to buy 1,000 shares of IBM stock (this is called a "market order" since it is to buy the stock at the current market price). Suppose another participant had placed an order to sell 1,000 shares of IBM at a price of $91 per share, and this was the lowest price of any "sell" order. The ECN would automatically match these two orders, execute the trade, and notify both participants that the trade has occurred. Participants can also post "limit orders," which might state that the participant is willing to buy 1,000 shares of IBM at $90 per share if the price falls that low during the next two hours. In other words, there are limits on the price and/or the duration of the order. The ECN will execute the limit order if the conditions are met, that is, if someone offers to sell IBM at a price of $90 or less during the next two hours. Two of the largest ECNs for trading U.S. stocks are Instinet (now owned by Nasdaq) and Archipelago (now owned by the NYSE). Other large ECNs include Eurex, a Swiss-German ECN that trades futures contracts, and SETS, a U.K. ECN that trades stocks.

SELF-TEST

What are the major differences between physical location exchanges and computer/telephone networks?
What are the differences among open outcry auctions, dealer markets, and ECNs?

1.9   Types of Stock Market Transactions

e-resource

For more on investment banking, see **Web Extension 1C** at the textbook's Web site, or see Chapter 19.

Because the primary objective of financial management is to maximize the firm's stock price, knowledge of the stock market is important to anyone involved in managing a business. We can classify stock market transactions into three distinct types.

Whenever stock is offered to the public for the first time, the company is said to be going public. This primary market transaction is called the initial public offering (IPO) market. If a company decides to sell (or issue) additional shares to raise new equity capital, this is still a primary market, but it is called a **seasoned equity offering.** Trading in the outstanding shares of established, publicly owned companies is a secondary market transaction. For example, if the owner of 100 shares of publicly held stock sells his or her stock, the trade is said to have occurred in the secondary market. Thus, the market for outstanding shares, or used shares, is the secondary market. The company receives no new money when sales occur in this market.

Following is a brief description of the recent IPO market; a more complete discussion of IPOs is in Chapter 19. Out of the 1,279 global IPOs in 2005, there were 237 U.S. IPOs that brought in a total of $36.1 billion. Although some U.S. IPOs were large, such as the $1.59 billion raised by Huntsman, no U.S. offerings were

Rational Exuberance

The Daily Planet Ltd. made history on May 1, 2003, by becoming the world's first publicly traded brothel. Technically, the Daily Planet only owns property, including a hotel with 18 rooms, each with a different theme, but all having multiperson showers and very large beds. The Daily Planet charges guests a room fee of A$115 per hour; clients also pay a fee of A$115 directly to individual members of the staff.

The IPO was for 7.5 million shares of stock, initially priced at A$0.50. However, the price ended the first day of trading at A$1.09, for a first-day return of 118%. The price closed the second day at A$1.56, for a 2-day return of 212%, one of the largest returns since the days of the dot-com boom. Institutional investors normally buy about 60% to 70% of IPO stock, but they didn't participate in this offering. The Daily Planet plans to use some of the proceeds to pay down debt and the rest for expansion, possibly through franchising.

The company is named after the fictitious newspaper where comic strip character Clark Kent was a reporter. All receptionists have "Lois Lane" nametags, and there is a telephone box in the lobby. What would Superman think!

in the global top ten largest (the biggest was the China Construction Bank Corp.'s IPO of $9.2 billion). In the United States the average first-day return was 9%, although some firms had spectacular first-day price run-ups. For example, Baidu.com was up 327.8% on its first day of trading, and Citi Trends gained 204.9% for the year. However, not all companies fared so well—Nuvim was down 88% its first day, and Refco lost a total of 98% for the year. Even if you are able to identify a "hot" issue, it is often difficult to purchase shares in the initial offering. These deals are generally oversubscribed, which means that the demand for shares at the offering price exceeds the number of shares issued. In such instances, investment bankers favor large institutional investors (who are their best customers), and small investors find it hard, if not impossible, to get in on the ground floor. They can buy the stock in the aftermarket, but evidence suggests that if you do not get in on the ground floor, the average IPO underperforms the overall market over the long run.[7]

For updates on IPO activity, see **http://www.ipomonitor.com** or **http://www.hoovers.com/global/ipoc/index.xhtml**. *The Wall Street Journal* also provides IPO data in its Year End Review of Markets & Finance at **http://online.wsj.com**.

Before you conclude that it isn't fair to let only the best customers have the stock in an initial offering, think about what it takes to become a best customer. Best customers are usually investors who have done lots of business in the past with the investment banking firm's brokerage department. In other words, they have paid large sums as commissions in the past, and they are expected to continue doing so in the future. As is so often true, there is no free lunch—most of the investors who get in on the ground floor of an IPO have in fact paid for this privilege.

SELF-TEST

Differentiate between an IPO, a seasoned equity offering, and a secondary transaction. Why is it often difficult for the average investor to make money during an IPO?

1.10 The Secondary Stock Markets

The two leading U.S. stock markets today are the New York Stock Exchange and the Nasdaq stock market.

---

[7]See Jay R. Ritter, "The Long-Run Performance of Initial Public Offerings," *Journal of Finance*, March 1991, 3–27.

You can access the home pages of the major U.S. stock markets at **http://www.nyse.com** or **http://www.nasdaq.com**. These sites provide background information as well as the opportunity to obtain individual stock quotes.

e-resource

For more on stock markets, see **Web Extension 1C** at the textbook's Web site.

The New York Stock Exchange

Before March of 2006, the **New York Stock Exchange (NYSE)** was a privately held firm owned by its members. It then merged with Archipelago, a publicly traded company that was one of the world's largest ECNs. NYSE members received approximately 70% of the shares in the combined firm, with Archipelago shareholders receiving the remainder. The combined firm, which also owns the Pacific Exchange, is now known as The NYSE Group, Inc. and is traded publicly under the ticker symbol NYX. It continues to operate the New York Stock Exchange (a physical location exchange located on Wall Street) and Arca (composed of the Pacific Exchange and the ECN formerly known as Archipelago).

The NYSE still has over 300 member organizations, which are corporations, partnerships, or LLCs. Membership prices were as high as $3.15 million in 2005. Member organizations are registered broker–dealers but may not conduct trading on the floor of the exchange unless they also hold a trading license issued by the NYSE. Before going public, the equivalent to a trading license was called a seat (although there is very little sitting on the floor of the exchange) and sold for up to $4 million in 2005. Trading licenses are now leased by member organizations from the exchange, with an annual fee of $54,219 in 2006. In early 2006, there were 1,274 licenses that had been leased.

Most of the larger investment banking houses operate *brokerage departments* and are members of the NYSE with leased trading rights. The NYSE is open on all normal working days, with the members meeting in large rooms equipped with electronic equipment that enables each member to communicate with his or her firm's offices throughout the country. For example, Merrill Lynch (the largest brokerage firm) might receive an order in its Atlanta office from a customer who wants to buy shares of AT&T stock. Simultaneously, Morgan Stanley's Denver office might receive an order from a customer wishing to sell shares of AT&T. Each broker communicates electronically with the firm's representative on the NYSE. Other brokers throughout the country are also communicating with their own exchange members. The exchange members with *sell orders* offer the shares for sale, and they are bid for by the members with *buy orders*. Thus, the NYSE operates as an *auction market*.[8]

---

[8]The NYSE is actually a modified auction market, wherein people (through their brokers) bid for stocks. Originally—about 200 years ago—brokers would literally shout, "I have 100 shares of Erie for sale; how much am I offered?" and then sell to the highest bidder. If a broker had a buy order, he or she would shout, "I want to buy 100 shares of Erie; who'll sell at the best price?" The same general situation still exists, although the exchanges now have members known as *specialists* who facilitate the trading process by keeping an inventory of shares of the stocks in which they specialize. If a buy order comes in at a time when no sell order arrives, the specialist will sell off some inventory. Similarly, if a sell order comes in, the specialist will buy and add to inventory. The specialist sets a *bid price* (the price the specialist will pay for the stock) and an *asked price* (the price at which shares will be sold out of inventory). The bid and asked prices are set at levels designed to keep the inventory in balance. If many buy orders start coming in because of favorable developments or sell orders come in because of unfavorable events, the specialist will raise or lower prices to keep supply and demand in balance. Bid prices are somewhat lower than asked prices, with the difference, or *spread*, representing the specialist's profit margin.

Special facilities are available to help institutional investors such as mutual funds or pension funds sell large blocks of stock without depressing their prices. In essence, brokerage houses that cater to institutional clients will purchase blocks (defined as 10,000 or more shares) and then resell the stock to other institutions or individuals. Also, when a firm has a major announcement that is likely to cause its stock price to change sharply, it will ask the exchanges to halt trading in its stock until the announcement has been made and digested by investors.

e-resource

See **Web Extension 1C** at the textbook's Web site for more on specialists and trading off the exchange floor.

Measuring the Market

A *stock index* is designed to show the performance of the stock market. Here are some leading indexes:

Dow Jones Industrial Average

Unveiled in 1896 by Charles H. Dow, the Dow Jones Industrial Average (DJIA) provided a benchmark for comparing individual stocks with the overall market and for comparing the market with other economic indicators. The industrial average began with just 10 stocks, was expanded in 1916 to 20 stocks, and then to 30 in 1928. Also, in 1928 *The Wall Street Journal* editors began adjusting it for stock splits and making substitutions. Today, the DJIA still includes 30 companies. They represent almost a fifth of the market value of all U.S. stocks, and all are both leading companies in their industries and widely held by individual and institutional investors. See **http://www.dowjones.com** for more information.

S&P 500 Index

Created in 1926, the S&P 500 Index is widely regarded as the standard for measuring large-cap U.S. stock market performance. The stocks in the S&P 500 are selected by the Standard & Poor's Index Committee for being the leading companies in the leading industries and for accurately reflecting the U.S. stock market. It is value weighted, so the largest companies (in terms of value) have the greatest influence. The S&P 500 Index is used as a comparison benchmark by 97% of all U.S. money managers and pension plan sponsors, and approximately $700 billion is managed so as to obtain the same performance as this index (that is, in indexed funds). See **http://www2.standardandpoors.com** for more information.

Nasdaq Composite Index

The Nasdaq Composite Index measures the performance of all common stocks listed on the Nasdaq stock market. Currently, it includes more than 5,000 companies, and because many of the technology-sector companies are traded on the computer-based Nasdaq exchange, this index is generally regarded as an economic indicator of the high-tech industry. Microsoft, Intel, and Cisco Systems are the three largest Nasdaq companies, and they comprise a high percentage of the index's value-weighted market capitalization. For this reason, substantial movements in the same direction by these three companies can move the entire index. See **http://www.nasdaq.com** for more information.

NYSE Composite Index

The NYSE Composite Index measures the performance of all common stocks listed on the NYSE. It is a value-weighted index composed of just over 2,000 stocks representing 77% of the total market capitalization of all publicly traded companies in the United States. See **http://www.nyse.com** for more information.

Trading the Market

Through the use of exchange traded funds (ETFs), it is now possible to buy and sell the market in much the same way as an individual stock. For example, the Standard & Poor's depository receipt (SPDR) is a share of a fund composed of the stocks in the S&P 500. SPDRs trade during regular market hours, making it possible to buy or sell the S&P 500 any time during the day. There are hundreds of other ETFs, including ones for the Nasdaq and Dow Jones Industrial Average.

Recent Performance

Go to the Web site **http://finance.yahoo.com/**. Enter the symbol for any of the indexes (^DJI for the Dow Jones, ^SPC for the S&P 500, ^IXIC for the Nasdaq, and ^NYA for the NYSE) and click GO. This will bring up the current value of the index, shown in a table. Click Basic Chart in the panel on the left, and it will bring up a chart showing the historical performance of the index. Directly above the chart is a series of buttons that allows you to choose the number of years and to plot the relative performance of several indexes on the same chart. You can even download the historical data in spreadsheet form by clicking Historical Prices in the left panel.

The Nasdaq Stock Market

The **National Association of Securities Dealers (NASD)** is a self-regulatory body that licenses brokers and oversees trading practices. The computerized network used by the NASD is known as the NASD Automated Quotation System, or Nasdaq. Nasdaq started as just a quotation system, but it has grown to become an organized securities market with its own listing requirements. Nasdaq lists about 5,000 stocks, although not all trade through the same Nasdaq system. For example, the Nasdaq National Market lists the larger Nasdaq stocks, such as Microsoft and Intel, while the Nasdaq SmallCap Market lists smaller companies with the potential for high growth. Nasdaq also operates the Nasdaq OTC Bulletin Board, which lists quotes for stock that is registered with the Securities Exchange Commission (SEC) but that is not listed on any exchange, usually because the company is too small or too unprofitable.[9] Finally, Nasdaq operates the Pink Sheets, which provide quotes on companies that are not registered with the SEC.

"Liquidity" is the ability to trade quickly at a net price (that is, after any commissions) that is very close to the security's recent market value. In a dealer market, such as Nasdaq, a stock's liquidity depends on the number and quality of the dealers who make a market in the stock. Nasdaq has more than 400 dealers, most making markets in a large number of stocks. The typical stock has about 10 market makers, but some stocks have more than 50 market makers. Obviously, there are more market makers, and liquidity, for the Nasdaq National Market than for the SmallCap Market. There is very little liquidity for stocks on the OTC Bulletin Board or the Pink Sheets.

Competition in the Secondary Markets

There is intense competition between the NYSE and Nasdaq. Since most of the largest companies trade on the NYSE, the market capitalization of NYSE-traded stocks is much higher than for stocks traded on Nasdaq (about $13.3 trillion compared with $3.6 trillion in 2005). However, reported volume (number of shares traded) is often larger on Nasdaq, and more companies are listed on Nasdaq.[10] For comparison, the market capitalizations for global exchanges are $4.6 trillion in Tokyo, $3.1 trillion in London, and $1.2 trillion in Germany.

Interestingly, many high-tech companies such as Microsoft and Intel have remained on Nasdaq even though they easily meet the listing requirements of the NYSE. At the same time, however, other high-tech companies such as Gateway 2000, America Online, and Iomega have left Nasdaq for the NYSE. Despite these defections, Nasdaq's growth over the past decade has been impressive. In an effort to become even more competitive with the NYSE and with international markets, Nasdaq acquired one of the leading stock ECNs, Instinet, in 2005. In April of 2006, Nasdaq was finalizing its plans to become a publicly traded company. It made an offer to acquire the London Stock Exchange (LSE), withdrew the

---

[9]OTC stands for over-the-counter. Before Nasdaq, the quickest way to trade a stock that was not listed at a physical location exchange was to find a brokerage firm that kept shares of that stock in inventory. The stock certificates were actually kept in a safe and were literally passed over the counter when bought or sold. Nowadays the certificates for almost all listed stocks and bonds in the United States are stored in a vault beneath Manhattan, operated by the Depository Trust and Clearing Corporation (DTCC). Most brokerage firms have an account with the DTCC, and most investors leave their stocks with their brokers. Thus, when stocks are sold, the DTCC simply adjusts the accounts of the brokerage firms that are involved, and no stock certificates are actually moved.

[10]One transaction on Nasdaq generally shows up as two separate trades (the buy and the sell). This "double counting" makes it difficult to compare the volume between stock markets.

Figure 1-3

Relative Changes in Value for the NYSE and Nasdaq Stock Indexes

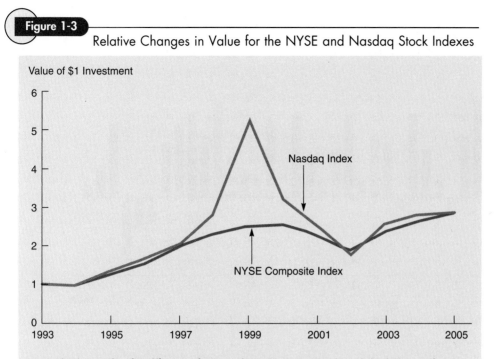

Notes: The data are from **http://finance.yahoo.com**. The NYSE Composite Index includes the impact of gains due to dividends, while the Nasdaq Index does not. However, most Nasdaq stocks pay little or no dividends, so the relative changes in value of the two indexes are reasonably comparable.

offer, but retained the right to make a subsequent offer and was busily acquiring additional shares of stock in the LSE. No matter how the LSE situation is resolved, one thing is clear—there will be a continued consolidation in the securities exchange industry, with a blurring of the lines between physical location exchanges and electronic exchanges.

Figure 1-3 shows the relative gains in value made by composite stock indexes of the two markets during the past 13 years. Although an investor would have ended up with roughly the same wealth, the Nasdaq Composite Index was much more affected by the technology boom and bust around the turn of the century.

SELF-TEST

What are some major differences between the NYSE and the Nasdaq stock market?

1.11 Stock Market Returns

Figure 1-3 shows the cumulative changes in wealth due to investing in the stock market, but it doesn't highlight the year-to-year risk. Figure 1-4 shows the annual returns of the S&P 500 Index. Notice that stocks have had positive returns in most years, but there have been several years with large losses. Stocks lost a total of over 40% of their value during the 1973–1974 period, and again during 2000–2002.

Figure 1-4

S&P 500 Index, Total Returns: Dividend Yield + Capital Gain or Loss

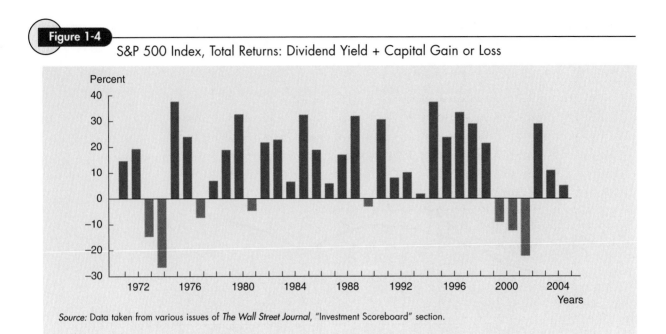

Source: Data taken from various issues of *The Wall Street Journal*, "Investment Scoreboard" section.

We will examine risk in more detail later in the book, but a cursory glance at Figure 1-4 shows just how risky stocks can be.

The U.S. stock market amounts to only about 40% of the world stock market, and this is prompting many U.S. investors to also hold foreign stocks. Analysts have long touted the benefits of investing overseas, arguing that foreign stocks improve diversification and provide good growth opportunities. Table 1-2 shows how stocks in different countries performed in 2005. The numbers on the right indicate how stocks in each country performed in terms of its local currency, while the numbers on the left show how the country's stocks performed in terms of the U.S. dollar. For example, in 2005 Swiss stocks rose by 33.18%, but the Swiss franc fell by about 18.27% versus the U.S. dollar. Therefore, if U.S. investors had bought Swiss stocks, they would have made 33.18% in Swiss franc terms, but those Swiss francs would have bought 18.27% fewer U.S. dollars, so the effective return in dollars would have been 14.91%. As this example shows, the results of foreign investments depend in part on what happens to the exchange rate. Indeed, when you invest overseas, you are making two bets: (1) that foreign stocks will increase in their local markets and (2) that the currencies in which you will be paid will rise relative to the dollar.

Even though foreign stocks have exchange rate risk, this by no means suggests that investors should avoid foreign stocks. Foreign investments improve diversification, and it is inevitable that there will be years when foreign stocks outperform domestic stocks. When this occurs, U.S. investors will be glad they put some of their money in overseas markets.

SELF-TEST

Explain how exchange rates affect the rate of return on international investments.

Table 1-2

2005 Performance of Selected Dow Jones Global Stock Indexes

Country	U.S. Dollars	Local Currency	Country	U.S. Dollars	Local Currency
Latvia	91.99%	120.95%	France	9.11%	25.73%
South Korea	58.41	54.69	Indonesia	8.93	15.47
Cyprus	53.70	75.18	Germany	8.46	24.99
Brazil	47.98	30.12	Sweden	8.43	29.86
Mexico	39.97	33.57	Hong Kong	6.94	6.68
Canada	25.48	22.34	U.K.	4.97	17.39
Japan	25.32	44.35	United States	4.49	4.49
South Africa	23.48	39.01	Taiwan	3.93	7.71
Austria	20.89	39.31	Belgium	3.33	19.08
Hungary	15.36	36.62	Spain	3.19	18.92
Switzerland	14.91	33.18	Malaysia	−1.02	−1.56
Australia	11.33	18.97	Italy	−1.96	12.98
Singapore	11.12	13.19	New Zealand	−3.32	2.54
Chile	10.88	2.17	Portugal	−4.38	10.18
Netherlands	10.82	27.70	Venezuela	−19.33	−19.09

Source: Adapted from *The Wall Street Journal Online,* **http://online.wsj.com/documents/ye05-djglobalindexes.htm**.

1.12   A Preview of What Is Ahead

A manager's primary job is to increase the fundamental value of his or her company. Equation 1-1 shows that a firm's fundamental value is the present value of its expected free cash flows when discounted at the weighted average cost of capital. This single valuation equation provides a good preview for the rest of the book. Chapter 2 shows how to determine the value today of a future cash flow, a topic called the time value of money. Chapter 3 explains financial statements and how to calculate free cash flows, along with taxation and its role in valuation. Chapter 4 shows how to use financial statements to identify a firm's strengths and risks. In Part 2, Chapters 5–8 discuss bonds, the risk–return relationship, and stocks. Chapter 9 discusses financial options, which often play an important role in managerial compensation, agency costs, and valuation. In Part 3, Chapter 10 ties these concepts together in estimating the weighted average cost of capital. Chapters 11–13 apply the valuation concepts of Equation 1-1 to individual projects, including extensive risk analysis and real options.

Part 4 explicitly addresses corporate valuation. Chapter 14 develops techniques for forecasting future financial statements and free cash flows. Chapter 15 directly uses the concepts in Equation 1-1 to determine a corporation's value, including the value of its stock. Chapter 15 also discusses corporate governance, which has a direct effect on how much value companies create for their shareholders.

Part 5 discusses basic corporate financing decisions, including capital structure choices (decision of how much debt versus equity the firm should use) and distribution policy (how much free cash flow should be paid out to shareholders, either as dividends or share repurchases). In Part 6, we address special topics that draw on the earlier chapters, including working capital management, risk management, bankruptcies, mergers, and multinational financial management.

e-Resources

The textbook's Web site contains several types of files:

1. It contains *Excel* files, called Tool Kits, that provide well-documented models for almost all of the text's calculations. Not only will these Tool Kits help you with this finance course, but they will serve as tool kits for you in other courses and in your career.
2. There are problems at the end of the chapters that require spreadsheets, and the Web site contains the models you will need to begin work on these problems.

e-resource

When we think it might be helpful for you to look at one of the Web site's files, we'll show an icon in the margin like the one that is shown here.

Other resources are also on the Web site, including Cyberproblems and problems that use the ThomsonONE—Business School Edition Web site. The textbook's Web site also contains an electronic library which contains Adobe PDF files for "extensions" to many chapters that cover additional useful material related to the chapter. This electronic library also has several additional complete chapters, as shown in the table of contents. In addition, the CengageNOW Web site also has a Learning Path that allows you to assess your level of understanding and to identify specific material that will help you address any areas of weakness. Your instructor may also choose to use the homework/quizzing feature at CengageNOW.

Summary

This chapter provided an overview of financial management and the financial environment. It explained the fundamental determinants of a firm's value and provided an overview of financial securities, financial institutions, and financial markets, with an emphasis on stock markets. The key concepts covered are listed below:

- The three main forms of business organization are the **proprietorship,** the **partnership,** and the **corporation.**
- Although each form of organization offers advantages and disadvantages, **corporations conduct much more business than the other forms.**
- The primary objective of management should be to **maximize stockholders' wealth,** and this means **maximizing the company's fundamental,** or

intrinsic, stock price. Legal actions that maximize stock prices usually increase social welfare.

- Firms increase cash flows by creating value for **customers, suppliers,** and **employees.**
- **Free cash flows (FCFs)** are the cash flows available for distribution to all of a firm's investors (shareholders and creditors) after the firm has paid all expenses (including taxes) and made the required investments in operations to support growth.
- The **value of a firm** depends on the **size of the firm's free cash flows,** the **timing of those flows,** and **their risk.**
- The **weighted average cost of capital (WACC)** is the average return required by all of the firm's investors. It is determined by the firm's **capital structure** (the firm's relative amounts of debt and equity), **interest rates,** the firm's **risk,** and the **market's attitude toward risk.**
- A **firm's fundamental,** or **intrinsic, value** is defined by:

$$\text{Value} = \frac{\text{FCF}_1}{(1 + \text{WACC})^1} + \frac{\text{FCF}_2}{(1 + \text{WACC})^2}$$

$$+ \frac{\text{FCF}_3}{(1 + \text{WACC})^3} + \cdots + \frac{\text{FCF}_\infty}{(1 + \text{WACC})^\infty}.$$

- Transfers of capital between borrowers and savers take place (1) by **direct transfers** of money and securities; (2) by transfers through **investment banking houses,** which act as middlemen; and (3) by transfers through **financial intermediaries,** which create new securities.
- Capital is allocated through the price system—a price must be paid to "rent" money. Lenders charge **interest** on funds they lend, while equity investors receive **dividends** and **capital gains** in return for letting firms use their money.
- Four fundamental factors affect the cost of money: (1) **production opportunities,** (2) **time preferences for consumption,** (3) **risk,** and (4) **inflation.**
- There are many different types of **financial securities.** Primitive securities represent claims on cash flows, such as stocks and bonds. **Derivatives** are claims on other traded securities, such as options.
- Major financial institutions include **commercial banks, savings and loan associations, mutual savings banks, credit unions, pension funds, life insurance companies,** and **mutual funds.**
- One result of ongoing regulatory changes has been a blurring of the distinctions between the different financial institutions. The trend in the United States has been toward **financial service corporations** that offer a wide range of financial services, including investment banking, brokerage operations, insurance, and commercial banking.
- There are many different types of **financial markets.** Each market serves a different region or deals with a different type of security.
- **Physical asset markets,** also called tangible or real asset markets, are those for such products as wheat, autos, and real estate. **Financial asset markets** are for primitive securities and derivative securities.
- **Spot markets** and **futures markets** are terms that refer to whether the assets are bought or sold for "on-the-spot" delivery or for delivery at some future date.

- **Money markets** are the markets for debt securities with maturities of less than 1 year. **Capital markets** are the markets for long-term debt and corporate stocks.
- **Primary markets** are the markets in which corporations raise new capital. **Secondary markets** are markets in which existing, already outstanding securities are traded among investors.
- Orders from buyers and sellers can be matched in one of three ways: (1) in an open outcry **auction,** (2) through **dealers,** and (3) automatically through an **electronic communications network (ECN).**
- There are two basic types of markets—the physical location exchanges (such as the NYSE) and computer/telephone networks (such as Nasdaq).

Questions

(1-1) Define each of the following terms:
   a. Proprietorship; partnership; corporation
   b. Limited partnership; limited liability partnership; professional corporation
   c. Stockholder wealth maximization
   d. Money market; capital market; primary market; secondary market
   e. Private markets; public markets; derivatives
   f. Investment banker; financial service corporation; financial intermediary
   g. Mutual fund; money market fund
   h. Physical location exchanges; computer/telephone network
   i. Open outcry auction; dealer market; electronic communications network (ECN)
   j. Production opportunities; time preferences for consumption
   k. Foreign trade deficit

(1-2) What are the three principal forms of business organization? What are the advantages and disadvantages of each?

(1-3) What is a firm's fundamental, or intrinsic, value? What might cause a firm's intrinsic value to be different than its actual market value?

(1-4) The president of Eastern Semiconductor Corporation (ESC) made this statement in the company's annual report: "ESC's primary goal is to increase the value of our common stockholders' equity." Later in the report, the following announcements were made:
   a. The company contributed $1.5 million to the symphony orchestra in Bridgeport, Connecticut, its headquarters' city.
   b. The company is spending $500 million to open a new plant and expand operations in China. No profits will be produced by the Chinese operation for 4 years, so earnings will be depressed during this period versus what they would have been had the decision not been made to expand in that market.

Discuss how ESC's stockholders might view each of these actions, and how the actions might affect the stock price.

(1-5)   Edmund Enterprises recently made a large investment to upgrade its technology. While these improvements won't have much of an impact on performance in the short run, they are expected to reduce future costs significantly. What impact will this investment have on Edmund Enterprises' earnings per share this year? What impact might this investment have on the company's intrinsic value and stock price?

(1-6)   Describe the different ways in which capital can be transferred from suppliers of capital to those who are demanding capital.

(1-7)   What are financial intermediaries, and what economic functions do they perform?

(1-8)   Suppose the population of Area Y is relatively young while that of Area O is relatively old, but everything else about the two areas is equal.
     a.   Would interest rates likely be the same or different in the two areas? Explain.
     b.   Would a trend toward nationwide branching by banks and savings and loans, and the development of nationwide diversified financial corporations affect your answer to part a?

(1-9)   Suppose a new and much more liberal Congress and administration were elected, and their first order of business was to take away the independence of the Federal Reserve System and to force the Fed to greatly expand the money supply. What effect would this have on the level of interest rates immediately after the announcement?

(1-10)   Is an initial public offering an example of a primary or a secondary market transaction?

(1-11)   Differentiate between dealer markets and stock markets that have a physical location.

(1-12)   Identify and briefly compare the two leading stock exchanges in the United States today.

---

e-resource

Cyberproblem

Please go to the textbook's Web site to access any Cyberproblems.

Mini Case

Assume that you recently graduated and have just reported to work as an investment advisor at the brokerage firm of Balik and Kiefer Inc. One of the firm's clients is Michelle DellaTorre, a professional tennis player who has just come to the United States from Chile. DellaTorre is a highly ranked tennis player who would like to start a company to produce and market apparel that she designs. She also expects to invest substantial amounts of money through Balik and Kiefer. DellaTorre is very bright, and, therefore, she would like to understand in general terms what will happen to her money. Your boss has developed the following set of questions that you must ask and answer to explain the U.S. financial system to DellaTorre.

a. Why is corporate finance important to all managers?

b. Describe the organizational forms a company might have as it evolves from a start-up to a major corporation. List the advantages and disadvantages of each form.

c. How do corporations go public and continue to grow? What are agency problems? What is corporate governance?

d. What should be the primary objective of managers?
   (1) Do firms have any responsibilities to society at large?
   (2) Is stock price maximization good or bad for society?
   (3) Should firms behave ethically?

e. What three aspects of cash flows affect the value of any investment?

f. What are free cash flows?

g. What is the weighted average cost of capital?

h. How do free cash flows and the weighted average cost of capital interact to determine a firm's value?

i. Who are the providers (savers) and users (borrowers) of capital? How is capital transferred between savers and borrowers?

j. What do we call the price that a borrower must pay for debt capital? What is the price of equity capital? What are the four most fundamental factors that affect the cost of money, or the general level of interest rates, in the economy?

k. What are some economic conditions (including international aspects) that affect the cost of money?

l. What are financial securities? Describe some financial instruments.

m. List some financial institutions.

n. What are some different types of markets?

o. How are secondary markets organized?
   (1) List some physical location markets and some computer/telephone networks.
   (2) Explain the differences between open outcry auctions, dealer markets, and electronic communications networks (ECNs).

chapter 2

Time Value of Money

In 2006, the U.S. pension system was significantly underfunded—companies in the S&P 500 needed an additional $40 billion to cover their pension commitments. This same situation existed in the U.K. and many other nations. Several factors contributed to this problem, including questionable applications of the time value of money.

First, note that there are two types of pension plans—"defined contribution plans," where a company provides a specific amount of money, often based on profits, to help its employees when they retire, and "defined benefit plans," where the company promises to make specific lifetime pension payments to employees when they retire. The payments depend on each employee's final pay at retirement, years of service with the company, and how long the employees live. Actuaries can estimate these factors, but the company's future obligations still are uncertain under a defined benefit plan.

As we noted in Chapter 1, a dollar in the future is worth less than a dollar today. Using the time value of money tools in this chapter, we can estimate how much is needed today to make the promised future payments. The amount needed today is actually the present value of the future payments. This present value is called the "pension liability," because it represents a claim against the company. Under our pension laws, the company is supposed to set aside enough money each year to meet these future claims. The amount of money that has been set aside, which is invested in a portfolio of stocks, bonds, real estate, and other assets, is called the "pension asset." If the pension asset is less than the pension liability, then a defined benefit plan is said to be underfunded.

When a company with an underfunded pension plan goes bankrupt, the pension obligations are assumed by the Pension Benefit Guarantee Corporation, a government agency that is implicitly backed by the U.S. government, which means taxpayers. When many companies are underfunded, a very real possibility exists that you, as a taxpayer, will have to bail out the system. Note too that limits exist on the payments to each employee, so if you are highly paid and your employer goes bankrupt, you will also be a loser.

How does the time value of money fit into all this? To see the connection, suppose a plan's pension assets are initially exactly equal to its liabilities, and then interest rates decline. As you will see, falling interest rates cause the present value of liabilities to increase. Simultaneously, the future earning power of the pension assets will probably be reduced, so unless the company increases its annual contributions the plan will become underfunded. This is exactly what happened during the early 2000s. Interest rates fell, pension plans became underfunded, companies that were having operating problems were unable to meet their funding requirements, and as a result many companies failed. This is but one of the many uses of time value analysis, but keep the pension fund example in mind as you go through the chapter.

In Chapter 1, we saw that the primary objective of financial management is to maximize the value of the firm's stock. We also saw that stock values depend in part on the timing of the cash flows investors expect from an investment—a dollar expected soon is worth more than a dollar expected in the distant future. Therefore, it is essential for financial managers to have a clear understanding of the time value of money and its impact on stock prices. These concepts are discussed in this chapter, where we show how the timing of cash flows affects asset values and rates of return.

The principles of time value analysis have many applications, ranging from setting up schedules for paying off loans to decisions about whether to acquire new equipment. *In fact, of all the concepts used in finance, none is more important than the* **time value of money,** *also called* **discounted cash flow (DCF) analysis.** Since time value concepts are used throughout the remainder of the book, it is vital that you understand the material in Chapter 2 and are able to work the chapter problems before you move on to other topics.[1]

2.1 Time Lines

The first step in time value analysis is to set up a **time line,** which will help you visualize what's happening in a particular problem. To illustrate, consider the following diagram, where PV represents $100 that is on hand today and FV is the value that will be in the account on a future date:

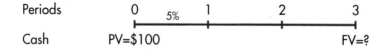

The intervals from 0 to 1, 1 to 2, and 2 to 3 are time periods such as years or months. Time 0 is today, and it is the beginning of Period 1; Time 1 is one period from today, and it is both the end of Period 1 and the beginning of Period 2; and so on. Although the periods are often years, periods can also be quarters or months or even days. Note that each tick mark corresponds to both the *end* of one period and the *beginning* of the next one. Thus, if the periods are years, the tick mark at Time 2 represents both the *end* of Year 2 and the *beginning* of Year 3.

Cash flows are shown directly below the tick marks, and the relevant interest rate is shown just above the time line. Unknown cash flows, which you are trying

---

[1]Calculator manuals tend to be long and complicated, partly because they cover a number of topics that aren't required in the basic finance course. Therefore, we provide, on the textbook's Web site, tutorials for the most commonly used calculators. The tutorials are keyed to this chapter, and they show exactly how to do the required calculations. If you don't know how to use your calculator, go to the Web site, get the relevant tutorial, and go through it as you study the chapter.

to find, are indicated by question marks. Here the interest rate is 5%; a single cash outflow, $100, is invested at Time 0; and the Time 3 value is an unknown inflow. In this example, cash flows occur only at Times 0 and 3, with no flows at Times 1 or 2. Note that in our example the interest rate is constant for all three years. That condition is generally true, but if it were not then we would show different interest rates for the different periods.

Time lines are essential when you are first learning time value concepts, but even experts use them to analyze complex finance problems, and we use them throughout the book. We begin each problem by setting up a time line to show what's happening, after which we provide an equation that must be solved to find the answer, and then we explain how to use a regular calculator, a financial calculator, and a spreadsheet to find the answer.

SELF-TEST

Do time lines deal only with years or could other periods be used?

Set up a time line to illustrate the following situation: You currently have $2,000 in a 3-year certificate of deposit (CD) that pays a guaranteed 4% annually.

2.2 Future Values

A dollar in hand today is worth more than a dollar to be received in the future because, if you had it now, you could invest it, earn interest, and end up with more than a dollar in the future. The process of going to **future values (FVs)** from **present values (PVs)** is called **compounding.** To illustrate, refer back to our 3-year time line and assume that you plan to deposit $100 in a bank that pays a guaranteed 5% interest each year. How much would you have at the end of Year 3? We first define some terms, after which we set up a time line and show how the future value is calculated.

PV = Present value, or beginning amount. In our example, $PV = \$100$.

FV_N = Future value, or ending amount, of your account after N periods. Whereas PV is the value now, or the *present value*, FV_N is the value N periods into the *future*, after the interest earned has been added to the account.

CF_t = Cash flow. Cash flows can be positive or negative. The cash flow for a particular period is often given a subscript, CF_t, where t is the period. Thus, $CF_0 = PV$ = the cash flow at Time 0, whereas CF_3 would be the cash flow at the end of Period 3.

I = Interest rate earned per year. Sometimes a lowercase i is used. Interest earned is based on the balance at the beginning of each year, and we assume that it is paid at the end of the year. Here $I = 5\%$, or, expressed as a decimal, 0.05. Throughout this chapter, we designate the interest rate as I because that symbol (or I/YR, for interest rate per year) is used on most financial calculators. Note, though, that in later chapters we use the symbol "r" to denote rates because r (for rate of return) is used more often in the finance literature. Note too that in this chapter we generally assume that interest payments are guaranteed by the U.S. government; hence they are certain. In later chapters we will consider risky investments, where the interest rate actually earned might differ from its expected level.

INT = Dollars of interest earned during the year = beginning amount times I. In our example, $INT = \$100(0.05) = \$5$.

N = Number of periods involved in the analysis. In our example, $N = 3$. Sometimes the number of periods is designated with a lowercase n, so both N and n indicate number of periods.

Corporate Valuation and the Time Value of Money

In Chapter 1, we told you that managers should strive to make their firms more valuable and that the value of a firm is determined by the size, timing, and risk of its free cash flows (FCF). Recall that free cash flows are the cash flows available for distribution to all of a firm's investors (stockholders and creditors) and that the weighted average cost of capital is the average rate of return required by all of the firm's investors. We showed you a formula, the same as the one below, for calculating value. That formula takes future cash flows and adjusts them to show how much those future risky cash flows are worth today. That formula is based on time value of money concepts, which we explain in this chapter.

$$\text{Value} = \frac{FCF_1}{(1 + WACC)^1} + \frac{FCF_2}{(1 + WACC)^2} + \frac{FCF_3}{(1 + WACC)^3} + \cdots + \frac{FCF_\infty}{(1 + WACC)^\infty}$$

We can use four different procedures to solve time value problems.[2] These methods are described in the following sections.

Step-by-Step Approach

The time line used to find the FV of $100 compounded for 3 years at 5%, along with some calculations, is shown below:

Time	0		1	2	3
		5%			
Amount at beginning of period	$100.00--→		$105.00----→	$110.25----→	$115.76

You start with $100 in the account—this is shown at t = 0. Then multiply the initial amount, and each succeeding amount, by (1 + I) = (1.05).

- You earn $100(0.05) = $5 of interest during the first year, so the amount at the end of Year 1 (or t = 1) is

$$
\begin{aligned}
FV_1 &= PV + INT \\
&= PV + PV(I) \\
&= PV(1 + I) \\
&= \$100(1 + 0.05) = \$100(1.05) = \$105.
\end{aligned}
$$

- You begin the second year with $105, earn 0.05($105) = $5.25 on the now larger beginning-of-period amount, and end the year with $110.25. Interest during Year 2 is $5.25, and it is higher than the first year's interest, $5, because you earned $5(0.05) = $0.25 interest on the first year's interest. This is called "compounding," and interest earned on interest is called "compound interest."
- This process continues, and because the beginning balance is higher in each successive year, the interest earned each year increases.
- The total interest earned, $15.76, is reflected in the final balance, $115.76.

---

[2]A fifth procedure is called the tabular approach. It used tables showing "interest factors" and was used before financial calculators and computers became available. Now, though, calculators and spreadsheets such as *Excel* are programmed to calculate the specific factor needed for a given problem and then to use it to find the FV. This is much more efficient than using the tables. Moreover, calculators and spreadsheets can handle fractional periods and fractional interest rates. For these reasons, tables are not used in business today; hence we do not discuss them in the text. For an explanation of the tabular approach, see **Web Extension 2C** at the textbook's Web site.

The step-by-step approach is useful because it shows exactly what is happening. However, this approach is time-consuming, especially if a number of years are involved, so streamlined procedures have been developed.

Formula Approach

In the step-by-step approach above, we multiply the amount at the beginning of each period by $(1 + I) = (1.05)$. Notice that the value at the end of Year 2 is

$$\begin{aligned} FV_2 &= FV_1(1 + I) \\ &= PV(1 + I)(1 + I) \\ &= PV(1 + I)^2 \\ &= 100(1.05)^2 = \$110.25. \end{aligned}$$

If N = 3, then we multiply PV by $(1 + I)$ three different times, which is the same as multiplying the beginning amount by $(1 + I)^3$. This concept can be extended, and the result is this key equation:

$$FV_N = PV(1 + I)^N. \tag{2-1}$$

We can apply Equation 2-1 via the formula approach to find the FV in our example:

$$FV_3 = \$100(1.05)^3 = \$115.76.$$

Equation 2-1 can be used with any calculator that has an exponential function, making it easy to find FVs, no matter how many years are involved.

Financial Calculators

Financial calculators are extremely helpful when working time value problems. First, note that financial calculators have five keys that correspond to the five variables in the basic time value equations. We show the inputs for our example above the keys and the output, the FV, below its key. Since there are no periodic payments, we enter 0 for PMT. We describe the keys in more detail below the diagram.

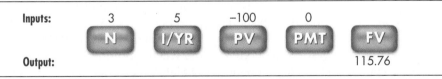

N = Number of periods. Some calculators use n rather than N.

I/YR = Interest rate per period. Some calculators use i or I rather than I/YR.

PV = Present value. In our example we begin by making a deposit, which is an outflow, so the PV should be entered with a negative sign. On most calculators you must enter the 100, then press the +/− key to switch from +100 to −100. If you enter −100 directly, this will subtract 100 from the last number in the calculator and give you an incorrect answer.

PMT = Payment. This key is used if we have a series of equal, or constant, payments. Since there are no such payments in our illustrative problem, we enter PMT = 0. We will use the PMT key when we discuss annuities later in this chapter.

> FV = Future value. In this example, the FV is positive because we entered the PV as a negative number. If we had entered the 100 as a positive number, then the FV would have been negative.

As noted in our example, you first enter the known values (N, I/YR, PMT, and PV) and then press the FV key to get the answer, 115.76.

Here are some tips for setting up financial calculators. Refer to your calculator manual or to our calculator tutorial on the CengageNOW Web site for details on how to set up your specific calculator.

One Payment per Period. Many calculators "come out of the box" assuming that 12 payments are made per year, i.e., they assume monthly payments. However, in this book we generally deal with problems where only 1 payment is made each year. *Therefore, you should set your calculator at 1 payment per year and leave it there.*

End Mode. With most contracts, payments are made at the end of each period. However, some contracts call for payments at the beginning of each period. You can switch between "End Mode" and "Begin Mode," depending on the problem you are solving. *Since most of the problems in this book call for end-of-period payments, you should return your calculator to End Mode after you work a problem where payments are made at the beginning of periods.*

Number of Decimal Places to Display. Most calculators use all significant digits in all calculations, but display only the number of decimal places that you specify. When working with dollars, we generally specify two decimal places. When dealing with interest rates, we generally specify two places if the rate is expressed as a percentage, like 5.25%, but we specify four places if the rate is expressed as a decimal, like 0.0525.

When students are first learning how to use financial calculators, two mistakes are common. First, students often forget that one cash flow must be negative. Mathematically, financial calculators solve a version of this equation:

$$PV(1 + I)^N + FV_N = 0. \qquad (2\text{-}2)$$

Notice that for reasonable values of I, either PV or FV_N must be negative and the other must be positive to make the equation true. Intuitively, this is because in all realistic situations, one cash flow is an outflow (which should have a negative sign) and one is an inflow (which should have a positive sign). The bottom line is that one of your inputs for a cash flow must be negative and one must be positive.

The second common mistake often occurs when inputting interest rates. For arithmetic operations with a nonfinancial calculator, the value "5.25%" would be entered as "0.0525." But with a financial calculator, the value "5.25%" should be entered as "5.25."

Spreadsheets

Spreadsheet programs are ideally suited for solving many financial problems, including time value of money problems.[3] With very little effort, the spreadsheet itself becomes a time line. Figure 2-1 shows how our problem would look in a spreadsheet.

---

[3] The textbook's Web site file **FM12 Ch 02 Tool Kit.xls** does the various calculations using *Excel*. We *highly recommend* that you go through the models. This will give you practice with *Excel*, which will help tremendously in later courses, in the job market, and in the workplace. Also, going through the models will enhance your understanding of financial concepts.

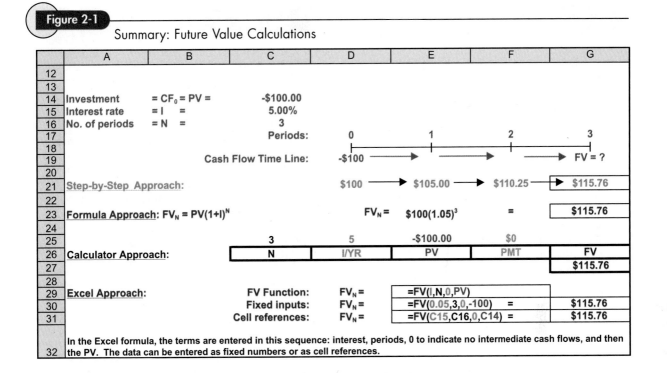

Figure 2-1

Summary: Future Value Calculations

	A	B	C	D	E	F	G
12							
13							
14	Investment	= CF₀ = PV =	-$100.00				
15	Interest rate	= I =	5.00%				
16	No. of periods	= N =	3				
17				Periods:	0	1	2	3
18								
19			Cash Flow Time Line:	-$100			FV = ?
20							
21	Step-by-Step Approach:			$100	$105.00	$110.25	$115.76
22							
23	Formula Approach: FVₙ = PV(1+I)ᴺ			FVₙ =	$100(1.05)³	=	$115.76
24							
25			3	5	-$100.00	$0	
26	Calculator Approach:		N	I/YR	PV	PMT	FV
27							$115.76
28							
29	Excel Approach:		FV Function:	FVₙ =	=FV(I,N,0,PV)		
30			Fixed inputs:	FVₙ =	=FV(0.05,3,0,-100)	=	$115.76
31			Cell references:	FVₙ =	=FV(C15,C16,0,C14)	=	$115.76
32	In the Excel formula, the terms are entered in this sequence: interest, periods, 0 to indicate no intermediate cash flows, and then the PV. The data can be entered as fixed numbers or as cell references.						

We used *Excel* to create Figure 2-1, which summarizes the four methods for finding the FV. Note that spreadsheets can be used to do calculations, but they can also be used like a word processor to create exhibits like Figure 2-1, which includes text, drawings, and calculations. The letters across the top designate columns, the numbers to the left designate rows, and the rows and columns jointly designate cells.

It is a good practice to put a problem's inputs in the same section. For example, in Figure 2-1, C14 is the cell where we specify the −$100 investment, C15 shows the interest rate, and C16 shows the number of periods.

Drawing a time line is an important step in solving finance problems. When we work a problem by hand we usually draw a time line. When we work a problem in *Excel*, we usually put in a time line. For example, in Figure 2-1 the time line is in Rows 17 to 19. Notice how easy it is in *Excel* to put in a time line, with each column designating a different period on the time line.

In Row 21 we have *Excel* go through the step-by-step calculations, multiplying the beginning-of-year values by (1 + I) to find the compounded value at the end of each period. Cell G21 shows the final result of the step-by-step approach.

We illustrate the formula approach in Row 23, using *Excel* to solve Equation 2-1 and find the FV. Cell G23 shows the formula result, $115.76.

Rows 25 to 27 illustrate the inputs and result from using a financial calculator.

The last section of Figure 2-1 illustrates *Excel*'s FV function. You can access the function wizard by clicking the f_x symbol in *Excel*'s formula bar, or you can go to the menu bar, select Insert, and then select Function from the drop-down menu. Select the category for Financial functions, and then select the FV function. The function is =FV(I,N,0,PV), as shown in Cell E29.[4] Cell E30 shows how the formula would look

FM

e-resource

See *FM12 Ch 02 Tool Kit.xls* for all calculations.

---

[4]The third entry in the FV function is zero in this example, to indicate that there are no periodic payments. Later in this chapter we will use the function in situations where we do have periodic payments.

The Power of Compound Interest

Suppose you are 26 years old and just received your MBA. After reading the introduction to this chapter, you decide to start investing in the stock market for your retirement. Your goal is to have $1 million when you retire at age 65. Assuming you earn a 10% annual rate on your stock investments, how much must you invest at the end of each year in order to reach your goal?

The answer is $2,490.98, but this amount depends critically on the return earned on your investments. If returns drop to 8%, your required annual contributions will rise to $4,185.13. If returns rise to 12%, you will need to put away only $1,461.97 per year.

What if you are like most of us and wait until later to worry about retirement? If you wait until age 40, you will need to save $10,168 per year to reach your $1 million goal, assuming you earn 10%, and $13,679 per year if you earn only 8%. If you wait until age 50 and then earn 8%, the required amount will be $36,830 per year.

While $1 million may seem like a lot of money, it won't be when you get ready to retire. If inflation averages 5% a year over the next 39 years, your $1 million nest egg will be worth only $149,148 in today's dollars. At an 8% rate of return, and assuming you live for 20 years after retirement, your annual retirement income in today's dollars will be only $15,191 before taxes. So, after celebrating graduation and your new job, start saving!

with numbers as inputs; the actual function itself is in Cell G30. Cell E31 shows how the formula would look with cell references as inputs, with the actual function in Cell G31. We always recommend using cell references as inputs to functions, because this makes it easy to change inputs and see the effects on the output.

Notice that when entering interest rates in *Excel*, you must input the actual number. For example, in cell C15, we input "0.05," and then formatted it as a percentage. In the function itself, you can enter "0.05" or "5%," but if you enter "5," *Excel* will think you mean 500%. This is exactly opposite the convention for financial calculators.

Comparing the Procedures

The first step in solving any time value problem is to understand the verbal description of the problem well enough to diagram it on a time line. Woody Allen said that 90% of success is just showing up. With time value problems, 90% of success is correctly setting up the time line.

FM
e-resource

See *FM12 Ch 02 Tool Kit.xls* for all calculations.

After you diagram the problem on a time line, your next step is to pick an approach to solve the problem. Which of the approaches should you use? The answer depends on the particular situation.

All business students should know Equation 2-1 by heart and should also know how to use a financial calculator. So, for simple problems such as finding the future value of a single payment, it is probably easiest and quickest to use either the formula approach or a financial calculator.

For problems with more than a couple of cash flows, the formula approach is usually too time-consuming, so here either the calculator or spreadsheet approaches would generally be used. Calculators are portable and quick to set up, but if many calculations of the same type must be done, or if you want to see how changes in an input such as the interest rate affect the future value, the spreadsheet approach is generally more efficient. If the problem has many irregular cash flows, or if you want to analyze many scenarios with different cash flows, then the spreadsheet approach is definitely the most efficient.

The important thing is that you understand the various approaches well enough to make a rational choice, given the nature of the problem and the equipment you have available. In any event, you must understand the concepts behind the calculations and know how to set up time lines in order to work complex problems. This is true for stock and bond valuation, capital budgeting, lease analysis, and many other important financial problems.

Graphic View of the Compounding Process

Figure 2-2 shows how a $1 investment grows over time at different interest rates. We made the curves by solving Equation 2-1 with different values for N and I. The interest rate is a growth rate: If a sum is deposited and earns 5% interest per year, then the funds on deposit will grow by 5% per year. Note also that time value concepts can be applied to anything that grows—sales, population, earnings per share, or your future salary.

Figure 2-2

Growth of $1 at Various Interest Rates and Time Periods

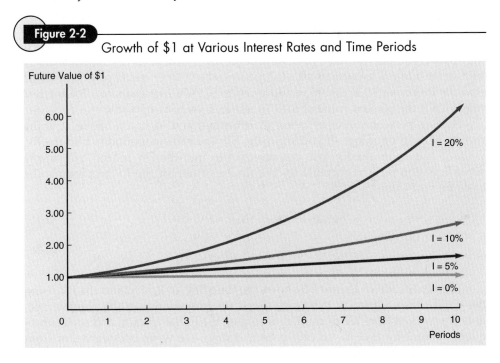

SELF-TEST

Explain why this statement is true: "A dollar in hand today is worth more than a dollar to be received next year."

What is compounding? What would the future value of $100 be after 5 years at 10% *compound* interest? ($161.05)

Suppose you currently have $2,000 and plan to purchase a 3-year certificate of deposit (CD) that pays 4% interest compounded annually. How much will you have when the CD matures? How would your answer change if the interest rate were 5%, or 6%, or 20%? ($2,249.73; $2,315.25; $2,382.03; $3,456.00) (Hint: With a calculator, enter N = 3, I/YR = 4, PV = −2000, and PMT = 0, then press FV to get 2,249.73. Then, enter I/YR = 5 to override the 4% and press FV again to get the second answer. In general, you can change one input at a time to see how the output changes.)

A company's sales in 2005 were $100 million. If sales grow at 8%, what will they be 10 years later, in 2015? ($215.89 million)

How much would $1, growing at 5% per year, be worth after 100 years? What would FV be if the growth rate were 10%? ($131.50; $13,780.61)

2.3 Present Values

Suppose you have some extra money to invest. A broker offers to sell you a security that will pay a guaranteed $115.76 three years from now. Banks are currently offering a guaranteed 5% interest on 3-year certificates of deposit (CDs), and if you don't buy the security you will buy a CD. The 5% rate paid on the CD is defined as your **opportunity cost,** or the rate of return you could earn on an alternative investment of similar risk. Given these conditions, what's the most you should pay for the security?

First, recall from the future value example in the last section that if you invested $100 at 5% it would grow to $115.76 in 3 years. You would also have $115.76 after 3 years if you bought the broker's security. Therefore, the most you should pay for the security is $100—this is its "fair price." This is also equal to the intrinsic, or fundamental, value of the security. If you could buy the security for *less than* $100, you should buy it rather than invest in the CD. Conversely, if its price were *more than* $100, you should buy the CD. If the security's price were exactly $100, you should be indifferent between the security and the CD.

The $100 is defined as the present value, or PV, of $115.76 due in 3 years when the appropriate interest rate is 5%. In general, *the present value of a cash flow due N years in the future is the amount which, if it were on hand today, would grow to equal the given future amount.* Since $100 would grow to $115.76 in 3 years at a 5% interest rate, $100 is the present value of $115.76 due in 3 years at a 5% rate.

Finding present values is called **discounting,** and as noted above, it is the reverse of compounding—if you know the PV, you can compound to find the FV, while if you know the FV, you can discount to find the PV. Indeed, we simply solve Equation 2-1, the formula for the future value, for the PV to produce the basic present value equation, 2-3:

$$\text{Future value} = FV_N = PV(1 + I)^N, \tag{2-1}$$

$$\text{Present value} = PV = \frac{FV_N}{(1 + I)^N}. \tag{2-3}$$

The top section of Figure 2-3 shows the time line and calculates the PV using the step-by-step approach. When we found the future value in the previous section, we worked from left to right, multiplying the initial amount and each subsequent amount by $(1 + I)$. To find present values, we work backwards, or from right to left, dividing the future value and each subsequent amount by $(1 + I)$. This procedure shows exactly what's happening, and that can be quite useful when you are working complex problems. However, it's inefficient, especially if you are dealing with a number of years.

With the formula approach we use Equation 2-3, simply dividing the future value by $(1 + I)^N$. This is more efficient than the step-by-step approach, and it gives the same result, as shown in Figure 2-3, Row 73.

Equation 2-2 is built into financial calculators, and as shown in Figure 2-3, Row 76, we can find the PV by entering values for N = 3, I/YR = 5, PMT = 0, and FV = 115.76, and then pressing the PV key to get −100.

e-resource

See **FM12 Ch 02 Tool Kit.xls** for all calculations.

e-resource

See **FM12 Ch 02 Tool Kit.xls** for all calculations.

---

[5]The third entry in the PV function is zero to indicate that there are no intermediate payments in this particular example.

Figure 2-3

Summary: Present Value Calculations

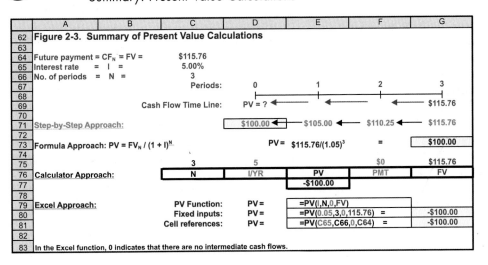

	A	B	C	D	E	F	G
62	Figure 2-3. Summary of Present Value Calculations						
63							
64	Future payment = CF_N = FV =		$115.76				
65	Interest rate = I =		5.00%				
66	No. of periods = N =		3				
67			Periods:	0	1	2	3
68							
69			Cash Flow Time Line:	PV = ? ←	←	←	$115.76
70							
71	Step-by-Step Approach:			$100.00 ←	$105.00 ←	$110.25 ←	$115.76
72							
73	Formula Approach: PV = FV_N / (1 + I)^N				PV= $115.76/(1.05)^3	=	$100.00
74							
75				3	5	$0	$115.76
76	Calculator Approach:			N	I/YR	PV	PMT	FV
77						-$100.00		
78								
79	Excel Approach:		PV Function:	PV =	=PV(I,N,0,FV)		
80			Fixed inputs:	PV =	=PV(0.05,3,0,115.76) =		-$100.00
81			Cell references:	PV =	=PV(C65,C66,0,C64) =		-$100.00
82							
83	In the Excel function, 0 indicates that there are no intermediate cash flows.						

Spreadsheets also have a function that solves Equation 2-2. In *Excel*, this is the PV function, and it is written as **=PV(I,N,0,FV).**[5] Cell E79 shows the inputs to this function. Cell E80 shows the function with fixed numbers as inputs, with the actual function and the resulting −$100 in Cell G80. Cell E81 shows the function with cell references as inputs, with the actual function and the resulting −$100 in Cell G81.

The fundamental goal of financial management is to maximize the firm's value, and the value of a business (or any asset, including stocks and bonds) is the *present value* of its expected future cash flows. Since present value lies at the heart of the valuation process, we will have much more to say about it in the remainder of this chapter and throughout the book.

Graphic View of the Discounting Process

Figure 2-4 shows that the present value of a sum to be received in the future decreases and approaches zero as the payment date is extended further and further into the future, and also that the present value falls faster the higher the interest rate. At relatively high rates, funds due in the future are worth very little today, and even at relatively low rates present values of sums due in the very distant future are quite small. For example, at a 20% discount rate, $1 million due in 100 years would be worth only about 1 cent today. (However, 1 cent would grow to almost $1 million in 100 years at 20%.)

SELF-TEST

What is "discounting," and how is it related to compounding? How is the future value equation (2-1) related to the present value equation (2-3)?

How does the present value of a future payment change as the time to receipt is lengthened? As the interest rate increases?

(continued)

SELF-TEST

Suppose a U.S. government bond promises to pay $2,249.73 three years from now. If the going interest rate on 3-year government bonds is 4%, how much is the bond worth today? How would your answer change if the bond matured in 5 rather than 3 years? What if the interest rate on the 5-year bond were 6% rather than 4%? ($2,000; $1,849.11; $1,681.13)

How much would $1,000,000 due in 100 years be worth today if the discount rate were 5%? If the discount rate were 20%? ($7,604.49; $0.0121)

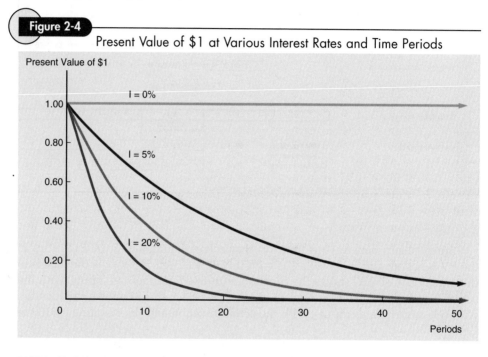

Figure 2-4

Present Value of $1 at Various Interest Rates and Time Periods

2.4 Finding the Interest Rate, I

Thus far we have used Equations 2-1, 2-2, and 2-3 to find future and present values. Those equations have four variables, and if we know three of them, we can solve for the fourth. Thus, if we know PV, I, and N, then we can solve Equation 2-2 for FV, while if we know FV, I, and N we can solve Equation 2-2 to find PV. That's what we did in the preceding two sections.

Now suppose we know PV, FV, and N, and we want to find I. For example, suppose we know that a given security has a cost of $100 and that it will return $150 after 10 years. Thus, we know PV, FV, and N, and we want to find the rate of return we will earn if we buy the security. Here's the solution using Equation 2-1:

FM
e-resource

See **FM12 Ch 02 Tool
Kit.xls** for all calculations.

$$FV = PV(1 + I)^N$$

$$\$150 = \$100(1 + I)^{10}$$

$$\$150/\$100 = (1 + I)^{10}$$

$$(1 + I)^{10} = 1.5$$

$$(1 + I) = 1.5^{(1/10)}$$

$$(1 + I) = 1.0414$$

$$I = 0.0414 = 4.14\%.$$

Finding the interest rate by solving the formula takes a little time, but financial calculators and spreadsheets can find interest rates almost instantly. Here's the calculator setup:

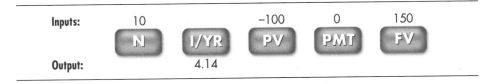

Enter N = 10, PV = −100, PMT = 0 because there are no payments until the security matures, and FV = 150. Then, when you press the I/YR key, the calculator gives the answer, 4.14%. Notice that the PV is a negative value because it is a cash outflow (an investment) and the FV is positive because it is a cash inflow (a return of the investment). If you enter both PV and FV as positive numbers (or both as negative numbers), your calculator will be unable to solve for the interest rate.

In *Excel*, the RATE function can be used to find the interest rate: **=RATE (N,PMT,PV,FV)**. For this example, the function would be **=RATE(3,0,−100,150)** = 0.414 = 4.14%. See the file ***FM12 Ch 02 Tool Kit.xls*** at the textbook's Web site for an example.

SELF-TEST
The U.S. Treasury offers to sell you a bond for $585.43. No payments will be made until the bond matures 10 years from now, at which time it will be redeemed for $1,000. What interest rate would you earn if you bought this bond for $585.43? What rate would you earn if you could buy the bond for $550? For $600? (5.5%; 6.16%; 5.24%)

Microsoft earned $0.12 per share in 1994. Ten years later, in 2004, it earned $1.04. What was the growth rate in Microsoft's earnings per share (EPS) over the 10-year period? If EPS in 2004 had been $0.65 rather than $1.04, what would the growth rate have been? (24.1%; 18.41%)

2.5 Finding the Number of Years, N

We sometimes need to know how long it will take to accumulate a sum of money, given our beginning funds and the rate we will earn on those funds. For example, suppose we now have $500,000 and the interest rate is 4.5%. How long will it take to grow to $1 million?

Here is Equation 2-1:

$$\$1,000,000 = \$500,000(1 + 0.045)^N.$$

Transform this to

$$\$1,000,000/\$500,000 = 2 = (1 + 0.045)^N.$$

Take the natural log of both sides, and then solve for N:

$$N[\ln(1.045)] = \ln(2)$$
$$N = \ln(2)/\ln(1.045).$$

Find the logs with a calculator, and complete the solution:

$$N = 0.6931/0.0440$$
$$= 15.7473.$$

e-resource

See **FM12 Ch 02 Tool Kit.xls** for all calculations.

Therefore, it takes $500,000 about 15.7473 years to grow to $1,000,000 if the interest rate is 4.5%.

As you might expect, financial calculators and spreadsheets can find N very quickly. Here's the calculator setup:

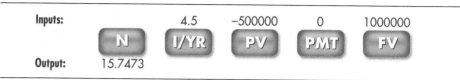

Enter I/YR = 4.5, PV = −500000, PMT = 0, and FV = 1000000. When we press the N key, we get the answer, 15.7473 years.

In *Excel*, the NPER function can be used to find the number of periods: **=NPER(I,PMT,PV,FV).** For this example, the function would be **=RATE(0.045,0,−500000, 1000000)** = 15.7473. See the file **FM12 Ch 02 Tool Kit.xls** at the textbook's Web site for an example.

SELF-TEST

How long would it take $1,000 to double if it were invested in a bank that pays 6% per year? How long would it take if the rate were 10%? (11.9 years; 7.27 years)

Microsoft's 2004 earnings per share were $1.04, and its growth rate during the prior 10 years was 24.1% per year. If that growth rate were maintained, how long would it take for Microsoft's EPS to double? (3.21 years)

2.6 Annuities

Thus far we have dealt with single payments, or "lump sums." However, many assets provide a series of cash inflows over time, and many obligations like auto loans, student loans, and mortgages require a series of payments. If the payments are equal and are made at fixed intervals, then the series is an **annuity.** For example, $100 paid at the end of each of the next 3 years is a 3-year annuity.

If payments occur at the *end* of each period, then we have an **ordinary** (or **deferred**) **annuity.** Payments on mortgages, car loans, and student loans are examples of ordinary annuities. If the payments are made at the *beginning* of each period, then we have an **annuity due.** Rental payments for an apartment, life insurance premiums, and lottery payoffs (if you are lucky enough to win one!) are examples of annuities due. Ordinary annuities are more common in finance, so when we use the term "annuity" in this book, assume that the payments occur at the ends of the periods unless otherwise noted.

Here are the time lines for a $100, 3-year, 5%, ordinary annuity and for the same annuity on an annuity due basis. With the annuity due, each payment is shifted back to the left by 1 year. A $100 deposit will be made each year, so we show the payments with minus signs.

Ordinary Annuity:

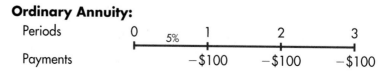

Annuity Due:

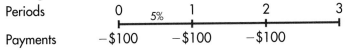

As we demonstrate in the following sections, we can find an annuity's future and present values, the interest rate built into annuity contracts, and how long it takes to reach a financial goal using an annuity. Keep in mind that annuities must have *constant payments* and a *fixed number of periods*. If these conditions don't hold, then we don't have an annuity.

SELF-TEST

What is the difference between an ordinary annuity and an annuity due?

Why should you rather receive an annuity due for $10,000 per year for 10 years than an otherwise similar ordinary annuity?

2.7 Future Value of an Ordinary Annuity

Consider the ordinary annuity diagrammed previously, where you deposit $100 at the end of each year for 3 years and earn 5% per year. Figure 2-5 calculates the **future value of the annuity, FVA$_N$,** using each of the approaches we used for single cash flows.

As shown in the step-by-step section of Figure 2-5, we compound each payment out to Time 3, then sum those compounded values to find the annuity's FV, FVA$_3$ = $315.25. The first payment earns interest for two periods, the second for one period, and the third earns no interest at all because it is made at the end of the annuity's life. This approach is straightforward, but if the annuity extends out for many years, it is cumbersome and time-consuming.

As you can see from the time line diagram, with the step-by-step approach we apply the following equation, with N = 3 and I = 5%:

$$FVA_N = PMT(1 + I)^{N-1} + PMT(1 + I)^{N-2} + PMT(1 + I)^{N-3}$$

$$= \$100(1.05)^2 + \$100(1.05)^1 + \$100(1.05)^0$$

$$= \$315.25.$$

For the general case, the future value of an annuity is

$$FVA_N = PMT(1 + I)^{N-1} + PMT(1 + I)^{N-2}$$

$$+ PMT(1 + I)^{N-3} + \ldots + PMT(1 + I)^0.$$

As shown in **Web Extension 2A** at the textbook's Web site, the future value of an annuity can be written as[6]

$$FVA_N = PMT\left[\frac{(1 + I)^N}{I} - \frac{1}{I}\right]. \qquad \text{(2-4)}$$

---

[6]Section 2.11 shows that the present value of an infinitely long annuity, called a perpetuity, is equal to PMT/I. The cash flows of an ordinary annuity of N periods are equal to the cash flows of a perpetuity minus the cash flows of a perpetuity that begins at year N + 1. Therefore, the future value of an N-period annuity is equal to the future value (as of year N) of a perpetuity minus the value (as of year N) of a perpetuity that begins at year N + 1. See **Web Extension 2A** at the textbook's Web site for details of this derivation.

Figure 2-5

Summary: Future Value of an Ordinary Annuity

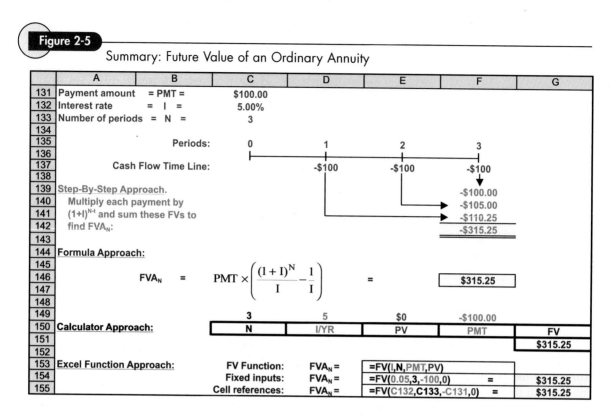

Using this formula, the future value of the annuity is

$$FVA_3 = \$100\left[\frac{(1 + 0.05)^3}{0.05} - \frac{1}{0.05}\right] = \$315.25.$$

Annuity problems are much easier to solve with financial calculators and spreadsheets. The following formula is built into financial calculators and spreadsheets:

FM

e-resource

See **FM12 Ch 02 Tool Kit.xls** for all calculations.

$$PV(1 + I)^N + PMT\left[\frac{(1 + I)^N}{I} - \frac{1}{I}\right] + FV = 0. \qquad (2\text{-}5)$$

When solving an annuity problem with a financial calculator, the presence of recurring payments means that we use the PMT key. Here's the calculator setup for our illustrative annuity:

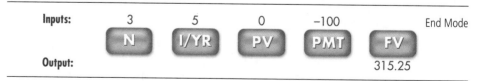

Inputs:	3	5	0	−100	End Mode
	N	I/YR	PV	PMT	FV
Output:					315.25

We enter PV = 0 because we start off with nothing, and we enter PMT = −100 because we plan to deposit this amount in the account at the end of each year. When we press the FV key we get the answer, FVA$_3$ = 315.25.

Since this is an ordinary annuity, with payments coming at the *end* of each year, we must set the calculator appropriately. As noted earlier, calculators "come out of the box" set to assume that payments occur at the end of each period, that is, to deal with ordinary annuities. However, there is a key that enables us to switch between ordinary annuities and annuities due. For ordinary annuities, the designation is "End Mode" or something similar, while for annuities due the designator is "Begin," "Begin Mode," or "Due" or something similar. If you make a mistake and set your calculator on Begin Mode when working with an ordinary annuity, then each payment will earn interest for one extra year, which will cause the compounded amounts, and thus the FVA, to be too large.

The last approach in Figure 2-5 shows the spreadsheet solution, using *Excel's* built-in FV function: **=FV(I,N,PMT,PV)**. In our example, we have **=FV(0.05,3, −100,0)**, with a resulting value of $315.25.

SELF-TEST

For an ordinary annuity with 5 annual payments of $100 and a 10% interest rate, how many years will the 1st payment earn interest, and what will this payment's value be at the end? Answer this same question for the 5th payment. (4 years, $146.41; 0 years, $100)

Assume that you plan to buy a condo 5 years from now, and you estimate that you can save $2,500 per year. You plan to deposit the money in a bank that pays 4% interest, and you will make the first deposit at the end of the year. How much will you have after 5 years? How would your answer change if the interest rate were increased to 6%? Lowered to 3%? ($13,540.81; $14,092.73; $13,272.84)

2.8 Future Value of an Annuity Due

Since each payment occurs one period earlier with an annuity due, the payments will all earn interest for one additional period. Therefore, the FV of an annuity due will be greater than that of a similar ordinary annuity.

If you went through the step-by-step procedure, you would see that our illustrative annuity due has an FV of $331.01 versus $315.25 for the ordinary annuity. See *FM12 Ch 02 Tool Kit.xls* at the textbook's Web site for a summary of these calculations.

With the formula approach, we first use Equation 2-4, but since each payment occurs one period earlier, we multiply the Equation 2-4 result by $(1 + I)$:

$$FVA_{due} = FVA_{ordinary}(1 + I). \tag{2-6}$$

e-resource

See *FM12 Ch 02 Tool Kit.xls* for all calculations.

Thus, for the annuity due, $FVA_{due} = \$315.25(1.05) = \$331.01$, which is the same result as found using the step-by-step approach.

With a calculator we input the variables just as we did with the ordinary annuity, but now we set the calculator to Begin Mode to get the answer, $331.01.

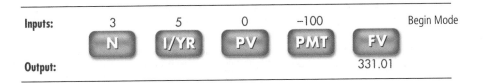

In *Excel*, we still use the FV function, but we must indicate that we have an annuity due. The function is **=FV(I,N,PMT,PV,Type),** where Type indicates the type of annuity. If Type is omitted, *Excel* assumes that it is zero, which indicates an ordinary annuity. For an annuity due, Type = 1. As shown in *FM12 Ch 02 Tool Kit.xls* at the textbook's Web site, the function is **=FV(0.05,3,−100,0,1)** = $331.01.

Why does an annuity due always have a higher future value than an ordinary annuity?

If you calculated the value of an ordinary annuity, how could you find the value of the corresponding annuity due?

Assume that you plan to buy a condo 5 years from now, and you need to save for a down payment. You plan to save $2,500 per year, with the first payment made *immediately*, and you will deposit the funds in a bank account that pays 4%. How much will you have after 5 years? How much would you have if you made the deposits at the end of each year? ($14,082.44; $13,540.81)

2.9 Present Value of an Ordinary Annuity and of an Annuity Due

The present value of an annuity, **PVA$_N$**, can be found using the step-by-step, formula, calculator, or spreadsheet methods. We begin with an ordinary annuity.

Present Value of an Ordinary Annuity

e-resource

See *FM12 Ch 02 Tool Kit.xls* for all calculations.

See Figure 2-6 for a summary of the different approaches for calculating the present value of an ordinary annuity.

As shown in the step-by-step section of Figure 2-6, we discount each payment back to Time 0, then sum those discounted values to find the annuity's PV, PVA$_3$ = $272.32. This approach is straightforward, but if the annuity extends out for many years, it is cumbersome and time-consuming.

The time line diagram shows that with the step-by-step approach we apply the following equation, with N = 3 and I = 5%:

$$PVA_N = PMT/(1 + I)^1 + PMT/(1 + I)^2 + \cdots + PMT/(1 + I)^N.$$

As shown in **Web Extension 2A** at the textbook's Web site, the present value of an annuity can be written as[7]

e-resource

See *FM12 Ch 02 Tool Kit.xls* for all calculations.

$$PVA_N = PMT\left[\frac{1}{I} - \frac{1}{I(1 + I)^N}\right]. \qquad (2\text{-}7)$$

For our annuity, this present value is

$$PVA_3 = PMT\left[\frac{1}{0.05} - \frac{1}{0.05(1 + 0.05)^3}\right] = \$272.32.$$

---

[7]Section 2.11 shows that the present value of an infinitely long annuity, called a perpetuity, is equal to PMT/I. The cash flows of an ordinary annuity of N periods are equal to the cash flows of a perpetuity minus the cash flows of a perpetuity that begins at year N + 1. Therefore, the present value of an N-period annuity is equal to the present value of a perpetuity minus the present value of a perpetuity that begins at year N + 1. See **Web Extension 2A** at the textbook's Web site for details of this derivation.

Figure 2-6

Summary: Present Value of an Ordinary Annuity

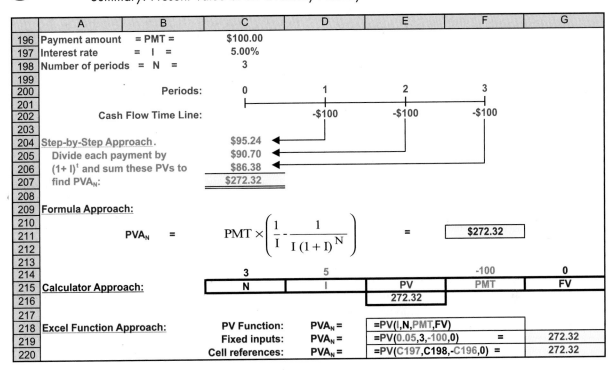

	A	B	C	D	E	F	G
196	Payment amount	= PMT =	$100.00				
197	Interest rate	= I =	5.00%				
198	Number of periods	= N =	3				
199							
200		Periods:	0	1	2	3	
201							
202		Cash Flow Time Line:		-$100	-$100	-$100	
203							
204	Step-by-Step Approach.		$95.24				
205	Divide each payment by		$90.70				
206	(1+ I)^t and sum these PVs to		$86.38				
207	find PVA$_N$:		$272.32				
208							
209	Formula Approach:						
210							
211		PVA$_N$ =	$PMT \times \left(\dfrac{1}{I} - \dfrac{1}{I\,(1+I)^N} \right)$		=	$272.32	
212							
213							
214			3	5		-100	0
215	Calculator Approach:		N	I	PV	PMT	FV
216					272.32		
217							
218	Excel Function Approach:		PV Function:	PVA$_N$ =	=PV(I,N,PMT,FV)		
219			Fixed inputs:	PVA$_N$ =	=PV(0.05,3,-100,0)	=	272.32
220			Cell references:	PVA$_N$ =	=PV(C197,C198,-C196,0) =		272.32

Financial calculators are programmed to solve Equation 2-5, so we merely input the variables and press the PV key, *making sure the calculator is set to End Mode.* The calculator setup is shown below:

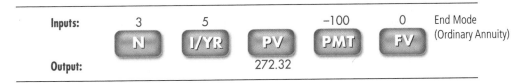

Inputs:	3	5		−100	0	End Mode
	N	I/YR	PV	PMT	FV	(Ordinary Annuity)
Output:			272.32			

The last approach in Figure 2-6 shows the spreadsheet solution, using *Excel's* built-in PV function: **=PV(I,N,PMT,FV)**. In our example, we have **=PV(0.05,3, −100,0)**, with a resulting value of $272.32.

Present Value of Annuities Due

Since each payment for an annuity due occurs one period earlier, the payments will all be discounted for one less period. Therefore, the PV of an annuity due will be greater than that of a similar ordinary annuity.

If you went through the step-by-step procedure, you would see that our illustrative annuity due has a PV of $285.94 versus $272.32 for the ordinary annuity. See *FM12 Ch 02 Tool Kit.xls* at the textbook's Web site for a summary of these calculations.

FM
e-resource
See *FM12 Ch 02 Tool Kit.xls* for all calculations.

With the formula approach, we first use Equation 2-7, but since each payment occurs one period earlier, we multiply the Equation 2-7 result by $(1 + I)$:

$$PVA_{due} = PVA_{ordinary}(1 + I). \qquad (2\text{-}8)$$

Thus, for the annuity due, $PVA_{due} = \$272.32(1.05) = \$285.94$, which is the same result as found using the step-by-step approach.

With a financial calculator, the inputs are the same as for an ordinary annuity, except you must set the calculator to the Begin Mode.

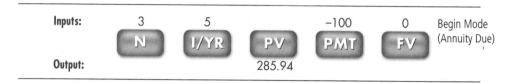

Inputs:	3	5		−100	0	Begin Mode
	N	I/YR	PV	PMT	FV	(Annuity Due)
Output:			285.94			

In *Excel*, we still use the PV function, but we must indicate that we have an annuity due. The function is **=PV(I,N,PMT,FV,Type)**, where Type indicates the type of annuity. If Type is omitted, *Excel* assumes that it is zero, which indicates an ordinary annuity. For an annuity due, Type = 1. As shown in **FM12 Ch 02 Tool Kit.xls** at the CengageNOW Web site, the function for this example is **=PV(0.05,3,−100,0,1)** = \$285.94.

Why does an annuity due have a higher present value than an ordinary annuity?

If you know the present value of an ordinary annuity, how can you find the PV of the corresponding annuity due?

What is the PVA of an ordinary annuity with 10 payments of \$100 if the appropriate interest rate is 10%? What would PVA be if the interest rate were 4%? What if the interest rate were 0%? How would the PVA values differ if we were dealing with annuities due? (\$614.46; \$811.09; \$1,000.00; \$675.90; \$843.53; \$1,000.00)

Assume that you are offered an annuity that pays \$100 at the end of each year for 10 years. You could earn 8% on your money in other investments with equal risk. What is the most you should pay for the annuity? If the payments began immediately, how much would the annuity be worth? (\$671.01; \$724.69)

2.10 Finding Annuity Payments, Periods, and Interest Rates

We can find payments, periods, and interest rates for annuities. Five variables come into play: N, I, PMT, FV, and PV. If we know any four, we can find the fifth. It is not too difficult to solve Equation 2-5 for the payment if you know all of the other inputs. But when trying to find the interest rate or number of periods, Equation 2-5 usually must be solved by trial-and-error. Therefore, we present only the solution approaches using a financial calculator or spreadsheet.

Finding Annuity Payments, PMT

Suppose we need to accumulate $10,000 and have it available five years from now. Suppose further that we can earn a return of 6% on our savings, which are currently zero. Thus, we know that FV = 10,000, PV = 0, N = 5, and I/YR = 6. We can enter these values in a financial calculator and then press the PMT key to find how large our deposits must be. The answer will, of course, depend on whether we make deposits at the end of each year (ordinary annuity) or at the beginning (annuity due). Here are the results for each type of annuity:

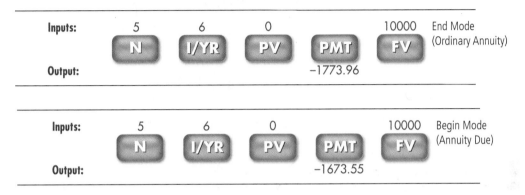

Thus, you must save $1,773.96 per year if you make payments at the *end* of each year, but only $1,673.55 if the payments begin *immediately*. Note that the required payment for the annuity due is the ordinary annuity payment divided by (1 + I): $1,773.96/1.06 = $1,673.55.

Spreadsheets can also be used to find annuity payments. To find end-of-year payments, we use the PMT function: **=PMT(I,N,PV,FV)**. In our example, this is **=PMT(0.06,5,0,10000)** = $1,773.96. For the payments of an annuity due (payments at the beginning of the period), the same formula is used, except we must specify the type of annuity, with Type = 1 indicating an annuity due: **=PMT(I,N,PV,FV,Type)** **=PMT(0.06,5,0,10000,1)** = $1,673.55.

e-resource
See **FM12 Ch 02 Tool Kit.xls** for all calculations.

Finding the Number of Periods, N

Suppose you decide to make end-of-year deposits, but you can only save $1,200 per year. Again assuming that you would earn 6%, how long would it take you to reach your $10,000 goal? Here is the calculator setup:

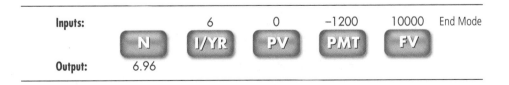

With these smaller deposits, it would take 6.96 years to reach the $10,000 target. If you began the deposits immediately, then you would have an annuity due and N would be a bit less, 6.63 years.

In *Excel*, you can use the NPER function: **=NPER(I,PMT,PV,FV)**. For this example, the function is **=NPER(0.06,−1200,0,10000)** = 6.96.

e-resource
See **FM12 Ch 02 Tool Kit.xls** for all calculations.

Finding the Interest Rate, I

Now suppose you can only save $1,200 annually, but you still want to have the $10,000 in five years. What rate of return would enable you to achieve your goal? Here is the calculator setup:

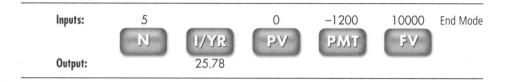

Inputs:	5		0	−1200	10000	End Mode
	N	I/YR	PV	PMT	FV	
Output:		25.78				

You would need to earn a whopping 25.78%! About the only possible (but risky) way to get such a high return would be to invest in speculative stocks or head to Las Vegas and a casino. Of course, speculative stocks and gambling aren't like making deposits in a bank with a guaranteed rate of return, so there's a good chance you'd end up with nothing. We'd recommend that you change your plans—save more, lower your $10,000 target, or extend your time horizon. It might be appropriate to seek a somewhat higher return, but trying to earn 25.78% in a 6% market would require taking on more risk than would be prudent.

In *Excel*, you can use the RATE function: **=RATE(N,PMT,PV,FV)**. For this example, the function is **=RATE(3,−1200,0,10000)** = 0.2578 = 25.78 percent.

SELF-TEST

Suppose you inherited $100,000 and invested it at 7% per year. How much could you withdraw at the *end* of each of the next 10 years? How would your answer change if you made withdrawals at the *beginning* of each year? ($14,237.75; $13,306.31)

If you had $100,000 that was invested at 7% and you wanted to withdraw $10,000 at the end of each year, how long would your funds last? How long would they last if you earned 0%? How long would they last if you earned the 7% but limited your withdrawal to $7,000 per year? (17.8 years; 10 years; forever)

Your rich uncle named you as the beneficiary of his life insurance policy. The insurance company gives you a choice of $100,000 today or a 12-year annuity of $12,000 at the end of each year. What rate of return is the insurance company offering? (6.11%)

Assume that you just inherited an annuity that will pay you $10,000 per year for 10 years, with the first payment being made today. A friend of your mother offers to give you $60,000 for the annuity. If you sell it, what rate of return will your mother's friend earn on the investment? If you think a "fair" return would be 6%, how much should you ask for the annuity? (13.70%; $78,016.92)

2.11 Perpetuities

In the last section we dealt with annuities whose payments continue for a specific number of periods—for example, $100 per year for 10 years. However, some securities promise to make payments forever. For example, in 1749 the British government issued some bonds whose proceeds were used to pay off other British bonds, and since this action consolidated the government's debt, the new bonds were called consols. Since **consols** promise to pay interest perpetually, they are perpetuities. The interest rate on the consols was 2.5%, so a bond with a face value of $1,000 would pay $25 per year in perpetuity.[8]

---

[8] The consols actually pay interest in pounds, but we discuss them in dollar terms for simplicity.

A **perpetuity** is simply an annuity with an extended life. Since the payments go on forever, you can't apply the step-by-step approach. However, it's easy to find the PV of a perpetuity with the following formula:[9]

$$\text{PV of a perpetuity} = \frac{\text{PMT}}{\text{I}}. \qquad\qquad \textbf{(2-9)}$$

Now we can use Equation 2-9 to find the value of a British consol with a face value of $1,000 that pays $25 per year in perpetuity. The answer depends on the interest rate. In 1888, the "going rate" as established in the financial marketplace was 2.5%, so at that time the consol's value was $1,000:

$$\text{Consol value}_{1888} = \$25/0.025 = \$1,000.$$

In 2006, 118 years later, the annual payment was still $25, but the going interest rate had risen to 5.2%, causing the consol's value to fall to $480.77:

$$\text{Consol value}_{2006} = \$25/0.052 = \$480.77.$$

Note, though, that if interest rates decline in the future, say to 2%, the value of the consol will rise:

$$\text{Consol value if rates decline to } 2\% = \$25/0.02 = \$1,250.00.$$

These examples demonstrate an important point: *When interest rates change, the prices of outstanding bonds also change. Bond prices decline if rates rise and increase if rates fall.* We will discuss this point in more detail in Chapter 5, where we cover bonds in depth.

SELF-TEST

What is the present value of a perpetuity that pays $1,000 per year, beginning 1 year from now, if the appropriate interest rate is 5%? What would the value be if the annuity began its payments immediately? ($20,000, $21,000). (Hint: Just add the $1,000 to be received immediately to the value of the annuity.)

What happens to the value of a bond if interest rates go up? If rates go down?

2.12 Uneven Cash Flows

The definition of an annuity includes the term *constant payment*—in other words, annuities involve payments that are equal in every period. Although many financial decisions do involve constant payments, many others involve **nonconstant, or uneven, cash flows.** For example, the dividends on common stocks typically increase over time, and investments in capital equipment almost always generate uneven cash flows. Throughout the book, we reserve the term **payment (PMT)** for annuities with their equal payments in each period and use the term **cash flow (CF_t)** to denote uneven cash flows, where the t designates the period in which the cash flow occurs.

There are two important classes of uneven cash flows: (1) a stream that consists of a series of annuity payments plus an additional final lump sum and (2) all other uneven streams. Bonds represent the best example of the first type, while

---

[9]See **Web Extension 2A** at the textbook's Web site for a derivation of the perpetuity formula.

stocks and capital investments illustrate the other type. Here are numerical examples of the two types of flows:

1. Annuity plus additional final payment:

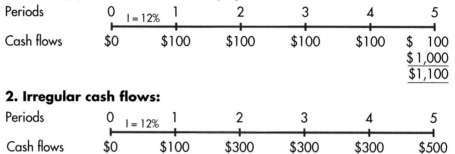

Periods	0	1	2	3	4	5
		I = 12%				
Cash flows	$0	$100	$100	$100	$100	$ 100
						$ 1,000
						$1,100

2. Irregular cash flows:

Periods	0	1	2	3	4	5
		I = 12%				
Cash flows	$0	$100	$300	$300	$300	$500

We can find the PV of either stream by using Equation 2-10 and following the step-by-step procedure, where we discount each cash flow and then sum them to find the PV of the stream:

FM
e-resource
See **FM12 Ch 02 Tool Kit.xls** for all calculations.

$$PV = \frac{CF_1}{(1 + I)^1} + \frac{CF_2}{(1 + I)^2} + \cdots + \frac{CF_N}{(1 + I)^N} = \sum_{t=1}^{N} \frac{CF_t}{(1 + I)^t}. \qquad (2\text{-}10)$$

If we did this, we would find the PV of Stream 1 to be $927.90 and the PV of Stream 2 to be $1,016.35.

The step-by-step procedure is straightforward, but if we have a large number of cash flows it is time-consuming. However, financial calculators and spreadsheets speed up the process considerably.

First, consider Stream 1, and notice that it is a 5-year, 12%, ordinary annuity plus a final payment of $1,000. We could find the PV of the annuity, then find the PV of the final payment, and then sum them to get the PV of the stream. However, financial calculators do this in one simple step—use the five TVM keys, enter the data as shown below, and then press the PV key to get the answer, $927.90.

Inputs:	5	12		100	1000
	N	I/YR	PV	PMT	FV
Output:			−927.90		

Similarly, we could use the PV function in *Excel*: **=PV(I,N,PMT,FV)**. This is similar to our previous solutions for an annuity, except we now have a nonzero value for FV. Applying the PV function, we get **=PV(0.12,5,100,1000)** = −$927.90.

Now consider the second uneven stream shown in Figure 2-7. The top section shows the time line and an application of the step-by-step approach.

Because the cash flows do not represent an annuity, you can't use the annuity feature on your financial calculator to find the present value. However, your financial calculator does have a feature that allows you to find the present value. First, you input the individual cash flows, in chronological order, into the cash flow register. [10] Cash flows are usually designated CF_0, CF_1, CF_2, CF_3, and so on.

---

[10]We cover the calculator mechanics in the tutorial, and we discuss the process in more detail in Chapter 11, where we use the NPV calculation to analyze proposed projects. If you don't know how to do the calculation with your calculator, it will be worthwhile to go to our tutorial or your calculator manual, learn the steps, and be sure you can make this calculation. You will have to learn to do it eventually, and now is a good time.

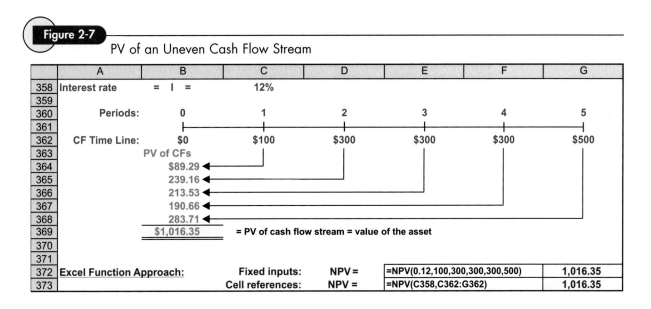

Figure 2-7   PV of an Uneven Cash Flow Stream

	A	B	C	D	E	F	G
358	Interest rate	= I =	12%				
359							
360	Periods:	0	1	2	3	4	5
361							
362	CF Time Line:	$0	$100	$300	$300	$300	$500
363		PV of CFs					
364		$89.29					
365		239.16					
366		213.53					
367		190.66					
368		283.71					
369		$1,016.35	= PV of cash flow stream = value of the asset				
370							
371							
372	**Excel Function Approach:**		Fixed inputs:	NPV =	=NPV(0.12,100,300,300,300,500)		1,016.35
373			Cell references:	NPV =	=NPV(C358,C362:G362)		1,016.35

Next, you enter the interest rate, I. At this point, you have substituted in all the known values of Equation 2-10, so you only need to press the NPV key to find the present value of the stream. The calculator has been programmed to find the PV of each cash flow and then to sum these values to find the PV of the entire stream. To input the cash flows for this problem, enter 0 (because $CF_0 = 0$), 100, 300, 300, 300, and 500 in that order into the cash flow register, enter I = 12, and then press NPV to obtain the answer, $1,016.35.

Two points should be noted. First, when dealing with the cash flow register, the calculator uses the term "NPV" rather than "PV." The N stands for "net," so NPV is the abbreviation for "Net Present Value," which is simply the net present value of a series of positive and negative cash flows, including the cash flow at time zero.

The second point to note is that repeated cash flows with identical values can be entered into the cash flow register more efficiently by using the Nj key. In this illustration, you would enter $CF_0 = 0$, $CF_1 = 100$, $CF_2 = 300$, Nj = 3 (which tells the calculator that the 300 occurs 3 times), and $CF_5 = 500$.[11] Then enter I = 12, press the NPV key, and 1,016.35 will appear in the display. Also, note that amounts entered into the cash flow register remain in the register until they are cleared. Thus, if you had previously worked a problem with eight cash flows, and then moved to a problem with only four cash flows, the calculator would simply add the cash flows from the second problem to those of the first problem. Therefore, you must be sure to clear the cash flow register before starting a new problem.

Spreadsheets are especially useful for solving problems with uneven cash flows. Just as with a financial calculator, you must enter the cash flows in the spreadsheet, as shown in Figure 2-7. To find the PV of these cash flows with *Excel*, you can use the NPV function. Put your cursor on Cell G373, click the function wizard, click Financial, scroll down to NPV, and click OK to get the dialog box.

---

[11]On some calculators, instead of entering $CF_5 = 500$, you enter $CF_3 = 500$, because this is the next *different* cash flow.

Then enter C358 or 0.12 for Rate and the range of cells containing the cash flows, C362:G362, for Value 1. Be very careful when entering the range of cash flows. With a financial calculator, you begin by entering the Time 0 cash flow. With *Excel*, you do *not* include the Time 0 cash flow; instead, you begin with the Year 1 cash flow. Now, when you click OK, you get the PV of the stream, $1,016.35. Note that you can use the PV function if the payments are constant but you must use the NPV function if the cash flows are not constant. Note too that one of the advantages of spreadsheets over financial calculators is that you can see the cash flows, which makes it easy to spot any typing errors.

SELF-TEST

Could you use Equation 2-3, once for each cash flow, to find the PV of an uneven stream of cash flows?

What is the present value of a 5-year ordinary annuity of $100 plus an additional $500 at the end of Year 5 if the interest rate is 6%? How would the PV change if the $100 payments occurred in Years 1 through 10 and the $500 came at the end of Year 10? ($794.87; $1,015.21)

What is the present value of the following uneven cash flow stream: $0 at Time 0, $100 in Year 1 (or at Time 1), $200 in Year 2, $0 in Year 3, and $400 in Year 4 if the interest rate is 8%? ($558.07)

Would a typical common stock provide cash flows more like an annuity or more like an uneven cash flow stream?

2.13 Future Value of an Uneven Cash Flow Stream

The future value of an uneven cash flow stream (sometimes called the **terminal value**) is found by compounding each payment to the end of the stream and then summing the future values:

$$FV = CF_0(1 + I)^N + CF_1(1 + I)^{N-1} + CF_2(1 + I)^{N-2} + \cdots + CF_{N-1}(1 + I) + CF_N$$

$$= \sum_{t=0}^{N} CF_t(1 + I)^{N-t} \qquad \text{(2-11)}$$

FM

e-resource

See **FM12 Ch 02 Tool Kit.xls** for all calculations.

The future value of our illustrative uneven cash flow stream is $1,791.15, as shown in Figure 2-8.

Some financial calculators have a net future value (NFV) key which, after the cash flows and interest rate have been entered, can be used to obtain the future value of an uneven cash flow stream. Even if your calculator doesn't have the NFV feature, you can use the cash flow stream's net present value to find its net future value: NFV = NPV(1 + I)^N. Thus, in our example, you could find the PV of the stream, then find the FV of that PV, compounded for N periods at I%. In the illustrative problem, find PV = 1,016.35 using the cash flow register and I = 12. Then enter N = 5, I = 12, PV = −1016.35, and PMT = 0. Press FV to find FV = 1,791.15, which equals the NFV shown on the time line in Figure 2-8. A similar procedure can be used in *Excel*: First find the NPV, then find its FV. See **FM12 Ch 02 Tool Kit.xls** for details.

SELF-TEST

What is the future value of this cash flow stream: $100 at the end of 1 year, $150 due after 2 years, and $300 due after 3 years if the appropriate interest rate is 15%? ($604.75)

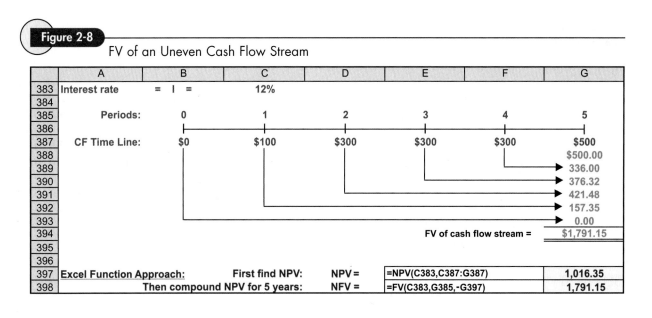

Figure 2-8

FV of an Uneven Cash Flow Stream

	A	B	C	D	E	F	G
383	Interest rate	= I =	12%				
384							
385	Periods:	0	1	2	3	4	5
386							
387	CF Time Line:	$0	$100	$300	$300	$300	$500
388							$500.00
389							336.00
390							376.32
391							421.48
392							157.35
393							0.00
394						FV of cash flow stream =	$1,791.15
395							
396							
397	**Excel Function Approach:**		**First find NPV:**	NPV =	=NPV(C383,C387:G387)		1,016.35
398			**Then compound NPV for 5 years:**	NFV =	=FV(C383,G385,-G397)		1,791.15

2.14 Solving for I with Uneven Cash Flows

Before financial calculators and spreadsheets existed, it was *extremely difficult* to find I if the cash flows were uneven. With spreadsheets and financial calculators, though, it's relatively easy to find I. If you have an annuity plus a final lump sum, you can input values for N, PV, PMT, and FV into the calculator's TVM registers and then press the I/YR key. Here is the setup for Stream 1 from Section 2.12, assuming we must pay $927.90 to buy the asset. The rate of return on the $927.90 investment is 12%, as shown below:

e-resource

See **FM12 Ch 02 Tool Kit.xls** for all calculations.

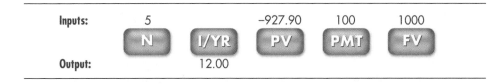

Inputs:	5		−927.90	100	1000
	N	I/YR	PV	PMT	FV
Output:		12.00			

Finding the interest rate for an uneven cash flow stream is a bit more complicated. Figure 2-9 shows Stream 2 from Section 2.12, assuming CF_0 is −$1,000. First, note that there is no simple procedure for finding the rate of return—finding the rate requires a trial-and-error process, which means that one really needs a financial calculator or a spreadsheet. With a calculator, we would enter the CFs into the cash flow register and then press the IRR key to get the answer. IRR stands for "internal rate of return," and it is the rate of return the investment provides. The investment is the cash flow at Time 0, and it must be entered as a negative number. When we enter those cash flows in the calculator's

Figure 2-9

IRR of an Uneven Cash Flow Stream

	A	B	C	D	E	F	G
421	Periods:	0	1	2	3	4	5
422							
423	CF Time Line:	-$1,000	$100	$300	$300	$300	$500
424							
425	Excel Function Approach:		Cell references:	IRR =	=IRR(B423:G423)		12.55%

cash flow register and press the IRR key, we get the rate of return on the $1,000 investment, 12.55%.

You would get the same answer using *Excel's* IRR function, as shown in Figure 2-9. Notice that with the IRR function, you must include all cash flows, including the Time 0 cash flow; with the NPV function, you do not include the Time 0 cash flow.

SELF-TEST

An investment costs $465 and is expected to produce cash flows of $100 at the end of each of the next 4 years, then an extra lump sum payment of $200 at the end of the 4th year. What is the expected rate of return on this investment? (9.05%)

An investment costs $465 and is expected to produce cash flows of $100 at the end of Year 1, $200 at the end of Year 2, and $300 at the end of Year 3. What is the expected rate of return on this investment? (11.71%)

2.15 Semiannual and Other Compounding Periods

In almost all of our examples thus far, we have assumed that interest is compounded once a year, or annually. This is called **annual compounding.** Suppose, however, that you put $100 into a bank that states it pays a 6% annual interest rate but that interest is credited each 6 months. This is called **semiannual compounding.** How much would you have accumulated at the end of 1 year, 2 years, or some other period under semiannual compounding? Note that virtually all bonds pay interest semiannually, most stocks pay dividends quarterly, and most mortgages, student loans, and auto loans require monthly payments. Therefore, it is essential that you understand how to deal with nonannual compounding.

Types of Interest Rates

Compounding involves three types of interest rates: nominal rates, I_{NOM}; periodic rates, I_{PER}; and effective annual rates, EAR or EFF%.

Nominal, or Quoted, Rate, I_{NOM} [12] This is the rate that is quoted by banks, brokers, and other financial institutions. So, if you talk with a banker, broker, mortgage lender, auto finance company, or student loan officer about rates, the nominal rate is the one he or she will normally quote you. However, to be meaningful, the quoted nominal rate must also include the number of compounding periods per year. For example, a bank might offer 6%, compounded quarterly, on CDs; or a mutual fund might offer 5%, compounded monthly, on its money market account.

---

[12]The term *nominal rate* as it is used here has a different meaning than the way it was used in Chapter 1. There, nominal interest rates referred to stated market rates as opposed to real (zero inflation) rates. In this chapter, the term *nominal rate* means the stated, or quoted, annual rate as opposed to the effective annual rate, which we explain later. In both cases, though, *nominal* means *stated*, or *quoted*, as opposed to some adjusted rate.

The nominal rate on loans to consumers is also called the **Annual Percentage Rate (APR).** For example, if a credit card issuer quotes an annual rate of 18%, this is the APR.

Note that the nominal rate is never shown on a time line, and it is never used as an input in a financial calculator, unless compounding occurs only once a year. If more frequent compounding occurs, you should use the periodic rate as discussed below.

Periodic Rate, I_{PER} This is the rate charged by a lender or paid by a borrower each period. It can be a rate per year, per 6-month period, per quarter, per month, per day, or per any other time interval. For example, a bank might charge 1.5% per month on its credit card loans, or a finance company might charge 3% per quarter on installment loans. We find the periodic rate as follows:

$$\text{Periodic rate, } I_{PER} = I_{NOM}/M, \qquad \text{(2-12)}$$

which implies that

$$\text{Nominal annual rate} = I_{NOM} = (\text{Periodic rate})(M). \qquad \text{(2-13)}$$

Here I_{NOM} is the nominal annual rate and M is the number of compounding periods per year. To illustrate, consider a finance company loan at 3% per quarter:

$$\text{Nominal annual rate} = I_{NOM} = (\text{Periodic rate})(M) = (3\%)(4) = 12\%,$$

or

$$\text{Periodic rate} = I_{NOM}/M = 12\%/4 = 3\% \text{ per quarter.}$$

If there is only one payment per year, or if interest is added only once a year, then M = 1, and the periodic rate is equal to the nominal rate.

The periodic rate is the rate that is generally shown on time lines and used in calculations.[13] To illustrate use of the periodic rate, suppose you invest $100 in an account that pays a nominal rate of 12%, compounded quarterly. How much would you have after 2 years?

For compounding more frequently than annually, we use the following modification of Equation 2-1:

$$FV_N = PV(1 + I_{PER})^{\text{Number of periods}} = PV\left(1 + \frac{I_{NOM}}{M}\right)^{MN}. \qquad \text{(2-14)}$$

For the example of $100 compounded quarterly at an annual nominal rate of 12% for 2 years, the time line is

[13]The only exception is in situations where (1) annuities are involved and (2) the payment periods do not correspond to the compounding periods. If an annuity is involved and if its payment periods do not correspond to the compounding periods—for example, if you are making quarterly payments into a bank account to build up a specified future sum, but the bank pays interest on a daily basis—then the calculations are more complicated. For such problems, one can proceed in two alternative ways. (1) Determine the periodic (daily) interest rate by dividing the nominal rate by 365 (or 360 if the bank uses a 360-day year), then compound each payment over the exact number of days from the payment date to the terminal point, and then sum the compounded payments to find the future value of the annuity. This is what would generally be done in the real world, because with a computer it would be a simple process. (2) Calculate the EAR, as defined later in this section, based on daily compounding, then find the corresponding nominal rate based on quarterly compounding (because the annuity payments are made quarterly), then find the quarterly periodic rate, and use that rate with standard annuity procedures. The second procedure is faster with a calculator, but hard to explain and generally not used in practice given the ready availability of computers.

Using Equation 2-14,

$$FV = \$100(1 + 0.03)^8$$

$$= \$126.68.$$

With a financial calculator, we work the problem with inputs $N = 2 \times 4 = 8$, $I = 12/4 = 3$, $PV = -100$, and $PMT = 0$. The result is $FV = \$126.68$.

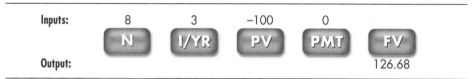

Inputs:	8	3	−100	0	
	N	I/YR	PV	PMT	FV
Output:					126.68

Most financial calculators have a feature that allows you to set the number of payments per year and then use the nominal annual interest rate. However, in our experience, students make fewer errors when using the periodic rate with their calculators set for one payment per year (i.e., per period), so this is what we recommend.

Effective (or Equivalent) Annual Rate (EAR or EFF%) This is the annual rate that produces the same result as if we had compounded at a given periodic rate M times per year. The EAR, also called EFF% (for effective percentage), is found as follows:

$$\text{Effective annual rate (EFF\%)} = \left(1 + \frac{I_{NOM}}{M}\right)^M - 1.0. \qquad \textbf{(2-15)}$$

You could also use the interest conversion feature of a financial calculator.[14]

In the EAR equation, I_{NOM}/M is the periodic rate, and M is the number of periods per year. For example, suppose you could borrow using either a credit card that charges 1% per month or a bank loan with a 12% quoted nominal interest rate that is compounded quarterly. Which should you choose? To answer this question, the cost rate of each alternative must be expressed as an EAR:

$$\text{Credit card loan: EFF\%} = (1 + 0.01)^{12} - 1.0 = (1.01)^{12} - 1.0$$

$$= 1.126825 - 1.0 = 0.126825 = 12.6825\%.$$

$$\text{Bank loan: EFF\%} = (1 + 0.03)^4 - 1.0 = (1.03)^4 - 1.0$$

$$= 1.125509 - 1.0 = 0.125509 = 12.5509\%.$$

FM

e-resource

See **FM12 Ch 02 Tool Kit.xls** for all calculations.

Thus, the credit card loan is slightly more costly than the bank loan. This result should have been intuitive to you—both loans have the same 12% nominal rate, yet you would have to make monthly payments on the credit card versus quarterly payments under the bank loan.

The EFF% rate is not used in calculations. However, it should be used to compare the effective cost or rate of return on loans or investments when payment periods differ, as in the credit card versus bank loan example.

[14]Most financial calculators are programmed to find the EFF% or, given the EFF%, to find the nominal rate. This is called "interest rate conversion." You enter the nominal rate and the number of compounding periods per year and then press the EFF% key to find the effective annual rate. However, we generally use Equation 2-15 because it's as easy to use as the interest conversion feature is, and the equation reminds us of what we are really doing. If you use the interest rate conversion feature on your calculator, don't forget to reset your calculator settings. Interest conversion is discussed in the tutorials.

The Result of Frequent Compounding

Suppose you plan to invest $100 for 5 years at a nominal annual rate of 10%. What will happen to the future value of your investment if interest is compounded more frequently than once a year? Because interest will be earned on interest more often, you might expect the future value to increase as the frequency of compounding increases. Similarly, you might also expect the effective annual rate to increase with more frequent compounding. As Table 2-1 shows, you would be correct—the future value and EAR do in fact increase as the frequency of compounding increases. Notice that the biggest increases in FV and EAR occur when compounding goes from annual to semiannual, and that moving from monthly to daily compounding has a relatively small impact. Although Table 2-1 shows daily compounding as the smallest interval, it is possible to compound even more frequently. At the limit, one can have **continuous compounding.** This is explained in *Web Extension 2B* at the textbook's Web site.

Table 2-1

The Impact of Frequent Compounding

Frequency of Compounding	Nominal Annual Rate	Effective Annual Rate (EFF%)[a]	Future Value of $100 Invested for 5 Years[b]
Annual	10.00%	10.000%	$161.05
Semiannual	10.00	10.250	162.89
Quarterly	10.00	10.381	163.86
Monthly	10.00	10.471	164.53
Daily[c]	10.00	10.516	164.86

[a]The EAR is calculated using Equation 2-14.
[b]The future value is calculated using Equation 2-13.
[c]The daily calculations assume 365 days per year.

SELF-TEST

Would you rather invest in an account that pays 7% with annual compounding or 7% with monthly compounding? Would you rather borrow at 7% and make annual or monthly payments? Why?

What is the *future value* of $100 after 3 years if the appropriate interest rate is 8%, compounded annually? Compounded monthly? ($125.97; $127.02)

What is the *present value* of $100 due in 3 years if the appropriate interest rate is 8%, compounded annually? Compounded monthly? ($79.38; $78.73)

Define the terms "Annual Percentage Rate, or APR," "effective annual rate, or EFF%," and "nominal interest rate, I_{NOM}."

A bank pays 5% with daily compounding on its savings accounts. Should it advertise the nominal or effective rate if it is seeking to attract new deposits?

Credit card issuers must by law print their Annual Percentage Rate (APR) on their monthly statements. A common APR is 18%, with interest paid monthly. What is the EFF% on such a loan? (EFF% = $(1 + 0.18/12)^{12} - 1 = 0.1956 = 19.56\%$.)

Some years ago banks didn't have to reveal the rate they charged on credit cards. Then Congress passed a "truth in lending" law that required them to publish their APR. Is the APR really the "most truthful" rate, or would the EFF% be "more truthful?"

2.16 Fractional Time Periods

Thus far we have assumed that payments occur at either the beginning or the end of periods, but not *within* periods. However, we often encounter situations that require compounding or discounting over fractional periods. For example, suppose you deposited $100 in a bank that pays a nominal rate of 10% but adds interest daily, based on a 365-day year. How much would you have after 9 months? The answer is $107.79, found as follows:[15]

$$\text{Periodic rate} = I_{PER} = 0.10/365 = 0.000273973 \text{ per day.}$$

$$\text{Number of days} = (9/12)(365) = 0.75(365)$$

$$= 273.75 \text{ rounded to } 274.$$

$$\text{Ending amount} = \$100(1.000273973)^{274} = \$107.79.$$

Now suppose you borrow $100 from a bank whose nominal rate is 10% per year "simple interest," which means that interest is not earned on interest. If the loan is outstanding for 274 days, how much interest would you have to pay? Here we would calculate a daily interest rate, I_{PER}, as above, but multiply it by 274 rather than use the 274 as an exponent:

$$\text{Interest owed} = \$100(0.000273973)(274) = \$7.51 \text{ interest.}$$

You would owe the bank a total of $107.51 after 274 days. This is the procedure most banks actually use to calculate interest on loans, except that they require borrowers to pay the interest on a monthly basis rather than after 274 days.

SELF-TEST

Suppose a company borrowed $1 million at a rate of 9%, simple interest, with interest paid at the end of each month. The bank uses a 360-day year. How much interest would the firm have to pay in a 30-day month? What would the interest be if the bank used a 365-day year? [(0.09/360)(30)($1,000,000) = $7,500 interest for the month. For the 365-day year, (0.09/365)(30)($1,000,000) = $7,397.26 of interest. The use of a 360-day year raises the interest cost by $102.74. That's why banks like to use it on loans.]

(Continued)

---

[15]Bank loan contracts specifically state whether they are based on a 360- or a 365-day year. If a 360-day year is used, then the daily rate is higher, so the effective rate is also higher. Here we assumed a 365-day year. Also, note that in real-world calculations, banks' computers have built-in calendars, so they can calculate the exact number of days, taking account of 30-day, 31-day, and 28- or 29-day months.

SELF-TEST

Suppose you deposited $1,000 in a credit union that pays 7% with daily compounding and a 365-day year. What is the EFF%, and how much could you withdraw after 7 months, assuming this is 7/12 of a year? [EFF% = $(1 + 0.07/365)^{365} - 1 = 0.07250098 = 7.250098\%$. Thus, your account would grow from $1,000 to $1,000(1.07250098)^{0.583333} = \$1,041.67$, and you could withdraw that amount.]

2.17 Amortized Loans

An important application of compound interest involves loans that are paid off in installments over time. Included are automobile loans, home mortgage loans, student loans, and many business loans. A loan that is to be repaid in equal amounts on a monthly, quarterly, or annual basis is called an **amortized loan**.[16]

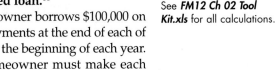

FM

e-resource

See **FM12 Ch 02 Tool Kit.xls** for all calculations.

Table 2-2 illustrates the amortization process. A homeowner borrows $100,000 on a mortgage loan, and the loan is to be repaid in 5 equal payments at the end of each of the next 5 years.[17] The lender charges 6% on the balance at the beginning of each year.

Our first task is to determine the payment the homeowner must make each year. Here's a picture of the situation:

The payments must be such that the sum of their PVs equals $100,000:

$$\$100{,}000 = \frac{\text{PMT}}{(1.06)^1} + \frac{\text{PMT}}{(1.06)^2} + \frac{\text{PMT}}{(1.06)^3} + \frac{\text{PMT}}{(1.06)^4} + \frac{\text{PMT}}{(1.06)^5} = \sum_{t=1}^{5} \frac{\text{PMT}}{(1.06)^t}$$

It is possible to use the annuity formula in Equation 2-7, but it is much easier to use a financial calculator or spreadsheet. With a financial calculator, we insert values into a calculator as shown below to get the required payments, $23,739.64:

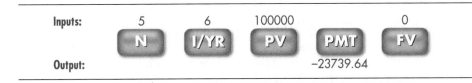

Inputs:	5	6	100000		0
	N	I/YR	PV	PMT	FV
Output:				−23739.64	

Therefore, the borrower must pay the lender $23,739.64 per year for the next 5 years.

With *Excel*, you would use the PMT function: **=PMT(I,N,PV,FV)** = **PMT(0.06,5,100000,0)** = −$23,739.64.

Each payment will consist of two parts—interest and repayment of principal. This breakdown is shown on an **amortization schedule** such as the one in Table 2-2. The interest component is relatively high in the first year, but it declines as the loan balance decreases. For tax purposes, the borrower would deduct the interest component while the lender would report the same amount as taxable income.

---

[16]The word *amortized* comes from the Latin *mors*, meaning "death," so an amortized loan is one that is "killed off" over time.
[17]Most mortgage loans call for monthly payments over 10 to 30 years, but we use a shorter period to simplify the example.

Table 2-2

Loan Amortization Schedule, $100,000 at 6% for 5 Years

Year	Beginning Amount (1)	Payment (2)	Interest[a] (3)	Repayment of Principal[b] (2) − (3) = (4)	Ending Balance (1) − (4) = (5)
1	$100,000.00	$23,739.64	$6,000.00	$17,739.64	$82,260.36
2	$82,260.36	$23,739.64	$4,935.62	$18,804.02	$63,456.34
3	$63,456.34	$23,739.64	$3,807.38	$19,932.26	$43,524.08
4	$43,524.08	$23,739.64	$2,611.44	$21,128.20	$22,395.89
5	$22,395.89	$23,739.64	$1,343.75	$22,395.89	$0.00

[a]Interest in each period is calculated by multiplying the loan balance at the beginning of the year by the interest rate. Therefore, interest in Year 1 is $100,000(0.06) = $6,000; in Year 2 it is $82,260.36(0.06) = $4,935.62; and so on.
[b]Repayment of principal is equal to the payment of $23,739.64 minus the interest charged for the year.

SELF-TEST

Suppose you borrowed $30,000 on a student loan at a rate of 8% and now must repay it in 3 equal installments at the end of each of the next 3 years. How large would your payments be, how much of the first payment would represent interest, how much would be principal, and what would your ending balance be after the first year? (PMT = $11,641.01; Interest = $2,400; Principal = $9,241.01; Balance at end of Year 1 = $20,758.99)

2.18 Growing Annuities

Normally, an annuity is defined as a series of *constant* payments to be received over a specified number of periods. However, the term **growing annuity** is used to describe a series of payments that grow at a constant rate.

Example 1: Finding a Constant Real Income. Growing annuities are often used in the area of financial planning, where a prospective retiree wants to determine the maximum constant *real*, or *inflation-adjusted*, withdrawals he or she can make over a specified number of years. For example, suppose a 65-year-old is contemplating retirement, expects to live for another 20 years, has a $1 million nest egg, expects to earn 8% on his or her investments, expects inflation to average 3% per year, and wants to withdraw a constant *real* amount annually over the next remaining 20 years. If the first withdrawal is to be made today, what is the amount of this initial withdrawal?

This problem can be solved in three ways. (1) Set up a spreadsheet model that is similar to an amortization table, where the account earns 8% per year, withdrawals rise at the 3% inflation rate, and *Excel*'s Goal Seek function is used to find the initial inflation-adjusted withdrawal, and a zero balance remains at the end of the 20th year. (2) Use a financial calculator, where we first calculate the real rate of return, adjusted for inflation, and use it for I/YR when finding the payment for an annuity due. (3) Use a relatively complicated and obtuse formula to find this same amount.[18] We illustrate the first two procedures in the chapter model, *FM12 Ch 02 Tool Kit.xls.* The financial calculator approach is easiest to use, but the spreadsheet model provides the clearest picture of what is happening. It shows the value of the retirement portfolio, the earning, and each withdrawal over the 20-year planning horizon. Also, the spreadsheet model creates graphs that make it easy to explain things to people who are planning their financial futures.

e-resource

See *FM12 Ch 02 Tool Kit.xls* for all calculations.

To implement the calculator approach, we first find the expected real, or inflation adjusted, rate of return, where r_r is the real rate of return and r_{NOM} the nominal rate of return:

$$\text{Real rate} = r_r = [(1 + r_{NOM})/(1 + \text{Inflation})] - 1.0 \qquad (2\text{-}16)$$
$$= [1.08/1.03] - 1.0 = 0.048543689 = 4.8543689\%.$$

Next, we set the calculator to Begin Mode, after which we input N = 20, I = real rate = 4.8543689, PV = −1,000,000, and FV = 0, then press PMT to get $75,585.53. This is the value at Time 0, today, and the initial withdrawal will increase at the inflation rate, 3%. With this initial withdrawal, the retiree will have a constant real income over the next 20 years.

In our example we assumed that the first withdrawal would be made immediately. The procedure would be slightly different if we wanted to make end-of-year withdrawals. First, we would find the real rate the same way and enter the same inputs into the calculator as shown above. Second, we would the calculator set to End Mode. The calculated PMT would be $79,254.73. However, that value is in beginning-of-year terms, and since inflation of 3% will occur during the year, we must make the following adjustment to find the inflation-adjusted initial payment:

$$\text{Initial withdrawal} = \$79,254.73(1 + \text{Inflation})$$

$$= \$79,254.73(1.03)$$

$$= \$81,632.38.$$

The first withdrawal, at the end of the year, would thus be $81,632.38, it would grow by 3% per year, and after the 20th withdrawal (at the end of the 20th year) the balance in the retirement fund would be zero.

The end-of-year payment is also analyzed in *FM12 Ch 02 Tool Kit.xls.* There we set up an amortization table that shows the beginning balance, the annual withdrawals, the annual earnings, and the ending balance for each of the 20 years. This analysis confirms the $81,632.38 initial withdrawal found above.

Example 2: Initial Deposit to Accumulate a Future Sum. As another example of a growing annuity, suppose you need to accumulate $100,000 in 10 years. You plan to make a deposit now, at Time 0, and then to make 9 more deposits at the beginning of the following 9 years, for a total of 10 deposits. The bank pays 6% interest, and you expect to increase your initial deposit amount by the 2% inflation rate each year. How much would you need to deposit initially? First, we calculate the real rate:

$$\text{Real rate} = r_r = [1.06/1.02] - 1.0 = 0.0392157 = 3.92157\%.$$

---

[18]For example, the formula used to find the payment for a growing ordinary annuity is shown below. If g = annuity growth rate and I = rate of return on investment, then

$$\text{PVIF of a growing annuity} = \text{PVIFGA} = [1 - [(1 + g)/(1 + I)]^N]/[(I - g)/(1 + g)].$$

$$\text{PMT} = \text{PV/PVIFGA}.$$

Next, since inflation is expected to be 2% per year, then in 10 years the target $100,000 will have a purchasing power of:

$$\$100,000/(1 + 0.02)^{10} = \$82,034.83.$$

Now we can find the size of the required initial payment by setting a financial calculator to the "BEG" mode and then inputting $N = 10$, $I/YR = 3.92157$, $PV = 0$, and $FV = 82,034.83$. Then, when we press the PMT key, we get $PMT = -6,598.87$. Thus, a deposit of $6,598.87 made at time zero and growing by 2 percent per year will accumulate to $100,000 by Year 10 if the interest rate is 6%. Again, this result is confirmed in the chapter model. The key to this analysis is to express I/YR, PV, and PMT in real, inflation-adjusted terms.

SELF-TEST

Differentiate between a "regular" and a growing annuity.

What three methods can be used to deal with growing annuities?

If the nominal interest rate is 10% and the expected inflation rate is 5%, what is the expected real rate of return? (4.7619%)

Summary

Most financial decisions involve situations in which someone pays money at one point in time and receives money at some later time. Dollars paid or received at two different points in time are different, and this difference is recognized and accounted for by *time value of money (TVM) analysis*.

- **Compounding** is the process of determining the **future value (FV)** of a cash flow or a series of cash flows. The compounded amount, or future value, is equal to the beginning amount plus the interest earned.
- Future value of a single payment: $FV_N = PV(1 + I)^N$.
- **Discounting** is the process of finding the **present value (PV)** of a future cash flow or a series of cash flows; discounting is the reciprocal, or reverse, of compounding.
- Present value of a single payment: $PV = \dfrac{FV_N}{(1 + I)^N}$.
- An **annuity** is defined as a series of equal periodic payments (PMT) for a specified number of periods.
- Future value of an annuity:

$$FVA_N = PMT\left[\frac{(1 + I)^N}{I} - \frac{1}{I}\right].$$

- Present value of an annuity:

$$PVA_N = PMT\left[\frac{1}{I} - \frac{1}{I(1 + I)^N}\right].$$

- An annuity whose payments occur at the *end* of each period is called an **ordinary annuity.** The formulas above are for ordinary annuities.
- If each payment occurs at the beginning of the period rather than at the end, then we have an **annuity due.** The PV of each payment would be larger,

because each payment would be discounted back one year less, so the PV of the annuity would also be larger. Similarly, the FV of the annuity due would also be larger because each payment would be compounded for an extra year. The following formulas can be used to convert the PV and FV of an ordinary annuity to an annuity due:

$$\text{PVA (annuity due)} = \text{PVA of an ordinary annuity} \times (1 + I),$$

$$\text{FVA (annuity due)} = \text{FVA of an ordinary annuity} \times (1 + I).$$

- A **perpetuity** is an annuity with an infinite number of payments.

$$\text{Value of a perpetuity} = \frac{\text{PMT}}{\text{I}}.$$

- To find the PV or FV of an uneven series, find the PV or FV of each individual cash flow and then sum them.
- If you know the cash flows and the PV (or FV) of a cash flow stream, you can **determine the interest rate.**
- When compounding occurs more frequently than once a year, the nominal rate must be converted to a periodic rate, and the number of years must be converted to periods.

$$I_{PER} = \text{Nominal annual rate/Periods per year}$$

$$\text{Periods} = \text{Years} \times \text{Periods per year}$$

The periodic rate and number of periods would be used for calculations and shown on time lines.

- If comparing the costs of loans that require payments more than once a year, or the rates of return on investments that pay interest more frequently, then the comparisons should be based on **equivalent** (or **effective**) rates of return using this formula:

$$\text{Effective annual rate (EFF\%)} = \left(1 + \frac{I_{NOM}}{M}\right)^M - 1.0.$$

- The general equation for finding the future value for any number of compounding periods per year is

$$FV_N = PV(1 + I_{PER})^{\text{Number of periods}} = PV\left(1 + \frac{I_{NOM}}{M}\right)^{MN}$$

where

$$I_{NOM} = \text{Nominal quoted interest rate,}$$

$$M = \text{Number of compounding periods per year,}$$

$$N = \text{Number of years.}$$

- An **amortized loan** is one that is paid off in equal payments over a specified period. An **amortization schedule** shows how much of each payment constitutes interest, how much is used to reduce the principal, and the unpaid balance at each point in time.

Questions

(2-1) Define each of the following terms:
   a. PV; I; INT; FV_N; PVA_N; FVA_N; PMT; M; I_{NOM}
   b. Opportunity cost rate
   c. Annuity; lump sum payment; cash flow; uneven cash flow stream
   d. Ordinary (deferred) annuity; annuity due
   e. Perpetuity; consol
   f. Outflow; inflow; time line; terminal value
   g. Compounding; discounting
   h. Annual, semiannual, quarterly, monthly, and daily compounding
   i. Effective annual rate (EAR); nominal (quoted) interest rate; APR; periodic rate
   j. Amortization schedule; principal versus interest component of a payment; amortized loan

(2-2) What is an *opportunity cost rate?* How is this rate used in discounted cash flow analysis, and where is it shown on a time line? Is the opportunity rate a single number that is used in all situations?

(2-3) An *annuity* is defined as a series of payments of a fixed amount for a specific number of periods. Thus, $100 a year for 10 years is an annuity, but $100 in Year 1, $200 in Year 2, and $400 in Years 3 through 10 does *not* constitute an annuity. However, the second series *contains* an annuity. Is this statement true or false?

(2-4) If a firm's earnings per share grew from $1 to $2 over a 10-year period, the *total growth* would be 100%, but the *annual growth rate* would be *less than* 10%. True or false? Explain.

(2-5) Would you rather have a savings account that pays 5% interest compounded semiannually or one that pays 5% interest compounded daily? Explain.

Self-Test Problems   Solutions Appear in Appendix A

(ST-1)
Future Value

Assume that 1 year from now, you will deposit $1,000 into a savings account that pays 8%.
   a. If the bank compounds interest annually, how much will you have in your account 4 years from now?
   b. What would your balance 4 years from now be if the bank used quarterly compounding rather than annual compounding?
   c. Suppose you deposited the $1,000 in 4 payments of $250 each at Year 1, Year 2, Year 3, and Year 4. How much would you have in your account at Year 4, based on 8% annual compounding?
   d. Suppose you deposited 4 equal payments in your account at Year 1, Year 2, Year 3, and Year 4. Assuming an 8% interest rate, how large would each of your payments have to be for you to obtain the same ending balance as you calculated in part a?

(ST-2)
Time Value of Money

Assume that 4 years from now you will need $1,000. Your bank compounds interest at an 8% annual rate.

a. How much must you deposit 1 year from now to have a balance of $1,000 4 years from now?

b. If you want to make equal payments at Years 1 through 4 to accumulate the $1,000, how large must each of the 4 payments be?

c. If your father were to offer either to make the payments calculated in part b ($221.92) or to give you a lump sum of $750 1 year from now, which would you choose?

d. If you have only $750 1 year from now, what interest rate, compounded annually, would you have to earn to have the necessary $1,000 4 years from now?

e. Suppose you can deposit only $186.29 each at Years 1 through 4, but you still need $1,000 at Year 4. What interest rate, with annual compounding, must you seek out to achieve your goal?

f. To help you reach your $1,000 goal, your father offers to give you $400 1 year from now. You will get a part-time job and make 6 additional payments of equal amounts each 6 months thereafter. If all of this money is deposited in a bank that pays 8%, compounded semiannually, how large must each of the 6 payments be?

g. What is the effective annual rate being paid by the bank in part f?

(ST-3)
Effective Annual Rates

Bank A pays 8% interest, compounded quarterly, on its money market account. The managers of Bank B want its money market account to equal Bank A's effective annual rate, but interest is to be compounded on a monthly basis. What nominal, or quoted, rate must Bank B set?

Easy Problems 1–8

Problems   Answers Appear in Appendix B

(2-1)
**Future Value
of a Single Payment**

If you deposit $10,000 in a bank account that pays 10% interest annually, how much will be in your account after 5 years?

(2-2)
**Present Value of a
Single Payment**

What is the present value of a security that will pay $5,000 in 20 years if securities of equal risk pay 7% annually?

(2-3)
**Interest Rate
of a Single Payment**

Your parents will retire in 18 years. They currently have $250,000, and they think they will need $1,000,000 at retirement. What annual interest rate must they earn to reach their goal, assuming they don't save any additional funds?

(2-4)
**Number of Periods
of a Single Payment**

If you deposit money today in an account that pays 6.5% annual interest, how long will it take to double your money?

(2-5)
**Number of Periods
for an Annuity**

You have $42,180.53 in a brokerage account, and you plan to deposit an additional $5,000 at the end of every future year until your account totals $250,000. You expect to earn 12% annually on the account. How many years will it take to reach your goal?

(2-6)
**Future Value: Annuity
versus Annuity Due**

What is the future value of a 7%, 5-year ordinary annuity that pays $300 each year? If this were an annuity due, what would its future value be?

(2-7)
**Present and Future
Value of an Uneven
Cash Flow Stream**

An investment will pay $100 at the end of each of the next 3 years, $200 at the end of Year 4, $300 at the end of Year 5, and $500 at the end of Year 6. If other investments of equal risk earn 8% annually, what is its present value? Its future value?

(2-8)

Annuity Payment and EAR

You want to buy a car, and a local bank will lend you $20,000. The loan would be fully amortized over 5 years (60 months), and the nominal interest rate would be 12%, with interest paid monthly. What would be the monthly loan payment? What would be the loan's EAR?

Intermediate Problems 9–30

(2-9)

Present and Future Values of Single Cash Flows for Different Periods

Find the following values, *using the equations*, and then work the problems using a financial calculator to check your answers. Disregard rounding differences. (Hint: If you are using a financial calculator, you can enter the known values and then press the appropriate key to find the unknown variable. Then, without clearing the TVM register, you can "override" the variable that changes by simply entering a new value for it and then pressing the key for the unknown variable to obtain the second answer. This procedure can be used in parts b and d, and in many other situations, to see how changes in input variables affect the output variable.)

a.   An initial $500 compounded for 1 year at 6%.
b.   An initial $500 compounded for 2 years at 6%.
c.   The present value of $500 due in 1 year at a discount rate of 6%.
d.   The present value of $500 due in 2 years at a discount rate of 6%.

(2-10)

Present and Future Values of Single Cash Flows for Different Interest Rates

Use equations and a financial calculator to find the following values. See the hint for Problem 2-9.

a.   An initial $500 compounded for 10 years at 6%..
b.   An initial $500 compounded for 10 years at 12%.
c.   The present value of $500 due in 10 years at a 6% discount rate.
d.   The present value of $500 due in 10 years at a 12% discount rate.

(2-11)

Time for a Lump Sum to Double

To the closest year, how long will it take $200 to double if it is deposited and earns the following rates? [Notes: (1) See the hint for Problem 2-9. (2) This problem cannot be solved exactly with some financial calculators. For example, if you enter PV = −200, PMT = 0, FV = 400, and I = 7 in an HP-12C, and then press the N key, you will get 11 years for part a. The correct answer is 10.2448 years, which rounds to 10, but the calculator rounds up. However, the HP-10B gives the correct answer.]

a.   7%.
b.   10%.
c.   18%.
d.   100%.

(2-12)

Future Value of an Annuity

Find the *future value* of the following annuities. The first payment in these annuities is made at the *end* of Year 1; that is, they are *ordinary annuities*. (Notes: See the hint to Problem 2-9. Also, note that you can leave values in the TVM register, switch to "BEG," press FV, and find the FV of the annuity due.)

a. $400 per year for 10 years at 10%.
b. $200 per year for 5 years at 5%.
c. $400 per year for 5 years at 0%.
d.   Now rework parts a, b, and c assuming that payments are made at the *beginning* of each year; that is, they are *annuities due*.

(2-13)

Present Value of an Annuity

Find the *present value* of the following *ordinary annuities* (see note to Problem 2-9):

a. $400 per year for 10 years at 10%.
b. $200 per year for 5 years at 5%.
c. $400 per year for 5 years at 0%.
d.   Now rework parts a, b, and c assuming that payments are made at the *beginning* of each year; that is, they are *annuities due*.

(2-14)
Uneven Cash
Flow Stream

a. Find the present values of the following cash flow streams. The appropriate interest rate is 8%. (Hint: It is fairly easy to work this problem dealing with the individual cash flows. However, if you have a financial calculator, read the section of the manual that describes how to enter cash flows such as the ones in this problem. This will take a little time, but the investment will pay huge dividends throughout the course. Note, if you do work with the cash flow register, then you must enter $CF_0 = 0$.)

Year	Cash Stream A	Cash Stream B
1	$100	$300
2	400	400
3	400	400
4	400	400
5	300	100

b. What is the value of each cash flow stream at a 0% interest rate?

(2-15)
Effective Rate of Interest

Find the interest rates, or rates of return, on each of the following:
a. You *borrow* $700 and promise to pay back $749 at the end of 1 year.
b. You *lend* $700 and receive a promise to be paid $749 at the end of 1 year.
c. You borrow $85,000 and promise to pay back $201,229 at the end of 10 years.
d. You borrow $9,000 and promise to make payments of $2,684.80 per year for 5 years.

(2-16)
Future Value for Various
Compounding Periods

Find the amount to which $500 will grow under each of the following conditions:
a. 12% compounded annually for 5 years.
b. 12% compounded semiannually for 5 years.
c. 12% compounded quarterly for 5 years.
d. 12% compounded monthly for 5 years.

(2-17)
Present Value for Various
Compounding Periods

Find the present value of $500 due in the future under each of the following conditions:
a. 12% nominal rate, semiannual compounding, discounted back 5 years.
b. 12% nominal rate, quarterly compounding, discounted back 5 years.
c. 12% nominal rate, monthly compounding, discounted back 1 year.

(2-18)
Future Value of an
Annuity for Various
Compounding Periods

Find the future values of the following ordinary annuities:
a. FV of $400 each 6 months for 5 years at a nominal rate of 12%, compounded semiannually.
b. FV of $200 each 3 months for 5 years at a nominal rate of 12%, compounded quarterly.
c. The annuities described in parts a and b have the same amount of money paid into them during the 5-year period and both earn interest at the same nominal rate, yet the annuity in part b earns $101.75 more than the one in part a over the 5 years. Why does this occur?

(2-19)
Effective versus Nominal
Interest Rates

Universal Bank pays 7% interest, compounded annually, on time deposits. Regional Bank pays 6% interest, compounded quarterly.
a. Based on effective interest rates, in which bank would you prefer to deposit your money?
b. Could your choice of banks be influenced by the fact that you might want to withdraw your funds during the year as opposed to at the end of the year? In answering this question, assume that funds must be left on deposit during the entire compounding period in order for you to receive any interest.

(2-20)
Amortization Schedule

a. Set up an amortization schedule for a $25,000 loan to be repaid in equal installments at the end of each of the next 5 years. The interest rate is 10%.

b. How large must each annual payment be if the loan is for $50,000? Assume that the interest rate remains at 10% and that the loan is paid off over 5 years.

c. How large must each payment be if the loan is for $50,000, the interest rate is 10%, and the loan is paid off in equal installments at the end of each of the next 10 years? This loan is for the same amount as the loan in part b, but the payments are spread out over twice as many periods. Why are these payments not half as large as the payments on the loan in part b?

(2-21)
Growth Rates

Hanebury Corporation's current sales were $12 million. Sales were $6 million 5 years earlier.

a. To the nearest percentage point, at what rate have sales been growing?

b. Suppose someone calculated the sales growth for Hanebury Corporation in part a as follows: "Sales doubled in 5 years. This represents a growth of 100% in 5 years, so, dividing 100% by 5, we find the growth rate to be 20% per year." Explain what is wrong with this calculation.

(2-22)
Expected Rate of Return

Washington-Pacific invests $4 million to clear a tract of land and to set out some young pine trees. The trees will mature in 10 years, at which time Washington-Pacific plans to sell the forest at an expected price of $8 million. What is Washington-Pacific's expected rate of return?

(2-23)
Effective Rate of Interest

A mortgage company offers to lend you $85,000; the loan calls for payments of $8,273.59 per year for 30 years. What interest rate is the mortgage company charging you?

(2-24)
Required Lump Sum
Payment

To complete your last year in business school and then go through law school, you will need $10,000 per year for 4 years, starting next year (that is, you will need to withdraw the first $10,000 one year from today). Your rich uncle offers to put you through school, and he will deposit in a bank paying 7% interest a sum of money that is sufficient to provide the 4 payments of $10,000 each. His deposit will be made today.

a. How large must the deposit be?

b. How much will be in the account immediately after you make the first withdrawal? After the last withdrawal?

(2-25)
Repaying a Loan

While Mary Corens was a student at the University of Tennessee, she borrowed $12,000 in student loans at an annual interest rate of 9%. If Mary repays $1,500 per year, how long, to the nearest year, will it take her to repay the loan?

(2-26)
Reaching a Financial
Goal

You need to accumulate $10,000. To do so, you plan to make deposits of $1,250 per year, with the first payment being made a year from today, in a bank account that pays 12% annual interest. Your last deposit will be less than $1,250 if less is needed to round out to $10,000. How many years will it take you to reach your $10,000 goal, and how large will the last deposit be?

(2-27)
Present Value of a
Perpetuity

What is the present value of a perpetuity of $100 per year if the appropriate discount rate is 7%? If interest rates in general were to double and the appropriate discount rate rose to 14%, what would happen to the present value of the perpetuity?

(2-28)
PV and Effective
Annual Rate

Assume that you inherited some money. A friend of yours is working as an unpaid intern at a local brokerage firm, and her boss is selling securities that call for 4 payments, $50 at the end of each of the next 3 years, plus a payment of $1,050 at the end of Year 4. Your friend says she can get you some of these securities at a cost of $900 each. Your money is now invested in a bank that pays an 8% nominal (quoted) interest rate but with quarterly compounding. You regard the securities as being just as safe, and as liquid, as your bank deposit, so your required effective annual rate of return on the securities is the same as that on your bank deposit. You must calculate the value of the securities to decide whether they are a good investment. What is their present value to you?

(2-29)
Loan Amortization

Assume that your aunt sold her house on December 31 and that she took a mortgage in the amount of $10,000 as part of the payment. The mortgage has a quoted (or nominal) interest rate of 10%, but it calls for payments every 6 months, beginning on June 30, and the mortgage is to be amortized over 10 years. Now, 1 year later, your aunt must inform the IRS and the person who bought the house of the interest that was included in the two payments made during the year. (This interest will be income to your aunt and a deduction to the buyer of the house.) To the closest dollar, what is the total amount of interest that was paid during the first year?

(2-30)
Loan Amortization

Your company is planning to borrow $1,000,000 on a 5-year, 15%, annual payment, fully amortized term loan. What fraction of the payment made at the end of the second year will represent repayment of principal?

**Challenging
Problems 31–34**
(2-31)
**Nonannual
Compounding**

a.   It is now January 1. You plan to make 5 deposits of $100 each, one every 6 months, with the first payment being made *today*. If the bank pays a nominal interest rate of 12% but uses semiannual compounding, how much will be in your account after 10 years?

b.   You must make a payment of $1,432.02 10 years from today. To prepare for this payment, you will make 5 equal deposits, beginning today and for the next 4 quarters, in a bank that pays a nominal interest rate of 12%, quarterly compounding. How large must each of the 5 payments be?

(2-32)
Nominal Rate of Return

Anne Lockwood, manager of Oaks Mall Jewelry, wants to sell on credit, giving customers 3 months in which to pay. However, Anne will have to borrow from her bank to carry the accounts payable. The bank will charge a nominal 15%, but with monthly compounding. Anne wants to quote a nominal rate to her customers (all of whom are expected to pay on time) that will exactly cover her financing costs. What nominal annual rate should she quote to her credit customers?

(2-33)
**Required Annuity
Payments**

Assume that your father is now 50 years old, that he plans to retire in 10 years, and that he expects to live for 25 years after he retires, that is, until he is 85. He wants his first retirement payment to have the same purchasing power at the time he retires as $40,000 has today. He wants all his subsequent retirement payments to be equal to his first retirement payment (do not let the retirement payments grow with inflation: he realizes that the real value of his retirement income will decline year by year after he retires). His retirement income will begin the day he retires, 10 years from today, and he will then get 24 additional annual payments. Inflation is expected to be 5% per year from today forward; he currently has $100,000 saved up; and he expects to earn a return on his savings of 8% per year, annual compounding. To the nearest dollar, how much must he save during each of the next 10 years (with equal deposits being made at the end of each year) to meet his retirement goal? (Hint: Neither the amount he saves nor the amount he withdraws upon retirement is a growing annuity.)

(2-34)
Growing Annuity Payments

You wish to accumulate $1 million by your retirement date, which is 25 years from now. You will make 25 deposits in your bank, with the first occurring today. The bank pays 8% interest, compounded annually. You expect to get an annual raise of 3%, so you will let the amount you deposit each year also grow by 3% (i.e., your second deposit will be 3% greater than your first, the third will be 3% greater than the second, etc.). How much must your first deposit be to meet your goal?

e-resource

Spreadsheet Problem

(2-35)
Build a Model: The Time Value of Money

Start with the partial model in the file *FM12 Ch 02 P35 Build a Model.xls* from the textbook's Web site. Answer the following questions, using a spreadsheet model to do the calculations.

a.   Find the FV of $1,000 invested to earn 10% after 5 years. Answer this question by using a math formula and also by using the *Excel* function wizard.

b.   Now create a table that shows the FV at 0%, 5%, and 20% for 0, 1, 2, 3, 4, and 5 years. Then create a graph with years on the horizontal axis and FV on the vertical axis to display your results.

c.   Find the PV of $1,000 due in 5 years if the discount rate is 10%. Again, work the problem with a formula and also by using the function wizard.

d.   A security has a cost of $1,000 and will return $2,000 after 5 years. What rate of return does the security provide?

e.   Suppose California's population is 30 million people, and its population is expected to grow by 2% per year. How long would it take for the population to double?

f.   Find the PV of an annuity that pays $1,000 at the end of each of the next 5 years if the interest rate is 15%. Then find the FV of that same annuity.

g.   How would the PV and FV of the annuity change if it were an annuity due rather than an ordinary annuity?

h.   What would the FV and PV for parts a and c be if the interest rate were 10% with semiannual compounding rather than 10% with annual compounding?

i.   Find the PV and FV of an investment that makes the following end-of-year payments. The interest rate is 8%.

Year	Payment
1	$100
2	200
3	400

j.   Suppose you bought a house and took out a mortgage for $50,000. The interest rate is 8%, and you must amortize the loan over 10 years with equal end-of-year payments. Set up an amortization schedule that shows the annual payments and the amount of each payment that goes to pay off the principal and the amount that constitutes interest expense to the borrower and interest income to the lender.

   (1)   Create a graph that shows how the payments are divided between interest and principal repayment over time.

   (2)   Suppose the loan called for 10 years of monthly payments, with the same original amount and the same nominal interest rate. What would the amortization schedule show now?

Cyberproblem

Please go to the textbook's Web site to access any Cyberproblems.

Mini Case

Assume that you are nearing graduation and that you have applied for a job with a local bank. As part of the bank's evaluation process, you have been asked to take an examination that covers several financial analysis techniques. The first section of the test addresses discounted cash flow analysis. See how you would do by answering the following questions.

a.   Draw time lines for (1) a $100 lump sum cash flow at the end of Year 2, (2) an ordinary annuity of $100 per year for 3 years, and (3) an uneven cash flow stream of −$50, $100, $75, and $50 at the end of Years 0 through 3.

b.   (1) What is the future value of an initial $100 after 3 years if it is invested in an account paying 10% annual interest?
     (2) What is the present value of $100 to be received in 3 years if the appropriate interest rate is 10%?

c.   We sometimes need to find how long it will take a sum of money (or anything else) to grow to some specified amount. For example, if a company's sales are growing at a rate of 20% per year, how long will it take sales to double?

d.   If you want an investment to double in 3 years, what interest rate must it earn?

e.   What is the difference between an ordinary annuity and an annuity due? What type of annuity is shown below? How would you change it to the other type of annuity?

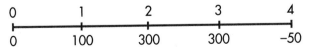

f.   (1) What is the future value of a 3-year ordinary annuity of $100 if the appropriate interest rate is 10%?
     (2) What is the present value of the annuity?
     (3) What would the future and present values be if the annuity were an annuity due?

g.   What is the present value of the following uneven cash flow stream? The appropriate interest rate is 10%, compounded annually.

0	1	2	3	4
0	100	300	300	−50

h.   (1) Define (a) the stated, or quoted, or nominal rate (I_{NOM}) and (b) the periodic rate (I_{PER}).
     (2) Will the future value be larger or smaller if we compound an initial amount more often than annually, for example, every 6 months, or *semiannually*, holding the stated interest rate constant? Why?

    (3) What is the future value of $100 after 5 years under 12% annual compounding? Semiannual compounding? Quarterly compounding? Monthly compounding? Daily compounding?

    (4) What is the effective annual rate (EFF%)? What is the EFF% for a nominal rate of 12%, compounded semiannually? Compounded quarterly? Compounded monthly? Compounded daily?

i.   Will the effective annual rate ever be equal to the nominal (quoted) rate?

j.   (1) Construct an amortization schedule for a $1,000, 10% annual rate loan with 3 equal installments.

    (2) What is the annual interest expense for the borrower, and the annual interest income for the lender, during Year 2?

k.   Suppose on January 1 you deposit $100 in an account that pays a nominal, or quoted, interest rate of 11.33463%, with interest added (compounded) daily. How much will you have in your account on October 1, or after 9 months?

l.   (1) What is the value at the end of Year 3 of the following cash flow stream if the quoted interest rate is 10%, compounded semiannually?

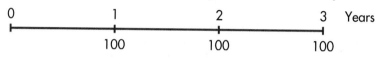

    (2) What is the PV of the same stream?

    (3) Is the stream an annuity?

    (4) An important rule is that you should never show a nominal rate on a time line or use it in calculations unless what condition holds? (Hint: Think of annual compounding, when I_{NOM} = EFF% = I_{PER}.) What would be wrong with your answer to Questions l-(1) and l-(2) if you used the nominal rate (10%) rather than the periodic rate ($I_{NOM}/2$ = 10%/2 = 5%)?

m.   Suppose someone offered to sell you a note calling for the payment of $1,000 fifteen months from today. They offer to sell it to you for $850. You have $850 in a bank time deposit that pays a 6.76649% nominal rate with daily compounding, which is a 7% effective annual interest rate, and you plan to leave the money in the bank unless you buy the note. The note is not risky—you are sure it will be paid on schedule. Should you buy the note? Check the decision in three ways: (1) by comparing your future value if you buy the note versus leaving your money in the bank, (2) by comparing the PV of the note with your current bank account, and (3) by comparing the EFF% on the note versus that of the bank account.

chapter 3

Financial Statements, Cash Flow, and Taxes

When evaluating a company, who can you trust? The analysts at top brokerage firms rate companies, using terms such as buy, hold, or sell. Maybe you think you can trust their ratings, since these analysts are highly trained and have access to great data sources. Think again. When the market was in the middle of a long, steady decline in the early 2000s, these analysts made 7,033 buy recommendations, but only 57 sells. What could possibly cause such optimism? How about their own personal compensation and their own firms' profits, rather than their clients' best interests? Most brokerage firms are members of a corporate family that includes an investment bank. If an analyst gives a company a negative rating, the company will take its investment banking business to a banking firm that gives it a better rating. To prevent this defection, analysts are pressured to refrain from making low, offensive ratings. Indeed, analysts who don't fall in line are often fired, such as Mike Mayo, formerly of Credit Suisse First Boston, who gave honest (and subsequently shown to be

accurate) negative ratings. In fact, at CSFB, the analysts actually reported to investment bankers, and internal e-mails revealed that analysts were often replaced to keep investment banking clients happy.

At Merrill Lynch, e-mail revealed an even more disturbing situation. Analysts consistently gave positive ratings to firms, but then blasted the firms in internal e-mails. For example, analysts gave one company a strong buy rating but wrote that the company was "a piece of junk" in their internal e-mails. That's actually better than the e-mail for another positively rated company, which was called a "piece of s—t." Another company was rated "Neutral in the short term/Minimum 40% appreciation long term," but e-mails stated that there was nothing interesting about the company, "except banking fees."

New York attorney general Eliot Spitzer brought action against a number of Wall Street firms, which eventually settled for $1.4 billion (but which didn't stop the many suits brought against the firms by individual investors who lost money after acting on

Sources: Jeremy Kahn, "Frank Quattrone's Heavy Hand," *Fortune*, December 30, 2002, 78; Jeremy Kahn and Nelson D. Schwartz, "A New Investor Era? Ha!" *Fortune*, November 25, 2002, 35–38; David Rynecki, "The Price of Being Right," *Fortune*, February 4, 2001, 126–141; Nelson D. Schwartz and Jeremy Kahn, "Can This Bull Run Again," *Fortune*, December 30, 2002, 68–82; and Alynda Wheat, "Hall of Shame: Merrill Lynch-to-English Dictionary," *Fortune*, April 29, 2002, 28.

the analysts' recommendations). These legal actions are getting some results. For example, CSFB has reassigned analysts so that they report to its general counsel instead of its securities division, and Morgan Stanley's analysts have actually increased the number of unfavorable ratings from 2% to over 22%.

Who can you trust? Your best bet is to learn how to analyze a company, starting with this chapter, and then trust yourself.

e-resource

The textbook's Web site contains an *Excel* file that will guide you through the chapter's calculations. The file for this chapter is *FM12 Ch 03 Tool Kit.xls* and we encourage you to open the file and follow along as you read the chapter.

A manager's primary goal is to maximize the value of his or her firm's stock. Value is based on the stream of cash flows the firm will generate in the future. But how does an investor go about estimating future cash flows, and how does a manager decide which actions are most likely to increase cash flows? The answers to both questions lie in a study of the financial statements that publicly traded firms must provide to investors. Here, "investors" include both institutions (banks, insurance companies, pension funds, and the like) and individuals. Thus, this chapter begins with a discussion of what the basic financial statements are, how they are used, and what kinds of financial information users need.

The value of any business asset—whether it is a *financial asset* such as a stock or a bond, or a *real (physical) asset* such as land, buildings, and equipment—depends on the usable, after-tax cash flows the asset is expected to produce. Therefore, this chapter also explains the difference between accounting income and cash flow. Finally, since it is *after-tax* cash flow that is important, this chapter provides an overview of the federal income tax system.

3.1 Financial Statements and Reports

A source for links to the annual reports of many companies is **http://www .annualreportservice .com.**

Of the various reports corporations issue to their stockholders, the **annual report** is probably the most important. Two types of information are provided in an annual report. First, there is a verbal section, often presented as a letter from the chairman, that describes the firm's operating results during the past year and then discusses new developments that will affect future operations. Second, the annual report presents four basic financial statements—the *balance sheet*, the *income statement*, the *statement of retained earnings*, and the *statement of cash flows*. Taken together, these statements give an accounting picture of the firm's operations and financial position. Detailed data are provided for the two or three most recent years, along with historical summaries of key operating statistics for the past 5 or 10 years.[1]

The quantitative and verbal materials are equally important. The financial statements report *what has actually happened* to assets, earnings, and dividends over the past few years, whereas the verbal statements attempt to explain why things turned out the way they did.

For illustrative purposes, we use data on MicroDrive Inc., a producer of disk drives for microcomputers. Formed in 1982, MicroDrive has grown steadily and has earned a reputation for being one of the best firms in the microcomputer

---

[1]Firms also provide less comprehensive quarterly reports. Larger firms file even more detailed statements, giving breakdowns for each major division or subsidiary, with the Securities and Exchange Commission (SEC). These reports, called *10-K reports*, are available on the SEC's Web site at **http://www.sec.gov** under the heading "EDGAR."

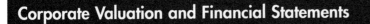

Corporate Valuation and Financial Statements

In Chapter 1, we told you that managers should strive to make their firms more valuable, and that the value of a firm is determined by the size, timing, and risk of its free cash flows (FCF). This chapter shows you how to use a company's financial statements to calculate FCF.

$$\text{Value} = \frac{\text{FCF}_1}{(1 + \text{WACC})^1} + \frac{\text{FCF}_2}{(1 + \text{WACC})^2} + \frac{\text{FCF}_3}{(1 + \text{WACC})^3} + \cdots + \frac{\text{FCF}_\infty}{(1 + \text{WACC})^\infty}$$

components industry. MicroDrive's earnings dropped a bit in the most recent year, and management blamed a three-month strike that kept the firm from fully utilizing a new plant that had been financed mostly with debt. However, management went on to paint a more optimistic picture for the future, stating that full operations had been resumed, that several new products had been introduced, and that profits were expected to rise sharply. Of course, the profit increase may not occur, and analysts should compare management's past statements with subsequent results when judging the credibility of the projected improvement. In any event, *the information contained in an annual report is used by investors to help form expectations about future earnings and dividends.*

SELF-TEST

What is the annual report, and what two types of information are given in it?
Why is the annual report of great interest to investors?
What four types of financial statements are typically included in the annual report?

3.2 The Balance Sheet

Table 3-1 shows MicroDrive's most recent **balance sheets,** which represent "snapshots" of its financial position on the last day of each year. Although most companies report their balance sheets only on the last day of a given period, the "snapshot" actually changes daily as inventories are bought and sold, as fixed assets are added or retired, or as bank loan balances are increased or paid down. Moreover, a retailer will have much larger inventories before Christmas than later in the spring, so balance sheets for the same company can look quite different at different times during the year.

The left side of a balance sheet lists assets, which are the "things" the company owns. They are listed in order of "liquidity," or length of time it typically takes to convert them to cash at fair market values. The right side lists the claims that various groups have against the company's value, listed in the order in which they must be paid. For example, suppliers may have a claim called "accounts payable" that is due within 30 days, banks may have claims called "notes payable" that are due within 90 days, and bondholders may have claims that are not due for 20 years or more. Stockholders come last, for two reasons. First, their claim represents ownership (or equity) and need never be "paid off." Second, they

Table 3-1

MicroDrive Inc.: December 31 Balance Sheets (Millions of Dollars)

Assets	2007	2006	Liabilities and Equity	2007	2006
Cash and equivalents	$ 10	$ 15	Accounts payable	$ 60	$ 30
Short-term investments	0	65	Notes payable	110	60
Accounts receivable	375	315	Accruals	140	130
Inventories	615	415	Total current liabilities	$ 310	$ 220
Total current assets	$1,000	$ 810	Long-term bonds	754	580
Net plant and equipment	1,000	870	Total liabilities	$1,064	$ 800
			Preferred stock (400,000 shares)	40	40
			Common stock (50,000,000 shares)	130	130
			Retained earnings	766	710
			Total common equity	$ 896	$ 840
Total assets	$2,000	$1,680	Total liabilities and equity	$2,000	$1,680

FM

e-resource

See **FM12 Ch 03 Tool Kit.xls** for all details.

have a residual claim in the sense that they may receive payments only if the other claimants have already been paid. The nonstockholder claims are liabilities from the stockholders' perspective. The amounts shown on the balance sheets are called **book values** since they are based on the amounts recorded by bookkeepers when assets are purchased or liabilities are issued. As you will see throughout this textbook, book values may be very different from **market values,** which are the current values as determined in the marketplace.

The following sections provide more information about specific asset, liability, and equity accounts.

Assets

Cash, short-term investments, accounts receivable, and inventories are listed as current assets, because MicroDrive is expected to convert them into cash within a year. All assets are stated in dollars, but only cash represents actual money that can be spent. Some marketable securities mature very soon, and can be converted quickly into cash at prices close to their book values. These securities are called "cash equivalents," and they are included with cash. Therefore, MicroDrive could write checks for a total of $10 million. Other types of marketable securities have a longer time until maturity, and their market values are less predictable. These securities are classified as "short-term investments."

When MicroDrive sells its products to a customer but doesn't demand immediate payment, the customer then has an obligation called an "account receivable." The $375 million shown in accounts receivable is the amount of sales for which MicroDrive has not yet been paid.

Inventories show the dollars MicroDrive has invested in raw materials, work-in-process, and finished goods available for sale. MicroDrive uses the **FIFO (first-in, first-out)** method to determine the inventory value shown on its balance sheet ($615 million). It could have used the **LIFO (last-in, first-out)** method.

During a period of rising prices, by taking out old, low-cost inventory and leaving in new, high-cost items, FIFO will produce a higher balance sheet inventory value but a lower cost of goods sold on the income statement. (This is strictly used for accounting; companies actually use older items first.) Because MicroDrive uses FIFO, and because inflation has been occurring, (1) its balance sheet inventories are higher than they would have been had it used LIFO, (2) its cost of goods sold is lower than it would have been under LIFO, and (3) its reported profits are therefore higher. In MicroDrive's case, if the company had elected to switch to LIFO, its balance sheet would have inventories of $585 million rather than $615 million, and its earnings (discussed in the next section) would have been reduced by $18 million. Thus, the inventory valuation method can have a significant effect on financial statements, which is important to know when comparing different companies.

Rather than treat the entire purchase price of a long-term asset (such as a factory, plant, or equipment) as an expense in the purchase year, accountants "spread" the purchase cost over the asset's useful life.[2] The amount they charge each year is called the **depreciation** expense. Some companies report an amount called "gross plant and equipment," which is the total cost of the long-term assets they have in place, and another amount called "accumulated depreciation," which is the total amount of depreciation that has been charged on those assets. Some companies, such as MicroDrive, only report net plant and equipment, which is gross plant and equipment less accumulated depreciation. Chapter 12 provides a more detailed explanation of depreciation methods.

Liabilities and Equity

Accounts payable, notes payable, and accruals are listed as current liabilities, because MicroDrive is expected to pay them within a year. When MicroDrive purchases supplies but doesn't immediately pay for them, it takes on an obligation called an account payable. Similarly, when MicroDrive takes out a loan that must be repaid within a year, it signs an IOU called a note payable. MicroDrive doesn't pay its taxes or its employees' wages daily, and the amount it owes on these items at any point in time is called an "accrual," or an "accrued expense." Long-term bonds are also liabilities because they, too, reflect a claim held by someone other than a stockholder.

Preferred stock is a hybrid, or a cross between common stock and debt. In the event of bankruptcy, preferred stock ranks below debt but above common stock. Also, the preferred dividend is fixed, so preferred stockholders do not benefit if the company's earnings grow. Most firms do not use much, or even any, preferred stock, so "equity" usually means "common equity" unless the words "total" or "preferred" are included.

When a company sells shares of stock, the proceeds are recorded in the common stock account.[3] Retained earnings are the cumulative amount of earnings that have not been paid out as dividends. The sum of common stock and retained earnings is called "common equity," or sometimes just equity. If a company's assets could actually be sold at their book value, and if the liabilities and preferred

---

[2]This is called *accrual accounting*, which attempts to match revenues to the periods in which they are earned and expenses to the periods in which the effort to generate income occurred. Students sometimes call this "a cruel rule" because it can be confusing.

[3]Companies sometimes break the total proceeds into two parts, one called "par" and the other called "paid-in-capital" or "capital surplus." For example, if a company sells shares of stock for $10, it might record $1 of par and $9 of paid-in-capital. For most purposes, the distinction between par and paid-in-capital is not important, and most companies use no-par stock.

stock were actually worth their book values, then a company could sell its assets, pay off its liabilities and preferred stock, and the remaining cash would belong to common stockholders. Therefore, common equity is sometimes called **net worth**—it's the assets net of the liabilities.

SELF-TEST

What is the balance sheet, and what information does it provide?
How is the order of the information shown on the balance sheet determined?
Why might a company's December 31 balance sheet differ from its June 30 balance sheet?
A firm has $8 million in total assets. It has $3 million in current liabilities, $2 million in long-term debt, and $1 million in preferred stock. What is the total value of common equity? ($2 million)

3.3 The Income Statement

Table 3-2 gives the **income statements** for MicroDrive, which show its financial performance over each of the last 2 years. Income statements can cover any period of time, but they are usually prepared monthly, quarterly, and annually. Unlike the balance sheet, which is a snapshot of a firm at a point in time, the income statement reflects performance during the period.

Subtracting operating costs from net sales but excluding depreciation and amortization results in **EBITDA**, which stands for earnings before interest, taxes, depreciation, and amortization. Depreciation and amortization are annual charges that reflect the estimated costs of the assets used up each year. Depreciation applies to tangible assets, such as plant and equipment, whereas amortization applies to intangible assets such as patents, copyrights, trademarks, and goodwill.[4] Because neither depreciation nor amortization is paid in cash, some analysts claim that EBITDA is a better measure of financial strength than is net income. However, as we show later in the chapter, EBITDA is not as important as free cash flow. In fact, some financial wags have stated that EBITDA really stands for "earnings before anything bad happens."

The net income available to common shareholders, which is revenues less expenses, taxes, and preferred dividends (but before paying common dividends), is generally referred to as **net income,** although it is also called **profit** or **earnings,** particularly in the news or financial press. Dividing net income by the number of shares outstanding gives earnings per share (EPS), which is often called "the bottom line." Throughout this book, unless otherwise indicated, net income means net income available to common stockholders.[5]

---

[4]The accounting treatment of goodwill resulting from mergers has changed in recent years. Rather than an annual charge, companies are required to periodically evaluate the value of goodwill and reduce net income only if the goodwill's value has decreased materially ("become impaired," in the language of accountants). For example, in 2002 AOL Time Warner wrote off almost $100 billion associated with the AOL merger. It doesn't take too many $100 billion expenses to really hurt net income!

[5]Companies report "comprehensive income" as well as net income. Comprehensive income is equal to net income plus several comprehensive income items. One example of comprehensive income is the unrealized gain or loss that occurs when a marketable security, classified as "available for sale," is marked-to-market. For our purposes, we assume that there are no comprehensive income items, so we present only basic income statements throughout the text. Although not required, some companies also report "pro forma income." For example, if a company incurs an expense that it doesn't expect to recur, such as the closing of a plant, it might calculate pro forma income as though it had not incurred the one-time expense. There are no hard and fast rules for calculating pro forma income, and companies report it on a voluntary basis. As a result, it is often subject to abuse, with many companies finding ingenious ways to make pro forma income higher than traditional income. The SEC and the Public Company Accounting Oversight Board (PCAOB) are taking steps to reduce deceptive uses of pro forma reporting.

Table 3-2

MicroDrive Inc.: Income Statements for Years Ending December 31
(Millions of Dollars, Except for Per-Share Data)

	2007	2006
Net sales	$3,000.0	$2,850.0
Operating costs excluding depreciation and amortization	2,616.2	2,497.0
Earnings before interest, taxes, depreciation, and amortization (EBITDA)	$ 383.8	$ 353.0
Depreciation	100.0	90.0
Amortization	0.0	0.0
Depreciation and amortization	$ 100.0	$ 90.0
Earnings before interest and taxes (EBIT, or operating income)	$ 283.8	$ 263.0
Less interest	88.0	60.0
Earnings before taxes (EBT)	$ 195.8	$ 203.0
Taxes (40%)	78.3	81.2
Net income before preferred dividends	$ 117.5	$ 121.8
Preferred dividends	4.0	4.0
Net income	$ 113.5	$ 117.8
Common dividends	$ 57.5	$ 53.0
Addition to retained earnings	$ 56.0	$ 64.8
Per-Share Data		
Common stock price	$ 23.00	$ 26.00
Earnings per share (EPS)[a]	$ 2.27	$ 2.36
Dividends per share (DPS)[a]	$ 1.15	$ 1.06
Book value per share (BVPS)[a]	$ 17.92	$ 16.80
Cash flow per share (CFPS)[a]	$ 4.27	$ 4.16

[a]There are 50,000,000 shares of common stock outstanding. Note that EPS is based on earnings after preferred dividends—that is, on net income available to common stockholders. Calculations of the most recent EPS, DPS, BVPS, and CFPS are shown below:

$$\text{Earnings per share} = \text{EPS} = \frac{\text{Net income}}{\text{Common shares outstanding}} = \frac{\$113,500,000}{50,000,000} = \$2.27.$$

$$\text{Dividends per share} = \text{DPS} = \frac{\text{Dividends paid to common stockholders}}{\text{Common shares outstanding}} = \frac{\$57,500,000}{50,000,000} = \$1.15.$$

$$\text{Book value per share} = \text{BVPS} = \frac{\text{Total common equity}}{\text{Common shares outstanding}} = \frac{\$896,000,000}{50,000,000} = \$17.92.$$

$$\text{Cash flow per share} = \text{CFPS} = \frac{\text{Net income} + \text{Depreciation} + \text{Amortization}}{\text{Common shares outstanding}} = \frac{\$213,500,000}{50,000,000} = \$4.27.$$

SELF-TEST

What is an income statement, and what information does it provide?

Why is earnings per share called "the bottom line"?

What is EBITDA?

Regarding the time period reported, how does the income statement differ from the balance sheet?

A firm has $2 million in earnings before taxes. The firm has an interest expense of $300,000 and depreciation of $200,000; it has no amortization. What is its EBITDA? ($2.5 million)

3.4   Statement of Retained Earnings

Table 3-3, the **statement of retained earnings,** shows that MicroDrive began 2007 with $710 million of retained earnings, that during the year it earned $113.5 million and paid out $57.5 in dividends, and that it plowed the difference, $56 million, back into the business. These "corporate savings" caused retained earnings to increase from $710 million at the end of 2006 to $766 million at the end of 2007.

Note that "retained earnings" represents a *claim against assets*, not an asset per se. In 2007 MicroDrive's stockholders allowed it to reinvest $56 million instead of distributing the money as dividends, and management spent this money on new assets. Thus, retained earnings as reported on the balance sheet does not represent cash and is not "available" for the payment of dividends or anything else.[6]

e-resource

See **FM12 Ch 03 Tool Kit.xls** for all details.

Table 3-3

MicroDrive Inc.: Statement of Retained Earnings for Year Ending December 31, 2007 (Millions of Dollars)

Balance of retained earnings, December 31, 2006	$710.0
Add: Net income, 2007	113.5
Less: Dividends to common stockholders	(57.5)[a]
Balance of retained earnings, December 31, 2007	$766.0

[a]Here, and throughout the book, parentheses are used to denote negative numbers.

SELF-TEST

What is the statement of retained earnings, and what information does it provide?

Why do changes in retained earnings occur?

Explain why the following statement is true: "Retained earnings as reported on the balance sheet does not represent cash and is not 'available' for the payment of dividends or anything else."

A firm had a retained earnings balance of $3 million in the previous year. In the current year, its net income is $2.5 million. If it pays $1 million in common dividends in the current year, what is its resulting retained earnings balance? ($4.5 million)

---

[6]The amount reported in the retained earnings account is *not* an indication of the amount of cash the firm has. Cash (as of the balance sheet date) is found in the cash account, an asset account. A positive number in the retained earnings account indicates only that in the past the firm earned some income, but its dividends paid were less than its earnings. Even though a company reports record earnings and shows an increase in its retained earnings account, it still may be short of cash.

The same situation holds for individuals. You might own a new BMW (no loan), lots of clothes, and an expensive stereo, hence have a high net worth, but if you have only 23 cents in your pocket plus $5 in your checking account, you will still be short of cash.

3.5 Net Cash Flow

Many financial analysts focus on **net cash flow.** A business's *net cash flow* generally differs from its *accounting profit* because some of the revenues and expenses listed on the income statement were not received or paid in cash during the year. The relationship between net cash flow and net income can be expressed as follows:

$$\text{Net cash flow} = \text{Net income} - \text{Noncash revenues} + \text{Noncash charges.} \quad \text{(3-1)}$$

The primary examples of noncash charges are depreciation and amortization. These items reduce net income but are not paid out in cash, so we add them back to net income when calculating net cash flow. Another example of a noncash charge is deferred taxes. In some instances, companies are allowed to defer tax payments to a later date even though the tax payment is reported as an expense on the income statement. Therefore, deferred tax payments are added to net income when calculating net cash flow.[7] At the same time, some revenues may not be collected in cash during the year, and these items must be subtracted from net income when calculating net cash flow.

Typically, depreciation and amortization are by far the largest noncash items, and in many cases the other noncash items roughly net out to zero. For this reason, many analysts assume that net cash flow equals net income plus depreciation and amortization:

$$\text{Net cash flow} = \text{Net income} + \text{Depreciation and amortization.} \quad \text{(3-2)}$$

To keep things simple, we will generally assume that Equation 3-2 holds. However, you should remember that Equation 3-2 will not accurately reflect net cash flow in those instances where there are significant noncash items beyond depreciation and amortization.

We can illustrate Equation 3-2 with 2007 data for MicroDrive taken from Table 3-2:

$$\text{Net cash flow} = \$113.5 + \$100.0 = \$213.5 \text{ million.}$$

To illustrate depreciation's effect, suppose a machine with a life of 5 years and a zero expected salvage value was purchased in 2006 for $100,000 and placed into service in 2007. This $100,000 cost is not expensed in the purchase year; rather, it is charged against production over the machine's 5-year depreciable life. If the depreciation expense were not taken, profits would be overstated, and taxes would be too high. So, the annual depreciation charge is deducted from sales revenues, along with such other costs as labor and raw materials, to determine income. However, because the $100,000 was actually expended back in 2006, the depreciation charged against income in 2007 and subsequent years is not a cash outlay, as are labor or raw materials charges. Depreciation is a noncash charge, so it must be added back to net income to obtain the net cash flow. If we assume that all other noncash items (including amortization) sum to zero, then net cash flow is simply equal to net income plus depreciation.

---

[7]Deferred taxes may arise, for example, if a company uses accelerated depreciation for tax purposes but straight-line depreciation for reporting its financial statements to investors.

Financial Analysis on the Internet

A wide range of valuable financial information is available on the Internet. With just a couple of clicks, an investor can easily find the key financial statements for most publicly traded companies. Here's a partial (but by no means a complete) list of places you can go to get started:

- One of the very best sources of financial information is Thomson Financial. Go to the textbook's Web site and follow the directions to access ThomsonONE—Business School Edition. An especially useful feature is the ability to download up to 10 years of financial statements in spreadsheet form. First, enter the ticker for a company and click GO. From the top tab (in dark blue), select Financials. This will show a second row of items (in light blue). Selecting More from this row will reveal a drop-down menu. Select SEC Database Reports & Charts. This will bring up another drop-down menu which includes the ten-year balance sheets, income statements, and statement of cash flows. To download the financial statements into a spreadsheet, first select one of the statements, such as the 10YR Balance Sheet. The balance sheets will then be displayed on your browser page. To download, click on the *Excel* icon toward the right of the light blue row at the top of the ThomsonONE panel. This will bring up a dialog box that lets you download the *Excel* file to your computer.
- Try Yahoo's finance Web site, **http://finance.yahoo.com**. Here you will find updated market information along with links to a variety of interesting research sites. Enter a stock's ticker symbol, click GO, and you will see the stock's current price, along with recent news about the company. The panel on the left has links to key statistics, the company's income statement, balance sheet, statement of cash flows, and more. The Yahoo site also has a list of insider transactions, so you can tell if a company's CEO and other key insiders are buying or selling their company's stock. In addition, there is a message board where investors share opinions about the company, and there is a link to the company's filings with the Securities and Exchange Commission (SEC). Note that, in most cases, a more complete list of the SEC filings can be found at **http://www.sec.gov**.

- Other sources for up-to-date market information are **http://money.cnn.com,** and **http://www.zacks.com**. These sites also provide financial statements in standardized formats.
- Both **http://www.bloomberg.com** and **http://www.marketwatch.com** have areas where you can obtain stock quotes along with company financials, links to Wall Street research, and links to SEC filings.
- If you are looking for charts of key accounting variables (for example, sales, inventory, depreciation and amortization, and reported earnings), along with the financial statements, take a look at **http://www.smartmoney.com**.
- Another good place to look is **http://www.investor.reuters.com**. Here you can find links to analysts' research reports along with the key financial statements.
- Zacks (shown above) and **http://www.hoovers.com** each has free research available along with more detailed information provided to subscribers.

Once you have accumulated all of this information, you may be looking for sites that provide opinions regarding the direction of the overall market and views regarding individual stocks. Two popular sites in this category are The Motley Fool's Web site, **http://www.fool.com**, and the Web site for The Street.com, **http://www.thestreet.com**.

SELF-TEST

Differentiate between net cash flow and accounting profit.

In accounting, the emphasis is on net income. What is emphasized in finance, and why is that item emphasized?

A firm has net income of $5 million. Assuming that depreciation of $1 million is its only noncash expense, what is the firm's net cash flow? ($6 million)

3.6 Statement of Cash Flows

Even if a company reports a large net income during a year, the *amount of cash* reported on its year-end balance sheet may be the same or even lower than its beginning cash. The reason is that its net income can be used in a variety of ways, not just kept as cash in the bank. For example, the firm may use its net income to pay dividends, to increase inventories, to finance accounts receivable, to invest in fixed assets, to reduce debt, or to buy back common stock. Indeed, the company's *cash position* as reported on its balance sheet is affected by a great many factors, including the following:

1. **Net income before preferred dividends.** Other things held constant, a positive net income will lead to more cash in the bank. However, as we discuss below, other things generally are not held constant.
2. **Noncash adjustments to net income.** To calculate cash flow, it is necessary to adjust net income to reflect noncash revenues and expenses, such as depreciation and deferred taxes, as shown above in the calculation of net cash flow.
3. **Changes in working capital.** Increases in current assets other than cash, such as inventories and accounts receivable, decrease cash, whereas decreases in these accounts increase cash. For example, if inventories are to increase, the firm must use some of its cash to acquire the additional inventory. Conversely, if inventories decrease, this generally means the firm is selling inventories and not replacing all of them, hence generating cash. On the other hand, if payables increase, the firm has received additional credit from its suppliers, which saves cash, but if payables decrease, this means it has used cash to pay off its suppliers. Therefore, increases in current liabilities such as accounts payable increase cash, whereas decreases in current liabilities decrease cash.
4. **Investments**. If a company invests in fixed assets or short-term financial investments, this will reduce its cash position. On the other hand, if it sells some fixed assets or short-term investments, this will increase cash.
5. **Security transactions and dividend payments**. If a company issues stock or bonds during the year, the funds raised will increase its cash position. On the other hand, if the company uses cash to buy back outstanding stock or to pay off debt, or if it pays dividends to its shareholders, this will reduce cash.

Each of the above factors is reflected in the **statement of cash flows,** which summarizes the changes in a company's cash position. The statement separates activities into three categories, plus a summary section:

1. **Operating activities,** which includes net income, depreciation, changes in current assets and liabilities other than cash, short-term investments, and short-term debt.
2. **Investing activities,** which includes investments in or sales of fixed assets and short-term financial investments.
3. **Financing activities,** which includes raising cash by issuing short-term debt, long-term debt, or stock. Also, because both dividends paid and cash used to buy back outstanding stock or bonds reduce the company's cash, such transactions are included here.

Accounting texts explain how to prepare the statement of cash flows, but the statement is used to help answer questions such as these: Is the firm generating enough cash to purchase the additional assets required for growth? Is the firm generating any extra cash that can be used to repay debt or to invest in new products? Such information is useful both for managers and investors, so the statement of cash flows is an important part of the annual report.

Table 3-4

MicroDrive Inc.: Statement of Cash Flows for 2007 (Millions of Dollars)

FM

e-resource

See **FM12 Ch 03 Tool Kit.xls** for all details.

	Cash Provided or Used
Operating Activities	
Net income before preferred dividends	$117.5
Adjustments:	
Noncash adjustments:	
Depreciation[a]	100.0
Due to changes in working capital:[b]	
Increase in accounts receivable	(60.0)
Increase in inventories	(200.0)
Increase in accounts payable	30.0
Increase in accruals	10.0
Net cash provided by operating activities	($ 2.5)
Investing Activities	
Cash used to acquire fixed assets[c]	($230.0)
Sale of short-term investments	$ 65.0
Net cash provided by investing activities	($165.0)
Financing Activities	
Increase in notes payable	$ 50.0
Increase in bonds outstanding	174.0
Payment of preferred and common dividends	(61.5)
Net cash provided by financing activities	$162.5
Summary	
Net change in cash	($ 5.0)
Cash at beginning of year	15.0
Cash at end of year	$ 10.0

[a]Depreciation is a noncash expense that was deducted when calculating net income. It must be added back to show the correct cash flow from operations.
[b]An increase in a current asset *decreases* cash. An increase in a current liability *increases* cash. For example, inventories increased by $200 million and therefore reduced cash by a like amount.
[c]The net increase in fixed assets is $130 million; however, this net amount is after a deduction for the year's depreciation expense. Depreciation expense would have to be added back to find the increase in gross fixed assets. From the company's income statement, we see that the 2007 depreciation expense is $100 million; thus, expenditures on fixed assets were actually $230 million.

Table 3-4 shows MicroDrive's statement of cash flows as it would appear in the company's annual report. The top section shows cash generated by and used in operations—for MicroDrive, operations provided net cash flows of *minus* $2.5 million. This subtotal, the minus $2.5 million net cash flow provided by operating activities, is in many respects the most important figure in any of the financial statements. Profits as reported on the income statement can be "doctored" by such tactics as depreciating assets too slowly, not recognizing bad debts promptly, and the like. However, it is far more difficult to simultaneously doctor profits and the working capital accounts. Therefore, it is not uncommon for a company to report positive net income right up to the day it declares bankruptcy. In such cases, however, the net cash flow from operations almost always began to deteriorate much earlier, and analysts who kept an eye on cash flow could have predicted trouble. Therefore, if you are ever analyzing a company and are pressed for time, look first at the trend in net cash flow provided by operating activities, because it will tell you more than any other number.

The second section shows investing activities. MicroDrive purchased fixed assets totaling $230 million and sold $65 million of short-term investment, for a net cash flow from investing activities of *minus* $165 million.

The third section, financing activities, includes borrowing from banks (notes payable), selling new bonds, and paying dividends on common and preferred stock. MicroDrive raised $224 million by borrowing, but it paid $61.5 million in preferred and common dividends. Therefore, its net inflow of funds from financing activities was $162.5 million.

In the summary, where all of these sources and uses of cash are totaled, we see that MicroDrive's cash outflows exceeded its cash inflows by $5 million during 2007; that is, its net change in cash was a *negative* $5 million.

MicroDrive's statement of cash flows should be worrisome to its managers and to outside analysts. The company had a $2.5 million cash shortfall from operations, it spent an additional $230 million on new fixed assets, and it paid out another $61.5 million in dividends. It covered these cash outlays by borrowing heavily and by liquidating $65 million of short-term investments. Obviously, this situation cannot continue year after year, so something will have to be done. Later in the chapter we consider some of the actions MicroDrive's financial staff might recommend to ease the cash flow problem.[8]

SELF-TEST

What types of questions does the statement of cash flows answer?

Identify and briefly explain the three different categories of activities shown in the statement of cash flows.

A firm has inventories of $2 million for the previous year and $1.5 million for the current year. What impact does this have on net cash provided by operations? (Increase of $500,000)

3.7 Modifying Accounting Data for Managerial Decisions

Thus far in the chapter we have focused on financial statements as they are presented in the annual report. However, these statements are designed more for use by creditors and tax collectors than for managers and stock analysts. Therefore, certain modifications are needed for use in corporate decision making.

---

[8]For a more detailed discussion of financial statement analysis, see Lyn M. Fraser and Aileen Ormiston, *Understanding Financial Statements*, 8th ed. (Upper Saddle River, NJ: Prentice-Hall, 2007).

In the following sections we discuss how financial analysts combine stock prices and accounting data to make the statements more useful.

Operating Assets and Total Net Operating Capital

Different firms have different financial structures, different tax situations, and different amounts of nonoperating assets. These differences affect traditional accounting measures such as the rate of return on equity. They can cause two firms, or two divisions within a single firm, that actually have similar operations to appear to be operated with different efficiency. This is important, because if managerial compensation systems are to function properly, operating managers must be judged and compensated for those things that are under their control, not on the basis of things outside their control. Therefore, to judge managerial performance, we need to compare managers' ability to generate *operating income* (*EBIT*) with the *operating assets* under their control.

The first step in modifying the traditional accounting framework is to divide total assets into two categories, **operating assets,** which consist of the assets necessary to operate the business, and **nonoperating assets,** which include cash and short-term investments above the level required for normal operations, investments in subsidiaries, land held for future use, and the like. Moreover, operating assets are further divided into **operating current assets,** such as inventory, and **long-term operating assets,** such as plant and equipment. Obviously, if a manager can generate a given amount of profit and cash flow with a relatively small investment in operating assets, then the amount of capital investors must put up is reduced and the rate of return on that capital increases.

Most capital used in a business is supplied by investors—stockholders, bondholders, and lenders such as banks. Investors must be paid for the use of their money, with payment coming as interest in the case of debt and as dividends plus capital gains in the case of stock. So, if a company buys more assets than it actually needs, and thus raises too much capital, then its capital costs will be unnecessarily high.

Must all of the capital used to acquire assets be obtained from investors? The answer is no, because some of the funds are provided as a normal consequence of operations. For example, some funds will come from suppliers and be reported as *accounts payable*, while other funds will come as *accrued wages and accrued taxes*, which amount to short-term loans from workers and tax authorities. Such funds are called **operating current liabilities.** Therefore, if a firm needs $100 million of assets, but it has $10 million of accounts payable and another $10 million of accrued wages and taxes, then its *investor-supplied capital* would be only $80 million.

Net operating working capital is defined as operating current assets minus operating current liabilities. In other words, net operating working capital is the working capital acquired with investor-supplied funds. Here is the definition in equation form:

$$\text{Net operating} \atop \text{working capital} = \text{Operating current} \atop \text{assets} - \text{Operating current} \atop \text{liabilities} . \qquad (3\text{-}3)$$

Now think about how these concepts can be used in practice. First, all companies must carry some cash to "grease the wheels" of their operations. Companies continuously receive checks from customers and write checks to suppliers, employees, and so on. Because inflows and outflows do not coincide perfectly, a company must keep some cash in its bank account. In other words, some cash is required to conduct operations. The same is true for most other current assets, such as inventory and accounts receivable, which are required for normal operations. However, any short-term securities the firm holds generally result from investment decisions made by the treasurer, and they are not used in the core operations. Therefore, short-term investments are normally excluded when calculating net operating working capital.[9]

Some current liabilities—especially accounts payable and accruals—arise in the normal course of operations. Moreover, each dollar of such current liabilities is a dollar that the company does not have to raise from investors to acquire current assets. Therefore, to calculate net operating working capital, we deduct these operating current liabilities from the operating current assets. Other current liabilities that charge interest, such as notes payable to banks, are treated as investor-supplied capital and thus are not deducted when calculating net working capital.

If you are ever uncertain about an item, ask yourself whether it is a natural consequence of operations or if it is a discretionary choice, such as a particular method of financing, or an investment in a financial asset. If it is discretionary, it is not an operating asset or liability.

We can apply these definitions to MicroDrive, using the balance sheet data given in Table 3-1. Here is the net operating working capital for 2007:

$$\text{Net operating working capital} = (\text{Cash} + \text{Accounts receivable} + \text{Inventories})$$
$$- (\text{Accounts payable} + \text{Accruals})$$
$$= (\$10 + \$375 + \$615) - (\$60 + \$140)$$
$$= \$800 \text{ million.}$$

MicroDrive's total net operating capital at year-end 2007 was the sum of its net operating working capital and its operating long-term assets (which consist only of net plant and equipment):

$$\text{Total net operating capital} = (\text{Net operating working capital})$$
$$+ (\text{Operating long–term assets})$$
$$= \$800 + \$1,000 \quad\quad \text{(3-4)}$$
$$= \$1,800 \text{ million.}$$

For the previous year, net operating working capital was

$$\text{Net operating working capital} = (\$15 + \$315 + \$415) - (\$30 + \$130)$$
$$= \$585 \text{ million.}$$

---

[9]If the marketable securities are held as a substitute for cash, and therefore reduce the cash requirements, then they may be classified as part of operating working capital. Generally, though, large holdings of marketable securities are held as a reserve for some contingency or else as a temporary "parking place" for funds prior to an acquisition, a major capital investment program, or the like.

Adding the $870 million of fixed assets, its total operating capital at year-end 2006 was

$$\text{Total net operating capital} = \$585 + \$870$$

$$= \$1,455 \text{ million.}$$

Notice that we have defined total net operating capital as the sum of net operating working capital and operating long-term assets. In other words, our definition is in terms of operating assets and liabilities. However, we can also calculate total net operating capital by adding up the funds provided by investors, such as notes payable, long-term bonds, preferred stock, and common equity. For MicroDrive, the total capital provided by investors at year-end 2006 was $60 + $580 + $40 + $840 = $1,520 million. Of this amount, $65 million was tied up in short-term investments, which are not directly related to MicroDrive's operations. Therefore, only $1,520 − $65 = $1,455 million of investor-supplied capital was used in operations. Notice that this is exactly the same value as calculated above. This shows that we can calculate total net operating capital either from net operating working capital and operating long-term assets or from the investor-supplied funds. We usually base our calculations upon the first definition since it is possible to perform this calculation for a division, whereas it is not possible to do so using the definition based on investor-supplied capital.

We use the terms total net operating capital, operating capital, net operating assets, and capital to mean the same thing. Unless we specifically say "investor-supplied capital," we are referring to total net operating capital.

MicroDrive increased its operating capital to $1,800 from $1,455 million, or by $345 million, during 2007. Furthermore, most of this increase went into working capital, which rose from $585 to $800 million, or by $215 million. This 37% increase in net operating working capital versus a sales increase of only 5% (from $2,850 to $3,000 million) should set off warning bells in your head: Why did MicroDrive tie up so much additional cash in working capital? Is the company gearing up for a big increase in sales, or are inventories not moving and receivables not being collected? We will address these questions in detail in Chapter 4, when we cover ratio analysis.

Net Operating Profit After Taxes (NOPAT)

If two companies have different amounts of debt, hence different amounts of interest charges, they could have identical operating performances but different net incomes—the one with more debt would have a lower net income. Net income is certainly important, but it does not always reflect the true performance of a company's operations or the effectiveness of its operating managers. A better measurement for comparing managers' performance is **net operating profit after taxes,** or **NOPAT,** which is the amount of profit a company would generate if it had no debt and held no financial assets. NOPAT is defined as follows:[10]

$$\text{NOPAT} = \text{EBIT}(1 - \text{Tax rate}). \tag{3-5}$$

---

[10]For firms with a more complicated tax situation, it is better to define NOPAT as follows: NOPAT = (Net income before preferred dividends) + (Net interest expense)(1 − Tax rate). Also, if firms are able to defer paying some of their taxes, perhaps by the use of accelerated depreciation, then NOPAT should be adjusted to reflect the taxes that the company actually paid on its operating income. See P. Daves, M. Ehrhardt, and R. Shrieves, *Corporate Valuation: A Guide for Managers and Investors* (Mason, OH: Thomson South-Western, 2004) for a detailed explanation of these and other adjustments. Also see Tim Koller, Marc Goedhart, and David Wessels, *Valuation: Measuring and Managing the Value of Companies* (Hoboken, N.J.: John Wiley & Sons, Inc., 2005) and G. Bennett Stewart, *The Quest for Value* (New York: Harper Collins, 1991).

Financial Bamboozling: How to Spot It

Recent accounting frauds by Enron, WorldCom, Xerox, Merck, Arthur Andersen, Tyco, and many others have shown that analysts can no longer blindly assume that a firm's published financial statements are the best representation of its financial position. Clearly, many companies were "pushing the envelope" if not outright lying in an effort to make their companies look better.

A recent *Fortune* article points out that there are only three basic ways to manipulate financial statements: moving earnings from the future to the present, avoiding taxes, or hiding debt. For example, suppose one telecom firm (think WorldCom or Global Crossing) sold the right to use parts of its fiber-optic network for 10 years to another telecom firm for $100 million. The seller would immediately record revenues of $100 million. The buyer, however, could spread the expense over 10 years and report an expense of only $10 million this year. The buyer would simultaneously sell similar rights to the original seller for $100 million. This way, no cash changes hands, both companies report an extra $100 million in revenue, but each reports a cost of only $10 million. Thus, both companies "created" an extra $90 million in pre-tax profits, without doing anything. Of course, both companies will have to report an extra $10 million expense each year for the remaining 9 years, but they have each boosted short-term profits and thus this year's exec-utive bonuses. To boost earnings next year, all they have to do is play the same game, but on a bigger scale.

For hiding debt, it's hard to beat Enron's special purpose entities (SPEs). These SPEs owed hundreds of millions of dollars, and it turned out that Enron was responsible for this debt, even though it never showed up on Enron's financial statements.

How can you spot bamboozling? Here are some tips. When companies have lots of write-offs or charges for restructuring, it could be that they are planning on managing earnings in the future. In other words, they sandbag this year to pad next year's earnings. Beware of serial acquirers, especially if they use their own stock to buy other companies. This can increase reported earnings, but it often erodes value since the acquirer usually pays a large premium for the target. Watch out for companies that depreciate their assets much slower than others in the industry (this is shown in the financial statement's footnotes). This causes their current earnings to look larger than their competitors', even though they aren't actually performing any better. Perhaps the best evidence of bamboozling is if earnings are consistently growing faster than cash flows, which almost always indicates a financial scam.

Sources: Geoffrey Colvin, "Bamboozling: A Field Guide," *Fortune*, July 8, 2002, 51; and Shawn Tully, "Don't Get Burned," *Fortune*, February 18, 2002, 87–90.

Using data from the income statements of Table 3-2, MicroDrive's 2007 NOPAT is found to be

$$\text{NOPAT} = \$283.8(1 - 0.4) = \$283.8(0.6) = \$170.3 \text{ million.}$$

This means MicroDrive generated an after-tax operating profit of $170.3 million, a little better than its previous NOPAT of $263(0.6) = $157.8 million. However, the income statements in Table 3-2 show that MicroDrive's earnings per share actually declined. This decrease in EPS was caused by an increase in interest expense, and not by a decrease in operating profit. Moreover, the balance sheets in Table 3-1 show an increase in debt. But why did MicroDrive increase its debt? As we just saw, its investment in operating capital increased dramatically during 2007, and that increase was financed primarily with debt.

Free Cash Flow

Earlier in this chapter, we defined net cash flow as net income plus noncash adjustments, which typically means net income plus depreciation. Note, though, that cash flows cannot be maintained over time unless depreciated fixed assets are replaced, so management is not completely free to use net cash flows however it chooses. Therefore, we now define another term, **free cash flow (FCF),** which is the cash flow actually available for distribution to investors *after the company has made all the investments in fixed assets and working capital necessary to sustain ongoing operations.*

When you studied income statements in accounting, the emphasis was probably on the firm's net income, which is its **accounting profit.** However, the value of a company's operations is determined by the stream of cash flows that the operations will generate now and in the future. To be more specific, the value of operations depends on all the future expected free cash flows (FCF), defined as after-tax operating profit minus the amount of new investment in working capital and fixed assets necessary to sustain the business. Thus, free cash flow represents the cash that is actually available for distribution to investors. *Therefore, the way for managers to make their companies more valuable is to increase free cash flow.*

Calculating Free Cash Flow

As shown earlier in the chapter, MicroDrive had $1,455 million of total net operating capital at the end of 2006, but $1,800 million at the end of 2007. Therefore, during 2007, it made a **net investment in operating capital** of

Net investment in operating capital = $1,800 − $1,455 = $345 million.

MicroDrive's free cash flow in 2007 was

$$\begin{aligned} FCF &= NOPAT - \text{Net investment in operating capital} \\ &= \$170.3 - \$345 \\ &= -\$174.7 \text{ million.} \end{aligned} \tag{3-6}$$

Net fixed assets rose from $870 to $1,000 million, or by $130 million. However, MicroDrive reported $100 million of depreciation, so its gross investment in fixed assets was $130 + $100 = $230 million for the year. With this background, we find the **gross investment in operating capital** as follows:

$$\begin{aligned} \begin{matrix} \text{Gross investment in} \\ \text{operating capital} \end{matrix} &= \begin{matrix} \text{Net investment in} \\ \text{operating capital} \end{matrix} + \text{Depreciation} \\ &= \$345 + \$100 = \$445 \text{ million.} \end{aligned} \tag{3-7}$$

Because depreciation is a noncash expense, some analysts calculate **operating cash flow** as

$$\text{Operating cash flow} = NOPAT + \text{Depreciation.} \tag{3-8}$$

MicroDrive's most recent operating cash flow is

Operating cash flow = NOPAT + Depreciation = $170.3 + $100 = $270.3.

An algebraically equivalent expression for free cash flow in terms of operating cash flow and gross investment in operating capital is

$$FCF = \text{Operating cash flow} - \text{Gross investment in operating capital}$$
$$= (\$170.3 + \$100) - \$445 \tag{3-9}$$
$$= -\$174.7 \text{ million.}$$

Equations 3-6 and 3-9 are equivalent because depreciation is added to both NOPAT and net investment in Equation 3-6 to arrive at Equation 3-9. We usually use Equation 3-6, because it saves us this step.

The Uses of FCF

Recall that free cash flow (FCF) is the amount of cash that is available for distribution to all investors, including both shareholders and debtholders. There are five good uses for FCF:

1. Pay interest to debtholders, keeping in mind that the net cost to the company is the after-tax interest expense.
2. Repay debtholders, that is, pay off some of the debt.
3. Pay dividends to shareholders.
4. Repurchase stock from shareholders.
5. Buy short-term investments or other nonoperating assets.

Recall that the company does not have to use FCF to acquire operating assets since, by definition, FCF already takes into account the purchase of all operating assets needed to support growth. Unfortunately, there is evidence to suggest that some companies with high FCF tend to make unnecessary investments that don't add value, such as paying too much to acquire some other company. Thus, high FCF can cause waste if managers fail to act in the best interest of shareholders. As discussed in Chapter 1, this is called an agency cost, since managers are hired as agents to act on behalf of stockholders. We discuss agency costs and ways to control them in Chapter 15, where we discuss value-based management and corporate governance, and in Chapter 16, where we discuss the choice of capital structure.

In practice, most companies combine these five uses in such a way that the net total is equal to FCF. For example, a company might pay interest and dividends, issue new debt, and also sell some of its marketable securities. Some of these activities are cash outflows (for example, paying interest and dividends) and some are cash inflows (for example, issuing debt and selling marketable securities), but the net cash flow from these five activities is equal to FCF.

FCF and Corporate Value

FCF is the amount of cash available for distribution to investors, and, as a result, the value of a company depends on the present value of its expected future FCFs, discounted at the company's weighted average cost of capital (WACC). Subsequent chapters will develop the tools needed to forecast FCFs and evaluate their risk. Chapter 15 ties all this together with a model that is used to calculate the value of a company. Even though you do not yet have all the tools to apply the model, it's important that you understand this basic concept: *FCF is the cash available for distribution to investors. Therefore, the value of a firm primarily depends on its expected future FCFs.*

Evaluating FCF, NOPAT, and Operating Capital

Even though MicroDrive had a positive NOPAT, its very high investment in operating assets resulted in a negative free cash flow. Because free cash flow is what is available for distribution to investors, not only was there nothing for investors, but investors actually had to provide *additional* money to keep the business going. Investors provided most of this new money as debt.

Is a negative free cash flow always bad? The answer is, "Not necessarily; it depends on why the free cash flow was negative." If FCF was negative because NOPAT was negative, that is a bad sign, because then the company is probably experiencing operating problems. However, many high-growth companies have positive NOPAT but negative free cash flow because they are making large investments in operating assets to support growth. There is nothing wrong with profitable growth, even if it causes negative cash flows.

One way to determine whether growth is profitable is by examining the **return on invested capital (ROIC),** which is the ratio of NOPAT to total operating capital. If the ROIC exceeds the rate of return required by investors, then a negative free cash flow caused by high growth is nothing to worry about. Chapter 15 discusses this in detail.

To calculate the ROIC, we first calculate NOPAT and operating capital. The return on invested capital (ROIC) is a performance measure that indicates how much NOPAT is generated by each dollar of operating capital:

$$\text{ROIC} = \frac{\text{NOPAT}}{\text{Operating capital}}. \tag{3-10}$$

If ROIC is greater than the rate of return investors require, which is the weighted average cost of capital (WACC), then the firm is adding value.

As noted earlier, a negative current FCF is not necessarily bad, provided it is due to high growth. For example, during the late 1990s Home Depot had negative FCF due to its rapid growth, but it also had a very high ROIC, and this high ROIC resulted in a high market value for the stock.

MicroDrive had an ROIC in 2007 of 9.46% ($170.3/$1,800 = 0.0946). Is this enough to cover its cost of capital? We'll answer that question in the next section.

SELF-TEST

What is net operating working capital? Why does it exclude most short-term investments and also notes payable?

What is total net operating capital? Why is it important for managers to calculate a company's capital requirements?

Why is NOPAT a better performance measure than net income?

What is free cash flow? Why is it important?

A firm's total net operating capital for the previous year was $2 million. For the current year, its total net operating capital is $2.5 million and its NOPAT is $1.2 million. What is its free cash flow for the current year? ($700,000)

3.8 MVA and EVA

Neither traditional accounting data nor the modified data discussed in the preceding section incorporates stock prices, even though the primary goal of management is to maximize the firm's stock price. Financial analysts have therefore developed two additional performance measures, MVA, or Market Value Added, and EVA, or Economic Value Added. These concepts are discussed in this section.[11]

Market Value Added (MVA)

The primary goal of most firms is to maximize shareholders' wealth. This goal obviously benefits shareholders, but it also helps to ensure that scarce resources are allocated efficiently, which benefits the economy. Shareholder wealth is maximized by maximizing the *difference* between the market value of the firm's stock and the amount of equity capital that was supplied by shareholders. This difference is called the **Market Value Added (MVA):**

For an updated estimate of Coca-Cola's MVA, go to **http://finance.yahoo .com**, enter KO, and click GO. This shows the market value of equity, called Mkt Cap. To get the book value of equity, select Balance Sheet from the left panel.

$$\text{MVA} = \text{Market value of stock} - \text{Equity capital supplied by shareholders}$$
$$= (\text{Shares outstanding})(\text{Stock price}) - \text{Total common equity}. \qquad \text{(3-11)}$$

To illustrate, consider Coca-Cola. In May 2006, its total market equity value was $104.8 billion, while its balance sheet showed that stockholders had put up only $16.4 billion. Thus, Coca-Cola's MVA was $104.8 − $16.4 = $88.4 billion. This $88.4 billion represents the difference between the money that Coca-Cola's stockholders have invested in the corporation since its founding—including retained earnings—versus the cash they could get if they sold the business. The higher its MVA, the better the job management is doing for the firm's shareholders.

Sometimes MVA is defined as the total market value of the company minus the total amount of investor-supplied capital:

$$\text{MVA} = \text{Total market value} - \text{Total investor supplied capital}$$
$$= (\text{Market value of stock} + \text{Market value of debt}) \qquad \text{(3-11a)}$$
$$- \text{Total investor supplied capital}.$$

For most companies, the total amount of investor-supplied capital is the sum of equity, debt, and preferred stock. We can calculate the total amount of investor-supplied capital directly from their reported values in the financial statements. The total market value of a company is the sum of the market values of common equity, debt, and preferred stock. It is easy to find the market value of equity, since stock prices are readily available, but it is not always easy to find the market value of debt. Hence, many analysts use the value of debt that is reported in the financial statements, the debt's book value, as an estimate of its market value.

---

[11]The concepts of EVA and MVA were developed by Joel Stern and Bennett Stewart, co-founders of the consulting firm Stern Stewart & Company. Stern Stewart copyrighted the terms "EVA" and "MVA," so other consulting firms have given other names to these values. Still, EVA and MVA are the terms most commonly used in practice.

For Coca-Cola, the total amount of reported debt was about $5.7 billion, and Coca-Cola had no preferred stock. Using this as an estimate of the market value of debt, Coke's total market value was $104.8 + $5.7 = $110.5 billion. The total amount of investor-supplied funds was $16.4 + $5.7 = $22.1 billion. Using these total values, the MVA was $110.5 − $22.1 = $88.4 billion. Note that this is the same answer that we got using the previous definition of MVA. Both methods will give the same result if the market value of debt is approximately equal to its book value.

Economic Value Added (EVA)

Whereas MVA measures the effects of managerial actions since the very inception of a company, **Economic Value Added (EVA)** focuses on managerial effectiveness in a given year. The basic EVA formula is as follows:

$$
\begin{aligned}
\text{EVA} &= \text{Net operating profit after taxes (NOPAT)} \\
&\quad - \text{After-tax dollar cost of capital used to support operations} \quad \text{(3-12)} \\
&= \text{EBIT}(1 - \text{Tax rate}) - (\text{Total net operating capital})(\text{WACC}).
\end{aligned}
$$

We can also calculate EVA in terms of ROIC:

$$
\text{EVA} = (\text{Operating capital})(\text{ROIC} - \text{WACC}). \qquad \text{(3-13)}
$$

As this equation shows, a firm adds value—that is, has a positive EVA—if its ROIC is greater than its WACC. If WACC exceeds ROIC, then new investments in operating capital will reduce the firm's value.

EVA is an estimate of a business's true economic profit for the year, and it differs sharply from accounting profit.[12] EVA represents the residual income that remains after the cost of *all* capital, including equity capital, has been deducted, whereas accounting profit is determined without imposing a charge for equity capital. As we discuss in Chapter 10, equity capital has a cost, because funds provided by shareholders could have been invested elsewhere, where they would have earned a return. Shareholders give up the opportunity to invest elsewhere when they provide capital to the firm. The return they could earn elsewhere in investments of equal risk represents the cost of equity capital. This cost is an *opportunity cost* rather than an *accounting cost*, but it is quite real nevertheless.

Note that when calculating EVA we do not add back depreciation. Although it is not a cash expense, depreciation is a cost since worn-out assets must be replaced, and it is therefore deducted when determining both net income and EVA. Our calculation of EVA assumes that the true economic depreciation of the company's fixed assets exactly equals the depreciation used for accounting and tax purposes. If this were not the case, adjustments would have to be made to obtain a more accurate measure of EVA.

---

[12]The most important reason EVA differs from accounting profit is that the cost of equity capital is deducted when EVA is calculated. Other factors that could lead to differences include adjustments that might be made to depreciation, to research and development costs, to inventory valuations, and so on. These other adjustments also can affect the calculation of investor-supplied capital, which affects both EVA and MVA. See Stewart, *The Quest for Value*, cited in footnote 10.

Table 3-5

MVA and EVA for MicroDrive, Inc. (Millions of Dollars)

e-resource

See **FM12 Ch 03 Tool Kit.xls** for all details.

	2007	2006
MVA Calculation		
Price per share	$ 23.0	$ 26.0
Number of shares (millions)	50.0	50.0
Market value of equity = Share price (Number of shares)	$1,150.0	$1,300.0
Book value of equity	$ 896.0	$ 840.0
MVA = Market value − Book value	$ 254.0	$ 460.0
EVA Calculation		
EBIT	$ 283.8	$ 263.0
Tax rate	40%	40%
NOPAT = EBIT(1 − T)	$ 170.3	$ 157.8
Total investor-supplied operating capital[a]	$1,800.0	$1,455.0
Weighted average cost of capital, WACC (%)	11.0%	10.8%
Dollar cost of capital = Operating capital (WACC)	$ 198.0	$157.1
EVA = NOPAT − Dollar cost of capital	($ 27.7)	$ 0.7
ROIC = NOPAT/Operating capital	9.46%	10.85%
ROIC − Cost of capital = ROIC − WACC	(1.54%)	0.05%
EVA = (Operating capital)(ROIC − WACC)	($ 27.7)	$ 0.7

[a]Investor-supplied operating capital equals the sum of notes payable, long-term debt, preferred stock, and common equity, less short-term investments. It could also be calculated as total liabilities and equity minus accounts payable, accruals, and short-term investments. It is also equal to total net operating capital.

EVA measures the extent to which the firm has increased shareholder value. Therefore, if managers focus on EVA, this will help to ensure that they operate in a manner that is consistent with maximizing shareholder wealth. Note too that EVA can be determined for divisions as well as for the company as a whole, so it provides a useful basis for determining managerial performance at all levels. Consequently, EVA is being used by an increasing number of firms as the primary basis for determining managerial compensation.

Table 3-5 shows how MicroDrive's MVA and EVA are calculated. The stock price was $23 per share at year-end 2007, down from $26 per share the previous year. Its WACC, which is the percentage after-tax cost of capital, was 10.8% in 2006 and 11.0% in 2007, and its tax rate was 40%. Other data in Table 3-5 were given in the basic financial statements provided earlier in the chapter.

Note first that the lower stock price and the higher book value of equity (due to retaining earnings during 2007) combined to reduce the MVA. The 2007 MVA is still positive, but $460 − $254 = $206 million of stockholders' value was lost during the year.

EVA for 2006 was just barely positive, and in 2007 it was negative. Operating income (NOPAT) rose, but EVA still declined, primarily because the amount of capital rose more sharply than NOPAT—by about 26% versus 8%—and the cost of this additional capital pulled EVA down.

Sarbanes-Oxley and Financial Fraud

Investors need to be cautious when they review financial statements. While companies are required to follow GAAP, managers still have quite a lot of discretion in deciding how and when to report certain transactions. Consequently, two firms in exactly the same operating situation may report financial statements that convey different impressions about their financial strength. Some variations may stem from legitimate differences of opinion about the correct way to record transactions. In other cases, managers may choose to report numbers in a way that helps them present either higher earnings or more stable earnings over time. As long as they follow GAAP, such actions are not illegal, but these differences make it harder for investors to compare companies and gauge their true performances.

Unfortunately, there have also been cases where managers overstepped the bounds and reported fraudulent statements. Indeed, a number of high-profile executives have faced criminal charges because of their misleading accounting practices. For example, in June 2002 it was discovered that WorldCom (now called MCI) had committed the most

massive accounting fraud of all time by recording over $7 billion of ordinary operating costs as capital expenditures, thus overstating net income by the same amount.

WorldCom's published financial statements fooled most investors—investors bid the stock price up to $64.50, and banks and other lenders provided the company with more than $30 billion of loans. Arthur Andersen, the firm's auditor, was faulted for not detecting the fraud. WorldCom's CFO and CEO were convicted and Arthur Andersen went bankrupt. But that didn't help the investors who relied on the published financial statements.

In response to these and other abuses, Congress passed the Sarbanes-Oxley Act of 2002. One of its provisions requires both the CEO and the CFO to sign a statement certifying that the "financial statements and disclosures fairly represent, in all material respects, the operations and financial condition" of the company. This will make it easier to haul off in handcuffs a CEO or CFO who has been misleading investors. Whether this will prevent future financial fraud remains to be seen.

Recall also that net income fell, but not nearly so dramatically as the decline in EVA. Net income does not reflect the amount of equity capital employed, but EVA does. Because of this omission, net income is not as useful as EVA for setting corporate goals and measuring managerial performance.

We will have more to say about both MVA and EVA later in the book, but we can close this section with two observations. First, there is a relationship between MVA and EVA, but it is not a direct one. If a company has a history of negative EVAs, then its MVA will probably be negative, and vice versa if it has a history of positive EVAs. However, the stock price, which is the key ingredient in the MVA calculation, depends more on expected future performance than on historical performance. Therefore, a company with a history of negative EVAs could have a positive MVA, provided investors expect a turnaround in the future.

The second observation is that when EVAs or MVAs are used to evaluate managerial performance as part of an incentive compensation program, EVA is the measure that is typically used. The reasons are (1) EVA shows the value added during a given year, whereas MVA reflects performance over the company's entire life, perhaps even including times before the current managers were born, and (2) EVA can be applied to individual divisions or other units of a large corporation, whereas MVA must be applied to the entire corporation.

SELF-TEST

Define "Market Value Added (MVA)" and "Economic Value Added (EVA)."

How does EVA differ from accounting profit?

A firm has $100 million in total net operating capital. Its return on invested capital is 14% and its weighted average cost of capital is 10%. What is its EVA? ($400,000)

3.9 The Federal Income Tax System

The value of any financial asset (including stocks, bonds, and mortgages), as well as most real assets such as plants or even entire firms, depends on the stream of cash flows produced by the asset. Cash flows from an asset consist of *usable* income plus depreciation, and usable income means income *after taxes*. The following sections describe the key features of corporate and individual taxation.

Corporate Income Taxes

The corporate tax structure, shown in Table 3-6, is relatively simple. The **marginal tax rate** is the rate paid on the last dollar of income, while the **average tax rate** is the average rate paid on all income. To illustrate, if a firm had $65,000 of taxable income, its tax bill would be

$$\text{Taxes} = \$7,500 + 0.25(\$65,000 - \$50,000)$$

$$= \$7,500 + \$3,750 = \$11,250.$$

Its marginal rate would be 25%, and its average tax rate would be $11,250/$65,000 = 17.3%. Note that corporate income above $18,333,333 has an average and marginal tax rate of 35%.[13]

Interest and Dividend Income Received by a Corporation Interest income received by a corporation is taxed as ordinary income at regular corporate tax rates. *However, 70% of the dividends received by one corporation from another is excluded from taxable income, while the remaining 30% is taxed at the ordinary tax rate.*[14] Thus, a corporation earning more than $18,333,333 and paying a 35% marginal tax rate would pay only (0.30)(0.35) = 0.105 = 10.5% of its dividend income as taxes, so its effective tax rate on dividends received would be 10.5%. If this firm had $10,000 in pre-tax dividend income, its after-tax dividend income would be $8,950:

$$
\begin{aligned}
\text{After-tax income} &= \text{Before-tax income} - \text{Taxes} \\
&= \text{Before-tax income} - (\text{Before-tax income})(\text{Effective tax rate}) \\
&= \text{Before-tax income}(1 - \text{Effective tax rate}) \\
&= \$10,000[1 - (0.30)(0.35)] \\
&= \$10,000(1 - 0.105) = \$10,000(0.895) = \$8,950.
\end{aligned}
$$

---

[13]Prior to 1987, many large, profitable corporations such as General Electric and Boeing paid no income taxes. The reasons for this were as follows: (1) expenses, especially depreciation, were defined differently for calculating taxable income than for reporting earnings to stockholders, so some companies reported positive profits to stockholders but losses—hence no taxes—to the Internal Revenue Service; and (2) some companies that did have tax liabilities used various tax credits to offset taxes that would otherwise have been payable. This situation was effectively eliminated in 1987.

The principal method used to eliminate this situation is the Alternative Minimum Tax (AMT). Under the AMT, both corporate and individual taxpayers must figure their taxes in two ways, the "regular" way and the AMT way, and then pay the higher of the two. The AMT is calculated as follows: (1) Figure your regular taxes. (2) Take your taxable income under the regular method and then add back certain items, especially income on certain municipal bonds, depreciation in excess of straight-line depreciation, certain research and drilling costs, itemized or standard deductions (for individuals), and a number of other items. (3) The income determined in (2) is defined as AMT income, and it must then be multiplied by the AMT tax rate to determine the tax due under the AMT system. An individual or corporation must then pay the higher of the regular tax or the AMT tax. In 2006, there were two AMT tax rates for individuals (26% and 28%, depending on the level of AMT income and filing status). Most corporations have an AMT of 20%. However, there is no AMT for very small companies, defined as those that have had average sales of less than $7.5 million for the last 3 years.

[14]The size of the dividend exclusion actually depends on the degree of ownership. Corporations that own less than 20% of the stock of the dividend-paying company can exclude 70% of the dividends received; firms that own more than 20% but less than 80% can exclude 80% of the dividends; and firms that own more than 80% can exclude the entire dividend payment. We will, in general, assume a 70% dividend exclusion.

Table 3-6

Corporate Tax Rates as of January 2006

If a Corporation's Taxable Income Is	It Pays This Amount on the Base of the Bracket	Plus this Percentage on the Excess over the Base	Average Tax Rate at Top of Bracket
Up to $50,000	$0	15%	15.0%
$50,000–$75,000	$7,500	25	18.3
$75,000–$100,000	$13,750	34	22.3
$100,000–$335,000	$22,250	39	34.0
$335,000–$10,000,000	$113,900	34	34.0
$10,000,000–$15,000,000	$3,400,000	35	34.3
$15,000,000–$18,333,333	$5,150,000	38	35.0
Over $18,333,333	$6,416,667	35	35.0

FM

e-resource

See **FM12 Ch 03 Tool Kit.xls** for all details.

If the corporation pays its own after-tax income out to its stockholders as dividends, the income is ultimately subjected to *triple taxation:* (1) the original corporation is first taxed, (2) the second corporation is then taxed on the dividends it received, and (3) the individuals who receive the final dividends are taxed again. This is the reason for the 70% exclusion on intercorporate dividends.

If a corporation has surplus funds that can be invested in marketable securities, the tax factor favors investment in stocks, which pay dividends, rather than in bonds, which pay interest. For example, suppose GE had $100,000 to invest, and it could buy either bonds that paid interest of $8,000 per year or preferred stock that paid dividends of $7,000. GE is in the 35% tax bracket; therefore, its tax on the interest, if it bought bonds, would be 0.35($8,000) = $2,800, and its after-tax income would be $5,200. If it bought preferred (or common) stock, its tax would be 0.35[(0.30)($7,000)] = $735, and its after-tax income would be $6,265. Other factors might lead GE to invest in bonds, but the tax factor certainly favors stock investments when the investor is a corporation.[15]

Interest and Dividends Paid by a Corporation A firm's operations can be financed with either debt or equity capital. If it uses debt, it must pay interest on this debt, whereas if it uses equity, it is expected to pay dividends to the equity investors (stockholders). The interest *paid* by a corporation is deducted from its operating income to obtain its taxable income, but dividends paid are not deductible. Therefore, a firm needs $1 of pre-tax income to pay $1 of interest, but if it is in the 40% federal-plus-state tax bracket, it must earn $1.67 of pre-tax income to pay $1 of dividends:

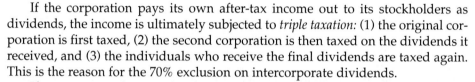

$$\frac{\text{Pre-tax income needed}}{\text{to pay \$1 of dividends}} = \frac{\$1}{1 - \text{Tax rate}} = \frac{\$1}{0.60} = \$1.67.$$

[15]This illustration demonstrates why corporations favor investing in lower-yielding preferred stocks over higher-yielding bonds. When tax consequences are considered, the yield on the preferred stock, [1 − 0.35(0.30)](7.0%) = 6.265%, is higher than the yield on the bond, (1 − 0.35)(8.0%) = 5.2%. Also, note that corporations are restricted in their use of borrowed funds to purchase other firms' preferred or common stocks. Without such restrictions, firms could engage in *tax arbitrage*, whereby the interest on borrowed funds reduces taxable income on a dollar-for-dollar basis, but taxable income is increased by only $0.30 per dollar of dividend income. Thus, current tax laws reduce the 70% dividend exclusion in proportion to the amount of borrowed funds used to purchase the stock.

Table 3-7

Apex Corporation: Calculation of $12 Million Loss Carryback and Amount Available for Carryforward

	Past Year 2005	Past Year 2006	Current Year 2007
Original taxable income	$2,000,000	$2,000,000	−$12,000,000
Carryback credit	2,000,000	2,000,000	
Adjusted profit	$ 0	$ 0	
Taxes previously paid (40%)	800,000	800,000	
Difference = Tax refund due	$ 800,000	$ 800,000	
Total tax refund received			$1,600,000
Amount of loss carryforward available			
Current loss			−$12,000,000
Carryback losses used			4,000,000
Carryforward losses still available			−$8,000,000

Working backward, if a company has $1.67 in pre-tax income, it must pay $0.67 in taxes [(0.4)($1.67) = $0.67]. This leaves it with after-tax income of $1.00.

Of course, it is generally not possible to finance exclusively with debt capital, and the risk of doing so would offset the benefits of the higher expected income. *Still, the fact that interest is a deductible expense has a profound effect on the way businesses are financed—our corporate tax system favors debt financing over equity financing.* This point is discussed in more detail in Chapters 10 and 16.

Corporate Capital Gains Before 1987, corporate long-term capital gains were taxed at lower rates than corporate ordinary income, so the situation was similar for corporations and individuals. Under current law, however, corporations' capital gains are taxed at the same rates as their operating income.

Corporate Loss Carryback and Carryforward Ordinary corporate operating losses can be carried back (**carryback**) to each of the preceding 2 years and forward (**carryforward**) for the next 20 years and used to offset taxable income in those years. For example, an operating loss in 2007 could be carried back and used to reduce taxable income in 2005 and 2006, and forward, if necessary, and used in 2008, 2009, and so on, to the year 2027. After carrying back 2 years, any remaining loss is typically carried forward first to the next year, then to the one after that, and so on, until losses have been used up or the 20-year carryforward limit has been reached.[16]

To illustrate, suppose Apex Corporation had $2 million of *pre-tax* profits (taxable income) in 2005 and 2006, and then, in 2007, Apex lost $12 million. Also, assume that Apex's federal-plus-state tax rate is 40%. As shown in Table 3-7, the company would use the carryback feature to recompute its taxes for 2005, using

---

[16]In the wake of the terrorist attacks on the World Trade Center and Pentagon on September 11, 2001, Congress temporarily changed the carryback provision in the Tax Code. The new provision allows operating losses incurred in tax years ending in 2001 or 2002 to be carried back 5 years rather than the normal 2 years. This provision is set to expire before this edition goes to print, so we will use a 2-year carryback provision in all of the examples.

c. Now assume that Wendt does not receive the interest income but does receive an additional $1 million as dividends on some stock it owns. What is the tax on this dividend income?

(3-9) ✓
Corporate After-Tax Yield
The Shrieves Corporation has $10,000 that it plans to invest in marketable securities. It is choosing among AT&T bonds, which yield 7.5%, state of Florida muni bonds, which yield 5%, and AT&T preferred stock, with a dividend yield of 6%. Shrieves's corporate tax rate is 35%, and 70% of the dividends received are tax exempt. Find the after-tax returns on both securities.

(3-10) ✓
Cash Flows
The Moore Corporation has operating income (EBIT) of $750,000. The company's depreciation expense is $200,000. Moore is 100% equity financed, and it faces a 40% tax rate. What is the company's net income? What is its net cash flow?

(3-11) ✓
Income and Cash Flow Analysis
The Berndt Corporation expects to have sales of $12 million. Costs other than depreciation are expected to be 75% of sales, and depreciation is expected to be $1.5 million. All sales revenues will be collected in cash, and costs other than depreciation must be paid for during the year. Berndt's federal-plus-state tax rate is 40%. Berndt has no debt.

a. Set up an income statement. What is Berndt's expected net cash flow?
b. Suppose Congress changed the tax laws so that Berndt's depreciation expenses doubled. No changes in operations occurred. What would happen to reported profit and to net cash flow?
c. Now suppose that Congress, instead of doubling Berndt's depreciation, reduced it by 50%. How would profit and net cash flow be affected?
d. If this were your company, would you prefer Congress to cause your depreciation expense to be doubled or halved? Why?

Challenging Problems 12–13

(3-12) (✓)
Free Cash Flows
You have just obtained financial information for the past 2 years for Bridgewater Equine Corporation. Answer the following questions.
a. What is the net operating profit after taxes (NOPAT) for 2007?
b. What are the amounts of net operating working capital for both years?
c. What are the amounts of total net operating capital for both years?
d. What is the free cash flow for 2007?
e. How can you explain the large increase in dividends in 2007?

Bridgewater Equine Corporation: Income Statements for Year Ending December 31 (Millions of Dollars)

	2007	2006
Sales	$1,200.0	$1,000.0
Operating costs excluding depreciation	1,020.0	850.0
Depreciation	30.0	25.0
Earnings before interest and taxes	$ 150.0	$ 125.0
Less interest	21.7	20.2
Earnings before taxes	$ 128.3	$ 104.8
Taxes (40%)	51.3	41.9
Net income available to common stockholders	$ 77.0	$ 62.9
Common dividends	$ 60.5	$ 4.4

Bridgewater Equine Corporation: Balance Sheets as of December 31 (Millions of Dollars)

	2007	2006
Assets		
Cash and equivalents	$ 12.0	$ 10.0
Short-term investments	0.0	0.0
Accounts receivable	180.0	150.0
Inventories	180.0	200.0
Total current assets	$372.0	$360.0
Net plant and equipment	300.0	250.0
Total assets	$672.0	$610.0
Liabilities and Equity		
Accounts payable	$108.0	$90.0
Notes payable	67.0	51.5
Accruals	72.0	60.0
Total current liabilities	$247.0	$201.5
Long-term bonds	150.0	150.0
Total liabilities	$397.0	$351.5
Common stock (50 million shares)	50.0	50.0
Retained earnings	225.0	208.5
Common equity	$275.0	$258.5
Total liabilities and equity	$672.0	$610.0

(3-13)

Loss Carryback and Carryforward

The Bookbinder Company has made $150,000 before taxes during each of the last 15 years, and it expects to make $150,000 a year before taxes in the future. However, in 2007 the firm incurred a loss of $650,000. The firm will claim a tax credit at the time it files its 2007 income tax return, and it will receive a check from the U.S. Treasury. Show how it calculates this credit, and then indicate the firm's tax liability for each of the next 5 years. Assume a 40% tax rate on *all* income to ease the calculations.

e-resource

Spreadsheet Problem

(3-14)

Build a Model: Financial Statements, EVA, and MVA

Start with the partial model in the file *FM12 Ch 03 P14 Build a Model.xls* at the textbook's Web site. Cumberland Industries' most recent balance sheets (in thousands of dollars) are shown below and in the partial model in the file:

	2007	2006
Cash	$ 91,450	$ 74,625
Short-term investments	11,400	15,100
Accounts receivable	103,365	85,527
Inventories	38,444	34,982
Total current assets	$244,659	$210,234
Net fixed assets	67,165	42,436
Total assets	$311,824	$252,670
Accounts payable	$ 30,761	$23,109
Accruals	30,477	22,656
Notes payable	16,717	14,217
Total current liabilities	$ 77,955	$59,982
Long-term debt	76,264	63,914
Total liabilities	$154,219	$123,896
Common stock	100,000	90,000
Retained earnings	57,605	38,774
Total common equity	$157,605	$128,774
Total liabilities and equity	$311,824	$252,670

a. The company's sales for 2007 were $455,150,000, and EBITDA was 15% of sales. Furthermore, depreciation amounted to 11% of net fixed assets, interest charges were $8,575,000, the state-plus-federal corporate tax rate was 40%, and Cumberland pays 40% of its net income out in dividends. Given this information, construct Cumberland's 2007 income statement. (Hint: Start with the partial model in the file.)

b. Next, construct the firm's statement of retained earnings for the year ending December 31, 2007, and then its 2007 statement of cash flows.

c. Calculate net operating working capital, total net operating capital, net operating profit after taxes, and free cash flow for 2007.

d. Calculate the firm's EVA and MVA for 2007. Assume that Cumberland had 10 million shares outstanding, that the year-end closing stock price was $17.25 per share, and its after-tax cost of capital (WACC) was 12%.

e-resource

Cyberproblem

Please go to the textbook's Web site to access any Cyberproblems.

Mini Case

Donna Jamison, a graduate of the University of Tennessee with 4 years of banking experience, was recently brought in as assistant to the chairman of the board of Computron Industries, a manufacturer of electronic calculators.

The company doubled its plant capacity, opened new sales offices outside its home territory, and launched an expensive advertising campaign. Computron's results were not satisfactory, to put it mildly. Its board of directors, which consisted of its president and vice-president plus its major stockholders (who were all local businesspeople), was most upset when directors learned how the expansion was going. Suppliers were being paid late and were unhappy, and the bank was complaining about the deteriorating situation and threatening to cut off credit. As a result, Al Watkins, Computron's president, was informed that changes would have to be made, and quickly, or he would be fired. Also, at the board's insistence Donna Jamison was brought in and given the job of assistant to Fred Campo, a retired banker who was Computron's chairman and largest stockholder. Campo agreed to give up a few of his golfing days and to help nurse the company back to health, with Jamison's help.

Jamison began by gathering financial statements and other data.

Balance Sheets	2006	2007
Assets		
Cash	$ 9,000	$ 7,282
Short-term investments	48,600	20,000
Accounts receivable	351,200	632,160
Inventories	715,200	1,287,360
Total current assets	$1,124,000	$1,946,802
Gross fixed assets	491,000	1,202,950
Less: Accumulated depreciation	146,200	263,160
Net fixed assets	$344,800	$ 939,790
Total assets	$1,468,800	$2,886,592
Liabilities and Equity		
Accounts payable	$ 145,600	$ 324,000
Notes payable	200,000	720,000
Accruals	136,000	284,960
Total current liabilities	$ 481,600	$1,328,960
Long-term debt	323,432	1,000,000
Common stock (100,000 shares)	460,000	460,000
Retained earnings	203,768	97,632
Total equity	$ 663,768	$ 557,632
Total liabilities and equity	$1,468,800	$2,886,592

Income Statements	2006	2007
Sales	$3,432,000	$5,834,400
Cost of goods sold	2,864,000	4,980,000
Other expenses	340,000	720,000
Depreciation	18,900	116,960
Total operating costs	$3,222,900	$5,816,960
EBIT	$ 209,100	$17,440
Interest expense	62,500	176,000
EBT	$ 146,600	($ 158,560)
Taxes (40%)	58,640	(63,424)
Net income	$ 87,960	($ 95,136)

Other Data

Stock price	$ 8.50	$ 6.00
Shares outstanding	100,000	100,000
EPS	$ 0.880	($ 0.951)
DPS	$ 0.220	$ 0.110
Tax rate	40%	40%

Statement of Retained Earnings, 2007

Balance of retained earnings, 12/31/2006	$ 203,768
Add: Net income, 2007	(95,136)
Less: Dividends paid, 2007	(11,000)
Balance of retained earnings, 12/31/2007	$ 97,632

Statement of Cash Flows, 2007

Operating Activities

Net income	($ 95,136)
Adjustments:	
Noncash adjustments:	
Depreciation	116,960
Changes in working capital:	
Change in accounts receivable	(280,960)
Change in inventories	(572,160)
Change in accounts payable	178,400
Change in accruals	148,960
Net cash provided by operating activities	($ 503,936)

Statement of Cash Flows, 2007—continued	2007
Investing Activities	
Cash used to acquire fixed assets	($ 711,950)
Change in short-term investments	28,600
Net cash provided by investing activities	($ 683,350)
Financing Activities	
Change in notes payable	520,000
Change in long-term debt	676,568
Change in common stock	—
Payment of cash dividends	(11,000)
Net cash provided by financing activities	$1,185,568
Summary	
Net change in cash	($ 1,718)
Cash at beginning of year	9,000
Cash at end of year	$ 7,282

Assume that you are Jamison's assistant, and you must help her answer the following questions for Campo.

a. What effect did the expansion have on sales and net income? What effect did the expansion have on the asset side of the balance sheet? What effect did it have on liabilities and equity?

b. What do you conclude from the statement of cash flows?

c. What is free cash flow? Why is it important? What are the five uses of FCF?

d. What are operating current assets? What are operating current liabilities? How much net operating working capital and total net operating capital does Computron have?

e. What are Computron's net operating profit after taxes (NOPAT) and free cash flow (FCF)?

f. Calculate Computron's return on invested capital. Computron has a 10% cost of capital (WACC). Do you think Computron's growth added value?

g. Jamison also has asked you to estimate Computron's EVA. She estimates that the after-tax cost of capital was 10% in both years.

h. What happened to Computron's Market Value Added (MVA)?

i. Assume that a corporation has $100,000 of taxable income from operations plus $5,000 of interest income and $10,000 of dividend income. What is the company's federal tax liability?

j. Assume that you are in the 25% marginal tax bracket and that you have $5,000 to invest. You have narrowed your investment choices down to California bonds with a yield of 7% or equally risky ExxonMobil bonds with a yield of 10%. Which one should you choose and why? At what marginal tax rate would you be indifferent to the choice between California and ExxonMobil bonds?

chapter 4

Analysis of Financial Statements

To guide or not to guide, that is the question. Or at least it's the question many companies are wrestling with regarding earnings forecasts. Should a company provide earnings estimates to investors? In 2006, Best Buy answered this question by announcing that it would no longer provide quarterly earnings forecasts. It's no coincidence that Best Buy's decision came shortly after its actual earnings came in just 2 cents below the forecast, yet its stock price fell by 12%. Coca-Cola, Motorola, and Citigroup are among the growing number of companies that no longer provide quarterly earnings forecasts.

Virtually no one disputes that investors need as much information as possible to accurately evaluate a company, and academic studies show that companies with greater transparency have higher valuations. However, greater disclosure often brings the possibility of lawsuits if investors have reason to believe that the disclosure is fraudulent. The Private Securities Litigation Reform Act of 1995 helped prevent "frivolous" lawsuits, but still,

before 2000, many companies provided earnings information to brokerage firms' analysts, and the analysts then forecast their own earnings expectations. In 2000 the SEC adopted Reg FD (Regulation Fair Disclosure), which prevented companies from disclosing information only to select groups, such as analysts. Reg FD led many companies to begin providing quarterly earnings forecasts directly to the public, and a survey by the National Investors Relations Institute showed that 95% of respondents in 2006 provided either annual or quarterly earnings forecasts, up from 45% in 1999.

Two trends are now in evidence. First, the number of companies reporting quarterly earnings forecasts is falling, but the number reporting annual forecasts is increasing. Second, many companies are providing other types of forward-looking information, including key operating ratios plus qualitative information about the company and its industry. Ratio analysis can help investors use such information, so keep that in mind as you read this chapter.

Sources: Adapted from Joseph McCafferty, "Guidance Lite," *CFO*, June 2006, 16–17, and William F. Coffin and Crocker Coulson, "Is Earnings Guidance Disappearing in 2006?" 2006, White Paper, available at **http://www.ccgir.com/ccgir/white_papers/pdf/Earnings %20Guidance%202006.pdf**.

Financial statement analysis involves (1) comparing the firm's performance with that of other firms in the same industry and (2) evaluating trends in the firm's financial position over time. This analysis helps managers identify deficiencies and then take actions to improve performance. The real value of financial statements lies in the fact that they can be used to help predict future earnings, dividends, and free cash flow. From an investor's standpoint, *predicting the future is what financial statement analysis is all about*, while from management's standpoint, *financial statement analysis is useful both to help anticipate future conditions and, more important, as a starting point for planning actions that will improve the firm's future performance.*[1]

FM

e-resource

The textbook's Web site contains an *Excel* file that will guide you through the chapter's calculations. The file for this chapter is **FM12 Ch 04 Tool Kit.xls** and we encourage you to open the file and follow along as you read the chapter.

4.1 Ratio Analysis

Financial ratios are designed to help evaluate financial statements. For example, Firm A might have debt of $5,248,760 and interest charges of $419,900, while Firm B might have debt of $52,647,980 and interest charges of $3,948,600. Which company is stronger? The burden of these debts, and the companies' ability to repay them, can best be evaluated by comparing (1) each firm's debt to its assets and (2) the interest it must pay to the income it has available for payment of interest. Such comparisons are made by *ratio analysis*.

We will calculate the Year 2007 financial ratios for MicroDrive Inc., using data from the balance sheets and income statements given in Table 4-1. We will also evaluate the ratios in relation to the industry averages. Note that dollar amounts are in millions.

4.2 Liquidity Ratios

A **liquid asset** is one that trades in an active market and hence can be quickly converted to cash at the going market price, and a firm's "liquidity ratios" deal with this question: Will the firm be able to pay off its debts as they come due over the next year or so? As shown in Table 4-1, MicroDrive has current liabilities of $310

FM

e-resource

See **FM12 Ch 04 Tool Kit.xls** for details.

Corporate Valuation and Analysis of Financial Statements

The value of a firm is determined by the size, timing, and risk of its expected future free cash flows (FCF). This chapter shows you how to use financial statements to evaluate a company's risk and its ability to generate free cash flows.

$$\text{Value} = \frac{FCF_1}{(1 + WACC)^1} + \frac{FCF_2}{(1 + WACC)^2} + \frac{FCF_3}{(1 + WACC)^3} + \cdots + \frac{FCF_\infty}{(1 + WACC)^\infty}$$

---

[1]Widespread accounting fraud has cast doubt on whether all firms' published financial statements can be trusted. New regulations by the SEC and the exchanges, and new laws enacted by Congress, have both improved oversight of the accounting industry and increased the criminal penalties on management for fraudulent reporting.

Table 4-1

MicroDrive Inc.: Balance Sheets and Income Statements for Years Ending December 31 (Millions of Dollars, Except for Per Share Data)

Assets	2007	2006	Liabilities and Equity	2007	2006
Cash and equivalents	$ 10	$ 15	Accounts payable	$ 60	$ 30
Short-term investments	0	65	Notes payable	110	60
Accounts receivable	375	315	Accruals	140	130
Inventories	615	415	Total current liabilities	$ 310	$ 220
Total current assets	$1,000	$ 810	Long-term bonds[a]	754	580
Net plant and equipment	1,000	870	Total liabilities	$ 1,064	$ 800
			Preferred stock		
			(400,000 shares)	40	40
			Common stock		
			(50,000,000 shares)	130	130
			Retained earnings	766	710
			Total common equity	$ 896	$ 840
Total assets	$2,000	$1,680	Total liabilities and equity	$ 2,000	$ 1,680

	2007	2006
Net sales	$3,000.0	$2,850.0
Operating costs excluding depreciation and amortization[b]	2,616.2	2,497.0
Earnings before interest, taxes, depreciation, and amortization (EBITDA)	$ 383.8	$ 353.0
Depreciation	100.0	90.0
Amortization	0.0	0.0
Depreciation and amortization	$ 100.0	$ 90.0
Earnings before interest and taxes (EBIT, or operating income)	$ 283.8	$ 263.0
Less interest	88.0	60.0
Earnings before taxes (EBT)	$ 195.8	$ 203.0
Taxes (40%)	78.3	81.2
Net income before preferred dividends	$ 117.5	$ 121.8
Preferred dividends	4.0	4.0
Net income	$ 113.5	$ 117.8
Common dividends	$ 57.5	$ 53.0
Addition to retained earnings	$ 56.0	$ 64.8
Per-Share Data		
Common stock price	$ 23.00	$ 26.00
Earnings per share (EPS)	$ 2.27	$ 2.36
Book value per share (BVPS)	$ 17.92	$ 16.80
Cash flow per share (CFPS)	$ 4.27	$ 4.16

[a]The bonds have a sinking fund requirement of $20 million a year.
[b]The costs include lease payments of $28 million a year.

million that must be paid off within the coming year. Will it have trouble satisfying those obligations? A full liquidity analysis requires the use of cash budgets, but by relating the amount of cash and other current assets to current obligations, ratio analysis provides a quick, easy-to-use measure of liquidity. Two commonly used **liquidity ratios** are discussed in this section.

Ability to Meet Short-term Obligations: The Current Ratio

The **current ratio** is calculated by dividing current assets by current liabilities:

$$\text{Current ratio} = \frac{\text{Current assets}}{\text{Current liabilities}}$$

$$= \frac{\$1,000}{\$310} = 3.2 \text{ times.}$$

$$\text{Industry average} = 4.2 \text{ times.}$$

Current assets normally include cash, marketable securities, accounts receivable, and inventories. Current liabilities consist of accounts payable, short-term notes payable, current maturities of long-term debt, accrued taxes, and other accrued expenses (principally wages).

MicroDrive has a lower current ratio than the average for its industry. Is this good or bad? Sometimes the answer depends on who is asking the question. For example, suppose a supplier is trying to decide whether to extend credit to MicroDrive. In general, creditors like to see a high current ratio. If a company is getting into financial difficulty, it will begin paying its bills (accounts payable) more slowly, borrowing from its bank, and so on, so its current liabilities will be increasing. If current liabilities are rising faster than current assets, the current ratio will fall, and this could spell trouble. Because the current ratio provides the best single indicator of the extent to which the claims of short-term creditors are covered by assets that are expected to be converted to cash fairly quickly, it is the most commonly used measure of short-term solvency.

Now consider the current ratio from the perspective of a shareholder. A high current ratio could mean that the company has a lot of money tied up in non-productive assets, such as excess cash or marketable securities. Or perhaps the high current ratio is due to large inventory holdings, which might well become obsolete before they can be sold. Thus, shareholders might not want a high current ratio.

An industry average is not a magic number that all firms should strive to maintain—in fact, some very well-managed firms will be above the average while other good firms will be below it. However, if a firm's ratios are far removed from the averages for its industry, this is a red flag, and analysts should be concerned about why the variance occurs. For example, suppose a low current ratio is traced to low inventories. Is this a competitive advantage resulting from the firm's mastery of just-in-time inventory management, or an Achilles' heel that is causing the firm to miss shipments and lose sales? Ratio analysis doesn't answer such questions, but it does point to areas of potential concern.

Quick, or Acid Test, Ratio

The **quick**, or **acid test, ratio** is calculated by deducting inventories from current assets and then dividing the remainder by current liabilities:

$$\text{Quick, or acid test, ratio} = \frac{\text{Current assets} - \text{Inventories}}{\text{Current liabilities}}$$

$$= \frac{\$385}{\$310} = 1.2 \text{ times.}$$

$$\text{Industry average} = 2.1 \text{ times.}$$

Inventories are typically the least liquid of a firm's current assets; hence they are the current assets on which losses are most likely to occur in a bankruptcy. Therefore, a measure of the firm's ability to pay off short-term obligations without relying on the sale of inventories is important.

The industry average quick ratio is 2.1, so MicroDrive's 1.2 ratio is low in comparison with other firms in its industry. Still, if the accounts receivable can be collected, the company can pay off its current liabilities without having to liquidate its inventory.

SELF-TEST

Identify two ratios that are used to analyze a firm's liquidity position, and write out their equations.
What are the characteristics of a liquid asset? Give some examples.
Which current asset is typically the least liquid?
A company has current liabilities of $800 million, and its current ratio is 2.5. What is its level of current assets? ($2,000 million) If this firm's quick ratio is 2, how much inventory does it have? ($400 million)

4.3   Asset Management Ratios

The second group of ratios, the **asset management ratios,** measures how effectively the firm is managing its assets. These ratios are designed to answer this question: Does the total amount of each type of asset as reported on the balance sheet seem reasonable, too high, or too low in view of current and projected sales levels? If a company has excessive investments in assets, then its operating assets and capital will be unduly high, which will reduce its free cash flow and its stock price. On the other hand, if a company does not have enough assets, it will lose sales, which will hurt profitability, free cash flow, and the stock price. Therefore, it is important to have the *right* amount invested in assets. Ratios that analyze the different types of assets are described in this section.

Evaluating Inventories: The Inventory Turnover Ratio

The **inventory turnover ratio** is defined as sales divided by inventories:

$$\text{Inventory turnover ratio} = \frac{\text{Sales}}{\text{Inventories}}$$

$$= \frac{\$3,000}{\$615} = 4.9 \text{ times.}$$

$$\text{Industry average} = 9.0 \text{ times.}$$

As a rough approximation, each item of MicroDrive's inventory is sold out and restocked, or "turned over," 4.9 times per year. "Turnover" is a term that originated many years ago with the old Yankee peddler, who would load up his wagon with goods and then go off to peddle his wares. The merchandise was called "working capital" because it was what he actually sold, or "turned over," to produce his profits, whereas his "turnover" was the number of trips he took each year. Annual sales divided by inventory equaled turnover, or trips per year. If he made 10 trips per year, stocked 100 pans, and made a gross profit of $5 per pan, his annual gross profit would be (100)($5)(10) = $5,000. If he went faster and made 20 trips per year, his gross profit would double, other things held constant. So, his turnover directly affected his profits.

MicroDrive's turnover of 4.9 times is much lower than the industry average of 9 times. This suggests that MicroDrive is holding too much inventory. Excess inventory is, of course, unproductive, and it represents an investment with a low or zero rate of return. MicroDrive's low inventory turnover ratio also makes us question the current ratio. With such a low turnover, we must wonder whether the firm is actually holding obsolete goods not worth their stated value.[2]

Note that sales occur over the entire year, whereas the inventory figure is for one point in time. For this reason, it is better to use an average inventory measure.[3] If the firm's business is highly seasonal, or if there has been a strong upward or downward sales trend during the year, it is especially useful to make some such adjustment. To maintain comparability with industry averages, however, we did not use the average inventory figure.

Evaluating Receivables: The Days Sales Outstanding

Days sales outstanding (DSO), also called the "average collection period" (ACP), is used to appraise accounts receivable, and it is calculated by dividing accounts receivable by average daily sales to find the number of days' sales that are tied up in receivables.[4] Thus, the DSO represents the average length of time that the firm must wait after making a sale before receiving cash, which is the average collection period. MicroDrive has 46 days sales outstanding, well above the 36-day industry average:

$$\text{DSO} = \begin{matrix} \text{Days} \\ \text{sales} \\ \text{outstanding} \end{matrix} = \frac{\text{Receivables}}{\text{Average sales per day}} = \frac{\text{Receivables}}{\text{Annual sales/365}}$$

$$= \frac{\$375}{\$3,000 > 365} = \frac{\$375}{\$8.2192} = 45.6 \text{ days} \approx 46 \text{ days.}$$

$$\text{Industry average} = 36 \text{ days.}$$

The DSO can also be evaluated by comparison with the terms on which the firm sells its goods. For example, MicroDrive's sales terms call for payment within 30 days. The fact that 45 days of sales are outstanding indicates that customers, on the average, are not paying their bills on time. This deprives MicroDrive of funds that it could use to invest in productive assets. Moreover, in some instances the

---

[2]A problem arises when calculating and analyzing the inventory turnover ratio. Sales are stated at market prices, so if inventories are carried at cost, as they generally are, the calculated turnover overstates the true turnover ratio. Therefore, it would be more appropriate to use cost of goods sold in place of sales in the formula's numerator. However, established compilers of financial ratio statistics such as Dun & Bradstreet use the ratio of sales to inventories carried at cost. To develop a figure that can be compared with those published by Dun & Bradstreet and similar organizations, it is necessary to measure inventory turnover with sales in the numerator, as we do here.

[3]Preferably, the average inventory value should be calculated by summing the monthly figures during the year and dividing by 12. If monthly data are not available, one can add the beginning and ending annual figures and divide by 2. However, most industry ratios are calculated as above, using end-of-year values.

[4]It would be better to use *average* receivables, but we used year-end values for comparability with the industry average.

fact that a customer is paying late may signal that the customer is in financial trouble, in which case MicroDrive may have a hard time ever collecting the receivable. Therefore, if the trend in DSO over the past few years has been rising, but the credit policy has not been changed, this would be strong evidence that steps should be taken to expedite the collection of accounts receivable.

Evaluating Fixed Assets: The Fixed Assets Turnover Ratio

The **fixed assets turnover ratio** measures how effectively the firm uses its plant and equipment. It is the ratio of sales to net fixed assets:

$$\text{Fixed assets turnover ratio} = \frac{\text{Sales}}{\text{Net fixed assets}}$$

$$= \frac{\$3,000}{\$1,000} = 3.0 \text{ times.}$$

$$\text{Industry average} = 3.0 \text{ times.}$$

MicroDrive's ratio of 3.0 times is equal to the industry average, indicating that the firm is using its fixed assets about as intensively as are other firms in its industry. Therefore, MicroDrive seems to have about the right amount of fixed assets in relation to other firms.

A potential problem can exist when interpreting the fixed assets turnover ratio. Recall from accounting that fixed assets reflect the historical costs of the assets. Inflation has caused the value of many assets that were purchased in the past to be seriously understated. Therefore, if we were comparing an old firm that had acquired many of its fixed assets years ago at low prices with a new company that had acquired its fixed assets only recently, we would probably find that the old firm had the higher fixed assets turnover ratio. However, this would be more reflective of the difficulty accountants have in dealing with inflation than of any inefficiency on the part of the new firm. Financial analysts must recognize that this problem exists and deal with it judgmentally.

Evaluating Total Assets: The Total Assets Turnover Ratio

The final asset management ratio, the **total assets turnover ratio,** measures the turnover of all the firm's assets; it is calculated by dividing sales by total assets:

$$\text{Total assets turnover ratio} = \frac{\text{Sales}}{\text{Total assets}}$$

$$= \frac{\$3,000}{\$2,000} = 1.5 \text{ times.}$$

$$\text{Industry average} = 1.8 \text{ times.}$$

MicroDrive's ratio is somewhat below the industry average, indicating that the company is not generating a sufficient volume of business given its total asset investment. Sales should be increased, some assets should be sold, or a combination of these steps should be taken.

4.4 Debt Management Ratios

The extent to which a firm uses debt financing, or **financial leverage,** has three important implications: (1) By raising funds through debt, stockholders can maintain control of a firm without increasing their investment. (2) If the firm earns more on investments financed with borrowed funds than it pays in interest, then its shareholders' returns are magnified, or "leveraged," but their risks are also magnified. (3) Creditors look to the equity, or owner-supplied funds, to provide a margin of safety, so the higher the proportion of funding supplied by stockholders, the less risk creditors face. Chapter 16 explains the first two points in detail, while the following ratios examine leverage from a creditor's point of view.

How the Firm Is Financed: Total Liabilities to Total Assets

The ratio of total liabilities to total assets is called the **debt ratio,** or sometimes the **total debt ratio.** It measures the percentage of funds provided by current liabilities and long-term debt:

$$\text{Debt ratio} = \frac{\text{Total liabilities}}{\text{Total assets}}$$

$$= \frac{\$310 + \$754}{\$2,000} = \frac{\$1,064}{\$2,000} = 53.2\%.$$

$$\text{Industry average} = 40.0\%.$$

Creditors prefer low debt ratios because the lower the ratio, the greater the cushion against creditors' losses in the event of liquidation. Stockholders, on the other hand, may want more leverage because it magnifies expected earnings.

MicroDrive's debt ratio is 53.2%, which means that its creditors have supplied more than half the total financing. As we will discuss in Chapter 16, a variety of factors determine a company's optimal debt ratio. Nevertheless, the fact that MicroDrive's debt ratio exceeds the industry average raises a red flag and may make it costly for MicroDrive to borrow additional funds without first raising more equity capital. Creditors may be reluctant to lend the firm more money, and management would probably be subjecting the firm to the risk of bankruptcy if it increased the debt ratio by borrowing additional funds.

If you use a debt ratio that you did not calculate yourself, be sure to find out how the ratio was defined. Some sources provide the ratio of long-term debt to total assets, and some provide the ratio of debt to equity, so be sure to check the source's definition.[5]

---

[5]The debt-to-assets (D/A) and debt-to-equity (D/E) ratios are simply transformations of each other when debt is defined as total liabilities:

$$D/E = \frac{D/A}{1 - D/A} \text{ and } D/A = \frac{D/E}{1 + D/E}.$$

Ability to Pay Interest: Times-Interest-Earned

The **times-interest-earned (TIE) ratio** is determined by dividing earnings before interest and taxes (EBIT in Table 4-1) by the interest charges:

$$\text{Times-interest-earned (TIE) ratio} = \frac{\text{EBIT}}{\text{Interest charges}}$$

$$= \frac{\$283.8}{\$88} = 3.2 \text{ times.}$$

$$\text{Industry average} = 6 \text{ times.}$$

The TIE ratio measures the extent to which operating income can decline before the firm is unable to meet its annual interest costs. Failure to meet this obligation can bring legal action by the firm's creditors, possibly resulting in bankruptcy. Note that earnings before interest and taxes, rather than net income, is used in the numerator. Because interest is paid with pre-tax dollars, the firm's ability to pay current interest is not affected by taxes.

MicroDrive's interest is covered 3.2 times. Since the industry average is 6 times, MicroDrive is covering its interest charges by a relatively low margin of safety. Thus, the TIE ratio reinforces the conclusion from our analysis of the debt ratio that MicroDrive would face difficulties if it attempted to borrow additional funds.

Ability to Service Debt: EBITDA Coverage Ratio

The TIE ratio is useful for assessing a company's ability to meet interest charges on its debt, but this ratio has two shortcomings: (1) Interest is not the only fixed financial charge—companies must also reduce debt on schedule, and many firms lease assets and thus must make lease payments. If they fail to repay debt or meet lease payments, they can be forced into bankruptcy. (2) EBIT does not represent all the cash flow available to service debt, especially if a firm has high depreciation and/or amortization charges. To account for these deficiencies, bankers and others have developed the **EBITDA coverage ratio,** defined as follows:[6]

$$\text{EBITDA coverage ratio} = \frac{\text{EBITDA + Lease payments}}{\text{Interest + Principal payments + Lease payments}}$$

$$= \frac{\$383.8 + \$28}{\$88 + \$20 + \$28} = \frac{\$411.8}{\$136} = 3.0 \text{ times.}$$

$$\text{Industry average} = 4.3 \text{ times.}$$

MicroDrive had $383.8 million of earnings before interest, taxes, depreciation, and amortization (EBITDA). Also, lease payments of $28 million were deducted while calculating EBITDA. That $28 million was available to meet financial charges; hence it must be added back, bringing the total available to cover fixed financial charges to $411.8 million. Fixed financial charges consisted of $88 million of interest, $20 million of sinking fund payments, and $28 million for lease payments, for

[6]Different analysts define the EBITDA coverage ratio in different ways. For example, some would omit the lease payment information, and others would "gross up" principal payments by dividing them by $(1 - T)$ because these payments are not tax deductions, and hence must be made with after-tax cash flows. We included lease payments because, for many firms, they are quite important, and failing to make them can lead to bankruptcy just as surely as can failure to make payments on "regular" debt. We did not gross up principal payments because, if a company is in financial difficulty, its tax rate will probably be zero; so the gross up is not necessary whenever the ratio is really important.

International Accounting Differences Create Headaches for Investors

You must be a good financial detective to analyze financial statements, especially if the company operates overseas. Despite attempts to standardize accounting practices, there are many differences in the way financial information is reported in different countries, and these differences create headaches for investors trying to make cross-border company comparisons.

A study by two Rider College accounting professors demonstrated that huge differences can exist. The professors developed a computer model to evaluate the net income of a hypothetical but typical company operating in different countries. Applying the standard accounting practices of each country, the hypothetical company would have reported net income of $34,600 in the United States, $260,600 in the United Kingdom, and $240,600 in Australia.

Such variances occur for a number of reasons. In most countries, including the United States, an asset's balance sheet value is reported at original cost less any accumulated depreciation. However, in some countries, asset values are adjusted to reflect current market prices. Also, inventory valuation methods vary from country to country, as does the treatment of goodwill. Other differences arise from the treatment of leases, research and development costs, and pension plans.

These differences arise from a variety of legal, historical, cultural, and economic factors. For example, in Germany and Japan large banks are the key source of both debt and equity capital, whereas in the United States public capital markets are most important. As a result, U.S. corporations disclose a great deal of information to the public, while German and Japanese corporations use very conservative accounting practices that appeal to the banks.

There are two basic trends regarding international accounting standards. The first is a movement toward a single set of accounting standards. For example, the European Union now requires all EU-listed companies to comply with standards defined by the International Accounting Standards Board (IASB). There are also ongoing discussions between the IASB and the U.S. Financial Accounting Standards Board (FASB) to develop a single set of financial standards for all companies worldwide. Second, IASB standards rely on general principles, while FASB standards are rules based. As the recent accounting scandals demonstrate, many U.S. companies have been able to comply with U.S. rules while violating the principle, or intent, underlying the rules. This is fueling a debate over the relative effectiveness of principles-based versus rules-based standards.

Sources: See the Web sites of the IASB and the FASB: **http://www.iasb.org.uk** and **http://www.fasb.org**.

---

a total of $136 million.[7] Therefore, MicroDrive covered its fixed financial charges by 3.0 times. However, if EBITDA declines, the coverage will fall, and EBITDA certainly can decline. Moreover, MicroDrive's ratio is well below the industry average, so again, the company seems to have a relatively high level of debt.

The EBITDA coverage ratio is most useful for relatively short-term lenders such as banks, which rarely make loans (except real estate–backed loans) for longer than about 5 years. Over a relatively short period, depreciation-generated funds can be used to service debt. Over a longer time, those funds must be reinvested to maintain the plant and equipment or else the company cannot remain in business. Therefore, banks and other relatively short-term lenders focus on the EBITDA coverage ratio, whereas long-term bondholders focus on the TIE ratio.

SELF-TEST

How does the use of financial leverage affect current stockholders' control position?

In what way do taxes influence a firm's willingness to finance with debt?

In what way does the use of debt involve a risk-versus-return trade-off?

Explain the following statement: "Analysts look at both balance sheet and income statement ratios when appraising a firm's financial condition."

Name three ratios that are used to measure the extent to which a firm uses financial leverage, and write out their equations.

A company has EBITDA of $600 million, interest payments of $60 million, lease payments of $40 million, and required principal payments (due this year) of $30 million. What is its EBITDA coverage ratio? (4.9)

---

[7] A sinking fund is a required annual payment designed to reduce the balance of a bond or preferred stock issue.

4.5 Profitability Ratios

Profitability is the net result of a number of policies and decisions. The ratios examined thus far provide useful clues as to the effectiveness of a firm's operations, but the **profitability ratios** go on to show the combined effects of liquidity, asset management, and debt on operating results.

Profit Margin on Sales

The **profit margin on sales,** calculated by dividing net income by sales, gives the profit per dollar of sales:

$$\text{Profit margin on sales} = \frac{\text{Net income available to common stockholders}}{\text{Sales}}$$

$$= \frac{\$113.5}{\$3,000} = 3.8\%.$$

$$\text{Industry average} = 5.0\%.$$

MicroDrive's profit margin is below the industry average of 5%. This sub-par result occurs because costs are too high. High costs, in turn, generally occur because of inefficient operations. However, MicroDrive's low profit margin is also a result of its heavy use of debt. Recall that net income is income *after interest*. Therefore, if you consider two firms that have identical operations in the sense that their sales, operating costs, and EBIT are the same, then the firm that uses more debt will have higher interest charges. Those interest charges will pull net income down, and since sales are constant, the result will be a relatively low profit margin. In such a case, the low profit margin would not indicate an operating problem—rather, it would indicate a difference in financing strategies. Thus, the firm with the low profit margin might end up with a higher rate of return on its stockholders' investment due to its use of financial leverage. We will see exactly how profit margins and the use of debt interact to affect the return on stockholders' equity later in the chapter, when we examine the Du Pont model.

Basic Earning Power (BEP)

The **basic earning power (BEP) ratio** is calculated by dividing earnings before interest and taxes (EBIT) by total assets:

$$\text{Basic earning power (BEP) ratio} = \frac{\text{EBIT}}{\text{Total assets}}$$

$$= \frac{\$283.8}{\$2,000} = 14.2\,\%.$$

$$\text{Industry average} = 18.0\%.$$

This ratio shows the raw earning power of the firm's assets, before the influence of taxes and leverage, and it is useful for comparing firms with different tax situations and different degrees of financial leverage. Because of its low turnover ratios and low profit margin on sales, MicroDrive is not getting as high a return on its assets as is the average company in its industry.[8]

Return on Total Assets

The ratio of net income to total assets measures the **return on total assets (ROA)** after interest and taxes:

$$\text{Return on total assets} = \text{ROA} = \frac{\text{Net income available to common stockholders}}{\text{Total assets}}$$

$$= \frac{\$113.5}{\$2,000} = 5.7\%.$$

Industry average = 9.0%.

MicroDrive's 5.7% return is well below the 9% average for the industry. This low return results from (1) the company's low basic earning power plus (2) high interest costs resulting from its above-average use of debt, both of which cause its net income to be relatively low.

Return on Common Equity

Ultimately, the most important, or "bottom line," accounting ratio is the ratio of net income to common equity, which measures the **return on common equity (ROE):**

$$\text{Return on common equity} = \text{ROE} = \frac{\text{Net income available to common stockholders}}{\text{Common equity}}$$

$$= \frac{\$113.5}{\$896} = 12.7\%.$$

Industry average = 15.0%.

Stockholders invest to get a return on their money, and this ratio tells how well they are doing in an accounting sense. MicroDrive's 12.7% return is below the 15% industry average, but not as far below as the return on total assets. This somewhat better result is due to the company's greater use of debt, a point that is analyzed in detail later in the chapter.

SELF-TEST

Identify and write out the equations for four ratios that show the combined effects of liquidity, asset management, and debt management on profitability.
Why is the basic earning power ratio useful?
Why does the use of debt lower the ROA?
What does ROE measure? Since interest expense lowers profits, does using debt lower ROE?
A company has $200 billion of sales and $10 billion of net income. Its total assets are $100 billion, financed half by debt and half by common equity. What is its profit margin? (5%) What is its ROA? (10%) What is its ROE? (20%) Would ROA increase if the firm used less leverage? (yes) Would ROE increase? (no)

---

[8]Notice that EBIT is earned throughout the year, whereas the total assets figure is an end-of-the-year number. Therefore, it would be conceptually better to calculate this ratio as EBIT/Average assets = EBIT/[(Beginning assets + Ending assets)/2]. We have not made this adjustment because the published ratios used for comparative purposes do not include it. However, when we construct our own comparative ratios, we do make the adjustment. Incidentally, the same adjustment would also be appropriate for the next two ratios, ROA and ROE.

4.6 Market Value Ratios

A final group of ratios, the **market value ratios,** relates the firm's stock price to its earnings, cash flow, and book value per share. These ratios give management an indication of what investors think of the company's past performance and future prospects. If the liquidity, asset management, debt management, and profitability ratios all look good, then the market value ratios will be high, and the stock price will probably be as high as can be expected.

Price/Earnings Ratio

The **price/earnings (P/E) ratio** shows how much investors are willing to pay per dollar of reported profits. MicroDrive's stock sells for $23, so with an EPS of $2.27 its P/E ratio is 10.1:

$$\text{Price/earnings (P/E) ratio} = \frac{\text{Price per share}}{\text{Earnings per share}}$$

$$= \frac{\$23.00}{\$2.27} = 10.1 \text{ times.}$$

$$\text{Industry average} = 12.5 \text{ times.}$$

P/E ratios are higher for firms with strong growth prospects, other things held constant, but they are lower for riskier firms. Because MicroDrive's P/E ratio is below the average, this suggests that the company is regarded as being somewhat riskier than most, as having poorer growth prospects, or both. In the spring of 2006, the average P/E ratio for firms in the S&P 500 was 21.52, indicating that investors were willing to pay $21.52 for every dollar of earnings.

Price/Cash Flow Ratio

In some industries, stock price is tied more closely to cash flow than to net income. Consequently, investors often look at the **price/cash flow ratio,** where cash flow is defined as net income plus depreciation and amortization:

$$\text{Price/cash flow ratio} = \frac{\text{Price per share}}{\text{Cash flow per share}}$$

$$= \frac{\$23.00}{\$4.27} = 5.4 \text{ times.}$$

$$\text{Industry average} = 6.8 \text{ times.}$$

MicroDrive's price/cash flow ratio is also below the industry average, once again suggesting that its growth prospects are below average, its risk is above average, or both.

Note that some analysts look at multiples beyond just the price/earnings and the price/cash flow ratios. For example, depending on the industry, some may look at measures such as price/sales, price/customers, or price/EBITDA per share. Ultimately, though, value depends on free cash flows, so if these "exotic" ratios do not forecast future free cash flow, they may turn out to be misleading.

This was true in the case of the dot-com retailers before they crashed and burned in 2000, costing investors many billions.

Market/Book Ratio

The ratio of a stock's market price to its book value gives another indication of how investors regard the company. Companies with relatively high rates of return on equity generally sell at higher multiples of book value than those with low returns. First, we find MicroDrive's book value per share:

$$\text{Book value per share} = \frac{\text{Common equity}}{\text{Shares outstanding}}$$

$$= \frac{\$896}{50} = \$17.92.$$

Now we divide the market price by the book value to get a **market/book (M/B) ratio** of 1.3 times:

$$\text{Market/book ratio} = \text{M/B} = \frac{\text{Market price per share}}{\text{Book value per share}}$$

$$= \frac{\$23.00}{\$17.92} = 1.3 \text{ times.}$$

$$\text{Industry average} = 1.7 \text{ times.}$$

Investors are willing to pay relatively little for a dollar of MicroDrive's book value.

The average company in the S&P 500 had a market/book ratio of about 4.03 in the spring of 2006. Since M/B ratios typically exceed 1.0, this means that investors are willing to pay more for stocks than their accounting book values. The book value is a record of the past, showing the cumulative amount that stockholders have invested, either directly by purchasing newly issued shares or indirectly through retaining earnings. In contrast, the market price is forward-looking, incorporating investors' expectations of future cash flows. For example, in May 2006 Alaska Air had a market/book ratio of only 1.69, reflecting the crisis in the airlines industry caused by the terrorist attacks and oil price increases, whereas Dell Computer's market/book ratio was 14.79, indicating that investors expected Dell's past successes to continue.

Table 4-2 summarizes MicroDrive's financial ratios. As the table indicates, the company has many problems.

SELF-TEST

Describe three ratios that relate a firm's stock price to its earnings, cash flow, and book value per share, and write out their equations.

How do market value ratios reflect what investors think about a stock's risk and expected rate of return?

What does the price/earnings (P/E) ratio show? If one firm's P/E ratio is lower than that of another, what are some factors that might explain the difference?

How is book value per share calculated? Explain why book values often deviate from market values.

A company has $6 billion of net income, $2 billion of depreciation and amortization, $80 billion of common equity, and 1 billion shares of stock. If its stock price is $96 per share, what is its price/earnings ratio? (16) Its price/cash flow ratio? (12) Its market/book ratio? (1.2)

Table 4-2

MicroDrive Inc.: Summary of Financial Ratios (Millions of Dollars)

Ratio	Formula	Calculation	Ratio	Industry Average	Comment
Liquidity					
Current	$\dfrac{\text{Current assets}}{\text{Current liabilities}}$	$\dfrac{\$1,000}{\$310}$	=3.2×	4.2×	Poor
Quick	$\dfrac{\text{Current assets} - \text{Inventories}}{\text{Current liabilities}}$	$\dfrac{\$385}{\$310}$	=1.2×	2.1×	Poor
Asset management					
Inventory turnover	$\dfrac{\text{Sales}}{\text{Inventories}}$	$\dfrac{\$3,000}{\$615}$	=4.9×	9.0×	Poor
Days sales outstanding (DSO)	$\dfrac{\text{Receivables}}{\text{Annual sales}/365}$	$\dfrac{\$375}{\$8.219}$	=46 days	36 days	Poor
Fixed assets turnover	$\dfrac{\text{Sales}}{\text{Net fixed assets}}$	$\dfrac{\$3,000}{\$1,000}$	=3.0×	3.0×	OK
Total assets turnover	$\dfrac{\text{Sales}}{\text{Total assets}}$	$\dfrac{\$3,000}{\$2,000}$	=1.5×	1.8×	Somewhat low
Debt Management					
Total debt to total assets	$\dfrac{\text{Total liabilities}}{\text{Total assets}}$	$\dfrac{\$1,064}{\$2,000}$	=53.2%	40.0%	High (risky)
Times-interest-earned (TIE)	$\dfrac{\text{Earnings before interest and taxes (EBIT)}}{\text{Interest charges}}$	$\dfrac{\$283.8}{\$88}$	=3.2×	6.0×	Low (risky)
EBITDA coverage	$\dfrac{\text{EBITDA} + \text{Lease payments}}{\text{Interest} + \text{Principal payments} + \text{Lease payments}}$	$\dfrac{\$411.8}{\$136}$	=3.0×	4.3×	Low (risky)
Profitability					
Profit margin on sales	$\dfrac{\text{Net income available to common stockholders}}{\text{Sales}}$	$\dfrac{\$113.5}{\$3,000}$	=3.8%	5.0%	Poor
Basic earning power (BEP)	$\dfrac{\text{Earnings before interest and taxes (EBIT)}}{\text{Total assets}}$	$\dfrac{\$283.8}{\$2,000}$	=14.2%	17.2%	Poor
Return on total assets (ROA)	$\dfrac{\text{Net income available to common stockholders}}{\text{Total assets}}$	$\dfrac{\$113.5}{\$2,000}$	=5.7%	9.0%	Poor
Return on common equity (ROE)	$\dfrac{\text{Net income available to common stockholders}}{\text{Common equity}}$	$\dfrac{\$113.5}{\$896}$	=12.7%	15.0%	Poor
Market Value					
Price/earnings (P/E)	$\dfrac{\text{Price per share}}{\text{Earnings per share}}$	$\dfrac{\$23.00}{\$2.27}$	=10.1×	12.5×	Low
Price/cash flow	$\dfrac{\text{Price per share}}{\text{Cash flow per share}}$	$\dfrac{\$23.00}{\$4.27}$	=5.4×	6.8×	Low
Market/book (M/B)	$\dfrac{\text{Market price per share}}{\text{Book value per share}}$	$\dfrac{\$23.00}{\$17.92}$	=1.3×	1.7×	Low

4.7 Trend Analysis, Common Size Analysis, and Percent Change Analysis

It is important to analyze trends in ratios as well as their absolute levels, for trends give clues as to whether a firm's financial condition is likely to improve or to deteriorate. To do a **trend analysis,** one simply plots a ratio over time, as shown in Figure 4-1. This graph shows that MicroDrive's rate of return on common equity has been declining since 2004, even though the industry average has been relatively stable. All the other ratios could be analyzed similarly.

Common size analysis and **percent change analysis** are two other techniques that can be used to identify trends in financial statements. Common size analysis is also useful in comparative analysis, and some sources of industry data, such as Risk Management Associates, are presented exclusively in common size form.[9]

In a common size analysis, all income statement items are divided by sales, and all balance sheet items are divided by total assets. Thus, a common size income statement shows each item as a percentage of sales, and a common size balance sheet shows each item as a percentage of total assets. The advantage of common size analysis is that it facilitates comparisons of balance sheets and income statements over time and across companies.

Common size statements are very easy to generate if the financial statements are in a spreadsheet. In fact, if you obtain your financial statements from a source with standardized financial statements, then it is easy to cut and paste the data for a new company over your original company's data, and all of your spreadsheet

Figure 4-1

Rate of Return on Common Equity, 2003–2007

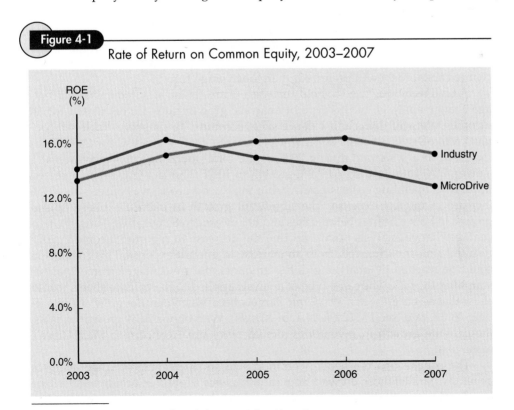

[9]Risk Management Associates was formerly known as Robert Morris Associates.

Table 4-3

MicroDrive Inc.: Common Size Income Statement

	A	B	C	D	E	F	G
165				**2007**			
166				**Industry Composite**	**2007**	**2006**	
167	Net sales			100.0%	100.0%	100.0%	
168	Operating costs			87.6%	87.2%	87.6%	
169	Earnings before interest, taxes, depr. & amort. (EBITDA)			2.8%	12.8%	12.4%	
170	Depreciation and amortization			90.4%	3.3%	3.2%	
171	Earnings before interest and taxes (EBIT)			9.6%	9.5%	9.2%	
172	Less interest			1.3%	2.9%	2.1%	
173	Earnings before taxes (EBT)			8.3%	6.5%	7.1%	
174	Taxes (40%)			3.3%	2.6%	2.8%	
175	Net Income before preferred dividends			5.0%	3.9%	4.3%	
176	Preferred dividends			0.0%	0.1%	0.1%	
177	Net Income available to common stockholders (profit margin)			5.0%	3.8%	4.1%	
178							

Note: Percentages may not total exactly due to rounding when printed.

e-resource

See **FM12 Ch 04 Tool Kit.xls** for all details.

formulas will be valid for the new company. We generated Table 4-3 in the *Excel* file **FM12 Ch 04 Tool Kit.xls**. This table contains MicroDrive's 2006 and 2007 common size income statements, along with the composite statement for the industry. (Note: Rounding may cause addition/subtraction differences in Tables 4-3 and 4-4.) MicroDrive's operating costs are slightly above average, as are its interest expenses, but its taxes are relatively low because of its low EBIT. The net effect of all these forces is a relatively low profit margin.

Table 4-4 shows MicroDrive's common size balance sheets, along with the industry average. Its accounts receivable are significantly higher than the industry average, its inventories are significantly higher, and it uses far more fixed charge capital (debt and preferred) than the average firm.

A final technique used to help analyze a firm's financial statements is percentage change analysis. In this type of analysis, growth rates are calculated for all income statement items and balance sheet accounts. To illustrate, Table 4-5 contains MicroDrive's income statement percentage change analysis for 2007. Sales increased at a 5.3% rate during 2007, while total operating costs increased at a slower 4.8% rate, leading to 7.9% growth in EBIT. The fact that sales increased faster than operating costs is positive, but this "good news" was offset by a 46.7% increase in interest expense. The significant growth in interest expense caused growth in both earnings before taxes and net income to be negative. Thus, the percentage change analysis points out that the decrease in reported income in 2007 resulted almost exclusively from an increase in interest expense. This conclusion could be reached by analyzing dollar amounts, but percentage change analysis simplifies the task. The same type of analysis applied to the balance sheets would show that assets grew at a 19.0% rate, largely because inventories grew at a whopping 48.2% rate (see **FM12 Ch 04 Tool Kit.xls**). With only a 5.3% growth in sales, the extreme growth in inventories should be of great concern to MicroDrive's managers.

The conclusions reached in common size and percentage change analyses generally parallel those derived from ratio analysis. However, occasionally a serious deficiency is highlighted by only one of the three analytical techniques. Also, it is often useful to have all three and to drive home to management, in slightly

e-resource

See **FM12 Ch 04 Tool Kit.xls** for all details.

Table 4-4

MicroDrive Inc.: Common Size Balance Sheet

	A	B	C	D	E	F
187			**2007**			
188			**Industry Composite**	**2007**	**2006**	
189	*Assets*					
190	Cash and equivalents		1.0%	0.5%	0.9%	
191	Short-term investments		2.2%	0.0%	3.9%	
192	Accounts receivable		17.8%	18.8%	18.8%	
193	Inventories		<u>19.8%</u>	<u>30.8%</u>	<u>24.7%</u>	
194	Total current assets		40.8%	50.0%	48.2%	
195	Net plant and equipment		<u>59.2%</u>	<u>50.0%</u>	<u>51.8%</u>	
196	Total assets		<u>100.0%</u>	<u>100.0%</u>	<u>100.0%</u>	
197						
198	*Liabilities and equity*					
199	Accounts payable		1.8%	3.0%	1.8%	
200	Notes payable		4.4%	5.5%	3.6%	
201	Accruals		<u>3.6%</u>	<u>7.0%</u>	<u>7.7%</u>	
202	Total current liabilities		9.8%	15.5%	13.1%	
203	Long-term bonds		<u>30.2%</u>	<u>37.7%</u>	<u>34.5%</u>	
204	Total liabilities		40.0%	53.2%	47.6%	
205	Preferred stock		0.0%	2.0%	2.4%	
206	Total common equity		<u>60.0%</u>	<u>44.8%</u>	<u>50.0%</u>	
207	Total liabilities and equity		<u>100.0%</u>	<u>100.0%</u>	<u>100.0%</u>	
208						

Note: Percentages may not total exactly due to rounding when printed.

Table 4-5

MicroDrive Inc.: Income Statement Percentage Change Analysis

	A	B	C	D	E
218	Base year =	2006		**Percent Change in**	
219				**2007**	
220	Net sales			5.3%	
221	Operating costs			<u>4.8%</u>	
222	Earnings before interest, taxes, depr. & amort. (EBITDA)			8.7%	
223	Depreciation and amortization			<u>11.1%</u>	
224	Earnings before interest and taxes (EBIT)			7.9%	
225	Less interest			<u>46.7%</u>	
226	Earnings before taxes (EBT)			(3.5%)	
227	Taxes (40%)			<u>(3.5%)</u>	
228	Net Income before preferred dividends			(3.5%)	
229	Preferred dividends			<u>0.0%</u>	
230	Net Income available to common stockholders			<u>(3.7%)</u>	
231					

Note: Percentages may not total exactly due to rounding when printed.

different ways, the need to take corrective actions. Thus, a thorough financial statement analysis will include ratio, percentage change, and common size analyses, as well as a Du Pont analysis, as described next.

4.8 Tying the Ratios Together: The Du Pont Equation

In ratio analysis, it is sometimes easy to miss the forest for all the trees. Managers often need a framework that ties together a firm's profitability, its asset usage efficiency, and its use of debt. This section provides just such a model. The profit margin times the total assets turnover is called the **Du Pont equation,** and it gives the rate of return on assets (ROA):

$$ROA = \text{Profit margin} \times \text{Total assets turnover}$$
$$= \frac{\text{Net income}}{\text{Sales}} \times \frac{\text{Sales}}{\text{Total assets}}. \tag{4-1}$$

For MicroDrive, the ROA is

$$ROA = 3.8\% \times 1.5 = 5.7\%.$$

MicroDrive made 3.8%, or 3.8 cents, on each dollar of sales, and its assets were turned over 1.5 times during the year. Therefore, the company earned a return of 5.7% on its assets.

To find the return on equity (ROE), multiply the rate of return on assets (ROA) by the *equity multiplier,* which is the ratio of assets to common equity:

$$\text{Equity multiplier} = \frac{\text{Total assets}}{\text{Common equity}}. \tag{4-2}$$

Firms that have a lot of leverage (i.e., a lot of liabilities or preferred stock) will necessarily have a high equity multiplier—the more leverage, the less the equity, hence the higher the equity multiplier. For example, if a firm has $1,000 of assets and is financed with $800 (or 80%) liabilities and preferred stock, then its equity will be $200, and its equity multiplier will be $1,000/$200 = 5. Had it used only $200 of liabilities and preferred stock, then its equity would have been $800, and its equity multiplier would have been only $1,000/$800 = 1.25.[10]

Therefore, the return on equity (ROE) depends on the ROA and the use of leverage:

---

[10]Expressed algebraically,

$$\text{Debt ratio} = \frac{D}{A} = \frac{A - E}{A} = \frac{A}{A} - \frac{E}{A} = 1 - \frac{1}{\text{Equity multiplier}}.$$

Here we use D to denote all debt, other liabilities, and preferred stock; in other words, D is all financing other than common equity, E is common equity, A is total assets, and A/E is the equity multiplier.

$$ROE = ROA \times \text{Equity multiplier}$$

$$= \frac{\text{Net income}}{\text{Total assets}} \times \frac{\text{Total assets}}{\text{Common equity}}. \qquad \text{(4-3)}$$

MicroDrive's ROE is

$$ROE = 5.7\% \times \frac{\$2,000}{\$896}$$

$$= 5.7\% \times 2.23$$

$$= 12.7\%$$

Now we can combine Equations 4-1 and 4-3 to form the *extended Du Pont equation*, which shows how the profit margin, the assets turnover ratio, and the equity multiplier combine to determine the ROE:

$$ROE = (\text{Profit margin})(\text{Total assets turnover})(\text{Equity multiplier})$$

$$= \frac{\text{Net income}}{\text{Sales}} \times \frac{\text{Sales}}{\text{Total assets}} \times \frac{\text{Total assets}}{\text{Common equity}}. \qquad \text{(4-4)}$$

For MicroDrive, we have

$$ROE = (3.8\%)(1.5)(2.23)$$

$$= 12.7\%.$$

The 12.7% rate of return could, of course, be calculated directly: both Sales and Total assets cancel, leaving Net income/Common equity = $113.5/$896 = 12.7%. However, the Du Pont equation shows how the profit margin, the total assets turnover, and the use of debt interact to determine the return on equity.

The insights provided by the Du Pont model are valuable, and it can be used for "quick and dirty" estimates of the impact that operating changes have on returns. For example, holding all else equal, if MicroDrive can drive up its ratio of sales/total assets to 1.8, then its ROE will improve to (3.8%)(1.8)(2.23) = 15.25%. For a more complete "what if" analysis, most companies use a forecasting model such as the one described in Chapter 14.

SELF-TEST Explain how the extended, or modified, Du Pont equation can be used to reveal the basic determinants of ROE.

What is the equity multiplier?

A company has a profit margin of 6%, a total asset turnover ratio of 2, and an equity multiplier of 1.5. What is its ROE? (18%)

4.9 Comparative Ratios and Benchmarking

Ratio analysis involves comparisons—a company's ratios are compared with those of other firms in the same industry, that is, with industry average figures. However, like most firms, MicroDrive's managers go one step further—they also compare their ratios with those of a smaller set of the leading computer companies. This technique is called **benchmarking,** and the companies used for the comparison are called **benchmark companies.** For example, MicroDrive benchmarks against five other firms that its management considers to be the best-managed companies with operations similar to its own.

Table 4-6

Comparative Ratios for Dell Computer Corporation, the Computer Hardware Industry, the Technology Sector, and the S&P 500

Ratio	Dell	Computer Hardware Industry[a]	Technology Sector[b]	S&P 500
P/E ratio	17.96	27.13	32.75	21.52
Market to book	14.79	9.13	5.60	4.03
Price to tangible book	14.79	9.71	7.47	7.02
Price to cash flow	16.18	28.39	26.57	15.76
Net profit margin	6.39	6.26	14.82	14.02
Quick ratio	0.91	1.48	2.73	1.29
Current ratio	1.11	1.85	3.22	1.80
Long-term debt to equity	0.12	0.08	0.21	0.55
Total debt to equity	0.12	0.09	0.24	0.69
Interest coverage (TIE)[c]	—	5.87	12.99	14.21
Return on assets	15.60	11.82	11.05	7.96
Return on equity	67.22	35.60	18.60	19.32
Inventory turnover	86.06	61.88	12.77	12.54
Asset turnover	2.44	1.86	0.84	0.96

[a]The computer hardware industry is composed of 50 firms, including IBM, Dell, Apple, Sun Microsystems, Gateway, and Silicon Graphics.
[b]The technology sector contains 11 industries, including communications equipment, computer hardware, computer networks, semiconductors, and software and programming.
[c]Dell had more interest income than interest expense.
Source: Adapted from **http://www.investor.reuters.com**, May 2, 2006.

Many companies also benchmark various parts of their overall operation against top companies, whether they are in the same industry or not. For example, MicroDrive has a division that sells hard drives directly to consumers through catalogs and the Internet. This division's shipping department benchmarks against L.L. Bean, even though they are in different industries, because L.L. Bean's shipping department is one of the best. MicroDrive wants its own shippers to strive to match L.L. Bean's record for on-time shipments.

Comparative ratios are available from a number of sources, including *Value Line*, Dun and Bradstreet (D&B), and the *Annual Statement Studies* published by Risk Management Associates, which is the national association of bank loan officers. Table 4-6 reports selected ratios from Reuters.

Each data-supplying organization uses a somewhat different set of ratios designed for its own purposes. For example, D&B deals mainly with small firms, many of which are proprietorships, and it sells its services primarily to banks and other lenders. Therefore, D&B is concerned largely with the creditor's viewpoint, and its ratios emphasize current assets and liabilities, not market value ratios. So, when you select a comparative data source, you should be sure that your emphasis is similar to that of the agency whose ratios you plan to use. Additionally, there are often definitional differences in the ratios presented by different sources, so before using a source, be sure to verify the exact definitions of the ratios to ensure consistency with your own work.

Ratio Analysis on the Web

A great source for comparative ratios is **http://www .investor.reuters.com**. You have to register to use the site, but registration is free. Once you register and log in, this web page contains a field to enter a company's ticker symbol. Once you do this, click the "Symbol" ratio button, and then click the "Go" but-

ton. This brings up a table with the stock quote, some company information, and some additional links. Select "Ratios," which brings up a page with a detailed ratio analysis for the company and includes comparative ratios for other companies in the same sector, the same industry, and the S&P 500.

SELF-TEST

Differentiate between trend analysis and comparative ratio analysis.
Why is it useful to do a comparative ratio analysis?
What is benchmarking?

4.10 Uses and Limitations of Ratio Analysis

To find quick information about a company, go to **http://www.investor .reuters.com**. Here you can find company profiles, stock price and share information, and several key ratios.

Ratio analysis is used by three main groups: (1) *managers*, who employ ratios to help analyze, control, and thus improve their firms' operations; (2) *credit analysts*, including bank loan officers and bond rating analysts, who analyze ratios to help ascertain a company's ability to pay its debts; and (3) *stock analysts*, who are interested in a company's efficiency, risk, and growth prospects. In later chapters we will look more closely at the basic factors that underlie each ratio, which will give you a better idea about how to interpret and use ratios. Note, though, that while ratio analysis can provide useful information concerning a company's operations and financial condition, it does have limitations that necessitate care and judgment. Some potential problems are listed below:

1. Many large firms operate different divisions in different industries, and for such companies it is difficult to develop a meaningful set of industry averages. Therefore, ratio analysis is more useful for small, narrowly focused firms than for large, multidivisional ones.
2. Most firms want to be better than average, so merely attaining average performance is not necessarily good. As a target for high-level performance, it is best to focus on the industry leaders' ratios. Benchmarking helps in this regard.
3. Inflation may have badly distorted firms' balance sheets—recorded values are often substantially different from "true" values. Further, because inflation affects both depreciation charges and inventory costs, profits are also affected. Thus, a ratio analysis for one firm over time, or a comparative analysis of firms of different ages, must be interpreted with judgment.
4. Seasonal factors can also distort a ratio analysis. For example, the inventory turnover ratio for a food processor will be radically different if the balance sheet figure used for inventory is the one just before versus just after the close of the canning season. This problem can be minimized by using monthly averages for inventory (and receivables) when calculating turnover ratios.
5. Firms can employ **"window dressing" techniques** to make their financial statements look stronger. To illustrate, a Chicago builder borrowed on a two-year basis in late December. Because the loan was for more than 1 year, it was not included in current liabilities. The builder held the proceeds of the loan as cash. This improved his current and quick ratios, and made his year-end balance sheet look stronger. However, the improvement was strictly window dressing; a week later the builder paid off the loan and the balance sheet was back at the old level.

6. Different accounting practices can distort comparisons. As noted earlier, inventory valuation and depreciation methods can affect financial statements and thus distort comparisons among firms. Also, if one firm leases a substantial amount of its productive equipment, then its assets may appear low relative to sales because leased assets often do not appear on the balance sheet. At the same time, the liability associated with the lease obligation may not be shown as debt. Therefore, leasing can artificially improve both the turnover and the debt ratios.

7. It is difficult to generalize about whether a particular ratio is "good" or "bad." For example, a high current ratio may indicate a strong liquidity position, which is good, or excessive cash, which is bad (because excess cash in the bank is a nonearning asset). Similarly, a high fixed assets turnover ratio may denote either that a firm uses its assets efficiently or that it is undercapitalized and cannot afford to buy enough assets.

8. A firm may have some ratios that look "good" and others that look "bad," making it difficult to tell whether the company overall is strong or weak. However, statistical procedures can be used to analyze the *net effects* of a set of ratios. Many banks and other lending organizations use discriminant analysis, a statistical technique, to analyze firms' financial ratios, and then classify the firms according to their probability of getting into financial trouble.

9. Effective use of financial ratios requires that the financial statements on which they are based be accurate. Revelations in 2001 and 2002 of accounting fraud by such industry giants as WorldCom and Enron showed that financial statements are not always accurate; hence information based on reported data can be misleading.

Ratio analysis is useful, but analysts should be aware of these problems and make adjustments as necessary. Ratio analysis conducted in a mechanical, unthinking manner is dangerous, but used intelligently and with good judgment, it can provide useful insights into a firm's operations. Your judgment in interpreting a set of ratios is bound to be weak at this point, but it will improve as you go through the remainder of the book.

SELF-TEST

List three types of users of ratio analysis. Would the different users emphasize the same or different types of ratios?

List several potential problems with ratio analysis.

4.11 Looking Beyond the Numbers

Hopefully, working through this chapter has helped your understanding of financial statements and improved your ability to interpret accounting numbers. These important and basic skills are necessary when making business decisions, evaluating performance, and forecasting likely future developments.

Sound financial analysis involves more than just calculating numbers—good analysis requires that certain qualitative factors be considered when evaluating a company. These factors, as summarized by the American Association of Individual Investors (AAII), include the following:

1. **Are the company's revenues tied to one key customer?** If so, the company's performance may decline dramatically if the customer goes elsewhere.

2. **To what extent are the company's revenues tied to one key product?** Companies that rely on a single product may be more efficient and focused, but a lack of diversification increases risk.

3. **To what extent does the company rely on a single supplier?** Depending on a single supplier may lead to unanticipated shortages and thus to lower profits.

4. **What percentage of the company's business is generated overseas?** Companies with a large percentage of overseas business are often able to realize higher growth and larger profit margins. However, firms with large overseas operations also find that the value of their operations depends in large part on the value of the local currency. Thus, fluctuations in currency markets create additional risks for firms with large overseas operations. In addition, the political stability of the region is important.

5. **What about the competition?** It is important to consider both the likely actions of the current competition and the likelihood of new competitors in the future.

6. **What are the company's future prospects?** Does the company invest heavily in research and development? If so, its future prospects may depend critically on the success of products currently in the pipeline.

7. **How does the legal and regulatory environment affect the company?** It is crucial to factor in the effects of proposed regulations and pending or likely lawsuits.

SELF-TEST   What are some qualitative factors analysts should consider when evaluating a company's likely future financial performance?

Summary

The primary purpose of this chapter was to discuss techniques used by investors and managers to analyze financial statements. The key concepts covered are listed below.

- **Financial statement analysis** generally begins with a set of **financial ratios** designed to reveal a company's strengths and weaknesses as compared with other companies in the same industry, and to show whether its financial position has been improving or deteriorating over time.

- **Liquidity ratios** show the relationship of a firm's current assets to its current liabilities, and thus its ability to meet maturing debts. Two commonly used liquidity ratios are the **current ratio** and the **quick,** or **acid test, ratio.**

- **Asset management ratios** measure how effectively a firm is managing its assets. These ratios include **inventory turnover, days sales outstanding, fixed assets turnover,** and **total assets turnover.**

- **Debt management ratios** reveal (1) the extent to which the firm is financed with debt and (2) its likelihood of defaulting on its debt obligations. They include the **debt ratio, times-interest-earned ratio,** and **EBITDA coverage ratio.**

- **Profitability ratios** show the combined effects of liquidity, asset management, and debt management policies on operating results. They include the **profit margin on sales,** the **basic earning power ratio,** the **return on total assets,** and the **return on common equity.**

- **Market value ratios** relate the firm's stock price to its earnings, cash flow, and book value per share, thus giving management an indication of what investors think of the company's past performance and future prospects. These include the **price/earnings ratio, price/cash flow ratio,** and the **market/book ratio.**

- **Trend analysis,** where one plots a ratio over time, is important, because it reveals whether the firm's condition has been improving or deteriorating over time.

- The **Du Pont system** is designed to show how the profit margin on sales, the assets turnover ratio, and the use of debt interact to determine the rate of return on equity. The firm's management can use the Du Pont system to analyze ways of improving performance.
- **Benchmarking** is the process of comparing a particular company with a group of similar, successful companies.

Ratio analysis has limitations, but used with care and judgment, it can be very helpful.

Questions

(4-1) Define each of the following terms:
  a. Liquidity ratios: current ratio; quick, or acid test, ratio
  b. Asset management ratios: inventory turnover ratio; days sales outstanding (DSO); fixed assets turnover ratio; total assets turnover ratio
  c. Financial leverage: debt ratio; times-interest-earned (TIE) ratio; coverage ratio
  d. Profitability ratios: profit margin on sales; basic earning power (BEP) ratio; return on total assets (ROA); return on common equity (ROE)
  e. Market value ratios: price/earnings (P/E) ratio; price/cash flow ratio; market/book (M/B) ratio; book value per share
  f. Trend analysis; comparative ratio analysis; benchmarking
  g. Du Pont equation; window dressing; seasonal effects on ratios

(4-2) Financial ratio analysis is conducted by managers, equity investors, long-term creditors, and short-term creditors. What is the primary emphasis of each of these groups in evaluating ratios?

(4-3) Over the past year, M. D. Ryngaert & Co. has realized an increase in its current ratio and a drop in its total assets turnover ratio. However, the company's sales, quick ratio, and fixed assets turnover ratio have remained constant. What explains these changes?

(4-4) Profit margins and turnover ratios vary from one industry to another. What differences would you expect to find between a grocery chain such as Safeway and a steel company? Think particularly about the turnover ratios, the profit margin, and the Du Pont equation.

(4-5) How might (a) seasonal factors and (b) different growth rates distort a comparative ratio analysis? Give some examples. How might these problems be alleviated?

(4-6) Why is it sometimes misleading to compare a company's financial ratios with those of other firms that operate in the same industry?

Self-Test Problems   Solutions Appear in Appendix A

(ST-1)
Debt Ratio
Argent Corporation had earnings per share of $4 last year, and it paid a $2 dividend. Total retained earnings increased by $12 million during the year, while book value per share at year-end was $40. Argent has no preferred stock, and no new common

stock was issued during the year. If Argent's year-end debt (which equals its total liabilities) was $120 million, what was the company's year-end debt/assets ratio?

(ST-2)
Ratio Analysis

The following data apply to Jacobus and Associates (millions of dollars):

Cash and marketable securities	$100.00
Fixed assets	$283.50
Sales	$1,000.00
Net income	$50.00
Quick ratio	2.0×
Current ratio	3.0×
DSO	40.55 days
ROE	12%

Jacobus has no preferred stock—only common equity, current liabilities, and long-term debt.
a. Find Jacobus's (1) accounts receivable (A/R), (2) current liabilities, (3) current assets, (4) total assets, (5) ROA, (6) common equity, and (7) long-term debt.
b. In part a, you should have found Jacobus's accounts receivable (A/R) = $111.1 million. If Jacobus could reduce its DSO from 40.55 days to 30.4 days while holding other things constant, how much cash would it generate? If this cash were used to buy back common stock (at book value), thus reducing the amount of common equity, how would this affect (1) the ROE, (2) the ROA, and (3) the total debt/total assets ratio?

Easy
Problems 1–5

Problems   Answers Appear in Appendix B

(4-1)
Days Sales Outstanding

Greene Sisters has a DSO of 20 days. The company's average daily sales are $20,000. What is the level of its accounts receivable? Assume there are 365 days in a year.

(4-2)
Debt Ratio

Vigo Vacations has an equity multiplier of 2.5. The company's assets are financed with some combination of long-term debt and common equity. What is the company's debt ratio?

(4-3)
Market/Book Ratio

Winston Washers' stock price is $75 per share. Winston has $10 billion in total assets. Its balance sheet shows $1 billion in current liabilities, $3 billion in long-term debt, and $6 billion in common equity. It has 800 million shares of common stock outstanding. What is Winston's market/book ratio?

(4-4)
Price/Earnings Ratio

A company has an EPS of $1.50, a cash flow per share of $3.00, and a price/cash flow ratio of 8.0 times. What is its P/E ratio?

(4-5)
ROE

Needham Pharmaceuticals has a profit margin of 3% and an equity multiplier of 2.0. Its sales are $100 million and it has total assets of $50 million. What is its ROE?

Intermediate
Problems 6–10

(4-6) ✓
Du Pont Analysis

Donaldson & Son has an ROA of 10%, a 2% profit margin, and a return on equity equal to 15%. What is the company's total assets turnover? What is the firm's equity multiplier?

(4-7)
Current and Quick Ratios

Ace Industries has current assets equal to $3 million. The company's current ratio is 1.5, and its quick ratio is 1.0. What is the firm's level of current liabilities? What is the firm's level of inventories?

(4-8) ✓
Profit Margin and Debt Ratio

Assume you are given the following relationships for the Clayton Corporation:

$$\text{Sales/total assets} \qquad 1.5\times$$
$$\text{Return on assets (ROA)} \quad 3\%$$
$$\text{Return on equity (ROE)} \quad 5\%$$

Calculate Clayton's profit margin and debt ratio.

(4-9)
Current and Quick Ratios

The Nelson Company has $1,312,500 in current assets and $525,000 in current liabilities. Its initial inventory level is $375,000, and it will raise funds as additional notes payable and use them to increase inventory. How much can Nelson's short-term debt (notes payable) increase without pushing its current ratio below 2.0? What will be the firm's quick ratio after Nelson has raised the maximum amount of short-term funds?

(4-10) ✓
Times-Interest-Earned Ratio

The Manor Corporation has $500,000 of debt outstanding, and it pays an interest rate of 10% annually: Manor's annual sales are $2 million, its average tax rate is 30%, and its net profit margin on sales is 5%. If the company does not maintain a TIE ratio of at least 5 times, its bank will refuse to renew the loan, and bankruptcy will result. What is Manor's TIE ratio?

**Challenging
Problems 11–14**

(4-11)
Balance Sheet Analysis

Complete the balance sheet and sales information in the table that follows for Hoffmeister Industries using the following financial data:

Debt ratio: 50%

Quick ratio: 0.80×

Total assets turnover: 1.5×

Days sales outstanding: 36.5 days[a]

Gross profit margin on sales: (Sales − Cost of goods sold)/Sales = 25%

Inventory turnover ratio: 5×

[a]Calculation is based on a 365-day year.

Balance Sheet

Cash		Accounts payable	
Accounts receivable		Long-term debt	60,000
Inventories		Common stock	
Fixed assets		Retained earnings	97,500
Total assets	$300,000	Total liabilities and equity	
Sales		Cost of goods sold	

(4-12)
Comprehensive Ratio Calculations

The Kretovich Company had a quick ratio of 1.4, a current ratio of 3.0, an inventory turnover of 6 times, total current assets of $810,000, and cash and marketable securities of $120,000. What were Kretovich's annual sales and its DSO? Assume a 365-day year.

(4-13) ✓ Data for Morton Chip Company and its industry averages follow.

Comprehensive Ratio Analysis

a. Calculate the indicated ratios for Morton.
b. Construct the extended Du Pont equation for both Morton and the industry.
c. Outline Morton's strengths and weaknesses as revealed by your analysis.
d. Suppose Morton had doubled its sales as well as its inventories, accounts receivable, and common equity during 2007. How would that information affect the validity of your ratio analysis? (Hint: Think about averages and the effects of rapid growth on ratios if averages are not used. No calculations are needed.)

Morton Chip Company: Balance Sheet as of December 31, 2007 (In Thousands)

Cash	$77,500	Accounts payable	$129,000
Receivables	336,000	Notes payable	84,000
Inventories	241,500	Other current liabilities	117,000
Total current assets	$655,000	Total current liabilities	$330,000
Net fixed assets	292,500	Long-term debt	256,500
		Common equity	361,000
Total assets	$947,500	Total liabilities and equity	$947,500

Morton Chip Company: Income Statement for Year Ended December 31, 2007 (In Thousands)

Sales	$1,607,500
Cost of goods sold	1,392,500
Selling, general, and administrative expenses	145,000
Earnings before interest and taxes (EBIT)	$ 70,000
Interest expense	24,500
Earnings before taxes (EBT)	$ 45,500
Federal and state income taxes (40%)	18,200
Net income	$ 27,300

Ratio	Morton	Industry Average
Current assets/current liabilities	_____	2.0×
Days sales outstanding[a]	_____	35.0 days
Sales/inventory	_____	6.7×
Sales/fixed assets	_____	12.1×
Sales/total assets	_____	3.0×
Net income/sales	_____	1.2%
Net income/total assets	_____	3.6%
Net income/common equity	_____	9.0%
Total debt/total assets	_____	60.0%

[a]Calculation is based on a 365-day year.

(4-14)

Comprehensive Ratio Analysis

The Jimenez Corporation's forecasted 2008 financial statements follow, along with some industry average ratios.

a. Calculate Jimenez's 2008 forecasted ratios, compare them with the industry average data, and comment briefly on Jimenez's projected strengths and weaknesses.

b. What do you think would happen to Jimenez's ratios if the company initiated cost-cutting measures that allowed it to hold lower levels of inventory and substantially decreased the cost of goods sold? No calculations are necessary. Think about which ratios would be affected by changes in these two accounts.

Jimenez Corporation: Forecasted Balance Sheet as of December 31, 2008

Cash	$ 72,000
Accounts receivable	439,000
Inventories	894,000
Total current assets	$ 1,405,000
Fixed assets	431,000
Total assets	$ 1,836,000
Accounts and notes payable	$ 432,000
Accruals	170,000
Total current liabilities	$602,000
Long-term debt	404,290
Common stock	575,000
Retained earnings	254,710
Total liabilities and equity	$ 1,836,000

Jimenez Corporation: Forecasted Income Statement for 2008

Sales	$4,290,000
Cost of goods sold	3,580,000
Selling, general, and administrative expenses	370,320
Depreciation	159,000
Earnings before taxes (EBT)	$ 180,680
Taxes (40%)	72,272
Net income	$ 108,408

Per-Share Data

EPS	$4.71
Cash dividends per share	$0.95
P/E ratio	5×
Market price (average)	$23.57
Number of shares outstanding	23,000

Industry Financial Ratios (2007)[a]

Quick ratio	1.0×
Current ratio	2.7×
Inventory turnover[b]	7.0×
Days sales outstanding[c]	32 days
Fixed assets turnover[b]	13.0×
Total assets turnover[b]	2.6×
Return on assets	9.1%
Return on equity	18.2%
Debt ratio	50.0%
Profit margin on sales	3.5%
P/E ratio	6.0×
P/cash flow ratio	3.5×

[a]Industry average ratios have been constant for the past 4 years.
[b]Based on year-end balance sheet figures.
[c]Calculation is based on a 365-day year.

e-resource

Spreadsheet Problem

(4-15)
Build a Model:
Ratio Analysis

Start with the partial model in the file *FM12 Ch 04 P15 Build a Model.xls* from the textbook's Web site. This problem requires you to further analyze the financial data given for Cumberland Industries in the Build a Model problem for Chapter 3.

Cumberland Industries' common stock has increased in price from $14.75 to $17.25 from the end of 2006 to the end of 2007, and its shares outstanding increased from 9 to 10 million shares during that same period. Cumberland has annual lease payments of $75,000 (which are included in operating costs on the income statement), but no sinking fund payments are required. Now answer the following questions.

Using Cumberland's financial statements as given in the Chapter 3 Build a Model problem, perform a ratio analysis for 2006 and 2007. Consider its liquidity, asset management, debt management, profitability, and market value ratios.

a. Has Cumberland's liquidity position improved or worsened? Explain.
b. Has Cumberland's ability to manage its assets improved or worsened? Explain.
c. How has Cumberland's profitability changed during the last year?
d. Perform an extended Du Pont analysis for Cumberland for 2006 and 2007.
e. Perform a common size analysis. What has happened to the composition (that is, percentage in each category) of assets and liabilities?
f. Perform a percent change analysis. What does this tell you about the change in profitability and asset utilization?

e-resource

Cyberproblem

Please go to the textbook's Web site to access any Cyberproblems.

Mini Case

The first part of the case, presented in Chapter 3, discussed the situation that Computron Industries was in after an expansion program. Thus far, sales have not been up to the forecasted level, costs have been higher than were projected, and a large loss occurred in 2007, rather than the expected profit. As a result, its managers, directors, and investors are concerned about the firm's survival.

Donna Jamison was brought in as assistant to Fred Campo, Computron's chairman, who had the task of getting the company back into a sound financial position. Computron's 2006 and 2007 balance sheets and income statements, together with projections for 2008, are shown in the following tables. Also, the tables show the 2006 and 2007 financial ratios, along with industry average data. The 2008 projected financial statement data represent Jamison's and Campo's best guess for 2008 results, assuming that some new financing is arranged to get the company "over the hump."

Balance Sheets	2006	2007	2008E
Assets			
Cash	$ 9,000	$ 7,282	$ 14,000
Short-term investments	48,600	20,000	71,632
Accounts receivable	351,200	632,160	878,000
Inventories	715,200	1,287,360	1,716,480
Total current assets	$1,124,000	$1,946,802	$2,680,112
Gross fixed assets	491,000	1,202,950	1,220,000
Less: Accumulated depreciation	146,200	263,160	383,160
Net fixed assets	$ 344,800	$ 939,790	$ 836,840
Total assets	$1,468,800	$2,886,592	$3,516,952
Liabilities and Equity			
Accounts payable	$ 145,600	$ 324,000	$ 359,800
Notes payable	200,000	720,000	300,000
Accruals	136,000	284,960	380,000
Total current liabilities	$ 481,600	$1,328,960	$1,039,800
Long-term debt	323,432	1,000,000	500,000
Common stock (100,000 shares)	460,000	460,000	1,680,936
Retained earnings	203,768	97,632	296,216
Total equity	$ 663,768	$ 557,632	$1,977,152
Total liabilities and equity	$1,468,800	$2,886,592	$3,516,952

Note: "E" indicates estimated. The 2008 data are forecasts.

Income Statements	2006	2007	2008E
Sales	$3,432,000	$5,834,400	$7,035,600
Cost of goods sold	2,864,000	4,980,000	5,800,000
Other expenses	340,000	720,000	612,960
Depreciation	18,900	116,960	120,000
Total operating costs	$3,222,900	$5,816,960	$6,532,960
EBIT	$ 209,100	$ 17,440	$ 502,640
Interest expense	62,500	176,000	80,000
EBT	$ 146,600	($ 158,560)	$ 422,640
Taxes (40%)	58,640	(63,424)	169,056
Net income	$ 87,960	($ 95,136)	$ 253,584
Other Data			
Stock price	$8.50	$6.00	$12.17
Shares outstanding	100,000	100,000	250,000
EPS	$0.880	($0.951)	$1.014
DPS	$0.220	0.110	0.220
Tax rate	40%	40%	40%
Book value per share	$6.638	$5.576	$7.909
Lease payments	$40,000	$40,000	$40,000

Note: "E" indicates estimated. The 2008 data are forecasts.

Ratio Analysis

	2006	2007	2008E	Industry Average
Current	2.3×	1.5×	—	2.7×
Quick	0.8×	0.5×	—	1.0×
Inventory turnover	4.8×	4.5×	—	6.1×
Days sales outstanding	37.3	39.6	—	32.0
Fixed assets turnover	10.0×	6.2×	—	7.0×
Total assets turnover	2.3×	2.0×	—	2.5×
Debt ratio	54.8%	80.7%	—	50.0%
TIE	3.3×	0.1×	—	6.2×
EBITDA coverage	2.6×	0.8×	—	8.0×
Profit margin	2.6%	21.6%	—	3.6%
Basic earning power	14.2%	0.6%	—	17.8%
ROA	6.0%	23.3%	—	9.0%
ROE	13.3%	217.1%	—	17.9%
Price/earnings (P/E)	9.7×	26.3×	—	16.2×
Price/cash flow	8.0×	27.5×	—	7.6×
Market/book	1.3×	1.1×	—	2.9×

Note: "E" indicates estimated. The 2008 data are forecasts.

Jamison examined monthly data for 2007 (not given in the case), and she detected an improving pattern during the year. Monthly sales were rising, costs were falling, and large losses in the early months had turned to a small profit by

December. Thus, the annual data looked somewhat worse than final monthly data. Also, it appeared to be taking longer for the advertising program to get the message across, for the new sales offices to generate sales, and for the new manufacturing facilities to operate efficiently. In other words, the lags between spending money and deriving benefits were longer than Computron's managers had anticipated. For these reasons, Jamison and Campo see hope for the company—provided it can survive in the short run.

Jamison must prepare an analysis of where the company is now, what it must do to regain its financial health, and what actions should be taken. Your assignment is to help her answer the following questions. Provide clear explanations, not yes or no answers.

a. Why are ratios useful? What are the five major categories of ratios?

b. Calculate the 2008 current and quick ratios based on the projected balance sheet and income statement data. What can you say about the company's liquidity position in 2006, 2007, and as projected for 2008? We often think of ratios as being useful (1) to managers to help run the business, (2) to bankers for credit analysis, and (3) to stockholders for stock valuation. Would these different types of analysts have an equal interest in the liquidity ratios?

c. Calculate the 2008 inventory turnover, days sales outstanding (DSO), fixed assets turnover, and total assets turnover. How does Computron's utilization of assets stack up against that of other firms in its industry?

d. Calculate the 2008 debt, times-interest-earned, and EBITDA coverage ratios. How does Computron compare with the industry with respect to financial leverage? What can you conclude from these ratios?

e. Calculate the 2008 profit margin, basic earning power (BEP), return on assets (ROA), and return on equity (ROE). What can you say about these ratios?

f. Calculate the 2008 price/earnings ratio, price/cash flow ratio, and market/book ratio. Do these ratios indicate that investors are expected to have a high or low opinion of the company?

g. Perform a common size analysis and percent change analysis. What do these analyses tell you about Computron?

h. Use the extended Du Pont equation to provide a summary and overview of Computron's financial condition as projected for 2008. What are the firm's major strengths and weaknesses?

i. What are some potential problems and limitations of financial ratio analysis?

j. What are some qualitative factors analysts should consider when evaluating a company's likely future financial performance?

Selected Additional Cases

The following cases from Textchoice, Cengage Learning's online library, cover many of the concepts discussed in this chapter and are available at *http://www.textchoice2.com.*

Klein-Brigham Series:

Case 35, "Mark X Company (A)," which illustrates the use of ratio analysis in the evaluation of a firm's existing and potential financial positions.

Case 36, "Garden State Container Corporation," which is similar in content to Case 35.

Case 51, "Safe Packaging Corporation," which updates Case 36.

Case 68, "Sweet Dreams Inc.," which also updates Case 36.

Case 71, "Swan-Davis, Inc.," which illustrates how financial analysis, based on both historical statements and forecasted statements, is used for internal management and lending decisions.

part 2

Securities and Their Valuation

chapter 5

Bonds, Bond Valuation, and Interest Rates

A lot of U.S. bonds have been issued, and we mean a LOT! According to the Federal Reserve, there are about $4.8 trillion of outstanding U.S. Treasury securities, more than $2.2 trillion of municipal securities, $3.0 trillion of corporate bonds, and more than $947 billion of foreign bonds held in the United States. Not only is the dollar amount mind-boggling, so is the variety. Bonds come in many shapes and flavors, with a number of new varieties introduced each year. For instance, two of the most interesting bonds don't pay any interest, and one actually has a negative interest rate.

How can a bond not pay interest? An investor might buy such a bond today for $558 in exchange for the promise of $1,000 in 10 years. The investor would not receive any cash interest payments, but the 10-year increase from the original purchase price to the $1,000 repayment would provide a 6% annual return on the investment. Although there are no annual cash interest payments, the government still allows corporate issuers to deduct an imputed annual interest expense from their taxable income based on the bond's annual appreciation in value. Thus, the company gets a tax deduction each year, even though it isn't making actu-al interest payments. Of course, the downside is that the company will have to come up with the full $1,000 per bond in 10 years to pay off the bondholders, plus the bondholders must report the imputed interest and pay taxes on it.

Even more interesting, Berkshire Hathaway (chaired by Warren Buffett) issued bonds with a negative interest rate in 2002. Technically, Berkshire's bonds called for a 3% interest payment, but they also had an attached warrant that allows an investor to purchase shares of Berkshire Hathaway stock at a fixed price in the future. If the stock price rises above the specified price, then investors can profit by exercising the warrants. However, Berkshire Hathaway didn't just give away the warrants—it required investors to make annual installment payments equal to 3.75% of the bond's face value. Thus, investors receive a 3% interest payment, but they must then pay a 3.75% warrant fee, for a net interest rate of negative 0.75%. Berkshire Hathaway can deduct the 3% interest payment for tax purposes, but the 3.75% warrant fee is not taxable, further increasing Berkshire Hathaway's annual after-tax cash flow.

Think about the implications of these and other bonds as you read this chapter.

Source: http://www.federalreserve.gov/releases/Z1/current/, "Flow of Funds Accounts of the United States, Section L.2, Credit Market Debt Owed by Nonfinancial Sectors."

e-resource

The textbook's Web site contains an *Excel* file that will guide you through the chapter's calculations. The file for this chapter is **FM12 Ch 05 Tool Kit.xls,** and we encourage you to open the file and follow along as you read the chapter.

Growing companies must acquire land, buildings, equipment, inventory, and other operating assets. The debt markets are a major source of funding for such purchases. Therefore, every manager should have a working knowledge of the types of bonds companies and government agencies issue, the terms that are contained in bond contracts, the types of risks to which both bond investors and issuers are exposed, and procedures for determining the values of and rates of return on bonds.

5.1 Who Issues Bonds?

A **bond** is a long-term contract under which a borrower agrees to make payments of interest and principal, on specific dates, to the holders of the bond. For example, on January 5, 2008, MicroDrive Inc. borrowed $50 million by issuing $50 million of bonds. For convenience, we assume that MicroDrive sold 50,000 individual bonds for $1,000 each. Actually, it could have sold one $50 million bond, 10 bonds with a $5 million face value, or any other combination that totals to $50 million. In any event, MicroDrive received the $50 million, and in exchange it promised to make annual interest payments and to repay the $50 million on a specified maturity date.

Investors have many choices when investing in bonds, but bonds are classified into four main types: Treasury, corporate, municipal, and foreign. Each type differs with respect to expected return and degree of risk.

Treasury bonds, sometimes referred to as government bonds, are issued by the U.S. federal government.[1] It is reasonable to assume that the federal government will make good on its promised payments, so these bonds have no default risk. However, Treasury bond prices decline when interest rates rise, so they are not free of all risks.

Corporate bonds, as the name implies, are issued by corporations. Unlike Treasury bonds, corporate bonds are exposed to default risk—if the issuing company gets into trouble, it may be unable to make the promised interest and principal payments. Different corporate bonds have different levels of default risk, depending on the issuing company's characteristics and the terms of the specific bond. Default risk often is referred to as "credit risk," and the larger the default or credit risk, the higher the interest rate the issuer must pay.

Municipal bonds, or "munis," are issued by state and local governments. Like corporate bonds, munis have default risk. However, munis offer one major advantage over all other bonds: The interest earned on most municipal bonds is exempt from federal taxes and also from state taxes if the holder is a resident of the issuing state. Consequently, municipal bonds carry interest rates that are considerably lower than those on corporate bonds with the same default risk.

Foreign bonds are issued by foreign governments or foreign corporations. Foreign corporate bonds are, of course, exposed to default risk, and so are some foreign government bonds. An additional risk exists if the bonds are denominated

---

[1]The U.S. Treasury actually issues three types of securities: "bills," "notes," and "bonds." A bond makes an equal payment every 6 months until it matures, at which time it makes an additional lump sum payment. If the maturity at the time of issue is less than 10 years, it is called a note rather than a bond. A T-bill has a maturity of 52 weeks or less at the time of issue, and it makes no payments at all until it matures. Thus, bills are sold initially at a discount to their face, or maturity, value.

effective maturity of a bond declines each year after it has been issued. Thus, MicroDrive's bonds had a 15-year original maturity, but in 2009, a year later, they will have a 14-year maturity, and so on.

Provisions to Call or Redeem Bonds

Most corporate bonds contain a **call provision,** which gives the issuing corporation the right to call the bonds for redemption.[4] The call provision generally states that the company must pay the bondholders an amount greater than the par value if they are called. The additional sum, which is termed a **call premium,** is often set equal to one year's interest if the bonds are called during the first year, and the premium declines at a constant rate of INT/N each year thereafter, where INT = annual interest and N = original maturity in years. For example, the call premium on a $1,000 par value, 10-year, 10% bond would generally be $100 if it were called during the first year, $90 during the second year (calculated by reducing the $100, or 10%, premium by one-tenth), and so on. However, bonds are often not callable until several years (generally 5 to 10) after they are issued. This is known as a **deferred call,** and the bonds are said to have **call protection.**

Suppose a company sold bonds when interest rates were relatively high. Provided the issue is callable, the company could sell a new issue of low-yielding securities if and when interest rates drop. It could then use the proceeds of the new issue to retire the high-rate issue and thus reduce its interest expense. This process is called a **refunding operation.**

A call provision is valuable to the firm but potentially detrimental to investors. If interest rates go up, the company will not call the bond, and the investor will be stuck with the original coupon rate on the bond, even though interest rates in the economy have risen sharply. However, if interest rates fall, the company *will* call the bond and pay off investors, who then must reinvest the proceeds at the current market interest rate, which is lower than the rate they were getting on the original bond. In other words, the investor loses when interest rates go up, but he or she doesn't reap the gains when rates fall. To induce an investor to take this type of risk, a new issue of callable bonds must provide a higher interest rate than an otherwise similar issue of noncallable bonds. For example, Pacific Timber Company issued bonds yielding 9.5%; these bonds were callable immediately. On the same day, Northwest Milling Company sold an issue with similar risk and maturity that yielded 9.2%, but these bonds were noncallable for 10 years. Investors were willing to accept a 0.3% lower interest rate on Northwest's bonds for the assurance that the 9.2% interest rate would be earned for at least 10 years. Pacific, on the other hand, had to incur a 0.3% higher annual interest rate to obtain the option of calling the bonds in the event of a subsequent decline in rates.

Bonds that are **redeemable at par** at the holder's option protect investors against a rise in interest rates. If rates rise, the price of a fixed-rate bond declines. However, if holders have the option of turning their bonds in and having them redeemed at par, they are protected against rising rates. Examples of such debt include Transamerica's $50 million issue of 25-year, 8½% bonds. The bonds are not callable by the company, but holders can turn them in for redemption at par 5 years after the date of issue. If interest rates have risen, holders will turn in the

---

[4]A majority of municipal bonds also contain call provisions. Although the U.S. Treasury no longer issues callable bonds, some past Treasury issues were callable.

bonds and reinvest the proceeds at a higher rate. This feature enabled Transamerica to sell the bonds with an 8½% coupon at a time when other similarly rated bonds had yields of 9%.

In late 1988, the corporate bond markets were sent into turmoil by the leveraged buyout of RJR Nabisco. RJR's bonds dropped in value by 20% within days of the LBO announcement, and the prices of many other corporate bonds also plunged, because investors feared that a boom in LBOs would load up many companies with excessive debt, leading to lower bond ratings and declining bond prices. All this led to a resurgence of concern about **event risk,** which is the risk that some sudden event, such as an LBO, will occur and increase the credit risk of the company, hence lowering the firm's bond rating and the value of its outstanding bonds. Investors' concern over event risk meant that those firms deemed most likely to face events that could harm bondholders had to pay dearly to raise new debt capital, if they could raise it at all. In an attempt to control debt costs, a new type of protective covenant was devised to minimize event risk. This covenant, called a **super poison put,** enables a bondholder to turn in, or "put" a bond back to the issuer at par in the event of a takeover, merger, or major recapitalization.

Poison puts have actually been around since 1986, when the leveraged buyout trend took off. However, the earlier puts proved to be almost worthless because they allowed investors to "put" their bonds back to the issuer at par value only in the event of an unfriendly takeover. But because almost all takeovers are eventually approved by the target firm's board, mergers that started as hostile generally ended as friendly. Also, the earlier poison puts failed to protect investors from voluntary recapitalizations, in which a company sells a big issue of bonds to pay a big, one-time dividend to stockholders or to buy back its own stock. The "super" poison puts that were used following the RJR buyout announcement protected against both of these actions. This is a good illustration of how quickly the financial community reacts to changes in the marketplace.

Finally, some bonds have a **make-whole call provision.** This allows a company to call the bond, but it must pay a call price that is essentially equal to the market value of a similar noncallable bond. This provides companies with an easy way to repurchase bonds as part of a financial restructuring, such as a merger.

Sinking Funds

Some bonds also include a **sinking fund provision** that facilitates the orderly retirement of the bond issue. On rare occasions the firm may be required to deposit money with a trustee, which invests the funds and then uses the accumulated sum to retire the bonds when they mature. Usually, though, the sinking fund is used to buy back a certain percentage of the issue each year. A failure to meet the sinking fund requirement causes the bond to be thrown into default, which may force the company into bankruptcy. Obviously, a sinking fund can constitute a significant cash drain on the firm.

In most cases, the firm is given the right to handle the sinking fund in either of two ways:

1. The company can call in for redemption (at par value) a certain percentage of the bonds each year; for example, it might be able to call 5% of the total original amount of the issue at a price of $1,000 per bond. The bonds are numbered

serially, and those called for redemption are determined by a lottery administered by the trustee.

2. The company may buy the required number of bonds on the open market.

The firm will choose the least-cost method. If interest rates have risen, causing bond prices to fall, it will buy bonds in the open market at a discount; if interest rates have fallen, it will call the bonds. Note that a call for sinking fund purposes is quite different from a refunding call as discussed above. A sinking fund call typically requires no call premium, but only a small percentage of the issue is normally callable in any one year.[5]

Although sinking funds are designed to protect bondholders by ensuring that an issue is retired in an orderly fashion, you should recognize that sinking funds can work to the detriment of bondholders. For example, suppose the bond carries a 10% interest rate, but yields on similar bonds have fallen to 7.5%. A sinking fund call at par would require an investor to give up a bond that pays $100 of interest and then to reinvest in a bond that pays only $75 per year. This obviously harms those bondholders whose bonds are called. On balance, however, bonds that have a sinking fund are regarded as being safer than those without such a provision, so at the time they are issued sinking fund bonds have lower coupon rates than otherwise similar bonds without sinking funds.

Other Features

Several other types of bonds are used sufficiently often to warrant mention. First, **convertible bonds** are bonds that are convertible into shares of common stock, at a fixed price, at the option of the bondholder. Convertibles have a lower coupon rate than nonconvertible debt, but they offer investors a chance for capital gains in exchange for the lower coupon rate. Bonds issued with **warrants** are similar to convertibles. Warrants are options that permit the holder to buy stock for a stated price, thereby providing a capital gain if the price of the stock rises. Bonds that are issued with warrants, like convertibles, carry lower coupon rates than straight bonds.

Another type of bond is an **income bond,** which pays interest only if the interest is earned. These securities cannot bankrupt a company, but from an investor's standpoint they are riskier than "regular" bonds. Yet another bond is the **indexed,** or **purchasing power, bond,** which first became popular in Brazil, Israel, and a few other countries plagued by high inflation rates. The interest rate paid on these bonds is based on an inflation index such as the consumer price index, so the interest paid rises automatically when the inflation rate rises, thus protecting the bondholders against inflation. In January 1997, the U.S. Treasury began issuing indexed bonds, and they currently pay a rate that is roughly 1 to 4% plus the rate of inflation during the past year.

Bond Markets

Corporate bonds are traded primarily in the over-the-counter market rather than in organized exchanges. Most bonds are owned by and traded among the large financial institutions (for example, life insurance companies, mutual funds, and pension funds, all of which deal in very large blocks of securities), and it is rela-

---

[5]Some sinking funds require the issuer to pay a call premium.

tively easy for the over-the-counter bond dealers to arrange the transfer of large blocks of bonds among the relatively few holders of the bonds.

Information on bond trades in the over-the-counter market is not widely published, but a representative group of bonds is listed and traded on the bond division of the NYSE and is reported on the bond market page of *The Wall Street Journal*. Bond data are also available on the Internet, at sites such as **http://www.bondpage.com** and **http://finance.yahoo.com**.

SELF-TEST

Define "floating-rate bonds" and "zero coupon bonds."
Why is a call provision advantageous to a bond issuer?
What are the two ways a sinking fund can be handled? Which method will be chosen by the firm if interest rates have risen? If interest rates have fallen?
Are securities that provide for a sinking fund regarded as being riskier than those without this type of provision? Explain.
What are income bonds and indexed bonds?
Why do bonds with warrants and convertible bonds have lower coupons than similarly rated bonds that do not have these features?

5.3 Bond Valuation

The value of any financial asset—a stock, a bond, a lease, or even a physical asset such as an apartment building or a piece of machinery—is simply the present value of the cash flows the asset is expected to produce. The cash flows from a specific bond depend on its contractual features as described above. For a standard coupon-bearing bond such as the one issued by MicroDrive, the cash flows consist of interest payments during the life of the bond, plus the amount borrowed when the bond matures (usually a $1,000 par value). In the case of a floating-rate bond, the interest payments vary over time. In the case of a zero coupon bond, there are no interest payments, only the face amount when the bond matures. For a "regular" bond with a fixed coupon rate, here is the situation:

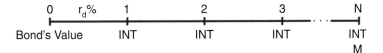

The notation in the time line is explained below:

r_d = The bond's required rate of return, which is the market rate of interest for that type of bond. This is the discount rate that is used to calculate the present value of the bond's cash flows. It is also called the "yield" or "going rate of interest." Note that r_d is *not* the coupon interest rate. It is equal to the coupon rate only if (as in this case) the bond is selling at par. Generally, most coupon bonds are issued at par, which implies that the coupon rate is set at r_d. Thereafter, interest rates, as measured by r_d, will fluctuate, but the coupon rate is fixed, so r_d will equal the coupon rate only by chance. We use the term "i" or "I" to designate the interest rate for many calculations because those terms are used on financial calculators but "r," with the subscript "d" to designate the rate on a debt security, is normally used in finance.[6]

---

[6]The appropriate interest rate on a bond depends on its risk, liquidity, and years to maturity, as well as supply and demand conditions in the capital markets.

> N = Number of years before the bond matures. Note that N declines each year after the bond was issued, so a bond that had a maturity of 15 years when it was issued (original maturity = 15) will have N = 14 after 1 year, N = 13 after 2 years, and so on. Note also that at this point we assume that the bond pays interest once a year, or annually, so N is measured in years. Later on, we will deal with semiannual payment bonds, which pay interest each 6 months.
>
> INT = Dollars of interest paid each year = Coupon rate × Par value. For a bond with a 10% coupon and a $1,000 par value, the annual interest is 0.10($1,000) = $100. In calculator terminology, INT = PMT = 100. If the bond had been a semiannual payment bond, the payment would have been $50 every 6 months. The payment would vary if the bond was a "floater."
>
> M = Par, or maturity, value of the bond. This amount must be paid off at maturity, and it is often equal to $1,000.

The following general equation, written in several forms, can be used to find the value of any bond, V_B:

$$V_B = \frac{INT}{(1 + r_d)^1} + \frac{INT}{(1 + r_d)^2} + \cdots + \frac{INT}{(1 + r_d)^N} + \frac{M}{(1 + r_d)^N}$$

$$= \sum_{t=1}^{N} \frac{INT}{(1 + r_d)^t} + \frac{M}{(1 + r_d)^N} \qquad (5\text{-}1)$$

$$= INT\left[\frac{1}{r_d} - \frac{1}{r_d(1 + r_d)^N}\right] + \frac{M}{(1 + r_d)^N}.$$

Notice that the cash flows consist of an annuity of N years plus a lump sum payment at the end of Year N, and this fact is reflected in Equation 5-1. Further, Equation 5-1 can be solved by one of three procedures: (1) with a formula, (2) with a financial calculator, and (3) with a spreadsheet.

Solving for the Bond Price

Recall that MicroDrive issued a 15-year bond with an annual coupon rate of 10% and a par value of $1,000. To find the value of MicroDrive's bond with a formula, we insert values for MicroDrive's bond into Equation 5-1:

$$V_B = \sum_{t=1}^{15} \frac{\$100}{(1 + 0.10)^t} + \frac{\$1,000}{(1 + 0.10)^{15}}$$

$$= \$100\left[\frac{1}{0.10} - \frac{1}{0.10(1 + 0.10)^{15}}\right] + \frac{\$1,000}{(1 + 0.10)^{15}} \qquad (5\text{-}1a)$$

$$= \$1,000.$$

We could use the first row of Equation 5-1 to discount each cash flow back to the present and then sum these PVs to find the bond's value; see Figure 5-1. This procedure is not very efficient, especially if the bond has many years to maturity.

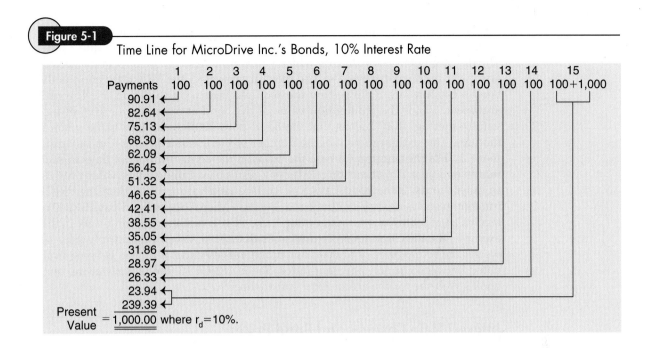

Figure 5-1

Time Line for MicroDrive Inc.'s Bonds, 10% Interest Rate

Alternatively, you could use the formula in the second row of Equation 5-1a with a simple or scientific calculator, although this would still be somewhat cumbersome.

A financial calculator is ideally suited for finding bond values. Here is the setup for MicroDrive's bond:

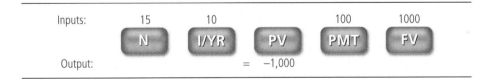

Input N = 15, I/YR = r_d = 10, INT = PMT = 100, M = FV = 1000, and then press the PV key to find the value of the bond, $1,000. Since the PV is an outflow to the investor, it is shown with a negative sign. The calculator is programmed to solve Equation 5-1: It finds the PV of an annuity of $100 per year for 15 years, discounted at 10%, then it finds the PV of the $1,000 maturity payment, and then it adds these two PVs to find the value of the bond. Notice that even though the time line in Figure 5-1 shows a total of $1,100 at Year 15, you should not enter FV = 1100! When you entered N = 15 and PMT = 100, you told the calculator that there is a $100 payment at Year 15. Thus, the FV = 1000 accounts for any *extra* payment at Year 15, above and beyond the $100 payment.

With *Excel*, it is easiest to use the same PV function that we used in Chapter 2: **=PV(I,N,PMT,FV,0).** For MicroDrive's bond, the function is **=PV(0.10,15,100,1000,0)** with a result of −$1,000. Like the financial calculator solution, the bond value is negative because PMT and FV are positive.

Excel also provides specialized functions for bond prices based on actual dates. For example, in *Excel* you could find the MicroDrive bond value as of the date it was issued by using the function wizard to enter this formula:

=PRICE(DATE(2008,1,5),DATE(2023,1,5),10%,10%,100,1,0)

FM

e-resource

See **FM12 Ch 05 Tool Kit.xls** at the textbook's Web site.

The first two arguments in the function are *Excel's* DATE function. The DATE function takes the year, month, and date as inputs and converts them into a date. The first argument is the date on which you want to find the price, and the second argument is the maturity date. The third argument in the PRICE function is the bond's coupon rate, followed by the required return on the bond, r_d. The fifth argument, 100, is the redemption value of the bond at maturity per $100 of face value; entering "100" means that the bond pays 100% of its face value when it matures. The sixth argument is the number of payments per year. The last argument, 1, tells the program to base the price on the actual number of days in each month and year. This function produces a result based upon a face value of $100. In other words, if the bond pays $100 of face value at maturity, then the PRICE function result is the price of the bond. Because MicroDrive's bond pays $1,000 of face value at maturity, we must multiply the PRICE function's result by 10. In this example, the PRICE function returns a result of $100. When we multiply it by 10, we get the actual price of $1,000. This function is essential if a bond is being evaluated between coupon payment dates. See *FM12 Ch 05 Tool Kit.xls* at the textbook's Web site for the actual *Excel* spreadsheet.[7]

Interest Rate Changes and Bond Prices

In this example the bond is selling at a price equal to its par value. Whenever the going market rate of interest, r_d, is equal to the coupon rate, a *fixed-rate* bond will sell at its par value. Normally, the coupon rate is set at the going rate when a bond is issued, causing it to sell at par initially.

The coupon rate remains fixed after the bond is issued, but interest rates in the market move up and down. Looking at Equation 5-1, we see that an *increase* in the market interest rate (r_d) will cause the price of an outstanding bond to *fall*, whereas a *decrease* in rates will cause the bond's price to *rise*. For example, if the market interest rate on MicroDrive's bond increased to 15% immediately after it was issued, we would recalculate the price with the new market interest rate as follows:

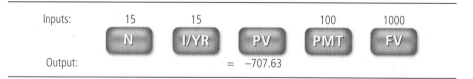

		15	15		100	1000
Inputs:		N	I/YR	PV	PMT	FV
Output:				= −707.63		

The price would fall to $707.63. Notice that the bond would then sell at a price below its par value. Whenever the going rate of interest *rises above* the coupon rate, a fixed-rate bond's price will fall *below* its par value, and it is called a **discount bond.**

---

[7]The bond prices quoted by brokers are calculated as described. However, if you bought a bond between interest payment dates, you would have to pay the basic price plus accrued interest. Thus, if you purchased a MicroDrive bond 6 months after it was issued, your broker would send you an invoice stating that you must pay $1,000 as the basic price of the bond plus $50 interest, representing one-half the annual interest of $100. The seller of the bond would receive $1,050. If you bought the bond the day before its interest payment date, you would pay $1,000 + (364/365)($100) = $1,099.73. Of course, you would receive an interest payment of $100 at the end of the next day. For more on the valuation of bonds between payment dates, see Richard Taylor, "The Valuation of Semiannual Bonds between Interest Payment Dates," *The Financial Review*, August 1988, pp. 365–368, and K. S. Maurice Tse and Mark A. White, "The Valuation of Semiannual Bonds between Interest Payment Dates: A Correction," *Financial Review*, November 1990, pp. 659–662.

On the other hand, bond prices rise when market interest rates fall. For example, if the market interest rate on MicroDrive's bond decreased to 5%, we would once again recalculate its price:

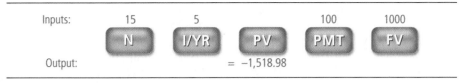

Inputs: 15   5   100   1000
          N   I/YR   PV   PMT   FV

Output: = −1,518.98

In this case the price rises to $1,518.98. In general, whenever the going interest rate *falls below* the coupon rate, a fixed-rate bond's price will rise *above* its par value, and it is called a **premium bond.**

SELF-TEST

Why do the prices of fixed-rate bonds fall if expectations for inflation rise?

What is a "discount bond?" A "premium bond?"

A bond that matures in 6 years has a par value of $1,000, an annual coupon payment of $80, and a market interest rate of 9%. What is its price? ($955.14)

A bond that matures in 18 years has a par value of $1,000, an annual coupon of 10%, and a market interest rate of 7%. What is its price? ($1,301.77)

5.4 Bond Yields

Unlike the coupon interest rate, which is fixed, the bond's *yield* varies from day to day depending on current market conditions. Moreover, the yield can be calculated in three different ways, and three "answers" can be obtained. These different yields are described in the following sections.

Yield to Maturity

Suppose you were offered a 14-year, 10% annual coupon, $1,000 par value bond at a price of $1,494.93. What rate of interest would you earn on your investment if you bought the bond and held it to maturity? This rate is called the bond's **yield to maturity (YTM),** and it is the interest rate generally discussed by investors when they talk about rates of return. The yield to maturity is usually the same as the market rate of interest, r_d, and to find it, all you need to do is solve Equation 5-1 for r_d:

$$V_B = \$1,494.93 = \frac{\$100}{(1 + r_d)^1} + \cdots + \frac{\$100}{(1 + r_d)^{14}} + \frac{\$1,000}{(1 + r_d)^{14}}.$$

You can substitute values for r_d until you find a value that "works" and forces the sum of the PVs on the right side of the equal sign to equal $1,494.93. Alternatively, you can substitute values of r_d into the third form of Equation 5-1 until you find a value that works.

Finding r_d = YTM by trial-and-error would be a tedious, time-consuming process, but as you might guess, it is easy with a financial calculator. Here is the setup:

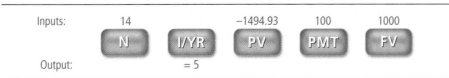

Inputs: 14   −1494.93   100   1000
          N   I/YR   PV   PMT   FV

Output: = 5

Simply enter N = 14, PV = −1494.93, PMT = 100, and FV = 1000, and then press the I/YR key. The answer, 5%, will then appear.

You could also find the YTM with a spreadsheet. In *Excel*, you would use the RATE function for this bond, inputting N = 14, PMT = 100, PV = −1494.93, FV = 1000, 0 for Type, and leave Guess blank: =**RATE(14,100,−1494.93,1000,0)**. The result is 5%. The RATE function only works if the current date is immediately after either the issue date or a coupon payment date. To find bond yields on other dates, use *Excel's* YIELD function. See the **FM12 Ch 05 Tool Kit.xls** file for an example.

The yield to maturity can be viewed as the bond's *promised rate of return*, which is the return that investors will receive if all the promised payments are made. However, the yield to maturity equals the *expected rate of return* only if (1) the probability of default is zero and (2) the bond cannot be called. If there is some default risk, or if the bond may be called, then there is some probability that the promised payments to maturity will not be received, in which case the calculated yield to maturity will differ from the expected return.

The YTM for a bond that sells at par consists entirely of an interest yield, but if the bond sells at a price other than its par value, the YTM will consist of the interest yield plus a positive or negative capital gains yield. Note also that a bond's yield to maturity changes whenever interest rates in the economy change, and this is almost daily. One who purchases a bond and holds it until it matures will receive the YTM that existed on the purchase date, but the bond's calculated YTM will change frequently between the purchase date and the maturity date.

Yield to Call

If you purchased a bond that was callable and the company called it, you would not have the option of holding the bond until it matured. Therefore, the yield to maturity would not be earned. For example, if MicroDrive's 10% coupon bonds were callable, and if interest rates fell from 10% to 5%, then the company could call in the 10% bonds, replace them with 5% bonds, and save $100 − $50 = $50 interest per bond per year. This would be beneficial to the company, but not to its bondholders.

If current interest rates are well below an outstanding bond's coupon rate, then a callable bond is likely to be called, and investors will estimate its expected rate of return as the **yield to call (YTC)** rather than as the yield to maturity. To calculate the YTC, solve this equation for r_d:

$$\text{Price of bond} = \sum_{t=1}^{N} \frac{\text{INT}}{(1 + r_d)^t} + \frac{\text{Call price}}{(1 + r_d)^N}. \tag{5-2}$$

Here N is the number of years until the company can call the bond; call price is the price the company must pay in order to call the bond (it is often set equal to the par value plus one year's interest); and r_d is the YTC.

To illustrate, suppose MicroDrive's bonds had a provision that permitted the company, if it desired, to call the bonds 10 years after the issue date at a price of $1,100. Suppose further that interest rates had fallen, and one year after issuance the going interest rate had declined, causing the price of the bonds to rise to $1,494.93. Here is the time line and the setup for finding the bond's YTC with a financial calculator:

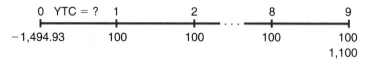

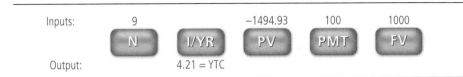

Inputs:	9		−1494.93	100	1000
	N	I/YR	PV	PMT	FV
Output:		4.21 = YTC			

The YTC is 4.21%—this is the return you would earn if you bought the bond at a price of $1,494.93 and it was called 9 years from today. (The bond could not be called until 10 years after issuance, and 1 year has gone by, so there are 9 years left until the first call date.)

Do you think MicroDrive *will* call the bonds when they become callable? MicroDrive's actions would depend on what the going interest rate is when the bonds become callable. If the going rate remains at $r_d = 5\%$, then MicroDrive could save $10\% - 5\% = 5\%$, or $50 per bond per year, by calling them and replacing the 10% bonds with a new 5% issue. There would be costs to the company to refund the issue, but the interest savings would probably be worth the cost, so MicroDrive would probably refund the bonds. Therefore, you would probably earn YTC = 4.21% rather than YTM = 5% if you bought the bonds under the indicated conditions.

In the balance of this chapter, we assume that bonds are not callable unless otherwise noted, but some of the end-of-chapter problems deal with yield to call.

Current Yield

If you examine brokerage house reports on bonds, you will often see reference to a bond's **current yield.** The current yield is the annual interest payment divided by the bond's current price. For example, if MicroDrive's bonds with a 10% coupon were currently selling at $985, the bond's current yield would be 10.15% ($100/$985).

Unlike the yield to maturity, the current yield does not represent the rate of return that investors should expect on the bond. The current yield provides information regarding the amount of cash income that a bond will generate in a given year, but since it does not take account of capital gains or losses that will be realized if the bond is held until maturity (or call), it does not provide an accurate measure of the bond's total expected return.

The fact that the current yield does not provide an accurate measure of a bond's total return can be illustrated with a zero coupon bond. Since zeros pay no annual income, they always have a current yield of zero. This indicates that the bond will not provide any cash interest income, but since the bond will appreciate in value over time, its total rate of return clearly exceeds zero.

SELF-TEST

Explain the difference between the yield to maturity and the yield to call.
How does a bond's current yield differ from its total return?
Could the current yield exceed the total return?
A bond currently sells for $850. It has an 8-year maturity, an annual coupon of $80, and a par value of $1,000. What is its yield to maturity? (10.90%) What is its current yield? (9.41%)
A bond currently sells for $1,250. It pays a $110 annual coupon and has a 20-year maturity, but it can be called in 5 years at $1,110. What are its YTM and its YTC? (8.38%, 6.85%) Is it likely to be called if interest rates don't change?

5.5 Changes in Bond Values Over Time

At the time a coupon bond is issued, the coupon is generally set at a level that will cause the market price of the bond to equal its par value. If a lower coupon were set, investors would not be willing to pay $1,000 for the bond, while if a higher coupon were set, investors would clamor for the bond and bid its price up over $1,000. Investment bankers can judge quite precisely the coupon rate that will cause a bond to sell at its $1,000 par value.

A bond that has just been issued is known as a **new issue.** (Investment bankers classify a bond as a new issue for about one month after it has first been issued. New issues are usually actively traded, and are called "on-the-run" bonds.) Once the bond has been on the market for a while, it is classified as an **outstanding bond,** also called a **seasoned issue.** Newly issued bonds generally sell very close to par, but the prices of seasoned bonds vary widely from par. Except for floating-rate bonds, coupon payments are constant, so when economic conditions change, a bond with a $100 coupon that sold at par when it was issued will sell for more or less than $1,000 thereafter.

MicroDrive's bonds with a 10% coupon rate were originally issued at par. If r_d remained constant at 10%, what would the value of the bond be 1 year after it was issued? Now the term to maturity is only 14 years—that is, N = 14. With a financial calculator, just override N = 15 with N = 14, press the PV key, and you find a value of $1,000. If we continued, setting N = 13, N = 12, and so forth, we would see that the value of the bond will remain at $1,000 as long as the going interest rate remains constant at the coupon rate, 10%.

Now suppose interest rates in the economy fell after the MicroDrive bonds were issued, and, as a result, r_d *fell below the coupon rate,* decreasing from 10 to 5%. Both the coupon interest payments and the maturity value remain constant, but now 5% would have to be used for r_d in Equation 5-1. The value of the bond at the end of the first year would be $1,494.93:

$$V_B = \sum_{t=1}^{14} \frac{\$100}{(1 + 0.05)^t} + \frac{\$1,000}{(1 + 0.10)^{14}}$$

$$= \$100 \left[\frac{1}{0.05} - \frac{1}{0.05(1 + 0.05)^{14}} \right] + \frac{\$1,000}{(1 + 0.05)^{14}}$$

$$= \$1,494.93.$$

With a financial calculator, just change r_d = I/YR from 10 to 5, and then press the PV key to get the answer, $1,494.93. Thus, if r_d fell *below* the coupon rate, the bond would sell above par, or at a **premium.**

The arithmetic of the bond value increase should be clear, but what is the logic behind it? The fact that r_d has fallen to 5% means that if you had $1,000 to invest, you could buy new bonds like MicroDrive's (every day some 10 to 12 companies sell new bonds), except that these new bonds would pay $50 of interest each year rather than $100. Naturally, you would prefer $100 to $50, so you would be willing to pay more than $1,000 for a MicroDrive bond to obtain its higher coupons. All investors would react similarly, and as a result, the MicroDrive bonds would be bid up in price to $1,494.93, at which point they would provide the same 5% rate of return to a potential investor as the new bonds.

Assuming that interest rates remain constant at 5% for the next 14 years, what would happen to the value of a MicroDrive bond? It would fall gradually from $1,494.93 at present to $1,000 at maturity, when MicroDrive will redeem each bond for $1,000. This point can be illustrated by calculating the value of the bond 1 year later, when it has 13 years remaining to maturity. With a financial calculator, simply input the values for N, I, PMT, and FV, now using N = 13, and press the PV key to find the value of the bond, $1,469.68. Thus, the value of the bond will have fallen from $1,494.93 to $1,469.68, or by $25.25. If you were to calculate the value of the bond at other future dates, the price would continue to fall as the maturity date approached.

Note that if you purchased the bond at a price of $1,494.93 and then sold it 1 year later with r_d still at 5%, you would have a capital loss of $25.25, or a total return of $100.00 − $25.25 = $74.75. Your percentage rate of return would consist of an **interest yield** (also called a **current yield**) plus a **capital gains yield**, calculated as follows:

$$\text{Interest, or current, yield} = \$100/\$1{,}494.93 \quad = \quad 0.0669 = \quad 6.69\%$$
$$\text{Capital gains yield} = -\$25.25/\$1{,}494.93 = -0.0169 = -\underline{1.69\%}$$
$$\text{Total rate of return, or yield} = \$74.75/\$1{,}494.93 \quad = \quad 0.0500 = \quad \underline{5.00\%}$$

Had interest rates risen from 10 to 15% during the first year after issue rather than fallen from 10 to 5%, then you would enter N = 14, I/YR = 15, PMT = 100, and FV = 1000, and then press the PV key to find the value of the bond, $713.78. In this case, the bond would sell below its par value, or at a discount. The total expected future return on the bond would again consist of a current yield and a capital gains yield, but now the capital gains yield would be *positive*. The total return would be 15%. To see this, calculate the price of the bond with 13 years left to maturity, assuming that interest rates remain at 15%. With a calculator, enter N = 13, I = 15, PMT = 100, and FV = 1000, and then press PV to obtain the bond's value, $720.84.

Note that the capital gain for the year is the difference between the bond's value at Year 2 (with 13 years remaining) and the bond's value at Year 1 (with 14 years remaining), or $720.84 − $713.78 = $7.06. The interest yield, capital gains yield, and total yield are calculated as follows:

$$\text{Interest, or current, yield} = \$100/\$713.78 \quad = 0.1401 = 14.01\%$$
$$\text{Capital gains yield} = \$7.06/\$713.78 \quad = 0.0099 = \quad \underline{0.99\%}$$
$$\text{Total rate of return, or yield} = \$107.06/\$713.78 = 0.1500 = \underline{\underline{15.00\%}}$$

Figure 5-2 graphs the value of the bond over time, assuming that interest rates in the economy (1) remain constant at 10%, (2) fall to 5% and then remain constant at that level, or (3) rise to 15% and remain constant at that level. Of course, if interest rates do *not* remain constant, then the price of the bond will fluctuate. However, regardless of what future interest rates do, the bond's price will approach $1,000 as it nears the maturity date (barring bankruptcy, in which case the bond's value might fall dramatically).

Figure 5-2 illustrates the following key points:

1. Whenever the going rate of interest, r_d, is equal to the coupon rate, a *fixed-rate* bond will sell at its par value. Normally, the coupon rate is set equal to the going rate when a bond is issued, causing it to sell at par initially.
2. Interest rates do change over time, but the coupon rate remains fixed after the bond has been issued. Whenever the going rate of interest *rises above* the coupon rate, a fixed-rate bond's price will *fall below* its par value. Such a bond is called a discount bond.
3. Whenever the going rate of interest *falls below* the coupon rate, a fixed-rate bond's price will *rise above* its par value. Such a bond is called a premium bond.
4. Thus, an *increase* in interest rates will cause the prices of outstanding bonds to *fall*, whereas a *decrease* in rates will cause bond prices to *rise*.

Drinking Your Coupons

In 1996 Chateau Teyssier, an English vineyard, was looking for some cash to purchase additional vines and to modernize its production facilities. Their solution? With the assistance of a leading underwriter, Matrix Securities, the vineyard issued 375 bonds, each costing 2,650 British pounds. The issue raised nearly 1 million pounds, or roughly $1.5 million.

What makes these bonds interesting is that, instead of getting paid with something boring like money, these bonds paid their investors back with wine. Each June until 2002, when the bond matured,

investors received their "coupons." Between 1997 and 2001, each bond provided six cases of the vineyard's rosé or claret. Starting in 1998 and continuing through maturity in 2002, investors also received four cases of its prestigious Saint Emilion Grand Cru. Then, in 2002, they got their money back.

The bonds were not without risk. The vineyard's owner, Jonathan Malthus, acknowledges that the quality of the wine "is at the mercy of the gods."

Source: Steven Irvine, "My Wine Is My Bond, and I Drink My Coupons," *Euromoney,* July 1996, p. 7.

5. The market value of a bond will always approach its par value as its maturity date approaches, provided the firm does not go bankrupt.

These points are very important, for they show that bondholders may suffer capital losses or make capital gains, depending on whether interest rates rise or fall after the bond is purchased.

SELF-TEST

What is meant by the terms "new issue" and "seasoned issue"?

Last year a firm issued 30-year, 8% annual coupon bonds at a par value of $1,000. (1) Suppose that one year later the going rate drops to 6%. What is the new price of the bonds, assuming that they now have 19 years to maturity? ($1,271.81) (2) Suppose instead that one year after issue the going interest rate increases to 10% (rather than falling to 6%). What is the price? ($812.61)

Figure 5-2

Time Path of the Value of a 10% Coupon, $1,000 Par Value Bond When Interest Rates Are 5%, 10%, and 15%

FM
e-resource
See **FM12 Ch 05 Tool Kit.xls** for all calculations.

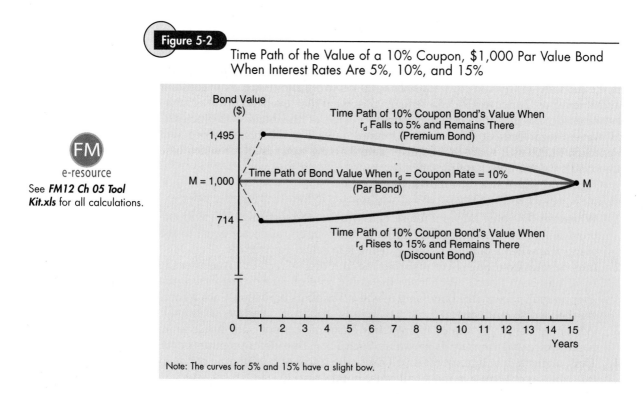

Note: The curves for 5% and 15% have a slight bow.

5.8 The Real Risk-Free Rate of Interest, r*

The **real risk-free rate of interest, r***, is defined as the interest rate that would exist on a riskless security if no inflation were expected, and it may be thought of as the rate of interest on *short-term* U.S. Treasury securities in an inflation-free world. The real risk-free rate is not static—it changes over time depending on economic conditions, especially (1) on the rate of return corporations and other borrowers expect to earn on productive assets and (2) on people's time preferences for current versus future consumption.[10]

In addition to its regular bond offerings, in 1997 the U.S. Treasury began issuing **indexed bonds,** with payments linked to inflation. These bonds are called **TIPS,** short for **Treasury Inflation-Protected Securities.** Because the payments (including the principal) are tied to inflation, the yield on a TIPS is a good estimate of the risk-free rate. In June 2006, the TIPS with a 7-month remaining maturity had a 2.64% yield. This is a pretty good estimate of the real risk-free rate, r*, although ideally we would prefer a TIPS with an even shorter time until maturity. We will have more to say about how to use TIPS when we discuss the inflation premium in the next section. For details on how TIPS are adjusted, see *Web Extension 5B* at the textbook's Web site.

FM
e-resource

SELF-TEST ――――――――――――――――――――――――――――――――
What security provides a good estimate of the real risk-free rate?

5.9 The Inflation Premium (IP)

Inflation has a major effect on interest rates because it erodes the purchasing power of the dollar and lowers the real rate of return on investments. To illustrate, suppose you saved $1,000 and invested it in a Treasury bill that matures in 1 year and pays a 5% interest rate. At the end of the year, you will receive $1,050—your original $1,000 plus $50 of interest. Now suppose the inflation rate during the year is 10%, and it affects all items equally. If gas had cost $1 per gallon at the beginning of the year, it would cost $1.10 at the end of the year. Therefore, your $1,000 would have bought $1,000/$1 = 1,000 gallons at the beginning of the year, but only $1,050/$1.10 = 955 gallons at the end. In *real terms,* you would be worse off— you would receive $50 of interest, but it would not be sufficient to offset inflation. You would thus be better off buying 1,000 gallons of gas (or some other storable asset) than buying the Treasury bill.

Investors are well aware of inflation's effects on interest rates, so when they lend money, they build in an **inflation premium (IP)** equal to the average expected inflation rate over the life of the security. For a short-term, default-free U.S. Treasury bill, the actual interest rate charged, $r_{T\text{-bill}}$, would be the real risk-free rate, r*, plus the inflation premium (IP):

$$r_{T\text{-bill}} = r_{RF} = r^* + IP.$$

―――

[10]The real rate of interest as discussed here is different from the *current* real rate as often discussed in the press. The current real rate is often estimated as the current interest rate minus the current (or most recent) inflation rate, while the real rate, as used here (and in the fields of finance and economics generally) without the word "current," is the current interest rate minus the *expected future* inflation rate over the life of the security. For example, suppose the current quoted rate for a one-year Treasury bill is 5%, inflation during the latest year was 2%, and inflation expected for the coming year is 4%. Then the *current* real rate would be approximately 5% − 2% = 3%, but the *expected* real rate would be approximately 5% − 4% = 1%.

Therefore, if the real short-term risk-free rate of interest were r* = 0.6%, and if inflation were expected to be 1.0% (and hence IP = 1.0%) during the next year, then the quoted rate of interest on 1-year T-bills would be 0.6% + 1.0% = 1.6%.

It is important to note that the inflation rate built into interest rates is *the inflation rate expected in the future*, not the rate experienced in the past. Thus, the latest reported figures might show an annual inflation rate of 2%, but that is for the *past* year. If people on average expect a 6% inflation rate in the future, then 6% would be built into the current interest rate.

Note also that the inflation rate reflected in the quoted interest rate on any security is the *average rate of inflation expected over the security's life*. Thus, the inflation rate built into a 1-year bond is the expected inflation rate for the next year, but the inflation rate built into a 30-year bond is the average rate of inflation expected over the next 30 years. If I_t is the expected inflation during year t, the inflation premium for an N-year bond's yield can be approximated as

$$IP_N = \frac{I_1 + I_2 + \cdots + I_N}{N}. \tag{5-5}$$

For example, if investors expect inflation to average 3% during Year 1 and 5% during Year 2, then the inflation premium built into a 2-year bond's yield can be approximated by

$$IP_2 = \frac{I_1 + I_2}{2} = \frac{3\% + 5\%}{2} = 4\%.$$

In the previous section we saw that the yield on an inflation-indexed Treasury bond (TIPS) is a good estimate of the real interest rate. We can also use TIPS to estimate inflation premiums. For example, in June 2006, the yield on a 5-year nonindexed T-bond was 5.18% and the yield on a 5-year TIPS was 2.50%. Thus, the 5-year inflation premium was 5.18% − 2.50% = 2.68%, implying that investors expected inflation to average 2.68% over the next 5 years.[11] Similarly, the rate on a 22-year nonindexed T-bond was 5.33% and the rate on a 22-year indexed T-bond was 2.56%. Thus, the long-term inflation premium was approximately 5.33% − 2.56% = 2.77%, implying that investors expected inflation to average 2.77% over the next three decades.[12] These calculations are summarized below:

	Maturity	
	5 Years	22 Years
Nonindexed U.S. Treasury bond	5.18%	5.33%
TIPS	2.50	2.56
Inflation premium	2.68%	2.77%

Expectations for future inflation are closely, but not perfectly, correlated with rates experienced in the recent past. Therefore, if the inflation rate reported for last month increases, people often raise their expectations for future inflation, and this change in expectations will cause an increase in interest rates.

---

[11]To be theoretically precise, we should use a *geometric average* by solving the following equation: $(1 + IP)^5(1.0518)^5 = 1.0250^5$. Solving for IP gives IP = 2.55%, which is very close to our approximation.

[12]There are several other sources for the estimated inflation premium. The Congressional Budget Office regularly updates the estimates of inflation that it uses in its forecasted budgets; see **http://www.cbo.gov/**, select Current Economic Projections. A second source is the University of Michigan's Institute for Social Research, which regularly polls consumers regarding their expectations for price increases during the next year; see **http://www.isr.umich .edu/src/projects.html**, select the Surveys of Consumers, and then select the table for Expected Change in Prices. We prefer using inflation premiums derived from indexed and nonindexed Treasury securities, as described in the text, since these are based on how investors actually spend their money, not on theoretical models or opinions.

Note that Germany, Japan, and Switzerland have, over the past several years, had lower inflation rates than the United States, so their interest rates have generally been lower than ours. South Africa and most South American countries have experienced higher inflation, and that is reflected in their interest rates.

SELF-TEST

Explain how a TIPS and a nonindexed Treasury security can be used to estimate the inflation premium. The yield on a 15-year TIPS is 3% and the yield on a 15-year Treasury bond is 5%. What is the inflation premium for a 15-year security? (2%)

5.10 The Nominal, or Quoted, Risk-Free Rate of Interest, r_{RF}

The **nominal**, or **quoted, risk-free rate, r_{RF}**, is the real risk-free rate plus a premium for expected inflation: $r_{RF} = r^* + IP$. To be strictly correct, the risk-free rate should mean the interest rate on a totally risk-free security—one that has no risk of default, no maturity risk, no liquidity risk, no risk of loss if inflation increases, and no risk of any other type. There is no such security, so there is no observable truly risk-free rate. If the term "risk-free rate" is used without either the modifier "real" or the modifier "nominal," people generally mean the quoted (nominal) rate, and we will follow that convention in this book. Therefore, when we use the term "risk-free rate, r_{RF}," we mean the nominal risk-free rate, which includes an inflation premium equal to the average expected inflation rate over the life of the security. In general, we use the T-bill rate to approximate the short-term risk-free rate, and the T-bond rate to approximate the long-term risk-free rate (even though it also includes a maturity premium). So, whenever you see the term "risk-free rate," assume that we are referring either to the quoted U.S. T-bill rate or to the quoted T-bond rate.

Since $r_{RF} = r^* + IP$, we can rewrite Equation 5-4 as follows:

$$\text{Nominal, or quoted, rate} = r_d = r_{RF} + DRP + LP + MRP. \qquad (5\text{-}6)$$

Therefore, when discussing the rate on a bond, we often start with the short-term risk-free rate and make adjustments for the default risk premium, the liquidity premium, and the maturity risk premium.

SELF-TEST

What security is a good approximation of the nominal risk-free rate?

5.11 The Default Risk Premium (DRP)

If the issuer defaults on a payment, investors receive less than the promised return on the bond. The quoted interest rate includes a default risk premium (DRP)—the greater the default risk, the higher the bond's yield to maturity.[13] The default risk on Treasury securities is zero, but default risk can be substantial for corporate and municipal bonds. In this section we consider some issues related to default risk.

---

[13]Suppose two bonds have the same promised cash flows, coupon rate, maturity, liquidity, and inflation exposure, but one bond has more default risk than the other. Investors will naturally pay less for the bond with the greater chance of default. As a result, bonds with higher default risk will have higher interest rates.

Bond Contract Provisions That Influence Default Risk

Default risk is affected by both the financial strength of the issuer and the terms of the bond contract, especially whether collateral has been pledged to secure the bond. Several types of contract provisions are discussed below.

Bond Indentures   An **indenture** is a legal document that spells out the rights of both bondholders and the issuing corporation, and a **trustee** is an official (usually a bank) who represents the bondholders and makes sure the terms of the indenture are carried out. The indenture may be several hundred pages in length, and it will include **restrictive covenants** that cover such points as the conditions under which the issuer can pay off the bonds prior to maturity, the levels at which certain ratios must be maintained if the company is to issue additional debt, and restrictions against the payment of dividends unless earnings meet certain specifications.

The Securities and Exchange Commission (1) approves indentures and (2) makes sure that all indenture provisions are met before allowing a company to sell new securities to the public. A firm will have different indentures for each of the major types of bonds it issues, but a single indenture covers all bonds of the same type. For example, one indenture will cover a firm's first mortgage bonds, another its debentures, and a third its convertible bonds.

Mortgage Bonds   Under a **mortgage bond,** the corporation pledges certain assets as security for the bond. To illustrate, in 2007 Billingham Corporation needed $10 million to build a major regional distribution center. Bonds in the amount of $4 million, secured by a *first mortgage* on the property, were issued. (The remaining $6 million was financed with equity capital.) If Billingham defaults on the bonds, the bondholders can foreclose on the property and sell it to satisfy their claims.

If Billingham were to choose, it could issue *second mortgage bonds* secured by the same $10 million of assets. In the event of liquidation, the holders of these second mortgage bonds would have a claim against the property, but only after the first mortgage bondholders had been paid off in full. Thus, second mortgages are sometimes called *junior mortgages,* because they are junior in priority to the claims of *senior mortgages,* or *first mortgage bonds.*

All mortgage bonds are subject to an indenture. The amount of new bonds that can be issued is virtually always limited to a specified percentage of the firm's total "bondable property," which generally includes all land, plant, and equipment.

Debentures and Subordinated Debentures   A **debenture** is an unsecured bond, and as such it provides no lien against specific property as security for the obligation. Debenture holders are, therefore, general creditors whose claims are protected by property not otherwise pledged. In practice, the use of debentures depends both on the nature of the firm's assets and on its general credit strength. Extremely strong companies often use debentures; they simply do not need to put up property as security for their debt. Debentures are also issued by weak companies that have already pledged most of their assets as collateral for mortgage loans. In this latter case, the debentures are quite risky, and they will bear a high interest rate.

The term *subordinate* means "below," or "inferior to," and, in the event of bankruptcy, subordinated debt has claims on assets only after senior debt has been paid off. **Subordinated debentures** may be subordinated either to designated notes payable (usually bank loans) or to all other debt. In the event of liquidation or reorganization, holders of subordinated debentures cannot be paid until all senior debt, as named in the debentures' indentures, has been paid.

Table 5-1
───

Moody's and S&P Bond Ratings

	Investment Grade				Junk Bonds			
Moody's	Aaa	Aa	A	Baa	Ba	B	Caa	C
S&P	AAA	AA	A	BBB	BB	B	CCC	D

Note: Both Moody's and S&P use "modifiers" for bonds rated below triple-A. S&P uses a plus and minus system; thus, A+ designates the strongest A-rated bonds and A− the weakest. Moody's uses a 1, 2, or 3 designation, with 1 denoting the strongest and 3 the weakest; thus, within the double-A category, Aa1 is the best, Aa2 is average, and Aa3 is the weakest.

Development Bonds   Some companies may be in a position to benefit from the sale of either **development bonds** or **pollution control bonds.** State and local governments may set up both *industrial development agencies* and *pollution control agencies.* These agencies are allowed, under certain circumstances, to sell **tax-exempt bonds,** then to make the proceeds available to corporations for specific uses deemed (by Congress) to be in the public interest. Thus, an industrial development agency in Florida might sell bonds to provide funds for a paper company to build a plant in the Florida Panhandle, where unemployment is high. Similarly, a Detroit pollution control agency might sell bonds to provide Ford with funds to be used to purchase pollution control equipment. In both cases, the income from the bonds would be tax exempt to the holders, so the bonds would sell at relatively low interest rates. Note, however, that these bonds are guaranteed by the corporation that will use the funds, not by a governmental unit, so their rating reflects the credit strength of the corporation using the funds.

Municipal Bond Insurance   Municipalities can have their bonds insured, which means that an insurance company guarantees to pay the coupon and principal payments should the issuer default. This reduces risk to investors, who will thus accept a lower coupon rate for an insured bond vis-à-vis an uninsured one. Even though the municipality must pay a fee to get its bonds insured, its savings due to the lower coupon rate often make insurance cost effective. Keep in mind that the insurers are private companies, and the value added by the insurance depends on the creditworthiness of the insurer. However, the larger ones are strong companies, and their own ratings are AAA. Therefore, the bonds they insure are also rated AAA, regardless of the credit strength of the municipal issuer. Bond ratings are discussed in the next section.

Bond Ratings

Since the early 1900s, bonds have been assigned quality ratings that reflect their probability of going into default. The three major rating agencies are Moody's Investors Service (Moody's), Standard & Poor's Corporation (S&P), and Fitch Investors Service. Moody's and S&P's rating designations are shown in Table 5-1.[14] The triple- and double-A bonds are extremely safe. Single-A and triple-B bonds are also strong enough to be called **investment grade bonds,** and they are the

---

[14]In the discussion to follow, reference to the S&P code is intended to imply the Moody's and Fitch's codes as well. Thus, triple-B bonds mean both BBB and Baa bonds; double-B bonds mean both BB and Ba bonds; and so on.

lowest-rated bonds that many banks and other institutional investors are permitted by law to hold. Double-B and lower bonds are speculative, or **junk bonds.** These bonds have a significant probability of going into default. A later section discusses junk bonds in more detail.

Bond ratings are based on both qualitative and quantitative factors, some of which are listed below:

1. *Various ratios,* including the debt ratio, the times-interest-earned ratio, and the EBITDA coverage ratio. The better the ratios, the higher the rating.
2. *Mortgage provisions:* Is the bond secured by a mortgage? If it is, and if the property has a high value in relation to the amount of bonded debt, the bond's rating is enhanced.
3. *Subordination provisions:* Is the bond subordinated to other debt? If so, it will be rated at least one notch below the rating it would have if it were not subordinated. Conversely, a bond with other debt subordinated to it will have a somewhat higher rating.
4. *Guarantee provisions:* Some bonds are guaranteed by other firms. If a weak company's debt is guaranteed by a strong company (usually the weak company's parent), the bond will be given the strong company's rating.
5. *Sinking fund:* Does the bond have a sinking fund to ensure systematic repayment? This feature is a plus factor to the rating agencies.
6. *Maturity:* Other characteristics the same, a bond with a shorter maturity will be judged less risky than a longer-term bond, and this will be reflected in the ratings.
7. *Stability:* Are the issuer's sales and earnings stable?
8. *Regulation:* Is the issuer regulated, and could an adverse regulatory climate cause the company's economic position to decline? Regulation is especially important for utilities and telephone companies.
9. *Antitrust:* Are any antitrust actions pending against the firm that could erode its position?
10. *Overseas operations:* What percentage of the firm's sales, assets, and profits are from overseas operations, and what is the political climate in the host countries?
11. *Environmental factors:* Is the firm likely to face heavy expenditures for pollution control equipment?
12. *Product liability:* Are the firm's products safe? The tobacco companies today are under pressure, and so are their bond ratings.
13. *Pension liabilities:* Does the firm have unfunded pension liabilities that could pose a future problem?
14. *Labor unrest:* Are there potential labor problems on the horizon that could weaken the firm's position? As this is written, a number of airlines face this problem, and it has caused their ratings to be lowered.
15. *Accounting policies:* If a firm uses relatively conservative accounting policies, its reported earnings will be of "higher quality" than if it uses less conservative procedures. Thus, conservative accounting policies are a plus factor in bond ratings.

Representatives of the rating agencies have consistently stated that no precise formula is used to set a firm's rating; all the factors listed, plus others, are taken into account, but not in a mathematically precise manner. Nevertheless, as we see in Table 5-2, there is a strong correlation between bond ratings and many of the ratios

Table 5-2

Bond Rating Criteria: Median Financial Ratios for Different Bond Rating Classifications

Ratios	AAA	AA	A	BBB	BB	B	CCC
EBIT interest coverage (EBIT/Interest)	23.83	13.63	6.93	4.23	2.33	0.93	0.43
EBITDA interest coverage (EBITDA/Interest)	25.33	17.13	9.43	5.93	3.13	1.63	0.93
Funds from operations/Total debt	167.8%	77.5%	43.2%	34.6%	20.0%	10.1%	2.9%
Free operating cash flow/Total debt	104.1%	41.1%	25.4%	16.9%	7.9%	2.6%	20.9%
Total debt/EBITDA	0.23	1.13	1.73	2.43	3.83	5.63	7.43
Return on capital	35.1%	26.9%	16.8%	13.4%	10.3%	6.7%	2.3%
Total debt/Total capital	6.23%	34.83%	39.83%	45.63%	57.23%	74.23%	101.23%

Source: Standard & Poor's 2004 Corporate Ratings Criteria, October 28, 2004. For ratio definitions and updates, go to **http://www. standardandpoors.com;** select Credit Ratings, then Industrials (under Browse By Sector), then Criteria and Definitions, then the Corporate Criteria Book. Scroll down until you come to the Ratings and Ratios; Ratio Medians; Ratio Guidelines link. The ratios require a free registration.

described in Chapter 4. Not surprisingly, companies with lower debt ratios, higher cash flow to debt, higher returns on capital, higher EBITDA interest coverage ratios, and EBIT interest coverage ratios typically have higher bond ratings.

Bond Ratings and the Default Risk Premium

Bond ratings are important both to firms and to investors. First, most bonds are purchased by institutional investors rather than individuals, and many institutions are restricted to investment-grade securities. Thus, if a firm's bonds fall below BBB, it will have a difficult time selling new bonds because many potential purchasers will not be allowed to buy them. Second, many bond covenants stipulate that the coupon rate on the bond automatically increases if the rating falls below a specified level. Third, because a bond's rating is an indicator of its default risk, the rating has a direct, measurable influence on the bond's yield. A **bond spread** is the difference between a bond's yield and the yield on some other security of the same maturity, as shown in Table 5-3. Unless specified differently, the term "spread" generally means the difference between a bond's yield and the yield on a similar maturity Treasury bond.

Notice in Column (1) of Table 5-3 that yields increase monotonically as ratings become lower. In other words, investors demand higher required rates of return, r_d, as risk increases. Column (2) shows the spread of each bond's yield above that of the U.S. Treasury bond. Notice the AAA spread is about 1.01% above a T-bond. The two bonds are very similar except with respect to default risk and liquidity (which we discuss in the next section). Because AAA bonds often have good liquidity, this spread is a pretty good estimate of the default risk premium for AAA bonds. Even though lower-rated bonds usually have less liquidity (and therefore higher liquidity premiums), the spread between a bond and a Treasury bond of a similar maturity is often used as an approximation of the default risk premium for the bond. Therefore, it would be reasonable to estimate the default risk premium for a BBB bond as about 1.35%.

For updates, find the yields for AAA, AA, and A bonds at **http://finance.yahoo.com/bonds/composite_bond_rates.** Representative yields for BBB, BB, B, and CCC bonds can be found using the bond screener at **http://screen .yahoo .com/bonds.html.** Also, Vanguard has a table of yields for selected bonds at **http://flagship2 .vanguard.com/VGApp/ hnw/FundsBondsMarket SummaryTable.**

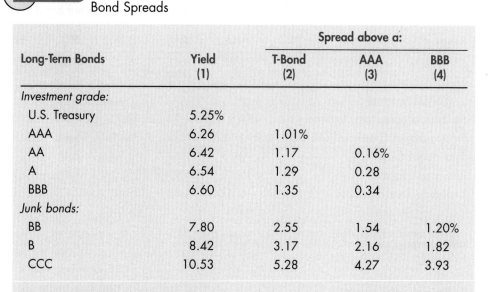

Table 5-3				
Bond Spreads				
			Spread above a:	
Long-Term Bonds	**Yield (1)**	**T-Bond (2)**	**AAA (3)**	**BBB (4)**
Investment grade:				
U.S. Treasury	5.25%			
AAA	6.26	1.01%		
AA	6.42	1.17	0.16%	
A	6.54	1.29	0.28	
BBB	6.60	1.35	0.34	
Junk bonds:				
BB	7.80	2.55	1.54	1.20%
B	8.42	3.17	2.16	1.82
CCC	10.53	5.28	4.27	3.93

Source Adapted from Yahoo!, June 23, 2006.

Note: The spreads in Column (2) are found by taking the yields in Column (1) and subtracting the yield on the U.S. Treasury bond. The spreads in Column (3) are found by taking the yields in Column (1) and subtracting the yield on the AAA bond. The spreads in Column (4) are found by taking the yields in Column (1) and subtracting the yield on the BBB bond.

Just as we talk about the spread of a bond relative to a T-bond, we can also talk about the spread between any two corporate bonds. For example, Column (3) shows the spreads above a AAA bond and Column (4) shows the spreads above a BBB bond. Notice that spreads increase dramatically for junk bonds, which reflects their risk and the fact that institutional investors are not allowed to hold junk bonds.

Not only do spreads vary with the rating of the security, but they vary with respect to maturity. For example, a 5-year AAA bond had a spread of only 0.55% while the 20-year AAA bond in Table 5-3 had a spread of 1.01%. As this illustrates, spreads increase as maturity increases. This should make sense. If a bond matures soon, investors are able to forecast the company's performance fairly well. But if a bond has a long time until it matures, investors have a difficult time forecasting the likelihood that the company will fall into financial distress, so investors demand a higher required return.

Spreads also vary over time. As shown in Column (2), the spread of a AAA bond was about 1.01% in June 2006. This is close to the historical average of about 1%. But at times the spread has fallen to 0.20% and at times it has risen to 2.06%. As explained in Chapter 1, investors are risk averse, and their risk aversion can change over time. As investors become more risk averse, spreads increase. For example, spreads were quite large after the 9/11/2001 terrorist attacks. In contrast, spreads were quite narrow in the early 1990s as the U.S. economy was beginning a long period of growth.

As you might expect, changes in a firm's bond rating affect the default risk premium on its debt and the ability of the firm to borrow long-term capital. Rating agencies review outstanding bonds on a periodic basis, occasionally upgrading or downgrading a bond as a result of its issuer's changed circumstances. For example,

See the Standard & Poor's Web site, **http://www .standardandpoors.com,** or the Moody's, Web site, **http://www.moodys .com,** for updates on changes in ratings.

Verizon Wireless's long-term debt was upgraded to an A2 by Moody's in June 2006. Moody's stated that the reason was strong operating results and growing cash flows.

Ratings agencies generally do a good job of measuring the average credit risk of bonds, and they do their best to change ratings whenever they perceive a change in credit quality. At the same time, it is important to understand that ratings do not adjust immediately to changes in credit quality, and in some cases there can be a considerable lag between a change in credit quality and a change in rating. For example, the rating agencies were caught off guard by Enron's rapid decline. Enron declared bankruptcy on a Sunday in December 2001, and the preceding Friday its bonds still carried an investment-grade rating.

SELF-TEST

Differentiate between mortgage bonds and debentures.
Name the major rating agencies, and list some factors that affect bond ratings.
What is a bond spread?
How do bond ratings affect the default risk premium?
A 10-year T-bond has a yield of 6%. A corporate bond with a rating of AA has a yield of 4.5%. If the corporate bond has excellent liquidity, what is an estimate of the corporate bond's default risk premium? (1.5%)

5.12 The Liquidity Premium (LP)

A "liquid" asset can be converted to cash quickly and at a "fair market value." Financial assets are generally more liquid than real assets. Because liquidity is important, investors include **liquidity premiums (LPs)** when market rates of securities are established. Although it is difficult to accurately measure liquidity premiums, a differential of at least two and probably four or five percentage points exists between the least liquid and the most liquid financial assets of similar default risk and maturity. Corporate bonds issued by small companies are traded less frequently than those issued by large companies, so small company bonds tend to have a higher liquidity premium.

SELF-TEST

Which bond usually will have a higher liquidity premium, one issued by a large company or one issued by a small company?

5.13 The Maturity Risk Premium (MRP)

All bonds, even Treasury bonds, are exposed to two additional sources of risk: interest rate risk and reinvestment risk. The net effect of these two sources of risk upon a bond's yield is called the **maturity risk premium, MRP.** The following sections explain how interest rate risk and reinvestment risk affect a bond's yield.

Interest Rate Risk

Interest rates go up and down over time, and an increase in interest rates leads to a decline in the value of outstanding bonds. This risk of a decline in bond values due to rising interest rates is called **interest rate risk.** To illustrate, suppose you bought some 10% MicroDrive bonds at a price of $1,000, and interest rates in the following year rose to 15%. As we saw earlier, the price of the bonds would fall to

e-resource

For more on bond risk, including duration analysis, see **Web Extension 5C** at the textbook's Web site.

$713.78, so you would have a loss of $286.22 per bond.[15] Interest rates can and do rise, and rising rates cause a loss of value for bondholders. Thus, people or firms who invest in bonds are exposed to risk from changing interest rates.

One's exposure to interest rate risk is higher on bonds with long maturities than on those maturing in the near future.[16] This point can be demonstrated by showing how the value of a 1-year bond with a 10% annual coupon fluctuates with changes in r_d, and then comparing these changes with those on a 25-year bond. The 1-year bond's value for $r_d = 5\%$ is shown below:

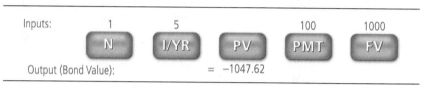

Using either a calculator or a spreadsheet, you could calculate the bond values for a 1-year and 25-year bond at several current market interest rates; these results are summarized and plotted in Figure 5-3. Note how much more sensitive the price of the 25-year bond is to changes in interest rates. At a 10% interest rate, both the 25-year and the 1-year bonds are valued at $1,000. When rates rise to 15%, the 25-year bond falls to $676.79, but the 1-year bond falls only to $956.52.

For bonds with similar coupons, this differential sensitivity to changes in interest rates always holds true—the longer the maturity of the bond, the more its price changes in response to a given change in interest rates. Thus, even if the risk of default on two bonds is exactly the same, the one with the longer maturity is exposed to more risk from a rise in interest rates.

The explanation for this difference in interest rate risk is simple. Suppose you bought a 25-year bond that yielded 10%, or $100 a year. Now suppose interest rates on comparable-risk bonds rose to 15%. You would be stuck with only $100 of interest for the next 25 years. On the other hand, had you bought a 1-year bond, you would have a low return for only 1 year. At the end of the year, you would get your $1,000 back, and you could then reinvest it and receive a 15% return ($150) for the next year. Thus, interest rate risk reflects the length of time one is committed to a given investment.

Reinvestment Rate Risk

As we saw in the preceding section, an *increase* in interest rates will hurt bondholders because it will lead to a decline in the value of a bond portfolio. But can a *decrease* in interest rates also hurt bondholders? The answer is yes, because if interest rates fall, a bondholder will probably suffer a reduction in his or her income. For example, consider a retiree who has a portfolio of bonds and lives off the income they produce. The bonds, on average, have a coupon rate of 10%. Now

---

[15]You would have an *accounting* (and tax) loss only if you sold the bond; if you held it to maturity, you would not have such a loss. However, even if you did not sell, you would still have suffered a *real economic loss in an opportunity cost sense* because you would have lost the opportunity to invest at 15% and would be stuck with a 10% bond in a 15% market. In an economic sense, "paper losses" are just as bad as realized accounting losses.

[16]Actually, a bond's maturity and coupon rate both affect interest rate risk. Low coupons mean that most of the bond's return will come from repayment of principal, whereas on a high coupon bond with the same maturity, more of the cash flows will come in during the early years due to the relatively large coupon payments. A measurement called "duration," which finds the average number of years the bond's PV of cash flows remains outstanding, has been developed to combine maturity and coupons. A zero coupon bond, which has no interest payments and whose payments all come at maturity, has a duration equal to the bond's maturity. Coupon bonds all have durations that are shorter than maturity, and the higher the coupon rate, the shorter the duration. Bonds with longer duration are exposed to more interest rate risk. *Excel's* DURATION function provides an easy way to calculate a bond's duration. See **Web Extension 5C** and **FM12 Ch 05 Tool Kit.xls** for more on duration.

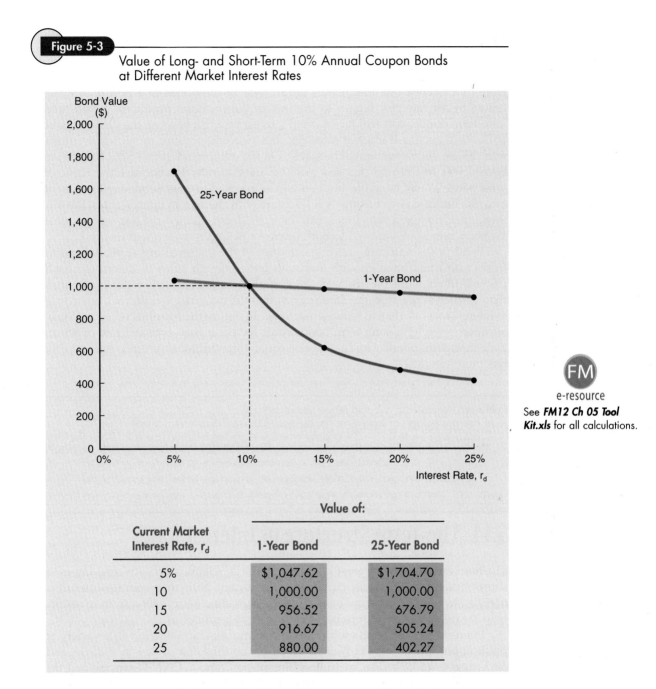

Figure 5-3

Value of Long- and Short-Term 10% Annual Coupon Bonds at Different Market Interest Rates

	Value of:	
Current Market Interest Rate, r_d	1-Year Bond	25-Year Bond
5%	$1,047.62	$1,704.70
10	1,000.00	1,000.00
15	956.52	676.79
20	916.67	505.24
25	880.00	402.27

FM

e-resource

See **FM12 Ch 05 Tool Kit.xls** for all calculations.

suppose interest rates decline to 5%. Many of the bonds will be called, and as calls occur, the bondholder will have to replace 10% bonds with 5% bonds. Even bonds that are not callable will mature, and when they do, they will have to be replaced with lower-yielding bonds. Thus, our retiree will suffer a reduction of income.

The risk of an income decline due to a drop in interest rates is called **reinvestment rate risk.** Reinvestment rate risk is obviously high on callable bonds. It is also high on short maturity bonds, because the shorter the maturity of a bond, the fewer the years when the relatively high old interest rate will be earned, and the sooner the funds will have to be reinvested at the new low rate. Thus, retirees whose primary holdings are short-term securities, such as bank CDs and short-term bonds, are hurt badly by a decline in rates, but holders of long-term bonds continue to enjoy their old high rates.

Comparing Interest Rate and Reinvestment Rate Risk: The Maturity Risk Premium

Note that interest rate risk relates to the *value* of the bonds in a portfolio, while reinvestment rate risk relates to the *income* the portfolio produces. If you hold long-term bonds, you will face a lot of interest rate risk because the value of your bonds will decline if interest rates rise, but you will not face much reinvestment rate risk, so your income will be stable. On the other hand, if you hold short-term bonds, you will not be exposed to much interest rate risk because the value of your portfolio will be stable, but you will be exposed to considerable reinvestment rate risk because your income will fluctuate with changes in interest rates. We see, then, that no fixed-rate bond can be considered totally riskless—even most Treasury bonds are exposed to both interest rate and reinvestment rate risk.[17]

Bond prices reflect the trading activities of the marginal investors, defined as those who trade often enough and with large enough sums to determine bond prices. Although one particular investor might be more averse to reinvestment risk than to interest rate risk, the data suggest that the marginal investor is more averse to interest rate risk than to reinvestment risk. To induce the marginal investor to take on interest rate risk, long-term bonds must have a higher expected rate of return than short-term bonds. Holding all else equal, this additional return is the maturity risk premium (MRP).

SELF-TEST   Differentiate between interest rate risk and reinvestment rate risk.
To which type of risk are holders of long-term bonds more exposed? Short-term bondholders?
Assume that the real risk-free rate is r* = 3% and the average expected inflation rate is 2.5% for the fore-seeable future. The DRP and LP for a bond are each 1%, and the applicable MRP is 2%. What is the bond's yield? (9.5%)

5.14 The Term Structure of Interest Rates

The **term structure of interest rates** describes the relationship between long- and short-term rates. The term structure is important both to corporate treasurers deciding whether to borrow by issuing long- or short-term debt and to investors who are deciding whether to buy long- or short-term bonds.

Interest rates for bonds with different maturities can be found in a variety of publications, including *The Wall Street Journal* and the *Federal Reserve Bulletin*, and on a number of Web sites, including Bloomberg, Yahoo!, CNN Financial, and the Federal Reserve Board. Using interest rate data from these sources, we can determine the term structure at any given point in time. For example, the tabular section below Figure 5-4 presents interest rates for different maturities on three different dates. The set of data for a given date, when plotted on a graph such as Figure 5-4, is called the **yield curve** for that date.

As the figure shows, the yield curve changes both in position and in slope over time. In March 1980, all rates were quite high because high inflation was expected. However, the rate of inflation was expected to decline, so the inflation premium (IP) was larger for short-term bonds than for long-term bonds. This caused short-

---

[17]Note, though, that indexed Treasury bonds are almost riskless, but they pay a relatively low real rate. Also, risks have not disappeared—they are simply transferred from bondholders to taxpayers.

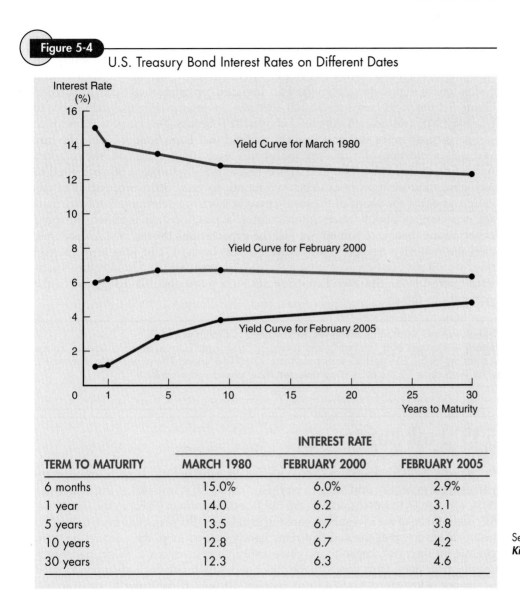

Figure 5-4

U.S. Treasury Bond Interest Rates on Different Dates

| | INTEREST RATE | | |
TERM TO MATURITY	MARCH 1980	FEBRUARY 2000	FEBRUARY 2005
6 months	15.0%	6.0%	2.9%
1 year	14.0	6.2	3.1
5 years	13.5	6.7	3.8
10 years	12.8	6.7	4.2
30 years	12.3	6.3	4.6

e-resource
See *FM12 Ch 05 Tool Kit.xls* for all calculations.

term yields to be higher than long-term yields, resulting in a *downward-sloping* yield curve. By February 2000, inflation had indeed declined and thus all rates were lower. The yield curve had become **humped**—medium-term rates were higher than either short- or long-term rates. By February 2005, all rates had fallen below the 2000 levels, and because short-term rates had dropped below long-term rates, the yield curve was *upward sloping*. As we write this in June 2006, the term structure was virtually flat at about 5.2%.

Figure 5-4 shows yield curves for U.S. Treasury securities, but we could have constructed curves for bonds issued by GE, IBM, Delta Airlines, or any other company that borrows money over a range of maturities. Had we constructed such corporate yield curves and plotted them on Figure 5-4, they would have been above those for Treasury securities because corporate yields include default risk premiums and somewhat higher liquidity premiums than Treasury bonds. However, the corporate yield curves would have had the same general shape as the Treasury curves. Also, the riskier the corporation, the higher its yield curve, so Delta, which is in bankruptcy, would have a higher yield curve than GE or IBM.

Historically, long-term rates are generally above short-term rates because of the maturity risk premium, so the yield curve usually slopes upward. For this reason, people often call an upward-sloping yield curve a **"normal" yield curve** and a yield curve that slopes downward an **inverted**, or **"abnormal" curve.** Thus, in Figure 5-4 the yield curve for March 1980 was inverted, while the yield curve in February 2005 was normal. As stated above, the February 2000 curve was humped.

A few academics and practitioners contend that large bond traders who buy and sell securities of different maturities each day dominate the market. According to this view, a bond trader is just as willing to buy a 30-year bond to pick up a short-term profit as to buy a 3-month security. Strict proponents of this view argue that the shape of the yield curve is therefore determined only by market expectations about future interest rates, a position that is called the **pure expectations theory,** or sometimes just the **expectations theory.** If this were true, then the maturity risk premium (MRP) would be zero, and long-term interest rates would simply be a weighted average of current and expected future short-term interest rates. See *Web Extension 5D* for a more detailed discussion of the expectations theory.

FM
e-resource

Go to the textbook's Web site for a discussion of the expectations theory in *Web Extension 5D.*

SELF-TEST

What is a yield curve, and what information would you need to draw this curve?
Distinguish among the shapes of a "normal" yield curve, an "abnormal" curve, and a "humped" curve.
If the interest rates on 1-, 5-, 20-, and 30-year bonds are 4%, 5%, 6%, and 7%, respectively, how would you describe the yield curve? If the rates were reversed, how would you describe it?

5.15 Junk Bonds

Prior to the 1980s, fixed-income investors such as pension funds and insurance companies were generally unwilling to buy risky bonds, so it was almost impossible for risky companies to raise capital in the public bond markets. Then, in the late 1970s, Michael Milken of the investment banking firm Drexel Burnham Lambert, relying on historical studies that showed that risky bonds yielded more than enough to compensate for their risk, began to convince institutional investors of the merits of purchasing risky debt. Thus was born the junk bond, a high-risk, high-yield bond issued to finance a leveraged buyout, a merger, or a troubled company.[18] For example, Public Service of New Hampshire financed construction of its troubled Seabrook nuclear plant with junk bonds, and junk bonds were used by Ted Turner to finance the development of CNN and Turner Broadcasting. In junk bond deals, the debt ratio is generally extremely high, so the bondholders must bear as much risk as stockholders normally would. The bonds' yields reflect this fact—a promised return of 25% per annum was required to sell some Public Service of New Hampshire bonds.

The emergence of junk bonds as an important type of debt is another example of how the investment banking industry adjusts to and facilitates new developments in capital markets. In the 1980s, mergers and takeovers increased dramatically. People like T. Boone Pickens and Henry Kravis thought that certain old-line, established companies were run inefficiently and were financed too conservatively, and they wanted to take these companies over and restructure them. Michael Milken and his staff at Drexel Burnham Lambert began an active campaign to persuade certain institutions (often S&Ls) to purchase high-yield bonds. Milken

---

[18]Another type of junk bond is one that was highly rated when it was issued but whose rating has fallen because the issuing corporation has fallen on hard times. Such bonds are called "fallen angels."

developed expertise in putting together deals that were attractive to the institutions yet feasible in the sense that projected cash flows were sufficient to meet the required interest payments. The fact that interest on the bonds was tax deductible, combined with the much higher debt ratios of the restructured firms, also increased after-tax cash flows and helped make the deals feasible.

The development of junk bond financing has done much to reshape the U.S. financial scene. The existence of these securities contributed to the loss of independence of Gulf Oil and hundreds of other companies, and it led to major shake-ups in such companies as CBS, Union Carbide, and USX (formerly U.S. Steel). It also caused Drexel Burnham Lambert to leap from essentially nowhere in the 1970s to become the most profitable investment banking firm during the 1980s.

The phenomenal growth of the junk bond market was impressive, but controversial. In 1989, Drexel Burnham Lambert was forced into bankruptcy, and "junk bond king" Michael Milken, who had earned $500 million 2 years earlier, was sent to jail. Those events led to the collapse of the junk bond market in the early 1990s. Since then, however, the junk bond market has rebounded, and junk bonds are here to stay as an important form of corporate financing for many companies.

SELF-TEST

What are junk bonds?

5.16 Bankruptcy and Reorganization

During recessions, bankruptcies normally rise, and recent recessions are no exception. The 2001 recession claimed WorldCom, Enron, Conseco, Global Crossing, United Airlines, Adelphia Communications, Pacific Gas and Electric, Kmart, and the FINOVA Group. The total assets of these companies, prior to filing for bankruptcy, were about $355 billion! The recessions didn't end in 2001, with some giant companies, such as Delta Airlines, recently filing for bankruptcy. A brief discussion of bankruptcy follows, while a more detailed discussion appears in Chapter 24.

When a business becomes *insolvent*, it does not have enough cash to meet its interest and principal payments. A decision must then be made whether to dissolve the firm through *liquidation* or to permit it to *reorganize* and thus stay alive. These issues are addressed in Chapters 7 and 11 of the federal bankruptcy statutes, and the final decision is made by a federal bankruptcy court judge.

The decision to force a firm to liquidate versus permit it to reorganize depends on whether the value of the reorganized firm is likely to be greater than the value of the firm's assets if they are sold off piecemeal. In a reorganization, the firm's creditors negotiate with management on the terms of a potential reorganization. The reorganization plan may call for a *restructuring* of the firm's debt, in which case the interest rate may be reduced, the term to maturity lengthened, or some of the debt may be exchanged for equity. The point of the restructuring is to reduce the financial charges to a level that the firm's cash flows can support. Of course, the common stockholders also have to give up something—they often see their position diluted as a result of additional shares being given to debtholders in exchange for accepting a reduced amount of debt principal and interest. In fact, the original common stockholders often end up with nothing. A trustee may be appointed by the court to oversee the reorganization, but generally the existing management is allowed to retain control.

Liquidation occurs if the company is deemed to be too far gone to be saved— if it is worth more dead than alive. If the bankruptcy court orders a liquidation, assets are sold off and the cash obtained is distributed as specified in Chapter 7 of the Bankruptcy Act. Here is the priority of claims:

1. Past-due property taxes.
2. Secured creditors are entitled to the proceeds from the sale of the specific property that was used to support their loans.
3. The trustee's costs of administering and operating the bankrupt firm are next in line.
4. Expenses incurred after bankruptcy was filed come next.
5. Wages due workers, up to a limit of $2,000 per worker, follow.
6. Claims for unpaid contributions to employee benefit plans are next. This amount, together with wages, cannot exceed $2,000 per worker.
7. Unsecured claims for customer deposits up to $900 per customer are next.
8. Federal, state, and local taxes due come next.
9. Unfunded pension plan liabilities are next although some limitations exist.
10. General unsecured creditors are tenth on the list.
11. Preferred stockholders come next, up to the par value of their stock.
12. Common stockholders are finally paid, if anything is left, which is rare.

The key points for you to know are (1) the federal bankruptcy statutes govern both reorganization and liquidation, (2) bankruptcies occur frequently, and (3) a priority of the specified claims must be followed when distributing the assets of a liquidated firm.

SELF-TEST ──
Differentiate between a Chapter 7 liquidation and a Chapter 11 reorganization.
List the priority of claims for the distribution of a liquidated firm's assets.

Summary

This chapter described the different types of bonds governments and corporations issue, explained how bond prices are established, and discussed how investors estimate the rates of return they can expect to earn. We also discussed the various types of risks that investors face when they buy bonds. The key concepts covered are summarized below.

- A **bond** is a long-term promissory note issued by a business or governmental unit. The issuer receives money in exchange for promising to make interest payments and to repay the principal on a specified future date.
- Some recent innovations in long-term financing include **zero coupon bonds**, which pay no annual interest, but are issued at a discount; **floating-rate debt**, whose interest payments fluctuate with changes in the general level of interest rates; and **junk bonds**, which are high-risk, high-yield instruments issued by firms that use a great deal of financial leverage.
- A **call provision** gives the issuing corporation the right to redeem the bonds prior to maturity under specified terms, usually at a price greater than the maturity value (the difference is a **call premium**). A firm will typically call a bond if interest rates fall substantially below the coupon rate.
- A **redeemable bond** gives the investor the right to sell the bond back to the issuing company at a previously specified price. This is a useful feature (for investors) if interest rates rise or if the company engages in unanticipated risky activities.

- A **sinking fund** is a provision that requires the corporation to retire a portion of the bond issue each year. The purpose of the sinking fund is to provide for the orderly retirement of the issue. A sinking fund typically requires no call premium.

- There are many different types of bonds with different sets of features. These include **convertible bonds, bonds with warrants, income bonds, purchasing power (indexed) bonds, mortgage bonds, debentures, subordinated debentures, junk bonds, development bonds,** and **insured municipal bonds**. The return required on each type of bond is determined by the bond's riskiness.

- The **value of a bond** is found as the present value of an **annuity** (the interest payments) plus the present value of a lump sum (the **principal**). The bond is evaluated at the appropriate periodic interest rate over the number of periods for which interest payments are made.

- The equation used to find the value of an annual coupon bond is

$$V_B = \sum_{t=1}^{N} \frac{INT}{(1 + r_d)^t} + \frac{M}{(1 + r_d)^N}.$$

- An adjustment to the formula must be made if the bond pays interest **semi-annually:** divide INT and r_d by 2, and multiply N by 2.

- The return earned on a bond held to maturity is defined as the bond's **yield to maturity (YTM)**. If the bond can be redeemed before maturity, it is **callable**, and the return investors receive if it is called is defined as the **yield to call (YTC)**. The YTC is found as the present value of the interest payments received while the bond is outstanding plus the present value of the call price (the par value plus a call premium).

- The **nominal** (or **quoted**) **interest rate** on a debt security, r_d, is composed of the real risk-free rate, r*, plus premiums that reflect inflation (IP), default risk (DRP), liquidity (LP), and maturity risk (MRP):

$$r_d = r^* + IP + DRP + LP + MRP.$$

- The **risk-free rate of interest, r_{RF},** is defined as the real risk-free rate, r*, plus an inflation premium, IP: $r_{RF} = r^* + IP$.

- The longer the maturity of a bond, the more its price will change in response to a given change in interest rates; this is called **interest rate risk**. However, bonds with short maturities expose investors to high **reinvestment rate risk**, which is the risk that income from a bond portfolio will decline because cash flows received from bonds will be rolled over at lower interest rates.

- Corporate and municipal bonds have **default risk**. If an issuer defaults, investors receive less than the promised return on the bond. Therefore, investors should evaluate a bond's default risk before making a purchase.

- Bonds are assigned **ratings** that reflect the probability of their going into default. The highest rating is AAA, and they go down to D. The higher a bond's rating, the lower its risk and therefore its interest rate.

- The relationship between the yields on securities and the securities' maturities is known as the **term structure of interest rates**, and the **yield curve** is a graph of this relationship.

- The shape of the yield curve depends on two key factors: (1) **expectations about future inflation** and (2) **perceptions about the relative risk of securities with different maturities**.

- The yield curve is normally **upward sloping**—this is called a **normal yield curve**. However, the curve can slope downward (an **inverted yield curve**) if the inflation rate is expected to decline. The yield curve also can be **humped,** which means that interest rates on medium-term maturities are higher than rates on both short- and long-term maturities.

Questions

(5-1)   Define each of the following terms:
a.   Bond; Treasury bond; corporate bond; municipal bond; foreign bond
b.   Par value; maturity date; coupon payment; coupon interest rate
c.   Floating-rate bond; zero coupon bond; original issue discount bond (OID)
d.   Call provision; redeemable bond; sinking fund
e.   Convertible bond; warrant; income bond; indexed, or purchasing power, bond
f.   Premium bond; discount bond
g.   Current yield (on a bond); yield to maturity (YTM); yield to call (YTC)
h.   Reinvestment risk; interest rate risk; default risk
i.   Indentures; mortgage bond; debenture; subordinated debenture
j.   Development bond; municipal bond insurance; junk bond; investment-grade bond
k.   Real risk-free rate of interest, r^*; nominal risk-free rate of interest, r_{RF}
l.   Inflation premium (IP); default risk premium (DRP); liquidity; liquidity premium (LP)
m.   Interest rate risk; maturity risk premium (MRP); reinvestment rate risk
n.   Term structure of interest rates; yield curve
o.   "Normal" yield curve; inverted ("abnormal") yield curve

(5-2)   "The values of outstanding bonds change whenever the going rate of interest changes. In general, short-term interest rates are more volatile than long-term interest rates. Therefore, short-term bond prices are more sensitive to interest rate changes than are long-term bond prices." Is this statement true or false? Explain.

(5-3)   The rate of return you would get if you bought a bond and held it to its maturity date is called the bond's yield to maturity. If interest rates in the economy rise after a bond has been issued, what will happen to the bond's price and to its YTM? Does the length of time to maturity affect the extent to which a given change in interest rates will affect the bond's price?

(5-4)   If you buy a *callable* bond and interest rates decline, will the value of your bond rise by as much as it would have risen if the bond had not been callable? Explain.

(5-5)   A sinking fund can be set up in one of two ways:
(1)   The corporation makes annual payments to the trustee, who invests the proceeds in securities (frequently government bonds) and uses the accumulated total to retire the bond issue at maturity.
(2)   The trustee uses the annual payments to retire a portion of the issue each year, either calling a given percentage of the issue by a lottery and paying a specified price per bond or buying bonds on the open market, whichever is cheaper.

Discuss the advantages and disadvantages of each procedure from the viewpoint of both the firm and its bondholders.

Self-Test Problem   Solution Appears in Appendix A

(ST-1)
Bond Valuation

The Pennington Corporation issued a new series of bonds on January 1, 1984. The bonds were sold at par ($1,000), had a 12% coupon, and matured in 30 years, on December 31, 2013. Coupon payments are made semiannually (on June 30 and December 31).

a.   What was the YTM on January 1, 1984?

b.   What was the price of the bonds on January 1, 1989, 5 years later, assuming that interest rates had fallen to 10%?

c.   Find the current yield, capital gains yield, and total return on January 1, 1989, given the price as determined in part b.

d.   On July 1, 2007, 5½ years before maturity, Pennington's bonds sold for $916.42. What were the YTM, the current yield, the capital gains yield, and the total return at that time?

e.   Now, assume that you plan to purchase an outstanding Pennington bond on March 1, 2007, when the going rate of interest given its risk is 15.5%. How large a check must you write to complete the transaction? This is a hard question.

Problems   Answers Appear in Appendix B

Easy Problems 1–6

(5-1)
Bond Valuation with
Annual Payments

Jackson Corporation's bonds have 12 years remaining to maturity. Interest is paid annually, the bonds have a $1,000 par value, and the coupon interest rate is 8%. The bonds have a yield to maturity of 9%. What is the current market price of these bonds?

(5-2)
Yield to Maturity for
Annual Payments

Wilson Wonders' bonds have 12 years remaining to maturity. Interest is paid annually, the bonds have a $1,000 par value, and the coupon interest rate is 10%. The bonds sell at a price of $850. What is their yield to maturity?

(5-3)
Current Yield for Annual
Payments

Heath Foods' bonds have 7 years remaining to maturity. The bonds have a face value of $1,000 and a yield to maturity of 8%. They pay interest annually and have a 9% coupon rate. What is their current yield?

(5-4)
Determinant of Interest
Rates

The real risk-free rate of interest is 4%. Inflation is expected to be 2% this year and 4% during the next 2 years. Assume that the maturity risk premium is zero. What is the yield on 2-year Treasury securities? What is the yield on 3-year Treasury securities?

(5-5)
Default Risk Premium

A Treasury bond that matures in 10 years has a yield of 6%. A 10-year corporate bond has a yield of 9%. Assume that the liquidity premium on the corporate bond is 0.5%. What is the default risk premium on the corporate bond?

(5-6)
Maturity Risk Premium

The real risk-free rate is 3%, and inflation is expected to be 3% for the next 2 years. A 2-year Treasury security yields 6.3%. What is the maturity risk premium for the 2-year security?

Intermediate
Problems 7–20

(5-7)
Bond Valuation with
Semiannual Payments

Renfro Rentals has issued bonds that have a 10% coupon rate, payable semiannually. The bonds mature in 8 years, have a face value of $1,000, and a yield to maturity of 8.5%. What is the price of the bonds?

(5-8)
Yield to Maturity and Call
with Semiannual
Payments

Thatcher Corporation's bonds will mature in 10 years. The bonds have a face value of $1,000 and an 8% coupon rate, paid semiannually. The price of the bonds is $1,100. The bonds are callable in 5 years at a call price of $1,050. What is their yield to maturity? What is their yield to call?

(5-9) ✓
Bond Valuation and
Interest Rate Risk

The Garraty Company has two bond issues outstanding. Both bonds pay $100 annual interest plus $1,000 at maturity. Bond L has a maturity of 15 years, and Bond S a maturity of 1 year.
a.   What will be the value of each of these bonds when the going rate of interest is (1) 5%, (2) 8%, and (3) 12%? Assume that there is only one more interest payment to be made on Bond S.
b.   Why does the longer-term (15-year) bond fluctuate more when interest rates change than does the shorter-term bond (1 year)?

(5-10) ✓
Yield to Maturity and
Required Returns

The Brownstone Corporation bonds have 5 years remaining to maturity. Interest is paid annually; the bonds have a $1,000 par value; and the coupon interest rate is 9%.
a.   What is the yield to maturity at a current market price of (1) $829 or (2) $1,104?
b.   Would you pay $829 for one of these bonds if you thought that the appropriate rate of interest was 12%—that is, if $r_d = 12\%$? Explain your answer.

(5-11)
Yield to Call and
Realized Rates of Return

Seven years ago, Goodwynn & Wolf Incorporated sold a 20-year bond issue with a 14% annual coupon rate and a 9% call premium. Today, G&W called the bonds. The bonds originally were sold at their face value of $1,000. Compute the realized rate of return for investors who purchased the bonds when they were issued and who surrender them today in exchange for the call price.

(5-12)
Bond Yields and
Rates of Return

A 10-year, 12% semiannual coupon bond with a par value of $1,000 may be called in 4 years at a call price of $1,060. The bond sells for $1,100. (Assume that the bond has just been issued.)
a.   What is the bond's yield to maturity?
b.   What is the bond's current yield?
c.   What is the bond's capital gain or loss yield?
d.   What is the bond's yield to call?

(5-13)
Yield to Maturity and
Current Yield

You just purchased a bond that matures in 5 years. The bond has a face value of $1,000 and has an 8% annual coupon. The bond has a current yield of 8.21%. What is the bond's yield to maturity?

(5-14)
Current Yield with
Semiannual Payments

A bond that matures in 7 years sells for $1,020. The bond has a face value of $1,000 and a yield to maturity of 10.5883%. The bond pays coupons semiannually. What is the bond's current yield?

(5-15)
Yield to Call, Yield to
Maturity, and
Market Rates

Absolom Motors' 14% coupon rate, semiannual payment, $1,000 par value bonds that mature in 30 years are callable 5 years from now at a price of $1,050. The bonds sell at a price of $1,353.54, and the yield curve is flat. Assuming that interest rates in the economy are expected to remain at their current level, what is the best estimate of the nominal interest rate on new bonds?

(5-16) ✓
Interest Rate Sensitivity

A bond trader purchased each of the following bonds at a yield to maturity of 8%. Immediately after she purchased the bonds, interest rates fell to 7%. What is the percentage change in the price of each bond after the decline in interest rates? Fill in the following table:

	Price @ 8%	Price @ 7%	Percentage Change
10-year, 10% annual coupon	_____	_____	_____
10-year zero	_____	_____	_____
30-year zero	_____	_____	_____
$100 perpetuity	_____	_____	_____

(5-17)
Bond Value as
Maturity Approaches

An investor has two bonds in his portfolio. Each bond matures in 4 years, has a face value of $1,000, and has a yield to maturity equal to 9.6%. One bond, Bond C, pays an annual coupon of 10%; the other bond, Bond Z, is a zero coupon bond. Assuming that the yield to maturity of each bond remains at 9.6% over the next 4 years, what will be the price of each of the bonds at the following time periods? Fill in the following table:

t	Price of Bond C	Price of Bond Z
0	_____	_____
1	_____	_____
2	_____	_____
3	_____	_____
4	_____	_____

(5-18)
Determinants of Interest
Rates

The real risk-free rate is 2%. Inflation is expected to be 3% this year, 4% next year, and then 3.5% thereafter. The maturity risk premium is estimated to be $0.0005 \times (t - 1)$, where t = number of years to maturity. What is the nominal interest rate on a 7-year Treasury security?

(5-19)
Maturity Risk Premiums

Assume that the real risk-free rate, r*, is 3% and that inflation is expected to be 8% in Year 1, 5% in Year 2, and 4% thereafter. Assume also that all Treasury securities are highly liquid and free of default risk. If 2-year and 5-year Treasury notes both yield 10%, what is the difference in the maturity risk premiums (MRPs) on the two notes; that is, what is MRP_5 minus MRP_2?

(5-20)
Inflation Risk Premiums

Due to a recession, the inflation rate expected for the coming year is only 3%. However, the inflation rate in Year 2 and thereafter is expected to be constant at some level above 3%. Assume that the real risk-free rate is r* = 2% for all maturities and that there are no maturity premiums. If 3-year Treasury notes yield 2 percentage points more than 1-year notes, what inflation rate is expected after Year 1?

**Challenging Problems
21–23**

(5-21)
Bond Valuation and
Changes in Maturity and
Required Returns

Suppose Hillard Manufacturing sold an issue of bonds with a 10-year maturity, a $1,000 par value, a 10% coupon rate, and semiannual interest payments.
a. Two years after the bonds were issued, the going rate of interest on bonds such as these fell to 6%. At what price would the bonds sell?
b. Suppose that, 2 years after the initial offering, the going interest rate had risen to 12%. At what price would the bonds sell?

c. Suppose that the conditions in part a existed—that is, interest rates fell to 6% 2 years after the issue date. Suppose further that the interest rate remained at 6% for the next 8 years. What would happen to the price of the bonds over time?

(5-22)
Yield to Maturity and Yield to Call

Arnot International's bonds have a current market price of $1,200. The bonds have an 11% annual coupon payment, a $1,000 face value, and 10 years left until maturity. The bonds may be called in 5 years at 109% of face value (call price = $1,090).

a. What is the yield to maturity?
b. What is the yield to call, if they are called in 5 years?
c. Which yield might investors expect to earn on these bonds, and why?
d. The bond's indenture indicates that the call provision gives the firm the right to call them at the end of each year beginning in Year 5. In Year 5, they may be called at 109% of face value, but in each of the next 4 years the call percentage will decline by 1 percentage point. Thus, in Year 6 they may be called at 108% of face value, in Year 7 they may be called at 107% of face value, and so on. If the yield curve is horizontal and interest rates remain at their current level, when is the latest that investors might expect the firm to call the bonds?

(5-23)
Determinants of Interest Rates

Suppose you and most other investors expect the inflation rate to be 7% next year, to fall to 5% during the following year, and then to remain at a rate of 3% thereafter. Assume that the real risk-free rate, r*, will remain at 2% and that maturity risk premiums on Treasury securities rise from zero on very short-term securities (those that mature in a few days) to a level of 0.2 percentage point for 1-year securities. Furthermore, maturity risk premiums increase 0.2 percentage point for each year to maturity, up to a limit of 1.0 percentage point on 5-year or longer-term T-notes and T-bonds.

a. Calculate the interest rate on 1-, 2-, 3-, 4-, 5-, 10-, and 20-year Treasury securities, and plot the yield curve.
b. Now suppose ExxonMobil's bonds, rated AAA, have the same maturities as the Treasury bonds. As an approximation, plot an ExxonMobil yield curve on the same graph with the Treasury bond yield curve. (Hint: Think about the default risk premium on ExxonMobil's long-term versus its short-term bonds.)
c. Now plot the approximate yield curve of Long Island Lighting Company, a risky nuclear utility.

e-resource

Spreadsheet Problem

(5-24)
Build a Model: Bond Valuation

Start with the partial model in the file *FM12 Ch 05 P24 Build a Model.xls* from the textbook's Web site. Rework Problem 5-12. After completing parts a through d, answer the following related questions.

e. How would the price of the bond be affected by changing interest rates? (Hint: Conduct a sensitivity analysis of price to changes in the yield to maturity, which is also the going market interest rate for the bond. Assume that the bond will be called if and only if the going rate of interest *falls below* the coupon rate. That is an oversimplification, but assume it anyway for purposes of this problem.)

f. Now assume that the date is October 25, 2007. Assume further that our 12%, 10-year bond was issued on July 1, 2007, is callable on July 1, 2011, at $1,060, will mature on June 30, 2017, pays interest semiannually (January 1 and July 1), and sells for $1,100. Use your spreadsheet to find (1) the bond's yield to maturity and (2) its yield to call.

Cyberproblem

e-resource

Please go to the textbook's Web site to access any Cyberproblems.

Mini Case

Sam Strother and Shawna Tibbs are vice presidents of Mutual of Seattle Insurance Company and codirectors of the company's pension fund management division. An important new client, the North-Western Municipal Alliance, has requested that Mutual of Seattle present an investment seminar to the mayors of the represented cities, and Strother and Tibbs, who will make the actual presentation, have asked you to help them by answering the following questions. Because the Boeing Company operates in one of the league's cities, you are to work Boeing into the presentation.

a. What are the key features of a bond?
b. What are call provisions and sinking fund provisions? Do these provisions make bonds more or less risky?
c. How is the value of any asset whose value is based on expected future cash flows determined?
d. How is the value of a bond determined? What is the value of a 10-year, $1,000 par value bond with a 10% annual coupon if its required rate of return is 10%?
e. (1) What would be the value of the bond described in part d if, just after it had been issued, the expected inflation rate rose by 3 percentage points, causing investors to require a 13% return? Would we now have a discount or a premium bond?

    (2) What would happen to the bond's value if inflation fell, and r_d declined to 7%? Would we now have a premium or a discount bond?

    (3) What would happen to the value of the 10-year bond over time if the required rate of return remained at 13%, or if it remained at 7%? [Hint: With a financial calculator, enter PMT, I/YR, FV, and N, and then change (override) N to see what happens to the PV as the bond approaches maturity.]

f. (1) What is the yield to maturity on a 10-year, 9%, annual coupon, $1,000 par value bond that sells for $887.00? That sells for $1,134.20? What does the fact that a bond sells at a discount or at a premium tell you about the relationship between r_d and the bond's coupon rate?

   (2) What are the total return, the current yield, and the capital gains yield for the discount bond? (Assume the bond is held to maturity and the company does not default on the bond.)

g. How does the equation for valuing a bond change if semiannual payments are made? Find the value of a 10-year, semiannual payment, 10% coupon bond if nominal $r_d = 13\%$.

h. Suppose a 10-year, 10%, semiannual coupon bond with a par value of $1,000 is currently selling for $1,135.90, producing a nominal yield to maturity of 8%. However, the bond can be called after 5 years for a price of $1,050.

   (1) What is the bond's *nominal yield to call (YTC)*?

   (2) If you bought this bond, do you think you would be more likely to earn the YTM or the YTC? Why?

i. Write a general expression for the yield on any debt security (r_d) and define these terms: real risk-free rate of interest (r^*), inflation premium (IP), default risk premium (DRP), liquidity premium (LP), and maturity risk premium (MRP).

j. Define the nominal risk-free rate (r_{RF}). What security can be used as an estimate of r_{RF}?

k. Describe a way to estimate the inflation premium (IP) for a T-Year bond.

l. What is a bond spread and how is it related to the default risk premium? How are bond ratings related to default risk? What factors affect a company's bond rating?

m. What is *interest rate (or price) risk?* Which bond has more interest rate risk, an annual payment 1-year bond or a 10-year bond? Why?

n. What is *reinvestment rate risk?* Which has more reinvestment rate risk, a 1-year bond or a 10-year bond?

o. How are interest rate risk and reinvestment rate risk related to the maturity risk premium?

p. What is the term structure of interest rates? What is a yield curve?

q. At any given time, how would the yield curve facing a AAA-rated company compare with the yield curve for U.S. Treasury securities? At any given time, how would the yield curve facing a BB-rated company compare with the yield curve for U.S. Treasury securities?

r. Briefly describe bankruptcy law. If a firm were to default on the bonds, would the company be immediately liquidated? Would the bondholders be assured of receiving all of their promised payments?

Selected Additional Cases

The following cases from Textchoice, *Cengage Learning's online library, cover many of the concepts discussed in this chapter and are available at* *http://www.textchoice2.com.*

Klein-Brigham Series:
Case 3, "Peachtree Securities, Inc. (B)."
Case 72, "Swan Davis."
Case 78, "Beatrice Peabody."

Brigham-Buzzard Series:
Case 3, "Powerline Network Corporation (Bonds and Preferred Stock)."

chapter 6

Risk, Return, and the
Capital Asset Pricing Model

Skill or luck? That's the question *The Wall Street Journal's* Investment Dartboard Contest sought to answer by comparing the actual investment results of professional analysts against amateurs and dart throwers. Here's how the contest worked. First, *The Wall Street Journal* (*WSJ*) picked four professional analysts, and each of those pros formed a portfolio by picking four stocks. The stocks had to trade on the NYSE, AMEX, or Nasdaq; have a market capitalization of at least $50 million and a stock price of at least $2; and have average daily trades of at least $100,000. Second, amateurs could enter the contest by e-mailing their pick of a single stock to the *WSJ*, which then picked four amateurs at random and combined their choices to make a four-stock portfolio. Third, a group of *WSJ* editors formed a portfolio by throwing four darts at the stock tables. At the beginning of each contest, the *WSJ* announced the six resulting portfolios, and at the end of six months, the paper announced the results. The top two pros were invited back for the next contest.

Since 1990 there have been 142 completed contests. The pros beat the darts 87 times and lost 55 times. The pros also beat the Dow Jones Industrial Average in 54% of the contests. The pros had an average six-month portfolio return of 10.2%, much higher than either the

DJIA six-month average of 5.6% or the darts' return of only 3.5%. The readers, meantime, lost an average of 4% versus a same-period (30 contests) gain of 7.2% for the pros.

Do these results mean that skill is more important than luck when it comes to investing in stocks? Not necessarily, according to Burton Malkiel, an economics professor at Princeton and the author of the widely read book, *A Random Walk Down Wall Street*. Since the dart-selected portfolios consist of randomly chosen stocks, they should have average risk. However, the pros have consistently picked high-risk stocks. Because there was a bull market during most of the contest, one would expect high-risk stocks to outperform the average stock. According to Malkiel, the pros' performance could be due to a rising market rather than superior analytical skills. The *WSJ* stopped that contest in 2002, so we won't know for sure whether Malkiel was right or wrong.

The *WSJ* now runs a new contest, pitting six amateurs against six darts. In the recently completed Contest No. 21, the darts trounced the readers by gaining 20% versus the readers' loss of −4.1% (the Dow Jones Industrial Average was up 5.1%). Overall, readers have won 8 contests, while the darts have won 13. If you would like to enter the contest, e-mail your stock pick to **sundaydartboard@wsj.com**.

In this chapter, we start from the basic premise that investors like returns and dislike risk. Therefore, people will invest in riskier assets only if they expect to receive higher returns. We define precisely what the term *risk* means as it relates to investments. We examine procedures managers use to measure risk, and we discuss the relationship between risk and return. In later chapters we extend these relationships to show how risk and return interact to determine security prices. Managers must understand and apply these concepts as they plan the actions that will shape their firms' futures.

e-resource
The textbook's Web site contains an *Excel* file that will guide you through the chapter's calculations. The file for this chapter is **FM12 Ch 06 Tool Kit.xls,** and we encourage you to open the file and follow along as you read the chapter.

6.1 Investment Returns

With most investments, an individual or business spends money today with the expectation of earning even more money in the future. The concept of *return* provides investors with a convenient way to express the financial performance of an investment. To illustrate, suppose you buy 10 shares of a stock for $1,000. The stock pays no dividends, but at the end of one year, you sell the stock for $1,100. What is the return on your $1,000 investment?

One way to express an investment return is in *dollar terms*. The dollar return is simply the total dollars received from the investment less the amount invested:

$$\text{Dollar return} = \text{Amount received} - \text{Amount invested}$$

$$= \$1,100 - \$1,000$$

$$= 100.$$

If, at the end of the year, you sell the stock for only $900, your dollar return will be −$100.

Although expressing returns in dollars is easy, two problems arise: (1) To make a meaningful judgment about the return, you need to know the scale (size) of the investment; a $100 return on a $100 investment is a good return (assuming the investment is held for 1 year), but a $100 return on a $10,000 investment would be a poor return. (2) You also need to know the timing of the return; a $100 return on a $100 investment is a very good return if it occurs after one year, but the same dollar return after 20 years is not very good.

The solution to the scale and timing problems is to express investment results as *rates of return*, or *percentage returns*. For example, the rate of return on the 1-year stock investment, when $1,100 is received after 1 year, is 10%:

$$\text{Rate of return} = \frac{\text{Amount received} - \text{Amount invested}}{\text{Amount invested}}$$

$$= \frac{\text{Dollar return}}{\text{Amount invested}} = \frac{\$100}{\$1,000}$$

$$= 0.10 = 10\%.$$

The rate of return calculation "standardizes" the return by considering the annual return per unit of investment. Although this example has only one outflow and one inflow, the annualized rate of return can easily be calculated in situations where multiple cash flows occur over time by using time value of money concepts.

Corporate Valuation and Risk

In Chapter 1, we told you that managers should strive to make their firms more valuable, and that the value of a firm is determined by the size, timing, and risk of its free cash flows (FCF). This chapter shows you how to measure a firm's risk and the rate of return expected by shareholders, which affects the weighted average cost of capital (WACC). All else held equal, higher risk increases the WACC, which reduces the firm's value.

$$\text{Value} = \frac{FCF_1}{(1 + WACC)^1} + \frac{FCF_2}{(1 + WACC)^2} + \frac{FCF_3}{(1 + WACC)^3} + \cdots + \frac{FCF_\infty}{(1 + WACC)^\infty}$$

SELF-TEST

Differentiate between dollar returns and rates of return.

Why are rates of return superior to dollar returns in terms of accounting for the size of investment and the timing of cash flows?

Suppose you pay $500 for an investment that returns $600 in 1 year. What is the annual rate of return? (20%)

6.2 Stand-Alone Risk

Risk is defined in *Webster's* as "a hazard; a peril; exposure to loss or injury." Thus, risk refers to the chance that some unfavorable event will occur. If you go skydiving, you are taking a chance with your life—skydiving is risky. If you bet on the horses, you are risking your money. If you invest in speculative stocks (or, really, *any* stock), you are taking a risk in the hope of earning an appreciable return.

An asset's risk can be analyzed in two ways: (1) on a stand-alone basis, where the asset is considered in isolation, and (2) on a portfolio basis, where the asset is held as one of a number of assets in a portfolio. Thus, an asset's **stand-alone risk** is the risk an investor would face if he or she held only this one asset. Obviously, most assets are held in portfolios, but it is necessary to understand stand-alone risk in order to understand risk in a portfolio context.

To illustrate the risk of financial assets, suppose an investor buys $100,000 of short-term Treasury bills with an expected return of 5%. In this case, the rate of return on the investment, 5%, can be estimated quite precisely, and the investment is defined as being essentially *risk free*. However, if the $100,000 were invested in the stock of a company just being organized to prospect for oil in the mid-Atlantic, then the investment's return could not be estimated precisely. One might analyze the situation and conclude that the *expected* rate of return, in a statistical sense, is 20%, but the investor should recognize that the *actual* rate of return could range from, say, +1,000% to −100%. Because there is a significant danger of actually earning much less than the expected return, the stock would be relatively risky.

No investment should be undertaken unless the expected rate of return is high enough to compensate the investor for the perceived risk of the investment. In our example, it is clear that few if any investors would be willing to buy the oil company's stock if its expected return were the same as that of the T-bill.

Table 6-1

Probability Distributions for Sale.com and Basic Foods

Demand for the Company's Products	Probability of This Demand Occurring	Rate of Return on Stock if This Demand Occurs	
		Sale.com	Basic Foods
Strong	0.3	100%	40%
Normal	0.4	15	15
Weak	0.3	(70)	(10)
	1.0		

Risky assets rarely actually produce their expected rates of return; generally, risky assets earn either more or less than was originally expected. Indeed, if assets always produced their expected returns, they would not be risky. Investment risk, then, is related to the probability of actually earning a low or negative return: The greater the chance of a low or negative return, the riskier the investment. However, risk can be defined more precisely, and we do so in the next section.

Probability Distributions

An event's *probability* is defined as the chance that the event will occur. For example, a weather forecaster might state, "There is a 40% chance of rain today and a 60% chance that it will not rain." If all possible events, or outcomes, are listed, and if a probability is assigned to each event, the listing is called a **probability distribution.** Keep in mind that the probabilities must sum to 1.0, or 100%.

With this in mind, consider the possible rates of return due to dividends and stock price changes that you might earn next year on a $10,000 investment in the stock of either Sale.com or Basic Foods Inc. Sale.com is an Internet company offering deep discounts on factory seconds and overstocked merchandise. Because it faces intense competition, its new services may or may not be competitive in the marketplace, so its future earnings cannot be predicted very well. Indeed, some new company could develop better services and literally bankrupt Sale.com. Basic Foods, on the other hand, distributes essential food staples to grocery stores, and its sales and profits are relatively stable and predictable.

The rate-of-return probability distributions for the two companies are shown in Table 6-1. There is a 30% chance of strong demand, in which case both companies will have high earnings, pay high dividends, and enjoy capital gains. There is a 40% probability of normal demand and moderate returns, and there is a 30% probability of weak demand, which will mean low earnings and dividends as well as capital losses. Notice, however, that Sale.com's rate of return could vary far more widely than that of Basic Foods. There is a fairly high probability that the value of Sale.com's stock will drop substantially, resulting in a 70% loss, while there is a much smaller possible loss for Basic Foods.

Note that the following discussion of risk applies to all random variables, not just stock returns.

e-resource

See **FM12 Ch 06 Tool Kit.xls** at the textbook's Web site for all calculations.

Table 6-2

Calculation of Expected Rates of Return: Payoff Matrix

		Sale.com		Basic Foods	
Demand for the Company's Products (1)	Probability of This Demand Occurring (2)	Rate of Return if This Demand Occurs (3)	Product: (2) × (3) = (4)	Rate of Return if This Demand Occurs (5)	Product: (2) × (5) = (6)
Strong	0.3	100%	30%	40%	12%
Normal	0.4	15	6	15	6
Weak	0.3	(70)	(21)	(10)	(3)
	1.0		$\hat{r} = 15\%$		$\hat{r} = 15\%$

Expected Rate of Return

If we multiply each possible outcome by its probability of occurrence and then sum these products, as in Table 6-2, we have a *weighted average* of outcomes. The weights are the probabilities, and the weighted average is the **expected rate of return, $\hat{r}$,** called "r-hat."[1] The expected rates of return for both Sale.com and Basic Foods are shown in Table 6-2 to be 15%. This type of table is known as a *payoff matrix.*

The expected rate of return calculation can also be expressed as an equation that does the same thing as the payoff matrix table:[2]

$$\text{Expected rate of return} = \hat{r} = P_1 r_1 + P_2 r_2 + \cdots + P_n r_n = \sum_{i=1}^{n} P_i r_i. \qquad (6\text{-}1)$$

Here r_i is the *i*th possible outcome, P_i is the probability of the *i*th outcome, and n is the number of possible outcomes. Thus, $\hat{r}$ is a weighted average of the possible outcomes (the r_i values), with each outcome's weight being its probability of occurrence. Using the data for Sale.com, we obtain its expected rate of return as follows:

$$\hat{r} = P_1(r_1) + P_2(r_2) + P_3(r_3)$$

$$= 0.3(100\%) + 0.4(15\%) + 0.3(-70\%)$$

$$= 15\%.$$

Basic Foods' expected rate of return is also 15%:

$$\hat{r} = 0.3(40\%) + 0.4(15\%) + 0.3(-10\%)$$

$$= 15\%.$$

We can graph the rates of return to obtain a picture of the variability of possible outcomes; this is shown in the Figure 6-1 bar charts. The height of each bar signifies the probability that a given outcome will occur. The range of probable

---

[1] In later chapters, we will use $\hat{r}_d$ and $\hat{r}_s$ to signify the returns on bonds and stocks, respectively. However, this distinction is unnecessary in this chapter, so we just use the general term, $\hat{r}$, to signify the expected return on an investment.

[2] This equation is valid for any random variable with a discrete probability distribution, not just for stock returns.

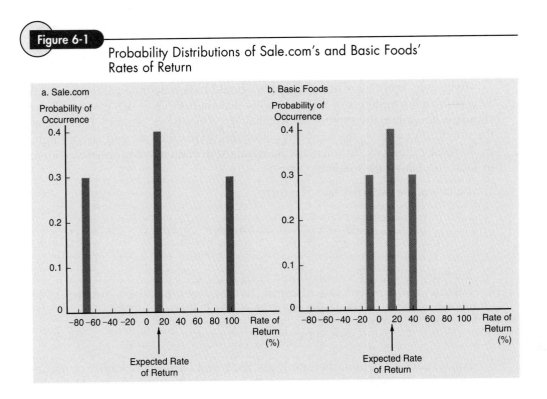

Figure 6-1

Probability Distributions of Sale.com's and Basic Foods' Rates of Return

returns for Sale.com is from −70 to +100%, with an expected return of 15%. The expected return for Basic Foods is also 15%, but its range is much narrower.

Thus far, we have assumed that only three situations can exist: strong, normal, and weak demand. Actually, of course, demand could range from a deep depression to a fantastic boom, and there are unlimited possibilities in between. Suppose we had the time and patience to assign a probability to each possible level of demand (with the sum of the probabilities still equaling 1.0) and to assign a rate of return to each stock for each level of demand. We would have a table similar to Table 6-1, except it would have many more entries in each column. This table could be used to calculate expected rates of return as shown previously, and the probabilities and outcomes could be approximated by continuous curves such as those presented in Figure 6-2. Here we have changed the assumptions so that there is essentially a zero probability that Sale.com's return will be less than −70% or more than 100%, or that Basic Foods' return will be less than −10% or more than 40%, but virtually any return within these limits is possible.

The tighter, or more peaked, the probability distribution, the more likely it is that the actual outcome will be close to the expected value, and, consequently, the less likely it is that the actual return will end up far below the expected return. Thus, the tighter the probability distribution, the lower the risk assigned to a stock. Since Basic Foods has a relatively tight probability distribution, its *actual return* is likely to be closer to its 15% *expected return* than that of Sale.com.

Measuring Stand-Alone Risk: The Standard Deviation

Risk is a difficult concept to grasp, and a great deal of controversy has surrounded attempts to define and measure it. However, a common definition, and one that is satisfactory for many purposes, is stated in terms of probability distributions such as those presented in Figure 6-2: *The tighter the probability distribution of expected future returns, the smaller the risk of a given investment.* According to this definition, Basic Foods is less risky than Sale.com because there is a smaller chance that its actual return will end up far below its expected return.

To be most useful, any measure of risk should have a definite value—we need a measure of the tightness of the probability distribution. One such measure is the **standard deviation,** the symbol for which is σ, pronounced "sigma." The smaller the standard deviation, the tighter the probability distribution, and, accordingly, the less risky the stock. To calculate the standard deviation, we proceed as shown in Table 6-3, taking the following steps:[3]

1. Calculate the expected rate of return:

$$\text{Expected rate of return} = \hat{r} = \sum_{i=1}^{n} P_i r_i.$$

   For Sale.com, we previously found $\hat{r} = 15\%$.

2. Subtract the expected rate of return ($\hat{r}$) from each possible outcome (r_i) to obtain a set of deviations about $\hat{r}$ as shown in Column 1 of Table 6-3:

$$\text{Deviation}_i = r_i - \hat{r}.$$

3. Square each deviation, then multiply the result by the probability of occurrence for its related outcome, and then sum these products to obtain the

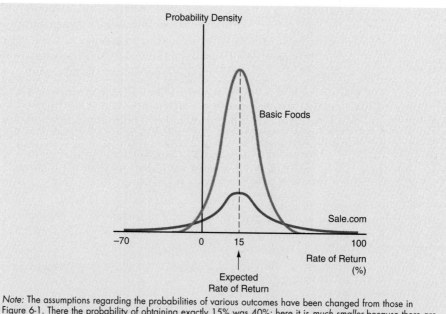

Figure 6-2

Continuous Probability Distributions of Sale.com's and Basic Foods' Rates of Return

Note: The assumptions regarding the probabilities of various outcomes have been changed from those in Figure 6-1. There the probability of obtaining exactly 15% was 40%; here it is *much smaller* because there are many possible outcomes instead of just three. With continuous distributions, it is more appropriate to ask what the probability is of obtaining at least some specified rate of return than to ask what the probability is of obtaining exactly that rate. This topic is covered in detail in statistics courses.

---

[3]These equations are valid for any random variable from a discrete probability distribution, not just for returns.

See **FM12 Ch 06 Tool Kit.xls** at the textbook's Web site for all calculations.

Table 6-3		
Calculating Sale.com's Standard Deviation		

(Values for r_i and $\hat{r}$ are percentages.)

$r_i - \hat{r}$ (1)	$(r_i - \hat{r})^2$ (2)	$(r_i - \hat{r})^2 P_i$ (3)
$100 - 15 = \quad 85\%$	$7{,}225\%$	$(7{,}225)(0.3) = 2{,}167.5\%$
$15 - 15 = \quad 0$	0	$(0)(0.04) = \quad\quad 0.0$
$-70 - 15 = -85$	$7{,}225$	$(7{,}225)(0.3) = \underline{2{,}167.5}$
		Variance $= \sigma^2 = \underline{4{,}335.0\%}$

$$\text{Standard deviation} = \sigma = \sqrt{\sigma^2} = \sqrt{4{,}335\%} = 65.84\%$$

variance of the probability distribution as shown in Columns 2 and 3 of the table:

$$\text{Variance} = \sigma^2 = \sum_{i=1}^{n} (r_i - \hat{r})^2 P_i. \tag{6-2}$$

4. Finally, find the square root of the variance to obtain the standard deviation:

$$\text{Standard deviation} = \sigma = \sqrt{\sum_{i=1}^{n} (r_i - \hat{r})^2 P_i}. \tag{6-3}$$

Thus, the standard deviation is essentially a weighted average of the deviations from the expected value, and it provides an idea of how far above or below the expected value the actual value is likely to be. Sale.com's standard deviation is seen in Table 6-3 to be $\sigma = 65.84\%$. Using these same procedures, we find Basic Foods' standard deviation to be 19.36%. Sale.com has the larger standard deviation, which indicates a greater variation of returns and thus a greater chance that the actual return may be substantially lower than the expected return. Therefore, Sale.com is a riskier investment than Basic Foods when held alone.[4]

If a probability distribution is normal, the *actual* return will be within ± 1 standard deviation of the *expected* return 68.26 percent of the time. Figure 6-3 illustrates this point, and it also shows the situation for $\pm 2\ \sigma$ and $\pm 3\ \sigma$. For Sale.com, $\hat{r} = 15\%$ and $\sigma = 65.84\%$, whereas $\hat{r} = 15\%$ and $\sigma = 19.36\%$ for Basic Foods. Thus, if the two distributions were normal, there would be a 68.26% probability that Sale.com's actual return would be in the range of $15 \pm 65.84\%$, or from –50.84 to 80.84%. For Basic Foods, the 68.26% range is $15 \pm 19.36\%$, or from -4.36 to 34.36%. For the average firm listed on the New York Stock Exchange, σ has generally been in the range of 35 to 40% in recent years.

---

[4]Most financial calculators have no built-in formula for finding the expected value or variance for discrete probability distributions, except for the special case in which the probabilities for all outcomes are equal. Therefore, you must go through the processes outlined in Tables 6-2 and 6-3 (i.e., Equations 6-1 and 6-3). For an example of this process using a financial calculator, see Richard W. Taylor, "Discrete Probability Analysis with the BAII Plus Professional Calculator," *Journal of Financial Education*, Winter 2005, pp. 100–106. *Excel* also has no built-in formula for discrete distributions, although it is possible to find free add-ins on the Web that do the calculations for discrete distributions.

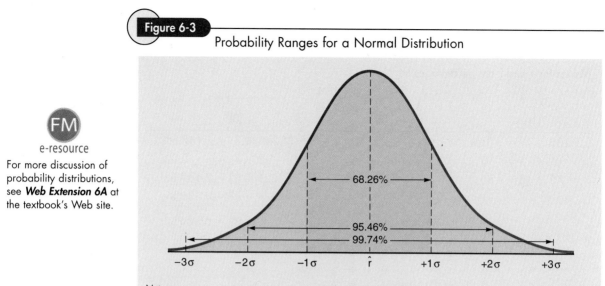

FM

e-resource

For more discussion of probability distributions, see **Web Extension 6A** at the textbook's Web site.

Figure 6-3

Probability Ranges for a Normal Distribution

Notes:

a.   The area under the normal curve always equals 1.0, or 100%. Thus, the areas under any pair of normal curves drawn on the same scale, whether they are peaked or flat, must be equal.

b.   Half of the area under a normal curve is to the left of the mean, indicating that there is a 50% probability that the actual outcome will be less than the mean, and half is to the right of $\hat{r}$, indicating a 50% probability that it will be greater than the mean.

c.   Of the area under the curve, 68.26% is within $\pm 1\sigma$ of the mean, indicating that the probability is 68.26% that the actual outcome will be within the range $\hat{r} - \sigma$ to $\hat{r} + \sigma$.

Using Historical Data to Measure Risk

In the previous example, we described the procedure for finding the mean and standard deviation when the data are in the form of a known probability distribution. Suppose only sample returns data over some past period are available. The past **realized rate of return** in period t is denoted by $\bar{r}_t$ ("r bar t"). The average annual return over the last n years is $\bar{r}_{Avg}$:

$$\bar{r}_{Avg} = \frac{\sum_{t=1}^{n} \bar{r}_t}{n}. \tag{6-4}$$

The standard deviation of a sample of returns can be estimated using this formula:

$$\text{Estimated } \sigma = S = \sqrt{\frac{\sum_{t=1}^{n} (\bar{r}_t - \bar{r}_{Avg})^2}{n-1}}. \tag{6-5}$$

When estimated from past data, the standard deviation is often denoted by S. Here is an example:[5]

---

[5]Because we are estimating the standard deviation from a sample of observations, the denominator in Equation 6-5 is "n − 1" and not just "n." Equations 6-4 and 6-5 are built into all financial calculators. For example, to find the sample standard deviation, enter the rates of return into the calculator and press the key marked S (or S_x) to get the standard deviation. See our tutorials or your calculator manual for details.

Year	$\bar{r}_t$
2005	15%
2006	−5
2007	20

$$\bar{r}_{Avg} = \frac{(15 - 5 + 20)}{3} = 10.0\%,$$

$$\text{Estimated } \sigma \text{ (or S)} = \sqrt{\frac{(15 - 10)^2 + (-5 - 10)^2 + (20 - 10)^2}{3 - 1}}$$

$$= \sqrt{\frac{350}{2}} = 13.2\%.$$

In *Excel*, the average can be found using a built-in function: **=AVERAGE(0.15,−0.05,0.20)** = 10.0%. For the sample standard deviation, the function is **=STDEV(0.15,−0.05,0.20)** = 13.2%.

The historical σ is often used as an estimate of the future σ. Because past variability is likely to be repeated, S may be a reasonably good estimate of future risk. However, it is usually incorrect to use $\bar{r}_{Avg}$ for some past period as an estimate of $\hat{r}$, the expected future return. For example, just because a stock had a 75% return in the past year, there is no reason to expect a 75% return this year.

e-resource
See **FM12 Ch 06 Tool Kit.xls** at the textbook's Web site for all calculations.

Measuring Stand-Alone Risk: The Coefficient of Variation

If a choice has to be made between two investments that have the same expected returns but different standard deviations, most people would choose the one with the lower standard deviation and, therefore, the lower risk. Similarly, given a choice between two investments with the same risk (standard deviation) but different expected returns, investors would generally prefer the investment with the higher expected return. To most people, this is common sense—return is "good," risk is "bad," and consequently investors want as much return and as little risk as possible. But how do we choose between two investments if one has a higher expected return but the other a lower standard deviation? To help answer this question, we often use another measure of risk, the **coefficient of variation (CV)**, which is the standard deviation divided by the expected return:

$$\text{Coefficient of variation} = CV = \frac{\sigma}{\hat{r}}. \qquad (6\text{-}6)$$

The coefficient of variation shows the risk per unit of return, and it provides a more meaningful basis for comparison when the expected returns on two alternatives are not the same. Since Basic Foods and Sale.com have the same expected return, the coefficient of variation is not necessary in this case. The firm with the larger standard deviation, Sale.com, must have the larger coefficient of variation when the means are equal. In fact, the coefficient of variation for Sale.com is 65.84/15 = 4.39 and that for Basic Foods is 19.36/15 = 1.29. Thus, Sale.com is more than three times as risky as Basic Foods on the basis of this criterion. Because the coefficient of variation captures the effects of both risk and return, it is a better measure than just standard deviation for evaluating stand-alone risk in situations where two or more investments have substantially different expected returns.

financial assets are actually held as parts of portfolios. Banks, pension funds, insurance companies, mutual funds, and other financial institutions are required by law to hold diversified portfolios. Even individual investors—at least those whose security holdings constitute a significant part of their total wealth—generally hold portfolios, not the stock of only one firm. This being the case, from an investor's standpoint the fact that a particular stock goes up or down is not very important; *what is important is the return on his or her portfolio, and the portfolio's risk. Logically, then, the risk and return of an individual security should be analyzed in terms of how that security affects the risk and return of the portfolio in which it is held.*

To illustrate, Pay Up Inc. is a collection agency that operates nationwide through 37 offices. The company is not well known, its stock is not very liquid, its earnings have fluctuated quite a bit in the past, and it doesn't pay a dividend. All this suggests that Pay Up is risky and that the required rate of return on its stock, r, should be relatively high. However, Pay Up's required rate of return in 2006, and all other years, was quite low in relation to those of most other companies. This indicates that investors regard Pay Up as being a low-risk company in spite of its uncertain profits. The reason for this counterintuitive fact has to do with diversification and its effect on risk. Pay Up's earnings rise during recessions, whereas most other companies' earnings tend to decline when the economy slumps. It's like fire insurance—it pays off when other things go badly. Therefore, adding Pay Up to a portfolio of "normal" stocks tends to stabilize returns on the entire portfolio, thus making the portfolio less risky.

Portfolio Returns

The **expected return on a portfolio, $\hat{r}_p$,** is simply the weighted average of the expected returns on the individual assets in the portfolio, with the weights being the fraction of the total portfolio invested in each asset:

$$\hat{r}_p = w_1\hat{r}_1 + w_2\hat{r}_2 + \cdots + w_n\hat{r}_n$$
$$= \sum_{i=1}^{n} w_i\hat{r}_i. \qquad (6\text{-}7)$$

Here the $\hat{r}_i$'s are the expected returns on the individual stocks, the w_i's are the weights, and there are n stocks in the portfolio. Note that (1) w_i is the fraction of the portfolio's dollar value invested in Stock i (that is, the value of the investment in Stock i divided by the total value of the portfolio) and (2) the w_i's must sum to 1.0.

Assume that in August 2007, a security analyst estimated that the following returns could be expected on the stocks of four large companies:

	Expected Return, $\hat{r}$
Southwest Airlines	15.0%
Starbucks	12.0
FedEx	10.0
Dell	9.0

If we formed a $100,000 portfolio, investing $25,000 in each stock, the expected portfolio return would be 11.5%:

$$\hat{r}_p = w_1\hat{r}_1 + w_2\hat{r}_2 + w_3\hat{r}_3 + w_4\hat{r}_4$$
$$= 0.25(15\%) + 0.25(12\%) + 0.25(10\%) + 0.25(9\%)$$
$$= 11.5\%.$$

Of course, the actual realized rates of return will almost certainly be different from their expected values, so the realized portfolio return, $\bar{r}_p$, will be different from the expected return. For example, Starbucks might double and provide a return of $+100\%$, whereas Dell might have a terrible year, fall sharply, and have a return of -75%. Note, though, that those two events would be somewhat offsetting, so the portfolio's return might still be close to its expected return, even though the individual stocks' actual returns were far from their expected returns.

Portfolio Risk

As we just saw, the expected return on a portfolio is simply the weighted average of the expected returns on the individual assets in the portfolio. However, unlike returns, the risk of a portfolio, σ_p, is generally not the weighted average of the standard deviations of the individual assets in the portfolio; the portfolio's risk will almost always be smaller than the weighted average of the assets' σ's. In fact, it is theoretically possible to combine stocks that are individually quite risky as measured by their standard deviations to form a portfolio that is completely riskless, with $\sigma_p = 0$.

To illustrate the effect of combining assets, consider the situation in Figure 6-4. The bottom section gives data on rates of return for Stocks W and M individually, as well as for a portfolio invested 50% in each stock. The three graphs plot the data in a time series format. The two stocks would be quite risky if they were held in isolation, but when they are combined to form Portfolio WM, they are not risky at all. (Note: These stocks are called W and M because the graphs of their returns in Figure 6-4 resemble a W and an M.)

The reason Stocks W and M can be combined to form a riskless portfolio is that their returns move countercyclically to each other—when W's returns fall, those of M rise, and vice versa. The tendency of two variables to move together is called **correlation,** and the **correlation coefficient** measures this tendency.[7] The symbol for the correlation coefficient is the Greek letter rho, ρ (pronounced roe). In statistical terms, we say that the returns on Stocks W and M are *perfectly negatively correlated*, with $\rho = -1.0$.

The estimate of correlation from a sample of historical data is often called "R." Here is the formula to estimate the correlation between stocks i and j ($\bar{r}_{i,t}$ is the actual return for Stock i in period t, and $\bar{r}_{i,\text{Avg}}$ is the average return during the n-period sample; similar notation is used for Stock j):

$$\text{Estimated } \rho = R = \frac{\sum\limits_{t=1}^{n} (\bar{r}_{i,t} - \bar{r}_{i,\text{Avg}})(\bar{r}_{j,t} - \bar{r}_{j,\text{Avg}})}{\sqrt{\sum\limits_{t=1}^{n} (\bar{r}_{i,t} - \bar{r}_{i,\text{Avg}})^2} \sqrt{\sum\limits_{t=1}^{n} (\bar{r}_{j,t} - \bar{r}_{j,\text{Avg}})^2}}. \qquad \text{(6-8)}$$

Fortunately, it is easy to estimate the correlation coefficients with a financial calculator. Simply enter the returns on the two stocks and then press a key labeled "r."[8] In *Excel*, use the CORREL function. See *FM12 Ch 06 Tool Kit.xls* for the calculation of correlation between Stocks W and M.

The opposite of perfect negative correlation, with $\rho = -1.0$, is *perfect positive correlation*, with $\rho = +1.0$. Returns on two perfectly positively correlated stocks

---

[7]The correlation coefficient, ρ, can range from $+1.0$, denoting that the two variables move up and down in perfect synchronization, to -1.0, denoting that the variables always move in exactly opposite directions. A correlation coefficient of zero indicates that the two variables are not related to each other—that is, changes in one variable are independent of changes in the other.

[8]See our tutorial or your calculator manual for the exact steps. Also, note that the correlation coefficient is often denoted by the term "r." We use ρ here to avoid confusion with r as used to denote the rate of return.

Figure 6-4

Rates of Return for Two Perfectly Negatively Correlated Stocks ($\rho = -1.0$)
and for Portfolio WM

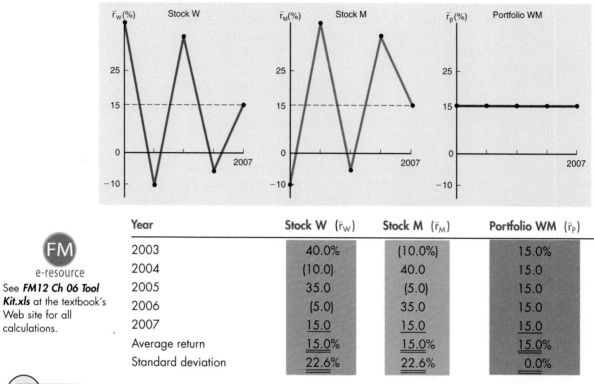

Year	Stock W ($\bar{r}_W$)	Stock M ($\bar{r}_M$)	Portfolio WM ($\bar{r}_P$)
2003	40.0%	(10.0%)	15.0%
2004	(10.0)	40.0	15.0
2005	35.0	(5.0)	15.0
2006	(5.0)	35.0	15.0
2007	15.0	15.0	15.0
Average return	15.0%	15.0%	15.0%
Standard deviation	22.6%	22.6%	0.0%

Figure 6-5

Rates of Return for Two Perfectly Positively Correlated Stocks ($\rho = +1.0$)
and for Portfolio MM'

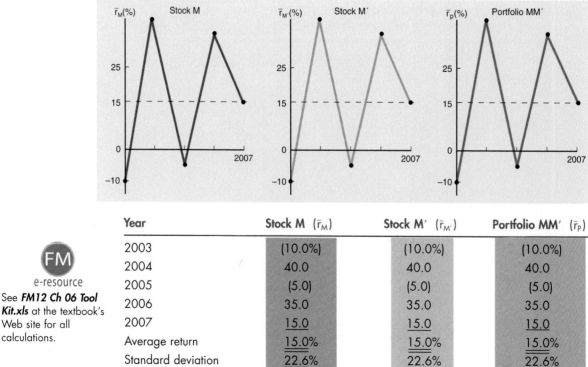

Year	Stock M ($\bar{r}_M$)	Stock M' ($\bar{r}_{M'}$)	Portfolio MM' ($\bar{r}_P$)
2003	(10.0%)	(10.0%)	(10.0%)
2004	40.0	40.0	40.0
2005	(5.0)	(5.0)	(5.0)
2006	35.0	35.0	35.0
2007	15.0	15.0	15.0
Average return	15.0%	15.0%	15.0%
Standard deviation	22.6%	22.6%	22.6%

(M and M′) would move up and down together, and a portfolio consisting of two such stocks would be exactly as risky as each individual stock. This point is illustrated in Figure 6-5, where we see that the portfolio's standard deviation is equal to that of the individual stocks. *Thus, diversification does nothing to reduce risk if the portfolio consists of perfectly positively correlated stocks.*

Figures 6-4 and 6-5 demonstrate that when stocks are perfectly negatively correlated ($\rho = -1.0$), all risk can be diversified away, but when stocks are perfectly positively correlated ($\rho = +1.0$), diversification does no good whatsoever. In reality, virtually all stocks are positively correlated, but not perfectly so. Past studies have estimated that on average the correlation coefficient for the monthly returns on two randomly selected stocks is about 0.3.[9] *Under this condition, combining stocks into portfolios reduces risk but does not completely eliminate it.* Figure 6-6 illustrates this point with two stocks whose correlation coefficient is $\rho = +0.35$. The portfolio's average return is 15%, which is exactly the same as the average return for our other two illustrative portfolios, but its standard deviation is 18.6%, which is between the other two portfolios' standard deviations.

These examples demonstrate that in one extreme case ($\rho = -1.0$), risk can be completely eliminated, while in the other extreme case ($\rho = +1.0$), diversification does no good whatsoever. The real world lies between these extremes, so combining stocks into portfolios reduces, but does not eliminate, the risk inherent in the individual stocks. Also, we should note that in the real world, it is *impossible* to find stocks like W and M, whose returns are expected to be perfectly negatively correlated. *Therefore, it is impossible to form completely riskless stock portfolios.* Diversification can reduce risk but not eliminate it, so the real world is similar to the situation depicted in Figure 6-6.

What would happen if we included more than two stocks in the portfolio? *As a rule, the risk of a portfolio will decline as the number of stocks in the portfolio increases.* If we added enough partially correlated stocks, could we completely eliminate risk? In general, the answer is no, but the extent to which adding stocks to a portfolio reduces its risk depends on the *degree of correlation* among the stocks: The smaller the positive correlation coefficients, the lower the risk in a large portfolio. If some stocks had correlations of -1.0, all risk could be eliminated. *In the real world, where the correlations among the individual stocks are generally positive but less than $+1.0$, some, but not all, risk can be eliminated.*

In general, there are higher correlations between the returns on two companies in the same industry than for two companies in different industries. Thus, to minimize risk, portfolios should be diversified across industries.

Diversifiable Risk versus Market Risk

As noted above, it is difficult if not impossible to find stocks whose expected returns are negatively correlated—most stocks tend to do well when the national economy is strong and badly when it is weak. Thus, even very large portfolios end up with a substantial amount of risk, but not as much risk as if all the money were invested in only one stock.

---

[9]A recent study by Chan, Karceski, and Lakonishok (1999) estimated that the average correlation coefficient between two randomly selected stocks was 0.28, while the average correlation coefficient between two large-company stocks was 0.33. The time period of their sample was 1968 to 1998. See Louis K. C. Chan, Jason Karceski, and Josef Lakonishok, "On Portfolio Optimization: Forecasting Covariance and Choosing the Risk Model," *The Review of Financial Studies*, Vol. 12, No. 5, Winter 1999, pp. 937–974. A study by Campbell, Lettau, Malkiel, and Xu found that the average correlation fell from around 0.35 in the late 1970s to less than 0.10 by the late 1990s; see John Y. Campbell, Martin Lettau, Burton G. Malkiel, and Yexiao Xu, "Have Individual Stocks Become More Volatile? An Empirical Exploration of Idiosyncratic Risk," *Journal of Finance*, February 2001, pp. 1–43.

Figure 6-6

Rates of Return for Two Partially Correlated Stocks ($\rho = +0.35$) and for Portfolio WY

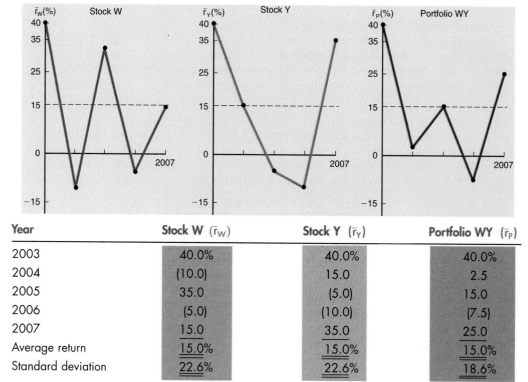

Year	Stock W ($\bar{r}_W$)	Stock Y ($\bar{r}_Y$)	Portfolio WY ($\bar{r}_P$)
2003	40.0%	40.0%	40.0%
2004	(10.0)	15.0	2.5
2005	35.0	(5.0)	15.0
2006	(5.0)	(10.0)	(7.5)
2007	15.0	35.0	25.0
Average return	15.0%	15.0%	15.0%
Standard deviation	22.6%	22.6%	18.6%

To see more precisely how portfolio size affects portfolio risk, consider Figure 6-7, which shows how portfolio risk is affected by forming larger and larger portfolios of randomly selected New York Stock Exchange (NYSE) stocks. Standard deviations are plotted for an average one-stock portfolio, a two-stock portfolio, and so on, up to a portfolio consisting of all 2,000-plus common stocks that were listed on the NYSE at the time the data were graphed. The graph illustrates that, in general, the risk of a portfolio consisting of large-company stocks tends to decline and to approach some limit as the size of the portfolio increases. According to data accumulated in recent years, σ_1, the standard deviation of a one-stock portfolio (or an average stock), is approximately 35%. A portfolio consisting of all stocks, which is called the **market portfolio,** would have a standard deviation, σ_M, of about 20%, which is shown as the horizontal dashed line in Figure 6-7.

Thus, almost half of the risk inherent in an average individual stock can be eliminated if the stock is held in a reasonably well-diversified portfolio, which is one containing 40 or more stocks in a number of different industries. Some risk always remains, however, so it is virtually impossible to diversify away the effects of broad stock market movements that affect almost all stocks.

The part of a stock's risk that *can* be eliminated is called *diversifiable risk*, while the part that *cannot* be eliminated is called *market risk*.[10] The fact that a large part of the risk of any individual stock can be eliminated is vitally important, because rational investors *will* eliminate it and thus render it irrelevant.

---

[10]Diversifiable risk is also known as *company-specific*, or *unsystematic*, risk. Market risk is also known as *nondiversifiable, systematic*, or *beta*, risk; it is the risk that remains after diversification.

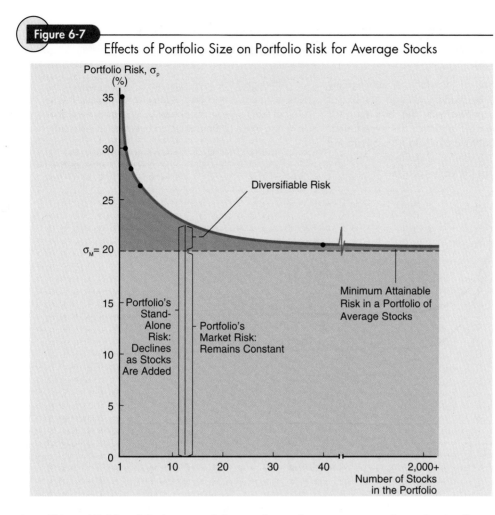

Figure 6-7

Effects of Portfolio Size on Portfolio Risk for Average Stocks

Diversifiable risk is caused by such random events as lawsuits, strikes, successful and unsuccessful marketing programs, the winning or losing of a major contract, and other events that are unique to a particular firm. Because these events are random, their effects on a portfolio can be eliminated by diversification—bad events in one firm will be offset by good events in another. **Market risk,** on the other hand, stems from factors that systematically affect most firms: war, inflation, recessions, and high interest rates. Since most stocks are negatively affected by these factors, market risk cannot be eliminated by diversification.

We know that investors demand a premium for bearing risk; that is, the higher the risk of a security, the higher its expected return must be to induce investors to buy (or to hold) it. However, if investors are primarily concerned with the risk of their *portfolios* rather than the risk of the individual securities in the portfolio, how should the risk of an individual stock be measured? One answer is provided by the **Capital Asset Pricing Model (CAPM),** an important tool used to analyze the relationship between risk and rates of return.[11] The primary conclusion of the CAPM is this: *The relevant risk of an individual stock is its contribution to the risk of a well-diversified portfolio.* A stock might be quite risky if held by itself, but if half of its risk can be eliminated by diversification, then its **relevant risk,** which is its *contribution to the portfolio's risk*, is much smaller than its stand-alone risk.

---

[11]Indeed, the 1990 Nobel Prize was awarded to the developers of the CAPM, Professors Harry Markowitz and William F. Sharpe. The CAPM is a relatively complex theory, and only its basic elements are presented in this chapter. A more in-depth presentation appears in Chapter 7.

The Benefits of Diversifying Overseas

Figure 6-7 shows that an investor can significantly reduce portfolio risk by holding a large number of stocks. The figure accompanying this box suggests that investors may be able to reduce risk even further by holding a large portfolio of stocks from all around the world, because the returns of domestic and international stocks are not perfectly correlated.

Although U.S. investors have traditionally been relatively reluctant to hold international assets, it is a safe bet that in the years ahead U.S. investors will shift more and more of their assets to overseas investments.

Source: For further reading, see Kenneth Kasa, "Measuring the Gains from International Portfolio Diversification," *Federal Reserve Bank of San Francisco Weekly Letter,* no. 94-14 (April 8, 1994).

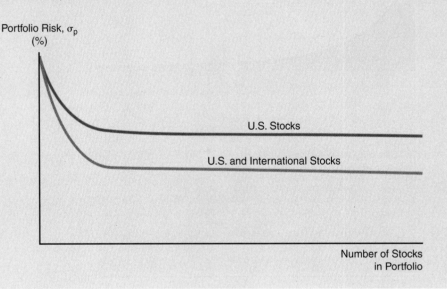

A simple example will help make this point clear. Suppose you are offered the chance to flip a coin once. If it's heads, you win $20,000, but if it's tails, you lose $16,000. This is a good bet—the expected return is 0.5($20,000) + 0.5(−$16,000) = $2,000. However, it is a highly risky proposition, because you have a 50% chance of losing $16,000. Thus, you might well refuse to make the bet. Alternatively, suppose you were offered the chance to flip a coin 100 times, and you would win $200 for each head but lose $160 for each tail. It is theoretically possible that you would flip all heads and win $20,000, and it is also theoretically possible that you would flip all tails and lose $16,000, but the chances are very high that you would actually flip about 50 heads and about 50 tails, winning a net of about $2,000. Although each individual flip is a risky bet, collectively you have a low-risk proposition because most of the risk has been diversified away. This is the idea behind holding portfolios of stocks rather than just one stock, except that with stocks all of the risk cannot be eliminated by diversification—those risks related to broad, systematic changes in the stock market will remain.

Are all stocks equally risky in the sense that adding them to a well-diversified portfolio will have the same effect on the portfolio's riskiness? The answer is no. Different stocks will affect the portfolio differently, so different securities have different degrees of relevant risk. How can the relevant risk of an individual stock be measured? As we have seen, all risk except that related to broad market movements can, and presumably will, be diversified away. After all, why accept risk that can be easily eliminated? *The risk that remains after diversifying is market risk, or the risk that is inherent in the market, and it can be measured by the degree to which a given stock tends to move up or down with the market*. In the next section, we develop a meas-ure of a stock's market risk, and then, in a later section, we introduce an equation for determining the required rate of return on a stock, given its market risk.

Contribution to Market Risk: Beta

As we noted above, the primary conclusion of the CAPM is that the relevant risk of an individual stock is the amount of risk the stock contributes to a well-diversified portfolio. The benchmark for a well-diversified stock portfolio is the market port-folio, which is a portfolio containing all stocks. Therefore, the relevant risk of an individual stock, which is called its **beta coefficient,** is defined under the CAPM as the amount of risk that the stock contributes to the market portfolio. In CAPM terminology, ρ_{iM} is the correlation between the ith stock's return and the return on the market, σ_i is the standard deviation of the ith stock's return, and σ_M is the stan-dard deviation of the market's return. The beta coefficient of the ith stock, denot-ed by b_i, is defined as follows:

$$b_i = \left(\frac{\sigma_i}{\sigma_M}\right)\rho_{iM}. \qquad (6\text{-}9)$$

This tells us that a stock with a high standard deviation, σ_i, will tend to have a high beta, which means that it contributes a relatively large amount of risk to a well-diversified portfolio. This makes sense, because if all other things are equal, a stock with high stand-alone risk will contribute a lot of risk to the portfolio. Note too that a stock with a high correlation with the market, ρ_{iM}, will also have a large beta, and hence be risky. This also makes sense, because a high correlation means that diversification is not helping much; hence the stock contributes a lot of risk to the portfolio.

The **covariance between stock i and the market, COV$_{iM}$,** is defined as[12]

$$COV_{iM} = \rho_{iM}\,\sigma_i\,\sigma_M. \qquad (6\text{-}10)$$

Substituting Equation 6-10 into 6-9 provides another frequently used expression for beta:

$$b_i = \frac{COV_{iM}}{\sigma_M^2}. \qquad (6\text{-}11)$$

Calculators and spreadsheets can calculate the components of Equation 6-9 (ρ_{iM}, σ_i, and σ_M), which can then be used to calculate beta, but there is another way. Suppose you plotted the stock's returns on the y-axis of a graph and the market portfolio's returns on the x-axis, as shown in Figure 6-8. The formula for the slope

---

[12]Using historical data, the sample covariance can be calculated as

$$\text{Sample covariance from historical data} = COV_{iM} = \frac{\sum_{t=1}^{n}(\bar{r}_{i,t} - \bar{r}_{i,\,Avg})(\bar{r}_{M,t} - \bar{r}_{M,\,Avg})}{n-1}.$$

Calculating the covariance is somewhat easier than calculating the correlation. So if you have already calculated the standard deviations, then it is easier to calculate the covariance and then calculate the correlation as: $\rho_{iM} = COV_{iM}/(\sigma_i\sigma_M)$.

of a regression line is exactly equal to the formula for beta in Equation 6-11. Therefore, to estimate beta for a security, you can just estimate a regression with the stock's returns on the y-axis and the market's returns on the x-axis.

Individual Stock Betas

The tendency of a stock to move up and down with the market is reflected in its beta coefficient. An *average-risk stock* is defined as one with a beta equal to 1.0. Such a stock's returns tend to move up and down, on average, with the market, which is measured by some index such as the Dow Jones Industrials, the S&P 500, or the New York Stock Exchange Composite Index. A portfolio of such b = 1.0 stocks will move up and down with the broad market indexes, and it will be just as risky as the indexes. A portfolio of b = 0.5 stocks will be half as risky as the market. On the other hand, a portfolio of b = 2.0 stocks will be twice as risky as the market.

Figure 6-8 shows a graph of the historical returns of three stocks and the market. The data below the graph assume that in Year 1 the "market," defined as a portfolio consisting of all stocks, had a total return (dividend yield plus capital gains yield) of $\bar{r}_M = 10\%$ and Stocks H, A, and L (for High, Average, and Low risk) also all had returns of 10%. In Year 2, the market went up sharply, and the return on the market portfolio was $\bar{r} = 20\%$. Returns on the three stocks also went up: H soared to 30%; A went up to 20%, the same as the market; and L only went up to 15%. The market dropped in Year 3, and the market return was $\bar{r}_M = -10\%$. The three stocks' returns also fell, H plunging to -30%, A falling to -10%, and L going down to $\bar{r}_L = 0\%$. Thus, the three stocks all moved in the same direction as the market, but H was by far the most volatile; A was just as volatile as the market; and L was less volatile.

Beta measures a stock's volatility relative to the market, which by definition has b = 1.0. As we noted above, the slope of a regression line shows how a stock moves in response to a movement in the general market. Most stocks have betas in the range of 0.50 to 1.50, and the average beta for all stocks is 1.0 by definition.

Theoretically, it is possible for a stock to have a negative beta. In this case, the stock's returns would tend to rise whenever the returns on other stocks fall. In practice, very few stocks have a negative beta. Keep in mind that a stock in a given period may move counter to the overall market, even though the stock's beta is positive. If a stock has a positive beta, we would *expect* its return to increase whenever the overall stock market rises. However, company-specific factors may cause the stock's realized return to decline, even though the market's return is positive.

Portfolio Betas

A very important feature of beta is that the beta of a portfolio is a weighted average of its individual securities' betas:

$$b_p = w_1b_1 + w_2b_2 + \cdots + w_nb_n$$
$$= \sum_{i=1}^{n} w_ib_i.$$

(6-12)

Here b_p is the beta of the portfolio, and it shows how volatile the portfolio is in relation to the market; w_i is the fraction of the portfolio invested in the

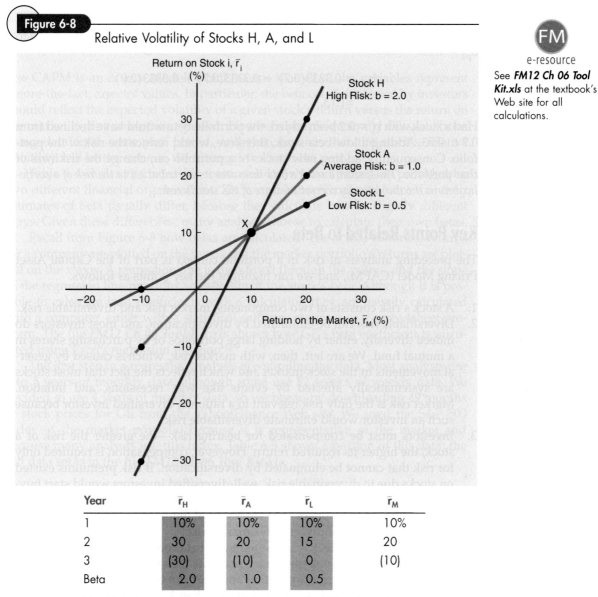

Figure 6-8

Relative Volatility of Stocks H, A, and L

Year	$\bar{r}_H$	$\bar{r}_A$	$\bar{r}_L$	$\bar{r}_M$
1	10%	10%	10%	10%
2	30	20	15	20
3	(30)	(10)	0	(10)
Beta	2.0	1.0	0.5	

Note: These three stocks plot exactly on their regression lines. This indicates that they are exposed only to market risk. Mutual funds that concentrate on stocks with betas of 2.0, 1.0, and 0.5 will have patterns similar to those shown in the graph.

*i*th stock; and b_i is the beta coefficient of the *i*th stock. For example, if an investor holds a $100,000 portfolio consisting of $33,333.33 invested in each of three stocks, and if each of the stocks has a beta of 0.7, then the portfolio's beta will be $b_p = 0.7$:

$$b_p = 0.3333(0.7) + 0.3333(0.7) + 0.3333(0.7) = 0.7.$$

Such a portfolio will be less risky than the market, so it should experience relatively narrow price swings and have relatively small rate-of-return fluctuations. In terms of Figure 6-8, the slope of its regression line would be 0.7, which is less than that for a portfolio of average stocks.

Table 6-5

Stock Return Data for General Electric

Date	Market Level (S&P 500 Index)	Market Return	GE Adjusted Stock Price	GE Return
May 2006	1,280.16	−2.3%	34.33	−0.8%
April 2006	1,310.61	1.2	34.59	−0.5
March 2006	1,294.87	1.1	34.78	5.8
February 2006	1,280.66	0.0	32.87	1.1
.				
.				
.				
August 2002	916.07	0.5	27.30	−6.4
July 2002	911.62	−7.9	29.16	10.8
June 2002	989.82	−7.2	26.31	−6.1
May 2002	1,067.14	NA	28.02	NA
Average return (annual)		5.4%		6.9%
Standard deviation (annual)		13.0%		19.1%
Correlation between GE and the market		0.49		

Check out **http://finance
.yahoo.com** for General
Electric using its ticker
symbol of GE. You can
also download data for
the S&P 500 Index using
its symbol of ^SPX.

The second step is to convert the stock prices into rates of return. For example, to find the May 2006 return for GE, we find the percentage change from the previous month: ($34.59 − $34.33)/$34.59 = −0.0008 = −0.83%.[14] We also find the percent change of the S&P Index level, and use this as the market return.

As Table 6-5 shows, GE had an average annual return of 6.9% during this 4-year period, while the market had an average annual return of 5.4%. As we noted before, it is usually unreasonable to think that the future expected return for a stock will equal its average historical return over a relatively short period, such as 4 years. However, we might well expect past volatility to be a reasonable estimate of future volatility, at least during the next couple of years. Note that the standard deviation for GE's return during this period was 19.1% versus 13.0% for the market. Thus, the market's volatility is less than that of GE. This is what we would expect, since the market is a well-diversified portfolio and thus much of its risk has been diversified away. The correlation between GE's stock returns and the market returns is about 0.49, which is a little higher than the correlation for a typical stock.

Figure 6-9 shows a plot of GE's returns against the market returns. As you will notice if you look in the file *FM12 Ch 06 Tool Kit.xls,* we used the *Excel* Chart

[14]The prices reported in Yahoo!Finance are adjusted for dividends and stock splits so we can calculate the return as the percentage change in the adjusted price. If you use a source that reports actual market prices, then you have to make the adjustment yourself when calculating returns. For example, suppose the stock price is $100 in July, the company has a 2-for-1 split, and the actual price is then $60 in August. The reported adjusted price for August would be $60, but the reported price for July would be lowered to $50 to reflect the stock split. This gives an accurate stock return of 20%: ($60 − $50)/$50 = 20%, the same as if there had not been a split, in which case the return would have been ($120 − $100)/$100 = 20%. Or suppose the actual price in September was $50, the company paid a $10 dividend, and the actual price in October was $60. Shareholders have earned a return of ($60 + $10 − $50)/$50 = 40%. Yahoo!Finance reports an adjusted price of $60 for October, and an adjusted price of $42.857 for September, which gives a return of ($60 − $42.857)/$42.857 = 40%. Again, the percentage change in the adjusted price accurately reflects the actual return.

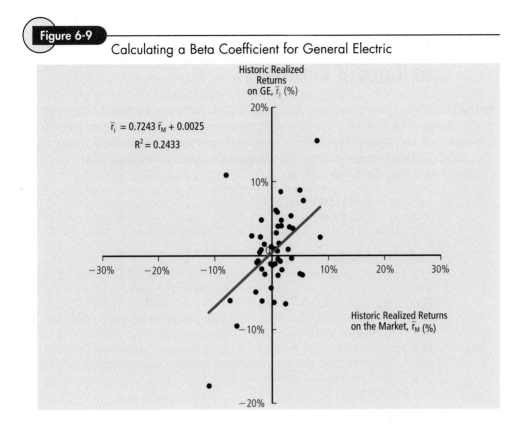

Figure 6-9

Calculating a Beta Coefficient for General Electric

feature to add a trend line and to display the equation and R^2 value on the chart itself. Alternatively, we could have used the *Excel* regression analysis feature, which would have provided more detailed data.

Figure 6-9 shows that GE's beta is about 0.72, as shown by the slope coefficient in the regression equation displayed on the chart. This means that GE's beta is less than the 1.0 average beta. Thus, GE moves up and down less than the market. Note, however, that the points are not clustered very tightly around the regression line. Sometimes GE does much better than the market, while at other times it does much worse. The R^2 value shown in the chart measures the degree of dispersion about the regression line. Statistically speaking, it measures the percentage of the variance that is explained by the regression equation. An R^2 of 1.0 indicates that all points lie exactly on the line, hence that all of the variance of the y-variable is explained by the x-variable. GE's R^2 is about 0.24, which is fairly typical for an individual stock. This indicates that about 24% of the variance in GE's returns is explained by the market returns. If we had done a similar analysis for a portfolio of 40 randomly selected stocks, then the points would probably have been clustered tightly around the regression line, and the R^2 would have probably been over 0.9.

Finally, note that the intercept shown in the regression equation on the chart is about 0.0025. Since the regression equation is based on monthly data, this means that over this period GE's stock earned about 0.25% more per month than an average stock as a result of factors other than a general increase in stock prices.

SELF-TEST

What types of data are needed to calculate a beta coefficient for an actual company? What does the R^2 measure? What is the R^2 for a typical company?

6.5 The Relationship between Risk and Rates of Return

In the preceding section, we saw that under the CAPM theory, beta is the appropriate measure of a stock's relevant risk. Now we must specify the relationship between risk and return: For a given level of risk as measured by beta, what rate of return should investors require to compensate them for bearing that risk? To begin, let us define the following terms:

$\hat{r}_i$ = *expected* rate of return on the *i*th stock.

r_i = *required* rate of return on the *i*th stock. This is the minimum expected return that is required to induce an average investor to purchase the stock.

$\bar{r}$ = realized, after-the-fact return.

r_{RF} = risk-free rate of return. In this context, r_{RF} is generally measured by the expected return on long-term U.S. Treasury bonds.

b_i = beta coefficient of the *i*th stock.

r_M = required rate of return on a portfolio consisting of all stocks, which is called the *market portfolio*.

RP_M = risk premium on "the market." $RP_M = (r_M - r_{RF})$ is the additional return over the risk-free rate required to induce an average investor to invest in the market portfolio.

RP_i = risk premium on the *i*th stock: $RP_i = (RP_M)b_i$.

The **market risk premium, RP_M,** shows the premium investors require for bearing the risk of an average stock, and it depends on the degree of risk aversion that investors on average have. Let us assume that Treasury bonds yield $r_{RF} = 6\%$, and the market has a required return of $r_M = 11\%$. The market risk premium is 5%:

$$RP_M = r_M - r_{RF} = 11\% - 6\% = 5\%.$$

We can measure a stock's relative riskiness by its beta coefficient. The risk premium for the *i*th stock is

Risk premium for Stock i = $RP_i = (RP_M)b_i$. (6-13)

If we know the market risk premium, RP_M, and the stock's risk as measured by its beta coefficient, b_i, we can find the stock's risk premium as the product $(RP_M)b_i$. For example, if $b_i = 0.5$ and $RP_M = 5\%$, then RP_i is 2.5%:

$$RP_i = (5\%)(0.5)$$
$$= 2.5\%.$$

The required return for any investment can be expressed in general terms as

Required return = Risk-free return + Premium for risk.

Here the risk-free return includes a premium for expected inflation, and we assume that the assets under consideration have similar maturities and liquidity. Under these conditions, the relationship between the required return and risk is called the **Security Market Line (SML):**

| SML Equation: | $\dfrac{\text{Required return}}{\text{on Stock i}} = \dfrac{\text{Risk-free}}{\text{rate}} + \left(\dfrac{\text{Market risk}}{\text{premium}}\right)\left(\dfrac{\text{Stock i's}}{\text{beta}}\right)$ | |

$$r_i = r_{RF} + (r_M - r_{RF})b_i \qquad (6\text{-}14)$$
$$= r_{RF} + (RP_M)b_i.$$

The required return for Stock i can be written as follows:

$$r_i = 6\% + 5\%(0.5)$$
$$= 8.5\%.$$

If some other Stock j were riskier than Stock i and had $b_j = 2.0$, then its required rate of return would be 16%:

$$r_j = 6\% + (5\%)2.0 = 16\%.$$

An average stock, with $b = 1.0$, would have a required return of 11%, the same as the market return:

$$r_A = 6\% + (5\%)\,1.0 = 11\% = r_M.$$

As noted above, Equation 6-14 is called the Security Market Line (SML) equation, and it is often expressed in graph form, as in Figure 6-10, which shows the SML when $r_{RF} = 6\%$ and $RP_M = 5\%$. Note the following points:

1. Required rates of return are shown on the vertical axis, while risk as measured by beta is shown on the horizontal axis. This graph is quite different from the one shown in Figure 6-8, where the returns on individual stocks were plotted on the vertical axis and returns on the market index were shown on the horizontal axis. The slopes of the three lines in Figure 6-8 were used to calculate the three stocks' betas, and those betas were then plotted as points on the horizontal axis of Figure 6-10.

2. Riskless securities have $b_i = 0$; therefore, r_{RF} appears as the vertical axis intercept in Figure 6-10. If we could construct a portfolio that had a beta of zero, it would have a required return equal to the risk-free rate.

3. The slope of the SML (5% in Figure 6-10) reflects the degree of risk aversion in the economy—the greater the average investor's aversion to risk, then (a) the steeper the slope of the line, (b) the greater the risk premium for all stocks, and (c) the higher the required rate of return on all stocks.[15] These points are discussed further in a later section.

4. The values we worked out for stocks with $b_i = 0.5$, $b_i = 1.0$, and $b_i = 2.0$ agree with the values shown on the graph for r_L, r_A, and r_H.

5. Negative betas are rare but can occur. For example, some stocks associated with gold, such as a mining operation, occasionally have a negative beta. Based on the SML, a stock with a negative beta should have a required return less than the risk-free rate. In fact, a stock with a very large but negative beta might have negative required return! This means that when the market is doing well, this stock will do poorly. But it also implies the opposite: When the market is doing poorly, a negative beta stock should have a positive return. In other words, the negative beta stock acts as insurance. Therefore, an

---

[15]Students sometimes confuse beta with the slope of the SML. This is a mistake. The slope of any straight line is equal to the "rise" divided by the "run," or $(Y_1 - Y_0)/(X_1 - X_0)$. Consider Figure 6-10. If we let $Y = r$ and $X = $ beta, and we go from the origin to $b = 1.0$, we see that the slope is $(r_M - r_{RF})/(b_M - b_{RF}) = (11\% - 6\%)/(1 - 0) = 5\%$. Thus, the slope of the SML is equal to $(r_M - r_{RF})$, the market risk premium. In Figure 6-10, $r_i = 6\% + 5\%b_i$, so an increase of beta from 1.0 to 2.0 would produce a 5 percentage point increase in r_i.

Figure 6-10

The Security Market Line (SML)

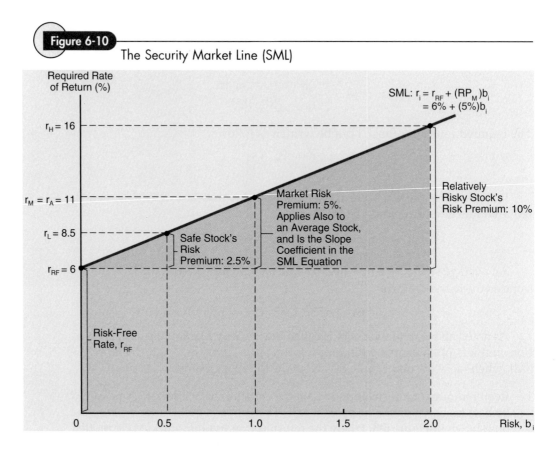

investor might be willing to accept a negative return on the stock during the good times if it is likely to provide a positive return in bad times.

Both the Security Market Line and a company's position on it change over time due to changes in interest rates, investors' aversion to risk, and individual companies' betas. Such changes are discussed in the following sections.

The Impact of Inflation

Interest is the same as "rent" on borrowed money, or the price of money. Thus, r_{RF} is the price of money to a riskless borrower. The risk-free rate as measured by the rate on U.S. Treasury securities is called the *nominal*, or *quoted, rate*, and it consists of two elements: (1) a *real inflation-free rate of return, r**, and (2) an *inflation premium, IP*, equal to the anticipated rate of inflation.[16] Thus, $r_{RF} = r^* + IP$. The real rate on long-term Treasury bonds has historically ranged from 2% to 4%, with a mean of about 3%. Therefore, if no inflation were expected, long-term Treasury bonds would yield about 3%. However, as the expected rate of inflation increases, a premium must be added to the real risk-free rate of return to compensate investors for the loss of purchasing power that results from inflation. Therefore, the 6% r_{RF} shown in Figure 6-10 might be thought of as consisting of a 3% real risk-free rate of return plus a 3% inflation premium: $r_{RF} = r^* + IP = 3\% + 3\% = 6\%$.

If the expected inflation rate rose by 2%, to 3% + 2% = 5%, this would cause r_{RF} to rise to 8%. Such a change is shown in Figure 6-11. Notice that under the CAPM, the

---

[16]Long-term Treasury bonds also contain a maturity risk premium, MRP. Here we include the MRP in r* to simplify the discussion. See Chapter 5 for more on bond pricing and bond risk premiums.

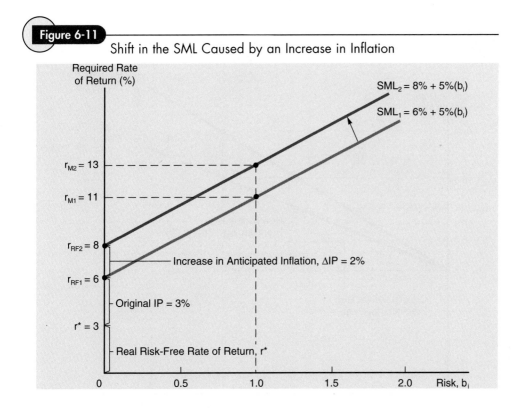

Figure 6-11

Shift in the SML Caused by an Increase in Inflation

increase in r_{RF} leads to an *equal* increase in the rate of return on all risky assets, because the same inflation premium is built into the required rate of return of both riskless and risky assets. For example, the rate of return on an average stock, r_M, increases from 11 to 13%. Other risky securities' returns also rise by 2 percentage points.

The discussion above also applies to any change in the nominal risk-free interest rate, whether it is caused by a change in expected inflation or in the real interest rate. The key point to remember is that a change in r_{RF} will not necessarily cause a change in the market risk premium, which is the required return on the market, r_M, minus the risk-free rate, r_{RF}. In other words, as r_{RF} changes, so may the required return on the market, keeping the market risk premium stable. Think of a sailboat floating in a harbor. The distance from the ocean floor to the ocean surface is like the risk-free rate, and it moves up and down with the tides. The distance from the top of the ship's mast to the ocean floor is like the required market return: It, too, moves up and down with the tides. But the distance from the mast-top to the ocean surface is like the market risk premium—it generally stays the same, even though tides move the ship up and down. In other words, a change in the risk-free rate also causes a change in the required market return, r_M, resulting in a relatively stable market risk premium, $r_M - r_{RF}$.

Changes in Risk Aversion

The slope of the Security Market Line reflects the extent to which investors are averse to risk—the steeper the slope of the line, the greater the average investor's risk aversion. Suppose investors were indifferent to risk; that is, they were not risk averse. If r_{RF} were 6%, then risky assets would also provide an expected return of 6%, because if there were no risk aversion, there would be no risk premium, and the SML would be plotted as a horizontal line. As risk aversion increases, so does the risk premium, and this causes the slope of the SML to become steeper.

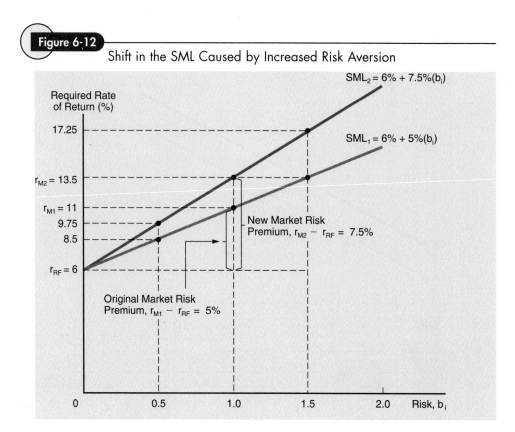

Figure 6-12

Shift in the SML Caused by Increased Risk Aversion

Figure 6-12 illustrates an increase in risk aversion. The market risk premium rises from 5 to 7.5%, causing r_M to rise from $r_{M1} = 11\%$ to $r_{M2} = 13.5\%$. The returns on other risky assets also rise, and the effect of this shift in risk aversion is more pronounced on riskier securities. For example, the required return on a stock with $b_i = 0.5$ increases by only 1.25 percentage points, from 8.5 to 9.75%, whereas that on a stock with $b_i = 1.5$ increases by 3.75 percentage points, from 13.5 to 17.25%.

Changes in a Stock's Beta Coefficient

As we shall see later in the book, a firm can influence its market risk, hence its beta, through changes in the composition of its assets and also through its use of debt. A company's beta can also change as a result of external factors such as increased competition in its industry, the expiration of basic patents, and the like. When such changes occur, the required rate of return also changes.

SELF-TEST

Differentiate among the expected rate of return ($\hat{r}$), the required rate of return (r), and the realized, after-the-fact return ($\bar{r}$) on a stock. Which would have to be larger to get you to buy the stock, $\hat{r}$ or r? Would $\hat{r}$, r, and $\bar{r}$ typically be the same or different for a given company?

What are the differences between the relative volatility graph (Figure 6-8), where "betas are made," and the SML graph (Figure 6-10), where "betas are used"? Discuss both how the graphs are constructed and the information they convey.

What happens to the SML graph in Figure 6-10 when inflation increases or decreases?

What happens to the SML graph when risk aversion increases or decreases? What would the SML look like if investors were indifferent to risk, that is, had zero risk aversion?

How can a firm influence its market risk as reflected in its beta?

A stock has a beta of 1.4. Assume that the risk-free rate is 5.5% and the market risk premium is 5%. What is the stock's required rate of return? (12.5%)

6.6 The CAPM, Risk, and Return: Is Something Missing?

The Holy Grail of finance is the search for the relationship between risk and required rates of return. This relationship affects the securities purchased and sold by investors, the strategies chosen by portfolio managers, and the projects selected by corporate managers. In fact, most decisions in finance boil down to the trade-off between risk and return: Does the security or project in question have enough return to justify its risk? To answer this question, you must be able to specify the relationship between required return and risk. If the security or project provides at least the required return, then it is acceptable.

The Capital Asset Pricing Model (CAPM) was the first theory of risk and return to become widely used by analysts, investors, and corporations. One of its key contributions is the insight that required returns should not be affected by diversifiable risk and that only nondiversifiable risk matters. Indeed, investors have become more diversified as the CAPM has become more widely known.[17] However, despite the CAPM's intuitive appeal, a number of studies have raised concerns about its validity. In particular, a study by Eugene Fama of the University of Chicago and Kenneth French of Yale casts doubt on the CAPM.[18] Fama and French found two variables that are consistently related to stock returns: (1) the firm's size and (2) its market/book ratio. After adjusting for other factors, they found that smaller firms have provided relatively high returns and that returns are relatively high on stocks with low market/book ratios. At the same time, and contrary to the CAPM, they found no relationship between a stock's beta and its return.

As an alternative to the traditional CAPM, researchers and practitioners have begun to look to more general multifactor models that expand on the CAPM and address its shortcomings. The multifactor model is an attractive generalization of the traditional CAPM model's insight that market risk, or the risk that cannot be diversified away, underlies the pricing of assets. In a multifactor model, market risk is measured relative to a set of risk factors that determine the behavior of asset returns, whereas the CAPM gauges risk only relative to the market return. It is important to note that the risk factors in the multifactor models are all nondiversifiable sources of risk. Empirical research investigating the relationship between economic risk factors and security returns is ongoing, but it has discovered several risk factors—including the bond default premium, the bond term structure premium, and inflation—that affect most securities.

An underlying assumption of the CAPM (and most other risk-return models) is that investors are rational, or at least the large investors whose buying and selling actions determine security prices are rational. However, psychologists have long known that humans aren't always rational, and this has led to a new field in finance called behavioral finance. Behavioral finance seeks to explain why investors and managers make certain decisions, even if those decisions seem to contradict rational pricing models such as the CAPM.

We discuss the Fama-French models, the multifactor models, and behavioral finance in more detail in Chapter 7. And as we will discuss in Chapter 10, it is not

---

[17]There is evidence suggesting that investors still do not diversify enough. See Meir Statman, "The Diversification Puzzle," *Financial Analysts Journal*, 2004, pp. 44–53.
[18]See Eugene F. Fama and Kenneth R. French, "The Cross-Section of Expected Stock Returns," *Journal of Finance*, 1992, pp. 427–465; and Eugene F. Fama and Kenneth R. French, "Common Risk Factors in the Returns on Stocks and Bonds," *Journal of Financial Economics*, 1993, pp. 3–56.

always easy to estimate beta or the market risk premium for the CAPM. Despite these issues, however, the CAPM is still the most widely used risk-return model for corporate finance applications.

SELF-TEST

Are there any reasons to question the validity of the CAPM? Explain.

Summary

In this chapter, we described the trade-off between risk and return. We began by discussing how to calculate risk and return for both individual assets and portfolios. In particular, we differentiated between stand-alone risk and risk in a portfolio context, and we explained the benefits of diversification. Finally, we developed the CAPM, which explains how risk affects rates of return. In the chapters that follow, we will give you the tools to estimate the required rates of return for bonds, preferred stock, and common stock, and we will explain how firms use these returns to develop their costs of capital. As you will see, the cost of capital is an important element in the firm's capital budgeting process. The key concepts covered in this chapter are listed below.

- **Risk** can be defined as the chance that some unfavorable event will occur.
- The risk of an asset's cash flows can be considered on a **stand-alone basis** (each asset by itself) or in a **portfolio context,** where the investment is combined with other assets and its risk is reduced through **diversification.**
- Most rational investors hold **portfolios of assets,** and they are more concerned with the riskiness of their portfolios than with the risk of individual assets.
- The **expected return** on an investment is the mean value of its probability distribution of returns.
- The **greater the probability** that the actual return will be far below the expected return, the **greater the stand-alone risk** associated with an asset.
- The average investor is **risk averse,** which means that he or she must be compensated for holding risky assets. Therefore, riskier assets have higher required returns than less risky assets.
- An asset's risk consists of (1) **diversifiable risk,** which can be eliminated by diversification, plus (2) **market risk,** which cannot be eliminated by diversification.
- The **relevant risk** of an individual asset is its contribution to the riskiness of a well-diversified **portfolio,** which is the asset's **market risk.** Since market risk cannot be eliminated by diversification, investors must be compensated for bearing it.
- A stock's **beta coefficient, b,** is a measure of its market risk. Beta measures the extent to which the stock's returns move relative to the market.
- A **high-beta stock** is more volatile than an average stock, while a **low-beta stock** is less volatile than an average stock. An average stock has b = 1.0.
- The **beta of a portfolio** is a **weighted average** of the betas of the individual securities in the portfolio.
- The **Security Market Line (SML)** equation shows the relationship between a security's market risk and its required rate of return. The return required for any security i is equal to the **risk-free rate** plus the **market risk premium** times the security's beta: $r_i = r_{RF} + (RP_M)b_i$.
- Even though the expected rate of return on a stock is generally equal to its required return, a number of things can happen to cause the required rate of

return to change: (1) **the risk-free rate can change** because of changes in either real rates or anticipated inflation, (2) **a stock's beta can change**, and (3) **investors' aversion to risk can change**.

- Because returns on assets in different countries are not perfectly correlated, **global diversification** may result in lower risk for multinational companies and globally diversified portfolios.

Questions

(6-1) Define the following terms, using graphs or equations to illustrate your answers wherever feasible:
   a. Stand-alone risk; risk; probability distribution
   b. Expected rate of return, $\hat{r}$
   c. Continuous probability distribution
   d. Standard deviation, σ; variance, σ^2; coefficient of variation, CV
   e. Risk aversion; realized rate of return, $\bar{r}$
   f. Risk premium for Stock i, RP_i; market risk premium, RP_M
   g. Capital Asset Pricing Model (CAPM)
   h. Expected return on a portfolio, $\hat{r}_p$; market portfolio
   i. Correlation coefficient, ρ; correlation
   j. Market risk; diversifiable risk; relevant risk
   k. Beta coefficient, b; average stock's beta, b_A
   l. Security Market Line (SML); SML equation
   m. Slope of SML as a measure of risk aversion

(6-2) The probability distribution of a less risky return is more peaked than that of a riskier return. What shape would the probability distribution have for (a) completely certain returns and (b) completely uncertain returns?

(6-3) Security A has an expected return of 7%, a standard deviation of returns of 35%, a correlation coefficient with the market of -0.3, and a beta coefficient of -1.5. Security B has an expected return of 12%, a standard deviation of returns of 10%, a correlation with the market of 0.7, and a beta coefficient of 1.0. Which security is riskier? Why?

(6-4) Suppose you owned a portfolio consisting of $250,000 worth of long-term U.S. government bonds.
   a. Would your portfolio be riskless?
   b. Now suppose you hold a portfolio consisting of $250,000 worth of 30-day Treasury bills. Every 30 days your bills mature, and you reinvest the principal ($250,000) in a new batch of bills. Assume that you live on the investment income from your portfolio and that you want to maintain a constant standard of living. Is your portfolio truly riskless?
   c. Can you think of any asset that would be completely riskless? Could someone develop such an asset? Explain.

(6-5) If investors' aversion to risk increased, would the risk premium on a high-beta stock increase more or less than that on a low-beta stock? Explain.

(6-6) If a company's beta were to double, would its expected return double?

(6-7)   Is it possible to construct a portfolio of stocks which has an expected return equal to the risk-free rate?

Self-Test Problems   Solutions Appear in Appendix A

(ST-1)
Realized Rates of Return

Stocks A and B have the following historical returns:

Year	Stock A's Returns, $\bar{r}_A$	Stock B's Returns, $\bar{r}_B$
2003	(18%)	(24%)
2004	44	24
2005	(22)	(4)
2006	22	8
2007	34	56

a. Calculate the average rate of return for each stock during the 5-year period. Assume that someone held a portfolio consisting of 50% of Stock A and 50% of Stock B. What would have been the realized rate of return on the portfolio in each year? What would have been the average return on the portfolio during this period?

b. Now calculate the standard deviation of returns for each stock and for the portfolio. Use Equation 6-5.

c. Looking at the annual returns data on the two stocks, would you guess that the correlation coefficient between returns on the two stocks is closer to 0.8 or to −0.8?

d. If you added more stocks at random to the portfolio, which of the following is the most accurate statement of what would happen to σ_p?

(1) σ_p would remain constant.
(2) σ_p would decline to somewhere in the vicinity of 20%.
(3) σ_p would decline to zero if enough stocks were included.

(ST-2)
Beta and Required
Rate of Return

ECRI Corporation is a holding company with four main subsidiaries. The percentage of its business coming from each of the subsidiaries, and their respective betas, are as follows:

Subsidiary	Percentage of Business	Beta
Electric utility	60%	0.70
Cable company	25	0.90
Real estate	10	1.30
International/special projects	5	1.50

a. What is the holding company's beta?

b. Assume that the risk-free rate is 6% and the market risk premium is 5%. What is the holding company's required rate of return?

c. ECRI is considering a change in its strategic focus: it will reduce its reliance on the electric utility subsidiary, so the percentage of its business from this subsidiary will be 50%. At the same time, ECRI will increase its reliance on the international/special projects division, so the percentage of its business from that subsidiary will rise to 15%. What will be the shareholders' required rate of return if they adopt these changes?

Problems   Answers Appear in Appendix B

Easy Problems 1–3

(6-1)
Portfolio Beta
An individual has $35,000 invested in a stock which has a beta of 0.8 and $40,000 invested in a stock with a beta of 1.4. If these are the only two investments in her portfolio, what is her portfolio's beta?

(6-2)
Required Rate of Return
Assume that the risk-free rate is 6% and the expected return on the market is 13%. What is the required rate of return on a stock that has a beta of 0.7?

(6-3)
Expected and Required
Rates of Return
Assume that the risk-free rate is 5% and the market risk premium is 6%. What is the expected return for the overall stock market? What is the required rate of return on a stock that has a beta of 1.2?

Intermediate Problems 4–9

(6-4)
Expected Return—
Discrete Distribution
A stock's return has the following distribution:

Demand for the Company's Products	Probability of This Demand Occurring	Rate of Return if This Demand Occurs
Weak	0.1	(50%)
Below average	0.2	(5)
Average	0.4	16
Above average	0.2	25
Strong	0.1	60
	1.0	

Calculate the stock's expected return, standard deviation, and coefficient of variation.

(6-5)
Expected Returns—
Discrete Distribution
The market and Stock J have the following probability distributions:

Probability	r_M	r_J
0.3	15%	20%
0.4	9	5
0.3	18	12

a. Calculate the expected rates of return for the market and Stock J.
b. Calculate the standard deviations for the market and Stock J.
c. Calculate the coefficients of variation for the market and Stock J.

(6-6)
Required Rate of Return
Suppose $r_{RF} = 5\%$, $r_M = 10\%$, and $r_A = 12\%$.

a. Calculate Stock A's beta.
b. If Stock A's beta were 2.0, what would be A's new required rate of return?

(6-7)
Required Rate of Return
Suppose $r_{RF} = 9\%$, $r_M = 14\%$, and $b_i = 1.3$.

a. What is r_i, the required rate of return on Stock i?
b. Now suppose r_{RF} (1) increases to 10% or (2) decreases to 8%. The slope of the SML remains constant. How would this affect r_M and r_i?

c. Now assume r_{RF} remains at 9% but r_M (1) increases to 16% or (2) falls to 13%. The slope of the SML does not remain constant. How would these changes affect r_i?

(6-8)
Portfolio Beta
Suppose you hold a diversified portfolio consisting of a $7,500 investment in each of 20 different common stocks. The portfolio beta is equal to 1.12. Now, suppose you have decided to sell one of the stocks in your portfolio with a beta equal to 1.0 for $7,500 and to use these proceeds to buy another stock for your portfolio. Assume the new stock's beta is equal to 1.75. Calculate your portfolio's new beta.

(6-9)
Portfolio Required Return
Suppose you are the money manager of a $4 million investment fund. The fund consists of four stocks with the following investments and betas:

Stock	Investment	Beta
A	$ 400,000	1.50
B	600,000	(0.50)
C	1,000,000	1.25
D	2,000,000	0.75

If the market required rate of return is 14% and the risk-free rate is 6%, what is the fund's required rate of return?

Challenging
Problems 10–13

(6-10)
Portfolio Beta
You have a $2 million portfolio consisting of a $100,000 investment in each of 20 different stocks. The portfolio has a beta equal to 1.1. You are considering selling $100,000 worth of one stock which has a beta equal to 0.9 and using the proceeds to purchase another stock which has a beta equal to 1.4. What will be the new beta of your portfolio following this transaction?

(6-11)
Required Rate of Return
Stock R has a beta of 1.5, Stock S has a beta of 0.75, the expected rate of return on an average stock is 13%, and the risk-free rate of return is 7%. By how much does the required return on the riskier stock exceed the required return on the less risky stock?

(6-12) ✓
Historical Realized
Rates of Return
Stocks A and B have the following historical returns:

Year	Stock A's Returns, $\bar{r}_A$	Stock B's Returns, $\bar{r}_B$
2003	(18.00%)	(14.50%)
2004	33.00	21.80
2005	15.00	30.50
2006	(0.50)	(7.60)
2007	27.00	26.30

a. Calculate the average rate of return for each stock during the 5-year period.
b. Assume that someone held a portfolio consisting of 50% of Stock A and 50% of Stock B. What would have been the realized rate of return on the portfolio in each year? What would have been the average return on the portfolio during this period?
c. Calculate the standard deviation of returns for each stock and for the portfolio.
d. Calculate the coefficient of variation for each stock and for the portfolio.
e. If you are a risk-averse investor, would you prefer to hold Stock A, Stock B, or the portfolio? Why?

(6-13) ✓ You have observed the following returns over time:

Historical Returns:
Expected and Required
Rates of Return

Year	Stock X	Stock Y	Market
2003	14%	13%	12%
2004	19	7	10
2005	(16)	25	(12)
2006	3	1	1
2007	20	11	15

Assume that the risk-free rate is 6% and the market risk premium is 5%.
a.   What are the betas of Stocks X and Y?
b.   What are the required rates of return for Stocks X and Y?
c.   What is the required rate of return for a portfolio consisting of 80% of Stock X and 20% of Stock Y?
d.   If Stock X's expected return is 22%, is Stock X under- or overvalued?

Spreadsheet Problem

(6-14)
Evaluating Risk
and Return

e-resource

Start with the partial model in the file *FM12 Ch 06 P14 Build a Model.xls* from the textbook's Web site. Bartman Industries' and Reynolds Incorporated's stock prices and dividends, along with the Market Index, are shown below. Stock prices are reported for December 31 of each year, and dividends reflect those paid during the year. The market data are adjusted to include dividends.

Year	Bartman Industries Stock Price	Dividend	Reynolds Incorporated Stock Price	Dividend	Market Index includes Divs.
2007	$17.250	$1.15	$48.750	$3.00	11,663.98
2006	14.750	1.06	52.300	2.90	8,785.70
2005	16.500	1.00	48.750	2.75	8,679.98
2004	10.750	0.95	57.250	2.50	6,434.03
2003	11.375	0.90	60.000	2.25	5,602.28
2002	7.625	0.85	55.750	2.00	4,705.97

a.   Use the data given to calculate annual returns for Bartman, Reynolds, and the Market Index, and then calculate average returns over the 5-year period. (Hint: Remember, returns are calculated by subtracting the beginning price from the ending price to get the capital gain or loss, adding the dividend to the capital gain or loss, and dividing the result by the beginning price. Assume that dividends are already included in the index. Also, you cannot calculate the rate of return for 2002 because you do not have 2001 data.)
b.   Calculate the standard deviations of the returns for Bartman, Reynolds, and the Market Index. (Hint: Use the sample standard deviation formula given in the chapter, which corresponds to the STDEV function in *Excel*.)
c.   Now calculate the coefficients of variation for Bartman, Reynolds, and the Market Index.
d.   Construct a scatter diagram graph that shows Bartman's and Reynolds's returns on the vertical axis and the Market Index's returns on the horizontal axis.

e. Estimate Bartman's and Reynolds's betas as the slope of a regression with stock return on the vertical axis (y-axis) and market return on the horizontal axis (x-axis). (Hint: use *Excel*'s SLOPE function.) Are these betas consistent with your graph?

f. The risk-free rate on long-term Treasury bonds is 6.04%. Assume that the market risk premium is 5%. What is the expected return on the market? Now use the SML equation to calculate the two companies' required returns.

g. If you formed a portfolio that consisted of 50% of Bartman stock and 50% of Reynolds stock, what would be its beta and its required return?

h. Suppose an investor wants to include Bartman Industries' stock in his or her portfolio. Stocks A, B, and C are currently in the portfolio, and their betas are 0.769, 0.985, and 1.423, respectively. Calculate the new portfolio's required return if it consists of 25% of Bartman, 15% of Stock A, 40% of Stock B, and 20% of Stock C.

---

e-resource

Cyberproblem

Please go to the textbook's Web site to access any Cyberproblems.

Mini Case

Assume that you recently graduated with a major in finance, and you just landed a job as a financial planner with Barney Smith Inc., a large financial services corporation. Your first assignment is to invest $100,000 for a client. Because the funds are to be invested in a business at the end of 1 year, you have been instructed to plan for a 1-year holding period. Further, your boss has restricted you to the investment alternatives shown in the table with their probabilities and associated outcomes. (Disregard for now the items at the bottom of the data; you will fill in the blanks later.)

Returns on Alternative Investments

State of the Economy	Probability	T-Bills	Alta Industries	Repo Men	American Foam	Market Portfolio	2-Stock Portfolio
				Estimated Rate of Return			
Recession	0.1	8.0%	(22.0%)	28.0%	10.0%ª	(13.0%)	3.0%
Below average	0.2	8.0	(2.0)	14.7	(10.0)	1.0	
Average	0.4	8.0	20.0	0.0	7.0	15.0	10.0
Above average	0.2	8.0	35.0	(10.0)	45.0	29.0	
Boom	0.1	8.0	50.0	(20.0)	30.0	43.0	15.0
$\hat{r}$			1.7%	13.8%	15.0%		
σ		0.0		13.4	18.8	15.3	
CV			7.9	1.4	1.0		
b			−0.86	0.68			

ªNote that the estimated returns of American Foam do not always move in the same direction as the overall economy. For example, when the economy is below average, consumers purchase fewer mattresses than they would if the economy were stronger. However, if the economy is in a flat-out recession, a large number of consumers who were planning to purchase a more expensive inner spring mattress may purchase, instead, a cheaper foam mattress. Under these circumstances, we would expect American Foam's stock price to be higher if there is a recession than if the economy was just below average.

Barney Smith's economic forecasting staff has developed probability estimates for the state of the economy, and its security analysts have developed a
sophisticated computer program that was used to estimate the rate of return on
each alternative under each state of the economy. Alta Industries is an electronics
firm; Repo Men Inc. collects past-due debts; and American Foam manufactures
mattresses and various other foam products. Barney Smith also maintains an
"index fund" which owns a market-weighted fraction of all publicly traded
stocks; you can invest in that fund, and thus obtain average stock market results.
Given the situation as described, answer the following questions.

a. What are investment returns? What is the return on an investment that costs
    $1,000 and is sold after 1 year for $1,100?
b. (1) Why is the T-bill's return independent of the state of the economy? Do
    T-bills promise a completely risk-free return? (2) Why are Alta Industries'
    returns expected to move with the economy whereas Repo Men's are expected
    to move counter to the economy?
c. Calculate the expected rate of return on each alternative and fill in the blanks
    in the row for $\hat{r}$ in the table.
d. You should recognize that basing a decision solely on expected returns is
    appropriate only for risk-neutral individuals. Because your client, like virtu-
    ally everyone, is risk averse, the riskiness of each alternative is an important
    aspect of the decision. One possible measure of risk is the standard deviation
    of returns. (1) Calculate this value for each alternative, and fill in the blank in
    the row for σ in the table. (2) What type of risk is measured by the standard
    deviation? (3) Draw a graph that shows *roughly* the shape of the probability
    distributions for Alta Industries, American Foam, and T-bills.
e. Suppose you suddenly remembered that the coefficient of variation (CV) is
    generally regarded as being a better measure of stand-alone risk than the stan-
    dard deviation when the alternatives being considered have widely differing
    expected returns. Calculate the missing CVs, and fill in the blanks in the row
    for CV in the table. Does the CV produce the same risk rankings as the standard
    deviation?
f. Suppose you created a 2-stock portfolio by investing $50,000 in Alta Industries
    and $50,000 in Repo Men. (1) Calculate the expected return ($\hat{r}_p$), the standard
    deviation (σ_p), and the coefficient of variation (CV_p) for this portfolio and fill in
    the appropriate blanks in the table. (2) How does the risk of this 2-stock portfo-
    lio compare with the risk of the individual stocks if they were held in isolation?
g. Suppose an investor starts with a portfolio consisting of one randomly selected
    stock. What would happen (1) to the risk and (2) to the expected return of the
    portfolio as more and more randomly selected stocks were added to the port-
    folio? What is the implication for investors? Draw a graph of the two portfo-
    lios to illustrate your answer.
h. (1) Should portfolio effects impact the way investors think about the risk of
    individual stocks? (2) If you decided to hold a 1-stock portfolio, and conse-
    quently were exposed to more risk than diversified investors, could you expect
    to be compensated for all of your risk; that is, could you earn a risk premium
    on that part of your risk that you could have eliminated by diversifying?
i. How is market risk measured for individual securities? How are beta coeffi-
    cients calculated?
j. Suppose you have the following historical returns for the stock market and for
    another company, P. Q. Unlimited. Explain how to calculate beta, and use the
    historical stock returns to calculate the beta for PQU. Interpret your results.

Year	Market	PQU
1	25.7%	40.0%
2	8.0	215.0
3	211.0	215.0
4	15.0	35.0
5	32.5	10.0
6	13.7	30.0
7	40.0	42.0
8	10.0	210.0
9	210.8	225.0
10	213.1	25.0

k. The expected rates of return and the beta coefficients of the alternatives as supplied by Barney Smith's computer program are as follows:

Security	Return ($\hat{r}$)	Risk (Beta)
Alta Industries	17.4%	1.29
Market	15.0	1.00
American Foam	13.8	0.68
T-bills	8.0	0.00
Repo Men	1.7	(0.86)

(1) Do the expected returns appear to be related to each alternative's market risk? (2) Is it possible to choose among the alternatives on the basis of the information developed thus far?

l. (1) Write out the Security Market Line (SML) equation, use it to calculate the required rate of return on each alternative, and then graph the relationship between the expected and required rates of return. (2) How do the expected rates of return compare with the required rates of return? (3) Does the fact that Repo Men has an expected return that is less than the T-bill rate make any sense? (4) What would be the market risk and the required return of a 50–50 portfolio of Alta Industries and Repo Men? Of Alta Industries and American Foam?

m. (1) Suppose investors raised their inflation expectations by 3 percentage points over current estimates as reflected in the 8% T-bill rate. What effect would higher inflation have on the SML and on the returns required on high- and low-risk securities? (2) Suppose instead that investors' risk aversion increased enough to cause the market risk premium to increase by 3 percentage points. (Inflation remains constant.) What effect would this have on the SML and on returns of high- and low-risk securities?

Selected Additional Cases

The following cases from Textchoice, Cengage Learning's online library, cover many of the concepts discussed in this chapter and are available at *http://www.textchoice2.com*.

Klein-Brigham Series:
Case 2, "Peachtree Securities, Inc. (A)."
Brigham-Buzzard Series:
Case 2, "Powerline Network Corporation (Risk and Return)."

Portfolio Theory and Other Asset Pricing Models

Americans love mutual funds. By 1985, they had invested about $495 billion in mutual funds, which is not exactly chicken feed. By mid-2006, however, they had invested more than $9 trillion in mutual funds! Not only has the amount of money invested in mutual funds skyrocketed, but the variety of funds is astounding. You can buy funds that specialize in virtually any type of asset, funds that specialize in stocks from a particular industry, a particular continent, or a particular country. There are money market funds that invest only in Treasury bills and other short-term securities, and there are even funds that hold municipal bonds from a specific state.

For those of you with a social conscience, you can buy funds that refuse to own stocks of companies that pollute, sell tobacco products, or have workforces that are not culturally diverse. For others, there is the "Vice Fund," which invests only in brewers, defense contractors, tobacco companies, and the like.

You can also buy "market neutral funds," which sell some stocks short, invest in others, and promise (perhaps falsely) to do well no matter which way the market goes. There

is the Undiscovered Managers Behavioral fund that picks stocks by psychoanalyzing Wall Street analysts. And then there is the Tombstone fund, which owns stocks only from the funeral industry.

You can buy an index fund, which simply holds a portfolio of stocks in an index such as the S&P 500 and doesn't try to beat the market. Instead, index funds strive for low expenses and pass the savings on to investors. An Exchange Traded Fund, or ETF, actually has its own stock that is traded on a stock exchange. Different ETFs hold widely varied portfolios, ranging from the S&P 500 to gold mining companies to Middle Eastern oil companies, and their fees to long-term investors are quite low. At the other extreme, hedge funds, which are pools of money provided by institutions and wealthy individuals, are extremely actively managed—even to the extent of taking over and then operationally managing firms in the portfolio—and have relatively high expenses.

As you read this chapter, think about how portfolio theory, which became widely understood about 30 years ago, has influenced the mutual fund industry.

Sources: The Securities Industry and Financial Markets Association, June 2006, http://www.sia.com/research/pdf/keystats.pdf; "The Many New Faces of Mutual Funds," Fortune, July 6, 1998, pp. 217–218; and "Street Myths," Fortune, May 24, 1999, p. 320.

In Chapter 6 we presented the key elements of risk and return analysis. There we saw that much of a stock's risk can be eliminated by diversification, so rational investors should hold portfolios of stocks rather than just one stock. We also introduced the Capital Asset Pricing Model (CAPM), which links risk and required rates of return, using a stock's beta coefficient as the relevant measure of risk. In this chapter, we extend these concepts and explain portfolio theory. We then present an in-depth treatment of the CAPM, including a more detailed look at how betas are calculated. We discuss two other asset pricing models, the Arbitrage Pricing Theory model and the Fama-French three-factor model. Last, we introduce a new but fast-growing field, behavioral finance.

7.1 Efficient Portfolios

e-resource

The textbook's Web site contains an *Excel* file that will guide you through the chapter's calculations. The file for this chapter is *FM12 Ch 07 Tool Kit.xls,* and we encourage you to open the file and follow along as you read the chapter.

Recall from Chapter 6 the important role that the correlation between assets plays in portfolio risk. One important use of portfolio risk concepts is to select **efficient portfolios,** defined as those portfolios that provide the highest expected return for any degree of risk, or the lowest degree of risk for any expected return. We begin with the two-asset case and then extend it to the general case of N assets.

The Two-Asset Case

Consider two assets, A and B. Suppose we have estimated the expected returns $(\hat{r}_A$ and $\hat{r}_B)$, the standard deviations $(\sigma_A$ and $\sigma_B)$ of returns, and the correlation coefficient (ρ_{AB}) for returns.[1] The expected return and standard deviation for a portfolio containing these two assets are

$$\hat{r}_p = w_A\hat{r}_A + (1 - w_A)\hat{r}_B \qquad (7\text{-}1)$$

and

$$\text{Portfolio SD} = \sigma_p = \sqrt{w_A^2\sigma_A^2 + (1 - w_A)^2\sigma_B^2 + 2w_A(1 - w_A)\rho_{AB}\sigma_A\sigma_B}. \qquad (7\text{-}2)$$

Here w_A is the fraction of the portfolio invested in Security A, so $(1 - w_A)$ is the fraction invested in Security B.

To illustrate, suppose we can allocate our funds between A and B in any proportion. Suppose Security A has an expected rate of return of $\hat{r}_A = 5\%$ and a standard deviation of returns $\sigma_A = 4\%$, while $\hat{r}_B = 8\%$ and $\sigma_B = 10\%$. Our first task is to determine the set of *attainable* portfolios, and then from this attainable set to select the *efficient* subset.

To construct the attainable set, we need data on the degree of correlation between the two securities' expected returns, ρ_{AB}. Let us work with three different assumed degrees of correlation, $\rho_{AB} = +1.0, \rho_{AB} = 0,$ and $\rho_{AB} = -1.0,$ and use

---

[1]See Chapter 6 for definitions using historical data to estimate the expected return, standard deviation, covariance, and correlation.

Corporate Valuation and Risk

In Chapter 1, we told you that managers should strive to make their firms more valuable and that the value of a firm is determined by the size, timing, and risk of its free cash flows (FCF). This chapter provides additional insights into how to measure a firm's risk, which affects its WACC and its value.

$$Value = \frac{FCF_1}{(1 + WACC)^1} + \frac{FCF_2}{(1 + WACC)^2} + \frac{FCF_3}{(1 + WACC)^3} + \cdots + \frac{FCF_\infty}{(1 + WACC)^\infty}$$

them to develop the portfolios' expected returns, $\hat{r}_p$, and standard deviations, σ_p. (Of course, only one correlation can exist; our example simply shows three alternative situations that might exist.)

To calculate $\hat{r}_p$, we use Equation 7-1, substituting the given values for $\hat{r}_A$ and $\hat{r}_B$, and then calculating $\hat{r}_p$ for different values of w_A. For example, when w_A equals 0.75, then $\hat{r}_p = 5.75\%$:

$$\hat{r}_p = w_A\hat{r}_A + (1 - w_A)\hat{r}_B$$
$$= 0.75(5\%) + 0.25(8\%) = 5.75\%.$$

Other values of $\hat{r}_p$ were found similarly, and they are shown in the $\hat{r}_p$ column of Table 7-1.

Next, we use Equation 7-2 to find σ_p. Substitute the given values for σ_A, σ_B, and ρ_{AB}, and then calculate σ_p for different values of w_A. For example, in the case where $\rho_{AB} = 0$ and $w_A = 0.75$, then $\sigma_p = 3.9\%$:

$$\sigma_p = \sqrt{w_A^2\sigma_A^2 + (1 - w_A)^2\sigma_B^2 + 2w_A(1 - w_A)\rho_{AB}\sigma_A\sigma_B}$$
$$= \sqrt{(0.5625)(0.0016) + (0.0625)(0.01) + 2(0.75)(0.25)(0)(0.04)(0.10)}$$
$$= \sqrt{0.0009 + 0.000625} = \sqrt{0.001525} = 0.039 = 3.9\%.$$

Table 7-1

$\hat{r}_p$ and σ_p under Various Assumptions

Proportion of Portfolio in Security A (Value of w_A)	Proportion of Portfolio in Security B (Value of $1 - w_A$)	$\hat{r}_p$	σ_p Case I ($\rho_{AB} = +1.0$)	σ_p Case II ($\rho_{AB} = 0$)	σ_p Case III ($\rho_{AB} = -1.0$)
1.00	0.00	5.00%	4.0%	4.0%	4.0%
0.75	0.25	5.75	5.5	3.9	0.5
0.50	0.50	6.50	7.0	5.4	3.0
0.25	0.75	7.25	8.5	7.6	6.5
0.00	1.00	8.00	10.0	10.0	10.0

FM

e-resource

See *FM12 Ch 07 Tool Kit.xls* at the textbook's Web site for all calculations.

Table 7-1 gives $\hat{r}_p$ and σ_p values for w_A = 1.00, 0.75, 0.50, 0.25, and 0.00, and Figure 7-1 plots $\hat{r}_p$, σ_p, and the attainable set of portfolios for each correlation. In both the table and the graphs, note the following points:

1. The three graphs across the top row of Figure 7-1 designate Case I, where the two assets are perfectly positively correlated; that is, ρ_{AB} = +1.0. The three graphs in the middle row are for the zero correlation case, and the three in the bottom row are for perfect negative correlation.
2. We rarely encounter ρ_{AB} = −1.0, 0.0, or +1.0. Generally, ρ_{AB} is in the range of +0.5 to +0.7 for most stocks. Case II (zero correlation) produces graphs which, pictorially, most closely resemble real-world examples.
3. The left column of graphs shows how the *expected portfolio returns* vary with different combinations of A and B. We see that these graphs are identical in each of the three cases: The portfolio return, $\hat{r}_p$, is a linear function of w_A, and it does not depend on the correlation coefficients. This is also seen from the single $\hat{r}_p$ column in Table 7-1.
4. The middle column of graphs shows how risk is affected by the portfolio mix. Starting from the top, we see that portfolio risk, σ_p, increases linearly in Case I, where ρ_{AB} = +1.0; it is nonlinear in Case II; and Case III shows that risk can be completely diversified away if ρ_{AB} = −1.0. Thus σ_p, unlike $\hat{r}_p$, *does* depend on correlation.

Figure 7-1

Illustrations of Portfolio Returns, Risk, and the Attainable Set of Portfolios

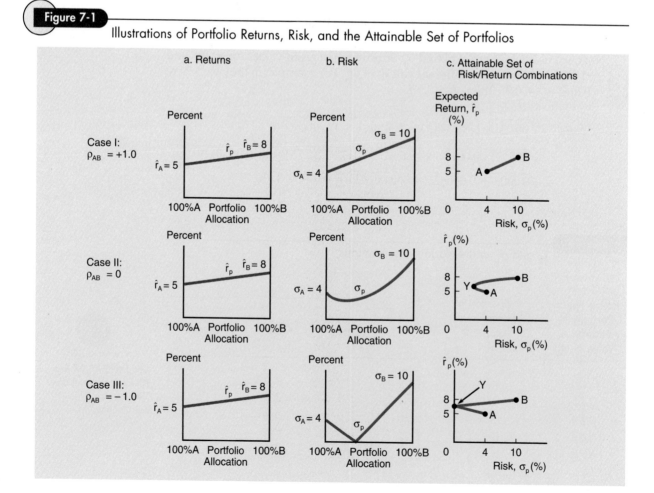

5. Note that in both Cases II and III, but not in Case I, someone holding only Stock A could sell some A, buy some B, and both increase his or her expected return and lower risk.

6. The right column of graphs shows the attainable, or feasible, set of portfolios constructed with different mixes of Securities A and B. Unlike the other columns, which plotted return and risk versus the portfolio's composition, each of the three graphs here was plotted from pairs of $\hat{r}_p$ and σ_p as shown in Table 7-1. For example, Point A in the upper right graph is the point $\hat{r}_p = 5\%$, $\sigma_p = 4\%$ from the Case I data. All other points on the curves were plotted similarly. With only two securities in the portfolio, the attainable set is a curve or line, and we can achieve each risk/return combination on the relevant curve by some allocation of our investment funds between Securities A and B.

7. Are all combinations on the attainable set equally good? The answer is no. Only that part of the attainable set from Y to B in Cases II and III is defined to be efficient. The part from A to Y is inefficient because for any degree of risk on the line segment AY, a higher return can be found on segment YB. Thus, no rational investor would hold a portfolio that lies on segment AY. In Case I, however, the entire feasible set is efficient—no combination of the securities can be ruled out.

From these examples we see that in one extreme case ($\rho = -1.0$), risk can be completely eliminated, while in the other extreme case ($\rho = +1.0$), diversification does no good whatsoever. In between these extremes, combining two stocks into a portfolio reduces but does not eliminate the risk inherent in the individual stocks. If we differentiate Equation 7-2, set the derivative equal to zero, and then solve for w_A, we obtain the fraction of the portfolio that should be invested in Security A if we wish to form the least-risky portfolio. Here is the equation:

$$\text{Minimum risk portfolio: } w_A = \frac{\sigma_B(\sigma_B - \rho_{AB}\sigma_A)}{\sigma_A^2 + \sigma_B^2 - 2\rho_{AB}\sigma_A\sigma_B}. \qquad (7\text{-}3)$$

As a rule, we limit w_A to the range 0 to $+1.0$; that is, if the solution value is $w_A > 1.0$, set $w_A = 1.0$, and if w_A is negative, set $w_A = 0.0$. A w_A value that is negative means that Security A is sold short; if w_A is greater than 1.0, B is sold short. In a short sale, you borrow a stock and then sell it, expecting to buy it back later (at a lower price) in order to repay the person from whom the stock was borrowed. If you sell short and the stock price rises, you lose, but you win if the price declines.

The N-Asset Case

The same principles from the two-asset case also apply when the portfolio is composed of N assets. Here is the notation for the N-asset case: The percentage of the investment in asset i (the portfolio weight) is w_i, the expected return for asset i is $\hat{r}_i$, the standard deviation of asset i is σ_i, and the correlation between asset i and asset j is ρ_{ij}. The expected return for a portfolio with N assets is

$$\hat{r}_p = \sum_{i=1}^{N} (w_i \hat{r}_i) \qquad (7\text{-}4)$$

and the variance of the portfolio is

$$\sigma_p^2 = \sum_{i=1}^{N} \sum_{j=1}^{N} (w_i w_j \sigma_i \sigma_j \rho_{ij}). \tag{7-5}$$

For the case in which $i = j$, the correlation is $\rho_{ii} = 1$. Notice also that when $i = j$, the product $\sigma_i \sigma_i = \sigma_i^2$.

One way to apply Equation 7-5 is to set up a table, with a row and column for each asset. Give the rows and columns labels showing the assets' weights and standard deviations. Then fill in each cell in the table by multiplying the values in the row and column headings by the correlation between the assets, as shown below:

	$w_1\sigma_1$ (1)	$w_2\sigma_2$ (2)	$w_3\sigma_3$ (3)
$w_1\sigma_1$ (1)	$w_1\sigma_1 w_1\sigma_1 \rho_{11} = w_1^2\sigma_1^2$	$w_1\sigma_1 w_2\sigma_2 \rho_{12}$	$w_1\sigma_1 w_3\sigma_3 \rho_{13}$
$w_2\sigma_2$ (2)	$w_2\sigma_2 w_1\sigma_1 \rho_{21}$	$w_2\sigma_2 w_2\sigma_2 \rho_{22} = w_2^2\sigma_2^2$	$w_2\sigma_2 w_3\sigma_3 \rho_{23}$
$w_3\sigma_3$ (3)	$w_3\sigma_3 w_1\sigma_1 \rho_{31}$	$w_3\sigma_3 w_2\sigma_2 \rho_{32}$	$w_3\sigma_3 w_3\sigma_3 \rho_{33} = w_3^2\sigma_3^2$

The portfolio variance is the sum of the nine cells. For the diagonals, we have substituted the values for the case in which $i = j$. Notice that some of the cells have identical values. For example, the cell for Row 1 and Column 2 has the same value as the cell for Column 1 and Row 2. This suggests an alternative formula:

$$\sigma_p^2 = \sum_{i=1}^{N} w_i^2\sigma_i^2 + \sum_{i=1}^{N} \sum_{\substack{j=1 \\ j \neq i}}^{N} 2w_i\sigma_i w_j\sigma_j \rho_{ij}. \tag{7-5a}$$

The main thing to remember when calculating portfolio standard deviations is to not leave out any terms. Using a table like the one above can help.

SELF-TEST

What is meant by the term "attainable, or feasible, set"?

Within the attainable set, which portfolios are "efficient"?

Stock A has an expected return of 10% and a standard deviation of 35%. Stock B has an expected return of 14% and a standard deviation of 45%. The correlation coefficient between Stock A and B is 0.3. What are the expected return and standard deviation of a portfolio invested 60% in Stock A and 40% in Stock B? (12.0%; 31.5%)

7.2   Choosing the Optimal Portfolio

With only two assets, the feasible set of portfolios is a line or curve as shown in the third column of graphs back in Figure 7-1. However, if we were to increase the number of assets, we would obtain an area like the shaded area in Figure 7-2. The points A, H, G, and E represent single securities (or portfolios containing only one security). All the other points in the shaded area and its boundaries, which comprise the feasible set, represent portfolios of two or more securities. Each point in this area represents a particular portfolio with a risk of σ_p and an expected return of $\hat{r}_p$. For example, point X represents one such portfolio's risk and expected return, as do B, C, and D.

Figure 7-2

The Efficient Set of Investments

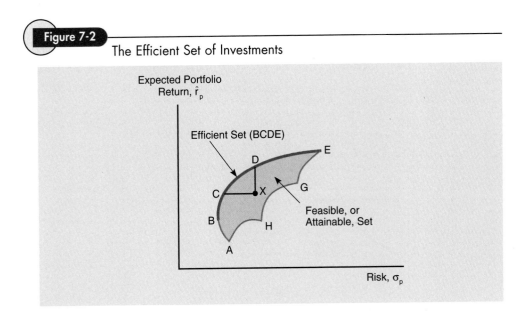

The Efficient Frontier

Given the full set of potential portfolios that could be constructed from the available assets, which portfolio should actually be held? This choice involves two separate decisions: (1) determining the efficient set of portfolios and (2) choosing from the efficient set the single portfolio that is best for the specific investor.

The Efficient Frontier

In Figure 7-2, the boundary line BCDE defines the efficient set of portfolios, which is also called the **efficient frontier**.[2] Portfolios to the left of the efficient set are not possible because they lie outside the attainable set. Portfolios to the right of the boundary line (interior portfolios) are inefficient because some other portfolio would provide either a higher return for the same degree of risk or a lower risk for the same rate of return. For example, Portfolio X is dominated by Portfolios C and D.

Risk/Return Indifference Curves

Given the efficient set of portfolios, which specific portfolio should an investor choose? To determine the optimal portfolio for a particular investor, we must know the investor's attitude toward risk as reflected in his or her risk/return trade-off function, or **indifference curve.**

An investor's risk/return trade-off function is based on the standard economic concepts of utility theory and indifference curves, which are illustrated in Figure 7-3. The curves labeled I_Y and I_Z represent the indifference curves of Individuals Y and Z. Ms. Y is indifferent between the riskless 5% portfolio, a portfolio with an expected return of 6% but a risk of $\sigma_p = 1.4\%$, and so on. Mr. Z is indifferent between a riskless 5% return, an expected 6% return with risk of $\sigma_p = 3.3\%$, and so on.

---

[2]A computational procedure for determining the efficient set of portfolios was developed by Harry Markowitz and first reported in his article "Portfolio Selection," *Journal of Finance*, March 1952. In this article, Markowitz developed the basic concepts of portfolio theory, and he later won the Nobel Prize in economics for his work.

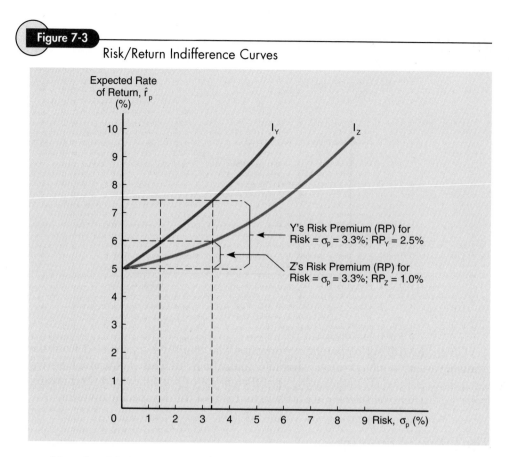

Figure 7-3

Risk/Return Indifference Curves

Note that Ms. Y requires a higher expected rate of return as compensation for any given amount of risk; thus, Ms. Y is said to be more **risk averse** than Mr. Z. Her higher risk aversion causes Ms. Y to require a higher **risk premium**—defined here as the difference between the 5% riskless return and the expected return required to compensate for any specific amount of risk—than Mr. Z requires. Thus, Ms. Y requires a risk premium (RP_Y) of 2.5% to compensate for a risk of $\sigma_p = 3.3\%$, while Mr. Z's risk premium for this degree of risk is only $RP_Z = 1.0\%$. *As a generalization, the steeper the slope of an investor's indifference curve, the more risk averse the investor.* Thus, Ms. Y is more risk averse than Mr. Z.

Each individual has a "map" of indifference curves; the indifference maps for Ms. Y and Mr. Z are shown in Figure 7-4. The higher curves denote a greater level of satisfaction (or utility). Thus, I_{Z2} is better than I_{Z1} because, for any level of risk, Mr. Z has a higher expected return, hence greater utility. An infinite number of indifference curves could be drawn in the map for each individual, and each individual has a unique map.

The Optimal Portfolio for an Investor

Figure 7-4 also shows the feasible set of portfolios for the two-asset case, under the assumption that $\rho_{AB} = 0$, as it was developed in Figure 7-1. The optimal portfolio for each investor is found at the tangency point between the efficient set of portfolios and one of the investor's indifference curves. This tangency point marks the highest level of satisfaction the investor can attain. Ms. Y, who is more risk averse than Mr. Z, chooses a portfolio with a lower expected return (about 6%) but a risk

Figure 7-4

Selecting the Optimal Portfolio of Risky Assets

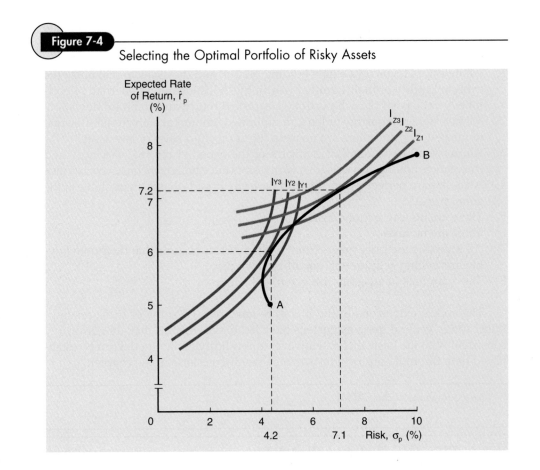

of only $\sigma_p = 4.2\%$. Mr. Z picks a portfolio that provides an expected return of about 7.2%, but it has a risk of about $\sigma_p = 7.1\%$. Ms. Y's portfolio is more heavily weighted with the less risky security, while Mr. Z's portfolio contains a larger proportion of the more risky security.[3]

SELF-TEST

What is the efficient frontier?
What are indifference curves?
Conceptually, how does an investor choose his or her optimal portfolio?

7.3 The Basic Assumptions of the Capital Asset Pricing Model

The **Capital Asset Pricing Model (CAPM),** which was introduced in the last chapter, specifies the relationship between risk and required rates of return on assets

---

[3]Ms. Y's portfolio would contain 67% of Security A and 33% of Security B, whereas Mr. Z's portfolio would consist of 27% of Security A and 73% of Security B. These percentages can be determined with Equation 7-1 by simply seeing what percentage of the two securities is consistent with $\hat{r}_p = 6.0\%$ and 7.2%. For example, $w_A(5\%) + (1 - w_A)(8\%) = 7.2\%$, and solving for w_A, we obtain $w_A = 0.27$ and $(1 - w_A) = 0.73$.

when they are held in well-diversified portfolios. The assumptions underlying the CAPM's development are summarized in the following list:[4]

1. All investors focus on a single holding period, and they seek to maximize the expected utility of their terminal wealth by choosing among alternative portfolios on the basis of each portfolio's expected return and standard deviation.
2. All investors can borrow or lend an unlimited amount at a given risk-free rate of interest, r_{RF}, and there are no restrictions on short sales of any asset.[5]
3. All investors have identical estimates of the expected returns, variances, and covariances among all assets (that is, investors have homogeneous expectations).
4. All assets are perfectly divisible and perfectly liquid (that is, marketable at the going price).
5. There are no transactions costs.
6. There are no taxes.
7. All investors are price takers (that is, all investors assume that their own buying and selling activity will not affect stock prices).
8. The quantities of all assets are given and fixed.

Theoretical extensions in the literature have relaxed some of these assumptions, and in general these extensions have led to conclusions that are reasonably consistent with the basic theory. However, the validity of any model can be established only through empirical tests, which we discuss later in the chapter.

SELF-TEST

What are the key assumptions of the CAPM?

7.4   The Capital Market Line and the Security Market Line

Figure 7-4 showed the set of portfolio opportunities for the two-asset case, and it illustrated how indifference curves can be used to select the optimal portfolio from the feasible set. In Figure 7-5, we show a similar diagram for the many-asset case, but here we also include a risk-free asset with a return r_{RF}. The riskless asset by definition has zero risk, $\sigma = 0\%$, so it is plotted on the vertical axis.

The figure shows both the feasible set of portfolios of risky assets (the shaded area) and a set of indifference curves (I_1, I_2, I_3) for a particular investor. Point N, where indifference curve I_1 is tangent to the efficient set, represents a possible portfolio choice; it is the point on the efficient set of risky portfolios where the investor obtains the highest possible return for a given amount of risk and the smallest degree of risk for a given expected return.

However, the investor can do better than Portfolio N; he or she can reach a higher indifference curve. In addition to the feasible set of risky portfolios, we now have a risk-free asset that provides a riskless return, r_{RF}. Given the risk-free asset, investors can create new portfolios that combine the risk-free asset with a

---

[4]The CAPM was originated by William F. Sharpe in his article "Capital Asset Prices: A Theory of Market Equilibrium under Conditions of Risk," which appeared in the September 1964 issue of the *Journal of Finance*. Note that Professor Sharpe won the Nobel Prize in economics for his capital asset pricing work. The assumptions inherent in Sharpe's model were spelled out by Michael C. Jensen in "Capital Markets: Theory and Evidence," *Bell Journal of Economics and Management Science*, Autumn 1972, pp. 357–398.
[5]With no restrictions on short sales, an asset's weight in the portfolio may be negative or greater than 1 as long as the sum of all asset weights equals 1.

Figure 7-5

Investor Equilibrium: Combining the Risk-Free Asset with the Market Portfolio

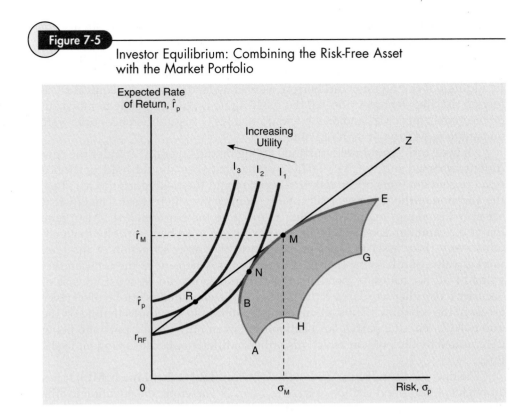

portfolio of risky assets. This enables them to achieve any combination of risk and return on the straight line connecting r_{RF} with M, the point of tangency between that straight line and the efficient frontier of risky asset portfolios.[6] Some portfolios on the line $r_{RF}MZ$ will be preferred to most risky portfolios on the efficient frontier BNME, so the points on the line $r_{RF}MZ$ now represent the best attainable combinations of risk and return.

Given the new opportunities along line $r_{RF}MZ$, our investor will move from Point N to Point R, which is on his or her highest attainable risk/return

---

[6]The risk/return combinations between a risk-free asset and a risky asset (a single stock or a portfolio of stocks) will always be linear. To see this, consider the following equations, which were developed earlier, for return, $\hat{r}_p$, and risk, σ_p, for any combination w_{RF} and $(1 - w_{RF})$:

$$\hat{r}_p = w_{RF}\, r_{RF} + (1 - w_{RF})\, \hat{r}_M \qquad (7\text{-}1a)$$

and

$$\sigma_P = \sqrt{w_{RF}^2\sigma_{RF}^2 + (1 - w_{RF})^2\sigma_M^2 + 2w_{RF}(1 - w_{RF})\rho_{RF,M}\sigma_{RF}\sigma_M}. \qquad (7\text{-}2a)$$

Equation 7-1a is linear. As for Equation 7-2a, we know that r_{RF} is the risk-free asset, so $\sigma_{RF} = 0$; hence, σ_{RF}^2 is also zero. Using this information, we can simplify Equation 7-2a as follows:

$$\sigma_P = \sqrt{(1 - w_{RF})^2\sigma_M^2} = (1 - w_{RF})\sigma_M. \qquad (7\text{-}2b)$$

Thus, σ_p is also linear when a riskless asset is combined with a portfolio of risky assets.

If expected returns, as measured by $\hat{r}_p$, and risk, as measured by σ_p, are both linear functions of w_{RF}, then the relationship between $\hat{r}_p$ and σ_p, when graphed as in Figure 7-5, must also be linear. For example, if 100% of the portfolio is invested in r_{RF} with a return of 8%, the portfolio return will be 8% and σ_p will be 0. If 100% is invested in M, with $r_M = 12\%$ and $\sigma_M = 10\%$, then $\sigma_p = 1.0(10\%) = 10\%$, and $\hat{r}_p = 0(8\%) + 1.0(12\%) = 12\%$. If 50% of the portfolio is invested in M and 50% in the risk-free asset, then $\sigma_p = 0.5(10\%) = 5\%$, and $\hat{r}_p = 0.5(8\%) + 0.5(12\%) = 10\%$. Plotting these points will reveal the linear relationship given as $r_{RF}MZ$ in Figure 7-5.

indifference curve. Note that any point on the old efficient frontier BNME (except the point of tangency M) is dominated by some point along the line $r_{RF}MZ$. In general, since investors can include both the risk-free security and a fraction of the risky portfolio, M, in a portfolio, it will be possible to move to a point such as R. In addition, if the investor can borrow as well as lend (lending is equivalent to buying risk-free debt securities) at the riskless rate r_{RF}, it is possible to move out on the line segment MZ, and one would do so if his or her indifference curve were tangent to $r_{RF}MZ$ to the right of Point M.[7]

All investors should hold portfolios lying on the line $r_{RF}MZ$ under the conditions assumed in the CAPM. This implies that they should hold portfolios that are combinations of the risk-free security and the risky portfolio M. Thus, the addition of the risk-free asset totally changes the efficient set: The efficient set now lies along line $r_{RF}MZ$ rather than along the curve BNME. Also, note that if the capital market is to be in equilibrium, M must be a portfolio that contains every risky asset in exact proportion to that asset's fraction of the total market value of all assets; that is, if Security i is X percent of the total market value of all securities, X percent of the market portfolio M must consist of Security i. (In other words, M is the market-value-weighted portfolio of *all* risky assets in the economy.) Thus, all investors should hold portfolios that lie on the line $r_{RF}MZ$, with the particular location of a given individual's portfolio being determined by the point at which his or her indifference curve is tangent to the line.

The line $r_{RF}MZ$ in Figure 7-5 is called the **Capital Market Line (CML).** It has an intercept of r_{RF} and a slope of $(\hat{r}_M - r_{RF})/\sigma_M$.[8] Therefore, the equation for the Capital Market Line may be expressed as follows:

$$\text{CML: } \hat{r}_p = r_{RF} + \left(\frac{\hat{r}_M - r_{RF}}{\sigma_M} \right) \sigma_p. \qquad (7\text{-}6)$$

The expected rate of return *on an efficient portfolio* is equal to the riskless rate plus a risk premium that is equal to $(\hat{r}_M - r_{RF})/\sigma_M$ multiplied by the portfolio's standard deviation, σ_p. Thus, the CML specifies a linear relationship between an efficient portfolio's expected return and risk, with the slope of the CML being equal to the expected return on the market portfolio of risky stocks, $\hat{r}_M$, minus the risk-free rate, r_{RF}, which is called the **market risk premium,** all divided by the standard deviation of returns on the market portfolio, σ_M:

$$\text{Slope of the CML} = (\hat{r}_M - r_{RF})/\sigma_M.$$

---

[7]An investor who is highly averse to risk will have a steep indifference curve and will end up holding only the riskless asset, or perhaps a portfolio at a point such as R, holding some of the risky market portfolio and some of the riskless asset. An investor only slightly averse to risk will have a relatively flat indifference curve, which will cause him or her to move out beyond M toward Z, borrowing to do so. This investor might buy stocks on margin, which means borrowing and using the stocks as collateral. If individuals' borrowing rates are higher than r_{RF}, then the line $r_{RF}MZ$ will tilt down (that is, be less steep) beyond M. This condition would invalidate the basic CAPM, or at least require it to be modified. Therefore, the assumption of being able to borrow or lend at the same rate is crucial to CAPM theory.

[8]Recall that the slope of any line is measured as $\Delta Y/\Delta X$, or the change in height associated with a given change in horizontal distance. r_{RF} is at 0 on the horizontal axis, so $\Delta X = \sigma_M - 0 = \sigma_M$. The vertical axis difference associated with a change from r_{RF} to $\hat{r}_M$ is $\hat{r}_M - r_{RF}$. Therefore, slope $= \Delta Y/\Delta X = (\hat{r}_M - r_{RF})/\sigma_M$.

For example, suppose $r_{RF} = 10\%$, $\hat{r}_M = 15\%$, and $\sigma_M = 15\%$. Then, the slope of the CML would be $(15\% - 10\%)/15\% = 0.33\%$, and if a particular efficient portfolio had $\sigma_p = 10\%$, then its $\hat{r}_p$ would be

$$\hat{r}_p = 10\% + 0.33(10\%) = 13.3\%.$$

A riskier portfolio with $\sigma_p = 20\%$ would have $\hat{r}_p = 10\% + 0.33(20\%) = 16.6\%$.

The CML is graphed in Figure 7-6. It is a straight line with an intercept at r_{RF} and a slope equal to the market risk premium $(r_M - r_{RF})$ divided by σ_M. The slope of the CML reflects the aggregate attitude of investors toward risk.

Note that an efficient portfolio is one that is well diversified; hence all of its unsystematic risk has been eliminated and its only remaining risk is market risk. Therefore, unlike individual stocks, the risk of an efficient portfolio is measured by its standard deviation, σ_p. The CML equation specifies the relationship between risk and return for such efficient portfolios, that is, for portfolios that lie on the CML, and in the CML equation and graph, risk is measured by portfolio standard deviation.

The CML specifies the relationship between risk and return for an efficient portfolio, but investors and managers are more concerned about the relationship between risk and return for *individual assets*. To develop the risk/return relationship for individual securities, note in Figure 7-5 that all investors are assumed to hold portfolio M, so M must be the market portfolio, that is, the one that contains all stocks. Note also that M is an *efficient* portfolio. Thus, the CML defines the relationship between the market portfolio's expected return and its standard deviation. Equations 7-4 and 7-5 show the formulas for the expected return and standard deviation for a multi-asset portfolio, including the market portfolio. It is possible to take the equations for the expected return and standard deviation of a multi-asset portfolio and show that the required return for each individual stock i

---

Figure 7-6

The Capital Market Line (CML)

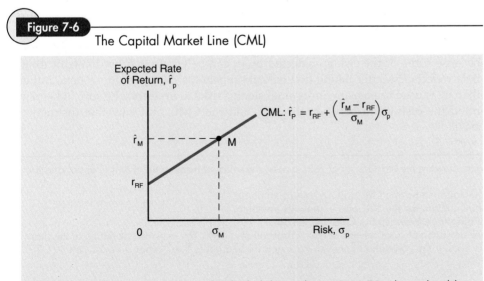

Note: We did not draw it in, but you can visualize the shaded space shown in Figure 7-5 in this graph and the CML as the line formed by connecting r_{RF} with the tangent to the shaded space.

must conform to the following equation in order for the CML to hold for the market portfolio:[9]

$$r_i = r_{RF} + \frac{(r_M - r_{RF})}{\sigma_M}\left(\frac{Cov(r_i, r_M)}{\sigma_M}\right)$$

$$= r_{RF} + (r_M - r_{RF})\left(\frac{Cov(r_i, r_M)}{\sigma_M^2}\right). \tag{7-7}$$

The CAPM defines the beta coefficient of company i, b_i, as follows:

$$b_i = \frac{\text{Covariance between Stock i and the market}}{\text{Variance of market returns}} = \frac{Cov(r_i, r_M)}{\sigma_M^2}$$

$$= \frac{\rho_{iM}\sigma_i\sigma_M}{\sigma_M^2} = \rho_{iM}\left(\frac{\sigma_i}{\sigma_M}\right). \tag{7-8}$$

Recall that the risk premium for the market, RP_M, is $r_M - r_{RF}$. Using this definition and substituting Equation 7-8 into Equation 7-7 gives the **Security Market Line (SML):**

$$\text{SML: } r_i = r_{RF} + (r_M - r_{RF})b_i$$

$$= r_{RF} + (RP_M)b_i. \tag{7-9}$$

The SML tells us that an individual stock's required return is equal to the risk-free rate plus a premium for bearing risk. The premium for risk is equal to the risk premium for the market, RP_M, multiplied by the risk of the individual stock, as measured by its beta coefficient. The beta coefficient measures the amount of risk that the stock contributes to the market portfolio.

Unlike the CML for a well-diversified portfolio, the SML tells us that the standard deviation (σ_i) of an individual stock should not be used to measure its risk, because some of the risk as reflected by σ_i can be eliminated by diversification. Beta reflects risk after taking diversification benefits into account, so beta, rather than σ_i, is used to measure individual stocks' risks to investors. Be sure to keep in mind the distinction between the SML and the CML, and why that distinction exists.

SELF-TEST

Draw a graph showing the feasible set of risky assets, the efficient frontier, the risk-free asset, and the CML.

Write out the equation for the CML and explain its meaning.

Write out the equation for the SML and explain its meaning.

What is the difference between the CML and the SML?

The standard deviation of stock returns of Park Corporation is 60%. The standard deviation of the market return is 20%. If the correlation between Park and the market is 0.40, what is Park's beta? (1.2)

---

[9]For consistency with most investments textbooks, we let $Cov(r_i, r_M)$ denote the covariance between the returns of assets i and M. Using the notation in Chapter 6, we would have denoted the covariance as COV_{iM}.

7.5   Calculating Beta Coefficients

Equation 7-7 defines beta, but recall from Chapter 6 that this equation for beta is also the formula for the slope coefficient in a regression of the stock return against the market return. Therefore, beta can be calculated by plotting the historical returns of a stock on the y-axis of a graph versus the historical returns of the market portfolio on the x-axis, and fitting the regression line. In his 1964 article that set forth the CAPM, Sharpe called this regression line the **characteristic line.** Thus, a stock's beta is the slope of its characteristic line. In Chapter 6 we used this approach to calculate the beta for General Electric. In this chapter, we perform a more detailed analysis of the calculation of beta for General Electric, and we also perform a similar analysis for a portfolio of stocks, Fidelity's Magellan Fund.

Calculating the Beta Coefficient for a Single Stock: General Electric

Table 7-2 shows a summary of the data used in this analysis; the full data set is in the file **FM12 Ch 07 Tool Kit.xls**. Table 7-2 shows the market returns (defined as the percentage price change of the S&P 500), the stock returns for GE, and the returns on the Magellan Fund (which is a well-diversified portfolio). The table also shows the risk-free rate, defined as the rate on a short-term (3-month) U.S. Treasury bill, which we will use later in this analysis.

FM
e-resource
See **FM12 Ch 07 Tool Kit.xls** at the textbook's Web site.

As Table 7-2 shows, GE had an average annual return of 6.9% during this 4-year period (June 2002 through May 2006), while the market had an average annual return of 5.4%. As we noted before, it is usually unreasonable to think that the future expected return for a stock will equal its average historical return over a relatively short period, such as 4 years. However, we might well expect past volatility to be a reasonable estimate of future volatility, at least during the next couple of years. Note that the standard deviation for GE's return during this period was 19.1% versus 13.0% for the market. Thus, the market's volatility is less than that of GE. This is what we would expect, since the market is a well-diversified portfolio and thus much of its risk has been diversified away. The correlation between GE's stock returns and the market returns is about 0.49, which is a little higher than the correlation for a typical stock.

Table 7-2

Summary of Data for Calculating Beta (June 2002–May 2006)

	r_M, Market Return (S&P 500 Index)	r_i, GE Return	r_p, Fidelity Megellan Fund Return	r_{RF}, Risk-Free Rate (Monthly Return on 3-Month T-Bill)
Average return (annual)	5.4%	6.9%	5.7%	2.1%
Standard deviation (annual)	13.0%	19.1%	13.5%	0.4%
Correlation with market return, ρ		0.49	0.98	−0.04

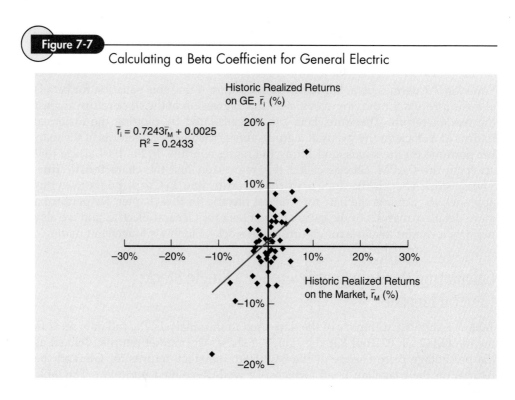

Figure 7-7

Calculating a Beta Coefficient for General Electric

$\bar{r}_i = 0.7243\bar{r}_M + 0.0025$
$R^2 = 0.2433$

Historic Realized Returns on GE, $\bar{r}_i$ (%)

Historic Realized Returns on the Market, $\bar{r}_M$ (%)

Figure 7-7 shows a plot of GE's returns against the market's returns. As you will notice if you look in the file **FM12 Ch 07 Tool Kit.xls**, we used the *Excel* chart feature to add a trend line and to display the equation and R^2 value on the chart itself. We also used the *Excel* regression analysis feature, which provides additional data.

Table 7-3 reports some of the regression results for GE. Its estimated beta, which is the slope coefficient, is about 0.72. This means that GE's beta is less than the average beta of 1.0. Therefore, GE moves up and down, on average, by less than the same percent as the market. As with all regression results, 0.72 is just an estimate of beta, and not necessarily the true value of beta. Table 7-3 also shows the t statistic and the probability that the true beta is zero. For GE, this probability is approximately equal to zero. This means that there is virtually a zero chance that the true beta is equal to zero. Since this probability is less than 5%, statisticians would say that the slope coefficient, beta, is "statistically significant." The output of the regression analysis also gives us the 95% confidence interval for the estimate of beta. For GE, the results tell us that we can be 95% confident that the true beta is between 0.35 and 1.10. This is an extremely wide range, but it is typical for most individual stocks. Therefore, the regression estimate for the beta of any single company is highly uncertain.

Note also that the points in Figure 7-7 are not clustered very tightly around the regression line. Sometimes GE does much better than the market; other times it does much worse. The R^2 value shown in the chart measures the degree of dispersion about the regression line. Statistically speaking, it measures the percent of variance that is explained by the regression equation. An R^2 of 1.0 indicates that all points lie exactly on the line, hence that all of the variance of the y-variable is explained by the x-variable. The R^2 for GE is about 0.24, which is typical for most individual stocks. This indicates that about 24% of the variance in GE's returns is explained by the market return.

Table 7-3

Regression Results for Calculating Beta

	Regression Coefficient	t Statistic	Probability of t Statistic	Lower 95% Confidence Interval	Upper 95% Confidence Interval
Panel a: General Electric (Market model)					
Intercept	0.00	0.35	0.73	−0.01	0.02
Slope	0.72	3.85	0.00	0.35	1.10
Panel b: Magellan Fund (Market model)					
Intercept	0.00	0.16	0.88	0.00	0.00
Slope	1.01	31.86	0.00	0.95	1.08
Panel c: General Electric (CAPM: Excess returns)					
Intercept	0.00	0.29	0.78	−0.01	0.02
Slope	0.73	3.87	0.00	0.35	1.11

Note: The market model uses actual historical returns; the CAPM model uses returns in excess of the risk-free rate.

Finally, note that the intercept shown in the regression equation displayed on the chart is about 0.0025. Since the regression equation is based on monthly data, this means that GE had a 3% average monthly return that was not explained by the CAPM model. However, the regression results in Table 7-3 also show that the probability of the t statistic is greater than 5%, meaning that the "true" intercept might be zero. Therefore, most statisticians would say that this intercept is not statistically significant—the returns of GE are so volatile that we cannot be sure that the true intercept is not equal to zero. Translating statistician-talk into English, this means that the part of GE's average monthly return that is not explained by the CAPM could very well be zero. Thus, the CAPM might very well explain all of GE's average monthly returns.

The Market Model versus the CAPM

Note that when we estimated beta, we used the following regression equation:

$$\bar{r}_{i,t} = a_i + b_i\bar{r}_{M,t} + e_{i,t} \tag{7-10}$$

where

$\bar{r}_{i,t}$ = historical (realized) rate of return on Stock i in period t.
$\bar{r}_{M,t}$ = historical (realized) rate of return on the market in period t.
a_i = vertical axis intercept term for Stock i.
b_i = slope, or beta coefficient, for Stock i.
$e_{i,t}$ = random error, reflecting the difference between the actual return on Stock i in a given period and the return as predicted by the regression line.

Equation 7-10 is called the **market model,** because it regresses the stock's return against the market's return. However, the SML of the CAPM for realized returns is a little different from Equation 7-10, as is shown below:

$$\text{SML for realized returns: } \bar{r}_{i,t} = \bar{r}_{RF,t} + b_i(\bar{r}_{M,t} - \bar{r}_{RF,t}) + e_{i,t}, \qquad \textbf{(7-11)}$$

where $\bar{r}_{RF,t}$ is the historical (realized) risk-free rate in period t.

To use the CAPM to estimate beta, we must rewrite Equation 7-11 to be a regression equation by adding an intercept, a_i. The resulting regression equation is

$$(\bar{r}_i - \bar{r}_{RF,t}) = a_i + b_i(\bar{r}_{M,t} - \bar{r}_{RF,t}) + e_{i,t}. \qquad \textbf{(7-12)}$$

Therefore, to be theoretically correct when estimating beta, we should use the stock's return in excess of the risk-free rate as the y-variable and the market's return in excess of the risk-free rate as the x-variable. We did this for GE using the data in Table 7-2, and the results are reported in Panel c of Table 7-3. Note that there are no appreciable differences between the results in Panel a, the market model, and in Panel c, the CAPM model. This typically is the case, so we will use the market model in the rest of this book.

Calculating the Beta Coefficient for a Portfolio: The Magellan Fund

Let's calculate beta for the Magellan Fund, which is a well-diversified portfolio. Figure 7-8 shows the plot of Magellan's monthly returns versus the market's monthly returns. Note the differences between this chart and the one for GE shown in Figure 7-7. The points for Magellan are tightly clustered around the regression line, indicating that the vast majority of Magellan's volatility is explained by the stock market. The R^2 of over 0.95 confirms this visual conclusion. We can also see from Table 7-2 that the Magellan Fund has a standard deviation of 13.5%, which is only slightly higher than the 13.0% standard deviation of the market.

As Table 7-3 shows, the estimated beta is 1.01, and the 95% confidence interval is from 0.95 to 1.08, which is much tighter than the one for GE. The intercept is virtually zero, and the probability of the intercept's t statistic is greater than 5%. Therefore, the intercept is statistically insignificant, indicating that the CAPM explains the average monthly return of the Magellan Fund very well.

Mutual fund managers are often evaluated by their risk-adjusted performance. The three most widely used measures are *Jensen's alpha, Sharpe's reward-to-variability ratio,* and *Treynor's reward-to-volatility ratio.* **Jensen's alpha,** which is the intercept in a CAPM regression of excess returns, is 0.25% per year for Magellan, which seems to indicate that the Magellan fund had slightly superior performance. However, this intercept was not statistically significantly different from zero. Its t statistic is 0.18, which is so low a value that it could happen about 86% of the time by chance even if the intercept is truly zero. If this probability is greater than 5%, as is the case for Magellan, most statisticians will be reluctant to conclude that Magellan's excess return of 0.25% is truly better than zero, not just a result of pure chance.

e-resource

See **FM12 Ch 07 Tool Kit.xls** at the textbook's Web site for all calculations for these measures.

Figure 7-8

Calculating a Beta Coefficient for Fidelity's Magellan Fund

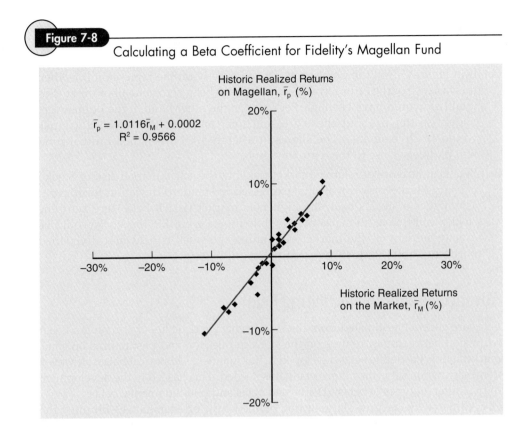

$$\bar{r}_p = 1.0116\bar{r}_M + 0.0002$$
$$R^2 = 0.9566$$

Historic Realized Returns
on Magellan, $\bar{r}_p$ (%)

Historic Realized Returns
on the Market, $\bar{r}_M$ (%)

Sharpe's reward-to-variability ratio is defined as the portfolio's average return (in excess of the risk-free rate) divided by its standard deviation. Sharpe's ratio for Magellan during the past 4 years is 0.27, which is almost the same as the S&P's measure of 0.26.

Treynor's reward-to-volatility ratio is defined as the portfolio's average return (in excess of the risk-free rate) divided by its beta. For Magellan, this is 3.6%, which is a little better than the S&P 500's ratio 3.3%. All in all, the Magellan fund seems to have slightly outperformed the market, but perhaps not by a statistically significant amount. While it is not clear whether or not Magellan "beat the market," it did dramatically reduce the risk faced by investors vis-à-vis the risk inherent in a randomly chosen individual stock.

Additional Insights into Risk and Return

The CAPM provides some additional insights into the relationship between risk and return.

1. The relationship between a stock's total risk, market risk, and diversifiable risk can be expressed as follows:

Total risk = Variance = Market risk + Diversifiable risk

$$\sigma_i^2 = b_i^2 \sigma_M^2 + \sigma_{e_i}^2.$$

(7-13)

Here σ_i^2 is the variance (or total risk) of Stock i, σ_M^2 is the variance of the market, b_i is Stock i's beta coefficient, and $\sigma_{e_i}^2$ is the variance of Stock i's regression error term.

2. If in Figure 7-7 all the points had plotted exactly on the regression line, then the variance of the error term, $\sigma_{e_i}^2$, would have been zero, and all of the stock's total risk would have been market risk. On the other hand, if the points were widely scattered about the regression line, much of the stock's total risk would be diversifiable. The shares of a large, well-diversified mutual fund will plot very close to the regression line.

3. Beta is a measure of relative market risk, but the *actual* market risk of Stock i is $b_i^2\sigma_M^2$. Market risk can also be expressed in standard deviation form, $b_i\sigma_M$. The higher a stock's beta, the higher its market risk. If beta were zero, the stock would have no market risk, while if beta were 1.0, the stock would be exactly as risky as the market—assuming the stock is held in a diversified portfolio—and the stock's market risk would be σ_M.

Advanced Issues in Calculating Beta

Betas are generally estimated from the stock's characteristic line by running a linear regression between past returns on the stock in question and past returns on some market index. We define betas developed in this manner as **historical betas**. However, in most situations, it is the *future* beta that is needed. This has led to the development of two different types of betas: (1) adjusted betas and (2) fundamental betas.

Adjusted betas grew largely out of the work of Marshall E. Blume, who showed that true betas tend to move toward 1.0 over time.[10] Therefore, we can begin with a firm's pure historical statistical beta, make an adjustment for the expected future movement toward 1.0, and produce an adjusted beta that will, on average, be a better predictor of the future beta than would the unadjusted historical beta. *Value Line* publishes betas based on approximately this formula:

$$\text{Adjusted beta} = 0.67(\text{Historical beta}) + 0.35(1.0).$$

Consider American Camping Corporation, a retailer of supplies for outdoor activities. ACC's historical beta is 1.2. Therefore, its adjusted beta is

$$\text{Adjusted beta} = 0.67(1.2) + 0.35(1.0) = 1.15.$$

Other researchers have extended the adjustment process to include such fundamental risk variables as financial leverage, sales volatility, and the like. The end product here is a **fundamental beta**.[11] These betas are constantly adjusted to reflect changes in a firm's operations and capital structure, whereas with historical betas (including adjusted ones), such changes might not be reflected until several years after the company's "true" beta had changed.

Adjusted betas are obviously heavily dependent on unadjusted historical betas, and so are fundamental betas as they are actually calculated. Therefore, the plain old historical beta, calculated as the slope of the characteristic line, is important even if

[10]See Marshall E. Blume, "Betas and Their Regression Tendencies," *Journal of Finance*, June 1975, pp. 785–796, and Marshall E. Blume, "On the Assessment of Risk," *Journal of Finance*, March 1971, pp. 1–10.
[11]See Barr Rosenberg and James Guy, "Beta and Investment Fundamentals," *Financial Analysts Journal*, May–June 1976, pp. 60–72. Rosenberg, then a professor at the University of California at Berkeley, later founded a company that calculates fundamental betas by a proprietary procedure and then sells them to institutional investors.

one goes on to develop a more exotic version. With this in mind, it should be noted that several different sets of data can be used to calculate historical betas, and the different data sets produce different results. Here are some points to note:

1. Betas can be based on historical periods of different lengths. For example, data for the past 1, 2, 3, and so on, years may be used. Most people who calculate betas today use 5 years of data, but this choice is arbitrary, and different lengths of time usually alter significantly the calculated beta for a given company.
2. Returns may be calculated over holding periods of different lengths—a day, a week, a month, a quarter, a year, and so on. For example, if it has been decided to analyze data on NYSE stocks over a 5-year period, then we might obtain 52(5) = 260 weekly returns on each stock and on the market index. We could also use 12(5) = 60 monthly returns, or 1(5) = 5 annual returns. The set of returns on each stock, however large the set turns out to be, would then be regressed on the corresponding market returns to obtain the stock's beta. In statistical analysis, it is generally better to have more rather than fewer observations, because using more observations generally leads to greater statistical confidence. This suggests the use of weekly returns, and, say, 5 years of data, for a sample size of 260, or even daily returns for a still larger sample size. However, the shorter the holding period, the more likely the data are to exhibit random "noise." Also, the greater the number of years of data, the more likely it is that the company's basic risk position has changed. Thus, the choice of both the number of years of data and the length of the holding period for calculating rates of return involves trade-offs between a desire to have many observations versus a desire to rely on recent and consequently more relevant data.
3. The value used to represent "the market" is also an important consideration, as the index used can have a significant effect on the calculated beta. Many analysts today use the New York Stock Exchange Composite Index (based on more than 2,000 common stocks, weighted by the value of each company), but others use the S&P 500 Index. In theory, the broader the index, the better the beta. Indeed, the index should really include returns on all stocks, bonds, leases, private businesses, real estate, and even "human capital." As a practical matter, however, we cannot get accurate returns data on most other types of assets, so measurement problems largely restrict us to stock indexes.

Where does this leave financial managers regarding the proper beta? They must "pay their money and take their choice." Some managers calculate their own betas, using whichever procedure seems most appropriate under the circumstances. Others use betas calculated by organizations such as Yahoo!Finance or *Value Line*, perhaps using one service or perhaps averaging the betas of several services. The choice is a matter of judgment and data availability, for there is no "right" beta. Generally, though, the betas derived from different sources will, for a given company, be reasonably close together. If they are not, then our confidence in using the CAPM will be diminished.

SELF-TEST

Explain the meaning and significance of a stock's beta coefficient. Illustrate your explanation by drawing, on one graph, the characteristic lines for stocks with low, average, and high risk. (Hint: Let your three characteristic lines intersect at $\bar{r}_i = \bar{r}_M = 6\%$, the assumed risk-free rate.)

What is a typical R^2 for the characteristic line of an individual stock? For a portfolio?

What is the market model? How is it different from the SML for the CAPM?

How are stand-alone risk, market risk, and diversifiable risk related?

7.6 Empirical Tests of the CAPM

Does the CAPM's SML produce reasonable estimates for a stock's required return? The literature dealing with empirical tests of the CAPM is quite extensive, so we can give here only a synopsis of some of the key work.

Tests of the Stability of Beta Coefficients

According to the CAPM, the beta used to estimate a stock's market risk should reflect investors' estimates of the stock's *future* volatility in relation to that of the market. Obviously, we do not know now how a stock will be related to the market in the future, nor do we know how the average investor views this expected future relative volatility. All we have are data on past volatility, which we can use to plot the characteristic line and to calculate *historical betas*. If historical betas have been stable over time, then there would seem for reason for investors to use past betas as estimators of future volatility. For example, if Stock i's beta had been stable in the past, then its historical b_i would probably be a good proxy for its *ex ante*, or expected, beta. By "stable" we mean that if b_i were calculated with data from the period of, say, 2002 to 2006, then this same beta (approximately) should be found from 2007 to 2011.

Robert Levy, Marshall Blume, and others have studied the question of beta stability in depth.[12] Levy calculated betas for individual securities, as well as for portfolios of securities, over a range of time intervals. He concluded (1) that the betas of individual stocks are unstable, hence that past betas for *individual securities* are *not* good estimators of their future risk, but (2) that betas of portfolios of 10 or more randomly selected stocks are reasonably stable, hence that past *portfolio* betas are good estimators of future portfolio volatility. In effect, the errors in individual securities' betas tend to offset one another in a portfolio. The work of Blume and others supports this position.

The conclusion that follows from the beta stability studies is that the CAPM is a better concept for structuring investment portfolios than it is for estimating the required return for individual securities.[13]

Tests of the CAPM Based on the Slope of the SML

The CAPM states that a linear relationship exists between a security's required rate of return and its beta. Further, when the SML is graphed, the vertical axis intercept should be r_{RF}, and the required rate of return for a stock (or portfolio) with b = 1.0 should be r_M, the required rate of return on the market. Various researchers have attempted to test the validity of the CAPM by calculating betas and realized rates of return, plotting these values in graphs such as that in Figure 7-9, and then observing whether or not (1) the intercept is equal to r_{RF}, (2) the plot is linear, and (3) the line passes through the point b = 1.0, r_M. Monthly or daily historical rates of return are generally used for stocks, and both 30-day Treasury bill rates and long-term Treasury bond rates have been used to estimate the value

---

[12]See Robert A. Levy, "On the Short-Term Stationarity of Beta Coefficients," *Financial Analysts Journal*, November–December 1971, pp. 55–62; and Marshall E. Blume, "Betas and Their Regression Tendencies," *Journal of Finance*, June 1975, pp. 785–796.

[13]For more on beta stability, see Robert W. Kolb and Ricardo J. Rodriguez, "The Regression Tendencies of Betas: A Reappraisal," *The Financial Review*, May 1989, pp. 319–334. Also see Robert Kolb, "Is the Distribution of Betas Stationary?" *Journal of Financial Research*, Winter 1990, pp. 279–283.

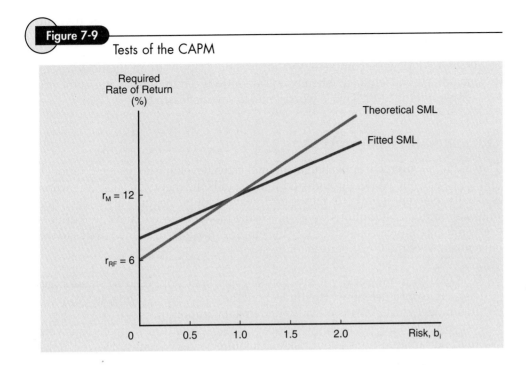

Figure 7-9

Tests of the CAPM

Required Rate of Return (%)

Theoretical SML

Fitted SML

$r_M = 12$

$r_{RF} = 6$

0   0.5   1.0   1.5   2.0   Risk, b_i

of r_{RF}. Also, most of the studies actually analyzed portfolios rather than individual securities because security betas are so unstable.

Before discussing the results of the tests, it is critical to recognize that although the CAPM is an ex ante, or forward-looking, model, the data used to test it are entirely historical. This presents a problem, for there is no reason to believe that *realized* rates of return over past holding periods are necessarily equal to the rates of return people *expect* in the future. Also, historical betas may or may not reflect expected future risk. This lack of ex ante data makes it extremely difficult to test the CAPM, but for what it is worth, here is a summary of the key results:

1. The evidence generally shows a significant positive relationship between realized returns and beta. However, the slope of the relationship is usually less than that predicted by the CAPM.
2. The relationship between risk and return appears to be linear. Empirical studies give no evidence of significant curvature in the risk/return relationship.
3. Tests that attempt to assess the relative importance of market and company-specific risk do not yield conclusive results. The CAPM implies that company-specific risk should not be relevant, yet both kinds of risk appear to be positively related to security returns; that is, higher returns seem to be required to compensate for diversifiable as well as market risk. However, it may be that the observed relationships reflect statistical problems rather than the true nature of capital markets.
4. Richard Roll has questioned whether it is even conceptually possible to test the CAPM.[14] Roll showed that the linear relationship that prior researchers had observed in graphs like Figure 7-9 resulted from the mathematical properties of the models being tested, hence that a finding of linearity proved nothing

---

[14]See Richard Roll, "A Critique of the Asset Pricing Theory's Tests," *Journal of Financial Economics*, March 1977, pp. 129–176.

whatsoever about the validity of the CAPM. Roll's work did not disprove the CAPM, but he did show that it is virtually impossible to prove that investors behave in accordance with its predictions.

5. If the CAPM were completely valid, it should apply to all financial assets, including bonds. In fact, when bonds are introduced into the analysis, they *do not* plot on the SML. This is worrisome, to say the least.

Current Status of the CAPM

The CAPM is extremely appealing at an intellectual level: It is logical and rational, and once someone works through and understands the theory, his or her reaction is usually to accept it without question. However, doubts begin to arise when one thinks about the assumptions upon which the model is based, and these doubts are as much reinforced as reduced by the empirical tests. Our own views as to the current status of the CAPM are as follows:

1. The CAPM framework, with its focus on market as opposed to stand-alone risk, is clearly a useful way to think about the risk of assets. Thus, as a conceptual model, the CAPM is of truly fundamental importance.

2. When applied in practice, the CAPM appears to provide neat, precise answers to important questions about risk and required rates of return. However, the answers are less clear than they seem. The simple truth is that we do not know precisely how to measure any of the inputs required to implement the CAPM. These inputs should all be ex ante, yet only ex post data are available. Further, historical data on $\bar{r}_M$, r_{RF}, and betas vary greatly depending on the time period studied and the methods used to estimate them. Thus, although the CAPM appears precise, estimates of r_i found through its use are subject to potentially large errors.[15]

3. Because the CAPM is logical in the sense that it represents the way risk-averse people ought to behave, the model is a useful conceptual tool.

4. It is appropriate to think about many financial problems in a CAPM framework. However, it is important to recognize the limitations of the CAPM when using it in practice.

SELF-TEST

What are the two major types of tests that have been performed to test the validity of the CAPM? Explain their results. (Beta stability and slope of the SML.)
Are there any reasons to question the validity of the CAPM? Explain.

7.7   Arbitrage Pricing Theory

The CAPM is a single-factor model. That is, it specifies risk as a function of only one factor, the security's beta coefficient. Perhaps the risk/return relationship is more complex, with a stock's required return a function of more than one factor. For example, what if investors, because personal tax rates on capital gains are lower than those on dividends, value capital gains more highly than dividends? Then, if two stocks had the same market risk, the stock paying the higher dividend would have the higher required rate of return. In that case, required returns would be a function of two factors, market risk and dividend policy.

---

[15]For an article supporting a positive link between market risk and expected return, see Felicia Marston and Robert S. Harris, "Risk and Return: A Revisit Using Expected Returns," *Financial Review*, February 1993, pp. 117–137.

Further, what if many factors are required to specify the equilibrium risk/return relationship rather than just one or two? Stephen Ross has proposed an approach called the **Arbitrage Pricing Theory (APT).**[16] The APT can include any number of risk factors, so the required return could be a function of two, three, four, or more factors. We should note at the outset that the APT is based on complex mathematical and statistical theory that goes far beyond the scope of this text. Also, although the APT model is widely discussed in academic literature, practical usage to date has been limited. However, usage may increase, so students should at least have an intuitive idea of what the APT is all about.

The SML states that each stock's required return is equal to the risk-free rate plus the product of the market risk premium times the stock's beta coefficient. Assuming stocks are in equilibrium, the required return will be equal to the expected return:

$$\hat{r}_i = r_i = r_{RF} + (r_M - r_{RF})b_i.$$

The historical realized return, $\bar{r}_i$, which will generally be different from the expected return, can be expressed as follows:[17]

$$\bar{r}_i = \hat{r}_i + (\bar{r}_M - \hat{r}_M)b_i + e_i. \tag{7-14}$$

Thus, the realized return, $\bar{r}_i$, will be equal to the expected return, $\hat{r}_i$, plus a positive or negative increment, $(\bar{r}_M - \hat{r}_M)b_i$, which depends jointly on the stock's beta and whether the market did better or worse than was expected, plus a random error term, e_i.

The market's realized return, $\bar{r}_M$, is in turn determined by a number of factors, including domestic economic activity as measured by gross domestic product (GDP), the strength of the world economy, the level of inflation, changes in tax laws, and so forth. Further, different groups of stocks are affected in different ways by these fundamental factors. So, rather than specifying a stock's return as a function of one factor (return on the market), one could specify required and realized returns on individual stocks as a function of various fundamental economic factors. If this were done, we would transform Equation 7-14 into 7-15:

$$\bar{r}_i = \hat{r}_i + (\bar{F}_1 - \hat{F}_1)b_{i1} + \cdots + (\bar{F}_j - \hat{F}_j)b_{ij} + e_i. \tag{7-15}$$

Here,

$\bar{r}_i$ = realized rate of return on Stock i.
$\hat{r}_i$ = expected rate of return on Stock i.
$\bar{F}_j$ = realized value of economic Factor j.
$\hat{F}_j$ = expected value of Factor j.
b_{ij} = sensitivity of Stock i to economic Factor j.
e_i = effect of unique events on the realized return of Stock i.

---

[16]See Stephen A. Ross, "The Arbitrage Theory of Capital Asset Pricing," *Journal of Economic Theory*, December 1976, pp. 341–360.
[17]To avoid cluttering the notation, we have dropped the subscript t to denote a particular time period.

Equation 7-15 shows that the realized return on any stock is equal to (1) the stock's expected return, (2) increases or decreases that depend on unexpected changes in fundamental economic factors times the sensitivity of the stock to these changes, and (3) a random term that reflects changes unique to the firm.

Certain stocks or groups of stocks are most sensitive to Factor 1, others to Factor 2, and so forth, and every portfolio's returns depend on what happened to the different fundamental factors. Theoretically, one could construct a portfolio such that (1) the portfolio was riskless and (2) the net investment in it was zero (some stocks would be sold short, with the proceeds from the short sales being used to buy the stocks held long). Such a zero investment portfolio must have a zero expected return, or else arbitrage operations would occur and cause the prices of the underlying assets to change until the portfolio's expected return was zero. Using some complex mathematics and a set of assumptions including the possibility of short sales, the APT equivalent of the CAPM's Security Market Line can be developed from Equation 7-15:[18]

$$r_i = r_{RF} + (r_1 - r_{RF})b_{i1} + \cdots + (r_j - r_{RF})b_{ij}. \qquad \text{(7-16)}$$

Here r_j is the required rate of return on a portfolio that is sensitive only to the jth economic factor ($b_{pj} = 1.0$) and has zero sensitivity to all other factors. Thus, for example, $(r_2 - r_{RF})$ is the risk premium on a portfolio with $b_{p2} = 1.0$ and all other $b_{pj} = 0.0$. Note that Equation 7-16 is identical in form to the SML, but it permits a stock's required return to be a function of multiple factors.

To illustrate the APT concept, assume that all stocks' returns depend on only three risk factors: inflation, industrial production, and the aggregate degree of risk aversion (the cost of bearing risk, which we assume is reflected in the spread between the yields on Treasury and low-grade bonds). Further, suppose (1) the risk-free rate is 8.0%; (2) the required rate of return is 13% on a portfolio with unit sensitivity ($b = 1.0$) to inflation and zero sensitivities ($b = 0.0$) to industrial production and degree of risk aversion; (3) the required return is 10% on a portfolio with unit sensitivity to industrial production and zero sensitivities to inflation and degree of risk aversion; and (4) the required return is 6% on a portfolio (the risk-bearing portfolio) with unit sensitivity to the degree of risk aversion and zero sensitivities to inflation and industrial production. Finally, assume that Stock i has factor sensitivities (betas) of 0.9 to the inflation portfolio, 1.2 to the industrial production portfolio, and −0.7 to the risk-bearing portfolio. Stock i's required rate of return, according to the APT, would be 16.3%:

$$r_i = 8\% + (13\% - 8\%)0.9 + (10\% - 8\%)1.2 + (6\% - 8\%)(-0.7)$$
$$= 16.3\%.$$

Note that if the required rate of return on the market were 15.0% and Stock i had a CAPM beta of 1.1, then its required rate of return, according to the SML, would be 15.7%:

$$r_i = 8\% + (15\% - 8\%)1.1 = 15.7\%.$$

---

[18]See Thomas E. Copeland, J. Fred Weston, and Kuldeep Shastri, *Financial Theory and Corporate Policy*, 4th Edition (Reading, MA: Addison-Wesley, 2005).

The primary theoretical advantage of the APT is that it permits several economic factors to influence individual stock returns, whereas the CAPM assumes that the effect of all factors, except those unique to the firm, can be captured in a single measure, the volatility of the stock with respect to the market portfolio. Also, the APT requires fewer assumptions than the CAPM and hence is more general. Finally, the APT does not assume that all investors hold the market portfolio, which is a CAPM requirement that clearly is not met in practice.

However, the APT faces several major hurdles in implementation, the most severe being that the APT does not identify the relevant factors. Thus, the APT does not tell us what factors influence returns, nor does it even indicate how many factors should appear in the model. There is some empirical evidence that only three or four factors are relevant: perhaps inflation, industrial production, the spread between low- and high-grade bonds, and the term structure of interest rates, but no one knows for sure.

The APT's proponents argue that it is not actually necessary to identify the relevant factors. Researchers use a statistical procedure called **factor analysis** to develop the APT parameters. Basically, they start with hundreds, or even thousands, of stocks and then create several different portfolios, where the returns on each portfolio are not highly correlated with returns on the other portfolios. Thus, each portfolio is apparently more heavily influenced by one of the unknown factors than are the other portfolios. Then, the required rate of return on each portfolio becomes the estimate for that unknown economic factor, shown as r_j in Equation 7-16. The sensitivities of each individual stock's returns to the returns on that portfolio are the factor sensitivities (betas). Unfortunately, the results of factor analysis are not easily interpreted; hence it does not provide significant insights into the underlying economic determinants of risk.[19]

SELF-TEST

What is the primary difference between the APT and the CAPM?

What are some disadvantages of the APT?

An analyst has modeled the stock of Brown Kitchen Supplies using a two-factor APT model. The risk-free rate is 5%, the required return on the first factor (r_1) is 10%, and the required return on the second factor (r_2) is 15%. If $b_{i1} = 0.5$ and $b_{i2} = 1.3$, what is Brown's required return? (20.5%)

7.8 The Fama-French Three-Factor Model

As we mentioned in Chapter 6, the results of two studies by Eugene F. Fama and Kenneth R. French of the University of Chicago seriously challenge the CAPM.[20] In the first of these studies, published in 1992, Fama and French hypothesized that the SML should have three factors. The first is the stock's CAPM beta, which measures the market risk of the stock. The second is the size of the company, measured by the market value of its equity (MVE), because if small companies are riskier than large companies, then we might expect small companies to have higher stock returns than large companies. The third factor is the book value of equity

---

[19]For additional discussion of the APT, see Eward L. Bubnys, "Simulating and Forecasting Utility Stock Returns: Arbitrage Pricing Theory vs. Capital Asset Pricing Model," *The Financial Review*, February 1990, pp. 1–23; David H. Goldenberg and Ashok J. Robin, "The Arbitrage Pricing Theory and Cost-of-Capital Estimation: The Case of Electric Utilities," *Journal of Financial Research*, Fall 1991, pp. 181–196; and Ashok Robin and Ravi Shukla, "The Magnitude of Pricing Errors in the Arbitrage Pricing Theory," *Journal of Financial Research*, Spring 1991, pp. 65–82.

[20]See Eugene F. Fama and Kenneth R. French, "The Cross-Section of Expected Stock Returns," *Journal of Finance*, 1992, pp. 427–465. Also see Eugene F. Fama and Kenneth R. French, "Common Risk Factors in the Returns on Stocks and Bonds," *Journal of Financial Economics*, 1993, pp. 3–56.

divided by the market value of equity, or the book-to-market ratio (B/M). If the market value is larger than the book value, then investors are optimistic about the stock's future. On the other hand, if the book value is larger than the market value, then investors are pessimistic about the stock's future, and it is likely that a ratio analysis will reveal that the company is experiencing sub-par operating performance and possibly even financial distress. In other words, a stock with a high B/M ratio might be risky, in which case investors would require a higher expected return to induce them to invest in such a stock.

When Fama and French tested their hypotheses, they found that small companies and companies with high B/M ratios had higher rates of return than the average stock, just as they hypothesized. Somewhat surprisingly, however, they found no relation between beta and return. After taking into account the returns due to the company's size and B/M ratio, high-beta stocks did not have higher-than-average returns, and low-beta stocks did not have lower-than-average returns.

In the second of their two studies, published in 1993, Fama and French developed a three-factor model based on their previous results. The first factor in the **Fama-French three-factor model** is the market risk premium, which is the market return, $\bar{r}_M$, minus the risk-free rate, $\bar{r}_{RF}$. Thus, their model begins like the CAPM, but they go on to add a second and third factor.[21] To form the second factor, they ranked all actively traded stocks by size and then divided them into two portfolios, consisting of small and big stocks. They calculated the return on each of these two portfolios, and created a third portfolio by subtracting the return on the big portfolio from that of the small one. They called this the SMB portfolio (for small size minus big size). This portfolio is designed to measure the variation in stock returns that is caused by the size effect.

To form the third factor, they ranked all stocks according to their book-to-market ratios (B/M). They placed the 30% of stocks with the highest ratios into a portfolio that they called the H portfolio (for high B/M ratios). They placed the 30% of stocks with the lowest ratios into a portfolio called the L portfolio (for low B/M ratios). They subtracted the return of the L portfolio from the H portfolio, and they called the result the HML portfolio (for high-B/M ratio minus low-B/M ratio). Their resulting model is shown here:

$$(\bar{r}_i - \bar{r}_{RF}) = a_i + b_i(\bar{r}_M - \bar{r}_{RF}) + c_i(\bar{r}_{SMB}) + d_i(\bar{r}_{HML}) + e_i, \qquad (7\text{-}17)$$

where

$\bar{r}_i$ = historical (realized) rate of return on Stock i.

$\bar{r}_{RF}$ = historical (realized) rate of return on the risk-free rate.

$\bar{r}_M$ = historical (realized) rate of return on the market.

$\bar{r}_{SMB}$ = historical (realized) rate of return on the small-size portfolio minus the big-size portfolio.

$\bar{r}_{HML}$ = historical (realized) rate of return on the high-B/M portfolio minus the low-B/M portfolio.

a_i = vertical axis intercept term for Stock i.

b_i, c_i, and d_i = slope coefficients for Stock i.

e_i = random error, reflecting the difference between the actual return on Stock i in a given period and the return as predicted by the regression line.

---

[21]Although our description captures the essence of their process for forming factors, their actual process is a little more complicated. The interested reader should see their 1993 paper as referenced in Footnote 20.

The Fama-French three-factor model version of the CAPM Security Market Line for the required return on a stock is

$$r_i = r_{RF} + a_i + b_i(r_M - r_{RF}) + c_i(r_{SMB}) + d_i(r_{HML}), \qquad \text{(7-18)}$$

where $r_M - r_{RF}$ is the market risk premium, r_{SMB} is the expected value (i.e., premium) for the size factor, and r_{HML} is the expected value (i.e., premium) for the book/market factor.

Here is how you might apply this model. Suppose you ran the regression in Equation 7-17 for a stock, and estimated the following regression coefficients: $a_i = 0.0$, $b_i = 0.9$, $c_i = 0.2$, and $d_i = 0.3$. Assume that the expected market risk premium is 6% (that is, $r_M - r_{RF} = 6\%$) and that the risk-free rate is 6.5%. Suppose the expected value of r_{SMB} is 3.2% and the expected value of r_{HML} is 4.8%.[22] Using the Fama-French three-factor model, the required return is

$$
\begin{aligned}
r_i &= r_{RF} + a_i + b_i(r_M - r_{RF}) + c_i(r_{SMB}) + d_i(r_{HML}) \\
&= 6.5\% + 0.0\% + 0.9(6\%) + 0.2(3.2\%) + 0.3(4.8\%) \qquad \text{(7-18a)} \\
&= 13.98\%.
\end{aligned}
$$

To date, the Fama-French three-factor model has been used primarily by academic researchers rather than by managers at actual companies, the majority of whom are still using the CAPM. Part of this difference was due at one time to the lack of available data. Most professors had access to the type of data required to calculate the factors, but data for the size factor and the B/M factor were not readily available to the general public. Partially to address this problem, Professor French has made the required historical data available at his Web site.[23] However, there is still difficulty in estimating the expected values of the size factor and the B/M factor. Although we know the historical average returns for these factors, we don't know whether the past historical returns are good estimators of the future expected returns for these factors. In other words, we don't know the risk premium associated with the size and book/market sources of risk. Finally, many managers choose to wait and adopt a new theory only after it has been widely accepted by the academic community.

And that isn't the case right now. In fact, there are a number of subsequent studies indicating that the Fama-French model is not correct.[24] Several of these studies suggest that the size effect is no longer having an effect on stock returns, that there never was a size effect (the previous results were caused by peculiarities in the data sources), or that the size effect doesn't apply to most

---

[22]These are the average returns Fama and French found in their sample period for r_{SMB} and r_{HML}.

[23]Professor French's web site, **http://mba.tuck.dartmouth.edu/pages/faculty/ken.french/data_library .html#Research,** now provides time series data for the returns on the factors ($\bar{r}_M - \bar{r}_{RF}$, $\bar{r}_{SMB}$, and $\bar{r}_{HML}$).

[24]See Peter J. Knez and Mark J. Ready, "On the Robustness of Size and Book-to-Market in the Cross-Sectional Regressions," *Journal of Finance*, September 1997, pp. 1355–1382; Dongcheol Kim, "A Reexamination of Firm Size, Book-to-Market, and Earnings Price in the Cross-Section of Expected Stock Returns," *Journal of Financial and Quantitative Analysis*, December 1997, pp. 463–489; Tyler Shumway and Vincent A. Warther, "The Delisting Bias in CRSP's Nasdaq Data and Its Implications for the Size Effect," *Journal of Finance*, December 1999, pp. 2361–2379; Tim Loughran, "Book-to-Market Across Firm Size, Exchange, and Seasonality: Is There an Effect?" *Journal of Financial and Quantitative Analysis*, September 1997, pp. 249–268; and Ilia D. Dichev, "Is the Risk of Bankruptcy a Systematic Risk?" *Journal of Finance*, June 1998, pp. 1131–1147.

companies. Other studies suggest that the book-to-market effect is not as significant as first supposed and that the book-to-market effect is not caused by risk. Another recent study shows that if the composition of a company's assets were changing over time with respect to the mix of physical assets and growth opportunities (such as R&D, patents, etc.), then it would appear as though there were size and book-to-market effects. In other words, even if the returns on the individual assets conform to the CAPM, changes in the mix of assets would cause the firm's beta to change over time in such a way that the firm would appear to have size and book-to-market effects.[25]

SELF-TEST

What are the factors in the Fama-French model?

How can the model be used to estimate the required return on a stock?

Why isn't the model widely used by managers at actual companies?

An analyst has modeled the stock of a company using a Fama-French three-factor model. The risk-free rate is 5%, the required market return is 11%, the risk premium for small stocks (r_{SMB}) is 3.2%, and the risk premium for value stocks (r_{HML}) is 4.8%. If $a_i = 0$, $b_i = 0.7$, $c_i = 1.2$, and $d_i = 0.7$, what is the stock's required return? (16.4%)

7.9 An Alternative Theory of Risk and Return: Behavioral Finance

The Efficient Markets Hypothesis (EMH) is one of the cornerstones of modern finance theory. It implies that, on average, assets trade at prices equal to their intrinsic values. As we note in Chapter 8, the logic behind the EMH is straightforward. If a stock's price is "too low," rational traders will quickly take advantage of this opportunity and will buy the stock. Their actions will quickly push prices back to their equilibrium level. Likewise, if prices are "too high," rational traders will sell the stock, pushing the price down to its equilibrium level. Proponents of the EMH argue that prices cannot be systematically wrong unless you believe that market participants are unable or unwilling to take advantage of profitable trading opportunities.

While the logic behind the EMH is compelling, some events seem to be inconsistent with the EMH. First, there is some evidence that stocks may have short-term momentum. Stocks that perform poorly tend to continue performing poorly over the next 3 to 12 months, and stocks that perform well tend to continue performing well in the short-term future. On the other hand, there is some evidence that stocks have long-term reversals. In particular, stocks that have the lowest returns in a 5-year period tend to outperform the market during the next 5 years. The opposite is true for stocks that outperform the market during a 5-year period: They tend to have lower than average returns during the next 5-year period.[26]

In response to such observations, a number of researchers are blending psychology with finance, creating a new field called **behavioral finance.** There is a large body of evidence in the field of psychology indicating that people don't behave rationally in many areas of their lives, so some argue that we should not expect people to behave rationally with their investments.[27] Pioneers in this field

---

[25]See Jonathan B. Berk, Richard C. Green, and Vasant Naik, "Optimal Investment, Growth Options, and Security Returns," *Journal of Finance*, October 1999, pp. 1553–1608.

[26]N. Jegadeesh and S. Titman, "Returns to Buying Winners and Selling Losers: Implications for Stock Market Efficiency," *Journal of Finance*, March 1993, pp. 69–91; and W. F. M. DeBondt and R. H. Thaler, "Does the Stock Market Overreact?" *Journal of Finance*, July 1985, pp. 793–808.

[27]See Brian O'Reilly, "Why Johnny Can't Invest," *Fortune*, November 9, 1998, pp. 173–178.

include psychologists Daniel Kahneman and Amos Tversky, along with University of Chicago finance professor Richard Thaler. Their work has encouraged a growing number of scholars to work in this promising area of research.

Professor Thaler and his colleague, Nicholas Barberis, have summarized much of this research in a recent article.[28] They argue that behavioral finance theory rests on two important building blocks. First, they argue that mispricing can persist because it is often difficult or risky for traders to take advantage of mispriced assets. For example, even if it was clear that a stock's price is too low because investors have overreacted to recent bad news, a trader with limited capital may be reluctant to buy the stock for fear that the same forces that pushed the price down may work to keep it artificially low for a long period of time. On the other side, during the recent stock market bubble that burst in 2000, many traders who believed (correctly!) that stock prices were too high lost a lot of money selling stocks in the early stages of the bubble because stock prices went even higher before they eventually collapsed. In other words, there is no safe way to take advantage of mispricing.

While the first building block explains *why* mispricings may persist, the second tries to understand *how* mispricings can occur in the first place. This is where the insights from psychology come into play. For example, Kahneman and Tversky suggested that individuals view potential losses and potential gains very differently. If you ask an average person whether he or she would rather have $500 with certainty or flip a fair coin and receive $1,000 if heads comes up and nothing if it comes out tails, most would prefer the certain $500 gain, which suggests an aversion to risk. However, if you ask the same person whether he or she would rather pay $500 with certainty or flip a coin and pay $1,000 if it's heads and nothing if it's tails, most would indicate that they prefer to flip the coin. But this implies a preference for risk. In other words, people appear to dislike risk when it comes to gains, but will take on risk in order to avoid a sure loss. Other experiments have reinforced this idea that most people experience "loss aversion," or a strong desire to avoid realizing losses. In irrational, but common, mental bookkeeping, a loss isn't really a loss until the losing investment is actually sold. This leads investors to sell losers much less frequently than winners even though this is suboptimal for tax purposes.[29]

Not only do most people view risky gains and losses differently, but other studies suggest that people's willingness to take a gamble depends on recent past performance. Gamblers who are ahead tend to take on more risks (i.e., they are playing with the house's money), whereas those who are behind tend to become more conservative. These experiments suggest that investors and managers behave differently in down markets than they do in up markets, in which they are playing with the "house's" money.

Many psychological tests also show that people are overconfident with respect to their own abilities relative to the abilities of others, which is the basis of Garrison Keillor's joke about a town where all the children are above average. Barberis and Thaler point out that:

> Overconfidence may in part stem from two other biases, self attribution bias and hindsight bias. Self attribution bias refers to people's tendency to ascribe any success they have in some activity to their own talents, while blaming failure on bad luck, rather than on their ineptitude. Doing this repeatedly will lead people to the pleasing but erroneous

---

[28]Nicholas Barberis and Richard Thaler, "A Survey of Behavioral Finance," Chapter 18, *Handbook of the Economics of Finance*, edited by George Constantinides, Milt Harris, and René Stulz, part of the Handbooks in Economics Series, Elsevier/North-Holland, 2003.

[29]See Terrance Odean, "Are Investors Reluctant to Realize Their Losses?" *Journal of Finance*, October 1998, pp. 1775–1798.

conclusion that they are very talented. For example, investors might become overconfident after several quarters of investing success [Gervais and Odean (2001)[30]]. Hindsight bias is the tendency of people to believe, after an event has occurred, that they predicted it before it happened. If people think they predicted the past better than they actually did, they may also believe that they can predict the future better than they actually can.

Some researchers have hypothesized that the combination of overconfidence and biased self-attribution leads to overly volatile stock markets, short-term momentum, and long-term reversals.[31] In other words, stock returns reflect the irrational, but predictable, behavior of humans. Behavioral finance also has implications for corporate finance. Recent research by Ulrike Malmendier of the Stanford Graduate School of Business and Geoffrey Tate of the Wharton School suggests that overconfidence leads managers to overestimate their abilities and the quality of their projects.[32] This result may explain why so many corporate projects fail to live up to their stated expectations.

SELF-TEST

What is short-term momentum? What are long-term reversals? What is behavioral finance?

Summary

Chapter 7 completes our discussion of risk and return for traded securities. The primary goal of this chapter was to extend your knowledge of risk and return concepts. The key concepts covered are listed below:

- The **feasible set** of portfolios represents all portfolios that can be constructed from a given set of assets.
- An **efficient portfolio** is one that offers the most return for a given amount of risk, or the least risk for a given amount of return.
- The **optimal portfolio** for an investor is defined by the investor's highest possible **indifference curve** that is tangent to the **efficient set** of portfolios.
- The **Capital Asset Pricing Model (CAPM)** describes the relationship between market risk and required rates of return.
- The **Capital Market Line (CML)** describes the risk/return relationship for efficient portfolios, that is, for portfolios that consist of a mix of the market portfolio and a riskless asset.
- The **Security Market Line (SML)** is an integral part of the CAPM, and it describes the risk/return relationship for individual assets. The required rate of return for any Stock i is equal to the **risk-free rate** plus the **market risk premium** times the stock's **beta coefficient**: $r_i = r_{RF} + (r_M - r_{RF})b_i$.
- Stock i's **beta coefficient, b_i,** is a measure of the stock's **market risk.** Beta measures the **volatility** of returns on a security **relative to returns on the market,** which is the portfolio of all risky assets.

---

[30]See Terrance Odean and Simon Gervais, "Learning to Be Overconfident," *Review of Financial Studies*, Spring 2001, pp. 1–27.

[31]See Terrance Odean, "Volume, Volatility, Price, and Profit When All Traders Are Above Average," *Journal of Finance*, December 1998, pp. 1887–1934; and Kent Daniel, David Hirshleifer, and Avanidhar Subrahmanyam, "Investor Psychology and Security Market Under- and Overreactions," *Journal of Finance*, December 1998, pp. 1839–1885.

[32]See Ulrike Malmendier and Geoffrey Tate, "CEO Overconfidence and Corporate Investment," *Journal of Finance*, December 2005, pp. 2661–2700.

- The beta coefficient is measured by the slope of the stock's **characteristic line,** which is found by regressing historical returns on the stock versus historical returns on the market.
- Although the CAPM provides a convenient framework for thinking about risk and return issues, it *cannot be proven empirically,* and its parameters are very difficult to estimate. Thus, the required rate of return for a stock as estimated by the CAPM may not be exactly equal to the true required rate of return.
- Deficiencies in the CAPM have motivated theorists to seek other risk/return equilibrium models, and the **Arbitrage Pricing Theory (APT)** is one important new model.
- The **Fama-French three-factor model** has one factor for the **market return,** a second factor for the **size effect,** and a third factor for the **book-to-market effect.**
- **Behavioral finance** assumes that investors don't always behave rationally.

In the next two chapters, we will see how a security's required rate of return affects its value.

Questions

(7-1)   Define the following terms, using graphs or equations to illustrate your answers wherever feasible:
    a.   Portfolio; feasible set; efficient portfolio; efficient frontier
    b.   Indifference curve; optimal portfolio
    c.   Capital Asset Pricing Model (CAPM); Capital Market Line (CML)
    d.   Characteristic line; beta coefficient, b
    e.   Arbitrage Pricing Theory (APT); Fama-French three-factor model; behavioral finance

(7-2)   Security A has an expected rate of return of 6%, a standard deviation of returns of 30%, a correlation coefficient with the market of −0.25, and a beta coefficient of −0.5. Security B has an expected return of 11%, a standard deviation of returns of 10%, a correlation with the market of 0.75, and a beta coefficient of 0.5. Which security is more risky? Why?

Self-Test Problem   Solution Appears in Appendix A

(ST-1)   You are planning to invest $200,000. Two securities, A and B, are available, Risk and Return   and you can invest in either of them or in a portfolio with some of each. You estimate that the following probability distributions of returns are applicable for A and B:

Security A		Security B	
P_A	r_A	P_B	r_B
0.1	−10%	0.1	−30%
0.2	5	0.2	0
0.4	15	0.4	20
0.2	25	0.2	40
0.1	40	0.1	70
	$\hat{r}_A = ?$		$\hat{r}_B = 20.0\%$
	$\sigma_A = ?$		$\sigma_B = 25.7\%$

a. The expected return for Security B is $\hat{r}_B = 20\%$, and $\sigma_B = 25.7\%$. Find $\hat{r}_A$ and σ_A.
b. Use Equation 7-3 to find the value of w_A that produces the minimum risk portfolio. Assume $\rho_{AB} = -0.5$ for parts b and c.
c. Construct a table giving $\hat{r}_p$ and σ_p for portfolios with $w_A = 1.00, 0.75, 0.50, 0.25,$ 0.0, and the minimum risk value of w_A. (Hint: For $w_A = 0.75$, $\hat{r}_p = 16.25\%$ and $\sigma_p = 8.5\%$; for $w_A = 0.5$, $\hat{r}_p = 17.5\%$ and $\sigma_p = 11.1\%$; for $w_A = 0.25$, $\hat{r}_p = 18.75\%$ and $\sigma_p = 17.9\%$.)
d. Graph the feasible set of portfolios and identify the efficient frontier of the feasible set.
e. Suppose your risk/return trade-off function, or indifference curve, is tangent to the efficient set at the point where $\hat{r}_p = 18\%$. Use this information, plus the graph constructed in part d, to locate (approximately) your optimal portfolio. Draw in a reasonable indifference curve, indicate the percentage of your funds invested in each security, and determine the optimal portfolio's σ_p and $\hat{r}_p$. (Hint: Estimate σ_p and $\hat{r}_p$ graphically, and then use the equation for $\hat{r}_p$ to determine w_A.)
f. Now suppose a riskless asset with a return $\hat{r}_{RF} = 10\%$ becomes available. How would this change the investment opportunity set? Explain why the efficient frontier becomes linear.
g. Given the indifference curve in part e, would you change your portfolio? If so, how? (Hint: Assume the indifference curves are parallel.)
h. What are the beta coefficients of Stocks A and B? [Hints: (1) Recognize that $r_i = r_{RF} + b_i(r_M - r_{RF})$ and solve for b_i, and (2) assume that your preferences match those of most other investors.]

Problems Answers Appear in Appendix B

Easy
Problems 1–3

(7-1)
Beta
The standard deviation of stock returns for Stock A is 40%. The standard deviation of the market return is 20%. If the correlation between Stock A and the market is 0.70, what is Stock A's beta?

(7-2)
APT
An analyst has modeled the stock of Crisp Trucking using a two-factor APT model. The risk-free rate is 6%, the expected return on the first factor (r_1) is 12%, and the expected return on the second factor (r_2) is 8%. If $b_{i1} = 0.7$ and $b_{i2} = 0.9$, what is Crisp's required return?

(7-3)
Fama-French
Three-Factor
Model

An analyst has modeled the stock of a company using a Fama-French three-factor model. The risk-free rate is 5%, the required market return is 10%, the risk premium for small stocks (r_{SMB}) is 3.2%, and the risk premium for value stocks (r_{HML}) is 4.8%. If $a_i = 0$, $b_i = 1.2$, $c_i = -0.4$, and $d_i = 1.3$, what is the stock's required return?

**Intermediate
Problems 4–6**

(7-4)
Two-Asset
Portfolio

Stock A has an expected return of 12% and a standard deviation of 40%. Stock B has an expected return of 18% and a standard deviation of 60%. The correlation coefficient between Stocks A and B is 0.2. What are the expected return and standard deviation of a portfolio invested 30% in Stock A and 70% in Stock B?

(7-5)
SML and CML
Comparison

The beta coefficient of an asset can be expressed as a function of the asset's correlation with the market as follows:

$$b_i = \frac{\rho_{i,M}\sigma_i}{\sigma_M}.$$

a. Substitute this expression for beta into the Security Market Line (SML), Equation 7-9. This results in an alternative form of the SML.
b. Compare your answer to part a with the Capital Market Line (CML), Equation 7-6. What similarities are observed? What conclusions can be drawn?

(7-6)
CAPM and the
Fama-French
Three-Factor
Model

Suppose you are given the following information. The beta of company i, b_i, is 1.1, the risk-free rate, r_{RF}, is 7%, and the expected market premium, $r_M - r_{RF}$, is 6.5%. (Assume that $a_i = 0.0$.)

a. Use the Security Market Line (SML) of CAPM to find the required return for this company.
b. Because your company is smaller than average and more successful than average (that is, it has a low book-to-market ratio), you think the Fama-French three-factor model might be more appropriate than the CAPM. You estimate the additional coefficients from the Fama-French three-factor model: The coefficient for the size effect, c_i, is 0.7, and the coefficient for the book-to-market effect, d_i, is −0.3. If the expected value of the size factor is 5% and the expected value of the book-to-market factor is 4%, what is the required return using the Fama-French three-factor model?

**Challenging
Problems 7–8**

(7-7)
Characteristic
Line and
Security
Market Line

You are given the following set of data:

| | **Historical Rates of Return** | |
Year	NYSE	Stock X
1	(26.5%)	(14.0%)
2	37.2	23.0
3	23.8	17.5
4	(7.2)	2.0
5	6.6	8.1
6	20.5	19.4
7	30.6	18.2

a. Use a spreadsheet (or a calculator with a linear regression function) to determine Stock X's beta coefficient.

b. Determine the arithmetic average rates of return for Stock X and the NYSE over the period given. Calculate the standard deviations of returns for both Stock X and the NYSE.

c. Assuming (1) that the situation during Years 1 to 7 is expected to hold true in the future (that is, $\hat{r}_X = \bar{r}_X$; $\hat{r}_M = \bar{r}_M$; and both σ_X and b_X in the future will equal their past values), and (2) that Stock X is in equilibrium (that is, it plots on the Security Market Line), what is the risk-free rate?

d. Plot the Security Market Line.

e. Suppose you hold a large, well-diversified portfolio and are considering adding to the portfolio either Stock X or another stock, Stock Y, that has the same beta as Stock X but a higher standard deviation of returns. Stocks X and Y have the same expected returns; that is, $\hat{r}_X = \hat{r}_Y = 10.6\%$. Which stock should you choose?

(7-8)   You are given the following set of data:

Characteristic
Line

| Year | Historical Rates of Return | |
	NYSE	Stock Y
1	4.0%	3.0%
2	14.3	18.2
3	19.0	9.1
4	(14.7)	(6.0)
5	(26.5)	(15.3)
6	37.2	33.1
7	23.8	6.1
8	(7.2)	3.2
9	6.6	14.8
10	20.5	24.1
11	30.6	18.0
	Mean = 9.8%	9.8%
	$\sigma = 19.6\%$	13.8%

a. Construct a scatter diagram showing the relationship between returns on Stock Y and the market. Use a spreadsheet or a calculator with a linear regression function to estimate beta.

b. Give a verbal interpretation of what the regression line and the beta coefficient show about Stock Y's volatility and relative risk as compared with those of other stocks.

c. Suppose the scatter of points had been more spread out, but the regression line was exactly where your present graph shows it. How would this affect (1) the firm's risk if the stock is held in a one-asset portfolio and (2) the actual risk premium on the stock if the CAPM holds exactly?

d. Suppose the regression line had been downward sloping and the beta coefficient had been negative. What would this imply about (1) Stock Y's relative risk, (2) its correlation with the market, and (3) its probable risk premium?

Spreadsheet Problem

e-resource

(7-9)
Feasible
Portfolios

Start with the partial model in the file *FM12 Ch 07 P09 Build a Model.xls* from the textbook's Web site. Following is information for the required returns and standard deviations of returns for A, B, and C.

Stock	r_i	σ_i
A	7.0%	33.11%
B	10.0%	53.85%
C	20.0%	89.44%

The correlation coefficients for each pair are shown below in a matrix, with each cell in the matrix showing the correlation between the stock in the same row and column. For example, $\rho_{AB} = 0.1571$ is in the row for A and the column for B. Notice that the diagonal values are equal to 1, because a variable is always perfectly positively correlated with itself.

	A	B	C
A	1.0000	0.1571	0.1891
B	0.1571	1.0000	0.1661
C	0.1891	0.1661	1.0000

a. Suppose a portfolio has 30% invested in A, 50% in B, and 20% in C. What are the expected return and standard deviation of the portfolio?
b. The partial model lists 66 different combinations of portfolio weights. For each combination of weights, find the required return and standard deviation.
c. The partial model provides a scatter diagram showing the required returns and standard deviations calculated above. This provides a visual indicator of the feasible set. If you would like a return of 10.50%, what is the smallest standard deviation that you must accept?

e-resource

Cyberproblem

Please go to the textbook's Web site to access any Cyberproblems.

Mini Case

To begin, briefly review the Chapter 6 Mini Case. Then, extend your knowledge of risk and return by answering the following questions:

a. Suppose Asset A has an expected return of 10% and a standard deviation of 20%. Asset B has an expected return of 16% and a standard deviation of 40%. If the correlation between A and B is 0.35, what are the expected return and standard deviation for a portfolio comprised of 30% Asset A and 70% Asset B?

b. Plot the attainable portfolios for a correlation of 0.35. Now plot the attainable portfolios for correlations of +1.0 and −1.0.

c. Suppose a risk-free asset has an expected return of 5%. By definition, its standard deviation is zero, and its correlation with any other asset is also zero. Using only Asset A and the risk-free asset, plot the attainable portfolios.

d. Construct a reasonable, but hypothetical, graph that shows risk, as measured by portfolio standard deviation, on the x-axis and expected rate of return on the y-axis. Now add an illustrative feasible (or attainable) set of portfolios, and show what portion of the feasible set is efficient. What makes a particular portfolio efficient? Don't worry about specific values when constructing the graph—merely illustrate how things look with "reasonable" data.

e. Now add a set of indifference curves to the graph created for part b. What do these curves represent? What is the optimal portfolio for this investor? Finally, add a second set of indifference curves that leads to the selection of a different optimal portfolio. Why do the two investors choose different portfolios?

f. What is the Capital Asset Pricing Model (CAPM)? What are the assumptions that underlie the model?

g. Now add the risk-free asset. What impact does this have on the efficient frontier?

h. Write out the equation for the Capital Market Line (CML) and draw it on the graph. Interpret the CML. Now add a set of indifference curves, and illustrate how an investor's optimal portfolio is some combination of the risky portfolio and the risk-free asset. What is the composition of the risky portfolio?

i. What is a characteristic line? How is this line used to estimate a stock's beta coefficient? Write out and explain the formula that relates total risk, market risk, and diversifiable risk.

j. What are two potential tests that can be conducted to verify the CAPM? What are the results of such tests? What is Roll's critique of CAPM tests?

k. Briefly explain the difference between the CAPM and the Arbitrage Pricing Theory (APT).

l. Suppose you are given the following information. The beta of a company, b_i, is 0.9; the risk-free rate, r_{RF}, is 6.8%; and the expected market premium, $r_M - r_{RF}$, is 6.3%. Because your company is larger than average and more successful than average (that is, it has a lower book-to-market ratio), you think the Fama-French three-factor model might be more appropriate than the CAPM. You estimate the additional coefficients from the Fama-French three-factor model: The coefficient for the size effect, c_i, is -0.5, and the coefficient for the book-to-market effect, d_i, is -0.3. If the expected value of the size factor is 4% and the expected value of the book-to-market factor is 5%, what is the required return using the Fama-French three-factor model? (Assume that $a_i = 0.0$.) What is the required return using CAPM?

Selected Additional Cases

The following case from Textchoice, *Cengage Learning's online library, covers many of the concepts discussed in this chapter and is available at* **http://www.textchoice2.com.**

Klein-Brigham Series:
Case 2, "Peachtree Securities, Inc. (A)."

chapter 8

Stocks, Stock Valuation, and Stock Market Equilibrium

From slightly less than 4,000 in early 1995, the Dow Jones Industrial Average surged to 11,723 in early 2000. To put this remarkable 7,723-point rise in perspective, consider that the Dow first reached 1,000 in 1965, then took another 22 years to hit 2,000, then 4 more years to reach 3,000, and another 4 to get to 4,000 (in 1995). Then, in just over 5 years, it reached 11,723. Thus, in those 5 years investors made almost twice as much in the stock market as they made in the previous 70 years!

That bull market made it possible for many people to take early retirement, buy expensive homes, and afford large expenditures such as college tuition. Encouraged by this performance, more and more investors flocked to the market, and today more than 79 million Americans own stock. Moreover, a rising stock market made it easier and cheaper for corporations to raise equity capital, which facilitated economic growth.

However, some observers were concerned that many investors did not realize just how risky the stock market is. Indeed, the Dow fell all the way to 8,236 in the days following the terrorist attacks of September 11, 2001. It surged back up to 10,635 in early 2002, but fell to 7,286 by late 2002. In mid-2006, the market stood at about 10,989.

Note too that while all boats may rise with the tide, the same does not hold for stock markets—regardless of the trend, some individual stocks always make huge gains while others suffer substantial losses. Even though the overall market was up 1.7% in 2005, many individual stocks performed much better while others performed worse. For example, Apple Computer rose more than 123%, but GM was down 51.5%. In terms of market value, Genentech added more than $40 billion to its stockholders' wealth, while Dell's shareholders saw more than $28 billion of wealth evaporate.

Although it is difficult to predict prices, we are not completely in the dark when it comes to valuing stocks. Indeed, after studying this chapter, you should have a reasonably good understanding of the factors that influence stock prices. With that knowledge—and a little luck—you may be able to find the next Apple or Genentech and avoid future GMs.

In Chapters 6 and 7 we examined risk and required stock returns. In this chapter we will use those results to estimate the intrinsic value of a stock with the dividend growth model. The concepts and models developed here will also be used when we estimate the cost of capital in Chapter 10. In subsequent chapters, we will demonstrate how the cost of capital is used to help make many important decisions, especially the decision to invest or not invest in new assets. Consequently, it is critically important that you understand the basics of stock valuation.

Some companies are so small that their common stocks are not actively traded; they are owned by only a few people, usually the companies' managers. The stock in such firms is said to be **closely held.** In contrast, the stocks of most larger companies are owned by a large number of investors, most of whom are not active in management. Such stock is called **publicly held stock.** Institutions, such as pension plans, mutual funds, foreign investors, insurance companies, and brokerage firms, buy and sell relatively actively, so they account for about 75% of all transactions. Thus, institutional investors have a heavy influence on the valuation of individual stocks. But before plunging into stock valuation, we begin with a closer look at what it means to be a stockholder.

e-resource

The textbook's Web site contains an *Excel* file that will guide you through the chapter's calculations. The file for this chapter is *FM12 Ch 08 Tool Kit.xls,* and we encourage you to open the file and follow along as you read the chapter.

8.1 Legal Rights and Privileges of Common Stockholders

The common stockholders are the *owners* of a corporation, and as such they have certain rights and privileges as discussed in this section.

Control of the Firm

A firm's common stockholders have the right to elect its directors, who, in turn, elect the officers who manage the business. In a small firm, the largest stockholder typically assumes the positions of president and chairperson of the board of directors. In a large, publicly owned firm, the managers typically have some stock, but their personal holdings are generally insufficient to give them voting control. Thus, the managements of most publicly owned firms can be removed by the stockholders if the management team is not effective.

State and federal laws stipulate how stockholder control is to be exercised. First, corporations must hold an election of directors periodically, usually once a year, with the vote taken at the annual meeting. Frequently, one-third of the directors are elected each year for a 3-year term. Each share of stock has one vote; thus, the owner of 1,000 shares has 1,000 votes for each director.[1] Stockholders can appear at the annual meeting and vote in person, but typically they transfer their right to vote to a second party by means of a **proxy.** Management always solicits stockholders' proxies and usually gets them. However, if earnings are poor and stockholders are dissatisfied, an outside group may solicit the proxies in an effort to overthrow management and take control of the business. This is known as a **proxy fight.** Proxy fights are discussed in detail in Chapter 15.

---

[1]In the situation described, a 1,000-share stockholder could cast 1,000 votes for each of three directors if there were three contested seats on the board. An alternative procedure that may be prescribed in the corporate charter calls for *cumulative voting.* Here the 1,000-share stockholder would get 3,000 votes if there were three vacancies, and he or she could cast all of them for one director. Cumulative voting helps small groups get representation on the board.

Corporate Valuation and Stock Risk

In Chapter 1, we told you that managers should strive to make their firms more valuable and that the value of a firm is determined by the size, timing, and risk of its free cash flows (FCF):

$$V_{Firm} = \frac{FCF_1}{(1 + WACC)^1} + \frac{FCF_2}{(1 + WACC)^2} + \frac{FCF_3}{(1 + WACC)^3} + \cdots + \frac{FCF_\infty}{(1 + WACC)^\infty}.$$

The FCFs are the cash flows available to all investors and the WACC is the return required by all investors, so the present value of the FCFs is the value of the firm to all investors. In Chapter 15 we will use the equation above to estimate the intrinsic value of stock, but in this chapter we use an alternative approach. Instead of discounting the cash flows to all investors at the rate of return required by all investors, we discount the cash flows to stockholders (dividends, D_t) at the rate required by stockholders (r_s). The result is the intrinsic value to stockholders:

$$V_{Stock} = \frac{D_1}{(1 + r_s)^1} + \frac{D_2}{(1 + r_s)^2} + \cdots + \frac{D_\infty}{(1 + r_s)^\infty}.$$

The Preemptive Right

Common stockholders often have the right, called the **preemptive right,** to purchase any additional shares sold by the firm. In some states, the preemptive right is automatically included in every corporate charter; in others, it is necessary to insert it specifically into the charter.

The preemptive right enables current stockholders to maintain control and prevents a transfer of wealth from current stockholders to new stockholders. If it were not for this safeguard, the management of a corporation could issue a large number of additional shares at a low price and purchase these shares itself. Management could thereby seize control of the corporation and steal value from the current stockholders. For example, suppose 1,000 shares of common stock, each with a price of $100, were outstanding, making the total market value of the firm $100,000. If an additional 1,000 shares were sold at $50 a share, or for $50,000, this would raise the total market value to $150,000. When total market value is divided by new total shares outstanding, a value of $75 a share is obtained. The old stockholders thus lose $25 per share, and the new stockholders have an instant profit of $25 per share. Thus, selling common stock at a price below the market value would dilute its price and transfer wealth from the present stockholders to those who were allowed to purchase the new shares. The preemptive right prevents such occurrences.

SELF-TEST

What is a proxy fight?
What are the two primary reasons for the existence of the preemptive right?

8.2 Types of Common Stock

Although most firms have only one type of common stock, in some instances **classified stock** is used to meet the special needs of the company. Generally, when special classifications are used, one type is designated *Class A*, another *Class B*, and so on. Small, new companies seeking funds from outside sources frequently use different types of common stock. For example, when Genetic Concepts went public, its Class A stock was sold to the public and paid a dividend, but this stock had no voting rights for 5 years. Its Class B stock, which was retained by the organizers of the company, had full voting rights for 5 years, but the legal terms stated that dividends could not be paid on the Class B stock until the company had established its earning power by building up retained earnings to a designated level. The use of classified stock thus enabled the public to take a position in a conservatively financed growth company without sacrificing income, while the founders retained absolute control during the crucial early stages of the firm's development. At the same time, outside investors were protected against excessive withdrawals of funds by the original owners. As is often the case in such situations, the Class B stock was called **founders' shares.**

Note that "Class A," "Class B," and so on, have no standard meanings. Most firms have no classified shares, but a firm that does could designate its Class B shares as founders' shares and its Class A shares as those sold to the public, while another could reverse these designations. Still other firms could use stock classifications for entirely different purposes. For example, when General Motors acquired Hughes Aircraft for $5 billion, it paid in part with a new Class H common, GMH, which had limited voting rights and whose dividends were tied to Hughes's performance as a GM subsidiary. The reasons for the new stock were reported to be (1) that GM wanted to limit voting privileges on the new classified stock because of management's concern about a possible takeover and (2) that Hughes's employees wanted to be rewarded more directly on Hughes's own performance than would have been possible through regular GM stock.

GM's deal posed a problem for the NYSE, which had a rule against listing a company's common stock if the company had any nonvoting common stock outstanding. GM made it clear that it was willing to delist if the NYSE did not change its rules. The NYSE concluded that such arrangements as GM had made were logical and were likely to be made by other companies in the future, so it changed its rules to accommodate GM. In reality, though, the NYSE had little choice. In recent years, the Nasdaq market has proven that it can provide a deep, liquid market for common stocks, and the defection of GM would have hurt the NYSE much more than GM.

As these examples illustrate, the right to vote is often a distinguishing characteristic between different classes of stock. Suppose two classes of stock differ in but one respect: One class has voting rights but the other does not. As you would expect, the stock with voting rights would be more valuable. In the United States, which has a legal system with fairly strong protection for minority stockholders (that is, noncontrolling stockholders), voting stock typically sells at a price 4% to 6% above that of otherwise similar nonvoting stock. Thus, if a stock with no voting rights sold for $50, then one with voting rights would probably sell for $52 to $53. In countries with legal systems that provide less protection for minority stockholders, the right to vote is far more valuable. For example, voting stock on average sells for 45% more than nonvoting stock in Israel and for 82% more in Italy.

As we noted above, General Motors created its Class H common stock as a part of its acquisition of Hughes Aircraft. This type of stock, with dividends tied to a particular part of a company, is called **tracking stock.** It also is called **target stock.** Although GM used its tracking stock in an acquisition, other companies are attempting to use such stock to increase shareholder value. For example, in 1995 US West had several business areas with very different growth prospects, ranging from slow-growth local telephone services to high-growth cellular, cable television, and directory services. US West felt that investors were unable to correctly value its

Note that **http://finance .yahoo.com** provides an easy way to find stocks meeting specified criteria. Under the section on Stock Research, select Stock Screener. To find the largest companies in terms of market value, for example, choose More Preset Screens, then select Largest Market Cap. You can also create custom screens to find stocks meeting other criteria.

high-growth lines of business, since cash flows from slow-growth and high-growth businesses were mingled. To separate the cash flows and to allow separate valuations, the company issued tracking stocks. Similarly, Georgia-Pacific Corp. issued tracking stock for its timber business, and in 2002 Loews Corporation, a holding company with property and casualty insurance, oil and gas drilling, and tobacco subsidiaries, issued Carolina Group tracking stock tied to the performance of its Lorillard tobacco subsidiary. Despite this trend, many analysts are skeptical as to whether tracking stock increases a company's total market value. Companies still report consolidated financial statements for the entire company, and they have considerable leeway in allocating costs and reporting the financial results for the various divisions, even those with tracking stock. Thus, a tracking stock is not the same as the stock of an independent, stand-alone company.

SELF-TEST

What are some reasons a company might use classified stock?

8.3   Stock Market Reporting

Up until a couple of years ago, the best source of stock quotations was the business section of a daily newspaper, such as *The Wall Street Journal*. One problem with newspapers, however, is that they are printed only once a day. Now it is possible to get quotes all during the day from a wide variety of Internet sources.[2] One of the best is provided by Bloomberg at **http://www.bloomberg.com**. Figure 8-1 shows a quote for Abbott Labs, which is traded on the NYSE under the symbol ABT. As Figure 8-1 shows, Abbott Labs' stock ended the day at $41.95, for a loss of $0.09, which is a 0.21% decrease from the previous day. The data also show that Abbott opened the current day at $41.75, reached a high during the day of $42.20, and fell as low as $41.56. During the past year, the price has been as high as $50.00 and as low as $37.50. More than 3.9 million shares traded during the day. If this quote had been during trading hours, it would also have provided information about the quotes at which the stock could be bought (the Ask quote) or sold (the

Figure 8-1

Stock Quote for Abbott Labs, June 23, 2006

ABT:US Abbott Laboratories

More on ABT:US   Detailed Quote ⬍

6/23   11:52   NEW YORK   CURRENCY: USD   INDUSTRY: Medical-Drugs

Price	Change	% Change	Bid	Ask	Open	Volume
41.950	-0.090	-0.214	N.A.	N.A.	41.750	3,941,700

High	Low	52-Week High (7/12/05)		52-Week Low (11/30/05)		1-Year Return
42.200	41.560	50.00		37.50		12.171%

Source: **http://www.bloomberg.com.**

---

[2]Most free sources actually provide quotes that are delayed by 20 minutes.

Bid quote). In addition to this information, the Web page has links to research and much more detailed data for Abbott Labs.

SELF-TEST

What data are often provided in a stock quotation?

8.4 Common Stock Valuation

Common stocks provide an expected future cash flow stream, and a stock's value is found in the same manner as the values of other financial assets—namely, as the present value of the expected future cash flow stream. The expected cash flows consist of two elements: (1) the dividends expected in each year and (2) the price investors expect to receive when they sell the stock. The expected final stock price includes the return of the original investment plus an expected capital gain.

Definitions of Terms Used in Stock Valuation Models

We saw in Chapter 1 that managers seek to maximize the values of their firms' stocks. A manager's actions affect both the stream of income to investors and the riskiness of that stream. Therefore, managers need to know how alternative actions are likely to affect stock prices. At this point we develop some models to help show how the value of a share of stock is determined. We begin by defining the following terms:

D_t = Dividend the stockholder *expects* to receive at the end of Year t. D_0 is the most recent dividend, which has already been paid; D_1 is the first dividend expected, and it will be paid at the end of this year; D_2 is the dividend expected at the end of 2 years; and so forth. D_1 represents the first cash flow a new purchaser of the stock will receive. Note that D_0, the dividend that has just been paid, is known with certainty. However, all future dividends are expected values, so the estimate of D_t may differ among investors.[3]

P_0 = Actual **market price** of the stock today.

$\hat{P}_t$ = Expected price of the stock at the end of each Year t (pronounced "P hat t"). $\hat{P}_0$ is the **intrinsic,** or **fundamental, value** of the stock today as seen by the particular investor doing the analysis; $\hat{P}_1$ is the price expected at the end of one year; and so on. Note that $\hat{P}_0$ is the intrinsic value of the stock today based on a particular investor's estimate of the stock's expected dividend stream and the risk of that stream. Hence, whereas the market price P_0 is fixed and is identical for all investors, $\hat{P}_0$ could differ among investors depending on how optimistic they are regarding the company. The caret, or "hat," is used to indicate that $\hat{P}_t$ is an estimated value. $\hat{P}_0$, the individual investor's estimate of the intrinsic value today, could be above or below P_0, the current stock price, but an investor would buy the stock only if his or her estimate of $\hat{P}_0$ were equal to or greater than P_0.

Since there are many investors in the market, there can be many values for $\hat{P}_0$. However, we can think of a group of "average," or "marginal,"

---

[3]Stocks generally pay dividends quarterly, so theoretically we should evaluate them on a quarterly basis. However, in stock valuation, most analysts work on an annual basis because the data generally are not precise enough to warrant refinement to a quarterly model. For additional information on the quarterly model, see Charles M. Linke and J. Kenton Zumwalt, "Estimation Biases in Discounted Cash Flow Analysis of Equity Capital Cost in Rate Regulation," *Financial Management*, Autumn 1984, pp. 15–21. Also see Robert Brooks and Billy Helms, "An N-Stage, Fractional Period, Quarterly Dividend Discount Model," *Financial Review*, November 1990, pp. 651–657.

investors whose actions actually determine the market price. For these marginal investors, P_0 must equal $\hat{P}_0$; otherwise, a disequilibrium would exist, and buying and selling in the market would change P_0 until $P_0 = \hat{P}_0$ for the marginal investor.

$D_1/P_0 =$ Expected **dividend yield** during the coming year. If the stock is expected to pay a dividend of $D_1 = \$1$ during the next 12 months, and if its current price is $P_0 = \$10$, then the expected dividend yield is $\$1/\$10 = 0.10 = 10\%$.

$\dfrac{\hat{P}_1 - P_0}{P_0} =$ Expected **capital gains yield** during the coming year. If the stock sells for $10 today, and if it is expected to rise to $10.50 at the end of one year, then the expected capital gain is $\hat{P}_1 - P_0 = \$10.50 - \$10.00 = \$0.50$, and the expected capital gains yield is $\$0.50/\$10 = 0.05 = 5\%$.

$g =$ Expected **growth rate** in dividends as predicted by a marginal investor. If dividends are expected to grow at a constant rate, g is also equal to the expected rate of growth in earnings and in the stock's price. Different investors may use different g's to evaluate a firm's stock, but the market price, P_0, is set on the basis of the g estimated by marginal investors.

$r_s =$ Minimum acceptable, or **required, rate of return** on the stock, considering both its riskiness and the returns available on other investments. Again, this term generally relates to marginal investors. The primary determinants of r_s include the real rate of return, expected inflation, and risk.

$\hat{r}_s =$ **Expected rate of return** that an investor who buys the stock expects to receive in the future. $\hat{r}_s$ (pronounced "r hat s") could be above or below r_s, but one would buy the stock only if $\hat{r}_s$ were equal to or greater than r_s. $\hat{r}_s$ is equal to the expected dividend yield (D_1/P_0) plus expected capital gains yield [$(\hat{P}_1 - P_0)/P_0$]. In our example, $\hat{r}_s = 10\% + 5\% = 15\%$.

$\bar{r}_s =$ **Actual**, or **realized**, *after-the-fact* **rate of return**, pronounced "r bar s." You may *expect* to obtain a return of $\hat{r}_s = 15\%$ if you buy ExxonMobil today, but if the market goes down, you may end up next year with an actual realized return that is much lower, perhaps even negative.

Expected Dividends as the Basis for Stock Values

Like all financial assets, equilibrium stock prices are the present value of a stream of cash flows. What are the cash flows that corporations provide to their stockholders? First, think of yourself as an investor who buys a stock with the intention of holding it (in your family) forever. In this case, all that you (and your heirs) will receive is a stream of dividends, and the value of the stock today is calculated as the present value of an infinite stream of dividends:

$$\text{Value of stock} = \hat{P}_0 = \text{PV of expected future dividends}$$

$$= \frac{D_1}{(1 + r_s)^1} + \frac{D_2}{(1 + r_s)^2} + \cdots + \frac{D_\infty}{(1 + r_s)^\infty} \quad \textbf{(8-1)}$$

$$= \sum_{t=1}^{\infty} \frac{D_t}{(1 + r_s)^t}.$$

What about the more typical case, where you expect to hold the stock for a finite period and then sell it—what is the value of $\hat{P}_0$ in this case? Unless the company is likely to be liquidated or sold and thus to disappear, *the value of the stock is again determined by Equation 8-1.* To see this, recognize that for any individual investor, the expected cash flows consist of expected dividends plus the expected sale price of the stock. However, the sale price the current investor receives will depend on the dividends some future investor expects. Therefore, for all present and future investors in total, expected cash flows must be based on expected future dividends. Put another way, unless a firm is liquidated or sold to another concern, the cash flows it provides to its stockholders will consist only of a stream of dividends; therefore, the value of a share of its stock must be the present value of that expected dividend stream.

The general validity of Equation 8-1 can also be confirmed by asking the following question: Suppose I buy a stock and expect to hold it for 1 year. I will receive dividends during the year plus the value $\hat{P}_1$ when I sell out at the end of the year. But what will determine the value of $\hat{P}_1$? The answer is that it will be determined as the present value of the dividends expected during Year 2 plus the stock price at the end of that year, which, in turn, will be determined as the present value of another set of future dividends and an even more distant stock price. This process can be continued ad infinitum, and the ultimate result is Equation 8-1.[4]

SELF-TEST

What are the two parts of most stocks' expected total return?

How does one calculate the capital gains yield and the dividend yield of a stock?

If D_1 = \$3.00, P_0 = \$50, and $\hat{P}_1$ = \$52, what is the stock's expected dividend yield, capital gains yield, and total expected return for the coming year? (6%, 4%, 10%)

8.5 Constant Growth Stocks

Equation 8-1 is a generalized stock valuation model in the sense that the time pattern of D_t can be anything: D_t can be rising, falling, fluctuating randomly, or it can even be zero for several years, and Equation 8-1 will still hold. With a computer spreadsheet we can easily use this equation to find a stock's intrinsic value for any pattern of dividends.[5] In practice, the hard part is getting an accurate forecast of the future dividends. However, in many cases, the stream of dividends is expected to grow at a constant rate. If this is the case, Equation 8-1 may be rewritten as follows:[6]

$$\hat{P}_0 = \frac{D_0(1 + g)^1}{(1 + r_s)^1} + \frac{D_0(1 + g)^2}{(1 + r_s)^2} + \cdots + \frac{D_0(1 + g)^\infty}{(1 + r_s)^\infty}$$

$$= D_0 \sum_{t=1}^{\infty} \frac{(1 + g)^t}{(1 + r_s)^t}$$

$$= \frac{D_0(1 + g)}{r_s - g} = \frac{D_1}{r_s - g}.$$

(8-2)

FM
e-resource

The last term in Equation 8-2 is derived in **Web Extension 8A,** available on the textbook's Web site.

---

[4]We should note that investors periodically lose sight of the long-run nature of stocks as investments and forget that in order to sell a stock at a profit, one must find a buyer who will pay the higher price. If you analyze a stock's value in accordance with Equation 8-1, conclude that the stock's market price exceeds a reasonable value, and then buy the stock anyway, then you would be following the "bigger fool" theory of investment—you think that you may be a fool to buy the stock at its excessive price, but you also think that when you get ready to sell it, you can find someone who is an even bigger fool. The bigger fool theory was widely followed in the spring of 2000, just before the Nasdaq market lost more than one-third of its value.

[5]Actually, we can find an approximate price. If we project dividends for 100 years or more, the present value of that finite dividend stream is approximately equal to the present value of the infinite dividend stream.

[6]The last term in Equation 8-2 is derived in **Web Extension 8A** at the textbook's Web site.

The last term of Equation 8-2 is called the **constant growth model**, or the **Gordon model** after Myron J. Gordon, who did much to develop and popularize it.

A necessary condition for the validity of Equation 8-2 is that r_s be greater than g. Look back at the second form of Equation 8-2. If g is larger than r_s, then $(1 + g)^t/(1 + r_s)^t$ must always be greater than 1. In this case, the second line of Equation 8-2 is the sum of an infinite number of terms, with each term being a number larger than 1. Therefore, if the constant g were greater than r_s, the resulting stock price would be infinite! Since no company is worth an infinite price, it is impossible to have a constant growth rate that is greater than r_s. Occasionally, a student will plug a value for g greater than r_s into the last form of Equation 8-2 and report a negative stock price. This is nonsensical. The last form of Equation 8-2 is valid only when g is less than r_s. *If g is greater than r_s the constant growth model cannot be used and the answer you would get from using Equation 8-2 would be wrong and misleading.*

Illustration of a Constant Growth Stock

Assume that MicroDrive just paid a dividend of $1.15 (that is, $D_0 = \$1.15$). Its stock has a required rate of return, r_s, of 13.4%, and investors expect the dividend to grow at a constant 8% rate in the future. The estimated dividend 1 year hence would be $D_1 = \$1.15(1.08) = \$1.24$; D_2 would be $1.34; and the estimated dividend 5 years hence would be $1.69:

$$D_t = D_0(1 + g)^t = \$1.15(1.08)^5 = \$1.69.$$

We could use this procedure to estimate each future dividend, and then use Equation 8-1 to determine the current stock value, $\hat{P}_0$. In other words, we could find each expected future dividend, calculate its present value, and then sum all the present values to find the intrinsic value of the stock.

Such a process would be time consuming, but we can take a short cut—just insert the illustrative data into Equation 8-2 to find the stock's intrinsic value, $23:

$$\hat{P}_0 = \frac{\$1.15(1.08)}{0.134 - 0.08} = \frac{\$1.242}{0.054} = \$23.00.$$

The concept underlying the valuation process for a constant growth stock is graphed in Figure 8-2. Dividends are growing at the rate g = 8%, but because $r_s > g$, the present value of each future dividend is declining. For example, the dividend in Year 1 is $D_1 = D_0(1 + g)^1 = \$1.15(1.08) = \$1.242$. However, the present value of this dividend, discounted at 13.4%, is $PV(D_1) = \$1.242/(1.134)^1 = \$1.095$. The dividend expected in Year 2 grows to $1.242(1.08) = \$1.341$, but the present value of this dividend falls to $1.043. Continuing, $D_3 = \$1.449$ and $PV(D_3) = \$0.993$, and so on. Thus, the expected dividends are growing, but the present value of each successive dividend is declining, because the dividend growth rate (8%) is less than the rate used for discounting the dividends to the present (13.4%).

If we summed the present values of each future dividend, this summation would be the value of the stock, $\hat{P}_0$. When g is a constant, this summation is equal to $D_1/(r_s - g)$, as shown in Equation 8-2. Therefore, if we extended the lower step function curve in Figure 8-2 on out to infinity and added up the present values of each future dividend, the summation would be identical to the value given by Equation 8-2, $23.00.

Figure 8-2

Present Value of Dividends of a Constant Growth Stock
where $D_0 = \$1.15$, $g = 8\%$, $r_s = 13.4\%$

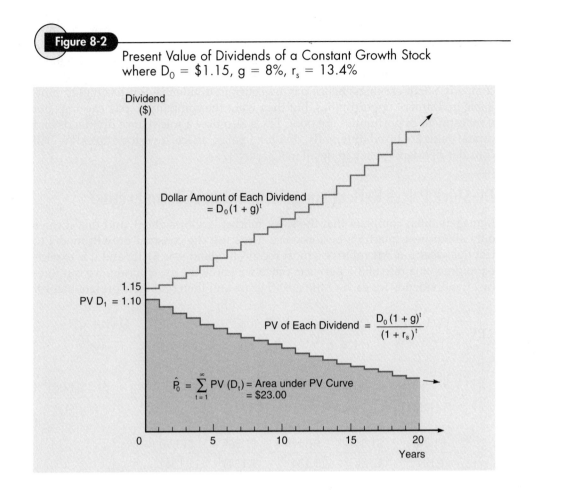

Although Equation 8-2 assumes that dividends grow to infinity, most of the value is based on dividends during a relatively short time period. In our example, 70% of the value is attributed to the first 25 years, 91% to the first 50 years, and 99.4% to the first 100 years. So, companies don't have to live forever for the Gordon growth model to be used.

Dividend and Earnings Growth

Growth in dividends occurs primarily as a result of growth in *earnings per share (EPS)*. Earnings growth, in turn, results from a number of factors, including (1) inflation, (2) the amount of earnings the company retains and reinvests, and (3) the rate of return the company earns on its equity (ROE). Regarding inflation, if output (in units) is stable, but both sales prices and input costs rise at the inflation rate, then EPS will also grow at the inflation rate. Even without inflation, EPS will also grow as a result of the reinvestment, or plowback, of earnings. If the firm's earnings are not all paid out as dividends (that is, if some fraction of earnings is retained), the dollars of investment behind each share will rise over time, which should lead to growth in earnings and dividends.

Even though a stock's value is derived from expected dividends, this does not necessarily mean that corporations can increase their stock prices by simply raising the current dividend. Shareholders care about *all* dividends, both current and those expected in the future. Moreover, there is a trade-off between current dividends and future dividends. Companies that pay high current dividends necessarily retain and reinvest less of their earnings in the business, and that reduces future earnings and dividends. So, the issue is this: Do shareholders prefer higher current dividends at the cost of lower future dividends, the reverse, or are stockholders indifferent? There is no simple answer to this question. Shareholders prefer to have the company retain earnings, hence pay less current dividends, if it has highly profitable investment opportunities, but they want the company to pay earnings out if investment opportunities are poor. Taxes also play a role—since dividends and capital gains are taxed differently, dividend policy affects investors' taxes. We will consider dividend policy in detail in Chapter 17.

Do Stock Prices Reflect Long-Term or Short-Term Events?

Managers often complain that the stock market is shortsighted, and that it cares only about next quarter's performance. Let's use the constant growth model to test this assertion. MicroDrive's most recent dividend was $1.15, and it is expected to grow at a rate of 8% per year. Since we know the growth rate, we can forecast the dividends for each of the next 5 years and then find their present values:

$$PV = \frac{D_0(1 + g)^1}{(1 + r_s)^1} + \frac{D_0(1 + g)^2}{(1 + r_s)^2} + \frac{D_0(1 + g)^3}{(1 + r_s)^3} + \frac{D_0(1 + g)^4}{(1 + r_s)^4} + \frac{D_0(1 + g)^5}{(1 + r_s)^5}$$

$$= \frac{\$1.15(1.08)^1}{(1.134)^1} + \frac{\$1.15(1.08)^2}{(1.134)^2} + \frac{\$1.15(1.08)^3}{(1.134)^3} + \frac{\$1.15(1.08)^4}{(1.134)^4} + \frac{\$1.15(1.08)^5}{(1.134)^5}$$

$$= \frac{\$1.242}{(1.134)^1} + \frac{\$1.341}{(1.134)^2} + \frac{\$1.449}{(1.134)^3} + \frac{\$1.565}{(1.134)^4} + \frac{\$1.690}{(1.134)^5}$$

$$= 1.095 + 1.043 + 0.993 + 0.946 + 0.901$$

$$\approx \$5.00.$$

Recall that MicroDrive's stock price is $23.00. Therefore, only $5.00, or 22%, of the $23.00 stock price is attributable to short-term cash flows. This means that MicroDrive's managers will have a bigger effect on the stock price if they work to increase long-term cash flows rather than focus on short-term flows. This situation holds for most companies. Indeed, a number of professors and consulting firms have used actual company data to show that more than 80% of a typical company's stock price is due to cash flows expected more than 5 years in the future.

This brings up an interesting question. If most of a stock's value is due to long-term cash flows, why do managers and analysts pay so much attention to quarterly earnings? Part of the answer lies in the information conveyed by short-term earnings. For example, if actual quarterly earnings are lower than expected, not because of fundamental problems but only because a company has increased its research and development (R&D) expenditures, studies have shown that the stock price probably won't decline and may actually increase. This makes sense, because R&D should increase future cash flows. On the other hand, if quarterly earnings are lower than expected because customers don't like the company's new products, then this new information will have negative implications for future values of g, the long-term growth rate. As we show later in this chapter, even small changes in g can lead to large changes in stock prices. Therefore, quarterly earnings themselves might not be very important, but the information they convey about future prospects can be terribly important.

Another reason many managers focus on short-term earnings is that some firms pay managerial bonuses on the basis of current earnings rather than stock prices (which reflect future earnings). For these managers, the concern with quarterly earnings is not due to their effect on stock prices—it's due to their effect on bonuses.[7]

When Can the Constant Growth Model Be Used?

The constant growth model is often appropriate for mature companies with a stable history of growth. Expected growth rates vary somewhat among companies, but dividend growth for most mature firms is generally expected to continue in the future at about the same rate as nominal gross domestic product (real GDP plus inflation). On this basis, one might expect the dividends of an average, or "normal," company to grow at a rate of 5% to 8% a year.

Note too that Equation 8-2 is sufficiently general to handle the case of a **zero growth stock,** where the dividend is expected to remain constant over time. If $g = 0$, Equation 8-2 reduces to Equation 8-3:

$$\hat{P}_0 = \frac{D}{r_s}. \qquad (8\text{-}3)$$

This is essentially the equation for a perpetuity, and it is simply the dividend divided by the discount rate.

SELF-TEST

Write out and explain the valuation formula for a constant growth stock.
Are stock prices affected more by long-term or short-term events?
A stock is expected to pay a dividend of $2 at the end of the year. The required rate of return is $r_s = 12\%$. What would the stock's price be if the constant growth rate in dividends were 4%? What would the price be if $g = 0\%$? ($25.00; $16.67)

8.6 Expected Rate of Return on a Constant Growth Stock

We can solve Equation 8-2 for r_s, again using the hat to indicate that we are dealing with an expected rate of return:[8]

$$\begin{matrix} \text{Expected rate} \\ \text{of return} \end{matrix} = \begin{matrix} \text{Expected} \\ \text{dividend} \\ \text{yield} \end{matrix} + \begin{matrix} \text{Expected growth} \\ \text{rate, or capital} \\ \text{gains yield} \end{matrix} \qquad (8\text{-}4)$$

$$\hat{r}_s = \frac{D_1}{P_0} + g.$$

---

[7]Many apparent puzzles in finance can be explained either by managerial compensation systems or by peculiar features of the Tax Code. So, if you can't explain a firm's behavior in terms of economic logic, look to bonuses or taxes as possible explanations.

[8]The r_s value in Equation 8-2 is a *required* rate of return, but when we solve for r_s to obtain Equation 8-4, we are finding an *expected* rate of return. Obviously, the solution requires that $r_s = \hat{r}_s$. This equality holds if the stock market is in equilibrium, a condition that will be discussed later in the chapter.

Thus, if you buy a stock for a price $P_0 = \$23$, and if you expect the stock to pay a dividend $D_1 = \$1.242$ 1 year from now and to grow at a constant rate $g = 8\%$ in the future, then your expected rate of return will be 13.4%:

$$\hat{r}_s = \frac{\$1.242}{\$23} + 8\% = 5.4\% + 8\% = 13.4\%.$$

In this form, we see that $\hat{r}_s$ is the *expected total return* and that it consists of an *expected dividend yield*, $D_1/P_0 = 5.4\%$, plus an *expected growth rate or capital gains yield*, $g = 8\%$.

Suppose this analysis had just been conducted, with the current price, P_0, equal to $\$23$ and the Year 1 expected dividend, D_1, equal to $\$1.242$. What is the expected price at the end of the first year, immediately after D_1 has been paid? We would again apply Equation 8-2, but this time we would use the Year 2 dividend, $D_2 = D_1(1 + g) = \$1.242(1.08) = \$1.3414$:

$$\hat{P}_1 = \frac{D_2}{r_s - g} = \frac{\$1.3414}{0.134 - 0.08} = \$24.84.$$

Now, note that $24.84 is 8% larger than P_0, the $23 price found 1 year earlier:

$$\$23(1.08) = \$24.84.$$

Thus, we would expect a capital gain of $\$24.84 - \$23.00 = \$1.84$ during the year, which would provide a capital gains yield of 8%:

$$\text{Capital gains yield} = \frac{\text{Capital gain}}{\text{Beginning price}} = \frac{\$1.84}{\$23.00} = 0.08 = 8\%.$$

We could extend the analysis, and in each future year the expected capital gains yield would always equal g, the expected dividend growth rate.

The dividend yield during the year could be estimated as follows:

$$\text{Dividend yield} = \frac{D_2}{\hat{P}_1} = \frac{\$1.3414}{\$24.84} = 0.054 = 5.4\%.$$

The popular Motley Fool Web site http://www.fool.com/school/introductiontovaluation.htm provides a good description of some of the benefits and drawbacks of a few of the more commonly used valuation procedures.

The dividend yield for the next year could also be calculated, and again it would be 5.4%. Thus, *for a constant growth stock*, the following conditions must hold:

1. The dividend is expected to grow forever at a constant rate, g.
2. The stock price is expected to grow at this same rate.
3. The expected dividend yield is constant.
4. The expected capital gains yield is also constant, and it is equal to g.
5. The expected total rate of return, $\hat{r}_s$, is equal to the expected dividend yield plus the expected growth rate: $\hat{r}_s = \text{dividend yield} + g$.

The term *expected* should be clarified—it means expected in a probabilistic sense, as the "statistically expected" outcome. Thus, if we say the growth rate is expected to remain constant at 8%, we mean that the best prediction for the growth rate in any future year is 8%, not that we literally expect the growth rate to be exactly 8% in each future year. In this sense, the constant growth assumption is a reasonable one for many large, mature companies.

SELF-TEST

What conditions must hold if a stock is to be evaluated using the constant growth model?

What does the term "expected" mean when we say "expected growth rate"?

If $D_0 = \$4.00$, $r_s = 9\%$, and $g = 5\%$ for a constant growth stock, what is the stock's expected dividend yield and capital gains yield for the coming year? (4%, 5%)

8.7 Valuing Stocks That Have a Nonconstant Growth Rate

For many companies, it is inappropriate to assume that dividends will grow at a constant rate. Firms typically go through *life cycles*. During the early part of their lives, their growth is much faster than that of the economy as a whole; then they match the economy's growth; and finally their growth is slower than that of the economy.[9] Automobile manufacturers in the 1920s, computer software firms such as Microsoft in the 1990s, and technology firms such as Cisco in the 2000s are examples of firms in the early part of the cycle; these firms are called **supernormal, or nonconstant, growth** firms. Figure 8-3 illustrates nonconstant growth and also compares it with normal growth, zero growth, and negative growth.[10]

In the figure, the dividends of the supernormal growth firm are expected to grow at a 30% rate for 3 years, after which the growth rate is expected to fall to 8%, the assumed average for the economy. The value of this firm, like any other, is the present value of its expected future dividends as determined by Equation 8-1. When D_t is growing at a constant rate, we simplify Equation 8-1 to $\hat{P}_0 = D_1/(r_s - g)$. In the supernormal case, however, the expected growth rate is not a constant—it declines at the end of the period of supernormal growth.

Because Equation 8-2 requires a constant growth rate, we obviously cannot use it to value stocks that have nonconstant growth. However, assuming that a company currently enjoying supernormal growth will eventually slow down and become a constant growth stock, we can find its value. First, we assume that the dividend will grow at a nonconstant rate (generally a relatively high rate) for N periods, after which it will grow at a constant rate, g. N is often called the **terminal date,** or **horizon date.**

We can use the constant growth formula, Equation 8-2, what the stock's value will be at period N, to determine what the stock's **horizon,** or **terminal, value** will be N periods from today:

---

[9]The concept of life cycles could be broadened to *product cycle*, which would include both small start-up companies and large companies like Procter & Gamble, which periodically introduce new products that give sales and earnings a boost. We should also mention *business cycles*, which alternately depress and boost sales and profits. The growth rate just after a major new product has been introduced, or just after a firm emerges from the depths of a recession, is likely to be much higher than the "expected long-run average growth rate," which is the proper number for a DCF analysis.

[10]A negative growth rate indicates a declining company. A mining company whose profits are falling because of a declining ore body is an example. Someone buying such a company would expect its earnings, and consequently its dividends and stock price, to decline each year, and this would lead to capital losses rather than capital gains. Obviously, a declining company's stock price will be relatively low, and its dividend yield must be high enough to offset the expected capital loss and still produce a competitive total return. Students sometimes argue that they would never be willing to buy a stock whose price was expected to decline. However, if the annual dividends are large enough to *more than offset* the falling stock price, the stock could still provide a good return.

Figure 8-3

Illustrative Dividend Growth Rates

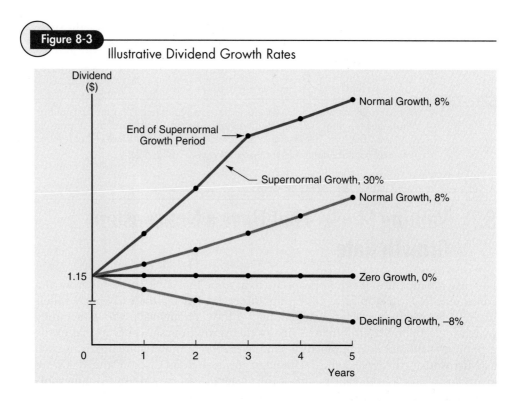

$$\text{Horizon value} = \hat{P}_N = \frac{D_{N+1}}{r_s - g} = \frac{D_N(1 + g)}{r_s - g}. \qquad (8\text{-}5)$$

The stock's intrinsic value today, $\hat{P}_0$, is the present value of the dividends during the nonconstant growth period plus the present value of the horizon value:

$$\hat{P}_0 = \underbrace{\frac{D_1}{(1 + r_s)^1} + \frac{D_2}{(1 + r_s)^2} + \cdots + \frac{D_N}{(1 + r_s)^N}}_{\substack{\text{PV of dividends during the} \\ \text{nonconstant growth period} \\ t = 1, \ldots, N}} + \underbrace{\frac{D_{N+1}}{(1 + r_s)^{N+1}} + \cdots + \frac{D_\infty}{(1 + r_s)^\infty}}_{\substack{\text{PV of dividends during the} \\ \text{constant growth period} \\ t = N + 1, \ldots, \infty}}.$$

$$\hat{P}_0 = \underbrace{\frac{D_1}{(1 + r_s)^1} + \frac{D_2}{(1 + r_s)^2} + \cdots + \frac{D_N}{(1 + r_s)^N}}_{\substack{\text{PV of dividends during the} \\ \text{nonconstant growth period} \\ t = 1, \ldots, N}} + \underbrace{\frac{\hat{P}_N}{(1 + r_s)^N}}_{\substack{\text{PV of horizon} \\ \text{value } \hat{P}_N: \\ \frac{[(D_{N+1})/(r_s - g)]}{(1 + r_s)^N}.}} \qquad (8\text{-}6)$$

Figure 8-4

Process for Finding the Value of a Supernormal Growth Stock

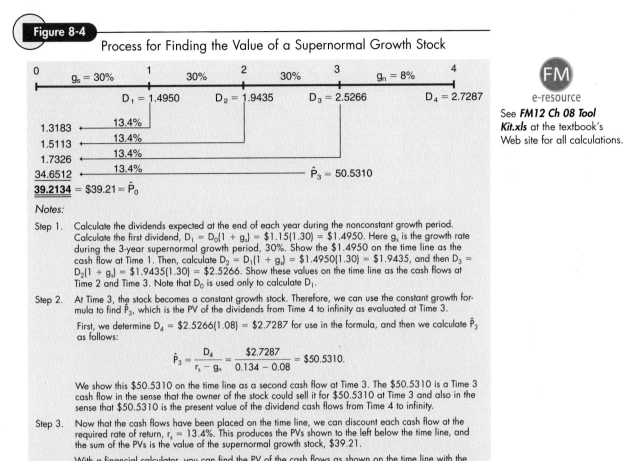

FM
e-resource
See **FM12 Ch 08 Tool Kit.xls** at the textbook's Web site for all calculations.

Notes:

Step 1.   Calculate the dividends expected at the end of each year during the nonconstant growth period. Calculate the first dividend, $D_1 = D_0(1 + g_s) = \$1.15(1.30) = \$1.4950$. Here g_s is the growth rate during the 3-year supernormal growth period, 30%. Show the \$1.4950 on the time line as the cash flow at Time 1. Then, calculate $D_2 = D_1(1 + g_s) = \$1.4950(1.30) = \$1.9435$, and then $D_3 = D_2(1 + g_s) = \$1.9435(1.30) = \$2.5266$. Show these values on the time line as the cash flows at Time 2 and Time 3. Note that D_0 is used only to calculate D_1.

Step 2.   At Time 3, the stock becomes a constant growth stock. Therefore, we can use the constant growth formula to find $\hat{P}_3$, which is the PV of the dividends from Time 4 to infinity as evaluated at Time 3.

First, we determine $D_4 = \$2.5266(1.08) = \$2.7287$ for use in the formula, and then we calculate $\hat{P}_3$ as follows:

$$\hat{P}_3 = \frac{D_4}{r_s - g_n} = \frac{\$2.7287}{0.134 - 0.08} = \$50.5310.$$

We show this \$50.5310 on the time line as a second cash flow at Time 3. The \$50.5310 is a Time 3 cash flow in the sense that the owner of the stock could sell it for \$50.5310 at Time 3 and also in the sense that \$50.5310 is the present value of the dividend cash flows from Time 4 to infinity.

Step 3.   Now that the cash flows have been placed on the time line, we can discount each cash flow at the required rate of return, $r_s = 13.4\%$. This produces the PVs shown to the left below the time line, and the sum of the PVs is the value of the supernormal growth stock, \$39.21.

With a financial calculator, you can find the PV of the cash flows as shown on the time line with the cash flow (CFLO) register of your calculator. Enter 0 for CF_0 because you get no cash flow at Time 0, $CF_1 = 1.495$, $CF_2 = 1.9435$, and $CF_3 = 2.5266 + 50.531 = 53.0576$. Then enter I = 13.4, and press the NPV key to find the value of the stock, \$39.21.

To implement Equation 8-6, we go through the following three steps:

1.   Estimate the expected dividends for each year during the period of nonconstant growth.
2.   Find the expected price of the stock at the end of the nonconstant growth period, at which point it has become a constant growth stock.
3.   Find the present values of the expected dividends during the nonconstant growth period and the present value of the expected stock price at the end of the nonconstant growth period. Their sum is the intrinsic value of the stock, $\hat{P}_0$.

Figure 8-4 can be used to illustrate the process for valuing nonconstant growth stocks. Here we make the following assumptions:

r_s = Stockholders' required rate of return = 13.4%. This rate is used to discount the cash flows.

N = Years of supernormal growth = 3.

g_s = Rate of growth in both earnings and dividends during the supernormal growth period = 30%. This rate is shown directly on the time line. (Note: The growth rate during the supernormal growth period could vary from year to year. Also, there could be several different supernormal growth periods, e.g., 30% for 3 years, then 20% for 3 years, and then a constant 8%.)

g_n = Rate of normal, constant growth after the supernormal period = 8%. This rate is also shown on the time line, between Periods 3 and 4.

D_0 = Last dividend the company paid = $1.15.

The valuation process as diagrammed in Figure 8-4 is explained in the steps set forth below the time line. The estimated value of the supernormal growth stock is $39.21.

SELF-TEST

Explain how one would find the value of a supernormal growth stock.

Explain what is meant by "horizon (terminal) date" and "horizon (terminal) value."

Suppose D_0 = $5.00 and r_s = 9%. The expected growth rate from Year 0 to Year 1 ($g_{0 \text{ to } 1}$) = 20%, the expected growth rate from Year 1 to Year 2 ($g_{1 \text{ to } 2}$) = 10%, and the constant rate beyond Year 2 is g_n = 5%. What are the expected dividends for Year 1 and Year 2? What is the expected horizon value price at Year 2 ($\hat{P}_2$)? What is $\hat{P}_0$? ($6.00 and $6.60; $138.60; $125.45)

8.8 Stock Valuation by the Free Cash Flow Approach

The box at the beginning of the chapter showed that the value of a firm is the present value of its future expected free cash flows (FCFs), discounted at the weighted average cost of capital (WACC). Following is a simple example illustrating this approach to stock valuation.

Suppose a firm had a free cash flow of $200 million at the end of the most recent year. Chapter 14 shows how to forecast financial statements and free cash flows, but for now let's assume that the firm's FCFs are expected to grow at a constant rate of 5% per year forever. Chapter 10 explains how to estimate the weighted average cost of capital, but for now let's assume that the firm's WACC is 9%. The present value of the expected future free cash flows is the PV of a growing annuity, so we can use a variation of Equation 8-2, the value of a constantly growing stream of dividends:

$$V = \frac{FCF(1 + g)}{WACC - g} = \frac{\$200(1.05)}{0.09 - 0.05} = \$5,250 \text{ million.} \qquad \text{(8-7)}$$

FCFs are the cash flow available for distribution to *all* of the firm's investors, not just the shareholders. The WACC is the average rate of return required by *all* of the firm's investors, not just shareholders. Therefore, V is the value of the entire firm's operations, not just the value of its equity. If the firm had any nonoperating assets, such as short-term investments in marketable securities, we would add them to V to find the total value. The firm in this example has no nonoperating assets, so its total value is $5,250 million. To find the value of equity, subtract the value of claims held by all groups other than common shareholders, such as debtholders and preferred stockholders. If the value of debt and preferred stock equals $2,000 million, then the firm's equity has a value of $5,250 − $2,000 = $3,250 million. If 325 million shares of stock are outstanding, then the intrinsic stock value $3,250/325 = $10 per share. This example should give you the general idea behind the free cash flow approach to stock valuation, but see Chapter 15 for a more comprehensive example, including the situation where free cash flows are growing initially at a nonconstant rate.

Explain how to find the stock price using the free cash flow approach.

8.9 Market Multiple Analysis

Another method of stock valuation is **market multiple analysis,** which applies a market-determined multiple to net income, earnings per share, sales, book value, or, for businesses such as cable TV or cellular telephone systems, the number of subscribers. While the discounted dividend method applies valuation concepts in a precise manner, focusing on expected cash flows, market multiple analysis is more judgmental. To illustrate the concept, suppose that a company's forecasted earnings per share are $7.70. The average price per share to earnings per share (P/E) ratio for similar publicly traded companies is 12.

To estimate the company's stock value using the market P/E multiple approach, simply multiply its $7.70 earnings per share by the market multiple of 12 to obtain the value of $7.70(12) = $92.40. This is its estimated stock price per share.

Note that measures other than net income can be used in the market multiple approach. For example, another commonly used measure is *earnings before interest, taxes, depreciation, and amortization (EBITDA).* The EBITDA multiple is the total value of a company (the market value of equity plus debt) divided by EBITDA. This multiple is based on total value, since EBITDA measures the entire firm's performance. Therefore, it is called an **entity multiple.** The EBITDA market multiple is the average EBITDA multiple for similar publicly traded companies. Multiplying a company's EBITDA by the market multiple gives an estimate of the company's total value. To find the company's estimated stock price per share, subtract debt from total value, and then divide by the number of shares of stock.

As noted above, in some businesses such as cable TV and cellular telephone, an important element in the valuation process is the number of customers a company has. For example, telephone companies have been paying about $2,000 per customer when acquiring cellular operators. Managed care companies such as HMOs have applied similar logic in acquisitions, basing their valuations on the number of people insured. Some Internet companies have been valued by the number of "eyeballs," which is the number of hits on the site.

What is market multiple analysis?
What is an entity multiple?

8.10 Preferred Stock

Preferred stock is a *hybrid*—it is similar to bonds in some respects and to common stock in others. Like bonds, preferred stock has a par value and a fixed amount of dividends that must be paid before dividends can be paid on the common stock. However, if the preferred dividend is not earned, the directors can omit (or "pass") it without throwing the company into bankruptcy. So, although preferred stock has a fixed payment like bonds, a failure to make this payment will not lead to bankruptcy.

As noted above, a preferred stock entitles its owners to regular, fixed dividend payments. If the payments last forever, the issue is a perpetuity whose value, V_{ps}, is found as follows:

$$V_{ps} = \frac{D_{ps}}{r_{ps}}. \tag{8-8}$$

V_{ps} is the value of the preferred stock, D_{ps} is the preferred dividend, and r_{ps} is the required rate of return. MicroDrive has preferred stock outstanding that pays a dividend of $10 per year. If the required rate of return on this preferred stock is 10%, then its value is $100, found by solving Equation 8-8 as follows:

$$V_{ps} = \frac{\$10.00}{0.103} = \$100.00.$$

If we know the current price of a preferred stock and its dividend, we can solve for the expected rate of return as follows:

$$\hat{r}_{ps} = \frac{D_{ps}}{V_{ps}}. \tag{8-8a}$$

Some preferred stocks have a stated maturity date, say, 50 years. If a firm's preferred stock matures in 50 years, pays a $10 annual dividend, has a par value of $100, and has a required return of 8%, then we can find its price as follows: Enter N = 50, I/YR = 8, PMT = 10, and FV = 100. Then press PV to find the price, V_{ps} = $124.47. If r_{ps} = I = 10%, change I = 8 to I = 10, and find P = V_{ps} = PV = $100. If you know the price of a share of preferred stock, you can solve for I/YR to find the expected rate of return, $\hat{r}_{ps}$.

Most preferred stocks pay dividends quarterly. This is true for MicroDrive, so we could find the effective rate of return on its preferred stock (perpetual or maturing) as follows:

$$EFF\% = EAR_p = \left(1 + \frac{r_{Nom}}{m}\right)^m - 1 = \left(1 + \frac{0.10}{4}\right)^4 - 1 = 10.38\%.$$

If an investor wanted to compare the returns on MicroDrive's bonds and its preferred stock, it would be best to convert the nominal rates on each security to effective rates and then compare these "equivalent annual rates."

8.11 Stock Market Equilibrium

Recall that r_i, the required return on Stock i, can be found using the Security Market Line (SML) equation as it was developed in our discussion of the Capital Asset Pricing Model (CAPM) back in Chapter 6:

$$r_i = r_{RF} + (RP_M)b_i.$$

If the risk-free rate of return is 8%, the market risk premium, RP_M, is 4%, and Stock i has a beta of 2, then the marginal investor will require a return of 16% on Stock i:

$$r_i = 8\% + (4\%)2.0$$
$$= 16\%.$$

The **marginal investor** will want to buy Stock i if its expected rate of return is more than 16%, will want to sell it if the expected rate of return is less than 16%, and will be indifferent, hence will hold but not buy or sell, if the expected rate of return is exactly 16%. Now suppose the investor's portfolio contains Stock i, and he or she analyzes the stock's prospects and concludes that its earnings, dividends, and price can be expected to grow at a constant rate of 5% per year. The last dividend was $D_0 = \$2.8571$, so the next expected dividend is

$$D_1 = \$2.8571(1.05) = \$3.$$

Our marginal investor observes that the present price of the stock, P_0, is $30. Should he or she purchase more of Stock i, sell the stock, or maintain the present position?

The investor can calculate Stock i's *expected rate of return* as follows:

$$\hat{r}_i = \frac{D_1}{P_0} + g = \frac{\$3}{\$30} + 5\% = 15\%.$$

Because the expected rate of return is less than the required return of 16%, this marginal investor would want to sell the stock, as would most other holders. However, few people would want to buy at the $30 price, so the present owners would be unable to find buyers unless they cut the price of the stock. Thus, the price would decline, and this decline would continue until the price reached $27.27, at which point the stock would be in **equilibrium,** defined as the price at which the expected rate of return, 16%, is equal to the required rate of return:

$$\hat{r}_i = \frac{\$3}{\$27.27} + 5\% = 11\% + 5\% = 16\% = r_i.$$

Had the stock initially sold for less than $27.27, say, $25, events would have been reversed. Investors would have wanted to buy the stock because its expected rate of return would have exceeded its required rate of return, and buy orders would have driven the stock's price up to $27.27.

To summarize, in equilibrium two related conditions must hold:

1. A stock's expected rate of return as seen by the marginal investor must equal its required rate of return: $\hat{r}_i = r_i$.
2. The actual market price of the stock must equal its intrinsic value as estimated by the marginal investor: $P_0 = \hat{P}_0$.

Of course, some individual investors may believe that $\hat{r}_i > r_i$ and $\hat{P}_0 > P_0$; hence they would invest in the stock, while other investors may have an opposite view and would sell all of their shares. However, it is the marginal investor who establishes the actual market price, and for this investor, we must have $\hat{r}_i = r_i$ and $P_0 = \hat{P}_0$. If these conditions do not hold, trading will occur until they do.

Changes in Equilibrium Stock Prices and Market Volatility

Stock prices are not constant—they undergo violent changes at times. For example, on September 17, 2001, the first day of trading after the terrorist attacks of September 11, the Dow Jones average dropped 685 points. This was the largest decline ever in the Dow, but not the largest percentage loss, which was -24.4% on December 12, 1914. More recently, the Dow fell by 22.6% on October 19, 1987. The Dow has also had some spectacular increases. In fact, its eighth-largest increase was 368 points on September 24, 2001, shortly after its largest-ever decline. The Dow's largest increase ever was 499 points on April 16, 2000, and its largest percentage gain of 15.4% occurred on March 15, 1933. At the risk of understatement, the stock market is volatile!

To see how such changes can occur, assume that Stock i is in equilibrium, selling at a price of $27.27. If all expectations were exactly met, during the next year the price would gradually rise to $28.63, or by 5%. However, many different events could occur to cause a change in the equilibrium price. To illustrate, consider again the set of inputs used to develop Stock i's price of $27.27, along with a new set of assumed input variables:

	Variable Value	
	Original	New
Risk-free rate, r_{RF}	8%	7%
Market risk premium, $r_M - r_{RF}$	4%	3%
Stock i's beta coefficient, b_i	2.0	1.0
Stock i's expected growth rate, g_i	5%	6%
D_0	$2.8571	$2.8571
Price of Stock i	$27.27	?

Now give yourself a test: How would the indicated change in each variable, by itself, affect the price, and what is your guess as to the new stock price?

Every change, taken alone, would lead to an *increase* in the price. Taken together, the first three changes lower r_i, which declines from 16 to 10%:

$$\text{Original } r_i = 8\% + 4\%(2.0) = 16\%;$$

$$\text{New } r_i = 7\% + 3\%(1.0) = 10\%.$$

Using these values, together with the new g value, we find that $\hat{P}_0$ rises from $27.27 to $75.71:[11]

---

[11]A price change of this magnitude is by no means rare for an individual stock. The prices of *many* stocks double or halve during a year. For example, Ciena, a phone equipment maker, fell by 76.1% in 1998, increased by 183% in 2000, declined by 84% in 2001, and declined by another 64% in 2002. In 2004 alone, Ciena declined by 79% and then increased by 102%.

$$\text{Original } \hat{P}_0 = \frac{\$2.8571(1.05)}{0.16 - 0.05} = \frac{\$3}{0.11} = \$27.27;$$

$$\text{New } \hat{P}_0 = \frac{\$2.8571(1.06)}{0.10 - 0.06} = \frac{\$3.0285}{0.04} = \$75.71.$$

At the new price, the expected and required rates of return are equal:[12]

$$\hat{r}_i = \frac{\$3.0285}{\$75.71} + 6\% = 10\% = r_i.$$

As this example illustrates, even small changes in the size or risk of expected future dividends can cause large changes in stock prices. What might cause investors to change their expectations about future dividends? It could be new information about the company, such as preliminary results for an R&D program, initial sales of a new product, or the discovery of harmful side effects from the use of an existing product. Or, new information that will affect many companies could arrive, such as a tightening of interest rates by the Federal Reserve. Given the existence of computers and telecommunications networks, new information hits the market on an almost continuous basis, and it causes frequent and sometimes large changes in stock prices. In other words, *ready availability of information causes stock prices to be volatile!*

If a stock's price is stable, that probably means that little new information is arriving. But if you think it's risky to invest in a volatile stock, imagine how risky it would be to invest in a company that rarely released new information about its sales or operations. It may be bad to see your stock's price jump around, but it would be a lot worse to see a stable quoted price most of the time and then to see huge moves on the rare days when new information was released. Fortunately, in our economy timely information is readily available, and evidence suggests that stocks, especially those of large companies, adjust rapidly to new information. Consequently, equilibrium ordinarily exists for any given stock, and required and expected returns are generally equal. Stock prices certainly change, sometimes violently and rapidly, but this simply reflects changing conditions and expectations. There are, of course, times when a stock appears to react for several months to favorable or unfavorable developments. However, this does not signify a long adjustment period; rather, it simply indicates that as more new pieces of information about the situation become available, the market adjusts to them. The ability of the market to adjust to new information is discussed in the next section.

SELF-TEST

What two conditions must hold for a stock to be in equilibrium?
Why doesn't a volatile stock price imply irrational pricing?

8.12 The Efficient Markets Hypothesis

As we briefly discussed in Chapter 7, a body of theory called the **Efficient Markets Hypothesis (EMH)** holds (1) that stocks are always in equilibrium and

---

[12]It should be obvious by now that *actual realized* rates of return are not necessarily equal to expected and required returns. Thus, an investor might have *expected* to receive a return of 15% if he or she had bought Ciena stock, but after the fact, the realized return was far above 15% in 2000 and was far below in 1998, 2001, and 2002.

should we expect them to be rational in their financial decisions? For example, studies show that investors tend to hold on too long to stocks that have performed poorly in the past (i.e., losers), but that they sell winners too quickly. This field of study is called behavioral finance, and Chapter 7 discusses it in more detail.[15]

Keep in mind that the EMH does not assume that all investors are rational. Instead, it assumes that stock market prices reflect intrinsic values. As we described earlier, new information should cause a stock's current intrinsic value to move to a new intrinsic value based on that new information. The EHM further assumes that whenever stock prices deviate from their intrinsic values due to a lag in the incorporation of new information, investors will *quickly* take advantage of mispricing by buying undervalued stocks and selling overvalued stocks. Thus, investors' actions work to drive prices to their new equilibrium level based on new information. Even if some investors behave irrationally, such as holding losers too long and selling winners too quickly, that does not imply that the markets are not efficient. Thus, it is possible to have irrational investors in a rational market.

On the other hand, if the market itself is irrational (i.e., consistently mispriced), rational investors can lose a lot of money even if they are ultimately proven to be correct. For example, a "rational" investor in mid-1999 might have concluded that the Nasdaq was overvalued when it was trading at 3,000. If that investor had acted on that assumption and sold stock short, he or she would have lost a lot of money the following year when the Nasdaq soared to over 5,000 as "irrational exuberance" pushed the prices of already overvalued stocks to even higher levels. Ultimately, if our "rational investor" had the courage, patience, and financial resources to hold on for the run, he or she would have been vindicated, because the Nasdaq subsequently fell to about 1,300. But as the economist John Maynard Keynes said, "In the long run we are all dead."

What is the bottom line on market efficiency? Based on our reading of the evidence, we believe that for most stocks, for most of the time, it is generally safe to assume that the market is reasonably efficient in the sense that the intrinsic price is approximately equal to the actual market price ($\hat{P}_0 \approx P_0$).

Implications of Market Efficiency for Financial Decisions

What bearing does the EMH have on financial decisions? First, many investors have given up trying to beat the market because the professionals who manage mutual fund portfolios, on average, do not outperform the overall stock market as measured by an index like the S&P 500.[16] Indeed, the relatively poor performance of actively managed mutual funds helps explain the growing popularity of indexed funds, where administrative costs are relatively low. Rather than spending time and money trying to find undervalued stocks, index funds try instead to match overall market returns by buying the basket of stocks that makes up a particular index, such as the S&P 500.

Second, market efficiency also has important implications for managerial decisions, especially stock issues, stock repurchases, and tender offers. If the

---

[15]Three noteworthy sources for students interested in behavioral finance are Richard H. Thaler, Editor, *Advances in Behavioral Finance* (New York: Russell Sage Foundation, 1993); Andrei Shleifer, *Inefficient Markets: An Introduction to Behavioral Finance* (New York: Oxford University Press, 2000); and Nicholas Barberis and Richard Thaler, "A Survey of Behavioral Finance," Chapter 18, *Handbook of the Economics of Finance*, edited by George Constantinides, Milt Harris, and René Stulz, part of the Handbooks in Economics Series (Elsevier/North-Holland, 2003). Students interested in learning more about the Efficient Markets Hypothesis should consult Burton G. Malkiel, *A Random Walk Down Wall Street* (New York: W.W. Norton & Company, 1999).
[16]For a discussion of the recent performance of actively managed funds, see Jonathan Clements, "Resisting the Lure of Managed Funds," *The Wall Street Journal*, February 27, 2001, C1.

market prices stocks fairly, then managerial decisions based on the premise that a stock is undervalued or overvalued might not make sense. Managers may have better information about their own companies than outsiders, but they cannot use this information for their own advantage, nor can they deliberately defraud any investors.

Summary

Corporate decisions should be analyzed in terms of how alternative courses of action are likely to affect a firm's value. However, it is necessary to know how stock prices are established before attempting to measure how a given decision will affect a specific firm's value. This chapter showed how stock values are determined, and also how investors go about estimating the rates of return they expect to earn. The key concepts covered are listed below:

- A **proxy** is a document that gives one person the power to act for another, typically the power to vote shares of common stock. A **proxy fight** occurs when an outside group solicits stockholders' proxies in an effort to vote a new management team into office.
- A **takeover** occurs when a person or group succeeds in ousting a firm's management and takes control of the company.
- Stockholders often have the right to purchase any additional shares sold by the firm. This right, called the **preemptive right,** protects the control of the present stockholders and prevents dilution of their value.
- Although most firms have only one type of common stock, in some instances **classified stock** is used to meet the special needs of the company. One type is **founders' shares.** This is stock owned by the firm's founders that carries sole voting rights but restricted dividends for a specified number of years.
- **Closely held stock** is owned by a few individuals who are typically associated with the firm's management.
- **Publicly owned stock** is owned by a relatively large number of individuals who are not actively involved in the firm's management.
- The **intrinsic value of a share of stock** is calculated as the **present value of the stream of dividends** the stock is expected to provide in the future.
- The equation used to find the **intrinsic, or expected, value of a constant growth stock** is

$$\hat{P}_0 = \frac{D_1}{r_s - g}.$$

- The **expected total rate of return** from a stock consists of an **expected dividend yield** plus an **expected capital gains yield.** For a constant growth firm, both the expected dividend yield and the expected capital gains yield are constant.

- The equation for $\hat{r}_s$, the **expected rate of return on a constant growth stock,** can be expressed as follows:

$$\hat{r}_s = \frac{D_1}{P_0} + g.$$

- A **zero growth stock** is one whose future dividends are not expected to grow at all, while a **supernormal growth stock** is one whose earnings and dividends are expected to grow much faster than the economy as a whole over some specified time period and then to grow at the "normal" rate.
- To find the **present value of a supernormal growth stock,** (1) find the dividends expected during the supernormal growth period, (2) find the price of the stock at the end of the supernormal growth period, (3) discount the dividends and the projected price back to the present, and (4) sum these PVs to find the current intrinsic, or expected, value of the stock, $\hat{P}_0$.
- The **horizon (terminal) date** is the date when individual dividend forecasts are no longer made because the dividend growth rate is assumed to be constant.
- The **horizon (terminal) value** is the value at the horizon date of all future dividends after that date.
- **Preferred stock** is a hybrid security having some characteristics of debt and some of equity.
- Most preferred stocks are **perpetuities,** and the value of a share of perpetual preferred stock is found as the dividend divided by the required rate of return:

$$V_{ps} = \frac{D_{ps}}{r_{ps}}.$$

- **Maturing preferred stock** is evaluated with a formula that is identical in form to the bond value formula.
- The **marginal investor** is a representative investor whose actions reflect the beliefs of those people who are currently trading a stock. It is the marginal investor who determines a stock's price.
- **Equilibrium** is the condition under which the expected return on a security as seen by the marginal investor is just equal to its required return, $\hat{r}_s = r_s$. Also, the stock's intrinsic value must be equal to its market price, $\hat{P}_0 = P_0$.
- The **Efficient Markets Hypothesis (EMH)** holds (1) that stocks are always in equilibrium and (2) that it is impossible for an investor who does not have inside information to consistently "beat the market." Therefore, according to the EMH, stocks are always fairly valued ($\hat{P}_0 = P_0$), the required return on a stock is equal to its expected return ($r_s = \hat{r}_s$), and all stocks' expected returns plot on the SML.

Questions

(8-1) Define each of the following terms:
   a. Proxy; proxy fight; takeover; preemptive right; classified stock; founders' shares
   b. Closely held stock; publicly owned stock
   c. Intrinsic value ($\hat{P}_0$); market price (P_0)

    d. Required rate of return, r_s; expected rate of return, $\hat{r}_s$; actual, or realized, rate of return, $\bar{r}_s$

    e. Capital gains yield; dividend yield; expected total return

    f. Normal, or constant, growth; supernormal, or nonconstant, growth; zero growth stock

    g. Preferred stock

    h. Equilibrium; Efficient Markets Hypothesis (EMH); three forms of EMH

(8-2) Two investors are evaluating General Motors' stock for possible purchase. They agree on the expected value of D_1 and also on the expected future dividend growth rate. Further, they agree on the risk of the stock. However, one investor normally holds stocks for 2 years, while the other normally holds stocks for 10 years. On the basis of the type of analysis done in this chapter, they should both be willing to pay the same price for General Motors' stock. True or false? Explain.

(8-3) A bond that pays interest forever and has no maturity date is a perpetual bond. In what respect is a perpetual bond similar to a no-growth common stock, and to a share of preferred stock?

Self-Test Problems   Solutions Appear in Appendix A

(ST-1)
Constant Growth Stock
Valuation

Ewald Company's current stock price is $36, and its last dividend was $2.40. In view of Ewald's strong financial position and its consequent low risk, its required rate of return is only 12%. If dividends are expected to grow at a constant rate, g, in the future, and if r_s is expected to remain at 12%, what is Ewald's expected stock price 5 years from now?

(ST-2)
Supernormal Growth
Stock Valuation

Snyder Computer Chips Inc. is experiencing a period of rapid growth. Earnings and dividends are expected to grow at a rate of 15% during the next 2 years, at 13% in the third year, and at a constant rate of 6% thereafter. Snyder's last dividend was $1.15, and the required rate of return on the stock is 12%.

    a. Calculate the value of the stock today.

    b. Calculate $\hat{P}_1$ and $\hat{P}_2$.

    c. Calculate the dividend yield and capital gains yield for Years 1, 2, and 3.

Problems   Answers Appear in Appendix B

Easy Problems 1–5

(8-1)
DPS Calculation

Thress Industries just paid a dividend of $1.50 a share (i.e., $D_0 = \$1.50$). The dividend is expected to grow 5% a year for the next 3 years, and then 10% a year thereafter. What is the expected dividend per share for each of the next 5 years?

(8-2)
Constant Growth
Valuation

Boehm Incorporated is expected to pay a $1.50 per share dividend at the end of the year (i.e., $D_1 = \$1.50$). The dividend is expected to grow at a constant rate of 7% a year. The required rate of return on the stock, r_s, is 15%. What is the value per share of the company's stock?

(8-3)
Constant Growth
Valuation

Woidtke Manufacturing's stock currently sells for $20 a share. The stock just paid a dividend of $1.00 a share (i.e., $D_0 = \$1.00$). The dividend is expected to grow at a constant rate of 10% a year. What stock price is expected 1 year from now? What is the required rate of return on the company's stock?

(8-4)
Preferred Stock Valuation

Basil Pet Products has preferred stock outstanding which pays a dividend of $5 at the end of each year. The preferred stock sells for $50 a share. What is the preferred stock's required rate of return?

(8-5)
Nonconstant Growth
Valuation

A company currently pays a dividend of $2 per share, $D_0 = \$2$. It is estimated that the company's dividend will grow at a rate of 20% per year for the next 2 years, then the dividend will grow at a constant rate of 7% thereafter. The company's stock has a beta equal to 1.2, the risk-free rate is 7.5%, and the market risk premium is 4%. What is your estimate of the stock's current price?

Intermediate
Problems 6–16

(8-6)
Constant Growth Rate, g

A stock is trading at $80 per share. The stock is expected to have a year-end dividend of $4 per share ($D_1 = \$4$), which is expected to grow at some constant rate g throughout time. The stock's required rate of return is 14%. If you are an analyst who believes in efficient markets, what is your forecast of g?

(8-7)
Constant Growth
Valuation

You are considering an investment in the common stock of Crisp's Cookware. The stock is expected to pay a dividend of $2 a share at the end of the year ($D_1 = \$2.00$). The stock has a beta equal to 0.9. The risk-free rate is 5.6%, and the market risk premium is 6%. The stock's dividend is expected to grow at some constant rate g. The stock currently sells for $25 a share. Assuming the market is in equilibrium, what does the market believe will be the stock price at the end of 3 years? (That is, what is $\hat{P}_3$?)

(8-8)
Preferred Stock Rate of
Return

What will be the nominal rate of return on a preferred stock with a $100 par value, a stated dividend of 8% of par, and a current market price of (a) $60, (b) $80, (c) $100, and (d) $140?

(8-9)
Declining Growth Stock
Valuation

Brushy Mountain Mining Company's ore reserves are being depleted, so its sales are falling. Also, its pit is getting deeper each year, so its costs are rising. As a result, the company's earnings and dividends are declining at the constant rate of 4% per year. If $D_0 = \$5$ and $r_s = 15\%$, what is the value of Brushy Mountain's stock?

(8-10)
Rates of Return and
Equilibrium

The beta coefficient for Stock C is $b_C = 0.4$, whereas that for Stock D is $b_D = -0.5$. (Stock D's beta is negative, indicating that its rate of return rises whenever returns on most other stocks fall. There are very few negative beta stocks, although collection agency stocks are sometimes cited as an example.)

a. If the risk-free rate is 9% and the expected rate of return on an average stock is 13%, what are the required rates of return on Stocks C and D?

b. For Stock C, suppose the current price, P_0, is $25; the next expected dividend, D_1, is $1.50; and the stock's expected constant growth rate is 4%. Is the stock in equilibrium? Explain, and describe what will happen if the stock is not in equilibrium.

(8-11)
Nonconstant Growth
Stock Valuation

Assume that the average firm in your company's industry is expected to grow at a constant rate of 6% and its dividend yield is 7%. Your company is about as risky as the average firm in the industry, but it has just successfully completed some R&D work that leads you to expect that its earnings and dividends will grow at a rate of 50% [$D_1 = D_0(1 + g) = D_0(1.50)$] this year and 25% the following year, after which growth should match the 6% industry average rate. The last dividend paid (D_0) was $1. What is the value per share of your firm's stock?

(8-12)
Nonconstant Growth
Stock Valuation

Simpkins Corporation is expanding rapidly, and it currently needs to retain all of its earnings; hence it does not pay any dividends. However, investors expect Simpkins to begin paying dividends, with the first dividend of $1.00 coming 3 years from today. The dividend should grow rapidly—at a rate of 50% per year—during Years 4 and 5. After Year 5, the company should grow at a constant rate of 8% per year. If the required return on the stock is 15%, what is the value of the stock today?

(8-13)
Preferred Stock Valuation

Rolen Riders issued preferred stock with a stated dividend of 10% of par. Preferred stock of this type currently yields 8%, and the par value is $100. Assume dividends are paid annually.
a.   What is the value of Rolen's preferred stock?
b.   Suppose interest rate levels rise to the point where the preferred stock now yields 12%. What would be the value of Rolen's preferred stock?

(8-14)
Return on Common Stock

You buy a share of The Ludwig Corporation stock for $21.40. You expect it to pay dividends of $1.07, $1.1449, and $1.2250 in Years 1, 2, and 3, respectively, and you expect to sell it at a price of $26.22 at the end of 3 years.
a.   Calculate the growth rate in dividends.
b.   Calculate the expected dividend yield.
c.   Assuming that the calculated growth rate is expected to continue, you can add the dividend yield to the expected growth rate to get the expected total rate of return. What is this stock's expected total rate of return?

(8-15)
Constant Growth Stock
Valuation

Investors require a 15% rate of return on Brooks Sisters' stock ($r_s = 15\%$).
a.   What will be Brooks Sisters' stock value if the previous dividend was $D_0 = \$2$ and if investors expect dividends to grow at a constant compound annual rate of (1) −5%, (2) 0%, (3) 5%, and (4) 10%?
b.   Using data from part a, what is the Gordon (constant growth) model value for Brooks Sisters' stock if the required rate of return is 15% and the expected growth rate is (1) 15% or (2) 20%? Are these reasonable results? Explain.
c.   Is it reasonable to expect that a constant growth stock would have $g > r_s$?

(8-16)
Equilibrium Stock Price

The risk-free rate of return, r_{RF}, is 11%; the required rate of return on the market, r_M, is 14%; and Schuler Company's stock has a beta coefficient of 1.5.
a.   If the dividend expected during the coming year, D_1, is $2.25, and if g = a constant 5%, at what price should Schuler's stock sell?
b.   Now, suppose the Federal Reserve Board increases the money supply, causing the risk-free rate to drop to 9% and r_M to fall to 12%. What would this do to the price of the stock?
c.   In addition to the change in part b, suppose investors' risk aversion declines; this fact, combined with the decline in r_{RF}, causes r_M to fall to 11%. At what price would Schuler's stock sell?

d. Now, suppose Schuler has a change in management. The new group institutes policies that increase the expected constant growth rate to 6%. Also, the new management stabilizes sales and profits, and thus causes the beta coefficient to decline from 1.5 to 1.3. Assume that r_{RF} and r_M are equal to the values in part c. After all these changes, what is Schuler's new equilibrium price? (Note: D_1 goes to $2.27.)

**Challenging
Problems 17–19**

(8-17)
Constant Growth Stock
Valuation

Suppose a firm's common stock paid a dividend of $2 *yesterday*. You expect the dividend to grow at the rate of 5% per year for the next 3 years, and, if you buy the stock, you plan to hold it for 3 years and then sell it.

a. Find the expected dividend for each of the next 3 years; that is, calculate D_1, D_2, and D_3. Note that $D_0 = $2.

b. Given that the appropriate discount rate is 12% and that the first of these dividend payments will occur 1 year from now, find the present value of the dividend stream; that is, calculate the PV of D_1, D_2, and D_3, and then sum these PVs.

c. You expect the price of the stock 3 years from now to be $34.73; that is, you expect $\hat{P}_3$ to equal $34.73. Discounted at a 12% rate, what is the present value of this expected future stock price? In other words, calculate the PV of $34.73.

d. If you plan to buy the stock, hold it for 3 years, and then sell it for $34.73, what is the most you should pay for it?

e. Use Equation 8-2 to calculate the present value of this stock. Assume that $g = 5\%$, and it is constant.

f. Is the value of this stock dependent on how long you plan to hold it? In other words, if your planned holding period were 2 years or 5 years rather than 3 years, would this affect the value of the stock today, $\hat{P}_0$?

(8-18)
Nonconstant Growth
Stock Valuation

Reizenstein Trucking (RT) has just developed a solar panel capable of generating 200% more electricity than any solar panel currently on the market. As a result, RT is expected to experience a 15% annual growth rate for the next 5 years. By the end of 5 years, other firms will have developed comparable technology, and RT's growth rate will slow to 5% per year indefinitely. Stockholders require a return of 12 % on RT's stock. The most recent annual dividend (D_0), which was paid yesterday, was $1.75 per share.

a. Calculate RT's expected dividends for $t = 1$, $t = 2$, $t = 3$, $t = 4$, and $t = 5$.

b. Calculate the value of the stock today, $\hat{P}_0$. Proceed by finding the present value of the dividends expected at $t = 1$, $t = 2$, $t = 3$, $t = 4$, and $t = 5$ plus the present value of the stock price which should exist at $t = 5$, $\hat{P}_5$. The $\hat{P}_5$ stock price can be found by using the constant growth equation. Notice that to find $\hat{P}_5$, you use the dividend expected at $t = 6$, which is 5% greater than the $t = 5$ dividend.

c. Calculate the expected dividend yield, $D_1/\hat{P}_0$, the capital gains yield expected during the first year, and the expected total return (dividend yield plus capital gains yield) during the first year. (Assume that $\hat{P}_0 = P_0$, and recognize that the capital gains yield is equal to the total return minus the dividend yield.) Also calculate these same three yields for $t = 5$ (e.g., $D_6/\hat{P}_5$).

(8-19)
Supernormal Growth
Stock Valuation

Taussig Technologies Corporation (TTC) has been growing at a rate of 20% per year in recent years. This same growth rate is expected to last for another 2 years.

a. If $D_0 = $1.60, $r_s = 10\%$, and $g_n = 6\%$, what is TTC's stock worth today? What are its expected dividend yield and capital gains yield at this time?

b. Now assume that TTC's period of supernormal growth is to last another 5 years rather than 2 years. How would this affect its price, dividend yield, and capital gains yield? Answer in words only.

c. What will be TTC's dividend yield and capital gains yield once its period of supernormal growth ends? (Hint: These values will be the same regardless of whether you examine the case of 2 or 5 years of supernormal growth; the calculations are very easy.)

d. Of what interest to investors is the changing relationship between dividend yield and capital gains yield over time?

Spreadsheet Problem

e-resource

(8-20)
Build a Model:
Supernormal Growth
and Corporate Valuation

Start with the partial model in the file *FM12 Ch 08 P20 Build a Model.xls* from the textbook's Web site. Rework Problem 8–19, parts a, b, and c, using a spreadsheet model. For part b, calculate the price, dividend yield, and capital gains yield as called for in the problem.

Cyberproblem

e-resource

Please go to the textbook's Web site to access any Cyberproblems.

Mini Case

Sam Strother and Shawna Tibbs are senior vice presidents of Mutual of Seattle. They are co-directors of the company's pension fund management division, with Strother having responsibility for fixed income securities (primarily bonds) and Tibbs responsible for equity investments. A major new client, the Northwestern Municipal Alliance, has requested that Mutual of Seattle present an investment seminar to the mayors of the represented cities, and Strother and Tibbs, who will make the actual presentation, have asked you to help them.

To illustrate the common stock valuation process, Strother and Tibbs have asked you to analyze the Temp Force Company, an employment agency that supplies word processor operators and computer programmers to businesses with temporarily heavy workloads. You are to answer the following questions:

a. Describe briefly the legal rights and privileges of common stockholders.

b. (1) Write out a formula that can be used to value any stock, regardless of its dividend pattern.

  (2) What is a constant growth stock? How are constant growth stocks valued?

  (3) What happens if a company has a constant g that exceeds its r_s? Will many stocks have expected $g > r_s$ in the short run (i.e., for the next few years)? In the long run (i.e., forever)?

c. Assume that Temp Force has a beta coefficient of 1.2, that the risk-free rate (the yield on T-bonds) is 7.0%, and that the market risk premium is 5%. What is the required rate of return on the firm's stock?

d. Assume that Temp Force is a constant growth company whose last dividend (D_0, which was paid yesterday) was $2.00 and whose dividend is expected to grow indefinitely at a 6% rate.
   (1) What is the firm's expected dividend stream over the next 3 years?
   (2) What is the firm's current stock price?
   (3) What is the stock's expected value 1 year from now?
   (4) What are the expected dividend yield, the capital gains yield, and the total return during the first year?

e. Now assume that the stock is currently selling at $30.29. What is the expected rate of return on the stock?

f. What would the stock price be if its dividends were expected to have zero growth?

g. Now assume that Temp Force is expected to experience supernormal growth of 30% for the next 3 years, then to return to its long-run constant growth rate of 6%. What is the stock's value under these conditions? What is its expected dividend yield and capital gains yield in Year 1? In Year 4?

h. Is the stock price based more on long-term or short-term expectations? Answer this by finding the percentage of Temp Force's current stock price based on dividends expected more than 3 years in the future.

i. Suppose Temp Force is expected to experience zero growth during the first 3 years and then to resume its steady-state growth of 6% in the fourth year. What is the stock's value now? What is its expected dividend yield and its capital gains yield in Year 1? In Year 4?

j. Finally, assume that Temp Force's earnings and dividends are expected to decline by a constant 6% per year, that is, $g = -6\%$. Why would anyone be willing to buy such a stock, and at what price should it sell? What would be the dividend yield and capital gains yield in each year?

k. What is market multiple analysis?

l. Temp Force recently issued preferred stock. It pays an annual dividend of $5, and the issue price was $50 per share. What is the expected return to an investor on this preferred stock?

m. Why do stock prices change? Suppose the expected D_1 is $2, the growth rate is 5%, and r_s is 10%. Using the constant growth model, what is the price? What is the impact on stock price if g is 4% or 6%? If r_s is 9% or 11%?

n. What does market equilibrium mean?

o. If equilibrium does not exist, how will it be established?

p. What is the Efficient Markets Hypothesis, what are its three forms, and what are its implications?

Selected Additional Cases

The following cases from Textchoice, Cengage Learning's online library, cover many of the concepts discussed in this chapter and are available at *http://www.textchoice2.com.*

Klein-Brigham Series:
Case 3, "Peachtree Securities, Inc. (B)"; Case 71,

"Swan Davis"; Case 78, "Beatrice Peabody"; and Case 101, "TECO Energy."

Brigham-Buzzard Series:
Case 4, "Powerline Network Corporation (Stocks)."

Financial Options and Applications in Corporate Finance

Microsoft has granted options to buy more than 800 million shares to its employees, or about 16,000 options per person.[1] Of course, many employees have fewer options and some have more, but any way you cut it, that's a lot of options. Microsoft isn't the only company with mega-grants: Bank of America, Citigroup, IBM, JPMorgan Chase, and Ford are among the many companies that have granted options to buy more than 100 million shares to their employees. Whether your next job is with a high-tech firm, a financial service company, or a manufacturer, you will probably receive stock options, so it's important that you understand them.

In a typical grant, you receive options allowing you to purchase shares of stock at a fixed price, which is called the "strike" price, on or before a stated expiration date. Most plans have a vesting period, during which you can't exercise the options. For example,

suppose you are granted 1,000 options with a strike price of $50, an expiration date 10 years from now, and a vesting period of 3 years. Even if the stock price rises above $50 during the first 3 years, you can't exercise the options due to the vesting requirement. After 3 years, if you are still with the company, you have the right to exercise the options. For example, if the stock goes up to $110, you could pay the company $50(1,000) = $50,000 and receive 1,000 shares of stock worth $110,000. However, if you don't exercise the options within 10 years, they will expire and thus be worthless.

Even though the vesting requirement prevents you from exercising the options the moment they are granted to you, the options clearly have some immediate value. Therefore, if you are choosing between different job offers where options are involved, you will need a way to determine the value of the alternative options. This chapter explains how to value options, so read on.

---

[1]Interestingly, Microsoft and some other companies stopped granting options after a change in accounting regulations that requires that the estimated value of options be "expensed," or taken as a cost at the time they are granted. We discuss expensing options later in this chapter.

e-resource

The textbook's Web site contains an *Excel* file that will guide you through the chapter's calculations. The file for this chapter is **FM12 Ch 09 Tool Kit.xls,** and we encourage you to open the file and follow along as you read the chapter.

Every manager should understand the basic principles of option pricing. First, many projects allow managers to make strategic or tactical changes in plans as market conditions change. The existence of these "embedded options" often means the difference between a successful project and a failure. Understanding basic financial options can help you manage the value inherent in these real options. Second, many companies use derivatives, which are in essence financial options, to manage risk, so an understanding of financial options is necessary before tackling derivatives. Third, option pricing theory provides insights into the optimal debt/equity choice, especially when convertible securities are involved. And fourth, understanding financial options will help you deal better with any employee stock options that you receive.

9.1 Financial Options

An **option** is a contract that gives its holder the right to buy (or sell) an asset at some predetermined price within a specified period of time. The following sections explain the different features that affect an option's value.

Option Types and Markets

There are many types of options and option markets.[2] To illustrate how options work, suppose you owned 100 shares of General Computer Corporation (GCC), which on January 9, 2007, sold for $53.50 per share. You could sell to someone the right to buy your 100 shares at any time until May 18, 2007, at a price of, say, $55 per share. This is called an **American option,** because it can be exercised any time before it expires. By contrast, a **European option** can only be exercised on its expiration date. The $55 is called the **strike,** or **exercise, price.** The last day that the option can be exercised is called the **expiration date.** Such options exist, and they are traded on a number of exchanges, with the Chicago Board Options Exchange (CBOE) being the oldest and the largest. This type of option is defined as a **call option,** because the buyer has a "call" on 100 shares of stock. The seller of an option is called the option *writer.* An investor who "writes" call options against stock held in his or her portfolio is said to be selling **covered options.** Options sold without the stock to back them up are called **naked options.** When the strike price exceeds the current stock price, a call option is said to be **out-of-the-money.** When the strike price is less than the current price of the stock, the option is **in-the-money.**

You can also buy an option that gives you the right to *sell* a stock at a specified price within some future period—this is called a **put option.** For example, suppose you think GCC's stock price is likely to decline from its current level of $53.50 sometime during the next 4 months. A put option will give you the right to sell at a fixed price even after the market price declines. You could then buy at the new lower market price, sell at the higher fixed price, and earn a profit. Table 9-1 provides data on GCC's options. You could buy the 4-month May put option for $218.75 ($2³⁄₁₆ × 100). That would give you the right to sell 100 shares (that you would not necessarily own) at a price of $50 per share ($50 is the strike price). Suppose you bought this 100-share contract for $218.75 and then GCC's stock fell

[2]For an in-depth treatment of options, see Don M. Chance, *An Introduction to Derivatives and Risk Management* (Mason, OH: Thomson/South-Western, 2004) or John C. Hull, *Options, Futures, and Other Derivatives* (Upper Saddle River, NJ: Prentice-Hall, 2006).

Table 9-1

January 9, 2007, Listed Options Quotations

		CALLS—LAST QUOTE			PUTS—LAST QUOTE		
Closing Price	**Strike Price**	**February**	**March**	**May**	**February**	**March**	**May**
General Computer Corporation (GCC)							
53½	50	4¼	4¾	5½	⅝	1⅜	2 3/16
53½	55	1 5/16	2 1/16	3⅛	2⅝	r	4½
53½	60	5/16	11/16	1½	6⅝	r	8
U.S. Medical							
56⅝	55	4¼	5⅛	7	2¼	3¾	r
Sport World							
53⅛	55	½	1⅛	r	2⅛	r	r

Note: r means not traded on January 9.

to $45. You could buy the stock on the open market at $45 and exercise your put option by selling the stock at $50. Your profit from exercising the option would be ($50 − $45)(100) = $500. After subtracting the $218.75 you paid for the option, your profit (before taxes and commissions) would be $281.25.

Table 9-1 contains an extract from the Listed Options Quotations Table as it would appear the next day in a daily newspaper. Sport World's February $55 call option sold for $0.50. Thus, for $0.50(100) = $50 you could buy options that would give you the right to buy 100 shares of Sport World stock at a price of $55 per share from January until February, or during the next month.[3] If the stock price stayed below $55 during that period, you would lose your $50, but if it rose to $65, your $50 investment would increase in value to ($65 − $55)(100) = $1,000 in less than 30 days. That translates into a very healthy annualized rate of return. Incidentally, if the stock price did go up, you would not actually exercise your options and buy the stock—rather, you would sell the options, which would then have a value of at least $1,000 versus the $50 you paid, to another option buyer or to the original seller.

The Chicago Board Options Exchange provides 20-minute delayed quotes for equity, index, and LEAPS options at **http://www.cboe.com.**

In addition to options on individual stocks, options are also available on several stock indexes such as the NYSE Index and the S&P 100 Index. Index options permit one to hedge (or bet) on a rise or fall in the general market as well as on individual stocks.

Option trading is one of the hottest financial activities in the United States. The leverage involved makes it possible for speculators with just a few dollars to make a fortune almost overnight. Also, investors with sizable portfolios can sell options against their stocks and earn the value of the option (less brokerage commissions),

[3]The expiration date is the Friday before the third Saturday of the exercise month. Also, note that option contracts are generally written in 100-share multiples.

even if the stock's price remains constant. Most important, though, options can be used to create *hedges* that protect the value of an individual stock or portfolio.[4]

Conventional options are generally written for 6 months or less, but a type of option called a **Long-Term Equity AnticiPation Security (LEAPS)** is different. Like conventional options, LEAPS are listed on exchanges and are available on both individual stocks and stock indexes. The major difference is that LEAPS are long-term options, having maturities of up to 2½ years. One-year LEAPS cost about twice as much as the matching 3-month option, but because of their much longer time to expiration, LEAPS provide buyers with more potential for gains and offer better long-term protection for a portfolio.

Corporations on whose stocks options are written have nothing to do with the option market. Corporations do not raise money in the option market, nor do they have any direct transactions in it. Moreover, option holders do not vote for corporate directors or receive dividends. There have been studies by the SEC and others as to whether option trading stabilizes or destabilizes the stock market, and whether this activity helps or hinders corporations seeking to raise new capital. The studies have not been conclusive, but option trading is here to stay, and many regard it as the most exciting game in town.

Table 9-1 can provide some insights into call option valuation. First, we see that at least three factors affect a call option's value:

1. *Market price versus strike price.* The higher the stock's market price in relation to the strike price, the higher will be the call option price. Thus, Sport World's $55 February call option sells for $0.50, whereas U.S. Medical's $55 February option sells for $4.25. This difference arises because U.S. Medical's current stock price is $56⅝ versus only $53⅛ for Sport World.
2. *Level of strike price.* The higher the strike price, the lower the call option price. Thus, all of GCC's call options, regardless of exercise month, decline as the strike price increases.
3. *Length of option.* The longer the option period, the higher the option price. This occurs because the longer the time before expiration, the greater the chance that the stock price will climb substantially above the exercise price. Thus, option prices increase as the expiration date is lengthened.

Other factors that affect option values, especially the volatility of the underlying stock, are discussed in later sections.

Exercise Value versus Option Price

How is the actual price of a call option determined in the market? In a later section, we present a widely used model (the Black-Scholes model) for pricing call options, but first it is useful to establish some basic concepts. To begin, we define a call option's **exercise value** as follows:[5]

$$\text{Exercise value} = \text{MAX[Current price of the stock} - \text{Strike price, 0]}.$$

---

[4]Insiders who trade illegally generally buy options rather than stock because the leverage inherent in options increases the profit potential. Note, though, that it is illegal to use insider information for personal gain, and an insider using such information would be taking advantage of the option seller. Insider trading, in addition to being unfair and essentially equivalent to stealing, hurts the economy: Investors lose confidence in the capital markets and raise their required returns because of an increased element of risk, and this raises the cost of capital and thus reduces the level of real investment.

[5]MAX means choose the maximum. For example, MAX[15, 0] = 15, and MAX[−10, 0] = 0.

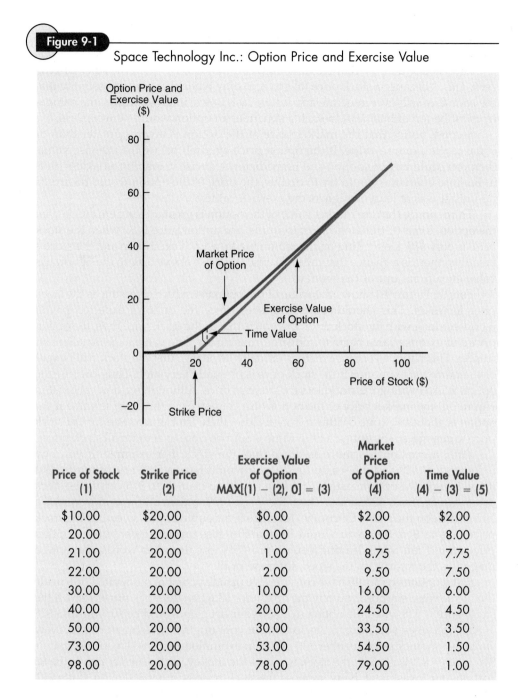

Figure 9-1

Space Technology Inc.: Option Price and Exercise Value

Price of Stock (1)	Strike Price (2)	Exercise Value of Option MAX[(1) − (2), 0] = (3)	Market Price of Option (4)	Time Value (4) − (3) = (5)
$10.00	$20.00	$0.00	$2.00	$2.00
20.00	20.00	0.00	8.00	8.00
21.00	20.00	1.00	8.75	7.75
22.00	20.00	2.00	9.50	7.50
30.00	20.00	10.00	16.00	6.00
40.00	20.00	20.00	24.50	4.50
50.00	20.00	30.00	33.50	3.50
73.00	20.00	53.00	54.50	1.50
98.00	20.00	78.00	79.00	1.00

The exercise value is what the option would be worth if it expired immediately. For example, if a stock sells for $50 and its option has a strike price of $20, then you could buy the stock for $20 by exercising the option. You would own a stock worth $50, but you would have to pay only $20. Therefore, the option would be worth $30 if you had to exercise it immediately. The minimum exercise value is zero, because no one would exercise an out-of-the-money option.

Figure 9-1 presents some data on Space Technology Inc. (STI), a company that recently went public and whose stock price has fluctuated widely during its short history. The third column in the tabular data shows the exercise values for STI's call option when the stock was selling at different prices; the fourth column gives the actual market prices for the option; and the fifth column shows the time value, which is the excess of the actual option price over its exercise value.[6]

First, notice that the market value of the option is zero when the stock price is zero. This is because a stock price falls to zero only when there is no possibility that the company will ever generate any future cash flows; in other words, the company must be out of business. In such a situation, an option would be worthless.

Second, notice that the market price of the option is always greater than or equal to the exercise value. If the option price ever fell below the exercise value, then you could buy the option and immediately exercise it, reaping a riskless profit. Because everyone would try to do this, the price of the option would be driven up until it was at least as high as the exercise value.

Third, notice that the market value of the option is greater than zero even when the option is out-of-the-money. For example, the option price is $2 when the stock price is only $10. Depending on the remaining time until expiration and the stock's volatility, there is a chance that the stock price will rise above $20, so the option has value even if it is out-of-the-money.

Fourth, Figure 9-1 shows the value of the option steadily increasing as the stock price increases. This shouldn't be surprising, since the option's expected payoff increases along with the stock price. But notice that as the stock price rises, the option price and exercise value begin to converge, causing the time value to get smaller and smaller. This happens because there is virtually no chance that the stock will be out-of-the-money at expiration if the stock price is presently very high. Thus, owning the option is like owning the stock, less the exercise price. Although we don't show it in Figure 9-1, the market price of the option also converges to the exercise value if the option is about to expire. With expiration close, there isn't much time for the stock price to change, so the option's time value would be close to zero for all stock prices.

Fifth, an option has more leverage than the stock. For example, if you buy STI's stock at $20 and it goes up to $30, you would have a 50% rate of return. But if you bought the option instead, its price would go from $8 to $16 versus the stock price increase from $20 to $30. Thus, there is a 100% return on the option versus a 50% return on the stock. Of course, leverage is a double-edged sword: If the stock price falls to $10, then you would have a 50% loss on the stock, but the option price would fall to $2, leaving you with a 75% loss. In other words, the option magnifies the returns on the stock, for good or ill.

Sixth, options typically have considerable upside potential but limited downside risk. To see this, suppose you buy the option for $8 when the stock price is $20. If the stock price is $28 when the option expires, your net gain would be $0: you gain $28 − $20 = $8 when you exercise the option, but your original investment was $8. Now suppose the stock price is either $30 or $20 at expiration. If it's $30, your net gain is $10 − $8 = $2. If it's $20, the stock is out-of-the-money, and your net loss is the $8 cost of your investment. Now suppose the stock price is either $50 or $5. If it's $50, your net gain is $30 − $8 = $22; if $5, your net loss is still your $8 initial investment. As this example shows, the payoffs from the option aren't symmetric. The most you can lose is $8, and this happens whether the stock price at expiration is $20, $10, or even $1. On the other hand, every dollar of stock price above $20 yields an extra dollar of payoff from the option, and every dollar above $28 is a dollar of net profit.

---

[6]Among traders an option's market price is also called its "premium." This is particularly confusing since for all other securities the term *premium* means the excess of the market price over some base price. To avoid confusion, we will not use the term *premium* to refer to the option price. Also, the difference between an option's market price and its exercise value is called its "time value" because this represents the extra amount over the option's immediate exercise value a purchaser will pay for the chance the stock price will appreciate over time.

Financial Reporting for Employee Stock Options

When granted to executives and other employees, options are a "hybrid" form of compensation. At some companies, especially small ones, option grants may be a substitute for cash wages—employees are willing to take lower cash salaries if they have options. Options also provide an incentive for employees to work harder. Whether issued to motivate employees or to conserve cash, options clearly have value at the time they are granted, and they transfer wealth from existing shareholders to employees to the extent that they do not reduce cash expenditures or increase employee productivity sufficiently to offset their value at the time of issue.

Companies like the fact that an option grant requires no immediate cash expenditure, although it might dilute shareholder wealth if it is later exercised. Employees, and especially CEOs, like the potential wealth that they receive when they are granted options. When option grants were relatively small, they didn't show up on investors' radar screens. However, as the high-tech sector began making mega-grants in the 1990s, and as other industries followed suit in the heavy use of options, stockholders began to realize that large grants were making some CEOs filthy rich at the stockholders' expense.

Before 2005, option grants were not very visible in companies' financial reports. Even though such grants are clearly a wealth transfer to employees, companies were only required to footnote the grants and could ignore them when reporting their income statements and balance sheets. The Financial Accounting Standards Board now requires companies to show option grants as an expense on the income statement. To do this, the value of the grant is estimated at the time of the grant and then expensed during the vesting period. For example, if the initial value is $100 million and the vesting period is 2 years, the company would report a $50 million expense for each of the next 2 years. This approach isn't perfect because it isn't a cash expense, and it does not take into account changes in the option's value after it is initially granted. However, it does make the option grant more visible to investors, which is a good thing.

In addition to the stock price and the exercise price, the price of an option depends on three other factors: (1) the option's term to maturity, (2) the variability of the stock price, and (3) the risk-free rate. We will explain precisely how these factors affect call option prices later, but for now, note these points:

1. The longer a call option has to run, the greater its value and the larger its time value. If an option expires at 4 P.M. today, there is not much chance that the stock price will go up very much, so the option will sell at close to its exercise value and its time value will be small. On the other hand, if the expiration date is a year away, the stock price could rise sharply, pulling the option's value up with it.
2. An option on an extremely volatile stock is worth more than one on a very stable stock. If the stock price rarely moves, then there is little chance of a large gain on the stock; hence the option will not be worth much. However, if the stock is highly volatile, the option could easily become very valuable. At the same time, losses on options are limited—you can make an unlimited amount, but you can lose only what you paid for the option. Therefore, a large decline in a stock's price does not have a corresponding bad effect on option holders. As a result of the unlimited upside but limited downside potential, the more volatile a stock, the higher the value of its options.
3. Options will be exercised in the future, and part of a call option's value depends on the present value of the cost to exercise it. If interest rates are high, then the present value of the cost to exercise is low, which increases the option's value.

Because of Points 1 and 2, a graph such as Figure 9-1 will show that the longer an option's life, the higher its market price line will be above the exercise value line. Similarly, the more volatile the price of the underlying stock, the higher the market price line. We will see precisely how these factors, and also the risk-free rate, affect option values when we discuss the Black-Scholes model.

SELF-TEST

What is an option? A call option? A put option?

Define a call option's exercise value. Why is the actual market price of a call option usually above its exercise value?

What are some factors that affect a call option's value?

Brighton Memory's stock is currently trading at $50 a share. A call option on the stock with a $35 strike price currently sells for $21. What are the exercise value and the time value of the call option? ($15.00; $6.00)

9.2 Introduction to Option Pricing Models: The Binomial Approach

All option pricing models are based on the concept of a **riskless hedge.** The purpose of such a hedge isn't to create a riskless security—you can buy Treasury securities for that—but, instead, to determine how much an option is worth. To see how this works, suppose a hypothetical investor, we'll call her the *hedger*, buys some shares of stock and simultaneously writes a call option on the stock. As a result of writing the call option, our hedger (1) receives a payment from the call option's purchaser and (2) assumes an obligation to satisfy the purchaser if he or she chooses to exercise the option. Let's focus only on the hedger's portfolio, which contains stock and the obligation to satisfy the option's purchaser (we'll solve for the amount the hedger receives for selling the option in just a bit). If the stock price goes up, the hedger will earn a profit on the stock. However, the option holder will then exercise the option, our hedger will have to sell a share of stock to the option holder at the strike price (which is below the market price), and that will reduce our hedger's profit on the stock's gain. Conversely, if the stock goes down, our hedger will lose on her stock investment, but she won't lose as much in satisfying the option: If the stock goes down a lot, the option holder won't exercise the option, and the hedger will owe nothing; if the stock goes down a little, then the hedger might still have to sell a share at a below-market price to satisfy the option holder, but the market price will be closer to the strike price, so the hedger will lose less. As we will soon show, it is possible to create the portfolio such that the hedger will end up with a riskless position—the value of the portfolio will be the same regardless of what the stock does.

If the portfolio is riskless, then its return must be equal to the riskless rate in order to keep the market in equilibrium. If the portfolio offered a higher rate of return than the riskless rate, arbitrageurs would buy the portfolio and in the process push the price up and the rate of return down, and vice versa if it offered less than the riskless rate. Given the price of the stock, its volatility, the option's exercise price, the life of the option, and the risk-free rate, there is a single option price that satisfies the equilibrium condition, namely, that the portfolio will earn the riskless rate.

The following example applies the **binomial approach,** so named because we assume the stock price can take on only one of two possible values at the end of each period. The stock of Western Cellular, a manufacturer of cell phones, sells for $40 per share. Options exist that permit the holder to buy one share of Western at

e-resource

See **Web Extension 9A** at the textbook's Web site for more discussion of the binomial approach.

an exercise price of $35. These options will expire at the end of 1 year. The steps to the binomial approach are shown below.

Step 1. Define the possible ending prices of the stock. Let's assume that Western's stock will be selling at one of two prices at the end of the year, either $50 or $32. If there is a 70% chance of the $50 price, then Western's expected price is 0.7($50) + 0.3($32) = $44.6.[7] Because the current stock price is $40, Western has an 11.5% expected return: ($44.6 − $40)/$40 = 0.115 = 11.5%. If Western were a riskier stock, then we would have assumed different ending prices that had a wider range and possibly a higher expected return. See **Web Extension 9A** for a more detailed explanation of the relationship between the stock's risk and the possible ending stock prices. Figure 9-2 illustrates the stock's possible price paths and contains additional information that is explained below.

Step 2. Find the range of values at expiration. When the option expires at the end of the year, Western's stock will sell for either $50 or $32, a range of $50 − $32 = $18. As shown in Figure 9-2, the option will pay $15 if the stock is $50, because this is above the strike price of $35: $50 − $35 = $15. The option will pay nothing if the stock price is $32, because this is below the strike price. The range of option payoffs is $15 − $0 = $15. The hedger's portfolio consists of the stock and the obligation to satisfy the option holder, so the value of the portfolio in 1 year is the stock price minus the option payoff.

Step 3. Buy exactly enough stock to equalize the range of payoffs for the stock and the option. Figure 9-2 shows that the range of payoffs for the stock is $18 and the range for the option is $15. To construct the riskless portfolio, we need to equalize these ranges so that the profits from the stock exactly offset the losses in satisfying the option holder. We do so by buying $15/$18 = 0.8333 share and selling one option (or 8,333 shares and 10,000 options).

Here is why equalizing ranges gives the correct number of shares of stock. Let P_u be the stock price if it goes up, P_d the stock price if it goes down, C_u the call option payoff if the stock goes up, C_d the call option payoff if the stock goes down, and N the number of shares of stock. We want the portfolio value to be the same whether the stock goes up or down. The portfolio value for an up stock price is $N(P_u) − C_u$, and the value for a down stock price is $N(P_d) − C_d$. Setting these equal and solving for N yields

$$N = \frac{C_u - C_d}{P_u - P_d},$$ (9-1)

which is the same as equalizing the ranges. For the stock in this example, we have

$$N = \frac{\$15 - \$0}{\$50 - \$32} = 0.8333,$$

which is the same answer we got before.

FM
e-resource
See **FM12 Ch 09 Tool Kit.xls** at the textbook's Web site for all calculations.

[7]As we'll soon show, we don't have to specify the probability of the ending prices to calculate the option price.

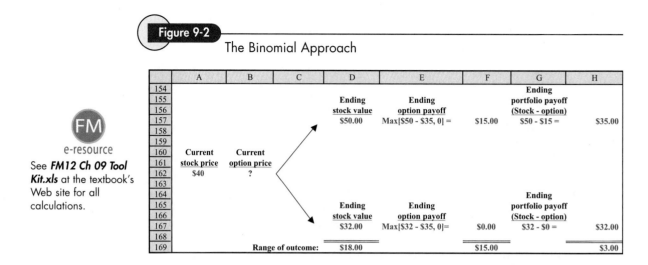

Figure 9-2

The Binomial Approach

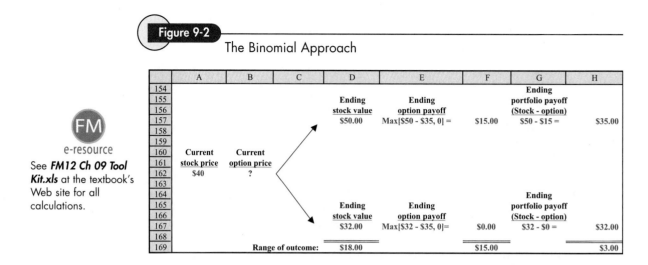

e-resource

See **FM12 Ch 09 Tool Kit.xls** at the textbook's Web site for all calculations.

With N = 0.8333, the current value of the stock in the portfolio is $40(0.8333) = $33.33. The value of the portfolio's stock at the end of the year will be either $50(0.8333) = $41.67 or $32(0.8333) = $26.67. As shown in Figure 9-3, the range of the stock's ending value is now $41.67 − $26.67 = $15.

Step 4. **Create a riskless hedged investment.** We created a riskless portfolio by buying 0.8333 share of the stock and selling one call option, as shown in Figure 9-3. The stock in the portfolio will have a value of either $41.67 or $26.67, depending on the ending price of Western's stock. The call option that was sold will have no effect on the value of the portfolio if Western's price falls to $32 because it will not be exercised—it will expire worthless. However, if the stock price ends at $50, the holder of the option will exercise it, paying the $35 strike price for stock that would cost $50 on the open market. The option holder's profit is the option writer's loss, so the option will cost the hedger $15. Now note that the value of the portfolio is $26.67 regardless of whether Western's stock goes up or down, so the portfolio is riskless. A hedge has been created that protects against both increases and decreases in the price of the stock.

Step 5. **Find the call option's price.** To this point, we have not mentioned the price of the call option that was sold to create the riskless hedge. What is the *fair*, or *equilibrium*, price? The value of the portfolio will be $26.67 at the end of the year, regardless of what happens to the price of the stock. This $26.67 is riskless, and so the portfolio should earn the risk-free rate, which is 8%. If the risk-free rate is compounded daily, the present value of the portfolio's ending value is[8]

$$PV = \frac{\$26.67}{\left(1 + \dfrac{0.08}{365}\right)^{365}} = \$24.62.$$

This means that the current value of the portfolio must be $24.62 to ensure that the portfolio earns the risk-free rate of return. The current value of the portfolio is equal to the value of the stock minus the value of the obligation to cover the call option. At the time the call option is sold, the obligation's value is exactly

---

[8]To be technically correct, we should discount the ending value using a continuously compounded interest rate, as discussed in **Web Extension 2B**.

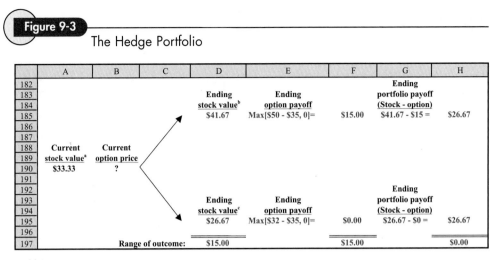

Figure 9-3

The Hedge Portfolio

	A	B	C	D	E	F	G	H
182							Ending	
183				Ending	Ending		portfolio payoff	
184				stock value[b]	option payoff		(Stock - option)	
185				$41.67	Max[$50 - $35, 0]=	$15.00	$41.67 - $15 =	$26.67
186								
187								
188	Current	Current						
189	stock value[a]	option price						
190	$33.33	?						
191								
192							Ending	
193				Ending	Ending		portfolio payoff	
194				stock value[c]	option payoff		(Stock - option)	
195				$26.67	Max[$32 - $35, 0]=	$0.00	$26.67 - $0 =	$26.67
196								
197		Range of outcome:		$15.00		$15.00		$0.00

Notes:
[a]The portfolio contains 0.8333 share of stock, with a stock price of $40, so its value is 0.8333($40) = $33.33.
[b]The ending stock price is $50, so the value is 0.8333($50) = $41.67.
[c]The ending stock price is $32, so the value is 0.8333($32) = $26.67.

FM e-resource
See **FM12 Ch 09 Tool Kit.xls** for all calculations. Also, **Web Extension 9A** provides more discussion of the binomial approach.

equal to the price of the option. Because Western's stock is currently selling for $40, and because the portfolio contains 0.8333 share, the value of the stock in the portfolio is 0.8333($40) = $33.33. What remains is the price of the option:

$$\text{PV of portfolio} = \text{Current value of stock in portfolio} - \text{Current option price}$$

$$\text{Current option price} = \text{Current value of stock in portfolio} - \text{PV of portfolio}$$

$$= \$33.33 - \$24.62 = \$8.71.$$

If this option sold at a price higher than $8.71, other investors could create riskless portfolios as described above and earn more than the riskless rate. Investors (especially the large investment banking firms) would create such portfolios and sell options until their price fell to $8.71, at which point the market would be in equilibrium. Conversely, if the options sold for less than $8.71, investors would create an "opposite" portfolio by buying a call option and selling short the stock.[9] The resulting supply shortage would drive the price up to $8.71. Thus, investors (or arbitrageurs) would buy and sell in the market until the options were priced at their equilibrium level.

Clearly, this example is unrealistic. Although you could duplicate the purchase of 0.8333 share by buying 8,333 shares and selling 10,000 options, the stock price assumptions are unrealistic; Western's stock price could be almost anything after 1 year, not just $50 or $32. However, if we allowed the stock to move up or down more often during the year, then a more realistic range of ending prices would result. For

---

[9]Suppose an investor (or speculator) does not own any IBM stock. If the investor anticipates a rise in the stock price and consequently buys IBM stock, he or she is said to have *gone long* in IBM. On the other hand, if the investor thinks IBM's stock is likely to fall, he or she could *go short*, or *sell IBM short*. Because the short seller has no IBM stock, he or she would have to borrow the shares from a broker and sell the borrowed shares. If the stock price falls, the short seller could, later on, buy shares on the open market and pay back the ones borrowed from the broker. The short seller's profit, before commissions and taxes, would be the difference between the price received from the short sale and the price paid later to purchase the replacement stock.

Figure 9-4

The Binomial Lattice

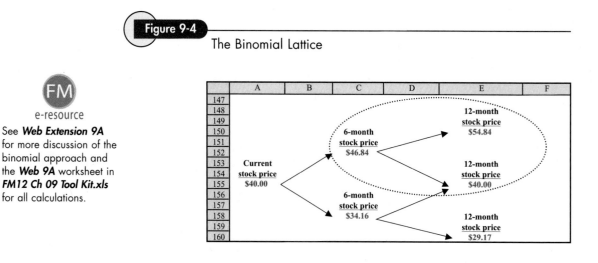

example, suppose we allowed stock prices to change every 6 months, with Western's stock price either going up to $46.84 or down to $34.16. If the price goes up in the first 6 months to $46.84, then suppose it either goes up to $54.84 or down to $40 by the end of the year. If the price falls to $34.16 during the first 6 months, then suppose it either goes up to $40 or down to $29.17 by the end of the year. This pattern of stock price movements is called a **binomial lattice** and is shown in Figure 9-4.

If we focus only on the upper right portion of the lattice shown inside the oval, it is very similar to the problem we just solved in Figures 9-2 and 9-3. We can apply the same solution procedure to find the value of the option at the end of 6 months, given a 6-month stock price of $46.84. As explained in *Web Extension 9A*, the value of the option at the end of 6 months is $13.21, given that the stock price goes up to $46.84; see the *Web 9A* worksheet in *FM12 Ch 09 Tool Kit.xls* for all calculations. Applying the same approach to the lower right portion of the lattice, the *Web Extension* and *Tool Kit* show that the option value at the end of 6 months is $2.83, given a 6-month stock price of $34.16. These values are shown in Figure 9-5. Using the values in Figure 9-5 and the same approach as before, we can calculate the current price, which is $8.60. Notice that by solving three binomial problems, we are able to find the current option price.

If we break the year into smaller periods and allow the stock price to move up or down more often, the lattice would have a more realistic range of possible outcomes. Of course, estimating the current option price would require solving lots of binomial problems within the lattice, but each problem is very simple, and computers can solve them rapidly. With more outcomes, the resulting estimated option price is more accurate. For example, if we divide the year into 10 periods, the estimated price is $8.38. With 100 periods, the price is $8.41. With 1,000, it is still $8.41, which shows that the solution converges to its final value with a relatively small number of steps. In fact, as we break the year into smaller and smaller periods, the solution for the binomial approach converges to the Black-Scholes solution, which is described in the next section.

The binomial approach is widely used to value options with more complicated payoffs than the call option in our example, such as employee stock options. This is beyond the scope of a financial management textbook, but if you are interested in learning more about the binomial approach, take a look at the textbooks by Don Chance or John Hull.[10]

---

[10]See the books by Chance or Hull, cited in Footnote 2.

Figure 9-5

Six-Month Stock Prices and Option Values for the First Section
of the Binomial Lattice

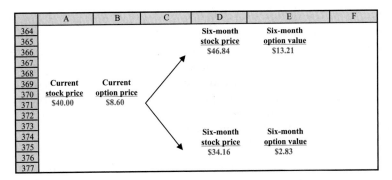

SELF-TEST

Describe how a risk-free portfolio can be created using stocks and options.

How can such a portfolio be used to help estimate a call option's value?

Lett Incorporated's stock price is now $50 but it is expected to either go up to $75 or down to $35 by the end of the year. There is a call option on Lett's stock with a strike price of $55 and an expiration date 1 year from now. What are the call option's payoffs if the stock price goes up? If the stock price goes down? If we sell one call option, how many shares of Lett's stock must we buy to create a riskless hedged portfolio consisting of the option position and the stock? What is the payoff of this portfolio? If the annual risk free rate is 6%, how much is the riskless portfolio worth today (assuming daily compounding)? What is the current value of the call option? ($20; $0; 0.5; $17.50; $16.48; $8.52)

9.3 The Black-Scholes Option Pricing Model (OPM)

The **Black-Scholes Option Pricing Model (OPM),** developed in 1973, helped give rise to the rapid growth in options trading. This model, which has even been programmed into some handheld and Web-based calculators, is widely used by option traders.

OPM Assumptions and Equations

In deriving their option pricing model, Fischer Black and Myron Scholes made the following assumptions:

1. The stock underlying the call option provides no dividends or other distributions during the life of the option.
2. There are no transaction costs for buying or selling either the stock or the option.
3. The short-term, risk-free interest rate is known and is constant during the life of the option.
4. Any purchaser of a security may borrow any fraction of the purchase price at the short-term, risk-free interest rate.
5. Short selling is permitted, and the short seller will receive immediately the full cash proceeds of today's price for a security sold short.

For a Web-based option calculator, see **http://www.cboe.com/LearnCenter/OptionCalculator.aspx.**

6. The call option can be exercised only on its expiration date.
7. Trading in all securities takes place continuously, and the stock price moves randomly.

The derivation of the Black-Scholes model rests on the concept of a riskless hedge such as the one we set up in the last section. By buying shares of a stock and simultaneously selling call options on that stock, an investor can create a risk-free investment position, where gains on the stock will exactly offset losses on the option. This riskless hedged position must earn a rate of return equal to the risk-free rate. Otherwise, an arbitrage opportunity will exist, and people trying to take advantage of this opportunity will drive the price of the option to the equilibrium level as specified by the Black-Scholes model.

The Black-Scholes model consists of the following three equations:

$$V = P[N(d_1)] - Xe^{-r_{RF}t}[N(d_2)] \qquad (9\text{-}2)$$

$$d_1 = \frac{\ln(P/X) + [r_{RF} + (\sigma^2/2)]t}{\sigma\sqrt{t}} \qquad (9\text{-}3)$$

$$d_2 = d_1 - \sigma\sqrt{t}. \qquad (9\text{-}4)$$

Here,

V = Current value of the call option.

P = Current price of the underlying stock.

$N(d_i)$ = Probability that a deviation less than d_i will occur in a standard normal distribution. Thus, $N(d_1)$ and $N(d_2)$ represent areas under a standard normal distribution function.

X = Strike price of the option.

$e \approx 2.7183$.

r_{RF} = Risk-free interest rate.[11]

t = Time until the option expires (the option period).

$\ln(P/X)$ = Natural logarithm of P/X.

σ^2 = Variance of the rate of return on the stock.

Note that the value of the option is a function of the variables we discussed earlier: (1) P, the stock's price; (2) t, the option's time to expiration; (3) X, the strike price; (4) σ^2, the variance of the underlying stock; and (5) r_{RF}, the risk-free rate. We do not derive the Black-Scholes model—the derivation involves some extremely complicated mathematics that go far beyond the scope of this text. However, it is

Robert's Online Option Pricer can be accessed at **http://www.intrepid.com/ ~robertl/optionpricer.html.** The site is designed to provide a financial service over the Internet to small investors for option pricing, giving anyone a means to price option trades without having to buy expensive software and hardware.

---

[11]The risk-free rate should be expressed as a continuously compounded rate. If r is a continuously compounded rate, then the effective annual yield is $e^r - 1.0$. An 8% continuously compounded rate of return yields $e^{0.08} - 1 = 8.33\%$. In all of the Black-Scholes option pricing model examples, we will assume that the rate is expressed as a continuously compounded rate.

not difficult to use the model. Under the assumptions set forth previously, if the option price is different from the one found by Equation 9-2, this would provide the opportunity for arbitrage profits, which would force the option price back to the value indicated by the model.[12] As we noted earlier, the Black-Scholes model is widely used by traders, so actual option prices conform reasonably well to values derived from the model.

Loosely speaking, the first term of Equation 9-2, $P[N(d_1)]$, can be thought of as the expected present value of the terminal stock price, given that $P > X$ and the option will be exercised. The second term, $Xe^{-r_{RF}t}[N(d_2)]$, can be thought of as the present value of the exercise price, given that the option will be exercised. However, rather than try to figure out exactly what the equations mean, it is more productive to plug in some numbers to see how changes in the inputs affect the value of an option. The following example is also in the file *FM12 Ch 09 Tool Kit.xls*.

FM
e-resource

See *FM12 Ch 09 Tool Kit.xls* at the textbook's Web site.

OPM Illustration

The current stock price, P, the exercise price, X, and the time to maturity, t, can all be obtained from a newspaper such as *The Wall Street Journal*. The risk-free rate, r_{RF}, is the yield on a Treasury bill with a maturity equal to the option expiration date. The annualized variance of stock returns, σ^2, can be estimated by multiplying the variance of the percentage change in daily stock prices for the past year [that is, the variance of $(P_t - P_{t-1})/P_{t-1}$] by 365 days.

Assume that the following information has been obtained:

$$P = \$20.$$
$$X = \$20.$$
$$t = 3 \text{ months or } 0.25 \text{ year.}$$
$$r_{RF} = 6.4\% = 0.064.$$
$$\sigma^2 = 0.16. \text{ Note that if } \sigma^2 = 0.16, \text{ then } \sigma = \sqrt{0.16} = 0.4.$$

FM
e-resource

See *FM12 Ch 09 Tool Kit.xls* at the textbook's Web site for all calculations.

Given this information, we can now use the OPM by solving Equations 9-2, 9-3, and 9-4. Since d_1 and d_2 are required inputs for Equation 9-2, we solve Equations 9-3 and 9-4 first:

$$d_1 = \frac{\ln(\$20/\$20) + [0.064 + (0.16/2)](0.25)}{0.40(0.50)}$$

$$= \frac{0 + 0.036}{0.20} = 0.180$$

$$d_2 = d_1 - 0.4\sqrt{0.25} = 0.180 - 0.20 = -0.020.$$

Note that $N(d_1) = N(0.180)$ and $N(d_2) = N(-0.020)$ represent areas under a standard normal distribution function. From the table in Appendix D, or from the *Excel*

---

[12]*Programmed trading*, in which stocks are bought and options are sold, or vice versa, is an example of arbitrage between stocks and options.

Table 9-2

Effects of OPM Factors on the Value of a Call Option

	INPUT FACTORS					OUTPUT
Case	P	X	t	r_{RF}	σ^2	V
Base case	$20	$20	0.25	6.4%	0.16	$1.74
Increase P by $5	**25**	20	0.25	6.4	0.16	5.57
Increase X by $5	20	**25**	0.25	6.4	0.16	0.34
Increase t to 6 months	20	20	**0.50**	6.4	0.16	2.54
Increase r_{RF} to 9%	20	20	0.25	**9.0**	0.16	1.81
Increase σ^2 to 0.25	20	20	0.25	6.4	**0.25**	2.13

function NORMSDIST, we see that the value $d_1 = 0.180$ implies a probability of $0.0714 + 0.5000 = 0.5714$, so $N(d_1) = 0.5714$. Since d_2 is negative, $N(d_2) = 0.500 - 0.0080 = 0.4920$. We can use those values to solve Equation 9-2:

$$V = \$20[N(d_1)] - \$20e^{-(0.064)(0.25)}[N(d_2)]$$
$$= \$20[N(0.180)] - \$20(0.9841)[N(-0.020)]$$
$$= \$20(0.5714) - \$19.68(0.4920)$$
$$= \$11.43 - \$9.69 = \$1.74.$$

Thus the value of the option, under the assumed conditions, is $1.74. Suppose the actual option price was $2.25. Arbitrageurs could simultaneously sell the option, buy the underlying stock, and earn a riskless profit. Such trading would occur until the price of the option was driven down to $1.74. The reverse would occur if the option sold for less than $1.74. Thus, investors would be unwilling to pay more than $1.74 for the option, and they could not buy it for less, so $1.74 is the *equilibrium value* of the option.

To see how the five OPM factors affect the value of the option, consider Table 9-2. Here the top row shows the base-case input values that were used above to illustrate the OPM and the resulting option value, V = $1.74. In each of the subsequent rows, the boldfaced factor is increased, while the other four are held constant at their base-case levels. The resulting value of the call option is given in the last column. Now let's consider the effects of the changes:

1. **Current stock price.** If the current stock price, P, increases from $20 to $25, the option value increases from $1.74 to $5.57. Thus, the value of the option increases as the stock price increases, but by less than the stock price increase, $3.83 versus $5.00. Note, though, that the percentage increase in the option value, ($5.57 − $1.74)/$1.74 = 220%, far exceeds the percentage increase in the stock price, ($25 − $20)/$20 = 25%.
2. **Exercise price.** If the exercise price, X, increases from $20 to $25, the value of the option declines. Again, the decrease in the option value is less than the exercise price increase, but the percentage change in the option value, ($0.34 − $1.74)/$1.74 = −78%, exceeds the percentage change in the exercise price, ($25 − $20)/$20 = 25%.

Taxes and Stock Options

If an employee stock option grant meets certain conditions, it is called a "tax-qualifying grant," or sometimes an "Incentive Stock Option;" otherwise, it is a "nonqualifying grant." For example, suppose you receive a grant of 1,000 options with an exercise price of $50. If the stock price goes to $110 and you exercise the options, you must pay $50(1,000) = $50,000 for stock that is worth $110,000, which is a sweet deal. But what is your tax liability? If you receive a nonqualifying grant, you are liable for ordinary income taxes on 1,000($110 − $50) = $60,000 when you exercise the option. If it is a tax-qualified grant, you owe no regular taxes when exercised. If you then wait at least a year and sell the stock, say, for $150, you would have a long-term capital gain of 1,000($150 − $50) = $100,000, which would be taxed at the lower capital gains rate.

Before you gloat over your newfound wealth, you had better consult your accountant. Your "profit" when you exercise the tax-qualified options isn't taxable under the regular tax code, but it is under the Alternative Minimum Tax (AMT) code. With an AMT tax rate of up to 28%, you might owe as much as 0.28($110 − $50)(1,000) = $16,800. Here's where people get into trouble. The AMT tax isn't due until the following April, so you might think about waiting until then to sell some stock to pay your AMT

tax (so that the sale will qualify as a long-term capital gain).

But what happens if the stock price falls to $5 by next April? You can sell your stock, which raises only $5(1,000) = $5,000 in cash. Without getting into the details, you have a long-term capital loss of 1,000($50 − $5) = $45,000, but IRS regulations limit your net capital loss in a single year to $3,000. In other words, the cash from the sale and the tax benefit from the capital loss aren't nearly enough to cover the AMT tax. You may be able to reduce your taxes in future years because of the AMT tax you pay this year and the carry forward of the remaining long-term capital loss, but that doesn't help right now. You lost $45,000 of your original $50,000 investment, you now have very little cash, and, adding insult to injury, the IRS will insist that you also pay the $16,800 AMT tax.

This is exactly what happened to many people who made paper fortunes in the dot-com boom only to see them evaporate in the ensuing bust. They were left with worthless stock but multi-million-dollar AMT tax obligations. In fact, many still have IRS liens garnishing their wages until they eventually pay their AMT tax. So if you receive stock options, we congratulate you. But unless you want to be the next poster child for poor financial planning, we advise you to settle your AMT tax when you incur it.

---

3. **Option period.** As the time to expiration increases from $t = 3$ months (or 0.25 year) to $t = 6$ months (or 0.50 year), the value of the option increases from $1.74 to $2.54. This occurs because the value of the option depends on the chances for an increase in the price of the underlying stock, and the longer the option has to go, the higher the stock price may climb. Thus, a 6-month option is worth more than a 3-month option.

4. **Risk-free rate.** As the risk-free rate increases from 6.4% to 9%, the value of the option increases slightly, from $1.74 to $1.81. Equations 9-1, 9-2, and 9-3 suggest that the principal effect of an increase in r_{RF} is to reduce the present value of the exercise price, $Xe^{-r_{RF}t}$, hence to increase the current value of the option.[13] The risk-free rate also plays a role in determining the values of the normal distribution functions $N(d_1)$ and $N(d_2)$, but this effect is of secondary importance. Indeed, option prices in general are not very sensitive to interest rate changes, at least not to changes within the ranges normally encountered.

---

[13]At this point, you may be wondering why the first term in Equation 9-2, $P[N(d_1)]$, is not discounted. In fact, it has been, because the current stock price, P, already represents the present value of the expected stock price at expiration. In other words, P is a discounted value, and the discount rate used in the market to determine today's stock price includes the risk-free rate. Thus, Equation 9-2 can be thought of as the present value of the end-of-period-option spread between the stock price and the strike price, adjusted for the probability that the stock price will be higher than the strike price.

5. **Variance.** As the variance increases from the base case 0.16 to 0.25, the value of the option increases from $1.74 to $2.13. Therefore, the riskier the underlying security, the more valuable the option. This result is logical. First, if you bought an option to buy a stock that sells at its exercise price, and if $\sigma^2 = 0$, then there would be a zero probability of the stock going up, hence a zero probability of making money on the option. On the other hand, if you bought an option on a high-variance stock, there would be a higher probability that the stock would go way up, hence that you would make a large profit on the option. Of course, a high-variance stock could go way down, but as an option holder, your losses would be limited to the price paid for the option—only the right-hand side of the stock's probability distribution counts. Put another way, an increase in the price of the stock helps option holders more than a decrease hurts them, so the greater the variance, the greater the value of the option. This makes options on risky stocks more valuable than those on safer, low-variance stocks.

Myron Scholes and Robert Merton were awarded the 1997 Nobel Prize in Economics, and Fischer Black would have been a co-recipient had he still been living. Their work provided analytical tools and methodologies that are widely used to solve many types of financial problems, not just option pricing. Indeed, the entire field of modern risk management is based primarily on their contributions. Although the Black-Scholes model was derived for a European option that can be exercised only on its maturity date, it also applies to American options that don't pay any dividends prior to expiration. The textbooks by Don Chance and John Hull that we listed in Footnote 2 show adjusted models for dividend-paying stocks.

SELF-TEST

What is the purpose of the Black-Scholes Option Pricing Model?

Explain what a "riskless hedge" is and how the riskless hedge concept is used in the Black-Scholes OPM.

Describe the effect of a change in each of the following factors on the value of a call option: (1) stock price; (2) exercise price; (3) option life; (4) risk-free rate; and (5) stock return variance, that is, risk of stock.

What is the value of a call option with these data: P = $35, X = $25, r_{RF} = 6%, t = 0.5 (6 months), and σ^2 = 0.36? ($12.05)

9.4   The Valuation of Put Options

A put option gives its owner the right to sell a share of stock. If the stock pays no dividends and the option can only be exercised upon its expiration date, what is its value? Rather than reinventing the wheel, consider the payoffs for two portfolios at expiration date T, as shown in Table 9-3. The first portfolio consists of a put option and a share of stock; the second has a call option (with the same strike price and expiration date as the put option) and some cash. The amount of cash is equal to the present value of the exercise cost, discounted at the continuously compounded risk-free rate, which is $Xe^{-r_{RF}t}$. At expiration, the value of this cash will equal the exercise cost, X.

If the stock price at expiration date T, P_T, is less than the strike price, X, when the option expires, then the value of the put option at expiration is $X - P_T$. Therefore, the value of Portfolio 1, which contains the put and the stock, is equal to $X - P_T$ plus P_T, or just X. For Portfolio 2, the value of the call is zero at expiration

Table 9-3

Portfolio Payoffs

	STOCK PRICE AT EXPIRATION IF:	
	$P_T < X$	$P_T \geq X$
Put	$X - P_T$	0
Stock	P_T	P_T
Portfolio 1:	X	P_T
Call	0	$P_T - X$
Cash	X	X
Portfolio 2:	X	P_T

(because the call option is out-of-the-money), and the value of the cash is X, for a total value of X. Notice that both portfolios have the same payoffs if the stock price is less than the strike price.

What if the stock price is greater than the strike price at expiration? In this case, the put is worth nothing, so the payoff of Portfolio 1 is equal to the stock price at expiration, P_T. The call option is worth $P_T - X$, and the cash is worth X, so the payoff of Portfolio 2 is P_T. Therefore, the payoffs of the two portfolios are equal, whether the stock price is below or above the strike price.

If the two portfolios have identical payoffs, they must have identical values. This is known as the **put-call parity relationship:**

Put option + Stock = Call option + PV of exercise price.

If V is the Black-Scholes value of the call option, then the value of a put is[14]

$$\text{Put option} = V - P + Xe^{-r_{RF}t}. \qquad (9\text{-}5)$$

For example, consider a put option written on the stock discussed in the previous section. If the put option has the same exercise price and expiration date as the call, its price is

$$\text{Put option} = \$1.74 - \$20 + \$20\,e^{-0.064(0.25)}$$

$$= \$1.74 - \$20 + \$19.68 = 1.42.$$

SELF-TEST

In words, what is put-call parity?

A put option written on the stock of Taylor Enterprises (TE) has an exercise price of $25 and 6 months remaining until expiration. The risk-free rate is 6%. A call option written on TE has the same exercise price and expiration date as the put option. TE's stock price is $35. If the call option has a price of $12.05, what is the price (i.e., value) of the put option? ($1.26)

---

[14]This model cannot be applied to an American put option or to a European option on a stock that pays a dividend prior to expiration. For an explanation of valuation approaches in these situations, see the books by Chance or Hull cited in Footnote 2.

9.5 Applications of Option Pricing in Corporate Finance

Option pricing is used in four major areas in corporate finance: (1) real options analysis for project evaluation and strategic decisions, (2) risk management, (3) capital structure decisions, and (4) compensation plans.

Real Options

Suppose a company has a 1-year proprietary license to develop a software application for use in a new generation of wireless cellular telephones. Hiring programmers and marketing consultants to complete the project will cost $30 million. The good news is that if consumers love the new cell phones, there will be a tremendous demand for the new software. The bad news is that if sales of the new cell phones are low, the software project will be a disaster. Should the company spend the $30 million and develop the software?

Because the company has a license, it has the option of waiting for a year, at which time it might have a much better insight into market demand for the new cell phones. If demand is high in a year, then the company can spend the $30 million and develop the software. If demand is low, it can avoid losing the $30 million development cost by simply letting the license expire. Notice that the license is analogous to a call option: It gives the company the right to buy something (in this case, software for the new cell phones) at a fixed price ($30 million) at any time during the next year. The license gives the company a **real option,** because the underlying asset (the software) is a real asset and not a financial asset.

There are many other types of real options, including the option to increase capacity at a plant, to expand into new geographical regions, to introduce new products, to switch inputs (such as gas versus oil), to switch outputs (such as producing sedans versus SUVs), and to abandon a project. Many companies now evaluate real options with techniques similar to those described earlier in the chapter for pricing financial options. Real options are described in greater depth in Chapter 13.

Risk Management

Suppose a company plans to issue $400 million of bonds in 6 months to pay for a new plant now under construction. The plant will be profitable if interest rates remain at current levels, but if rates rise, it will be unprofitable. To hedge against rising rates, the company could purchase a put option on Treasury bonds. If interest rates go up, the company would "lose" because its bonds would carry a high interest rate, but it would have an offsetting gain on its put options. Conversely, if rates fall, the company would "win" when it issues its own low-rate bonds, but it would lose on the put options. By purchasing puts, the company has hedged the risk it would otherwise face due to possible interest rate changes.

Another example of risk management is a firm that bids on a foreign contract. For example, suppose a winning bid means the firm will receive a payment of 12 million euros in 9 months. At a current exchange rate of $1.04 per euro, the project would be profitable. But if the exchange rate falls to $0.80 per euro, the project would be a loser. To avoid exchange rate risk, the firm could take a short position in a forward contract, which would allow it to convert 12 million euros into dollars at a fixed rate of $1.00 per euro in 9 months, which would still ensure a profitable project. This eliminates exchange rate risk if the firm wins the contract, but what if the firm loses the contract? It would still be obligated to sell 12 million euros at a price of $1.00 per euro, which could be a disaster. For example, if the exchange rate rises to $1.25 per euro, the firm would have to spend $15 million to purchase 12 million euros at a price of $1.25/€ and then sell the euros for $12 million = ($1.00/€)(€12 million), a loss of $3 million.

To eliminate this risk, the firm could also purchase a currency call option that allows it to buy 12 million euros at a fixed price of $1.00 per euro. If the company wins the bid, it will let the option expire, but it will use the forward contract to convert the euros at the forward contract's rate of $1.00 per euro. If the firm loses the bid, then it will exercise the call option and purchase 12 million euros for $1.00 per euro. It will then use those proceeds to close out the forward contract. Thus, the company is able to lock in the future exchange rate if it wins the bid and avoid any net payments at all if it loses the bid. The total cost in either scenario is equal to the initial cost of the option. In other words, the cost of the option is like insurance that guarantees the exchange rate if the company wins the bid and guarantees no net obligations if it loses the bid.

Many other applications of risk management involve futures contracts and other complex derivatives rather than calls and puts. However, the principles used in pricing derivatives are similar to those used earlier in this chapter for pricing options. Thus, financial options and their valuation techniques play key roles in risk management. Derivatives and their use in risk management are discussed in greater depth in Chapter 23.

Capital Structure Decisions

Decisions regarding the mix of debt and equity used to finance operations are quite important. One interesting aspect of the capital structure decision is based on option pricing. For example, consider a firm with debt requiring a final principal payment of $60 million in 1 year. If the company's value 1 year from now is $61 million, then it can pay off the debt and have $1 million left for stockholders. If the firm's value is less than $60 million, then it might well file for bankruptcy and turn over its assets to the creditors, resulting in stockholders' equity of zero. In other words, the value of the stockholders' equity is analogous to a call option: The equity holders have the right to buy the assets for $60 million (which is the face value of the debt) in 1 year (when the debt matures).

Suppose the firm's owner-managers are considering two projects. One has very little risk, and it will result in an asset value of either $59 million or $61 million. The other has high risk, and it will result in an asset value of either $20 million or $100 million. Notice that the equity will be worth zero if the assets are worth less than $60 million, so the stockholders will be hurt no worse if the assets end up at $20 million than if they end up at $59 million. On the other hand, the stockholders would benefit much more if the assets were worth $100 million rather than $61 million. Thus, the owner-managers have an incentive to choose risky projects, which is consistent with an option's value rising with the risk of the underlying asset. Potential lenders recognize this situation, so they build covenants into loan agreements that restrict managers from making excessively risky investments.

Not only does option pricing theory help explain why managers might want to choose risky projects (for example, think about Enron) and why debtholders might want very restrictive covenants, but options also play a direct role in capital structure choices. For example, a firm might choose to issue convertible debt,

chapter 10

The Cost of Capital

General Electric has long been recognized as one of the world's best-managed companies, and it has rewarded its shareholders with outstanding returns. During its corporate life, GE has raised a cumulative $109 billion in capital from its stockholders, but it has turned that $109 billion into stock worth more than $346 billion. Its Market Value Added (MVA), which is the difference between its stock's market capitalization and the amount shareholders originally put up, is a whopping $237 billion! Not surprisingly, GE is always at or near the top of all companies in MVA.

When investors provide a corporation with funds, they expect the company to generate an appropriate return on that capital. From the company's perspective, the investors' expected return is a cost of using the capital, and it is called the "cost of capital." A variety of factors influence a firm's cost of capital. Some, such as the level of interest rates, state and federal tax policies, and the regulatory environment, are outside the firm's control. However, both the degree of risk in the projects it undertakes and the types of funds it raises are under the company's control, and both have a profound effect on its cost of capital.

GE's overall cost of capital (the weighted average cost of its debt and equity) has been estimated to be about 8%. Therefore, to satisfy its investors, GE must generate a return on an average project of at least 8%. Some of GE's projects are "home grown" in the sense that the company has developed a new product or entered a new geographic market. For example, GE's appliance division introduced the Advantium speed-cooking oven and the ultra-quiet Triton dishwasher, and GE began Lexan® polycarbonate production at a new plastics plant in Cartagena, Spain. Sometimes GE creates completely new lines of business, as when it began providing e-commerce services. When GE evaluates potential projects such as these, it must determine whether the return on the capital it must invest in the project will exceed the cost of that capital.

GE also invests by acquiring other companies. Since 2002, GE has spent over $65 billion to acquire hundreds of companies, such as its acquisition of Everest VIT, a company specializing in remote visual inspection technology. Again, GE must estimate the expected return on capital, and the cost of that capital, for each of these acquisitions, and then make the investment only if the expected return is greater than the cost.

How has GE done with its investments? We estimate that it has a 17.7% return on capital, well above its 8% estimated cost of capital. With such a large differential, it's no wonder GE has created a great deal of value for its investors.

Most important business decisions require capital, including decisions to develop new products, build factories and distribution centers, install information technology, expand internationally, and acquire other companies. For each of these decisions, a company must estimate the total investment that is required and decide whether the expected rate of return exceeds the cost of the capital. The cost of capital is also used in many compensation plans, with bonuses dependent on whether the company's return on invested capital exceeds the cost of capital. The cost of capital is also a key factor in choosing the mixture of debt and equity used to finance the firm and in decisions to lease rather than buy assets. As these examples illustrate, the cost of capital is a critical element in business decisions.[1]

FM
e-resource
The textbook's Web site contains an *Excel* file that will guide you through the chapter's calculations. The file for this chapter is **FM12 Ch 10 Tool Kit.xls,** and we encourage you to open the file and follow along as you read the chapter.

10.1 The Weighted Average Cost of Capital

What precisely do the terms "cost of capital" and "weighted average cost of capital" mean? To begin, note that it is possible to finance a firm entirely with common equity. However, most firms employ several types of capital, called **capital components,** with common and preferred stock, along with debt, being the three most frequently used types. All capital components have one feature in common: The investors who provided the funds expect to receive a return on their investment.

If a firm's only investors were common stockholders, then the cost of capital would be the required rate of return on equity. However, most firms employ different types of capital, and, due to differences in risk, these different securities have different required rates of return. The required rate of return on each capital component is called its **component cost,** and the cost of capital used to analyze capital budgeting decisions should be a *weighted average* of the various components' costs. We call this weighted average just that, the **weighted average cost of capital,** or **WACC.**

Corporate Valuation and the Cost of Capital

In Chapter 1, we told you that managers should strive to make their firms more valuable and that the value of a firm is determined by the size, timing, and risk of its free cash flows (FCF). In particular, a firm's value is the present value of its FCFs, discounted at the weighted average cost of capital (WACC). In the previous chapters, we examined the major sources of financing (stocks, bonds, and preferred stock) on an individual basis. In this chapter, we put those pieces together and estimate the WACC.

$$\text{Value} = \frac{\text{FCF}_1}{(1 + \text{WACC})^1} + \frac{\text{FCF}_2}{(1 + \text{WACC})^2} + \frac{\text{FCF}_3}{(1 + \text{WACC})^3} + \cdots + \frac{\text{FCF}_\infty}{(1 + \text{WACC})^\infty}$$

[1]The cost of capital is also an important factor in the regulation of electric, gas, and telephone companies. These utilities are natural monopolies in the sense that one firm can supply service at a lower cost than could two or more firms. Because it has a monopoly, your electric or telephone company could, if it were unregulated, exploit you. Therefore, regulators (1) determine the cost of the capital investors have provided the utility and (2) then set rates designed to permit the company to earn its cost of capital, no more and no less.

Most firms set target percentages for the different financing sources. For example, National Computer Corporation (NCC) plans to raise 30% of its required capital as debt, 10% as preferred stock, and 60% as common equity. This is its **target capital structure.** We discuss how targets are established in Chapter 16, but for now simply accept NCC's 30/10/60 debt, preferred, and common percentages as given.

The following sections discuss each of the component costs in more detail, and then we show how to combine them to calculate the weighted average cost of capital.[2]

What are the three major capital components?

What is a component cost?

What is a target capital structure?

10.2 Cost of Debt, $r_d(1 - T)$

The first step in estimating the cost of debt is to determine the rate of return debtholders require, or r_d. Although estimating r_d is conceptually straightforward, some problems arise in practice. Companies use both fixed- and floating-rate debt, straight and convertible debt, and debt with and without sinking funds, and each form has a somewhat different cost.

It is unlikely that the financial manager will know at the start of a planning period the exact types and amounts of debt that will be used during the period. The type or types used will depend on the specific assets to be financed and on capital market conditions as they develop over time. Even so, the financial manager does know what types of debt are typical for his or her firm. For example, NCC typically issues commercial paper to raise short-term money to finance working capital, and it issues 30-year bonds to raise long-term debt used to finance its capital budgeting projects. Since the WACC is used primarily in capital budgeting, NCC's treasurer uses the cost of 30-year bonds in her WACC estimate.

Assume that it is January 2008, and NCC's treasurer is estimating the WACC for the coming year. How should she calculate the component cost of debt? Most financial managers begin by discussing current and prospective interest rates with their investment bankers. Assume that NCC's bankers believe that a new 30-year, noncallable, straight bond issue will require an 11% coupon rate with semiannual payments, and that it can be offered to the public at its $1,000 par value. Therefore, their estimate of r_d is equal to 11%.[3]

Note that the 11% is the cost of **new, or marginal, debt,** and it will probably not be the same as the average rate on NCC's previously issued debt, which is called the **historical, or embedded, rate.** The embedded cost is important for some decisions but not for others. For example, the average cost of all the capital raised in the past and still outstanding is used by regulators when they determine the rate of return a public utility should be allowed to earn. However, in financial management the WACC is used primarily to make investment decisions, and these decisions hinge on projects' expected future returns versus the cost of new, or marginal, capital. *Thus, for our purposes, the relevant cost is the marginal cost of new debt to be raised during the planning period.*

---

[2]For a comprehensive treatment of the cost of capital, see Michael C. Ehrhardt, *The Search for Value: Measuring the Company's Cost of Capital* (Boston: Harvard Business School Press, 1994).

[3]The effective annual rate is $(1 + 0.11/2)^2 - 1 = 11.3\%$, but NCC and most other companies use nominal rates for all component costs.

Suppose NCC had issued debt in the past and the bonds are publicly traded. The financial staff could use the market price of the bonds to find their yield to maturity (or yield to call if the bonds sell at a premium and are likely to be called). The yield is the rate of return the existing bondholders expect to receive, and it is also a good estimate of r_d, the rate of return that new bondholders will require.

For example, suppose NCC has outstanding bonds with a 9% annual coupon rate, 22 years remaining until maturity, and a face value of $1,000. The bonds make semiannual coupon payments and currently are trading in the market at a price of $835.42. We can find the yield to maturity using a financial calculator with these inputs: N = 44, PV = −835.42, PMT = 45, and FV = 1,000. Solving for the rate, we find I/YR = 5.500%. This is a semiannual periodic rate, so the nominal annual rate is 11.00%. This is consistent with the investment bankers' estimated rate, so 11% is a reasonable estimate for r_d.

If NCC had no publicly traded debt, its staff could look at yields on publicly traded debt of similar firms. This too should provide a reasonable estimate of r_d.

The required return to debtholders, r_d, is not equal to the company's cost of debt because interest payments are deductible, which means the government in effect pays part of the total cost. As a result, the cost of debt to the firm is less than the rate of return required by debtholders.

The **after-tax cost of debt, $r_d(1 - T)$,** is used to calculate the weighted average cost of capital, and it is the interest rate on debt, r_d, less the tax savings that result because interest is deductible. This is the same as r_d multiplied by $(1 - T)$, where T is the firm's marginal tax rate.[4]

$$\text{After-tax component cost of debt} = \text{Interest rate} - \text{Tax savings}$$
$$= r_d - r_d T \qquad \text{(10-1)}$$
$$= r_d(1 - T).$$

Suppose NCC has a marginal federal-plus-state tax rate of 40%. NCC's after-tax cost of debt is 6.6%:[5]

$$r_d(1 - T) = 11\%(1.0 - 0.4)$$
$$= 11\%(0.6)$$
$$= 6.6\%.$$

Most debt offerings have very low flotation costs, especially for privately placed debt. Because the flotation costs usually are low, most analysts ignore them when estimating the after-tax cost of debt. The following example illustrates the procedure for incorporating flotation costs and their impact on the after-tax cost of debt.

Suppose NCC can issue 30-year debt with an annual coupon rate of 11%, with coupons paid semiannually. The flotation costs, F, are equal to 1% of the value of

---

[4]The federal tax rate for most corporations is 35%. However, most corporations are also subject to state income taxes, so the marginal tax rate on most corporate income is about 40%. For illustrative purposes, we assume that the effective federal-plus-state tax rate on marginal income is 40%. The effective tax rate is *zero* for a firm with such large current or past losses that it does not pay taxes. In this situation the after-tax cost of debt is equal to the pre-tax interest rate.

[5]Strictly speaking, the after-tax cost of debt should reflect the *expected* cost of debt. While NCC's bonds have a promised return of 11%, there is some chance of default, so its bondholders' expected return (and consequently NCC's cost) is a bit less than 11%. However, for a relatively strong company such as NCC, this difference is quite small.

the issue. Instead of finding the pre-tax yield based upon pre-tax cash flows and then adjusting it to reflect taxes, as we did in the example above, we can find the after-tax cost of debt based upon after-tax cash flows using this formula:

$$M(1 - F) = \sum_{t=1}^{N} \frac{INT(1 - T)}{[1 + r_d(1 - T)]^t} + \frac{M}{[1 + r_d(1 - T)]^N}. \qquad (10\text{-}2)$$

Here M is the bond's par value, F is the **percentage flotation cost** (i.e., the percentage of proceeds), N is the number of payments, T is the firm's tax rate, INT is the dollars of interest per period, and $r_d(1 - T)$ is the after-tax cost of debt adjusted for flotation costs. With a financial calculator, enter N = 60, PV = −1000(1 − 0.01) = −990, PMT = 55(1 − 0.40) = 33, and FV = 1000. Solving for I/YR, we find I/YR = $r_d(1 - T)$ = 3.38%, which is the semiannual after-tax component cost of debt. The nominal after-tax cost of debt is 6.68%. Note that this is quite close to the original 6.60% after-tax cost, so in this instance adjusting for flotation costs doesn't make much difference.[6]

However, the flotation adjustment would be higher if F were larger or if the bond's life were shorter. For example, if F were 10% rather than 1%, then the nominal annual flotation-adjusted $r_d(1 - T)$ would be 7.44%. With N at 1 year rather than 30 years, and F still equal to 1%, then the nominal annual $r_d(1 - T)$ = 7.66%. Finally, if F = 10% and N = 1, then the nominal annual $r_d(1 - T)$ = 17.97%. In all of these cases, the differential would be too high to ignore.

As an alternative to adjusting the cost of debt for flotation costs, in some situations it makes sense to instead adjust the project's cash flows. For example, **project financing** is a special situation in which a large project, such as an oil refinery, is financed with debt and other securities that have a specific claim on the project's cash flows. Notice that this is different from the usual debt offering, in which the debt has a claim on the corporation's cash flows. Because project financing is funded by securities with claims tied to a particular project, the flotation costs can be included with the project's other cash flows when evaluating the value of the project. However, project financing is relatively rare, so when we incorporate the impact of flotation costs, we usually do so by adjusting the component cost of new financing.

SELF-TEST

Why is the after-tax cost of debt rather than the before-tax cost used to calculate the weighted average cost of capital?

Is the relevant cost of debt the interest rate on already *outstanding* debt or that on *new* debt? Why?

A company has outstanding long-term bonds with a face value of $1,000, a 10% coupon rate, 25 years remaining until maturity, and a current market value of $1,214.82. If it pays interest semiannually, what is the nominal annual pre-tax cost of debt? If the company's tax rate is 40%, what is the after-tax cost of debt? (8%; 4.8%)

10.3 Cost of Preferred Stock, r_{ps}

A number of firms, including NCC, use preferred stock as part of their permanent financing mix. Preferred dividends are not tax deductible. Therefore, the company bears their full cost, and *no tax adjustment is used when calculating the cost of preferred stock*. Note too that while some preferred stocks are issued without a stated maturity date, today most have a sinking fund that effectively limits their life. Finally,

[6]Equation 10-2 produces the correct after-tax cost of debt only for bonds issued at par. For bonds with a price other than par, the after-tax cash flows must be adjusted to take into account the actual taxation of the discount or premium. See **Web Extension 5A** at the textbook's Web site for a discussion of the taxation of original issue discount bonds.

although it is not mandatory that preferred dividends be paid, firms generally have every intention of doing so, because otherwise (1) they cannot pay dividends on their common stock, (2) they will find it difficult to raise additional funds in the capital markets, and (3) in some cases preferred stockholders can take control of the firm.

The **component cost of preferred stock, r_{ps},** is the cost used in weighted average cost of capital calculation. For preferred stock with a stated maturity date, we use the same approach as in the previous section for the cost of debt, keeping in mind that a firm has no tax saving with preferred stock. For preferred stock without a stated maturity date, r_{ps} is

$$\text{Component cost of preferred stock} = r_{ps} = \frac{D_{ps}}{P_{ps}(1 - F)}, \qquad \text{(10-3)}$$

where D_{ps} is the preferred dividend, P_{ps} is the preferred stock price, and F is flotation cost as a percentage of proceeds.

To illustrate the calculation, assume that NCC has preferred stock that pays a $10 dividend per share and sells for $100 per share. If NCC issued new shares of preferred, it would incur an underwriting (or flotation) cost of 2.5%, or $2.50 per share, so it would net $97.50 per share. Therefore, NCC's cost of preferred stock is 10.3%:

$$r_{ps} = \$10/\$97.50 = 10.3\%.$$

If we had not incorporated flotation costs, we would have incorrectly estimated $r_{ps} = \$10/\$100 = 10.0\%$, which is too big a difference to ignore. Therefore, analysts usually include flotation costs when estimating the cost of preferred stock.

SELF-TEST

Does the component cost of preferred stock include or exclude flotation costs? Explain.

Why is no tax adjustment made to the cost of preferred stock?

A company's preferred stock currently trades at $50 per share and pays a $3 annual dividend per share. Flotation costs are equal to 3% of the proceeds. If the company issues preferred stock, what is cost of the newly issued preferred stock? (6.19%)

10.4 Cost of Common Stock, r_s

Companies can raise common equity in two ways: (1) directly, by issuing new shares, and (2) indirectly, by reinvesting, or retaining, earnings. If new shares are issued, what rate of return must the company earn to satisfy the new stockholders? In Chapter 6, we saw that investors require a return of r_s. However, a company must earn more than r_s on new external equity to provide this rate of return to investors because there are commissions and fees, called flotation costs, when a firm issues new equity.

Few mature firms issue new shares of common stock through public offerings.[7] In fact, less than 2% of all new corporate funds come from the external public equity market. There are three reasons for this:

1. Flotation costs can be quite high, as we show later in this chapter.
2. Investors perceive issuing equity as a negative signal about the true value of the company's stock. Investors believe that managers have superior knowledge

---

[7]A few companies issue new shares through new-stock dividend reinvestment plans, which we discuss in Chapter 18. Also, quite a few companies sell stock to their employees, and companies occasionally issue stock to finance huge projects or mergers.

about companies' future prospects, and that managers are most likely to issue new stock when they think the current stock price is higher than the true value. Therefore, if a mature company announces plans to issue additional shares, this typically causes its stock price to decline.

3. An increase in the supply of stock will put pressure on the stock's price, forcing the company to sell the new stock at a lower price than existed before the new issue was announced.

Therefore, we assume that the companies in the following examples do not plan to issue new shares.[8] We will address the impact of flotation costs on the cost of equity later in the chapter.

Does new equity capital raised indirectly by retaining earnings have a cost? The answer is a resounding yes. If some earnings are retained, then stockholders will incur an **opportunity cost**—the earnings could have been paid out as dividends (or used to repurchase stock), in which case stockholders could then have reinvested the money in other investments. *Thus, the firm should earn on its reinvested earnings at least as much as its stockholders themselves could earn on alternative investments of equivalent risk.*

What rate of return can stockholders expect to earn on equivalent-risk investments? The answer is r_s, because they expect to earn that return by simply buying the stock of the firm in question or that of a similar firm. *Therefore, r_s is the cost of common equity raised internally by reinvesting earnings.* If a company cannot earn at least r_s on reinvested earnings, then it should pass those earnings on to its stockholders and let them invest the money themselves in assets that do provide r_s.

Whereas debt and preferred stock are contractual obligations that have easily determined costs, it is more difficult to estimate r_s. However, we can employ the principles described in Chapters 6, 7, and 8 to produce reasonably good cost of equity estimates. Three methods typically are used: (1) the Capital Asset Pricing Model (CAPM), (2) the discounted cash flow (DCF) method, and (3) the bond-yield-plus-risk-premium approach. These methods are not mutually exclusive. When faced with the task of estimating a company's cost of equity, we generally use all three methods and then choose among them on the basis of our confidence in the input data available for the specific case at hand.

SELF-TEST

What are the two sources of equity capital?

Why do most established firms not issue additional shares of common equity?

Explain why there is a cost to using reinvested earnings; that is, why aren't reinvested earnings a free source of capital?

10.5 The CAPM Approach

To estimate the cost of common stock using the Capital Asset Pricing Model (CAPM) as discussed in Chapter 6, we proceed as follows:

Step 1. Estimate the risk-free rate, r_{RF}.

Step 2. Estimate the current expected market risk premium, RP_M, which is the expected market return minus the risk-free rate.

Step 3. Estimate the stock's beta coefficient, b_i, and use it as an index of the stock's risk. The i signifies the ith company's beta.

---

[8]There are times when companies should issue stock in spite of these problems; hence we discuss stock issues and the cost of equity later in the chapter.

Step 4. Substitute the preceding values into the CAPM equation to estimate the required rate of return on the stock in question:

$$r_s = r_{RF} + (RP_M)b_i. \tag{10-4}$$

Equation 10-4 shows that the CAPM estimate of r_s begins with the risk-free rate, r_{RF}, to which is added a risk premium set equal to the risk premium on the market, RP_M, scaled up or down to reflect the particular stock's risk as measured by its beta coefficient. The following sections explain how to implement the four-step process.

Estimating the Risk-Free Rate

The starting point for the CAPM cost of equity estimate is r_{RF}, the risk-free rate. There is really no such thing as a truly riskless asset in the U.S. economy. Treasury securities are essentially free of default risk, but nonindexed long-term T-bonds will suffer capital losses if interest rates rise, and a portfolio of short-term T-bills will provide a volatile earnings stream because the rate earned on T-bills varies over time.

Since we cannot in practice find a truly riskless rate upon which to base the CAPM, what rate should we use? A survey of highly regarded companies shows that about two-thirds of the companies use the rate on long-term Treasury bonds.[9] We agree with their choice, and here are our reasons:

To find the rate on a T-bond, go to **http://www.federalreserve.gov.** Select "Economic Research and Data," and then select "Statistics: Releases and Historical Data." Click on "Daily" for H.15, "Interest Rates."

1. Common stocks are long-term securities, and although a particular stockholder may not have a long investment horizon, most stockholders do invest on a long-term basis. Therefore, it is reasonable to think that stock returns embody long-term inflation expectations similar to those reflected in bonds rather than the short-term expectations in bills.
2. Treasury bill rates are more volatile than are Treasury bond rates and, most experts agree, more volatile than r_s.[10]
3. In theory, the CAPM is supposed to measure the expected return over a particular holding period. When it is used to estimate the cost of equity for a project, the theoretically correct holding period is the life of the project. Since many projects have long lives, the holding period for the CAPM also should be long. Therefore, the rate on a long-term T-bond is a logical choice for the risk-free rate.

In light of the preceding discussion, we believe that the cost of common equity is more closely related to Treasury bond rates than to T-bill rates. This leads us to favor T-bonds as the base rate, or r_{RF}, in a CAPM cost of equity analysis. T-bond rates can be found in *The Wall Street Journal* or the *Federal Reserve Bulletin*. Many analysts use the yield on a 10-year T-bond as a proxy for the risk-free rate, although the yields on a 20-year or 30-year T-bond are also reasonable proxies.

---

[9]See Robert E. Bruner, Kenneth M. Eades, Robert S. Harris, and Robert C. Higgins, "Best Practices in Estimating the Cost of Capital: Survey and Synthesis," *Financial Practice and Education*, Spring/Summer 1998, pp. 13–28.
[10]Economic events usually have a larger impact on short-term rates than on long-term rates. For example, see the analysis of the 1995–1996 federal debt limit disagreement between the White House and Congress provided in Srinivas Nippani, Pu Liu, and Craig T. Schulman, "Are Treasury Securities Free of Default?" *Journal of Financial and Quantitative Analysis*, June 2001, pp. 251–266.

Estimating the Market Risk Premium

The market risk premium, RP_M, is the expected market return minus the risk-free rate. This is also called the **equity risk premium,** or just the **equity premium.** It is caused by investor risk aversion: Since most investors are averse to risk, they require a higher expected return (a risk premium) to induce them to invest in risky equities versus relatively low-risk debt. The premium can be estimated on the basis of (1) historical data or (2) forward-looking data.

Historical Risk Premium Historical risk premium data for U.S. securities, updated annually, are available from Ibbotson Associates.[11] Their study includes historical data on stocks, T-bills, T-bonds, and corporate bonds from 1926 through the latest year (2005 currently). Ibbotson calculates the actual realized rates of return on each set of securities and defines the historical market risk premium on common stocks as the difference between the historical realized returns on stocks and T-bonds. Ibbotson's latest study reports a 6.6% arithmetic average historical risk premium and a 5.1% geometric average historical risk premium. If investor risk aversion had actually been constant during their sample period, then the arithmetic average would be the best estimate for next year's risk premium, while the geometric average would be the best estimate for the longer-term risk premium, say, for the next 20 years.

For many years, academic researchers and corporate analysts used the Ibbotson historical risk premium to estimate the current equity risk premium, under the assumption that the risk premium doesn't change over time. However, this approach has come under fire in recent years. For example, in 2000, 2001, and 2002, bonds had higher returns than stocks. This caused negative realized risk premiums during those years, which reduced the historical average risk premium. However, most knowledgeable observers believe that the true equity risk premium actually increased during the 2000–2002 period and that the increasing premium contributed to the declining stock market during those years; an increasing risk premium caused higher costs of equity, lower stock prices, and, thus, lower stock returns. As this shows, an increase in the current risk premium causes a decrease in the historical premium, and vice versa. Thus, greater risk aversion by investors will cause a lower historical risk premium as reported by Ibbotson, the exact opposite of its true effect. If risk aversion does vary over time, as many experts believe, it throws a lot of cold water on those who use the historical risk premium to estimate the current premium.

Go to **http://investor .reuters.com,** enter the ticker symbol for any company, and then click Go. Select "Ratios" from the column on the left. This page provides current values for the dividend yield of the company, industry, sector, and the S&P 500. The link "Estimates" at the bottom of the page takes you to forecasts of growth rates in sales, dividends, and earnings for the next 5 years for the company.

Forward-Looking Risk Premiums An alternative to the historical risk premium is to estimate a forward-looking, or ex ante, risk premium. The market risk premium, RP_M, can be estimated as $r_M - r_{RF}$. The risk-free rate is observable, so the key is to estimate the required return on the market. The most common approach is to use the discounted cash flow (DCF) model to estimate the expected market rate of return, $\hat{r}_M$. If the market is in equilibrium, then the expected return is equal to the required return: $\hat{r}_M = r_M$:

$$\begin{array}{c}\text{Expected} \\ \text{rate of return}\end{array} = \hat{r}_M = \frac{D_1}{P_0} + g = r_{RF} + RP_M = r_M = \begin{array}{c}\text{Required} \\ \text{rate of return.}\end{array}$$

---

[11]See *Stocks, Bonds, Bills, and Inflation: Valuation Edition 2006 Yearbook* (Chicago: Ibbotson Associates, 2006).

In words, the required return on the market is the sum of the expected dividend yield plus the expected growth rate. Note that the expected dividend yield, D_1/P_0, can be found using the current dividend yield and the expected growth rate: $D_1/P_0 = D_0(1 + g)/P_0$. Therefore, to estimate the required return on the market, all you need are estimates of the current dividend yield and the expected growth rate in dividends. Several data sources report the current dividend yield on the market, as measured by the S&P 500. For example, in mid-2006 Reuters.com reports a current dividend yield of 2.22% for the S&P 500.

It is much more difficult to obtain an estimate of the expected dividend growth rate. What we really need is the long-run dividend growth rate that a marginal investor expects to obtain if he or she buys a broad portfolio of stocks. Since we cannot identify the marginal investors, let alone get inside their heads, it is impossible to obtain a direct estimate of the relevant growth rate. Faced with these data limitations, analysts usually estimate the expected dividend growth rate in one of two ways: (1) the historical dividend growth rate or (2) analysts' forecasts for earnings growth rates as an approximation for expected dividend growth.

For example, Reuters.com reports a 9.58% annual growth rate of dividends for the S&P 500 during the past 5 years. Using the current dividend yield of 2.22%, the estimated market return is

$$r_M = \left[\frac{D_0}{P_0}(1 + g) \right] + g$$

$$= [0.0222(1 + 0.0958)] + 0.0958$$

$$= 0.1201 = 12.01\%.$$

Given a current (mid-2006) long-term T-bond rate of around 5.2%, the estimated forward-looking risk premium from this approach is about $12.01\% - 5.2\% = 6.81\%$. However, the problems here are similar to those encountered with historical risk premiums—there is no compelling reason to believe that investors expect future growth to be exactly like past growth, and past growth rates are extremely sensitive to the period over which growth is measured. In addition, many companies have small dividend payments but repurchase stock as a way to return free cash flow to investors. We discuss this more in Chapter 18, but the implication here is that historical dividend growth rates don't truly reflect the cash distributions to investors.

The second approach for estimating the expected dividend growth rate is to obtain published forecasts from security analysts. Unfortunately, analysts generally forecast earnings growth rates, not dividend growth rates, and the longest forecast period is typically 5 years.[12] For example, Yahoo!Finance reports a 10.68% forecasted earnings 5-year growth rate for the S&P 500. If we use this earnings growth rate as an approximation of the dividend growth rate, then the estimated market return is

$$r_M = \left[\frac{D_0}{P_0}(1 + g) \right] + g$$

$$= [0.0222(1 + 0.1068)] + 0.1068$$

$$= 0.1314 = 13.14\%.$$

To find an estimate of earnings growth, go to **http://finance.yahoo.com,** get a quote for any stock, and then select "Analyst Estimates" from the column on the left.

---

[12]In theory, the constant growth rate for sales, earnings, and dividends ought to be equal. However, this has not been true for past growth rates. For example, the S&P 500 has had past 5-year annual average growth rates of 9.59% for sales, 13.6% for earnings per share, and 9.58% for dividends.

Given a current long-term T-bond rate of 5.2%, the estimated forward-looking risk premium from this approach is 13.14% − 5.2% = 7.94%. Notice that this is quite a bit higher than our previous estimate based on the historical dividend growth rate.

Unfortunately, there are problems with this approach, too. (1) Earnings growth rates and dividend growth rates are not always identical. (2) The accuracy (and truthfulness) of analysts who work for investment banking firms has been questioned in recent years. This suggests that it might be better to use the forecasts of independent analysts, such as those who work for publications like *Value Line*, rather than those who work for the large investment banking firms. (3) Different analysts have different opinions, leading to very different growth rate estimates.

To muddy the water a bit further, some academics have recently argued for a much lower market risk premium. Eugene Fama and Kenneth French examined earnings and dividend growth rates during the period from 1951 to 2000 and found the forward-looking market risk premium to be 2.55%. Jay Ritter argues that the forward-looking market risk premium should be based on inflation-adjusted expected returns and should be even lower—closer to 1%.[13]

Our View on the Market Risk Premium After reading the previous sections, you might well be confused about the correct market risk premium, since the different approaches give different results. Here is our opinion. The risk premium is driven primarily by investors' attitudes toward risk, and there are good reasons to believe that investors are less risk averse today than 50 years ago. The advent of pension plans, Social Security, health insurance, and disability insurance means that people today can take more chances with their investments, which should make them less risk averse. Also, many households have dual incomes, which also allows investors to take more chances. Finally, the historical average return on the market as Ibbotson measures it is probably too high due to a survivorship bias. Putting it all together, we conclude that the true risk premium in 2006 is lower than the long-term historical average.

But how much lower is the current premium? In our consulting, we typically use a risk premium of about 5%, but we would have a hard time arguing with someone who used a risk premium in the range of 3.5 to 6.5%. We believe that investor risk aversion is relatively stable but not absolutely constant from year to year. When market prices are relatively high, then investors are feeling less risk averse, so we use a risk premium at the low end of our range. Conversely, we use a risk premium at the high end of our range when market prices are relatively low. The bottom line is that there is no way to prove that a particular risk premium is either right or wrong, although we would be suspicious of an estimated market premium that is less than 3.5% or greater than 6.5%.[14]

Estimating Beta

Recall from Chapter 6 that beta is usually estimated as the slope coefficient in a regression, with the company's stock returns on the y-axis and market returns on the x-axis. The resulting beta is called the *historical beta*, since it is based on historical data.

---

[13]See Eugene F. Fama and Kenneth R. French, "The Equity Premium," *Journal of Finance*, April 2002, pp. 637–659; and Jay Ritter, "The Biggest Mistakes We Teach," *Journal of Financial Research*, Summer 2002, pp. 159–168.
[14]For more on estimating the risk premium, see Eugene F. Brigham and Steve R. Vinson, "The Risk Premium Approach to Measuring a Utility's Cost of Equity," *Financial Management*, Spring 1985, pp. 33–45; and Robert S. Harris and Felicia C. Marston, "Estimating Shareholder Risk Premia Using Analysts' Growth Forecasts," *Financial Management*, Summer 1992, pp. 63–70.

Although this approach is conceptually straightforward, complications quickly arise in practice.

First, there is no theoretical guidance as to the correct holding period over which to measure returns. The returns for a company can be calculated using daily, weekly, or monthly time periods, and the resulting estimates of beta will differ. Beta is also sensitive to the number of observations used in the regression. With too few observations, the regression loses statistical power, but with too many, the "true" beta may have changed during the sample period. In practice, it is common to use either 4 to 5 years of monthly returns or 1 to 2 years of weekly returns.

Second, the market return should, theoretically, reflect every asset, even the human capital being built by students. In practice, however, it is common to use only an index of common stocks such as the S&P 500, the NYSE Composite, or the Wilshire 5000. Even though these indexes are highly correlated with one another, using different indexes in the regression will often result in different estimates of beta.

Third, some organizations modify the calculated historical beta in order to produce what they deem to be a more accurate estimate of the "true" beta, where the true beta is the one that reflects the risk perceptions of the marginal investor. One modification, called an *adjusted beta*, attempts to correct a possible statistical bias by adjusting the historical beta to make it closer to the average beta of 1.0. A second modification, called a *fundamental beta*, incorporates information about the company, such as changes in its product lines and capital structure.

Fourth, even the best estimates of beta for an individual company are statistically imprecise. The average company has an estimated beta of 1.0, but the 95% confidence interval ranges from about 0.6 to 1.4. For example, if your regression produces an estimated beta of 1.0, then you can be 95% sure that the true beta is in the range of 0.6 to 1.4.

The preceding discussion refers to conditions in the United States and other countries with well-developed financial markets, where relatively good data are available. Still, as we have seen, beta can only be estimated within a fairly wide range. When we move on to countries with less-developed financial markets, we are even less certain about the true size of a company's beta.

Moreover, further complications arise when we are dealing with multinational companies, especially those that raise equity capital in different parts of the world. We might, for example, be relatively confident in the beta calculated for the parent company in its home country but less confident of the betas for subsidiaries located in other countries. When such complications arise, we are often forced to make "educated guesses" as to the appropriate beta. It would, of course, be nice to have exact, precise numbers for everything and thus be able to make decisions with a great deal of confidence. However, that's just not the way the world is—we are often forced to use judgment, and our discussion should help improve your judgment regarding the choice of beta for use in cost of capital studies.

To find an estimate of beta, go to **http://investor.reuters.com** and enter the ticker symbol for a stock quote. Or go to Thomson ONE—Business School Edition. Beta is shown in the section of Key Fundamentals.

An Illustration of the CAPM Approach

To illustrate the CAPM approach for NCC, assume that $r_{RF} = 8\%$, $RP_M = 6\%$, and $b_i = 1.1$, indicating that NCC is somewhat riskier than average. Therefore, NCC's cost of equity is 14.6%:

$$r_s = 8\% + (6\%)(1.1)$$
$$= 8\% + 6.6\%$$
$$= 14.6\%.$$

It should be noted that although the CAPM approach appears to yield an accurate, precise estimate of r_s, it is hard to know the correct estimates of the inputs required to make it operational because (1) it is hard to estimate precisely the beta that investors expect the company to have in the future, and (2) it is difficult to estimate the market risk premium. Despite these difficulties, surveys indicate that CAPM is the preferred choice for the vast majority of companies.

SELF-TEST

What is generally considered to be the most appropriate estimate of the risk-free rate, the yield on a short-term T-bill or the yield on a long-term T-bond?

Explain the two methods for estimating the market risk premium, that is, the historical data approach and the forward-looking approach.

What are some of the problems encountered when estimating beta?

A company's beta is 1.4. The yield on a long-term T-bond is 5%. If the market risk premium is 5.5%, what is r_s? (12.7%)

10.6 Dividend-Yield-Plus-Growth-Rate, or Discounted Cash Flow (DCF), Approach

In Chapter 8, we saw that if dividends are expected to grow at a constant rate, then the price of a stock is

$$P_0 = \frac{D_1}{r_s - g}. \tag{10-5}$$

Here P_0 is the current price of the stock, D_1 is the dividend expected to be paid at the end of Year 1, and r_s is the required rate of return. We can solve for r_s to obtain the required rate of return on common equity, which for the marginal investor is also equal to the expected rate of return:

$$r_s = \hat{r}_s = \frac{D_1}{P_0} + \text{Expected g}. \tag{10-6}$$

Thus, investors expect to receive a dividend yield, D_1/P_0, plus a capital gain, g, for a total expected return of $\hat{r}_s$. In equilibrium this expected return is also equal to the required return, r_s. This method of estimating the cost of equity is called the **discounted cash flow, or DCF, method.** Henceforth, we will assume that markets are at equilibrium (which means that $r_s = \hat{r}_s$), so we can use the terms r_s and $\hat{r}_s$ interchangeably.

Estimating Inputs for the DCF Approach

Three inputs are required to use the DCF approach: the current stock price, the current dividend, and the expected growth in dividends. Of these inputs, the growth rate is by far the most difficult to estimate. The following sections describe the most commonly used approaches for estimating the growth rate: (1) historical growth rates, (2) the retention growth model, and (3) analysts' forecasts.

Historical Growth Rates   First, if earnings and dividend growth rates have been relatively stable in the past, and if investors expect these trends to continue, then the past realized growth rate may be used as an estimate of the expected future growth rate.

We explain several different methods for estimating historical growth rates in **Web Extension 10A**. For NCC, these different methods produce estimates of historical growth ranging from 4.6% to 11.0%, with most estimates fairly close to 7%.

As the *Tool Kit* shows, one can take a given set of historical data and, depending on the years and the calculation method used, obtain a large number of quite different growth rates. Now recall our purpose in making these calculations: We are seeking the future dividend growth rate that investors expect, and we reasoned that, if past growth rates have been stable, then investors might base future expectations on past trends. This is a reasonable proposition, but, unfortunately, we rarely find much historical stability. Therefore, the use of historical growth rates in a DCF analysis must be applied with judgment, and also be used (if at all) in conjunction with other growth estimation methods, as discussed next.

e-resource
See **Web Extension 10A** at the textbook's Web site. The **Web 10A** worksheet in the file **FM12 Ch 10 Tool Kit.xls** shows all calculations.

Retention Growth Model Most firms pay out some of their net income as dividends and reinvest, or retain, the rest. The payout ratio is the percent of net income that the firm pays out as a dividend, defined as total dividends divided by net income; see Chapter 4 for more details on ratios. The retention ratio is the complement of the payout ratio: Retention ratio = (1 − Payout ratio). ROE is the return on equity, defined as net income available for common stockholders divided by common equity. Although we don't prove it here, you should find it reasonable that the growth rate of a firm will depend on the amount of net income that it retains and the rate it earns on the retentions. Using this logic, we can write the **retention growth model:**

$$g = ROE(\text{Retention ratio}). \qquad \text{(10-7)}$$

Equation 10-7 produces a constant growth rate, but when we use it we are, by implication, making four important assumptions: (1) We expect the payout rate, and thus the retention rate, to remain constant; (2) we expect the return on equity on new investment to remain constant; (3) the firm is not expected to issue new common stock, or, if it does, we expect this new stock to be sold at a price equal to its book value; and (4) future projects are expected to have the same degree of risk as the firm's existing assets.

NCC has had an average return on equity of about 14.5% over the past 15 years. The ROE has been relatively steady, but even so it has ranged from a low of 11.0% to a high of 17.6%. In addition, NCC's dividend payout rate has averaged 0.52 over the past 15 years, so its retention rate has averaged 1.0 − 0.52 = 0.48. Using Equation 10-7, we estimate g to be 7%:[15]

$$g = 14.5\%(0.48) = 7\%.$$

Analysts' Forecasts A third technique calls for using security analysts' forecasts. Analysts publish earnings' growth rate estimates for most of the larger publicly owned companies. For example, *Value Line* provides such forecasts on 1,700

---

[15]The retention growth model can also be applied to find the market's growth rate by using the market's payout ratio and ROE. For example, in mid-2006, Reuters reports a dividend payout ratio of 28.63% and current ROE of 19.8% for the S&P 500. This implies g = 0.198(1 − 0.2863) = 0.1413 = 14.13% for the market.

For example, see **http://www.zacks.com.**

e-resource

See **Web Extension 10B** at the textbook's Web site for an explanation of this approach; all calculations are in the worksheet **Web 10B** in the file **FM12 Ch 10 Tool Kit.xls.**

companies, and all of the larger brokerage houses provide similar forecasts. Further, several companies compile analysts' forecasts on a regular basis and provide summary information such as the median and range of forecasts on widely followed companies. These growth rate summaries, such as those compiled by Zack's or by Thomson ONE, can be found on the Internet. These earnings' growth rates are often used as estimates of dividend growth rates.

However, these forecasts often involve nonconstant growth. For example, some analysts were forecasting that NCC would have a 10.4% annual growth rate in earnings and dividends over the next 5 years, but a growth rate after 5 years of 6.5%.

This nonconstant growth forecast can be used to develop a proxy constant growth rate. Computer simulations indicate that dividends beyond Year 50 contribute very little to the value of any stock—the present value of dividends beyond Year 50 is virtually zero, so for practical purposes, we can ignore anything beyond 50 years. If we consider only a 50-year horizon, we can develop a weighted average growth rate and use it as a constant growth rate for cost of capital purposes. In the NCC case, we assumed a growth rate of 10.4% for 5 years followed by a growth rate of 6.5% for 45 years. We weight the short-term growth by 5/50 = 10% and the long-term growth by 45/50 = 90%. This produces an average growth rate of 0.10(10.4%) + 0.90(6.5%) = 6.9%.

Rather than convert nonconstant growth estimates into an approximate average growth rate, it is possible to use the nonconstant growth estimates to directly estimate the required return on common stock.

Illustration of the Discounted Cash Flow Approach

To illustrate the DCF approach, suppose NCC's stock sells for $32; its next expected dividend is $2.40; and its expected growth rate is 7%. NCC's expected and required rate of return, hence its cost of common stock, would then be 14.5%:

$$\hat{r}_s = r_s = \frac{\$2.40}{\$32.00} + 7.0\%$$

$$= 7.5\% + 7.0\%$$

$$= 14.5\%.$$

Evaluating the Methods for Estimating Growth

Note that the DCF approach expresses the cost of common equity as the dividend yield (the expected dividend divided by the current price) plus the growth rate. The dividend yield can be estimated with a high degree of certainty, but uncertainty in the growth estimate induces uncertainty in the DCF cost estimate. We discussed three methods for estimating future growth: (1) historical growth rates, (2) retention growth model, and (3) analysts' forecasts. Of these three methods, studies have shown that analysts' forecasts usually represent the best source of growth rate data for DCF cost of capital estimates.[16]

---

[16]See Robert Harris, "Using Analysts' Growth Rate Forecasts to Estimate Shareholder Required Rates of Return," *Financial Management*, Spring 1986, pp. 58–67. Analysts' forecasts are the best predictors of actual future growth, and also the growth rate investors say they use in valuing stocks. Also see Stephen G. Timme and Peter C. Eisemann, "On the Use of Consensus Forecasts of Growth in the Constant Growth Model: The Case of Electric Utilities," *Financial Management*, Winter 1989, pp. 23–35.

What inputs are required for the DCF method?

What are the ways to estimate the dividend growth rate?

Which of these methods provides the best estimate?

A company's estimated growth rate in dividends is 6%. Its current stock price is $40 and its expected annual dividend is $2. Using the DCF approach, what is r_s? (11%)

10.7 Bond-Yield-Plus-Risk-Premium Approach

Some analysts use a subjective, ad hoc procedure to estimate a firm's cost of common equity: They simply add a judgmental risk premium of 3 to 5 percentage points to the interest rate on the firm's own long-term debt. It is logical to think that firms with risky, low-rated, and consequently high-interest-rate debt will also have risky, high-cost equity, and the procedure of basing the cost of equity on a readily observable debt cost utilizes this logic. In this approach,

$$r_s = \text{Bond yield} + \text{Bond risk premium.} \qquad \text{(10-8)}$$

The bonds of NCC have a yield of 11.0%. If its bond risk premium is estimated as 3.7%, its estimated cost of equity is 14.7%:

$$r_s = 11.0\% + 3.7\% = 14.7\%.$$

Because the 3.7% risk premium is a judgmental estimate, the estimated value of r_s is also judgmental. Empirical work suggests that the risk premium over a firm's own bond yield has generally ranged from 3 to 5 percentage points, with recent values close to 3%. With such a large range, this method is not likely to produce a precise cost of equity. However, it can get us "into the right ballpark."

What is the reasoning behind the bond-yield-plus-risk-premium approach?

A company's bond yield is 7%. If the appropriate bond risk premium is 3.5%, what is r_s, based on the bond-yield-plus-risk-premium approach? (10.5%)

10.8 Comparison of the CAPM, DCF, and Bond-Yield-Plus-Risk-Premium Methods

We have discussed three methods for estimating the required return on common stock. For NCC, the CAPM estimate is 14.6%, the DCF constant growth estimate is 14.5%, and the bond-yield-plus-risk-premium is 14.7%. The overall average of these three methods is (14.6% + 14.5% + 14.7%)/3 = 14.6%. These results are unusually consistent, so it would make little difference which one we used. However, if the methods produced widely varied estimates, then a financial analyst would have to use his or her judgment as to the relative merits of each estimate and then choose the estimate that seemed most reasonable under the circumstances.

Recent surveys found that the CAPM approach is by far the most widely used method. Although most firms use more than one method, almost 74% of respondents in one survey, and 85% in the other, used the CAPM.[17] This is in sharp contrast to a 1982 survey, which found that only 30% of respondents used the CAPM.[18] Approximately 16% now use the DCF approach, down from 31% in 1982. The bond-yield-plus-risk-premium is used primarily by companies that are not publicly traded.

People experienced in estimating the cost of equity recognize that both careful analysis and sound judgment are required. It would be nice to pretend that judgment is unnecessary and to specify an easy, precise way of determining the exact cost of equity capital. Unfortunately, this is not possible—finance is in large part a matter of judgment, and we simply must face that fact.

SELF-TEST

Which approach for estimating the required return on common stock is used most often by businesses today?

10.9 Adjusting the Cost of Stock for Flotation Costs

As explained earlier, most mature companies rarely issue new public equity. However, for those that do, the **cost of new common equity, r_e,** or external equity, is higher than the cost of equity raised internally by reinvesting earnings, r_s, because of **flotation costs** involved in issuing new common stock. What rate of return must be earned on funds raised by selling new stock to make issuing stock worthwhile? To put it another way, what is the cost of new common stock?

The answer for a constant growth stock is found by applying this formula:

$$r_e = \hat{r}_e = \frac{D_1}{P_0(1 - F)} + g. \tag{10-9}$$

In Equation 10-9, F is the percentage flotation cost incurred in selling the new stock, so $P_0(1 - F)$ is the net price per share received by the company.

Using the same inputs as before when we estimated NCC's cost of stock using the DCF approach, but assuming that NCC has a flotation cost of 10%, its cost of new outside equity is computed as follows:

$$r_e = \frac{\$2.40}{\$32(1 - 0.10)} + 7.0\%$$

$$= \frac{\$2.40}{\$28.00} + 7.0\%$$

$$= 8.6\% + 7.0\% = 15.6\%.$$

As we calculated earlier using the DCF model but ignoring flotation costs, NCC's stockholders require a return of $r_s = 14.5\%$. However, because of flotation costs the company must earn *more* than 14.5% on the net funds obtained by selling stock if

[17]See John R. Graham and Campbell Harvey, "The Theory and Practice of Corporate Finance: Evidence from the Field," *Journal of Financial Economics*, 2001, pp. 187–243, and the paper cited in Footnote 9. Interestingly, a growing number of firms (about 34%) also are using CAPM-type models with more than one factor. Of these firms, over 40% include factors for interest-rate risk, foreign exchange risk, and business cycle risk (proxied by gross domestic product). More than 20% of these firms include a factor for inflation, size, and exposure to particular commodity prices. Less than 20% of these firms make adjustments due to distress factors, book-to-market ratios, or momentum factors.
[18]See Lawrence J. Gitman and Vincent Mercurio, "Cost of Capital Techniques Used by Major U.S. Firms: Survey Analysis of *Fortune's* 1000," *Financial Management*, 1982, pp. 21–29.

Table 10-1

Average Flotation Costs for Debt and Equity

Amount of Capital Raised (Millions of Dollars)	Average Flotation Cost for Common Stock (% of Total Capital Raised)	Average Flotation Cost for New Debt (% of Total Capital Raised)
2–9.99	13.28	4.39
10–19.99	8.72	2.76
20–39.99	6.93	2.42
40–59.99	5.87	2.32
60–79.99	5.18	2.34
80–99.99	4.73	2.16
100–199.99	4.22	2.31
200–499.99	3.47	2.19
500 and up	3.15	1.64

Source: Inmoo Lee, Scott Lochhead, Jay Ritter, and Quanshui Zhao, "The Costs of Raising Capital," *The Journal of Financial Research*, Spring 1996, pp. 59–74. Reprinted with permission.

investors are to receive a 14.5% return on the money they put up. Specifically, if the firm earns 15.6% on funds obtained by issuing new stock, then earnings per share will remain at the previously expected level, the firm's expected dividend can be maintained, and, as a result, the price per share will not decline. If the firm earns less than 15.6%, then earnings, dividends, and growth will fall below expectations, causing the stock price to decline. If the firm earns more than 15.6%, the stock price will rise.

As we noted earlier, most analysts use the CAPM to estimate the cost of equity. In an earlier section, we estimated NCC's CAPM cost of equity as 14.6%. How could the analyst incorporate flotation costs? In the example above, application of the DCF methodology gives a cost of equity of 14.5% if flotation costs are ignored and a cost of equity of 15.6% if flotation costs are included. Therefore, flotation costs add 1.1 percentage points to the cost of equity (15.6 − 14.5 = 1.1). To incorporate flotation costs into the CAPM estimate, you would add the 1.1 percentage points to the 14.6% CAPM estimate, resulting in a 15.7% estimated cost of external equity. As an alternative, you could find the average of the CAPM, DCF, and bond-yield-plus-risk-premium costs of equity ignoring flotation costs, and then add to it the 1.1 percentage points due to flotation costs.

Table 10-1 shows the average flotation cost for debt and equity issued by U.S. corporations in the 1990s. The common stock flotation costs are for non-IPOs. Costs associated with IPOs are even higher—about 17% of gross proceeds for common equity if the amount raised is less than $10 million and about 6% if more than $500 million is raised. The data include both utility and nonutility companies. If utilities were excluded, flotation costs would be even higher. Notice that flotation costs are higher for equity than for debt, and that flotation costs (as a percent of capital raised) fall as the amount of capital raised increases.

SELF-TEST
What are flotation costs?

Are flotation costs higher for debt or equity?

A firm has common stock with $D_1 = \$3.00$; $P_0 = \$30$; $g = 5\%$; and $F = 4\%$. If the firm must issue new stock, what is its cost of external equity, r_e? (15.42%)

10.10 Composite, or Weighted Average, Cost of Capital, WACC

As we will see in Chapter 15, each firm has an optimal capital structure, defined as that mix of debt, preferred, and common equity that causes its stock price to be maximized. Therefore, a value-maximizing firm will establish a *target (optimal) capital structure* and then raise new capital in a manner that will keep the actual capital structure on target over time. In this chapter, we assume that the firm has identified its optimal capital structure, that it uses this optimum as the target, and that it finances so as to remain constantly on target. How the target is established is examined in Chapter 15.

The target proportions of debt, preferred stock, and common equity, along with the component costs of capital, are used to calculate the firm's WACC. To illustrate, suppose NCC has a target capital structure calling for 30% debt, 10% preferred stock, and 60% common equity. Its before-tax cost of debt, r_d, is 11%; its after-tax cost of debt is $r_d(1 - T) = 11\%(0.6) = 6.6\%$; its cost of preferred stock, r_{ps}, is 10.3%; its cost of common equity, r_s, is 14.6%; its marginal tax rate is 40%; and all of its new equity will come from retained earnings. We can calculate NCC's weighted average cost of capital, WACC, as follows:

$$\begin{aligned} \text{WACC} &= w_d r_d(1 - T) + w_{ps}r_{ps} + w_{ce}r_s \\ &= 0.3(11.0\%)(0.6) + 0.1(10.3\%) + 0.6(14.6\%) \qquad \textbf{(10-10)} \\ &= 11.76\% \approx 11.8\%. \end{aligned}$$

Here w_d, w_{ps}, and w_{ce} are the weights used for debt, preferred, and common equity, respectively.

Every dollar of new capital that NCC obtains will on average consist of 30 cents of debt with an after-tax cost of 6.6%, 10 cents of preferred stock with a cost of 10.3%, and 60 cents of common equity with a cost of 14.6%. The average cost of each whole dollar, the WACC, is 11.8%.

Two points should be noted. First, the WACC is the current weighted average cost the company would face for a new, or *marginal*, dollar of capital—it is not the average cost of dollars raised in the past. Second, the percentages of each capital component, called weights, should be based on management's target capital structure, which is presumably an estimate of the firm's optimal capital structure. Here are the rationales for those points.

The required rates of return for a company's investors, whether they are new or old, are always marginal rates. For example, a stockholder might have invested in a company last year when the risk-free interest rate was 6% and might have had a required return on equity of 12%. If the risk-free rate subsequently falls and is now 4%, then the investor's required return on equity is now 10% (holding all else constant). This is the same required rate of return that a new equity holder would have, whether the new investor bought stock in the secondary market or through a new equity offering. In other words, whether the shareholders are already equity holders or are brand new equity holders, all have the same required rate of return, which is the current required rate of return on equity. The same reasoning applies for the firm's bondholders. All bondholders, whether old or new, have a required

Global Variations in the Cost of Capital

For U.S. firms to be competitive with foreign companies, they must have a cost of capital no greater than that faced by their international competitors. In the past, many experts argued that U.S. firms were at a disadvantage. In particular, Japanese firms enjoyed a very low cost of capital, which lowered their total costs and thus made it hard for U.S. firms to compete. Recent events, however, have considerably narrowed cost of capital differences between U.S. and Japanese firms. In particular, the U.S. stock market has outperformed the Japanese market in the last decade, which has made it easier and cheaper for U.S. firms to raise equity capital.

As capital markets become increasingly integrated, cross-country differences in the cost of capital are disappearing. Today, most large corporations raise capital throughout the world; hence we are moving toward one global capital market rather than distinct capital markets in each country. Although government policies and market conditions can affect the cost of capital within a given country, this primarily affects smaller firms that do not have access to global capital markets, and even these differences are becoming less important as time goes by. What matters most is the risk of the individual firm, not the market in which it raises capital.

rate of return equal to the yield on the firm's debt, which is based on current market conditions.

Because all investors have required rates of return based on current market conditions rather than the past market conditions at the investments' purchase dates, the cost of capital depends on current conditions, not on historic or past market conditions. It is in this sense that the cost of capital is a marginal cost, since it depends on current market rates, which are the rates the company would pay on any new capital (ignoring flotation costs, which we discuss later in the chapter).

We have heard managers (and students!) say, "We are only raising debt this year, and it has a 5% after-tax cost, so we should use this, and not our 10% WACC, to evaluate this year's projects." Here is the flaw in that line of reasoning: Although some investors, such as debtholders, have higher-priority claims relative to other investors, *all* investors have claims on *all* future cash flows. For example, if a company raises debt and also invests in a new project that same year, the new debtholders don't have a specific claim on that specific project's cash flows (assuming it is not nonrecourse project financing). In fact, new debtholders receive a claim on the cash flows being generated by existing as well as new projects, while old debtholders (and equity holders) have claims on both new and existing projects. Thus, the decision to take on a new project should depend on the project's ability to satisfy all of the company's investors, not just the new debtholders, even if only debt is being raised that year.

An investor expects to receive a rate of return on the full amount that is at stake, which is the current market value of the investment. Therefore, the weights used in estimating the WACC should be based on market values, not book values. Recall from Chapter 4 that a firm's risk, as measured by its bond rating, affects its cost of debt. Recall also that the bond rating depends in part on the percentage of the firm that is financed with debt. As we show in Chapter 16, this also affects the cost of equity. In other words, the costs of debt and equity depend on the capital structure weights. However, these costs depend more on the future weights that investors expect than the current weights, which fluctuate due to market conditions and the most recent form of external financing (debt or equity). Thus, the weights used in calculating the WACC should also be based on the expected future weights, which are the firm's target weights.

SELF-TEST

How is the weighted average cost of capital calculated? Write out the equation.

On what should the weights be based?

A firm has the following data: Target capital structure of 25% debt, 10% preferred stock, and 65% common equity; Tax rate = 40%; r_d = 7%; r_{ps} = 7.5%; and r_s = 11.5%. Assume the firm will not issue new stock. What is this firm's WACC? (9.28%)

10.11 Factors That Affect the Weighted Average Cost of Capital

The cost of capital is affected by a number of factors. Some are beyond the firm's control, but others are influenced by its financing and investment policies.

Factors the Firm Cannot Control

The three most important factors that are beyond a firm's direct control are (1) the level of interest rates, (2) the market risk premium, and (3) tax rates.

The Level of Interest Rates If interest rates in the economy rise, the cost of debt increases because firms will have to pay bondholders a higher interest rate to obtain debt capital. Also, recall from our discussion of the CAPM that higher interest rates increase the costs of common and preferred equity. During the 1990s, interest rates in the United States declined significantly and are still relatively low in mid-2006. This reduced the cost of both debt and equity capital for all firms, which encouraged additional investment. Lower interest rates also enabled U.S. firms to compete more effectively with German and Japanese firms, which in the past had enjoyed relatively low costs of capital.

Market Risk Premium The perceived risk inherent in stocks and investors' aversion to risk determine the market risk premium. Individual firms have no control over this factor, but it affects the cost of equity and, through a substitution effect, the cost of debt, and thus the WACC.

Tax Rates Tax rates, which are largely beyond the control of an individual firm (although firms do lobby for more favorable tax treatment), have an important effect on the cost of capital. Tax rates are used in the calculation of the cost of debt as used in the WACC, and there are other, less obvious ways in which tax policy affects the cost of capital. For example, lowering the capital gains tax rate relative to the rate on ordinary income would make stocks more attractive, which would reduce the cost of equity relative to that of debt. That would, as we see in Chapter 16, lead to a change in a firm's optimal capital structure toward less debt and more equity.

Factors the Firm Can Control

A firm can affect its cost of capital through (1) its capital structure policy, (2) its dividend policy, and (3) its investment (capital budgeting) policy.

Capital Structure Policy In this chapter, we assume that a firm has a given target capital structure, and we use weights based on that target structure to calculate the WACC. It is clear, though, that a firm can change its capital structure, and such a change can affect its cost of capital. First, beta is a function of financial leverage, so capital structure affects the cost of equity. Second, the after-tax cost of debt is lower than the cost of equity. Therefore, if the firm decides to use more debt and less common equity, this change in the weights in the WACC equation will tend to lower the WACC. However, an increase in the use of debt will increase the risk of both the debt and the equity, and increases in component costs will tend to offset the effects of the change in the weights. In Chapter 16 we discuss this in more depth, and we demonstrate that a firm's optimal capital structure is the one that minimizes its cost of capital.

Dividend Policy As we see in Chapter 18, the percentage of earnings paid out in dividends may affect a stock's required rate of return, r_s. Also, if a firm's payout ratio is so high that it must issue new stock to fund its capital budget, this will force it to incur flotation costs, and this too will affect its cost of capital. This second point is discussed in detail earlier in this chapter and also in Chapter 17.

Investment Policy When we estimate the cost of capital, we use as the starting point the required rates of return on the firm's outstanding stock and bonds. Those rates reflect the risk of the firm's existing assets. Therefore, we have implicitly been assuming that new capital will be invested in assets with the same degree of risk as existing assets. This assumption is generally correct, as most firms do invest in assets similar to those they currently use. However, it would be incorrect if a firm dramatically changed its investment policy. For example, if a firm invests in an entirely new line of business, its marginal cost of capital should reflect the risk of that new business. To illustrate, Time Warner's merger with AOL undoubtedly increased its risk and cost of capital.

SELF-TEST

What three factors that affect the cost of capital are generally beyond the firm's control?

What three policies under the firm's control are likely to affect its cost of capital?

Explain how a change in interest rates in the economy would affect each component of the weighted average cost of capital.

10.12 Adjusting the Cost of Capital for Risk

As we have calculated it, the cost of capital reflects the average risk and overall capital structure of the entire firm. But what if a firm has divisions in several business lines that differ in risk? Or what if a company is considering a project that is much riskier than its typical project? It doesn't make sense for a company to use its overall cost of capital to discount divisional or project-specific cash flows that don't have the same risk as the company's average cash flows. The following sections explain how to adjust the cost of capital for divisions and for specific projects.

The Divisional Cost of Capital

Consider Starlight Sandwich Shops, a company with two divisions—a bakery operation and a chain of cafes. The bakery division is low risk and has a 10% cost of capital. The cafe division is riskier and has a 14% cost of capital. Each division is approximately the same size, so Starlight's overall cost of capital is 12%. The bakery manager has a project with an 11% expected rate of return, and the cafe division manager has a project with a 13% expected return. Should these projects be accepted or rejected? Starlight can create value if it accepts the bakery's project, since its rate of return is greater than its cost of capital (11% > 10%), but the cafe project's rate of return is less than its cost of capital (13% < 14%), so it should be rejected. However, if one simply compared the two projects' returns with Starlight's 12% overall cost of capital, then the bakery's value-adding project would be rejected while the cafe's value-destroying project would be accepted.

Many firms use the CAPM to estimate the cost of capital for specific divisions. To begin, recall that the Security Market Line equation expresses the risk/return relationship as follows:

$$r_s = r_{RF} + (RP_M)b_i.$$

As an example, consider the case of Huron Steel Company, an integrated steel producer operating in the Great Lakes region. For simplicity, assume that Huron has only one division and uses only equity capital, so its cost of equity is also its corporate cost of capital, or WACC. Huron's beta = b = 1.1; r_{RF} = 7%; and RP_M = 6%. Thus, Huron's cost of equity is 13.6%:

$$r_s = 7\% + (6\%)1.1 = 13.6\%.$$

This suggests that investors should be willing to give Huron money to invest in average-risk projects if the company expects to earn 13.6% or more on this money. By average risk we mean projects having risk similar to the firm's existing division.

Now suppose Huron creates a new transportation division consisting of a fleet of barges to haul iron ore, and barge operations have betas of 1.5 rather than 1.1. The barge division, with b = 1.5, has a 16.0% cost of capital:

$$r_{Barge} = 7\% + (6\%)1.5 = 16.0\%.$$

On the other hand, if Huron adds a low-risk division, such as a new distribution center with a beta of only 0.5, its divisional cost of capital would be 10%:

$$r_{Center} = 7\% + (6\%)0.5 = 10.0\%.$$

A firm itself may be regarded as a "portfolio of assets," and since the beta of a portfolio is a weighted average of the betas of its individual assets, adding the barge and distribution center divisions will change Huron's overall beta. The exact value of the new beta would depend on the relative size of the investment in the new divisions versus Huron's original steel operations. If 70% of Huron's total value ends up in the steel division, 20% in the barge division, and 10% in the distribution center, then its new corporate beta would be

$$New\ beta = 0.7(1.1) + 0.2(1.5) + 0.1(0.5) = 1.12.$$

Thus, investors in Huron's stock would have a required return of

$$r_{Huron} = 7\% + (6\%)1.12 = 13.72\%.$$

Even though the investors require an overall return of 13.72%, they expect a rate of return in each division at least as good as the division's required return based on the SML. In particular, they expect a return of at least 13.6% from the steel division, 16.0% from the barge division, and 10.0% from the distribution center.

Techniques for Measuring Divisional Betas

In Chapter 6 we discussed the estimation of betas for stocks and indicated the difficulties in estimating beta. The estimation of divisional betas is much more difficult because divisions do not have their own publicly traded stock.[19] Therefore, we must estimate the beta that the division would have if it were a separate publicly traded company. Two approaches can be used to estimate individual assets' betas—the pure play method and the accounting beta method.

The Pure Play Method In the **pure play method,** the company tries to find several single-product companies in the same line of business as the division being evaluated, and it then averages those companies' betas to determine the cost of capital for its own division. For example, suppose Huron could find three existing single-product firms that operate barges, and suppose also that Huron's management believes its barge division would be subject to the same risks as those firms. Huron could then determine the betas of those firms, average them, and use this average beta as a proxy for the barge division's beta.[20]

The Accounting Beta Method As noted above, it may be impossible to find single-product, publicly traded firms suitable for the pure play approach. If that is the case, we may be able to use the **accounting beta method.** Betas normally are found by regressing the returns of a particular company's *stock* against returns on a *stock market index.* However, we could run a regression of the division's *accounting return on assets* against the *average return on assets* for a large sample of companies, such as those included in the S&P 500. Betas determined in this way (that is, by using accounting data rather than stock market data) are called **accounting betas.**

Estimating the Cost of Capital for Individual Projects

Although it is intuitively clear that riskier projects have a higher cost of capital, it is difficult to estimate project risk. First, note that three separate and distinct types of risk can be identified:

1. **Stand-alone risk** is the variability of the project's expected returns.
2. **Corporate,** or **within-firm, risk** is the variability the project contributes to the corporation's returns, giving consideration to the fact that the project represents only one asset of the firm's portfolio of assets, hence that some of its risk effects will be diversified away.
3. **Market,** or **beta, risk** is the risk of the project as seen by a well-diversified stockholder. Market risk is measured by the project's effect on the firm's beta coefficient.

Taking on a project with a high degree of either stand-alone or corporate risk will not necessarily affect the firm's beta. However, if the project has highly uncertain returns, and if those returns are highly correlated with returns on the firm's other assets and with most other assets in the economy, then the project will have a high degree of all types of risk. For example, suppose General Motors decides to undertake a major expansion to build electric autos. GM is not sure how its

---

[19]This same problem applies to privately held companies, which we discuss in a later section.
[20]If the pure play firms employ different capital structures than that of Huron, this fact must be dealt with by adjusting the beta coefficients. See Chapter 16 for a discussion of this aspect of the pure play method. For a technique that can be used when pure play firms are not available, see Yatin Bhagwat and Michael Ehrhardt, "A Full Information Approach for Estimating Divisional Betas," *Financial Management,* Summer 1991, pp. 60–69.

technology will work on a mass production basis, so there is much risk in the venture—its stand-alone risk is high. Management also estimates that the project will do best if the economy is strong, for then people will have more money to spend on the new autos. This means that the project will tend to do well if GM's other divisions are doing well and will tend to do badly if other divisions are doing badly. This being the case, the project will also have high corporate risk. Finally, since GM's profits are highly correlated with those of most other firms, the project's beta will also be high. Thus, this project will be risky under all three definitions of risk.

Of the three measures, market risk is theoretically the most relevant because of its direct effect on stock prices. Unfortunately, the market risk for a project is also the most difficult to estimate. In practice, most decision makers consider all three risk measures in a judgmental manner.

The first step is to determine the divisional cost of capital, and then to group divisional projects into subjective risk categories. Then, using the divisional WACC as a starting point, **risk-adjusted costs of capital** are developed for each category. For example, a firm might establish three risk classes—high, average, and low—then assign average-risk projects the divisional cost of capital, higher-risk projects an above-average cost, and lower-risk projects a below-average cost. Thus, if a division's WACC were 10%, its managers might use 10% to evaluate average-risk projects in the division, 12% for high-risk projects, and 8% for low-risk projects. While this approach is better than not risk adjusting at all, these risk adjustments are necessarily subjective and somewhat arbitrary. Unfortunately, given the data, there is no completely satisfactory way to specify exactly how much higher or lower we should go in setting risk-adjusted costs of capital.

SELF-TEST

Based on the CAPM, how would one find the required return for a low-risk division and for a high-risk division?

Describe the pure play and the accounting beta methods for estimating divisional betas.

What are the three types of project risk?

Which type of risk is theoretically the most relevant? Why?

Describe a procedure firms can use to develop costs of capital for projects with differing degrees of risk.

10.13 Privately Owned Firms and Small Businesses

Up until now, our discussion of the cost of stock has been focused on publicly owned corporations. When we estimated the rate of return required by public stockholders, we used stock prices as input data for the DCF method and stock returns to estimate beta as an input for the CAPM approach. But how should one measure the cost of stock for a firm whose stock is not traded? Most analysts begin by identifying one or more publicly traded firms that are in the same industry and that are approximately the same size as the privately owned firm.[21] The analyst then estimates the betas for these publicly traded firms and uses their average beta as an estimate of the beta of the privately owned firm. Note that this is similar to the pure play method for estimating divisional betas that we discussed earlier. With an estimate of beta, the cost of stock can be estimated with the CAPM approach.

---

[21] In Chapter 16 we show how to adjust for differences in capital structures.

The liquidity of an ownership stake in a privately held firm is less than the liquidity of publicly held stock. Just as the yield on a thinly traded bond has a liquidity premium, the required return on stock in a privately held firm should reflect a liquidity premium.[22] Many analysts make an ad hoc adjustment to reflect this lack of liquidity by adding 1 to 3 percentage points to the firm's cost of equity. This "rule of thumb" is not very satisfying theoretically because we don't know exactly how large a liquidity premium to add, but it is very common in practice. In fact, some analysts make a similar liquidity adjustment for any small firm's cost of stock, even if the firm is publicly traded.

In addition to difficulty in estimating the cost of equity for small firms and privately held firms, there are also problems in estimating the capital structure weights. These weights should be based on the target market-value weights. However, a privately held firm can't observe its market value. If a firm doesn't know its current market weights, that makes it difficult for the firm to estimate its target weights. To resolve this problem, many analysts begin by making a trial guess as to the value of the firm's equity. The analysts then use this estimated value of equity to estimate the cost of capital, then use the cost of capital to estimate the value of the firm, and complete the circle by using the estimated value of the firm to estimate the value of its equity.[23] If this newly estimated equity value is different than their trial guess, analysts repeat the process but start the iteration with the newly estimated equity value as the trial value of equity. After several iterations, the trial value of equity and the resulting estimated equity value usually converge. Although somewhat tedious, this process provides a good estimate of the weights and the cost of capital.

SELF-TEST

Identify some problems that occur when estimating the cost of capital for a privately held firm. What are some solutions to these problems?

10.14 Four Mistakes to Avoid

We often see managers and students make the following mistakes when estimating the cost of capital. Although we have discussed these errors previously at separate places in the chapter, they are worth repeating here:

1. *Never use the coupon rate on a firm's existing debt as the pre-tax cost of debt.* The relevant pre-tax cost of debt is the interest rate the firm would pay if it issued debt today.
2. *When estimating the market risk premium for the CAPM method, never use the historical average return on stocks in conjunction with the current risk-free rate.* The historical average return on common stocks has been about 12.4%, the historical return on long-term Treasury bonds about 5.8%, and the difference between them, which is the **historical risk premium**, is 6.6%. The **current risk premium** is found as the difference between an estimate of the current expected rate of return on common stocks and the current expected yield on T-bonds. To illustrate, suppose an estimate of the future return on common stock is 10%, and the current rate on long-term T-bonds is 4%. This implies that you expect to earn 10% if you buy stock today and 4% if you buy bonds. Therefore, this implies a current market risk premium of 10% − 4% = 6%. A case could be made for

---

[22]See Yakov Amihud and Haim Mendelson, "Liquidity and Cost of Capital: Implications for Corporate Management," *Journal of Applied Corporate Finance*, Fall 1989, pp. 65–73.
[23]See Chapter 15 for more discussion on estimating the value of a firm.

using either the historical or the current risk premium, but it would be wrong to take the *historical* rate of return on the market, 12.4%, subtract from it the *current* 4% rate on T-bonds, and then use 12.4% − 4% = 8.4% as the risk premium.

3. *Never use the book value of equity when estimating the capital structure weights for the WACC.* Your first choice should be to use the target capital structure to determine the weights. If you are an outside analyst and do not know the target weights, it is better to estimate weights based on the current market values of the capital components than on their book values. This is especially true for equity. For example, the stock of an average S&P 500 firm in mid-2006 had a market value that was about 3.74 times its book value, and in general, stocks' market values are rarely close to their book values. If the company's debt is not publicly traded, then it is reasonable to use the book value of debt to estimate the weights, since book and market values of debt, especially short-term debt, are usually close to one another. To summarize, if you don't know the target weights, then use market values of equity rather than book values to obtain the weights used to calculate WACC.

4. *Always remember that capital components are funds that come from investors.* If it's not from an investor, then it's not a capital component. Sometimes the argument is made that accounts payable and accruals are sources of funding and should be included in the calculation of the WACC. However, these accounts are due to operating relationships with suppliers and employees, and they are deducted when determining the investment requirement for a project. Therefore, they should not be included in the WACC. Of course, they are not ignored in either corporate valuation or capital budgeting. As we saw in Chapter 3, current liabilities do affect cash flow, hence have an effect on corporate valuation. Moreover, in Chapter 12 we show that the same is true for capital budgeting, namely, that current liabilities affect the cash flows of a project, but not its WACC.

To find the current S&P 500 market-to-book ratio, go to **http://investor.reuters.com**, get the stock quote for any company, and select "Ratios." Then look for the Price to Book ratio.

SELF-TEST

What are four common mistakes people make when estimating the WACC?

Summary

This chapter showed how the cost of capital is developed for use in capital budgeting. The key concepts covered are listed below.

- The cost of capital used in capital budgeting is a **weighted average** of the types of capital the firm uses, typically debt, preferred stock, and common equity.
- The **component cost of debt** is the **after-tax cost of new debt.** It is found by multiplying the cost of new debt by $(1 - T)$, where T is the firm's marginal tax rate: $r_d(1 - T)$.
- **Flotation cost adjustments** should be made for debt if the flotation costs are relatively large. Reduce the bond's issue price by the flotation expenses, reduce the bond's cash flows to reflect taxes, and then solve for the after-tax yield to maturity.
- The **component cost of preferred stock** is calculated as the preferred dividend divided by the net issuing price, where the net issuing price is the price the firm receives after deducting flotation costs: $r_{ps} = D_{ps}/[P_{ps}(1 - F)]$. Flotation costs are usually relatively large for preferred stock issues, so we typically include the impact of flotation costs when estimating r_{ps}.

- The **cost of common equity, r_s,** is also called the **cost of common stock.** It is the rate of return required by the firm's stockholders, and it can be estimated by three methods: (1) the **CAPM approach,** (2) the **dividend-yield-plus-growth-rate,** or **DCF, approach,** and (3) the **bond-yield-plus-risk-premium approach.**

- To use the **CAPM approach,** (1) estimate the firm's beta, (2) multiply this beta by the market risk premium to determine the firm's risk premium, and (3) add the firm's risk premium to the risk-free rate to obtain the cost of common stock: $r_s = r_{RF} + (RP_M)b_i$.

- The best proxy for the **risk-free rate** is the yield on long-term T-bonds.

- To use the **dividend-yield-plus-growth-rate approach,** which is also called the **discounted cash flow (DCF) approach,** add the firm's expected growth rate to its expected dividend yield: $r_s = \hat{r}_s = D_1/P_0 + g$.

- The growth rate can be estimated from **historical earnings and dividends** or by use of the **retention growth model, g = (1 − Payout)(Return on equity),** or it can be based on **analysts' forecasts.**

- The **bond-yield-plus-risk-premium approach** calls for adding a risk premium of from 3 to 5 percentage points to the firm's interest rate on long-term debt: $r_s = $ Bond yield + Bond RP.

- When calculating the **cost of new common stock, r_e,** the DCF approach can be adapted to account for flotation costs. For a constant growth stock, this cost can be expressed as $r_e = \hat{r}_e = D_1/[P_0(1 − F)] + g$. Note that flotation costs cause r_e to be greater than r_s.

- Each firm has a **target capital structure,** defined as that mix of debt, preferred stock, and common equity that minimizes its **weighted average cost of capital (WACC):**

$$WACC = w_d r_d(1 − T) + w_{ps} r_{ps} + w_{ce} r_s.$$

- **Various factors affect a firm's cost of capital.** Some of these factors are determined by the financial environment, but the firm influences others through its financing, investment, and dividend policies.

- Many firms estimate a **divisional cost of capital** for each division that reflects that division's risk and capital structure.

- The **pure play** and **accounting beta methods** can sometimes be used to estimate betas for large projects or for divisions.

- A project's **stand-alone risk** is the risk the project would have if it were the firm's only asset and if stockholders held only that one stock. Stand-alone risk is measured by the variability of the asset's expected returns.

- **Corporate,** or **within-firm, risk** reflects the effects of a project on the firm's risk, and it is measured by the project's effect on the firm's earnings variability.

- **Market,** or **beta, risk** reflects the effects of a project on the risk of stockholders, assuming they hold diversified portfolios. Market risk is measured by the project's effect on the firm's beta coefficient.

- Most decision makers consider all three risk measures in a judgmental manner and then classify projects into subjective risk categories. Using the divisional WACC as a starting point, risk-adjusted costs of capital are developed for each category. The **risk-adjusted cost of capital** is the cost of capital appropriate for a given project, given the risk of that project. The greater the risk, the higher the cost of capital.

- Firms may be able to use the **CAPM** to estimate the cost of capital for specific projects or divisions. However, estimating betas for projects is difficult.

The cost of capital as developed in this chapter is used in the following chapters to determine the value of a corporation and to evaluate capital budgeting projects. In addition, we extend the concepts developed here in Chapter 16, where we consider the effect of the capital structure on the cost of capital.

Questions

(10-1) Define each of the following terms:
a. Weighted average cost of capital, WACC; after-tax cost of debt, $r_d(1 - T)$
b. Cost of preferred stock, r_{ps}; cost of common equity or cost of common stock, r_s
c. Target capital structure
d. Flotation cost, F; cost of new external common equity, r_e

(10-2) In what sense is the WACC an average cost? A marginal cost?

(10-3) How would each of the following affect a firm's cost of debt, $r_d(1 - T)$; its cost of equity, r_s; and its weighted average cost of capital, WACC? Indicate by a plus (+), a minus (−), or a zero (0) if the factor would raise, lower, or have an indeterminate effect on the item in question. Assume other things are held constant. Be prepared to justify your answer, but recognize that several of the parts probably have no single correct answer; these questions are designed to stimulate thought and discussion.

	Effect On		
	$r_d(1 - T)$	r_s	WACC
a. The corporate tax rate is lowered.			
b. The Federal Reserve tightens credit.			
c. The firm uses more debt.			
d. The firm doubles the amount of capital it raises during the year.			
e. The firm expands into a risky new area.			
f. Investors become more risk averse.			

(10-4) Distinguish between beta (or market) risk, within-firm (or corporate) risk, and stand-alone risk for a potential project. Of the three measures, which is theoretically the most relevant, and why?

(10-5) Suppose a firm estimates its cost of capital for the coming year to be 10%. What might be reasonable costs of capital for average-risk, high-risk, and low-risk projects?

Self-Test Problem   Solution Appears in Appendix A

(ST-1)
WACC

Longstreet Communications Inc. (LCI) has the following capital structure, which it considers to be optimal: debt = 25%, preferred stock = 15%, and common stock = 60%. LCI's tax rate is 40% and investors expect earnings and dividends to grow at a constant rate of 6% in the future. LCI paid a dividend of $3.70 per share last year (D_0), and its stock currently sells at a price of $60 per share. Treasury bonds yield 6%, the market risk premium is 5%, and LCI's beta is 1.3. These terms would apply to new security offerings:

Preferred: New preferred could be sold to the public at a price of $100 per share, with a dividend of $9. Flotation costs of $5 per share would be incurred.

Debt: Debt could be sold at an interest rate of 9%.

a. Find the component costs of debt, preferred stock, and common stock. Assume LCI does not have to issue any additional shares of common stock.

b. What is the WACC?

Problems   Answers Appear in Appendix B

Easy
Problems 1–8

(10-1)
After-Tax Cost of Debt

Calculate the after-tax cost of debt under each of the following conditions:
a.   Interest rate, 13%; tax rate, 0%.
b.   Interest rate, 13%; tax rate, 20%.
c.   Interest rate, 13%; tax rate, 35%.

(10-2)
After-Tax Cost of Debt

LL Incorporated's currently outstanding 11% coupon bonds have a yield to maturity of 8%. LL believes it could issue at par new bonds that would provide a similar yield to maturity. If its marginal tax rate is 35%, what is LL's after-tax cost of debt?

(10-3)
Cost of Preferred Stock

Duggins Veterinary Supplies can issue perpetual preferred stock at a price of $50 a share. The issue is expected to pay a constant annual dividend of $4.50 a share. Ignoring flotation costs, what is the company's cost of preferred stock, r_{ps}?

(10-4)
Cost of Preferred Stock with Flotation Costs

Burnwood Tech plans to issue some $60 par preferred stock with a 6% dividend. The stock is selling on the market for $70.00, and Burnwood must pay flotation costs of 5% of the market price. What is the cost of the preferred stock?

(10-5)
Cost of Equity: DCF

Summerdahl Resorts' common stock is currently trading at $36 a share. The stock is expected to pay a dividend of $3.00 a share at the end of the year ($D_1 = $3.00), and the dividend is expected to grow at a constant rate of 5% a year. What is the cost of common equity?

(10-6)
Cost of Equity: CAPM

Booher Book Stores has a beta of 0.8. The yield on a 3-month T-bill is 4% and the yield on a 10-year T-bond is 6%. The market risk premium is 5.5%, but the stock market return in the previous years was 15%. What is the estimated cost of common equity using the CAPM?

(10-7)
WACC

Shi Importers' balance sheet shows $300 million in debt, $50 million in preferred stock, and $250 million in total common equity. Shi faces a 40% tax rate and the following data: $r_d = 6\%$, $r_{ps} = 5.8\%$, and $r_s = 12\%$. If Shi has a target capital structure of 30% debt, 5% preferred stock, and 65% common stock, what is Shi's WACC?

(10-8)
WACC

David Ortiz Motors has a target capital structure of 40% debt and 60% equity. The yield to maturity on the company's outstanding bonds is 9%, and the company's tax rate is 40%. Ortiz's CFO has calculated the company's WACC as 9.96%. What is the company's cost of equity capital?

Intermediate Problems 9–14

(10-9)
Bond Yield and After-Tax Cost of Debt

A company's 6% coupon rate, semiannual payment, $1,000 par value bond that matures in 30 years sells at a price of $515.16. The company's federal-plus-state tax rate is 40%. What is the firm's component cost of debt for purposes of calculating the WACC? (Hint: Base your answer on the *nominal* rate.)

(10-10)
Cost of Equity

The earnings, dividends, and stock price of Shelby Inc. are expected to grow at 7% per year in the future. Shelby's common stock sells for $23 per share, its last dividend was $2.00, and the company will pay a dividend of $2.14 at the end of the current year.
a. Using the discounted cash flow approach, what is its cost of equity?
b. If the firm's beta is 1.6, the risk-free rate is 9%, and the expected return on the market is 13%, what will be the firm's cost of equity using the CAPM approach?
c. If the firm's bonds earn a return of 12%, what will r_s be using the bond-yield-plus-risk-premium approach? (Hint: Use the midpoint of the risk premium range.)
d. On the basis of the results of parts a through c, what would you estimate Shelby's cost of equity to be?

(10-11)
Cost of Equity

Radon Homes' current EPS is $6.50. It was $4.42 5 years ago. The company pays out 40% of its earnings as dividends, and the stock sells for $36.
a. Calculate the past growth rate in earnings. (Hint: This is a 5-year growth period.)
b. Calculate the *next* expected dividend per share, D_1 [$D_0 = 0.4(\$6.50) = \$2.60$]. Assume that the past growth rate will continue.
c. What is the cost of equity, r_s, for Radon Homes?

(10-12)
Calculation of g and EPS

Spencer Supplies' stock is currently selling for $60 a share. The firm is expected to earn $5.40 per share this year and to pay a year-end dividend of $3.60.
a. If investors require a 9% return, what rate of growth must be expected for Spencer?

b.   If Spencer reinvests earnings in projects with average returns equal to the stock's expected rate of return, what will be next year's EPS? [Hint: g = ROE(Retention ratio).]

(10-13)
The Cost of Equity and Flotation Costs

Messman Manufacturing will issue common stock to the public for $30. The expected dividend and growth in dividends are $3.00 per share and 5%, respectively. If the flotation cost is 10% of the issue proceeds, what is the cost of external equity, r_e?

(10-14)
The Cost of Debt and Flotation Costs

Suppose a company will issue new 20-year debt with a par value of $1,000 and a coupon rate of 9%, paid annually. The tax rate is 40%. If the flotation cost is 2% of the issue proceeds, what is the after-tax cost of debt?

Challenging Problems 15–17

(10-15)
WACC Estimation

On January 1, the total market value of the Tysseland Company was $60 million. During the year, the company plans to raise and invest $30 million in new projects. The firm's present market value capital structure, shown below, is considered to be optimal. Assume that there is no short-term debt.

Debt	$30,000,000
Common equity	30,000,000
Total capital	$60,000,000

New bonds will have an 8% coupon rate, and they will be sold at par. Common stock is currently selling at $30 a share. Stockholders' required rate of return is estimated to be 12%, consisting of a dividend yield of 4% and an expected constant growth rate of 8%. (The next expected dividend is $1.20, so $1.20/$30 = 4%.) The marginal corporate tax rate is 40%.

a.   To maintain the present capital structure, how much of the new investment must be financed by common equity?

b.   Assume that there is sufficient cash flow such that Tysseland can maintain its target capital structure without issuing additional shares of equity. What is the WACC?

c.   Suppose now that there is not enough internal cash flow and the firm must issue new shares of stock. Qualitatively speaking, what will happen to the WACC?

(10-16)
Market Value Capital Structure

Suppose the Schoof Company has this *book value* balance sheet:

Current assets	$30,000,000	Current liabilities	$10,000,000
Fixed assets	50,000,000	Long-term debt	30,000,000
		Common equity	
		Common stock	
		(1 million shares)	1,000,000
		Retained earnings	39,000,000
Total assets	$80,000,000	Total claims	$80,000,000

The current liabilities consist entirely of notes payable to banks, and the interest rate on this debt is 10%, the same as the rate on new bank loans. The long-term debt consists of 30,000 bonds, each of which has a par value of $1,000, carries an annual coupon interest rate of 6%, and matures in 20 years. The going rate of interest on new long-term debt, r_d, is 10%, and this is the present yield to maturity on the bonds. The common stock sells at a price of $60 per share. Calculate the firm's market value capital structure.

(10-17)   A summary of the balance sheet of Travellers Inn Inc. (TII), a company that was
WACC Estimation   formed by merging a number of regional motel chains and that hopes to rival Holiday Inn on the national scene, is shown in the table:

Travellers Inn: December 31, 2006 (Millions of Dollars)

Cash	$ 10	Accounts payable	$ 10
Accounts receivable	20	Accruals	10
Inventories	20	Short-term debt	5
Current assets	$ 50	Current liabilities	$ 25
Net fixed assets	50	Long-term debt	30
		Preferred stock	5
		Common equity	
		Common stock	$ 10
		Retained earnings	30
		Total common equity	$ 40
Total assets	$100	Total liabilities and equity	$100

These facts are also given for TII:

(1) Short-term debt consists of bank loans that currently cost 10%, with interest payable quarterly. These loans are used to finance receivables and inventories on a seasonal basis, so in the off-season, bank loans are zero.

(2) The long-term debt consists of 20-year, semiannual payment mortgage bonds with a coupon rate of 8%. Currently, these bonds provide a yield to investors of $r_d = 12\%$. If new bonds were sold, they would yield investors 12%.

(3) TII's perpetual preferred stock has a $100 par value, pays a quarterly dividend of $2, and has a yield to investors of 11%. New perpetual preferred would have to provide the same yield to investors, and the company would incur a 5% flotation cost to sell it.

(4) The company has 4 million shares of common stock outstanding. $P_0 = \$20$, but the stock has recently traded in the range of $17 to $23. $D_0 = \$1$ and $EPS_0 = \$2$. ROE based on average equity was 24% in 2006, but management expects to increase this return on equity to 30%; however, security analysts are not aware of management's optimism in this regard.

(5) Betas, as reported by security analysts, range from 1.3 to 1.7; the T-bond rate is 10%; and RP_M is estimated by various brokerage houses to be in the range of 4.5% to 5.5%. Brokerage house reports forecast growth rates in the range of 10% to 15% over the foreseeable future. However, some analysts do not explicitly forecast growth rates, but they indicate to their clients that they expect TII's historical trends, as shown in the table in fact (9), to continue.

(6) At a recent conference, TII's financial vice president polled some pension fund investment managers on the minimum rate of return they would have to expect on TII's common to make them willing to buy the common rather than TII bonds, when the bonds yielded 12%. The responses suggested a risk premium over TII bonds of 4 to 6 percentage points.

(7) TII is in the 40% federal-plus-state tax bracket.

(8) TII's principal investment banker, Henry, Kaufman & Company, predicts a decline in interest rates, with r_d falling to 10% and the T-bond rate to 8%, although Henry, Kaufman & Company acknowledges that an increase in the expected inflation rate could lead to an increase rather than a decrease in rates.

(9) Here is the historical record of EPS and DPS:

Year	EPS	DPS	Year	EPS	DPS
1992	$0.09	$0.00	2000	$0.78	$0.00
1993	−0.20	0.00	2001	0.80	0.00
1994	0.40	0.00	2002	1.20	0.20
1995	0.52	0.00	2003	0.95	0.40
1996	0.10	0.00	2004	1.30	0.60
1997	0.57	0.00	2005	1.60	0.80
1998	0.61	0.00	2006	2.00	1.00
1999	0.70	0.00			

Assume that you are a recently hired financial analyst, and your boss, the treasurer, has asked you to estimate the company's WACC; assume no new equity will be issued. Your cost of capital should be appropriate for use in evaluating projects which are in the same risk class as the firm's average assets now on the books.

e-resource

Spreadsheet Problem

(10-18)
Build a Model: WACC

Start with the partial model in the file **FM12 Ch 10 P18 Build a Model.xls** from the textbook's Web site. The stock of Gao Computing sells for $50, and last year's dividend was $2.10. A flotation cost of 10% would be required to issue new common stock. Gao's preferred stock pays a dividend of $3.30 per share, and new preferred could be sold at a price to net the company $30 per share. Security analysts are projecting that the common dividend will grow at a rate of 7% a year. The firm can also issue additional long-term debt at an interest rate (or before-tax cost) of 10%, and its marginal tax rate is 35%. The market risk premium is 6%, the risk-free rate is 6.5%, and Gao's beta is 0.83. In its cost-of-capital calculations, Gao uses a target capital structure with 45% debt, 5% preferred stock, and 50% common equity.

a. Calculate the cost of each capital component (that is, the after-tax cost of debt), the cost of preferred stock (including flotation costs), and the cost of equity (ignoring flotation costs) with the DCF method and the CAPM method.

b. Calculate the cost of new stock using the DCF model.

c. What is the cost of new common stock, based on the CAPM? (Hint: Find the difference between r_e and r_s as determined by the DCF method and add that differential to the CAPM value for r_s.)

d. Assuming that Gao will not issue new equity and will continue to use the same target capital structure, what is the company's WACC?

e. Suppose Gao is evaluating three projects with the following characteristics:

(1) Each project has a cost of $1 million. They will all be financed using the target mix of long-term debt, preferred stock, and common equity. The cost of the common equity for each project should be based on the beta estimated for the project. All equity will come from retained earnings.

(2) Equity invested in Project A would have a beta of 0.5 and an expected return of 9.0%.

(3) Equity invested in Project B would have a beta of 1.0 and an expected return of 10.0%.

(4) Equity invested in Project C would have a beta of 2.0 and an expected return of 11.0%.

f. Analyze the company's situation and explain why each project should be accepted or rejected.

Cyberproblem

e-resource

Please go to the textbook's Web site to access any Cyberproblems.

Mini Case

During the last few years, Harry Davis Industries has been too constrained by the high cost of capital to make many capital investments. Recently, though, capital costs have been declining, and the company has decided to look seriously at a major expansion program that has been proposed by the marketing department. Assume that you are an assistant to Leigh Jones, the financial vice president. Your first task is to estimate Harry Davis's cost of capital. Jones has provided you with the following data, which she believes may be relevant to your task:

(1) The firm's tax rate is 40%.

(2) The current price of Harry Davis's 12% coupon, semiannual payment, non-callable bonds with 15 years remaining to maturity is $1,153.72. Harry Davis does not use short-term interest-bearing debt on a permanent basis. New bonds would be privately placed with no flotation cost.

(3) The current price of the firm's 10%, $100 par value, quarterly dividend, perpetual preferred stock is $116.95. Harry Davis would incur flotation costs equal to 5% of the proceeds on a new issue.

(4) Harry Davis's common stock is currently selling at $50 per share. Its last dividend (D_0) was $4.19, and dividends are expected to grow at a constant rate of 5% in the foreseeable future. Harry Davis's beta is 1.2, the yield on T-bonds is

7%, and the market risk premium is estimated to be 6%. For the bond-yield-plus-risk-premium approach, the firm uses a 4 percentage point risk premium.

(5) Harry Davis's target capital structure is 30% long-term debt, 10% preferred stock, and 60% common equity.

To structure the task somewhat, Jones has asked you to answer the following questions.

a. (1) What sources of capital should be included when you estimate Harry Davis's weighted average cost of capital (WACC)?

(2) Should the component costs be figured on a before-tax or an after-tax basis?

(3) Should the costs be historical (embedded) costs or new (marginal) costs?

b. What is the market interest rate on Harry Davis's debt and its component cost of debt?

c. (1) What is the firm's cost of preferred stock?

(2) Harry Davis's preferred stock is riskier to investors than its debt, yet the preferred's yield to investors is lower than the yield to maturity on the debt. Does this suggest that you have made a mistake? (Hint: Think about taxes.)

d. (1) What are the two primary ways companies raise common equity?

(2) Why is there a cost associated with reinvested earnings?

(3) Harry Davis doesn't plan to issue new shares of common stock. Using the CAPM approach, what is Harry Davis's estimated cost of equity?

e. (1) What is the estimated cost of equity using the discounted cash flow (DCF) approach?

(2) Suppose the firm has historically earned 15% on equity (ROE) and retained 35% of earnings, and investors expect this situation to continue in the future. How could you use this information to estimate the future dividend growth rate, and what growth rate would you get? Is this consistent with the 5% growth rate given earlier?

(3) Could the DCF method be applied if the growth rate was not constant? How?

f. What is the cost of equity based on the bond-yield-plus-risk-premium method?

g. What is your final estimate for the cost of equity, r_s?

h. What is Harry Davis's weighted average cost of capital (WACC)?

i. What factors influence a company's WACC?

j. Should the company use the composite WACC as the hurdle rate for each of its divisions?

k. What procedures are used to determine the risk-adjusted cost of capital for a particular division? What approaches are used to measure a division's beta?

l. Harry Davis is interested in establishing a new division, which will focus primarily on developing new Internet-based projects. In trying to determine the cost of capital for this new division, you discover that stand-alone firms involved in similar projects have on average the following characteristics:

- Their capital structure is 10% debt and 90% common equity.
- Their cost of debt is typically 12%.
- The beta is 1.7.

Given this information, what would your estimate be for the division's cost of capital?

m. What are three types of project risk? How is each type of risk used?

n. Explain in words why new common stock that is raised externally has a higher percentage cost than equity that is raised internally by reinvesting earnings.

o. (1) Harry Davis estimates that if it issues new common stock, the flotation cost will be 15%. Harry Davis incorporates the flotation costs into the DCF approach. What is the estimated cost of newly issued common stock, taking into account the flotation cost?

  (2) Suppose Harry Davis issues 30-year debt with a par value of $1,000 and a coupon rate of 10%, paid annually. If flotation costs are 2%, what is the after-tax cost of debt for the new bond issue?

p. What four common mistakes in estimating the WACC should Harry Davis avoid?

Selected Additional Cases

The following cases from Textchoice, *Cengage Learning's online library, cover many of the concepts discussed in this chapter and are available at* **http://www.textchoice2.com.**

Klein-Brigham Series:

Case 42, "West Coast Semiconductor"; Case 54, "Ace Repair"; Case 55, "Premier Paint & Body";

Case 6, "Randolph Corporation"; Case 75, "The Western Company"; and Case 81, "Pressed Paper Products."

Brigham-Buzzard Series:

Case 5, "Powerline Network Corporation (Determining the Cost of Capital)."

chapter 11

The Basics of Capital Budgeting: Evaluating Cash Flows

In 1970, the Adolph Coors Company was a small brewer serving a regional market, but because of its quality products and aggressive marketing, by 1990 Coors had risen to the number three brand in the U.S. beer market. During this high-growth phase, the corporate emphasis was on marketing, technology, engineering, and capacity additions. When investing in new equipment or factories, Coors always went "the Cadillac route," with little scrutiny of proposed projects. In effect, their motto was "If you build it, they will come," and indeed, for two decades consumers did come to Coors.

However, the brewing industry began to experience major problems in the 1990s. Many consumers were drawn to wine, causing growth in beer sales to fall below 1% per year. In addition, large numbers of microbreweries opened, providing beer drinkers with an alternative to the national brands. These events proved particularly painful to Coors, whose lack of financial discipline had led to a frivolous use of capital and thus to a high-cost infrastructure.

In 1995 Coors hired a new CFO, Timothy Wolf, who soon learned that Coors had a low return on invested capital, a negative free cash flow, and an unreliable planning/forecasting process. Wolf quickly created an in-house education program to teach managers and engineers how to conduct rational project analyses. Even more important, he began to shift the corporate culture from a focus on undisciplined growth and high-technology engineering to creating shareholder value. This new focus was put to the test when Coors reexamined its plans for a major new bottle-washing facility in Virginia. Using the capital budgeting processes established by Wolf, the project team was able to reduce the cost of the investment by 25% even as they implemented design changes that led to lower operating costs.

In 2005, Coors merged with Molson Inc. to form Coors Molson Brewing Company, and Wolf became the Global CFO of the combined brewery. With a continued focus on free cash flow and return on invested capital, the value of a share of Coors' stock has climbed from about $14 when Wolf joined in 1995 to over $68 in July 2006, an annualized average gain of more than 15%.

Capital budgeting is the process of evaluating a company's potential investments and deciding which ones to accept. This chapter provides an overview of the capital budgeting process and explains the basic techniques used to evaluate potential projects, given that their expected cash flows have already been estimated. Chapter 12 then explains how to estimate a project's cash flows and analyze its risk.

11.1　Overview of Capital Budgeting

Capital budgeting is the decision process that managers use to identify those projects that add to the firm's value, and as such it is perhaps the most important task faced by financial managers and their staffs. First, a firm's capital budgeting decisions define its strategic direction because moves into new products, services, or markets must be preceded by capital expenditures. Second, the results of capital budgeting decisions continue for many years, reducing flexibility. Third, poor capital budgeting can have serious financial consequences. If the firm invests too much, it will waste investors' capital on excess capacity. On the other hand, if it does not invest enough, its equipment and computer software may not be sufficiently modern to enable it to produce competitively. Also, if it has inadequate capacity, it may lose market share to rival firms, and regaining lost customers requires heavy selling expenses, price reductions, or product improvements, all of which are costly.

A firm's growth, and even its ability to remain competitive and to survive, depends on a constant flow of ideas for new products, for ways to make existing products better, and for ways to operate at a lower cost. Accordingly, a well-managed firm will go to great lengths to encourage good capital budgeting proposals from its employees. If a firm has capable and imaginative executives and employees, and if its incentive system is working properly, many ideas for capital investment will be advanced. Some ideas will be good ones, but others will not.

Corporate Valuation and Capital Budgeting

You can calculate the free cash flows (FCF) for a project in much the same way as for a firm. When the project's free cash flows are discounted at the appropriate risk-adjusted rate, the result is the project's value. One difference between valuing a firm and valuing a project is the rate that is used to discount cash flows. For a firm, it is the overall weighted cost of capital; for a project, it is r, the project's risk-adjusted cost of capital.

Subtracting the initial cost of the project gives the net present value (NPV). If a project has a positive NPV, then it adds value to the firm. In fact, the firm's market value added (MVA) is the sum of all its projects' NPVs. Therefore, the process for evaluating projects, called **capital budgeting,** is critical for a firm's success.

$$NPV = \left[\frac{FCF_1}{(1 + r)^1} + \frac{FCF_2}{(1 + r)^2} + \cdots + \frac{FCF_N}{(1 + r)^N} \right] - \text{Initial cost}$$

Therefore, companies must screen projects for those that add value, the primary topic of this chapter.

Screening capital expenditure proposals is not a costless operation—analysis provides benefits, but it also has a cost in terms of the time it requires. Larger investments and riskier projects require increasingly detailed analysis and approval at a higher level within the firm. Thus, a plant manager might be authorized to approve routine maintenance expenditures up to $10,000 on the basis of a relatively unsophisticated analysis, but the full board of directors might have to approve decisions that involve either amounts over $1 million or expansions into new products or markets.

Six key methods are used to evaluate projects and to decide whether or not they should be accepted: (1) net present value (NPV), (2) internal rate of return (IRR), (3) modified internal rate of return (MIRR), (4) profitability index (PI), (5) payback, and (6) discounted payback. We explain how each method is applied, and then we evaluate how well each performs in terms of identifying those projects that will maximize the firm's stock price.

The first, and most difficult, step in project analysis is estimating the relevant cash flows, a step that Chapter 12 explains in detail. Our present focus is on the different evaluation methods, so we provide the cash flows used in this chapter, starting with the expected cash flows of Projects S and L in Panel A of Figure 11-1 (we will explain Panel B when we discuss the evaluation methods shown in the next sections). These projects are equally risky, and the cash flows for each year, CF_t, reflect purchase cost, investments in working capital, taxes, depreciation, and salvage values. As we show in Chapter 12, this definition of project cash flows is equivalent to the definition of free cash flows as defined in Chapter 3, except the

FM
e-resource

Web Extension 11A at the textbook's Web site explains a seventh method, the accounting rate of return (ARR) approach. The ARR approach has major flaws, and the Web Extension explains why it should not be used.

Figure 11-1

Net Cash Flows and Selected Evaluation Criteria for Projects S and L (CF_t)

	A	B	C	D	E	F
23	**Panel A: Project Cash Flows and Cost of Capital**					
24						
25	**Project S:**	**0**	**1**	**2**	**3**	**4**
26						
27		-$1,000	$500	$400	$300	$100
28						
29	**Project L:**	**0**	**1**	**2**	**3**	**4**
30						
31		-$1,000	$100	$300	$400	$600
32						
33		**Project cost of capital = r =**		10%		
34						
35	**Panel B: Summary of Selected Evaluation Criterion**					
36						
37			**Project**			
38			**S**	**L**		
39		**NPV:**	$78.82	$49.18		
40		**IRR:**	14.5%	11.8%		
41		**MIRR:**	12.1%	11.3%		
42		**PI:**	1.08	1.05		

FM
e-resource

See **FM12 Ch 11 Tool Kit.xls** at the textbook's Web site for all calculations.

cash flows are for the project and not the entire firm. Finally, we assume that all cash flows occur at the end of the designated year. Incidentally, the S stands for *short* and the L for *long*: Project S is a short-term project in the sense that its cash inflows come in sooner than L's.

Why are capital budgeting decisions so important?

What are some ways firms get ideas for capital projects?

Which types of projects receive the most analysis?

11.2 Net Present Value (NPV)

The **net present value (NPV) method** is based upon the **discounted cash flow (DCF) technique.** To implement this approach, we proceed as follows:

1. Find the present value of each cash flow, including the initial cash flow, discounted at the project's cost of capital, r.
2. Sum these discounted cash flows; this sum is defined as the project's NPV.

The equation for the NPV is as follows:

$$NPV = CF_0 + \frac{CF_1}{(1+r)^1} + \frac{CF_2}{(1+r)^2} + \cdots + \frac{CF_N}{(1+r)^N}$$

$$= \sum_{t=0}^{N} \frac{CF_t}{(1+r)^t}.$$

(11-1)

Here CF_t is the expected net cash flow at Period t, r is the project's cost of capital, and n is its life. Cash outflows (expenditures such as the cost of buying equipment or building factories) are treated as *negative* cash flows. In evaluating Projects S and L, only CF_0 is negative, but for many large projects such as the Alaska Pipeline, an electric generating plant, or a new Boeing jet aircraft, outflows occur for several years before operations begin and cash flows turn positive.

Application of the NPV Method

At a 10% cost of capital, Project S's NPV is $78.82:

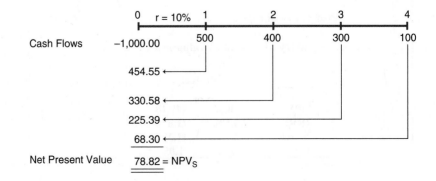

By a similar process, we find $NPV_L = \$49.18$.

If the projects were *mutually exclusive*, the one with the higher NPV should be accepted and the other rejected. S would be ranked over L and thus accepted because S has the higher NPV. **Mutually exclusive** means that if one project is taken on, the other must be rejected. For example, a conveyor-belt system to move goods in a warehouse and a fleet of forklifts for the same purpose illustrates mutually exclusive projects—accepting one implies rejecting the other. **Independent projects** are those whose cash flows are independent of one another. If Wal-Mart were considering a new store in Boise and another in Atlanta, those projects would be independent of one another. If our Projects S and L were independent, then both should be accepted because both have a positive NPV and thus add value to the firm. If they were mutually exclusive, then S should be chosen because it has the higher NPV.

Calculating the NPV by using Equation 11-1 and a regular calculator becomes tedious and error-prone for projects with many cash flows. It is much more efficient to use a financial calculator or a spreadsheet. Different calculators are set up somewhat differently, but they all have a section of memory called the "cash flow register" that is used for uneven cash flows such as those in Projects S and L (as opposed to equal annuity cash flows). A solution process for Equation 11-1 is literally programmed into financial calculators, and all you have to do is enter the cash flows (being sure to observe the signs), along with the value of $r = I/YR$. At that point, you have (in your calculator) this equation:

$$NPV_S = -1,000 + \frac{500}{(1.10)^1} + \frac{400}{(1.10)^2} + \frac{300}{(1.10)^3} + \frac{100}{(1.10)^4}.$$

Note that the equation has one unknown, NPV. Now all you need to do is to ask the calculator to solve the equation for you, which you do by pressing the NPV button (and, on some calculators, the "compute" button). The answer, 78.82, will appear on the screen.[1]

Most projects last for more than 4 years, and, as you will see in Chapter 12, we must go through quite a few steps to develop the estimated cash flows. Therefore, financial analysts generally use spreadsheets for project analysis. The cash flows for Projects S and L are shown in the spreadsheet in Panel A of Figure 11-1. In Panel B, we used the *Excel* NPV function to calculate the projects' NPVs. To access the NPV function in *Excel*, you can click the function wizard, f_x, then Financial, then NPV, and then OK. Input D33 as the first argument in the NPV function; this is the rate for *Excel* to use in discounting the cash flows. Then input the range of future cash flows, C27:F27, in the NPV function as "Value 1." Click OK, and the result is $1,078.82. Despite its name, the NPV function actually finds the PV of future cash flows, not the NPV. To find the NPV, edit the cell by adding B27 to the NPV result. The resulting formula in Cell C39 is $=$**B27$+$NPV(D33,C27:F27)**, and it gives a value of $78.82. Note that you cannot enter the initial cash flow of $-\$1,000$ as part of the NPV range because the *Excel* NPV function assumes that the first cash flow in the range occurs at $t = 1$. Also be aware that if you input a value for the rate, it must be the actual number. For example, we could have entered a rate of "0.10" or "10%," but if we entered "10," *Excel* would interpret it as 1000%. This is exactly opposite the convention used in financial calculators, where you would enter 10.

e-resource

See **FM12 Ch 11 Tool Kit.xls** at the textbook's Web site for all calculations.

---

[1]The keystrokes for finding the NPV are shown for several calculators in the calculator tutorials provided at the textbook's Web site.

Figure 11-3

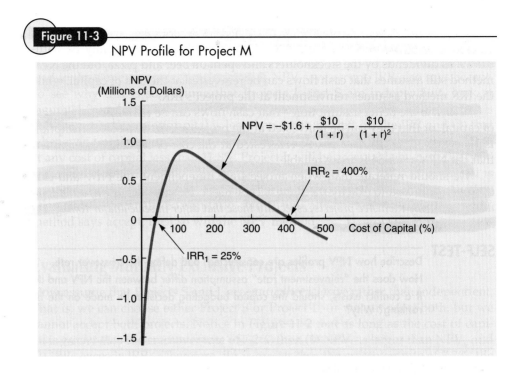

NPV Profile for Project M

restore the land to its original condition. Therefore, the project's expected net cash flows are as follows (in millions of dollars):

Expected Net Cash Flows

Year 0	End of Year 1	End of Year 2
−$1.6	+$10	−$10

These values can be substituted into Equation 11-2 to derive the IRR for the investment:

$$NPV = \frac{-\$1.6 \text{ million}}{(1 + IRR)^0} + \frac{\$10 \text{ million}}{(1 + IRR)^1} + \frac{-\$10 \text{ million}}{(1 + IRR)^2} = 0.$$

When solved, we find that NPV = 0 when IRR = 25% and also when IRR = 400%.[6] Therefore, the IRR of the investment is both 25% and 400%. This relationship is depicted graphically in Figure 11-3. Note that no dilemma would arise if the NPV method were used; we would simply use Equation 11-1, find the NPV, and use the result to evaluate the project. If Proje%ct M's cost of capital were 10%, then its NPV would be −$0.77 million, and the project should be rejected. If r were between 25 and 400%, the NPV would be positive.

e-resource

See **FM12 Ch 11 Tool Kit.xls** at the textbook's Web site for all calculations.

---

[6]If you attempted to find the IRR of Project M with many financial calculators, you would get an error message. This same message would be given for all projects with multiple IRRs. However, you can still find Project M's IRR by first calculating its NPV using several different values for r and then plotting the NPV profile. The intersection with the x-axis gives a rough idea of the IRR value. Finally, you can use trial and error to find the exact value of r that forces NPV = 0.

The IRR function in spreadsheets begins its trial-and-error search for a solution with an initial guess. If you omit the initial guess, the *Excel* default starting point is 10%. Now suppose the values −1.6, +10, and −10 were in Cells A1:C1. You could use this *Excel* formula, =**IRR(A1:C1,10%)**, where 10% is the initial guess, and it would produce a result of 25%. If you used a guess of 300%, you would have this formula, =**IRR(A1:C1,300%)**, and it would produce a result of 400%.

The example illustrates how multiple IRRs can arise when a project has non-normal cash flows. In contrast, the NPV criterion can easily be applied, and this method leads to conceptually correct capital budgeting decisions.

SELF-TEST

Explain the difference between normal and nonnormal cash flows, and their relationship to the "multiple IRR problem."

A project has the following cash flows: $CF_0 = -\$1,100$, $CF_1 = \$2,100$, $CF_2 = \$2,100$, and $CF_3 = =\$3,600$. How many positive IRRs might this project have? If you set the starting trial value to 10% in either your calculator or an *Excel* spreadsheet, what is the IRR? If you set the starting trial value to 400%? What is the NPV of the project with a very low cost of capital, such as $r = 0\%$? Does this suggest that the project should or should not be accepted? (18.2%; 106.7%; $-\$500$)

11.6 Modified Internal Rate of Return (MIRR)

In spite of a strong academic preference for NPV, surveys indicate that many executives prefer IRR over NPV. Apparently, managers find it intuitively more appealing to evaluate investments in terms of percentage rates of return than dollars of NPV. Given this fact, can we devise a percentage evaluator that is better than the regular IRR? The answer is yes—we can modify the IRR and make it a better indicator of relative profitability, hence better for use in capital budgeting. The new measure is called the **modified IRR,** or **MIRR,** and it is defined as follows:

$$\sum_{t=0}^{N} \frac{COF_t}{(1+r)^t} = \frac{\sum_{t=0}^{N} CIF_t(1+r)^{N-1}}{(1+MIRR)^N}$$

$$PV \text{ of costs} = \frac{Terminal\ value}{(1+MIRR)^N}$$

$$= PV \text{ of terminal value.}$$

(11-3)

Here COF refers to cash outflows (negative numbers) or the cost of the project, CIF refers to cash inflows (positive numbers), and r is the cost of capital. The left term is simply the present value of the investment outlays when discounted at the cost of capital, and the numerator of the right term is the compounded future value of the inflows, assuming that the cash inflows are reinvested at the cost of capital. The compounded future value of the cash inflows is also called the **terminal value,** or **TV.** The discount rate that forces the present value of the TV to equal the present value of the costs is defined as the MIRR.[7]

---

[7]There are several alternative definitions for the MIRR. The differences primarily relate to whether negative cash flows that occur after positive cash flows begin should be compounded and treated as part of the TV or discounted and treated as a cost. A related issue is whether negative and positive flows in a given year should be netted or treated separately. For a complete discussion, see William R. McDaniel, Daniel E. McCarty, and Kenneth A. Jessell, "Discounted Cash Flow with Explicit Reinvestment Rates: Tutorial and Extension," *The Financial Review,* August 1988, pp. 369–385; and David M. Shull, "Interpreting Rates of Return: A Modified Rate of Return Approach," *Financial Practice and Education,* Fall 1993, pp. 67–71.

FM
e-resource
See **FM12 Ch 11 Tool Kit.xls** at the textbook's Web site for all calculations.

We can illustrate the calculation with Project S:

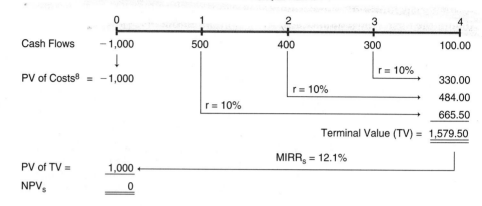

Using the cash flows as set out on the time line, first find the terminal value by compounding each cash inflow at the 10% cost of capital. Then enter N = 4, PV = −1000, PMT = 0, FV = 1579.5, and then press the I/YR button to find $MIRR_S$ = 12.1%. Similarly, we find $MIRR_L$ = 11.3%.

Excel has a function for the MIRR. Using the cash flows in Panel A of Figure 11-1, the formula in C41 is **=MIRR(B27:F27,D33,D33)**. The first argument in the function is the range of cash flows, beginning with CF_0. The second argument is the cost of capital used for discounting cash outflows, and the third argument is the rate used for compounding inflows (i.e., the reinvestment rate). In our definition of the MIRR, we assume that reinvestment is at the cost of capital, so we enter the project cost of capital percent twice. The result is an MIRR of 12.1%.

The modified IRR has a significant advantage over the regular IRR. MIRR assumes that cash flows from all projects are reinvested at the cost of capital, while the regular IRR assumes that the cash flows from each project are reinvested at the project's own IRR. Because reinvestment at the cost of capital is generally more correct, the modified IRR is a better indicator of a project's true profitability. The MIRR also eliminates the multiple IRR problem. To illustrate, with r = 10%, Project M (the strip mine project) has MIRR = 5.6% versus its 10% cost of capital, so it should be rejected. This is consistent with the decision based on the NPV method, because at r = 10%, NPV = −$0.77 million.

Is MIRR as good as NPV for choosing between mutually exclusive projects? If two projects are of equal size and have the same life, then NPV and MIRR will always lead to the same decision. Thus, for any set of projects like our Projects S and L, if $NPV_S > NPV_L$, then $MIRR_S > MIRR_L$, and the kinds of conflicts we encountered between NPV and the regular IRR will not occur. Also, if the projects are of equal size, but differ in lives, the MIRR will always lead to the same decision as the NPV if the MIRRs are both calculated using as the terminal year the life of the longer project. (Just fill in zeros for the shorter project's missing cash flows.) However, if the projects differ in size, then conflicts can still occur. For example, if we were choosing between a large project and a small mutually exclusive one, then we might find $NPV_L > NPV_S$, but $MIRR_S > MIRR_L$.

Our conclusion is that the MIRR is superior to the regular IRR as an indicator of a project's "true" rate of return, or "expected long-term rate of return," but the NPV method is still the best way to choose among competing projects because

---

[8]In this example, the only negative cash flow occurs at t = 0, so the PV of costs is equal to CF_0.

it provides the best indication of how much each project will add to the value of the firm.

SELF-TEST
Describe how the modified IRR (MIRR) is calculated.

What are the primary differences between the MIRR and the regular IRR?

What condition can cause the MIRR and NPV methods to produce conflicting rankings?

A project has the following expected cash flows: $CF_0 = -\$500$, $CF_1 = \$200$, $CF_2 = \$200$, and $CF_3 = \$400$. Using a 10% discount rate and reinvestment rate, what is the MIRR? (19.9%)

11.7 Profitability Index

Another method used to evaluate projects is the **profitability index (PI)**:

$$PI = \frac{\text{PV of future cash flows}}{\text{Initial cost}} = \frac{\sum_{t=1}^{N} \dfrac{CF_t}{(1+r)^t}}{CF_0}. \tag{11-4}$$

Here CF_t represents the expected future cash flows, and CF_0 represents the initial cost. The PI shows the *relative* profitability of any project, or the present value per dollar of initial cost. The PI for Project S, based on a 10% cost of capital, is 1.08:

$$PI_S = \frac{\$1078.82}{\$1000} = 1.08.$$

Thus, on a present value basis, Project S is expected to produce $1.08 for each $1 of investment. Project L, with a PI of 1.05, should produce $1.05 for each dollar invested.

In Panel B of Figure 11-1, we calculate the PI using the NPV function. Our formula in Cell C42 is **=NPV(D33,C27:F27)/(−B27).**

A project is acceptable if its PI is greater than 1.0, and the higher the PI, the higher the project's ranking. Therefore, both S and L would be accepted by the PI criterion if they were independent, and S would be ranked ahead of L if they were mutually exclusive.

Mathematically, the NPV, IRR, MIRR, and PI methods will always lead to the same accept/reject decisions for *independent* projects: If a project's NPV is positive, its IRR and MIRR will always exceed r, and its PI will always be greater than 1.0. However, these methods can give conflicting rankings for *mutually exclusive* projects, for the same reasons that IRR can give conflicting rankings.

FM
e-resource

See *FM12 Ch 11 Tool Kit.xls* at the textbook's Web site for all calculations.

SELF-TEST
Explain how the PI is calculated. What does it measure?

A project has the following expected cash flows: $CF_0 = -\$500$, $CF_1 = \$200$, $CF_2 = \$200$, and $CF_3 = \$400$. If the project's cost of capital is 9%, what is the PI? (1.32)

11.8 Payback Methods

NPV and IRR are the most widely used methods today, but the earliest selection criterion was the payback methods. We now discuss the regular payback period and the discounted payback period.

Payback Period

The **payback period,** defined as the expected number of years required to recover the original investment, was the first formal method used to evaluate capital budgeting projects. The basic idea is to start with the project's cost, determine the number of years prior to full recovery of the cost, and then determine the fraction of the next year that is required for full recovery, assuming cash flows occur evenly during the year:

$$\text{Payback} = \begin{array}{c} \text{Number of} \\ \text{years prior to} \\ \text{full recovery} \end{array} + \frac{\text{Unrecovered cost at start of year}}{\text{Cash flow during full recovery year}}. \qquad \text{(11-5)}$$

The payback calculation for Project S is diagrammed in Figure 11-4 and is explained below.

The cumulative net cash flow at $t = 0$ is just the initial cost of $-\$1,000$. At Year 1 the cumulative net cash flow is the previous cumulative of $-\$1,000$ plus the Year 1 cash flow of $\$500$: $-\$1,000 + \$500 = -\$500$. Similarly, the cumulative for Year 2 is the previous cumulative of $-\$500$ plus the Year 2 inflow of $\$400$, resulting in $-\$100$. We see that by the end of Year 3 the cumulative inflows have more than recovered the initial outflow. Thus, the payback occurred during the third year. If the $\$300$ of inflows comes in evenly during Year 3, then the exact payback period can be found as follows:

$$\text{Payback}_\text{S} = 2 + \frac{\$100}{\$300} = 2.33 \text{ years.}$$

Applying the same procedure to Project L, we find $\text{Payback}_\text{L} = 3.33$ years.

The shorter the payback period, the better. If the projects were mutually exclusive, S would be ranked over L because S has the shorter payback.

The payback has three main flaws: (1) Dollars received in different years are all given the same weight—a dollar in Year 4 is assumed to be just as valuable as a dollar in Year 1. (2) Cash flows beyond the payback year are given no consideration whatsoever, regardless of how large they might be. (3) Unlike the NPV, which tells

e-resource

See **FM12 Ch 11 Tool Kit.xls** at the textbook's Web site for all calculations.

Figure 11-4

Payback Period for Projects S and L

	A	B	C	D	E	F	G	H
398	Project S		Year:	0	1	2	3	4
399								
400			Cash flow:	-1,000	500	400	300	100
401			Cumulative cash flow:	-1,000	-500	-100	200	300
402			Percent of year required for payback:		1.00	1.00	0.33	0.00
403			Payback =	2.33				
404								
405	Project L		Year:	0	1	2	3	4
406								
407			Cash flow:	-1,000	100	300	400	600
408			Cumulative cash flow:	-1,000	-900	-600	-200	400
409			Percent of year required for payback:		1.00	1.00	1.00	0.33
410			Payback =	3.33				

us by how much the project should increase shareholder wealth, and the IRR, which tells us how much a project yields over the cost of capital, the payback merely tells us when we get our investment back. There is no necessary relationship between a given payback and investor wealth maximization, so we don't know how to set the "right" payback.

Discounted Payback Period

Some firms use a variant of the regular payback, the **discounted payback period,** which is similar to the regular payback period except that the expected cash flows are discounted by the project's cost of capital. Thus, the discounted payback period is defined as the number of years required to recover the investment from *discounted* net cash flows. Figure 11-5 contains the discounted net cash flows for Projects S and L, assuming both projects have a cost of capital of 10%. To construct Figure 11-5, each cash inflow is divided by $(1 + r)^t = (1.10)^t$, where t is the year in which the cash flow occurs and r is the project's cost of capital. After 3 years, Project S will have generated $1,011 in discounted cash inflows. Because the cost is $1,000, the discounted payback is just under 3 years, or, to be precise, 2 + ($214.9/$225.4) = 2.95 years. Project L's discounted payback is 3.88 years:

$$\text{Discounted payback}_S = 2.0 + \$214.9/\$225.4 = 2.95 \text{ years.}$$

$$\text{Discounted payback}_L = 3.0 + \$360/\$410 = 3.88 \text{ years.}$$

For Projects S and L, the rankings are the same regardless of which payback method is used; that is, Project S is preferred to Project L. Often, however, the regular and the discounted paybacks produce conflicting rankings.

Evaluating Payback and Discounted Payback

The discounted payback approach corrects the first flaw of the regular payback method because it considers the time value of the cash flows. However, it too fails

Figure 11-5

Projects S and L: Discounted Payback Period

	A	B	C	D	E	F	G	H
422	Figure 11-5. Projects S and L: Discounted Payback Period (r = 10%)							
423								
424	Project S		Year:	0	1	2	3	4
425								
426			Cash flow:	(1,000)	500	400	300	100
427			Discounted cash flow:	(1,000)	455	331	225	68
428			Cumulative discounted CF:	(1,000)	(545)	(215)	11	79
429			Percent of year required for payback:		1.00	1.00	0.95	0.00
430			Discounted Payback:	2.95				
431								
432	Project L		Year:	0	1	2	3	4
433								
434			Cash flow:	(1,000)	100	300	400	600
435			Discounted cash flow:	(1,000)	91	248	301	410
436			Cumulative discounted CF:	(1,000)	(909)	(661)	(361)	49
437			Percent of year required for payback:		1.00	1.00	1.00	0.88
438			Discounted Payback:	3.88				

e-resource

See **FM12 Ch 11 Tool Kit.xls** at the textbook's Web site for all calculations.

to consider cash flows occurring after the payback year and, as with regular payback, there is no relationship between discounted payback and wealth maximization.

Although the payback methods have serious faults as ranking criteria, they do provide information on how long funds will be tied up in a project. Thus, the shorter the payback period, other things held constant, the greater the project's *liquidity*. Also, since cash flows expected in the distant future are generally riskier than near-term cash flows, the payback is often used as an indicator of a project's *risk*.

SELF-TEST

What two pieces of information does the payback convey that are absent from the other capital budgeting decision methods?

What three flaws does the regular payback have? Does the discounted payback correct these flaws?

A project has the following expected cash flows: $CF_0 = -\$500$, $CF_1 = \$200$, $CF_2 = \$200$, and $CF_3 = \$400$. If the project's cost of capital is 9%, what are the project's payback period and discounted payback period? (2.25; 2.48)

11.9 Conclusions on Capital Budgeting Methods

We have discussed six capital budgeting decision methods, compared the methods with one another, and highlighted their relative strengths and weaknesses. In the process, we probably created the impression that "sophisticated" firms should use only one method in the decision process, NPV. However, virtually all capital budgeting decisions are analyzed by computer, so it is easy to calculate and list all the decision measures: payback and discounted payback, NPV, IRR, modified IRR (MIRR), and profitability index (PI). In making the accept/reject decision, most large, sophisticated firms calculate and consider all of the measures, because each one provides decision makers with a somewhat different piece of relevant information.

NPV is important because it gives a direct measure of the dollar benefit of the project to shareholders. Therefore, we regard NPV as the best single measure of *profitability*. IRR also measures profitability, but here it is expressed as a percentage rate of return, which many decision makers prefer. Further, IRR contains information concerning a project's "safety margin." To illustrate, consider the following two projects: Project S (for small) costs $10,000 and is expected to return $16,500 at the end of one year, while Project L (for large) costs $100,000 and has an expected payoff of $115,500 after one year. At a 10% cost of capital, both projects have an NPV of $5,000, so by the NPV rule we should be indifferent between them. However, Project S has a much larger margin for error. Even if its realized cash inflow were 39% below the $16,500 forecast, the firm would still recover its $10,000 investment. On the other hand, if Project L's inflows fell by only 13% from the forecasted $115,500, the firm would not recover its investment. Further, if no inflows were generated at all, the firm would lose only $10,000 with Project S, but $100,000 if it took on Project L.

The NPV provides no information about either of these factors—the "safety margin" inherent in the cash flow forecasts or the amount of capital at risk. However, the IRR does provide "safety margin" information—Project S's IRR is a whopping 65%, while Project L's IRR is only 15.5%. As a result, the realized return could fall substantially for Project S, and it would still make money. The modified IRR has all the virtues of the IRR, but (1) it incorporates a better reinvestment rate assumption, and (2) it avoids the multiple rate of return problem.

The PI measures profitability relative to the cost of a project—it shows the "bang per buck." Like the IRR, it gives an indication of the project's risk, because a high PI means that cash flows could fall quite a bit and the project would still be profitable.

Payback and discounted payback provide an indication of both the *risk* and the *liquidity* of a project: A long payback means (1) that the investment dollars will be locked up for many years—hence the project is relatively illiquid—and (2) that the project's cash flows must be forecasted far out into the future—hence the project is probably quite risky. A good analogy for this is the bond valuation process. An investor should never compare the yields to maturity on two bonds without also considering their terms to maturity, because a bond's risk is affected by its maturity.

The different measures provide different types of information to decision makers. Since it is easy to calculate all of them, all should be considered in the decision process. For any specific decision, more weight might be given to one measure than another, but it would be foolish to ignore the information provided by any of the methods.

Just as it would be foolish to ignore these capital budgeting methods, it would also be foolish to make decisions based *solely* on them. One cannot know at Time 0 the exact cost of future capital, or the exact future cash flows. These inputs are simply estimates, and if they turn out to be incorrect, then so will be the calculated NPVs and IRRs. *Thus, quantitative methods provide valuable information, but they should not be used as the sole criteria for accept/reject decisions* in the capital budgeting process. Rather, managers should use quantitative methods in the decision-making process but also consider the likelihood that actual results will differ from the forecasts. Qualitative factors, such as the chances of a tax increase, or a war, or a major product liability suit, should also be considered. *In summary, quantitative methods such as NPV and IRR should be considered as an aid to informed decisions but not as a substitute for sound managerial judgment.*

In this same vein, managers should ask sharp questions about any project that has a large NPV, a high IRR, or a high PI. In a perfectly competitive economy, there would be no positive NPV projects—all companies would have the same opportunities, and competition would quickly eliminate any positive NPV. Therefore, positive NPV projects must be predicated on some imperfection in the marketplace, and the longer the life of the project, the longer that imperfection must last. Therefore, managers should be able to identify the imperfection and explain why it will persist before accepting that a project will really have a positive NPV. Valid explanations might include patents or proprietary technology, which is how pharmaceutical and software firms create positive NPV projects. Pfizer's Lipitor® (a cholesteral-reducing medicine) and Microsoft's Windows XP® operating system are examples. Companies can also create positive NPV by being the first entrant into a new market or by creating new products that meet some previously unidentified consumer needs. The Post-it® notes invented by 3M are an example. Similarly, Dell developed procedures for direct sales of microcomputers, and in the process created projects with enormous NPV. Also, companies such as Southwest Airlines have managed to train and motivate their workers better than their competitors, and this has led to positive NPV projects. In all of these cases, the companies developed some source of competitive advantage, and that advantage resulted in positive NPV projects.

This discussion suggests three things: (1) If you can't identify the reason a project has a positive projected NPV, then its actual NPV will probably not be positive. (2) Positive NPV projects don't just happen—they result from hard work to develop some competitive advantage. At the risk of oversimplification, the primary job of a manager is to find and develop areas of competitive advantage. (3) Some competitive advantages last longer than others, with their durability depending on competitors' ability to replicate them. Patents, the control of scarce resources, or large size in an industry where strong economies of scale exist can keep competitors at bay. However, it is relatively easy to replicate nonpatentable features on products. The bottom line is that managers should strive to develop nonreplicable sources of competitive advantage, and if such an advantage cannot be demonstrated, then you should question projects with high NPV, especially if they have long lives.

SELF-TEST

Describe the advantages and disadvantages of the six capital budgeting methods discussed in this chapter.

Should capital budgeting decisions be made solely on the basis of a project's NPV?

What are some possible reasons that a project might have a large NPV?

11.10 Business Practices

Surveys designed to find out which of the criteria managers actually use have been taken over the years. Surveys taken prior to 1999 asked companies to indicate their primary criterion (the method they gave the most weight to), while the most recent one, in 1999, asked what method or methods managers calculated and used. The summary of the results as shown in Table 11-1 reveals some interesting trends.

First, the NPV criterion was not used significantly before the 1980s, but by 1999 it was close to the top in usage. Moreover, informal discussions with companies suggest that if 2005 data were available, NPV would have moved to the top. Second, the IRR method is widely used, but its recent growth is much less dramatic than that of NPV. Third, payback was the most important criterion 40 years ago, but its use as the primary criterion had fallen drastically by 1980. Companies still use payback because it is easy to calculate and it does provide some information,

Table 11-1

Capital Budgeting Methods Used in Practice

	Primary Criterion			Calculate and Use
	1960	1970	1980	1999
NPV	0%	0%	15%	75%
IRR	20	60	65	76
Payback	35	15	5	57
Discounted Payback	NA	NA	NA	29
Other	45	25	15	NA
Totals	100%	100%	100%	

Sources: The 1999 data are from John R. Graham and Campbell R. Harvey, "The Theory and Practice of Corporate Finance: Evidence from the Field," *Journal of Financial Economics,* 2001, pp. 187–244. Data from prior years are our estimates based on averaging data from these studies: J. S. Moore and A. K. Reichert, "An Analysis of the Financial Management Techniques Currently Employed by Large U.S. Corporations," *Journal of Business Finance and Accounting,* Winter 1983, pp. 623–645; and M. T. Stanley and S. B. Block, "A Survey of Multinational Capital Budgeting," *The Financial Review,* March 1984, pp. 36–51.

but it is rarely used today as the primary criterion. Fourth, "other methods," which are generally offshoots of NPV and/or IRR, have been fading as a primary criterion due to the increased use of IRR and especially NPV.

These trends are consistent with our evaluation of the various methods. NPV is the best single criterion, but all of the methods provide useful information, all are easy to calculate, and thus all are used, along with judgment and common sense.[9]

SELF-TEST   What trends in capital budgeting methodology can be seen from Table 11-1?

11.11 Special Applications of Cash Flow Evaluation

Misapplication of the NPV method can lead to errors when two mutually exclusive projects have unequal lives. There are also situations in which an asset should not be operated for its full life. The following sections explain how to evaluate cash flows in these situations.[10]

Comparing Projects with Unequal Lives

Note that a replacement decision involves comparing two mutually exclusive projects: retaining the old asset versus buying a new one. When choosing between two mutually exclusive alternatives with significantly different lives, an adjustment is necessary. For example, suppose a company is planning to modernize its production facilities, and it is considering either a conveyor system (Project C) or some forklift trucks (Project F) for moving materials. The first two sections of Figure 11-6 show the expected net cash flows, NPVs, and IRRs for these two mutually exclusive alternatives. We see that Project C, when discounted at the firm's 11.5% cost of capital, has the higher NPV and thus appears to be the better project.

Although the NPV shown in Figure 11-6 suggests that Project C should be selected, this analysis is incomplete, and the decision to choose Project C is actually incorrect. If we choose Project F, we will have an opportunity to make a similar investment in 3 years, and if cost and revenue conditions continue at the Figure 11-6 levels, this second investment will also be profitable. However, if we choose Project C, we cannot make this second investment. Two different approaches can be used to correctly compare Projects C and F, as shown below.

Replacement Chains The key to the **replacement chain (common life) approach** is to analyze both projects using a common life. In this example, we will find the NPV of Project F over a 6-year period, and then compare this extended NPV with

---

[9]For additional articles that discuss capital budgeting methods used in practice, see Suk H. Kim, Trevor Crick, and Seung H. Kim, "Do Executives Practice What Academics Preach?" *Management Accounting*, November 1986, pp. 49–52; Tarun K. Mukherjee, "Capital Budgeting Surveys: The Past and the Future," *Review of Business and Economic Research*, Spring 1987, pp. 37–56.; Tarun K. Mukherjee, "The Capital Budgeting Process of Large U.S. Firms: An Analysis of Capital Budgeting Manuals," *Managerial Finance*, Number 2/3, 1988, pp. 28–35; Marc Ross, "Capital Budgeting Practices of Twelve Large Manufacturers," *Financial Management*, Winter 1986, pp. 15–22; L. R. Runyan, "Capital Expenditure Decision Making in Small Firms," *Journal of Business Research*, September 1983, pp. 389–397; and Samuel C. Weaver, Donald Peters, Roger Cason, and Joe Daleiden, "Capital Budgeting," *Financial Management*, Spring 1989, pp. 10–17.

[10]For additional discussion of other special applications, see Paul K. Chaney, "Moral Hazard and Capital Budgeting," *Journal of Financial Research*, Summer 1989, pp. 113–128; Edward M. Miller, "Safety Margins and Capital Budgeting Criteria," *Managerial Finance*, Number 2/3, 1988, pp. 1–8; and John C. Woods and Maury R. Randall, "The Net Present Value of Future Investment Opportunities: Its Impact on Shareholder Wealth and Implications for Capital Budgeting Theory," *Financial Management*, Summer 1989, pp. 85–92.

(11-2) What types of projects require more detailed analysis in the capital budgeting process?

(11-3) Explain why the NPV of a relatively long-term project, defined as one for which a high percentage of its cash flows are expected in the distant future, is more sensitive to changes in the cost of capital than is the NPV of a short-term project.

(11-4) Explain why, if two mutually exclusive projects are being compared, the short-term project might have the higher ranking under the NPV criterion if the cost of capital is high, but the long-term project might be deemed better if the cost of capital is low. Would changes in the cost of capital ever cause a change in the IRR ranking of two such projects?

(11-5) In what sense is a reinvestment rate assumption embodied in the NPV, IRR, and MIRR methods? What is the assumed reinvestment rate of each method?

(11-6) Suppose a firm is considering two mutually exclusive projects. One has a life of 6 years and the other a life of 10 years. Would the failure to employ some type of replacement chain analysis bias an NPV analysis against one of the projects? Explain.

Self-Test Problem   Solution Appears in Appendix A

(ST-1)
Project Analysis

You are a financial analyst for the Hittle Company. The director of capital budgeting has asked you to analyze two proposed capital investments, Projects X and Y. Each project has a cost of $10,000, and the cost of capital for each project is 12%. The projects' expected net cash flows are as follows:

	Expected Net Cash Flows	
Year	Project X	Project Y
0	($10,000)	($10,000)
1	6,500	3,500
2	3,000	3,500
3	3,000	3,500
4	1,000	3,500

a. Calculate each project's payback period, net present value (NPV), internal rate of return (IRR), and modified internal rate of return (MIRR).
b. Which project or projects should be accepted if they are independent?
c. Which project should be accepted if they are mutually exclusive?
d. How might a change in the cost of capital produce a conflict between the NPV and IRR rankings of these two projects? Would this conflict exist if r were 5%? (Hint: Plot the NPV profiles.)
e. Why does the conflict exist?

Problems   Answers Appear in Appendix B

Easy Problems 1–7

(11-1)
NPV

A project has an initial cost of $52,125, expected net cash inflows of $12,000 per year for 8 years, and a cost of capital of 12%. What is the project's NPV? (Hint: Begin by constructing a time line.)

(11-2)
IRR

Refer to Problem 11-1. What is the project's IRR?

(11-3)
MIRR

Refer to Problem 11-1. What is the project's MIRR?

(11-4)
Profitability Index

Refer to Problem 11-1. What is the project's PI?

(11-5)
Payback

Refer to Problem 11-1. What is the project's payback period?

(11-6)
Discounted Payback

Refer to Problem 11-1. What is the project's discounted payback period?

(11-7)
NPV

Your division is considering two investment projects, each of which requires an up-front expenditure of $15 million. You estimate that the investments will produce the following net cash flows:

Year	Project A	Project B
1	$ 5,000,000	$20,000,000
2	10,000,000	10,000,000
3	20,000,000	6,000,000

What are the two projects' net present values, assuming the cost of capital is 10%? 5%? 15%?

Intermediate Problems 8–18

(11-8)
NPVs, IRRs, and MIRRs for Independent Projects

Edelman Engineering is considering including two pieces of equipment, a truck and an overhead pulley system, in this year's capital budget. The projects are independent. The cash outlay for the truck is $17,100, and that for the pulley system is $22,430. The firm's cost of capital is 14%. After-tax cash flows, including depreciation, are as follows:

Year	Truck	Pulley
1	$5,100	$7,500
2	5,100	7,500
3	5,100	7,500
4	5,100	7,500
5	5,100	7,500

Calculate the IRR, the NPV, and the MIRR for each project, and indicate the correct accept/reject decision for each.

(11-9)
NPVs and IRRs for Mutually Exclusive Projects

Davis Industries must choose between a gas-powered and an electric-powered forklift truck for moving materials in its factory. Since both forklifts perform the same function, the firm will choose only one. (They are mutually exclusive investments.) The electric-powered truck will cost more, but it will be less expensive to operate; it will cost $22,000, whereas the gas-powered truck will cost $17,500. The cost of capital that applies to both investments is 12%. The life for both types of truck is estimated to be 6 years, during which time the net cash flows for the electric-powered truck will be $6,290 per year and those for the gas-powered truck will be $5,000 per year. Annual net cash flows include depreciation expenses. Calculate the NPV and IRR for each type of truck, and decide which to recommend.

(11-10)
Capital Budgeting Methods

Project S has a cost of $10,000 and is expected to produce benefits (cash flows) of $3,000 per year for 5 years. Project L costs $25,000 and is expected to produce cash flows of $7,400 per year for 5 years. Calculate the two projects' NPVs, IRRs, MIRRs, and PIs, assuming a cost of capital of 12%. Which project would be selected, assuming they are mutually exclusive, using each ranking method? Which should actually be selected?

(11-11)
MIRR and NPV

Your company is considering two mutually exclusive projects, X and Y, whose costs and cash flows are shown below:

Year	X	Y
0	($1,000)	($1,000)
1	100	1,000
2	300	100
3	400	50
4	700	50

The projects are equally risky, and their cost of capital is 12%. You must make a recommendation, and you must base it on the modified IRR (MIRR). What is the MIRR of the better project?

(11-12)
NPV and IRR Analysis

After discovering a new gold vein in the Colorado mountains, CTC Mining Corporation must decide whether to mine the deposit. The most cost-effective method of mining gold is sulfuric acid extraction, a process that results in environmental damage. To go ahead with the extraction, CTC must spend $900,000 for new mining equipment and pay $165,000 for its installation. The gold mined will net the firm an estimated $350,000 each year over the 5-year life of the vein. CTC's cost of capital is 14%. For the purposes of this problem, assume that the cash inflows occur at the end of the year.
a. What are the NPV and IRR of this project?
b. Should this project be undertaken, ignoring environmental concerns?
c. How should environmental effects be considered when evaluating this, or any other, project? How might these effects change your decision in part b?

(11-13)
NPV and IRR Analysis

Cummings Products Company is considering two mutually exclusive investments. The projects' expected net cash flows are as follows:

	Expected Net Cash Flows	
Year	Project A	Project B
0	($300)	($405)
1	(387)	134
2	(193)	134
3	(100)	134
4	600	134
5	600	134
6	850	134
7	(180)	0

a. Construct NPV profiles for Projects A and B.

b. What is each project's IRR?

c. If you were told that each project's cost of capital was 10%, which project should be selected? If the cost of capital was 17%, what would be the proper choice?

d. What is each project's MIRR at a cost of capital of 10%? At 17%? (Hint: Consider Period 7 as the end of Project B's life.)

e. What is the crossover rate, and what is its significance?

(11-14)
Timing Differences

The Ewert Exploration Company is considering two mutually exclusive plans for extracting oil on property for which it has mineral rights. Both plans call for the expenditure of $10,000,000 to drill development wells. Under Plan A, all the oil will be extracted in 1 year, producing a cash flow at t = 1 of $12,000,000, while under Plan B, cash flows will be $1,750,000 per year for 20 years.

a. What are the annual incremental cash flows that will be available to Ewert Exploration if it undertakes Plan B rather than Plan A? (Hint: Subtract Plan A's flows from B's.)

b. If the firm accepts Plan A, then invests the extra cash generated at the end of Year 1, what rate of return (reinvestment rate) would cause the cash flows from reinvestment to equal the cash flows from Plan B?

c. Suppose a company has a cost of capital of 10%. Is it logical to assume that it would take on all available independent projects (of average risk) with returns greater than 10%? Further, if all available projects with returns greater than 10% have been taken, would this mean that cash flows from past investments would have an opportunity cost of only 10%, because all the firm could do with these cash flows would be to replace money that has a cost of 10%? Finally, does this imply that the cost of capital is the correct rate to assume for the reinvestment of a project's cash flows?

d. Construct NPV profiles for Plans A and B, identify each project's IRR, and indicate the crossover rate of return.

(11-15)
Scale Differences

The Pinkerton Publishing Company is considering two mutually exclusive expansion plans. Plan A calls for the expenditure of $50 million on a large-scale, integrated plant which will provide an expected cash flow stream of $8 million per year for 20 years. Plan B calls for the expenditure of $15 million to build a somewhat less efficient, more labor-intensive plant which has an expected cash flow stream of $3.4 million per year for 20 years. The firm's cost of capital is 10%.

    a.   Calculate each project's NPV and IRR.

    b.   Set up a Project Δ by showing the cash flows that will exist if the firm goes with the large plant rather than the smaller plant. What are the NPV and the IRR for this Project Δ?

    c.   Graph the NPV profiles for Plan A, Plan B, and Project Δ.

    d.   Give a logical explanation, based on reinvestment rates and opportunity costs, as to why the NPV method is better than the IRR method when the firm's cost of capital is constant at some value such as 10%.

(11-16)
Unequal Lives

Shao Airlines is considering two alternative planes. Plane A has an expected life of 5 years, will cost $100 million, and will produce net cash flows of $30 million per year. Plane B has a life of 10 years, will cost $132 million, and will produce net cash flows of $25 million per year. Shao plans to serve the route for 10 years. Inflation in operating costs, airplane costs, and fares is expected to be zero, and the company's cost of capital is 12%. By how much would the value of the company increase if it accepted the better project (plane)? What is the equivalent annual annuity for each plane?

(11-17)
Unequal Lives

The Perez Company has the opportunity to invest in one of two mutually exclusive machines that will produce a product it will need for the foreseeable future. Machine A costs $10 million but realizes after-tax inflows of $4 million per year for 4 years. After 4 years, the machine must be replaced. Machine B costs $15 million and realizes after-tax inflows of $3.5 million per year for 8 years, after which it must be replaced. Assume that machine prices are not expected to rise because inflation will be offset by cheaper components used in the machines. The cost of capital is 10%. By how much would the value of the company increase if it accepted the better machine? What is the equivalent annual annuity for each machine?

(11-18)
Unequal Lives

Filkins Fabric Company is considering the replacement of its old, fully depreciated knitting machine. Two new models are available: Machine 190-3, which has a cost of $190,000, a 3-year expected life, and after-tax cash flows (labor savings and depreciation) of $87,000 per year; and Machine 360-6, which has a cost of $360,000, a 6-year life, and after-tax cash flows of $98,300 per year. Knitting machine prices are not expected to rise, because inflation will be offset by cheaper components (microprocessors) used in the machines. Assume that Filkins' cost of capital is 14%. Should the firm replace its old knitting machine, and, if so, which new machine should it use? By how much would the value of the company increase if it accepted the better machine? What is the equivalent annual annuity for each machine?

**Challenging
Problems 19–22**

(11-19)
Multiple Rates of
Return

The Ulmer Uranium Company is deciding whether or not it should open a strip mine, the net cost of which is $4.4 million. Net cash inflows are expected to be $27.7 million, all coming at the end of Year 1. The land must be returned to its natural state at a cost of $25 million, payable at the end of Year 2.

    a.   Plot the project's NPV profile.

    b.   Should the project be accepted if $r = 8\%$? If $r = 14\%$? Explain your reasoning.

    c.   Can you think of some other capital budgeting situations where negative cash flows during or at the end of the project's life might lead to multiple IRRs?

d. What is the project's MIRR at r = 8%? At r = 14%? Does the MIRR method lead to the same accept/reject decision as the NPV method?

The Aubey Coffee Company is evaluating the within-plant distribution system for its new roasting, grinding, and packing plant. The two alternatives are (1) a conveyor system with a high initial cost, but low annual operating costs, and (2) several forklift trucks, which cost less, but have considerably higher operating costs. The decision to construct the plant has already been made, and the choice here will have no effect on the overall revenues of the project. The cost of capital for the plant is 8%, and the projects' expected net costs are listed in the table:

	Expected Net Cost	
Year	Conveyor	Forklift
0	($500,000)	($200,000)
1	(120,000)	(160,000)
2	(120,000)	(160,000)
3	(120,000)	(160,000)
4	(120,000)	(160,000)
5	(20,000)	(160,000)

a. What is the IRR of each alternative?
b. What is the present value of costs of each alternative? Which method should be chosen?

Your division is considering two investment projects, each of which requires an upfront expenditure of $25 million. You estimate that the cost of capital is 10% and that the investments will produce the following after-tax cash flows (in millions of dollars):

Year	Project A	Project B
1	5	20
2	10	10
3	15	8
4	20	6

a. What is the regular payback period for each of the projects?
b. What is the discounted payback period for each of the projects?
c. If the two projects are independent and the cost of capital is 10%, which project or projects should the firm undertake?
d. If the two projects are mutually exclusive and the cost of capital is 5%, which project should the firm undertake?
e. If the two projects are mutually exclusive and the cost of capital is 15%, which project should the firm undertake?
f. What is the crossover rate?
g. If the cost of capital is 10%, what is the modified IRR (MIRR) of each project?

The Scampini Supplies Company recently purchased a new delivery truck. The new truck cost $22,500, and it is expected to generate net after-tax operating cash flows, including depreciation, of $6,250 per year. The truck has a 5-year expected life. The expected salvage values after tax adjustments for the truck are given below. The company's cost of capital is 10%.

Year	Annual Operating Cash Flow	Salvage Value
0	($22,500)	$22,500
1	6,250	17,500
2	6,250	14,000
3	6,250	11,000
4	6,250	5,000
5	6,250	0

a. Should the firm operate the truck until the end of its 5-year physical life, or, if not, what is its optimal economic life?

b. Would the introduction of salvage values, in addition to operating cash flows, ever *reduce* the expected NPV and/or IRR of a project?

Spreadsheet Problem

(11-23)
Build a Model: Capital Budgeting Tools

e-resource

Start with the partial model in the file *FM12 Ch 11 P23 Build a Model.xls* from the textbook's Web site. Gardial Fisheries is considering two mutually exclusive investments. The projects' expected net cash flows are as follows:

	Expected Net Cash Flows	
Year	Project A	Project B
0	($375)	($575)
1	(300)	190
2	(200)	190
3	(100)	190
4	600	190
5	600	190
6	926	190
7	(200)	0

a. If you were told that each project's cost of capital was 12%, which project should be selected? If the cost of capital was 18%, what would be the proper choice?

b. Construct NPV profiles for Projects A and B.

c. What is each project's IRR?

d. What is the crossover rate, and what is its significance?

e. What is each project's MIRR at a cost of capital of 12%? At r = 18%? (Hint: Consider Period 7 as the end of Project B's life.)

f. What is the regular payback period for these two projects?

g. At a cost of capital of 12%, what is the discounted payback period for these two projects?

h. What is the profitability index for each project if the cost of capital is 12%?

Cyberproblem

e-resource

Please go to the textbook's Web site to access any Cyberproblems.

Mini Case

You have just graduated from the MBA program of a large university, and one of your favorite courses was "Today's Entrepreneurs." In fact, you enjoyed it so much you have decided you want to "be your own boss." While you were in the master's program, your grandfather died and left you $1 million to do with as you please. You are not an inventor, and you do not have a trade skill that you can market; however, you have decided that you would like to purchase at least one established franchise in the fast-foods area, maybe two (if profitable). The problem is that you have never been one to stay with any project for too long, so you figure that your time frame is 3 years. After 3 years you will go on to something else.

You have narrowed your selection down to two choices: (1) Franchise L, Lisa's Soups, Salads, & Stuff, and (2) Franchise S, Sam's Fabulous Fried Chicken. The net cash flows shown below include the price you would receive for selling the franchise in Year 3 and the forecast of how each franchise will do over the 3-year period. Franchise L's cash flows will start off slowly but will increase rather quickly as people become more health conscious, while Franchise S's cash flows will start off high but will trail off as other chicken competitors enter the marketplace and as people become more health conscious and avoid fried foods. Franchise L serves breakfast and lunch, while Franchise S serves only dinner, so it is possible for you to invest in both franchises. You see these franchises as perfect complements to one another: You could attract both the lunch and dinner crowds and the health conscious and not so health conscious crowds without the franchises directly competing against one another.

Here are the net cash flows (in thousands of dollars):

	Expected Net Cash Flow	
Year	Franchise L	Franchise S
0	($100)	($100)
1	10	70
2	60	50
3	80	20

Depreciation, salvage values, net working capital requirements, and tax effects are all included in these cash flows.

You also have made subjective risk assessments of each franchise and concluded that both franchises have risk characteristics that require a return of 10%. You must now determine whether one or both of the franchises should be accepted.

a. What is capital budgeting?

b. What is the difference between independent and mutually exclusive projects?

c. (1) Define the term *net present value (NPV)*. What is each franchise's NPV?

    (2) What is the rationale behind the NPV method? According to NPV, which franchise or franchises should be accepted if they are independent? Mutually exclusive?

    (3) Would the NPVs change if the cost of capital changed?

d. (1) Define the term *internal rate of return (IRR)*. What is each franchise's IRR?

    (2) How is the IRR on a project related to the YTM on a bond?

    (3) What is the logic behind the IRR method? According to IRR, which franchises should be accepted if they are independent? Mutually exclusive?

    (4) Would the franchises' IRRs change if the cost of capital changed?

e. (1) Draw NPV profiles for Franchises L and S. At what discount rate do the profiles cross?

(2) Look at your NPV profile graph without referring to the actual NPVs and IRRs. Which franchise or franchises should be accepted if they are independent? Mutually exclusive? Explain. Are your answers correct at any cost of capital less than 23.6%?

f. (1) What is the underlying cause of ranking conflicts between NPV and IRR?

(2) What is the "reinvestment rate assumption," and how does it affect the NPV versus IRR conflict?

(3) Which method is the best? Why?

g. (1) Define the term *modified IRR (MIRR)*. Find the MIRRs for Franchises L and S.

(2) What are the MIRR's advantages and disadvantages vis-à-vis the regular IRR? What are the MIRR's advantages and disadvantages vis-à-vis the NPV?

h. As a separate project (Project P), you are considering sponsoring a pavilion at the upcoming World's Fair. The pavilion would cost $800,000, and it is expected to result in $5 million of incremental cash inflows during its 1 year of operation. However, it would then take another year, and $5 million of costs, to demolish the site and return it to its original condition. Thus, Project P's expected net cash flows look like this (in millions of dollars):

Year	Net Cash Flows
0	($0.8)
1	5.0
2	(5.0)

The project is estimated to be of average risk, so its cost of capital is 10%.

(1) What are normal and nonnormal cash flows?

(2) What is Project P's NPV? What is its IRR? Its MIRR?

(3) Draw Project P's NPV profile. Does Project P have normal or nonnormal cash flows? Should this project be accepted?

i. What does the profitability index (PI) measure? What are the PI's of Franchises S and L?

j. (1) What is the payback period? Find the paybacks for Franchises L and S.

(2) What is the rationale for the payback method? According to the payback criterion, which franchise or franchises should be accepted if the firm's maximum acceptable payback is 2 years, and if Franchises L and S are independent? If they are mutually exclusive?

(3) What is the difference between the regular and discounted payback periods?

(4) What is the main disadvantage of discounted payback? Is the payback method of any real usefulness in capital budgeting decisions?

k. In an unrelated analysis, you have the opportunity to choose between the following two mutually exclusive projects:

	Expected Net Cash Flow	
Year	Project S	Project L
0	($100,000)	($100,000)
1	60,000	33,500
2	60,000	33,500
3	—	33,500
4	—	33,500

The projects provide a necessary service, so whichever one is selected is expected to be repeated into the foreseeable future. Both projects have a 10% cost of capital.

(1) What is each project's initial NPV without replication?

(2) What is each project's equivalent annual annuity?

(3) Now apply the replacement chain approach to determine the projects' extended NPVs. Which project should be chosen?

(4) Now assume that the cost to replicate Project S in 2 years will increase to $105,000 because of inflationary pressures. How should the analysis be handled now, and which project should be chosen?

l. You are also considering another project that has a physical life of 3 years; that is, the machinery will be totally worn out after 3 years. However, if the project were terminated prior to the end of 3 years, the machinery would have a positive salvage value. Here are the project's estimated cash flows:

Year	Initial Investment and Operating Cash Flows	End-of-Year Net Salvage Value
0	($5,000)	$5,000
1	2,100	3,100
2	2,000	2,000
3	1,750	0

Using the 10% cost of capital, what is the project's NPV if it is operated for the full 3 years? Would the NPV change if the company planned to terminate the project at the end of Year 2? At the end of Year 1? What is the project's optimal (economic) life?

m. After examining all the potential projects, you discover that there are many more projects this year with positive NPVs than in a normal year. What two problems might this extra large capital budget cause?

Selected Additional Cases

The following cases from Textchoice, *Cengage Learning's online library, cover many of the concepts discussed in this chapter and are available at* **http://www.textchoice2.com.**

Klein-Brigham Series:
Case 11, "Chicago Valve Company."

Brigham-Buzzard Series:
Case 6, "Powerline Network Corporation (Basics of Capital Budgeting)."

chapter 12

Cash Flow Estimation and Risk Analysis

Home Depot Inc. grew phenomenally during the 1990s, and it is still growing rapidly. At the beginning of 1990, it had 118 stores and annual sales of $2.8 billion. It now (mid-2006) has more than 2,065 stores and sales of more than $84 billion. The stock has also performed quite well—a $10,000 investment in 1990 would now be worth about $129,200, for an annual return of more than 17%!

For a typical new store, Home Depot spends around $20 million to purchase land, construct a new store, and stock it with inventory. Each new store thus represents a major capital expenditure, so the company must use capital budgeting techniques to determine if a potential store's expected cash flows are sufficient to cover its costs. Home Depot uses information from its existing stores to forecast new stores' expected cash flows. Thus far, its forecasts have been outstanding, but there are always risks that must be considered.

First, sales might be less than projected if the economy weakens. Second, some of Home Depot's customers might in the future bypass it altogether and buy directly from manufacturers through the Internet or from competitors such as Lowe's. Third, new stores could take sales away from existing stores, or "cannibalize" them.

To broaden its customer base from do-it-yourself customers and professional contractors, Home Depot also operates its Expo Design Center chain, which provides decorating advice, materials, and installation for middle- and upper-income customers.

The decision to expand requires a detailed assessment of the forecasted cash flows, including the risk that the forecasted level of sales might not be realized. In this chapter, we describe techniques for estimating a project's cash flows and their associated risk. As you read this chapter, think about how Home Depot might use these techniques to evaluate its capital budgeting decisions.

The basic principles of capital budgeting were covered in Chapter 11. Given a project's expected cash flows, it is easy to calculate its NPV, IRR, MIRR, PI, payback, and discounted payback. Unfortunately, cash flows are rarely just given—rather, managers must estimate them based on information collected from sources both inside and outside the company. Moreover, uncertainty surrounds the cash flow estimates, and some projects are riskier than others. In the first part of this chapter, we develop procedures for estimating the cash flows associated with capital budgeting projects. Then, in the second part, we discuss techniques used to measure and take account of project risk.

12.1 Estimating Cash Flows

e-resource

The textbook's Web site contains an *Excel* file that will guide you through the chapter's calculations. The file for this chapter is *FM12 Ch 12 Tool Kit.xls*, and we encourage you to open the file and follow along as you read the chapter.

The most important, but also the most difficult, step in capital budgeting is estimating **project cash flows.** Many variables are involved, and many individuals and departments participate in the process. For example, the forecasts of unit sales and sales prices are normally made by the marketing group, based on their knowledge of price elasticity, advertising effects, the state of the economy, competitors' reactions, and trends in consumers' tastes. Similarly, the capital outlays associated with a new product are generally obtained from the engineering and product development staffs, while operating costs are estimated by cost accountants, production experts, personnel specialists, purchasing agents, and so forth.

A proper analysis includes (1) obtaining information from various departments such as engineering and marketing, (2) ensuring that everyone involved with the forecast uses a consistent set of realistic economic assumptions, and (3) making sure that no biases are inherent in the forecasts. This last point is extremely important, because some managers become emotionally involved with pet projects, and others seek to build empires. Both problems cause cash flow forecast biases which make bad projects look good—on paper!

It is vital to identify the **relevant cash flows,** defined as the specific set of cash flows that should be considered in the decision at hand. Analysts often make errors in estimating cash flows, but two cardinal rules can help you minimize mistakes: (1) Capital budgeting decisions must be based on *cash flows*, not accounting income. (2) Only *incremental cash flows* are relevant.

Recall from Chapter 3 that **free cash flow (FCF)** is the cash flow available for distribution to investors. In a nutshell, the relevant cash flow for a project is the

---

Corporate Valuation, Cash Flows, and Risk Analysis

You can calculate the free cash flows (FCF) for a project in much the same way as for a firm. When the project's expected free cash flows are discounted at the project's appropriate risk-adjusted rate, r, the result is the project's value. This chapter focuses on how to estimate the size and risk of a project's cash flows.

$$NPV = \left[\frac{FCF_1}{(1 + r)^1} + \frac{FCF_2}{(1 + r)^2} + \frac{FCF_3}{(1 + r)^3} + \cdots + \frac{FCF_N}{(1 + r)^N} \right] - \text{Initial cost.}$$

additional free cash flow that the company can expect if it implements the project. This is also called the **incremental cash flow,** and it is the cash flow above and beyond what the company could expect if it doesn't implement the project. Chapter 3 defined FCF as:

$$\text{FCF} = \frac{\text{Net operating profit}}{\text{after taxes (NOPAT)}} - \frac{\text{Net investment in}}{\text{operating capital.}} \qquad (12\text{-}1)$$

When working with a company's financial statements, as we did in Chapter 3, the definition above is the most straightforward one to apply. But when estimating a project's cash flows, there are two reasons that make it more convenient to use a modified version of this equation. First, we are going to estimate the individual components that make up NOPAT and the net investment in operating capital. We can use these individual cash flow components directly in our analysis rather than taking the extra step to combine them so they appear exactly like a financial statement. Second, some of the cash flow components occur at the project's inception, some throughout its life, and some at the project's termination. Therefore, we typically show them in our analysis in roughly this order.

As shown in Chapter 3, NOPAT is equal to the earnings before interest and taxes (EBIT) that remain after paying operating taxes. By adding depreciation both to NOPAT and to the net investment in operating capital, an equivalent definition of FCF is

$$\text{FCF} = \text{EBIT}(1 - T)$$
$$+ \text{Depreciation} - \left(\frac{\text{Net investment in}}{\text{operating capital}} - \text{Depreciation} \right). \qquad (12\text{-}2)$$

Chapter 3 defined operating cash flow as the sum of depreciation and EBIT$(1 - T)$. That chapter also showed that the net investment in operating capital is the sum of the net investment in long-term fixed assets and the investment in net operating working capital (NOWC), where NOWC is defined as operating current assets less operating current liabilities. The net investment in long-term fixed assets is equal to the gross fixed asset expenditure minus depreciation. Using these relationships, we can rewrite Equation 12-2 as

$$\text{FCF} = \frac{\text{Operating}}{\text{cash flows}} - \frac{\text{Gross fixed asset}}{\text{expenditures}} - \left(\frac{\Delta\text{Operating current assets} -}{\Delta\text{Operating current liabilities}} \right). \qquad (12\text{-}3)$$

Some projects require expenditures on fixed assets at different times during their lives, but most require only an initial investment outlay in gross fixed assets. Also, the fixed assets of many projects have some salvage value at the end of the project. Therefore, it is common in capital budgeting analysis to break the gross fixed asset expenditures into the cash flows due to the initial investment outlay and the cash flows due to salvage. Substituting these definitions into Equation 12-3 gives us the usual approach to defining a project's free cash flows:

$$\text{FCF} = \frac{\text{Investment outlay}}{\text{cash flow}} + \frac{\text{Operating}}{\text{cash flow}} + \frac{\text{NOWC}}{\text{cash flow}} + \frac{\text{Salvage}}{\text{cash flow,}} \qquad (12\text{-}4)$$

where all cash flows are after taxes and the sign of the cash flow indicates whether it is an inflow or outflow. The project's free cash flows are also sometimes called **net cash flow,** and we will use the terms interchangeably.

It is worth mentioning that project analysis focuses on expected cash flows, not accounting net income. Accounting net income is based on the depreciation rate the firm's accountants choose, not necessarily the depreciation rates allowed by the IRS. Also, net income is measured after the deduction of interest expenses, whereas net cash flow focuses on operating cash flow. Moreover, the investment in working capital is not deducted from accounting income. For these and other reasons, net income is generally different from cash flow. Each has a role in financial management, *but for capital budgeting purposes it is the project's net cash flow, not its accounting net income, that is relevant.*

What is the most important step in a capital budgeting analysis?
What are the major components of a project's free cash flows?

12.2 Project Analysis: An Example

We illustrate the principles of capital budgeting analysis by examining a new project being considered by Regency Integrated Chips (RIC), a large Nashville-based technology company. This is a **new expansion project,** defined as one where the firm invests in new assets to increase sales. Following is some background information on the project.

Background on the Project

RIC's research and development department has been applying its expertise in microprocessor technology to develop a small computer designed to control home appliances. Once programmed, the computer will automatically control the heating and air-conditioning systems, security system, hot water heater, and even small appliances such as a coffee maker. By increasing a home's energy efficiency, the computer can cut costs enough to pay for itself within a few years. Development has now reached the stage where a decision must be made about whether or not to go forward with full-scale production.

RIC's marketing vice president believes that annual sales would be 20,000 units if the units were priced at $3,000 each, so annual sales are estimated at $60 million. RIC expects no growth in unit sales, and it believes that the unit price will rise by 2% each year. The engineering department has reported that the project will require additional manufacturing space, and RIC currently has an option to purchase an existing building, at a cost of $12 million, which would meet this need. The building would be bought and paid for on December 31, 2008. RIC bases depreciation on the Modified Accelerated Cost Recovery System (MACRS), which we explain in a later section. For depreciation purposes, the building falls into the MACRS 39-year class.

The necessary equipment would be purchased and installed in late 2008, and it would also be paid for on December 31, 2008. The equipment falls into the MACRS 5-year class. The equipment would cost $7.8 million and would require $0.2 million for shipping and installation. The depreciable basis under MACRS is equal to the purchase price of an asset plus any shipping and installation costs.

The basis is *not* adjusted for *salvage value* (which is the estimated market value of the asset at the end of its useful life), so the depreciation basis for the building is $7.8 + $0.2 = $8 million.[1]

The project's estimated economic life is 4 years. At the end of that time, the building is expected to have a market value of $7.5 million and a book value of $10.908 million, whereas the equipment would have a market value of $2 million and a book value of $1.36 million.

The production department has estimated that variable manufacturing costs would be $2,100 per unit and that fixed overhead costs, excluding depreciation, would be $8 million a year. They expect variable costs to rise by 2% per year, and fixed costs to rise by 1% per year. Depreciation expenses would be determined in accordance with MACRS rates.

RIC's marginal federal-plus-state tax rate is 40%; its cost of capital is 12%; and, for capital budgeting purposes, the company's policy is to assume that operating cash flows occur at the end of each year. Because the plant would begin operations on January 1, 2009, the first full year of operating cash flows would end on December 31, 2009.

Several other points should be noted: (1) RIC is a relatively large corporation, with sales of more than $4 billion, and it takes on many investments each year. Thus, if the computer control project does not work out, it will not bankrupt the company—management can afford to take a chance on the computer control project. (2) If the project is accepted, the company will be contractually obligated to operate it for its full 4-year life. Management must make this commitment to its component suppliers. (3) Returns on this project would be positively correlated with returns on RIC's other projects and also with the stock market—the project should do well if other parts of the firm and the general economy are strong.

Assume that you have been assigned to conduct the capital budgeting analysis. For now, assume that the project has the same risk as an average project and use the corporate weighted average cost of capital, 12%.

Estimation of the Cash Flows

Most projects are analyzed using a spreadsheet program such as *Excel*, and this one is no exception. The analysis is shown in Table 12-1 and is divided into five parts: (1) Input Data, (2) Depreciation Schedule, (3) Net Salvage Values, (4) Projected Net Cash Flows, and (5) Key Output. Note that numbers in the printed table are rounded from the actual numbers in the spreadsheet, although the spreadsheet uses the unrounded number for all calculations.

e-resource

See **FM12 Ch 12 Tool Kit.xls** at the textbook's Web site for all calculations.

Input Data (Part 1) Part 1 of Table 12-1, the Input Data section, provides the basic data used in the analysis. The inputs are really "assumptions"—thus, in the analysis we *assume* that 20,000 units can be sold at a price of $3 per unit (the sales price is actually $3,000, but for convenience we show all dollars in thousands). Some of the inputs are known with near certainty—for example, the 40% tax rate is not likely to change. Others are more speculative—units sold and the variable cost percentage are in this category. Obviously, if sales or costs are different from the assumed

---

[1] Regardless of whether accelerated or straight-line depreciation is used, the basis is not adjusted by the salvage value when calculating the depreciation that is used to determine taxable income.

levels, then profits and cash flows, hence NPV and IRR, will differ from their projected levels. Later in the chapter, we discuss how changes in the inputs affect the results. We usually show a key output, such as NPV, in the same section as the inputs, so that we can quickly see how a change in an input affects the output.

Table 12-1

Analysis of a New (Expansion) Project: Parts 1 and 2 (Dollars in Thousands)

	A	B	C	D	E	F	G	H	I
24	Part 1. Input Data								
25							Key Output: NPV	=	$5,809
26	Building cost (= Depreciable basis)			$12,000					
27	Equipment cost (= Depreciable basis)			$8,000		Market value of building at salvage			$7,500
28	Net Operating WC / Sales			10%		Market value of equip. at salvage			$2,000
29	First year sales (in units)			20,000		Tax rate			40%
30	Growth rate in units sold			0.0%		WACC			12.0%
31	Sales price per unit			$3.00		Inflation: growth in sales price			2.0%
32	Variable cost per unit			$2.10		Inflation: growth in VC per unit			2.0%
33	Fixed costs			$8,000		Inflation: growth in fixed costs			1.0%
34									
35	Part 2. Depreciation Schedule[a]					Years			
36					1	2	3	4	Cumulative
37					2009	2010	2011	2012	Depr'n
38	Building depr'n rate				1.3%	2.6%	2.6%	2.6%	
39	Building depr'n				$156	$312	$312	$312	$1,092
40	Ending book val: Cost - cum. depr'n				11,844	11,532	11,220	$10,908	
41									
42	Equipment depr'n rate				20.0%	32.0%	19.0%	12.0%	
43	Equipment depr'n				$1,600	$2,560	$1,520	$960	$6,640
44	Ending book val: Cost - cum. depr'n				6,400	3,840	2,320	$1,360	
45									
46	[a] The depreciation rates are multiplied by the depreciable basis ($12,000 for the building and $8,000 for the equipment) to determine the yearly depreciation								
47	expense. The correct depreciation percentages for the building depend upon the month that the building is put in service. Because this analysis assumes that								
48	all cash flows occur at the end of the year, and to prevent unnecessary complexity, we have rounded the depreciation percentages for the building. See the Tab								
49	named DeprTables for more details.								

Table 12-1

Analysis of a New (Expansion) Project: Part 3 (Dollars in Thousands)

	A	B	C	D	E	F	G	H	I
51	Part 3. Net Salvage Values at End of Project								
52					Building	Equipment	Total		
53	Market value when salvaged				$7,500	$2,000			
54	Book value when salvaged[b]				10,908	1,360			
55	Expected gain or loss[c]				-3,408	640			
56	Taxes paid or tax credit				-1,363	256			
57	Net cash flow from salvage[d]				$8,863	$1,744	$10,607		
58									
59	[b] Book value equals depreciable basis (initial cost in this case) minus accumulated MACRS depreciation. For the building, accumulated depreciation equals								
60	$1,092, so book value equals $12,000 - $1,092 = $10,908. For the equipment, accumulated depreciation equals $6,640, so book value equals $8,000 - $6,640 =								
61	$1,360.								
62									
63	[c] Building: $7,500 market value - $10,908 book value = -$3,408 a loss. This represents a shortfall in depreciation taken versus "true" depreciation, and it is								
64	treated as an operating expense for Year 4. Equipment: $2,000 market value- $1,360 book value = $640 profit. Here the depreciation charge exceeds the "true"								
65	depreciation, and the difference is called "depreciation recapture." It is taxed as ordinary income in Year 4. The actual book value at the time of disposition								
66	depends on the month of disposition. We have simplified the analysis and assumed that there will be a full year of depreciation in Year 4.								
67	[d] Net cash flow from salvage equals salvage (market) value minus taxes. For the building, the loss results in a tax credit, so net salvage value = $7,500 - (-$1,363)								
68	= $8,863.								

Depreciation Schedule (Part 2) Rows 38 and 42 give the yearly MACRS depreciation rates for the building and equipment; a later section explains why these are the appropriate rates, but for now we will just use them. Rows 39 and 43 give the annual depreciation expense, calculated as the depreciation rate multiplied by the asset's depreciable basis. Rows 40 and 44 show the book values at the end of each year, found by subtracting the accumulated annual depreciation from the depreciable basis.

Net Salvage Values (Part 3) See Part 3 of Table 12-1 for the calculation of after-tax salvage cash flows. Row 53 shows the salvage values for the building and equipment, which are the prices the company expects to receive when it sells the assets at the end of the project's life. Row 54 shows the book values at the end of Year 4; these values are calculated in Part 2. Row 55 shows the expected gain or loss, defined as the difference between the sale price and the book value. For tax purposes, gains and losses on depreciable assets are treated as ordinary income, not capital gains or losses.

RIC expects to sell the equipment for $2,000 even though it has a book value of only $1,360. To the IRS, this signifies that the depreciation rates were too high during the project's life, which allowed the company to shield too much of its earlier income from taxes. Therefore, the gain is called "depreciation recapture" by the IRS and is taxed as ordinary income. RIC's $640 gain on the sale of the equipment will be taxed at RIC's 40 percent corporate tax rate, resulting in a tax liability of $640(0.40) = $256, as shown in Row 56. Thus, RIC's net after-tax cash flow from the sale of the equipment is the salvage price minus the tax: $2,000 − $256 = $1,744.

As shown in Row 54, RIC's building will have a book value of $10,908 at the time of salvage, but the company expects to realize only $7,500 when it is sold. This would result in a loss of $3,408. This indicates that the building should have been depreciated at a faster rate—only if depreciation had been $3,408 larger would the book and market values have been equal. To compensate for the fact that not enough depreciation was charged during the building's life, the Tax Code stipulates that losses on the sale of operating assets can be used to reduce taxable ordinary income, just as depreciation reduces income. RIC expects to sell the building for $7,500 and receive a tax credit of $3,408(0.4) = $1,363. The resulting net after-tax cash flow is $7,500 + $1,336 = $8,863, as shown in Row 57.[2] Thus, RIC expects to net $8,863 from the sale of the building and $1,744 from the equipment, for a total of $10,607.[3]

Projected Net Cash Flows (Part 4) This section of Table 12-1 uses the information developed in Parts 1, 2, and 3 to find the projected cash flows over the project's life. Five periods are shown, from Year 0 to Year 4, in Columns E through I.

The initial investment outlays for long-term assets are shown as negative cash flows in Cells E75 and E76 for Year 0. Had there been additional fixed assets purchased during the project's life, their cash flows also would have been shown.

Rows 79 through 90 show the calculations for the operating cash flows. We begin with sales revenues, found as the product of units sold and the sales price. Next, we subtract variable costs, which were assumed to be $2.10 per unit. We then deduct fixed operating costs and depreciation to obtain taxable operating

---

[2]The formula in the spreadsheet subtracts the expected tax, but since the expected tax is negative, this is equivalent to adding a tax credit to the sales price.

[3]Note that if an asset is sold for exactly its book value, there will be no gain or loss, hence no tax liability or credit.

Table 12-1

Analysis of a New (Expansion) Project: Part 4 (Dollars in Thousands)

	A	B	C	D	E	F	G	H	I
71	Part 4. Projected Net Cash Flows				Years				
72					0	1	2	3	4
73					2008	2009	2010	2011	2012
74	*Investment Outlays: Long-Term Assets*								
75	Building				($12,000)				
76	Equipment				(8,000)				
77									
78	*Operating Cash Flows over the Project's Life*								
79	Units sold					20,000	20,000	20,000	20,000
80	Sales price					$3.00	$3.06	$3.12	$3.18
81	Sales revenue					$60,000	$61,200	$62,424	$63,672
82	Variable costs					42,000	42,840	43,697	44,571
83	Fixed operating costs					8,000	8,080	8,161	8,242
84	Depreciation (building)					156	312	312	312
85	Depreciation (equipment)					1,600	2,560	1,520	960
86	Oper. income before taxes (EBIT)					8,244	7,408	8,734	9,587
87	Taxes on operating income (40%)					3,298	2,963	3,494	3,835
88	Net operating profit after taxes (NOPAT)					4,946	4,445	5,241	5,752
89	Add back depreciation					1,756	2,872	1,832	1,272
90	Operating cash flow					$6,702	$7,317	$7,073	$7,024
91									
92	*Cash Flows Due to Net Operating Working Capital*								
93	Net operating working capital (based on sales)				$6,000	$6,120	$6,242	$6,367	$0
94	Cash flow due to investment in NOWC				($6,000)	($120)	($122)	($125)	$6,367
95									
96	*Salvage Cash Flows: Long-Term Assets*								
97	Net salvage cash flow: Building								$8,863
98	Net salvage cash flow: Equipment								1,744
99	Total salvage cash flows								$10,607
100									
101	Net cash flow (Time line of cash flows)				($26,000)	$6,582	$7,194	$6,948	$23,999
102									

income, or EBIT, in Row 86. When taxes (at a 40% rate) are subtracted, we are left with net operating profit after taxes, or NOPAT, in Row 88. We add back depreciation to obtain annual values for operating cash flow, as shown in Row 90.

RIC must purchase raw materials and replenish them each year as they are used. In Part 1 we assume that RIC must have an amount of NOWC on hand equal to 10% of the upcoming year's sales. For example, sales in Year 1 are $60,000, so RIC must have $6,000 in NOWC at Year 0, as shown in Cell E93. Because RIC had no NOWC prior to Year 0, it must make a $6,000 investment in NOWC at Year 0, as shown in Cell E94. Sales increase to $61,200 in Year 2, so RIC must have $6,120 of NOWC at Year 1. Because it already had $6,000 in NOWC on hand, its net investment at Year 1 is just $120, shown in Cell F94. Note that RIC will have no sales after Year 4, so it will require no NOWC at Year 4. Thus, it has a positive cash flow of $6,367 at Year 4 as working capital is sold but not replaced.

When the project's life ends, the company will receive the "Salvage Cash Flows" as shown in the column for Year 4 in Rows 97 and 98.[4] Thus, the total salvage cash flow amounts to $10,607 as shown in Row 99.

---

[4] These after-tax cash flows were estimated previously in Part 3.

Table 12-1

Analysis of a New (Expansion) Project: Part 5 (Dollars in Thousands)

	A	B	C	D	E	F	G	H	I
104	Part 5. Key Output and Appraisal of the Proposed Project (WACC = 12%)								
105									
106	Net Present Value			$5,809					
107	IRR			20.12%					
108	MIRR			17.79%					
109	PI			1.22					
110									
111							Years		
112					0	1	2	3	4
113	Cumulative cash flow for payback					(19,418)	(12,223)	(5,275)	18,723
114	Part of year required for payback:					1.00	1.00	1.00	0.22
115			Payback =	3.22					
116									
117							Years		
118					0	1	2	3	4
119	Discounted cash flow for payback:					5,877	5,735	4,945	15,252
120	Cumulative cash flow for payback					(20,123)	(14,388)	(9,442)	5,809
121	Part of year required for payback:					1.00	1.00	1.00	0.39
122			Payback =	3.39					

We sum the subtotals in Part 4 to obtain the net cash flows shown in Row 101. Those cash flows constitute a *cash flow time line*, and they are evaluated in Part 5 of Table 12-1.

Making the Decision

Part 5 of Table 12-1 shows the standard evaluation criteria—NPV, IRR, MIRR, PI, payback, and discounted payback—based on the cash flows shown in Row 101. The NPV is positive, the IRR and MIRR both exceed the 12% cost of capital, and the PI is greater than 1.0. Therefore, on the basis of the analysis thus far, it appears that the project should be accepted. Note, though, that we have been assuming that the project is about as risky as the company's average project. If the project were judged to be riskier than average, it would be necessary to increase the cost of capital, which might cause the NPV to become negative and leave the IRR and MIRR below the new WACC. Therefore, we cannot make a final decision until we evaluate the project's risk, the topic of a later section.

SELF-TEST   Refer to Table 12-1 and answer these questions:

a. If the WACC is 15%, what is the new NPV? ($3,454)

b. If the equipment were depreciated over a 10-year life rather than a 5-year life, but other aspects of the project were unchanged, would the NPV increase or decrease? Why?

12.3 Issues in Project Analysis

Now that you have seen an application of project analysis, here are some additional issues to keep in mind.

Purchase of Fixed Assets and Noncash Charges

Most projects require assets, and asset purchases represent *negative* cash flows. Even though the acquisition of assets results in a cash outflow, accountants do not show the purchase of fixed assets as a deduction from accounting income. Instead, they deduct a depreciation expense each year throughout the life of the asset. Depreciation shelters income from taxation, and this has an impact on cash flow, but depreciation itself is not a cash flow. Therefore, depreciation must be added to NOPAT when estimating a project's operating cash flow.

Depreciation is the most common noncash charge, but there are many other noncash charges that might appear on a company's financial statements. Just as with depreciation, all other noncash charges should be added back when calculating a project's net cash flow.

Changes in Net Operating Working Capital

Normally, additional inventories are required to support a new operation, and expanded sales tie up additional funds in accounts receivable. However, payables and accruals increase as a result of the expansion, and this reduces the cash needed to finance inventories and receivables. The difference between the required increase in operating current assets and the increase in operating current liabilities is the change in net operating working capital. If this change is positive, as it generally is for expansion projects, then additional financing, over and above the cost of the fixed assets, will be needed.

Toward the end of a project's life, inventories will be used but not replaced, and receivables will be collected without corresponding replacements. As these changes occur, the firm will receive cash inflows, and as a result, the investment in net operating working capital will be returned by the end of the project's life.

Interest Expenses Are Not Included in Project Cash Flows

Recall from Chapter 11 that we discount a project's cash flows by its cost of capital and that the cost of capital is a weighted average (WACC) of the costs of debt, preferred stock, and common equity, adjusted for the project's risk. This WACC is the rate of return necessary to satisfy all of the firm's investors, both stockholders and debtholders. A common mistake made by many students and financial managers is to subtract interest payments when estimating a project's cash flows. This is a mistake because the cost of debt is already embedded in the WACC, so subtracting interest payments from the project's cash flows would amount to double-counting interest costs.

If someone subtracted interest (or interest plus principal payments) from the project's cash flows, then they would be calculating the cash flows available to the equity holders, and these cash flows should be discounted at the cost of equity. This technique can give the correct answer, but in order for it to work you must be very careful to adjust the amount of debt outstanding each year in order to keep the risk of the equity cash flows constant. This process is very complicated, and we do not recommend it. Here is one final caution: If someone subtracts interest, then it is definitely wrong to discount the resulting cash flows by the WACC, and no amount of care can correct that error.

Therefore, you should not subtract interest expenses when finding a project's cash flows.

Sunk Costs

A **sunk cost** is an outlay that has already occurred, hence is not affected by the decision under consideration. Since sunk costs are not incremental costs, they should not be included in the analysis. For example, RIC spent $100,000 in 2007 for R&D to develop the technology for the integrated chips project. Is this 2007 expenditure a relevant cost with respect to the 2008 capital budgeting decision? The answer is no—the $100,000 is a *sunk cost*, and it will not affect future cash flows regardless of whether or not the new project is implemented. It often turns out that a particular project has a negative NPV if all the associated costs, including sunk costs, are considered. However, on an incremental basis, the project may be a good one because the *future incremental cash flows* are large enough to produce a positive NPV on the *incremental investment*.

Opportunity Costs

Opportunity costs are cash flows that could be generated from an asset the firm already owns, provided the asset is not used for the project in question. Instead of buying a new building, suppose that RIC already owns a building that could be used for the project. If RIC's managers decided to use this building rather than buy a new one, RIC would not incur the $12 million cash outlay to buy a new building. Would this mean that we should delete the $12 million expenditure from the analysis, which would obviously raise the estimated NPV well above the $5.8 million we found in Table 12-1?

The answer is that we should remove the cash flows related to the new building, but we should include the *opportunity cost* associated with the existing building as a cash cost. For example, if the building had a market value, after taxes and brokerage expenses, of $14 million, then RIC would be giving up $14 million if it used the building for the computer project. Therefore, we should charge the project the $14 million that would be forgone as an opportunity cost.

Effects on Other Parts of the Firm: Externalities

Economists define **externalities** as the effects a project has on other parts of the firm or on the environment. For example, Apple's introduction of the iPod nano caused some people who were planning to purchase a regular iPod to switch to a nano. The nano project generates positive cash flows, but it also reduces some of the company's current cash flows. This type of externality is called a **cannibalization effect,** because the new business eats into the company's existing business. The lost cash flows should be charged to the new project. However, it often turns out that if the one company does not produce a new product, some other company will, so the old cash flows would be lost anyway. In this case, no charge should be assessed against the new project. All this makes determining the cannibalization effect difficult, because it requires estimates of changes in sales and costs, and also the timing of when those changes will occur. Still, cannibalization can be important, so its potential effects should be considered.

Note that externalities can be positive as well as negative. For example, Apple's introduction of the nano has helped spur music sales at Apple's Music Store. When Apple was evaluating the nano project, it should have increased the project's cash flows by the expected cash flows due to additional music sales. It often turns out that a project's direct cash flows are insufficient to produce a positive NPV, but when indirect effects are considered, the project is deemed to be a good one.

Firms must also be concerned with *environmental externalities*. For example, it might be that RIC's new facility would give off noxious fumes that, while not bad enough to trigger governmental actions, would still cause ill feelings in the plant's neighborhood. Those ill feelings might not show up in the cash flow analysis, but they should still be considered. Perhaps a relatively small expenditure could correct the problem and keep the firm from suffering future ill will which might be costly in some hard-to-measure way.

Rather than focusing narrowly on the project at hand, analysts must anticipate the project's impact on the rest of the firm, which requires imagination and creative thinking. It is critical to identify and account for all externalities when evaluating a proposed project.

Replacement Projects

e-resource

For more discussion on replacement analysis decisions, refer to **Web Extension 12A** at the textbook's Web site.

A **replacement project** occurs when the firm replaces an existing asset with a new one. In this case, the incremental cash flows are the firm's *additional* inflows and outflows that result from investing in the new project. In a replacement analysis, the company is comparing its value if it takes on the new project to its value if it continues to use the existing asset. Thus, it is important to take into account all of the existing project's cash flow components, including depreciation and maintenance.

Timing of Cash Flows

We must account properly for the timing of cash flows. Accounting income statements are for periods such as years or months, so they do not reflect exactly when during the period cash revenues or expenses occur. Because of the time value of money, capital budgeting cash flows should in theory be analyzed exactly as they occur. Of course, there must be a compromise between accuracy and feasibility. A time line with daily cash flows would in theory be most accurate, but daily cash flow estimates would be costly to construct, unwieldy to use, and probably no more accurate than annual cash flow estimates because we simply cannot forecast well enough to warrant this degree of detail. Therefore, in most cases, we simply assume that all cash flows occur at the end of every year. However, for some projects, it may be useful to assume that cash flows occur at mid-year, or even quarterly or monthly.

SELF-TEST

What is the most common noncash charge that must be added back when finding project cash flows?

What is net operating working capital, and how does it affect a project's cash flows in capital budgeting?

Explain the following terms: sunk cost, opportunity cost, externality, and cannibalization.

12.4 Depreciation

We already discussed several issues associated with deprecation during the analysis of RIC's project, but there are additional topics that we discuss here.

Companies often calculate depreciation one way when figuring taxes and another way when reporting income to investors: Many use the **straight-line method** for stockholder reporting (or "book" purposes), but they use the fastest rate permitted by law for tax purposes. Under the straight-line method used for stockholder reporting, one normally takes the cost of the asset, subtracts its estimated salvage value, and divides the net amount by the asset's useful economic life. For example, consider an asset with a 5-year life that costs $100,000 and has a $12,500 salvage value; its annual straight-line depreciation charge is ($100,000 − $12,500)/5 = $17,500. Note, however, as we stated earlier, salvage value is a factor in financial reporting but it is *not* considered for tax depreciation purposes.

For tax purposes, Congress changes the permissible tax depreciation methods from time to time. Prior to 1954, the straight-line method was required for tax purposes, but in 1954 **accelerated methods** (double-declining balance and sum-of-years'-digits) were permitted. Then, in 1981, the old accelerated methods were replaced by a simpler procedure known as the Accelerated Cost Recovery System (ACRS). The ACRS system was changed again in 1986 as a part of the Tax Reform Act, and it is now known as the **Modified Accelerated Cost Recovery System (MACRS);** a 1993 tax law made further changes in this area.

Note that U.S. tax laws are very complicated, and in this text we can only provide an overview of MACRS designed to give you a basic understanding of the impact of depreciation on capital budgeting decisions. Further, the tax laws change so often that the numbers we present may be outdated before the book is even published. Thus, when dealing with tax depreciation in real-world situations, current Internal Revenue Service (IRS) publications or individuals with expertise in tax matters should be consulted.

For tax purposes, the entire cost of an asset is expensed over its depreciable life. Historically, an asset's depreciable life was set equal to its estimated useful economic life; it was intended that an asset would be fully depreciated at approximately the same time that it reached the end of its useful economic life. However, MACRS totally abandoned that practice and set simple guidelines that created several classes of assets, each with a more-or-less arbitrarily prescribed life called a *recovery period* or *class life*. The MACRS class lives bear only a rough relationship to assets' expected useful economic lives.

A major effect of the MACRS system has been to shorten the depreciable lives of assets, thus giving businesses larger tax deductions early in the assets' lives, and thereby increasing the present value of the cash flows. Table 12-2 describes the types of property that fit into the different class life groups, and Table 12-3 sets forth the MACRS recovery allowance percentages (depreciation rates) for selected classes of investment property.

Consider Table 12-2, which gives the MACRS class lives and the types of assets that fall into each category. Property in the 27.5- and 39-year categories (real estate) must be depreciated by the straight-line method, but 3-, 5-, 7-, and 10-year

Table 12-2

Major Classes and Asset Lives for MACRS

Class	Type of Property
3-year	Certain special manufacturing tools
5-year	Automobiles, light-duty trucks, computers, and certain special manufacturing equipment
7-year	Most industrial equipment, office furniture, and fixtures
10-year	Certain longer-lived types of equipment
27.5-year	Residential rental real property such as apartment buildings
39-year	All nonresidential real property, including commercial and industrial buildings

property (personal property) can be depreciated either by the accelerated method set forth in Table 12-3 or by the straight-line method.[5]

As we saw earlier in the chapter, higher depreciation expenses result in lower taxes in the early years, hence a higher present value of cash flows. Therefore, since a firm has the choice of using straight-line rates or the accelerated rates shown in Table 12-3, most elect to use the accelerated rates.

Table 12-3

Recovery Allowance Percentage for Personal Property

Ownership Year	Class of Investment			
	3-Year	5-Year	7-Year	10-Year
1	33%	20%	14%	10%
2	45	32	25	18
3	15	19	17	14
4	7	12	13	12
5		11	9	9
6		6	9	7
7			9	7
8			4	7
9				7
10				6
11				3
	100%	100%	100%	100%

Notes:

[a] We developed these recovery allowance percentages based on the 200% declining balance method prescribed by MACRS, with a switch to straight-line depreciation at some point in the asset's life. For example, consider the 5-year recovery allowance percentages. The straight-line percentage would be 20% per year, so the 200% declining balance multiplier is 2.0(20%) = 40% = 0.4. However, because the half-year convention applies, the MACRS percentage for Year 1 is 20%. For Year 2, there is 80% of the depreciable basis remaining to be depreciated, so the recovery allowance percentage is 0.40(80%) = 32%. In Year 3, 20% + 32% = 52% of the depreciation has been taken, leaving 48%, so the percentage is 0.4(48%) ≈ 19%. In Year 4, the percentage is 0.4(29%) ≈ 12%. After 4 years, straight-line depreciation exceeds the declining balance depreciation, so a switch is made to straight-line (this is permitted under the law). However, the half-year convention must also be applied at the end of the class life, and the remaining 17% of depreciation must be taken (amortized) over 1.5 years. Thus, the percentage in Year 5 is 17%/1.5 ≈ 11%, and in Year 6, 17% − 11% = 6%. Although the tax tables carry the allowance percentages out to two decimal places, we have rounded to the nearest whole number for ease of illustration.

[b] Residential rental property (apartments) is depreciated over a 27.5-year life, whereas commercial and industrial structures are depreciated over 39 years. In both cases, straight-line depreciation must be used. The depreciation allowance for the first year is based, pro rata, on the month the asset was placed in service, with the remainder of the first year's depreciation being taken in the 28th or 40th year. A half-month convention is assumed; that is, an asset placed in service in February would receive 10.5 months of depreciation in the first year.

---

[5] The Tax Code currently (for 2006) permits companies to *expense*, which is equivalent to depreciating over 1 year, up to $108,000 of equipment; see IRS Publication 946 for details. This is a benefit primarily for small companies. Thus, if a small company bought one asset worth up to $108,000, it could write the asset off in the year it was acquired. This is called "Section 179 expensing." We shall disregard this provision throughout the book. Also, Congress enacted the Job Creation and Worker Assistance Act of 2002 following the terrorist attacks on the World Trade Center and Pentagon. This act, among other things, temporarily changed how depreciation is charged for property acquired after September 10, 2001, and before September 11, 2004, and put in service before January 1, 2005. We shall disregard this provision throughout the book as well.

The yearly recovery allowance, or depreciation expense, is determined by multiplying each asset's *depreciable basis* by the applicable recovery percentage shown in Table 12-3. You might be wondering why 4 years of deprecation rates are shown for property in the 3-year class. Under MACRS, the assumption is generally made that property is placed in service in the middle of the first year. Thus, for 3-year-class property, the recovery period begins in the middle of the year the asset is placed in service and ends 3 years later. The effect of the *half-year convention* is to extend the recovery period out one more year, so 3-year-class property is depreciated over 4 calendar years, 5-year property is depreciated over 6 calendar years, and so on. This convention is incorporated into Table 12-3's recovery allowance percentages.[6]

SELF-TEST

What do the acronyms ACRS and MACRS stand for?

Briefly describe the tax depreciation system under MACRS.

12.5 Adjusting for Inflation

Inflation is a fact of life in the United States and most other nations, so it must be considered in any sound capital budgeting analysis.

Inflation-Induced Bias

Note that *in the absence of inflation*, the real rate, r_r, would be equal to the nominal rate, r_{NOM}. Moreover, the real and nominal expected net cash flows—RCF_t and NCF_t—would also be equal. Remember that *real* interest rates and cash flows do not include inflation effects, while *nominal* rates and flows do reflect the effects of inflation. In particular, an inflation premium, IP, is built into all nominal market interest rates.

Suppose the expected rate of inflation is positive, and we expect *all* of the project's cash flows—including those related to depreciation—to rise at the rate i. Further, assume that this same inflation rate, i, is built into the market cost of capital as an inflation premium, IP = i. In this situation, the nominal net cash flow, NCF_t, will increase annually at the rate of i percent, producing this result:

$$NCF_t = RCF_t(1 + i)^t.$$

For example, if we expected a net cash flow of $100 in Year 5 in the absence of inflation, then with a 5% annual rate of inflation, $NCF_5 = \$100(1.05)^5 = \$127.63$.

In general, the cost of capital used as the discount rate in capital budgeting analysis is based on the market-determined costs of debt and equity, so it is a nominal rate. To convert a real interest rate, r_r, to a nominal rate, r_{NOM}, when the inflation rate is i, we use this formula:

$$(1 + r_{NOM}) = (1 + r_r)(1 + i).$$

[6]The half-year convention also applies if the straight-line alternative is used, with half of one year's depreciation taken in the first year, a full year's depreciation taken in each of the remaining years of the asset's class life, and the remaining half-year's depreciation taken in the year following the end of the class life. You should recognize that virtually all companies have computerized depreciation systems. Each asset's depreciation pattern is programmed into the system at the time of its acquisition, and the computer aggregates the depreciation allowances for all assets when the accountants close the books and prepare financial statements and tax returns.

Sensitivity Analysis

Intuitively, we know that many of the variables that determine a project's cash flows could turn out to be different from the values used in the analysis. We also know that a change in a key input variable, such as units sold, will cause the NPV to change. **Sensitivity analysis** is a technique that indicates how much NPV will change in response to a given change in an input variable, other things held constant.

Sensitivity Tables and Graphs

Sensitivity analysis begins with a *base-case* situation, which is developed using the *expected* values for each input. To illustrate, consider the data given back in Table 12-1, where projected cash flows for RIC's computer project were shown. The values used to develop the table, including unit sales, sales price, fixed costs, and variable costs, are all most likely, or base-case, values, and the resulting $5.809 million NPV shown in Table 12-1 is called the **base-case NPV.** Now we ask a series of "what if" questions: What if unit sales fall 15% below the most likely level? What if the sales price per unit falls? What if variable costs are $2.50 per unit rather than the expected $2.10? Sensitivity analysis is designed to provide decision makers with answers to questions such as these.

In a sensitivity analysis, each variable is changed by several percentage points above and below the expected value, holding all other variables constant. Then a new NPV is calculated using each of these values. Finally, the set of NPVs is plotted to show how sensitive NPV is to changes in each variable. Figure 12-1 shows the computer project's sensitivity graphs for six of the input variables. The table below the graph gives the NPVs that were used to construct the graph. The slopes of the lines in the graph show how sensitive NPV is to changes in each of the inputs: *The steeper the slope, the more sensitive the NPV is to a change in the variable.* From the figure and the table, we see that the project's NPV is very sensitive to changes in the sales price and variable costs, fairly sensitive to changes in the growth rate and units sold, and not very sensitive to changes in either fixed costs or the cost of capital.

If we were comparing two projects, the one with the steeper sensitivity lines would be riskier, because for that project a relatively small error in estimating a variable such as unit sales would produce a large error in the project's expected NPV. Thus, sensitivity analysis can provide useful insights into the risk of a project.

Spreadsheet computer programs such as *Excel* are ideally suited for sensitivity analysis. We used the Data Table feature in the file ***FM12 Ch 12 Tool Kit.xls*** to generate the data for the graph in Figure 12-1. To conduct such an analysis by hand would be extremely time-consuming.

NPV Breakeven Analysis

A special application of sensitivity analysis is called **NPV breakeven analysis.** In a breakeven analysis, we find the level of an input that produces an NPV of exactly zero. We used *Excel's* Goal Seek feature to do this.

Table 12-4 shows the values of the inputs discussed above that produce a zero NPV. For example, the unit sales price can drop to $2.84 before the project's NPV falls to zero. Breakeven analysis is helpful in determining how bad things can get before the project has a negative NPV.

Scenario Analysis

Although sensitivity analysis is probably the most widely used risk analysis technique, it does have limitations. For example, we saw earlier that the computer

e-resource

See ***FM12 Ch 12 Tool Kit.xls*** for all calculations.

e-resource

See ***FM12 Ch 12 Tool Kit.xls*** at the textbook's Web site.

Figure 12-1

Evaluating Risk: Sensitivity Analysis (Dollars in Thousands)

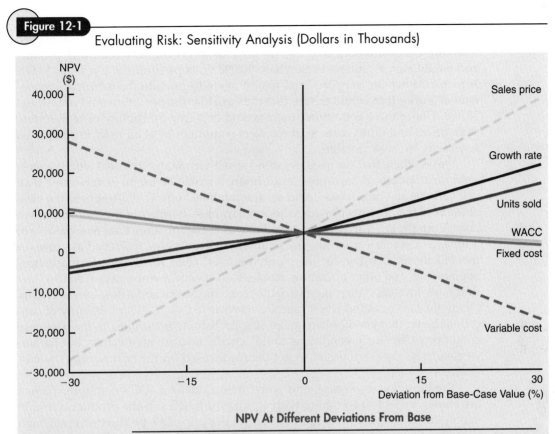

NPV At Different Deviations From Base

Deviation from Base Case	Sales Price	Variable Cost/Unit	Growth Rate	Year 1 Units Sold	Fixed Cost	WACC
−30%	($27,223)	$29,404	($ 4,923)	($ 3,628)	$10,243	$9,030
−15	(10,707)	17,607	(115)	1,091	8,026	7,362
0	5,809	5,809	5,809	5,809	5,809	5,809
15	22,326	(5,988)	12,987	10,528	3,593	4,363
30	38,842	(17,785)	21,556	15,247	1,376	3,014
Range	$66,064	$47,189	$26,479	$18,875	$ 8,867	$6,016

Table 12-4

NPV Breakeven Analysis (Dollars in Thousands)

Input	Input Value that Produces Zero NPV
Sales price	$2.84
Variable cost/unit	$2.26
Growth rate	−14.7%
Year 1 units sold	16,307
Fixed cost	$11,145
WACC	20.1%

project's NPV is highly sensitive to changes in the sales price and the variable cost per unit. Those sensitivities suggest that the project is risky. Suppose, however, that Home Depot or Circuit City was anxious to get the new computer product and would sign a contract to purchase 20,000 units per year for 4 years at $3,000 per unit. Moreover, suppose Intel would agree to provide the principal component at a price that would ensure that the variable cost per unit would not exceed $2,100. Under these conditions, there would be a low probability of high or low sales prices and input costs, so the project would not be at all risky in spite of its sensitivity to those variables.

We see, then, that we need to extend sensitivity analysis to deal with the *probability distributions* of the inputs. In addition, it would be useful to vary more than one variable at a time so we could see the combined effects of changes in the variables. Scenario analysis provides these extensions—it brings in the probabilities of changes in the key variables, and it allows us to change more than one variable at a time. In a scenario analysis, the financial analyst begins with the **base case,** or most likely set of values for the input variables. Then, he or she asks marketing, engineering, and other operating managers to specify a **worst-case scenario** (low unit sales, low sales price, high variable costs, and so on) and a **best-case scenario.** Often, the best case and worst case are set so as to have a 25% probability of conditions being that good or bad, and a 50% probability is assigned to the base-case conditions. Obviously, conditions could actually take on other values, but parameters such as these are useful to get people focused on the central issues in risk analysis.

The best-case, base-case, and worst-case values for RIC's computer project are shown in Table 12-5, along with a plot of the NPVs. If the product is highly successful, then the combination of a high sales price, low production costs, high first year sales, and a strong growth rate in future sales will result in a very high NPV, $146 million. However, if things turn out badly, then the NPV will be −$37 million. The graph shows a very wide range of possibilities, indicating that this is indeed a very risky project. If the bad conditions materialize, this will not bankrupt the company—this is just one project for a large company. Still, losing $37 million would certainly not help the stock price or the career of the project's manager.

The scenario probabilities and NPVs constitute a probability distribution of returns like those we dealt with in Chapter 6, except that the returns are measured in dollars instead of percentages (rates of return). The expected NPV (in thousands of dollars) is $30,135:[8]

$$\text{Expected NPV} = \sum_{i=1}^{n} P_i(NPV_i)$$

$$= 0.25(\$146,180) + 0.50(\$5,809) + 0.25(-\$37,257)$$

$$= \$30,135.$$

FM
e-resource
See **FM12 Ch 12 Tool Kit.xls** for a scenario analysis using *Excel's* Scenario Manager.

---

[8]Note that the expected NPV, $30,135, is *not* the same as the base-case NPV, $5,809 (in thousands). This is because the two uncertain variables, sales volume and sales price, are multiplied together to obtain dollar sales, and this process causes the NPV distribution to be skewed to the right. A big number times another big number produces a very big number, which, in turn, causes the average, or expected value, to increase.

Table 12-5

Scenario Analysis (Dollars in Thousands)

Scenario	Probability	Sales Price	Unit Sales	Variable Costs	Growth Rate	NPV
Best case	25%	$3.90	26,000	$1.47	30%	$146,180
Base case	50	3.00	20,000	2.10	0	5,809
Worst case	25	2.10	14,000	2.73	−30	(37,257)
					Expected NPV =	$30,135
					Standard deviation =	$69,267
				Coefficient of variation = Standard deviation/Expected NPV =		2.30

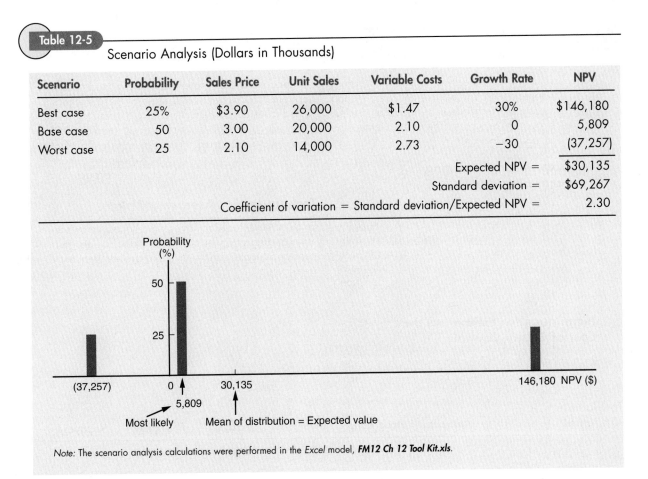

Note: The scenario analysis calculations were performed in the *Excel* model, *FM12 Ch 12 Tool Kit.xls*.

The standard deviation of the NPV is $69,267 (in thousands of dollars):

$$\sigma_{NPV} = \sqrt{\sum_{i=1}^{n} P_i(NPV_i) - (\text{Expected NPV})^2}$$

$$= \sqrt{\begin{array}{l} 0.25(\$146,180 - \$30,135)^2 + 0.50(\$5,809 - \$30,135)^2 \\ + 0.25(-\$37,257 - \$30,135)^2 \end{array}}$$

$$= \$69.267.$$

e-resource

See *FM12 Ch 12 Tool Kit.xls* at the textbook's Web site.

Finally, the project's coefficient of variation is

$$CV_{NPV} = \frac{\sigma_{NPV}}{E(NPV)} = \frac{\$69,267}{\$30,135} = 2.30.$$

The project's coefficient of variation can be compared with the coefficient of variation of RIC's "average" project to get an idea of the relative risk of the proposed project. RIC's existing projects, on average, have a coefficient of variation of about 1.0, so, on the basis of this stand-alone risk measure, we conclude that this project is much riskier than an "average" project.

Scenario analysis provides useful information about a project's stand-alone risk. However, it is limited in that it considers only a few discrete outcomes

Capital Budgeting Practices in the Asia/Pacific Region

A recent survey of executives in Australia, Hong Kong, Indonesia, Malaysia, the Philippines, and Singapore asked several questions about companies' capital budgeting practices. The study yielded the results summarized below.

Techniques for Evaluating Corporate Projects

Consistent with U.S. companies, most companies in this region evaluate projects using IRR, NPV, and payback. IRR usage ranged from 96% (in Australia) to 86% (in Hong Kong). NPV usage ranged from 96% (in Australia) to 81% (in the Philippines). Payback usage ranged from 100% (in Hong Kong and the Philippines) to 81% (in Indonesia).

Techniques for Estimating the Cost of Equity Capital

Recall from Chapter 10 that three basic approaches can be used to estimate the cost of equity: CAPM,

dividend yield plus growth rate (DCF), and cost of debt plus a risk premium. The use of these methods varied considerably from country to country (see Table A). The CAPM is used most often by U.S. firms. This is also true for Australian firms, but not for the other Asian/Pacific firms, who instead more often use the DCF and risk premium approaches.

Techniques for Assessing Risk

Firms in the Asian/Pacific region rely heavily on scenario and sensitivity analyses. They also use decision trees and Monte Carlo simulation, but less frequently (see Table B).

Table A

Method	Australia	Hong Kong	Indonesia	Malaysia	Philippines	Singapore
CAPM	72.7%	26.9%	0.0%	6.2%	24.1%	17.0%
Dividend yield plus growth rate	16.4	53.8	33.3	50.0	34.5	42.6
Cost of debt plus risk premium	10.9	23.1	53.4	37.5	58.6	42.6

Table B

Risk Assessment Technique	Australia	Hong Kong	Indonesia	Malaysia	Philippines	Singapore
Scenario analysis	96%	100%	94%	80%	97%	90%
Sensitivity analysis	100	100	88	83	94	79
Decision tree analysis	44	58	50	37	33	46
Monte Carlo simulation	38	35	25	9	24	35

Source: Adapted from George W. Kester et al., "Capital Budgeting Practices in the Asia-Pacific Region: Australia, Hong Kong, Indonesia, Malaysia, Philippines, and Singapore," *Financial Practice and Education*, Spring/Summer 1999, pp. 25–33.

(NPVs), even though there are an infinite number of possibilities. We describe a more complete method of assessing a project's stand-alone risk in the next section.

Monte Carlo Simulation

Monte Carlo simulation ties together sensitivities and probability distributions. It grew out of work in the Manhattan Project to build the first atomic bomb and was so named because it utilized the mathematics of casino gambling. While Monte

Carlo simulation is considerably more complex than scenario analysis, simulation software packages make this process manageable. Many of these packages are included as add-ons to spreadsheet programs such as *Excel*.

In a simulation analysis, the computer begins by picking at random a value for each variable—sales in units, the sales price, the variable cost per unit, and so on. Then those values are combined, and the project's NPV is calculated and stored in the computer's memory. Next, a second set of input values is selected at random, and a second NPV is calculated. This process is repeated perhaps 1,000 times, generating 1,000 NPVs. The mean and standard deviation of the set of NPVs is determined. The mean, or average value, is used as a measure of the project's expected NPV, and the standard deviation (or coefficient of variation) is used as a measure of risk.

Using this procedure, we conducted a simulation analysis of RIC's proposed project. As in our scenario analysis, we simplified the illustration by specifying the distributions for only four key variables: (1) sales price, (2) variable cost, (3) Year 1 units sold, and (4) growth rate.

We assumed that sales price can be represented by a continuous normal distribution with an expected value of $3.00 and a standard deviation of $0.35. Recall from Chapter 6 that there is about a 68% chance that the actual price will be within one standard deviation of the expected price, which results in a range of $2.65 to $3.35. Put another way, there is only a 32% chance that the price will fall outside the indicated range. Note too that there is less than a 1% chance that the actual price will be more than three standard deviations away from the expected price, which gives us a range of $1.95 to $4.05. Therefore, the sales price is very unlikely to be less than $1.95 or more than $4.05.

RIC has existing labor contracts and strong relationships with some of its suppliers, which makes the variable cost less uncertain. In the simulation we assumed that the variable cost can be described by a triangular distribution, with a lower bound of $1.40, a most likely value of $2.10, and an upper bound of $2.50. Note that this is not a symmetric distribution. The lower bound is $0.70 less than the most likely value, but the upper bound is only $0.40 higher than the most likely value. This is because RIC has an active risk management program under which it hedges against increases in the prices of the commodities used in its production processes. The net effect is that RIC's hedging activities reduce its exposure to price increases but still allow it to take advantage of falling prices.

Based on preliminary purchase agreements with major customers, RIC is certain that sales in the first year will be at least 15,000 units. The marketing department believes the most likely demand will be 20,000 units, but it is possible that demand will be much higher. The plant can produce a maximum of 30,000 units in the first year, although production can be expanded in subsequent years if there is higher than expected demand. Therefore, we represented Year 1 unit sales with a triangular distribution with a lower bound of 15,000 units, a most likely value of 20,000 units, and an upper bound of 30,000 units.

The marketing department anticipates no growth in unit sales after the first year, but it recognizes that actual sales growth could be either positive or negative. Moreover, actual growth is likely to be positively correlated with units sold in the first year, which means that if demand is higher than expected in the first year, then growth will probably be higher than expected in subsequent years. We represented growth with a normal distribution having an expected value of 0 percent and a standard deviation of 15%. We also specified the correlation between Year 1 unit sales and growth in sales to be 0.65. Graphs of these probability distributions are shown in Figure 12-2.

Figure 12-2

Probability Distributions Used in the Monte Carlo Simulation

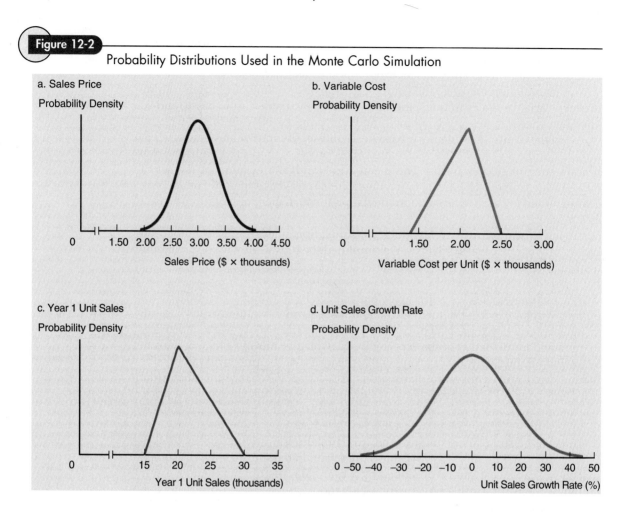

a. Sales Price

Probability Density

Sales Price ($ × thousands)

b. Variable Cost

Probability Density

Variable Cost per Unit ($ × thousands)

c. Year 1 Unit Sales

Probability Density

Year 1 Unit Sales (thousands)

d. Unit Sales Growth Rate

Probability Density

Unit Sales Growth Rate (%)

FM

e-resource

See *Explanation of Simulation.doc, Simtools.xla,* and *FM12 Ch 12 Tool Kit Simulation.xls* at the textbook's Web site.

We used these inputs and the model from *FM12 Ch 12 Tool Kit.xls* to conduct the simulation analysis. If you want to do the simulation yourself, you should first read the instructions in the file *Explanation of Simulation.doc*. This explains how to install an *Excel* add-in, *Simtools.xla*, which is necessary to run the simulation. After you have installed *Simtools.xla*, you can run the simulation analysis, which is in a separate spreadsheet, *FM12 Ch 12 Tool Kit Simulation.xls*.[9] Using this model, we simulated 1,000 outcomes for the capital budgeting project. Table 12-6 presents selected results from the simulation.

After running the simulation, the first thing to do is to verify that the results are consistent with our assumptions. The resulting mean and standard deviation of sales price are $3.01 and $0.35, respectively, which are virtually identical to our assumptions. Similarly, the resulting mean of −0.4% and standard deviation of 14.8% for growth are very close to our assumed distribution. The maximum for variable cost is $2.47, which is just under our specified maximum of $2.50, and the minimum is $1.40, which is equal to our specified minimum. Unit sales have a maximum of 29,741 and a minimum of 15,149, both of which are consistent with

---

[9]We are grateful to Professor Roger Myerson of Northwestern University for making *Simtools.xla* available to us. Note too that there are a number of commercially available simulation programs that can be used with *Excel*, including *@Risk* and *Crystal Ball*. Many universities and companies have such programs installed on their networks, and they can also be installed on PCs.

Table 12-6

Summary of Simulation Results (Thousands of Dollars)

	Risky Inputs				Output
	Sales Price	Variable Costs	Unit Sales	Growth	NPV
Mean	$3.01	$2.00	21,662	−0.4%	$13,867
Standard deviation	0.35	0.23	3,201	14.8	22,643
Maximum	4.00	2.47	29,741	42.7	124,091
Minimum	1.92	1.40	15,149	−51.5	−49,550
Median					10,607
Probability of NPV > 0					72.8%
Coefficient of variation					1.63

our assumptions. Finally, the resulting correlation between unit sales and growth is 0.664, which is very close to our assumed correlation of 0.65. Therefore, the results of the simulation are consistent with our assumptions.

Table 12-6 also reports summary statistics for the project's NPV. The mean is $13,867, which suggests that the project should be accepted. However, the range of outcomes is quite large, from a loss of $49,550 to a gain of $124,091, so the project is clearly risky. The standard deviation of $22,643 indicates that losses could easily occur, and this is consistent with this wide range of possible outcomes.[10] The coefficient of variation is 1.63, which is large compared with most of RIC's other projects. Table 12-6 also reports a median NPV of $10,607, which means that half the time the project will have an NPV greater than $10,607. The table also reports that 72.8% of the time we would expect the project to have a positive NPV.

A picture is worth a thousand words, and Figure 12-3 shows the probability distribution of the outcomes. Note that the distribution of outcomes is skewed to the right. As the figure shows, the potential downside losses are not as large as the potential upside gains. Our conclusion is that this is a very risky project, as indicated by the coefficient of variation, but it does have a positive expected NPV and the potential to be a home run.

SELF-TEST

List two reasons why, in practice, a project's stand-alone risk is important.

Differentiate between sensitivity and scenario analyses. What advantage does scenario analysis have over sensitivity analysis?

What is Monte Carlo simulation?

---

[10]Note that the standard deviation of NPV in the simulation is much smaller than the standard deviation in the scenario analysis. In the scenario analysis, we assumed that all of the poor outcomes would occur together in the worst-case scenario, and all of the positive outcomes would occur together in the best-case scenario. In other words, we implicitly assumed that all of the risky variables were perfectly positively correlated. In the simulation, we assumed that the variables were independent, with the exception of the correlation between unit sales and growth. The independence of variables in the simulation reduces the range of outcomes. For example, in the simulation, sometimes the sales price is high, but the sales growth is low. In the scenario analysis, a high sales price is always coupled with high growth. Because the scenario analysis's assumption of perfect correlation is unlikely, simulation may provide a better estimate of project risk. However, if the standard deviations and correlations used as inputs in the simulation are not estimated accurately, then the simulation output will likewise be inaccurate.

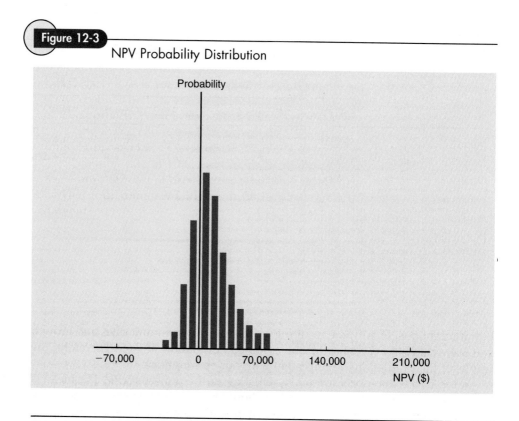

Figure 12-3

NPV Probability Distribution

12.7 Project Risk Conclusions

We have discussed the three types of risk normally considered in capital budgeting analysis—stand-alone risk, within-firm (or corporate) risk, and market risk—and we have discussed ways of assessing each. However, two important questions remain: (1) Should firms be concerned with stand-alone or corporate risk in their capital budgeting decisions, and (2) what do we do when the stand-alone, within-firm, and market risk assessments lead to different conclusions?

These questions do not have easy answers. From a theoretical standpoint, well-diversified investors should be concerned only with market risk, managers should be concerned only with stock price maximization, and this should lead to the conclusion that market (beta) risk ought to be given virtually all the weight in capital budgeting decisions. However, if investors are not well diversified, if the CAPM does not operate exactly as theory says it should, or if measurement problems keep managers from having confidence in the CAPM approach in capital budgeting, it may be appropriate to give stand-alone and corporate risk more weight than financial theory suggests. Note also that the CAPM ignores bankruptcy costs, even though such costs can be substantial, and the probability of bankruptcy depends on a firm's corporate risk, not on its beta risk. Therefore, even well-diversified investors should want a firm's management to give at least some consideration to a project's corporate risk instead of concentrating entirely on market risk.

Although it would be nice to reconcile these problems and to measure project risk on some absolute scale, the best we can do in practice is to estimate project risk in a somewhat nebulous, relative sense. For example, we can generally say with a fair degree of confidence that a particular project has more or less stand-alone risk than the firm's average project. Then, assuming that stand-alone and corporate risk are highly correlated (which is typical), the project's stand-alone risk will be a good measure of its corporate risk. Finally, assuming that market risk and corporate risk are highly correlated (as is true for most companies), a project with more corporate risk than average will also have more market risk, and vice versa for projects with low corporate risk.

SELF-TEST

In theory, should a firm be concerned with stand-alone and corporate risk? Should the firm be concerned with these risks in practice?

If a project's stand-alone, corporate, and market risk are highly correlated, would this make the task of measuring risk easier or harder? Explain.

12.8 Incorporating Project Risk into Capital Budgeting

As we described in Chapter 10, many firms calculate a cost of capital for each division, based on the division's market risk and capital structure. This is the first step toward incorporating risk analysis into capital budgeting decisions, but it is limited because it encompasses only market risk. Rather than directly estimating the corporate risk of a project, the risk management departments at many firms regularly assess the entire firm's likelihood of financial distress, based on current and proposed projects.[11] In other words, they assess a firm's corporate risk, given its portfolio of projects. This screening process will identify those projects that significantly increase corporate risk.

e-resource

See **Web Extension 12B** at the textbook's Web site, for a more detailed discussion of certainty equivalents and risk-adjusted discount rates.

Suppose a proposed project doesn't significantly affect a firm's likelihood of financial distress, but it does have greater stand-alone risk than the typical project in a division. Two methods are used to incorporate this project risk into capital budgeting. One is called the *certainty equivalent* approach. Here every cash inflow that is not known with certainty is scaled down, and the riskier the flow, the lower its certainty equivalent value. The other method, and the one we focus on here, is the **risk-adjusted discount rate** approach, under which differential project risk is dealt with by changing the discount rate. Average-risk projects are discounted at the firm's average cost of capital, higher-risk projects are discounted at a higher cost of capital, and lower-risk projects are discounted at a rate below the firm's average cost of capital. Unfortunately, there is no good way of specifying exactly *how much* higher or lower these discount rates should be. Given the present state of the art, risk adjustments are necessarily judgmental and somewhat arbitrary.[12]

SELF-TEST

How are risk-adjusted discount rates used to incorporate project risk into the capital budget decision process?

12.9 Managing Risk through Phased Decisions: Decision Trees

Up to this point we have focused primarily on techniques for estimating a project's stand-alone risk. Although this is an integral part of capital budgeting,

---

[11]These processes also measure the magnitude of the losses, which is often called *value at risk*.

[12]For more on risk adjustments, see Tarun K. Mukherjee, "Reducing the Uncertainty-Induced Bias in Capital Budgeting Decisions—A Hurdle Rate Approach," *Journal of Business Finance & Accounting*, September 1991, pp. 747–753; J. S. Butler and Barry Schachter, "The Investment Decision: Estimation Risk and Risk Adjusted Discount Rates," *Financial Management*, Winter 1989, pp. 13–22; and Samuel C. Weaver, Peter J. Clemmens III, Jack A. Gunn, and Bruce D. Danneburg, "Divisional Hurdle Rates and the Cost of Capital," *Financial Management*, Spring 1989, pp. 18–25.

managers are generally more interested in *reducing* risk than in *measuring* it. For example, sometimes projects can be structured so that expenditures do not have to be made all at one time, but, rather, can be made in stages over a period of years. This reduces risk by giving managers the opportunity to reevaluate decisions using new information and then either investing additional funds or terminating the project. Such projects can be evaluated using *decision trees*.

The Basic Decision Tree

Suppose United Robotics is considering the production of an industrial robot for the television manufacturing industry. The net investment for this project can be broken down into stages, as set forth in Figure 12-4:

STAGE 1.   At t = 0, which in this case is sometime in the near future, conduct a $500,000 study of the market potential for robots in television assembly lines.

STAGE 2.   If it appears that a sizable market does exist, then at t = 1 spend $1,000,000 to design and build a prototype robot. This robot would then be evaluated by television engineers, and their reactions would determine whether the firm should proceed with the project.

STAGE 3.   If reaction to the prototype robot is good, then at t = 2 build a production plant at a net cost of $10,000,000. If this stage were reached, the project would generate either high, medium, or low net cash flows over the following 4 years.

STAGE 4.   At t = 3 market acceptance will be known. If demand is low, the firm will terminate the project and avoid the negative cash flows in Years 4 and 5.

A **decision tree** such as the one in Figure 12-4 can be used to analyze such multistage, or sequential, decisions. Here we assume that 1 year goes by between decisions. Each circle represents a decision point, and it is called a **decision node.** The dollar value to the left of each decision node represents the net investment required at that decision point, and the cash flows shown under t = 3 to t = 5 represent the cash inflows if the project is pushed on to completion. Each diagonal line represents a **branch** of the decision tree, and each branch has an estimated probability. For example, if the firm decides to "go" with the project at Decision Point 1, it will spend $500,000 on a marketing study. Management estimates that

Figure 12-4

United Robotics: Decision Tree Analysis (Thousands of Dollars)

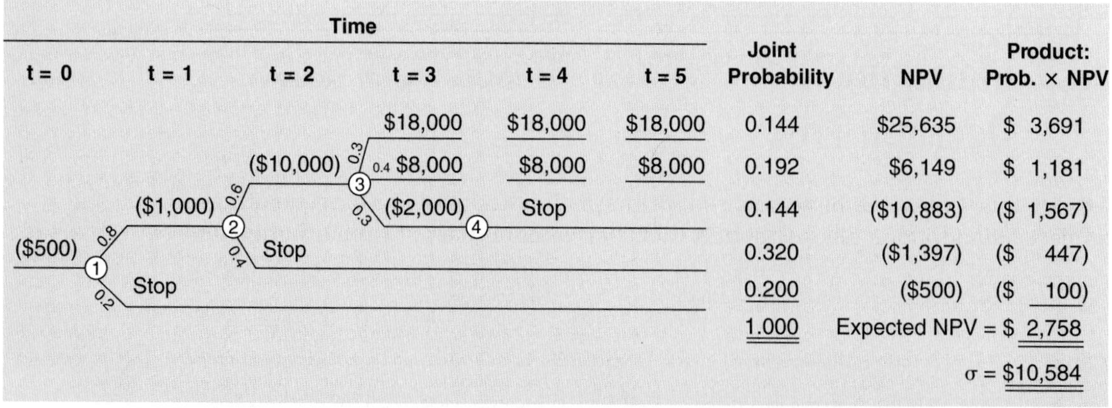

Time								
t = 0	t = 1	t = 2	t = 3	t = 4	t = 5	Joint Probability	NPV	Product: Prob. × NPV
			$18,000	$18,000	$18,000	0.144	$25,635	$ 3,691
		($10,000) 0.3 0.4 $8,000		$8,000	$8,000	0.192	$6,149	$ 1,181
	($1,000) 0.6		0.3 ($2,000)	Stop		0.144	($10,883)	($ 1,567)
($500) 0.8		0.4 Stop				0.320	($1,397)	($ 447)
	0.2 Stop					0.200	($500)	($ 100)
						1.000	Expected NPV =	$ 2,758
							σ =	$10,584

there is a 0.8 probability that the study will produce favorable results, leading to the decision to move on to Stage 2, and a 0.2 probability that the marketing study will produce negative results, indicating that the project should be canceled after Stage 1. If the project is canceled, the cost to the company will be the $500,000 for the initial marketing study, and it will be a loss.

If the marketing study yields positive results, then United Robotics will spend $1,000,000 on the prototype robot at Decision Point 2. Management estimates (before even making the initial $500,000 investment) that there is a 60% probability that the television engineers will find the robot useful and a 40% probability that they will not like it.

If the engineers like the robot, the firm will spend the final $10,000,000 to build the plant and go into production. If the engineers do not like the prototype, the project will be dropped. If the firm does go into production, the operating cash flows over the project's 4-year life will depend on how well the market accepts the final product. There is a 30% chance that acceptance will be quite good and net cash flows will be $18 million per year, a 40% probability of $8 million each year, and a 30% chance of losing $2 million. These cash flows are shown under Years 3 through 5.

In summary, the decision tree in Figure 12-4 defines the decision nodes and the branches that leave the nodes. There are two types of nodes, decision nodes and outcome nodes. Decision nodes are the points at which management can respond to new information. The first decision node is at $t = 1$, after the company has completed the marketing study (Decision Point 1 in Figure 12-4). The second decision node is at $t = 2$, after the company has completed the prototype study (Decision Point 2 in Figure 12-4). The outcome nodes show the possible results if a particular decision is taken. There is one relevant outcome node (Decision Point 3 in Figure 12-4), the one occurring at $t = 3$, and its branches show the possible cash flows if the company goes ahead with the industrial robot project. There is one more decision node, Decision Point 4, at which United Robotics terminates the project if acceptance is low. Note that the decision tree also shows the probabilities of moving into each branch that leaves a node.

The column of joint probabilities in Figure 12-4 gives the probability of occurrence of each branch, hence of each NPV. Each joint probability is obtained by multiplying together all probabilities on a particular branch. For example, the probability that the company will, if Stage 1 is undertaken, move through Stages 2 and 3, and that a strong demand will produce $18,000,000 per year of inflows, is $(0.8)(0.6)(0.3) = 0.144 = 14.4\%$.

The company has a cost of capital of 11.5%, and management assumes initially that the project is of average risk. The NPV of the top (most favorable) branch as shown in the next-to-last column is $25,635 (in thousands of dollars):

$$\text{NPV} = -\$500 - \frac{\$1,000}{(1.115)^1} - \frac{\$10,000}{(1.115)^2} + \frac{\$18,000}{(1.115)^3} + \frac{\$18,000}{(1.115)^4} + \frac{\$18,000}{(1.115)^5}$$

$$= \$25,635.$$

The NPVs for other branches were calculated similarly.

The last column in Figure 12-4 gives the product of the NPV for each branch times the joint probability of that branch, and the sum of these products is the project's expected NPV. Based on the expectations set forth in Figure 12-4 and a cost of capital of 11.5%, the project's expected NPV is $2.758 million.

As this example shows, decision tree analysis requires managers to explicitly articulate the types of risk a project faces and to develop responses to potential scenarios. Note also that our example could be extended to cover many other types of decisions and could even be incorporated into a simulation analysis. All in all, decision tree analysis is a valuable tool for analyzing project risk.[13]

SELF-TEST ───

What is a decision tree? A branch? A node?

12.10   Introduction to Real Options

According to traditional capital budgeting theory, a project's NPV is the present value of its expected future cash flows, discounted at a rate that reflects the riskiness of the expected future cash flows. Note, however, that this says nothing about actions that can be taken after the project has been accepted and placed in operation that might cause the cash flows to increase. In other words, traditional capital budgeting theory assumes that a project is like a roulette wheel. A gambler can choose whether or not to spin the wheel, but once the wheel has been spun, there is nothing he or she can do to influence the outcome. Once the game begins, the outcome depends purely on chance, with no skill involved.

Contrast roulette with other games, such as draw poker. Chance plays a role in poker, and it continues to play a role after the initial deal because players receive additional cards throughout the game. However, poker players are able to respond to their opponents' actions, so skillful players usually win.

Capital budgeting decisions have more in common with poker than roulette because (1) chance plays a continuing role throughout the life of the project but (2) managers can respond to changing market conditions and to competitors' actions. Opportunities to respond to changing circumstances are called **managerial options** because they give managers a chance to influence the outcome of a project. They are also called **strategic options** because they are often associated with large, strategic projects rather than routine maintenance projects. Finally, they are called **real options,** which are differentiated from financial options because they involve real, rather than financial, assets. The following sections describe several types of projects with **embedded options.**

Investment Timing Options

Conventional NPV analysis implicitly assumes that projects will either be accepted or rejected, which implies that they will be undertaken now or never. In practice, however, companies sometimes have a third choice—delay the decision until later, when more information is available. Such **investment timing options** can dramatically affect a project's estimated profitability and risk.

For example, suppose Sony plans to introduce an interactive DVD-TV system, and your software company has two alternatives: (1) immediately begin full-scale production of game software on DVDs for the new system or (2) delay investment in the project until you get a better idea of the size of the market for interactive DVDs. You might prefer delaying implementation. Keep in mind, though, that the *option to delay* is valuable only if it more than offsets any harm that might come from delaying. For example, if you delay, some other company might establish a loyal customer base that makes it difficult for your company to enter the market later. The

───

[13]In the United Robotics example we glossed over an important issue, namely, the appropriate cost of capital for the project. Adding decision nodes to a project clearly changes its risk, so we would expect the cost of capital for a project with few decision nodes to have a different risk than one with many nodes. If this were so, we would expect the projects to have different costs of capital. In fact, we might expect the cost of capital to change over time as the project moves to different stages, since the stages themselves differ in risk.

option to delay is usually most valuable to firms with proprietary technology, patents, licenses, or other barriers to entry, because these factors lessen the threat of competition. The option to delay is valuable when market demand is uncertain, but it is also valuable during periods of volatile interest rates, since the ability to wait can allow firms to delay raising capital for projects until interest rates are lower.

Growth Options

A **growth option** allows a company to increase its capacity if market conditions are better than expected. There are several types of growth options. One lets a company *increase the capacity of an existing product line*. A "peaking unit" power plant illustrates this type of growth option. Such units have high variable costs and are used to produce additional power only if demand and therefore prices are high.

The second type of growth option allows a company to *expand into new geographic markets*. Many companies are investing in Eastern Europe, Russia, and China even though standard NPV analysis produces negative NPVs. However, if these developing markets really take off, the option to open more facilities could be quite valuable.

The third type of growth option is the opportunity to *add new products*, including complementary products and successive "generations" of the original product. Toshiba probably lost money on its first laptop computers, but the manufacturing skills and consumer recognition it gained helped turn subsequent generations of laptops into money makers. In addition, Toshiba used its experience and name recognition in laptops as a springboard into the desktop computer market.

Abandonment Options

Many projects contain an **abandonment option.** When evaluating a potential project, standard DCF analysis assumes that the assets will be used over a specified economic life. While some projects must be operated over their full economic life, even though market conditions might deteriorate and cause lower than expected cash flows, others can be abandoned. For example, some contracts between automobile manufacturers and their suppliers specify the quantity and price of the parts that must be delivered. If a supplier's labor costs increase, then the supplier might well lose money on each part it ships. Including the option to abandon in such a contract might be quite valuable.

Note too that some projects can be structured so that they provide the option to *reduce capacity* or *temporarily suspend operations*. Such options are common in the natural resources industry, including mining, oil, and timber, and they should be reflected in the analysis when NPVs are being estimated.

Flexibility Options

Many projects offer **flexibility options** that permit the firm to alter operations depending on how conditions change during the life of the project. Typically, either inputs or outputs (or both) can be changed. BMW's Spartanburg, South Carolina, auto assembly plant provides a good example of output flexibility. BMW needed the plant to produce sports coupes. If it built the plant configured to produce only these vehicles, the construction cost would be minimized. However, the company thought that later on it might want to switch production to some other vehicle type, and that would be difficult if the plant were designed just for coupes. Therefore, BMW decided to spend additional funds to construct a more flexible plant—one that could produce different types of vehicles should demand patterns shift. Sure enough, things did change. Demand for coupes dropped a bit and that for sports utility vehicles soared. But BMW was ready, and the Spartanburg plant began spewing out hot-selling SUVs. The plant's cash flows are much higher than they would have been without the flexibility option that BMW "bought" by paying more to build a more flexible plant.

Electric power plants provide an example of input flexibility. Utilities can build plants that generate electricity by burning coal, oil, or natural gas. The prices of those fuels change over time, depending on events in the Middle East, changing environmental policies, and weather conditions. Some years ago, virtually all power plants were designed to burn just one type of fuel, because this resulted in the lowest construction cost. However, as fuel cost volatility increased, power companies began to build higher-cost but more flexible plants, especially ones that could switch from oil to gas and back again, depending on relative fuel prices.

Valuing Real Options

A full treatment of real option valuation is beyond the scope of this chapter, but there are some things we can say. First, if your project has an embedded real option, you should at least recognize and articulate its existence. Second, we know that a financial option is more valuable if it has a long time until maturity or if the underlying asset is very risky. If either of these characteristics applies to your real option, then you know that its value is relatively high, qualitatively speaking. Third, you might be able to model the real option along the lines of a decision tree. This will give you an approximate value, but keep in mind that you may not have a good estimate of the appropriate discount rate, because the real option changes the risk, and hence the required return, of the project.[14] We will discuss real options in more detail in Chapter 13.

SELF-TEST

Name some different types of real options.

Summary

Throughout the book, we have indicated that the value of any asset depends on the amount, timing, and risk of the cash flows it produces. In this chapter, we developed a framework for analyzing a project's cash flows and risk. The key concepts covered are listed below.

- The most important (and most difficult) step in analyzing a capital budgeting project is **estimating the incremental after-tax cash flows** the project will produce.
- **Project cash flow** is different from accounting income. Project cash flow reflects (1) **cash outlays for fixed assets,** (2) the **tax shield provided by depreciation,** and (3) cash flows due to **changes in net operating working capital.** Project cash flow does not include interest payments.
- In determining incremental cash flows, **opportunity costs** (the cash flows forgone by using an asset) must be included, but **sunk costs** (cash outlays that

---

[14]For more on real option valuation, see M. Amram and N. Kulatilaka, *Real Options: Managing Strategic Investment in an Uncertain World* (Boston: Harvard Business School Press, 1999); and M. Brennan and L. Trigeorgis, *Project Flexibility, Agency, and Competition: New Developments in the Theory and Application of Real Options* (New York: Oxford University Press, 2000).

have been made and that cannot be recouped) are not included. Any **externalities** (effects of a project on other parts of the firm) should also be reflected in the analysis.

- **Cannibalization** occurs when a new project leads to a reduction in sales of an existing product.
- **Tax laws** affect cash flow analysis in two ways: (1) They reduce operating cash flows, and (2) they determine the depreciation expense that can be taken in each year.
- Capital projects often require additional investments in **net operating working capital (NOWC).**
- The incremental cash flows from a typical project can be classified into three categories: (1) **initial investment outlay,** (2) **operating cash flows over the project's life,** and (3) **terminal year cash flows.**
- **Inflation effects** must be considered in project analysis. The best procedure is to build expected inflation into the cash flow estimates.
- Since stockholders are generally diversified, **market risk** is theoretically the most relevant measure of risk. Market, or beta, risk is important because beta affects the cost of capital, which, in turn, affects stock prices.
- **Corporate risk** is important because it influences the firm's ability to use low-cost debt, to maintain smooth operations over time, and to avoid crises that might consume management's energy and disrupt its employees, customers, suppliers, and community.
- **Sensitivity analysis** is a technique that shows how much a project's NPV will change in response to a given change in an input variable such as sales, other things held constant.
- **Scenario analysis** is a risk analysis technique in which the best- and worst-case NPVs are compared with the project's expected NPV.
- **Monte Carlo simulation** is a risk analysis technique that uses a computer to simulate future events and thus to estimate the profitability and riskiness of a project.
- The **risk-adjusted discount rate,** or **project cost of capital,** is the rate used to evaluate a particular project. It is based on the corporate WACC, which is increased for projects that are riskier than the firm's average project but decreased for less risky projects.
- **Decision tree analysis** shows how different decisions in a project's life affect its value.
- Opportunities to respond to changing circumstances are called **managerial options** because they give managers the option to influence the outcome of a project. They are also called **strategic options** because they are often associated with large, strategic projects rather than routine maintenance projects. Finally, they are also called **real options** because they involve "real," rather than "financial," assets. Many projects include a variety of **embedded options** that can dramatically affect the true NPV.
- An **investment timing option** involves not only the decision of *whether* to proceed with a project but also the decision of *when* to proceed with it. This opportunity to affect a project's timing can dramatically change its estimated value.
- A **growth option** occurs if an investment creates the opportunity to make other potentially profitable investments that would not otherwise be possible. These include (1) options to expand output, (2) options to enter a new geographical market, and (3) options to introduce complementary products or successive generations of products.

- The **abandonment option** is the ability to abandon a project if the operating cash flows and/or abandonment value turn out to be lower than expected. It reduces the risk of a project and increases its value. Instead of total abandonment, some options allow a company to reduce capacity or temporarily suspend operations.
- A **flexibility option** is the option to modify operations depending on how conditions develop during a project's life, especially the type of output produced or the inputs used.

Questions

(12-1) Define each of the following terms:
  a. Cash flow; accounting income
  b. Incremental cash flow; sunk cost; opportunity cost
  c. Net operating working capital changes; salvage value
  d. Real rate of return, r_r, versus nominal rate of return, r_{NOM}
  e. Sensitivity analysis; scenario analysis; Monte Carlo simulation analysis
  f. Risk-adjusted discount rate; project cost of capital
  g. Real options; managerial options; strategic options; embedded options
  h. Investment timing option; growth option; abandonment option; flexibility option

(12-2) Operating cash flows, rather than accounting profits, are listed in Table 12-1. What is the basis for this emphasis on cash flows as opposed to net income?

(12-3) Why is it true, in general, that a failure to adjust expected cash flows for expected inflation biases the calculated NPV downward?

(12-4) Explain why sunk costs should not be included in a capital budgeting analysis, but opportunity costs and externalities should be included.

(12-5) Explain how net operating working capital is recovered at the end of a project's life, and why it is included in a capital budgeting analysis.

(12-6) Define (a) simulation analysis, (b) scenario analysis, and (c) sensitivity analysis.

Self-Test Problems   Solutions Appear in Appendix A

(ST-1)
New Project Analysis

You have been asked by the president of the Farr Construction Company to evaluate the proposed acquisition of a new earth mover. The mover's basic price is $50,000, and it would cost another $10,000 to modify it for special use. Assume that the mover falls into the MACRS 3-year class, it would be sold after 3 years for $20,000, and it would require an increase in net working capital (spare parts inventory) of $2,000. The earth mover would have no effect on revenues, but it is expected to save the firm $20,000 per year in before-tax operating costs, mainly labor. The firm's marginal federal-plus-state tax rate is 40%.

  a. What is the net cost of the earth mover? (That is, what are the Year 0 cash flows?)
  b. What are the operating cash flows in Years 1, 2, and 3?

c. What are the additional (nonoperating) cash flows in Year 3?

d. If the project's cost of capital is 10%, should the earth mover be purchased?

(ST-2)
Corporate Risk Analysis

The staff of Porter Manufacturing has estimated the following net after-tax cash flows and probabilities for a new manufacturing process:

Net After-Tax Cash Flows

Year	P = 0.2	P = 0.6	P = 0.2
0	($100,000)	($100,000)	($100,000)
1	20,000	30,000	40,000
2	20,000	30,000	40,000
3	20,000	30,000	40,000
4	20,000	30,000	40,000
5	20,000	30,000	40,000
5*	0	20,000	30,000

Line 0 gives the cost of the process, Lines 1 through 5 give operating cash flows, and Line 5* contains the estimated salvage values. Porter's cost of capital for an average-risk project is 10%.

a. Assume that the project has average risk. Find the project's expected NPV. (Hint: Use expected values for the net cash flow in each year.)

b. Find the best-case and worst-case NPVs. What is the probability of occurrence of the worst case if the cash flows are perfectly dependent (perfectly positively correlated) over time? If they are independent over time?

c. Assume that all the cash flows are perfectly positively correlated, that is, there are only three possible cash flow streams over time: (1) the worst case, (2) the most likely, or base, case, and (3) the best case, with probabilities of 0.2, 0.6, and 0.2, respectively. These cases are represented by each of the columns in the table. Find the expected NPV, its standard deviation, and its coefficient of variation.

Problems   Answers Appear in Appendix B

Easy Problems 1–3

(12-1)
Investment Outlay

Johnson Industries is considering an expansion project. The necessary equipment could be purchased for $9 million, and the project would also require an initial $3 million investment in net operating working capital. The company's tax rate is 40%. What is the project's initial investment outlay?

(12-2)
Operating Cash Flow

Nixon Communications is trying to estimate the first-year operating cash flow (at t = 1) for a proposed project. The financial staff has collected the following information:

Projected sales	$10 million
Operating costs (not including depreciation)	$7 million
Depreciation	$2 million
Interest expense	$2 million

The company faces a 40% tax rate. What is the project's operating cash flow for the first year (t = 1)?

(12-3)
Net Salvage Value

Carter Air Lines is now in the terminal year of a project. The equipment originally cost $20 million, of which 80% has been depreciated. Carter can sell the used equipment today to another airline for $5 million, and its tax rate is 40%. What is the equipment's after-tax net salvage value?

Intermediate Problems 4–6

(12-4)
New Project Analysis

The Campbell Company is evaluating the proposed acquisition of a new milling machine. The machine's base price is $108,000, and it would cost another $12,500 to modify it for special use. The machine falls into the MACRS 3-year class, and it would be sold after 3 years for $65,000. The machine would require an increase in net working capital (inventory) of $5,500. The milling machine would have no effect on revenues, but it is expected to save the firm $44,000 per year in before-tax operating costs, mainly labor. Campbell's marginal tax rate is 35%.
   a. What is the net cost of the machine for capital budgeting purposes? (That is, what is the Year 0 net cash flow?)
   b. What are the net operating cash flows in Years 1, 2, and 3?
   c. What is the additional Year 3 cash flow (that is, the after-tax salvage and the return of working capital)?
   d. If the project's cost of capital is 12%, should the machine be purchased?

(12-5)
New Project Analysis

You have been asked by the president of your company to evaluate the proposed acquisition of a new spectrometer for the firm's R&D department. The equipment's basic price is $70,000, and it would cost another $15,000 to modify it for special use by your firm. The spectrometer, which falls into the MACRS 3-year class, would be sold after 3 years for $30,000. Use of the equipment would require an increase in net working capital (spare parts inventory) of $4,000. The spectrometer would have no effect on revenues, but it is expected to save the firm $25,000 per year in before-tax operating costs, mainly labor. The firm's marginal federal-plus-state tax rate is 40%.
   a. What is the net cost of the spectrometer? (That is, what is the Year 0 net cash flow?)
   b. What are the net operating cash flows in Years 1, 2, and 3?
   c. What is the additional (nonoperating) cash flow in Year 3?
   d. If the project's cost of capital is 10%, should the spectrometer be purchased?

(12-6)
Inflation Adjustments

The Rodriguez Company is considering an average-risk investment in a mineral water spring project that has a cost of $150,000. The project will produce 1,000 cases of mineral water per year indefinitely. The current sales price is $138 per case, and the current cost per case (all variable) is $105. The firm is taxed at a rate of 34%. Both prices and costs are expected to rise at a rate of 6% per year. The firm uses only equity, and it has a cost of capital of 15%. Assume that cash flows consist only of after-tax profits, since the spring has an indefinite life and will not be depreciated.
   a. Should the firm accept the project? (Hint: The project is a perpetuity, so you must use the formula for a perpetuity to find its NPV.)
   b. If total costs consisted of a fixed cost of $10,000 per year and variable costs of $95 per unit, and if only the variable costs were expected to increase with

inflation, would this make the project better or worse? Continue with the assumption that the sales price will rise with inflation.

**Challenging
Problems 7–10**

(12-7)
Scenario Analysis

Shao Industries is considering a proposed project for its capital budget. The company estimates that the project's NPV is $12 million. This estimate assumes that the economy and market conditions will be average over the next few years. The company's CFO, however, forecasts that there is only a 50% chance that the economy will be average. Recognizing this uncertainty, she has also performed the following scenario analysis:

Economic Scenario	Probability of Outcome	NPV
Recession	0.05	($70 million)
Below average	0.20	(25 million)
Average	0.50	12 million
Above average	0.20	20 million
Boom	0.05	30 million

What is the project's expected NPV, its standard deviation, and its coefficient of variation?

(12-8)
Risky Cash Flows

The Bartram-Pulley Company (BPC) must decide between two mutually exclusive investment projects. Each project costs $6,750 and has an expected life of 3 years. Annual net cash flows from each project begin 1 year after the initial investment is made and have the following probability distributions:

Project A		Project B	
Probability	Net Cash Flows	Probability	Net Cash Flows
0.2	$6,000	0.2	$ 0
0.6	6,750	0.6	6,750
0.2	7,500	0.2	18,000

BPC has decided to evaluate the riskier project at a 12% rate and the less risky project at a 10% rate.
a. What is the expected value of the annual net cash flows from each project? What is the coefficient of variation (CV)? (Hint: $\sigma_B = \$5,798$ and $CV_B = 0.76$.)
b. What is the risk-adjusted NPV of each project?
c. If it were known that Project B was negatively correlated with other cash flows of the firm, whereas Project A was positively correlated, how would this knowledge affect the decision? If Project B's cash flows were negatively correlated with gross domestic product (GDP), would that influence your assessment of its risk?

(12-9)
Simulation

Singleton Supplies Corporation (SSC) manufactures medical products for hospitals, clinics, and nursing homes. SSC may introduce a new type of X-ray scanner designed to identify certain types of cancers in their early stages. There are a number of uncertainties about the proposed project, but the following data are believed to be reasonably accurate.

	Probability	Value	Random Numbers
Developmental costs	0.3	$2,000,000	00–29
	0.4	4,000,000	30–69
	0.3	6,000,000	70–99
Project life	0.2	3 years	00–19
	0.6	8 years	20–79
	0.2	13 years	80–99
Sales in units	0.2	100	00–19
	0.6	200	20–79
	0.2	300	80–99
Sales price	0.1	$13,000	00–09
	0.8	13,500	10–89
	0.1	14,000	90–99
Cost per unit (excluding developmental costs)	0.3	$5,000	00–29
	0.4	6,000	30–69
	0.3	7,000	70–99

SSC uses a cost of capital of 15% to analyze average-risk projects, 12% for low-risk projects, and 18% for high-risk projects. These risk adjustments reflect primarily the uncertainty about each project's NPV and IRR as measured by the coefficients of variation of NPV and IRR. SSC is in the 40% federal-plus-state income tax bracket.

a. What is the expected IRR for the X-ray scanner project? Base your answer on the expected values of the variables. Also, assume the after-tax "profits" figure you develop is equal to annual cash flows. All facilities are leased, so depreciation may be disregarded. Can you determine the value of σ_{IRR} short of actual simulation or a fairly complex statistical analysis?

b. Assume that SSC uses a 15% cost of capital for this project. What is the project's NPV? Could you estimate σ_{NPV} without either simulation or a complex statistical analysis?

c. Show the process by which a computer would perform a simulation analysis for this project. Use the random numbers 44, 17; 16, 58, 1; 79, 83, 86; and 19, 62, 6 to illustrate the process with the first computer run. Actually calculate the first-run NPV and IRR. Assume that the cash flows for each year are independent of cash flows for other years. Also, assume that the computer operates as follows: (1) A developmental cost and a project life are estimated for the first run using the first two random numbers. (2) Next, sales volume, sales price, and cost per unit are estimated using the next three random numbers and used to derive a cash flow for the first year. (3) Then, the next three random numbers are used to estimate sales volume, sales price, and cost per unit for the second year, hence the cash flow for the second year. (4) Cash flows for other years are developed similarly, on out to the first run's estimated life. (5) With the developmental cost and the cash flow stream established, NPV and IRR for the first run are derived and stored in the computer's memory. (6) The process is repeated to generate perhaps 500 other NPVs and IRRs. (7) Frequency distributions for NPV and IRR are plotted by the computer, and the distributions' means and standard deviations are calculated.

(12-10)
Sequential Decisions

The Yoran Yacht Company (YYC), a prominent sailboat builder in Newport, may design a new 30-foot sailboat based on the "winged" keels first introduced on the 12-meter yachts that raced for the America's Cup.

First, YYC would have to invest $10,000 at t = 0 for the design and model tank testing of the new boat. YYC's managers believe that there is a 60% probability that this phase will be successful and the project will continue. If Stage 1 is not successful, the project will be abandoned with zero salvage value.

The next stage, if undertaken, would consist of making the molds and producing two prototype boats. This would cost $500,000 at t = 1. If the boats test well, YYC would go into production. If they do not, the molds and prototypes could be sold for $100,000. The managers estimate that the probability is 80% that the boats will pass testing, and that Stage 3 will be undertaken.

Stage 3 consists of converting an unused production line to produce the new design. This would cost $1,000,000 at t = 2. If the economy is strong at this point, the net value of sales would be $3,000,000, while if the economy is weak, the net value would be $1,500,000. Both net values occur at t = 3, and each state of the economy has a probability of 0.5. YYC's corporate cost of capital is 12%.

a. Assume that this project has average risk. Construct a decision tree and determine the project's expected NPV.

b. Find the project's standard deviation of NPV and coefficient of variation (CV) of NPV. If YYC's average project had a CV of between 1.0 and 2.0, would this project be of high, low, or average stand-alone risk?

Spreadsheet Problem

(12-11)
Build a Model: Issues in
Capital Budgeting

e-resource

Start with the partial model in the file *FM12 Ch 12 P11 Build a Model.xls* from the textbook's Web site. Webmasters.com has developed a powerful new server that would be used for corporations' Internet activities. It would cost $10 million to buy the equipment necessary to manufacture the server, and it would require net operating working capital equal to 10% of sales. The servers would sell for $24,000 per unit, and Webmasters believes that variable costs would amount to $17,500 per unit. After the first year the sales price and variable costs will increase at the inflation rate of 3%. The company's non-variable costs would be $1 million at Year 1 and would increase with inflation. It would take 1 year to buy the required equipment and set up operations, and the server project would have a life of 4 years. If the project is undertaken, it must be continued for the entire 4 years. Also, the project's returns are expected to be highly correlated with returns on the firm's other assets. The firm believes it could sell 1,000 units per year.

The equipment would be depreciated over a 5-year period, using MACRS rates. The estimated market value of the equipment at the end of the project's 4-year life is $500,000. Webmasters' federal-plus-state tax rate is 40%. Its cost of capital is 10% for average-risk projects, defined as projects with a coefficient of variation of NPV between 0.8 and 1.2. Low-risk projects are evaluated with a WACC of 8%, and high-risk projects at 13%.

a. Develop a spreadsheet model and use it to find the project's NPV, IRR, and payback.

b. Now conduct a sensitivity analysis to determine the sensitivity of NPV to changes in the sales price, variable costs per unit, and number of units sold.

Set these variables' values at 10% and 20% above and below their base-case values. Include a graph in your analysis.

c. Now conduct a scenario analysis. Assume that there is a 25% probability that best-case conditions, with each of the variables discussed in part b being 20% better than its base-case value, will occur. There is a 25% probability of worst-case conditions, with the variables 20% worse than base, and a 50% probability of base-case conditions.

d. If the project appears to be more or less risky than an average project, find its risk-adjusted NPV, IRR, and payback.

e. On the basis of information in the problem, would you recommend that the project be accepted?

e-resource

Cyberproblem

Please go to the textbook's Web site to access any Cyberproblems.

Mini Case

Shrieves Casting Company is considering adding a new line to its product mix, and the capital budgeting analysis is being conducted by Sidney Johnson, a recently graduated MBA. The production line would be set up in unused space in Shrieves's main plant. The machinery's invoice price would be approximately $200,000, another $10,000 in shipping charges would be required, and it would cost an additional $30,000 to install the equipment. The machinery has an economic life of 4 years, and Shrieves has obtained a special tax ruling that places the equipment in the MACRS 3-year class. The machinery is expected to have a salvage value of $25,000 after 4 years of use.

The new line would generate incremental sales of 1,250 units per year for 4 years at an incremental cost of $100 per unit in the first year, excluding depreciation. Each unit can be sold for $200 in the first year. The sales price and cost are both expected to increase by 3% per year due to inflation. Further, to handle the new line, the firm's net operating working capital would have to increase by an amount equal to 12% of sales revenues. The firm's tax rate is 40%, and its overall weighted average cost of capital is 10%.

a. Define "incremental cash flow."

(1) Should you subtract interest expense or dividends when calculating project cash flow?

(2) Suppose the firm had spent $100,000 last year to rehabilitate the production line site. Should this be included in the analysis? Explain.

(3) Now assume that the plant space could be leased out to another firm at $25,000 per year. Should this be included in the analysis? If so, how?

(4) Finally, assume that the new product line is expected to decrease sales of the firm's other lines by $50,000 per year. Should this be considered in the analysis? If so, how?

b. Disregard the assumptions in part a. What is Shrieves's depreciable basis? What are the annual depreciation expenses?

c. Calculate the annual sales revenues and costs (other than depreciation). Why is it important to include inflation when estimating cash flows?

d. Construct annual incremental operating cash flow statements.

e. Estimate the required net operating working capital for each year and the cash flow due to investments in net operating working capital.

f. Calculate the after-tax salvage cash flow.

g. Calculate the net cash flows for each year. Based on these cash flows, what are the project's NPV, IRR, MIRR, and payback? Do these indicators suggest that the project should be undertaken?

h. What does the term "risk" mean in the context of capital budgeting; to what extent can risk be quantified; and when risk is quantified, is the quantification based primarily on statistical analysis of historical data or on subjective, judgmental estimates?

i. (1) What are the three types of risk that are relevant in capital budgeting?
    (2) How is each of these risk types measured, and how do they relate to one another?
    (3) How is each type of risk used in the capital budgeting process?

j. (1) What is sensitivity analysis?
    (2) Perform a sensitivity analysis on the unit sales, salvage value, and cost of capital for the project. Assume that each of these variables can vary from its base-case, or expected, value by ±10%, 20%, and 30%. Include a sensitivity diagram, and discuss the results.
    (3) What is the primary weakness of sensitivity analysis? What is its primary usefulness?

k. Assume that Sidney Johnson is confident of her estimates of all the variables that affect the project's cash flows except unit sales and sales price. If product acceptance is poor, unit sales would be only 900 units a year and the unit price would only be $160; a strong consumer response would produce sales of 1,600 units and a unit price of $240. Johnson believes that there is a 25% chance of poor acceptance, a 25% chance of excellent acceptance, and a 50% chance of average acceptance (the base case).
    (1) What is scenario analysis?
    (2) What is the worst-case NPV? The best-case NPV?
    (3) Use the worst-, base-, and best-case NPVs and probabilities of occurrence to find the project's expected NPV, standard deviation, and coefficient of variation.

l. Are there problems with scenario analysis? Define simulation analysis, and discuss its principal advantages and disadvantages.

m. (1) Assume that Shrieves's average project has a coefficient of variation in the range of 0.2 to 0.4. Would the new line be classified as high risk, average risk, or low risk? What type of risk is being measured here?
    (2) Shrieves typically adds or subtracts 3 percentage points to the overall cost of capital to adjust for risk. Should the new line be accepted?
    (3) Are there any subjective risk factors that should be considered before the final decision is made?

n. What is a real option? What are some types of real options?

Selected Additional Cases

The following cases from Textchoice, *Cengage Learning's online library, cover many of the concepts discussed in this chapter and are available at* **http://www.textchoice2.com**.

Klein-Brigham Series:
Case 12, "Indian River Citrus Company (A)," Case 44, "Cranfield, Inc. (A)," and Case 14, "Robert Montoya, Inc.," focus on cash flow estimation. Case 13, "Indian River Citrus (B)," Case 45, "Cranfield, Inc. (B)," Case 58, "Tasty Foods (B)," Case 60, "Heavenly Foods," and Case 15, "Robert Montoya, Inc. (B)," illustrate project risk analysis. Cases 75, 76, and 77, "The Western Company (A and B)," are comprehensive cases.

Brigham-Buzzard Series:
Case 7, "Powerline Network Corporation (Risk and Real Options in Capital Budgeting)."

chapter 13

Real Options

When Hewlett-Packard sells a printer internationally, it customizes the printer for the particular country. This customization can be done either at the factory that produces the printers or in the field immediately prior to the sale. At one time HP customized almost all printers at the factory because it was much cheaper to do so. Now, however, HP ships unfinished printers to its warehouses and customizes them at locations nearer the point of sale. Why would HP choose the high-cost production method? Because it gives the company an option to match supply and demand. For example, if HP customizes at its factory and then ships printers to a French warehouse, it might be stuck with too many printers customized for French customers but not enough for Germans. However, if it ships unfinished printers to a warehouse close to the border, it can quickly customize them for French, German, or Swiss customers and thus meet unexpected shifts in demand. This flexibility is called a "real option," because it gives the company a better option for dealing with market conditions that differ from the original forecast.

Cadence Design Systems, which develops electronic products and services, provides another illustration of a real option. Rather than create all the necessary software itself, Cadence often contracts with specialized software developers. As a part of the license, Cadence must make a royalty payment to the software developer each time it sells a product that contains the software. Many of the software contracts include a floor that requires Cadence to make a specified minimum number of royalty payments, even if actual sales are lower than the floor. Because the demand for Cadence's products is uncertain, sales may be less than the floor, causing the company to make large payments without revenue to cover it. Of course, if sales are higher than expected, Cadence must make more royalty payments than expected, but it would then also have high revenues and thus could afford the payments.

In negotiating with its software suppliers, Cadence proposed an arrangement that had a relatively low floor but a higher per-unit royalty. Using a standard NPV analysis, Cadence's proposal produced a negative NPV. However, option pricing techniques showed that Cadence's proposed royalty arrangement would actually add value.

As you read this chapter and learn more about options, think about how option pricing techniques can lead to better capital budgeting decisions.

Sources: Peter Coy, "Exploiting Uncertainty: The 'Real-Option' Revolution in Decision-Making," *BusinessWeek*, June 7, 1999, p. 118; and S. L. Mintz, "Getting Real," *CFO*, November 1999, pp. 52–60.

Traditional discounted cash flow (DCF) analysis—where an asset's cash flows are estimated and then discounted to obtain the asset's NPV—has been the cornerstone for valuing all types of assets since the 1950s. Accordingly, most of our discussion of capital budgeting has focused on DCF valuation techniques. However, in recent years academics and practitioners have demonstrated that DCF valuation techniques do not always tell the complete story about a project's value, and that rote use of DCF can, at times, lead to incorrect capital budgeting decisions.[1]

DCF techniques were originally developed to value securities such as stocks and bonds. Securities are passive investments—once they have been purchased, most investors have no influence over the cash flows the assets produce. However, real assets are not passive investments—managerial actions after an investment has been made can influence its results. Furthermore, investing in a new project often brings with it the potential for increasing the firm's future investment opportunities. Such opportunities are, in effect, options—the right but not the obligation to take some action in the future. As we demonstrate in the next section, options are valuable, so projects that expand the firm's set of opportunities have positive **option values.** Similarly, any project that reduces the set of future opportunities destroys option value. Since a project's impact on the firm's opportunities, or its option value, may not be captured by conventional NPV analysis, this option value should be considered separately, as we do in this chapter.

13.1 Valuing Real Options

Recall from Chapter 12 that real options are opportunities for management to change the timing, scale, or other aspects of an investment in response to changes in market conditions. These opportunities are options in the sense that management can, if it is in the company's best interest, undertake some action; management is not required to undertake the action. These opportunities are real, as opposed to financial, because they involve decisions regarding real assets, such as plants, equipment, and land, rather than financial assets like stocks or bonds. Four examples of real options are investment timing options, growth options, abandonment options, and flexibility options. We give an example of how to value an investment timing option and a growth option. *Web Extension 13A,* available at the textbook's Web site, shows how to value an abandonment option.

Valuing a real option requires judgment, both to formulate the model and to estimate the inputs. Does this mean the answer won't be useful? Definitely not. For example, the models used by NASA only approximate the centers of gravity for the moon, the earth, and other heavenly bodies, yet even with these "errors" in their models, NASA has been able to put astronauts on the moon. As one professor said, "All models are wrong, but some are still quite useful." This is especially true for real options. We might not be able to find the exact value of a real option, but the value we find can be helpful in deciding whether or not to accept the project. Equally important, the process of looking for and then valuing real options often identifies critical issues that might otherwise go unnoticed.

---

[1]For an excellent general discussion of the problems inherent in discounted cash flow valuation techniques as applied to capital budgeting, see Avinash K. Dixit and Robert S. Pindyck, "The Options Approach to Capital Investment," *Harvard Business Review,* May–June 1995, pp. 105–115.

Five possible procedures can be used to deal with real options. Starting with the simplest, they are as follows:

1. Use discounted cash flow (DCF) valuation and ignore any real options by assuming their values are zero.
2. Use DCF valuation and include a qualitative recognition of any real option's value.
3. Use decision tree analysis.
4. Use a standard model for a financial option.
5. Develop a unique, project-specific model using financial engineering techniques.

The following sections illustrate these procedures.

SELF-TEST ───
List the five possible procedures for dealing with real options.

13.2 The Investment Timing Option: An Illustration

When we discussed capital budgeting in Chapters 11 and 12 we implicitly assumed that the projects we analyzed were "take it or leave it" endeavors. In reality, there is frequently an alternative to investing immediately—the decision to invest or not can be postponed until more information becomes available. By waiting, a better-informed decision can be made, and this investment timing option adds value to the project and reduces its risk.

e-resource
All calculations for the analysis of the investment timing option are shown in **FM12 Ch 13 Tool Kit.xls** at the textbook's Web site.

Murphy Systems is considering a project for a new type of handheld device that provides wireless Internet connections. The cost of the project is $50 million, but the future cash flows depend on the demand for wireless Internet connections, which is uncertain. Murphy believes there is a 25% chance that demand for the new device will be very high, in which case the project will generate cash flows of $33 million each year for 3 years. There is a 50% chance of average demand, with cash flows of $25 million per year, and a 25% chance that demand will be low and annual cash flows will be only $5 million. A preliminary analysis indicates that the project is somewhat riskier than average, so it has been assigned a cost of capital of 14% versus 12% for an average project at Murphy Systems. Here is a summary of the project's data:

Demand	Probability	Annual Cash Flow
High	0.25	$33 million
Average	0.50	25 million
Low	0.25	5 million
Expected annual cash flow		$22 million
Project's cost of capital		14%
Life of project		3 years
Required investment, or cost of project		$50 million

Murphy can accept the project and implement it immediately, but since the company has a patent on the device's core modules, it can also choose to delay the decision until next year, when more information about demand will be available. The cost will still be $50 million if Murphy waits, and the project will still be expected to generate the indicated cash flows, but each flow will be pushed back 1 year. However, if Murphy waits, it will know which of the demand conditions, hence which set of cash flows, will exist. If it waits, Murphy will of course make the investment only if demand is sufficient to provide a positive NPV.

Note that this real timing option resembles a call option on a stock. A call gives its owner the right to purchase a stock at a fixed strike price, but only if the stock's price is higher than the strike price will the owner exercise the option and buy the stock. Similarly, if Murphy defers implementation, then it will have the right to "purchase" the project by making the $50 million investment if the NPV as calculated next year, when new information is available, is positive.

Approach 1. DCF Analysis Ignoring the Timing Option

Based on probabilities for the different levels of demand, the expected annual cash flows are $22 million per year:

$$\text{Expected cash flow per year} = 0.25(\$33) + 0.50(\$25) + 0.25(\$5)$$

$$= \$22 \text{ million.}$$

Ignoring the investment timing option, the traditional NPV is $1.08 million, found as follows:

$$\text{NPV} = -\$50 + \frac{\$22}{(1 + 0.14)^1} + \frac{\$22}{(1 + 0.14)^2} + \frac{\$22}{(1 + 0.14)^3} = \$1.08.$$

The present value of the cash inflows is $51.08 million while the cost is $50 million, leaving an NPV of $1.08 million.

Based just on this DCF analysis, Murphy should accept the project. Note, though, that if the expected cash flows had been slightly lower, say, $21.5 million per year, the NPV would have been negative and the project would have been rejected. Also, note that the project is risky—there is a 25% probability that demand will be weak, in which case the NPV will turn out to be a negative $38.4 million.

Approach 2. DCF Analysis with a Qualitative Consideration of the Timing Option

The discounted cash flow analysis suggests that the project should be accepted, but just barely, and it ignores the existence of a possibly valuable real option. If Murphy implements the project now, it gains an expected (but risky) NPV of $1.08 million. However, accepting now means that it is also giving up the option to wait and learn more about market demand before making the commitment. Thus, the decision is this: Is the option Murphy would be giving up worth more or less than $1.08 million? If the option is worth more than $1.08 million, then Murphy should not give up the option, which means deferring the decision, and vice versa if the option is worth less than $1.08 million.

Based on the discussion of financial options in Chapter 9, what qualitative assessment can we make regarding the option's value? Put another way, without doing any additional calculations, does it appear that Murphy should go forward now or wait? In thinking about this decision, first note that the value of an option is higher if the current value of the underlying asset is high relative to its strike price, other things held constant. For example, a call option with a strike price of $50 on a stock with a current price of $50 is worth more than if the current price were $20. The strike price of the project is $50 million, while our first guess at the value of its cash flows is $51.08 million. We will calculate the exact value of Murphy's underlying asset later, but the DCF analysis does suggest that the underlying asset's value will be close to the strike price, so the option should be valuable. We also know that an option's value is higher the longer its time to expiration. Here the option has a 1-year life, which is fairly long for an option, and this too suggests that the option is probably valuable. Finally, we know that the value of an option increases with the risk of the underlying asset. The data used in the DCF analysis indicate that the project is quite risky, which again suggests that the option is valuable.

Thus, our qualitative assessment indicates that the option to delay might well be more valuable than the expected NPV of $1.08 if we undertake the project immediately. This is quite subjective, but the qualitative assessment should make Murphy's management pause, and then go on to make a quantitative assessment of the situation.

Approach 3. Scenario Analysis and Decision Trees

Part 1 of Figure 13-1 presents a scenario analysis similar to the ones in Chapter 12 except now the cash flows are shown as a decision tree diagram. Each possible outcome is shown as a "branch" on the tree. Each branch shows the cash flows and probability of a scenario, laid out as a time line. Thus, the top line, which gives the payoffs of the high-demand scenario, has positive cash flows of $33 million for the next 3 years, and its NPV is $26.61 million. The average-demand branch in the middle has an NPV of $8.04 million, while the NPV of the low-demand branch is a negative $38.39 million. Since Murphy will suffer a $38.39 million loss if demand is weak, and since there is a 25% probability of weak demand, the project is clearly risky.

The expected NPV is the weighted average of the three possible outcomes, with the weight for each outcome being its probability. The sum in the last column in Part 1 shows that the expected NPV is $1.08 million, the same as in the original DCF analysis. Part 1 also shows a standard deviation of $24.02 million for the NPV, and a coefficient of variation, defined as the ratio of standard deviation to the expected NPV, of 22.32, which is quite large. Clearly, the project is quite risky under the analysis thus far.

Part 2 is set up similarly to Part 1 except that it shows what happens if Murphy delays the decision and then implements the project only if demand turns out to be high or average. No cost is incurred now at Year 0—here the only action is to wait. Then, if demand is average or high, Murphy will spend $50 million at Year 1 and receive either $33 million or $25 million per year for the following 3 years. If demand is low, as shown on the bottom branch, Murphy will spend nothing at Year 1 and will receive no cash flows in subsequent years. The NPV of the high-demand branch is $23.35 million and that of the average-demand branch is $7.05 million. Because all cash flows under the low-demand scenario are zero, the NPV in this case will also be zero. The expected NPV if Murphy delays the decision is $9.36 million.

Figure 13-1

DCF and Decision Tree Analysis for the Investment Timing Option (Millions of Dollars)

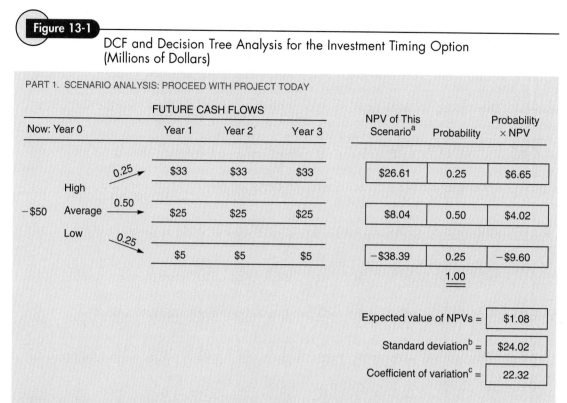

PART 1. SCENARIO ANALYSIS: PROCEED WITH PROJECT TODAY

Now: Year 0		FUTURE CASH FLOWS			NPV of This Scenario[a]	Probability	Probability × NPV
		Year 1	Year 2	Year 3			
	High	$33	$33	$33	$26.61	0.25	$6.65
−$50	Average	$25	$25	$25	$8.04	0.50	$4.02
	Low	$5	$5	$5	−$38.39	0.25	−$9.60
						1.00	

Expected value of NPVs = $1.08

Standard deviation[b] = $24.02

Coefficient of variation[c] = 22.32

PART 2. DECISION TREE ANALYSIS: IMPLEMENT NEXT YEAR ONLY IF OPTIMAL

Now: Year 0		FUTURE CASH FLOWS				NPV of This Scenario[d]	Probability	Probability × NPV
		Year 1	Year 2	Year 3	Year 4			
	High	−$50	$33	$33	$33	$23.35	0.25	$5.84
Wait	Average	−$50	$25	$25	$25	$7.05	0.50	$3.53
	Low	$0	$0	$0	$0	$0.00	0.25	$0.00
							1.00	

Expected value of NPVs = $9.36

Standard deviation[b] = $8.57

Coefficient of variation[c] = 0.92

Notes:
[a]The WACC is 14%.
[b]The standard deviation is calculated as explained in Chapter 6.
[c]The coefficient of variation is the standard deviation divided by the expected value.
[d]The NPV in Part 2 is as of Year 0. Therefore, each of the project cash flows is discounted back one more year than in Part 1.

This analysis shows that the project's expected NPV will be much higher if Murphy delays than if it invests immediately. Also, since there is no possibility of losing money under the delay option, this decision also lowers the project's risk. This clearly indicates that the option to wait is valuable, hence that Murphy should wait until Year 1 before deciding whether to proceed with the investment.

Before we conclude the discussion of decision trees, note that we used the same cost of capital, 14%, to discount cash flows in the "proceed immediately" scenario analysis in Part 1 and under the "delay 1 year" scenario in Part 2. However, for three reasons this is not appropriate. First, since there is no possibility of losing money if Murphy delays, the investment under that plan is clearly less risky than if Murphy charges ahead today. Second, the 14% cost of capital might be appropriate for risky cash flows, yet the investment in the project at Year 1 in Part 2 is known with certainty. Perhaps, then, we should discount it at the risk-free rate.[2] Third, the project's cash inflows (excluding the initial investment) are different in Part 2 than in Part 1 because the low-demand cash flows are eliminated. This suggests that if 14% is the appropriate cost of capital in the "proceed immediately" case, some lower rate would be appropriate in the "delay decision" case.

In Figure 13-2, Part 1, we repeat the "delay decision" analysis, with one exception. We continue to discount the operating cash flows in Year 2 through Year 4 at the 14% WACC, but now we discount the project's cost back at Year 1 with the risk-free rate, 6%. This increases the PV of the cost, which lowers the NPV from $9.36 million to $6.88 million. Note, though, that we really don't know precisely the appropriate WACC for the project—the 14% we used might be too high or too low for the operating cash flows in Year 2 through Year 4.[3] Therefore, in Part 2 of Figure 13-2 we show a sensitivity analysis of the NPV where the discount rates used for both the operating cash flows and for the project's cost vary. This sensitivity analysis shows that under all reasonable WACCs, the NPV of delaying is greater than $1.08 million, the NPV of immediate implementation. This means that the option to wait is more valuable than the $1.08 million resulting from immediate implementation. Therefore, Murphy should wait rather than implement the project immediately.

Approach 4. Valuing the Timing Option with the Black-Scholes Option Pricing Model

The decision tree approach, coupled with a sensitivity analysis, may provide enough information for a good decision. However, it is often useful to obtain additional insights into the real option's value, which means using the fourth procedure, an option pricing model. To do this, the analyst must find a standard financial option that resembles the project's real option.[4] As noted earlier, Murphy's option to delay the project is similar to a call option on a stock; hence the Black-Scholes Option Pricing Model can be used. This model requires five

---

[2]See Timothy A. Luehrman, "Investment Opportunities as Real Options: Getting Started on the Numbers," *Harvard Business Review*, July–August 1998, pp. 51–67, for a more detailed explanation of the rationale for using the risk-free rate to discount the project cost. This paper also provides a discussion of real option valuation. Professor Luehrman also has a follow-up paper that provides an excellent discussion of the ways real options affect strategy. See Timothy A. Luehrman, "Strategy as a Portfolio of Real Options," *Harvard Business Review*, September–October 1998, pp. 89–99.

[3]If we delay, the cash inflows might be considered more risky if there is a chance that the delay might cause those flows to decline due to the loss of Murphy's "first mover advantage." Put another way, we might gain information by waiting, and that could lower risk, but if a delay would enable others to enter and perhaps preempt the market, this could increase risk. In our example, we assumed that Murphy has a patent on critical components of the device, hence that no one could come in and preempt its position in the market.

[4]In theory, financial option pricing models apply only to assets that are continuously traded in a market. Even though real options usually don't meet this criterion, financial option models often provide a reasonably accurate approximation of the real option's value.

Figure 13-2

Decision Tree and Sensitivity Analysis for the Investment Timing Option
(Millions of Dollars)

PART 1. DECISION TREE ANALYSIS: IMPLEMENT IN ONE YEAR ONLY IF OPTIMAL (DISCOUNT COST AT THE RISK-FREE
RATE AND OPERATING CASH FLOWS AT THE WACC)

Now: Year 0		FUTURE CASH FLOWS				NPV of This Scenario[a]	Probability	Probability × NPV
		Year 1	Year 2	Year 3	Year 4			
Wait	High 0.25	−$50	$33	$33	$33	$20.04	0.25	$5.01
	Average 0.50	−$50	$25	$25	$25	$3.74	0.50	$1.87
	Low 0.25	$0	$0	$0	$0	$0.00	0.25	$0.00
							1.00	

Expected value of NPVs = $6.88

Standard deviation[b] = $7.75

Coefficient of variation[c] = 1.13

PART 2. SENSITIVITY ANALYSIS OF NPV TO CHANGES IN THE COST OF CAPITAL USED TO DISCOUNT COST
AND CASH FLOWS

	Cost of Capital Used to Discount the Year 1 Cost						
Cost of Capital Used to Discount the Year 2 through Year 4 Operating Cash Flows	3.0%	4.0%	5.0%	6.0%	7.0%	8.0%	9.0%
8.0%	$13.11	$13.46	$13.80	$14.14	$14.47	$14.79	$15.11
9.0%	11.78	12.13	12.47	12.81	13.14	13.47	13.78
10.0%	10.50	10.85	11.20	11.53	11.86	12.19	12.51
11.0%	9.27	9.62	9.97	10.30	10.64	10.96	11.28
12.0%	8.09	8.44	8.78	9.12	9.45	9.78	10.09
13.0%	6.95	7.30	7.64	7.98	8.31	8.64	8.95
14.0%	5.85	6.20	6.54	6.88	7.21	7.54	7.85
15.0%	4.79	5.14	5.48	5.82	6.15	6.48	6.79
16.0%	3.77	4.12	4.46	4.80	5.13	5.45	5.77
17.0%	2.78	3.13	3.47	3.81	4.14	4.46	4.78
18.0%	1.83	2.18	2.52	2.86	3.19	3.51	3.83

Notes:
[a]The operating cash flows in Year 2 through Year 4 are discounted at the WACC of 14%. The cost in Year 1 is discounted at the risk-free rate of 6%.
[b]The standard deviation is calculated as explained in Chapter 6.
[c]The coefficient of variation is the standard deviation divided by the expected value.

inputs: (1) the risk-free rate, (2) the time until the option expires, (3) the strike price, (4) the current price of the stock, and (5) the variance of the stock's rate of return. Therefore, we need to estimate values for those five inputs.

First, assuming that the rate on a 52-week Treasury bill is 6%, this rate can be used as the risk-free rate. Second, Murphy must decide within a year whether or not to implement the project, so there is 1 year until the option expires. Third, it will cost $50 million to implement the project, so $50 million can be used for the strike price. Fourth, we need a proxy for the value of the underlying asset, which in Black-Scholes is the current price of the stock. Note that a stock's current price is the present value of its expected future cash flows. For Murphy's real option, the underlying asset is the project itself, and its current "price" is the present value of its expected future cash flows. Therefore, as a proxy for the stock price we can use the present value of the project's future cash flows. And fifth, the variance of the project's expected return can be used to represent the variance of the stock's return in the Black-Scholes model.

Figure 13-3 shows how one can estimate the present value of the project's cash inflows. We need to find the current value of the underlying asset, that is, the project. For a stock, the current price is the present value of all expected future cash flows, including those that are expected even if we do not exercise the call option. Note also that the strike price for a call option has no effect on the stock's current price.[5] For our

Figure 13-3

Estimating the Input for Stock Price in the Option Analysis of the Investment Timing Option (Millions of Dollars)

Now: Year 0		Year 1	Year 2	Year 3	Year 4	PV of This Scenario[a]	Probability	Probability × PV
	High 0.25		$33	$33	$33	$67.21	0.25	$16.80
Wait	Average 0.50		$25	$25	$25	$50.91	0.50	$25.46
	Low 0.25		$5	$5	$5	$10.18	0.25	$2.55
							1.00	

Expected value of PVs[b] = $44.80

Standard deviation[c] = $21.07

Coefficient of variation[d] = 0.47

Notes:
[a]The WACC is 14%. All cash flows in this scenario are discounted back to Year 0.
[b]Here we find the PV, not the NPV, as the project's cost is ignored.
[c]The standard deviation is calculated as explained in Chapter 6.
[d]The coefficient of variation is the standard deviation divided by the expected value.

[5]The company itself is not involved with traded stock options. However, if the option were a warrant issued by the company, then the strike price would affect the company's cash flows, hence its stock price.

real option, the underlying asset is the delayed project, and its current "price" is the present value of all its future expected cash flows. Just as the price of a stock includes all of its future cash flows, the present value of the project should include all of its possible future cash flows. Moreover, since the price of a stock is not affected by the strike price of a call option, we ignore the project's "strike price," or cost, when we find its present value. Figure 13-3 shows the expected cash flows if the project is delayed. The PV of these cash flows as of now (Year 0) is $44.80 million, and this is the input we should use for the current price in the Black-Scholes model.

The last required input is the variance of the project's return. Three different approaches could be used to estimate this input. First, we could use judgment—an educated guess. Here we would begin by recalling that a company is a portfolio of projects (or assets), with each project having its own risk. Since returns on the company's stock reflect the diversification gained by combining many projects, we might expect the variance of the stock's returns to be lower than the variance of one of its average projects. The variance of an average company's stock return is about 12%, so we might expect the variance for a typical project to be somewhat higher, say, 15% to 25%. Companies in the Internet infrastructure industry are riskier than average, so we might subjectively estimate the variance of Murphy's project to be in the range of 18% to 30%.

The second approach, called the direct method, is to estimate the rate of return for each possible outcome and then calculate the variance of those returns. First, Part 1 in Figure 13-4 shows the PV for each possible outcome as of Year 1, the time when the option expires. Here we simply find the present value of all future operating cash flows discounted back to Year 1, using the WACC of 14%. The Year 1 present value is $76.61 million for high demand, $58.04 million for average demand, and $11.61 million for low demand. Then, in Part 2, we show the percentage return from the current time until the option expires for each scenario, based on the $44.80 million starting "price" of the project at Year 0 as calculated in Figure 13-3. If demand is high, we will obtain a return of 71.0%: ($76.61 − $44.80)/ $44.80 = 0.710 = 71.0%. Similar calculations show returns of 29.5% for average demand and −74.1% for low demand. The expected percentage return is 14%, the standard deviation is 53.6%, and the variance is 28.7%.[6]

The third approach for estimating the variance is also based on the scenario data, but the data are used in a different manner. First, we know that demand is not really limited to three scenarios—rather, a wide range of outcomes is possible. Similarly, the stock price at the time a call option expires could take on one of many values. It is reasonable to assume that the value of the project at the time when we must decide on undertaking it behaves similarly to the price of a stock at the time a call option expires. Under this assumption, we can use the expected value and standard deviation of the project's value to calculate the variance of its rate of return, σ^2, with this formula:[7]

$$\sigma^2 = \frac{\ln(CV^2 + 1)}{t}. \tag{13-1}$$

---

[6]Two points should be made about the percentage return. First, for use in the Black-Scholes model, we need a percentage return calculated as shown, not an IRR return. The IRR is not used in the option pricing approach. Second, the expected return turns out to be 14%, the same as the WACC. This is because the Year 0 price and the Year 1 PVs were all calculated using the 14% WACC, and because we are measuring return over only 1 year. If we measure the compound return over more than 1 year, then the average return generally will not equal 14%.
[7]See David C. Shimko, *Finance in Continuous Time* (Miami, FL: Kolb Publishing Company, 1992), for a more detailed explanation.

Figure 13-4

Estimating the Input for Variance in the Option Analysis of the Investment Timing Option (Millions of Dollars)

PART 1. FIND THE VALUE AND RISK OF FUTURE CASH FLOWS AT THE TIME THE OPTION EXPIRES

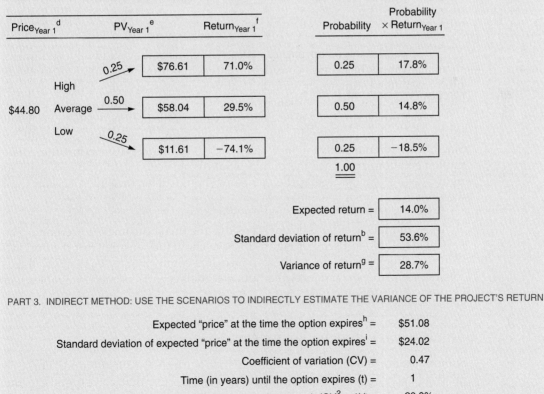

Now: Year 0		FUTURE CASH FLOWS				PV in Year 1 for This Scenario[a]	Probability	Probability × PV$_{Year 1}$
		Year 1	Year 2	Year 3	Year 4			
	High 0.25		$33	$33	$33	$76.61	0.25	$19.15
Wait	Average 0.50		$25	$25	$25	$58.04	0.50	$29.02
	Low 0.25		$5	$5	$5	$11.61	0.25	$2.90
							1.00	

Expected value of PV$_{Year 1}$ = $51.08

Standard deviation of PV$_{Year 1}$[b] = $24.02

Coefficient of variation of PV$_{Year 1}$[c] =   0.47

PART 2. DIRECT METHOD: USE THE SCENARIOS TO DIRECTLY ESTIMATE THE VARIANCE OF THE PROJECT'S RETURN

Price$_{Year 1}$[d]		PV$_{Year 1}$[e]	Return$_{Year 1}$[f]		Probability	Probability × Return$_{Year 1}$
	High 0.25	$76.61	71.0%		0.25	17.8%
$44.80	Average 0.50	$58.04	29.5%		0.50	14.8%
	Low 0.25	$11.61	−74.1%		0.25	−18.5%
					1.00	

Expected return =   14.0%

Standard deviation of return[b] =   53.6%

Variance of return[g] =   28.7%

PART 3. INDIRECT METHOD: USE THE SCENARIOS TO INDIRECTLY ESTIMATE THE VARIANCE OF THE PROJECT'S RETURN

Expected "price" at the time the option expires[h] = $51.08

Standard deviation of expected "price" at the time the option expires[i] = $24.02

Coefficient of variation (CV) =   0.47

Time (in years) until the option expires (t) =   1

Variance of the project's expected return = $\ln(CV^2 + 1)/t$ =   20.0%

(continued)

Figure 13-4

Estimating the Input for Variance in the Option Analysis of the Investment Timing Option (Millions of Dollars) (*continued*)

Notes:
[a]The WACC is 14%. The Year 2 through Year 4 cash flows are discounted back to Year 1.
[b]The standard deviation is calculated as explained in Chapter 6.
[c]The coefficient of variation is the standard deviation divided by the expected value.
[d]The Year 0 price is the expected PV from Figure 13-3.
[e]The Year 1 PVs are from Part 1.
[f]The returns for each scenario are calculated as $(PV_{Year\ 1} - Price_{Year\ 0})/Price_{Year\ 0}$.
[g]The variance of return is the standard deviation squared.
[h]The expected "price" at the time the option expires is taken from Part 1.
[i]The standard deviation of expected "price" at the time the option expires is taken from Part 1.

Here CV is the coefficient of variation of the underlying asset's price at the time the option expires and t is the time until the option expires. Thus, while the three scenarios are simplifications of the true condition, where there are an infinite number of possible outcomes, we can still use the scenario data to estimate the variance of the project's rate of return if it has an infinite number of possible outcomes.

For Murphy's project, this indirect method produces the following estimate of the variance of the project's return:

$$\sigma^2 = \frac{\ln(0.47^2 + 1)}{1} = 0.20 = 20\%. \tag{13-1a}$$

Which of the three approaches is best? Obviously, they all involve judgment, so an analyst might want to consider all three. In our example, all three methods produce similar estimates, but for illustrative purposes we will simply use 20% as our initial estimate for the variance of the project's rate of return.

In Part 1 of Figure 13-5 we calculate the value of the option to defer investment in the project based on the Black-Scholes model, and the result is $7.04 million. Since this is significantly higher than the $1.08 million NPV under immediate implementation, and since the option would be forfeited if Murphy goes ahead right now, we conclude that the company should defer the final decision until more information is available.

Note, though, that judgmental estimates were made at many points in the analysis, and it is useful to see how sensitive the final outcome is to certain of the key inputs. Thus, in Part 2 of Figure 13-5 we show the sensitivity of the option's value to different estimates of the variance. It is comforting to see that for all reasonable estimates of variance, the option to delay remains more valuable than immediate implementation.

Approach 5. Financial Engineering

Sometimes an analyst might not be satisfied with the results of a decision tree analysis and cannot find a standard financial option that corresponds to the real option. In such a situation the only alternative is to develop a unique model for the specific real option being analyzed, a process called **financial engineering.** When financial engineering is applied on Wall Street, where it

---

Figure 13-5

Estimating the Value of the Investment Timing Option Using a Standard Financial Option (Millions of Dollars)

PART 1. FIND THE VALUE OF A CALL OPTION USING THE BLACK-SCHOLES MODEL

Real Option

$r_{RF} =$	Risk-free interest rate	=	6%
$t =$	Time in years until the option expires	=	1
$X =$	Cost to implement the project	=	$50.00
$P =$	Current value of the project	=	$44.80[a]
$\sigma^2 =$	Variance of the project's rate of return	=	20.0%[b]
$d_1 =$	$\{\ln(P/X) + [r_{RF} + (\sigma^2/2)]t\}/(\sigma t^{1/2})$	=	0.112
$d_2 =$	$d_1 - \sigma(t^{1/2})$	=	−0.33
$N(d_1) =$		=	0.54
$N(d_2) =$		=	0.37
$V =$	$P[N(d_1)] - Xe^{-r_{RF}t}[N(d_2)]$	=	$7.04

PART 2. SENSITIVITY ANALYSIS OF OPTION VALUE TO CHANGES IN VARIANCE

Variance	Option Value
12.0%	$5.24
14.0	5.74
16.0	6.20
18.0	6.63
20.0	7.04
22.0	7.42
24.0	7.79
26.0	8.15
28.0	8.49
30.0	8.81
32.0	9.13

Notes:
[a]The current value of the project is taken from Figure 13-3.
[b]The variance of the project's rate of return is taken from Part 3 of Figure 13-4.

was developed, the result is a newly designed financial product.[8] When it is applied to real options, the result is the value of a project that contains embedded options.

Although financial engineering was originally developed on Wall Street, many financial engineering techniques have been applied to real options during the last 10 years. We expect this trend to continue, especially in light of the rapid improvements in computer processing speed and spreadsheet software capabilities. One financial engineering technique is called **risk-neutral valuation**. This technique uses simulation, and we discuss it in *Web Extension 13B*. Most other

---

[8]Financial engineering techniques are widely used for the creation and valuation of derivative securities.

financial engineering techniques are too complicated for a course in financial management, and so we leave a detailed discussion of them to a specialized course.

For an illustrative valuation of an abandonment option, see *Web Extension 13A*. The calculations are also shown in *FM12 Ch 13 Tool Kit.xls* available at the textbook's Web site.

SELF-TEST

What is a decision tree?
In a qualitative analysis, what factors affect the value of a real option?

13.3 The Growth Option: An Illustration

As we saw with the investment timing option, there is frequently an alternative to merely accepting or rejecting a static project. Many investment opportunities, if successful, lead to other investment opportunities. The production capacity of a successful product line can later be expanded to satisfy increased demand, or distribution can be extended to new geographic markets. A company with a successful name brand can capitalize on its success by adding complimentary or new products under the same brand. These growth options add value to a project and explain, for example, why companies are flocking to make inroads into the very difficult business environment in China.

Kidco Corporation designs and produces products aimed at the pre-teen market. Most of its products have a very short life, given the rapidly changing tastes of pre-teens. Kidco is now considering a project that will cost $30 million. Management believes there is a 25% chance that the project will "take off" and generate operating cash flows of $34 million in each of the next 2 years, after which pre-teen tastes will change and the project will be terminated. There is a 50% chance of average demand, in which case cash flows will be $20 million annually for 2 years. Finally, there is a 25% chance that the pre-teens won't like the product at all, and it will generate cash flows of only $2 million per year. The estimated cost of capital for the project is 14%.

Based on its experience with other projects, Kidco believes it will be able to launch a second-generation product if demand for the original product is average or above. This second-generation product will cost the same as the first product, $30 million, and the cost will be incurred at Year 2. However, given the success of the first-generation product, Kidco believes the second-generation product will be just as successful as the first-generation product.

This growth option resembles a call option on a stock, since it gives Kidco the opportunity to "purchase" a successful follow-on project at a fixed cost if the value of the project is greater than the cost. Otherwise, Kidco will let the option expire by not implementing the second-generation product.

The following sections apply the first four valuation approaches: (1) DCF, (2) DCF and qualitative assessment, (3) decision tree analysis, and (4) analysis with a standard financial option.

Approach 1. DCF Analysis Ignoring the Growth Option

Based on probabilities for the different levels of demand, the expected annual operating cash flows for the project are $19 million per year:

$$0.25(\$34) + 0.50(\$20) + 0.25(\$2) = \$19.00.$$

Ignoring the investment timing option, the traditional NPV is $1.29 million:

$$\text{NPV} = -\$30 + \frac{\$19}{(1 + 0.14)^1} + \frac{\$19}{(1 + 0.14)^2} = \$1.29.$$

Based on this DCF analysis, Kidco should accept the project.

Approach 2. DCF Analysis with a Qualitative Consideration of the Growth Option

Although the DCF analysis indicates that the project should be accepted, it ignores a potentially valuable real option. The option's time to maturity and the volatility of the underlying project provide qualitative insights into the option's value. Kidco's growth option has 2 years until maturity, which is a relatively long time, and the cash flows of the project are volatile. Taken together, this qualitative assessment indicates that the growth option should be quite valuable.

Approach 3. Decision Tree Analysis of the Growth Option

Part 1 of Figure 13-6 shows a scenario analysis for Kidco's project. The top line, which describes the payoffs for the high-demand scenario, has operating cash flows of $34 million for the next 2 years. The NPV of this branch is $25.99 million. The NPV of the average-demand branch in the middle is $2.93 million, and it is −$26.71 million for the low-demand scenario. The sum in the last column of Part 1 shows the expected NPV of $1.29 million. The coefficient of variation is 14.54, indicating that the project is very risky.

Part 2 of Figure 13-6 shows a decision tree analysis in which Kidco undertakes the second-generation product only if demand is average or high. In these scenarios, shown on the top two branches of the decision tree, Kidco will incur a cost of $30 million at Year 2 and receive operating cash flows of either $34 million or $20 million for the next 2 years, depending on the level of demand. If the demand is low, shown on the bottom branch, Kidco has no cost at Year 2 and receives no additional cash flows in subsequent years. All operating cash flows, which do not include the cost of implementing the second-generation project at Year 2, are discounted at the WACC of 14%. Because the $30 million implementation cost is known, it is discounted at the risk-free rate of 6%. As shown in Part 2 of Figure 13-6, the expected NPV is $4.70 million, indicating that the growth option is quite valuable.

The option itself alters the risk of the project, which means that 14% is probably not the appropriate cost of capital. Table 13-1 presents the results of a sensitivity analysis in which the cost of capital for the operating cash flows varies from 8% to 18%. The sensitivity analysis also allows the rate used to discount the implementation cost at Year 2 to vary from 3% to 9%. The NPV is positive for all reasonable combinations of discount rates.

Approach 4. Valuing the Growth Option with the Black-Scholes Option Pricing Model

The fourth approach is to use a standard model for a corresponding financial option. As we noted earlier, Kidco's growth option is similar to a call option on a

Figure 13-6

Scenario Analysis and Decision Tree Analysis for the Kidco Project (Millions of Dollars)

PART 1. SCENARIO ANALYSIS OF KIDCO'S FIRST-GENERATION PROJECT

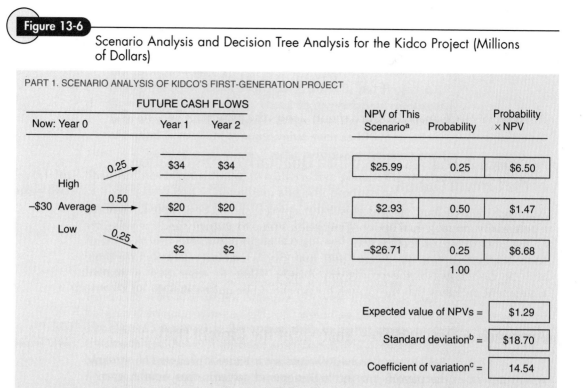

	FUTURE CASH FLOWS			NPV of This Scenario[a]	Probability	Probability × NPV
Now: Year 0		Year 1	Year 2			
High 0.25		$34	$34	$25.99	0.25	$6.50
−$30 Average 0.50		$20	$20	$2.93	0.50	$1.47
Low 0.25		$2	$2	−$26.71	0.25	$6.68
					1.00	

Expected value of NPVs =	$1.29
Standard deviation[b] =	$18.70
Coefficient of variation[c] =	14.54

PART 2. DECISION TREE ANALYSIS OF THE GROWTH OPTION

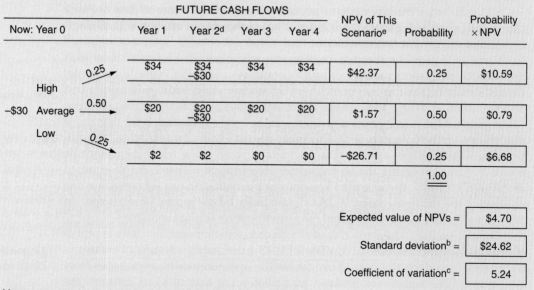

	FUTURE CASH FLOWS					NPV of This Scenario[e]	Probability	Probability × NPV
Now: Year 0		Year 1	Year 2[d]	Year 3	Year 4			
High 0.25		$34	$34 −$30	$34	$34	$42.37	0.25	$10.59
−$30 Average 0.50		$20	$20 −$30	$20	$20	$1.57	0.50	$0.79
Low 0.25		$2	$2	$0	$0	−$26.71	0.25	$6.68
							1.00	

Expected value of NPVs =	$4.70
Standard deviation[b] =	$24.62
Coefficient of variation[c] =	5.24

Notes:
[a]The operating cash flows are discounted by the WACC of 14%.
[b]The standard deviation is calculated as in Chapter 6.
[c]The coefficient of variation is the standard deviation divided by the expected value.
[d]The total cash flows at Year 2 are equal to the operating cash flows for the first-generation product minus the $30 million cost to implement the second-generation product, if it is optimal to do so. For example, the Year 2 cash flow in the high-demand scenario is $34 − $30 = $4 million. Based on Part 1, it is optional to implement the second-generation product only if demand is high or average.
[e]The operating cash flows in Year 1 through Year 2, which do not include the $30 million cost of implementing the second-generation project at Year 2 for the high-demand and average-demand scenarios, are discounted at the WACC of 14%. The $30 million implementation cost at Year 2 for the high-demand and average-demand scenarios is discounted at the risk-free rate of 6%.

Table 13-1

Sensitivity Analysis of the Kidco Decision Tree Analysis in Figure 13-6 (Millions of Dollars)

	Cost of Capital Used to Discount the $30 Million Implementation Cost at Year 2 of the Second-Generation Project						
	3.0%	4.0%	5.0%	6.0%	7.0%	8.0%	9.0%
8.0%	$10.96	$11.36	$11.76	$12.14	$12.51	$12.88	$13.23
9.0	9.61	10.01	10.41	10.79	11.16	11.52	11.88
10.0	8.30	8.71	9.10	9.49	9.86	10.22	10.57
11.0	7.04	7.45	7.84	8.23	8.60	8.96	9.31
12.0	5.83	6.23	6.63	7.01	7.38	7.75	8.10
13.0	4.65	5.06	5.45	5.84	6.21	6.57	6.92
14.0	3.52	3.92	4.32	4.70	5.07	5.44	5.79
15.0	2.42	2.83	3.22	3.61	3.98	4.34	4.69
16.0	1.36	1.77	2.16	2.54	2.92	3.28	3.63
17.0	0.33	0.74	1.13	1.52	1.89	2.25	2.60
18.0	−0.66	−0.25	0.14	0.52	0.90	1.26	1.61

(Left vertical axis label: Cost of Capital Used to Discount the Year 1 through Year 4 Operating Cash Flows (These do not include the $30 million implementation cost of the second-generation project at Year 2.))

stock, and so we will use the Black-Scholes model to find the value of the growth option. The time until the growth option expires is 2 years. The rate on a 2-year Treasury security is 6%, and this provides a good estimate of the risk-free rate. It will cost $30 million to implement the project, which is the strike price.

The input for stock price in the Black-Scholes model is the current value of the underlying asset. For the growth option, the underlying asset is the second-generation project, and its current value is the present value of its cash flows. The calculations in Figure 13-7 show that this is $24.07 million. Because the strike price of $30 million is greater than the current "price" of $24.07 million, the growth option is presently out of the money.

Figure 13-8 shows the estimates for the variance of the project's rate of return using the two methods described earlier in the chapter for the analysis of the investment timing option. The direct method, shown in Part 2, produces an estimate of 17.9% for the variance of return. The indirect method, in Part 3, estimates the variance as 15.3%. Both estimates are somewhat higher than the 12% variance of a typical company's stock return, which is consistent with the idea that a stock's variance is lower than a project's due to diversification effects. Thus, an estimated variance of 15% to 20% seems reasonable. We use an initial estimate of 15.3% in our initial application of the Black-Scholes model, shown in Part 1 of Figure 13-9.

Using the Black-Scholes model for a call option, Figure 13-9 shows a $4.34 million value for the growth option. The total NPV is the sum of the first-generation project's NPV and the value of the growth option: Total NPV = $1.29 + $4.34 = $5.63 million, which is much higher than the NPV of only the first-generation

Figure 13-7

Estimating the Input for Stock Price in the Growth Option Analysis of the Investment Timing Option (Millions of Dollars)

	FUTURE CASH FLOWS						
Now: Year 0	Year 1	Year 2	Year 3	Year 4	PV of This Scenario[a]	Probability	Probability × PV
High (0.25)			$34	$34	$43.08	0.25	$10.77
Average (0.50)			$20	$20	$25.34	0.50	$12.67
Low (0.25)			$2	$2	$2.53	0.25	$0.63
						1.00	

Expected value of PVs =	$24.07
Standard deviation[b] =	$14.39
Coefficient of variation[c] =	0.60

Notes:
[a]The WACC is 14%. All cash flows in this scenario are discounted back to Year 0.
[b]The standard deviation is calculated as in Chapter 6.
[c]The coefficient of variation is the standard deviation divided by the expected value.

Figure 13-8

Estimating the Input for Stock Return Variance in the Growth Option Analysis (Millions of Dollars)

PART 1. FIND THE VALUE AND RISK OF FUTURE CASH FLOWS AT THE TIME THE OPTION EXPIRES

	FUTURE CASH FLOWS						
Now: Year 0	Year 1	Year 2	Year 3	Year 4	PV of This Scenario[a]	Probability	Probability × PV
High (0.25)			$34	$34	$55.99	0.25	$14.00
Average (0.50)			$20	$20	$32.93	0.50	$16.47
Low (0.25)			$2	$2	$3.29	0.25	$0.82
						1.00	

Expected value of $PV_{Year\ 2}$ =	$31.29
Standard $deviation_{Year\ 2}$[b] =	$18.70
Coefficient of $variation_{Year\ 2}$[c] =	0.60

(continued)

Figure 13-8

Estimating the Input for Stock Return Variance in the Growth Option Analysis (Millions of Dollars) (*continued*)

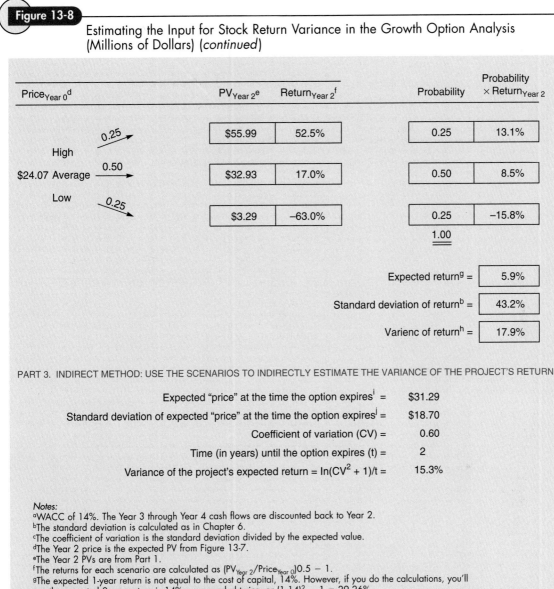

Price$_{Year\ 0}$[d]		PV$_{Year\ 2}$[e]	Return$_{Year\ 2}$[f]	Probability	Probability × Return$_{Year\ 2}$
High	0.25	$55.99	52.5%	0.25	13.1%
$24.07 Average	0.50	$32.93	17.0%	0.50	8.5%
Low	0.25	$3.29	−63.0%	0.25	−15.8%
				1.00	

Expected return[g] = **5.9%**

Standard deviation of return[b] = **43.2%**

Varienc of return[h] = **17.9%**

PART 3. INDIRECT METHOD: USE THE SCENARIOS TO INDIRECTLY ESTIMATE THE VARIANCE OF THE PROJECT'S RETURN

Expected "price" at the time the option expires[i] =	$31.29
Standard deviation of expected "price" at the time the option expires[j] =	$18.70
Coefficient of variation (CV) =	0.60
Time (in years) until the option expires (t) =	2
Variance of the project's expected return = $\ln(CV^2 + 1)/t$ =	15.3%

Notes:
[a]WACC of 14%. The Year 3 through Year 4 cash flows are discounted back to Year 2.
[b]The standard deviation is calculated as in Chapter 6.
[c]The coefficient of variation is the standard deviation divided by the expected value.
[d]The Year 2 price is the expected PV from Figure 13-7.
[e]The Year 2 PVs are from Part 1.
[f]The returns for each scenario are calculated as $(PV_{Year\ 2}/Price_{Year\ 0})0.5 - 1$.
[g]The expected 1-year return is not equal to the cost of capital, 14%. However, if you do the calculations, you'll see the expected 2-year return is 14% compounded twice, or $(1.14)^2 - 1 = 29.26\%$.
[h]The variance of return is the standard deviation squared.
[i]The expected "price" at the time the option expires is taken from Part 1.
[j]The standard deviation of the expected "price" at the time the option expires is taken from Part 1.

project. As this analysis shows, the growth option adds considerable value to the original project. In addition, sensitivity analysis in Part 2 of Figure 13-9 shows that the growth option's value is large for all reasonable values of variance. Thus, Kidco should accept the project.

SELF-TEST

Explain how growth options are like call options.

Figure 13-9

Estimating the Value of the Growth Option Using a Standard Financial Option (Millions of Dollars)

PART 1. FIND THE VALUE OF A CALL OPTION USING THE BLACK-SCHOLES MODEL

Real Option

r_{RF} =	Risk-free interest rate	=	6%
t =	Time (in years) until the option expires	=	2
X =	Cost to implement the project	=	$30.00
P =	Current value of the project	=	$24.07[a]
σ^2 =	Variance of project's rate of return	=	15.3%[b]
d_1 =	$\{\ln(P/X) + [r_{RF} + (\sigma^2/2)]t\}/(\sigma t^{1/2})$	=	0.096
d_2 =	$d_1 - \sigma(t^{1/2})$	=	−0.46
$N(d_1)$ =		=	0.54
$N(d_2)$ =		=	−0.32
V =	$P[N(d_1)] - Xe^{-r_{RF}t}[N(d_2)]$	=	$4.34

PART 2. SENSITIVITY ANALYSIS OF PUT OPTION VALUE TO CHANGES IN VARIANCE

Variance	Option Value
11.3%	$2.29
13.3	3.98
15.3	4.34
17.3	4.68
19.3	4.99
21.3	5.29
23.3	5.57
25.3	5.84
27.3	6.10
39.3	6.35
31.3	6.59

Notes:
[a]The current value of the project is taken from Figure 13-7.
[b]The variance of the project's rate of return is taken from Part 3 of Figure 13-8.

13.4 Concluding Thoughts on Real Options

We don't deny that real options can be pretty complicated. Keep in mind, however, that 50 years ago very few companies used NPV because it seemed too complicated. Now NPV is a basic tool used by virtually all companies and taught in all business schools. A similar, but more rapid, pattern of adoption is occurring with real options. Ten years ago very few companies used real options, but a recent survey

Growth Options at Dot-Com Companies

In September 2000, several dot-com companies had recently failed, including DEN (Digital Entertainment Network) and Boo.com, an e-tailer of clothing. Other dot-coms had incredible market valuations, such as Yahoo! ($58.2 billion), Amazon.com ($15.5 billion), and America Online ($126.9 billion).

What explained these wide variations in values? It was certainly not the physical assets the companies owned, since Yahoo! had enormous value but virtually no physical assets. We might be tempted to say the differences were explained by free cash flows. Perhaps dot-coms such as Amazon and Yahoo! had large expected future free cash flows, and their high values reflected this, but we certainly can't base that conclusion on their past results.

This is where real options come into play. Given its name recognition, infrastructure, and customer base, Amazon was in a position to grow into a variety of businesses, some of which might have been very profitable. The same was true for Yahoo!. In other words, it had many growth options with very low exercise prices. We know from our discussion of real options that an option is more valuable if the underlying source of risk is very volatile, and it's hard to imagine anything more volatile than the prospects of profitability in e-commerce. The field of e-commerce may end up being so competitive that there is little profit for the participating companies, or it may replace most existing forms of commerce, with the first movers having an enormous advantage. This uncertainty means that a growth option in e-commerce is very valuable. Therefore, companies with many growth options should have had high valuations.

Interestingly, it now (2006) looks as though Yahoo!'s and Amazon's options are in-the-money, while AOL's are out-of-the-money.

Source: Geoffrey Colvin, "You're Only as Good as Your Choices," *Fortune,* June 12, 2000, p. 75.

of CFOs reported that more than 26% of companies now use real option techniques when evaluating projects.[9] Just as with NPV, it's only a matter of time before virtually all companies use real option techniques.

We have provided you with some basic tools necessary for evaluating real options, starting with the ability to identify real options and make qualitative assessments regarding a real option's value. Decision trees are another important tool, since they facilitate an explicit identification of the embedded options, which is very important in the decision-making process. However, keep in mind that the decision tree should not use the original project's cost of capital. Although finance theory has not yet provided a way to estimate the appropriate cost of capital for a decision tree, sensitivity analysis can identify the effect that different costs of capital have on the project's value.

Many real options can be analyzed using a standard model for an existing financial option, such as the Black-Scholes model for calls and puts. There are also other financial models for a variety of options. These include the option to exchange one asset for another, the option to purchase the minimum or the maximum of two or more assets, the option on an average of several assets, and even an option on an option.[10] In fact, there are entire textbooks that describe even more options.[11]

---

[9]See John R. Graham and Campbell R. Harvey, "The Theory and Practice of Corporate Finance: Evidence from the Field," *Journal of Financial Economics,* 2001, pp. 187–243.
[10]See W. Margrabe, "The Value of an Option to Exchange One Asset for Another," *Journal of Finance,* March 1978, pp. 177–186; R. Stulz, "Options on the Minimum or Maximum of Two Risky Assets: Analysis and Applications," *Journal of Financial Economics,* 1982, pp. 161–185; H. Johnson, "Options on the Maximum or Minimum of Several Assets," *Journal of Financial and Quantitative Analysis,* September 1987, pp. 277–283; P. Ritchken, L. Sankarasubramanian, and A. M. Vijh, "Averaging Options for Capping Total Costs," *Financial Management,* Autumn 1990, pp. 35–41; and R. Geske, "The Valuation of Compound Options," *Journal of Financial Economics,* March 1979, pp. 63–81.
[11]See John C. Hull, *Options, Futures, and Other Derivatives,* 6th ed. (Upper Saddle River, NJ: Prentice-Hall, 2006).

Given the large number of standard models for existing financial options, it is often possible to find a financial option that resembles the real option being analyzed.

Sometimes there are some real options that don't resemble any financial options. But the good news is that many of these options can be valued using techniques from financial engineering. This is frequently the case if there is a traded financial asset that matches the risk of the real option. For example, many oil companies use oil futures contracts to price the real options that are embedded in various exploration and leasing strategies. With the explosion in the markets for derivatives, there are now financial contracts that span an incredible variety of risks. This means that an ever-increasing number of real options can be valued using these financial instruments. Most financial engineering techniques are beyond the scope of this book, but *Web Extension 13B*, available at the textbook's Web site, describes one particularly useful financial engineering technique called risk-neutral valuation.[12]

SELF-TEST

How widely used is real option analysis?
What techniques can be used to analyze real options?

Summary

In this chapter we discussed some topics that go beyond the simple capital budgeting framework, including the following:

- Investing in a new project often brings with it a potential increase in the firm's future opportunities. Opportunities are, in effect, options—the right but not the obligation to take some future action.
- A project may have an **option value** that is not accounted for in a conventional NPV analysis. Any project that expands the firm's set of opportunities has positive option value.
- **Real options** are opportunities for management to respond to changes in market conditions and involve "real" rather than "financial" assets. There are five possible procedures for valuing real options: (1) **DCF analysis only, and ignore the real option**, (2) **DCF analysis and a qualitative assessment of the real option's value**, (3) **decision tree analysis**, (4) **analysis with a standard model for an existing financial option**, and (5) **financial engineering techniques.**

---

[12]For more on real options, see Martha Amram, *Value Sweep: Mapping Corporate Growth Opportunities* (Boston: Harvard Business School Press, 2002); Martha Amram and Nalin Kulatilaka, *Real Options: Managing Strategic Investment in an Uncertain World* (Boston: Harvard Business School Press, 1999); Michael Brennan and Lenos Trigeorgis, *Project Flexibility, Agency, and Competition: New Developments in the Theory and Application of Real Options* (New York: Oxford University Press, 2000); Eduardo Schwartz and Lenos Trigeorgis, *Real Options and Investment Under Uncertainty* (Cambridge, MA: The MIT Press, 2001); Han T. J. Smit and Lenos Trigeorgis, *Strategic Investment: Real Options and Games* (Princeton, NJ: Princeton University Press, 2004); Lenos Trigeorgis, *Real Options in Capital Investment: Models, Strategies, and Applications* (Westport, CT: Praeger, 1995); and Lenos Trigeorgis, *Real Options: Managerial Flexibility and Strategy in Resource Allocation* (Cambridge, MA: The MIT Press, 1996).

Questions

(13-1) Define each of the following terms:
   a. Real options; managerial options; strategic options; embedded option
   b. Investment timing option; growth option; abandonment option; flexibility option
   c. Decision trees

(13-2) What factors should a company consider when it decides whether to invest in a project today or to wait until more information becomes available?

(13-3) In general, do timing options make it more or less likely that a project will be accepted today?

(13-4) If a company has an option to abandon a project, would this tend to make the company more or less likely to accept the project today?

Self-Test Problem   Solution Appears in Appendix A

(ST-1) Katie Watkins, an entrepreneur, believes consolidation is the key to profit in the
Real Options   fragmented recreational equine industry. In particular, she is considering start-ing a business that will develop and sell franchises to other owner-operators, who will then board and train hunter-jumper horses. The initial cost to develop and implement the franchise concept is $8 million. She estimates a 25% proba-bility of high demand for the concept, in which case she will receive cash flows of $13 million at the end of each year for the next 2 years. She estimates a 50% probability of medium demand, in which case the annual cash flows will be $7 million for 2 years, and a 25% probability of low demand with annual cash flow of $1 million for 2 years. She estimates the appropriate cost of capital is 15%. The risk-free rate is 6%.
   a. Find the NPV of each scenario, and then find the expected NPV.
   b. Now assume that the expertise gained by taking on the project will lead to an opportunity at the end of Year 2 to undertake a similar venture that will have the same cost as the original project. The new project's cash flows would follow whichever branch resulted for the original project. In other words, there would be an $8 million cost at the end of Year 2 and then cash flows of $13 million, $7 million, or $1 million for Years 3 and 4. Use decision tree analysis to estimate the combined value of the original project and the additional project (but implement the additional project only if it is optimal to do so). Assume the $8 million cost at Year 2 is known with certainty and should be discounted at the risk-free rate of 6%. [Hint: Do one decision tree that discounts the operating cash flows at the 15% cost of capital and another decision tree that discounts the costs of the projects (that is, the costs at Year 0 and Year 2) at the risk-free rate of 6%. Then sum the two decision trees to find the total NPV.]

c. Instead of using decision tree analysis, use the Black-Scholes model to estimate the value of the growth option. Assume the variance of the project's rate of return is 15%. Find the total value of the project with the option to expand (that is, the sum of the original expected value and the growth option). (Hint: You will need to find the expected present value of the additional project's operating cash flows to estimate the current price of the option's underlying asset.)

Problems   Answers Appear in Appendix B

Intermediate Problems 1–5

(13-1)
Investment Timing
Option: Decision Tree
Analysis

Kim Hotels is interested in developing a new hotel in Seoul. The company estimates that the hotel would require an initial investment of $20 million. Kim expects that the hotel will produce positive cash flows of $3 million a year at the end of each of the next 20 years. The project's cost of capital is 13%.
a. What is the project's net present value?
b. While Kim expects the cash flows to be $3 million a year, it recognizes that the cash flows could, in fact, be much higher or lower, depending on whether the Korean government imposes a large hotel tax. One year from now, Kim will know whether the tax will be imposed. There is a 50% chance that the tax will be imposed, in which case the yearly cash flows will be only $2.2 million. At the same time, there is a 50% chance that the tax will not be imposed, in which case the yearly cash flows will be $3.8 million. Kim is deciding whether to proceed with the hotel today or to wait 1 year to find out whether the tax will be imposed. If Kim waits a year, the initial investment will remain at $20 million. Assume that all cash flows are discounted at 13%. Using decision tree analysis, should Kim proceed with the project today or should it wait a year before deciding?

(13-2)
Investment Timing
Option: Decision Tree
Analysis

The Karns Oil Company is deciding whether to drill for oil on a tract of land that the company owns. The company estimates that the project would cost $8 million today. Karns estimates that once drilled, the oil will generate positive net cash flows of $4 million a year at the end of each of the next 4 years. While the company is fairly confident about its cash flow forecast, it recognizes that if it waits 2 years, it would have more information about the local geology as well as the price of oil. Karns estimates that if it waits 2 years, the project would cost $9 million. Moreover, if it waits 2 years, there is a 90% chance that the net cash flows would be $4.2 million a year for 4 years, and there is a 10% chance that the cash flows will be $2.2 million a year for 4 years. Assume that all cash flows are discounted at 10%.
a. If the company chooses to drill today, what is the project's net present value?
b. Using decision tree analysis, does it make sense to wait 2 years before deciding whether to drill?

(13-3)
Investment Timing
Option: Decision Tree
Analysis

Hart Lumber is considering the purchase of a paper company. Purchasing the company would require an initial investment of $300 million. Hart estimates that the paper company would provide net cash flows of $40 million at the end of each of the next 20 years. The cost of capital for the paper company is 13%.

a. Should Hart purchase the paper company?

b. While Hart's best guess is that cash flows will be $40 million a year, it recognizes that there is a 50% chance the cash flows will be $50 million a year, and a 50% chance that the cash flows will be $30 million a year. One year from now, it will find out whether the cash flows will be $30 million or $50 million. In addition, Hart also recognizes that if it wanted, it could sell the company at Year 3 for $280 million. Given this additional information, does using decision tree analysis indicate that it makes sense to purchase the paper company? Again, assume that all cash flows are discounted at 13%.

(13-4)
Real Options: Decision Tree Analysis

Utah Enterprises is considering buying a vacant lot that sells for $1.2 million. If the property is purchased, the company's plan is to spend another $5 million today (t = 0) to build a hotel on the property. The after-tax cash flows from the hotel will depend critically on whether the state imposes a tourism tax in this year's legislative session. If the tax is imposed, the hotel is expected to produce after-tax cash inflows of $600,000 at the end of each of the next 15 years. If the tax is not imposed, the hotel is expected to produce after-tax cash inflows of $1,200,000 at the end of each of the next 15 years. The project has a 12% cost of capital. Assume at the outset that the company does not have the option to delay the project. Use decision tree analysis to answer the following questions.

a. What is the project's expected NPV if the tax is imposed?

b. What is the project's expected NPV if the tax is not imposed?

c. Given that there is a 50% chance that the tax will be imposed, what is the project's expected NPV if they proceed with it today?

d. While the company does not have an option to delay construction, it does have the option to abandon the project 1 year from now if the tax is imposed. If it abandons the project, it would sell the complete property 1 year from now at an expected price of $6 million. Once the project is abandoned the company would no longer receive any cash inflows from it. Assuming that all cash flows are discounted at 12%, would the existence of this abandonment option affect the company's decision to proceed with the project today?

e. Finally, assume that there is no option to abandon or delay the project, but that the company has an option to purchase an adjacent property in 1 year at a price of $1.5 million. If the tourism tax is imposed, the net present value of developing this property (as of t = 1) is only $300,000 (so it wouldn't make sense to purchase the property for $1.5 million). However, if the tax is not imposed, the net present value of the future opportunities from developing the property would be $4 million (as of t = 1). Thus, under this scenario it would make sense to purchase the property for $1.5 million. Assume that these cash flows are discounted at 12%, and the probability that the tax will be imposed is still 50%. How much would the company pay today for the option to purchase this property 1 year from now for $1.5 million?

(13-5)
Growth Option: Decision Tree Analysis

Fethe's Funny Hats is considering selling trademarked curly orange-haired wigs for University of Tennessee football games. The purchase cost for a 2-year franchise to sell the wigs is $20,000. If demand is good (40% probability), then the net cash flows will be $25,000 per year for 2 years. If demand is bad (60% probability), then the net cash flows will be $5,000 per year for 2 years. Fethe's cost of capital is 10%.

a. What is the expected NPV of the project?

b. If Fethe makes the investment today, then it will have the option to renew the franchise fee for 2 more years at the end of Year 2 for an additional payment of $20,000. In this case, the cash flows that occurred in Years 1 and 2 will be repeated (so if demand was good in Years 1 and 2, then it will continue to be good in Years 3 and 4). Write out the decision tree and use decision tree analysis to calculate the expected NPV of this project including the option to continue on for an additional 2 years. Note: The franchise fee payment at the end of Year 2 is known, so it should be discounted at the risk-free rate, which is 6%.

Challenging Problems 6–8

(13-6)
Investment Timing Option: Option Analysis

Rework Problem 13-1 using the Black-Scholes model to estimate the value of the option. (Hint: Assume the variance of the project's rate of return is 6.87% and the risk-free rate is 8%.)

(13-7)
Investment Timing Option: Option Analysis

Rework Problem 13-2 using the Black-Scholes model to estimate the value of the option: The risk-free rate is 6%. (Hint: Assume the variance of the project's rate of return is 1.11%.)

(13-8)
Growth Option: Option Analysis

Rework Problem 13-5 using the Black-Scholes model to estimate the value of the option. The risk-free rate is 6%. (Hint: Assume the variance of the project's rate of return is 20.25%.)

Spreadsheet Problem

(13-9)
Build a Model: Real Options

e-resource

Start with the partial model in the file *FM12 Ch 13 P09 Build a Model.xls* from the textbook's Web site. Bradford Services Inc. (BSI) is considering a project that has a cost of $10 million and an expected life of 3 years. There is a 30% probability of good conditions, in which case the project will provide a cash flow of $9 million at the end of each year for 3 years. There is a 40% probability of medium conditions, in which case the annual cash flows will be $4 million, and there is a 30% probability of bad conditions and a cash flow of −$1 million per year. BSI uses a 12% cost of capital to evaluate projects like this.

a. Find the project's expected present value, NPV, and the coefficient of variation of the present value.

b. Now suppose that BSI can abandon the project at the end of the first year by selling it for $6 million. BSI will still receive the Year 1 cash flows, but will receive no cash flows in subsequent years.

c. Now assume that the project cannot be shut down. However, expertise gained by taking it on would lead to an opportunity at the end of Year 3 to undertake a venture that would have the same cost as the original project, and the new project's cash flows would follow whichever branch resulted for the original project. In other words, there would be a second $10 million cost at the end of Year 3, and then cash flows of either $9 million, $4 million, or −$1 million for the following 3 years. Use decision tree analysis to estimate the value of the project, including the opportunity to implement the new project at Year 3. Assume the $10 million cost at Year 3 is known with certainty and should be discounted at the risk-free rate of 6%.

d. Now suppose the original (no abandonment and no additional growth) project could be delayed a year. All the cash flows would remain unchanged, but information obtained during that year would tell the company exactly which set of demand conditions existed. Use decision tree analysis to estimate the value of the project if it is delayed by 1 year. (Hint: Discount the $10 million cost at the risk-free rate of 6% since it is known with certainty.)

e. Go back to part c. Instead of using decision tree analysis, use the Black-Scholes model to estimate the value of the growth option. The risk-free rate is 6%, and the variance of the project's rate of return is 22%.

Cyberproblems

Please go to the textbook's Web site to access any Cyberproblems.

Mini Case

Assume that you have just been hired as a financial analyst by Tropical Sweets Inc., a mid-sized California company that specializes in creating exotic candies from tropical fruits such as mangoes, papayas, and dates. The firm's CEO, George Yamaguchi, recently returned from an industry corporate executive conference in San Francisco, and one of the sessions he attended was on real options. Because no one at Tropical Sweets is familiar with the basics of real options, Yamaguchi has asked you to prepare a brief report that the firm's executives can use to gain at least a cursory understanding of the topic.

To begin, you gathered some outside materials on the subject and used these materials to draft a list of pertinent questions that need to be answered. In fact, one possible approach to the paper is to use a question-and-answer format. Now that the questions have been drafted, you have to develop the answers.

a. What are some types of real options?

b. What are five possible procedures for analyzing a real option?

c. Tropical Sweets is considering a project that will cost $70 million and will generate expected cash flows of $30 million per year for 3 years. The cost of capital for this type of project is 10% and the risk-free rate is 6%. After discussions with the marketing department, you learn that there is a 30% chance of high demand, with future cash flows of $45 million per year. There is a 40% chance of average demand, with cash flows of $30 million per year. If demand is low (a 30% chance), cash flows will be only $15 million per year. What is the expected NPV?

d. Now suppose this project has an investment timing option, since it can be delayed for a year. The cost will still be $70 million at the end of the year, and

chapter 14

Financial Planning and Forecasting Financial Statements

A recent survey of CFOs on financial planning found a paradox. On one hand, most respondents believe that financial planning is important, with the majority stating that budgeting is highly useful for allocating resources. On the other hand, many managers have doubts about the process, largely because they believe that the input data are rarely accurate enough to yield realistic results. In fact, 45% of the CFOs reported that budgeting is "contentious, political, and time-consuming." Even worse, 53% said that the budgeting process can encourage undesirable behavior among managers as they negotiate budgets to meet their own rather than the company's objectives.

What can CFOs do to improve the situation? Consider the budgeting process. It typically starts in July and ends in December, just prior to the forecasted year. The process begins with data acquisition, including historical information on sales, costs, inventories, batch sizes, defect rates, number of repeat customers, product mix by customer type, hours of employee training, and the like. Unfortunately, most larger companies have stand-alone software packages and spreadsheets that vary from division to division, making data acquisition time-consuming and error filled. Instead of basing growth and performance targets on analysis of the markets and competitors, targets are often set as last-year's-results-plus-a-percentage-increase.

To help solve this problem, companies are developing a variety of new strategies. "Demand-pull budgeting" links the budget to sales forecasts, and the sales forecasts are frequently updated to reflect changing economic conditions. A similar, but more regimented, procedure that is now used by 48% of the responding companies is the "rolling forecast." These companies make forecasts for 1-year ahead and 5-years ahead, but then modify them each quarter (or month) as new results become available. Also, some companies are now using "activity-based budgeting," which allocates costs and revenues by products and services rather than by traditional departments.

Another change is that the budgeting process at many companies is now focused on specific key items, which avoids wasting time and effort on things that have little effect on the firm's value. Yet another modification is to use performance targets based

Source: Don Durfee, "Alternative Budgeting," *CFO*, June 2006, p. 28.

on competitors' performances rather than the firm's own previous year, and then linking managerial compensation to these targets.

According to John McMahan of the Hackett Group, such changes are leading to greater forecast accuracy, higher employee satisfaction, and better corporate performance. Note too that these issues are often thought of more as "management" than as "finance," but this is a false distinction. Much of finance is numbers-oriented, but as any CFO will tell you, his or her primary job is to help the firm as a whole achieve good results. Think about all this as you go through the chapter.

Managers use **pro forma**, or **projected, financial statements** in four ways: (1) By looking at projected statements, they can assess whether the firm's anticipated performance is in line with the firm's own general targets and with investors' expectations. (2) Pro forma statements can be used to estimate the effect of proposed operating changes, enabling managers to conduct "what if" analyses. (3) Managers use pro forma statements to anticipate the firm's future financing needs. (4) Managers forecast free cash flows under different operating plans, forecast their capital requirements, and then choose the plan that maximizes shareholder value. Security analysts make the same types of projections, forecasting future earnings, cash flows, and stock prices.

e-resource

The texbook's Web site contains an *Excel* file that will guide you through the chapter's calculations. The file for this chapter is **FM12 Ch 14 Tool Kit.xls**, and we encourage you to open the file and follow along as you read the chapter.

14.1 Overview of Financial Planning

Our primary objective in this book is to explain what managers can do to make their companies more valuable. However, value creation is impossible unless the company has a well-articulated plan. As Yogi Berra once said, "You've got to be careful if you don't know where you're going, because you might not get there."

Strategic Plans

Strategic plans usually begin with a statement of the overall *corporate purpose.* Many companies are very clear about their corporate purpose: "Our mission is to maximize shareowner value over time."

This corporate purpose is increasingly common for U.S. companies, but that has not always been the case. For example, in 1990 Varian Associates, Inc. was regarded as one of the most technologically advanced electronics companies. However, Varian's management had been more concerned with developing new technology than with marketing it, and its stock price was lower than it had been 10 years earlier. Some of the larger stockholders were intensely unhappy with the state of affairs, and management was faced with the threat of a proxy fight or forced merger. In 1991, management announced a change in policy and stated that it would, in the future, emphasize both technological excellence *and* profitability, rather than focusing primarily on technology. Earnings improved dramatically, and the stock price rose after the change in corporate purpose.

Corporate Valuation and Financial Planning

The value of a firm is determined by the size, timing, and risk of its expected future free cash flows (FCF). This chapter shows you how to project the financial statements that are used to calculate expected future free cash flows. The next chapter shows you how to take those projected financial statements and estimate the value of the firm under different financial plans.

$$\text{Value} = \frac{FCF_1}{(1 + WACC)^1} + \frac{FCF_2}{(1 + WACC)^2} + \frac{FCF_3}{(1 + WACC)^3} + \cdots + \frac{FCF_\infty}{(1 + WACC)^\infty}$$

A corporate focus on creating wealth for the company's owners is not yet as common abroad as it is in the United States. For example, Veba AG, one of Germany's largest companies, created a stir in 1996 when it stated in its annual report that "Our commitment is to create value for you, our shareholders." This was quite different from the usual German model, in which companies have representatives from labor on their boards of directors and explicitly state their commitments to a variety of stakeholders. As one might expect, Veba's stock has consistently outperformed the average German stock. As the trend in international investing continues, more and more non–U.S. companies are adopting a corporate purpose similar to that of Varian and Veba.

Corporate scope defines a firm's lines of business and geographic area of operations. For example, Coca-Cola limits its products to soft drinks, but on a global scale. PepsiCo recently followed Coke's lead—it restricted its scope by spinning off its food service businesses. In fact, several studies have found that the market tends to value focused firms more highly than diversified firms.[1]

The corporate purpose states the general philosophy of the business, but it does not provide managers with operational objectives. The *statement of corporate objectives* sets forth specific goals to guide management. Most organizations have both qualitative and quantitative objectives. A typical quantitative objective might be attaining a 50% market share, a 20% ROE, a 10% earnings growth rate, or a $100 million Economic Value Added (EVA).

Once a firm has defined its purpose, scope, and objectives, it must develop a strategy for achieving its goals. *Corporate strategies* are broad approaches rather than detailed plans. For example, one airline may have a strategy of offering no-frills service among a limited number of cities, while another's strategy may be to offer "staterooms in the sky." Any such strategy should be compatible with the firm's purpose, scope, and objectives.

Operating Plans

Operating plans provide detailed implementation guidance to help meet the corporate objectives. These plans can be developed for any time horizon, but most companies use a 5-year horizon. A 5-year plan is detailed for the first year, with

---

[1]See, for example, Philip G. Berger and Eli Ofek, "Diversification's Effect on Firm Value," *Journal of Financial Economics*, 1995, pp. 39–66; and Larry Lang and René Stulz, "Tobin's Q, Corporate Diversification, and Firm Performance," *Journal of Political Economy*, 1994, pp. 1248–1280.

each succeeding year's plan becoming less specific. The plan explains who is responsible for each particular function, when specific tasks are to be accomplished, sales and profit targets, and the like.

Large, multidivisional companies such as General Electric break down their operating plans by divisions. Thus, each division has its own goals, mission, and plan for meeting its objectives, and these plans are then consolidated to form the corporate plan.

The Financial Plan

The financial planning process has five steps:

1. Project financial statements to analyze the effects of the operating plan on projected profits and financial ratios.
2. Determine the funds needed to support the 5-year plan.
3. Forecast the funds to be generated internally and identify those to be obtained from external sources, subject to any constraints due to borrowing covenants, such as restrictions on the debt ratio, the current ratio, and the coverage ratios.
4. Establish a performance-based management compensation system that rewards employees for creating shareholder wealth.
5. Monitor operations after implementing the plan, identify the cause of any deviations, and take corrective actions.

In the remainder of this chapter, we explain how to create a financial plan, including its three key components: (1) the sales forecast, (2) pro forma financial statements, and (3) the external financing plan. We discuss compensation in Chapter 15.

SELF-TEST

What are four ways that managers use pro forma statements?
Briefly explain the following terms: (1) corporate purpose, (2) corporate scope, (3) corporate objectives, and (4) corporate strategies.
Briefly describe the contents of an operating plan.
What are the steps of the financial planning process?

14.2 Sales Forecast

The **sales forecast** generally starts with a review of sales during the past 5 to 10 years, expressed in a graph such as that in Figure 14-1. The first part of the graph shows 5 years of historical sales for MicroDrive. The graph could have contained 10 years of sales data, but MicroDrive typically focuses on sales figures for the latest 5 years because the firm's studies have shown that its future growth is more closely related to recent events than to the distant past.

Entire courses are devoted to forecasting sales, so we can only touch on the basic elements here. However, forecasting the future sales growth rate always begins with a look at past growth. For example, the average of MicroDrive's recent annual growth rates is 10.3%. However, the compound growth rate from 2003 to 2007 is the solution value for g in the equation

$$\$2,058(1 + g)^4 = \$3,000,$$

e-resource

See ***FM12 Ch 14 Tool Kit.xls*** at the textbook's Web site for details.

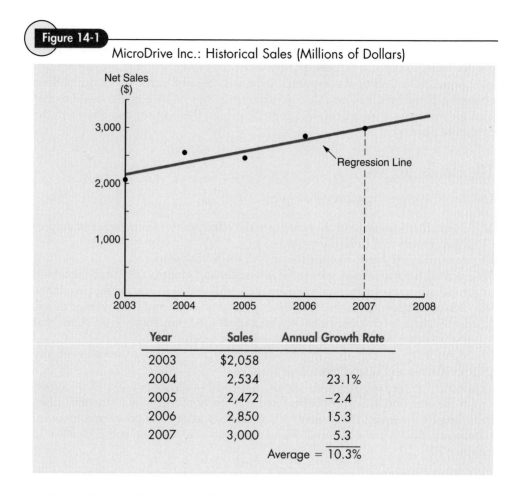

Figure 14-1

MicroDrive Inc.: Historical Sales (Millions of Dollars)

Year	Sales	Annual Growth Rate
2003	$2,058	
2004	2,534	23.1%
2005	2,472	−2.4
2006	2,850	15.3
2007	3,000	5.3
		Average = 10.3%

and it can be found by solving the equation or with a financial calculator, entering $N = 4$, $PV = -2058$, $PMT = 0$, $FV = 3000$, and then pressing I/YR to get $g = 9.9\%$.[2]

The preceding approaches are simple, but both can be poor representations of past growth. First, the arithmetic average procedure generally produces numbers that are too high. To illustrate why, suppose sales grew by 100% one year and then fell by −50% the next year. There would actually be zero growth over the 2 years, but the calculated average growth rate would be 25%. Similarly, the point-to-point procedure is not reliable because if either the beginning or ending year is an "outlier" in the sense of being above or below the trend line shown in Figure 14-1, then the calculated growth rate will not be representative of past growth. The solution to these problems is to use a regression approach, where a curve is fitted to the historic sales data and then the slope of that curve is used to measure historic growth. If we expect a constant growth rate (as opposed to a constant dollar amount, which would mean a declining growth rate), then the regression should be based on the natural log of sales, not sales itself. With a spreadsheet, this is not a difficult calculation, and by far the easiest way to calculate the growth rate is with *Excel*'s LOGEST function. Simply type the years and sales into a spreadsheet, click f_x on the menu bar, select Statistical functions, and then choose the LOGEST function. Highlight the sales range for the Y variable and the years range for X in the function dialog box, and then click OK. The result will be $1 + g$, so you finish by subtracting 1 to get the growth rate. For MicroDrive, the growth rate is 9.1%.

FM

e-resource

These approaches are demonstrated in the **FM12 Ch 14 Tool Kit.xls** at the textbook's Web site. Also, **Web Extension 10B** illustrates these approaches when estimating dividend growth rates.

---

[2]Unless we state differently, we will report values from MicroDrive's financial statements in units of a million dollars, as shown in Figure 14-1.

Although it is useful to calculate the past growth rate in sales, much more is involved in estimating future sales. Future sales will depend on the economy (both domestic and global), the industry's prospects, the company's current product line, proposed products that are in the pipeline, and marketing campaigns. When MicroDrive incorporated these issues into its analysis, it estimated 10% expected growth for the upcoming year.

If the sales forecast is off, the consequences can be serious. First, if the market expands by *more* than MicroDrive has anticipated, the company will not be able to meet demand. Its customers will end up buying competitors' products, and MicroDrive will lose market share. On the other hand, if its projections are overly optimistic, MicroDrive could end up with too much plant, equipment, and inventory, which hurts free cash flow and stock prices. If MicroDrive had financed an unnecessary expansion with debt, high interest charges would compound its problems. Thus, an accurate sales forecast is critical to the firm's well-being.

After much discussion and analysis, MicroDrive's managers decided to forecast a 10% increase in sales. How will MicroDrive's managers incorporate this increased level of sales into the financial plan? In particular, will MicroDrive have to raise any additional external funds in order to implement the plan? We will answer this question using two approaches: (1) the additional funds needed (AFN) formula, and (2) the forecasted financial statement method.

SELF-TEST

List some factors that should be considered when developing a sales forecast. Explain why an accurate sales forecast is critical to profitability.

14.3 The AFN Formula

If we assume that none of a firm's ratios will change (a heroic assumption!), we can use a simple approach to forecast financial requirements. Here is the logic. If sales increase, firms usually have to purchase assets (such as inventories, machines, etc.) in order to support the increased level of sales. Where will the firm get the money to purchase the projected increase in assets? There are three sources. First, some liabilities (such as accounts payable) usually increase when sales increase. Balance sheets require that total assets equal total liabilities and equity, which also means that the increase in assets must equal the increase in total liabilities and equity. Therefore, this spontaneous increase in liabilities is a source of funds for the projected increase in assets. Second, the firm should make a profit on the new sales. Part of this profit will be used to pay dividends, but the remaining profit can be used to help purchase the new assets. Recall that the net income not paid out as dividends is an addition to retained earnings. Therefore, this increase in equity is a source of financing for the projected increase in assets. Finally, any remaining increase in assets must be financed by additional external funds, such as additional bank loans, long-term debt, or stock issuances. The following formula applies this logic and defines the **additional funds needed (AFN)**:

Additional funds needed	=	Required asset increase	−	Spontaneous liability increase	−	Increase in retained earnings	(14-1)
AFN	=	$(A^*/S_0)\Delta S$	−	$(L^*/S_0)\Delta S$	−	$MS_1(RR).$	

The symbols in Equation 14-1 are defined below:

AFN = Additional funds needed.

A^* = Assets that are tied directly to sales, hence must increase if sales are to increase. Note that A designates total assets and A^* designates those assets that must increase if sales are to increase. When the firm is operating at full capacity, as is the case here, $A^* = A$. Often, though, A^* and A are not equal, and either the equation must be modified or we must use the projected financial statement method.

S_0 = Sales during the last year.

A^*/S_0 = Percentage of required assets to sales, which also shows the required dollar increase in assets per $1 increase in sales.

L^* = Liabilities that increase spontaneously. L^* is normally much less than total liabilities (L). Spontaneous liabilities include accounts payable and accruals, but not bank loans and bonds.

L^*/S_0 = Liabilities that increase spontaneously as a percentage of sales, or spontaneously generated financing per $1 increase in sales.

S_1 = Total sales projected for next year.

ΔS = Change in sales

M = Profit margin, or profit per $1 of sales.

RR = Retention ratio, which is the percentage of net income that is retained. The payout ratio is the percentage of net income paid out to shareholders. Because the retention ratio and the payout ratio must total to 1, RR is also equal to 1 − payout ratio.

Recall from the previous section that MicroDrive's managers forecast a 10% increase in sales, from $3,000 million to $3,300 million. Based on this projection, S_1 = $3,300 million and ΔS = $300 million. In the previous year, MicroDrive had $2,000 million in assets, which means that A^*/S_0 = $2,000/$3,000 = 0.6667.[3] If this ratio remains constant, as assumed in the AFN formula, assets must increase by about 67 cents for every $1 increase in sales.

In the previous year MicroDrive had $60 million in accounts payable and $140 million, for a total spontaneous liabilities, L^*, of $60 + $140 = $200 million. Therefore, L^*/S_0 = $200/$3,000 = 0.0667, which means that MicroDrive generates about 7 cents of spontaneous financing for every $1 increase in sales.

MicroDrive had $113.5 million in net income, for a profit margin of M = $113.5/$3,000 = 0.0378, which means that MicroDrive earns almost 3.8 cents on each dollar of sales. MicroDrive paid out $57.5 million in common dividends and retained $56 million, so RR = $56/$113.5 = 0.493.

Inserting MicroDrive's values into Equation 14-1, we find the additional funds needed to be $118 million:

$$\begin{matrix} \text{Additional} \\ \text{funds} \\ \text{needed} \end{matrix} = \begin{matrix} \text{Projected} \\ \text{increase in} \\ \text{assets} \end{matrix} - \begin{matrix} \text{Spontaneous} \\ \text{increase in} \\ \text{liabilities} \end{matrix} - \begin{matrix} \text{Increase in} \\ \text{retained} \\ \text{earnings} \end{matrix}$$

$$= 0.667(\Delta S) - 0.067(\Delta S) - 0.0378(S_1)(0.493)$$

$$= 0.667(\$300 \text{ million}) - 0.067(\$300 \text{ million})$$

$$- 0.0378(\$3,300 \text{ million})(0.493)$$

$$= \$200 \text{ million} - \$20 \text{ million} - \$61.58 \text{ million}$$

$$= \$118.42 \text{ million}.[4]$$

---

[3]For MicroDrive's financial statements, look back to Chapter 3 or look ahead to Tables 14-2 or 14-3.
[4]All calculations are done in the *Excel* file, **FM12 Ch 14 Tool Kit.xls**, available at the textbook's Web site. Because *Excel* doesn't round values in intermediate steps, there may be slight differences between the values from *Excel* and calculations based on the rounded intermediate values in the textbook.

To increase sales by $300 million, the formula suggests that MicroDrive must increase assets by $200 million. The $200 million of new assets must be financed in some manner. Of the total, $20 million will come from a spontaneous increase in liabilities, while another $61.58 million will be obtained from retained earnings. The remaining $118.42 million must be raised from external sources.

The AFN equation shows that external financing requirements depend on five key factors:

1. **Sales growth (ΔS).** Rapidly growing companies require large increases in assets and more external financing, other things held constant.
2. **Capital intensity (A*/S$_0$).** The amount of assets required per dollar of sales, A*/S$_0$ in Equation 14-1, is called the **capital intensity ratio.** This ratio has a major effect on capital requirements. Companies with higher assets-to-sales ratios require more assets for a given increase in sales, hence a greater need for external financing.
3. **Spontaneous liabilities-to-sales ratio (L*/S$_0$).** Companies that spontaneously generate a large amount of liabilities from accounts payable and accruals will have a relatively lower need for external financing.
4. **Profit margin (M).** The higher the profit margin, the larger the net income available to support increases in assets, hence the lower the need for external financing.
5. **Retention ratio (RR).** Companies that retain more of their earnings as opposed to paying them out as dividends will generate more retained earnings and thus have less need for external financing.

The logic behind the AFN formula and the insights above are important, but the AFN formula provides an accurate forecast only for companies whose ratios are all expected to remain constant. The AFN formula is useful for quickly obtaining a "back of the envelope" estimate of external financing requirements, but the percent of sales method, explained in the next section, is used by most companies for their more detailed financial planning.

SELF-TEST

If all ratios are expected to remain constant, a formula can be used to forecast AFN. Give the formula and briefly explain it.

How do the following factors affect external capital requirements: (1) retention ratio, (2) capital intensity, and (3) profit margin?

Suppose MicroDrive's growth rate in sales is forecast as 15%. If all ratios stay the same, what is the AFN? ($205.62 million)

14.4 The Forecasted Financial Statement (FFS) Method

Unlike the AFN formula, the **forecasted financial statement approach (FFS)** actually forecasts the complete set of financial statements. However, the logic of this approach is similar to that of the AFN formula. Before going into the details, let's take a look at the big picture. Just as with the AFN formula, we begin with the sales forecast. Similarly, we also forecast the assets that are required to support the sales. The AFN formula assumes all assets grow by the same proportion, but the forecasted financial statement approach allows different asset classes to grow at different rates. This additional level of detail makes this approach more realistic.

In addition, the result is a forecast of the entire asset side of the balance sheet, while the AFN formula only shows the net increase in assets.

Similar to the AFN formula, we forecast the spontaneous liabilities in the FFS approach. The AFN formula assumes each spontaneous liability grows at the same rate, but the FFS approach allows each spontaneous liability to grow at a different rate, providing a more realistic forecast. The AFN formula provides a forecast of the addition to retained earnings, based on the profit margin and the dividend retention ratio. In the FFS approach, we also forecast the addition to retained earnings, but we do this by first forecasting the entire income statement and dividend payment. We define the *specified sources of financing* as the total of spontaneous liabilities, existing financing (i.e., the current levels of debt and common equity), and the addition to retained earnings.

At this point in the process, we have a forecast of the projected income statements, a forecast of the asset side of the balance sheets, and a forecast of the liabilities and equity side of the balance sheets. If we are extraordinarily lucky, the balance sheets balance, which means that sources of financing (i.e., the liabilities and equity side of the balance sheets) are exactly equal to the required assets (i.e., the asset side of the balance sheets). If so, we have exactly enough financing to acquire the assets needed to support the forecasted level of sales. But in all our years of forecasting, we have never had this happen, and you probably won't be any luckier.

To make the balance sheets balance (ensuring enough financing to purchase the required assets), the FFS approach uses the **plug technique.** To use this technique, we define the AFN as the required assets minus the specified sources of financing, based on the projected balance sheets. If the AFN is positive, then we need to raise additional funds, so we "plug" this amount into the balance sheet as additional financing in the form of new notes payable, long-term debt, or equity.[5] For example, suppose the required assets equal $2,500 million and the specified sources of financing total $2,400 million. The required additional financing is $2,500 − $2,400 = $100 million. The firm might choose to raise this $100 million as new notes payable, thus increasing the old notes payable by $100 million.

If the AFN is negative, then the forecast has more financing (i.e., liabilities and equity) than needed to support the required assets. The firm could reduce its financing by paying off some debt, by repurchasing stock, or by paying higher dividends (which reduces the addition to retained earnings). However, many firms use short-term investments as a temporary repository for any extra cash, or as a "slush fund" for use in times when operating cash flows are lower than expected. Therefore, in our initial forecast, often we assume that any extra funds will be used to purchase additional short-term investments. We "plug" the amount of extra financing (the absolute value of the AFN) into short-term investments on the asset side of the balance sheet. For example, suppose the required assets equal only $2,200 million and the specified sources of financing total $2,400 million. The required additional financing is $2,200 − $2,400 = −$200 million. Thus, the firm would have an extra $200 million that it could use to purchase short-term investments. Notice that total assets would now equal $2,200 + $200 = $2,400 million, which is exactly equal to the total sources of financing.

Keep the big picture in mind as we forecast MicroDrive's financial statements.[6]

---

[5]We could even raise this additional financing by reducing dividend payments, which increases the addition to retained earnings. If the company has short-term investments, it might satisfy the AFN by selling some. But notice that if the company sells (or chooses not to purchase) operating assets, then the company will not be able to support the forecast sales. We'll discuss these issues later in the section.

[6]For a much more detailed treatment of financial forecasting, see P. Daves, M. Ehrhardt, and R. Shrieves, *Corporate Valuation: A Guide for Managers and Investors* (Mason, OH: Thomson/South-Western, 2004).

Step 1. Analyze the Historical Ratios

The first step is to analyze the historical ratios that will be used in the projections (see Table 14-1). This differs somewhat from the ratio analysis of Chapter 4, since the objective here is to forecast the future, or pro forma, financial statements. The next sections explain exactly why we need these particular ratios, but for now we will just describe the ratios and how to use them. Our illustration has only 2 years of data for MicroDrive, but a thorough analysis should have at least 5 years of historical data. In addition to MicroDrive's actual year-by-year ratios, the table also shows the historical average, which in this case is the average of the two prior years. The last column of the table shows the ratio for the industry composite, which is the sum of the financial statements for all firms in the industry.

Forecasting is as much art as science, but here are a few basic guidelines. First, are there trends in the ratios? In our experience, simple trends can help predict the future, because most companies, especially large ones, cannot turn on a dime. Second, how does a ratio compare with its historical average? Is any aberration caused by temporary factors, which means the ratio might revert back toward its average? Third, how does a ratio compare to the industry average? For example, in competitive industries, it is very difficult for a company to maintain a cost/sales ratio too much better than its peers. Fourth, what is happening in the economy and the firm's industry? For example, if a firm depends on oil as an input, then wars in the Middle East might drive up its costs. Fifth, what are the company's operating plans? For example, if the company is planning a major expansion, then its projected costs might be temporarily high as it has larger than normal advertising campaigns. Only after thinking about these questions and issues should a forecaster move on to the next step.

e-resource
See **FM12 Ch 14 Tool Kit.xls** at the textbook's Web site for details.

Step 2. Forecast the Income Statement

In this section we explain how to forecast the income statement and in the following section we forecast the balance sheet. Although we cover these topics in two separate sections, the forecasted financial statements are actually integrated with one another and with the previous year's statements. For example, the following

Table 14-1

Historical Ratios for MicroDrive Inc.

	Actual 2006	Actual 2007	Historical Average	Industry Average
Costs to sales	87.6%	87.2%	87.4%	87.1%
Depreciation to net plant and equipment	10.3	10.0	10.2	10.2
Cash to sales	0.5	0.3	0.4	1.0
Accounts receivable to sales	11.1	12.5	11.8	10.0
Inventory to sales	14.6	20.5	17.5	11.1
Net plant and equipment to sales	30.5	33.3	31.9	33.3
Accounts payable to sales	1.1	2.0	1.5	1.0
Accruals to sales	4.6	4.7	4.6	2.0

e-resource
See **FM12 Ch 14 Tool Kit.xls** at the textbook's Web site for details.

sections show that the income statement item "depreciation" depends on net plant and equipment, which is a balance sheet item. The balance sheet item "retained earnings" depends on the previous year's retained earnings, the forecasted net income, and the firm's dividend policy. Keep this interrelatedness in mind as you go through the forecast.

Forecast Sales   Table 14-2 shows the forecasted income statement. Management forecasts that sales will grow by 10%. Thus, forecasted sales, shown in Row 1, Column 3, is the product of the prior year's sales of $3,000 million and (1 + g): $3,000(1.1) = $3,300 million.

Forecast Earnings before Interest and Taxes (EBIT)   Table 14-1 shows that MicroDrive's ratio of costs to sales for the most recent year was 87.2% ($2,616/$3,000 = 0.872). Thus, to get a dollar of sales, MicroDrive had to incur 87.2 cents of costs. Initially, we assume that the cost structure will remain unchanged. Later on, we explore the impact of changes in the cost structure, but for now we assume that forecasted costs will equal 87.2% of forecasted sales. See Row 2 of Table 14-2.[7]

e-resource

See **FM12 Ch 14 Tool Kit.xls** at the textbook's Web site for details.

Because depreciation depends on the asset base, as described in Chapter 12, it is more reasonable to forecast depreciation as a percent of net plant and equipment rather than of sales. The most recent ratio of depreciation to net plant and equipment, shown in Table 14-1, was 10% ($100/$1,000 = 0.10), and MicroDrive's managers believe this is a good estimate of future depreciation rates. As we show

Table 14-2

MicroDrive Inc.: Actual and Projected Income Statements
(Millions of Dollars Except Per Share Data)

	Actual 2007 (1)	Forecast Basis (2)	Forecast for 2008 (3)
1. Sales	$3,000.0	110% × 2007 Sales =	$3,300.0
2. Costs except depreciation	2,616.2	87.2% × 2008 Sales =	2,877.6
3. Depreciation expense	100.0	10% × 2008 Net plant =	110.0
4. Total operating costs	$2,716.2		$2,987.6
5. EBIT	$ 283.8		$ 312.4
6. Less interest	88.0	(See text for explanation)	92.8
7. Earnings before taxes (EBT)	$ 195.8		$ 219.6
8. Taxes (40%)	78.3		87.8
9. NI before preferred dividends	$ 117.5		$ 131.8
10. Preferred dividends	4.0	Dividend rate × 2008 Pref. stk. =	4.0
11. NI available to common	$ 113.5		$ 127.8
12. Shares of common equity	50.0		50.0
13. Dividends per share	$ 1.15	108% × 2007 DPS =	$ 1.25
14. Dividends to common	$ 57.5	2008 DPS × Number of shares =	$ 62.5
15. Additions to retained earnings	$ 56.0		$ 65.3

[7]Notice that we don't forecast the growth rate in costs. Instead, we forecast the growth rate in sales and specify costs as a percent of sales.

later in Table 14-3, the forecasted net plant and equipment is $1,100 million. Therefore, forecasted depreciation is 0.10($1,100) = $110 million. Notice how a balance sheet item, net plant and equipment, affects the charge for depreciation, which is an income statement item.

Total operating costs, shown on Row 4, are the sum of costs of goods sold plus depreciation. EBIT is then found by subtraction.

Forecast Interest Expense   How should we forecast the interest charges? The actual net interest expense is the sum of a firm's daily interest charges less its daily interest income, if any, from short-term investments. Most companies have a variety of different debt obligations with different fixed interest rates and/or floating interest rates. For example, bonds issued in different years generally have different fixed rates, while most bank loans have rates that vary with interest rates in the economy. Given this situation, it is impossible to forecast the exact interest expense for the upcoming year, so we make two simplifying assumptions.

Assumption 1: Specifying the Balance of Debt for Computing Interest Expense. As noted above, interest on bank loans is calculated daily, based on the amount of debt at the beginning of the day, while bond interest depends on the amount of bonds outstanding. If debt remained constant all during the year, the correct balance to use when forecasting the annual interest expense would be the amount of debt at the beginning of the year, which is the same as the debt shown on the balance sheets at the end of the previous year. But how should you forecast the annual interest expense if debt is expected to change during the year, which is typical for most companies? One option would be to base the interest expense on the debt balance shown at the end of the forecasted year, but this has two disadvantages. First, it would charge a full year's interest on the additional debt, which would imply that the debt was put in place on January 1. Because this is usually not true, that forecast would overstate the most likely interest expense. Second, this assumption causes circularity in the spreadsheet. We discuss this in detail in **Web Extension 14A,** but the short explanation is that additional debt causes additional interest expense, which reduces the addition to retained earnings, which in turn requires a higher level of debt, which causes still more interest expense, and the cycle keeps repeating. This is called **financing feedback.** Spreadsheets can deal with this problem (see **Web Extension 14A**, available at the textbook's Web site), but add complexity to the model that might not be worth the benefits.

A similar approach would be to base the interest expense on the average of the debt at the beginning and end of the year. This approach would produce the correct interest expense only if debt were added evenly throughout the year, which is a big assumption. In addition, it also results in a circular model with all its complexity.

A third approach, which we illustrate below, works well for most situations. We base the interest expense on the amount of debt at the beginning of the year as shown on the previous year's balance sheet. However, since this will underestimate the true interest expense if debt increases throughout the year, as it usually does for most companies, we use an interest rate that is about 0.5% higher than the rate we actually expect. This approach provides reasonably accurate forecasts without greatly increasing the model's complexity. Keep in mind, though, that this simple approach might not work well in all situations, so see **Web Extension 14A** if you want to implement the more complex modeling technique.

Assumption 2: Specifying Interest Rates. As noted earlier, different loans have different interest rates. Rather than trying to specify the rate on each separate debt issue, we usually specify only two rates, one for short-term notes payable and one

FM
e-resource
See **FM12 Ch 14 Tool Kit.xls** at the textbook's Web site for details.

for long-term bonds. The interest rate on short-term debt usually floats, and because the best estimate of future rates is generally the current rate, it is most reasonable to apply the current market rate to short-term loans. For MicroDrive, the appropriate short-term rate is about 8.5%, which we rounded up to 9% because we will apply it to the debt balance at the beginning of the year.

Most companies' long-term debt consists of several different bond issues with different interest rates. During the course of the year, some of this debt may be paid off, and some new long-term debt may be added. Rather than try to estimate the interest expense for each particular issue, we apply a single interest rate to the total amount of long-term debt. This rate is an average of the rates on the currently outstanding long-term bonds and the rate that is expected on any new long-term debt. The average rate on MicroDrive's existing long-term bonds is about 10%, and it would have to pay about 10.5% on new long-term bonds. The average rate on old and new bonds is somewhere between 10% and 10.5%, which we round up to 11% because we are going to apply it to the debt at the beginning of the year, as explained above.

Calculating Interest Expense. The forecasted interest expense is the net interest paid on short-term financing plus the interest on long-term bonds. We estimate the net interest on short-term financing by first finding the interest expense on notes payable and then subtracting any interest income from short-term investments. We base interest charges on the amount of short-term debt at the beginning of the year (which is the debt at the end of the previous year), and we note that MicroDrive had no short-term investments. Therefore, MicroDrive's net short-term interest is 0.09($110) − 0.09($0) = $9.9 million. The interest on long-term bonds is 0.11($754.0) = $82.94, rounded to $82.9 million. Therefore, the total interest expense is $9.9 + $82.9 = $92.8 million.

Complete the Income Statement   Earnings before taxes (EBT) is calculated by subtracting interest from EBIT, and then we deduct taxes calculated at a 40% rate. The resulting net income before preferred dividends for 2008, which is $131.8 million, is shown in Row 9 of Table 14-2. MicroDrive's preferred stock pays a dividend of 10%. Based on the amount of preferred stock at the beginning of the year, the preferred dividends are 0.10($40) = $4 million. Thus, MicroDrive's forecasted net income available to common stock is $127.8 million, shown in Row 11.

Row 12 shows the number of shares of common stock, and Row 13 shows the most recent dividend per share, $1.15. MicroDrive does not plan to issue any new shares, but it does plan to increase the dividend by 8%, resulting in a forecasted dividend of 1.08($1.15) = $1.242, rounded up to $1.25 per share. With 50 million shares, the total forecasted dividend is 50($1.25) = $62.5 million. The forecasted addition to retained earnings is equal to the net income available to common stockholders minus the total dividends: $127.8 − $62.5 = $65.3 million, as shown in Row 15.

Step 3. Forecast the Balance Sheet

Let's start with the assets required to support sales.

Forecast Operating Assets   As noted earlier, MicroDrive's assets must increase if sales are to increase. MicroDrive writes and deposits checks every day. Because its managers don't know exactly when all of the checks will clear, they can't predict exactly what the balance in their checking accounts will be on any given day.

Therefore, they must maintain a balance of cash and cash equivalents (such as very short-term marketable securities) to avoid overdrawing their accounts. We discuss the issue of cash management in Chapter 22 and in *Web Chapter 28,* but for now we simply assume that the cash required to support a company's operations is proportional to its sales. MicroDrive's most recent ratio of cash to sales was approximately 0.33% ($10/$3,000 = 0.003333$), and management believes this ratio should remain constant. Therefore, the forecasted cash balance, shown in Row 1 of Table 14-3, is $0.003333(\$3,300) = \$11$ million.[8]

Unless a company changes its credit policy or has a change in its customer base, accounts receivable should be proportional to sales. The ratio of accounts receivable to sales was $\$375/\$3,000 = 0.125 = 12.5\%$. For now we assume that the credit policy and customers' paying patterns will remain constant, so the forecast for accounts receivable is $0.125(\$3,300) = \$412.5$ million, as shown in Row 3.

As sales increase, firms generally must carry more inventories. Chapter 22 and *Web Chapter 28* discuss inventory management in detail, but for now we assume that inventory will also be proportional to sales. The most recent inventory-to-sales ratio was $\$615/\$3,000 = 0.205 = 20.5\%$. Assuming no change in MicroDrive's inventory policy, the forecasted inventory is $0.205(\$3,300) = \$676.5$ million, as shown in Row 4.

It might be reasonable to assume that cash, accounts receivable, and inventories will be proportional to sales, but will the amount of net plant and equipment go up and down as sales go up and down? The correct answer could be either yes or no. When companies acquire plant and equipment, they often install more capacity than they currently need due to economies of scale in building capacity. Moreover, even if a plant is operating at its maximum rated capacity, most companies can produce additional units by reducing downtime for scheduled maintenance, by running machinery at a higher than optimal speed, or by adding a second or third shift. Therefore, at least in the short run, companies may not have a very close relationship between sales and net plant and equipment.

However, some companies do have a fixed relationship between sales and net plant and equipment, even in the short term. For example, new stores in many retail chains achieve the same sales during their first year as the chain's existing stores. The only way such retailers can grow (beyond inflation) is by adding new stores. Such companies therefore have a strong proportional relationship between fixed assets and sales.

Finally, in the long term there is a strong relationship between sales and net plant and equipment for virtually all companies: Few companies can continue to increase sales unless they eventually add capacity. Therefore, as a first approximation it is reasonable to assume that the long-term ratio of net plant and equipment to sales will be constant.

For the first years in a forecast, managers generally build in the actual planned expenditures on plant and equipment. If those estimates are not available, it is generally best to assume a constant ratio of net plant and equipment to sales.

For MicroDrive, the ratio of net plant and equipment to sales was $\$1,000/\$3,000 = 0.3333 = 33.33\%$. MicroDrive's net plant and equipment have grown fairly steadily in the past, and its managers expect steady future growth. Therefore, they forecast that they will need net plant and equipment of $0.3333(\$3,300) = \$1,100$ million.

---

[8]Notice that we do not specify a growth rate for cash. Instead, we specify a growth rate for sales and let cash equal a percent of sales. So the growth rate in cash depends on the sales growth rate and its percent of sales. If this percent of sales differs from the percentage in the previous year, then its growth rate will differ from the sales growth rate. Thus, items on the balance sheet may have different growth rates than the sales growth rate.

Table 14-3

MicroDrive Inc.: Actual and Projected Balance Sheets
(Millions of Dollars)

	Actual 2007 (1)	Forecast Basis (2)	Forecast for 2008 (3)
Assets			
1. Cash	$ 10.0	0.33% × 2008 Sales =	$ 11.0
2. Short-term investments	0.0	Previous plus "plug" if needed	0.0
3. Accounts receivable	375.0	12.50% × 2008 Sales =	412.5
4. Inventories	615.0	20.50% × 2008 Sales =	676.5
5. Total current assets	$1,000.0		$1,100.0
6. Net plant and equipment	1,000.0	33.33% × 2008 Sales =	1,100.0
7. Total assets	$2,000.0		$2,200.0
Liabilities and Equity			
8. Accounts payable	$ 60.0	2.00% × 2008 Sales =	$ 66.0
9. Accruals	140.0	4.67% × 2008 Sales =	154.0
10. Notes payable	110.0	Previous plus "plug" if needed	224.7
11. Total current liabilities	$ 310.0		$ 444.7
12. Long-term bonds	754.0	Same: no new issue	754.0
13. Total liabilities	$1,064.0		$1,198.7
14. Preferred stock	40.0	Same: no new issue	40.0
15. Common stock	130.0	Same: no new issue	130.0
16. Retained earnings	766.0	2007 RE + 2008 Additions to RE =	831.3
17. Total common equity	$ 896.0		$ 961.3
18. Total liabilities and equity	$2,000.0		$2,200.0
19. Required assets[a]			$2,200.0
20. Specified sources of financing[b]			2,085.3
21. Additional funds needed (AFN)			$ 114.7
22. Required additional notes payable			$ 114.7
23. Additional short-term investments			0.0

[a]Required assets include all of the forecasted operating assets, plus short-term investment from the previous year.

[b]Specified sources of financing include forecasted operating current liabilities, forecasted long-term bonds, forecasted preferred stock, forecasted common equity, and the amount of notes payable from the previous year.

For now, we make the temporary assumption that short-term investments will remain at their current level. We will return to this point after we forecast the rest of the balance sheet.

Forecast Operating Current Liabilities As sales increase, so will purchases of raw materials, and those additional purchases will spontaneously lead to a higher level of accounts payable. MicroDrive's most recent ratio of accounts payable to sales was $60/$3,000 = 0.02 = 2%. Assuming that the payables policy will not change, the forecasted level of accounts payable is 0.02($3,300) = $66 million, as shown in Row 8.

Higher sales require more labor, and higher sales normally result in higher taxable income and thus taxes. Therefore, accrued wages and taxes both increase as sales increase. MicroDrive's most recent ratio of accruals to sales was $140/$3,000 = 0.0467 = 4.67%. There is no reason to expect a change in this ratio, so the forecasted level of accruals is 0.0467($3,300) = $154 million.

Forecast Items Determined by Financial Policy Decisions Forecasting the remaining liability and equity depends on a firm's financial policies, which vary widely from firm to firm. We explain one fairly typical set of financial policies below, and we go through the calculations in detail in the chapter spreadsheet model, *FM12 Ch 14 Tool Kit.xls*. However, there are many other possible policies. *Web Extension 14B* describes a procedure that can be used to develop a model to fit any set of financial policies. Following is a brief discussion of financial policy decisions.

First, most mature companies rarely issue new common stock, so the forecast for common stock is usually the previous year's common stock; see Chapters 16 and 17 for more discussion. Second, most firms increase their dividends at a fairly steady rate, which allows us to forecast dividend payments; see Chapter 18 for a discussion of dividend policy. Subtracting forecasted dividends from forecasted net income gives the additions to retained earnings, which affects total common equity. Third, most firms do not use preferred stock, and those that already have preferred stock issue new preferred stock infrequently. Fourth, issuing more long-term bonds is a major event for most firms, and it often requires approval from the board of directors. Chapters 16 and 17 discuss long-term debt financing in detail. Fifth, many firms use short-term bank loans as a financial "shock absorber." When extra funding is needed, they draw down their lines of credit, thus increasing notes payable, until their short-term debt has risen to an unacceptably high level, at which point they arrange long-term financing. When they secure the long-term financing, they pay off some of their short-term debt to bring it down to an acceptable level.

With these typical financial policies in mind, let's turn back to MicroDrive. Initially we assume that MicroDrive will simply maintain its current level of notes payable; we will explain how to forecast the final level of notes payable shortly. In its initial financial plan, MicroDrive will keep long-term debt at the 2007 level, as shown in Row 12 of Table 14-3. The company's policy is not to issue any additional shares of preferred or common stock barring extraordinary circumstances. Therefore, its forecasts for preferred and common stock, shown in Rows 14 and 15, are the 2006 levels. MicroDrive plans to increase its dividend per share by about 8% per year. As shown in Row 15, this policy, when combined with the forecasted level of net income, results in a $65.3 million addition to retained earnings. On the balance sheet, the forecasted level of retained earnings is equal to the 2007 retained earnings plus the forecasted addition to retained earnings, or $766.0 + $65.3 = $831.3 million. Again, note that we make the temporary assumption that notes payable remain at their 2007 level.

Step 4. Raise the Additional Funds Needed

Based on the forecasted balance sheet, MicroDrive will need $2,200 million of operating assets to support its forecasted $3,300 million of sales. We define required assets as the sum of its forecasted operating assets plus the previous amount of short-term investments. Since MicroDrive had no short-term investments in 2007, its required assets are simply $2,200 million, as shown in Row 19 of Table 14-3.

We define the specified sources of financing as the sum of forecasted levels of operating current liabilities, long-term debt, preferred stock, and common equity, plus notes payable carried over from the previous year:

Accounts payable	$ 66.0
Accruals	154.0
Notes payable (carryover)	110.0
Long-term bonds	754.0
Preferred stock	40.0
Common stock	130.0
Retained earnings	831.3
Total	$2,085.3

Based on its required assets and specified sources of financing, MicroDrive's AFN is $2,200 − $2,085.3 = $114.7 million, as shown in Rows 19, 20, and 21 of Table 14-3. Because the AFN is positive, MicroDrive needs $114.7 million of additional financing, and its initial financial policy is to obtain these funds as notes payable. Therefore, we add $114.7 million into notes payable (Row 10 of Table 14-3), bringing the forecasted total to $110 + $114.7 = $224.7 million.

The plug approach that we used specifies the additional amount of *either* notes payable *or* short-term investments, but not both. If the AFN is positive, we assume that the firm will add to notes payable but leave short-term investments at their current level. If the AFN is negative, it will add to short-term investments but not to notes payable. Because we added notes payable, we don't add any short-term investment, and so this completes the initial forecast. Now it is time to analyze the plan and consider potential changes.

Analysis of the Forecast

The 2008 forecast as developed above is only the first part of MicroDrive's total forecasting process. We must next examine the projected statements and determine whether the forecast meets the financial targets as set forth in the 5-year financial plan. If the statements do not meet the targets, then elements of the forecast must be changed.

Table 14-4 shows MicroDrive's most recent actual ratios, its projected ratios, and the latest industry average ratios. (The table also shows a "Revised Forecast" in the third column, which we will discuss later. Disregard the revised data for now.) The firm's financial condition at the close of 2007 was weak, with many ratios being well below the industry averages. For example, MicroDrive's current ratio, based on Column 1 of Table 14-4, was only 3.2 versus 4.2 for an average competitor.

The "Inputs" section shown on the top three rows of the table provides data on three of the model's key drivers: (1) costs (excluding depreciation) as a percentage of sales, (2) accounts receivable as a percentage of sales, and (3) inventory as a percentage of sales. The preliminary forecast in Column 2 assumes these variables remain constant. While MicroDrive's cost-to-sales ratio is only slightly worse than the industry average, its ratios of accounts receivable to sales and inventory to sales are significantly higher than those of its competitors. Its investment in inventories

Table 14-4

Model Inputs, AFN, and Key Ratios (Millions of Dollars)

	Actual 2007 (1)	Preliminary Forecast for 2008 (2)	Revised Forecast for 2008 (3)	Industry Average 2007 (4)
Model Inputs				
Costs (excluding depreciation) as percentage of sales	87.2%	87.2%	86.0%	87.1%
Accounts receivable as percentage of sales	12.5	12.5	11.8	10.0
Inventory as percentage of sales	20.5	20.5	16.7	11.1
Model Outputs				
NOPAT (net operating profit after taxes)[a]	$170.3	$187.4	$211.2	
Net operating working capital[b]	$800.0	$880.0	$731.5	
Total operating capital[c]	$1,800.0	$1,980.0	$1,831.5	
Free cash flows (FCF)[d]	($174.7)	$7.4	$179.7	
AFN		$114.7	($57.5)	
Ratios				
Current ratio	3.2×	2.5×	3.1×	4.2×
Inventory turnover	4.9	1.9	6.0	9.0
Days sales outstanding	45.6	45.6	43.1	36.0
Total assets turnover	1.5	1.5	1.6	1.8
Debt ratio	53.2%	54.5%	51.4%	40.0%
Profit margin	3.8	3.9	4.6	5.0
Return on assets	5.7	5.8	7.2	9.0
Return on equity	12.7	13.3	15.4	15.0
Return on invested capital (NOPAT/Total operating capital)	9.5	9.5	11.5	11.4

[a]NOPAT = EBIT × (1 − T) from Table 14-2.
[b]Net operating working capital = Cash + Accounts receivable + Inventories − Accounts payable − Accruals from Table 14-3.
[c]Total operating capital = Net operating working capital + Net plant and equipment from Table 14-3.
[d]Free cash flow = NOPAT − Investment in total operating capital.

and receivables is too high, causing its returns on assets, equity, and invested capital as shown in the lower part of the table to be too low. Therefore, MicroDrive should make operational changes designed to reduce its current assets.

The "Ratios" section of Table 14-4 provides more details regarding the firm's weaknesses. MicroDrive's asset management ratios are much worse than the industry averages. For example, its total assets turnover ratio is 1.5 versus an industry average of 1.8. Its poor asset management ratios drag down the return on invested capital (9.5% for MicroDrive versus 11.4% for the industry average).

Furthermore, MicroDrive must carry more than the average amount of debt to support its excessive assets, and the extra interest expense reduces its profit margin to 3.9% versus 5.0% for the industry. Much of the debt is short term, and this results in a current ratio of 2.5 versus the 4.2 industry average. These problems will persist unless management takes action to improve things.

After reviewing its preliminary forecast, management decided to take three steps to improve its financial condition: (1) It decided to lay off some workers and close certain operations. It forecasted that these steps would lower operating costs (excluding depreciation) from the current 87.2% to 86% of sales as shown in Column 3 of Table 14-4. (2) By screening credit customers more closely and being more aggressive in collecting past-due accounts, the company believes it can reduce the ratio of accounts receivable to sales from 12.5% to 11.8%. (3) Finally, management thinks it can reduce the inventory-to-sales ratio from 20.5% to 16.7% through the use of tighter inventory controls.[9]

These projected operational changes were then used to create a revised set of forecasted statements for 2008. We do not show the new financial statements, but the revised ratios are shown in the third column of Table 14-4. You can see the details in the chapter spreadsheet model, *FM12 CH 14 Tool Kit.xls.* Here are the highlights of the revised forecast:

1. The reduction in operating costs improved the 2008 NOPAT, or net operating profit after taxes, by $23.8 million. Even more impressive, the improvements in the receivables policy and in inventory management reduced receivables and inventories by $148.5 million. The net result of the increase in NOPAT and the reduction of operating current assets was a very large increase in free cash flow for 2008, from a previously estimated $7.4 million to $179.7 million.
2. The profit margin improved to 4.6%. However, the firm's profit margin still lagged the industry average because its high debt ratio results in higher than average interest payments.
3. The increase in the profit margin resulted in an increase in projected retained earnings. More importantly, by tightening inventory controls and reducing the days sales outstanding, MicroDrive projected a reduction in inventories and receivables. Taken together, these actions resulted in a *negative* AFN of $57.5 million, which means that MicroDrive would actually generate $57.5 million more from internal operations and its financing plan than it needs for new assets. Under its current financial policy, MicroDrive would have $110 million in notes payable (the amount it carried over from the previous year) and $57.5 million in short-term investments. (Note: MicroDrive's managers considered using the $57.5 million to pay down some of the debt but decided instead to keep it as a liquid asset, which gives them the flexibility to quickly fund any new projects created by their R&D department.) The net effect is a significant reduction in MicroDrive's debt ratio, although it is still above the industry average.
4. These actions also raised the rate of return on assets from 5.8% to 7.2%, and they boosted the return on equity from 13.3% to 15.4%, which is even higher than the industry average.

Although MicroDrive's managers believed that the revised forecast was achievable, they were not sure of this. Accordingly, they wanted to know how variations in sales would affect the forecast. Therefore, they ran a spreadsheet model using several different sales growth rates and analyzed the results to see how the ratios would change under different growth scenarios. To illustrate, if the

---

[9]We will discuss receivables and inventory management in detail in Chapter 22.

sales growth rate increased from 10% to 20%, the AFN would change dramatically, from a $57.5 million *surplus* to an $89.8 million *shortfall* because more assets would be required to finance the additional sales.

The spreadsheet model was also used to evaluate dividend policy. If MicroDrive decided to reduce its dividend growth rate, then additional funds would be generated, and those funds could be invested in plant, equipment, and inventories; used to reduce debt; or used to repurchase stock.

We see, then, that forecasting is an iterative process. For planning purposes, the financial staff develops a preliminary forecast based on a continuation of past policies and trends. This provides a starting point, or "baseline" forecast. Next, the projections are modified to see what effects alternative operating plans would have on the firm's earnings and financial condition. This results in a revised forecast. Then alternative operating plans are examined under different sales growth scenarios, and the model is used to evaluate both dividend policy and capital structure decisions.

Finally, the projected statements can be used to estimate the effect of different plans on MicroDrive's stock price. This is called value-based management and is covered in Chapter 15.

SELF-TEST

List some factors that should be considered when developing a sales forecast.
What is the AFN, and how is the forecasted financial statements method used to estimate it?
Why do accounts payable and accruals provide "spontaneous funds" to a growing firm?

14.5 Forecasting Financial Requirements When the Balance Sheet Ratios Are Subject to Change

Both the AFN formula and the projected financial statement method as we initially used it assume that the ratios of assets and liabilities to sales (A^*/S_0 and L^*/S_0) remain constant over time. This, in turn, requires the assumption that each "spontaneous" asset and liability item increases at the same rate as sales. In graph form, this implies the type of relationship shown in Panel a of Figure 14-2, a relationship that is (1) linear and (2) passes through the origin. Under those conditions, if the company's sales increase from $200 million to $400 million, or by 100%, inventory will also increase by 100%, from $100 million to $200 million.

The assumption of constant ratios and identical growth rates is appropriate at times, but there are times when it is incorrect. Three such conditions are described in the following sections.

Economies of Scale

There are economies of scale in the use of many kinds of assets, and when economies occur, the ratios are likely to change over time as the size of the firm increases. For example, retailers often need to maintain base stocks of different inventory items, even if current sales are quite low. As sales expand, inventories may then grow less rapidly than sales, so the ratio of inventory to sales (I/S) declines. This situation is depicted in Panel b of Figure 14-2. Here we see that the inventory/sales ratio is 1.5, or 150%, when sales are $200 million, but the ratio declines to 1.0 when sales climb to $400 million.

The relationship in Panel b is linear, but nonlinear relationships often exist. Indeed, if the firm uses one popular model for establishing inventory levels (the EOQ model), its inventories will rise with the square root of sales. This situation

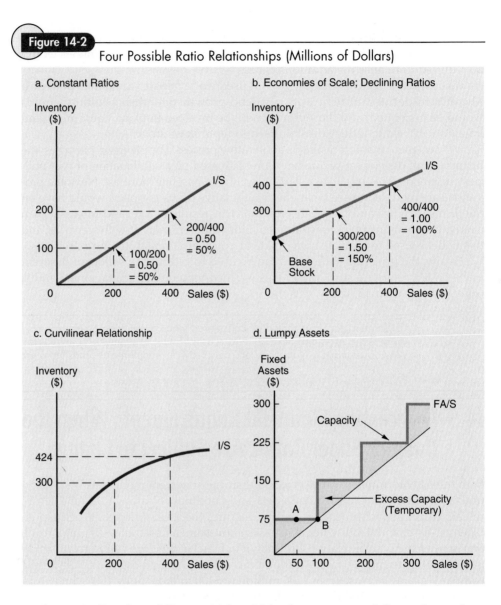

Figure 14-2

Four Possible Ratio Relationships (Millions of Dollars)

is shown in Panel c of Figure 14-2, which shows a curved line whose slope decreases at higher sales levels. In this situation, very large increases in sales would require very little additional inventory.

See *Web Extension 14B* for more on forecasting when variables are not proportional to sales.

Lumpy Assets

In many industries, technological considerations dictate that if a firm is to be competitive, it must add fixed assets in large, discrete units; such assets are often referred to as **lumpy assets.** In the paper industry, for example, there are strong economies of scale in basic paper mill equipment, so when a paper company expands capacity, it must do so in large, lumpy increments. This type of situation is depicted in Panel d of Figure 14-2. Here we assume that the minimum economically efficient plant has a cost of $75 million and that such a plant can produce enough output to reach a sales level of $100 million. If the firm is to be competitive, it simply must have at least $75 million of fixed assets.

Lumpy assets have a major effect on the fixed assets/sales (FA/S) ratio at different sales levels and, consequently, on financial requirements. At Point A in Panel d, which represents a sales level of $50 million, the fixed assets are $75 million, so the ratio FA/S = $75/$50 = 1.5. Sales can expand by $50 million, out to $100 million, with no additions to fixed assets. At that point, represented by Point B, the ratio FA/S = $75/$100 = 0.75. However, since the firm is operating at capacity (sales of $100 million), even a small increase in sales would require a doubling of plant capacity, so a small projected sales increase would bring with it a very large financial requirement.[10]

Excess Capacity Adjustments

Consider again the MicroDrive example set forth in Tables 14-2 and 14-3, but now assume that excess capacity exists in fixed assets. Specifically, assume that fixed assets in 2007 were being utilized to only 96% of capacity. If fixed assets had been used to full capacity, 2007 sales could have been as high as $3,125 million versus the $3,000 million in actual sales:

$$\text{Full capacity sales} = \frac{\text{Actual sales}}{\substack{\text{Percentage of capacity} \\ \text{at which fixed assets} \\ \text{were operated}}} \qquad (14\text{-}2)$$

$$= \frac{\$3,000 \text{ million}}{0.96} = \$3,125 \text{ million.}$$

This suggests that MicroDrive's target fixed assets/sales ratio should be 32% rather than 33.3%:

$$\text{Target fixed assets/Sales} = \frac{\text{Actual fixed assets}}{\text{Full capacity sales}} \qquad (14\text{-}3)$$

$$= \frac{\$1,000}{\$3,125} = 0.32 = 32\%.$$

Therefore, if sales are to increase to $3,300 million, then fixed assets would have to increase to $1,056 million:

$$\substack{\text{Required level} \\ \text{of fixed assets}} = (\text{Target fixed assets/Sales})(\text{Projected sales}) \qquad (14\text{-}4)$$

$$= 0.32(\$3,300) = \$1,056 \text{ million.}$$

We previously forecasted that MicroDrive would need to increase fixed assets at the same rate as sales, or by 10%. That meant an increase from $1,000 million to $1,100 million, or by $100 million. Now we see that the actual required increase is only from $1,000 million to $1,056 million, or by $56 million. Thus, the capacity-adjusted forecast is $100 million − $56 million = $44 million less than the earlier forecast. With a smaller fixed asset requirement, the projected AFN would decline from an estimated $118 million to $118 million − $44 million = $74 million.

---

[10]Several other points should be noted about Panel d of Figure 14-2. First, if the firm is operating at a sales level of $100 million or less, any expansion that calls for a sales increase above $100 million would require a *doubling* of the firm's fixed assets. A much smaller percentage increase would be involved if the firm were large enough to be operating a number of plants. Second, firms generally go to multiple shifts and take other actions to minimize the need for new fixed asset capacity as they approach Point B. However, these efforts can only go so far, and eventually a fixed asset expansion will be required. Third, firms often make arrangements to share excess capacity with other firms in their industry. For example, the situation in the electric utility industry is very much like that depicted in Panel d. However, electric companies often build jointly owned plants, or else they "take turns" building plants, and then they buy power from or sell power to other utilities to avoid building new plants that would be underutilized.

Note also that when excess capacity exists, sales can grow to the capacity sales as determined above with no increase in fixed assets, but sales beyond that level will require fixed asset additions as calculated in our example. The same situation could occur with respect to inventories, and the required additions would be determined in exactly the same manner as for fixed assets. Theoretically, the same situation could occur with other types of assets, but as a practical matter excess capacity normally exists only with respect to fixed assets and inventories.

SELF-TEST

Explain how economies of scale and lumpy asset acquisition affect financial forecasting.

Summary

The key concepts covered are listed below:

- **Financial forecasting** generally begins with a forecast of the firm's sales, in terms of both units and dollars.
- Either the **forecasted,** or **pro forma, financial statement method** or the **AFN formula method** can be used to forecast financial requirements. The financial statement method is more reliable, and it also provides ratios that can be used to evaluate alternative business plans.
- A firm can determine its **additional funds needed (AFN)** by estimating the amount of new assets necessary to support the forecasted level of sales and then subtracting from that amount the spontaneous funds that will be generated from operations. The firm can then plan how to raise the AFN most efficiently.
- The **higher a firm's sales growth rate,** the **greater** will be its need for additional financing. Similarly, the **smaller its retention ratio,** the **greater** its need for additional funds.
- Adjustments must be made if **economies of scale** exist in the use of assets, if **excess capacity** exists, or if assets must be added in **lumpy increments.**
- **Linear regression** and **excess capacity adjustments** can be used to forecast asset requirements in situations where assets are not expected to grow at the same rate as sales.

Questions

(14-1) Define each of the following terms:
a. Operating plan; financial plan; sales forecast
b. Pro forma financial statement; forecasted financial statement method
c. Spontaneously generated funds
d. Additional funds needed (AFN); AFN formula; capital intensity ratio
e. Lumpy assets

(14-2) Certain liability and net worth items generally increase spontaneously with increases in sales. Put a check (✓) by those items that typically increase spontaneously:

Accounts payable	_____	Mortgage bonds	_____
Notes payable to banks	_____	Common stock	_____
Accrued wages	_____	Retained earnings	_____
Accrued taxes	_____		

(14-3) The following equation can, under certain assumptions, be used to forecast financial requirements:

$$AFN = (A^*/S_0)(\Delta S) - (L^*/S_0)(\Delta S) - MS_1(RR).$$

Under what conditions does the equation give satisfactory predictions, and when should it *not* be used?

(14-4) Suppose a firm makes the following policy changes. If the change means that external, nonspontaneous financial requirements (AFN) will increase, indicate this by a (+); indicate a decrease by a (−); and indicate indeterminate or no effect by a (0). Think in terms of the immediate, short-run effect on funds requirements.
   a. The dividend payout ratio is increased. _____
   b. The firm decides to pay all suppliers on delivery, rather than after a 30-day delay, to take advantage of discounts for rapid payment. _____
   c. The firm begins to sell on credit (previously all sales had been on a cash basis). _____
   d. The firm's profit margin is eroded by increased competition; sales are steady. _____

Self-Test Problems   Solutions Appear in Appendix A

(ST-1)
Growth Rate

The Barnsdale Corporation has the following ratios: $A^*/S_0 = 1.6$; $L^*/S_0 = 0.4$; profit margin = 0.10; and dividend payout ratio = 0.45, or 45%. Sales last year were $100 million. Assuming that these ratios will remain constant, use the AFN formula to determine the maximum growth rate Barnsdale can achieve without having to employ nonspontaneous external funds.

(ST-2)
Additional Funds
Needed

Suppose Barnsdale's financial consultants (see Problem ST-1) report (1) that the inventory turnover ratio is sales/inventory = 3 times versus an industry average of 4 times and (2) that Barnsdale could reduce inventories and thus raise its turnover to 4 without affecting sales, the profit margin, or the other asset turnover ratios. Under these conditions, use the AFN formula to determine the amount of additional funds Barnsdale would require during each of the next 2 years if sales grew at a rate of 20% per year.

(ST-3)
Excess Capacity

Van Auken Lumber's 2007 financial statements are shown below.

Van Auken Lumber: Balance Sheet as of December 31, 2007 (Thousands of Dollars)

Cash	$ 1,800	Accounts payable	$ 7,200
Receivables	10,800	Notes payable	3,472
Inventories	12,600	Accruals	2,520
Total current assets	$25,200	Total current liabilities	$13,192
Net fixed assets	21,600	Mortgage bonds	5,000
		Common stock	2,000
		Retained earnings	26,608
Total assets	$46,800	Total liabilities and equity	$46,800

Van Auken Lumber: Income Statement for December 31, 2007 (Thousands of Dollars)

Sales	$36,000
Operating costs	30,783
Earnings before interest and taxes	$ 5,217
Interest	717
Earnings before taxes	$ 4,500
Taxes (40%)	1,800
Net income	$ 2,700
Dividends (60%)	$ 1,620
Addition to retained earnings	$ 1,080

a. Assume that the company was operating at full capacity in 2007 with regard to all items *except* fixed assets; fixed assets in 2007 were being utilized to only 75% of capacity. By what percentage could 2008 sales increase over 2007 sales without the need for an increase in fixed assets?

b. Now suppose 2008 sales increase by 25% over 2007 sales. How much additional external capital will be required? Assume that Van Auken cannot sell any fixed assets. (Hint: Use the forecasted financial statements method to develop a pro forma balance sheet and income statement as in Tables 14-2 and 14-3.) Assume that any required financing is borrowed as notes payable. Use a 12% interest rate for all debt at the beginning of the year to forecast interest expense (cash does not earn interest), and use a pro forma income statement to determine the addition to retained earnings. (Another hint: Notes payable = $6,021.)

Problems   Answers Appear in Appendix B

Easy
Problems 1–3

(14-1)
AFN Formula

Baxter Video Products' sales are expected to increase from $5 million in 2007 to $6 million in 2008 or by 20%. Its assets totaled $3 million at the end of 2007. Baxter is at full capacity, so its assets must grow at the same rate as projected sales. At the end of 2007, current liabilities were $1 million, consisting of $250,000 of accounts payable, $500,000 of notes payable, and $250,000 of accruals. The after-tax profit margin is forecasted to be 5%, and the forecasted payout ratio is 70%. Use the AFN formula to forecast Baxter's additional funds needed for the coming year.

(14-2)
AFN Formula

Refer to Problem 14-1. What would be the additional funds needed if the company's year-end 2007 assets had been $4 million? Assume that all other numbers are the same. Why is this AFN different from the one you found in Problem 14-1? Is the company's "capital intensity" the same or different?

(14-3)
AFN Formula

Refer to Problem 14-1. Return to the assumption that the company had $3 million in assets at the end of 2007, but now assume that the company pays no dividends. Under these assumptions, what would be the additional funds needed for the coming year? Why is this AFN different from the one you found in Problem 14-1?

Intermediate
Problems 4–6

(14-4)
Sales Increase

Bannister Legal Services generated $2.0 million in sales during 2007, and its year-end total assets were $1.5 million. Also, at year-end 2007, current liabilities were $500,000, consisting of $200,000 of notes payable, $200,000 of accounts payable, and $100,000 of accruals. Looking ahead to 2008, the company estimates that its assets must increase by 75 cents for every $1 increase in sales. Bannister's profit margin is 5%, and its payout ratio is 60%. How large a sales increase can the company achieve without having to raise funds externally?

(14-5)
Long-Term Financing Needed

At year-end 2007, total assets for Bertin Inc. were $1.2 million and accounts payable were $375,000. Sales, which in 2007 were $2.5 million, are expected to increase by 25% in 2008. Total assets and accounts payable are proportional to sales, and that relationship will be maintained. Bertin typically uses no current liabilities other than accounts payable. Common stock amounted to $425,000 in 2007, and retained earnings were $295,000. Bertin plans to sell new common stock in the amount of $75,000. The firm's profit margin on sales is 6%; 40% of earnings will be paid out as dividends.
a. What was Bertin's total debt in 2007?
b. How much new, long-term debt financing will be needed in 2008? (Hint: AFN − New stock = New long-term debt.) Do not consider any financing feedback effects.

(14-6)
Additional Funds Needed

The Booth Company's sales are forecasted to increase from $1,000 in 2007 to $2,000 in 2008. Here is the December 31, 2007, balance sheet:

Cash	$ 100	Accounts payable	$ 50
Accounts receivable	200	Notes payable	150
Inventories	200	Accruals	50
Net fixed assets	500	Long-term debt	400
		Common stock	100
		Retained earnings	250
Total assets	$1,000	Total liabilities and equity	$1,000

Booth's fixed assets were used to only 50% of capacity during 2007, but its current assets were at their proper levels. All assets except fixed assets increase at the same rate as sales, and fixed assets would also increase at the same rate if the current excess capacity did not exist. Booth's after-tax profit margin is forecasted to be 5%, and its payout ratio will be 60%. What is Booth's additional funds needed (AFN) for the coming year?

Challenging Problems 7–9

(14-7)
Pro Forma Statements and Ratios

Upton Computers makes bulk purchases of small computers, stocks them in conveniently located warehouses, and ships them to its chain of retail stores. Upton's balance sheet as of December 31, 2007, is shown here (millions of dollars).

Cash	$ 3.5	Accounts payable	$ 9.0
Receivables	26.0	Notes payable	18.0
Inventories	58.0	Accruals	8.5
Total current assets	$ 87.5	Total current liabilities	$ 35.5
Net fixed assets	35.0	Mortgage loan	6.0
		Common stock	15.0
		Retained earnings	66.0
Total assets	$122.5	Total liabilities and equity	$122.5

Sales for 2007 were $350 million, while net income for the year was $10.5 million. Upton paid dividends of $4.2 million to common stockholders. The firm is operating at full capacity. Assume that all ratios remain constant.
a. If sales are projected to increase by $70 million, or 20%, during 2008, use the AFN equation to determine Upton's projected external capital requirements.

b. Construct Upton's pro forma balance sheet for December 31, 2008. Assume that all external capital requirements are met by bank loans and are reflected in notes payable. Assume Upton's profit margin and dividend payout ratio remain constant.

(14-8)
Additional Funds
Needed

Stevens Textile's 2007 financial statements are shown below.

Stevens Textile: Balance Sheet as of December 31, 2007 (Thousands of Dollars)

Cash	$ 1,080	Accounts payable	$ 4,320
Receivables	6,480	Accruals	2,880
Inventories	9,000	Notes payable	2,100
Total current assets	$16,560	Total current liabilities	$ 9,300
Net fixed assets	12,600	Mortgage bonds	3,500
		Common stock	3,500
		Retained earnings	12,860
Total assets	$29,160	Total liabilities and equity	$29,160

Stevens Textile: Income Statement for December 31, 2007 (Thousands of Dollars)

Sales	$36,000
Operating costs	32,440
Earnings before interest and taxes	$ 3,560
Interest	460
Earnings before taxes	$ 3,100
Taxes (40%)	1,240
Net income	$ 1,860
Dividends (45%)	$ 837
Addition to retained earnings	$ 1,023

Suppose 2008 sales are projected to increase by 15% over 2007 sales. Determine the additional funds needed. Assume that the company was operating at full capacity in 2007, that it cannot sell off any of its fixed assets, and that any required financing will be borrowed as notes payable. Also, assume that assets, spontaneous liabilities, and operating costs are expected to increase by the same percentage as sales. Use the forecasted financial statements method to develop a pro forma balance sheet and income statement for December 31, 2008. Use an interest rate of 10% on the balance of debt at the beginning of the year to compute interest (cash pays no interest). Use the pro forma income statement to determine the addition to retained earnings.

(14-9)
Additional Funds
Needed

Garlington Technologies Inc.'s 2007 financial statements are shown below.

Garlington Technologies Inc.: Balance Sheet as of December 31, 2007

Cash	$ 180,000	Accounts payable	$ 360,000
Receivables	360,000	Notes payable	156,000
Inventories	720,000	Accruals	180,000
Total current assets	$1,260,000	Total current liabilities	$ 696,000
Fixed assets	1,440,000	Common stock	1,800,000
		Retained earnings	204,000
Total assets	$2,700,000	Total liabilities and equity	$2,700,000

Garlington Technologies Inc.: Income Statement for December 31, 2007

Sales	$3,600,000
Operating costs	3,279,720
EBIT	$ 320,280
Interest	18,280
EBT	$ 302,000
Taxes (40%)	120,800
Net income	$ 181,200
Dividends	$ 108,000

Suppose that in 2008 sales increase by 10% over 2007 sales and that 2008 dividends will increase to $112,000. Construct the pro forma financial statements using the percent of sales method. Assume the firm operated at full capacity in 2007. Use an interest rate of 13% on the debt balance at the beginning of the year. Assume that the AFN will be in the form of notes payable.

Spreadsheet Problem

(14-10)
Build a Model:
Forecasting Financial
Statements

e-resource

Start with the partial model in the file *FM12 Ch 14 P10 Build a Model.xls* from the textbook's Web site. Cumberland Industries' financial planners must forecast the company's financial results for the coming year. The forecast will be based on the forecasted financial statements method, and any additional funds needed will be obtained by using a mix of notes payable, long-term debt, and common stock. No preferred stock will be issued. Data for the problem, including Cumberland Industries' balance sheet and income statement, can be found in the spreadsheet problem for Chapter 3. Use these data to answer the following questions.

a. Cumberland Industries has had the following sales since 2002. Assuming the historical trend continues, what will sales be in 2008?

Year	Sales
2002	$129,215,000
2003	180,901,000
2004	235,252,000
2005	294,065,000
2006	396,692,000
2007	455,150,000

Base your forecast on a spreadsheet regression analysis of the 2002–2007 sales. By what percentage are sales predicted to increase in 2008 over 2007? Is the sales growth rate increasing or decreasing?

b. Cumberland's management believes that the firm will actually experience a 20% increase in sales during 2008. Construct the 2008 pro forma financial statements. Cumberland will not issue any new stock or long-term bonds. Assume Cumberland will carry forward its current amounts of short-term investments and notes payable, prior to calculating additional funds needed

(AFN). Assume that any AFN will be raised as notes payable (if AFN is negative, Cumberland will purchase additional short-term investments). Use an interest rate of 9% for short-term debt (and for the interest income on short-term investments) and a rate of 11% for long-term debt. No interest is earned on cash. Use the beginning-of-year debt balances to calculate net interest expense. Assume dividends grow at an 8% rate.

c. Now create a graph that shows the sensitivity of AFN to the sales growth rate. To make this graph, compare the AFN at sales growth rates of 5%, 10%, 15%, 20%, 25%, and 30%.

d. Calculate net operating working capital (NOWC), total operating capital, NOPAT, and operating cash flow (OCF) for 2007 and 2008. Also, calculate the free cash flow (FCF) for 2008.

e. Suppose Cumberland can reduce its inventory-to-sales ratio to 5% and its cost-to-sales ratio to 83%. What happens to AFN and FCF?

Cyberproblems

e-resource

Please go to the textbook's Web site to access any Cyberproblems.

Mini Case

Betty Simmons, the new financial manager of Southeast Chemicals (SEC), a Georgia producer of specialized chemicals for use in fruit orchards, must prepare a financial forecast for 2008. SEC's 2007 sales were $2 billion, and the marketing department is forecasting a 25% increase for 2008. Simmons thinks the company was operating at full capacity in 2007, but she is not sure about this. The 2007 financial statements, plus some other data, are shown below.

A. 2007 Balance Sheet (Millions of Dollars)

		Percent of Sales			Percent of Sales
Cash and securities	$ 20	1%	Accounts payable and accruals	$ 100	5%
Accounts receivable	240	12%	Notes payable	100	
Inventories	240	12%	Total current liabilities	$ 200	
Total current assets	$ 500		Long-term debt	100	
Net fixed assets	500	25%	Common stock	500	
			Retained earnings	200	
Total assets	$1,000		Total liabilities and equity	$1,000	

B. 2007 Income Statement (Millions of Dollars)

		Percent of Sales
Sales	$2,000.00	
Cost of goods sold (COGS)	1,200.00	60%
Sales, general, and administrative costs (SGA)	700.00	35%
Earnings before interest and taxes	$ 100.00	
Interest	10.00	
Earnings before taxes	$ 90.00	
Taxes (40%)	36.00	
Net income	$ 54.00	
Dividends (40%)	21.60	
Addition to retained earnings	$ 32.40	

C. Key Ratios

	SEC	Industry
Profit margin	2.70%	4.005
Return on equity	7.71	15.60
Days sales outstanding (365 days)	43.80 days	32.00 days
Inventory turnover	8.33×	11.00×
Fixed assets turnover	4.00	5.00
Debt/assets	30.00%	36.00%
Times interest earned	10.00×	9.40×
Current ratio	2.50	3.00
Return on invested capital (NOPAT/Operating capital)	6.67%	14.00%

Assume that you were recently hired as Simmons's assistant, and your first major task is to help her develop the forecast. She asked you to begin by answering the following set of questions.

a. Describe three ways that pro forma statements are used in financial planning.
b. Explain the steps in financial forecasting.
c. Assume (1) that SEC was operating at full capacity in 2007 with respect to all assets, (2) that all assets must grow proportionally with sales, (3) that accounts payable and accruals will also grow in proportion to sales, and (4) that the 2007 profit margin and dividend payout will be maintained. Under these conditions, what will the company's financial requirements be for the coming year? Use the AFN equation to answer this question.
d. How would changes in the following items affect the AFN? (1) Sales increase; (2) the dividend payout ratio increases; (3) the profit margin increases; (4) the capital intensity ratio increases; (5) SEC begins paying its suppliers sooner. (Consider each item separately and hold all other things constant.)
e. Briefly explain how to forecast financial statements using the forecasted financial statements approach. Be sure to explain how to forecast interest expenses.

f. Now estimate the 2008 financial requirements using the forecasted financial statements approach. Assume (1) that each type of asset, as well as payables, accruals, and fixed and variable costs, will be the same percent of sales in 2008 as in 2007; (2) that the payout ratio is held constant at 40%; (3) that external funds needed are financed 50% by notes payable and 50% by long-term debt (no new common stock will be issued); (4) that all debt carries an interest rate of 10%; and (5) that interest expenses should be based on the balance of debt at the beginning of the year.

g. Why does the forecasted financial statements approach produce somewhat different AFN than the equation approach? Which method provides the more accurate forecast?

h. Calculate SEC's forecasted ratios, and compare them with the company's 2007 ratios and with the industry averages. Calculate SEC's forecasted free cash flow and return on invested capital (ROIC).

i. Based on comparisons between SEC's days sales outstanding (DSO) and inventory turnover ratios with the industry average figures, does it appear that SEC is operating efficiently with respect to its inventory and accounts receivable? Suppose SEC were able to bring these ratios into line with the industry averages and reduce its SGA/Sales ratio to 33%. What effect would this have on its AFN and its financial ratios? What effect would this have on free cash flow and ROIC?

j. Suppose you now learn that SEC's 2007 receivables and inventories were in line with required levels, given the firm's credit and inventory policies, but that excess capacity existed with regard to fixed assets. Specifically, fixed assets were operated at only 75% of capacity.

    (1) What level of sales could have existed in 2007 with the available fixed assets?

    (2) How would the existence of excess capacity in fixed assets affect the additional funds needed during 2008?

k. The relationship between sales and the various types of assets is important in financial forecasting. The forecasted financial statements approach, under the assumption that each asset item grows at the same rate as sales, leads to an AFN forecast that is reasonably close to the forecast using the AFN equation. Explain how each of the following factors would affect the accuracy of financial forecasts based on the AFN equation: (1) economies of scale in the use of assets and (2) lumpy assets.

Selected Additional Cases

The following cases from Textchoice, Cengage Learning's online library, cover many of the concepts discussed in this chapter and are available at *http://www.textchoice2.com.*

Klein-Brigham Series:
Case 37, "Space-Age Materials, Inc."; Case 38, "Automated Banking Management, Inc."; Case 52, "Expert Systems"; and Case 69, "Medical Management Systems, Inc."

Corporate Valuation, Value-Based Management, and Corporate Governance

If you had invested $1,000 in the NYSE Composite Index 10 years ago, your investment would have grown to $2,254, resulting in an 8.5% annual rate of return. Had you put the $1,000 in Berkshire Hathaway, you would now have $2,960, which is an 11.5% annual return. And if you had been really smart (or lucky) and invested in Dell, you would now have $13,705, which translates into a whopping 29.9% annual return! Berkshire Hathaway and Dell compete in very different industries and utilize different strategies, yet both have beaten the market by sharing an operating philosophy: They have created value for shareholders by focusing on the free cash flows of their underlying businesses. When this focus is applied systematically throughout a company, it is called value-based management, which is the central theme of this chapter.

Berkshire Hathaway's primary strategy has been to grow through acquisitions. Warren Buffett, Berkshire's CEO, wrote in a recent letter to shareholders that he seeks to own "businesses that generate cash and consistently earn above-average returns on their capital." When evaluating a potential acquisition, Buffett says he compares its purchase price with its "intrinsic value," which he defines as "the discounted value of the cash that can be taken out of a business during its remaining life." Thus, Buffett's growth strategy is governed by the principles of value-based management.

Instead of growing primarily through acquisitions, Dell has chosen to grow "organically" by expanding its existing businesses and developing new products and markets. For most companies, rapid growth in sales requires rapid growth in operating capital, which reduces free cash flow. But Dell is relentless in minimizing the amount of operating capital required to support sales. In fact, during the last 5 years, Dell has had outstanding performance in the drivers of value-based management: (1) Its sales have grown faster than the industry average, (2) its profit margin has exceeded the industry average, and (3) its capital requirements have remained lower than the industry average.

Keep Berkshire Hathaway's and Dell's focus on cash flows in mind as you read this chapter.

Sources: Various annual reports of Berkshire Hathaway Inc. and Dell Computers.

As we have emphasized throughout the book, maximizing shareholder value should be management's primary objective. However, to maximize value, managers need a tool for estimating the effects of alternative strategies. In this chapter, we develop and illustrate such a tool—the **corporate valuation model,** which is the present value of expected future free cash flows, discounted at the weighted average cost of capital. In a sense, the corporate valuation model is the culmination of all the material covered thus far, because it pulls together financial statements, cash flows, financial projections, time value of money, risk, and the cost of capital. Companies practice **value-based management** by systematically using the corporate valuation model to guide their decisions. Finally, the degree to which a company employs principles of value-based management often depends on its **corporate governance,** which is the set of laws, rules, and procedures that influence its operations and the decisions made by its managers.

15.1 Overview of Corporate Valuation

As stated earlier, managers should evaluate the effects of alternative strategies on their firms' values. This really means forecasting financial statements under alternative strategies, finding the present value of each strategy's cash flow stream, and then choosing the strategy that provides the maximum value. The financial statements should be projected using the techniques and procedures discussed in Chapter 14, and the discount rate should be the risk-adjusted cost of capital as discussed in Chapter 10. But what model should managers use to discount the cash flows? One possibility is the dividend growth model from Chapter 8. However, that model is often unsuitable for managerial purposes. For example, suppose a start-up company is formed to develop and market a new product. Its managers will focus on product development, marketing, and raising capital. They will probably be thinking about an eventual IPO, or perhaps the sale of the company to a larger firm—Cisco, Microsoft, Intel, IBM, or another of the industry leaders that buy hundreds of successful new companies each year. For the managers of such a start-up, the decision to initiate dividend payments in the foreseeable future will be totally off the radar screen. Thus, the dividend growth model is not useful for valuing most start-up companies.

Also, many established firms pay no dividends. Investors may expect them to pay dividends sometime in the future, but when, and how much? As long as internal opportunities and acquisitions are so attractive, the initiation of dividends will be postponed, and this makes the dividend growth model of little use. Even Microsoft, one of the world's most successful companies, only started paying a dividend in 2003.

Finally, the dividend growth model is generally of limited use for internal management purposes, even for a dividend-paying company. If the firm consisted of just one big asset, and that asset produced all of the cash flows used to pay dividends, then alternative strategies could be judged through the use of the dividend growth model. However, most firms have several different divisions with many assets, so the corporation's value depends on the cash flows from many different assets, and on the actions of many managers. These managers need a way to measure the effects of their decisions on corporate value, but the discounted dividend model isn't very useful because individual divisions don't pay dividends.

Corporate Valuation: Putting the Pieces Together

The value of a firm is determined by the size, timing, and risk of its expected future free cash flows (FCF). Chapter 14 showed how to project financial statements, and Chapter 3 showed how to calculate free cash flows. Chapter 10 explained how to estimate the weighted average cost of capital. This chapter puts the pieces together and shows how to calculate the value of a firm. It also shows how to use the valuation model as a guide for choosing among different corporate strategies and operating tactics.

$$\text{Value} = \frac{\text{FCF}_1}{(1 + \text{WACC})^1} + \frac{\text{FCF}_2}{(1 + \text{WACC})^2} + \frac{\text{FCF}_3}{(1 + \text{WACC})^3} + \cdots + \frac{\text{FCF}_\infty}{(1 + \text{WACC})^\infty}$$

Fortunately, the corporate valuation model does not depend on dividends, and it can be applied to divisions and subunits as well as to the entire firm.

Another important aspect of value-based management is the concept of corporate governance. The corporate valuation model shows how corporate decisions affect *stockholders*. However, corporate decisions are made by managers, not stockholders, and maximizing shareholder wealth is not the same as individual managers maximizing their own "satisfaction."[1] Thus, a key aspect of value-based management is making sure that managers focus on the goal of stockholder wealth maximization. The set of laws, rules, and procedures that influence a company's operations and motivate its managers falls under the general heading of *corporate governance*.

This chapter discusses the corporate valuation model, value-based management, and corporate governance, beginning with the corporate valuation model.

SELF-TEST   Why is the corporate valuation model applicable in more circumstances than the dividend growth model?

What is value-based management?

What is corporate governance?

15.2 The Corporate Valuation Model

Corporate assets are of two types: **operating** and **nonoperating.** Operating assets, in turn, take two forms: **assets-in-place** and **growth options.** Assets-in-place include such tangible assets as land, buildings, machines, and inventory, plus intangible assets such as patents, customer lists, reputation, and general know-how. Growth options are opportunities to expand that arise from the firm's current operating knowledge, experience, and other resources. The assets-in-place provide an expected stream of cash flows, and so do the growth options. To illustrate, Wal-Mart owns stores, inventory, and other tangible assets; it has a well-known name and a good reputation; and it has a lot of business know-how. These assets produce current sales and cash flows, and they also provide opportunities for new investments that will produce additional cash flows in the future.

---

[1]A distinction is sometimes made between "executives" and "managers," with executives being corporate officers and other members of the top management team. We do not make that distinction in this book—all people with important decision-making powers are designated "managers."

Similarly, Merck owns manufacturing plants, patents, and other real assets, and it has a knowledge base that facilitates the development of new drugs and thus new cash flow streams.

Most companies also own some nonoperating assets, which come in two forms. The first is a marketable securities portfolio over and above the cash needed to operate the business. For example, Ford Motor Company's automotive operation had about $10.3 billion in short-term investments as of December 2005, and this was in addition to $13.4 billion in cash. Second, Ford also had $1.8 billion of investments in other businesses, which were reported on the asset side of the balance sheet as "Equity in Net Assets of Affiliated Companies." In total Ford had $10.3 + $1.8 = $12.1 billion of nonoperating assets, compared with its $113.8 billion of automotive assets, or 10.6% of the total. For most companies, the percentage is much lower. For example, as of the end of 2005 Wal-Mart's percentage of nonoperating assets was less than 1%, which is more typical.

We see, then, that for most companies operating assets are far more important than nonoperating assets. Moreover, companies can influence the values of their operating assets, but the values of nonoperating assets are largely out of their direct control. Therefore, value-based management, hence this chapter, focuses on operating assets.

Estimating the Value of Operations

Tables 15-1 and 15-2 contain the actual 2007 and projected 2008 to 2011 financial statements for MagnaVision Inc., which produces optical systems for use in medical photography. (See Chapter 14 for more details on how to project financial statements.) Growth has been rapid in the past, but the market is becoming saturated, so the sales growth rate is expected to decline from 21% in 2008 to a sustainable rate of 5% in 2011 and beyond. Profit margins are expected to improve as the production process becomes more efficient and because MagnaVision will no longer be incurring marketing costs associated with the introduction of a major product. All items on the financial statements are projected to grow at a 5% rate after 2011. Note that the company does not pay a dividend, but it is expected to start paying out about 75% of its earnings beginning in 2010. (Chapter 18 explains in more detail how companies decide how much to pay out in dividends.)

Recall that free cash flow (FCF) is the cash from operations that is actually available for distribution to investors, including stockholders, bondholders, and preferred stockholders. The value of operations is the present value of the free cash flows the firm is expected to generate out into the future. Therefore, MagnaVision's value can be calculated as the present value of its expected future free cash flows from operations, discounted at its weighted average cost of capital, WACC, plus the value of its nonoperating assets. Here is the equation for the value of operations, which is the firm's value as a going concern:

$$\text{Value of operations} = V_{op} = \text{PV of expected future free cash flow}$$

$$= \frac{FCF_1}{(1 + WACC)^1} + \frac{FCF_2}{(1 + WACC)^2} + \cdots + \frac{FCF_\infty}{(1 + WACC)^\infty}$$

$$= \sum_{t=1}^{\infty} \frac{FCF_t}{(1 + WACC)^t}. \tag{15-1}$$

Table 15-1

MagnaVision Inc.: Income Statements (Millions of Dollars, Except for Per Share Data)

	Actual	Projected			
	2007	**2008**	**2009ª**	**2010**	**2011**
Net sales	$700.0	$850.0	$1,000.0	$1,100.0	$1,155.0
Costs (except depreciation)	599.0	734.0	911.0	935.0	982.0
Depreciation	28.0	31.0	34.0	36.0	38.0
Total operating costs	$627.0	$765.0	$ 945.0	$ 971.0	$1,020.0
Earnings before interest and taxes (EBIT)	$ 73.0	$ 85.0	$ 55.0	$ 129.0	$ 135.0
Less: Net interestᵇ	13.0	15.0	16.0	17.0	19.0
Earnings before taxes	$ 60.0	$ 70.0	$ 39.0	$ 112.0	$ 116.0
Taxes (40%)	24.0	28.0	15.6	44.8	46.4
Net income before preferred dividends	$ 36.0	$ 42.0	$ 23.4	$ 67.2	$ 69.6
Preferred dividends	6.0	7.0	7.4	8.0	8.3
Net income available for common dividends	$ 30.0	$ 35.0	$ 16.0	$ 59.2	$ 61.3
Common dividends	—	—	—	$ 44.2	$ 45.3
Addition to retained earnings	$ 30.0	$ 35.0	$ 16.0	$ 15.0	$ 16.0
Number of shares	100	100	100	100	100
Dividends per share	—	—	—	$ 0.442	$ 0.453

Notes:

ªNet income is projected to decline in 2009. This is due to the projected cost for a one-time marketing program in that year.
ᵇ"Net interest" is interest paid on debt less interest earned on marketable securities. Both items could be shown separately on the income state-ments, but for this example we combine them and show net interest. MagnaVision pays more interest than it earns; hence its net interest is subtracted.

MagnaVision's cost of capital is 10.84%. To find its value of operations as a going concern, we use an approach similar to the nonconstant dividend growth model for stocks in Chapter 8, proceeding as follows:

1. Assume that the firm will experience nonconstant growth for N years, after which it will grow at some constant rate.
2. Calculate the expected free cash flow for each of the N nonconstant growth years.
3. Recognize that after Year N growth will be constant, so we can use the constant growth formula to find the firm's value at Year N. This is the sum of the PVs for year N + 1 and all subsequent years, discounted back to Year N.
4. Find the PV of the free cash flows for each of the N nonconstant growth years. Also, find the PV of the firm's value at Year N.
5. Now sum all the PVs, those of the annual free cash flows during the noncon-stant period plus the PV of the Year N value, to find the firm's value of operations.

Table 15-3 calculates free cash flow for each year, using procedures discussed in Chapter 3. Line 1, with data for 2007 from the balance sheets in Table 15-2,

e-resource

See *FM12 Ch 15 Tool Kit.xls* at the textbook's Web site for all calculations.

Table 15-2

MagnaVision Inc.: Balance Sheets (Millions of Dollars)

	Actual	Projected			
	2007	2008	2009	2010	2011
Assets					
Cash	$ 17.0	$ 20.0	$ 22.0	$ 23.0	$ 24.0
Marketable securities[a]	63.0	70.0	80.0	84.0	88.0
Accounts receivable	85.0	100.0	110.0	116.0	121.0
Inventories	170.0	200.0	220.0	231.0	243.0
Total current assets	$335.0	$390.0	$432.0	$454.0	$476.0
Net plant and equipment	279.0	310.0	341.0	358.0	376.0
Total assets	$614.0	$700.0	$773.0	$812.0	$852.0
Liabilities and Equity					
Accounts payable	$ 17.0	$ 20.0	$ 22.0	$ 23.0	$ 24.0
Notes payable	123.0	140.0	160.0	168.0	176.0
Accruals	43.0	50.0	55.0	58.0	61.0
Total current liabilities	$183.0	$210.0	$237.0	$249.0	$261.0
Long-term bonds	124.0	140.0	160.0	168.0	176.0
Preferred stock	62.0	70.0	80.0	84.0	88.0
Common stock[b]	200.0	200.0	200.0	200.0	200.0
Retained earnings	45.0	80.0	96.0	111.0	127.0
Common equity	$245.0	$280.0	$296.0	$311.0	$327.0
Total liabilities and equity	$614.0	$700.0	$773.0	$812.0	$852.0

Notes:
[a]All assets except marketable securities are operating assets required to support sales. The marketable securities are financial assets not required in operations.
[b]Par plus paid-in capital.

shows the required net operating working capital, or operating current assets minus operating current liabilities, for 2007:

$$\text{Required net operating working capital} = \left(\begin{array}{c}\text{Cash} + \\ \text{Accounts receivable} \\ + \text{Inventories}\end{array}\right) - \left(\begin{array}{c}\text{Accounts} \\ \text{payable} + \\ \text{Accruals}\end{array}\right)$$

$$= (\$17.00 + \$85.00 + \$170.00) - (\$17.00 + \$43.00)$$

$$= \$212.00.$$

Line 2 shows required net plant and equipment, and Line 3, which is the sum of Lines 1 and 2, shows the required net operating assets, also called total net operating capital, or just operating capital. For 2007, operating capital is $212 + $279 = $491 million.

Table 15-3

Calculating MagnaVision's Expected Free Cash Flow (Millions of Dollars)

	Actual	Projected			
	2007	**2008**	**2009**	**2010**	**2011**
Calculation of Free Cash Flow					
1. Required net operating working capital	$212.00	$ 250.00	$ 275.00	$289.00	$303.00
2. Required net plant and equipment	279.00	310.00	341.00	358.00	376.00
3. Required total net operating capital[a]	$491.00	$ 560.00	$ 616.00	$647.00	$679.00
4. Required net new investment in operating capital = change in total net operating capital from previous year		$ 69.00	$ 56.00	$ 31.00	$ 32.00
5. NOPAT [Net operating profit after taxes = EBIT × (1 − Tax rate)][b]		$ 51.00	$ 33.00	$ 77.40	$ 81.00
6. Less: Required investment in operating capital		69.00	56.00	31.00	32.00
7. Free cash flow		($ 18.00)	($ 23.00)	$ 46.40	$ 49.00

[a]The terms "total net operating capital," "operating capital," and "net operating assets" all mean the same thing.
[b]NOPAT declines in 2009 because of a marketing expenditure projected for that year. See Note a in Table 15-1.

Line 4 shows the required annual addition to operating capital, found as the change in operating capital from the previous year. For 2008, the required investment in operating capital is $560 − $491 = $69 million.

Line 5 shows NOPAT, or net operating profit after taxes. Note that EBIT is operating earnings *before* taxes, while NOPAT is operating earnings *after* taxes. Therefore, NOPAT = EBIT(1 − T). With 2008 EBIT of $85 as shown in Table 15-1 and a tax rate of 40%, NOPAT as projected for 2007 is $51 million:

$$\text{NOPAT} = \text{EBIT}(1 − T) = \$85(1.0 − 0.4) = \$51 \text{ million.}$$

Although MagnaVision's operating capital is projected to produce $51 million of after-tax profits in 2008, the company must invest $69 million in new operating capital in 2008 to support its growth plan. Therefore, the free cash flow for 2008, shown on Line 7, is a negative $18 million:

$$\text{Free cash flow (FCF)} = \$51 − \$69 = −\$18 \text{ million.}$$

This negative free cash flow in the early years is typical for young, high-growth companies. Even though net operating profit after taxes (NOPAT) is positive in all years, free cash flow is negative because of the need to invest in operating assets. The negative free cash flow means the company will have to obtain new funds from investors, and the balance sheets in Table 15-2 show that notes payable, long-term bonds, and preferred stock all increase from 2007 to 2008. Stockholders will also help fund MagnaVision's growth—they will receive no dividends until 2010, so all of the net income from 2008 and 2009 will be reinvested. However, as growth slows, free cash flow will become positive, and MagnaVision plans to use some of its FCF to pay dividends beginning in 2010.[2]

A variant of the constant growth dividend model is shown below as Equation 15-2. This equation can be used to find the value of MagnaVision's operations at time N, when its free cash flows stabilize and begin to grow at a constant rate. This is the value of all FCFs beyond time N, discounted back to time N, which is 2011 for MagnaVision.

$$V_{op(\text{at time N})} = \sum_{t=N+1}^{\infty} \frac{FCF_t}{(1 + WACC)^{t-N}}$$

$$= \frac{FCF_{N+1}}{WACC - g} = \frac{FCF_N(1 + g)}{WACC - g}. \tag{15-2}$$

Based on a 10.84% cost of capital, $49 million of free cash flow in 2011, and a 5% growth rate, the value of MagnaVision's operations as of December 31, 2011, is forecasted to be $880.99 million:

e-resource

See **FM12 Ch 15 Tool Kit.xls** at the textbook's Web site for all calculations.

$$V_{op(12/31/11)} = \frac{FCF_{12/31/11}(1 + g)}{WACC - g}$$

$$= \frac{\$49(1 + 0.05)}{0.1084 - 0.05} = \frac{\$51.45}{0.1084 - 0.05} = \$880.99. \tag{15-2a}$$

This $880.99 million figure is called the company's **terminal,** or **horizon, value,** because it is the value at the end of the forecast period. It is also sometimes called a **continuing value.** It is the amount that MagnaVision could expect to receive if it sold its operating assets on December 31, 2011.

Figure 15-1 shows the free cash flow for each year during the nonconstant growth period, along with the horizon value of operations in 2011. To find the value of operations as of "today," December 31, 2007, we find the PV of each annual cash flow in Figure 15-1, discounting at the 10.84% cost of capital. The sum of the PVs is approximately $615 million, and it represents an estimate of the price MagnaVision could expect to receive if it sold its operating assets today, December 31, 2007.

Estimating the Price per Share

The total value of any company is the value of its operations plus the value of its nonoperating assets.[3] As the December 31, 2007, balance sheet in Table 15-2 shows, MagnaVision had $63 million of marketable securities on that date. Unlike operating assets, we do not have to calculate a present value for marketable securities because short-term financial assets as reported on the balance sheet are at, or close to, their market value. Therefore, MagnaVision's total value on December 31, 2007, is $615.27 + $63.00 = $678.27 million.

If the company's total value on December 31, 2007, is $678.27 million, what is the value of its common equity? First, the sum of notes payable and long-term debt is $123 + $124 = $247 million, and these securities have the first claim on assets and income. Accounts payable and accruals were netted out earlier when calculating

---

[2]MagnaVision plans to increase its debt and preferred stock each year so as to maintain a constant capital structure. We discuss capital structure in detail in Chapter 16.
[3]The total value also includes the value of growth options not associated with assets-in-place, but MagnaVision has none.

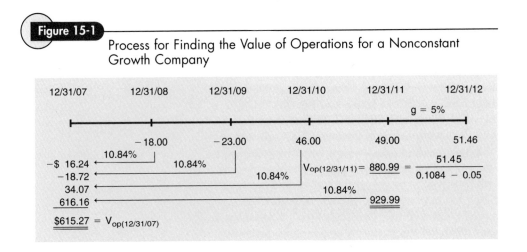

Figure 15-1

Process for Finding the Value of Operations for a Nonconstant Growth Company

free cash flow, so they have been accounted for. However, the preferred stock has a claim of $62 million, and it also ranks above the common. Therefore, the value left for common stockholders is $678.27 − $247 − $62 = $369.27 million.

Figure 15-2 is a bar chart that provides a breakdown of MagnaVision's value. The left bar shows the company's total value as the sum of its nonoperating assets plus its going concern value. Next, the middle bar shows the claim of each class of investors on that total value. Debtholders have the highest priority claim, and MagnaVision owes $123 million on notes payable and $124 million on long-term bonds, for a total of $247 million. The preferred stockholders have the next claim,

e-resource

See *FM12 Ch 15 Tool Kit.xls* at the textbook's Web site for all calculations.

Figure 15-2

MagnaVision's Value as of December 31, 2007

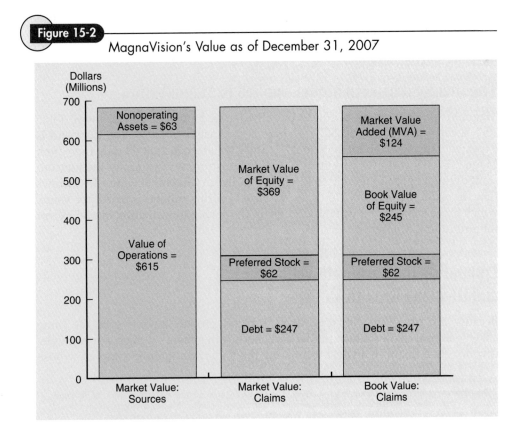

Table 15-4	Finding the Value of MagnaVision's Stock (Millions of Dollars, Except for Per Share Data)	
1. Value of operations (present value of free cash flows)		$615.27
2. Plus value of nonoperating assets		63.00
3. Total market value of the firm		$678.27
4. Less: Value of debt		247.00
Value of preferred stock		62.00
5. Value of common equity		$369.27
6. Divide by number of shares (in millions)		100.00
7. Value per share		$ 3.69

$62 million. The remaining value belongs to the common equity, and it amounts to $678.27 − $247.00 − $62.00 = $369.27 million.[4] In Chapter 3, we defined the Market Value Added (MVA) as the difference between the market value of stock and the equity capital supplied by shareholders. Here, we assume that the estimated market value of equity is approximately equal to the actual market value of equity; in other words, the intrinsic value of MagnaVision is equal to its market value. The bar on the right side of Figure 15-2 divides the market value of the equity into two components, the book value of equity, which represents the equity capital supplied by stockholders, and the MVA.

Table 15-4 summarizes the calculations used to find MagnaVision's stock value. There are 100 million shares outstanding, and their total value is $369.27 million. Therefore, the value of a single share is $369.27/100 = $3.69.

The Dividend Growth Model Applied to MagnaVision

MagnaVision has not yet begun to pay dividends. However, as we saw in Table 15-1, a cash dividend of $0.442 per share is forecasted for 2010. The dividend is expected to grow by about 2.5% in 2011, and then at a constant 5% rate thereafter. MagnaVision's cost of equity is 14%. In this situation, we can apply the nonconstant dividend growth model as developed earlier in Chapter 8. Figure 15-3 shows that the value of MagnaVision's stock, based on this model, is $3.70 per share, which is the same as the value found using the corporate valuation model except for a rounding difference.

Comparing the Corporate Valuation and Dividend Growth Models

Because the corporate valuation and dividend growth models give the same answer, does it matter which model you choose? In general, it does. For example, if you were a financial analyst estimating the value of a mature company whose

---

[4]When estimating the intrinsic market value of equity, it would be better to subtract the market values of debt and preferred stock rather than their book values. However, in most cases, including this one, the book values of fixed income securities are close to their market values. When this is true, one can simply use book values.

Figure 15-3

Using the DCF Dividend Model to Find MagnaVision's Stock Value

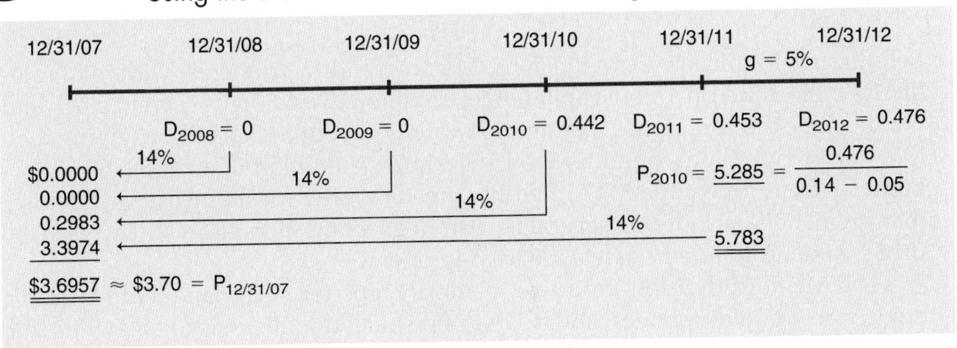

dividends are expected to grow steadily in the future, it would probably be more efficient to use the dividend growth model. Here you would only need to estimate the growth rate in dividends, not the entire set of pro forma financial statements.

However, if a company is paying a dividend but is still in the high-growth stage of its life cycle, you would need to project the future financial statements before you could make a reasonable estimate of future dividends. Then, because you would have already estimated future financial statements, it would be a toss-up as to whether the corporate valuation model or the dividend growth model would be easier to apply. Intel, which pays a dividend of about 40 cents per share versus earnings of about $1.11 per share, is an example of a company to which you could apply either model.

Now suppose you were trying to estimate the value of a company that has never paid a dividend, or a new firm that is about to go public, or a division that GE or some other large company is planning to sell. In all of these situations, you would have no choice: You would have to estimate future financial statements and use the corporate valuation model.

Actually, even if a company is paying steady dividends, much can be learned from the corporate valuation model; hence many analysts today use it for all types of valuations. The process of projecting the future financial statements can reveal quite a bit about the company's operations and financing needs. Also, such an analysis can provide insights into actions that might be taken to increase the company's value. This is value-based management, which we discuss in the next section.[5]

SELF-TEST

Give some examples of assets-in-place, growth options, and nonoperating assets.

Write out the equation for the value of operations.

What is the terminal, or horizon, value? Why is it also called the continuing value?

Explain how to estimate the price per share using the corporate valuation model.

A company expects a FCF of −$10 million at Year 1 and a FCF of $20 million at Year 2. FCF is expected to grow at a 5% rate after Year 2. If the WACC is 10%, what is the horizon value of operations; i.e., $V_{op(Year\ 2)}$? What is the current value of operations; i.e., $V_{op(Year\ 0)}$? ($420 million; $354.55 million)

A company has a current value of operations of $800 million. The company has $100 million in short-term investments. If the company has $400 million in debt and has 10 million shares outstanding, what is the price per share? ($50.00)

---

[5]For a more detailed explanation of corporate valuation, see P. Daves, M. Ehrhardt, and R. Shrieves, *Corporate Valuation: A Guide for Managers and Investors* (Mason, OH: Thomson/South-Western, 2004).

15.3 Value-Based Management

FM
e-resource
See **FM12 Ch 15 Tool Kit.xls** at the textbook's Web site for all calculations.

Bell Electronics Inc. has two divisions, Memory and Instruments, with total sales of $1.5 billion and operating capital of $1.07 billion. Based on its current stock and bond prices, the company's total market value is about $1.215 billion, giving it an MVA of $145 million, found as $1.215 − $1.070 = $0.145 billion = $145 million. Because it has a positive MVA, Bell has created value for its investors. Even so, management is considering several new strategic plans in its efforts to increase the firm's value. All of Bell's assets are used in operations.

The Memory division produces memory chips for such handheld electronic devices as cellular phones and PDAs (personal digital assistants), while the Instruments division produces devices for measuring and controlling sewage and water treatment facilities. Table 15-5 shows the latest financial results for the two divisions and for the company as a whole.

As Table 15-5 shows, Bell Memory is the larger of the two divisions, with higher sales and more operating capital. Bell Memory is also more profitable, with a NOPAT/Sales ratio of 7.9% versus 7.2% for Bell Instruments. This year, as in other recent years, the focus of the initial strategic planning sessions was on the Memory division. Bell Memory has grown rapidly because of the phenomenal growth in consumer electronics, and this division rocketed past Instruments several years ago. Although Memory's growth had tapered off, senior management generally agreed that this division would receive the lion's share of corporate attention and resources because it is larger, more profitable, and, frankly, more exciting. After all, Bell Memory is associated with the glamorous market for telecommunications and personal electronic devices, whereas Bell Instruments is associated with sewage and sludge.

The financial assumptions and projections associated with the preliminary strategic plans for the two divisions are shown in Tables 15-6 and 15-7. Based on the initial strategic plans, each division is projected to have 5% annual growth for the next 5 years and thereafter. The strategic plans also assume that the cost structures of the two divisions will remain unchanged from the current year, 2007. Only partial financial projections are shown in Tables 15-6 and 15-7, but when Bell's management decides on a final strategic plan, it will develop complete financial statements for the company as a whole and use them to determine financing requirements, as described in Chapter 14.

Table 15-5

Financial Results for Bell Electronics Inc. (Millions of Dollars, Except for Percentages)

	Division 1: Bell Memory	Division 2: Bell Instruments	Total Company
Sales	$1,000.0	$500.0	$1,500.0
Operating capital	870.0	200.0	1,070.0
Earnings before interest and taxes (EBIT)	131.0	60.0	191.0
Net operating profit after taxes (NOPAT)	78.6	36.0	114.6
Operating profitability (NOPAT/Sales)	7.9%	7.2%	7.6%

Table 15-6

Initial Projections for the Bell Memory Division (Millions of Dollars, Except for Percentages)

	Actual	Projected[a]				
	2007	**2008**	**2009**	**2010**	**2011**	**2012**
Panel A: Inputs						
Sales growth rate		5%	5%	5%	5%	5%
Costs/Sales	81%	81	81	81	81	81
Depreciation/Net plant	10	10	10	10	10	10
Cash/Sales	1	1	1	1	1	1
Accounts receivable/Sales	8	8	8	8	8	8
Inventories/Sales	30	30	30	30	30	30
Net plant/Sales	59	59	59	59	59	59
Accounts payable/Sales	5	5	5	5	5	5
Accruals/Sales	6	6	6	6	6	6
Tax rate	40	40	40	40	40	40
Panel B: Partial Income Statement						
Net sales	$1,000.0	$1,050.0	$1,102.5	$1,157.6	$1,215.5	$1,276.3
Costs (except depreciation)	$ 810.0	$ 850.5	$ 893.0	$ 937.7	$ 984.6	$1,033.8
Depreciation	59.0	62.0	65.0	68.3	71.7	75.3
Total operating costs	$ 869.0	$ 912.5	$ 958.1	$1,006.0	$1,056.3	$1,109.1
EBIT	$ 131.0	$ 137.6	$ 144.4	$ 151.6	$ 159.2	$ 167.2
Panel C: Partial Balance Sheets Operating Assets						
Cash	$ 10.0	$ 10.5	$ 11.0	$ 11.6	$ 12.2	$ 12.8
Accounts receivable	80.0	84.0	88.2	92.6	97.2	102.1
Inventories	300.0	315.0	330.8	347.3	364.7	382.9
Operating current assets	$ 390.0	$ 409.5	$ 430.0	$ 451.5	$ 474.0	$ 497.7
Net plant and equipment	$ 590.0	$ 619.5	$ 650.5	$ 683.0	$ 717.1	$ 753.0
Operating Liabilities						
Accounts payable	$ 50.0	$ 52.5	$ 55.1	$ 57.9	$ 60.8	$ 63.8
Accruals	60.0	63.0	66.2	69.5	72.9	76.6
Operating current liabilities	$ 110.0	$ 115.5	$ 121.3	$ 127.3	$ 133.7	$ 140.4

[a]Projected figures may not total exactly due to rounding.

> **Table 15-8**

Initial FCF Valuation of Each Division (Millions of Dollars, Except for Percentages)

	Actual	Projected				
	2007	2008	2009	2010	2011	2012
Panel A: FCF Valuation of the Bell Memory Division Calculation of FCF						
Net operating working capital	$ 280.0	$294.0	$308.7	$ 324.1	$ 340.3	$ 357.4
Net plant	590.0	619.5	650.5	683.0	717.1	753.0
Net operating capital	$ 870.0	$913.5	$959.2	$1,007.1	$1,057.5	$1,110.4
Investment in operating capital		$ 43.5	$ 45.7	$ 48.0	$ 50.4	$ 52.9
NOPAT	$ 78.6	$ 82.5	$ 86.7	$ 91.0	$ 95.5	$ 100.3
Free cash flow		$ 39.0	$ 41.0	$ 43.0	$ 45.2	$ 47.4
Growth in FCF			5.0%	5.0%	5.0%	5.0%
Value of Operations						
Horizon value						$ 905.7
Value of operations	$ 709.6					
Divisional MVA (Value of operations − Capital)	($160.4)					
Panel B: FCF Valuation of the Bell Instruments Division Calculation of FCF						
Net operating working capital	$ 50.0	$ 52.5	$ 55.1	$ 57.9	$ 60.8	$ 63.8
Net plant	150.0	157.5	165.4	173.6	182.3	191.4
Net operating capital	$ 200.0	$210.0	$220.5	$ 231.5	$ 243.1	$ 255.3
Investment in operating capital		$ 10.0	$ 10.5	$ 11.0	$ 11.6	$ 12.2
NOPAT	$ 36.0	$ 37.8	$ 39.7	$ 41.7	$ 43.8	$ 45.9
Free cash flow		$ 27.8	$ 29.2	$ 30.6	$ 32.2	$ 33.8
Growth in FCF			5.0%	5.0%	5.0%	5.0%
Value of Operations						
Horizon value						$ 645.1
Value of operations	$ 505.5					
Divisional MVA (Value of operations − Capital)	$305.5					

Notes: The WACC is 10.5% for each division. The horizon value (HV) at 2012 is calculated using Equation 15-2, the constant growth formula for free cash flows:

$$HV_{2011} = [FCF_{2012} \times (1 + g)] / (WACC - g).$$

The value of operations is the present value of the horizon value and the free cash flows discounted at the WACC, calculated in a manner similar to Figure 15-1. Projected figures may not total exactly due to rounding. See ***FM12 Ch 15 Took Kit.xls*** at the textbook's Web site for details.

the fourth factor, the WACC, also has a consistent effect—the lower it is, the higher the firm's value.

e-resource
See **FM12 Ch 15 Tool Kit.xls** at the textbook's Web site for details.

Another important metric in the corporate valuation model is the **expected return on invested capital (EROIC),** defined as the expected NOPAT for the coming year divided by the amount of operating capital at the beginning of the year (which is the end of the preceding year). Thus, EROIC represents the expected return on the capital that has already been invested. To illustrate, the EROIC of the Bell Memory division for 2012, the last year in the forecast period, is

$$\text{EROIC}_{2012} = \frac{\text{NOPAT}_{2013}}{\text{Capital}_{2012}} = \frac{\text{NOPAT}_{2012}(1+g)}{\text{Capital}_{2012}} = \frac{\$100.3(1.05)}{\$1,110.4} = 9.5\%.$$

To see exactly how the four value drivers and EROIC determine value for a constant growth firm, we can start with Equation 15-2,

$$V_{\text{op(at time N)}} = \frac{\text{FCF}_{N+1}}{\text{WACC} - g} \tag{15-2}$$

and rewrite it in terms of the value drivers:

$$V_{\text{op(at time N)}} = \text{Capital}_N + \left[\frac{\text{Sales}_N(1+g)}{\text{WACC}-g}\right]\left[\text{OP} - \text{WACC}\left(\frac{\text{CR}}{1+g}\right)\right]. \tag{15-3}$$

Equation 15-3 shows that the value of operations can be divided into two components: (1) the dollars of operating capital that investors have provided and (2) the additional value that management has added or subtracted, which is equivalent to MVA.

Note that the first bracket of Equation 15-3 shows the present value of growing sales, discounted at the WACC. This would be the MVA of a firm that has no costs and that never needs to invest additional capital. But firms do have costs and capital requirements, and their effect is shown in the second bracket. Here we see that, holding g constant, MVA will improve if operating profitability (OP) increases, capital requirements (CR) decrease, or WACC decreases.

Note that an increase in growth will not necessarily increase value. OP could be positive, but if CR is quite high, meaning that a lot of new capital is needed to support a given increase in sales, then the second bracket can be negative. In this situation, growth causes the term in the first bracket to increase, but it is being multiplied by a negative term in the second bracket, and the net result will be a decrease in MVA.

We can also rewrite Equation 15-2 in terms of EROIC:

$$V_{\text{op(at time N)}} = \text{Capital}_N + \frac{\text{Capital}_N(\text{EROIC}_N - \text{WACC})}{\text{WACC} - g}. \tag{15-4}$$

Equation 15-4 also breaks value into two components, the value of capital and the MVA, shown in the second term. This term for MVA shows that value depends on the spread between the expected return on invested capital, EROIC, and WACC. If EROIC is greater than WACC, then the return on capital is greater than the return investors expect, and management is adding value. In this case, an increase in the growth rate causes value to go up. If EROIC is exactly equal to WACC, then the firm is, in an economic sense, "breaking even." It has positive accounting profits and cash flow, but these cash flows are just sufficient to satisfy investors, causing value to exactly equal the amount of capital that has been provided. If EROIC is less than WACC, the term in brackets is negative, management is destroying value, and growth is harmful. Here the faster the growth rate is, the lower the firm's value.

We should also note that the insights from Equations 15-3 and 15-4 apply to all firms, but the equations themselves can only be applied to relatively stable firms whose growth has leveled out at a constant rate. For example, in 2001 Home Depot grew at around 20% per year, so at that time we could not apply Equations 15-3 and 15-4 directly (although we could always apply Equation 15-1). Home Depot's NOPAT/Sales ratio was 5.6%, which was excellent for its industry, but even though it was profitable, it had negative free cash flows. This is because Home Depot was still in its high-growth phase, which required enormous investments in operating capital. Since 2001, Home Depot's sales growth has slowed due to market saturation, and its free cash flows have become very large and positive.[7] Based on its 2005 financial statements, Home Depot's EROIC was about 21.5%, which is much larger than its WACC. This large spread contributes to its $45 billion MVA.

Table 15-9 shows the value drivers for Bell's two divisions, measured at 2012, the end of the forecast period. We report these for the end of the forecast period because ratios can change during the forecast period due to input changes. By the end of the forecast period, however, all inputs and ratios should be stable.

Table 15-9 shows that both divisions have the same growth rate and the same WACC. Bell Memory is more profitable, but it also has much higher capital requirements. The result is that Bell Memory's EROIC is only 9.5%, well below its 10.5% WACC. Thus, growth doesn't help Bell Memory—indeed, it lowers the division's value.

Based on this analysis, Bell Memory's managers decided not to request funds for a marketing campaign. Instead, they developed a plan to reduce capital requirements. The new plan called for spending $50 million on an integrated supply chain information system that would allow them to cut their Inventories/Sales ratio from 30% to 20% and also reduce the Net plant/Sales ratio from 59% to 50%. Table 15-10 shows operating results based on this new plan. The value of operations

Table 15-9

Bell Electronics' Forecasted Value Drivers for 2012

	Division 1: Bell Memory	Division 2: Bell Instruments
Growth: g	5.0%	5.0%
Profitability: (NOPAT$_{2012}$/Sales$_{2012}$)	7.9	7.2
Capital requirement: (Capital$_{2012}$/Sales$_{2012}$)	87.0	40.0
WACC	10.5	10.5
Expected return on invested capital, EROIC: [NOPAT$_{2012}$(1 + g)/Capital$_{2012}$]	9.5	18.9

[7]For example, in 2004 Home Depot generated almost $3.4 billion in FCF. FCF tumbled in 2005 due to several major acquisitions that required significant investments in operating capital. However, Home Depot's EROIC in 2005 was a robust 21.5%.

Table 15-10

Comparison of the Preliminary and Final Plans (Millions of Dollars, Except for Percentages)

	Bell Memory		Bell Instruments	
	Preliminary	Final	Preliminary	Final
Inputs				
Sales growth rate, g	5%	5%	5%	6%
Inventories/Sales	30	20	15	16
Net plant/Sales	59	50	30	30
Results				
EROIC (2012)[a]	9.5%	13.0%	18.9%	18.6%
Invested (operating) capital (2012)[a]	$1,110.4	$ 867.9	$255.3	$274.3
Current value of operations (2007)[b]	709.6	1,157.4	505.5	570.1
Current MVA (2007)[b]	(160.4)	287.4	305.5	370.1

Notes:

[a]We report EROIC and capital for the end of the forecast period because ratios can change during the forecast period if inputs change during the forecast period. By the end of the forecast period, however, all inputs and ratios should be stable.
[b]We report the value of operations and the MVA as of the current date, 2007, because we want to see the effect that the proposed plans have on the current value of the divisions.

increases from $709.6 million to $1.1574 billion, or by $447.8 million. Because this is well over the $50 million required to implement the plan, top management decided to approve the plan. Note also that MVA becomes positive at $287.4 million, and the divisional EROIC rises to 13.0%, well over the 10.5% WACC.

Bell Instruments' managers also used the valuation model to assess changes in plans for their division. Given their high EROIC, the Instruments division proposed (1) an aggressive marketing campaign and (2) an increase in inventories that would allow faster delivery and fewer stock-outs. Together, these changes would boost the growth rate from 5% to 6%. The direct cost to implement the plan was $20 million, but there was also an indirect cost in that significantly more inventories would have to be carried. Indeed, the ratio of inventories to sales was forecasted to increase from 15% to 16%.

Should Instruments' new plan be implemented? Table 15-10 shows the forecasted results. The capital requirements associated with the increased inventory caused the EROIC to fall from 18.9% to 18.6%, but (1) the 18.6% return greatly exceeds the 10.5% WACC, and (2) the spread between 18.6% and 10.5% would be earned on additional capital. This caused the forecasted value of operations to increase from $505.5 to $570.1 million, or by $64.6 million. An 18.6% return on $274.3 million of capital is more valuable than an 18.9% return on $255.3 million of capital.[8] You, or one of Bell's stockholders, would surely rather have an asset that provides a 50% return on an investment of $1,000 than one that provides a 100% return on an investment of $1. Therefore, the new plan should be accepted, even though it lowers the Instruments division's EROIC.

---

[8]A potential fly in the ointment is the possibility that Bell has a compensation plan based on rates of return and not on changes in wealth. In such a plan, which is fairly typical, the managers might reject the new proposed strategic plan if it lowers ROIC and, hence, their bonuses, even though the plan is good for the company's stockholders. We discuss the effect of compensation plans in more detail later in the chapter.

Value-Based Management in Practice

The corporate valuation model, in which free cash flows are discounted at the weighted average cost of capital to determine the value of the company, lies at the heart of value-based management. Therefore, before adopting value-based management, managers would be wise to ask if the corporate valuation model produces results that are consistent with actual market values. The answer, according to a study by Copeland, Koller, and Murrin of the consulting firm McKinsey & Company, is a resounding yes. They applied the model to 35 companies and found a 0.94 correlation between the model's estimated values and the actual market values. Additional evidence of the model's usefulness was provided by McCafferty's recent survey, in which CFOs rated the corporate valuation model as the most important technique for estimating the value of a potential acquisition.

Finally, a recent *Fortune* article described how much corporations are paying consultants to help them implement the model. Marakon Associates, a leading advocate of value-based management, prides itself on having a single-minded view that a company should have one, and only one, goal—to increase shareholder wealth. It often takes Marakon several years to fully implement a value-based management system at a company. One reason for the lengthy implementation period is that Marakon breaks the company into segments to determine where value is currently being created or destroyed. These segments might be divisions, product lines, customers, or even channels of distribution. "Deep drilling," as they call this process, is arduous and time consuming, and it requires a great deal of data and analysis. Also, and perhaps even more important, full implementation requires both a change in corporate culture and the creation of an "organization's collective ability to out-think its rivals." In other words, the skill-set to use value-based management must permeate the entire company.

Although Marakon is a relatively small firm, with only 275 consultants versus almost 5,000 for McKinsey, it generates about $475,000 in revenue per consultant, which ties it with McKinsey as the most expensive consulting company. Note, though, that its rates seem to be justified. During the late 1990s, Marakon's client companies created an additional $68 billion of wealth versus what they would have created had they matched their industry peers' results.

Sources: Thomas A. Stewart, "Marakon Runners," *Fortune*, September 28, 1998, pp. 153–158; Joseph McCafferty, "What Acquiring Minds Want to Know," *CFO*, February 1999, p. 1; and Tom Copeland, Tim Koller, and Jack Murrin, *Valuation: Measuring and Managing the Value of Companies* (New York: John Wiley & Sons, 1994), p. 83.

Sometimes companies focus on their profitability and growth, without giving adequate consideration to their capital requirements. This is a big mistake—all the wealth creation drivers, not just growth, must be taken into account. Fortunately for Bell's investors, the revised plan was accepted. However, as this example illustrates, it is easy for a company to mistakenly focus only on profitability and growth. They are important, but so are the other value drivers—capital requirements and the weighted average cost of capital. Value-based management explicitly includes the effects of all the value drivers because it uses the corporate valuation model, and they are all embodied in the model.[9]

SELF-TEST

What are the four value drivers?

How is it possible that sales growth would decrease the value of a profitable firm?

You are given the following forecasted information for a constant growth company: Sales = $10 million; Operating profitability (OP) = 5%; Capital requirements (CR) = 40%; Growth (g) = 6%; and the weighted average cost of capital (WACC) = 10%. What is the current level of capital? What is the current level of NOPAT? What is the EROIC? What is the value of operations? ($4 million; $0.5 million; 13.25%; $7.25 million)

---

[9]For more on corporate valuation and value-based management, see Tim Koller, Marc Goedhart, and David Wessels, *Valuation: Measuring and Managing the Value of Companies*, 4th ed. (Hoboken, NJ: John Wiley & Sons, 2005); John D. Martin and J. William Petty, *Value Based Management: The Corporate Response to the Shareholder Revolution* (Boston: Harvard Business School Press, 2000); James M. McTaggart, Peter W. Kontes, and Michael C. Mankins, *The Value Imperative* (New York: The Free Press, 1994); and G. Bennett Stewart, *The Quest for Value* (New York: Harper Collins, 1991).

15.4 Managerial Behavior and Shareholder Wealth

Shareholders want companies to hire managers who are able and willing to take whatever legal and ethical actions they can to maximize stock prices.[10] This obviously requires managers with technical competence, but it also requires managers who are willing to put forth the extra effort necessary to identify and implement value-adding activities. However, managers are people, and people have both personal and corporate goals. Logically, therefore, managers can be expected to act in their own self-interests, and if their self-interests are not aligned with those of stockholders, then corporate value will not be maximized. There are six ways in which a manager's behavior might harm a firm's intrinsic value.

See the Web pages of CalPERS (the California Public Employees' Retirement System), **http://www.calpers.org,** and TIAA–CREF (Teachers Insurance and Annuity Association College Retirement Equity Fund), **http://www.tiaa-cref.org,** for excellent discussions of corporate governance.

1. Managers might not expend the time and effort required to maximize firm value. Rather than focusing on corporate tasks, they might spend too much time on external activities, such as serving on boards of other companies, or on nonproductive activities, such as golfing, lunching, traveling, surfing the Net, and so forth.

2. Managers might use corporate resources on activities that benefit themselves rather than shareholders. For example, they might spend company money on such perquisites as lavish offices, memberships at country clubs, museum-quality art for corporate apartments, large personal staffs, and corporate jets. Because these perks are not actually cash payments to the managers, they are called **nonpecuniary benefits.**

3. Managers might avoid making difficult but value-enhancing decisions that harm friends in the company. For example, a manager might not close a plant or terminate a project if the manager has personal relationships with those who are adversely affected by such decisions, even if termination is the economically sound action.

4. Managers might take on too much risk or they might not take on enough risk. For example, a company might have the opportunity to undertake a risky project with a positive NPV. If the project turns out badly, then the manager's reputation will be harmed and the manager might even be fired. Thus, a manager might choose to avoid risky projects even if they are desirable from a shareholder's point of view. On the other hand, a manager might take on projects with too much risk. Consider a project that is not living up to expectations. A manager might be tempted to invest even more money in the project rather than admit that the project is a failure. Or a manager might be willing to take on a second project with a negative NPV if it has even a slight chance of a very positive outcome, since hitting a home run with this second project might cover up the first project's poor performance. In other words, the manager might throw good money after bad.

5. If a company is generating positive free cash flow, a manager might "stockpile" it in the form of marketable securities instead of returning FCF to

---

[10]Notice that we said both legal and ethical actions. The accounting frauds perpetrated by Enron, WorldCom, and others that were uncovered in 2002 raised stock prices in the short run, but only because investors were misled about the companies' financial positions. Then, when the correct financial information was finally revealed, the stocks tanked. Investors who bought shares based on the fraudulent financial statements lost tens of billions of dollars. Releasing false financial statements is illegal. Aggressive earnings management and the use of misleading accounting tricks to pump up reported earnings is unethical, and executives should and will go to jail as a result of their shenanigans. When we speak of taking actions to maximize stock prices, we mean making operational or financial changes designed to maximize intrinsic stock value, not fooling investors with false or misleading financial reports.

investors. This potentially harms investors because it prevents them from allocating these funds to other companies with good growth opportunities. Even worse, positive FCF often tempts a manager into paying too much for the acquisition of another company. In fact, most mergers and acquisitions end up as break-even deals, at best, for the acquiring company because the premiums paid for the targets are often very large. Why would a manager be reluctant to return cash to investors? First, extra cash on hand reduces the company's risk, which appeals to many managers. Second, a large distribution of cash to investors is an admission that the company doesn't have enough good investment opportunities. Slow growth is normal for a maturing company, but it isn't very exciting for a manager to admit this. Third, there is a lot of glamour associated with making a large acquisition, and this can provide a large boost to a manager's ego. Fourth, compensation usually is higher for executives at larger companies. Cash distributions to investors make a company smaller, not larger.

6.   Managers might not release all the information that is desired by investors. Sometimes they might withhold information to prevent competitors from gaining an advantage. At other times they might try to avoid releasing bad news. For example, they might "massage" the data or "manage the earnings" so that the news doesn't look so bad. If investors are unsure about the quality of information provided by managers, they tend to discount the company's expected free cash flows at a higher cost of capital, which reduces the company's intrinsic value.

If senior managers believe there is little chance that they will be removed, we say that they are *entrenched*. Such a company faces a high risk of being poorly run, because entrenched managers are able to act in their own interests rather than in the interests of shareholders.

SELF-TEST

Name six types of managerial behaviors that can reduce a firm's intrinsic value.

15.5 Corporate Governance

A key requirement for successful implementation of value-based management is to influence executives and other managers so that they do not behave in the ways described in the section above, but instead behave in a way that maximizes a firm's intrinsic value. Corporate governance can provide just such an influence. Corporate governance can be defined as the set of laws, rules, and procedures that influence a company's operations and the decisions made by its managers. At the risk of oversimplification, most corporate governance provisions come in two forms, sticks and carrots. The primary stick is the *threat of removal*, either as a decision by the board of directors or as the result of a hostile takeover. If a firm's managers are maximizing the value of the resources entrusted to them, they need not fear the loss of their jobs. On the other hand, if managers are not maximizing value, they should be removed by their own boards of directors, by dissident stockholders, or by other companies seeking to profit by installing a better management team. The main carrot is *compensation*. Managers have greater incentives to maximize intrinsic stock value if their compensation is linked to their firm's performance rather than being strictly in the form of salary.

Almost all corporate governance provisions affect either the threat of removal or compensation. Some provisions are internal to a firm and are under its control.[11] These internal provisions and features can be divided into five areas: (1) monitoring and discipline by the board of directors; (2) charter provisions and bylaws that affect the likelihood of hostile takeovers; (3) compensation plans; (4) capital structure choices; and (5) accounting control systems. In addition to the corporate governance provisions that are under a firm's control, there are also environmental factors outside of a firm's control, such as the regulatory environment, block ownership patterns, competition in the product markets, the media, and litigation. Our discussion begins with the internal provisions.

Monitoring and Discipline by the Board of Directors

Shareholders are a corporation's owners and they elect the board of directors to act as agents on their behalf. In the United States, it is the board's duty to monitor senior managers and discipline them, either by removal or by a reduction in compensation, if the managers do not act in the interests of shareholders.[12] This is not necessarily the case outside the United States. For example, many companies in Europe are required to have employee representatives on the board. Also, many European and Asian companies have bank representatives on the board. But even in the United States, many boards fail to act in the shareholders' best interests. How can this be?

Consider the election process. The ballot for a board position usually lists only one candidate. Although outside candidates can run a "write-in" campaign, only those candidates named by the board's nominating committee are on the ballot.[13] At many companies, the CEO is also the chairman of the board and has considerable influence on this nominating committee. This means that in practice it often is the CEO who in effect nominates candidates for the board. High compensation and prestige go with a position on the board of a major company, so board seats are prized possessions. Board members typically want to retain their positions, and they are grateful to whoever helped get them on the board. Thus, the nominating process often results in a board that is favorably disposed to the CEO.[14]

Many board members are "insiders," that is, people who hold managerial positions within the company, such as the CFO. Because insiders report to the CEO, it may be difficult for them to oppose the CEO at a board meeting.

---

[11]We have adapted this framework from the one provided by Stuart L. Gillan, "Recent Developments in Corporate Governance: An Overview," *Journal of Corporate Finance*, June 2006, pp. 381–402. Gillan provides an excellent discussion of the issues associated with corporate governance. We highly recommend this paper to the reader who is interested in an expanded discussion of the issues in this section.

[12]There are a few exceptions to this rule. For example, some states have laws allowing the board to take into consideration the interests of other stakeholders, such as employees and members of the community.

[13]There is currently (2006) a movement under way to allow shareholders to also nominate candidates for the board, but only time will tell whether this movement is successful.

[14]Voting procedures also affect the ability of outsiders to gain positions on the board. For example, boards can be elected by either cumulative or noncumulative voting. Under cumulative voting, each shareholder is given a number of votes equal to his or her shares times the number of board seats up for election. For example, the holder of 100 shares of stock will receive 1,000 votes if 10 seats are to be filled. Then, the shareholder can distribute his or her votes however he or she sees fit. One hundred votes could be cast for each of 10 candidates, or all 1,000 votes could be cast for one candidate. If noncumulative voting is used, our illustrative stockholder cannot concentrate his or her votes—no more than 100 votes can be cast for any one candidate.

With noncumulative voting, if management controls 51% of the shares, they can fill every seat on the board—dissident stockholders cannot put a representative on the board. With cumulative voting, however, if 10 seats are to be filled, dissidents can elect a representative, provided they hold 10% plus one share of the stock.

Note also that bylaws specify whether the entire board is to be elected annually or if directors are to have staggered terms, with, say, one-third of the seats to be filled each year and directors to serve 3-year terms. With staggered terms, fewer seats come up each year, making it harder for dissidents to gain representation on the board.

Even outside board members often have strong connections with the CEO through personal friendships, consulting, or other fee-generating activities. In fact, outsiders sometimes have very little expert business knowledge but have "celebrity" status from nonbusiness activities. Some companies also have **interlocking boards of directors,** where Company A's CEO sits on Company B's board and B's CEO sits on A's board. In these situations, even the outside directors are not truly independent and impartial.

Large boards (those with more than about ten to twelve members) often are less effective than smaller boards. As anyone who has been on a committee can attest, individual participation tends to fall as committee size increases. Thus, there is a greater likelihood that members of a large board will be less active than those on smaller boards.

The compensation of board members has an impact on the board's effectiveness. When board members have extraordinarily high compensation, the CEO also tends to have extremely high compensation. This suggests that such boards tend to be too lenient with the CEO.[15] The form of board compensation also affects board performance. Rather than compensating board members with only salary, many companies now include restricted stock grants or stock options in an effort to better align board members with stockholders.

Studies show that corporate governance usually improves if: (1) the CEO is not also the chairman of the board; (2) the board has a majority of true outsiders who bring some type of business expertise to the board; (3) the board is not too large; and (4) board members are compensated appropriately. The good news for the shareholder is that the boards at many companies have made significant improvements in these directions during the last decade. Fewer CEOs are also board chairmen, and as power has shifted from CEOs to boards as a whole there has been a tendency to replace insiders with strong, independent outsiders. Today, the typical board has about one-third insiders and two-thirds outsiders, and most outsiders are truly independent. Moreover, board members are compensated primarily with stock or options rather than a straight salary. These changes clearly have decreased the patience of boards with poorly performing CEOs. Within the past several years the CEOs of Procter & Gamble, Coca-Cola, GM, IBM, Mattel, Campbell Soup, and Xerox, to name just a few, have been removed by their boards. This would have been unheard of 30 years ago.

Charter Provisions and Bylaws That Affect the Likelihood of Hostile Takeovers

Hostile takeovers usually occur when managers have not been willing or able to maximize the profit potential of the resources under their control. In such a situation, another company can acquire the poorly performing firm, replace its managers, increase free cash flow, and improve MVA. The following paragraphs describe some provisions that can be included in a corporate charter to make it harder for poorly performing managers to remain in control.[16]

---

[15]See I. E. Brick, O. Palmon, and J. Wald, "CEO Compensation, Director Compensation, and Firm Performance: Evidence of Cronyism?" *Journal of Corporate Finance,* June 2006, pp. 403–423.

[16]Some states have laws that go further than others to protect management. This is one reason that many companies are incorporated in manager-friendly Delaware. Some companies have even shifted their state of incorporation to Delaware because their managers felt that a hostile takeover attempt was likely. Note that a "shareholder-friendly charter" could and would waive the company's right to strong anti-takeover protection, even if the state allowed it.

A shareholder-friendly charter should ban **targeted share repurchases,** also known as **greenmail.** For example, suppose a company's stock is selling for $20 per share. Now a hostile bidder, or raider, who plans to replace management if the takeover is successful, buys 5% of the company's stock at the $20 price.[17] The raider then makes an offer to purchase the remainder of the stock for $30 per share. The company might offer to buy back the bidder's stock at a price of, say, $35 per share. This is called a targeted share repurchase since the stock will be purchased only from the bidder and not from any other shareholders. Because the bidder paid only $20 per share for the stock, he or she would be making a quick profit of $15 per share, which could easily total several hundred million dollars. As a part of the deal, the raider would sign a document promising not to attempt to take over the company for a specified number of years; hence the buyback also is called greenmail. Greenmail hurts shareholders in two ways. First, they are left with $20 stock when they could have received $30 per share. Second, the company purchased stock from the bidder at $35 per share, which represents a direct loss by the remaining shareholders of $15 for each repurchased share.

Managers who buy back stock in targeted repurchases typically argue that their firms are worth more than the raiders offered, and that in time the "true value" will be revealed in the form of a much higher stock price. This situation might be true if a company were in the process of restructuring itself, or if new products with high potential were in the pipeline. But if the old management had been in power for a long time, and if it had a history of making empty promises, then one should question whether the true purpose of the buyback was to protect stockholders or management.

Another characteristic of a stockholder-friendly charter is that it does not contain a **shareholder rights provision,** better described as a **poison pill.** These provisions give the shareholders of target firms the right to buy a specified number of shares in the company at a very low price if an outside group or firm acquires a specified percentage of the firm's stock. Therefore, if a potential acquirer tries to take over a company, its other shareholders will be entitled to purchase additional shares of stock at a bargain price, thus seriously diluting the holdings of the raider. For this reason, these clauses are called poison pills, because if they are in the charter, the acquirer will end up swallowing a poison pill if the acquisition is successful. Obviously, the existence of a poison pill makes a takeover more difficult, and this helps to entrench management.

A third management entrenchment tool is a **restricted voting rights** provision, which automatically deprives a shareholder of voting rights if the shareholder owns more than a specified amount of stock. The board can grant voting rights to such a shareholder, but this is unlikely if the shareholder plans to take over the company.

Using Compensation to Align Managerial and Shareholder Interests

The typical CEO today receives a fixed salary, a cash bonus based on the firm's performance, and stock-based compensation, either in the form of stock grants or

---

[17]Someone can, under the law, acquire up to 5% of a firm's stock without announcing the acquisition. Once the 5% limit has been hit, the acquirer must "announce" the acquisition by filing a report with the SEC, and the report must list not only the acquirer's position but also his or her intentions, such as a passive investment or a takeover. These reports are monitored closely, so as soon as one is filed, management is alerted to the imminent possibility of a takeover.

option grants. Cash bonuses often are based upon short-run operating factors, such as this year's growth in earnings per share, or medium-term operating performance, such as earnings growth over the last 3 years.

Stock-based compensation is often in the form of options. Chapter 8 explains option valuation in detail, but we discuss here how a standard **stock option compensation plan** works. Suppose IBM decides to grant an option to an employee, allowing him or her to purchase a specified number of IBM shares at a fixed price, called the **exercise price,** regardless of the actual price of the stock. The exercise price is usually set equal to the current stock price at the time the option is granted. Thus, if IBM's current price were $100, then the option would have an exercise price of $100. Options usually cannot be exercised until after some specified period (the **vesting period**), which is usually 1 to 5 years. Moreover, they have an **expiration date,** usually 10 years after issue. For our IBM example, assume that the vesting period is 3 years and the expiration date is 10 years. Thus, the employee can exercise the option 3 years after issue or wait as long as 10 years. Of course, the employee would not exercise unless IBM's stock is above the $100 exercise price, and if the price never rose above $100, the option would expire unexercised. However, if the stock price were above $100 on the expiration date, the option would surely be exercised.

Suppose the stock price had grown to $134 after 5 years, at which point the employee decided to exercise the option. He or she would buy stock from IBM for $100, so IBM would get only $100 for stock worth $134. The employee would (probably) sell the stock the same day he or she exercised the option, hence would receive in cash the $34 difference between the $134 stock price and the $100 exercise price. People often time the exercise of options to the purchase of a new home or some other large expenditure.

In theory, stock options should align a manager's interests with those of shareholders, influencing the manager to behave in a way that maximizes the company's value. But in practice there are two reasons why this does not always occur.

First, suppose in the example above a CEO is granted options on 1 million shares. In this case, the executive would receive $34 for each option, or a total of $34 million. Keep in mind that this is in addition to an annual salary and cash bonuses. The logic behind employee options is that they motivate people to work harder and smarter, thus making the company more valuable and benefiting shareholders. But take a closer look at this example. If the risk-free rate is 5.5%, the market risk premium is 6%, and IBM's beta is 1.19, then the expected return, based on the CAPM, is 5.5% + 1.19(6%) = 12.64%. IBM's dividend yield is only 0.8%, so the expected annual price appreciation must be around 11.84% (12.64% − 0.8% = 11.84%). Now note that if IBM's stock price grew from $100 to $134 over 5 years, that would translate to an annual growth rate of only 6%, not the 11.84% shareholders expected. Thus, the executive would receive $34 million for helping run a company that performed below shareholders' expectations. As this example illustrates, standard stock options do not necessarily link executives' wealth with that of shareholders.

Even worse, the events of the early 2000s showed that some executives were willing to illegally falsify financial statements in order to drive up stock prices just prior to exercising their stock options. In some notable cases, the subsequent stock price drop and loss of investor confidence have forced firms into bankruptcy. This behavior is certainly not in shareholders' best interests![18]

---

[18]Several academic studies show that option-based compensation leads to a greater likelihood of earnings restatements and outright fraud. See A. Agrawal and S. Chadha, "Corporate Goverance and Accounting Scandals," *Journal of Law and Economics*, 2006, pp. 371–406; N. Burns and S. Kedia, "The Impact of Performance-Based Compensation on Misreporting," *Journal of Financial Economics*, January 2006, pp. 35–67; and D. J. Denis, P. Hanouna, and A. Sarin, "Is There a Dark Side to Incentive Compensation?" *Journal of Corporate Finance*, June 2006, pp. 467–488.

As a result, companies today are experimenting with different types of compensation plans, with different vesting periods and different measures of performance. For example, it is more difficult to legally manipulate EVA (Economic Value Added) than it is to manipulate earnings per share.[19] Just as "all ships rise in a rising tide," so too do most stocks rise in a bull market such as the one during the 1990s. In a strong market, even the stocks of companies whose performance ranks in the bottom 10% of their peer group can rise and thus trigger handsome executive bonuses. This situation is leading to compensation plans that are based on *relative* as opposed to *absolute* stock price performance. For example, some compensation plans have indexed options, whose exercise prices depend on the performance of the market or of a subset of competitors. Finally, the empirical results from academic studies show that the correlation between executive compensation and corporate performance is mixed. Some studies suggest that the type of compensation plan used affects company performance, while others suggest little if any effect.[20] But we can say with certainty that managerial compensation plans will continue to receive lots of attention from researchers, the popular press, and boards of directors.

Capital Structure and Internal Control Systems

Capital structure decisions can affect managerial behavior. As the debt level increases, so does the probability of bankruptcy. This increased threat of bankruptcy brings with it two effects on behavior. First, when times are good, managers may waste cash flow on perquisites and unnecessary expenditures as described earlier in this chapter. The good news is that an increasing threat of bankruptcy reduces such wasteful spending.

But the bad news is that a manager may become gun-shy and reject positive NPV projects if they are risky. From a stockholder's point of view it would be unfortunate if a risky project caused the company to go into bankruptcy, but note that other companies in the stockholder's portfolio may be taking on risky projects that turn out successfully. Since most stockholders are well diversified, they can afford for a manager to take on risky but positive NPV projects. But a manager's reputation and wealth are generally tied to a single company, so the project may be unacceptably risky from the manager's point of view. Thus, high debt can cause managers to forgo positive NPV projects unless they are extremely safe. This is called the **underinvestment problem,** and it is another type of agency cost. Notice that debt can reduce one aspect of agency costs (wasteful spending), but it may increase another (underinvestment), so the net effect on value isn't clear.

Internal control systems have become an increasingly important issue since the passage of the Sarbanes-Oxley Act of 2002. Section 404 of the act requires companies to establish effective internal control systems. The Securities Exchange Commission, which is charged with the implementation of Sarbanes-Oxley, defines an effective internal control system as one that provides "reasonable assurance regarding the reliability of financial reporting and the preparation of financial statements for external purposes in accordance with generally accepted accounting principles." In other words, investors should be able to trust a company's reported financial statements.

---

[19]For a discussion of EVA, see Al Ehrbar, *EVA: The Real Key to Creating Wealth* (New York; John Wiley & Sons, 1998); and Pamela P. Peterson and David R. Peterson, *Company Performance and Measures of Value Added* (The Research Foundation of the Institute of Chartered Financial Analysts, 1996).
[20]For example, see Jennifer Carpenter and David Yermack, eds. *Executive Compensation and Shareholder Value* (Boston: Kluwer Academic Publishers, 1999).

The Sarbanes-Oxley Act of 2002 and Corporate Governance

In 2002 Congress passed the Sarbanes-Oxley Act, known in the industry now as SOX, as a measure to improve transparency in financial accounting and to prevent fraud. SOX consists of eleven chapters, or *titles*, which establish wide-ranging new regulations for auditors, CEOs and CFOs, boards of directors, investment analysts, and investment banks. These regulations are designed to ensure that (a) companies that perform audits are sufficiently independent of the companies that they audit, (b) a key executive in each company *personally* certifies that the financial statements are complete and accurate, (c) the board of directors' audit committee is relatively independent of management, (d) financial analysts are relatively independent of the companies they analyze, and (e) companies publicly and promptly release all important information about their financial condition. The individual titles are briefly summarized below.

Title I establishes the Public Company Accounting Oversight Board, whose charge is to oversee auditors and establish quality control and ethical standards for audits.

Title II requires that auditors be independent of the companies that they audit. Basically this means they can't provide consulting services to the companies they audit. The purpose is to remove financial incentives for auditors to help management cook the books.

Title III requires that the board of directors' audit committee must be composed of "independent" members. Section 302 requires that the CEO and CFO must review the annual and quarterly financial statements and reports and personally certify that they are complete and accurate. Penalties for certifying reports executives know are false range up to a $5 million fine, 20 years in prison, or both. Under Section 304, if the financial statements turn out to be false and must be restated, then certain bonuses and equity-based compensation that executives earn must be reimbursed to the company.

Title IV's Section 401(a) requires prompt disclosure and more extensive reporting on off–balance sheet transactions. Section 404 requires that management evaluate its internal financial controls and report whether they are "effective." The external auditing firm must also indicate whether it agrees with management's evaluation of its internal controls. Section 409 requires that a company disclose to the public promptly and *in plain English* any material changes to its financial condition. Title IV also places restrictions on the loans that a company can make to its executives.

Title V addresses the relationship between financial analysts, the investment banks they work for, and the companies they cover. It requires that analysts and brokers who make stock recommendations disclose any conflicts of interest they might have with the stocks they recommend.

Titles VI and VII are technical in nature, dealing with the SEC's budget and powers and requiring that several studies be undertaken by the SEC.

Title VIII establishes penalties for destroying or falsifying audit records. It also provides "whistle-blower protection" for employees who report fraud.

Title IX increases the penalties for a variety of white-collar crimes associated with securities fraud, such as mail and wire fraud. Section 902 also makes it a crime to alter, destroy, or hide documents that might be used in an investigation. It also makes it a crime to conspire to do so.

Title X requires that the CEO sign the company's federal income tax return.

Title XI provides penalties for obstructing an investigation and grants the SEC authority to remove officers or directors from a company if they have committed fraud.

Environmental Factors Outside of a Firm's Control

As noted earlier, corporate governance is also affected by environmental factors that are outside of a firm's control, including the regulatory/legal environment, block ownership patterns, competition in the product markets, the media, and litigation.

Regulations and Laws The regulatory/legal environment includes the agencies that regulate financial markets, such as the SEC. Even though the fines and penalties levied on firms for financial misrepresentation by the SEC are relatively small, the damage to a firm's reputation can have significant costs, leading to extremely large reductions in the firm's value.[21] Thus, the regulatory system has an enormous impact on corporate governance and firm value.

The regulatory/legal environment also includes the laws and legal system under which a company operates. These vary greatly from country to country. Studies show that firms located in countries with strong legal protection for investors have stronger corporate governance, and that this is reflected in better access to financial markets, a lower cost of equity, increases in market liquidity, and less noise in stock prices.[22]

Block Ownership Patterns Prior to the 1960s, most U.S. stock was owned by a large number of individual investors, each of whom owned a diversified portfolio of stocks. Because these individuals owned a small amount of any given company's stock, they could do little to influence its operations. Also, with such a small investment, it was not cost effective for them to monitor companies closely. Indeed, if a stockholder was dissatisfied, he or she would typically just "vote with his or her feet," that is, sell his or her stock. This situation began to change as institutional investors such as pension and mutual funds gained control of a larger and larger share of investment capital, and as they then acquired a larger and larger percentage of all outstanding stock. Given their large block holdings, it now makes sense for institutional investors to monitor management, and they have the clout to influence the board. In some cases, they have actually elected their own representatives to the board. For example, when TIAA–CREF, a huge private pension fund, became frustrated with the performance and leadership of Furr's/Bishop, a cafeteria chain, the fund led a fight that ousted the entire board and then elected a new board, which consisted only of outsiders.

In general, activist investors with large blocks in companies have been good for all shareholders. They have searched for firms with poor profitability and then replaced management with new teams that are well-versed in value-based management techniques, and thereby have improved profitability. Not surprisingly, stock prices usually rise when the news comes out that a well-known activist investor has taken a major position in an underperforming company.

Note that activist investors can improve performance even if they don't go so far as to take over a firm. More often, they either elect their own representatives to the board or simply point out the firm's problems to other board members. In such cases, boards often change their attitudes and become less tolerant when they realize that the management team is not following the dictates of value-based management. Moreover, the firm's top managers recognize what will happen if they don't whip the company into shape, and they go about doing just that.

Competition in the Product Markets The degree of competition in a firm's product market has an impact on its corporate governance. For example, companies in industries with lots of competition don't have the luxury of tolerating poorly performing CEOs. As might be expected, CEO turnover is more likely in competitive industries than in those with less competition.[23] When most firms in an industry

[21]For example, see Jonathan M. Karpoff, D. Scott Lee, and Gerald S. Martin, "The Cost to Firms of Cooking the Books" (March 8, 2006). Available at SSRN: **http://ssrn.com/abstract=652121.**

[22]For example, see R. La Porta, F. Lopez-de-Silanes, A. Shleifer, and R. Vishny, "Legal Determinants of External Finance," *Journal of Finance*, 1997, pp.1131–1150; Hazem Daouk, Charles M. C. Lee, and David Ng, "Capital Market Governance: How Do Security Laws Affect Market Performance?" *Journal of Corporate Finance*, June 2006, pp. 560–593; and Li Jin and Stewart C. Myers, "R^2 Around the World: New Theory and New Tests," *Journal of Financial Economics*, 2006, pp. 257–292.

[23]See M. De Fond and C. Park, "The Effect of Competition on CEO Turnover," *Journal of Accounting and Economics*, 1999, pp. 35–56; and T. Fee and C. Hadlock, "Management Turnover and Product Market Competition: Empirical Evidence from the U.S. Newspaper Industry," *Journal of Business*, 2000, pp. 205–243.

International Corporate Governance

Corporate governance includes the following factors: (1) the likelihood that a poorly performing firm can be taken over; (2) whether the board of directors is dominated by insiders or outsiders; (3) the extent to which most of the stock is held by a few large "blockholders" versus many small shareholders; and (4) the size and form of executive compensation. A recent study compared corporate governance in Germany, Japan, and the United States.

First, note from the accompanying table that the threat of a takeover serves as a stick in the United States but not in Japan or Germany. This threat, which reduces management entrenchment, should benefit shareholders in the United States relative to the other two countries. Second, German and Japanese boards are larger than those in the United States, and Japanese boards consist primarily of insiders versus German and American boards, which have similar inside/outside mixes. It should be noted, though, that the boards of most large German corporations include representatives of labor, whereas U.S. boards represent just shareholders. Thus, it would appear that U.S. boards, with a higher percentage of outsiders, would have interests most closely aligned with those of shareholders.

German and Japanese firms are also more likely to be controlled by large blocks of stock than those in the United States. Although pension and mutual funds, as well as other institutional investors, are increasingly important in the United States, block ownership is still less prevalent than in Germany and Japan. In both Germany and Japan, banks often own large blocks of stock, something that is not permitted by law in the United States, and corporations also own large blocks of stock in other corporations. In Japan, combinations of companies, called **keiretsus,** have cross-ownership of stock among the member companies, and these interlocking blocks distort the definition of an outside board member. For example, when the performance of a company in a keiretsu deteriorates, new directors are often appointed from the staffs of other members of the keiretsu. Such appointees might be classified officially as insiders, but they represent interests other than those of the troubled company's CEO.

In general, large blockholders are better able to monitor management than are small investors, so one might expect the blockholder factor to favor German and Japanese shareholders. However, these blockholders have other relationships with the company that might be detrimental to outside shareholders. For example, if one company buys from another, transfer pricing might be used to shift wealth to a favored company, or a company might be forced to buy from a sister company in spite of the availability of lower-cost resources from outside the group.

Executive compensation packages differ dramatically across the three countries, with U.S. executives receiving by far the highest compensation. However, compensation plans are remarkably similar in terms of how sensitive total compensation is to corporate performance.

are fairly similar, then you might expect it to be easier to find a qualified replacement from another firm for a poorly performing CEO. This is exactly what the evidence shows: As industry homogeneity increases, so does the likelihood of CEO turnover.[24]

The Media and Litigation Corporate governance, especially compensation, is a hot topic in the media. The media can have a positive impact by discovering or reporting corporate problems, such as the Enron scandal. Another example is the extensive recent (2006) coverage being given to option backdating, in which the exercise prices of executive stock options are set *after* the options officially have been granted. Because the exercise prices are set at the lowest stock price during the quarter in which the options are granted, the options are in-the-money and more valuable when their "official" life begins. However, the media can also hurt corporate governance by focusing too much attention on a CEO. Such "superstar"

---

[24]See R. Parrino, "CEO Turnover and Outside Succession: A Cross-Sectional Analysis," *Journal of Financial Economics,* 1997, pp. 165–197.

Which country's system of corporate governance is best from the standpoint of a shareholder whose goal is stock price maximization? There is no definitive answer. U.S. stocks have had the best performance in recent years. Moreover, German and Japanese companies are slowly moving toward the U.S. system with respect to size of compensation, and compensation plans in all three countries are being linked ever more closely to performance. At the same time, though, U.S. companies are moving toward the others in the sense of having larger ownership blocks, and since those blocks are primarily held by pension and mutual funds rather than banks and related corporations, they better represent the interests of shareholders.

Source: Steven N. Kaplan, "Top Executive Incentives in Germany, Japan, and the USA: A Comparison," in *Executive Compensation and Shareholder Value*, Jennifer Carpenter and David Yermack, eds. (Boston: Kluwer Academic Publishers, 1999), pp. 3–12.

International Characteristics of Corporate Governance

	Germany	Japan	United States
Threat of a takeover	Moderate	Low	High
Board of directors			
Size of board	26	21	14
Percent insiders	27%	91%	33%
Percent outsiders	73%	9%	67%
Are large blocks of stock typically owned by			
A controlling family?	Yes	No	No
Another corporation?	Yes	Yes	No
A bank?	Yes	Yes	No
Executive compensation			
Amount of compensation	Moderate	Low	High
Sensitivity to performance	Low to moderate	Low to moderate	Low to moderate

CEOs often command excessive compensation packages and spend too much time on activities outside the company, resulting in too much pay for too little performance.[25]

In addition to penalties and fines from regulatory bodies such as the SEC, civil litigation also occurs when companies are suspected of fraud. The recent research indicates that such suits lead to improvements in corporate governance.[26]

SELF-TEST

What are two primary forms of corporate governance (that is, the carrot and the stick)?

What factors improve a board of directors' effectiveness?

What are three provisions in many corporate charters that deter takeovers?

Describe how a typical stock option plan works. What are some problems with a typical stock option plan?

---

[25]See U. Malmendier and G. A. Tate, "Superstar CEOs," Working Paper, Stanford University, 2005.

[26]For example, see D. B. Farber, "Restoring Trust after Fraud: Does Corporate Governance Matter?" *Accounting Review*, 2005, pp. 539–561; and Stephen P. Ferris, Tomas Jandik, Robert M. Lawless, and Anil Makhija, "Derivative Lawsuits as a Corporate Governance Mechanism: Empirical Evidence on Board Changes Surrounding Filings," *Journal of Financial and Quantitative Analysis*, forthcoming.

15.6 Employee Stock Ownership Plans (ESOPs)

See http://www
.esopassociation
.org for more on ESOPs.

Studies show that 90% of the employees who receive stock under option plans sell the stock as soon as they exercise their options, so the plans motivate employees only for a limited period.[27] Moreover, many companies limit their stock option plans to key managers and executives. To help provide long-term productivity gains, and also to help improve retirement incomes for all employees, Congress authorized the use of **Employee Stock Ownership Plans (ESOPs).** Today about 9,000 privately held companies and 1,000 publicly held firms have ESOPs, and more are being created every day. Typically, the ESOP's major asset is shares of the common stock of the company that created it, and of the 10,000 total ESOPs, about 2,500 of them actually own a majority of their company's stock.[28]

To illustrate how an ESOP works, consider Gallagher & Abbott Inc. (G&A), a Knoxville, Tennessee, construction company. G&A's simplified balance sheet is shown below:

G&A's Balance Sheet prior to ESOP (Millions of Dollars)

Assets		Liabilities and Equity	
Cash	$ 10	Debt	$100
Other	190	Equity (1 million shares)	100
Total	**$200**	**Total**	**$200**

Now G&A creates an ESOP, which is a new legal entity. The company issues 500,000 shares of new stock at $100 per share, or $50 million in total, which it sells to the ESOP. G&A's employees are the ESOP's stockholders, and each employee receives an ownership interest based on the size of his or her salary and years of service. The ESOP borrows the $50 million to buy the newly issued stock.[29] Financial institutions are willing to lend the ESOP the money because G&A signs a guarantee for the loan. Here is the company's new balance sheet:

G&A's Balance Sheet after the ESOP (Millions of Dollars)

Assets		Liabilities and Equity	
Cash	$ 60	Debt[a]	$100
Other	190	Equity (1.5 million shares)	150
Total	**$250**	**Total**	**$250**

[a]The company has guaranteed the ESOP's loan, and it has promised to make payments to the ESOP sufficient to retire the loan, but this does not show up on the balance sheet.

---

[27]See Gary Laufman, "To Have and Have Not," *CFO*, March 1998, pp. 58–66.
[28]See Eugene Pilotte, "Employee Stock Ownership Plans, Management Motives, and Shareholder Wealth: A Review of the Evidence," *Journal of Financial Education*, Spring 1997, pp. 41–46; and Daniel Eisenberg, "No ESOP Fable," *Time*, May 10, 1999, p. 95.
[29]Our description is somewhat simplified. Technically, the stock would be placed in a suspense account and then be allocated to employees as the debt is repaid.

The company now has an additional $50 million of cash and $50 million more of book equity, but it has a de facto liability due to its guarantee of the ESOP's debt. It could use the cash to finance an expansion, but many companies use the cash to repurchase their own common stock, so we assume that G&A will do likewise. The company's new balance sheets, and that of the ESOP, are shown below:

G&A's Balance Sheet after the ESOP and Share Repurchase
(Millions of Dollars)

Assets		Liabilities and Equity	
Cash	$ 10	Debt	$100
Other	190	Equity (1 million shares)	150
		Treasury stock	(50)
Total	$200	**Total**	$200

ESOP's Initial Balance Sheet (Millions of Dollars)

Assets		Liabilities and Equity	
Cash	$ 10	Debt	$100
Other	190	Equity (1 million shares)	100
Total	$200	**Total**	$200

Note that while the company's balance sheet looks exactly as it did initially, there is really a huge difference—the footnote that discloses that the company has guaranteed the ESOP's debt, hence that it has an off-balance-sheet liability of $50 million. Moreover, because the ESOP has no equity, the guarantee is very real indeed. Finally, note that operating assets have not been increased at all, but the total debt outstanding supported by those assets has increased by $50 million.[30]

If this were the whole story, there would be no reason to have an ESOP. However, G&A has promised to make payments to the ESOP in sufficient amounts to enable the ESOP to pay interest and principal charges on the debt so as to amortize the debt over 15 years. Thus, after 15 years the debt will be paid off, and the ESOP's equity holders, who are the employees, will have equity with a book value of $50 million and a market value that could be much higher if G&A's stock increases, as it should over time. Then, as employees retire, the ESOP will distribute a pro rata amount of the G&A stock to each employee, who can then use it as a part of his or her retirement plan.

An ESOP is clearly beneficial for employees, but why would a company want to establish one? There are five primary reasons:

1. Congress passed the enabling legislation in hopes of enhancing employees' productivity and thus making the economy more efficient. In theory, if an employee has equity in the enterprise, he or she will work harder and smarter. Note too that if employees are more productive and creative, this will benefit

---

[30]We assumed that the company used the $50 million paid to it by the ESOP to repurchase common stock and thus to increase its de facto debt. It could have used the $50 million to retire debt, in which case its true debt ratio would remain unchanged, or it could have used the money to support an expansion.

outside shareholders, because productivity enhancements that benefit ESOP shareholders also benefit outside shareholders.

2. The ESOP represents additional compensation to employees, because in our example there is a $50 million (or more) transfer of wealth from existing shareholders to employees over the 15-year period. Presumably, if the ESOP were not created, then some other form of compensation would have been required, and that alternative compensation might not have the secondary benefit of enhancing productivity. Note too that the ESOP's payments to employees (as opposed to the payment by the company) come primarily at retirement, and Congress wanted to boost retirement incomes.

3. Depending on when an employee's rights to the ESOP are vested, the ESOP may help the firm retain employees.

4. There are also strong tax incentives to encourage a company to form an ESOP. First, Congress decreed that in cases where the ESOP owns 50% or more of the company's common stock, the financial institutions that lend money to ESOPs can exclude from taxable income 50% of the interest they receive on the loan. This improves the financial institutions' after-tax returns, making them willing to lend to ESOPs at below-market rates. Therefore, a company that establishes an ESOP can borrow through the ESOP at a lower rate than would otherwise be available—in our example, the $50 million of debt would be at a reduced rate.

 There is also a second tax advantage. If the company were to borrow directly, it could deduct interest but not principal payments from its taxable income. However, companies typically make the required payments to their ESOPs in the form of cash dividends. Dividends are not normally deductible from taxable income, *but cash dividends paid on ESOP stock are deductible if the dividends are paid to plan participants or are used to repay the loan.* Thus, companies whose ESOPs own 50% of their stock can in effect borrow on ESOP loans at subsidized rates and then deduct both the interest and principal payments made on the loans. American Airlines and Publix Supermarkets are two of the many firms that have used ESOPs to obtain this benefit, along with motivating employees by giving them an equity interest in the enterprise.

5. A less desirable use of ESOPs is to help companies avoid being acquired by another company. The company's CEO, or someone appointed by the CEO, typically acts as trustee for its ESOP, and the trustee is supposed to vote the ESOP's shares according to the will of the plan participants. Moreover, the participants, who are the company's employees, usually oppose takeovers because they frequently involve labor cutbacks. Therefore, if an ESOP owns a significant percentage of the company's shares, then management has a powerful tool for warding off takeovers. This is not good for outside stockholders.

Are ESOPs good for a company's shareholders? In theory, ESOPs motivate employees by providing them with an ownership interest. That should increase productivity and thereby enhance stock values. Moreover, tax incentives mitigate the costs associated with some ESOPs. However, an ESOP can be used to help entrench management, and that could hurt stockholders. How do the pros and cons balance out? The empirical evidence is not entirely clear, but certain findings are worth noting. First, if an ESOP is established to help defend against a takeover, then the firm's stock price typically falls when plans for the ESOP are announced. The market does not like the prospect of entrenching management and having to give up the premium normally associated with a takeover. However, if the ESOP is established for tax purposes and/or to motivate employees, the stock price generally goes up at the time of the announcement. In these cases, the company typically has a subsequent improvement in sales per employee and other long-term performance measures, which stimulates the stock price. Indeed, a recent study showed that companies with ESOPs enjoyed a 26% average annual stock return versus a return of only 19% for peer companies without ESOPs.[31] Therefore, it appears that ESOPs, if used appropriately, can be a powerful tool to help create shareholder value.

SELF-TEST

What are ESOPs? What are some of their advantages and disadvantages?

Summary

- **Corporate assets** consist of operating assets and financial, or nonoperating, assets.
- **Operating assets** take two forms: assets-in-place and growth options.
- **Assets-in-place** include the land, buildings, machines, and inventory that the firm uses in its operations to produce products and services.
- **Growth options** refer to opportunities the firm has to increase sales. They include opportunities arising from R&D expenditures, customer relationships, and the like.
- **Financial,** or **nonoperating, assets** are distinguished from operating assets and include items such as investments in marketable securities and noncontrolling interests in the stock of other companies.
- The **value of nonoperating assets** is usually close to the figure reported on the balance sheet.
- The **value of operations** is the present value of all the future free cash flows expected from operations when discounted at the weighted average cost of capital:

$$V_{op(\text{at time } 0)} = \sum_{t=1}^{\infty} \frac{FCF_t}{(1 + WACC)^t}.$$

- The **terminal,** or **horizon, value** is the value of operations at the end of the explicit forecast period. It is also called the **continuing value,** and it is equal to the present value of all free cash flows beyond the forecast period, discounted back to the end of the forecast period at the weighted average cost of capital:

$$\text{Continuing value} = V_{op(\text{at time } N)} = \frac{FCF_{N+1}}{WACC - g} = \frac{FCF_N(1 + g)}{WACC - g}.$$

- The **corporate valuation model** can be used to calculate the total value of a company by finding the value of operations plus the value of nonoperating assets.
- The **value of equity** is the total value of the company minus the value of the debt and preferred stock. The **price per share** is the total value of the equity divided by the number of shares.

---

[31]See Daniel Eisenberg, "No ESOP Fable," *Time*, May 10, 1999, p. 95.

- **Value-based management** involves the systematic use of the corporate valuation model to evaluate a company's potential decisions.
- The four **value drivers** are (1) the growth rate in sales (g), (2) operating profitability (OP), which is measured by the ratio of NOPAT to sales, (3) capital requirements (CR) as measured by the ratio of operating capital to sales, and (4) the weighted average cost of capital (WACC).
- **Expected return on invested capital (EROIC)** is equal to expected NOPAT divided by the amount of capital that is available at the beginning of the year.
- A company creates value when the spread between EROIC and WACC is positive, that is, when EROIC − WACC > 0.
- **Corporate governance** involves the manner in which shareholders' objectives are implemented, and it is reflected in a company's policies and actions.
- The two primary mechanisms used in corporate governance are: (1) the threat of removal of a poorly performing CEO and (2) the type of plan used to compensate executives and managers.
- Poorly performing managers can be removed either by a takeover or by the company's own board of directors. Provisions in the corporate charter affect the difficulty of a successful takeover, and the composition of the board of directors affects the likelihood of a manager being removed by the board.
- **Managerial entrenchment** is most likely when a company has a weak board of directors coupled with strong anti-takeover provisions in its corporate charter. In this situation, the likelihood that badly performing senior managers will be fired is low.
- **Nonpecuniary benefits** are noncash perks such as lavish offices, memberships at country clubs, corporate jets, foreign junkets, and the like. Some of these expenditures may be cost effective, but others are wasteful and simply reduce profits. Such fat is almost always cut after a hostile takeover.
- **Targeted share repurchases,** also known as **greenmail,** occur when a company buys back stock from a potential acquirer at a higher than fair market price. In return, the potential acquirer agrees not to attempt to take over the company.
- **Shareholder rights provisions,** also known as **poison pills,** allow existing shareholders to purchase additional shares of stock at a lower than market value if a potential acquirer purchases a controlling stake in the company.
- A **restricted voting rights** provision automatically deprives a shareholder of voting rights if the shareholder owns more than a specified amount of stock.
- **Interlocking boards of directors** occur when the CEO of Company A sits on the board of Company B, and B's CEO sits on A's board.
- A **stock option** provides for the purchase of a share of stock at a fixed price, called the **exercise price,** no matter what the actual price of the stock is. Stock options have an **expiration date**, after which they cannot be exercised.
- An **Employee Stock Ownership Plan,** or **ESOP,** is a plan that facilitates employees' ownership of stock in the company for which they work.

Questions

(15-1)   Define each of the following terms:
   a.   Assets-in-place; growth options; nonoperating assets
   b.   Net operating working capital; operating capital; NOPAT; free cash flow
   c.   Value of operations; horizon value; corporate valuation model
   d.   Value-based management; value drivers; EROIC
   e.   Managerial entrenchment; nonpecuniary benefits
   f.   Greenmail; poison pills; restricted voting rights
   g.   Stock option; ESOP

(15-2)   Explain how to use the corporate valuation model to find the price per share of common equity.

(15-3)   Explain how it is possible for sales growth to decrease the value of a profitable company.

(15-4)   What are some actions an entrenched management might take that would harm shareholders?

(15-5)   How is it possible for an employee stock option to be valuable even if the firm's stock price fails to meet shareholders' expectations?

Self-Test Problem   Solution Appears in Appendix A

(ST-1)
Corporate Valuation

Watkins Inc. has never paid a dividend, and when it might begin paying dividends is unknown. Its current free cash flow is $100,000, and this FCF is expected to grow at a constant 7% rate. The weighted average cost of capital is WACC = 11%. Watkins currently holds $325,000 of nonoperating marketable securities. Its long-term debt is $1,000,000, but it has never issued preferred stock. Watkins has 50,000 shares of stock outstanding.
   a.   Calculate Watkins' value of operations.
   b.   Calculate the company's total value.
   c.   Calculate the value of its common equity.
   d.   Calculate the per share stock price.

Problems   Answers Appear in Appendix B

Easy Problems 1–5

(15-1)
Free Cash Flow

Use the following income statements and balance sheets to calculate Garnet Inc.'s free cash flow for 2008.

Garnet Inc.

	2008	2007
Income Statement		
Net sales	$530.0	$500.0
Costs (except depreciation)	400.0	380.0
Depreciation	30.0	25.0
Total operating costs	$430.0	$405.0
Earnings before interest and taxes (EBIT)	100.0	95.0
Less interest	23.0	21.0
Earnings before taxes	$ 77.0	$ 74.0
Taxes (40%)	30.8	29.6
Net income	$ 46.2	$ 44.4
Balance Sheet		
Assets		
Cash	$ 28.0	$ 27.0
Marketable securities	69.0	66.0
Accounts receivable	81.0	80.0
Inventories	112.0	106.0
Total current assets	$293.0	$279.0
Net plant and equipment	281.0	265.0
Total assets	$574.0	$544.0
Liabilities and Equity		
Accounts payable	$ 56.0	$ 52.0
Notes payable	138.0	130.0
Accruals	28.0	28.0
Total current liabilities	$222.0	$210.0
Long-term bonds	173.0	164.0
Common stock	100.0	100.0
Retained earnings	79.0	70.0
Common equity	$179.0	$170.0
Total liabilities and equity	$574.0	$544.0

(15-2)
Value of Operations of Constant Growth Firm

EMC Corporation has never paid a dividend. Its current free cash flow is $400,000 and is expected to grow at a constant rate of 5%. The weighted average cost of capital is WACC = 12%. Calculate EMC's value of operations.

(15-3)
Horizon Value

Current and projected free cash flows for Radell Global Operations are shown below. Growth is expected to be constant after 2009. The weighted average cost of capital is 11%. What is the horizon, or continuing, value at 2009?

	Actual		Projected	
	2007	2008	2009	2010
Free cash flow (millions of dollars)	$606.82	$667.50	$707.55	$750.00

(15-4)
EROIC and MVA of
Constant Growth Firm

A company has capital of $200,000,000. It has an EROIC of 9%, forecasted constant growth of 5%, and a WACC of 10%. What is its value of operations? What is its MVA? (Hint: Use Equation 15-4.)

(15-5)
Value Drivers and
Horizon Value of
Constant Growth Firm

You are given the following forecasted information for the year 2011: Sales = $300,000,000; Operating profitability (OP) = 6%; Capital requirements (CR) = 43%; Growth (g) = 5%; and the weighted average cost of capital (WACC) = 9.8%. If these values remain constant, what is the horizon value (that is, the 2011 value of operations)? (Hint: Use Equation 15-3.)

**Intermediate
Problems 6–7**

(15-6)
Value of Operations

Brooks Enterprises has never paid a dividend. Free cash flow is projected to be $80,000 and $100,000 for the next 2 years, respectively, and after the second year it is expected to grow at a constant rate of 8%. The company's weighted average cost of capital is WACC = 12%.
a. What is the terminal, or horizon, value of operations? (Hint: Find the value of all free cash flows beyond Year 2 discounted back to Year 2.)
b. Calculate the value of Brooks' operations.

(15-7)
Corporate Valuation

Dozier Corporation is a fast-growing supplier of office products. Analysts project the following free cash flows (FCFs) during the next 3 years, after which FCF is expected to grow at a constant 7% rate. Dozier's cost of capital is WACC = 13%.

	Year		
	1	2	3
Free cash flow ($ millions)	−$20	$30	$40

a. What is Dozier's terminal, or horizon, value? (Hint: Find the value of all free cash flows beyond Year 3 discounted back to Year 3.)
b. What is the current value of operations for Dozier?
c. Suppose Dozier has $10 million in marketable securities, $100 million in debt, and 10 million shares of stock. What is the price per share?

**Challenging
Problems 8–10**

(15-8)
Value of Equity

The balance sheet of Hutter Amalgamated is shown below. If the 12/31/2007 value of operations is $756 million, what is the 12/31/2007 value of equity?

Balance Sheet, December 31, 2007 (Millions of Dollars)

Assets		Liabilities and Equity	
Cash	$ 20.0	Accounts payable	$ 19.0
Marketable securities	77.0	Notes payable	151.0
Accounts receivable	100.0	Accruals	51.0
Inventories	200.0	Total current liabilities	$221.0
Total current assets	$397.0	Long-term bonds	190.0
Net plant and equipment	279.0	Preferred stock	76.0
		Common stock (par plus PIC)	100.0
		Retained earnings	89.0
		Common equity	$189.0
Total assets	$676.0	Total liabilities and equity	$676.0

(15-9)
Price per Share The balance sheet of Roop Industries is shown below. The 12/31/2007 value of operations is $651 million and there are 10 million shares of common equity. What is the price per share?

Balance Sheet, December 31, 2007 (Millions of Dollars)

Assets		Liabilities and Equity	
Cash	$ 20.0	Accounts payable	$ 19.0
Marketable securities	47.0	Notes payable	65.0
Accounts receivable	100.0	Accruals	51.0
Inventories	200.0	Total current liabilities	$135.0
Total current assets	$367.0	Long-term bonds	131.0
Net plant and equipment	279.0	Preferred stock	33.0
		Common stock (par plus PIC)	160.0
		Retained earnings	187.0
		Common equity	$347.0
Total assets	$646.0	Total liabilities and equity	$646.0

(15-10)
Corporate Valuation The financial statements of Lioi Steel Fabricators are shown below, with the actual results for 2007 and the projections for 2008. Free cash flow is expected to grow at a 6% rate after 2008. The weighted average cost of capital is 11%.
a. If operating capital as of 12/31/2007 is $502.2 million, what is the free cash flow for 12/31/2008?
b. What is the horizon value as of 12/31/2008?
c. What is the value of operations as of 12/31/2007?
d. What is the total value of the company as of 12/31/2007?
e. What is the price per share for 12/31/2007?

Income Statements for the Year Ending December 31
(Millions of Dollars Except for Per Share Data)

	Actual 2007	Projected 2008
Net sales	$500.0	$530.0
Costs (except depreciation)	360.0	381.6
Depreciation	37.5	39.8
Total operating costs	$397.5	$421.4
Earnings before interest and taxes	$102.5	$108.6
Less interest	13.9	16.0
Earnings before taxes	$ 88.6	$ 92.6
Taxes (40%)	35.4	37.0
Net income before preferred dividends	$ 53.2	$ 55.6
Preferred dividends	6.0	7.4
Net income available for common dividends	$ 47.2	$ 48.2
Common dividends	$ 40.8	$ 29.7
Addition to retained earnings	$ 6.4	$ 18.5
Number of shares	10	10
Dividends per share	$ 4.08	$ 2.97

Balance Sheets for December 31 (Millions of Dollars)

	Actual 2007	Projected 2008
Assets		
Cash	$ 5.3	$ 5.6
Marketable securities	49.9	51.9
Accounts receivable	53.0	56.2
Inventories	106.0	112.4
Total current assets	$214.2	$226.1
Net plant and equipment	375.0	397.5
Total assets	$589.2	$623.6
Liabilities and Equity		
Accounts payable	$ 9.6	$ 11.2
Notes payable	69.9	74.1
Accruals	27.5	28.1
Total current liabilities	$107.0	$113.4
Long-term bonds	140.8	148.2
Preferred stock	35.0	37.1
Common stock (par plus PIC)	160.0	160.0
Retained earnings	146.4	164.9
Common equity	$306.4	$324.9
Total liabilities and equity	$589.2	$623.6

Spreadsheet Problem

(15-11)
Build a Model:
Corporate
Valuation

Start with the partial model in the file *FM12 Ch 15 P11 Build a Model.xls* from the textbook's Web site. The Henley Corporation is a privately held company specializing in lawn care products and services. The most recent financial statements are shown below.

e-resource

Income Statement for the Year Ending December 31
(Millions of Dollars Except for Per Share Data)

	2007
Net sales	$800.0
Costs (except depreciation)	576.0
Depreciation	60.0
Total operating costs	$636.0
Earnings before interest and taxes	$164.0
Less interest	32.0
Earnings before taxes	$132.0
Taxes (40%)	52.8
Net income before preferred dividends	$ 79.2
Preferred dividends	1.4
Net income available for common dividends	$ 77.9
Common dividends	$ 31.1
Addition to retained earnings	$ 46.7
Number of shares (in millions)	10
Dividends per share	$ 3.11

Balance Sheet for December 31 (Millions of Dollars)

Assets	2007	Liabilities and Equity	2007
Cash	$ 8.0	Accounts payable	$ 16.0
Marketable securities	20.0	Notes payable	40.0
Accounts receivable	80.0	Accruals	40.0
Inventories	160.0	Total current liabilities	$ 96.0
Total current assets	$268.0	Long-term bonds	300.0
Net plant and equipment	600.0	Preferred stock	15.0
		Common stock (par plus PIC)	257.0
		Retained earnings	200.0
		Common equity	$457.0
Total assets	$868.0	Total liabilities and equity	$868.0

The ratios and selected information for the current and projected years are shown below.

	Actual	Projected			
	2007	2008	2009	2010	2011
Sales growth rate		15%	10%	6%	6%
Costs/Sales	72%	72	72	72	72
Depreciation/Net PPE	10	10	10	10	10
Cash/Sales	1	1	1	1	1
Accounts receivable/Sales	10	10	10	10	10
Inventories/Sales	20	20	20	20	20
Net PPE/Sales	75	75	75	75	75
Accounts payable/Sales	2	2	2	2	2
Accruals/Sales	5	5	5	5	5
Tax rate	40	40	40	40	40
Weighted average cost of capital (WACC)	10.5	10.5	10.5	10.5	10.5

a. Forecast the parts of the income statement and balance sheets necessary to calculate free cash flow.
b. Calculate free cash flow for each projected year. Also calculate the growth rates of free cash flow each year to ensure that there is constant growth (that is, the same as the constant growth rate in sales) by the end of the forecast period.
c. Calculate operating profitability (OP = NOPAT/Sales), capital requirements (CR = Operating capital/Sales), and expected return on invested capital (EROIC = Expected NOPAT/Operating capital at beginning of year). Based on the spread between EROIC and WACC, do you think that the company will have a positive Market Value Added (MVA = Market value of company − Book value of company = Value of operations − Operating capital)?
d. Calculate the value of operations and MVA. (Hint: First calculate the horizon value at the end of the forecast period, which is equal to the value of operations at the end of the forecast period. Assume that growth beyond the horizon is 6%.)
e. Calculate the price per share of common equity as of 12/31/2007.

Cyberproblem

Please go to the textbook's Web site to access any Cyberproblems.

Mini Case

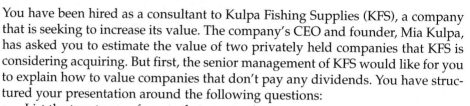

You have been hired as a consultant to Kulpa Fishing Supplies (KFS), a company that is seeking to increase its value. The company's CEO and founder, Mia Kulpa, has asked you to estimate the value of two privately held companies that KFS is considering acquiring. But first, the senior management of KFS would like for you to explain how to value companies that don't pay any dividends. You have structured your presentation around the following questions:

a. List the two types of assets that companies own.

b. What are assets-in-place? How can their value be estimated?

c. What are nonoperating assets? How can their value be estimated?

d. What is the total value of a corporation? Who has claims on this value?

e. The first acquisition target is a privately held company in a mature industry. The company currently has free cash flow of $20 million. Its WACC is 10% and it is expected to grow at a constant rate of 5%. The company has marketable securities of $100 million. It is financed with $200 million of debt, $50 million of preferred stock, and $210 million of book equity.

 (1) What is its value of operations?

 (2) What is its total corporate value? What is its value of equity?

 (3) What is its MVA (MVA = Total corporate value − Total book value)?

f. The second acquisition target is a privately held company in a growing industry. The target has recently borrowed $40 million to finance its expansion; it has no other debt or preferred stock. It pays no dividends and currently has no marketable securities. KFS expects the company to produce free cash flows of −$5 million in 1 year, $10 million in 2 years, and $20 million in 3 years. After 3 years, free cash flow will grow at a rate of 6%. Its WACC is 10% and it currently has 10 million shares of stock.

 (1) What is its horizon value (that is, its value of operations at Year 3)? What is its current value of operations (that is, at time zero)?

 (2) What is its value of equity on a price per share basis?

g. KFS is also interested in applying value-based management to its own divisions. Explain what value-based management is.

h. What are the four value drivers? How does each of them affect value?

i. What is expected return on invested capital (EROIC)? Why is the spread between EROIC and WACC so important?

j. KFS has two divisions. Both have current sales of $1,000, current expected growth of 5%, and a WACC of 10%. Division A has high profitability (OP = 6%) but high capital requirements (CR = 78%). Division B has low profitability (OP = 4%) but low capital requirements (CR = 27%). What is the MVA of each division, based on the current growth of 5%? What is the MVA of each division if growth is 6%?

k. What is the EROIC of each division for 5% growth and for 6% growth? How is this related to MVA?

l. List six potential managerial behaviors that can harm a firm's value.

m. The managers at KFS have heard that corporate governance can affect shareholder value. What is corporate governance? List five corporate governance provisions that are internal to a firm and are under its control.

n. What characteristics of the board of directors usually lead to effective corporate governance?

o.   List three provisions in the corporate charter that affect takeovers.
p.   Briefly describe the use of stock options in a compensation plan. What are some potential problems with stock options as a form of compensation?
q.   What is block ownership? How does it affect corporate governance?
r.   Briefly explain how regulatory agencies and legal systems affect corporate governance.

Selected Additional Cases

The following cases from Textchoice, *Cengage Learning's online library, cover many of the concepts discussed in this chapter and are available at* **http://www.textchoice2.com.**

Klein-Brigham Series:
Case 41, "Advanced Fuels Corporation," and Case 93, "Electro Technology Corporation," discuss financing and valuing a new venture.

Brigham-Buzzard Series:
Case 14, "Maris Distributing Company," discusses valuation techniques used in a court case.

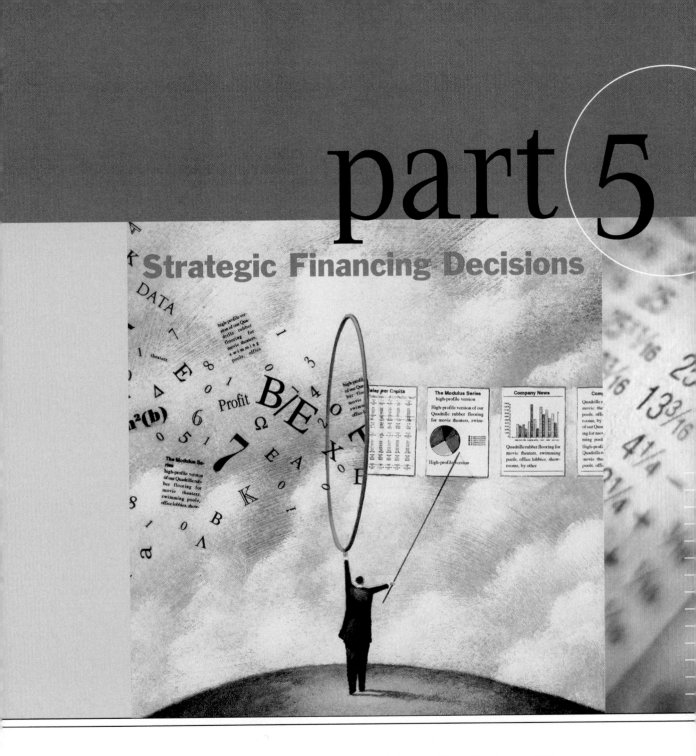

part 5

Strategic Financing Decisions

chapter 16

Capital Structure Decisions: The Basics

A company can obtain long-term financing in the form of equity, debt, or some combination. The accompanying table shows the long-term debt ratios for different business sectors, along with selected individual companies within those sectors. There are obvious differences between sectors' average debt ratios, with Technology having a very low average ratio (17%) and others, such as Utilities (60%), having much higher ratios. But notice that within each sector some companies have very low levels of debt, while others have very high levels. For example, the average debt ratio for Consumer/Noncyclical is 45%, but Starbucks has no long-term debt whereas Kellogg has 59%. Why do we see such variation across companies and business sectors, and can a company make itself more valuable through its choice of debt ratio? Keep these questions in mind as you read this chapter.

For updates on a company's ratio, go to http://www.reuters.com and enter the ticker symbol for a stock quote. Click on Ratios (on the left) for updates on the sector ratio. The long-term debt ratio in the table is the percent of long-term financing that comes from debt: (Long-term debt)/(Long-term debt + Equity).

Sector and Company	Long-Term Debt Ratio	Sector and Company	Long-Term Debt Ratio
Technology	17%	**Consumer/Noncyclical**	45%
Intuit Inc. (INTU)	0	Starbucks Corporation (SBUX)	0
IKON Office Solutions (IKN)	32	Kellogg Company (K)	59
Energy	25	**Conglomerates**	60
ExxonMobil Corporation (XOM)	6	Minnesota Mining & Mfg. (MMM)	10
Chesapeake Energy Corp. (CHK)	46	Olin Corp. (OLN)	36
Health Care	26	**Utilities**	60
Patterson Dental Company (PDCO)	15	Reliant Energy Inc. (RRI)	54
HCA Inc. (HCA)	70	CMS Energy Corporation (CMS)	73
Transportation	37	**Services**	45
United Parcel Service (UPS)	15	Administaff Inc. (ASF)	14
Continental Airlines Inc. (CAL)	89	Allied Waste Industries (AW)	67

(Continued)

Sector and Company	Long-Term Debt Ratio	Sector and Company	Long-Term Debt Ratio
Basic Materials	42	**Consumer Cyclical**	57
Anglo American PLC (AAUK)	21	Callaway Golf Company (ELY)	0
Century Aluminum Company (CENX)	89	Black & Decker Corp. (BDK)	37
Capital Goods	41		
Winnebago Industries (WGO)	0		
Caterpillar Inc. (CAT)	76		

As we saw in Chapters 14 and 15, all firms need operating capital to support their sales. To acquire that operating capital, funds must be raised, usually as a combination of equity and debt. The firm's mixture of debt and equity is called its **capital structure.** Although actual levels of debt and equity may vary somewhat over time, most firms try to keep their financing mix close to a **target capital structure.** A firm's **capital structure decision** includes its choice of a target capital structure, the average maturity of its debt, and the specific types of financing it decides to use at any particular time. As with operating decisions, managers should make capital structure decisions designed to maximize the firm's value.

e-resource

The textbook's Web site contains an *Excel* file that will guide you through the chapter's calculations. The file for this chapter is **FM12 Ch 16 Tool Kit.xls**, and we encourage you to open the file and follow along as you read the chapter.

16.1 A Preview of Capital Structure Issues

Recall from Chapter 15 that the value of a firm's operations is the present value of its expected future free cash flows (FCF), discounted at its weighted average cost of capital (WACC):

$$V_{op} = \sum_{t=1}^{\infty} \frac{FCF_t}{(1 + WACC)^t}. \qquad (16\text{-}1)$$

The WACC depends on the percentages of debt and equity (w_d and w_{ce}), the cost of debt (r_d), the cost of stock (r_s), and the corporate tax rate (T):

$$WACC = w_d(1 - T)r_d + w_{ce}r_s. \qquad (16\text{-}2)$$

As these equations show, the only way any decision can change a firm's value is by affecting either free cash flows or the cost of capital. We discuss below some of the ways that a higher proportion of debt can affect WACC and/or FCF.

Corporate Valuation and Capital Structure

A firm's financing choices obviously have a direct effect on its weighted average cost of capital (WACC). Financing choices also have an indirect effect because they change the risk and required return of debt and equity. This chapter focuses on the debt–equity choice and its effect on value.

$$\text{Value} = \frac{FCF_1}{(1 + WACC)^1} + \frac{FCF_2}{(1 + WACC)^2} + \frac{FCF_3}{(1 + WACC)^3} + \cdots + \frac{FCF_\infty}{(1 + WACC)^\infty}$$

Debt Increases the Cost of Stock, r_s

Debtholders have a prior claim on the company's cash flows relative to shareholders, who are entitled only to any residual cash flow after debtholders have been paid. As we show later in a numerical example, the "fixed" claim of the debtholders causes the "residual" claim of the stockholders to become less certain, and this increases the cost of stock, r_s.

Debt Reduces the Taxes a Company Pays

Imagine that a company's cash flows are a pie, and three different groups get pieces of the pie. The first piece goes to the government in the form of taxes, the second goes to debtholders, and the third to shareholders. Companies can deduct interest expenses when calculating taxable income, which reduces the government's piece of the pie and leaves more pie available to debtholders and investors. This reduction in taxes reduces the after-tax cost of debt, as shown in Equation 16-2.

The Risk of Bankruptcy Increases the Cost of Debt, r_d

As debt increases, the probability of financial distress, or even bankruptcy, goes up. With higher bankruptcy risk, debtholders will insist on a higher promised return, which increases the pre-tax cost of debt, r_d.

The Net Effect on the Weighted Average Cost of Capital

As Equation 16-2 shows, the WACC is a weighted average of relatively low-cost debt and high-cost equity. If we increase the proportion of debt, then the weight of low-cost debt (w_d) increases and the weight of high-cost equity (w_{ce}) decreases. If all else remained the same, then the WACC would fall and the value of the firm in Equation 16-1 would increase. But the previous paragraphs show that all else doesn't remain the same: both r_d and r_s increase. While it should be clear that changing the capital structure affects all the variables in the WACC equation, it's not easy to say whether those changes increase the WACC, decrease it, or balance out exactly and leave the WACC unchanged. We'll return to this issue later, when we discuss capital structure theory.

Bankruptcy Risk Reduces Free Cash Flow

As the risk of bankruptcy increases, some customers may choose to buy from another company, which hurts sales. This, in turn, decreases net operating profit after taxes (NOPAT), thus reducing FCF. Financial distress also hurts the productivity of workers and managers, as they spend more time worrying about their next job rather than their current job. Again, this reduces NOPAT and FCF. Finally, suppliers tighten their credit standards, which reduces accounts payable and causes net operating working capital to increase, thus reducing FCF. Therefore, the risk of bankruptcy can decrease FCF and reduce the value of the firm.

Bankruptcy Risk Affects Agency Costs

Higher levels of debt may affect the behavior of managers in two opposing ways. First, when times are good, managers may waste cash flow on perquisites and unnecessary expenditures. This is an agency cost, as described in Chapter 15. The good news is that the threat of bankruptcy reduces such wasteful spending, which increases FCF.

But the bad news is that a manager may become gun-shy and reject positive NPV projects if they are risky. From the stockholder's point of view it would be unfortunate if a risky project caused the company to go into bankruptcy, but note that other companies in the stockholder's portfolio may be taking on risky projects that turn out to be successful. Since most stockholders are well diversified, they can afford for a manager to take on risky but positive NPV projects. But a manager's reputation and wealth are generally tied to a single company, so the project may be unacceptably risky from the manager's point of view. Thus, high debt can cause managers to forgo positive NPV projects unless they are extremely safe. This is called the **underinvestment problem,** and it is another type of agency cost. Notice that debt can reduce one aspect of agency costs (wasteful spending) but may increase another (underinvestment), so the net effect on value isn't clear.

Issuing Equity Conveys a Signal to the Marketplace

Managers are in a better position to forecast a company's free cash flow than are investors, and academics call this **informational asymmetry.** Suppose a company's stock price is $50 per share. If managers are willing to issue new stock at $50 per share, investors reason that no one would sell anything for less than its true value. Therefore, the true value of the shares as seen by the managers with their superior information must be less than or equal to $50. Thus, investors perceive an equity issue as a negative signal, and this usually causes the stock price to fall.[1]

SELF-TEST Briefly describe some ways in which the capital structure decision can affect the WACC and FCF.

16.2 Business Risk and Financial Risk

In Chapter 6, when we examined risk from the viewpoint of a stock investor, we distinguished between *market risk*, which is measured by the firm's beta coefficient,

---

[1]An exception to this rule is any situation with little informational asymmetry, such as a regulated utility. Also, some companies, such as start-ups or high-tech ventures, are unable to find willing lenders and therefore must issue equity; we discuss this later in the chapter.

and *stand-alone risk*, which includes both market risk and an element of risk that can be eliminated by diversification. Now we introduce two new dimensions of risk: (1) *business risk*, or the risk of the firm's stock if it uses no debt, and (2) *financial risk*, which is the additional risk placed on the common stockholders as a result of the firm's decision to use debt.[2]

Conceptually, each firm has a certain amount of risk inherent in its operations—this is its business risk. If it uses any debt, then in effect it is partitioning its investors into two groups and concentrating its business risk on one class—the common stockholders. The additional risk the stockholders of a levered firm face, over the risk they would face if the firm used no debt, is the firm's financial risk. For example, if half of a firm's capital is raised as debt and half as common equity, then each common stockholder would bear about twice as much risk as if only equity were used. Naturally, a levered firm's stockholders will demand more compensation for bearing the additional (financial) risk, so the required rate of return on common equity will increase with the use of debt. *In other words, the greater the use of debt, the greater the concentration of risk on the stockholders, and the higher the cost of common equity.* In the balance of this section, we examine business and financial risk within a stand-alone risk framework, which ignores the effects of diversification. Later, we analyze the effects of diversification.

Business Risk

As noted above, **business risk** is the risk a firm's common stockholders would face if the firm had no debt. Business risk arises from uncertainty in projections of the firm's cash flows, which in turn means uncertainty about its operating profit and its capital (investment) requirements. In other words, we do not know for sure how large operating profits will be, nor do we know how much we will have to invest to develop new products, build new plants, and so forth. The return on invested capital (ROIC) combines these two sources of uncertainty, and its variability can be used to measure business risk on a stand-alone basis:

$$ROIC = \frac{NOPAT}{Capital} = \frac{EBIT(1-T)}{Capital}$$

$$= \frac{\text{Net income to common stockholders} + \text{After-tax interest payments}}{Capital}.$$

Here NOPAT is net operating profit after taxes, and capital is the required amount of operating capital, which is numerically equivalent to the sum of the firm's debt and common equity. Business risk can then be measured by the standard deviation of ROIC, σ_{ROIC}. If the firm's capital requirements are stable, then we can use the variability in EBIT, σ_{EBIT}, as an alternative measure of stand-alone business risk. Business risk depends on a number of factors, as described below:

1. *Demand variability.* The more stable the demand for a firm's products, other things held constant, the lower its business risk.
2. *Sales price variability.* Firms whose products are sold in highly volatile markets are exposed to more business risk than similar firms whose output prices are more stable.

---

[2]Preferred stock also adds to financial risk. To simplify matters, we concentrate on debt and common equity in this chapter.

3. *Input cost variability.* Firms whose input costs are highly uncertain are exposed to a high degree of business risk.
4. *Ability to adjust output prices for changes in input costs.* Some firms are better able than others to raise their own output prices when input costs rise. The greater the ability to adjust output prices to reflect cost conditions, the lower the business risk.
5. *Ability to develop new products in a timely, cost-effective manner.* Firms in such high-tech industries as drugs and computers depend on a constant stream of new products. The faster that products become obsolete, the greater the business risk.
6. *Foreign risk exposure.* Firms that generate a high percentage of their earnings overseas are subject to earnings declines due to exchange rate fluctuations. Also, if a firm operates in a politically unstable area, it may be subject to political risks. See Chapter 26 for a further discussion.
7. *The extent to which costs are fixed: operating leverage.* If a high percentage of its costs are fixed, hence do not decline when demand falls, then the firm is exposed to a relatively high degree of business risk. This factor is called *operating leverage,* and it is discussed at length in the next section.

Each of these factors is determined partly by the firm's industry characteristics, but each of them is also controllable to some extent by management. For example, most firms can, through their marketing policies, take actions to stabilize both unit sales and sales prices. However, this stabilization may require spending a great deal on advertising and/or price concessions to get commitments from customers to purchase fixed quantities at fixed prices in the future. Similarly, firms can reduce the volatility of future input costs by negotiating long-term labor and materials supply contracts, but they may have to pay prices above the current spot price to obtain these contracts. Many firms are also using hedging techniques to reduce business risk.

Operating Leverage

In physics, leverage implies the use of a lever to raise a heavy object with a small force. In politics, if people have leverage, their smallest word or action can accomplish a lot. *In business terminology, a high degree of* **operating leverage,** *other factors held constant, implies that a relatively small change in sales results in a large change in EBIT.*

Other things held constant, the higher a firm's fixed costs, the greater its operating leverage. Higher fixed costs are generally associated with more highly automated, capital intensive firms and industries. However, businesses that employ highly skilled workers who must be retained and paid even during recessions also have relatively high fixed costs, as do firms with high product development costs, because the amortization of development costs is an element of fixed costs.

Consider Strasburg Electronics Company, a debt-free (unlevered) firm. Figure 16-1 illustrates the concept of operating leverage by comparing the results that Strasburg could expect if it used different degrees of operating leverage. Plan A calls for a relatively small amount of fixed costs, $20,000. Here the firm would not have much automated equipment, so its depreciation, maintenance, property taxes, and so on would be low. However, the total operating costs line has a relatively steep slope, indicating that variable costs per unit are higher than they would be if the firm used more operating leverage. Plan B calls for a higher level

e-resource

See **FM12 Ch 16 Tool Kit.xls** at the textbook's Web site for all calculations.

Figure 16-1

Illustration of Operating Leverage

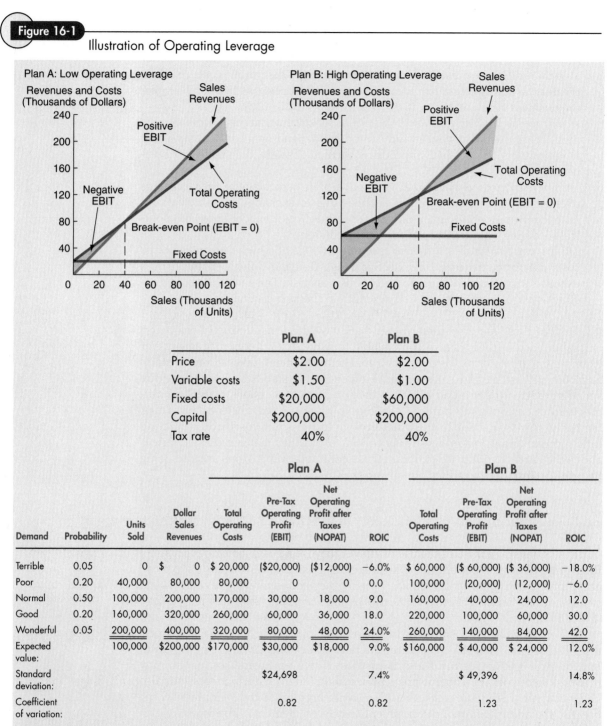

		Plan A	Plan B
	Price	$2.00	$2.00
	Variable costs	$1.50	$1.00
	Fixed costs	$20,000	$60,000
	Capital	$200,000	$200,000
	Tax rate	40%	40%

					Plan A				Plan B		
Demand	Probability	Units Sold	Dollar Sales Revenues	Total Operating Costs	Pre-Tax Operating Profit (EBIT)	Net Operating Profit after Taxes (NOPAT)	ROIC	Total Operating Costs	Pre-Tax Operating Profit (EBIT)	Net Operating Profit after Taxes (NOPAT)	ROIC
Terrible	0.05	0	$ 0	$ 20,000	($20,000)	($12,000)	−6.0%	$ 60,000	($ 60,000)	($ 36,000)	−18.0%
Poor	0.20	40,000	80,000	80,000	0	0	0.0	100,000	(20,000)	(12,000)	−6.0
Normal	0.50	100,000	200,000	170,000	30,000	18,000	9.0	160,000	40,000	24,000	12.0
Good	0.20	160,000	320,000	260,000	60,000	36,000	18.0	220,000	100,000	60,000	30.0
Wonderful	0.05	200,000	400,000	320,000	80,000	48,000	24.0%	260,000	140,000	84,000	42.0
Expected value:		100,000	$200,000	$170,000	$30,000	$18,000	9.0%	$160,000	$ 40,000	$ 24,000	12.0%
Standard deviation:					$24,698		7.4%		$ 49,396		14.8%
Coefficient of variation:					0.82		0.82		1.23		1.23

Notes:

^{a}Operating costs = Variable costs + Fixed costs.

^{b}The federal-plus-state tax rate is 40%, so NOPAT = EBIT(1 − Tax rate) = EBIT(0.6).

^{c}ROIC = NOPAT/Capital.

^{d}The break-even sales level for Plan B is not shown in the table, but it is 60,000 units or $120,000.

^{e}The expected value, standard deviations, and coefficients of variation were found using the procedures discussed in Chapter 6.

of fixed costs, $60,000. Here the firm uses automated equipment (with which one operator can turn out a few or many units at the same labor cost) to a much larger extent. The break-even point is higher under Plan B—breakeven occurs at 60,000 units under Plan B versus only 40,000 units under Plan A.

We can calculate the break-even quantity by recognizing that **operating breakeven** occurs when earnings before interest and taxes (EBIT) = 0:[3]

$$EBIT = PQ - VQ - F = 0. \qquad (16-3)$$

Here P is average sales price per unit of output, Q is units of output, V is variable cost per unit, and F is fixed operating costs. If we solve for the break-even quantity, Q_{BE}, we get this expression:

$$Q_{BE} = \frac{F}{P - V}. \qquad (16-4)$$

Thus for Plan A,

$$Q_{BE} = \frac{\$20,000}{\$2.00 - \$1.50} = 40,000 \text{ units,}$$

and for Plan B,

$$Q_{BE} = \frac{\$60,000}{\$2.00 - \$1.00} = 60,000 \text{ units.}$$

How does operating leverage affect business risk? *Other things held constant, the higher a firm's operating leverage, the higher its business risk.* The data in Figure 16-1 confirm this. Plan A's lower operating leverage gives rise to a much lower range of possible EBITs, from −$20,000 if demand is terrible to $80,000 if demand is wonderful, with a standard deviation of $24,698. Plan B's EBIT range is much larger, from −$60,000 to $140,000, and it has a standard deviation of $49,396. Plan A's ROIC range is lower as well, from −6.0% to 24.0%, with a standard deviation of 7.4%, versus Plan B's ROIC range of from −18% to 42%, with a standard deviation of 14.8%, which is twice as high as A's.

Even though Plan B is riskier, note also that it has a higher expected EBIT and ROIC: $40,000 and 12% versus A's $30,000 and 9%. Therefore, Strasburg must make a choice between a project with a higher expected return but more risk and one with less risk but a lower return. For the rest of this analysis, we assume that Strasburg has decided to go with Plan B because management believes that the higher expected return is sufficient to compensate for the higher risk.

To a large extent, operating leverage is determined by technology. Electric utilities, telephone companies, airlines, steel mills, and chemical companies simply *must* have large investments in fixed assets; this results in high fixed costs and operating leverage. Similarly, drug, auto, computer, and other companies must spend heavily to develop new products, and product-development costs increase operating leverage. Grocery stores, on the other hand, generally have significantly

---

[3]This definition of breakeven does not include any fixed financial costs because Strasburg is an unlevered firm. If there were fixed financial costs, the firm would suffer an accounting loss at the operating break-even point. We introduce financial costs shortly.

lower fixed costs, hence lower operating leverage. Although industry factors do exert a major influence, all firms have some control over their operating leverage. For example, an electric utility can expand its generating capacity by building either a gas-fired or a coal-fired plant. The coal plant would require a larger investment and would have higher fixed costs, but its variable operating costs would be relatively low. The gas-fired plant, on the other hand, would require a smaller investment and would have lower fixed costs, but the variable costs (for gas) would be high. Thus, by its capital budgeting decisions, a utility (or any other company) can influence its operating leverage, hence its business risk.[4]

Financial Risk

Financial risk is the additional risk placed on the common stockholders as a result of the decision to finance with debt. Conceptually, stockholders face a certain amount of risk that is inherent in a firm's operations—this is its business risk, which is defined as the uncertainty inherent in projections of future ROIC. If a firm uses debt (financial leverage), this concentrates its business risk on its common stockholders. To illustrate, suppose ten people decide to form a corporation to manufacture disk drives. There is a certain amount of business risk in the operation. If the firm is capitalized only with common equity, and if each person buys 10% of the stock, then each investor shares equally in the business risk. However, suppose the firm is capitalized with 50% debt and 50% equity, with five of the investors putting up their capital as debt and the other five putting up their money as equity. In this case, the five investors who put up the equity will have to bear *virtually all* of the business risk, so the common stock will be much riskier than it would have been had the firm been financed only with equity. Thus, the use of debt, or **financial leverage,** concentrates the firm's business risk on its stockholders. This concentration of business risk occurs because debtholders, who receive fixed interest payments, bear none of the business risk.[5]

e-resource

See **FM12 Ch 16 Tool Kit.xls** at the textbook's Web site for detailed calculations.

To illustrate the concentration of business risk, we can extend the Strasburg Electronics example. To date, the company has never used debt, but the treasurer is now considering a possible change in the capital structure. For now, assume that only two financing choices are being considered—remaining at zero debt, or shifting to $100,000 debt and $100,000 book equity.

First, focus on Section I of Table 16-1, which assumes that Strasburg uses no debt. Since debt is zero, interest is also zero; hence pre-tax income is equal to EBIT. Taxes at 40% are deducted to obtain net income, which is then divided by the $200,000 of book equity to calculate ROE. Note that Strasburg receives a tax credit if the demand is either terrible or poor (which are the two scenarios where net income is negative). Here we assume that Strasburg's losses can be carried back to offset income earned in the prior year. The ROE at each sales level is then multiplied by the probability of that sales level to calculate the 12% expected ROE. Note that this 12% is equal to the ROIC we found in Figure 16-1 for Plan B, since ROE is equal to ROIC if a firm has no debt.

Now let's look at the situation if Strasburg decides to use $100,000 of debt financing, shown in Section II of Table 16-1, with the debt costing 10%. Demand will not be affected, nor will operating costs; hence the EBIT columns are the same for the zero debt and $100,000 debt cases. However, the company will now have

---

[4]See **Web Extension 16A** for additional discussion of measuring the degree of operating leverage.
[5]Holders of corporate debt generally do bear some business risk, because they may lose some of their investment if the firm goes bankrupt. We discuss this in more depth later in the chapter.

Table 16-1

Effects of Financial Leverage: Strasburg Electronics Financed with Zero Debt or with $100,000 of Debt

Section I. Zero Debt

Debt   0
Book equity $200,000

Demand for Product (1)	Probability (2)	EBIT (3)	Interest (4)	Pre-Tax Income (5)	Taxes (40%) (6)	Net Income (7)	ROE (8)
Terrible	0.05	($ 60,000)	$0	($ 60,000)	($24,000)	($36,000)	−18.0%
Poor	0.20	(20,000)	0	(20,000)	(8,000)	(12,000)	−6.0
Normal	0.50	40,000	0	40,000	16,000	24,000	12.0
Good	0.20	100,000	0	100,000	40,000	60,000	30.0
Wonderful	0.05	140,000	0	140,000	56,000	84,000	42.0
Expected value:		$ 40,000	$0	$ 40,000	$16,000	$24,000	12.0%
Standard deviation:							14.8%
Coefficient of variation:							1.23

Section II. $100,000 of Debt

Debt $100,000
Book equity $100,000
Interest rate   10%

Demand for Product (1)	Probability (2)	EBIT (3)	Interest (4)	Pre-Tax Income (5)	Taxes (40%) (6)	Net Income (7)	ROE (8)
Terrible	0.05	($ 60,000)	$10,000	($ 70,000)	($28,000)	($42,000)	−42.0%
Poor	0.20	(20,000)	10,000	(30,000)	(12,000)	(18,000)	−18.0
Normal	0.50	40,000	10,000	30,000	12,000	18,000	18.0
Good	0.20	100,000	10,000	90,000	36,000	54,000	54.0
Wonderful	0.05	140,000	10,000	130,000	52,000	78,000	78.0
Expected value:		$ 40,000	$10,000	$ 30,000	$12,000	$18,000	18.0%
Standard deviation:							29.6%
Coefficient of variation:							1.65

Assumptions:

1. In terms of its operating leverage, Strasburg has chosen Plan B. The probability distribution and EBITs are obtained from Figure 16-1.
2. Sales and operating costs, hence EBIT, are not affected by the financing decision. Therefore, EBIT under both financing plans is identical, and it is taken from the EBIT column for Plan B in Figure 16-1.
3. All losses can be carried back to offset income in the prior year.

$100,000 of debt with a cost of 10%; hence its interest expense will be $10,000. This interest must be paid regardless of the state of the economy—if it is not paid, the company will be forced into bankruptcy, and stockholders will probably be wiped out. Therefore, we show a $10,000 cost in Column 4 as a fixed number for all demand conditions. Column 5 shows pre-tax income, Column 6 the applicable taxes, and Column 7 the resulting net income. When the net income figures are divided by the book equity—which will now be only $100,000 because $100,000 of the $200,000 total requirement was obtained as debt—we find the ROEs under each demand state. If demand is terrible and sales are zero, then a very large loss will be incurred, and the ROE will be −42.0%. However, if demand is wonderful, then ROE will be 78.0%. The probability-weighted average is the expected ROE, which is 18.0% if the company uses $100,000 of debt.

Typically, financing with debt increases the common stockholders' expected rate of return for an investment, but debt also increases the common stockholders' risk. This situation holds with our example—financial leverage raises the expected ROE from 12% to 18%, but it also increases the risk of the investment as seen by the increase in the standard deviation from 14.8% to 29.6% and the increase in the coefficient of variation from 1.23 to 1.65.[6]

We see, then, that using leverage has both good and bad effects: Higher leverage increases expected ROE, but it also increases risk. The next section discusses how this trade-off between risk and return affects the value of the firm.[7]

SELF-TEST

What is business risk, and how can it be measured?

What are some determinants of business risk?

How does operating leverage affect business risk?

What is financial risk, and how does it arise?

Explain this statement: "Using leverage has both good and bad effects."

A firm has fixed operating costs of $100,000 and variable costs of $4 per unit. If it sells the product for $6 per unit, what is the break-even quantity? (50,000)

16.3 Capital Structure Theory

In the previous section, we showed how capital structure choices affect a firm's ROE and its risk. For a number of reasons, we would expect capital structures to vary considerably across industries. For example, pharmaceutical companies generally have very different capital structures than airline companies. Moreover, capital structures vary among firms within a given industry. What factors explain these differences? In an attempt to answer this question, academics and practitioners have developed a number of theories, and the theories have been subjected to many empirical tests. The following sections examine several of these theories.[8]

---

[6]See Chapter 6 for a review of procedures for calculating the standard deviation and coefficient of variation. Recall that the advantage of the coefficient of variation is that it permits better comparisons when the expected values of ROE vary, as they do here for the two capital structures.

[7]For more on the links between market risk, operating risk, and financial leverage, see Carolyn M. Callahan and Rosanne M. Mohr, "The Determinants of Systematic Risk: A Synthesis," *The Financial Review*, May 1989, pp. 157–181; and Alexandros P. Prezas, "Effects of Debt on the Degrees of Operating and Financial Leverage," *Financial Management*, Summer 1987, pp. 39–44.

[8]For additional discussion of capital structure theories, see John C. Easterwood and Palani-Rajan Kadapakkam, "The Role of Private and Public Debt in Corporate Capital Structures," *Financial Management*, Autumn 1991, pp. 49–57; Gerald T. Garvey, "Leveraging the Underinvestment Problem: How High Debt and Management Shareholdings Solve the Agency Costs of Free Cash Flow," *Journal of Financial Research*, Summer 1992, pp. 149–166; Milton Harris and Artur Raviv, "Capital Structure and the Informational Role of Debt," *Journal of Finance*, June 1990, pp. 321–349; and Ronen Israel, "Capital Structure and the Market for Corporate Control: The Defensive Role of Debt Financing," *Journal of Finance*, September 1991, pp. 1391–1409.

Modigliani and Miller: No Taxes

Modern capital structure theory began in 1958, when Professors Franco Modigliani and Merton Miller (hereafter MM) published what has been called the most influential finance article ever written.[9] MM's study was based on some strong assumptions, including the following:

1. There are no brokerage costs.
2. There are no taxes.
3. There are no bankruptcy costs.
4. Investors can borrow at the same rate as corporations.
5. All investors have the same information as management about the firm's future investment opportunities.
6. EBIT is not affected by the use of debt.

If these assumptions hold true, MM proved that a firm's value is unaffected by its capital structure; hence the following situation must exist:

$$V_L = V_U = S_L + D. \tag{16-5}$$

Here V_L is the value of a levered firm, which is equal to V_U, the value of an identical but unlevered firm. S_L is the value of the levered firm's stock, and D is the value of its debt.

Recall that the WACC is a combination of the cost of debt and the relatively higher cost of equity, r_s. As leverage increases, more weight is given to low-cost debt, but equity gets riskier, driving up r_s. Under MM's assumptions, r_s increases by exactly enough to keep the WACC constant. Put another way, if MM's assumptions are correct, it does not matter how a firm finances its operations, so capital structure decisions would be irrelevant.

Despite the fact that some of these assumptions are obviously unrealistic, MM's irrelevance result is extremely important. By indicating the conditions under which capital structure is irrelevant, MM also provided us with clues about what is required for capital structure to be relevant and hence to affect a firm's value. MM's work marked the beginning of modern capital structure research, and subsequent research has focused on relaxing the MM assumptions in order to develop a more realistic theory of capital structure.

Another extremely important aspect of MM's work was their thought process. To make a long story short, they imagined two portfolios. The first contained all the equity of the unlevered firm, and it generated cash flows in the form of dividends. The second portfolio contained all the levered firm's stock and debt, so its cash flows were the levered firm's dividends and interest payments. Under MM's assumptions, the cash flows of the two portfolios would be identical. They then concluded that if two portfolios produce the same cash flows, they must have the same value.[10] As we showed in Chapter 9, this simple idea changed the entire

[9]Franco Modigliani and Merton H. Miller, "The Cost of Capital, Corporation Finance, and the Theory of Investment," *American Economic Review*, June 1958, pp. 261–297. Modigliani and Miller both won Nobel Prizes for their work.
[10]They actually showed that if the values of the two portfolios differed, then an investor could engage in riskless arbitrage: The investor could create a trading strategy (buying one portfolio and selling the other) that had no risk, required none of the investor's own cash, and resulted in a positive cash flow for the investor. This would be such a desirable strategy that everyone would try to implement it. But if everyone tries to buy the same portfolio, its price will be driven up by market demand, and if everyone tries to sell a portfolio, its price will be driven down. The net result of the trading activity would be to change the portfolio's values until they were equal and no more arbitrage was possible.

Yogi Berra on the MM Proposition

When a waitress asked Yogi Berra (Baseball Hall of Fame catcher for the New York Yankees) whether he wanted his pizza cut into four pieces or eight, Yogi replied: "Better make it four. I don't think I can eat eight."[a]

Yogi's quip helps convey the basic insight of Modigliani and Miller. The firm's choice of leverage "slices" the distribution of future cash flows in a way that is like slicing a pizza. MM recognized that if you fix a company's investment activities, it's like fixing

the size of the pizza; no information costs means that everyone sees the same pizza; no taxes means the IRS gets none of the pie; and no "contracting costs" means nothing sticks to the knife.

So, just as the substance of Yogi's meal is unaffected by whether the pizza is sliced into four pieces or eight, the economic substance of the firm is unaffected by whether the liability side of the balance sheet is sliced to include more or less debt, at least under the MM assumptions.

[a]Lee Green, *Sportswit* (New York: Fawcett Crest, 1984), p. 228.

Source: "Yogi Berra on the MM Proposition," *Journal of Applied Corporate Finance,* Winter 1995, p. 6. Reprinted by permission of Stern Stewart Management.

financial world because it led to the development of options and derivatives. Thus, their paper's approach was just as important as its conclusions.

Modigliani and Miller: The Effect of Corporate Taxes

MM published a follow-up paper in 1963 in which they relaxed the assumption that there are no corporate taxes.[11] The Tax Code allows corporations to deduct interest payments as an expense, but dividend payments to stockholders are not deductible. This differential treatment encourages corporations to use debt in their capital structures. This means that interest payments reduce the taxes paid by a corporation, and if a corporation pays less to the government, more of its cash flow is available for its investors. In other words, the tax deductibility of the interest payments shields the firm's pre-tax income.

As in their earlier paper, MM introduced a second important way of looking at the effect of capital structure: The value of a levered firm is the value of an otherwise identical unlevered firm plus the value of any "side effects." While others expanded on this idea, the only side effect MM considered was the tax shield:

$$V_L = V_U + \text{Value of side effects} = V_U + \text{PV of tax shield.} \qquad \text{(16-6)}$$

Under their assumptions, they showed that the present value of the tax shield is equal to the corporate tax rate, T, multiplied by the amount of debt, D:

$$V_L = V_U + TD. \qquad \text{(16-7)}$$

With a tax rate of about 40%, this implies that every dollar of debt adds about 40 cents of value to the firm, and this leads to the conclusion that the optimal capital

---

[11]Franco Modigliani and Merton H. Miller, "Corporate Income Taxes and the Cost of Capital: A Correction," *American Economic Review,* June 1963, pp. 433–443.

structure is virtually 100% debt. MM also showed that the cost of equity, r_s, increases as leverage increases, but that it doesn't increase quite as fast as it would if there were no taxes. As a result, under MM with corporate taxes the WACC falls as debt is added.

Miller: The Effect of Corporate and Personal Taxes

Merton Miller (this time without Modigliani) later brought in the effects of personal taxes.[12] He noted that all of the income from bonds is generally interest, which is taxed as personal income at rates (T_d) going up to 38.6%, while income from stocks generally comes partly from dividends and partly from capital gains. Further, long-term capital gains are taxed at a rate of 20%, and this tax is deferred until the stock is sold and the gain realized. If stock is held until the owner dies, no capital gains tax whatsoever must be paid. So, on average, returns on stocks are taxed at lower effective rates (T_s) than returns on debt.

Because of the tax situation, Miller argued that investors are willing to accept relatively low before-tax returns on stock relative to the before-tax returns on bonds. (The situation here is similar to that with tax-exempt municipal bonds as discussed in Chapter 5 and preferred stocks held by corporate investors as discussed in Chapter 8.) For example, an investor might require a return of 10% on Strasburg's bonds, and if stock income were taxed at the same rate as bond income, the required rate of return on Strasburg's stock might be 16% because of the stock's greater risk. However, in view of the favorable treatment of income on the stock, investors might be willing to accept a before-tax return of only 14% on the stock.

Thus, as Miller pointed out, (1) the *deductibility of interest* favors the use of debt financing, but (2) the *more favorable tax treatment of income from stock* lowers the required rate of return on stock and thus favors the use of equity financing.

Miller showed that the net impact of corporate and personal taxes is given by this equation:

$$V_L = V_U = \left[1 - \frac{(1 - T_c)(1 - T_s)}{(1 - T_d)} \right] D. \qquad \text{(16-8)}$$

Here T_c is the corporate tax rate, T_s is the personal tax rate on income from stocks, and T_d is the tax rate on income from debt. Miller argued that the marginal tax rates on stock and debt balance out in such a way that the bracketed term in Equation 16-8 is zero, so $V_L = V_U$, but most observers believe that there is still a tax advantage to debt. For example, with a 40% marginal corporate tax rate, a 30% marginal rate on debt, and a 12% marginal rate on stock, the advantage of debt financing is

$$V_L = V_U + \left[1 - \frac{(1 - 0.40)(1 - 0.12)}{(1 - 0.30)} \right] D \qquad \text{(16-8a)}$$

$$= V_U + 0.25D.$$

Thus it appears as though the presence of personal taxes reduces but does not completely eliminate the advantage of debt financing.

---

[12]Merton H. Miller, "Debt and Taxes," *Journal of Finance*, May 1977, pp. 261–275. Miller was president of the American Finance Association, and he delivered the paper as his presidential address.

Trade-Off Theory

MM's results also depend on the assumption that there are no **bankruptcy costs.** However, in practice bankruptcy can be quite costly. Firms in bankruptcy have very high legal and accounting expenses, and they also have a hard time retaining customers, suppliers, and employees. Moreover, bankruptcy often forces a firm to liquidate or sell assets for less than they would be worth if the firm were to continue operating. For example, if a steel manufacturer goes out of business, it might be hard to find buyers for the company's blast furnaces, even though they were quite expensive. Assets such as plant and equipment are often illiquid because they are configured to a company's individual needs and also because they are difficult to disassemble and move.

Note, too, that the *threat of bankruptcy*, not just bankruptcy per se, produces these problems. Key employees jump ship, suppliers refuse to grant credit, customers seek more stable suppliers, and lenders demand higher interest rates and impose more restrictive loan covenants if potential bankruptcy looms.

Bankruptcy-related problems are most likely to arise when a firm includes a great deal of debt in its capital structure. Therefore, bankruptcy costs discourage firms from pushing their use of debt to excessive levels.

Bankruptcy-related costs have two components: (1) the probability of financial distress and (2) the costs that would be incurred given that financial distress occurs. Firms whose earnings are more volatile, all else equal, face a greater chance of bankruptcy and, therefore, should use less debt than more stable firms. This is consistent with our earlier point that firms with high operating leverage, and thus greater business risk, should limit their use of financial leverage. Likewise, firms that would face high costs in the event of financial distress should rely less heavily on debt. For example, firms whose assets are illiquid and thus would have to be sold at "fire sale" prices should limit their use of debt financing.

The preceding arguments led to the development of what is called "the trade-off theory of leverage," in which firms trade off the benefits of debt financing (favorable corporate tax treatment) against the higher interest rates and bankruptcy costs. In essence, the **trade-off theory** says that the value of a levered firm is equal to the value of an unlevered firm plus the value of any side effects, which include the tax shield and the expected costs due to financial distress. A summary of the trade-off theory is expressed graphically in Figure 16-2. Here are some observations about the figure:

1. Under the assumptions of the Modigliani-Miller with-corporate-taxes paper, a firm's value will be maximized if it uses virtually 100% debt, and the line labeled "MM Result Incorporating the Effects of Corporate Taxation" in Figure 16-2 expresses the relationship between value and debt under their assumptions.

2. There is some threshold level of debt, labeled D_1 in Figure 16-2, below which the probability of bankruptcy is so low as to be immaterial. Beyond D_1, however, expected bankruptcy-related costs become increasingly important, and they reduce the tax benefits of debt at an increasing rate. In the range from D_1 to D_2, expected bankruptcy-related costs reduce but do not completely offset the tax benefits of debt, so the stock price rises (but at a decreasing rate) as the debt ratio increases. However, beyond D_2, expected bankruptcy-related costs exceed the tax benefits, so from this point on increasing the debt ratio lowers the value of the stock. Therefore, D_2 is the optimal capital structure. Of course, D_1 and D_2 vary from firm to firm, depending on their business risks and bankruptcy costs.

3. While theoretical and empirical work support the general shape of the curve in Figure 16-2, this graph must be taken as an approximation, not as a precisely defined function.

Figure 16-2

Effect of Leverage on Value

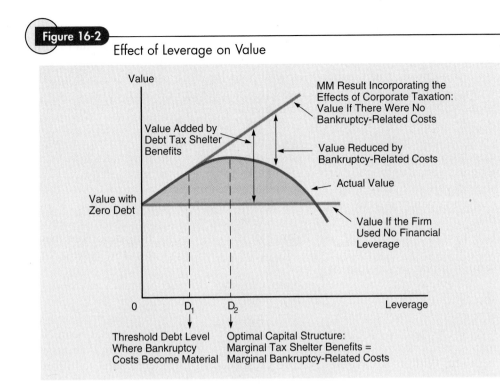

Signaling Theory

MM assumed that investors have the same information about a firm's prospects as its managers—this is called **symmetric information.** However, in fact managers often have better information than outside investors. This is called **asymmetric information,** and it has an important effect on the optimal capital structure. To see why, consider two situations, one in which the company's managers know that its prospects are extremely positive (Firm P) and one in which the managers know that the future looks negative (Firm N).

Suppose, for example, that Firm P's R&D labs have just discovered a non-patentable cure for the common cold. They want to keep the new product a secret as long as possible to delay competitors' entry into the market. New plants must be built to make the new product, so capital must be raised. How should Firm P's management raise the needed capital? If it sells stock, then, when profits from the new product start flowing in, the price of the stock would rise sharply, and the purchasers of the new stock would make a bonanza. The current stockholders (including the managers) would also do well, but not as well as they would have done if the company had not sold stock before the price increased, because then they would not have had to share the benefits of the new product with the new stockholders. *Therefore, one would expect a firm with very positive prospects to try to avoid selling stock and, rather, to raise any required new capital by other means, including using debt beyond the normal target capital structure.*[13]

Now let's consider Firm N. Suppose its managers have information that new orders are off sharply because a competitor has installed new technology

---

[13]It would be illegal for Firm P's managers to personally purchase more shares on the basis of their inside knowledge of the new product.

that has improved its products' quality. Firm N must upgrade its own facilities, at a high cost, just to maintain its current sales. As a result, its return on investment will fall (but not by as much as if it took no action, which would lead to a 100% loss through bankruptcy). How should Firm N raise the needed capital? Here the situation is just the reverse of that facing Firm P, which did not want to sell stock so as to avoid having to share the benefits of future developments. *A firm with negative prospects would want to sell stock, which would mean bringing in new investors to share the losses!*[14] The conclusion from all this is that firms with extremely bright prospects prefer not to finance through new stock offerings, whereas firms with poor prospects like to finance with outside equity. How should you, as an investor, react to this conclusion? You ought to say, "If I see that a company plans to issue new stock, this should worry me because I know that management would not want to issue stock if future prospects looked good. However, management *would* want to issue stock if things looked bad. Therefore, I should lower my estimate of the firm's value, other things held constant, if it plans to issue new stock."

If you gave the above answer, your views would be consistent with those of sophisticated portfolio managers. *In a nutshell, the announcement of a stock offering is generally taken as a* **signal** *that the firm's prospects as seen by its management are not bright. Conversely, a debt offering is taken as a positive signal.* Notice that Firm N's managers cannot make a false signal to investors by mimicking Firm P and issuing debt. With its unfavorable future prospects, issuing debt could soon force Firm N into bankruptcy. Given the resulting damage to the personal wealth and reputations of N's managers, they cannot afford to mimic Firm P. All of this suggests that when a firm announces a new stock offering, more often than not the price of its stock will decline. Empirical studies have shown that this situation does indeed exist.[15]

Reserve Borrowing Capacity

Because issuing stock emits a negative signal and thus tends to depress the stock price, even if the company's prospects are bright, it should, in normal times, maintain a **reserve borrowing capacity** that can be used in the event that some especially good investment opportunity comes along. *This means that firms should, in normal times, use more equity and less debt than is suggested by the tax benefit/bankruptcy cost trade-off model expressed in Figure 16-2.*

The Pecking Order Hypothesis

The presence of flotation costs and asymmetric information may cause a firm to raise capital according to a **pecking order.** In this situation a firm first raises capital internally by reinvesting its net income and selling off its short-term marketable securities. When that supply of funds has been exhausted, the firm will issue debt and perhaps preferred stock. Only as a last resort will the firm issue common stock.[16]

---

[14]Of course, Firm N would have to make certain disclosures when it offered new shares to the public, but it might be able to meet the legal requirements without fully disclosing management's worst fears.
[15]See Paul Asquith and David W. Mullins, Jr., "The Impact of Initiating Dividend Payments on Shareholders' Wealth," *Journal of Business,* January 1983, pp. 77–96.
[16]For more, see Jonathon Baskin, "An Empirical Investigation of the Pecking Order Hypothesis," *Financial Management,* Spring 1989, pp. 26–35.

Using Debt Financing to Constrain Managers

Agency problems may arise if managers and shareholders have different objectives. Such conflicts are particularly likely when the firm's managers have too much cash at their disposal. Managers often use excess cash to finance pet projects or for perquisites such as nicer offices, corporate jets, and sky boxes at sports arenas, all of which may do little to maximize stock prices. Even worse, managers might be tempted to pay too much for an acquisition, something that could cost shareholders hundreds of millions of dollars. By contrast, managers with limited "excess cash flow" are less able to make wasteful expenditures.

Firms can reduce excess cash flow in a variety of ways. One way is to funnel some of it back to shareholders through higher dividends or stock repurchases. Another alternative is to shift the capital structure toward more debt in the hope that higher debt service requirements will force managers to be more disciplined. If debt is not serviced as required, the firm will be forced into bankruptcy, in which case its managers would likely lose their jobs. Therefore, a manager is less likely to buy an expensive new corporate jet if the firm has large debt service requirements that could cost the manager his or her job. In short, high levels of debt **bond the cash flow,** since much of it is precommitted to servicing the debt.

A **leveraged buyout (LBO)** is one way to bond cash flow. In an LBO debt is used to finance the purchase of a company's shares, after which the firm "goes private." Many leveraged buyouts, which were especially common during the late 1980s, were designed specifically to reduce corporate waste. As noted, high debt payments force managers to conserve cash by eliminating unnecessary expenditures.

Of course, increasing debt and reducing the available cash flow has its downside: It increases the risk of bankruptcy. One professor has argued that adding debt to a firm's capital structure is like putting a dagger into the steering wheel of a car.[17] The dagger—which points toward your stomach—motivates you to drive more carefully, but you may get stabbed if someone runs into you, even if you are being careful. The analogy applies to corporations in the following sense: Higher debt forces managers to be more careful with shareholders' money, but even well-run firms could face bankruptcy (get stabbed) if some event beyond their control such as a war, an earthquake, a strike, or a recession occurs. To complete the analogy, the capital structure decision comes down to deciding how large a dagger stockholders should use to keep managers in line.

Finally, too much debt may overconstrain managers. A large portion of a manager's personal wealth and reputation is tied to a single company, so managers are not well diversified. When faced with a positive NPV project that is risky, a manager may decide that it's not worth taking on the risk, even when well-diversified stockholders would find the risk acceptable. As previously mentioned, this is an underinvestment problem. The more debt the firm has, the greater the likelihood of financial distress, and thus the greater the likelihood that managers will forgo risky projects even if they have positive NPVs.

The Investment Opportunity Set and Reserve Borrowing Capacity

Bankruptcy and financial distress are costly, and, as noted above, this can discourage highly levered firms from undertaking risky new investments. If potential new investments, although risky, have positive net present values, then high

[17]Ben Bernanke, "Is There Too Much Corporate Debt?" *Federal Reserve Bank of Philadelphia Business Review,* September/October 1989, pp. 3–13.

levels of debt can be doubly costly—the expected financial distress and bankruptcy costs are high, and the firm loses potential value by not making some potentially profitable investments. On the other hand, if a firm has very few profitable investment opportunities, then high levels of debt can keep managers from wasting money by investing in poor projects. For such companies, increases in the debt ratio can increase the value of the firm.

Thus, in addition to the tax, signaling, bankruptcy, and managerial constraint effects discussed earlier, the firm's optimal capital structure is related to its set of investment opportunities. Firms with many profitable opportunities should maintain their ability to invest by using low levels of debt, which is also consistent with maintaining reserve borrowing capacity. Firms with few profitable investment opportunities should use high levels of debt and thus have substantial interest payments, which means imposing managerial constraint through debt.[18]

Windows of Opportunity

If markets are efficient, then security prices should reflect all available information, so they are neither underpriced nor overpriced (except during the time it takes prices to move to a new equilibrium caused by the release of new information). The *windows of opportunity theory* states that managers don't believe this, but instead think that stock prices and interest rates are sometimes either too low or high relative to their true fundamental values. In particular, the theory suggests that managers issue equity when they believe stock market prices are abnormally high and issue debt when they believe interest rates are abnormally low. In other words, they try to time the market.[19] Notice that this differs from signaling theory because no asymmetric information is involved: These managers aren't basing their beliefs on insider information, just on a difference of opinion with the market consensus.

SELF-TEST
Why does the MM theory with corporate taxes lead to 100% debt?
Explain how *asymmetric information* and *signals* affect capital structure decisions.
What is meant by *reserve borrowing capacity*, and why is it important to firms?
How can the use of debt serve to discipline managers?

16.4 Capital Structure Evidence and Implications

There have been hundreds, perhaps even thousands, of papers testing the capital structure theories described in the previous section and we can only cover the highlights here.[20]

Empirical Evidence

Studies show that firms do benefit from the tax deductibility of interest payments, with a typical firm increasing in value by about $0.10 for every dollar of debt. This is much less than the corporate tax rate, so this supports the Miller model

---

[18]See Michael J. Barclay and Clifford W. Smith, Jr., "The Capital Structure Puzzle: Another Look at the Evidence," *Journal of Applied Corporate Finance*, Spring 1999, pp. 8–20.
[19]See Malcolm Baker and Jeffrey Wurgler, "Market Timing and Capital Structure," *Journal of Finance*, February 2002, pp. 1–32.
[20]This section also draws heavily from Barclay and Smith, "The Capital Structure Puzzle"; Jay Ritter, ed., *Recent Developments in Corporate Finance* (Northampton, MA: Edward Elgar Publishing Inc., 2005); and a presentation by Jay Ritter at the 2003 FMA meetings, "The Windows of Opportunity Theory of Capital Structure."

(with personal taxes) more than the MM model (with only corporate taxes). Recent evidence shows that the cost of bankruptcies can be as much as 10% to 20% of the firm's value.[21] Thus, the evidence shows the existence of tax benefits and financial distress costs, which provides support for the trade-off theory.

A particularly interesting study by Professors Mehotra, Mikkelson, and Partch examined the capital structure of firms that were spun off from their parents.[22] The financing choices of existing firms might be influenced by their past financing choices and by the costs of moving from one capital structure to another, but because spin-offs are newly created companies, managers can choose a capital structure without regard to these issues. The study finds that more profitable firms (which have a lower expected probability of bankruptcy) and more asset-intensive firms (which have better collateral and thus a lower cost of bankruptcy should one occur) have higher levels of debt. These findings support the trade-off theory.

However, there is also evidence that is inconsistent with a static optimal target capital structure as implied by the trade-off theory. For example, stock prices are very volatile, which causes a firm's actual market-based debt ratio to deviate frequently from its target. However, such deviations don't cause firms to immediately issue or repurchase securities in an effort to return to the target. This inertia indicates that if there is an optimal capital structure as implied by the trade-off theory, firms don't try to maintain it very closely.

In fact, if stock prices have a big run-up, which reduces the debt ratio, the trade-off theory suggests that firms should issue debt to return to their target. However, firms tend to do the opposite, and issue stock after big run-ups. This is much more consistent with the windows of opportunity theory, with managers trying to time the market by issuing stock when they perceive the market to be overvalued. Furthermore, firms tend to issue debt when stock prices and interest rates are low. The maturity of the issued debt seems to reflect an attempt to time interest rates: Firms tend to issue short-term debt if the term structure is upward sloping but long-term debt if the term structure is flat. Again, these facts suggest that managers try to time the market, which is consistent with the windows of opportunity theory.

Firms issue equity much less frequently than debt. On the surface, this seems to support both the pecking order hypothesis and the signaling hypothesis. The pecking order hypothesis predicts that firms with a high level of informational asymmetry, which causes equity issuances to be costly, should issue debt before issuing equity. However, we often see the opposite, with high-growth firms (which usually have greater informational asymmetry) issuing more equity than debt. Also, many highly profitable firms could afford to issue debt (which comes before equity in the pecking order) but instead choose to issue equity. With respect to the signaling hypothesis, consider the case of firms that have large increases in earnings that were unanticipated by the market. If managers have superior information, they will anticipate these upcoming performance improvements and issue debt before the increase. Such firms do, in fact, tend to issue debt slightly more frequently than other firms, but the difference isn't economically meaningful.

Many firms have less debt than might be expected, and many have large amounts of short-term investments. This is especially true for firms with high market/book ratios (which indicate many growth options and informational asymmetry problems). This behavior is consistent with the hypothesis that investment opportunities influence attempts to maintain reserve borrowing capacity. It is also consistent

---

[21]The *expected cost* of financial distress is the product of bankruptcy costs and the probability of bankruptcy. At moderate levels of debt with low probabilities of bankruptcy, the expected cost of financial distress would be much less than actual bankruptcy costs if the firm failed.
[22]See V. Mehotra, W. Mikkelson, and M. Partch, "The Design of Financial Policies in Corporate Spin-offs," *Review of Financial Studies,* Winter 2003, pp. 1359–1388.

Taking a Look at Global Capital Structures

To what extent does capital structure vary across different countries? The accompanying table, which is taken from a study by Raghuram Rajan and Luigi Zingales, both of the University of Chicago, shows the median debt ratios of firms in the largest industrial countries.

Rajan and Zingales also show that there is considerable variation in capital structure among firms within each of the seven countries. However, they also show that capital structures for the firms in each country are generally determined by a similar set of factors: firm size, profitability, market-to-book ratio, and the ratio of fixed assets to total assets. All in all, the Rajan–Zingales study suggests that the points developed in the chapter apply to firms all around the world.

Median Percentage of Debt to Total Assets in Different Countries

Country	Book Value Debt Ratio
Canada	32%
France	18
Germany	11
Italy	21
Japan	21
United Kingdom	10
United States	25

Source: Raghuram G. Rajan and Luigi Zingales, "What Do We Know about Capital Structure? Some Evidence from International Data," *The Journal of Finance*, December 1995, pp. 1421–1460.

with tax considerations, since low-growth firms, which have more debt, are more likely to be able to use the tax shield. This behavior is not consistent with the pecking order hypothesis, where low-growth firms, which often have high free cash flow, would be able to avoid issuing debt by raising funds internally.

Summarizing these results, it appears that firms try to capture debt's tax benefits while avoiding financial distress costs. However, they also allow their debt ratios to deviate from the static optimal target ratio implied by the trade-off theory. There is a little evidence indicating that firms follow a pecking order and use security issuances as signals, but there is much more evidence in support of the windows of opportunity theory. Finally, it appears that firms often maintain reserve borrowing capacity, especially those with many growth opportunities or problems with informational asymmetry.[23]

Implications for Managers

Managers should explicitly consider tax benefits when making capital structure decisions. Tax benefits obviously are more valuable for firms with high tax rates. Firms can utilize tax loss carryforwards and carrybacks, but the time value of

[23]For more on empirical tests of capital structure theory, see Gregor Andrade and Steven Kaplan, "How Costly Is Financial (Not Economic) Distress? Evidence from Highly Leveraged Transactions That Became Distressed," *Journal of Finance*, 1998, pp. 1443–1493; Malcolm Baker, Robin Greenwood, and Jeffrey Wurgler, "The Maturity of Debt Issues and Predictable Variation in Bond Returns," *Journal of Financial Economics*, November 2003, pp. 261–291; Murray Z. Frank and Vidhan K. Goyal, "Testing the Pecking Order Theory of Capital Structure," *Journal of Financial Economics*, February 2003, pp. 217–248; Michael Long and Ileen Malitz, "The Investment-Financing Nexus: Some Empirical Evidence," *Midland Corporate Finance Journal*, Fall 1985, pp. 53–59.

money means that tax benefits are more valuable for firms with stable, positive pre-tax income. Therefore, a firm whose sales are relatively stable can safely take on more debt and incur higher fixed charges than a company with volatile sales. Other things being equal, a firm with less operating leverage is better able to employ financial leverage because it will have less business risk and less volatile earnings.

Managers should also consider the expected cost of financial distress, which depends on the probability and cost of distress. Notice that stable sales and lower operating leverage provide tax benefits but also reduce the *probability* of financial distress. One *cost* of financial distress comes from lost investment opportunities. Firms with profitable investment opportunities need to be able to fund them, either by holding higher levels of marketable securities or by maintaining excess borrowing capacity. An astute corporate treasurer made this statement to the authors:

"Our company can earn a lot more money from good capital budgeting and operating decisions than from good financing decisions. Indeed, we are not sure exactly how financing decisions affect our stock price, but we know for sure that having to turn down a promising venture because funds are not available will reduce our long-run profitability."

Another cost of financial distress is the possibility of being forced to sell assets to meet liquidity needs. General-purpose assets that can be used by many businesses are relatively liquid and make good collateral, in contrast to special-purpose assets. Thus, real estate companies are usually highly levered, whereas companies involved in technological research are not.

Asymmetric information also has a bearing on capital structure decisions. For example, suppose a firm has just successfully completed an R&D program, and it forecasts higher earnings in the immediate future. However, the new earnings are not yet anticipated by investors, hence are not reflected in the stock price. This company should not issue stock—it should finance with debt until the higher earnings materialize and are reflected in the stock price. Then it could issue common stock, retire the debt, and return to its target capital structure.

Managers should consider conditions in the stock and bond markets. For example, during a recent credit crunch, the junk bond market dried up, and there was simply no market at a "reasonable" interest rate for any new long-term bonds rated below BBB. Therefore, low-rated companies in need of capital were forced to go to the stock market or to the short-term debt market, regardless of their target capital structures. When conditions eased, however, these companies sold bonds to get their capital structures back on target.

Finally, managers should always consider lenders' and rating agencies' attitudes. For example, one large utility was recently told by Moody's and Standard & Poor's that its bonds would be downgraded if it issued more debt. This influenced its decision to finance its expansion with common equity. This doesn't mean that managers should never increase debt if it will cause their bond rating to fall, but managers should always factor this into their decision making.[24]

SELF-TEST

Which capital structure theories does the empirical evidence seem to support?

What issues should managers consider when making capital structure decisions?

---

[24]For some insights into how practicing financial managers view the capital structure decision, see John Graham and Campbell Harvey, "The Theory and Practice of Corporate Finance: Evidence from the Field," *Journal of Financial Economics*, 2001, pp. 187–243; Ravindra R. Kamath, "Long-Term Financing Decisions: Views and Practices of Financial Managers of NYSE Firms," *Financial Review*, May 1997, pp. 331–356; Edgar Norton, "Factors Affecting Capital Structure Decisions," *Financial Review*, August 1991, pp. 431–446; J. Michael Pinegar and Lisa Wilbricht, "What Managers Think of Capital Structure Theory: A Survey," *Financial Management*, Winter 1989, pp. 82–91.

Table 16-3

Strasburg's Optimal Capital Structure

Percent Financed with Debt, w_d (1)	Market Debt/Equity, D/S (2)[a]	After-Tax Cost of Debt, $(1-T)r_d$ (3)[b]	Estimated Beta, b (4)[c]	Cost of Equity, r_s (5)[d]	WACC (6)[e]	Value of Operations, V_{op} (7)[f]
0%	0.00%	4.80%	1.00	12.0%	12.00%	$200,000
10	11.11	4.80	1.07	12.4	11.64	206,186
20	25.00	4.86	1.15	12.9	11.29	212,540
30	42.86	5.10	1.26	13.5	11.01	217,984
40	**66.67**	**5.40**	**1.40**	**14.4**	**10.80**	**222,222**
50	100.00	6.60	1.60	15.6	11.10	216,216
60	150.00	8.40	1.90	17.4	12.00	200,000

Notes:

[a]The D/S ratio is calculated as D/S = $w_d/(1 - w_d)$.
[b]The interest rates are shown in Table 16-2, and the tax rate is 40%.
[c]The beta is estimated using Hamada's formula in Equation 16-9.
[d]The cost of equity is estimated using the CAPM formula: $r_s = r_{RF} + (RP_M)b$, where the risk-free rate is 6% and the market risk premium is 6%.
[e]The weighted average cost of capital is calculated using Equation 16-2: WACC = $w_{ce}r_s + w_d r_d(1 - T)$, where $w_{ce} = (1 - w_d)$.
[f]The value of the firm's operations is calculated using the free cash flow valuation formula in Equation 16-1, modified to reflect the fact that since Strasburg has zero growth, V_{op} = FCF/WACC. Strasburg has zero growth, so it requires no investment in capital and its FCF is equal to its NOPAT. Using the EBIT shown in Table 16-1:

$$FCF = NOPAT - Investment \ in \ capital = EBIT(1 - T) - 0$$

$$= \$40,000(1 - 0.4) = \$24,000.$$

If Strasburg changes its capital structure by adding debt, this would increase the risk stockholders bear. That, in turn, would result in an additional risk premium. Conceptually, this situation would exist:

$$r_s = r_{RF} + Premium \ for \ business \ risk + Premium \ for \ financial \ risk.$$

Column 4 of Table 16-3 shows Strasburg's estimated beta for the capital structures under consideration. Figure 16-3 (using data calculated in Column 5 of Table 16-3) graphs Strasburg's required return on equity at different debt ratios. As the figure shows, r_s consists of the 6% risk-free rate, a constant 6% premium for business risk, and a premium for financial risk that starts at zero but rises at an increasing rate as the debt ratio increases.

3. Estimating the Weighted Average Cost of Capital, WACC

Column 6 of Table 16-3 shows Strasburg's weighted average cost of capital, WACC, at different capital structures. Currently, it has no debt, so its capital structure is 100% equity, and at this point WACC = r_s = 12%. As Strasburg begins to use debt (which has a lower cost than equity), the WACC declines. However, as the debt ratio increases, the costs of both debt and equity rise, at first slowly but

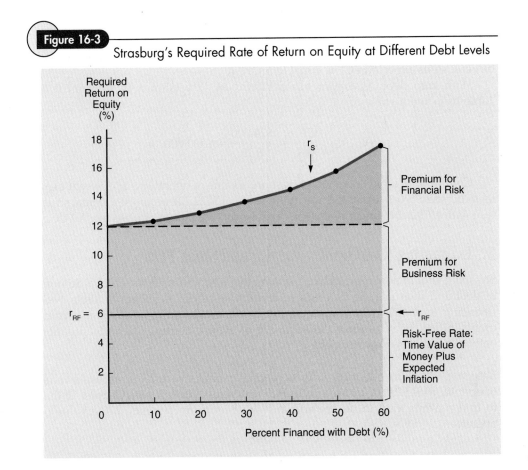

Figure 16-3

Strasburg's Required Rate of Return on Equity at Different Debt Levels

then at a faster and faster rate. Eventually, the increasing costs of the two components offset the fact that more debt (which is still less costly than equity) is being used. At 40% debt, Strasburg's WACC hits a minimum of 10.8%, and after that it rises with further increases in the debt ratio.

Note too that even though the component cost of equity is always higher than that of debt, using only lower-cost debt would not maximize value because of the feedback effects on the costs of debt and equity. If Strasburg were to issue more than 40% debt, the costs of both debt and equity would increase. Even though the cost of debt would be lower than the cost of equity, the overall WACC would increase because the costs of debt and equity increase.

4. Estimating the Firm's Value

We can estimate Strasburg's value of operations using Equation 16-1. Because Strasburg has zero growth, we can use the constant growth version of Equation 16-1:

$$V_{op} = \frac{FCF}{WACC}. \qquad \textbf{(16-1a)}$$

Recall that FCF is net operating profit after taxes (NOPAT) minus the required net investment in capital. Table 16-1 shows that Strasburg has an expected EBIT of

$40,000. With a tax rate of 40%, its expected NOPAT is $24,000 = $40,000 × (1 − 0.40). Since Strasburg has zero growth, its future net investments in operating assets will be zero, so its expected FCF is equal to NOPAT.

With zero debt, Strasburg has a WACC of 12% (shown in Column 6 of Table 16-3) and a value of

$$V_{op} = \frac{FCF}{WACC} = \frac{\$24,000}{0.12} = \$200,000.$$

Column 7 of Table 16-3 shows Strasburg's value of operations at different capital structures.[26] Notice that the maximum value of $222,222 occurs at a capital structure with 40% debt, which is also the capital structure that minimizes the WACC.

5. Estimating Shareholder Wealth and Stock Price

Strasburg should now **recapitalize,** meaning that it should issue the optimal amount of debt and then use the proceeds to repurchase stock. As shown in Table 16-3, financing with 40% debt is optimal. But before tackling the **recap,** as it is commonly called, let's consider the sequence of events, starting with the situation before Strasburg issues any debt.

Strasburg's Original Situation   At its original capital structure, Strasburg's value of operations is $200,000, based on its FCF and WACC. Recall from Chapter 15 that to find a firm's total value, we add any short-term investments to the value of operations:

$$\text{Total corporate value} = V_{op} + \text{Value of short-term investments.}$$

Strasburg has no short-term investments, so its total value is

$$\text{Total corporate value} = \$200,000 + \$0 = \$200,000.$$

To find the initial estimated market value of equity, S_0, we subtract debt from the total value:[27]

$$S_0 = \text{Total corporate value} - \text{Value of all debt.}$$

Strasburg has no debt, so its equity value is

$$S_0 = \$200,000 - \$0 = \$200,000.$$

To find the stock price, we divide the equity value by the initial number of shares, n_0. Strasburg has 10,000 shares, so its price per share is $200,000/10,000 = $20. These calculations are summarized in Column 1 of Table 16-4. Column 1 also shows the wealth of the shareholders. The shareholders own Strasburg's equity, which is worth $200,000. Strasburg has not yet made any cash distributions to shareholders, so the total wealth of shareholders is $200,000.

---

[26]In this analysis we assume that Strasburg's expected EBIT and FCF are constant for the various capital structures. In a more refined analysis we might try to estimate any possible declines in FCF at high levels of debt as the threat of bankruptcy becomes imminent.
[27]We would also subtract preferred stock if the company has any.

Table 16-4

Anatomy of·a Recapitalization

	Before Debt Issue (1)	After Debt Issue, But Before Repurchase (2)	After Repurchase (3)
V_{op}	$200,000	$222,222	$222,222
+ ST investments	0	88,889	0
V_{Total}	$200,000	$311,111	$222,222
− Debt	0	88,889	88,889
Value of equity (S)	$200,000	$222,222	$133,333
÷ No. shares	10,000	10,000	6,000
P	$20.00	$22.22	$22.22
Value of stock	$200,000	$222,222	$133,333
+ Cash distributed in repurchase	0	0	88,889
Wealth of shareholders	$200,000	$222,222	$222,222

Strasburg Issues New Debt The next step in the recap is to issue debt and announce the firm's intent to repurchase stock with the newly issued debt. We know the percent of debt in the new target capital structure and we know the resulting value of the firm, so we can find the dollar value of debt as follows:[28]

$$D = w_d V_{op}.$$

At the optimal capital structure of 40% debt, the value of the firm's operations is $222,222, as shown in Table 16-3. Therefore, the dollar value of debt in the optimal capital structure is about $88,889 = 0.40($222,222).[29] The amount of cash raised by issuing debt is

$$\text{Cash raised by issuing debt} = D - D_0,$$

where D_0 is the amount of debt the company has before any new debt is issued. Strasburg has no debt to start with, so Strasburg raises $88,889 with its debt issuance.

After issuing the debt but before repurchasing stock, Strasburg will temporarily put the cash proceeds from the debt issue into short-term investments until it is able to complete the repurchase, as shown in Column 2 of Table 16-4. Notice that the debt issuance has two major effects. First, the lower cost of capital causes the value of operations to increase to $222,222. Second, the firm temporarily has short-term investments equal to $88,889. Therefore, at the point in time after issuing debt but before repurchasing stock, Strasburg's total value is

$$\text{Total corporate value} = \$222,222 + \$88,889 = \$311,111.$$

---

[28]Strasburg does not plan on holding any short-term investments after the recap is completed. Therefore, after the recap the value of operations will also equal the total value of the firm.
[29]These calculations are shown in the *Excel* file **FM12 Ch 16 Tool Kit.xls** at the textbook's Web site. The values in the text are rounded, but the values used in calculations in the spreadsheet are not rounded.

The value of equity after the debt issue but prior to the repurchase, S_{Prior}, is

$$S_{Prior} = \text{Value of equity after the debt issue but prior to the repurchase}$$

$$= \text{Total corporate value} - \text{Value of all debt}$$

$$= \$311,111 - \$88,889 = \$222,222.$$

The price per share after issuing debt but prior to repurchasing stock, P_{Prior}, is

$$P_{Prior} = \text{Price per share after debt issue but prior to repurchase}$$

$$= \frac{\text{Value of equity after debt issue but prior to repurchase}}{\text{Number of shares outstanding prior to repurchase}}$$

$$= S_{Prior}/n_0.$$

Because Strasburg has not yet repurchased any stock, it still has 10,000 shares outstanding. Therefore, the price per share after the debt issue but prior to the repurchase is

$$P_{Prior} = S_{Prior}/n_0$$

$$= \$222,222/10,000 = \$22.22.$$

Column 2 of Table 16-4 summarizes these calculations. Column 2 also shows the wealth of the shareholders. The shareholders own Strasburg's equity, which is worth $222,222. Strasburg has not yet made any cash distributions to shareholders, so the total wealth of shareholders is $222,222. The new wealth of $222,222 is greater than the initial wealth of $200,000, so the recapitalization has added value to Strasburg's shareholders.

Comparing Column 2 of Table 16-4 with Column 1, we see that the issuance of debt and the resulting change to the optimal capital structure: (1) decreases the WACC, (2) increases the value of operations, (3) increases shareholder wealth, and (4) increases the stock price.

Strasburg Repurchases Stock   What happens to the stock price during the repurchase? The short answer is "nothing." It is true that the additional debt will change the WACC and the stock price prior to the repurchase, but the subsequent repurchase itself will not affect the stock price.[30] To see why this is true, suppose the stock price is expected to increase after the repurchase. If this were true, it would be possible for an investor to buy the stock the day before the repurchase and then reap a reward the very next day. Current stockholders would realize this and would refuse to sell the stock unless they were paid the price that is expected immediately after the repurchase. Now suppose the stock price is expected to fall immediately after the repurchase. If this were true, current shareholders would try to sell the stock prior to the repurchase, but their actions would drive the price down to the price that is expected after the repurchase. As this "thought experiment" shows, the repurchase itself does not change the stock price.

---

[30]As we discuss in Chapter 18, a stock repurchase may be a signal of a company's future prospects, or it may be the way a company "announces" a change in capital structure, and either of those situations could have an impact on estimated free cash flows or WACC. However, neither situation applies to Strasburg.

Therefore, the post-repurchase price, P, is equal to P_{Prior}, the stock price after the debt issue but prior to the repurchase:

$$P = P_{Prior}.$$

For Strasburg, the price prior to the repurchase is $22.22, and the price after the repurchase is $22.22. This is also the price Strasburg pays to repurchase shares during the repurchase.

Strasburg uses the entire amount of cash raised by the debt issue to repurchase stock. As shown earlier, the total cash raised is equal to $D_0 - D$. The number of shares repurchased is equal to the cash raised by issuing debt divided by the repurchase price:

$$\text{Number of shares repurchased} = \frac{\text{Cash raised by issuing debt}}{\text{Repurchase price}}$$

$$= \frac{D - D_0}{P}.$$

(16-11)

Strasburg repurchases ($88,889 - $0)/$22.22 = 4,000 shares of stock.

The number of remaining shares after the repurchase, n, is equal to the initial number of shares minus the number that is repurchased:

$$n = \text{Number of outstanding shares remaining after the repurchase}$$

$$= n_0 - \text{Number of shares repurchased}$$

$$= n_0 - \frac{D - D_0}{P}.$$

(16-12)

For Strasburg, the number of remaining shares after the repurchase is

$$n = n_0 - (D - D_0)/P$$

$$= 10,000 - (\$88,889 - \$0)/\$22.22$$

$$= 10,000 - 4,000 = 6,000.$$

Column 3 of Table 16-4 summarizes these post-repurchase results. The repurchase doesn't change the value of operations, which remains at $222,222. However, the short-term investments are sold and the cash is used to repurchase stock. Strasburg is left with no short-term investments, so its total value is $222,222. The repurchase doesn't affect the amount of debt, so Strasburg's value of equity is equal to its total value minus the debt:

$$S = \$222,222 - \$88,889 = \$133,333.$$

After the repurchase, Strasburg has 6,000 shares of stock. The price per share is

$$P = S/n = \$133,333/6,000 = \$22.22.$$

Shareholders now own an equity position in the company worth only $133,333, but they have received a cash distribution in the amount of $88,889, so their total wealth is equal to the value of their equity plus the amount of cash they received: $133,333 + $88,889 = $222,222.

Here are some points worth noting. As shown in Column 2 of Table 16-4, the change in capital structure clearly added wealth to the shareholders, increased the price per share, and increased the cash (in the form of short-term investments) temporarily held by the company. However, the repurchase itself did not affect shareholder wealth or the price per share. The repurchase did reduce the cash held by the company and the number of shares outstanding, but shareholder wealth stayed constant. After the repurchase, shareholders directly own the funds used in the repurchase; before the repurchase, shareholders indirectly own funds. In either case, shareholders own the funds. The repurchase simply takes them out of the company's account and puts them into the shareholders' personal accounts.

The approach described above is based on the corporate valuation model and it will always provide the correct value for S, S_{Prior}, and P. However, there is a quicker way. After the recap is completed, the percent of equity in the capital structure, based on market values, is equal to $1 - w_d$. Therefore, the value of equity after the repurchase is

$$
\begin{aligned}
S &= V_{op}(1 - w_d) \\
&= \$222{,}222(1 - 0.4) = \$133{,}333,
\end{aligned}
\tag{16-13}
$$

which is the same answer we obtained earlier.

The wealth of the shareholders after the debt is issued but prior to the repurchase is equal to S_{Prior}. Wealth doesn't change during the repurchase, so S_{Prior} is equal to the value of equity after completion of the recapitalization plus the cash shareholders receive in the repurchase. Therefore, S_{Prior} is

$$
\begin{aligned}
S_{Prior} &= S + (D - D_0) \\
&= \$133{,}333 + (\$88{,}889 - \$0) = \$222{,}222,
\end{aligned}
\tag{16-14}
$$

as we obtained earlier.

We can use these relationships to define P:[31]

$$
\begin{aligned}
P &= P_{Prior} \\
&= S_{Prior}/n_0 \\
&= [S + (D - D_0)]/n_0 \\
&= [\$133{,}333 + (\$88{,}889 - \$0)]/10{,}000 \\
&= \$22.22.
\end{aligned}
\tag{16-15}
$$

---

[31]There are other ways to obtain Equation 16-15. By definition, $P = S/n$. Since P is also the stock price immediately prior to the repurchase and all debt proceeds are used to repurchase stock, the dollar value of repurchased shares is $P(n_0 - n) = D - D_0$. We have two equations, one defining the price per share after the repurchase and one defining the dollar value of repurchased stock. We have two unknowns, n and P. We can solve for the repurchase price: $P = (S + D - D_0)/n_0$.

Table 16-5

Strasburg's Stock Price and Earnings per Share

Percent Financed with Debt, w_d (1)	Value of Operations, V_{op} (2)[a]	Market Value of Debt, D (3)[b]	Market Value of Equity, S (4)[c]	Stock Price, P (5)[d]	Number of Shares after Repurchase, n (6)[e]	Net Income, NI (7)[f]	Earnings per Share, EPS (8)[g]
0%	$200,000	$ 0	$200,000	$20.00	$10,000	$24,000	$2.40
10	206,186	20,619	185,567	20.62	9,000	23,010	2.56
20	212,540	42,508	170,032	21.25	8,000	21,934	2.74
30	217,984	65,395	152,589	21.80	7,000	20,665	2.95
40	222,222	88,889	133,333	22.22	6,000	19,200	3.20
50	216,216	108,108	108,108	21.62	5,000	16,865	3.37
60	200,000	120,000	80,000	20.00	4,000	13,920	3.48

Notes:
[a] The value of operations is taken from Table 16-3.
[b] The value of debt is found by multiplying w_d from Column 1 by V_{op} from Column 2.
[c] The value of equity is found by multiplying $(1 - w_d)$ by V_{op}.
[d] The number of outstanding shares prior to the recap is $n_0 = 10,000$. The stock price is $P = [S + (D - D_0)]/n_0 = [S + D]/10,000$.
[e] The number of shares after repurchase is $n = S/P$.
[f] Net income is $NI = (EBIT - r_dD)(1 - T)$, where $EBIT = $40,000$ (taken from Table 16-1), r_d comes from Table 16-2, and $T = 40\%$.
[g] $EPS = NI/n$.

Equations 16-13 and 16-15 provide exactly the same values for S and P as does the sequential corporate valuation approach of Table 16-4, but they do it more directly.

Analyzing the Results

Table 16-5 repeats the analysis above and reports the value of operations, value of debt, value of equity, stock price, number of remaining shares, net income, and earnings per share for different capital structures. Notice that the price per share also is maximized under the same capital structure that minimizes the WACC and maximizes the value of the firm.

We summarize the results graphically in Figure 16-4. Notice that the cost of equity and the cost of debt both increase as debt increases. The WACC initially falls, but the rapidly increasing costs of equity and debt cause WACC to increase when the debt ratio goes above 40%. As indicated earlier, the minimum WACC and maximum corporate value occur at the same capital structure.

Now look closely at the curve for the value of the firm, and notice how flat it is around the optimal level of debt. Thus, it doesn't make a great deal of difference whether Strasburg's capital structure has 30% debt or 50%. Also, notice that the maximum value is about 11% greater than the value with no debt. Although this example is for a single company, the results are typical: The optimal capital structure can add 10% to 20% more value relative to zero debt, and there is a fairly wide region (from about 20% debt to 55%) over which value changes very little.

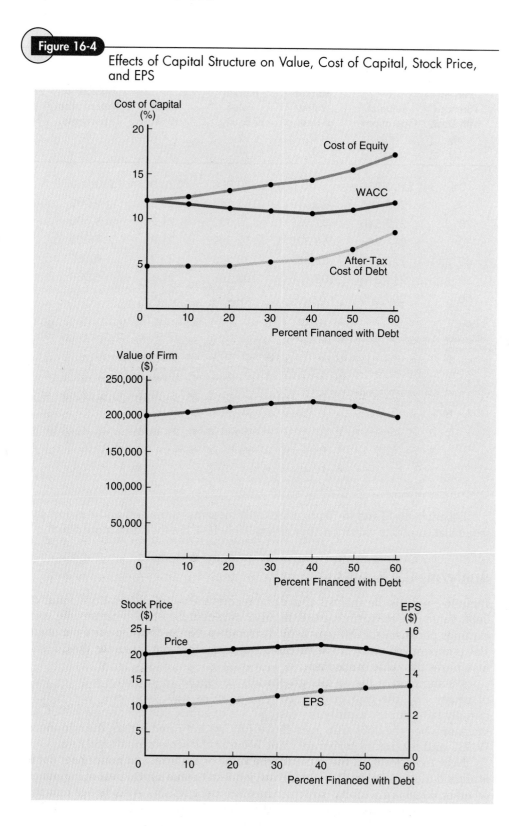

Figure 16-4

Effects of Capital Structure on Value, Cost of Capital, Stock Price, and EPS

In Chapter 15 we looked at value-based management and saw how companies can increase their value by improving their operations. There is good news and bad news regarding this. The good news is that small improvements in operations can lead to huge increases in value. But the bad news is that it's often very hard to improve operations, especially if the company is already well managed.

If instead you seek to increase a firm's value by changing its capital structure, we again have good news and bad news. The good news is that changing capital structure is very easy—just call an investment banker and issue debt (or the reverse if the firm has too much debt). The bad news is that this will add only a relatively small amount of value. Of course, any additional value is better than none, so it's hard to understand why there are some mature firms with zero debt.

Finally, Figure 16-4 shows that Strasburg's EPS steadily increases with leverage, while its stock price reaches a maximum and then begins to decline. For some companies there is a capital structure that maximizes EPS, but this is generally not the same capital structure that maximizes stock price. This is one additional reason we focus on cash flows and value rather than earnings.

SELF-TEST

What happens to the costs of debt and equity when the leverage increases? Explain.

Using the Hamada equation, show the effect of financial leverage on beta.

Using a graph and illustrative data, identify the premiums for financial risk and business risk at different debt levels. Do these premiums vary depending on the debt level? Explain.

Is expected EPS maximized at the optimal capital structure?

Use the Hamada equation to calculate the unlevered beta for JAB Industries, assuming the following data: $b_L = 1.4$; $T = 40\%$; $w_d = 0.45$. (0.939)

Suppose $r_{RF} = 6\%$ and $RP_M = 5\%$. What would the cost of equity be for JAB Industries if it has no debt? If w_d is 0.45? (10.70%; 13.0%)

A firm's value of operations is equal to $800 million after a recapitalization (the firm had no debt before the recap). The firm raised $200 million in new debt and used this to buy back stock. The firm had no short-term investments before or after the recap. After the recap, $w_d = 0.25$. The firm had 10 million shares before the recap. What is S (the value of equity after the recap)? What is P (the stock price) after the recap? What is n (the number of remaining shares) after the recap? (S = $600 million; P = $80; n = 7.5 million)

Summary

This chapter examined the effects of financial leverage on stock prices, earnings per share, and the cost of capital. The key concepts covered are listed below:

- A firm's **optimal capital structure** is that mix of debt and equity that maximizes the stock price. At any point in time, management has a specific **target capital structure** in mind, presumably the optimal one, although this target may change over time.
- Several factors influence a firm's capital structure. These include its (1) **business risk,** (2) **tax position,** (3) need for **financial flexibility,** (4) **managerial conservatism or aggressiveness,** and (5) **growth opportunities.**
- **Business risk** is the riskiness inherent in the firm's operations if it uses no debt. A firm will have little business risk if the demand for its products is stable, if the prices of its inputs and products remain relatively constant, if it can adjust its prices freely if costs increase, and if a high percentage of its costs are variable and hence will decrease if sales decrease. Other things the same, the lower a firm's business risk, the higher its optimal debt ratio.

- **Financial leverage** is the extent to which fixed-income securities (debt and preferred stock) are used in a firm's capital structure. **Financial risk** is the added risk borne by stockholders as a result of financial leverage.
- **Operating leverage** is the extent to which fixed costs are used in a firm's operations. In business terminology, a high degree of operating leverage, other factors held constant, implies that a relatively small change in sales results in a large change in ROIC.
- Robert Hamada used the underlying assumptions of the CAPM, along with the Modigliani and Miller model, to develop the **Hamada equation,** which shows the effect of financial leverage on beta as follows:

$$b = b_U[1 + (1 - T)(D/S)].$$

Firms can take their current beta, tax rate, and debt/equity ratio to arrive at their **unlevered beta, b_U,** as follows:

$$b_U = b/[1 + (1 - T)(D/S)].$$

- **Modigliani and Miller** and their followers developed a **trade-off theory of capital structure.** They showed that debt is useful because interest is **tax deductible,** but also that debt brings with it costs associated with actual or potential bankruptcy. The optimal capital structure strikes a balance between the tax benefits of debt and the costs associated with bankruptcy.
- An alternative (or, really, complementary) theory of capital structure relates to the **signals** given to investors by a firm's decision to use debt versus stock to raise new capital. A stock issue sets off a negative signal, while using debt is a positive, or at least a neutral, signal. As a result, companies try to avoid having to issue stock by maintaining a **reserve borrowing capacity,** and this means using less debt in "normal" times than the MM trade-off theory would suggest.
- A firm's owners may decide to use a relatively large amount of debt to constrain the managers. A **high debt ratio raises the threat of bankruptcy,** which not only carries a cost but also forces managers to be more careful and less wasteful with shareholders' money. Many of the corporate takeovers and leveraged buyouts in recent years were designed to improve efficiency by reducing the cash flow available to managers.

Although each firm has a theoretically optimal capital structure, as a practical matter we cannot estimate it with precision. Accordingly, financial executives generally treat the optimal capital structure as a range—for example, 40% to 50% debt—rather than as a precise point, such as 45%. The concepts discussed in this chapter help managers understand the factors they should consider when they set the target capital structure ranges for their firms.

Questions

(16-1) Define each of the following terms:
a. Capital structure; business risk; financial risk
b. Operating leverage; financial leverage, break-even point
c. Reserve borrowing capacity

(16-2)   What term refers to the uncertainty inherent in projections of future ROIC?

(16-3)   Firms with relatively high nonfinancial fixed costs are said to have a high degree of what?

(16-4)   "One type of leverage affects both EBIT and EPS. The other type affects only EPS." Explain this statement.

(16-5)   Why is the following statement true? "Other things being the same, firms with relatively stable sales are able to carry relatively high debt ratios."

(16-6)   Why do public utility companies usually have capital structures that are different from those of retail firms?

(16-7)   Why is EBIT generally considered to be independent of financial leverage? Why might EBIT actually be influenced by financial leverage at high debt levels?

(16-8)   If a firm went from zero debt to successively higher levels of debt, why would you expect its stock price to first rise, then hit a peak, and then begin to decline?

Self-Test Problems   Solutions Appear in Appendix A

(ST-1)
Optimal Capital Structure

The Rogers Company is currently in this situation: (1) EBIT = $4.7 million; (2) tax rate, T = 40%; (3) value of debt, D = $2 million; (4) r_d = 10%; (5) r_s = 15%; (6) shares of stock outstanding, n_0 = 600,000; and stock price, P_0 = $30. The firm's market is stable, and it expects no growth, so all earnings are paid out as dividends. The debt consists of perpetual bonds.
a.   What is the total market value of the firm's stock, S, and the firm's total market value, V?
b.   What is the firm's weighted average cost of capital?
c.   Suppose the firm can increase its debt so that its capital structure has 50% debt, based on market values (it will issue debt and buy back stock). At this level of debt, its cost of equity rises to 18.5% and its interest rate on all debt will rise to 12% (it will have to call and refund the old debt). What is the WACC under this capital structure? What is the total value? How much debt will it issue, and what is the stock price after the repurchase? How many shares will remain outstanding after the repurchase?

(ST-2)
Hamada Equation

Lighter Industrial Corporation (LIC) is considering a large-scale recapitalization. Currently, LIC is financed with 25% debt and 75% equity. LIC is considering increasing its level of debt until it is financed with 60% debt and 40% equity. The beta on its common stock at the current level of debt is 1.5, the risk-free rate is 6%, the market risk premium is 4%, and LIC faces a 40% federal-plus-state tax rate.
a.   What is LIC's current cost of equity?
b.   What is LIC's unlevered beta?
c.   What will be the new beta and new cost of equity if LIC recapitalizes?

Problems Answers Appear in Appendix B

Easy
Problems 1–6

(16-1)
Break-even Quantity

Shapland Inc. has fixed operating costs of $500,000 and variable costs of $50 per unit. If it sells the product for $75 per unit, what is the break-even quantity?

(16-2)
Unlevered Beta

Counts Accounting has a beta of 1.15. The tax rate is 40% and Counts is financed with 45% debt. What is Counts's unlevered beta?

(16-3)
Premium for Financial
Risk

Ethier Enterprise has an unlevered beta of 1.0. Ethier is financed with 50% debt and has a levered beta of 1.6. If the risk-free rate is 5.5% and the market risk premium is 6%, how much is the additional premium that Ethier's shareholders require to be compensated for financial risk?

(16-4)
Value of Equity after
Recapitalization

Nichols Corporation's value of operations is equal to $500 million after a recapitalization (the firm had no debt before the recap). It raised $200 million in new debt and used this to buy back stock. Nichols had no short-term investments before or after the recap. After the recap, $w_d = 0.4$. What is S (the value of equity after the recap)?

(16-5)
Stock Price after
Recapitalization

Lee Manufacturing's value of operations is equal to $900 million after a recapitalization (the firm had no debt before the recap). Lee raised $300 million in new debt and used this to buy back stock. Lee had no short-term investments before or after the recap. After the recap, $w_d = 1/3$. The firm had 30 million shares before the recap. What is P (the stock price after the recap)?

(16-6)
Shares Remaining after
Recapitalization

Dye Trucking raised $150 million in new debt and used this to buy back stock. After the recap, Dye's stock price is $7.5. If Dye had 60 million shares of stock before the recap, how many shares does it have after the recap?

Intermediate
Problems 7–9

(16-7)
Break-even Point

Schweser Satellites Inc. produces satellite earth stations that sell for $100,000 each. The firm's fixed costs, F, are $2 million; 50 earth stations are produced and sold each year; profits total $500,000; and the firm's assets (all equity financed) are $5 million. The firm estimates that it can change its production process, adding $4 million to investment and $500,000 to fixed operating costs. This change will (1) reduce variable costs per unit by $10,000 and (2) increase output by 20 units, but (3) the sales price on all units will have to be lowered to $95,000 to permit sales of the additional output. The firm has tax loss carryforwards that cause its tax rate to be zero, its cost of equity is 16%, and it uses no debt.

a. What is the incremental profit? To get a rough idea of the project's profitability, what is the project's expected rate of return for the next year (defined as the incremental profit divided by the investment)? Should the firm make the investment?

b. Would the firm's break-even point increase or decrease if it made the change?

c. Would the new situation expose the firm to more or less business risk than the old one?

(16-8)
Business and
Financial Risk

Here are the estimated ROE distributions for Firms A, B, and C:

	Probability				
	0.1	0.2	0.4	0.2	0.1
Firm A: ROE_A	0.0%	5.0%	10.0%	15.0%	20.0%
Firm B: ROE_B	(2.0)	5.0	12.0	19.0	26.0
Firm C: ROE_C	(5.0)	5.0	15.0	25.0	35.0

a. Calculate the expected value and standard deviation for Firm C's ROE. $ROE_A =$ 10.0%, $\sigma_A = 5.5\%$; $ROE_B = 12.0\%$, $\sigma_B = 7.7\%$.
b. Discuss the relative riskiness of the three firms' returns. (Assume that these distributions are expected to remain constant over time.)
c. Now suppose all three firms have the same standard deviation of basic earning power (EBIT/Total assets), $\sigma_A = \sigma_B = \sigma_C = 5.5\%$. What can we tell about the financial risk of each firm?

(16-9)
Capital Structure Analysis

The Rivoli Company has no debt outstanding, and its financial position is given by the following data:

Assets (book = market)	$3,000,000
EBIT	$500,000
Cost of equity, r_s	10%
Stock price, P_0	$15
Shares outstanding, n_0	200,000
Tax rate, T (federal-plus-state)	40%

The firm is considering selling bonds and simultaneously repurchasing some of its stock. If it moves to a capital structure with 30% debt based on market values, its cost of equity, r_s, will increase to 11% to reflect the increased risk. Bonds can be sold at a cost, r_d, of 7%. Rivoli is a no-growth firm. Hence, all its earnings are paid out as dividends, and earnings are expectationally constant over time.

a. What effect would this use of leverage have on the value of the firm?
b. What would be the price of Rivoli's stock?
c. What happens to the firm's earnings per share after the recapitalization?
d. The $500,000 EBIT given previously is actually the expected value from the following probability distribution:

Probability	EBIT
0.10	($ 100,000)
0.20	200,000
0.40	500,000
0.20	800,000
0.10	1,100,000

Determine the times-interest-earned ratio for each probability. What is the probability of not covering the interest payment at the 30% debt level?

**Challenging
Problems 10–12**

(16-10)
Capital Structure Analysis

Pettit Printing Company has a total market value of $100 million, consisting of 1 million shares selling for $50 per share and $50 million of 10% perpetual bonds now selling at par. The company's EBIT is $13.24 million, and its tax rate is 15%. Pettit can change its capital structure by either increasing its debt to 70% (based on market values) or decreasing it to 30%. If it decides to *increase* its use of leverage, it must call its old bonds and issue new ones with a 12% coupon. If it decides to *decrease* its leverage, it will call in its old bonds and replace them with new 8% coupon bonds. The company will sell or repurchase stock at the new equilibrium price to complete the capital structure change.

The firm pays out all earnings as dividends; hence, its stock is a zero growth stock. Its current cost of equity, r_s, is 14%. If it increases leverage, r_s will be 16%. If it decreases leverage, r_s will be 13%. What is the firm's WACC and total corporate value under each capital structure?

(16-11)
Optimal Capital Structure
with Hamada

Beckman Engineering and Associates (BEA) is considering a change in its capital structure. BEA currently has $20 million in debt carrying a rate of 8%, and its stock price is $40 per share with 2 million shares outstanding. BEA is a zero growth firm and pays out all of its earnings as dividends. EBIT is $14.933 million, and BEA faces a 40% federal-plus-state tax rate. The market risk premium is 4%, and the risk-free rate is 6%. BEA is considering increasing its debt level to a capital structure with 40% debt, based on market values, and repurchasing shares with the extra money that it borrows. BEA will have to retire the old debt in order to issue new debt, and the rate on the new debt will be 9%. BEA has a beta of 1.0.

a. What is BEA's unlevered beta? Use market value D/S when unlevering.
b. What are BEA's new beta and cost of equity if it has 40% debt?
c. What are BEA's WACC and total value of the firm with 40% debt?

(16-12)
WACC and Optimal
Capital Structure

Elliott Athletics is trying to determine its optimal capital structure, which now consists of only debt and common equity. The firm does not currently use preferred stock in its capital structure, and it does not plan to do so in the future. To estimate how much its debt would cost at different debt levels, the company's treasury staff has consulted with investment bankers and, on the basis of those discussions, has created the following table:

Market Debt-to-Value Ratio (w_d)	Market Equity-to-Value Ratio (w_{ce})	Market Debt-to-Equity Ratio (D/S)	Bond Rating	Before-Tax Cost of Debt (r_d)
0.0	1.0	0.00	A	7.0%
0.2	0.8	0.25	BBB	8.0
0.4	0.6	0.67	BB	10.0
0.6	0.4	1.50	C	12.0
0.8	0.2	4.00	D	15.0

Elliott uses the CAPM to estimate its cost of common equity, r_s. The company estimates that the risk-free rate is 5%, the market risk premium is 6%, and its tax rate is 40%. Elliott estimates that if it had no debt, its "unlevered" beta, b_U, would be 1.2. Based on this information, what is the firm's optimal capital structure, and what would the weighted average cost of capital be at the optimal capital structure?

Spreadsheet Problem

(16-13)
Build a Model: WACC
and Optimal Capital
Structure

e-resource

Start with the partial model in the file *FM12 Ch 16 P13 Build a Model.xls* from the textbook's Web site. Rework Problem 16-12 using a spreadsheet model. After completing the problem as it appears, answer the following related questions.

a. Plot a graph of the after-tax cost of debt, the cost of equity, and the WACC versus the debt/value ratio.

b. Would the optimal capital structure change if the unlevered beta changed? To answer this question, do a sensitivity analysis of WACC on b_U for different levels of b_U.

e-resource

Cyberproblem

Please go to the textbook's Web site to access any Cyberproblems.

Mini Case

Assume you have just been hired as business manager of PizzaPalace, a pizza restaurant located adjacent to campus. The company's EBIT was $500,000 last year, and since the university's enrollment is capped, EBIT is expected to remain constant (in real terms) over time. Since no expansion capital will be required, PizzaPalace plans to pay out all earnings as dividends. The management group owns about 50% of the stock, and the stock is traded in the over-the-counter market.

The firm is currently financed with all equity; it has 100,000 shares outstanding; and $P_0 = \$25$ per share. When you took your corporate finance course, your instructor stated that most firms' owners would be financially better off if the firms used some debt. When you suggested this to your new boss, he encouraged you to pursue the idea. As a first step, assume that you obtained from the firm's investment banker the following estimated costs of debt for the firm at different capital structures:

Percent Financed with Debt, w_d	r_d
0%	—
20	8.0%
30	8.5
40	10.0
50	12.0

If the company were to recapitalize, debt would be issued, and the funds received would be used to repurchase stock. PizzaPalace is in the 40%

state-plus-federal corporate tax bracket, its beta is 1.0, the risk-free rate is 6%, and the market risk premium is 6%.

a. Provide a brief overview of capital structure effects. Be sure to identify the ways in which capital structure can affect the weighted average cost of capital and free cash flows.

b. (1) What is business risk? What factors influence a firm's business risk?

(2) What is operating leverage, and how does it affect a firm's business risk? Show the operating break-even point if a company has fixed costs of $200, a sales price of $15, and variable costs of $10.

c. Now, to develop an example that can be presented to PizzaPalace's management to illustrate the effects of financial leverage, consider two hypothetical firms: Firm U, which uses no debt financing, and Firm L, which uses $10,000 of 12% debt. Both firms have $20,000 in assets, a 40% tax rate, and an expected EBIT of $3,000.

(1) Construct partial income statements, which start with EBIT, for the two firms.

(2) Now calculate ROE for both firms.

(3) What does this example illustrate about the impact of financial leverage on ROE?

d. Explain the difference between financial risk and business risk.

e. Now consider the fact that EBIT is not known with certainty, but rather has the following probability distribution:

Economic State	Probability	EBIT
Bad	0.25	$2,000
Average	0.50	3,000
Good	0.25	4,000

Redo the part a analysis for Firms U and L, but add basic earnings power (BEP), return on invested capital (ROIC, defined as $\text{NOPAT}/\text{Capital} = \text{EBIT}(1 - \text{T})/\text{TA}$ for this company), and the times-interest-earned (TIE) ratio to the outcome measures. Find the values for each firm in each state of the economy, and then calculate the expected values. Finally, calculate the standard deviations. What does this example illustrate about the impact of debt financing on risk and return?

f. What does capital structure theory attempt to do? What lessons can be learned from capital structure theory? Be sure to address the MM models.

g. What does the empirical evidence say about capital structure theory? What are the implications for managers?

h. With the above points in mind, now consider the optimal capital structure for PizzaPalace.

(1) For each capital structure under consideration, calculate the levered beta, the cost of equity, and the WACC.

(2) Now calculate the corporate value.

i. Describe the recapitalization process and apply it to PizzaPalace. Calculate the resulting value of the debt that will be issued, the resulting market value of equity, the price per share, the number of shares repurchased, and the remaining shares. Considering only the capital structures under analysis, what is PizzaPalace's optimal capital structure?

Selected Additional Cases

The following cases from Textchoice, *Cengage Learning's online library, cover many of the concepts discussed in this chapter and are available at* ***http://www.textchoice2.com***.

Klein-Brigham Series:
Case 9, "Kleen Kar, Inc.," Case 43, "Mountain Springs, Inc." and Case 57, "Greta Cosmetics, Inc.," which present a situation similar to the Strasburg example in the text. Case 74, "The Western Company," and Case 99, "Moore Plumbing Supply," explore capital structure policies.

Brigham-Buzzard Series:
Case 8, "Powerline Network Corporation (Operating Leverage, Financial Leverage, and the Optimal Capital Structure)."

chapter 17

Capital Structure Decisions: Extensions

At a meeting of the Financial Management Association, a panel session focused on how firms actually set their target capital structures. The participants included financial managers from Hershey Foods, Verizon, EG&G (a high-tech firm), and a number of other firms in various industries. Although there were minor differences in philosophy and procedures among the companies, several themes emerged.

First, in practice it is difficult to specify an optimal capital structure—indeed, managers even feel uncomfortable about specifying an optimal capital structure range. Thus, financial managers worry primarily about whether their firms are using too little or too much debt, not about the precise optimal amount of debt. Second, even if a firm's actual capital structure varies widely from the theoretical optimum, this might not have much effect on its stock price. Overall, financial managers believe that capital structure decisions are secondary in importance to operating decisions, especially those relating to capital budgeting and the strategic direction of the firm.

In general, financial managers focus on identifying a "prudent" level of debt rather than on setting a precise optimal level. A prudent level is defined as one that captures most of the benefits of debt yet (1) keeps financial risk at a manageable level, (2) ensures future financing flexibility, and (3) allows the firm to maintain a desirable credit rating. Thus, a prudent level of debt will protect the company against financial distress under all but the worst economic scenarios, and it will ensure access to money and capital markets under most conditions.

As you read this chapter, think about how you would make capital structure decisions if you had that responsibility. At the same time, don't forget the very important message from the FMA panel session: Establishing the right capital structure is an imprecise process at best, and it should be based on both informed judgment and quantitative analyses.

Chapter 16 presented basic material on capital structure, including an introduction to capital structure theory. We saw that debt concentrates a firm's business risk on its stockholders, thus raising stockholders' risk, but it also increases the expected return on equity. We also saw that there is some optimal level of debt that maximizes a company's stock price, and we illustrated this concept with a simple model. Now we go into more detail on capital structure theory. This will give you a deeper understanding of the benefits and costs associated with debt financing.

17.1 Capital Structure Theory: Arbitrage Proofs of the Modigliani-Miller Models

Until 1958, capital structure theory consisted of loose assertions about investor behavior rather than carefully constructed models that could be tested by formal statistical analysis. In what has been called the most influential set of financial papers ever published, Franco Modigliani and Merton Miller (MM) addressed capital structure in a rigorous, scientific fashion, and they set off a chain of research that continues to this day.[1]

FM

e-resource

The textbook's Web site contains an *Excel* file that will guide you through the chapter's calculations. The file for this chapter is *FM12 Ch 17 Tool Kit.xls*, and we encourage you to open the file and follow along as you read the chapter.

Assumptions

As we explain in this chapter, MM employed the concept of **arbitrage** to develop their theory. Arbitrage occurs if two similar assets—in this case, levered and unlevered stocks—sell at different prices. Arbitrageurs will buy the undervalued stock and simultaneously sell the overvalued stock, earning a profit in the process, and this will continue until market forces of supply and demand cause the prices of the two assets to be equal. For arbitrage to work, the assets must be equivalent, or nearly so. MM show that, under their assumptions, levered and unlevered stocks are sufficiently similar for the arbitrage process to operate.

No one, not even MM, believes that their assumptions are sufficiently correct to cause their models to hold exactly in the real world. However, their models do show how money can be made through arbitrage if one can find ways around problems with the assumptions. Here are the initial MM assumptions. Note that some of them were later relaxed:

1. There are *no taxes*, either personal or corporate.
2. Business risk can be measured by σ_{EBIT}, and firms with the same degree of business risk are said to be in a *homogeneous risk class*.
3. All present and prospective investors have identical estimates of each firm's future EBIT; that is, investors have *homogeneous expectations* about expected future corporate earnings and the riskiness of those earnings.

---

[1]See Franco Modigliani and Merton H. Miller, "The Cost of Capital, Corporation Finance and the Theory of Investment," *American Economic Review*, June 1958, pp. 261–297; "The Cost of Capital, Corporation Finance and the Theory of Investment: Reply," *American Economic Review*, September 1958, pp. 655–669; "Taxes and the Cost of Capital: A Correction," *American Economic Review*, June 1963, pp. 433–443; and "Reply," *American Economic Review*, June 1965, pp. 524–527. In a survey of Financial Management Association members, the original MM article was judged to have had the greatest impact on the field of finance of any work ever published. See Philip L. Cooley and J. Louis Heck, "Significant Contributions to Finance Literature," *Financial Management*, Tenth Anniversary Issue 1981, pp. 23–33. Note that both Modigliani and Miller won Nobel Prizes—Modigliani in 1985 and Miller in 1990.

Corporate Valuation and Capital Structure Decisions

A firm's financing choices obviously have a direct effect on its weighted average cost of capital (WACC). Financing choices also have an indirect effect because they change the risk and required return of debt and equity. This chapter focuses on the debt–equity choice and its effect on value.

$$\text{Value} = \frac{FCF_1}{(1 + WACC)^1} + \frac{FCF_2}{(1 + WACC)^2} + \frac{FCF_3}{(1 + WACC)^3} + \cdots + \frac{FCF_\infty}{(1 + WACC)^\infty}$$

4. Stocks and bonds are traded in *perfect capital markets*. This assumption implies, among other things, (a) that there are no brokerage costs and (b) that investors (both individuals and institutions) can borrow at the same rate as corporations.
5. *Debt is riskless.* This applies to both firms and investors, so the interest rate on all debt is the risk-free rate. Further, this situation holds regardless of how much debt a firm (or individual) uses.
6. All cash flows are *perpetuities*; that is, all firms expect zero growth, hence have an "expectationally constant" EBIT, and all bonds are perpetuities. "Expectationally constant" means that the best guess is that EBIT will be constant, but after the fact the realized level could be different from the expected level.

MM without Taxes

MM first analyzed leverage under the assumption that there are no corporate or personal income taxes. On the basis of their assumptions, they stated and algebraically proved two propositions:[2]

Proposition I   The value of any firm is established by capitalizing its expected net operating income (EBIT) at a constant rate (r_{sU}) that is based on the firm's risk class:

$$V_L = V_U = \frac{EBIT}{WACC} = \frac{EBIT}{r_{sU}}. \tag{17-1}$$

Here the subscript L designates a levered firm and U designates an unlevered firm. Both firms are assumed to be in the same business risk class, and r_{sU} is the required rate of return for an unlevered, or all-equity, firm of this risk class when there are no taxes. For our purposes, it is easiest to think in terms of a single firm that has the option of financing either with all equity or with some combination of debt and equity. Hence, L designates the firm if it uses some amount of debt, and U designates the firm if it uses no debt.

Because V as established by Equation 17-1 is a constant, *then under the MM model, when there are no taxes, the value of the firm is independent of its leverage.* As we shall see, this also implies the following:

1. The weighted average cost of capital, WACC, to the firm, is completely independent of its capital structure.

---

[2]MM actually stated and proved three propositions, but the third one is not material to our discussion here.

2. Regardless of the amount of debt the firm uses, its WACC is equal to the cost of equity that it would have if it used no debt.

Proposition II   When there are no taxes, the cost of equity to a levered firm, r_{sL}, is equal to (1) the cost of equity to an unlevered firm in the same risk class, r_{sU}, plus (2) a risk premium whose size depends on both the difference between an unlevered firm's costs of debt and equity and the amount of debt used:

$$r_{sL} = r_{sU} + \text{Risk premium} = r_{sU} + (r_{sU} - r_d)(D/S). \qquad \text{(17-2)}$$

Here D = market value of the firm's debt, S = market value of its equity, and r_d = the constant cost of debt. *Equation 17-2 states that as debt increases, the cost of equity also rises, and in a mathematically precise manner (even though the cost of debt does not rise).*

Taken together, the two MM propositions imply that using more debt in the capital structure will not increase the value of the firm, because the benefits of cheaper debt will be exactly offset by an increase in the riskiness of the equity, hence in its cost. *Thus, MM argue that in a world without taxes, both the value of a firm and its WACC would be unaffected by its capital structure.*

MM's Arbitrage Proof

MM used an *arbitrage proof* to support their propositions.[3] They showed that, under their assumptions, if two companies differed only (1) in the way they were financed and (2) in their total market values, then investors would sell shares of the higher-valued firm, buy those of the lower-valued firm, and continue this process until the companies had exactly the same market value. To illustrate, assume that two firms, L and U, are identical in all important respects except that Firm L has $4,000,000 of 7.5% debt while Firm U uses only equity. Both firms have EBIT = $900,000, and σ_{EBIT} is the same for both firms, so they are in the same business risk class.

MM assumed that all firms are in a zero-growth situation; that is, EBIT is expected to remain constant, which will occur if ROE is constant, all earnings are paid out as dividends, and there are no taxes. Under the constant EBIT assumption, the total market value of the common stock, S, is the present value of a perpetuity, which is found as follows:

$$S = \frac{\text{Dividends}}{r_{sL}} = \frac{\text{Net income}}{r_{sL}} = \frac{(\text{EBIT} - r_d D)}{r_{sL}}. \qquad \text{(17-3)}$$

Equation 17-3 is merely the value of a perpetuity whose numerator is the net income available to common stockholders, all of which is paid out as dividends, and whose denominator is the cost of common equity. Since there are no taxes, the numerator is not multiplied by $(1 - T)$ as it would be if we calculated NOPAT as in Chapters 3 and 15.

---

[3]By *arbitrage* we mean the simultaneous buying and selling of essentially identical assets that sell at different prices. The buying increases the price of the undervalued asset, and the selling decreases the price of the overvalued asset. Arbitrage operations will continue until prices have adjusted to the point where the arbitrageur can no longer earn a profit, at which point the market is in equilibrium. In the absence of transaction costs, equilibrium requires that the prices of the two assets be equal.

Assume that initially, *before any arbitrage occurs*, both firms have the same equity capitalization rate: $r_{sU} = r_{sL} = 10\%$. Under this condition, according to Equation 17-3, the following situation would exist:

Firm U:

$$\text{Value of Firm U's stock} = S_U = \frac{\text{EBIT} - r_d D}{r_{sU}}$$

$$= \frac{\$900,000 - \$0}{0.10} = \$9,000,000.$$

The total market value of Firm U $= V_U = D_U + S_U = \$0 + \$9,000,000$
$= \$9,000,000.$

Firm L:

$$\text{Value of Firm L's stock} = S_L = \frac{\text{EBIT} - r_d D}{r_{sL}}$$

$$= \frac{\$900,000 - 0.075(\$4,000,000)}{0.10} = \frac{\$600,000}{0.10}$$

$$= \$6,000,000.$$

The total market value of Firm L $= V_L = D_L + S_L = \$4,000,000 + \$6,000,000$
$= \$10,000,000.$

Thus before arbitrage, and assuming that $r_{sU} = r_{sL}$ (which implies that capital structure has no effect on the cost of equity), the value of the levered Firm L exceeds that of the unlevered Firm U.

MM argued that this is a disequilibrium situation that cannot persist. To see why, suppose you owned 10% of L's stock, so the market value of your investment was 0.10($6,000,000) = $600,000. According to MM, you could increase your income without increasing your exposure to risk. For example, suppose you (1) sold your stock in L for $600,000, (2) borrowed an amount equal to 10% of L's debt ($400,000), and then (3) bought 10% of U's stock for $900,000. Note that you would receive $1,000,000 from the sale of your 10% of L's stock plus your borrowing, and you would be spending only $900,000 on U's stock, so you would have an extra $100,000, which you could invest in riskless debt to yield 7.5%, or $7,500 annually. Now consider your income positions:

Old Income:	10% of L's $600,000 equity income	$60,000	
New Income:	10% of U's $900,000 equity income	$90,000	
	Less 7.5% interest on $400,000 loan	(30,000)	$60,000
	Plus 7.5% interest on extra $100,000		7,500
	Total new income		$67,500

Thus, your net income from common stock would be exactly the same as before, $60,000, but you would have $100,000 left over for investment in riskless debt, which would increase your income by $7,500. Therefore, the total return on your $600,000 net worth would rise to $67,500. Further, your risk, according to MM, would be the same as before, because you would have simply substituted $400,000 of "homemade" leverage for your 10% share of Firm L's $4 million of corporate leverage. Thus, neither your "effective" debt nor your risk would have changed. Therefore, you would have increased your income without raising your risk, which is obviously a desirable thing to do.

MM argued that this arbitrage process would actually occur, with sales of L's stock driving its price down and purchases of U's stock driving its price up, until the market values of the two firms were equal. Until this equality was established, gains could be obtained by switching from one stock to the other; hence the profit motive would force equality to be reached. When equilibrium is established, the values of Firms L and U, and their weighted average costs of capital, would be equal. Thus, according to Modigliani and Miller, both a firm's value and its WACC must be independent of capital structure.

Note that each of the assumptions listed at the beginning of this section is necessary for the arbitrage proof to work exactly. For example, if the companies did not have identical business risk, or if transactions costs were significant, then the arbitrage process could not be invoked. We discuss other implications of the assumptions later in the chapter.

Arbitrage with Short Sales

Even if you did not own any stock in L, you still could reap benefits if U and L did not have the same total market value. Your first step would be to sell short $600,000 of stock in L. To do this, your broker would let you borrow stock in L from another client. Your broker would then sell the stock for you and give you the proceeds, or $600,000 in cash. You would supplement this $600,000 by borrowing $400,000. With the $1 million total, you would buy 10% of the stock in U for $900,000, and have $100,000 remaining.

Your position would then consist of $100,000 in cash and two portfolios. The first portfolio would contain $900,000 of stock in U, and it would generate $90,000 of income. Because you own the stock, we'll call it the "long" portfolio. The other portfolio would consist of $600,000 of stock in L and $400,000 of debt. The value of this portfolio is $1 million, and it would generate $60,000 of dividends and $30,000 of interest. However, you would not own this second portfolio—you would "owe" it. Since you borrowed the $400,000, you would owe the $30,000 in interest. And since you borrowed the stock in L, you would "owe the stock" to the client from whom it was borrowed. Therefore, you would have to pay your broker the $60,000 of dividends paid by L, which the broker would then pass on to the client from whom the stock was borrowed. So, your net cash flow from the second portfolio would be a negative $90,000. Because you would "owe" this portfolio, we'll call it the "short" portfolio.

Where would you get the $90,000 that you must pay on the short portfolio? The good news is that this is exactly the amount of cash flow generated by your long portfolio. Because the cash flows generated by each portfolio are the same, the short portfolio "replicates" the long portfolio.

Here is the bottom line. You started out with no money of your own. By selling L short, borrowing $400,000, and purchasing stock in U, you ended up with $100,000 in cash plus the two portfolios. The portfolios mirror one another, so their net cash flow is zero. This is perfect arbitrage: You invest none of your own money, you have no risk, you have no future negative cash flows, but you end up with cash in your pocket.

Not surprisingly, many traders would want to do this. The selling pressure on L would cause its price to fall, and the buying pressure on U would cause its price to rise, until the two companies' values were equal. To put it another way, *if the long and short replicating portfolios have the same cash flows, then arbitrage will force them to have the same value.*

This is one of the most important ideas in modern finance. Not only does it give us insights into capital structure, but it is the fundamental building block underlying the valuation of real and financial options and derivatives as discussed in Chapters 9 and 23. Without the concept of arbitrage, the options and derivatives markets we have today simply would not exist.

MM with Corporate Taxes

MM's original work, published in 1958, assumed zero taxes. In 1963, they published a second article that incorporated corporate taxes. With corporate income taxes, they concluded that leverage will increase a firm's value. This occurs because interest is a tax-deductible expense; hence more of a levered firm's operating income flows through to investors.

Later in this chapter we present a proof of the MM propositions when personal taxes as well as corporate taxes are allowed. The situation when corporations are subject to income taxes, but there are no personal taxes, is a special case of the situation with both personal and corporate taxes, so we only present results here.

Proposition I   The value of a levered firm is equal to the value of an unlevered firm in the same risk class (V_U) *plus* the value of the tax shield ($V_{\text{Tax shield}}$) due to the tax deductibility of interest expenses. The value of the tax shield, which is often called the gain from leverage, is the present value of the annual tax savings. The annual tax saving is equal to the interest payment multiplied by the tax rate, T: Annual tax saving = $(r_d T)(D)$. MM assume a no-growth firm, so the present value of the annual tax saving is the present value of a perpetuity. They assume that the appropriate discount rate for the tax shield is the interest rate on debt, so the value of the tax shield is $V_{\text{Tax shield}} = (r_d T)(D)/r_d = TD$. Therefore, the value of a levered firm is

$$V_L = V_U + V_{\text{Tax shield}}$$
$$= V_U + TD. \tag{17-4}$$

The important point here is that when corporate taxes are introduced, the value of the levered firm exceeds that of the unlevered firm by the amount TD. Since the gain from leverage increases as debt increases, this implies that a firm's value is maximized at 100% debt financing.

Because all cash flows are assumed to be perpetuities, the value of the unlevered firm can be found by using Equation 17-3 and incorporating taxes. With zero debt (D = \$0), the value of the firm is its equity value:

$$V_U = S = \frac{\text{EBIT}(1 - T)}{r_{sU}}. \tag{17-5}$$

Note that the discount rate, r_{sU}, is not necessarily equal to the discount rate in Equation 17-1. The r_{sU} from Equation 17-1 is the required discount rate in a world with no taxes. The r_{sU} in Equation 17-5 is the required discount rate in a world with taxes.

Proposition II The cost of equity to a levered firm is equal to (1) the cost of equity to an unlevered firm in the same risk class plus (2) a risk premium whose size depends on the difference between the costs of equity and debt to an unlevered firm, the amount of financial leverage used, and the corporate tax rate:

$$r_{sL} = r_{sU} + (r_{sU} - r_d)(1 - T)(D/S). \qquad (17\text{-}6)$$

Note that Equation 17-6 is identical to the corresponding without-tax equation, 17-2, except for the term $(1 - T)$ in 17-6. Because $(1 - T)$ is less than 1, corporate taxes cause the cost of equity to rise less rapidly with leverage than it would in the absence of taxes. Proposition II, coupled with the fact that taxes reduce the effective cost of debt, is what produces the Proposition I result, namely, that the firm's value increases as its leverage increases.

As shown in Chapter 16, Professor Robert Hamada extended the MM analysis to define the relationship between a firm's beta, b, and the amount of leverage it has. The beta of an unlevered firm is denoted by b_U, and Hamada's equation is

$$b = b_U[1 + (1 - T)(D/S)]. \qquad (17\text{-}7)$$

Note that beta, like the cost of stock shown in Equation 17-6, increases with leverage.

Illustration of the MM Models

To illustrate the MM models, assume that the following data and conditions hold for Fredrickson Water Company, an old, established firm that supplies water to residential customers in several no-growth upstate New York communities:

1. Fredrickson currently has no debt; it is an all-equity company.
2. Expected EBIT = $2,400,000. EBIT is not expected to increase over time, so Fredrickson is in a no-growth situation.
3. Needing no new capital, Fredrickson pays out all of its income as dividends.
4. If Fredrickson begins to use debt, it can borrow at a rate $r_d = 8\%$. This borrowing rate is constant—it does not increase regardless of the amount of debt used. Any money raised by selling debt would be used to repurchase common stock, *so Fredrickson's assets would remain constant.*
5. The business risk inherent in Fredrickson's assets, and thus in its EBIT, is such that its beta is 0.80; this is called the unlevered beta, b_U, because Fredrickson has no debt. The risk-free rate is 8%, and the market risk premium (RP_M) is 5%. Using the Capital Asset Pricing Model (CAPM), Fredrickson's required rate of return on stock, r_{sU}, is 12% if no debt is used:

$$r_{sU} = r_{RF} + b_U(RP_M) = 8\% + 0.80(5\%) = 12\%.$$

FM

e-resource

See **FM12 Ch 17 Tool Kit.xls** at the textbook's Web site for all calculations.

With Zero Taxes To begin, assume that there are no taxes, so T = 0%. At any level of debt, Proposition I (Equation 17-1) can be used to find Fredrickson's value in an MM world, $20 million:

$$V_L = V_U = \frac{EBIT}{r_{sU}} = \frac{\$2.4 \text{ million}}{0.12} = \$20.0 \text{ million.}$$

If Fredrickson uses $10 million of debt, its stock's value must be $10 million:

$$S = V - D = \$20 \text{ million} - \$10 \text{ million} = \$10 \text{ million.}$$

We can also find Fredrickson's cost of equity, r_{sL}, and its WACC at a debt level of $10 million. First, we use Proposition II (Equation 17-2) to find r_{sL}, Fredrickson's levered cost of equity:

$$
\begin{aligned}
r_{sL} &= r_{sU} + (r_{sU} - r_d)(D/S) \\
&= 12\% + (12\% - 8\%)(\$10 \text{ million}/\$10 \text{ million}) \\
&= 12\% + 4.0\% = 16.0\%.
\end{aligned}
$$

Now we can find the company's weighted average cost of capital:

$$
\begin{aligned}
WACC &= (D/V)(r_d)(1 - T) + (S/V)r_{sL} \\
&= (\$10/\$20)(8\%)(1.0) + (\$10/\$20)(16.0\%) = 12.0\%.
\end{aligned}
$$

Fredrickson's value and cost of capital based on the MM model without taxes at various debt levels are shown in Panel a on the left side of Figure 17-1. Here we see that in an MM world without taxes, financial leverage simply does not matter: *The value of the firm, and its overall cost of capital, are both independent of the amount of debt.*

With Corporate Taxes To illustrate the MM model with corporate taxes, assume that all of the previous conditions hold except these two:

1. Expected EBIT = $4,000,000.[4]
2. Fredrickson has a 40% federal-plus-state tax rate, so T = 40%.

Other things held constant, the introduction of corporate taxes would lower Fredrickson's net income, hence its value, so we increased EBIT from $2.4 million to $4 million to make the comparison between the two models easier.

When Fredrickson has zero debt but pays taxes, Equation 17-5 can be used to find its value, $20 million:

$$V_U = \frac{EBIT(1 - T)}{r_{sU}} = \frac{\$4 \text{ million}(0.6)}{0.12} = \$20 \text{ million.}$$

---

[4]If we had left Fredrickson's EBIT at $2.4 million, the introduction of corporate taxes would have reduced the firm's value from $20 million to $12 million:

$$V_U = \frac{EBIT(1 - T)}{r_{sU}} = \frac{\$2.4 \text{ million}(0.6)}{0.12} = \$12.0 \text{ million.}$$

Corporate taxes reduce the amount of operating income available to investors in an unlevered firm by the factor (1 − T), so the value of the firm would be reduced by the same amount, holding r_{sU} constant.

Figure 17-1

Effects of Leverage: MM Models (Millions of Dollars)

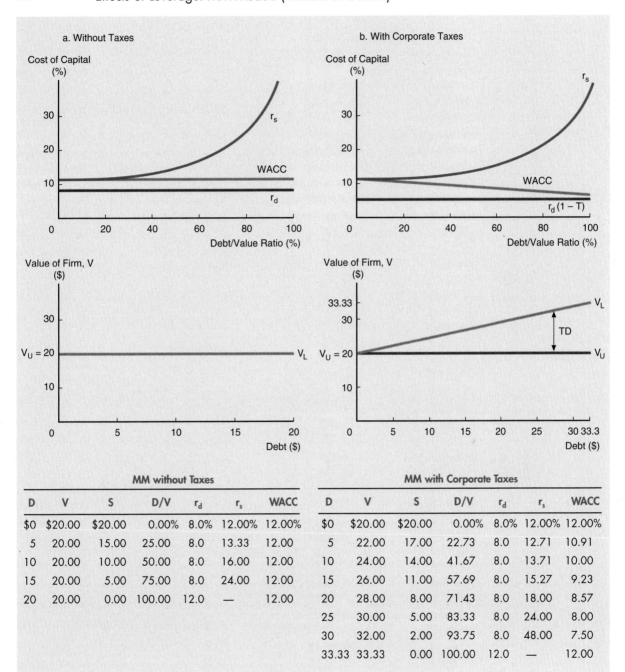

MM without Taxes						
D	V	S	D/V	r_d	r_s	WACC
$0	$20.00	$20.00	0.00%	8.0%	12.00%	12.00%
5	20.00	15.00	25.00	8.0	13.33	12.00
10	20.00	10.00	50.00	8.0	16.00	12.00
15	20.00	5.00	75.00	8.0	24.00	12.00
20	20.00	0.00	100.00	12.0	—	12.00

MM with Corporate Taxes						
D	V	S	D/V	r_d	r_s	WACC
$0	$20.00	$20.00	0.00%	8.0%	12.00%	12.00%
5	22.00	17.00	22.73	8.0	12.71	10.91
10	24.00	14.00	41.67	8.0	13.71	10.00
15	26.00	11.00	57.69	8.0	15.27	9.23
20	28.00	8.00	71.43	8.0	18.00	8.57
25	30.00	5.00	83.33	8.0	24.00	8.00
30	32.00	2.00	93.75	8.0	48.00	7.50
33.33	33.33	0.00	100.00	12.0	—	12.00

If Fredrickson now uses $10 million of debt in a world with taxes, we see by Proposition I (Equation 17-4) that its total market value rises to $24 million:

$$V_L = V_U + TD = \$20 \text{ million} + 0.4(\$10 \text{ million}) = \$24 \text{ million}.$$

Therefore, the implied value of Fredrickson's equity is $14 million:

$$S = V - D = \$24 \text{ million} - \$10 \text{ million} = \$14 \text{ million}.$$

We can also find Fredrickson's cost of equity, r_{sL}, and its WACC at a debt level of $10 million. First, we use Proposition II (Equation 17-6) to find r_{sL}, the levered cost of equity:

$$
\begin{aligned}
r_{sL} &= r_{sU} + (r_{sU} - r_d)(1 - T)(D/S) \\
&= 12\% + (12\% - 8\%)(0.6)(\$10 \text{ million}/\$14 \text{ million}) \\
&= 12\% + 1.71\% = 13.71\%.
\end{aligned}
$$

The company's weighted average cost of capital is 10%:

$$
\begin{aligned}
WACC &= (D/V)(r_d)(1 - T) + (S/V)r_{sL} \\
&= (\$10/\$24)(8\%)(0.6) + (\$14/\$24)(13.71\%) = 10.0\%.
\end{aligned}
$$

Note that we could also find the levered beta and then the levered cost of equity. First, we apply Hamada's equation to find the levered beta:

$$
\begin{aligned}
b &= b_U[1 + (1 - T)(D/S)] \\
&= 0.80[1 + (1 - 0.4)(\$10 \text{ million}/\$14 \text{ million})] \\
&= 1.1429.
\end{aligned}
$$

Applying the CAPM, the levered cost of equity is

$$r_{sL} = r_{RF} + b(RP_M) = 8\% + 1.1429(5\%) = 0.1371 = 13.71\%.$$

Notice that this is the same levered cost of equity that we obtained directly using Equation 17-6.

Fredrickson's value and cost of capital at various debt levels with corporate taxes are shown in Panel b on the right side of Figure 17-1. In an MM world with corporate taxes, financial leverage does matter: The value of the firm is maximized, and its overall cost of capital is minimized, if it uses almost 100% debt financing. The increase in value is due solely to the tax deductibility of interest payments, which lowers both the cost of debt and the equity risk premium by $(1 - T)$.[5]

---

[5]In the limiting case, where the firm used 100% debt financing, the bondholders would own the entire company; thus, they would have to bear all the business risk. (Up until this point, MM assume that the stockholders bear all the risk.) If the bondholders bear all the risk, then the capitalization rate on the debt should be equal to the equity capitalization rate at zero debt, $r_d = r_{sU} = 12\%$.

The income stream to the stockholders in the all-equity case was $\$4,000,000(1 - T) = \$2,400,000$, and the value of the firm was

$$V_U = \frac{\$2,400,000}{0.12} = \$20,000,000.$$

With all debt, the entire $4,000,000 of EBIT would be used to pay interest charges—r_d would be 12%, so $I = 0.12(\text{Debt}) = \$4,000,000$. Taxes would be zero, and investors (bondholders) would get the entire $4,000,000 of operating income; they would not have to share it with the government. Thus, at 100% debt, the value of the firm would be

$$V_L = \frac{\$4,000,000}{0.12} = \$33,333,333 = D.$$

There is, of course, a transition problem in all this—MM assume that $r_d = 8\%$ regardless of how much debt the firm has until debt reaches 100%, at which point r_d jumps to 12%, the cost of equity. As we shall see later in the chapter, r_d realistically rises as the use of financial leverage increases.

To conclude this section, compare the "Without Taxes" and "With Corporate Taxes" sections of Figure 17-1. Without taxes, both WACC and the firm's value (V) are constant. With corporate taxes, WACC declines and V rises as more and more debt is used, so the optimal capital structure, under MM with corporate taxes, is 100% debt.

SELF-TEST

Is there an optimal capital structure under the MM zero-tax model?

What is the optimal capital structure under the MM model with corporate taxes?

How does the Proposition I equation differ between the two models?

How does the Proposition II equation differ between the two models?

Why do taxes result in a "gain from leverage" in the MM model with corporate taxes?

An unlevered firm has a value of $100 million. An otherwise identical but levered firm has $30 million in debt. Under the MM zero-tax model, what is the value of the levered firm? Under the MM corporate tax model, what is the value of a levered firm if the corporate tax rate is 40%? ($100 million; $112 million)

17.2 Introducing Personal Taxes: The Miller Model

Although MM included *corporate taxes* in the second version of their model, they did not extend the model to include *personal taxes*. However, in his presidential address to the American Finance Association, Merton Miller presented a model to show how leverage affects firms' values when both personal and corporate taxes are taken into account.[6] To explain Miller's model, we begin by defining T_c as the corporate tax rate, T_s as the personal tax rate on income from stocks, and T_d as the personal tax rate on income from debt. Note that stock returns are expected to come partly as dividends and partly as capital gains, so T_s is a weighted average of the effective tax rates on dividends and capital gains. However, essentially all debt income comes from interest, which is effectively taxed at investors' top rates, so T_d is higher than T_s.

With personal taxes included, and under the same set of assumptions used in the earlier MM models, the value of an unlevered firm is found as follows:

$$V_U = \frac{EBIT(1 - T_c)}{r_{sU}} = \frac{EBIT(1 - T_c)(1 - T_s)}{r_{sU}(1 - T_s)}. \qquad (17\text{-}8)$$

The $(1 - T_s)$ term takes account of personal taxes. Note that to find the value of the unlevered firm we can either discount pre-personal-tax cash flows at the pre-personal-tax rate of r_{sU} or the after-personal-tax cash flows at the after-personal-tax rate of $r_{sU}(1 - T_s)$. Therefore, the numerator of the second form of Equation 17-8 shows how much of the firm's operating income is left after the unlevered firm pays corporate income taxes and its stockholders subsequently pay personal taxes on their equity income. Note also that the discount rate, r_{sU}, in Equation 17-8 is not

---

[6]See Merton H. Miller, "Debt and Taxes," *Journal of Finance*, May 1977, pp. 261–275.

necessarily equal to the discount rate in Equation 17-5. The r_{sU} from Equation 17-5 is the required discount rate in a world with corporate taxes but no personal taxes. The r_{sU} in Equation 17-8 is the required discount rate in a world with both corporate and personal taxes.

Miller's formula can be proved by an arbitrage proof similar to the one we presented earlier. However, the alternative proof shown below is easier to follow. To begin, we partition the levered firm's annual cash flows, CF_L, into those going to stockholders and those going to bondholders, after both corporate and personal taxes:

$$CF_L = \text{Net CF to stockholders} + \text{Net CF to bondholders}$$
$$= (EBIT - I)(1 - T_c)(1 - T_s) + I(1 - T_d). \qquad (17\text{-}9)$$

Here I is the annual interest payment. Equation 17-9 can be rearranged as follows:

$$CF_L = [EBIT(1 - T_c)(1 - T_s)] - [I(1 - T_c)(1 - T_s)] + [I(1 - T_d)]. \qquad (17\text{-}9a)$$

The first term in Equation 17-9a is identical to the after-personal-tax cash flow of an unlevered firm as shown in the numerator of Equation 17-8, and its present value is found by discounting the perpetual cash flow by $r_{sU}(1 - T_s)$. The second and third terms, which reflect leverage, result from the cash flows associated with debt financing, which under the MM assumptions are riskless. We can write the value of perpetual riskless debt as

$$D = \frac{I}{r_d} = \frac{I(1 - T_d)}{r_d(1 - T_d)}. \qquad (17\text{-}10)$$

We can either discount pre-personal-tax interest payments at the pre-personal-tax rate of r_d or we can discount after-personal-tax interest payments at the after-personal-tax rate $r_d(1 - T_d)$. Since they are after-personal-tax cash flows to debtholders, the present value of the two right-hand terms in Equation 17-9a can be obtained by discounting at the after-personal-tax cost of debt, $r_d(1 - T_d)$. Combining the present values of the three terms, we obtain this value for the levered firm:

$$V_L = \frac{EBIT(1 - T_c)(1 - T_s)}{r_{sU}(1 - T_s)} - \frac{I(1 - T_c)(1 - T_s)}{r_d(1 - T_d)} + \frac{I(1 - T_d)}{r_d(1 - T_d)}. \qquad (17\text{-}11)$$

The first term in Equation 17-11 is identical to V_U in Equation 17-8. Recognizing this, and when we consolidate the second two terms, we obtain this equation:

$$V_L = V_U + \frac{I(1 - T_d)}{r_d(1 - T_d)}\left[1 - \frac{(1 - T_c)(1 - T_s)}{(1 - T_d)}\right]. \qquad (17\text{-}11a)$$

Now recognize that the after-tax perpetual interest payment divided by the after-tax required rate of return on debt, $I(1 - T_d)/r_d(1 - T_d)$, equals the market value of the debt, D. Substituting D into the preceding equation and rearranging, we obtain this expression, called the **Miller model:**

$$\text{Miller model: } V_L = V_U + \left[1 - \frac{(1 - T_c)(1 - T_s)}{(1 - T_d)}\right]D. \qquad (17\text{-}12)$$

The Miller model provides an estimate of the value of a levered firm in a world with both corporate and personal taxes.

The Miller model has several important implications:

1. The term in brackets,

$$\left[1 - \frac{(1 - T_c)(1 - T_s)}{(1 - T_d)}\right],$$

   when multiplied by D, represents the gain from leverage. The bracketed term thus replaces the corporate tax rate, T, in the earlier MM model with corporate taxes, $V_L = V_U + TD$.

2. If we ignore all taxes, that is, if $T_c = T_s = T_d = 0$, then the bracketed term is zero, so in that case Equation 17-12 is the same as the original MM model without taxes.

3. If we ignore personal taxes, that is, if $T_s = T_d = 0$, then the bracketed term reduces to $[1 - (1 - T_c)] = T_c$, so Equation 17-12 is the same as the MM model with corporate taxes.

4. If the effective personal tax rates on stock and bond incomes were equal, that is, if $T_s = T_d$, then $(1 - T_s)$ and $(1 - T_d)$ would cancel, and the bracketed term would again reduce to T_c.

5. If $(1 - T_c)(1 - T_s) = (1 - T_d)$, then the bracketed term would be zero, and the value of using leverage would also be zero. This implies that the tax advantage of debt to the firm would be exactly offset by the personal tax advantage of equity. Under this condition, capital structure would have no effect on a firm's value or its cost of capital, so we would be back to MM's original zero-tax theory.

6. Because taxes on capital gains are lower than on ordinary income and can be deferred, the effective tax rate on stock income is normally less than that on bond income. This being the case, what would the Miller model predict as the gain from leverage? To answer this question, assume that the tax rate on corporate income is $T_c = 34\%$, the effective rate on bond income is $T_d = 28\%$, and the effective rate on stock income is $T_s = 15\%$.[7] Using these values in the Miller model, we find that a levered firm's value exceeds that of an unlevered firm by 22% of the market value of corporate debt:

$$\begin{aligned}\text{Gain from leverage} &= \left[1 - \frac{(1 - T_c)(1 - T_s)}{(1 - T_d)}\right]D \\ &= \left[1 - \frac{(1 - 0.34)(1 - 0.15)}{(1 - 0.28)}\right]D \\ &= (1 - 0.78)D \\ &= 0.22D.\end{aligned}$$

---

[7]In a 1978 article, Miller and Scholes described how investors could, theoretically, shelter or delay income from stock to the point where the effective personal tax rate on such income is essentially zero. See Merton H. Miller and Myron S. Scholes, "Dividends and Taxes," *Journal of Financial Economics,* December 1978, pp. 333–364. However, the 1986 changes in the tax law eliminated most of the shelters Miller and Scholes discussed.

Note that the MM model with corporate taxes would indicate a gain from leverage of $T_c(D) = 0.34D$, or 34% of the amount of corporate debt. Thus, with these assumed tax rates, adding personal taxes to the model lowers but does not eliminate the benefit from corporate debt. In general, whenever the effective tax rate on income from stock is less than the effective rate on income from bonds, the Miller model produces a lower gain from leverage than is produced by the MM with-tax model.

In his paper, Miller argued that firms in the aggregate would issue a mix of debt and equity securities such that the before-tax yields on corporate securities and the personal tax rates of the investors who bought these securities would adjust until an equilibrium was reached. At equilibrium, $(1 - T_d)$ would equal $(1 - T_c)(1 - T_s)$, so, as we noted earlier in point 5, the tax advantage of debt to the firm would be exactly offset by personal taxation, and capital structure would have no effect on a firm's value or its cost of capital. Thus, according to Miller, the conclusions derived from the original Modigliani-Miller zero-tax model are correct!

Others have extended and tested Miller's analysis. Generally, these extensions question Miller's conclusion that there is no advantage to the use of corporate debt. In fact, Equation 17-12 shows that both T_c and T_s must be less than T_d if there is to be zero gain from leverage. In the United States, for most corporations and investors, the effective tax rate on income from stock is less than on income from bonds; that is, $T_s < T_d$. However, many corporate bonds are held by tax-exempt institutions, and in those cases T_c is generally greater than T_d. Also, for those high-tax-bracket individuals with $T_d > T_c$, T_s may be large enough so that $(1 - T_c)(1 - T_s)$ is less than $(1 - T_d)$; hence there is an advantage to the use of corporate debt. Still, Miller's work does show that personal taxes offset some of the benefits of corporate debt, so the tax advantages of corporate debt are less than were implied by the earlier MM model, where only corporate taxes were considered.

As we note in the next section, both the MM and the Miller models are based on strong and unrealistic assumptions, so we should regard our examples as indicating the general effects of leverage on a firm's value, not a precise relationship.

SELF-TEST

How does the Miller model differ from the MM model with corporate taxes?

What are the implications of the Miller model if $T_c = T_s = T_d = 0$?

What are the implications if $T_s = T_d = 0$?

Considering the current tax structure in the United States, what is the primary implication of the Miller model?

An unlevered firm has a value of $100 million. An otherwise identical but levered firm has $30 million in debt. Under the Miller model, what is the value of a levered firm if the corporate tax rate is 40%, the personal tax rate on equity is 15%, and the personal tax rate on debt is 35%? ($106.46 million)

17.3 Criticisms of the MM and Miller Models

The conclusions of the MM and Miller models follow logically from their initial assumptions. However, both academicians and executives have voiced concerns over the validity of the MM and Miller models, and virtually no one believes they hold precisely. The MM zero-tax model leads to the conclusion that capital structure doesn't matter, yet we observe systematic capital structure patterns within industries. Further, when used with "reasonable" tax rates, both the MM model with corporate taxes and the Miller model lead to the conclusion that firms should use 100% debt financing, but firms do not (deliberately) go to that extreme.

People who disagree with the MM and Miller theories generally attack them on the grounds that their assumptions are not correct. Here are the main objections:

1. Both MM and Miller assume that personal and corporate leverage are perfect substitutes. However, an individual investing in a levered firm has less loss exposure as a result of corporate *limited liability* than if he or she used "home-made" leverage. For example, in our earlier illustration of the MM arbitrage argument, it should be noted that only the $600,000 our investor had in Firm L would be lost if that firm went bankrupt. However, if the investor engaged in arbitrage transactions and employed "homemade" leverage to invest in Firm U, then he or she could lose $900,000—the original $600,000 investment plus the $400,000 loan less the $100,000 investment in riskless bonds. This increased personal risk exposure would tend to restrain investors from engaging in arbitrage, and that could cause the equilibrium values of V_L, V_U, r_{sL}, and r_{sU} to be different from those specified by MM. Restrictions on institutional investors, who dominate capital markets today, may also retard the arbitrage process, because many institutional investors cannot legally borrow to buy stocks, hence are prohibited from engaging in homemade leverage.

   Note, though, that while limited liability may present a problem to individuals, it *does not* present a problem to corporations set up to undertake **leveraged buyouts (LBOs).** Thus, after MM's work became widely known, literally hundreds of LBO firms were established, and their founders made billions recapitalizing underleveraged firms. "Junk bonds" were created to aid in the process, and the managers of underleveraged firms who did not want their firms to be taken over increased debt usage on their own. Thus, MM's work raised the level of debt in corporate America, and that probably raised the level of economic efficiency.

2. If a levered firm's operating income declined, it would sell assets and take other measures to raise the cash necessary to meet its interest obligations and thus avoid bankruptcy. If our illustrative unlevered firm experienced the same decline in operating income, it would probably take the less drastic measure of cutting dividends rather than selling assets. If dividends were cut, investors who employed homemade leverage would not receive cash to pay the interest on their debt. Thus, homemade leverage puts stockholders in greater danger of bankruptcy than does corporate leverage.

3. Brokerage costs were assumed away by MM and Miller, making the switch from L to U costless. However, brokerage and other transaction costs do exist, and they too impede the arbitrage process.

4. MM initially assumed that corporations and investors can borrow at the risk-free rate. Although risky debt has been introduced into the analysis by others, to reach the MM and Miller conclusions it is still necessary to assume that both corporations and investors can borrow at the same rate. While major institutional investors probably can borrow at the corporate rate, many institutions are not allowed to borrow to buy securities. Further, most individual investors must borrow at higher rates than those paid by large corporations.

5. In his article, Miller concluded that an equilibrium would be reached, but to reach his equilibrium the tax benefit from corporate debt must be the same for all firms, and it must be constant for an individual firm regardless of the amount of leverage used. However, we know that tax benefits vary from firm to firm: Highly profitable companies gain the maximum tax benefit from leverage, while the benefits to firms that are struggling are much smaller. Further, some firms have other tax shields such as high depreciation, pension

plan contributions, and operating loss carryforwards, and these shields reduce the tax savings from interest payments.[8] It also appears simplistic to assume that the expected tax shield is unaffected by the amount of debt used. Higher leverage increases the probability that the firm will not be able to use the full tax shield in the future, because higher leverage increases the probability of future unprofitability and consequently lower tax rates. Note also that large, diversified corporations can use losses in one division to offset profits in another. Thus, the tax shelter benefit is more certain in large, diversified firms than in smaller, single-product companies. All things considered, it appears likely that the interest tax shield from corporate debt is more valuable to some firms than to others.

6. MM and Miller assume that there are no costs associated with financial distress, and they ignore agency costs. Further, they assume that all market participants have identical information about firms' prospects, which is also incorrect.

These six points all suggest that the MM and Miller models lead to questionable conclusions, and that the models would be better if certain of their assumptions could be relaxed. We discuss an extension of the models in the next section.

SELF-TEST

Should we accept that one of the models presented thus far (MM with zero taxes, MM with corporate taxes, or Miller) is correct? Why or why not?

Are any of the assumptions used in the models worrisome to you, and what does "worrisome" mean in this context?

17.4 An Extension to the MM Model: Nonzero Growth and a Risky Tax Shield

In this section we discuss an extension to the MM model that incorporates growth and different discount rates for the debt tax shield.[9]

MM assumed that firms pay out all of their earnings as dividends and therefore do not grow. However, most firms do grow, and growth affects the MM and Hamada results (as found in the first part of this chapter). Recall that for an unlevered firm, the WACC is just the unlevered cost of equity: WACC = r_{sU}. If g is the constant growth rate and FCF is the expected free cash flow, then the corporate value model from Chapter 15 shows that

$$V_U = \frac{FCF}{r_{sU} - g}.$$

(17-13)

---

[8]For a discussion of the impact of tax shields, see Harry DeAngelo and Ronald W. Masulis, "Optimal Capital Structure under Corporate and Personal Taxation," *Journal of Financial Economics*, March 1980, pp. 3–30; Thomas W. Downs, "Corporate Leverage and Nondebt Tax Shields: Evidence on Crowding-Out," *The Financial Review*, November 1993, pp. 549–583; John R. Graham, "Taxes and Corporate Finance: A Review," *The Review of Financial Studies*, Winter 2003, pp. 1075–1129; Moshe Ben-Horim, Shalom Hochman, and Oded Palmon, "The Impact of the 1986 Tax Reform Act on Corporate Financial Policy," *Financial Management*, Autumn 1987, pp. 29–35; Jeffrey K. Mackie-Mason, "Do Taxes Affect Corporate Financing Decisions?" *Journal of Finance*, December 1990, pp. 1471–1493; John M. Harris, Jr., Rodney L. Roenfeldt, and Philip L. Cooley, "Evidence of Financial Leverage Clienteles," *Journal of Finance*, September 1983, pp. 1125–1132; and Josef Zechner, "Tax Clienteles and Optimal Capital Structure under Uncertainty," *Journal of Business*, October 1990, pp. 465–491.
[9]See Phillip R. Daves and Michael C. Ehrhardt, "Corporate Valuation: The Combined Impact of Growth and the Tax Shield of Debt on the Cost of Capital and Systematic Risk," *Journal of Applied Finance*, Fall/Winter 2002, pp. 31–38.

As shown by Equation 17-4, the value of the levered firm is equal to the value of the unlevered firm plus gain from leverage, which is the value of the tax shield:

$$V_L = V_U + V_{\text{Tax shield}}. \qquad (17\text{-}4a)$$

However, when there is growth, the value of the tax shield is not equal to TD as it is in the MM model with corporate taxes. If the firm uses debt and g is positive, then, as the firm grows, the amount of debt will increase over time; hence the size of the annual tax shield will also increase at the rate g, provided the debt ratio remains constant. Moreover, the value of this growing tax shield is greater than the value of the constant tax shield in the MM analysis.

MM assumed that corporate debt was riskless and that the firm would always be able to use its tax savings. Therefore, they discounted the tax savings at the cost of debt, r_d, which is the risk-free rate. However, corporate debt is not risk free—firms do occasionally default on their loans. Also, a firm may not be able to use tax savings from debt in the current year if it already has a pre-tax loss from operations. Therefore, the flow of tax savings to the firm is not risk free; hence it should be discounted at a rate greater than the risk-free rate. In addition, since debt is safer than equity to an investor because it has a higher priority claim on the firm's cash flows, its discount rate should be no greater than the unlevered cost of equity. For now, assume that the appropriate discount rate for the tax savings is r_{TS}, which is greater than or equal to the cost of debt, r_d, and less than or equal to the unlevered cost of equity, r_{sU}.

If r_{TS} is the appropriate discount rate for the tax shield, r_d is the interest rate on the debt, T is the corporate tax rate, and D is the current amount of debt, then the present value of this growing tax shield is

$$V_{\text{Tax shield}} = \frac{r_d TD}{r_{TS} - g}. \qquad (17\text{-}14)$$

This formula is the same as the dividend growth formula from Chapter 8, with $r_d TD$ as the growing cash flow generated by the tax savings. Substituting Equation 17-14 into 17-4a provides a valuation equation that incorporates constant growth:

$$V_L = V_U + \left(\frac{r_d}{r_{TS} - g} \right) TD. \qquad (17\text{-}15)$$

The difference between Equation 17-15 for the value of the levered firm and the expression given in Equation 17-4 is the $r_d/(r_{TS} - g)$ term in parentheses, which reflects the added value of the tax shield due to growth. In the MM model, $r_{TS} = r_d = r_{RF}$ and $g = 0$ so the term in parentheses is equal to 1.0.

If $r_{TS} < r_{sU}$, growth can actually cause the levered cost of equity to be *less* than the unlevered cost of equity.[10] This happens because the combination of rapid growth and a low discount rate for the tax shield causes the value of the tax shield to dominate the unlevered value of the firm. If this were true, then high-growth

---

[10]See the paper by Daves and Ehrhardt in Footnote 9.

firms would tend to have larger amounts of debt than low-growth firms. However, this isn't consistent with either intuition or what we observe in the market: High-growth firms actually tend to have lower levels of debt. Regardless of the growth rate, firms with more debt should have a higher cost of equity than firms with no debt. These inconsistencies can be prevented if $r_{TS} = r_{sU}$. With this result, the value of the levered firm becomes[11]

$$V_L = V_U + \frac{r_d TD}{r_{sU} - g}. \tag{17-16}$$

Based on this valuation equation, the expressions for the levered cost of equity and the levered beta that correspond to Equations 17-6 and 17-7 are

$$r_{sL} = r_{sU} + (r_{sU} - r_d)\frac{D}{S} \tag{17-17}$$

and

$$b = b_U + (b_U - b_D)\frac{D}{S}. \tag{17-18}$$

As in Chapter 16, b_U is the beta of an unlevered firm and b is the beta of a levered firm. Because debt is not riskless, it has a beta, b_D.

Although the derivations of Equations 17-17 and 17-18 reflect corporate taxes and growth, neither of these expressions has the corporate tax rate or the growth rate in it. This means the expression for the levered required rate of return, Equation 17-17, is exactly the same as MM's expression for the levered required rate of return *without taxes*, Equation 17-2. And the expression for the levered beta, Equation 17-18, is exactly the same as Hamada's equation (with risky debt), but *without taxes*. The reason the tax rate and the growth rate drop out of these two expressions is that the growing tax shield is discounted at the unlevered cost of equity, r_{sU}, not at the cost of debt as in the MM model. The tax rate drops out because no matter how high the level of T, the total risk of the firm will not be changed since the unlevered cash flows and the tax shield are discounted at the same rate. The growth rate drops out for the same reason: An increasing debt level will not change the riskiness of the entire firm no matter what rate of growth prevails.[12]

Note that Equation 17-18 has the expression b_D. Since MM and Hamada assumed that corporate debt is riskless, its beta should be zero. However, if corporate debt is not riskless, then its beta, b_D, may not be zero. Assuming bonds lie on the Security Market Line, a bond's required return, r_d, can be expressed as $r_d = r_{RF} + b_D RP_M$. Solving for b_D gives $b_D = (r_d - r_{RF})/RP_M$.

---

[11]See Steven N. Kaplan and Richard S. Ruback, "The Valuation of Cash Flow Forecasts: An Empirical Analysis," *Journal of Finance*, September 1995, pp. 1059–1093, for a discussion of the *compressed APV* valuation method, which uses the assumption that $r_{TS} = r_{sU}$.

[12]Of course Equations 17-14, 17-15, and 17-16 also apply to firms that don't happen to be growing. In this special case, the difference between the Ehrhardt and Daves extension and the MM with taxes treatment is that MM assume that the tax shield should be discounted at the risk-free rate, while this extension to their model shows that it is more reasonable for the tax shield to be discounted at the unlevered cost of equity, r_{sU}. Because r_{sU} is greater than the risk-free rate, the value of a nongrowing tax shield will be lower when discounted at this higher rate, giving a lower value of the levered firm than what MM would predict.

Illustration of the MM Extension with Growth

Earlier in this chapter we examined Fredrickson Water Company, a zero-growth firm with unlevered value of $20 million. To see how growth affects the levered value of the firm and the levered cost of equity, let's look at Peterson Power Inc., which is similar to Fredrickson, except that it is growing. Peterson's expected free cash flow is $1 million, and the growth rate in free cash flow is 7%. Just like Fredrickson, its unlevered cost of equity is 12% and it faces a 40% tax rate. Peterson's unlevered value, $V_U = $1 million$/(0.12 − 0.07) = $20 million, just like Fredrickson.

Suppose now that Peterson, like Fredrickson, uses $10 million of debt with a cost of 8%. We see from Equation 17-16 that

$$V_L = \$20 \text{ million} + \left(\frac{0.08 \times 0.40 \times \$10 \text{ million}}{0.12 - 0.07} \right) = \$26.4 \text{ million}$$

and that the implied value of equity is

$$S = V_L - D = \$26.4 \text{ million} - \$10 \text{ million} = \$16.4 \text{ million}.$$

The increase in value due to leverage when there is 7% growth is $6.4 million, versus the increase in value of only $4 million for Fredrickson. The reason for this difference is that even though the debt tax shield is currently $(0.08)(0.40)(10 \text{ million}) = \$0.32$ million for each company, this tax shield will grow at a rate of 7% for Peterson, but it will remain fixed over time for Fredrickson. And even though Peterson and Fredrickson have the same initial dollar value of debt, their debt weights, w_D, are not the same. Peterson's $w_d = D/V_L = \$10/\$26.4 = 37.88\%$ while Fredrickson's w_d is $10/$24 = 41.67%.

With $10 million in debt, Peterson's new cost of equity is given by Equation 17-17:

$$r_{sL} = 12\% + (12\% - 8\%)\frac{0.3788}{0.6212} = 14.44\%.$$

This is higher than Fredrickson's levered cost of equity of 13.71%. Finally, Peterson's new WACC is $(1.0 - 0.3788)14.44\% + 0.3788(1 - 0.40)8\% = 10.78\%$ versus Fredrickson's WACC of 10.0%.

So, using the MM and Hamada models to calculate the value of a levered firm and its cost of capital when there is growth will (1) underestimate the value of the levered firm because they underestimate the value of the growing tax shield and (2) underestimate the levered WACC and levered cost of capital because, for a given initial amount of debt, they overestimate the firm's w_d.

SELF-TEST

Why is the value of the tax shield different when a firm grows?

Why would it be inappropriate to discount tax shield cash flows at the risk-free rate as MM do?

How will your estimates of the levered cost of equity be biased if you use the MM or Hamada models when growth is present? Why does this matter?

An unlevered firm has a value of $100 million. An otherwise identical but levered firm has $30 million in debt. Suppose that the firm is growing at a constant rate of 5%, the corporate tax rate is 40%, the cost of debt is 6%, and the unlevered cost of equity is 8% (assume r_{sU} is the appropriate discount rate for the tax shield). What is the value of the levered firm? What is the value of the stock? What is the levered cost of equity? ($124 million; $94 million; 8.64%)

17.5 Risky Debt and Equity as an Option

In the previous sections we evaluated equity and debt using the standard discounted cash flow techniques. However, we learned in Chapter 13 that if there is an opportunity for management to make a change as a result of new information after a project or investment has been started, there might be an option component to the project or investment being evaluated. This is the case with equity. To see why, consider Kunkel Inc., a small manufacturer of electronic wiring harnesses and instrumentation located in Minot, North Dakota. Kunkel's current value (debt plus equity) is $20 million, and its debt consists of $10 million face value of 5-year zero coupon debt. What decision does management make when the debt comes due? In most cases it would pay the $10 million that is due. But what if the company has done poorly and the firm is worth only $9 million? In that case, the firm is technically bankrupt, since its value is less than the amount of debt that is due. Management will choose to default on the loan—the firm will be liquidated or sold for $9 million, the debtholders will get all $9 million, and the stockholders will get nothing. Of course, if the firm is worth $10 million or more, management will choose to repay the loan. The ability to make this decision—to pay or not to pay—looks very much like an option, and the techniques we developed in Chapter 9 can be used to value it.

Using the Black-Scholes Option Pricing Model to Value Equity

To put this decision into an option context, suppose P is Kunkel's total value when the debt matures. Then if the debt is paid off, Kunkel's stockholders will receive the equivalent of P − $10 million if P > $10 million.[13] They will receive nothing if P ≤ $10 million since management will default on the bond. This can be rewritten as

$$\text{Payoff to stockholders} = \text{Max}(P - \$10 \text{ million}, 0).$$

See **FM12 Ch 17 Tool Kit.xls** at the textbook's Web site for all calculations.

This is exactly the same payoff as a European call option on the total value of the firm, P, with a strike, or exercise, price equal to the face value of the debt, $10 million. We can use the Black-Scholes Option Pricing Model from Chapter 9 to determine the value of this asset.

Recall from Chapter 9 that the value of a call option depends on five things: the price of the underlying asset, the strike price, the risk-free rate, the time to expiration, and the volatility of the market value of the underlying asset. Here the underlying asset is the total value of the firm. Assuming that volatility is 40% and the risk-free rate is 6%, here are the assumptions for the Black-Scholes model:

$$P = \$20 \text{ million}$$
$$X = \$10 \text{ million}$$
$$t = 5 \text{ years}$$
$$r_{RF} = 6\%$$
$$\sigma = 40\%$$

---

[13]Actually, rather than receive cash of P − $10 million, the stockholders will keep the company, which is worth P − $10 million, rather than turn it over to the bondholders.

The value of a European call option is given by Equations 9-2 to 9-4, which are repeated here:

$$V = P[(Nd_1)] - Xe^{-r_{RF}t}[N(d_2)] \qquad (17\text{-}19)$$

$$d_1 = \frac{\ln(P/X) + [r_{RF} + \sigma^2/2]t}{\sigma\sqrt{t}} \qquad (17\text{-}20)$$

$$d_2 = d_1 - \sigma\sqrt{t}. \qquad (17\text{-}21)$$

For Kunkel Inc.,

$$d_1 = \frac{\ln(20/10) + [0.06 + 0.40^2/2]5}{0.40\sqrt{5}} = 1.5576$$

$$d_2 = 1.5576 - 0.40\sqrt{5} = 0.6632.$$

Using the *Excel* NORMSDIST function, $N(d_1) = N(1.5576) = 0.9403$, $N(d_2) = N(0.6632) = 0.7464$, and $V = \$20(0.9403) - \$10e^{-0.06(5)}(0.7464) = \$13.28$ million. So, Kunkel's equity is worth $13.28 million, and its debt must be worth what is left over, $20 million − $13.28 million = $6.72 million. Since this is 5-year zero coupon debt, its yield must be

$$\text{Yield on debt} = \left(\frac{10}{6.72}\right)^{1/5} - 1 = 0.0827 = 8.27\%.$$

Thus, when Kunkel issued the debt, it received $6.72 million and the yield on the debt was 8.27%. Notice that the yield on the debt, 8.27%, is greater than the 6% risk-free rate. This is because the firm might default if its value falls enough, so the bonds are risky. Note also that the yield on the debt depends on the value of the option, and hence the riskiness of the firm. The debt will have a lower value, and a higher yield, the more the option is worth.

Managerial Incentives

The only decision an investor in a stock option can make, once the option is purchased, is whether and when to exercise it. However, this restriction does not apply to equity when it is viewed as an option on the total value of the firm. Management has some leeway to affect the riskiness of the firm through its capital budgeting and investment decisions, and it can affect the amount of capital invested in the firm through its dividend policy.

Capital Budgeting Decisions

When Kunkel issued the $10 million face value debt discussed above, the yield was determined in part by Kunkel's riskiness, which in turn was determined in part by what management intended to do with the $6.72 million it raised. We know from our analysis in Chapter 9 that options are worth more when volatility

Table 17-1

The Value of Kunkel's Debt and Equity
for Various Levels of Volatility

Standard Deviation	Equity	Debt	Debt Yield
20%	$12.62	$7.38	6.25%
30	12.83	7.17	6.89
40	**13.28**	**6.72**	**8.27**
50	13.86	6.14	10.25
60	14.51	5.49	12.74
70	15.17	4.83	15.66
80	15.81	4.19	18.99
90	16.41	3.59	22.74
100	16.96	3.04	26.92
110	17.46	2.54	31.56
120	17.90	2.10	36.68

FM

e-resource

See **FM12 Ch 17 Tool Kit.xls** at the textbook's Web site for details.

is higher. This means that if Kunkel's management can find a way to increase its riskiness without decreasing the total value of the firm, this will increase the value of the equity while decreasing the value of the debt. Management can do this by selecting risky rather than safe investment projects. Table 17-1 shows the value of the equity, debt, and the yield on the debt for a range of possible volatilities. The Tool Kit for this chapter shows the calculations.

Kunkel's current volatility is 40% so its equity is worth $13.28 million, and its debt is worth $6.72 million. However, if, after incurring the debt, management undertakes projects that increase its riskiness from a volatility of 40% to a volatility of 80%, the value of Kunkel's equity will increase by $2.53 million to $15.81 million, and the value of its debt will decrease by the same amount. This 19% increase in the value of the equity represents a transfer of wealth from the bondholders to the stockholders. A corresponding transfer of wealth from stockholders to bondholders would occur if Kunkel undertook projects that were safer than originally planned. Table 17-1 shows that if management undertakes safe projects and drives the volatility down to 30%, stockholders will lose (and bondholders will gain) $0.45 million.

Such a strategy of investing borrowed funds in risky assets is called **bait and switch** because the firm obtains the money, promising one investment policy, and then switches to another policy. The bait and switch problem is more severe when a firm's value is low relative to its level of debt. When Kunkel's total value was $20 million, doubling its volatility from 40% to 80% increased its equity value by 19%. But if Kunkel had done poorly in recent years and its total value were only $10 million, then the impact of increasing volatility would be much greater. Table 17-2 shows that if Kunkel's total value were only $10 million and if it issued $10 million face value of 5-year zero coupon debt, its equity would be worth $4.46 million at a volatility of 40%. Doubling the volatility to 80% would increase the value of the equity to $6.83 million, or by 53%. The incentive for management to "roll the dice" with borrowed funds can be enormous, and if management owns lots of stock options, their payoff from rolling the dice is even greater than the payoff to the stockholders!

Debt and Equity Values for Various Levels of
Volatility When the Total Value is $10 Million

Standard Deviation	Equity	Debt	Debt Yield
20%	$12.62	$7.38	6.25%
30	3.80	6.20	10.02
40	**4.46**	**5.54**	**12.52**
50	5.10	4.90	15.35
60	5.72	4.28	18.49
70	6.30	3.70	21.98
80	6.83	3.17	25.81
90	7.31	2.69	30.04
100	7.74	2.26	34.68
110	8.13	1.87	39.77
120	8.46	1.54	45.36

Bondholders are aware of these incentives and write covenants into debt issues that restrict management's ability to invest in riskier projects than originally promised. However, their attempts to protect themselves are not always successful, as the recent failures of Enron and Global Crossing demonstrate. The combination of a risky industry, high levels of debt, and option-based compensation has proven to be very dangerous!

Equity with Risky Coupon Debt

We have analyzed the simple case when a firm has zero coupon debt outstanding. The analysis becomes much more complicated when a firm has debt that requires periodic interest payments, because then management can decide whether or not to default on each interest payment date. For example, suppose Kunkel's $10 million of debt is a 1-year, 8% loan with semiannual payments. The scheduled payments are $400,000 in 6 months, and then $10.4 million at the end of the year. If management makes the scheduled $400,000 interest payment, then the stockholders will acquire the right to make the next payment of $10.4 million. If it does not make the $400,000 payment, the stockholders lose the right to make the next payment by defaulting, and hence they lose the firm.[14] In other words, at the beginning of the year the stockholders have an option to purchase an option. The option they own has an exercise price of $400,000 and it expires in 6 months, and if they exercise it, they will acquire an option to purchase the entire firm for $10.4 million in another 6 months.

If the debt were 2-year debt, then there would be four decision points for management, and the stockholders' position would be like an option on an option on

---

[14]Actually, bankruptcy is far more complicated than our example suggests. When a firm approaches default, it can take a number of actions, and even after filing for bankruptcy, stockholders can delay a takeover by bondholders for a long time, during which the value of the firm can deteriorate further. So, stockholders can often extract concessions from bondholders in situations where it looks like the bondholders should get all of the firm's value. Bankruptcy is discussed in more detail in Chapter 24.

an option on an option! These types of options are called **compound options,** and the techniques to value them are beyond the scope of this book. However, the incentives discussed above for the case when the firm has risky zero coupon debt still apply when the firm has to make periodic interest payments.[15]

SELF-TEST

Discuss how equity can be viewed as an option. Who has the option and what decision can they make?

Why would management want to increase the riskiness of the firm? Why would this make bondholders unhappy?

What can bondholders do to limit management's ability to bait and switch?

17.6 Capital Structure Theory: Our View

The great contribution of the capital structure models developed by MM, Miller, and their followers is that these models identified the specific benefits and costs of using debt—the tax benefits, financial distress costs, and so on. Prior to MM, no capital structure theory existed, so we had no systematic way of analyzing the effects of debt financing.

The trade-off model we discussed in Chapter 16 is summarized graphically in Figure 17-2. The top graph shows the relationships between the debt ratio and the cost of debt, the cost of equity, and the WACC. Both r_s and $r_d(1 - T_c)$ rise steadily with increases in leverage, but the rate of increase accelerates at higher debt levels, reflecting agency costs and the increased probability of financial distress. The WACC first declines, then hits a minimum at D/V^*, and then begins to rise. Note that the value of D in D/V^* in the upper graph is D^*, the level of debt in the lower graph that maximizes the firm's value. Thus, a firm's WACC is minimized and its value is maximized at the same capital structure. Note also that the general shapes of the curves apply regardless of whether we are using the modified MM with corporate taxes model, the Miller model, or a variant of these models.

Unfortunately, it is impossible to quantify accurately the costs and benefits of debt financing, so it is impossible to pinpoint D/V^*, the capital structure that maximizes a firm's value. Most experts believe such a structure exists for every firm, but that it changes over time as firms' operations and investors' preferences change. Most experts also believe that, as shown in Figure 17-2, the relationship between value and leverage is relatively flat over a fairly broad range, so large deviations from the optimal capital structure can occur without materially affecting the stock price.

Now consider signaling theory, which we discussed in Chapter 16. Because of asymmetric information, investors know less about a firm's prospects than its managers know. Further, managers try to maximize value for *current* stockholders, not new ones. Therefore, if the firm has excellent prospects, management will not want to issue new shares, but if things look bleak, then a new stock offering would benefit current stockholders. Consequently, investors take a stock offering to be a signal of bad news, so stock prices tend to decline when new issues are announced. As a result, new equity financings are relatively expensive. The net effect of signaling is to motivate firms to maintain a reserve borrowing capacity designed to permit future investment opportunities to be financed by debt if internal funds are not available.

---

[15]For more on viewing equity as an option, see D. Galai and R. Masulis, "The Option Pricing Model and the Risk Factor of Stock," *Journal of Financial Economics,* 1976, pp. 53–81. For a discussion on compound options, see Robert Geske, "The Valuation of Corporate Liabilities as Compound Options," *Journal of Financial and Quantitative Analysis,* June 1984, pp. 541–552.

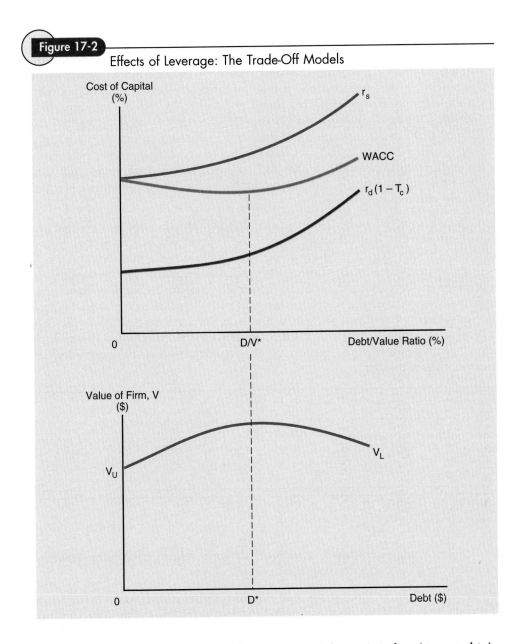

Figure 17-2

Effects of Leverage: The Trade-Off Models

By combining the trade-off and asymmetric information theories, we obtain this explanation for firms' behavior:

1. Debt financing provides benefits because of the tax deductibility of interest, so firms should have some debt in their capital structures.
2. However, financial distress and agency costs place limits on debt usage—beyond some point, these costs offset the tax advantage of debt. The costs of financial distress are especially harmful to firms whose values consist primarily of intangible growth options, such as research and development. Such firms should have lower levels of debt than firms whose asset bases consist mostly of tangible assets.
3. Because of problems resulting from asymmetric information and flotation costs, low-growth firms should follow a pecking order, by raising capital first from internal sources, then by borrowing, and finally by issuing new stock. In fact, such low-growth firms rarely need to issue external equity. High-growth

firms whose growth occurs primarily through increases in tangible assets should follow the same pecking order, but usually they will need to issue new stock as well as debt. High-growth firms whose values consist primarily of intangible growth options may run out of internally generated cash, but they should emphasize stock rather than debt due to the severe problems that financial distress imposes on such firms.

4. Finally, because of asymmetric information, firms should maintain a reserve of borrowing capacity in order to be able to take advantage of good investment opportunities without having to issue stock at low prices, and this reserve will cause the actual debt ratio to be lower than that suggested by the trade-off models.

There is some evidence that managers do attempt to behave in ways that are consistent with this view of capital structure. In a survey of CFOs, about two-thirds of the CFOs said that they follow a "hierarchy in which the most advantageous sources of funds are exhausted before other sources are used." The hierarchy usually followed the pecking order of first internally generated cash flow, then debt, and finally external equity, which is consistent with the predicted behavior of most low-growth firms. But there were occasions in which external equity was the first source of financing, which would be consistent with the theory for either high-growth firms or firms whose agency and financial distress costs have exceeded the benefit of the tax savings.[16]

SELF-TEST

Summarize the trade-off and signaling theories of capital structure.

Are the trade-off and signaling theories mutually exclusive; that is, might both be correct?

Does capital structure theory provide managers with a model that can be used to set a precise optimal capital structure?

Summary

In this chapter, we discussed a variety of topics related to capital structure decisions. The key concepts covered are listed below:

- In 1958, **Franco Modigliani and Merton Miller (MM)** proved, under a restrictive set of assumptions including zero taxes, that capital structure is irrelevant; that is, according to the original MM article, a firm's value is not affected by its financing mix.
- MM later added **corporate taxes** to their model and reached the conclusion that capital structure does matter. Indeed, their model led to the conclusion that firms should use 100% debt financing.
- MM's model with corporate taxes demonstrated that the primary benefit of debt stems from the **tax deductibility of interest payments.**

---

[16]For more on capital budgeting issues, see Ravindra R. Kamath, "Long-Term Financing Decisions: Views and Practices of Financial Managers of NYSE Firms," *Financial Review*, May 1997, pp. 350–356; Claire E. Crutchley and Robert S. Hansen, "A Test of the Agency Theory of Managerial Ownership, Corporate Leverage, and Corporate Dividends," *Financial Management*, Winter 1989, pp. 36–46; Michael T. Dugan and Keith A. Shriver, "An Empirical Comparison of Alternative Methods for Estimating the Degree of Operating Leverage," *Financial Review*, May 1992, pp. 309–321; Dilip K. Ghosh, "Optimum Capital Structure Redefined," *Financial Review*, August 1992, pp. 411–429; William A. Kelly, Jr., and James A. Miles, "Capital Structure Theory and the Fisher Effect," *Financial Review*, February 1989, pp. 53–73; J. Michael Pinegar and Lisa Wilbricht, "What Managers Think of Capital Structure Theory: A Survey," *Financial Management*, Winter 1989, pp. 82–91; Frederick C. Scherr, "A Multiperiod Mean-Variance Model of Optimal Capital Structure," *Financial Review*, February 1987, pp. 1–31.

- Later, Miller extended the theory to include **personal taxes.** The introduction of personal taxes reduces, but does not eliminate, the benefits of debt financing. Thus, the **Miller model** also leads to 100% debt financing.
- The introduction of growth changes the MM and Hamada results for the levered cost of equity and the levered beta.
- If the firm is growing at a constant rate, the debt tax shield is discounted at r_{sU}, and debt remains a constant proportion of the capital structure, then

$$r_{sL} = r_{sU} + (r_{sU} - r_d)\frac{D}{S}$$

and

$$b = b_U + (b_U - b_D)\frac{D}{S}.$$

- When debt is risky, management may choose to default on it. If the debt is zero coupon debt, then this makes equity like an option on the value of the firm with a strike price equal to the face value of the debt. If the debt has periodic interest payments, then the equity is like an option on an option, or a **compound option.**
- When a firm has risky debt and equity is like an option, management has an incentive to increase the firm's risk in order to increase the equity value at the expense of the debt value. This is called **bait and switch.**

Questions

(17-1)   Define each of the following terms:
  a.   MM Proposition I without taxes; with corporate taxes
  b.   MM Proposition II without taxes; with corporate taxes
  c.   Miller model
  d.   Financial distress costs
  e.   Agency costs
  f.   Trade-off model
  g.   Value of debt tax shield
  h.   Equity as an option

(17-2)   What term refers to the uncertainty inherent in projections of future ROIC?

(17-3)   Firms with relatively high nonfinancial fixed costs are said to have a high degree of what?

(17-4)   "One type of leverage affects both EBIT and EPS. The other type affects only EPS." Explain this statement.

(17-5)   Why is the following statement true? "Other things being the same, firms with relatively stable sales are able to carry relatively high debt ratios."

(17-6)   Why do public utility companies usually have capital structures that are different from those of retail firms?

(17-7)   Why is EBIT generally considered to be independent of financial leverage? Why might EBIT actually be influenced by financial leverage at high debt levels?

(17-8)   If a firm went from zero debt to successively higher levels of debt, why would you expect its stock price to first rise, then hit a peak, and then begin to decline?

Self-Test Problem   Solution Appears in Appendix A

(ST-1)
MM with Financial Distress Costs

B. Gibbs Inc. is an unleveraged firm, and it has constant expected operating earnings (EBIT) of $2 million per year. The firm's tax rate is 40%, and its market value is $V = S = \$12$ million. Management is considering the use of some debt financing. (Debt would be issued and used to buy back stock, so the size of the firm would remain constant.) Because interest expense is tax deductible, the value of the firm would tend to increase as debt is added to the capital structure, but there would be an offset in the form of a rising risk of financial distress. The firm's analysts have estimated, as an approximation, that the present value of any future financial distress costs is $8 million and that the probability of distress would increase with leverage according to the following schedule:

Value of Debt	Probability of Financial Distress
$ 2,500,000	0.00%
5,000,000	1.25
7,500,000	2.50
10,000,000	6.25
12,500,000	12.50
15,000,000	31.25
20,000,000	75.00

a. What is the firm's cost of equity and weighted average cost of capital at this time?
b. According to the "pure" MM with-tax model, what is the optimal level of debt?
c. What is the optimal capital structure when financial distress costs are included?
d. Plot the value of the firm, with and without distress costs, as a function of the level of debt.

Problems   Answers Appear in Appendix B

Easy Problems 1–3

(17-1)
MM Model with Zero Taxes

An unlevered firm has a value of $500 million. An otherwise identical but levered firm has $50 million in debt. Under the MM zero-tax model, what is the value of the levered firm?

(17-2)
MM Model with Corporate Taxes

An unlevered firm has a value of $800 million. An otherwise identical but levered firm has $60 million in debt. If the corporate tax rate is 35%, what is the value of the levered firm using the MM corporate-tax model?

(17-3)
Miller Model with Corporate and Personal Taxes

An unlevered firm has a value of $600 million. An otherwise identical but levered firm has $240 million in debt. Under the Miller model, what is the value of a levered firm if the corporate tax rate is 34%, the personal tax rate on equity is 10%, and the personal tax rate on debt is 35%?

Intermediate Problems 4–7

(17-4)
Business and Financial Risk—MM Model

Air Tampa has just been incorporated, and its board of directors is currently grappling with the question of optimal capital structure. The company plans to offer commuter air services between Tampa and smaller surrounding cities. Jaxair has been around for a few years, and it has about the same basic business risk as Air Tampa would have. Jaxair's market-determined beta is 1.8, and it has a current market value debt ratio (total debt/total assets) of 50% and a federal-plus-state tax rate of 40%. Air Tampa expects only to be marginally profitable at start-up; hence its tax rate would only be 25%. Air Tampa's owners expect that the total book and market value of the firm's stock, if it uses zero debt, would be $10 million. Air Tampa's CFO believes that the MM and Hamada formulas for the value of a levered firm and the levered firm's cost of capital should be used. These are given in Equations 17-4, 17-6, and 17-7.

a. Estimate the beta of an unlevered firm in the commuter airline business based on Jaxair's market-determined beta. (Hint: Jaxair's market-determined beta is a levered beta. Use Equation 17-7 and solve for b_U.)

b. Now assume that $r_d = r_{RF} = 10\%$ and the market risk premium, RP_M, is 5%. Find the required rate of return on equity for an unlevered commuter airline.

c. Air Tampa is considering three capital structures: (1) $2 million debt, (2) $4 million debt, and (3) $6 million debt. Estimate Air Tampa's r_s for these debt levels.

d. Calculate Air Tampa's r_s at $6 million debt assuming its federal-plus-state tax rate is now 40%. Compare this with your corresponding answer to part c. (Hint: The increase in the tax rate causes V_U to drop to $8 million.)

(17-5)
MM without Taxes

Companies U and L are identical in every respect except that U is unlevered while L has $10 million of 5% bonds outstanding. Assume (1) that all of the MM assumptions are met, (2) that there are no corporate or personal taxes, (3) that EBIT is $2 million, and (4) that the cost of equity to Company U is 10%.

a. What value would MM estimate for each firm?

b. What is r_s for Firm U? For Firm L?

c. Find S_L, and then show that $S_L + D = V_L = \$20$ million.

d. What is the WACC for Firm U? For Firm L?

e. Suppose $V_U = \$20$ million and $V_L = \$22$ million. According to MM, do these values represent an equilibrium? If not, explain the process by which equilibrium would be restored.

(17-6)
MM with Corporate Taxes

Companies U and L are identical in every respect except that U is unlevered while L has $10 million of 5% bonds outstanding. Assume that (1) all of the MM assumptions are met, (2) both firms are subject to a 40% federal-plus-state corporate tax rate, (3) EBIT is $2 million, and (4) the unlevered cost of equity is 10%.

a. What value would MM now estimate for each firm? (Use Proposition I.)

b. What is r_s for Firm U? For Firm L?

c. Find S_L, and then show that $S_L + D = V_L$ results in the same value as obtained in part a.

d. What is the WACC for Firm U? For Firm L?

(17-7)
Miller Model

Companies U and L are identical in every respect except that U is unlevered while L has $10 million of 5% bonds outstanding. Assume that (1) all of the MM assumptions are met, (2) both firms are subject to a 40% federal-plus-state corporate tax rate,

(3) EBIT is $2 million, (4) investors in both firms face a tax rate of $T_d = 28\%$ on debt income and $T_s = 20\%$, on average, on stock income, and (5) the appropriate required pre-personal-tax rate r_{sU} is 10%.

a. What is the value of the unlevered firm, V_U? (Note that V_U is now reduced by the personal tax on stock income; hence $V_U = \$12$ million as in Problem 17-6.)

b. What is the value of V_L?

c. What is the gain from leverage in this situation? Compare this with the gain from leverage in Problem 17-6.

d. Set $T_c = T_s = T_d = 0$. What is the value of the levered firm? The gain from leverage?

e. Now suppose $T_s = T_d = 0$, $T_c = 40\%$. What are the value of the levered firm and the gain from leverage?

f. Assume that $T_d = 28\%$, $T_s = 28\%$, and $T_c = 40\%$. Now what are the value of the levered firm and the gain from leverage?

Challenging Problems 8–10

(17-8)
MM Extension with Growth
Schwarzentraub Industries' expected free cash flow for the year is $500,000; in the future free cash flow is expected to grow at a rate of 9%. The company currently has no debt, and its cost of equity is 13%. Its tax rate is 40%. (Hint: Use Equations 17-16 and 17-17.)

a. Find V_U.

b. Find V_L and r_{sL} if Schwarzentraub uses $5 million in debt with a cost of 7%. Use the extension to the MM model that allows for growth.

c. Based on V_U from part a, find V_L and r_{sL} using the MM model (with taxes) if Schwarzentraub uses $5 million in 7% debt.

d. Explain the difference between the answers to parts b and c.

(17-9)
MM with and without Taxes
International Associates (IA) is just about to commence operations as an international trading company. The firm will have book assets of $10 million, and it expects to earn a 16% return on these assets before taxes. However, because of certain tax arrangements with foreign governments, IA will not pay any taxes; that is, its tax rate will be zero. Management is trying to decide how to raise the required $10 million. It is known that the capitalization rate for an all-equity firm in this business is 11%; that is, $r_U = 11\%$. Further, IA can borrow at a rate $r_d = 6\%$. Assume that the MM assumptions apply.

a. According to MM, what will be the value of IA if it uses no debt? If it uses $6 million of 6% debt?

b. What are the values of the WACC and r_s at debt levels of D = $0, D = $6 million, and D = $10 million? What effect does leverage have on firm value? Why?

c. Assume the initial facts of the problem ($r_d = 6\%$, EBIT = $1.6 million, $r_{sU} = 11\%$), but now assume that a 40% federal-plus-state corporate tax rate exists. Find the new market values for IA with zero debt and with $6 million of debt, using the MM formulas.

d. What are the values of the WACC and r_s at debt levels of D = $0, D = $6 million, and D = $10 million, assuming a 40% corporate tax rate? Plot the relationships between the value of the firm and the debt ratio, and between capital costs and the debt ratio.

e. What is the maximum dollar amount of debt financing that can be used? What is the value of the firm at this debt level? What is the cost of this debt?

Mini Case   **637**

f. How would each of the following factors tend to change the values you plotted in your graph?
   (1) The interest rate on debt increases as the debt ratio rises.
   (2) At higher levels of debt, the probability of financial distress rises.

(17-10)
Equity Viewed as an Option

A. Fethe Inc. is a custom manufacturer of guitars, mandolins, and other stringed instruments located near Knoxville, Tennessee. Fethe's current value of operations, which is also its value of debt plus equity, is estimated to be $5 million. Fethe has $2 million face-value zero coupon debt that is due in 2 years. The risk-free rate is 6%, and the standard deviation of returns for companies similar to Fethe is 50%. Fethe's owners view their equity investment as an option and would like to know the value of their investment.

a. Using the Black-Scholes Option Pricing Model, how much is Fethe's equity worth?

b. How much is the debt worth today? What is its yield?

c. How would the equity value and the yield on the debt change if Fethe's managers were able to use risk management techniques to reduce its volatility to 30%? Can you explain this?

Spreadsheet Problem

(17-11)
Build a Model: Equity Viewed as an Option

Start with the partial model in the file *FM12 Ch 17 P11 Build a Model.xls* at the textbook's Web site. Rework Problem 17-10 using a spreadsheet model. After completing the problem as it appears, answer the following related questions.

a. Graph the cost of debt versus the face value of debt for values of the face value from $0.5 to $8 million.

b. Graph the values of debt and equity for volatilities from 0.10 to 0.90 when the face value of the debt is $2 million.

c. Repeat part b, but instead using a face value of debt of $5 million. What can you say about the difference between the graphs in part b and part c?

e-resource
See *FM12 Ch 17 P11 Build a Model.xls* for details.

e-resource

Cyberproblem

Please go to the textbook's Web site to access any Cyberproblems.

Mini Case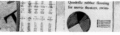

David Lyons, CEO of Lyons Solar Technologies, is concerned about his firm's level of debt financing. The company uses short-term debt to finance its temporary working capital needs, but it does not use any permanent (long-term) debt. Other solar technology companies average about 30% debt, and Mr. Lyons wonders why they use so much more debt and how it affects stock prices. To gain some insights into the matter, he poses the following questions to you, his recently hired assistant:

a. *BusinessWeek* recently ran an article on companies' debt policies, and the names Modigliani and Miller (MM) were mentioned several times as leading researchers on the theory of capital structure. Briefly, who are MM, and what assumptions are embedded in the MM and Miller models?

b. Assume that Firms U and L are in the same risk class, and that both have EBIT = $500,000. Firm U uses no debt financing, and its cost of equity is $r_{sU} = 14\%$. Firm L has $1 million of debt outstanding at a cost of $r_d = 8\%$. There are no taxes. Assume that the MM assumptions hold, and then:

   (1) Find V, S, r_s, and WACC for Firms U and L.

   (2) Graph (a) the relationships between capital costs and leverage as measured by D/V, and (b) the relationship between value and D.

c. Using the data given in part b, but now assuming that Firms L and U are both subject to a 40% corporate tax rate, repeat the analysis called for in b-(1) and b-(2) under the MM with-tax model.

d. Now suppose investors are subject to the following tax rates: $T_d = 30\%$ and $T_s = 12\%$.

   (1) What is the gain from leverage according to the Miller model?

   (2) How does this gain compare with the gain in the MM model with corporate taxes?

   (3) What does the Miller model imply about the effect of corporate debt on the value of the firm; that is, how do personal taxes affect the situation?

e. What capital structure policy recommendations do the three theories (MM without taxes, MM with corporate taxes, and Miller) suggest to financial managers? Empirically, do firms appear to follow any one of these guidelines?

f. How is the analysis in part c different if Firms U and L are growing? Assume that both firms are growing at a rate of 7% and that the investment in net operating assets required to support this growth is 10% of EBIT.

g. What if L's debt is risky? For the purpose of this example, assume that the value of L's operations is $4 million—which is the value of its debt plus equity. Assume also that its debt consists of 1-year zero coupon bonds with a face value of $2 million. Finally, assume that L's volatility is 0.60 ($\sigma = 0.60$) and that the risk-free rate is 6%.

h. What is the value of L's stock for volatilities between 0.20 and 0.95? What incentives might the manager of L have if she understands this relationship? What might debtholders do in response?

Selected Additional Cases

The following cases from Textchoice, Cengage Learning's online library, cover many of the concepts discussed in this chapter and are available at http://www.textchoice2.com.

Klein-Brigham Series:
Case 7, "Seattle Steel Products," Case 9, "Kleen Kar, Inc.," Case 10, "Aspeon Sparkling Water," Case 43, "Mountain Springs," Case 57, "Greta Cosmetics," Case 74, "The Western Company," Case 83, "Armstrong Production Company," and

Case 99, "Moore Plumbing Supply Company," focus on capital structure theory. Case 8, "Johnson Window Company," and Case 56, "Isle Marine Boat Company," cover operating and financial leverage.

Brigham-Buzzard Series:
Case 8, "Powerline Network Corporation," covers operating leverage, financial leverage, and the optimal capital structure.

chapter 18

Distributions to Shareholders: Dividends and Repurchases

Profitable companies regularly face three important questions: (1) How much of our free cash flow should we pass on to shareholders? (2) Should we provide this cash to stockholders by raising the dividend or by repurchasing stock? (3) Should we maintain a stable, consistent payment policy, or should we let the payments vary as conditions change?

In this chapter we will discuss many of the issues that affect firms' policies. As we will see, mature companies with stable cash flows and limited growth opportunities tend to return more of their cash to shareholders, either by paying dividends or by using the cash to repurchase common stock. By contrast, rapidly growing companies with good investment opportunities are prone to invest most of their available cash in new projects and thus are less likely to pay dividends or repurchase stock. Microsoft, which was long regarded as the epitome of a growth company, illustrates this tendency. Its sales grew from $786 million in 1989 to $28.365 billion as of June 30, 2002, which translates to an annual growth rate of nearly 32%. Much of this growth came from investments in new products and technology, and given its emphasis on growth, it paid no dividends.

Market saturation and competition (including piracy) have caused its sales growth to slow. In the fiscal year ending, June 30, 2006, Microsoft reported annual sales growth of about 11%, still respectable but far short of its spectacular earlier growth rates. As growth slowed, Microsoft's cash flows increased, and during 2006 its cash flow from operating activities was $14.4 billion.

As companies tend to do when growth slows and cash flows increase, Microsoft began paying a regular dividend in 2003, and it stunned the world with a huge special dividend in 2005, which, when combined with its regular dividend, totaled over $36 billion. Perhaps not coincidentally, Microsoft's decision to pay dividends coincided with a change in the Tax Code that lowered the tax rate on dividends from 35% to 15% for most investors.

In 2006, Microsoft paid regular dividends of $3.5 billion, but it also repurchased $17.1 billion in stock, for a total cash flow to shareholders of $20.6 billion. Microsoft still has over $34 billion in cash and marketable securities on its balance sheets, so investors are looking for more large cash distributions in the future.

e-resource

The textbook's Web site contains an *Excel* file that will guide you through the chapter's calculations. The file for this chapter is *FM12 Ch 18 Tool Kit.xls*, and we encourage you to open the file and follow along as you read the chapter.

Successful companies generate net operating profit after taxes (NOPAT). A company's growth opportunities and replacement requirements, identified through capital budgeting and financial planning, determine the amount that should be invested in operating capital. Subtracting the investment in operating capital from NOPAT results in free cash flow (FCF), which is the amount available for distribution to investors after paying expenses and taxes and making the necessary investments in operating capital. There are five potentially "good" uses for free cash flow: (1) to pay interest expenses, (2) to pay off debt, (3) to pay dividends, (4) to repurchase stock, and (5) to buy nonoperating assets such as Treasury bills or other marketable securities.[1] The capital structure choice determines the payments for interest expenses and debt principal, and the company's working capital policies (discussed in Chapter 22) determine its level of marketable securities. The remaining FCF should be distributed to shareholders, with the only choice being how much to distribute in the form of dividends versus stock repurchases.

Obviously, this is a simplification since companies (1) sometimes scale back their operating plans for sales and asset growth if such reductions are needed to maintain an existing dividend, (2) temporarily adjust their current financing mix in response to market conditions, and (3) often use marketable securities as shock absorbers for fluctuations in short-term cash flows. Still, there is interdependence among shareholder distributions, operating plans (which have the biggest impact on free cash flow), financing plans (which have the biggest impact on the cost of capital), and working capital policies (which determine the target level of marketable securities).

An excellent source of recent dividend news for major corporations is available at the Web site of Corporate Financials Online at **http://www .cfonews.com/scs**. By clicking the down arrow of the "News Category" box to the left of the screen, you may select "Dividends" to receive a list of companies with dividend news. Click on any company, and you will see its latest dividend news.

18.1 The Level of Distributions and Firm Value

Shareholder distributions for a wealth-maximizing firm affect the value of operations only to the extent that they change the cost of capital or investors' perceptions regarding expected free cash flow.[2] Here are the central issues addressed in this chapter: Can a company increase its value through (1) its choice of **distribution policy,** defined as the *level* of distributions, (2) the *form* of distributions (cash dividends versus stock repurchases), and (3) the *stability* of distributions?

The answer depends in part on investors' preferences for returns as dividend yields versus capital gains. The mix of yield return versus gains return is determined by the **target distribution ratio,** which is the percentage of net income distributed to shareholders through cash dividends or stock repurchases, and the **target payout ratio,** which is the percentage of net income paid as a cash dividend. Notice that the payout ratio must be less than the distribution ratio since the distribution ratio includes stock repurchases as well as cash dividends.

A high distribution ratio and a high payout ratio mean that a company pays large dividends and has small, or zero, stock repurchases. In this situation, the

---

[1]Recall from Chapter 3 that the company's cost of paying interest is on an after-tax basis. Recall also that a company doesn't *spend* FCF on operating assets (such as the acquisition of another company), because those expenditures were already deducted when calculating FCF. In other words, the purchase of an operating asset (even if it is another company) is not a *use* of FCF; instead, it is a *source* of FCF (albeit a "negative source"). Also, most growing companies actually issue new debt each year rather than repay debt. This "negative use" of FCF provides more FCF for the other uses.

[2]Shareholder distributions also affect the level of marketable securities, a nonoperating asset, which in turn affects the stock price.

Corporate Valuation and Distributions to Shareholders

Free cash flow is the amount of cash available for distribution to all investors (shareholders and debtholders) after paying expenses and taxes and making investments in the operating capital required to support the company's growth. Most of this book has focused on FCF generation, including its risk and expected level. In contrast, this chapter focuses on a use of FCF: How much FCF should be distributed to shareholders, and should it be distributed as dividends or stock repurchases? In addition, we show how distributions to shareholders are related to financing choices. Finally, we discuss ways that shareholders perceive distributions as signals regarding a firm's risk and expected future free cash flows.

dividend yield is relatively high and the expected capital gain is low. If a company has a large distribution ratio but a small payout ratio, then it pays low dividends but regularly repurchases stock, resulting in a low dividend yield but a relatively high expected capital gain yield. If a company has a low distribution ratio, then it must also have a relatively low payout ratio, again resulting in a low dividend yield and hopefully a relatively high capital gain. Therefore, a firm's **optimal distribution policy** must strike a balance between cash dividends and capital gains so as to maximize the stock price.

In this section we examine three theories of investor preferences for dividend yield versus capital gains: (1) the dividend irrelevance theory, (2) the "bird-in-the-hand" theory, and (3) the tax preference theory.

Dividend Irrelevance Theory

It has been argued that dividend policy has no effect on either the price of a firm's stock or its cost of capital. If dividend policy has no significant effects, then it would be *irrelevant*. The principal proponents of the **dividend irrelevance theory** are Merton Miller and Franco Modigliani (MM).[3] They argued that the firm's value is determined only by its basic earning power and its business risk. In other words, MM argued that the value of the firm depends only on the income produced by its assets, not on how this income is split between dividends and retained earnings.

To understand MM's argument, recognize that any shareholder can in theory construct his or her own dividend policy. For example, if a firm does not pay dividends, a shareholder who wants a 5% dividend can "create" it by selling 5% of his or her stock. Conversely, if a company pays a higher dividend than an investor desires, the investor can use the unwanted dividends to buy additional shares of the company's stock. If investors could buy and sell shares and thus create their own dividend policy without incurring costs, then the firm's dividend policy would truly be irrelevant. Note, though, that investors who want additional dividends must incur brokerage costs to sell shares and pay taxes on any capital gains. Investors who do not want dividends incur brokerage costs to purchase shares with their dividends. Because taxes and brokerage costs certainly exist, dividend policy may well be relevant.

---

[3]See Merton H. Miller and Franco Modigliani, "Dividend Policy, Growth, and the Valuation of Shares," *Journal of Business*, October 1961, pp. 411–433. However, their conclusion is valid only if investors expect managers eventually to pay out the equivalent of the present value of all future free cash flows; see Harry DeAngelo and Linda DeAngelo, "The Irrelevance of the MM Dividend Irrelevance Theorem," *Journal of Financial Economics*, 2006, pp. 293–315.

In developing their dividend theory, MM made a number of assumptions, especially the absence of taxes and brokerage costs. Obviously, taxes and brokerage costs do exist, so the MM irrelevance theory may not be true. However, MM argued (correctly) that all economic theories are based on simplifying assumptions, and that the validity of a theory must be judged by empirical tests, not by the realism of its assumptions. We will discuss empirical tests of MM's dividend irrelevance theory shortly.

Bird-in-the-Hand Theory: Dividends Are Preferred

The principal conclusion of MM's dividend irrelevance theory is that dividend policy does not affect the required rate of return on equity, r_s. This conclusion has been hotly debated in academic circles. In particular, Myron Gordon and John Lintner argued that r_s *decreases* as the dividend payout is increased because investors are less certain of receiving the capital gains that are supposed to result from retaining earnings than they are of receiving dividend payments.[4] Gordon and Lintner said, in effect, that investors value a dollar of expected dividends more highly than a dollar of expected capital gains because the dividend yield component is less risky than the expected capital gain.

MM disagreed. They argued that r_s is independent of dividend policy, which implies that investors are indifferent between dividends and capital gains. MM called the Gordon-Lintner argument the **bird-in-the-hand** fallacy because, in MM's view, most investors plan to reinvest their dividends in the stock of the same or similar firms, and, in any event, the risk of the firm's cash flows to investors in the long run is determined by the risk of operating cash flows, not by dividend payout policy.

Tax Preference Theory: Capital Gains Are Preferred

Before 2003, individual investors paid ordinary income taxes on dividends but lower rates on long-term capital gains. The Jobs and Growth Act of 2003 changed this and reduced the tax rate on dividend income to the same as on long-term capital gains.[5] However, there are two reasons stock price appreciation is taxed more favorably than dividend income. First, due to time value effects, a dollar of taxes paid in the future has a lower effective cost than a dollar paid today. So even if dividends and gains are taxed equally, capital gains are never taxed sooner than dividends. Second, if a stock is held by someone until he or she dies, no capital gains tax is due at all—the beneficiaries who receive the stock can use the stock's value on the death day as their cost basis and thus completely escape the capital gains tax.

---

[4]Myron J. Gordon, "Optimal Investment and Financing Policy," *Journal of Finance*, May 1963, pp. 264–272; and John Lintner, "Dividends, Earnings, Leverage, Stock Prices, and the Supply of Capital to Corporations," *Review of Economics and Statistics*, August 1962, pp. 243–269.

[5]Of course, nothing involving taxes is quite this simple. First, the dividend must be from a domestic company, and the investor must own the stock for more than 60 days during the 120-day period beginning 60 days before the ex-dividend date. There are other restrictions for dividends other than regular cash dividends. Under the new law, long-term capital gains are taxed at 5% for low-income investors (that is, those whose marginal tax rate is 15% or less) and at 15% for those with more income. Dividend income will be taxed at those same rates through 2007. In 2008, the 5% capital gains (and dividend rate) will drop to zero for low-income investors; there is no scheduled change for high-income investors in 2008. After 2008, the capital gains rates will revert to 10% and 20%, which were the capital gains rates in effect prior to the 2003 tax act. At the time this was written (2006), Congress was actively debating whether or not to extend the act.

Because of these tax advantages, investors may prefer to have companies minimize dividends. If so, investors would be willing to pay more for low-payout companies than for otherwise similar high-payout companies.[6]

Empirical Evidence and the Level of Shareholder Distributions

As Figure 18-1 shows, these three theories offer contradictory advice to corporate managers, so which, if any, should we believe? The most logical way to proceed is to test the theories empirically. Many such tests have been conducted, but their results have been unclear. There are two reasons for this: (1) For a valid statistical test, things other than distribution level must be held constant; that is, the sample companies must differ only in their distribution levels, and (2) we must be able to measure with a high degree of accuracy each firm's cost of equity. Neither of these two conditions holds: We cannot find a set of publicly owned firms that differ only in their distribution levels, nor can we obtain precise estimates of the cost of equity.

Figure 18-1

Dividend Irrelevance, Bird-in-the-Hand, and Tax Preference Dividend Theories

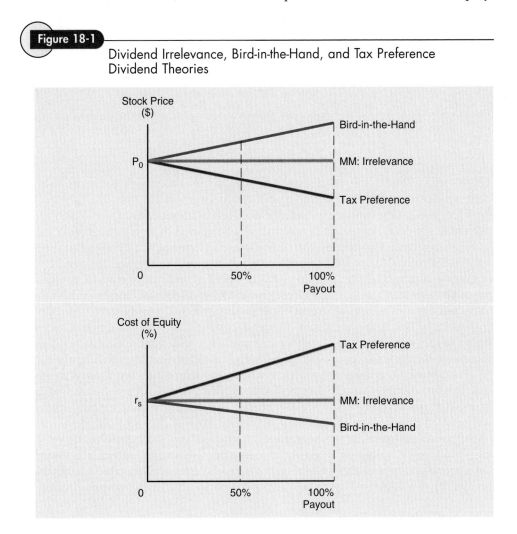

[6]For more on tax related issues, see Eli Talmor and Sheridan Titman, "Taxes and Dividend Policy," *Financial Management*, Summer 1990, pp. 32–35; and Rosita P. Chang and S. Ghon Rhee, "The Impact of Personal Taxes on Corporate Dividend Policy and Capital Structure Decisions," *Financial Management*, Summer 1990, pp. 21–31.

Dividend Yields Around the World

Dividend yields vary considerably in different stock markets throughout the world. In 1999 in the United States, dividend yields averaged 1.6% for the large blue chip stocks in the Dow Jones Industrials, 1.2% for a broader sample of stocks in the S&P 500, and 0.3% for stocks in the high-tech-dominated Nasdaq. Outside the United States, average dividend yields ranged from 5.7% in New Zealand to 0.7% in Taiwan. The accompanying table summarizes the dividend picture in 1999.

World Stock Market (Index)	Dividend Yield	World Stock Market (Index)	Dividend Yield
New Zealand	5.7%	United States (Dow Jones Industrials)	1.6%
Australia	3.1	Canada (TSE 300)	1.5
Britain FTSE 100	2.4	United States (S&P 500)	1.2
Hong Kong	2.4	Mexico	1.1
France	2.1	Japan Nikkei	0.7
Germany	2.1	Taiwan	0.7
Belgium	2.0	United States (Nasdaq)	0.3
Singapore	1.7		

Source: From Alexandra Eadie, "On the Grid Looking for Dividend Yield Around the World," *The Globe and Mail*, June 23, 1999, p. B16. Eadie's source was Bloomberg Financial Services. Reprinted with permission from *The Globe and Mail*.

Therefore, no one has yet identified a completely unambiguous relationship between distribution level and the cost of equity or firm value.

Here is what the empirical evidence does tell us about distributions. First, the percentage of dividend paying companies has declined during the last 30 years.[7] In 1978, about 66.5% of NYSE, AMEX, and Nasdaq firms paid a dividend. In 1999, only 20.8% paid a dividend. As a percent of net income, the average dividend payout ratio fell from 22.3% in 1974 to 13.8% in 1998. Second, the average repurchase payout as a percent of net income rose from 3.7% to 13.6%, causing the percent of total cash distributions as a percent of net income to remain fairly stable at around 26% to 28%. Third, the aggregate dividend payouts have become more concentrated in the sense that a relatively small number of older, more established, and more profitable firms accounts for most of the cash distributed as dividends.[8]

While total distributions as a percent of net income has been fairly steady, there is considerable variation in the level and form of payout among individual firms. We take a closer look at stock repurchases later in the chapter, but for now we focus on dividend payments.

Although investors in the aggregate cannot be shown to clearly prefer either higher or lower distribution levels, the evidence does show that individual investors have strong preferences. Evidence also shows that investors prefer stable, predictable dividend payouts (regardless of the payout level), and that they interpret dividend

[7]See Gustavo Grullon and Roni Michaely, "Dividends, Share Repurchases, and the Substitution Hypothesis," *Journal of Finance*, August 2002, pp. 1649–1684; or see Eugene Fama and Kenneth French, "Disappearing Dividends: Changing Firm Characteristics or Lower Propensity to Pay?" *Journal of Applied Corporate Finance*, Spring 2001, pp. 67–79.

[8]For example, see Harry DeAngelo, Linda DeAngelo, and Douglas J. Skinner, "Are Dividends Disappearing? Dividend Concentration and the Consolidation of Earnings," *Journal of Financial Economics*, 2004, pp. 425–456.

changes as signals about firms' future prospects. We discuss these issues in the next several sections.

SELF-TEST

What did Modigliani and Miller assume about taxes and brokerage costs when they developed their dividend irrelevance theory?

How did the bird-in-the-hand theory get its name?

What have been the results of empirical tests of the dividend theories?

18.2 Clientele Effect

As we indicated earlier, different groups, or *clienteles*, of stockholders prefer different dividend payout policies. For example, retired individuals, pension funds, and university endowment funds generally prefer cash income, so they may want the firm to pay out a high percentage of its earnings. Such investors are often in low or even zero tax brackets, so taxes are of no concern. On the other hand, stockholders in their peak earning years might prefer reinvestment, because they have less need for current investment income and would simply reinvest dividends received, after first paying income taxes on those dividends.

For updates of industry payout ratios, go to **http://yahoo.reuters.com**. After picking a company, select Ratios, then select Dividend.

If a firm retains and reinvests income rather than paying dividends, those stockholders who need current income would be disadvantaged. The value of their stock might increase, but they would be forced to go to the trouble and expense of selling off some of their shares to obtain cash. Also, some institutional investors (or trustees for individuals) would be legally precluded from selling stock and then "spending capital." On the other hand, stockholders who are saving rather than spending dividends might favor the low dividend policy, for the less the firm pays out in dividends, the less these stockholders will have to pay in current taxes, and the less trouble and expense they will have to go through to reinvest their after-tax dividends. Therefore, investors who want current investment income should own shares in high dividend payout firms, while investors with no need for current investment income should own shares in low dividend payout firms. For example, investors seeking high cash income might invest in electric utilities, which averaged a 49% payout in 2006, while those favoring growth could invest in the software industry, which paid out only 15% during the same time period.

To the extent that stockholders can switch firms, a firm can change from one dividend payout policy to another and then let stockholders who do not like the new policy sell to other investors who do. However, frequent switching would be inefficient because of (1) brokerage costs, (2) the likelihood that stockholders who are selling will have to pay capital gains taxes, and (3) a possible shortage of investors who like the firm's newly adopted dividend policy. Thus, management should be hesitant to change its dividend policy, because a change might cause current shareholders to sell their stock, forcing the stock price down. Such a price decline might be temporary, but it might also be permanent—if few new investors are attracted by the new dividend policy, then the stock price would remain depressed. Of course, the new policy might attract an even larger clientele than the firm had before, in which case the stock price would rise.

Evidence from several studies suggests that there is in fact a **clientele effect**.[9] MM and others have argued that one clientele is as good as another, so the existence

---

[9]For example, see R. Richardson Pettit, "Taxes, Transactions Costs and the Clientele Effect of Dividends," *Journal of Financial Economics*, December 1977, pp. 419–436.

of a clientele effect does not necessarily imply that one dividend policy is better than any other. MM may be wrong, though, and neither they nor anyone else can prove that the aggregate makeup of investors permits firms to disregard clientele effects. This issue, like most others in the dividend arena, is still up in the air.

SELF-TEST

Define the clientele effect and explain how it affects dividend policy.

18.3 Information Content, or Signaling, Hypothesis

When MM set forth their dividend irrelevance theory, they assumed that everyone—investors and managers alike—has identical information regarding a firm's future earnings and dividends. In reality, however, different investors have different views on both the level of future dividend payments and the uncertainty inherent in those payments, and managers have better information about future prospects than public stockholders.

It has been observed that an increase in the dividend is often accompanied by an increase in the price of a stock, while a dividend cut generally leads to a stock price decline. Some have argued that this indicates that investors prefer dividends to capital gains. However, MM argued differently. They noted the well-established fact that corporations are reluctant to cut dividends, hence do not raise dividends unless they anticipate higher earnings in the future. Thus, MM argued that a higher-than-expected dividend increase is a signal to investors that the firm's management forecasts good future earnings. Conversely, a dividend reduction, or a smaller-than-expected increase, is a signal that management is forecasting poor earnings in the future. Thus, MM argued that investors' reactions to changes in dividend policy do not necessarily show that investors prefer dividends to retained earnings. Rather, they argue that price changes following dividend actions simply indicate that there is an important **information,** or **signaling, content** in dividend announcements.

The initiation of a dividend by a firm that formerly paid no dividend is certainly a significant change in distribution policy. It appears that initiating firms' future earnings and cash flows are less risky than before the initiation. However, the evidence is mixed regarding the future profitability of initiating firms: Some studies find slightly higher earnings after the initiation, while others find no significant change in earnings.[10] What happens when firms with existing dividends unexpectedly increase or decrease the dividend? Early studies, using small data samples, concluded that unexpected dividend changes did not provide a signal about future earnings.[11] However, more recent data with larger samples provide mixed evidence.[12] On average, firms that cut dividends have had poor earnings in

---

[10]See Edward Dyl and Robert Weigand, "The Information Content of Dividend Initiations: Additional Evidence," *Financial Management*, Autumn 1998, pp. 27–35; P. Asquith and D. Mullins, "The Impact of Initiating Dividend Payments on Shareholders' Wealth," *Journal of Business*, January 1983, pp. 77–96; and P. Healy and K. Palepu, "Earnings Information Conveyed by Dividend Initiations and Omissions," *Journal of Financial Economics*, September 1988, pp. 149–175.

[11]For example, see N. Gonedes, "Corporate Signaling, External Accounting, and Capital Market Equilibrium: Evidence of Dividends, Income, and Extraordinary Items," *Journal of Accounting Research*, Spring 1978, pp. 26–79; and R. Watts, "The Information Content of Dividends," *Journal of Business*, April 1973, pp. 191–211.

[12]See Shlomo Benartzi, Roni Michaely, and Richard Thaler, "Do Changes in Dividends Signal the Future or the Past?" *Journal of Finance*, July 1997, pp. 1007–1034; and Yaron Brook, William Charlton, Jr., and Robert J. Hendershott, "Do Firms Use Dividends to Signal Large Future Cash Flow Increases?" *Financial Management*, Autumn 1998, pp. 46–57.

the years directly preceding the cut but have actually improved earnings in subsequent years. Firms that increase dividends have had earnings increases in the years preceding the increase but don't appear to have had subsequent earnings increases. However, they don't have subsequent declines in earnings either, so it appears that the increase in dividends signals that past earnings increases were not temporary. Also, a relatively large number of firms that expect a large permanent increase in cash flow (as opposed to earnings) do in fact increase their dividend payouts in the year prior to the cash flow increase.

All in all, there is clearly some information content in dividend announcements: Stock prices tend to fall when dividends are cut, even if they don't always rise when dividends are increased. However, this doesn't necessarily validate the signaling hypothesis since it is difficult to tell whether any stock price changes that follow changes in dividends reflect only signaling effects or both signaling and dividend preferences.

SELF-TEST

Define information content, and explain how it affects dividend policy.

18.4 Implications for Dividend Stability

The clientele effect and the information content in dividend announcements definitely have implications regarding the desirability of stable versus volatile dividends. For example, many stockholders rely on dividends to meet expenses, and they would be seriously inconvenienced if the dividend stream were unstable. Further, reducing dividends to make funds available for capital investment could send incorrect signals to investors, who might push down the stock price because they interpreted the dividend cut to mean that the company's future earnings prospects have been diminished. Thus, maximizing its stock price probably requires a firm to maintain a steady dividend policy. Because sales and earnings are expected to grow for most firms, a stable dividend policy means that a company's regular cash dividends should also grow at a steady, predictable rate.[13]

SELF-TEST

Why do the clientele effect and the information content hypotheses imply that investors prefer stable dividends?

18.5 Setting the Target Distribution Level: The Residual Distribution Model

When deciding how much cash to distribute to stockholders, two points should be kept in mind: (1) The overriding objective is to maximize shareholder value,

---

[13]For more on announcements and stability, see Jeffrey A. Born, "Insider Ownership and Signals—Evidence from Dividend Initiation Announcement Effects," *Financial Management*, Spring 1988, pp. 38–45; Chinmoy Ghosh and J. Randall Woolridge, "An Analysis of Shareholder Reaction to Dividend Cuts and Omissions," *Journal of Financial Research*, Winter 1988, pp. 281–294; C. Michael Impson and Imre Karafiath, "A Note on the Stock Market Reaction to Dividend Announcements," *Financial Review*, May 1992, pp. 259–271; James W. Wansley, C. F. Sirmans, James D. Shilling, and Young-jin Lee, "Dividend Change Announcement Effects and Earnings Volatility and Timing," *Journal of Financial Research*, Spring 1991, pp. 37–49; and J. Randall Woolridge and Chinmoy Ghosh, "Dividend Cuts: Do They Always Signal Bad News?" *Midland Corporate Finance Journal*, Summer 1985, pp. 20–32.

and (2) the firm's cash flows really belong to its shareholders, so management should refrain from retaining income unless they can reinvest it to produce returns higher than shareholders could themselves earn by investing the cash in investments of equal risk. On the other hand, recall from Chapter 10 that internal equity (reinvested earnings) is cheaper than external equity (new common stock issues) because it avoids flotation costs. This encourages firms to retain earnings so as to avoid having to issue new stock.

When establishing a distribution policy, one size does not fit all. Some firms produce a lot of cash but have limited investment opportunities—this is true for firms in profitable but mature industries where few opportunities for growth exist. Such firms typically distribute a large percentage of their cash to shareholders, thereby attracting investment clienteles that prefer high dividends. Other firms generate little or no excess cash since they have many good investment opportunities. Such firms generally distribute little or no cash but enjoy rising earnings and stock prices, thereby attracting investors who prefer capital gains.

As Table 18-1 suggests, dividend payouts and dividend yields for large corporations vary considerably. Generally, firms in stable, cash-producing industries such as utilities, financial services, and tobacco pay relatively high dividends, whereas companies in rapidly growing industries such as computer software tend to pay lower dividends.

For a given firm, the optimal distribution ratio is a function of four factors: (1) investors' preferences for dividends versus capital gains, (2) the firm's investment opportunities, (3) its target capital structure, and (4) the availability and cost of external capital. The last three elements are combined in what we call the **residual distribution model.** Under this model a firm follows these four steps when establishing its target distribution ratio: (1) It determines the optimal capital budget; (2) it determines the amount of equity needed to finance that budget, given its target capital structure; (3) it uses reinvested earnings to meet equity requirements to the extent possible; and (4) it pays dividends or repurchases stock only if more earnings are available than are needed to support the optimal capital budget. The word *residual* implies "leftover," and the residual policy implies that distributions are paid out of "leftover" earnings.

If a firm rigidly follows the residual distribution policy, then distributions paid in any given year can be expressed as follows:

$$
\begin{aligned}
\text{Distributions} &= \text{Net income} - \begin{array}{c}\text{Retained earnings needed to} \\ \text{finance new investments}\end{array} \qquad \text{(18-1)} \\
&= \text{Net income} - [(\text{Target equity ratio}) \times (\text{Total capital budget})].
\end{aligned}
$$

For example, suppose the target equity ratio is 60% and the firm plans to spend $50 million on capital projects. In that case, it would need $50(0.6) = $30 million of common equity. Then, if its net income were $100 million, its distributions would be $100 − $30 = $70 million. So, if the company had $100 million of earnings and a capital budget of $50 million, it would use $30 million of the retained earnings plus $50 − $30 = $20 million of new debt to finance the capital budget, and this would keep its capital structure on target. Note that the amount of equity needed to finance new investments might exceed the net income; in our example, this would happen if the capital budget were greater than $166.67 million. In that case, no distributions would be paid, and the company would have to issue new common stock in order to maintain its target capital structure.

Most firms have a target capital structure that calls for at least some debt, so new financing is done partly with debt and partly with equity. As long as the firm

Table 18-1

Dividend Payouts (July 2006)

Company	Industry	Dividend Payout	Dividend Yield
I. Companies That Pay High Dividends			
WD-40 Company (WDFC)	Household products	46%	2.8%
Empire District Electric (EDE)	Electric utility	130	6.2
Rayonier Inc. (RYN.N)	Forest products	68	5.1
Reynolds American Inc. (RAI)	Tobacco products	67	4.2
Regions Financial Corp. (RF)	Regional banks	60	4.1
Ingles Markets Inc. (IMKTA)	Retail (grocery)	48	4.0
Microsoft Corp (MSFT)	Software and programming	33	1.6
II. Companies That Pay Little or No Dividends			
Tiffany and Company (TIF)	Specialty retail	19%	1.3%
Harley-Davidson Inc. (HDI)	Recreational products	19	1.6
Aaron Rents Inc. (RNT)	Rental and leasing	4	0.3
Delta Air Lines Inc. (DALRQ)	Airline	NM[a]	0
Papa John's Intl. Inc. (PZZA)	Restaurants	0	0

[a]Reported a loss, so its dividend payout ratio is not meaningful.
Source: **http://yahoo.investor.reuters.com,** July 2006.

finances with the optimal mix of debt and equity, and provided it uses only internally generated equity (retained earnings), then the marginal cost of each new dollar of capital will be minimized. Internally generated equity is available for financing a certain amount of new investment, but beyond that amount, the firm must turn to more expensive new common stock. At the point where new stock must be sold, the cost of equity, and consequently the marginal cost of capital, rises.

To illustrate these points, consider the case of Texas and Western (T&W) Transport Company. T&W's overall composite cost of capital is 10%. However, this cost assumes that all new equity comes from retained earnings. If the company must issue new stock, its cost of capital will be higher. T&W has $60 million in net income and a target capital structure of 60% equity and 40% debt. Provided that it does not make any cash distributions, T&W could make net investments (investments in addition to asset replacements from depreciation) of $100 million, consisting of $60 million from reinvested earnings plus $40 million of new debt supported by the retained earnings, at a 10% marginal cost of capital. If the capital

Table 18-2

T&W's Distribution Ratio with $60 Million of Net Income and a 60% Target Equity Ratio When Faced with Different Investment Opportunities (Millions of Dollars)

	Investment Opportunities		
	Poor	**Average**	**Good**
Capital budget	$40	$70	$150
Net income	60	60	60
Required equity (0.6 × Capital budget)	24	42	90
Distributions paid (NI − Required equity)	$36	$18	−$30[a]
Distribution ratio (Dividend/NI)	60%	30%	0%

[a]With a $150 million capital budget, T&W would retain all of its earnings and also issue $30 million of new stock.

budget exceeded $100 million, the required equity component would exceed net income, which is of course the maximum amount of reinvested earnings. In this case, T&W would have to issue new common stock, thereby pushing its cost of capital above 10%.

At the beginning of its planning period, T&W's financial staff considers all proposed projects for the upcoming period. Independent projects are accepted if their estimated returns exceed the risk-adjusted cost of capital. In choosing among mutually exclusive projects, T&W chooses the project with the highest positive NPV. The capital budget represents the amount of capital that is required to finance all accepted projects. If T&W follows a strict residual distribution policy, we can see from Table 18-2 that there may be changes in the distribution ratio.

If T&W forecasts poor investment opportunities, its estimated capital budget will be only $40 million. To maintain the target capital structure, 40% of this capital ($16 million) must be raised as debt, and 60% ($24 million) must be equity. If it followed a strict residual policy, T&W would retain $24 million of its $60 million earnings to help finance new investments, then distribute the remaining $36 million to shareholders. Under this scenario, the company's distribution ratio would be $36 million/$60 million = 0.6 = 60%.

By contrast, if the company's investment opportunities are average, its optimal capital budget would rise to $70 million. Here it would require $42 million of retained earnings, so distributions would be $60 − $42 = $18 million, for a ratio of $18/$60 = 30%. Finally, if investment opportunities are good, the capital budget would be $150 million, which would require 0.6($150) = $90 million of equity. T&W would retain all of its net income ($60 million), thus make no distributions. Moreover, since the required equity exceeds the retained earnings, the company would have to issue some new common stock to maintain the target capital structure.

Since both investment opportunities and earnings will surely vary from year to year, strict adherence to the residual distribution policy would result in unstable distributions. One year the firm might make no distributions because it needed the money to finance good investment opportunities, but the next year it might make a large distribution because investment opportunities were poor and it therefore did not need to retain much. Similarly, fluctuating earnings could also lead to variable distributions, even if investment opportunities were stable. To this point, we have not said whether distributions should be in the form of dividends, stock repurchases, or some combination. The next sections discuss some specific issues associated with dividend payments and stock repurchases, followed by a comparison of their relative advantages and disadvantages.

SELF-TEST

Explain the logic of the residual dividend model and the steps a firm would take to implement it.

Hamilton Corporation has a target equity ratio of 65%. Its capital budget is $2 million. If Hamilton has net income of $1.6 million and follows a residual distribution model, how much will its distribution be? ($300,000)

18.6 Distributions in the Form of Dividends

This section explains how the volatile distributions implied by the residual model affect the use of dividends as a form of distribution. It also describes some of the institutional features associated with dividend payments.

Dividends and the Residual Model

If distributions were in the form of dividends, then rigidly following the residual policy would lead to fluctuating, unstable dividends. Since investors dislike volatile dividends, r_s would be high, and the stock price low. Therefore, firms should:

1. Estimate earnings and investment opportunities, on average, over the next five or so years.
2. Use this forecasted information and the target capital structure to find the average residual model distributions and dollars of dividends during the planning period.
3. Then set a *target payout ratio* based on the average projected data.

Thus, firms should use the residual policy to help set their long-run target distribution ratios, but not as a guide to the distribution in any one year.

Companies often use computerized financial forecasting models in conjunction with the residual distribution model as discussed above to help understand the determinants of an optimal dividend policy. Most larger corporations forecast their financial statements over the next 5 to 10 years. Information on projected capital expenditures and working capital requirements is entered into the model, along with sales forecasts, profit margins, depreciation, and the other elements required to forecast cash flows. The target capital structure is also specified, and the model shows the amount of debt and equity that will be required to meet the capital budgeting requirements while maintaining the target capital structure. Then, dividend payments are introduced. Naturally, the higher the payout ratio, the greater the required external equity. Most companies use the model to find a dividend pattern over the forecast period (generally 5 years) that will provide sufficient equity to support the capital budget without forcing them to sell new common stock or move the capital structure ratios outside the optimal range.

Some companies set a very low "regular" dividend and then supplement it with an "extra" dividend when times are good. General Motors, Ford, and other auto companies have followed the **low-regular-dividend-plus-extras policy** in the past. Each company announced a low regular dividend that it was sure could be maintained "through hell or high water," and stockholders could count on receiving that dividend under all conditions. Then, when times were good and profits and cash flows were high, the companies either paid a specially designated extra dividend or repurchased shares of stock. Investors recognized that the extras might not be maintained in the future, so they did not interpret them as a signal that the companies' earnings were going up permanently, nor did they take the elimination of the extra as a negative signal.

At times, however, companies must make substantial cuts in dividends in order to conserve cash. In October 2000, facing increasing competition, technology changes, a decline in its bond rating, and a cutoff from the commercial paper market, Xerox Corporation rolled back its quarterly dividend from $0.20 per share to $0.05 per share. This was a dividend rate not seen by Xerox shareholders since 1966. In the week prior to the dividend cut, the share price had declined significantly in response to an announcement that there would be a loss for the quarter rather than a modest profit and a warning that a dividend cut was being considered. Xerox took a substantial stock price hit when it conceded that cash flows would not be sufficient to cover the old dividend—the price declined from about $15 to about $8. However, some analysts viewed the cut as a positive action that would preserve cash and maintain Xerox's ability to service its debt.

Dividend Payment Procedures

Dividends are normally paid quarterly, and, if conditions permit, the dividend is increased once each year. For example, Katz Corporation paid $0.50 per quarter in 2007, or at an annual rate of $2.00. In common financial parlance, we say that in 2007 Katz's *regular quarterly dividend* was $0.50, and its *annual dividend* was $2.00. In late 2007, Katz's board of directors met, reviewed projections for 2008, and decided to keep the 2008 dividend at $2.00. The directors announced the $2 rate, so stockholders could count on receiving it unless the company experienced unanticipated operating problems.

The actual payment procedure is as follows:

1. *Declaration date.* On the **declaration date**—say, on November 8—the directors meet and declare the regular dividend, issuing a statement similar to the following: "On November 8, 2007, the directors of Katz Corporation met and declared the regular quarterly dividend of 50 cents per share, payable to holders of record on December 7, payment to be made on January 3, 2008." For accounting purposes, the declared dividend becomes an actual liability on the declaration date. If a balance sheet were constructed, the amount ($0.50)(Number of shares outstanding) would appear as a current liability, and retained earnings would be reduced by a like amount.

2. *Holder-of-record date.* At the close of business on the **holder-of-record date,** December 7, the company closes its stock transfer books and makes up a list of shareholders as of that date. If Katz Corporation is notified of the sale before 5 P.M. on December 7, then the new owner receives the dividend. However, if notification is received on or after December 8, the previous owner gets the dividend check.

3. *Ex-dividend date.* Suppose Jean Buyer buys 100 shares of stock from John Seller on December 4. Will the company be notified of the transfer in time to list

Buyer as the new owner and thus pay the dividend to her? To avoid conflict, the securities industry has set up a convention under which the right to the dividend remains with the stock until 2 business days prior to the holder-of-record date; on the second day before that date, the right to the dividend no longer goes with the shares. The date when the right to the dividend leaves the stock is called the **ex-dividend date.** In this case, the ex-dividend date is 2 days prior to December 7, or December 5:

Dividend goes with stock:	December 4
Ex-dividend date:	December 5
	December 6
Holder-of-record date:	December 7

Therefore, if Buyer is to receive the dividend, she must buy the stock on or before December 4. If she buys it on December 5 or later, Seller will receive the dividend because he will be the official holder of record.

Katz's dividend amounts to $0.50, so the ex-dividend date is important. Barring fluctuations in the stock market, we would normally expect the price of a stock to drop by approximately the amount of the dividend on the ex-dividend date. Thus, if Katz closed at $30.50 on December 4, it would probably open at about $30 on December 5.

4. *Payment date.* The company actually mails the checks to the holders of record on January 3, the **payment date.**

18.7 Distributions through Stock Repurchases

Stock repurchases, which occur when a company buys back some of its own outstanding stock, have become an important part of the financial landscape.[14] In fact, large companies have repurchased more shares than they have issued since 1985. Repurchases have also become the preferred method of initiating cash distributions to shareholders. In 1998, 81% of those firms initiating a distribution did so with a stock repurchase instead of a cash dividend, substantially higher than the 27% doing so in 1973.[15] Stock repurchases have also steadily replaced dividends as a form of distribution, with more cash returned to shareholders in repurchases than as dividend payments since 1998. This section discusses stock repurchases and their effect on value.

Three principal situations lead to stock repurchases. First, a company may decide to increase its leverage by issuing debt and using the proceeds to repurchase stock, as we described in Chapter 16. Second, many firms have given their

---

[14]The repurchased stock is called "treasury stock" and is shown as a negative value on the company's detailed balance sheet. On the consolidated balance sheet, treasury shares are deducted to find shares outstanding, and the price paid for the repurchased shares is deducted when determining common equity.
[15]See Gustavo Grullon and David Ikenberry, "What Do We Know about Stock Repurchases?" *Journal of Applied Corporate Finance,* Spring 2000, pp. 31–51.

employees stock options, and companies often repurchase their own stock to sell to employees when employees exercise the options. In this case, the number of outstanding shares reverts to its pre-repurchase level after the options are exercised. Third, a company may have excess cash. This may be due to a one-time cash inflow, such as the sale of a division, or it may simply be that the company is generating more free cash flow than it needs to service its debt.[16]

Stock repurchases are usually made in one of three ways: (1) A publicly owned firm can buy back its own stock through a broker on the open market.[17] (2) The firm can make a tender offer, under which it permits stockholders to send in (that is, "tender") shares in exchange for a specified price per share. In this case, the firm generally indicates that it will buy up to a specified number of shares within a stated time period (usually about 2 weeks). If more shares are tendered than the company wants to buy, purchases are made on a pro rata basis. (3) The firm can purchase a block of shares from one large holder on a negotiated basis. This is a targeted stock repurchase as discussed in Chapter 15.

The Effects of Stock Repurchases

Suppose a company has some extra cash, perhaps due to the sale of a division, and it plans to use that cash to repurchase stock.[18] To keep the example simple, we assume the company has no debt. The current stock price, P_0, is $20 and the company has 2 million outstanding shares, n_0, for a total market capitalization of $40 million. The company has $5 million in marketable securities (that is, extra cash) from the recent sale of a division. It has no other financial assets.

As described in the corporate valuation model of Chapter 15, the company's value of operations, V_{op}, is the present value of its expected future free cash flows, discounted at the WACC.[19] Notice that the repurchase will not affect the FCFs or the WACC, so the repurchase doesn't affect the value of operations. The total value of the company is the value of operations plus the value of the extra cash. We can find the price per share, P_0, by dividing the total value by the number of shares outstanding, n_0:

$$P_0 = \frac{V_{op} + \text{Extra cash}}{n_0}. \tag{18-2}$$

We can easily solve this for the value of operations: $V_{op} = P_0(n_0) - \text{Extra cash} = \$40 - \$5 = \$35$ million.

Now consider the repurchase. P is the repurchase price and n is the number of shares that will be outstanding after the repurchase. We can multiply the

[16]See Benton Gup and Doowoo Nam, "Stock Buybacks, Corporate Performance, and EVA," *Journal of Applied Corporate Finance,* Spring 2001, pp. 99–110, who show that firms that repurchase stock have a more superior operating performance than those that do not buy back stock, which is consistent with the notion that firms buy back stock when they generate additional free cash flow. Gup and Nam also show that the operating performance increases in the year after the buyback, indicating that the superior performance is sustainable.

[17]Many firms announce their plans to repurchase stock on the open market. For example, a company might announce that it plans to repurchase 4 million shares of stock. Interestingly, companies usually don't buy back all the shares they announce but instead repurchase only around 80% of the announced number. See Clifford Stephens and Michael Weisbach, "Actual Share Reacquisitions in Open-Market Repurchase Programs," *Journal of Finance,* February 1998, pp. 313–333.

[18]See Chapter 16 for a description of a stock repurchase as part of a recapitalization.

[19]The WACC is based on the company's capital used in operations and does not include any effects due to the extra cash.

unknown repurchase price by the number of shares that are repurchased, and this must equal the extra cash that is being used in the repurchase:

$$P(n_0 - n) = \text{Extra cash.} \qquad \text{(18-3)}$$

Since the company will have no extra cash after the repurchase, the stock price will be the value of operations divided by the remaining shares of stock:

$$P = \frac{V_{op}}{n}. \qquad \text{(18-4)}$$

We know the current price (P_0), the current number of shares (n_0), and the amount of extra cash. This leaves three remaining unknown variables (P, n, and V_{op}) and three equations, so we can solve for the unknown variables.[20] The solution shows that $P = P_0 = \$20$. In other words, the repurchase itself does not change the stock price. However, the repurchase does change the number of outstanding shares. Rewriting Equation 18-4,

$$n = \frac{V_{op}}{P} = \frac{\$35 \text{ million}}{\$20} = 1.75 \text{ million.} \qquad \text{(18-5)}$$

As a check, we can see that the total market capitalization before the repurchase was \$40 million, \$5 million was used to repurchase shares, and the total market capitalization after the repurchase is \$35 million = $P(n)$ = \$20(1.75 million). This should make sense, since the repurchase itself transferred \$5 million of corporate assets to the individual shareholders. Notice that the aggregate wealth of the shareholders didn't change. It was \$40 million prior to the repurchase, and it is \$40 million afterward (\$35 million in stock and \$5 million in cash). Notice also that a repurchase of 250,000 shares of stock at a price of \$20 equals the \$5 million in cash used to repurchase the shares.

To summarize, the events leading up to a repurchase (the sale of a division, a recapitalization, or the generation of higher than normal free cash flows) can certainly change the stock price, but the repurchase itself doesn't change the stock price.

A Tale of Two Cash Distributions: Dividends versus Stock Repurchases

Suppose a company's current earnings are \$400 million, it has 40 million shares of stock, and it pays out 50% of its earnings as dividends. Earnings are expected to grow at a constant rate of 5%, and the cost of equity is 10%. Its current dividend per share is 0.50(\$400/40) = \$5. Using the dividend growth model, the current stock price is

$$P_0 = \frac{D_1}{r_s - g} = \frac{D_0(1 + g)}{r_s - g} = \frac{\$5(1 + 0.05)}{0.10 - 0.05} = \frac{\$5.25}{0.05} = \$105.$$

---

[20]We can rewrite Equation 18-3 as Extra cash = $P(n_0) - P(n)$ and Equation 18-4 as $V_{op} = P(n)$. We then substitute these expressions for extra cash and V_{op} into Equation 18-2 and solve for P, which results in $P = P_0$.

Figure 18-2

Stock Repurchases versus Cash Dividends

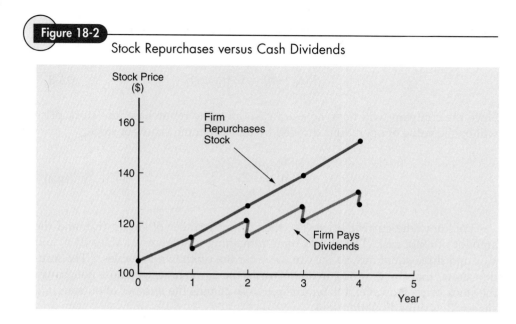

As the year progresses, the stock should climb in price by 10% to $115.5, but then fall by the amount of the dividend ($5.25) to $110.25 when the dividend is paid at Year 1.[21] This process will be repeated each year, as shown in Figure 18-2. Notice that the shareholders experience a 10% total return each year, with 5% as a dividend yield and 5% as a capital gain. Also, the total expected market value of equity after paying the dividend at the end of Year 1 is the price per share multiplied by the number of shares:

$$S_1 = \$110.25(40 \text{ million}) = \$4{,}410 \text{ million}.$$

Suppose the company decides to use 50% of its earnings to repurchase stock each year instead of paying dividends. To find the current price per share, we discount the total payments to shareholders and divide that by the current number of shares. These payments are exactly equal to the total dividend payments in the original scenario, so the current price is the same for both dividend policies, ignoring any taxes or signaling effects. But what happens when the end of the year arrives? The stock price has grown to $115.50, just as for the cash dividend policy. But unlike the case of cash dividends in which the stock price falls by the amount of the dividend, the price per share doesn't change when a company repurchases stock, as shown earlier in this section (see Figure 18-2). This means that the total rate of return for a shareholder under the repurchase policy is 10%, with a zero dividend yield and a 10% capital gain.

Year 1 earnings will be $400(1.05) = $420 million, and the total amount of cash used to repurchase stock is 0.50($420 million) = $210 million. Using Equation 18-3, we can solve for the number of shares remaining, n, after the repurchase at Year 1:

$$P(n_0 - n) = \text{Cash purchase}$$

$$\$115.5(40 - n) = \$210 \text{ million}$$

$$n = [\$115.5(40) - \$210]/\$115.5 = 38.182 \text{ million}.$$

---

[21]This assumes no tax effects.

The total market value of equity at Year 1, S_1, is the price per share multiplied by the number of shares,

$$S_1 = \$115.5(38.182 \text{ million}) = \$4,410 \text{ million},$$

which is identical to the market value of equity if the firm pays dividends instead of repurchasing stock.

This example illustrates three key results: (1) Ignoring possible tax effects and signals, the total market value of equity will be the same whether a firm pays dividends or repurchases stock. (2) The repurchase itself does not change the stock price (compared with using the cash to buy marketable securities), although it does reduce the number of outstanding shares. (3) The stock price for a company that repurchases its stock will climb faster than if it pays a dividend, but the total return to the shareholders will be the same.[22]

SELF-TEST

Explain how a repurchase changes the number of shares but not the stock price.

A firm has 2 million shares outstanding, with a $20 per share market price. The firm has $4 million in extra cash that it plans to use in a stock repurchase; the firm has no other financial investments. What is the firm's value of operations and how many shares will remain after the repurchase? ($36 million; 1.8 million)

18.8 Comparison of Dividends and Repurchases

The advantages of repurchases are as follows:

1. Repurchase announcements are viewed as positive signals by investors because the repurchase is often motivated by management's belief that the firm's shares are undervalued.
2. The stockholders have a choice when the firm distributes cash by repurchasing stock—they can sell or not sell. Thus, those stockholders who need cash can sell back some of their shares, while those who do not want additional cash can simply retain their stock. With a cash dividend, on the other hand, stockholders must accept a dividend payment.
3. Dividends are "sticky" in the short run because managements are reluctant to raise the dividend if the increase cannot be maintained in the future—managements dislike cutting cash dividends because of the negative signal a cut gives. Hence, if the excess cash flow is thought to be only temporary, management may prefer to make the distribution in the form of a stock repurchase rather than to declare an increased cash dividend that cannot be maintained.

---

[22]For more on repurchases, see David J. Denis, "Defensive Changes in Corporate Payout Policy: Share Repurchases and Special Dividends," *Journal of Finance*, December 1990, pp. 1433–1456; Gerald D. Gay, Jayant R. Kale, and Thomas H. Noe, "Share Repurchase Mechanisms: A Comparative Analysis of Efficacy, Shareholder Wealth and Corporate Control Effects," *Financial Management*, Spring 1991, pp. 44–59; April Klein and James Rosenfeld, "The Impact of Targeted Share Repurchases on the Wealth of Non-Participating Shareholders," *Journal of Financial Research*, Summer 1988, pp. 89–97; Jeffry M. Netter and Mark L. Mitchell, "Stock-Repurchase Announcements and Insider Transactions after the October 1987 Stock Market Crash," *Financial Management*, Autumn 1989, pp. 84–96; William Pugh and John S. Jahera, Jr., "Stock Repurchases and Excess Returns: An Empirical Examination," *The Financial Review*, February 1990, pp. 127–142; and James W. Wansley, William R. Lane, and Salil Sarkar, "Managements' View on Share Repurchase and Tender Offer Premiums," *Financial Management*, Autumn 1989, pp. 97–110.

4. Companies can use the residual model to set a *target cash distribution* level, then divide the distribution into a *dividend component* and a *repurchase component*. The dividend payout ratio will be relatively low, but the dividend itself will be relatively secure, and it will grow as a result of the declining number of shares outstanding. The company has more flexibility in adjusting the total distribution than it would if the entire distribution were in the form of cash dividends, because repurchases can be varied from year to year without giving off adverse signals. This procedure, which is what Florida Power & Light employed, has much to recommend it, and it is one reason for the dramatic increase in the volume of stock repurchases.

5. Repurchases can be used to produce large-scale changes in capital structures. For example, several years ago Consolidated Edison decided to borrow $400 million and use the funds to repurchase some of its common stock. Thus, Con Ed was able to quickly change its capital structure.

6. Companies that use stock options as an important component of employee compensation can repurchase shares and then use those shares when employees exercise their options. This avoids having to issue new shares and thus diluting earnings. Microsoft and other high-tech companies have used this procedure in recent years.

Disadvantages of repurchases include the following:

1. Stockholders may not be indifferent between dividends and capital gains, and the price of the stock might benefit more from cash dividends than from repurchases. Cash dividends are generally dependable, but repurchases are not.

2. The *selling* stockholders may not be fully aware of all the implications of a repurchase, or they may not have all the pertinent information about the corporation's present and future activities. However, firms generally announce repurchase programs before embarking on them to avoid potential stockholder suits.

3. The corporation may pay too much for the repurchased stock, to the disadvantage of remaining stockholders. If the firm seeks to acquire a relatively large amount of its stock, then the price may be bid above its equilibrium level and then fall after the firm ceases its repurchase operations.

When all the pros and cons on stock repurchases versus dividends have been totaled, where do we stand? Our conclusions may be summarized as follows:

1. Because of the deferred tax on capital gains, repurchases have a tax advantage over dividends as a way to distribute income to stockholders. This advantage is reinforced by the fact that repurchases provide cash to stockholders who want cash while allowing those who do not need current cash to delay its receipt. On the other hand, dividends are more dependable and are thus better suited for those who need a steady source of income.

2. Because of signaling effects, companies should not vary their dividends—that would lower investors' confidence in the company and adversely affect its cost of equity and its stock price. However, cash flows vary over time, as do investment opportunities, so the "proper" dividend in the residual model sense varies. To get around this problem, a company can set its dividend low enough to keep dividend payments from constraining operations and then use repurchases on a more or less regular basis to distribute excess cash. Such

a procedure will provide regular, dependable dividends plus additional cash flow to those stockholders who want it.

3. Repurchases are also useful when a firm wants to make a large shift in its capital structure, wants to distribute cash from a one-time event such as the sale of a division, or wants to obtain shares for use in an employee stock option plan.

SELF-TEST

What are some advantages and disadvantages of stock repurchases?

How can stock repurchases help a company operate in accordance with the residual distribution model?

18.9 Other Factors Influencing Distributions

In this section, we discuss several other factors that affect the dividend decision. These factors may be grouped into two broad categories: (1) constraints on dividend payments and (2) availability and cost of alternative sources of capital.

Constraints

1. *Bond indentures.* Debt contracts often limit dividend payments to earnings generated after the loan was granted. Also, debt contracts often stipulate that no dividends can be paid unless the current ratio, times-interest-earned ratio, and other safety ratios exceed stated minimums.

2. *Preferred stock restrictions.* Typically, common dividends cannot be paid if the company has omitted its preferred dividend. The preferred arrearages must be satisfied before common dividends can be resumed.

3. *Impairment of capital rule.* Dividend payments cannot exceed the balance sheet item "retained earnings." This legal restriction, known as the "impairment of capital rule," is designed to protect creditors. Without the rule, a company that is in trouble might distribute most of its assets to stockholders and leave its debtholders out in the cold. (*Liquidating dividends* can be paid out of capital, but they must be indicated as such, and they must not reduce capital below the limits stated in debt contracts.)

4. *Availability of cash.* Cash dividends can be paid only with cash, so a shortage of cash in the bank can restrict dividend payments. However, the ability to borrow can offset this factor.

5. *Penalty tax on improperly accumulated earnings.* To prevent wealthy individuals from using corporations to avoid personal taxes, the Tax Code provides for a special surtax on improperly accumulated income. Thus, if the IRS can demonstrate that a firm's dividend payout ratio is being deliberately held down to help its stockholders avoid personal taxes, the firm is subject to heavy penalties. This factor is generally relevant only to privately owned firms.

Alternative Sources of Capital

1. *Cost of selling new stock.* If a firm needs to finance a given level of investment, it can obtain equity by retaining earnings or by issuing new common stock. If flotation costs (including any negative signaling effects of a stock offering) are high, r_e will be well above r_s, making it better to set a low payout ratio and to

finance through retention rather than through the sale of new common stock. On the other hand, a high dividend payout ratio is more feasible for a firm whose flotation costs are low. Flotation costs differ among firms—for example, the flotation percentage is generally higher for small firms, so they tend to set low payout ratios.

2. *Ability to substitute debt for equity.* A firm can finance a given level of investment with either debt or equity. As noted above, low stock flotation costs permit a more flexible dividend policy because equity can be raised either by retaining earnings or by selling new stock. A similar situation holds for debt policy: If the firm can adjust its debt ratio without raising costs sharply, it can pay the expected dividend, even if earnings fluctuate, by increasing its debt ratio.

3. *Control.* If management is concerned about maintaining control, it may be reluctant to sell new stock; hence the company may retain more earnings than it otherwise would. However, if stockholders want higher dividends and a proxy fight looms, then the dividend will be increased.

SELF-TEST

What constraints affect dividend policy?

How does the availability and cost of outside capital affect dividend policy?

18.10 Overview of the Distribution Policy Decision

In practice, the distribution decision is made jointly with capital structure and capital budgeting decisions. The underlying reason for joining these decisions is asymmetric information, which influences managerial actions in two ways:

1. In general, managers do not want to issue new common stock. First, new common stock involves issuance costs—commissions, fees, and so on—and those costs can be avoided by using retained earnings to finance equity needs. Second, as we discussed in Chapter 16, asymmetric information causes investors to view new common stock issues as negative signals and thus lowers expectations regarding the firm's future prospects. The end result is that the announcement of a new stock issue usually leads to a decrease in the stock price. Considering the total costs involved, including both issuance and asymmetric information costs, managers prefer to use retained earnings as the primary source of new equity.

2. Dividend changes provide signals about managers' beliefs as to their firms' future prospects. Thus, dividend reductions generally have a significant negative effect on a firm's stock price. Since managers recognize this, they try to set dollar dividends low enough so that there is only a remote chance that the dividend will have to be reduced in the future.

The effects of asymmetric information suggest that, to the extent possible, managers should avoid both new common stock sales and dividend cuts, because both actions tend to lower stock prices. Thus, in setting distribution policy, managers should begin by considering the firm's future investment opportunities relative to its projected internal sources of funds. The target capital structure also plays a part, but because the optimal capital structure is a *range*, firms can vary their actual capital structures somewhat from year to year. Since it is best to avoid issuing new common stock, the target long-term payout ratio should be designed to permit the firm to meet all of its equity capital requirements with retained earnings. *In effect, managers should use the residual model to set dividends, but in a long-term framework.* Finally, the current dollar dividend should be set so that there is an extremely low probability that the dividend, once set, will ever have to be lowered or omitted.

Of course, the dividend decision is made during the planning process, so there is uncertainty about future investment opportunities and operating cash flows. Thus, the actual payout ratio in any year will probably be above or below the firm's long-range target. However, the dollar dividend should be maintained, or increased as planned, unless the firm's financial condition deteriorates to the point where the planned policy simply cannot be maintained. A steady or increasing stream of dividends over the long run signals that the firm's financial condition is under control. Further, investor uncertainty is decreased by stable dividends, so a steady dividend stream reduces the negative effect of a new stock issue, should one become absolutely necessary.

In general, firms with superior investment opportunities should set lower payouts, hence retain more earnings, than firms with poor investment opportunities. The degree of uncertainty also influences the decision. If there is a great deal of uncertainty regarding the forecasts of free cash flows, which are defined here as the firm's operating cash flows minus mandatory equity investments, then it is best to be conservative and to set a lower current dollar dividend. Also, firms with postponable investment opportunities can afford to set a higher dollar dividend, because in times of stress investments can be postponed for a year or two, thus increasing the cash available for dividends. Finally, firms whose cost of capital is largely unaffected by changes in the debt ratio can also afford to set a higher payout ratio, because they can, in times of stress, more easily issue additional debt to maintain the capital budgeting program without having to cut dividends or issue stock.

The net result of these factors is that many firms' dividend policies are consistent with the life-cycle theory in which younger firms with many investment opportunities but relatively low cash flows reinvest their earnings so that they can avoid the large flotation costs associated with raising external capital.[23] As firms mature and begin to generate more cash flow, they tend to pay more dividends and issue more debt as a way to bond their cash flows and thereby reduce the agency costs of free cash flow.

What do executives think? A recent survey indicates that financial executives believe it is extremely important to not reduce dividends, but that it is much less important to initiate dividend payments or to increase dividend payments. In general, they view the cash distribution decision as being much less important than capital budgeting decisions. Managers like the flexibility provided by repurchases instead of regular dividends. They tend to repurchase shares when they believe their stock price is undervalued, and they believe that shareholders view repurchases as positive signals. In general, the different taxation of dividends and repurchases is not a major factor when they choose how to distribute cash to investors.[24]

---

[23]For a test of the life-cycle theory, see Harry DeAngelo, Linda DeAngelo, and René Stulz, "Dividend Policy and the Earned/Contributed Capital Mix: A Test of the Life-Cycle Theory," *Journal of Financial Economics*, August 2006, pp. 227–254.
[24]See Alon Brav, John R. Graham, Campbell R. Harvey, and Roni Michaely, "Payout Policy in the 21st Century," *Journal of Financial Economics*, 2005, pp. 483–527.

Describe the decision process for distribution policy and dividend payout. Be sure to discuss all the factors that influence the decision.

18.11 Stock Splits and Stock Dividends

Stock splits and stock dividends are related to the firm's cash dividend policy. The rationale for stock splits and dividends can best be explained through an example. We will use Porter Electronic Controls Inc., a $700 million electronic components manufacturer, for this purpose. Since its inception, Porter's markets have been expanding, and the company has enjoyed growth in sales and earnings. Some of its earnings have been paid out in dividends, but some are also retained each year, causing its earnings per share and stock price to grow. The company began its life with only a few thousand shares outstanding, and, after some years of growth, the stock price was so high that few people could afford to buy a "round lot" of 100 shares. Porter's CFO thought this limited the demand for the stock and thus kept the total market value of the firm below what it would have been if more shares, at a lower price, had been outstanding. To correct this situation, Porter "split its stock," as described in the next section.

Stock Splits

Although there is little empirical evidence to support the contention, there is nevertheless a widespread belief in financial circles that an *optimal price range* exists for stocks. "Optimal" means that if the price is within this range, the firm's value will be maximized. Many observers, including Porter's management, believe that the best range for most stocks is from $20 to $80 per share. Accordingly, if the price of Porter's stock rose to $80, management would probably declare a 2-for-1 **stock split,** thus doubling the number of shares outstanding, halving the earnings and dividends per share, and thereby lowering the stock price. Each stockholder would have more shares, but each share would be worth less. If the post-split price were $40, Porter's stockholders would be exactly as well off as before the split. However, if the stock price were to stabilize above $40, stockholders would be better off. Stock splits can be of any size—for example, the stock could be split 2-for-1, 3-for-1, $1\frac{1}{2}$-for-1, or in any other way.

Sometimes a company will have a **reverse split.** For example, International Pictures Corp. (IPIX) developed the iPIX computer imaging technology, which allows a user to "walk through" a 360-degree view. Its stock price was in the $30 range prior to the dot-com crash of April 2000, but by August 2001 its price had fallen to $0.20 per share. One of Nasdaq's listing requirements is that the stock price must be above $1 per share, and Nasdaq was threatening to delist IPIX. To drive its price up, IPIX had a 1:10 reverse stock split before trading began on August 23, 2001, with its shareholders exchanging 10 shares of stock for a single new share. In theory, the stock price should have increased by a factor of 10, to around $2, but IPIX closed that day at a price of $1.46. Evidently, investors saw the reverse split as a negative signal.

Stock Dividends

Stock dividends are similar to stock splits in that they "divide the pie into smaller slices" without affecting the fundamental position of the current stockholders. On a 5% stock dividend, the holder of 100 shares would receive an additional 5 shares (without cost); on a 20% stock dividend, the same holder would receive 20 new shares; and so on. Again, the total number of shares is increased, so earnings, dividends, and price per share all decline.

If a firm wants to reduce the price of its stock, should it use a stock split or a stock dividend? Stock splits are generally used after a sharp price run-up to produce a large price reduction. Stock dividends used on a regular annual basis will keep the stock price more or less constrained. For example, if a firm's earnings and dividends were growing at about 10% per year, its stock price would tend to go up at about that same rate, and it would soon be outside the desired trading range. A 10% annual stock dividend would maintain the stock price within the optimal trading range. Note, though, that small stock dividends create bookkeeping problems and unnecessary expenses, so firms today use stock splits far more often than stock dividends.[25]

Effect on Stock Prices

If a company splits its stock or declares a stock dividend, will this increase the market value of its stock? Many empirical studies have sought to answer this question. Here is a summary of their findings.

1. On average, the price of a company's stock rises shortly after it announces a stock split or dividend.
2. However, these price increases are more the result of the fact that investors take stock splits/dividends as signals of higher future earnings and dividends than of a desire for stock dividends/splits per se. Because only companies whose managements think things look good tend to split their stocks, the announcement of a stock split is taken as a signal that earnings and cash dividends are likely to rise. Thus, the price increases associated with stock splits/dividends are probably the result of signals of favorable prospects for earnings and dividends, not a desire for stock splits/dividends per se.
3. If a company announces a stock split or stock dividend, its price will tend to rise. However, if during the next few months it does not announce an increase in earnings and dividends, then its stock price will drop back to the earlier level.
4. As we noted earlier, brokerage commissions are generally higher in percentage terms on lower-priced stocks. This means that it is more expensive to trade low-priced than high-priced stocks, and this, in turn, means that stock splits may reduce the liquidity of a company's shares. This particular piece of evidence suggests that stock splits/dividends might actually be harmful, although a lower price does mean that more investors can afford to trade in round lots (100 shares), which carry lower commissions than do odd lots (less than 100 shares).

What do we conclude from all this? From a purely economic standpoint, stock dividends and splits are just additional pieces of paper. However, they provide management with a relatively low-cost way of signaling that the firm's prospects

---

[25]Accountants treat stock splits and stock dividends somewhat differently. For example, in a two-for-one stock split, the number of shares outstanding is doubled and the par value is halved, and that is about all there is to it. With a stock dividend, a bookkeeping entry is made transferring "retained earnings" to "common stock."

look good.[26] Further, we should note that since few large, publicly owned stocks sell at prices above several hundred dollars, we simply do not know what the effect would be if Microsoft, Wal-Mart, Hewlett-Packard, and other highly successful firms had never split their stocks and consequently sold at prices in the thousands or even tens of thousands of dollars. All in all, it probably makes sense to employ stock dividends/splits when a firm's prospects are favorable, especially if the price of its stock has gone beyond the normal trading range.[27]

SELF-TEST

What are stock splits and stock dividends?

How do stock splits and dividends affect stock prices?

In what situations should managers consider the use of stock splits?

In what situations should managers consider the use of stock dividends?

Suppose you have 1,000 common shares of Burnside Bakeries. The EPS is $6.00, the DPS is $3.00, and the stock sells for $90 per share. Burnside announces a 3-for-1 split. Immediately after the split, how many shares will you have, what will the adjusted EPS and DPS be, and what would you expect the stock price to be? (3,000; $2; $1; $30)

18.12 Dividend Reinvestment Plans

During the 1970s, most large companies instituted **dividend reinvestment plans (DRIPs),** under which stockholders can choose to automatically reinvest their dividends in the stock of the paying corporation.[28] Today most larger companies offer DRIPs, and although participation rates vary considerably, about 25% of the average firm's shareholders are enrolled. There are two types of DRIPs: (1) plans that involve only "old stock" that is already outstanding and (2) plans that involve newly issued stock. In either case, the stockholder must pay taxes on the amount of the dividends, even though stock rather than cash is received.

Under both types of DRIPs, stockholders choose between continuing to receive dividend checks or having the company use the dividends to buy more stock in the corporation. Under the "old stock" type of plan, if a stockholder elects reinvestment, a bank, acting as trustee, takes the total funds available for reinvestment, purchases the corporation's stock on the open market, and allocates the shares purchased to the participating stockholders' accounts on a pro rata basis. The transaction costs of buying shares (brokerage costs) are low because of volume purchases, so these plans benefit small stockholders who do not need cash dividends for current consumption.

The "new stock" type of DRIP uses the reinvested funds to buy newly issued stock; hence these plans raise new capital for the firm. AT&T, Union Carbide, and

---

[26]For more on stock splits and stock dividends, see H. Kent Baker, Aaron L. Phillips, and Gary E. Powell, "The Stock Distribution Puzzle: A Synthesis of the Literature on Stock Splits and Stock Dividends," *Financial Practice and Education*, Spring/Summer 1995, pp. 24–37; Maureen McNichols and Ajay Dravid, "Stock Dividends, Stock Splits, and Signaling," *Journal of Finance*, July 1990, pp. 857–879; J. Randall Woolridge and Donald R. Chambers, "Reverse Splits and Shareholder Wealth," *Financial Management*, Autumn 1983, pp. 5–15; and David R. Peterson and Pamela P. Peterson, "A Further Understanding of Stock Distributions: The Case of Reverse Stock Splits," *Journal of Financial Research*, Fall 1992, pp. 189–205.

[27]It is interesting to note that Berkshire Hathaway, which is controlled by billionaire Warren Buffett, one of the most successful financiers of the 20th century, has never had a stock split, and its stock (BRKa) sold on the NYSE for $82,800 per share in April 2005. But, in response to investment trusts that were being formed to sell fractional units of the stock, and thus, in effect, split it, Buffett himself created a new class of Berkshire Hathaway stock (Class B) worth about 1/30 of a Class A (regular) share.

[28]See Richard H. Pettway and R. Phil Malone, "Automatic Dividend Reinvestment Plans," *Financial Management*, Winter 1973, pp. 11–18, for an old but still excellent discussion of the subject.

many other companies have had new stock plans in effect in recent years, using them to raise substantial amounts of new equity capital. No fees are charged to stockholders, and many companies offer stock at a discount of 3% to 5% below the actual market price. The companies offer discounts as a trade-off against flotation costs that would have been incurred if new stock had been issued through investment bankers rather than through the dividend reinvestment plans.

One interesting aspect of DRIPs is that they are forcing corporations to reexamine their basic dividend policies. A high participation rate in a DRIP suggests that stockholders might be better off if the firm simply reduced cash dividends, which would save stockholders some personal income taxes. Quite a few firms are surveying their stockholders to learn more about their preferences and to find out how they would react to a change in dividend policy. A more rational approach to basic dividend policy decisions may emerge from this research.

Note that companies start or stop using new stock DRIPs depending on their need for equity capital. Thus, both Union Carbide and AT&T recently stopped offering new stock DRIPs with a 5% discount because their needs for equity capital declined.

Some companies have expanded their DRIPs by moving to "open enrollment," whereby anyone can purchase the firm's stock directly and thus bypass brokers' commissions. ExxonMobil not only allows investors to buy their initial shares at no fee but also lets them pick up additional shares through automatic bank account withdrawals. Several plans, including ExxonMobil's, offer dividend reinvestment for individual retirement accounts, and some, such as U.S. West's, allow participants to invest weekly or monthly rather than on the quarterly dividend schedule. In all of these plans, and many others, stockholders can invest more than the dividends they are forgoing—they simply send a check to the company and buy shares without a brokerage commission. According to First Chicago Trust, which handles the paperwork for 13 million shareholder DRIP accounts, at least half of all DRIPs will offer open enrollment, extra purchases, and other expanded services within the next few years.[29]

SELF-TEST

What are dividend reinvestment plans?

What are their advantages and disadvantages from both the stockholders' and the firm's perspectives?

Summary

The key concepts covered in this chapter are listed below:

- **Distribution policy** involves three issues: (1) What fraction of earnings should be distributed? (2) Should the distribution be in the form of cash dividends or stock repurchases? (3) Should the firm maintain a steady, stable dividend growth rate?
- The **optimal distribution policy** strikes a balance between current dividends and future growth so as to maximize the firm's stock price.
- Miller and Modigliani developed the **dividend irrelevance theory,** which holds that a firm's dividend policy has no effect on either the value of its stock or its cost of capital.

---

[29]For more on DRIPs, see Pamela P. Peterson, David R. Peterson, and Norman H. Moore, "The Adoption of New-Issue Dividend Reinvestment Plans and Shareholder Wealth," *The Financial Review,* May 1987, pp. 221–232.

- The **bird-in-the-hand theory** holds that the firm's value will be maximized by a high dividend payout ratio, because investors regard cash dividends as being less risky than potential capital gains.
- The **tax preference theory** states that because long-term capital gains are subject to somewhat less onerous taxes than dividends, investors prefer to have companies retain earnings rather than pay them out as dividends.
- **Empirical tests** of the three theories **have been inconclusive.** Therefore, academicians cannot tell corporate managers how a given change in dividend policy will affect stock prices and capital costs.
- Dividend policy should take account of the **information content of dividends (signaling)** and the **clientele effect.** The information content, or signaling, effect relates to the fact that investors regard an unexpected dividend change as a signal of management's forecast of future earnings. The clientele effect suggests that a firm will attract investors who like the firm's dividend payout policy. Both factors should be considered by firms that are considering a change in dividend policy.
- In practice, dividend-paying firms follow a policy of paying a **steadily increasing dividend.** This policy provides investors with stable, dependable income, and departures from it give investors signals about management's expectations for future earnings.
- Most firms use the **residual distribution model** to set the long-run target distribution ratio at a level that will permit the firm to meet its equity requirements with retained earnings.
- Under a **stock repurchase plan,** a firm buys back some of its outstanding stock, thereby decreasing the number of shares, but leaving the stock price unchanged.
- **Legal constraints, investment opportunities, availability and cost of funds from other sources,** and **taxes** are also considered when firms establish dividend policies.
- A **stock split** increases the number of shares outstanding. Normally, splits reduce the price per share in proportion to the increase in shares because splits merely "divide the pie into smaller slices." However, firms generally split their stocks only if (1) the price is quite high and (2) management thinks the future is bright. Therefore, stock splits are often taken as positive signals and thus boost stock prices.
- A **stock dividend** is a dividend paid in additional shares rather than in cash. Both stock dividends and splits are used to keep stock prices within an "optimal" trading range.
- A **dividend reinvestment plan (DRIP)** allows stockholders to have the company automatically use dividends to purchase additional shares. DRIPs are popular because they allow stockholders to acquire additional shares without brokerage fees.

Questions

(18-1)   Define each of the following terms:
a.   Optimal distribution policy
b.   Dividend irrelevance theory; bird-in-the-hand theory; tax preference theory

    c.   Information content, or signaling, hypothesis; clientele effect

    d.   Residual distribution model; extra dividend

    e.   Declaration date; holder-of-record date; ex-dividend date; payment date

    f.   Dividend reinvestment plan (DRIP)

    g.   Stock split; stock dividend; stock repurchase

(18-2)   How would each of the following changes tend to affect aggregate (that is, the average for all corporations) payout ratios, other things held constant? Explain your answers.

    a.   An increase in the personal income tax rate

    b.   A liberalization of depreciation for federal income tax purposes—that is, faster tax write-offs

    c.   A rise in interest rates

    d.   An increase in corporate profits

    e.   A decline in investment opportunities

    f.   Permission for corporations to deduct dividends for tax purposes as they now do interest charges

    g.   A change in the Tax Code so that both realized and unrealized capital gains in any year were taxed at the same rate as dividends

(18-3)   What is the difference between a stock dividend and a stock split? As a stockholder, would you prefer to see your company declare a 100% stock dividend or a 2-for-1 split? Assume that either action is feasible.

(18-4)   One position expressed in the financial literature is that firms set their dividends as a residual after using income to support new investments.

    a.   Explain what a residual policy implies (assuming all distributions as dividends), illustrating your answer with a table showing how different investment opportunities could lead to different dividend payout ratios.

    b.   Think back to Chapter 16, in which we considered the relationship between capital structure and the cost of capital. If the WACC-versus-debt-ratio plot was shaped like a sharp V, would this have a different implication for the importance of setting dividends according to the residual policy than if the plot was shaped like a shallow bowl (or a flattened U)?

(18-5)   Indicate whether the following statements are true or false. If the statement is false, explain why.

    a.   If a firm repurchases its stock in the open market, the shareholders who tender the stock are subject to capital gains taxes.

    b.   If you own 100 shares in a company's stock and the company's stock splits 2-for-1, you will own 200 shares in the company following the split.

    c.   Some dividend reinvestment plans increase the amount of equity capital available to the firm.

    d.   The Tax Code encourages companies to pay a large percentage of their net income in the form of dividends.

    e.   If your company has established a clientele of investors who prefer large dividends, the company is unlikely to adopt a residual dividend policy.

    f.   If a firm follows a residual dividend policy, holding all else constant, its dividend payout will tend to rise whenever the firm's investment opportunities improve.

Self-Test Problem   Solution Appears in Appendix A

(ST-1)
Alternative Dividend
Payouts

Components Manufacturing Corporation (CMC) has an all-common-equity capital structure. It has 200,000 shares of $2 par value common stock outstanding. When CMC's founder, who was also its research director and most successful inventor, retired unexpectedly to the South Pacific in late 2007, CMC was left suddenly and permanently with materially lower growth expectations and relatively few attractive new investment opportunities. Unfortunately, there was no way to replace the founder's contributions to the firm. Previously, CMC found it necessary to plow back most of its earnings to finance growth, which averaged 12% per year. Future growth at a 5% rate is considered realistic, but that level would call for an increase in the dividend payout. Further, it now appears that new investment projects with at least the 14% rate of return required by CMC's stockholders ($r_s = 14\%$) would amount to only $800,000 for 2008 in comparison to a projected $2,000,000 of net income. If the existing 20% dividend payout were continued, retained earnings would be $1.6 million in 2008, but, as noted, investments that yield the 14% cost of capital would amount to only $800,000.

The one encouraging note is that the high earnings from existing assets are expected to continue, and net income of $2 million is still expected for 2008. Given the dramatically changed circumstances, CMC's management is reviewing the firm's dividend policy.

a.   Assuming that the acceptable 2008 investment projects would be financed entirely by earnings retained during the year, calculate DPS in 2008, assuming that CMC uses the residual distribution model and pays all distributions in the form of dividends.

b.   What payout ratio does your answer to part a imply for 2008?

c.   If a 60% payout ratio is maintained for the foreseeable future, what is your estimate of the present market price of the common stock? How does this compare with the market price that should have prevailed under the assumptions existing just before the news about the founder's retirement? If the two values of P_0 are different, comment on why.

Problems   Answers Appear in Appendix B

Easy Problems 1–5

(18-1)
Residual Distribution
Model

Axel Telecommunications has a target capital structure that consists of 70% debt and 30% equity. The company anticipates that its capital budget for the upcoming year will be $3,000,000. If Axel reports net income of $2,000,000 and it follows a residual distribution model with all distributions as dividends, what will be its dividend payout ratio?

(18-2)
Residual Distribution
Policy

Petersen Company has a capital budget of $1.2 million. The company wants to maintain a target capital structure which is 60% debt and 40% equity. The company forecasts that its net income this year will be $600,000. If the company follows a residual distribution model and pays all distributions as dividends, what will be its payout ratio?

(18-3)
Dividend Payout

The Wei Corporation expects next year's net income to be $15 million. The firm's debt ratio is currently 40%. Wei has $12 million of profitable investment opportunities, and it wishes to maintain its existing debt ratio. According to the residual distribution model (assuming all payments are in the form of dividends), how large should Wei's dividend payout ratio be next year?

(18-4)
Stock Repurchase

A firm has 10 million shares outstanding, with a $20 per share market price. The firm has $25 million in extra cash that it plans to use in a stock repurchase; the firm has no other financial investments. What is the firm's value of operations and how many shares will remain after the repurchase?

(18-5)
Stock Split

Gamma Medical's stock trades at $90 a share. The company is contemplating a 3-for-2 stock split. Assuming that the stock split will have no effect on the total market value of its equity, what will be the company's stock price following the stock split?

Intermediate Problems 6–9

(18-6)
External Equity Financing

Northern Pacific Heating and Cooling Inc. has a 6-month backlog of orders for its patented solar heating system. To meet this demand, management plans to expand production capacity by 40% with a $10 million investment in plant and machinery. The firm wants to maintain a 40% debt-to-total-assets ratio in its capital structure; it also wants to maintain its past dividend policy of distributing 45% of last year's net income. In 2007, net income was $5 million. How much external equity must Northern Pacific seek at the beginning of 2008 to expand capacity as desired?

(18-7)
Stock Split

Suppose you own 2,000 common shares of Laurence Incorporated. The EPS is $10.00, the DPS is $3.00, and the stock sells for $80 per share. Laurence announces a 2-for-1 split. Immediately after the split, how many shares will you have, what will the adjusted EPS and DPS be, and what would you expect the stock price to be?

(18-8)
Stock Split

After a 5-for-1 stock split, the Strasburg Company paid a dividend of $0.75 per new share, which represents a 9% increase over last year's pre-split dividend. What was last year's dividend per share?

(18-9)
Residual Distribution Policy

The Welch Company is considering three independent projects, each of which requires a $5 million investment. The estimated internal rate of return (IRR) and cost of capital for these projects are presented below:

Project H (high risk):   Cost of capital = 16%; IRR = 20%
Project M (medium risk):   Cost of capital = 12%; IRR = 10%
Project L (low risk):   Cost of capital = 8%; IRR = 9%

Note that the projects' cost of capital varies because the projects have different levels of risk. The company's optimal capital structure calls for 50% debt and 50% common equity. Welch expects to have net income of $7,287,500. If Welch bases its dividends on the residual model (all distributions are in the form of dividends), what will its payout ratio be?

Challenging Problems 10–11

(18-10)
Alternative Dividend Policies

In 2007 the Keenan Company paid dividends totaling $3,600,000 on net income of $10.8 million. 2007 was a normal year, and for the past 10 years, earnings have grown at a constant rate of 10%. However, in 2008, earnings are expected to jump to $14.4 million, and the firm expects to have profitable investment opportunities of $8.4 million. It is predicted that Keenan will not be able to maintain the 2008 level of earnings growth—the high 2008 earnings level is attributable to an exceptionally profitable new product line introduced that year—and the company will return to its previous 10% growth rate. Keenan's target debt ratio is 40%.

a. Calculate Keenan's total dividends for 2008 if it follows each of the following policies:

   (1) Its 2008 dividend payment is set to force dividends to grow at the long-run growth rate in earnings.

   (2) It continues the 2007 dividend payout ratio.

   (3) It uses a pure residual policy with all distributions in the form of dividends (40% of the $8.4 million investment is financed with debt).

   (4) It employs a regular-dividend-plus-extras policy, with the regular dividend being based on the long-run growth rate and the extra dividend being set according to the residual policy.

b. Which of the preceding policies would you recommend? Restrict your choices to the ones listed, but justify your answer.

c. Does a 2008 dividend of $9,000,000 seem reasonable in view of your answers to parts a and b? If not, should the dividend be higher or lower?

(18-11)
Residual Distribution Model
Buena Terra Corporation is reviewing its capital budget for the upcoming year. It has paid a $3.00 dividend per share (DPS) for the past several years, and its shareholders expect the dividend to remain constant for the next several years. The company's target capital structure is 60% equity and 40% debt; it has 1,000,000 shares of common equity outstanding; and its net income is $8 million. The company forecasts that it would require $10 million to fund all of its profitable (that is, positive NPV) projects for the upcoming year.

a. If Buena Terra follows the residual model and makes all distributions as dividends, how much retained earnings will it need to fund its capital budget?

b. If Buena Terra follows the residual model with all distributions in the form of dividends, what will be the company's dividend per share and payout ratio for the upcoming year?

c. If Buena Terra maintains its current $3.00 DPS for next year, how much retained earnings will be available for the firm's capital budget?

d. Can the company maintain its current capital structure, maintain the $3.00 DPS, and maintain a $10 million capital budget without having to raise new common stock?

e. Suppose that Buena Terra's management is firmly opposed to cutting the dividend; that is, it wishes to maintain the $3.00 dividend for the next year. Also assume that the company was committed to funding all profitable projects and was willing to issue more debt (along with the available retained earnings) to help finance the company's capital budget. Assume that the resulting change in capital structure has a minimal impact on the company's composite cost of capital, so that the capital budget remains at $10 million. What portion of this year's capital budget would have to be financed with debt?

f. Suppose once again that Buena Terra's management wants to maintain the $3.00 DPS. In addition, the company wants to maintain its target capital structure (60% equity, 40% debt), and maintain its $10 million capital budget. What is the minimum dollar amount of new common stock that the company would have to issue in order to meet each of its objectives?

g. Now consider the case where Buena Terra's management wants to maintain the $3.00 DPS and its target capital structure, but it wants to avoid issuing new common stock. The company is willing to cut its capital budget in order to meet its other objectives. Assuming that the company's projects are divisible, what will be the company's capital budget for the next year?

h. What actions can a firm that follows the residual distribution policy take when its forecasted retained earnings are less than the retained earnings required to fund its capital budget?

e-resource

Spreadsheet Problem

(18-12)

Build a Model: Residual Distribution Model

Start with the partial model in the file *FM12 Ch 18 P12 Build a Model.xls* from the textbook's Web site. Rework Problem 18-11, parts a through g, using a spreadsheet model.

e-resource

Cyberproblem

Please go to the textbook's Web site to access any Cyberproblems.

Mini Case

Southeastern Steel Company (SSC) was formed 5 years ago to exploit a new continuous-casting process. SSC's founders, Donald Brown and Margo Valencia, had been employed in the research department of a major integrated-steel company, but when that company decided against using the new process (which Brown and Valencia had developed), they decided to strike out on their own. One advantage of the new process was that it required relatively little capital in comparison with the typical steel company, so Brown and Valencia have been able to avoid issuing new stock, and thus they own all of the shares. However, SSC has now reached the stage where outside equity capital is necessary if the firm is to achieve its growth targets yet still maintain its target capital structure of 60% equity and 40% debt. Therefore, Brown and Valencia have decided to take the company public. Until now, Brown and Valencia have paid themselves reasonable salaries but routinely reinvested all after-tax earnings in the firm, so dividend policy has not been an issue. However, before talking with potential outside investors, they must decide on a dividend policy.

Assume that you were recently hired by Pierce Westerfield Carney (PWC), a national consulting firm, which has been asked to help SSC prepare for its public offering. Martha Millon, the senior PWC consultant in your group, has asked you to make a presentation to Brown and Valencia in which you review the theory of dividend policy and discuss the following questions.

a. (1) What is meant by the term "distribution policy"?

    (2) The terms "irrelevance," "bird-in-the-hand," and "tax preference" have been used to describe three major theories regarding the way dividend

payouts affect a firm's value. Explain what these terms mean, and briefly describe each theory.

(3) What do the three theories indicate regarding the actions management should take with respect to dividend payouts?

(4) What results have empirical studies of the dividend theories produced? How does all this affect what we can tell managers about dividend payouts?

b. Discuss (1) the information content, or signaling, hypothesis, (2) the clientele effect, and (3) their effects on distribution policy.

c. (1) Assume that SSC has an $800,000 capital budget planned for the coming year. You have determined that its present capital structure (60% equity and 40% debt) is optimal, and its net income is forecasted at $600,000. Use the residual distribution model approach to determine SSC's total dollar distribution. Assume for now that the distribution is in the form of a dividend. Then, explain what would happen if net income were forecasted at $400,000, or at $800,000.

(2) In general terms, how would a change in investment opportunities affect the payout ratio under the residual distribution policy?

(3) What are the advantages and disadvantages of the residual policy? (Hint: Don't neglect signaling and clientele effects.)

d. What are stock repurchases? Discuss the advantages and disadvantages of a firm repurchasing its own shares.

e. Describe the series of steps that most firms take in setting dividend policy in practice.

f. What are stock splits and stock dividends? What are the advantages and disadvantages of stock splits and stock dividends?

g. What is a dividend reinvestment plan (DRIP), and how does it work?

Selected Additional Cases

The following cases from Textchoice, *Cengage Learning's online library, cover many of the concepts discussed in this chapter and are available at* http://www.textchoice2.com:

Klein-Brigham Series:
Case 19, "Georgia Atlantic Company," Case 47, "Floral Fragrance, Inc.," Case 20, "Bessemer Steel

Products, Inc.," and Case 80, "The Western Company," which illustrate the dividend policy decision.

Brigham-Buzzard Series:
Case 9, "Powerline Network Corporation (Dividend Policy)."

part 6

Tactical Financing Decisions

chapter 19

Initial Public Offerings, Investment Banking, and Financial Restructuring

On any given day, thousands of businesses go to the market to raise capital. Following are some examples of securities sold during August 2006:

1. Aircastle Limited, a firm that leases jets to passenger and cargo airlines, sold 9.0909 million shares of common stock in an initial public offering. It planned to use the proceeds of this issue to repay debt that had been taken on under a senior secured revolving credit facility. Its lead underwriters, JPMorgan Chase & Co., Bear Stearns Cos., and Citigroup Inc., anticipated that the stock could be sold in the range of $21 to $23. The actual offering price was $23.00, and the stock closed on its first day of trading on the NYSE at $26.60. Although the initial investors paid $23 per share, Aircastle received only $21.39—the difference went to the underwriters as a fee for bringing the issue to market. Thus, out of the $209.091 million paid by investors, Aircastle received about $194.454 million, and the underwriters and their sales forces received $14.637 million. Because the stock ended the day $3.60 higher than the offering price, Aircastle left an additional $32.727 million "on the table." The initial investors who bought the stock gained this amount.

2. Leap Wireless International Inc. (the founder of Cricket cellular phone service), already a publicly traded company, announced plans to sell an additional 5.6 million shares of common stock at $42 per share. It planned to use the proceeds to purchase wireless spectrum soon to be auctioned by the FCC. Goldman, Sachs & Co. and Citigroup were the lead underwriters.

3. Cintas Corp. sold $250 million of callable 30-year bonds with a 6.15% coupon rate, using KeyBanc as the lead underwriter. The bonds were rated A2 by Moody's and A by Standard & Poor's. At the time of the issue, the bonds had a yield spread of 1.2 percentage points above the yield on 30-year U.S. Treasury bonds.

Although these three issues represent just a fraction of the securities issued that month, they do illustrate an initial public offering, an additional stock offering by an already-public company, and a debt offering. After reading this chapter, you should have a better understanding of the procedures these and other firms use to issue securities.

The previous three chapters described how a company makes capital structure and dividend policy decisions. Those decisions affect both the firm's need for new capital and the form or forms in which this capital is raised. We now discuss the actual process of raising capital, including the roles played by investment banks and regulatory agencies.

FM
e-resource
The textbook's Web site contains an *Excel* file that will guide you through the chapter's calculations. The file for this chapter is **FM12 Ch 19 Tool Kit.xls,** and we encourage you to open the file and follow along as you read the chapter.

19.1 The Financial Life Cycle of a Start-up Company

Most businesses begin life as proprietorships or partnerships, and if they become successful and grow, at some point they find it desirable to become corporations. Initially, most corporate stock is owned by the firms' founding managers and key employees. Even start-up firms that are ultimately successful usually begin with negative free cash flows due to their high growth rates and product development costs; hence, they must raise capital during these high-growth years. If the founding owners-managers have invested all of their own financial resources in the company, they must turn to outside sources of capital. Start-up firms generally have high growth opportunities relative to assets-in-place, and they suffer from especially large problems with asymmetric information. Therefore, as we discussed in Chapter 16, they must raise external capital primarily as equity rather than debt.

To protect investors from fraudulent stock issues, in 1933 Congress enacted the Securities Act, which created the **Securities and Exchange Commission (SEC)** to regulate the financial markets.[1] The Securities Act regulates interstate public offerings, which we explain later in this section, but it also provides several exemptions that allow companies to issue securities through **private placements** that are not registered with the SEC. The rules governing these exemptions are quite complex, but in general they restrict the number and type of investors who may participate in an issue. **Accredited investors** include the officers and directors of the company, high-wealth individuals, and institutional investors. In a nonregistered private placement, the company may issue securities to an unlimited number of accredited investors, but to only 35 nonaccredited investors. In addition, none of the investors can sell their securities in the secondary market to the general public.

Corporate Valuation, IPOs, and Financial Restructuring

Companies must make investments in operating capital before they can generate sales, net operating profit after taxes (NOPAT), and free cash flow. Some of these investments can be made from currently generated NOPAT, but rapid growth generally requires raising additional funds from the marketplace. This chapter explains how companies raise external funds to support their operations.

$$\text{Value} = \frac{\text{FCF}_1}{(1 + \text{WACC})^1} + \frac{\text{FCF}_2}{(1 + \text{WACC})^2} + \frac{\text{FCF}_3}{(1 + \text{WACC})^3} + \cdots + \frac{\text{FCF}_\infty}{(1 + \text{WACC})^\infty}$$

---

[1]In addition to federal statutes, which affect transactions that cross state borders, states have "Blue Sky" laws that regulate securities sold just within the state. These laws were designed to prevent unscrupulous dealers from selling something of little worth, such as blue sky, to naïve investors.

For most start-ups, the first round of external financing comes through a private placement of equity to one or two individual investors, called **angels.** In return for a typical investment in the range of $50,000 to $400,000, the angels receive stock and perhaps also a seat on the board of directors. Because angels can influence the strategic direction of the company, it is best that they bring experience and industry contacts to the table, not just cash.

As the company grows, its financing requirements may exceed the resources of individual investors, in which case it is likely to turn to a **venture capital fund.** A venture capital fund is a private limited partnership, which typically raises $30 million to $80 million from a relatively small group of primarily institutional investors, including pension funds, college endowments, and corporations.[2] The managers of a venture capital fund, called **venture capitalists,** or **VCs,** are usually very knowledgeable and experienced in a particular industry, such as health care. They screen hundreds of companies, and ultimately fund around a dozen, called **portfolio companies.** The venture fund buys shares of the portfolio companies, and the VCs sit on the companies' boards of directors. The venture capital fund usually has a prespecified life of 7 to 10 years, after which it is dissolved, either by selling the portfolio companies' stock and distributing the proceeds to the funds' investors or by directly distributing the stock to the investors.

SELF-TEST

What is a private placement?

What is an angel?

What is a venture capital fund? A VC?

19.2 The Decision to Go Public: Initial Public Offerings

Going public means selling some of a company's stock to outside investors and then letting the stock trade in public markets. For example, Celanese, Huntsman, Under Armour, Baidu.com, and many other companies took this step in 2005. The advantages and disadvantages of public stock ownership are discussed next.

Advantages of Going Public

1. *Increases liquidity and allows founders to harvest their wealth.* The stock of a private, or closely held, corporation is illiquid. It may be hard for one of the owners who wants to sell some shares to find a ready buyer, and even if a buyer is located, there is no established price on which to base the transaction.

2. *Permits founders to diversify.* As a company grows and becomes more valuable, its founders often have most of their wealth tied up in the company. By selling some of their stock in a public offering, they can diversify their holdings, thereby reducing the riskiness of their personal portfolios.

---

[2]The typical venture capital fund is a private limited partnership, with limited partners and a general partner. The limited partners contribute cash but are prohibited from being involved in the partnership's decision making. Because of their limited participation, they are not held liable for any of the partnership's liabilities, except to the extent of their original investment. The general partner usually contributes a relatively modest amount of cash, but acts as the partnership's manager. In return, the general partner normally receives annual compensation equal to 1% to 2% of the fund's assets plus a 20% share of the fund's eventual profits.

3. *Facilitates raising new corporate cash*. If a privately held company wants to raise cash by selling new stock, it must either go to its existing owners, who may not have any money or may not want to put more eggs in this particular basket, or else shop around for wealthy investors. However, it is usually quite difficult to get outsiders to put money into a closely held company, because if the outsiders do not have voting control (more than 50% of the stock), the inside stockholders/managers can take advantage of them. Going public, which brings with it both public disclosure of information and regulation by the SEC, greatly reduces this problem, and thus makes people more willing to invest in the company, which makes it easier for the firm to raise capital.

4. *Establishes a value for the firm*. If a company wants to give incentive stock options to key employees, it is useful to know the exact value of those options, and employees much prefer to own stock, or options on stock, that is publicly traded and therefore liquid. Also, when the owner of a privately owned business dies, state and federal tax appraisers must set a value on the company for estate tax purposes. Often, these appraisers set a higher value than that of a similar publicly traded company.

5. *Facilitates merger negotiations*. Having an established market price helps when a company is either being acquired or seeking to acquire another company where it will pay for the acquisition with stock.

6. *Increases potential markets*. Many companies report that it is easier to sell their products and services to potential customers after they become a publicly traded company.

Disadvantages of Going Public

1. *Cost of reporting*. A publicly owned company must file quarterly and annual reports with the SEC and/or various state agencies. These reports can be a costly burden, especially for small firms. In addition, compliance with Sarbanes-Oxley often requires considerable expense and manpower.

2. *Disclosure*. Management may not like the idea of reporting operating data, because these data will then be available to competitors. Similarly, the owners of the company may not want people to know their net worth, and since a publicly owned company must disclose the number of shares owned by its officers, directors, and major stockholders, it is easy enough for anyone to multiply shares held by price per share to estimate the net worth of the insiders.

3. *Self-dealings*. The owners-managers of closely held companies have many opportunities for various types of questionable but legal self-dealings, including the payment of high salaries, nepotism, personal transactions with the business (such as a leasing arrangement), and not-truly-necessary fringe benefits. Such self-dealings, which are often designed to minimize their personal tax liabilities, are much harder to arrange if a company is publicly owned.

4. *Inactive market/low price*. If the firm is very small, and if its shares are not traded frequently, its stock will not really be liquid, and the market price may not represent the stock's true value. Security analysts and stockbrokers simply will not follow the stock, because there will not be sufficient trading activity to generate enough brokerage commissions to cover the costs of following the stock.

5. *Control*. Because of possible tender offers and proxy fights, the managers of publicly owned firms who do not have voting control must be concerned about maintaining control. Further, there is pressure on such managers to produce annual earnings gains, even when it might be in the shareholders'

best long-term interests to adopt a strategy that reduces short-term earnings but raises them in future years. These factors have led a number of public companies to "go private" in "leveraged buyout" deals where the managers borrow the money to buy out the nonmanagement stockholders. We discuss the decision to go private in a later section.

6. *Investor relations.* Public companies must keep investors abreast of current developments. Many CFOs of newly public firms report that they spend two full days a week talking with investors and analysts.

Conclusions on Going Public

There are no hard-and-fast rules regarding if or when a company should go public. This is an individual decision that should be made on the basis of the company's and stockholders' own unique circumstances. If a company does decide to go public, either by selling newly issued stock to raise new capital or by the sale of stock by the current owners, the key issue is setting the price at which shares will be offered to the public. The company and its current owners should want to set the price as high as possible—the higher the offering price, the smaller the fraction of the company the current owners will have to give up to obtain any specified amount of money. On the other hand, potential buyers want the price set as low as possible. We return to the establishment of the offering price later in the chapter, after we describe some other aspects of common stock financing.

SELF-TEST

What are the major advantages of going public?

What are the major disadvantages?

19.3 The Process of Going Public

As the following sections show, the process of going public is a lot more complicated, expensive, and time-consuming than simply making the decision to go public.

Selecting an Investment Bank

After a company decides to go public, it faces the problem of how to sell its stock to a large number of investors. While most companies know how to sell their products, few have experience in selling securities. To help in this process, the company will interview a number of different **investment banks,** also called **underwriters,** and then select one to be the lead underwriter. To understand the factors that affect this choice, it helps to understand exactly what investment banks do.

First, the investment bank helps the firm determine the preliminary offering price, or price range, for the stock and the number of shares to be sold. The investment bank's reputation and experience in the company's industry are very important in convincing potential investors to purchase the stock at the offering price. In effect, the investment bank certifies that the stock is not overpriced, which obviously comforts investors. Second, the investment bank actually sells the shares to its existing clients, which include a mix of institutional investors and retail (that is, individual) customers. Third, the investment bank, through its associated brokerage house, will have an analyst "cover" the stock after it is issued. This analyst will regularly distribute reports to investors describing the stock's prospects, which will help to maintain an interest in the stock. Well-respected analysts increase the likelihood that there will be a liquid secondary market for the stock and that its price will reflect the company's true value.

The Underwriting Syndicate

The firm and its investment bank must next decide whether the bank will work on a **best efforts basis** or will **underwrite** the issue. In a best efforts sale, the bank does not guarantee that the securities will be sold or that the company will get the cash it needs, only that it will put forth its "best efforts" to sell the issue. On an underwritten issue, the company does get a guarantee, because the bank agrees to buy the entire issue and then resell the stock to its customers. Therefore, the bank bears significant risks in underwritten offerings. For example, on one IBM bond issue, interest rates rose sharply and bond prices fell, after the deal had been set but before the investment banks could sell the bonds to the ultimate purchasers. The banks lost somewhere between $10 million and $20 million. Had the offering been on a best efforts basis, IBM would have been the loser.

Except for extremely small issues, virtually all IPOs are underwritten. Investors are required to pay for securities within 10 days, and the investment bank must pay the issuing firm within 4 days of the official commencement of the offering. Typically, the bank sells the stock within a day or two after the offering begins, but on occasion, the bank miscalculates, sets the offering price too high, and thus is unable to move the issue. At other times, the market declines during the offering period, forcing the bank to reduce the price of the stock or bonds. In either instance, on an underwritten offering the firm receives the price that was agreed upon, so the bank must absorb any losses that are incurred.

Because they are exposed to large potential losses, investment banks typically do not handle the purchase and distribution of issues single-handedly unless the issue is a very small one. If the sum of money involved is large, investment banks form **underwriting syndicates** in an effort to minimize the risk each bank faces. The banking house that sets up the deal is called the **lead,** or **managing, under-writer.** Syndicated offerings are usually covered by more analysts, which contributes to greater liquidity in the post-IPO secondary market. Thus, syndication provides benefits to both underwriters and issuers.

In addition to the underwriting syndicate, on larger offerings still more investment banks are included in a **selling group,** which handles the distribution of securities to individual investors. The selling group includes all members of the underwriting syndicate plus additional dealers who take relatively small percentages of the total issue from the members of the underwriting syndicate. Thus, the underwriters act as wholesalers, while members of the selling group act as retailers. The number of houses in a selling group depends partly on the size of the issue, but is normally in the range of 10 to 15.

A new selling procedure has recently emerged that takes advantage of the trend toward institutional ownership of stock. In this type of sale, called an **unsyndicated stock offering,** the managing underwriter, acting alone, sells the issue entirely to a group of institutional investors, thus bypassing both retail stockbrokers and individual investors. In recent years, about 50% of all stock sold has been by unsyndicated offerings. Behind this phenomenon is a simple motivating force: money. The fees that issuers pay on a syndicated offering, which include commissions paid to retail brokers, can run a full percentage point higher than those on unsyndicated offerings. Further, although total fees are lower in unsyndicated offerings, managing underwriters usually come out ahead because they do not have to share the fees with an underwriting syndicate. However, some types of stock do not appeal to institutional investors, so not all firms can use unsyndicated offers.

Regulation of Securities Sales

Sales of new securities, and also sales in the secondary markets, are regulated by the Securities and Exchange Commission and, to a lesser extent, by each of the 50 states. Here are the primary elements of SEC regulation:

1. The SEC has jurisdiction over all **interstate public offerings** in amounts of $1.5 million or more.
2. Newly issued securities (stocks and bonds) must be registered with the SEC at least 20 days before they are publicly offered. The **registration statement,** called Form S-1, provides financial, legal, and technical information about the company to the SEC. A **prospectus,** which is embedded in the S-1, summarizes this information for investors. The SEC's lawyers and accountants analyze both the registration statement and the prospectus; if the information is inadequate or misleading, the SEC will delay or stop the public offering.[3]
3. After the SEC declares the registration to be effective, new securities may be advertised, but all sales solicitations must be accompanied by the prospectus. **Preliminary,** or **"red herring," prospectuses** may be distributed to potential buyers during the 20-day waiting period after the registration is effective, but no sales may be finalized during this time. The "red herring" prospectus contains all the key information that will appear in the final prospectus except the final price, which is generally set after the market closes the day before the new securities are actually offered to the public.
4. If the registration statement or prospectus contains **misrepresentations** or **omissions** of material facts, any purchaser who suffers a loss may sue for damages. Severe penalties may be imposed on the issuer or its officers, directors, accountants, engineers, appraisers, underwriters, and all others who participated in the preparation of the registration statement or prospectus.

The Roadshow and Book-Building

After the registration statement has been filed, the senior management team, the investment banks, and the company's lawyers go on a **roadshow.** The management team will make three to seven presentations each day to potential institutional investors, who are typically existing clients of the underwriters. The institutional investors ask questions during the presentation, but the management team may not give any information that is not in the registration statement due to the SEC-mandated **quiet period.** This quiet period begins when the registration statement is made effective and lasts for 25 days after the stock begins trading. Its purpose

---

[3]With the Internet, it is extremely easy to obtain the S-1 form, which typically has 50 to 200 pages of financial statements, a detailed discussion of the firm's business, the risks and opportunities the firm faces, details on its principal stockholders and managers, what will be done with the funds raised, and the like. This statement is filed with the SEC and is immediately available, through the Internet, to investors. The SEC staff reviews the filed S-1, and amendments may be issued, labeled S-1A, S-1B, etc. Most important, the likely range for the offering price will be reported, for example, $13 to $15 per share. If the market strengthens or weakens while the stock is undergoing SEC review, the price may be increased or decreased, right up to the last day. The SEC Web site is **http://www.sec.gov.**

is to create a level playing field for all investors, by ensuring that they all have access to the same information. It is not uncommon for the SEC to delay an IPO if managers violate the quiet period rules. The typical roadshow may last 10 to 14 days, with stops in 10 to 20 different cities. In many ways it resembles a coming-out party for the company, but it is much more grueling and has much higher stakes.

After a presentation, the investment banks ask the investor for an indication of interest, based on the offering price range shown in the registration statement. The investment bank records the number of shares that each investor is willing to buy, which is called **book-building.** As the roadshow progresses, the investment bank's "book" shows how demand for the offering is building. Many IPOs are **oversubscribed,** with investors wishing to purchase more shares than are available. In such a case the investment bank will allocate shares to the investors.[4] If demand is high enough, then sometimes they will increase the offering price. If demand is low, then they will either reduce the offering price or withdraw the IPO. Sometimes low demand is specifically due to concern over the company's future prospects, but sometimes low demand is caused by a fall in the general stock market. Thus, the timing of the roadshow and offering date are very important. As the old saying goes, sometimes it is better to be lucky than good.

If all goes well with the roadshow, the investment bank will finalize the offering price on the evening before the actual offering date.

The First Day of Trading

The first day of trading for many IPOs is wild and exciting. Table 19-1 shows the largest first-day returns for IPOs in 2005. Some stocks end the day with large gains, such as the 353.9% price increase of Baidu.com, as shown in Table 19-1. Others have a sharp run-up and then fall back by the end of the day. A few IPOs actually end their first day with a loss.

According to a study by Professors Tim Loughran and Jay Ritter of IPOs during 1990–1998, about 27.3% of the IPOs have an offer price that is lower than the low range in their initial registration filing, and these stocks have an average first-day return of 4.0%.[5] Even though the average return is positive, 47% of these stocks actually end the day with a loss or no gain. About 48.4% of IPOs have an offering price that is within the range of their initial filing. For such companies, the average first-day return was 10.8%. Due to indications of high demand during the roadshow, 24.3% of IPOs had a final offer price that was higher than their original range. These stocks had an average first-day return of 31.9%. Overall, the average first-day return was 14.1% during 1990–1998, with 75% of all IPOs having a positive return. During 1999, the average first-day return was an astronomical 70%!

You're probably asking yourself two questions: (1) How can you get in on these deals, and (2) why is the offering price so low? First, you probably can't get the chance to buy an IPO at its offering price, especially not a "hot" one. Virtually all sales go to institutional investors and preferred retail customers. There are a few Web-based investment banks who are trying to change this, such as the OpenIPO

---

[4]Most underwriting agreements contain an "overallotment option" that permits the underwriter to purchase additional shares up to 15% of the issue size to cover promises made to potential buyers. This is called a "green shoe" agreement because it was first used in the 1963 underwriting of a company named Green Shoe.

[5]See Tim Loughran and Jay R. Ritter, "Why Don't Issuers Get Upset about Leaving Money on the Table in IPOs?" *Review of Financial Studies,* 2002, pp. 413–444.

Table 19-1

Highest First-Day IPO Returns in 2005

Rank	Company (Symbol)	Offering Price	First-Day Closing Price	Gain
1	Baidu.com (BIDU)	$27.00	$122.54	353.9%
2	Under Armour Inc. (UA)	13.00	25.30	94.6
3	Int'l Securities Exchange (ISE)	18.00	30.40	68.9
4	Electro-Optical Sciences (MELA)	5.00	7.71	54.2
5	Adams Respiratory Therapeutics (ARXT)	17.00	25.75	51.5
6	IntercontinentalExchange (ICE)	26.00	39.25	51.0
7	Saifun Semiconductors (SFUN)	23.50	35.30	50.2
8	CBOT Holdings (BOT)	54.00	80.30	48.7
9	SunPower Corp (SPWR)	18.00	25.45	41.4
10	SunTech Power Holdings (STP)	15.00	21.20	41.3

Source: http://www.ipohome.com.

of W. R. Hambrecht & Co., but right now it is difficult for small investors to get in on the better first-day IPOs.

Various theories have been put forth to explain IPO underpricing. As long as issuing companies don't complain, investment banks have strong incentives to underprice the issue. First, underpricing increases the likelihood of oversubscription, which reduces the risk to the underwriter. Second, most investors who get to purchase the IPO at its offering price are preferred customers of the investment bank, and they became preferred customers because they generated lots of commissions in the investment bank's sister brokerage company. Therefore, the IPO is an easy way for the underwriter to reward customers for past and future commissions. Third, the underwriter needs an honest indication of interest when building the book prior to the offering, and underpricing is a possible way to secure this information from the institutional investors.

But why don't issuing companies object to underpricing? Some do, and are seeking alternative ways to issue securities, such as OpenIPO. However, most seem content to leave some money on the table. The best explanation seems to be that (1) the company wants to create excitement, and a price run-up on the first day does that; (2) only a small percentage of the company's stock is generally offered to the public, so current stockholders give away less due to underpricing than appears at first glance; and (3) IPO companies generally plan to have further offerings in the future, and the best way to ensure future success is to have a successful IPO, which underpricing guarantees.

Although IPOs on average provide large first-day returns, their long-term returns over the following 3 years are below average. For example, if you could not get in at the IPO price but purchased a portfolio of IPO stocks on their second day of trading, your 3-year return would have been lower than the return on a portfolio of similar but seasoned stocks. In summary, the offering price appears to be too low, but the first-day run-up is generally too high.

The Costs of Going Public

During recent years, virtually all investment banks have charged a 7% **spread** between the price they pay the issuing company and the price at which they sell shares to the public. Thus, they keep 7% of the offering price as their compensation. For example, in 2006 Aircastle Limited sold 9.0909 million shares at an offer price of $23.00 per share. In this IPO the underwriters' direct compensation was $1.61 per share. For 9.0909 million shares issued, these direct underwriting costs totaled about $14.637 million.

But there are other direct costs, such as lawyer's fees, accountant's costs, printing, engraving, and so on. These fees can easily amount to several hundred thousand dollars, which can be a large percentage of a small IPO.

Last, but not least, are the indirect costs. The money left on the table, which is equal to the number of shares multiplied by the difference in the closing price and the offering price, can be quite large. Aircastle experienced a first-day run-up to $26.60 from an offering price of $23.00, and so the indirect costs total 9.0909($26.60 − $23.00) = $32.727 million. In addition, senior managers spend an enormous amount of time working on the IPO rather than managing the business, which certainly carries a high cost, even if it cannot be easily measured.

Thus, Aircastle received proceeds of $194.454 million, and the underwriters and their sales forces received $14.637 million, with $32.727 million left on the table. There were undoubtedly other direct costs of several hundred thousand dollars, and indirect costs due to the diversion of the management team. As you can see, an IPO is quite expensive.[6]

The Importance of the Secondary Market

An active secondary market after the IPO provides the pre-IPO shareholders with a chance to convert some of their wealth into cash, makes it easier for the company to raise additional capital later, makes employee stock options more attractive, and makes it easier for the company to use its stock to acquire other companies. Without an active secondary market, there would be little reason to have an IPO. Thus, companies should try to ensure that their stock will trade in an active secondary market before they incur the high costs of an IPO.

There are several types of secondary markets: physical stock exchanges, dealer markets, and bulletin boards. We discuss each of these below.

The physical exchanges, such as the NYSE and AMEX, conduct their trading in an actual location. In general, the NYSE and AMEX provide excellent liquidity. In order to have its stock listed, a company must apply to an exchange, pay a relatively small fee, and meet the exchange's minimum requirements. These requirements relate to the size of the company's net income, its market value, and its "float," which is the number of shares outstanding and in the hands of outsiders (as opposed to the number held by insiders, who generally do not actively trade their stock). Also, the company must agree to disclose certain information to the exchange and to help the exchange track trading patterns and thus ensure that no

---

[6]For more on IPOs, see Roger G. Ibbotson, Jody L. Sindelar, and Jay R. Ritter, "Initial Public Offerings," *Journal of Applied Corporate Finance*, Summer 1988, pp. 37–45; Roger G. Ibbotson, Jody L. Sindelar, and Jay R. Ritter, "The Market's Problems with the Pricing of Initial Public Offerings," *Journal of Applied Corporate Finance*, Spring 1994, pp. 66–74; Chris J. Muscarella and Michael R. Vetsuypens, "The Underpricing of 'Second' Initial Public Offerings," *Journal of Financial Research*, Fall 1989, pp. 183–192; Jay R. Ritter, "The Long-Run Performance of Initial Public Offerings," *Journal of Finance*, March 1991, pp. 3–27; and Jay R. Ritter, "Initial Public Offerings," *Contemporary Finance Digest*, Spring 1998, pp. 5–30.

one is attempting to manipulate the stock's price. The size qualifications increase as a company moves from the AMEX to the NYSE.

Assuming a company qualifies, many believe that listing is beneficial to the company and to its stockholders. Listed companies receive a certain amount of free advertising and publicity, and their status as listed companies may enhance their prestige and reputation, which often leads to higher sales. Investors respond favorably to increased information, increased liquidity, and the confidence that the quoted price is not being manipulated. Listing provides investors with these benefits, which may help managers lower their firms' cost of equity and increase the value of their stock.[7]

The advantages of physical exchanges have been eroded—some would say eliminated—by computers and the Internet, which have benefited the dealer markets. The primary equity dealer markets are administered by Nasdaq, and they include the Nasdaq National Market and the Nasdaq SmallCap Market. Almost 85% of new IPO stocks trade in these markets. Unlike the physical exchanges, these consist of a network of dealers, with each dealer making a market in one or more stocks. A dealer makes a market in a company's stock by holding an inventory of the shares and then making offers to buy or sell the stock. Many stocks have excellent liquidity in these markets and remain there even though they easily meet the requirements for listing on the NYSE. Examples include Microsoft, Intel, Apple, and Cisco Systems.

Investment banks generally agree to make a market in a company's stock as part of their IPO duties. The diligence with which they carry out this task can have a huge effect on the stock's liquidity in the secondary market, and, thus, the success of the IPO.

Although the requirements for listing on the Nasdaq National Market or SmallCap Market are not as stringent as for the NYSE, some companies fail to maintain them and hence are "delisted." For these companies, offers to buy or sell the stock may be posted on the OTC Bulletin Board, an electronic bulletin board administered by Nasdaq. However, there is very little liquidity in these stocks, and an IPO would be considered a failure if the company's stock ended up on the OTC Bulletin Board.

Regulating the Secondary Market

As we stated earlier, a liquid and crime-free secondary market is critical to the success of an IPO or any other publicly traded security. So, in addition to regulating the process for issuing securities, the Securities Exchange Commission also has responsibilities in the secondary markets. The primary elements of SEC regulation are set forth below.

1. The SEC *regulates all national stock exchanges,* and companies whose securities are listed on an exchange must file annual reports similar to the registration statement with both the SEC and the exchange.
2. The SEC has control over trading by corporate *insiders.* Officers, directors, and major stockholders must file monthly reports of changes in their holdings of the stock of the corporation. Any short-term profits from such transactions must be turned over to the corporation.
3. The SEC has the power to *prohibit manipulation* by such devices as pools (large amounts of money used to buy or sell stocks to artificially affect prices)

---

[7]For additional discussion on the benefits of listing, see H. Kent Baker and Richard B. Edelman, "AMEX-to-NYSE Transfers, Market Microstructure, and Shareholder Wealth," *Financial Management,* Winter 1992, pp. 60–72; and Richard B. Edelman and H. Kent Baker, "Liquidity and Stock Exchange Listing," *The Financial Review,* May 1990, pp. 231–249.

or wash sales (sales between members of the same group to record artificial transaction prices).

4. The SEC has *control over the proxy statement* and the way the company uses it to solicit votes.

Control over credit used to buy securities is exercised by the Federal Reserve Board through **margin requirements,** which specify the maximum percentage of the purchase price someone can borrow. If a great deal of margin borrowing has persisted, then a decline in stock prices can result in inadequate coverages. This could force stockbrokers to issue **margin calls,** which require investors either to put up more money or have their margined stock sold to pay off their loans. Such forced sales further depress the stock market and thus can set off a downward spiral. The margin at the time a stock is purchased has been 50% since 1974 (subsequent "maintenance margins" are lower and are generally set by individual lenders).

The securities industry itself realizes the importance of stable markets, sound brokerage firms, and the absence of stock manipulation.[8] Therefore, the various exchanges work closely with the SEC to police transactions and to maintain the integrity and credibility of the system. Similarly, the **National Association of Securities Dealers (NASD)** cooperates with the SEC to police trading in its dealer and OTC markets. These industry groups also cooperate with regulatory authorities to set net worth and other standards for securities firms, to develop insurance programs to protect the customers of failed brokerage houses, and the like.

In general, government regulation of securities trading, as well as industry self-regulation, is designed to ensure (1) that investors receive information that is as accurate as possible, (2) that no one artificially manipulates the market price of a given stock, and (3) that corporate insiders do not take advantage of their position to profit in their companies' stocks at the expense of other stockholders. Neither the SEC, the state regulators, nor the industry itself can prevent investors from making foolish decisions or from having "bad luck," but they can and do help investors obtain the best data possible for making sound investment decisions.

Questionable IPO Practices

Among the many revelations to come out during 2002 regarding investment banking was the practice by some investment banking houses of letting CEOs and other high-ranking corporate executives in on "hot" IPOs. In these deals the demand for the new stock was far greater than supply at the offering price, so the investment banks were virtually certain that the stock would soar far above the offering price.

Some investment banks systematically allocated shares of hot IPOs to executives of companies that were issuing stocks and bonds—and thus generating fees to the banks who underwrote the deals. Bernie Ebbers, the chairman and CEO of WorldCom, one of the biggest providers of underwriting fees, was given huge allocations in hot IPOs, and he made millions on these deals. Ebbers is just one example— a lot of this was going on in the late 1990s, at the height of the tech/dot-com bubble.

Government regulators have been investigating this practice, called "spinning," and quite a few corporate executives and investment bankers may be charged with something that amounts to a kickback scheme under which those executives who favored particular investment banks were rewarded with allocations in hot IPOs.

---

[8]It is illegal for anyone to attempt to manipulate the price of a stock. During the 1920s and earlier, syndicates would buy and sell stocks back and forth at rigged prices so the public would believe that a particular stock was worth more or less than its true value. The exchanges, with the encouragement and support of the SEC, utilize sophisticated computer programs to help spot any irregularities that suggest manipulation, and they require disclosures to help identify manipulators. This same system helps to identify illegal insider trading. It is now illegal to manipulate a stock's price by spreading false news on the Internet.

Indeed, in 2004 Credit Suisse First Boston's Frank Quattrone was sentenced to 18 months in prison for obstructing a spinning investigation (however, the situation was still unresolved in late 2006 because Quattrone was granted a new trial with a new judge). Although the practice may or may not be illegal—this has yet to be determined—it is certainly unethical. The corporate executives were paid to work for their stockholders, so they should have turned over any IPO profits to their companies, not kept them for themselves. A suit filed by the New York Attorney General is seeking to force such profits to be "disgorged" by the executives and returned to the companies involved.

This kind of unethical and perhaps illegal behavior may help to explain IPO underpricing and "money left on the table." An executive might be more interested in getting a future hot IPO allocation than in whether or not the company gets the best terms from its investment bank. This situation would be exacerbated if the investment banks' analysts overstated prospects for the company and thereby pumped up its price just prior to the time when executives were to receive and exercise stock options.

In summary, we have a hard time justifying IPO underpricing during the late 1990s on rational economic grounds. People have come up with explanations for why companies let their investment banks price their stocks too low in IPOs, but those reasons seem rather weak. However, when coupled with what may have been a kickback scheme, the underpricing may make somewhat more sense. Before closing, though, we should make it clear that relatively few corporate executives were corrupt. However, just as one rotten apple can spoil a barrel of apples, a few bad executives, combined with lax regulation, can help a bad practice become "the industry standard" and thus become widespread.

SELF-TEST

What is the difference between "best efforts" and "underwriting"?

What are some SEC regulations regarding sales of new securities?

What is a roadshow? What is book-building?

What is underpricing? Leaving money on the table?

What are some of the costs of going public?

A company is planning an IPO. Its underwriters have said the stock will sell at $50 per share. The underwriters will charge a 7% spread. How many shares must the company sell to net $93 million, ignoring any other expenses? (2 million)

19.4 Equity Carve-Outs: A Special Type of IPO

A few years ago, Condec Corporation sold to the public about 20% of the equity in its wholly owned subsidiary, Unimation Inc. In this transaction, the subsidiary, like the parent, became publicly owned, but the parent retained full control of the subsidiary by retaining about 80% of the subsidiary's common stock. (Parent companies typically retain at least 80% of the subsidiary's common stock to preserve their ability to file a consolidated tax return.) This type of transaction is called an **equity carve-out** (or **partial public offering,** or **spin-out**). The market's response to Condec's carve-out announcement was very positive—the stock price rose 19% after correcting for the overall movement in the market.[9] Equity carve-outs raise

---

[9]For more information on equity carve-outs, see Roni Michaely and Wayne H. Shaw, "The Choice of Going Public: Spin-offs vs. Carve-outs," *Financial Management*, Autumn 1995, pp. 5–21; Katherine Schipper and Abbie Smith, "Equity Carve-Outs," *Midland Corporate Finance Journal*, Spring 1986, pp. 23–32; David M. Glassman, "Spin-Offs and Spin-Outs: Using 'Securitization' to Beat the Bureaucracy," *Journal of Applied Corporate Finance*, Fall 1988, pp. 82–89; and Anand Vijh, "Long-Term Returns from Equity Carve-outs," *Journal of Financial Economics*, (1999), pp. 273–308.

an interesting question: Why do carve-out announcements typically result in stock price increases while the announcements of new stock issues by parent corporations generally decrease stock prices?

One possible answer is that carve-outs facilitate the evaluation of corporate growth opportunities on a line-of-business basis. Thus, Condec, a conglomerate operating mostly in the defense industry, enabled investors to separately value its Unimation subsidiary, which manufactures industrial robots, by offering its stock to the public. Also, by creating a separate public market for Unimation's common stock, Condec offered investors a "pure play" in robotics, a relatively scarce commodity.

Another advantage to carve-outs is that they improve the ability of the parent to offer incentives to a subsidiary's managers. For example, McKesson Corporation, a $52 billion firm in the drug and health care industry, sold 17% of its Armor All subsidiary to the public. At the time, Neil Harlan, McKesson's chairman, said that Armor All is "different than most of our operations. It is heavily marketing-driven and entrepreneurial in nature." Creation of a public market for the shares of Armor All provided the opportunity for McKesson to offer incentive shares in the subsidiary to Armor All's top managers. Such shares, which hinge directly on the market value of Armor All, were clearly a better inducement to superior performance than a compensation plan tied to the parent corporation's stock price, since at the time Armor All accounted for only 2% of McKesson's total sales.

Another potential advantage of carve-outs is that they can increase the effectiveness of capital allocation. Internally, the competition for capital is often waged on political rather than economic grounds, and thus the use, and hence value, of new capital is very uncertain. After a carve-out, it is easier to measure the cost of capital for the different business units, and this can improve the capital budgeting process. Also, by selling an ownership interest in a narrowly focused line of business rather than offering a stake in the conglomerate parent, management can reduce the uncertainty faced by investors. This can lower the cost of capital for the various units and thus increase the aggregate value of the consolidated enterprise.

Equity carve-outs do have some associated costs. First, the underwriting commission involved in a carve-out is larger than for an equity offering by the parent. Second, because an equity carve-out is a type of initial public offering, there is a potential for underpricing the new offering. Third, key managers of the subsidiary must spend a significant amount of time marketing the new stock. Fourth, there are costs associated with the minority interest that is created in the carve-out. For example, the subsidiary's new board of directors must monitor all transactions between the subsidiary and the parent to ensure that the minority investors are not being exploited. Finally, there are additional costs including annual reports, SEC filings, analyst presentations, and so on, that must now be borne by both the parent and the subsidiary.

In summary, there are costs to equity carve-outs, but there are also benefits, and the benefits may make the carve-out an attractive option in many situations. In essence, a carve-out is a form of corporate **securitization,** which is the issuance of public securities backed by assets that have been segregated from the remaining assets of the company. By creating such securities, and a liquid market for trading them, a corporation can potentially reduce investor risk and increase the value of the firm as a whole. We cover securitization in more depth later in the chapter.

SELF-TEST

Explain what is meant by an equity carve-out.

On average, equity carve-outs have increased shareholder wealth. What are some potential explanations for this observed phenomenon?

19.5 Non-IPO Investment Banking Activities

FM

e-resource

See **Web Extension 19A** at the textbook's Web site for a discussion of rights offerings.

In addition to helping with IPOs, investment banks also help public companies raise additional debt and equity capital. As shown in Table 19-2, investment banks helped firms raise just over $6.5 trillion during 2005. In this section we describe some of the ways that investment banks and public companies work together to raise capital.[10]

Preliminary Decisions

Before raising capital, the firm makes some initial, preliminary decisions, including the following:

1. *Dollars to be raised.* How much new capital is needed?
2. *Type of securities used.* Should common, preferred, bonds, hybrid securities, or a combination, be used? Further, if common stock is to be issued, should it be done as a rights offering or by a direct sale to the general public?
3. *Competitive bid versus a negotiated deal.* Should the company simply offer a block of its securities for sale to the highest bidder, or should it negotiate a deal with an investment bank? These two procedures are called **competitive bids** and **negotiated deals,** respectively. Only about 100 of the largest firms listed on the NYSE, whose securities are already well-known to the investment banking community, are in a position to use the competitive bidding process. The investment banks must do a great deal of investigative work

Table 19-2 Top Five Underwriters of Global Debt and Equity in 2005	
Manager	**Proceeds (in Billions)**
Citigroup	$ 564.7
Lehman Brothers	420.8
Deutsche Bank AG	418.1
JPMorgan	414.6
Morgan Stanley	383.5
Industry total	$6,511.3

Source: The Wall Street Journal Online, January 3, 2006, p. R10.

[10]For an excellent discussion of the various procedures used to raise capital, see Jay R. Ritter, "Investment Banking and Securities Issuance," in *North-Holland Handbook of the Economics of Finance,* edited by George Constantinides, Milton Harris, and René Stulz (North-Holland, 2002). Also, see Bruce Jurin, "Raising Equity in an Efficient Market," *Midland Corporate Finance Journal,* Winter 1988, pp. 53–60; and Claudio Loderer, John W. Cooney, and Leonard D. Van Drunen, "The Price Elasticity of Demand for Common Stock," *Journal of Finance,* June 1991, pp. 621–651.

("due diligence") to bid on an issue unless they are already quite familiar with the firm, and such costs would be too high to make it worthwhile unless the bank was sure of getting the deal. Therefore, except for the largest firms, offerings of stock and bonds are generally on a negotiated basis.

4. *Selection of an investment bank.* Most deals are negotiated, so the firm must select an investment bank. This can be an important decision for a firm that is going public. On the other hand, an older firm that has already "been to market" will have an established relationship with an investment bank. However, it is easy to change banks if the firm is dissatisfied. Different investment banking houses are better suited for different companies. For example, Goldman Sachs and Morgan Stanley are the leading tech-IPO underwriters. Investment banking houses sell new issues largely to their own regular brokerage customers, so the nature of these customers has a major effect on the ability of the house to do a good job for corporate issuers. Finally, a major factor in choosing an underwriter is the reputation of the analyst who will cover the stock in the secondary market, since a strong buy recommendation from a well-respected analyst can trigger a sharp price run-up.

Private Placements

In a *private placement*, securities are sold to one or a few investors, generally institutional investors. Private placements are most common with bonds, but they also occur with stocks. The primary advantages of private placements are (1) lower flotation costs and (2) greater speed, since the shares do not have to go through the SEC registration process.

The most common type of private placement occurs when a company places securities directly with a financial institution, often an insurance company or a pension fund. In fact, Prudential Insurance Company has begun sending salespeople to call on businesses—not to sell them policies, but to sell them on raising funds privately from Prudential. To illustrate a private placement, AT&T sold 6.3 million shares of common stock worth about $650 million to Capital Group Inc., a Los Angeles institutional investor that manages both mutual and pension funds. The transaction was a blow to three Wall Street firms, Morgan Stanley, Dillon Reed, and Goldman Sachs, which wanted to sell the stock in a conventional public offering. AT&T's treasurer said selling the stock in a private placement saved about 2.5%, or $16.3 million, in underwriting expenses.

One type of private placement that is occurring with increasing frequency is when a large company makes an equity investment in a smaller supplier. For example, Comcast, Intel, Motorola, and Phillips, among others, invested several million dollars in Intellon Corporation, a telecommunications equipment manufacturer. Intellon needed capital for expansion, and the larger companies were all engaged in joint development ventures with Intellon and wanted it to have sufficient capital to move ahead quickly. Similar arrangements are quite common, and some of them go back many years. For example, Sears, Roebuck & Co., before its merger with Kmart, supplied equity capital to some of its major suppliers, including Johnson Controls, which furnished Sears with "Die-Hard" batteries, and DeSoto Chemical, which supplied most of the paints that Sears sold.

A potential disadvantage of a private placement is that if the securities are not registered with the SEC, they cannot be sold except to another large, "sophisticated" purchaser in the event the original buyer wants to sell them. However, many institutions meet this qualification so there is a large potential market for the securities. In addition, companies are increasingly choosing to register the securities they privately place to improve their marketability after placement. With improved marketability, private placements are becoming increasingly popular, and today they constitute almost 40% of all nonbank debt financing.

Shelf Registrations

The selling procedures described previously, including the 20-day waiting period after registration with the SEC, apply to most security sales. However, under the SEC's Rule 415, large, well-known public companies that issue securities frequently may file a master registration statement with the SEC and then update it with a short-form statement just prior to each individual offering. Under this procedure, a company can decide at 10 A.M. to sell securities and have the sale completed before noon. This procedure is known as **shelf registration** because, in effect, the company puts its new securities "on the shelf" and then sells them to investors when it feels the market is "right." Firms with less than $150 million in stock held by outside investors cannot use shelf registrations. The rationale for this distinction is to protect investors who may not be able to get adequate financial data about a little-known company in the short time between announcement of a shelf issue and its sale. Shelf registrations have two advantages over standard registrations: (1) lower flotation costs and (2) more control over the timing of the issue.[11]

Seasoned Equity Offerings

When a company with publicly traded stock issues additional shares, this is called a **seasoned equity offering,** also known as a *follow-on offering.* Because the stock is already publicly traded, the offering price will be based upon the existing market price of the stock. Typically, the investment bank buys the securities at a prescribed number of points below the closing price on the last day of registration. For example, suppose that in August 2007, the stock of Microwave Telecommunications Inc. (MTI) had a price of $28.60 per share, and the stock had traded between $25 and $30 per share during the previous 3 months. Suppose further that MTI and its underwriter agreed that the investment bank would buy 10 million new shares at $1 per share below the closing price on the last day of registration. If the stock closed at $25 on the day the SEC released the issue, MTI would receive $24 per share. Typically, such agreements have an escape clause that provides for the contract to be voided if the price of the securities drops below some predetermined figure. In the illustrative case, this "upset" price might be set at $24 per share. Thus, if the closing price of the shares on the last day of registration had been $23.50, MTI would have had the option of withdrawing from the agreement.

The investment bank will have an easier job if the issue is priced relatively low. However, the issuer naturally wants as high a price as possible. A conflict of interest on price therefore arises between the investment bank and the issuer. If the issuer is financially sophisticated and makes comparisons with similar security issues, the investment bank will be forced to price close to the market.

---

[11]For more on shelf registrations, see David J. Denis, "The Costs of Equity Issues Since Rule 415: A Closer Look," *Journal of Financial Research,* Spring 1993, pp. 77–88.

As we discussed in Chapter 16, the announcement of a new stock offering by a mature firm is often taken as a negative signal—if the firm's prospects were good, management would not want to issue new stock and thus share the rosy future with new stockholders. Therefore, the announcement of a new offering is taken as bad news. Consequently, the price will probably fall when the announcement is made, so the offering price will probably have to be set at a price below the preannouncement market price.

One final point is that *if negative signaling effects drive down the price of the stock, all shares outstanding, not just the new shares, are affected.* Thus, if MTI's stock should fall from \$28.60 to \$25 per share as a result of the financing, and if the price remains at the new level, then the company would incur a loss of \$3.60 on each of the 50 million shares previously outstanding, or a total market value loss of \$180 million. This loss, like underwriting expenses, is a flotation cost, and it should be considered as a cost associated with the stock issue. However, if the company's prospects really were poorer than investors thought, then the price decline would have occurred sooner or later anyway. On the other hand, if the company's prospects are really not all that bad (the signal was incorrect), then over time MTI's price should move back to its previous level. However, if the price does revert to its former level, there will have been a transfer of wealth from the original shareholders to the new shareholders. To prevent this, companies often sell additional shares of stock through a rights offering, which we explain in *Web Extension 19A*.

FM

e-resource

See *Web Extension 19A* at the textbook's Web site for a discussion of rights offerings.

SELF-TEST

What is the difference between a competitive bid and a negotiated deal?

What is a private placement?

What is shelf registration?

19.6 The Decision to Go Private

In a **going private** transaction, the entire equity of a publicly held firm is purchased by a small group of investors that usually includes the firm's current senior management.[12] In some of these transactions, the current management group acquires all of the equity of the company. In others, current management participates in the ownership with a small group of outside investors who typically place directors on the now-private firm's board and arrange for the financing needed to purchase the publicly held stock. Such deals almost always involve substantial borrowing, often up to 90%, and thus are commonly known as **leveraged buyouts (LBOs).**

Regardless of the structure of the deal, going private initially affects the right-hand side of the balance sheet, the liabilities and capital, and not the assets—going private simply rearranges the ownership structure. Thus, going private involves no obvious operating economies, yet the new owners are generally willing to pay a large premium over the stock's current price in order to take the firm private. For example, prior to its acquisition by Columbia, the managers of Hospital Corporation of America (HCA) paid \$51 a share to outside (public) shareholders although the stock was selling for only about \$31 before the LBO offer was made.

---

[12]See Harry DeAngelo, Linda DeAngelo, and Edward M. Rice, "Going Private: The Effects of a Change in Corporate Ownership," *Midland Corporate Finance Journal*, Summer 1984, pp. 35–43, for a more complete discussion of going private. The discussion in this section draws heavily from their work.

It is hard to believe that the managers of a company, who have the best information about the firm's potential profitability, would knowingly pay too much for the firm. Thus, HCA's managers must have regarded the firm as being grossly undervalued or else thought that they could significantly boost the firm's value under private ownership. This suggests that going private can increase the value of some firms sufficiently to enrich both managers and public stockholders. Other large companies going private recently include Georgia-Pacific (2005), Univision (2006), Kinder Morgan (2006), and G.M.A.C. (2006).

The primary advantages to going private are (1) administrative cost savings, (2) increased managerial incentives, (3) increased managerial flexibility, (4) increased shareholder participation, and (5) increased use of financial leverage, which of course reduces taxes. We discuss each of these advantages in more detail in the following paragraphs.

1. *Administrative cost savings.* Because going private takes the stock of a firm out of public hands, it saves on costs associated with securities registration, annual reports, SEC and exchange reporting, responding to stockholder inquiries, and so on. More important, the top managers of private firms are free from meetings with security analysts, government bodies, and other outside parties. Byron C. Radaker, CEO of Congoleum Corporation, a company that went private in the early 1980s, estimated the cost savings to his company from going private at between $6 million and $8 million per year.

2. *Increased managerial incentives.* An even larger potential gain comes from the improvement in incentives for high-level managerial performance. Their increased ownership means that the firm's managers benefit more directly from their own efforts; hence managerial efficiency tends to increase after going private. If the firm is highly successful, its managers can easily see their personal net worth increase ten- to twentyfold, while if the firm fails, its managers end up with nothing. Further, a highly leveraged position tends to drive the firm toward the extremes—large losses or large profits. The managers of companies that have gone through an LBO tell us that heavy interest payments, combined with a knowledge that success will bring great wealth, does a lot to cut fat and improve decisions.

3. *Increased managerial flexibility.* Another source of value stems from the increased flexibility available to managers of private firms. These managers do not have to worry about what a drop in next quarter's earnings will do to the firm's stock price; hence they can focus on long-term, strategic actions that ultimately will have the greatest positive impact on the firm's value. Managerial flexibility concerning asset sales is also greater in a private firm, since such sales do not have to be justified to a large number of shareholders with potentially diverse interests.

4. *Increased shareholder participation.* Going private typically results in replacing a dispersed, largely passive group of public shareholders with a small group of investors who take a much more active role in managing the firm. These new equity investors have a substantial position in the private firm; hence they have a greater motivation to monitor management and to provide incentives to management than do the typical stockholders of a public corporation. Further, the new nonmanagement equity investors, such as Kohlberg Kravis Roberts & Company (KKR), are typically represented on the board, and they bring both sophisticated financial expertise and hard-nosed attitudes to the new firm. These outsiders don't have good friends running money-losing divisions, so they are more willing to force major operating changes than are entrenched managers. For example, within a few weeks after KKR won the

battle for RJR Nabisco, the much touted but unprofitable Premier "smokeless" cigarette project was abandoned.

5. *Increased financial leverage.* Going private usually entails a drastic increase in the firm's use of debt financing, which has two effects. First, the firm's taxes are reduced because of the increase in deductible interest payments, so more of the operating income flows through to investors. Second, the increased debt servicing requirements force managers to hold costs down to ensure that the firm has sufficient cash flow to meet its obligations—a highly leveraged firm simply cannot afford any fat.

One might ask why all firms are not privately held. The answer is that while there are real benefits to private ownership, there are also benefits to being publicly owned. Most notably, public corporations have access to large amounts of equity capital on favorable terms, and for most companies, the advantage of access to public capital markets dominates the advantages of going private. Also, note that most companies that go private end up going public again after several years of operation as private firms. For example, HCA, which went private in 1987, again went public in 1992. During the private phase, management sheds inefficient businesses, cuts costs throughout the corporation, and, generally, rationalizes operations. These actions increase the value of the firm to investors. Once the company has been "straightened up," going public allows the private equity holders to recover their investment, take their profit, and move on to new ventures. Interestingly, in mid-2006 HCA announced plans to go private again.

Note too that the examples set by LBO companies are not lost on companies that maintain their publicly owned status. Thus, companies such as Phillips Petroleum and Union Carbide have changed their operations to the point where they resemble LBO companies. This has increased their value and thus made them less attractive to KKR and other LBO specialists, benefiting both managers and shareholders.

SELF-TEST

What is meant by the term "going private"?

What are the main benefits of going private?

Why don't all firms go private to capture these benefits?

19.7 Managing the Maturity Structure of Debt

Chapters 16 and 17 described the capital structure decision. But after a firm chooses the total amount of debt in its capital structure, it must still choose the maturities of the various securities that make up its debt. The following sections explain the factors associated with the choice of maturity structure.

Maturity Matching

Assume that Consolidated Tools, a Cincinnati machine tool manufacturer, made the decision to float a $25 million nonconvertible bond issue to help finance its 2007 capital budget. It must choose a maturity for the issue, taking into consideration the shape of the yield curve, management's own expectations about future interest rates, and the maturity of the assets being financed. To illustrate how asset maturities affect the choice of debt maturities, suppose Consolidated's capital projects consist primarily of new milling machinery. This machinery has an expected economic life of 10 years (even though it falls into the MACRS 5-year class life). Should Consolidated use debt with a 5-year, 10-year, 20-year, 30-year, or some other maturity?

Note that some of the new capital will come from common equity, which is permanent capital. On the other hand, debt maturities can be specified at the time of issue. If Consolidated financed its capital budget with 10-year sinking fund bonds, it would be matching asset and liability maturities. The cash flows resulting from the new machinery could be used to make the interest and sinking fund payments on the issue, so the bonds would be retired as the machinery wore out. If Consolidated used 1-year debt, it would have to pay off this debt with cash flows derived from assets other than the machinery in question. Conversely, if it used 20-year or 30-year debt, it would have to service the debt long after the assets that were purchased with the funds had been scrapped and had ceased providing cash flows. This would worry lenders.

Of course, the 1-year debt could probably be rolled over year after year, out to the 10-year asset maturity. However, if interest rates rose, Consolidated would have to pay a higher rate when it rolled over its debt, and if the company experienced difficulties, it might not be able to refund the debt at any reasonable rate.

For all these reasons, the safest all-around financing strategy is to match debt maturities with asset maturities. In recognition of this fact, firms generally place great emphasis on maturity matching, and this factor often dominates the debt maturity decision.

Some firms use zero coupon bonds as a tool in matching maturities. We explain these bonds in **Web Extension 5A.**

FM
e-resource
See **Web Extension 5A** at the textbook's Web site for more on zero coupon bonds.

Effects of Interest Rate Levels and Forecasts

Financial managers also consider interest rate levels and forecasts, both absolute and relative, when making financing decisions. For example, if long-term interest rates are high by historical standards and are expected to fall, managers will be reluctant to issue long-term debt, locking in those costs for long periods. We already know that one solution to this problem is to use a call provision—callability permits refunding should interest rates drop. However, there is a cost, because of the call premium and also because the firm must set a higher coupon on callable debt. Floating-rate debt could be used, but another alternative would be to finance with short-term debt whenever long-term rates are historically high, and then, assuming that interest rates subsequently fall, sell a long-term issue to replace the short-term debt. Of course, this strategy has its risks: If interest rates move even higher, the firm will be forced to renew its short-term debt at higher and higher rates, or to replace the short-term debt with a long-term bond that costs even more than it would have when the original decision was made.

We could argue that capital markets are efficient, hence that it is impossible to predict what future interest rates will be because these rates will be determined by information that is not now known. Thus, under the efficient markets hypothesis, it would be unproductive for firms to try to "beat the market" by forecasting future capital costs and then acting on these forecasts. According to this view, financial managers ought to arrange their capital structures in such a manner that they can ride out almost any economic storm, and this generally calls for (1) using some "reasonable" mix of debt and equity and (2) using debt with maturities that more or less match the maturities of the assets being financed.

Information Asymmetries

In Chapter 5, we discussed bond ratings and the effects of changes in ratings on the cost and availability of capital. If a firm's current financial condition is poor, its managers may be reluctant to issue new long-term debt because (1) a new debt issue would probably trigger a review by the rating agencies, and (2) debt issued when a firm is in poor financial shape would probably cost more and be subject to more severe restrictive covenants than debt issued from strength. Further, in Chapters 16 and 17 we pointed out that firms are reluctant to use new common stock financing, especially when this might be taken as a negative signal. Thus, a firm that is in a weakened condition, but whose internal forecasts indicate greater financial strength in the future, would be inclined to delay long-term financing of any type until things improved. Such a firm would be motivated to use short-term debt even to finance long-term assets, with the expectation of replacing the short-term debt in the future with cheaper, higher-rated long-term debt.

Conversely, a firm that is strong now but that forecasts a potentially bad time in the period just ahead would be motivated to finance long term now rather than to wait. Each of these scenarios implies either that the capital markets are inefficient or that investors do not have the same information regarding the firm's future as does its financial manager. The second situation undoubtedly is true at times, and the first one possibly is true at times.

The firm's earnings outlook, and the extent to which forecasted higher earnings per share are reflected in stock prices, also has an effect on the choice of securities. If a successful R&D program has just been concluded, and as a result management forecasts higher earnings than do most investors, then the firm would not want to issue common stock. It would use debt and then, once earnings rise and push up the stock price, sell common stock to restore the capital structure to its target level.

Amount of Financing Required

Obviously, the amount of financing required will influence the financing decision. This is mainly due to flotation costs. A $5 million debt financing, which is small in Wall Street terms, would most likely be done with a term loan or a privately placed bond issue, while a firm seeking $2 billion of new debt would most likely use a public offering of long-term bonds.

Availability of Collateral

Generally, secured debt is less costly than unsecured debt. Thus, firms with large amounts of marketable fixed assets are likely to use a relatively large amount of long-term debt, especially mortgage bonds. Additionally, each year's financing decision would be influenced by the amount of qualified assets available as security for new bonds.

SELF-TEST _What are some factors that financial managers consider when choosing the maturity structure of their debt?_
How do information asymmetries affect financing decisions?

19.8 Refunding Operations

A great deal of corporate debt was sold during the late 1980s at interest rates in the 9% to 12% range. Because the call protection on much of this debt has ended, and because interest rates have fallen since the debt was issued, many companies are analyzing the pros and cons of bond refundings. Refunding decisions actually involve two separate questions: (1) Is it profitable to call an outstanding issue in the current period and replace it with a new issue; and (2) even if refunding is currently profitable, would the firm's expected value be increased even more if the refunding were postponed to a later date? We consider both questions in this section.

Note that the decision to refund a security is analyzed in much the same way as a capital budgeting expenditure. The costs of refunding (the investment outlays) include (1) the call premium paid for the privilege of calling the old issue, (2) the costs of selling the new issue, (3) the tax savings from writing off the unexpensed flotation costs on the old issue, and (4) the net interest that must be paid while both issues are outstanding (the new issue is often sold prior to the refunding to ensure that the funds will be available). The annual cash flows, in a capital budgeting sense, are the interest payments that are saved each year plus the net tax savings that the firm receives for amortizing the flotation expenses. For example, if the interest expense on the old issue is $1,000,000, whereas that on the new issue is $700,000, the $300,000 reduction in interest savings constitutes an annual benefit.[13]

The net present value method is used to analyze the advantages of refunding: The future cash flows are discounted back to the present, and then this discounted value is compared with the cash outlays associated with the refunding. The firm should refund the bond only if the present value of the savings exceeds the cost—that is, if the NPV of the refunding operation is positive.

In the discounting process, the after-tax cost of the new debt, r_d, should be used as the discount rate. The reason is that there is relatively little risk to the savings—cash flows in a refunding decision are known with relative certainty, which is quite unlike the situation with cash flows in most capital budgeting decisions.

The easiest way to examine the refunding decision is through an example. Microchip Computer Company has a $60 million bond issue outstanding that has a 12% annual coupon interest rate and 20 years remaining to maturity. This issue, which was sold 5 years ago, had flotation costs of $3 million that the firm has been amortizing on a straight-line basis over the 25-year original life of the issue. The bond has a call provision that makes it possible for the company to retire the issue at this time by calling the bonds in at a 10% call premium. Investment banks have assured the company that it could sell an additional $60 million to $70 million worth of new 20-year bonds at an interest rate of 9%. To ensure that the funds required to pay off the old debt will be available, the new bonds will be sold 1 month before the old issue is called, so for 1 month, interest will have to be paid on two issues. Current short-term interest rates are 6%. Predictions are that long-term

---

[13]During the early 1980s, there was a flurry of work on the pros and cons of refunding bond issues that had fallen to deep discounts as a result of rising interest rates. At such times, the company could go into the market, buy its debt at a low price, and retire it. The difference between the bonds' par values and the prices the company paid would be reported as income, and taxes would have to be paid on it. The results of the research on the refunding of discount issues suggest that bonds should not, in general, be refunded after a rise in rates. See Andrew J. Kalotay, "On the Structure and Valuation of Debt Refundings," *Financial Management*, Spring 1982, pp. 41–42; and Robert S. Harris, "The Refunding of Discounted Debt: An Adjusted Present Value Analysis," *Financial Management*, Winter 1980, pp. 7–12.

interest rates are unlikely to fall below 9%.[14] Flotation costs on a new refunding issue will amount to $2,650,000, and the firm's marginal federal-plus-state tax rate is 40%. Should the company refund the $60 million of 12% bonds?

The following steps outline the decision process; they are summarized in the spreadsheet in Table 19-3. This spreadsheet is part of the spreadsheet model, *FM12 Ch 19 Tool Kit.xls*, developed for this chapter. The range of cells from A15 through H21 shows input data needed for the analysis, which were just discussed.

e-resource

See *FM12 Ch 19 Tool Kit.xls* at the textbook's Web site for details.

Step 1: Determine the Investment Outlay Required to Refund the Issue

Row 26.   *Call premium on old issue:*

$$\text{Before tax: } 0.10(\$60,000,000) = \$6,000,000$$

$$\text{After tax: } \$6,000,000(1 - T) = \$6,000,000(0.6)$$

$$= \$3,600,000.$$

Although Microchip must spend $6 million on the call premium, this is a deductible expense in the year the call is made. Because the company is in the 40% tax bracket, it saves $2.4 million in taxes; therefore, the after-tax cost of the call is only $3.6 million. This amount is shown in Row 26 of Table 19-3.

Row 27.   *Flotation costs on new issue:* Flotation costs on the new issue will be $2,650,000. This amount cannot be expensed for tax purposes, so it provides no immediate tax benefit.

Row 28.   *Flotation costs on old issue:* The old issue has an unamortized flotation cost of $(20/25)(\$3,000,000) = \$2,400,000$ at this time. If the issue is retired, the unamortized flotation cost may be recognized immediately as an expense, thus creating an after-tax savings of $\$2,400,000(T) = \$960,000$. Because this is a cash inflow, it is shown as a positive number in Row 28.

Rows 29 and 30.   *Additional interest:* One month's "extra" interest on the old issue, after taxes, costs $360,000:

$$(\text{Dollar amount})(1/12 \text{ of } 12\%)(1 - T) = \text{Interest cost}$$

$$(\$60,000,000)(0.01)(0.6) = \$360,000.$$

However, the proceeds from the new issue can be invested in short-term securities for 1 month. Thus, $60 million invested at a rate of 6% will return $180,000 in after-tax interest:

$$(\$60,000,000)(1/12 \text{ of } 6\%)(1 - T) = \text{Interest earned}$$

$$(\$60,000,000)(0.005)(0.6) = \$180,000.$$

---

[14]The firm's management has estimated that interest rates will probably remain at their present level of 9% or else rise; there is only a 25% probability that they will fall further.

Spreadsheet for the Bond Refunding Decision

	A	B	C	D	E	F	G	H
13	**Input Data (in thousands of dollars)**							
14								
15	Existing bond issue =			$60,000		New bond issue =		$60,000
16	Original flotation cost =			$3,000		New flotation cost =		$2,650
17	Maturity of original debt =			25		New bond maturity =		20
18	Years since old debt issue =			5		New cost of debt =		9.0%
19	Call premium (%) =			10.0%				
20	Original coupon rate =			12.0%		Tax rate =		40.0%
21	After-tax cost of new debt =			5.4%		Short-term interest rate =		6.0%
22								
23	**Schedule of cash flows**							
24						Before-tax	After-tax	
25	*Investment Outlay*							
26	Call premium on the old bond					($6,000.0)	($3,600.0)	
27	Flotation costs on new issue					($2,650.0)	($2,650.0)	
28	Immediate tax savings on old flotation cost expense					$2,400.0	$960.0	
29	Extra interest paid on old issue					($600.0)	($360.0)	
30	Interest earned on short-term investment					$300.0	$180.0	
31	Total after-tax investment						($5,470.0)	
32								
33	*Annual Flotation Cost Tax Effects: t=1 to 20*							
34	Annual tax savings from new issue flotation costs					$132.5	$53.0	
35	Annual lost tax savings from old issue flotation costs					($120.0)	($48.0)	
36	Net flotation cost tax savings =					$12.5	$5.0	
37								
38	*Annual Interest Savings Due to Refunding: t=1 to 20*							
39	Interest on old bond					$7,200.0	$4,320.0	
40	Interest on new bond					($5,400.0)	($3,240.0)	
41	Net interest savings					$1,800.0	$1,080.0	
42								
43	**Calculating the annual flotation cost tax effects and the annual interest savings**							
44								
45	Annual flotation Cost Tax Effects					Annual Interest Savings		
46	Maturity of the new bond (Nper)			20		Maturity of the new bond (Nper)		20
47	After-tax cost of new debt (Rate)			5.4%		After-tax cost of new debt (Rate)		5.4%
48	Annual flotation cost tax savings (Pmt)			$5		Annual interest savings (Pmt)		$1,080
49								
50	Since the annual flotation cost tax effects and interest savings occur for the next 20 years, they represent annuities. To evaluate							
51	this project, we must find the present values of these savings. Using the function wizard and solving for present value, we find							
52	that the present values of these annuities are:							
53								
54	NPV of annual flotation cost savings			$60.251		NPV of annual interest savings		$13,014.174
55								
56	Hence, the net present value of this bond refunding project will be the sum of the initial outlay and the present values of the							
57	annual flotation cost tax effects and interest savings.							
58								
59	Bond Refunding NPV =	Initial Outlay	+			PV of flotation costs +	PV of interest savings	
60	Bond Refunding NPV =	($5,470.000)	+			$60.251	+	$13,014.174
61								
62	Bond Refund NPV =	$7,604.425						

The net after-tax additional interest cost is thus $180,000:

Interest paid on old issue	($360,000)
Interest earned on short-term securities	180,000
Net additional interest	($180,000)

These figures are reflected in Rows 29 and 30 of Table 19-3.

Row 31.   *Total after-tax investment:* The total investment outlay required to refund the bond issue, which will be financed by debt, is thus $5,470,000.[15]

Call premium	($3,600,000)
Flotation costs, new	(2,650,000)
Flotation costs, old, tax savings	960,000
Net additional interest	(180,000)
Total investment	($5,470,000)

This total is shown in Row 31 of Table 19-3.

Step 2: Calculate the Annual Flotation Cost Tax Effects

Row 34.   *Tax savings on flotation costs on the new issue:* For tax purposes, flotation costs must be amortized over the life of the new bond, or for 20 years. Therefore, the annual tax deduction is

$$\frac{\$2,650,000}{20} = \$132,500.$$

Since our spreadsheet shows dollars in thousands, this number appears as $132.5 on the spreadsheet. Because the firm is in the 40% tax bracket, it has a tax savings of $132,500(0.4) = $53,000 a year for 20 years. This is an annuity of $53,000 for 20 years, and it is shown in Row 34.

Row 35.   *Tax benefits lost on flotation costs on the old issue:* The firm, however, will no longer receive a tax deduction of $120,000 a year for 20 years, so it loses an after-tax benefit of $48,000 a year. This is shown in Row 35.

Row 36.   *Net amortization tax effect:* The after-tax difference between the amortization tax effects of flotation on the new and old issues is $5,000 a year for 20 years. This is shown in Row 36.

Step 3: Calculate the Annual Interest Savings

Row 39.   *Interest on old bond, after tax:* The annual after-tax interest on the old issue is $4.32 million:

$$(\$60,000,000)(0.12)(0.6) = \$4,320,000.$$

This is shown in Row 39 of Table 19-3.

Row 40.   *Interest on new bond, after tax:* The new issue has an annual after-tax cost of $3,240,000:

$$(\$60,000,000)(0.09)(0.6) = \$3,240,000.$$

This is shown in Row 40.

[15]The investment outlay (in this case, $5,470,000) is usually obtained by increasing the amount of the new bond issue. In the example given, the new issue would be $65,470,000. However, the interest on the additional debt *should not* be deducted at Step 3 because the $5,470,000 itself will be deducted at Step 4. If additional interest on the $5,470,000 were deducted at Step 3, interest would, in effect, be deducted twice. The situation here is exactly like that in regular capital budgeting decisions. Even though some debt may be used to finance a project, interest on that debt is not subtracted when developing the annual cash flows. Rather, the annual cash flows are *discounted* at the project's cost of capital.

Row 41. *Net annual interest savings:* Thus, the net annual interest savings is $1,080,000:

Interest on old bonds, after tax	$4,620,000
Interest on new bonds, after tax	(3,240,000)
Annual interest savings, after tax	$1,080,000

This is shown in Row 41.

Step 4: Determine the NPV of the Refunding

Row 54. *PV of the benefits:* The PV of the annual after-tax flotation cost benefit can be found with a financial calculator, with N = 20, I/YR = 5.4, PMT = 5,000, and FV = 0. Solving for PV shows the flotation cost savings have a present value equal to $60,251. The PV of the $1,080,000 annual after-tax interest savings can be found with a financial calculator, with N = 20, I/YR = 5.4, PMT = 1,080,000 and FV = 0. Solving for PV shows the present value of after-tax interest cost savings is $13,014,174.

These values are used in Row 60 when finding the NPV of the refunding operation:

Amortization tax effects	$ 60,251
Interest savings	13,014,174
Net investment outlay	(5,470,000)
NPV from refunding	$ 7,604,425

Because the net present value of the refunding is positive, it would be profitable to refund the old bond issue.

We can summarize the data shown in Table 19-3 using a time line (amounts in thousands) as shown below:

Time Period	0	5.4%	1		2		20
After-tax investment	-5,470						
Flotation cost tax effects			5		5	...	5
Interest savings			1,080		1,080	...	1,080
Net cash flows	-5,470		1,085		1,085	...	1,085

$NPV_{5.4\%} = \$7,604.$

Several other points should be made. First, because the cash flows are based on differences between contractual obligations, their risk is the same as that of the underlying obligations. Therefore, the present values of the cash flows should be found by discounting at the firm's least risky rate—its after-tax cost of marginal debt. Second, since the refunding operation is advantageous to the firm, it must be disadvantageous to bondholders; they must give up their

TVA Ratchets Down Its Interest Expenses

In 1998, TVA raised $575 million in 30-year debt. If it had issued fixed-rate debt, it would be stuck with high coupon payments if interest rates in the market fall. If it had issued floating-rate debt, it would be stuck with high coupon payments if interest rates rise. If it had issued callable debt, then it could refinance if interest rates fall. But the costs of refunding are high, and TVA would have to agonize over the decision of whether to refund or wait in the hopes that rates will fall. None of these three choices seemed desirable, so TVA issued a new type of security that finesses these problems.

The new bonds are officially called Putable Automatic Rate Reset Securities (PARRS), but they are commonly known as ratchet bonds. After 2003, these bonds have a feature that resets the coupon rate each year to 94 basis points over the rate on the prevailing 30-year Treasury bond, if the new coupon would be lower than the ratchet bond's current coupon. In other words, the coupon on the bond will fall if interest rates fall, but will never increase from year to year, letting TVA lock in the lowest interest rates that prevail during the bond's life. In essence,

TVA gets to refund its debt in any year when rates fall, thus the term "ratchet."

The 94-basis-point spread is higher than the spread over Treasuries that normally exists on TVA's noncallable bonds, given its bond rating. However, if the bond rating deteriorates, then investors can "put" the bond by selling it back to TVA. The net effect is that investors are exposed to interest rate risk but not to credit risk, and they are compensated for interest rate risk by the relatively high spread.

These bonds were originally issued with a 6¾% coupon and on the first reset date, June 1, 2003, the rate ratcheted down to 5.952%, reflecting the decline in long-term interest rates since 1998. By June 1, 2005, long-term interest rates had fallen so that the coupon rate on the PARRS was ratcheted down to 5.49%. As of mid-2006, the rate was still 5.49%.

Source: Andrew Kalotay and Leslie Abreo, "Ratchet Bonds: Maximum Refunding Efficiency at Minimum Transaction Cost," *Journal of Applied Corporate Finance*, Vol. 41, no. 1 (Spring 1999), pp. 40–47, and TVA's Web site, **http://www.tva.gov**.

12% bonds and reinvest in new ones yielding 9%. This points out the danger of the call provision to bondholders, and it also explains why noncallable bonds command higher prices than callable bonds. Third, although it is not emphasized in the example, we assumed that the firm raises the investment required to undertake the refunding operation (the $5,470,000 shown in Row 31 of Table 19-3) as debt. This should be feasible because the refunding operation will improve the interest coverage ratio, even though a larger amount of debt is outstanding.[16] Fourth, we set up our example in such a way that the new issue had the same maturity as the remaining life of the old one. Often, the old bonds have a relatively short time to maturity (say, 5 to 10 years), whereas the new bonds have a much longer maturity (say, 25 to 30 years). In such a situation, the analysis should be set up similarly to a replacement chain analysis in capital budgeting, which was discussed in Chapter 11. Fifth, refunding decisions are

---

[16]See Aharon R. Ofer and Robert A. Taggart, Jr., "Bond Refunding: A Clarifying Analysis," *Journal of Finance*, March 1977, pp. 21–30, for a discussion of how the method of financing the refunding affects the analysis. Ofer and Taggart prove that if the refunding investment outlay is to be raised as common equity, the before-tax cost of debt is the proper discount rate, whereas if these funds are to be raised as debt, the after-tax cost of debt is the proper discount rate. Since a profitable refunding will virtually always raise the firm's debt-carrying capacity (because total interest charges after the refunding will be lower than before it), it is more logical to use debt than either equity or a combination of debt and equity to finance the operation. Therefore, firms generally do use additional debt to finance refunding operations.

Questions

(19-1)   Define each of the following terms:
  a. Going public; new issue market; initial public offering (IPO)
  b. Public offering; private placement
  c. Venture capitalists; roadshow; spread
  d. Securities and Exchange Commission (SEC); registration statement; shelf registration; margin requirement; insiders
  e. Prospectus; "red herring" prospectus
  f. National Association of Securities Dealers (NASD)
  g. Best efforts arrangement; underwritten arrangement
  h. Refunding; project financing; securitization; maturity matching

(19-2)   Is it true that the "flatter," or more nearly horizontal, the demand curve for a particular firm's stock and the less important investors regard the signaling effect of the offering, the more important the role of investment banks when the company sells a new issue of stock?

(19-3)   The SEC attempts to protect investors who are purchasing newly issued securities by making sure that the information put out by a company and its investment banks is correct and is not misleading. However, the SEC does not provide an opinion about the real value of the securities; hence, an investor might pay too much for some new stock and consequently lose heavily. Do you think the SEC should, as a part of every new stock or bond offering, render an opinion to investors on the proper value of the securities being offered? Explain.

(19-4)   How do you think each of the following items would affect a company's ability to attract new capital and the flotation costs involved in doing so?
  a. A decision of a privately held company to go public
  b. The increasing institutionalization of the "buy side" of the stock and bond markets
  c. The trend toward "financial conglomerates" as opposed to stand-alone investment banking houses
  d. Elimination of the preemptive right
  e. The introduction of shelf registrations in 1981

(19-5)   Before entering a formal agreement, investment banks carefully investigate the companies whose securities they underwrite; this is especially true of the issues of firms going public for the first time. Since the banks do not themselves plan to hold the securities but intend to sell them to others as soon as possible, why are they so concerned about making careful investigations?

Self-Test Problem   Solution Appears in Appendix A

(ST-1)   House Mountain Breweries (HMB) is planning an IPO. Its underwriters have said the stock will sell at $20 per share. The direct costs (legal fees, printing, etc.) will be $800,000. The underwriters will charge a 7% spread.

a. How many shares must HMB sell to net $30 million?
b. If the stock price closes the first day at $22, how much cash has HMB left on the table?
c. What are HMB's total costs (direct, indirect, and underwriting) for the IPO?

Problems   Answers Appear in Appendix B

Easy Problems 1–2

(19-1)
Profit or Loss on New Stock Issue

Security Brokers Inc. specializes in underwriting new issues by small firms. On a recent offering of Beedles Inc., the terms were as follows:

Price to public	$5 per share
Number of shares	3 million
Proceeds to Beedles	$14,000,000

The out-of-pocket expenses incurred by Security Brokers in the design and distribution of the issue were $300,000. What profit or loss would Security Brokers incur if the issue were sold to the public at an average price of
a. $5 per share?
b. $6 per share?
c. $4 per share?

(19-2)
Underwriting and Flotation Expenses

The Beranek Company, whose stock price is now $25, needs to raise $20 million in common stock. Underwriters have informed the firm's management that they must price the new issue to the public at $22 per share because of signaling effects. The underwriters' compensation will be 5% of the issue price, so Beranek will net $20.90 per share. The firm will also incur expenses in the amount of $150,000.
How many shares must the firm sell to net $20 million after underwriting and flotation expenses?

Intermediate Problem 3

(19-3)
New Stock Issue

The Edelman Gem Company, a small jewelry manufacturer, has been successful and has enjoyed a good growth trend. Now Edelman is planning to go public with an issue of common stock, and it faces the problem of setting an appropriate price on the stock. The company and its investment banks believe that the proper procedure is to select several similar firms with publicly traded common stock and to make relevant comparisons.

Several jewelry manufacturers are reasonably similar to Edelman with respect to product mix, asset composition, and debt/equity proportions. Of these companies, Kennedy Jewelers and Strasburg Fashions are most similar. When analyzing the following data, assume that 2002 and 2007 were reasonably "normal" years for all three companies—that is, these years were neither especially good nor especially bad in terms of sales, earnings, and dividends. At the time of the analysis, r_{RF} was 8% and RP_M was 4%. Kennedy is listed on the AMEX and Strasburg on the NYSE, while Edelman will be traded in the Nasdaq market.

	Kennedy	Strasburg	Edelman (Totals)
Earnings per share*			
2007	$ 4.50	$ 7.50	$1,200,000
2002	3.00	5.50	816,000
Price per share*			
2007	$36.00	$65.00	—
Dividends per share*			
2007	$ 2.25	$ 3.75	$ 600,000
2002	1.50	2.75	420,000
Book value per share, 2007*	$30.00	$55.00	$ 9 million
Market/book ratio, 2007	120%	118%	—
Total assets, 2007	$28 million	$ 82 million	$20 million
Total debt, 2007	$12 million	$ 30 million	$11 million
Sales, 2007	$41 million	$140 million	$37 million

*The data are on a per share basis for Kennedy and Strasburg, but are totals for Edelman.

a. Assume that Edelman has 100 shares of stock outstanding. Use this informa-
    tion to calculate earnings per share (EPS), dividends per share (DPS), and
    book value per share for Edelman. (Hint: Edelman's 2007 EPS = $12,000.)
b. Calculate earnings and dividend growth rates for the three companies. (Hint:
    Edelman's EPS growth rate is 8%.)
c. On the basis of your answer to part a, do you think Edelman's stock would
    sell at a price in the same "ballpark" as that of Kennedy and Strasburg, that is,
    in the range of $25 to $100 per share?
d. Assuming that Edelman's management can split the stock so that the 100
    shares could be changed to 1,000 shares, 100,000 shares, or any other number,
    would such an action make sense in this case? Why or why not?
e. Now assume that Edelman did split its stock and has 400,000 shares. Calculate
    new values for EPS, DPS, and book value per share. (Hint: Edelman's new
    2007 EPS is $3.00.)
f. Return on equity (ROE) can be measured as EPS/book value per share or as
    total earnings/total equity. Calculate ROEs for the three companies for 2007.
    (Hint: Edelman's 2007 ROE is 13.3%.)
g. Calculate dividend payout ratios for the three companies for both years.
    (Hint: Edelman's 2007 payout ratio is 50%.)
h. Calculate debt/total assets ratios for the three companies for 2007. (Hint:
    Edelman's 2007 debt ratio is 55%.)
i. Calculate the P/E ratios for Kennedy and Strasburg for 2007. Are these P/Es
    reasonable in view of relative growth, payout, and ROE data? If not, what
    other factors might explain them? (Hint: Kennedy's P/E = 8×.)
j. Now determine a range of values for Edelman's stock price, with 400,000
    shares outstanding, by applying Kennedy's and Strasburg's P/E ratios,
    price/dividends ratios, and price/book value ratios to your data for Edelman.
    For example, one possible price for Edelman's stock is (P/E Kennedy)(EPS
    Edelman) = 8($3) = $24 per share. Similar calculations would produce a

range of prices based on both Kennedy's and Strasburg's data. (Hint: Our range was $24 to $27.)

k. Using the equation $r_s = D_1/P_0 + g$, find approximate r_s values for Kennedy and Strasburg. Then use these values in the constant growth stock price model to find a price for Edelman's stock. (Hint: We averaged the EPS and DPS g's for Edelman.)

l. At what price do you think Edelman's shares should be offered to the public? You will want to select a price that will be low enough to induce investors to buy the stock but not so low that it will rise sharply immediately after it is issued. Think about relative growth rates, ROEs, dividend yields, and total returns ($r_s = D_1/P_0 + g$).

Challenging Problems 4–5

(19-4)

Refunding Analysis

Jan Volk, financial manager of Green Sea Transport (GST), has been asked by her boss to review GST's outstanding debt issues for possible bond refunding. Five years ago, GST issued $40,000,000 of 11%, 25-year debt. The issue, with semiannual coupons, is currently callable at a premium of 11%, or $110 for each $1,000 par value bond. Flotation costs on this issue were 6%, or $2,400,000.

Volk believes that GST could issue 20-year debt today with a coupon rate of 8%. The firm has placed many issues in the capital markets during the last 10 years, and its debt flotation costs are currently estimated to be 4% of the issue's value. GST's federal-plus-state tax rate is 40%.

Help Volk conduct the refunding analysis by answering the following questions:

a. What is the total dollar call premium required to call the old issue? Is it tax deductible? What is the net after-tax cost of the call?

b. What is the dollar flotation cost on the new issue? Is it immediately tax deductible? What is the after-tax flotation cost?

c. What amounts of old-issue flotation costs have not been expensed? Can these deferred costs be expensed immediately if the old issue is refunded? What is the value of the tax savings?

d. What is the net after-tax cash outlay required to refund the old issue?

e. What is the semiannual tax savings that arises from amortizing the flotation costs on the new issue? What is the forgone semiannual tax savings on the old-issue flotation costs?

f. What is the semiannual after-tax interest savings that would result from the refunding?

g. Thus far, Volk has identified two future cash flows: (1) the net of new-issue flotation cost tax savings and old-issue flotation cost tax savings that are lost if refunding occurs and (2) after-tax interest savings. What is the sum of these two semiannual cash flows? What is the appropriate discount rate to apply to these future cash flows? What is the present value of these cash flows? (Hint: The $PVIFA_{2.4\%,40} = 25.5309$.)

h. What is the NPV of refunding? Should GST refund now or wait until later?

(19-5)

Refunding Analysis

Mullet Technologies is considering whether or not to refund a $75 million, 12% coupon, 30-year bond issue that was sold 5 years ago. It is amortizing $5 million of flotation costs on the 12% bonds over the issue's 30-year life. Mullet's investment banks have indicated that the company could sell a new 25-year issue at an interest rate of 10% in today's market. Neither they nor Mullet's management anticipate that interest rates will fall below 10% any time soon, but there is a chance that rates will increase.

A call premium of 12% would be required to retire the old bonds, and flotation costs on the new issue would amount to $5 million. Mullet's marginal federal-plus-state tax rate is 40%. The new bonds would be issued 1 month before the old bonds are called, with the proceeds being invested in short-term government securities returning 6% annually during the interim period.

a. Perform a complete bond refunding analysis. What is the bond refunding's NPV?

b. What factors would influence Mullet's decision to refund now rather than later?

Spreadsheet Problem

(19-6)
Build a Model: Bond Refunding

Start with the partial model in the file *FM12 Ch 19 P 06 Build a Model.xls* from the textbook's Web site. Rework Problem 19-5, part a, using a spreadsheet model, and answer the following question:

e-resource

c. At what interest rate on the new debt is the NPV of the refunding no longer positive?

Cyberproblem

e-resource

Please go to the textbook's Web site to access any Cyberproblems.

Mini Case

Randy's, a family-owned restaurant chain operating in Alabama, has grown to the point where expansion throughout the entire Southeast is feasible. The proposed expansion would require the firm to raise about $15 million in new capital. Because Randy's currently has a debt ratio of 50%, and also because the family members already have all their personal wealth invested in the company, the family would like to sell common stock to the public to raise the $15 million. However, the family does want to retain voting control. You have been asked to brief the family members on the issues involved by answering the following questions:

a. What agencies regulate securities markets?

b. How are start-up firms usually financed?

c. Differentiate between a private placement and a public offering.

Selected Additional Cases **713**

d. Why would a company consider going public? What are some advantages and disadvantages?
e. What are the steps of an initial public offering?
f. What criteria are important in choosing an investment bank?
g. Would companies going public use a negotiated deal or a competitive bid?
h. Would the sale be on an underwritten or best efforts basis?
i. Without actually doing any calculations, describe how the preliminary offering range for the price of an IPO would be determined.
j. What is a roadshow? What is book-building?
k. Describe the typical first-day return of an IPO and the long-term returns to IPO investors.
l. What are the direct and indirect costs of an IPO?
m. What are equity carve-outs?
n. In what other ways are investment banks involved in issuing securities?
o. What is meant by "going private"? What are some advantages and disadvantages?
p. How do companies manage the maturity structure of their debt?
q. Under what conditions would a firm exercise a bond call provision?
r. Explain how firms manage the risk structure of their debt with
  (1) Project financing.
  (2) Securitization.

Selected Additional Cases

The following cases from Textchoice, *Cengage Learning's online library, cover many of the concepts discussed in this chapter and are available at* **http://www.textchoice2.com.**

Klein-Brigham Series:
Case 21, "Sun Coast Savings Bank," illustrates the decision to go public. Case 22, "Precision Tool Company," emphasizes the investment banking process. Case 23, "Art Deco Reproductions, Inc.," focuses on the analysis of a rights offering. Case 24, "Bay Area Telephone Company," Case 48, "Shenandoah Power Company," and Case 64, "Tucson Entertainment, Inc.," illustrate the bond refunding decision.

chapter 20

Lease Financing

Some of the biggest players in the airline business have never issued a ticket, lost a passenger's luggage, or landed a plane in bad weather. They are the aircraft leasing companies—the merchant bankers of aviation—and their role is to help finance aircraft and enable airlines to respond more quickly and efficiently to market changes. Among the major players in aircraft leasing are GPA Group, a closely held company based in Ireland, and International Lease Finance of Beverly Hills.

Aircraft leasing companies purchase airplanes from manufacturers such as Boeing and Airbus and then lease them, often on a relatively short-term basis, to carriers such as American, British Airways, Delta, Lufthansa, and United, as well as to small, regional companies all over the world. Leasing separates the risks and rewards of owning aircraft from those of operating them. Currently, leasing companies buy about 50% of all new commercial aircraft.

The airline industry has been undergoing major changes due to global deregulation. In the days of regulation, airlines knew precisely the routes they would serve, and they could raise prices to cover all cost increases. Thus, airlines could buy planes confident that route structures would be relatively stable and that revenues would cover financing costs. Now, however, airlines are constantly dropping and adding routes in response to changing competitive conditions. Because different types of aircraft are better suited for some routes than

others, airlines must frequently restructure their fleets for optimal operations. If an airline had purchased all of its aircraft, it would be more difficult to respond quickly to changing conditions. The leasing companies, on the other hand, lease all types of aircraft to all types of airlines, and there is usually some airline somewhere in the world that would be interested in a leased aircraft when it is returned to the leasing company. Therefore, leasing improves airlines' flexibility and efficiency.

Note, too, that global deregulation also spawned a host of start-up airlines in the United States, Europe, Africa, and Asia. Start-up airlines typically are in a precarious financial condition, and leasing companies are often more willing than banks and other lenders to take on the financing risk because lessors are in a relatively favorable legal position should the airline actually go bankrupt. Thus, it is easier for a leasing company to repossess and redeploy aircraft than it would be for a lender.

Interestingly, Airbus Industrie, the European aircraft consortium, has adopted short-term leases as a sales tool. In recent years, Delta and United "bought" aircraft from Airbus on "walkaway" leases under which airplanes with a 30-year life could be returned to the manufacturer in less than a year. U.S. manufacturers complained that Airbus can offer such terms only because it is subsidized by the four European countries that back the consortium.

Firms generally own fixed assets and report them on their balance sheets, but it is the use of assets that is important, not their ownership per se. One way to obtain the *use* of facilities and equipment is to buy them, but an alternative is to lease them. Prior to the 1950s, leasing was generally associated with real estate—land and buildings. Today, however, it is possible to lease virtually any kind of fixed asset, and currently over 30% of all new capital equipment is financed through lease arrangements.[1]

e-resource

The textbook's Web site contains an *Excel* file that will guide you through the chapter's calculations. The file for this chapter is ***FM12 Ch 20 Tool Kit.xls,*** and we encourage you to open the file and follow along as you read the chapter.

20.1 Types of Leases

Lease transactions involve two parties: the lessor, who owns the property, and the lessee, who obtains use of the property in exchange for one or more lease, or rental, payments. (Note that the term *lessee* is pronounced "less-ee," not "lease-ee," and *lessor* is pronounced "less-or.") Because both parties must agree before a lease transaction can be completed, this chapter discusses leasing from the perspectives of both the lessor and the lessee.

Leasing takes several different forms, the five most important being (1) operating leases, (2) financial, or capital, leases, (3) sale-and-leaseback arrangements, (4) combination leases, and (5) synthetic leases.

Operating Leases

Operating leases generally provide for both *financing* and *maintenance*. IBM was one of the pioneers of the operating lease contract, and computers and office copying machines, together with automobiles, trucks, and aircraft, are the primary types of equipment involved in operating leases. Ordinarily, operating leases require the lessor to maintain and service the leased equipment, and the cost of the maintenance is built into the lease payments.

Another important characteristic of operating leases is the fact that they are *not fully amortized*. In other words, the rental payments required under the lease contract are not sufficient for the lessor to recover the full cost of the asset. However, the lease contract is written for a period considerably shorter than the expected economic life of the asset, so the lessor can expect to recover all costs either by subsequent renewal payments, by releasing the asset to another lessee, or by selling the asset.

A final feature of operating leases is that they often contain a *cancellation clause* that gives the lessee the right to cancel the lease and return the asset before the expiration of the basic lease agreement. This is an important consideration to the lessee, for it means that the asset can be returned if it is rendered obsolete by technological developments or is no longer needed because of a change in the lessee's business.

Financial, or Capital, Leases

Financial leases, sometimes called **capital leases,** are differentiated from operating leases in that they (1) *do not* provide for maintenance service, (2) *are not*

[1]For a detailed treatment of leasing, see James S. Schallheim, *Lease or Buy? Principles for Sound Decision Making* (Boston: Harvard Business School Press, 1994).

cancellable, and (3) *are* fully amortized (that is, the lessor receives rental payments equal to the full price of the leased equipment plus a return on invested capital). In a typical arrangement, the firm that will use the equipment (the lessee) selects the specific items it requires and negotiates the price with the manufacturer. The user firm then arranges to have a leasing company (the lessor) buy the equipment from the manufacturer and simultaneously executes a lease contract. The terms of the lease generally call for full amortization of the lessor's investment, plus a rate of return on the unamortized balance that is close to the percentage rate the lessee would have paid on a secured loan. For example, if the lessee had to pay 10% for a loan, then a rate of about 10% would be built into the lease contract.

The lessee is generally given an option to renew the lease at a reduced rate upon expiration of the basic lease. However, the basic lease usually cannot be cancelled unless the lessor is paid in full. Also, the lessee generally pays the property taxes and insurance on the leased property. Since the lessor receives a return *after*, or *net of*, these payments, this type of lease is often called a "net, net" lease.

Sale-and-Leaseback Arrangements

Under a **sale-and-leaseback** arrangement, a firm that owns land, buildings, or equipment sells the property to another firm and simultaneously executes an agreement to lease the property back for a stated period under specific terms. The capital supplier could be an insurance company, a commercial bank, a specialized leasing company, the finance arm of an industrial firm, a limited partnership, or an individual investor. The sale-and-leaseback plan is an alternative to a mortgage.

Note that the seller immediately receives the purchase price put up by the buyer. At the same time, the seller-lessee retains the use of the property. The parallel to borrowing is carried over to the lease payment schedule. Under a mortgage loan arrangement, the lender would normally receive a series of equal payments just sufficient to amortize the loan and to provide a specified rate of return on the outstanding loan balance. Under a sale-and-leaseback arrangement, the lease payments are set up exactly the same way—the payments are just sufficient to return the full purchase price to the investor, plus a stated return on the lessor's investment.

Sale-and-leaseback arrangements are almost the same as financial leases, the major difference being that the leased equipment is used, not new, and the lessor buys it from the user-lessee instead of a manufacturer or a distributor. A sale-and-leaseback is thus a special type of financial lease.

Combination Leases

Many lessors now offer leases under a wide variety of terms. Therefore, in practice leases often do not fit exactly into the operating lease or financial lease category but combine some features of each. Such leases are called **combination leases.** To illustrate, cancellation clauses are normally associated with operating leases, but many of today's financial leases also contain cancellation clauses. However, in financial leases these clauses generally include prepayment provisions whereby the lessee must make penalty payments sufficient to enable the lessor to recover the unamortized cost of the leased property.

Synthetic Leases

A fifth type of lease, the synthetic lease, should also be mentioned. These leases were first used in the early 1990s, and they became very popular in the mid- to late-1990s, when companies such as Enron and Tyco, as well as "normal" companies, discovered that synthetic leases could be used to keep debt off their balance sheets. In a typical **synthetic lease,** a corporation that wanted to acquire an asset—generally real estate, with a very long life—with debt would first establish a *special-purpose entity,* or SPE. The SPE would then obtain financing, typically 97% debt provided by a financial institution and 3% equity provided by a party other than the corporation itself.[2] The SPE would then use the funds to acquire the property, and the corporation would lease the asset from the SPE, generally for a term of 3 to 5 years but with an option to extend the lease, which the firm generally expected to exercise. Because of the relatively short term of the lease, it was deemed to be an operating lease and hence did not have to be capitalized and shown on the balance sheet.

A corporation that set up SPEs was required to do one of three things when the lease expired: (1) pay off the SPE's 97% loan, (2) refinance the loan at the currently going interest rate, if the lender was willing to refinance at all, or (3) sell the asset and make up any shortfall between the sale price and the amount of the loan. Thus, the corporate user was guaranteeing the loan, yet it did not have to show an obligation on its balance sheet.

Synthetic leases stayed under the radar until 2001. As we discuss in the next section, long-term leases must be capitalized and shown on the balance sheet. Synthetic leases were designed to get around this requirement, and neither corporations such as Enron and Tyco that used them nor accounting firms such as Arthur Andersen that approved them wanted to have anyone look closely at them. However, after the scandals of the early 2000s, security analysts, the SEC, banking regulators, the FASB, and even corporate boards of directors began to seriously discuss SPEs and synthetic leases. Investors and bankers subjectively downgraded companies that made heavy use of them, and boards of directors began to tell their CFOs to stop using them and to close down the ones that existed. Moreover, the accounting regulatory bodies are in the process of revising the terms under which synthetic leases can be structured. It is not clear exactly how things will end up, but at this point the most likely outcomes are (1) that SPEs and synthetic leases will be much less important in the future than they were in the past; (2) that a lot more than 3% equity will be required to set up an SPE, meaning that the corporation will have less exposure and the lending institution more exposure; and (3) that some corporations with several synthetic leases outstanding are going to have difficulties in the near future, when those leases expire and the firms must either restructure the leases under more stringent terms or else pay off the SPE loans.

SELF-TEST

Who are the two parties to a lease transaction?

What is the difference between an operating lease and a financial, or capital, lease?

What is a sale-and-leaseback transaction?

What is a combination lease?

What is a synthetic lease?

---

[2]Enron's CFO, Andy Fastow, and other insiders provided the equity for many of Enron's SPEs. Also, a number of Merrill Lynch's executives provided SPE equity, allegedly to enable Merrill Lynch to obtain profitable investment banking deals. The very fact that SPEs are so well suited to conceal what's going on helped those who used them engage in shady deals that would have at least raised eyebrows had they been disclosed. In fact, Fastow pled guilty to two counts of conspiracy in connection with Enron's accounting fraud and ultimate bankruptcy. For more on this subject, see W. R. Pollert and E. J. Glickman, "Synthetic Leases Under Fire," at **http://www.strategicfinancemag.com**, October 2002.

20.2 Tax Effects

The full amount of the lease payments is a tax-deductible expense for the lessee *provided the Internal Revenue Service agrees that a particular contract is a genuine lease and not simply a loan called a lease.* This makes it important that a lease contract be written in a form acceptable to the IRS. A lease that complies with all IRS requirements is called a **guideline,** or **tax-oriented, lease,** and the tax benefits of ownership (depreciation and any investment tax credits) belong to the lessor. The main provisions of the tax guidelines are as follows:

1. The lease term (including any extensions or renewals at a fixed rental rate) must not exceed 80% of the estimated useful life of the equipment at the commencement of the lease transaction. Thus, an asset with a 10-year life can be leased for no more than 8 years. Further, the remaining useful life must not be less than 1 year. Note that an asset's expected useful life is normally much longer than its MACRS depreciation class life.
2. The equipment's estimated residual value (in constant dollars without adjustment for inflation) at the expiration of the lease must be at least 20% of its value at the start of the lease. This requirement can have the effect of limiting the maximum lease term.
3. Neither the lessee nor any related party can have the right to purchase the property at a predetermined fixed price. However, the lessee can be given an option to buy the asset at its fair market value.
4. Neither the lessee nor any related party can pay or guarantee payment of any part of the price of the leased equipment. Simply put, the lessee cannot make any investment in the equipment, other than through the lease payments.
5. The leased equipment must not be "limited use" property, defined as equipment that can be used only by the lessee or a related party at the end of the lease.

The reason for the IRS's concern about lease terms is that, without restrictions, a company could set up a "lease" transaction calling for very rapid payments, which would be tax deductible. The effect would be to depreciate the equipment over a much shorter period than its MACRS class life. For example, suppose a firm planned to acquire a $2 million computer that had a 3-year MACRS class life. The annual depreciation allowances would be $660,000 in Year 1, $900,000 in Year 2, $300,000 in Year 3, and $140,000 in Year 4. If the firm were in the 40% federal-plus-state tax bracket, the depreciation would provide a tax savings of $264,000 in Year 1, $360,000 in Year 2, $120,000 in Year 3, and $56,000 in Year 4, for a total savings of $800,000. At a 6% discount rate, the present value of these tax savings would be $714,567.

Now suppose the firm could acquire the computer through a 1-year lease arrangement with a leasing company for a payment of $2 million, with a $1 purchase option. If the $2 million payment were treated as a lease payment, it would be fully deductible, so it would provide a tax savings of $0.4($2,000,000) = $800,000 versus a present value of only $714,567 for the depreciation shelters. Thus, the lease payment and the depreciation would both provide the same total amount of tax savings (40% of $2,000,000, or $800,000), but the savings would come in faster, hence have a higher present value, with the 1-year lease. Therefore, if just any type of contract could be called a lease and given tax treatment as a lease, then the timing of the tax shelters could be speeded up as compared with ownership depreciation tax shelters. This speedup would benefit companies, but it would be costly to the government. For this reason, the IRS has established the rules described above for defining a lease for tax purposes.

Even though leasing can be used only within limits to speed up the effective depreciation schedule, there are still times when very substantial tax benefits can be derived from a leasing arrangement. For example, if a firm has incurred losses and hence has no current tax liabilities, then its depreciation shelters are not very useful. In this case, a leasing company set up by profitable companies such as GE or Philip Morris can buy the equipment, receive the depreciation shelters, and then share these benefits with the lessee by charging lower lease payments. This point will be discussed in detail later in the chapter, but the point now is that if firms are to obtain tax benefits from leasing, the lease contract must be written in a manner that will qualify it as a true lease under IRS guidelines. If there is any question about the legal status of the contract, the financial manager must be sure to have the firm's lawyers and accountants check the latest IRS regulations.[3]

Note that a lease that does not meet the tax guidelines is called a **non-tax-oriented lease.** For this type of lease, the lessee (1) is the effective owner of the leased property, (2) can depreciate it for tax purposes, and (3) can deduct only the interest portion of each lease payment.

SELF-TEST

What is the difference between a tax-oriented lease and a non-tax-oriented lease?

What are some lease provisions that would cause a lease to be classified as a non-tax-oriented lease?

Why does the IRS place limits on lease provisions?

20.3 Financial Statement Effects[4]

Under certain conditions, neither the leased assets nor the liabilities under the lease contract appear directly on the firm's balance sheet. For this reason, leasing is often called **off–balance sheet financing.** This point is illustrated in Table 20-1 by the balance sheets of two hypothetical firms, B (for "borrow") and L (for "lease"). Initially, the balance sheets of both firms are identical, and they both have debt ratios of 50%. Next, each firm decides to acquire a fixed asset costing $100. Firm B borrows $100 and buys the asset, so both an asset and a liability go on its balance sheet, and its debt ratio rises from 50% to 75%. Firm L leases the equipment. The lease may call for fixed charges as high as or even higher than the loan, and the obligations assumed under the lease may be equally or more dangerous from the standpoint of potential bankruptcy, but the firm's debt ratio remains at only 50%.

To correct this problem, the Financial Accounting Standards Board issued FASB Statement 13, which requires that, for an unqualified audit report, firms that enter into financial (or capital) leases must restate their balance sheets and report the leased asset as a fixed asset and the present value of the future lease payments as a liability. This process is called **capitalizing the lease,** and its net effect is to

---

[3]In 1981, Congress relaxed the normal IRS rules to permit *safe harbor leases*, which had virtually no IRS restrictions and which were explicitly designed to permit the transfer of tax benefits from unprofitable companies that could not use them to high-profit companies that could. The point of safe harbor leases was to provide incentives for capital investment to companies that had little or no tax liability—under safe harbor leasing, companies with no tax liability could sell the benefit to companies in a high marginal tax bracket. In 1981 and 1982, literally billions of dollars were paid by such profitable firms as IBM and Philip Morris for the tax shelters of such unprofitable ones as Ford and Eastern Airlines. However, in 1983, Congress curtailed the use of safe harbor leases.

[4]FASB Statement 13, "Accounting for Leases," spells out in detail both the conditions under which the lease must be capitalized and the procedures for capitalizing it. Also, see Schallheim, *op. cit.*, Chapter 4, for more on the accounting treatment of leases. However, note that lease accounting is currently under review, and FASB 13 will probably be replaced in the near future.

Table 20-1

Balance Sheet Effects of Leasing

Before Asset Increase				After Asset Increase							
Firms B and L				Firm B, Which Borrows and Buys				Firm L, Which Leases			
Current assets	$ 50	Debt	$ 50	Current assets	$ 50	Debt	$150	Current assets	$ 50	Debt	$ 50
Fixed assets	50	Equity	50	Fixed assets	150	Equity	50	Fixed assets	50	Equity	50
	$100		$100		$200		$200		$100		$100
Debt/assets ratio:			50%				75%				50%

cause Firms B and L to have similar balance sheets, both of which will, in essence, resemble the one shown for Firm B.

The logic behind Statement 13 is as follows. If a firm signs a financial lease contract, its obligation to make lease payments is just as binding as if it had signed a loan agreement—the failure to make lease payments can bankrupt a firm just as fast as the failure to make principal and interest payments on a loan. Therefore, for all intents and purposes, a financial lease is identical to a loan.[5] This being the case, if a firm signs a financial lease agreement, this has the effect of raising its true debt ratio, and thus its true capital structure is changed. Therefore, if the firm had previously established a target capital structure, and if there is no reason to think that the optimal capital structure has changed, then lease financing requires additional equity support, exactly like debt financing.

If disclosure of the lease in our Table 20-1 example were not made, then Firm L's investors could be deceived into thinking that its financial position is stronger than it really is. Thus, even before FASB Statement 13 was issued, firms were required to disclose the existence of long-term leases in footnotes to their financial statements. At that time, it was debated as to whether or not investors recognized fully the impact of leases and, in effect, would see that Firms B and L were in essentially the same financial position. Some people argued that leases were not fully recognized, even by sophisticated investors. If this were the case, then leasing could alter the capital structure decision in a significant manner—a firm could increase its true leverage through a lease arrangement, and this procedure would have a smaller effect on its cost of conventional debt, r_d, and on its cost of equity, r_s, than if it had borrowed directly and reflected this fact on its balance sheet. These benefits of leasing would accrue to existing investors at the expense of new investors who would, in effect, be deceived by the fact that the firm's balance sheet did not reflect its true financial leverage.

---

[5]There are, however, certain legal differences between loans and leases. In the event of liquidation in bankruptcy, a lessor is entitled to take possession of the leased asset, and if the value of the asset is less than the required payments under the lease, the lessor can enter a claim (as a general creditor) for one year's lease payments. Also, after bankruptcy has been declared but before the case has been resolved, lease payments may be continued, whereas all payments on debts are generally stopped. In a reorganization, the lessor receives the asset plus three years' lease payments if needed to cover the value of the lease. The lender under a secured loan arrangement has a security interest in the asset, meaning that if it is sold, the lender will be given the proceeds, and the full unsatisfied portion of the lender's claim will be treated as a general creditor obligation. It is not possible to state, as a general rule, whether a supplier of capital is in a stronger position as a secured creditor or as a lessor. However, in certain situations, lessors may bear less risk than secured lenders if financial distress occurs.

The question of whether investors were truly deceived was debated but never resolved. Those who believed strongly in efficient markets thought that investors were not deceived and that footnotes were sufficient, while those who questioned market efficiency thought that all leases should be capitalized. Statement 13 represents a compromise between these two positions, though one that is tilted heavily toward those who favor capitalization.

A lease is classified as a capital lease, hence must be capitalized and shown directly on the balance sheet, if one or more of the following conditions exist:

1. Under the terms of the lease, ownership of the property is effectively transferred from the lessor to the lessee.
2. The lessee can purchase the property at less than its true market value when the lease expires.
3. The lease runs for a period equal to or greater than 75% of the asset's life. Thus, if an asset has a 10-year life and the lease is written for 8 years, the lease must be capitalized.
4. The present value of the lease payments is equal to or greater than 90% of the initial value of the asset.[6]

These rules, together with strong footnote disclosure rules for operating leases, were supposed to be sufficient to ensure that no one would be fooled by lease financing. Thus, leases should be regarded as debt for capital structure purposes, and they should have the same effects as debt on r_d and r_s. Therefore, leasing is not likely to permit a firm to use more financial leverage than could be obtained with conventional debt.[7]

SELF-TEST

Why is lease financing sometimes referred to as off–balance sheet financing?

What is the intent of FASB Statement 13?

What is the difference in the balance sheet treatment of a lease that is capitalized versus one that is not?

20.4 Evaluation by the Lessee

Leases are evaluated by both the lessee and the lessor. The lessee must determine whether leasing an asset is less costly than buying it, and the lessor must decide whether the lease payments provide a satisfactory return on the capital invested in the leased asset. This section focuses on the lessee's analysis.

In the typical case, the events leading to a lease arrangement follow the sequence described below. We should note that a degree of uncertainty exists regarding the theoretically correct way to evaluate lease-versus-purchase decisions, and some very complex decision models have been developed to aid in the analysis. However, the simple analysis given here leads to the correct decision in all the cases we have ever encountered.

e-resource

See **FM12 Ch 20 Tool Kit.xls** at the textbook's Web site for all calculations.

1. The firm decides to acquire a particular building or piece of equipment; this decision is based on regular capital budgeting procedures. Whether or not to acquire the asset is *not* part of the typical lease analysis—in a lease analysis, we

---

[6]The discount rate used to calculate the present value of the lease payments must be the lower of (1) the rate used by the lessor to establish the lease payments (this rate is discussed later in the chapter) or (2) the rate of interest that the lessee would have to pay for new debt with a maturity equal to that of the lease. Also, note that any maintenance payments embedded in the lease payment must be stripped out prior to checking this condition.

[7]Note that Statement 13 was written many years before synthetic leases were developed. Synthetic leases can undercut FASB 13, but we anticipate new rules on lease accounting that will return the situation to that envisioned under FASB 13 at the time it was written.

are concerned simply with whether to obtain the use of the machine by lease or by purchase. Thus, for the lessee, the lease decision is typically just a financing decision. However, if the effective cost of capital obtained by leasing is substantially lower than the cost of debt, then the cost of capital used in the capital budgeting decision would have to be recalculated, and perhaps projects formerly deemed unacceptable might become acceptable. See *Web Extension 20B* at the textbook's Web site for more information on such feedback effects.

2. Once the firm has decided to acquire the asset, the next question is how to finance it. Well-run businesses do not have excess cash lying around, so capital to finance new assets must be obtained from some source.

3. Funds to purchase the asset could be obtained from internally generated cash flows, by borrowing, or by selling new equity. Alternatively, the asset could be leased. Because of the capitalization/disclosure provision for leases, leasing normally has the same capital structure effect as borrowing.

4. As indicated earlier, a lease is comparable to a loan in the sense that the firm is required to make a specified series of payments, and a failure to meet these payments could result in bankruptcy. If a company has a target capital structure, then $1 of lease financing displaces $1 of debt financing. Thus, the most appropriate comparison is lease financing versus debt financing. Note that the analysis should compare the cost of leasing with the cost of debt financing *regardless* of how the asset purchase is actually financed. The asset may be purchased with available cash or cash raised by issuing stock, but since leasing is a substitute for debt financing and has the same capital structure effect, the appropriate comparison would still be with debt financing.

To illustrate the basic elements of lease analysis, consider this simplified example (*FM12 Ch 20 Tool Kit.xls* at the textbook's Web site shows this analysis). The Thompson-Grammatikos Company (TGC) needs a 2-year asset that costs $100, and the company must choose between leasing and buying the asset. TGC's tax rate is 40%. If the asset is purchased, the bank would lend TGC the $100 at a rate of 10% on a 2-year, simple interest loan. Thus, the firm would have to pay the bank $10 in interest at the end of each year, plus return the $100 of principal at the end of Year 2. For simplicity, assume (1) that TGC could depreciate the asset over 2 years for tax purposes by the straight-line method if it is purchased, resulting in tax depreciation of $50 and tax savings of T(Depreciation) = 0.4($50) = $20 in each year, and (2) that the asset's value at the end of 2 years will be $0.

Alternatively, TGC could lease the asset under a guideline lease (by a special IRS ruling) for 2 years for a payment of $55 at the end of each year. The analysis for the lease-versus-borrow decision consists of (1) estimating the cash flows associated with borrowing and buying the asset, that is, the flows associated with debt financing; (2) estimating the cash flows associated with leasing the asset; and (3) comparing the two financing methods to determine which has the lower present value costs. Here are the borrow-and-buy flows, set up to produce a cash flow time line:

Cash Flows if TGC Buys	Year 0	Year 1	Year 2
Equipment cost	($100)		
Inflow from loan	100		
Interest expense		($10)	($ 10)
Tax savings from interest		4	4
Principal repayment			(100)
Tax savings from depreciation		20	20
Net cash flow (time line)	$ 0	$14	($ 86)

The net cash flow is zero in Year 0, positive in Year 1, and negative in Year 2. The operating cash flows are not shown, but they must, of course, have a PV greater than the PV of the financing costs or else TGC would not want to acquire the asset. Because the operating cash flows will be the same regardless of whether the asset is leased or purchased, they can be ignored.

Here are the cash flows associated with the lease:

Cash Flows if TGC Leases	Year 0	Year 1	Year 2
Lease payment		($55)	($55)
Tax savings from payment	—	22	22
Net cash flow (time line)	$0	($33)	($33)

Note that the two sets of cash flows reflect the tax deductibility of interest and depreciation if the asset is purchased, and the deductibility of lease payments if it is leased. Thus, the net cash flows include the tax savings from these items.[8]

To compare the cost streams of buying versus leasing, we must put them on a present value basis. As we explain later, the correct discount rate is the after-tax cost of debt, which for TGC is $10\%(1 - 0.4) = 6.0\%$. Applying this rate, we find the present value cost of buying to be $63.33 versus a present value cost of leasing of $60.50. Since leasing has the lower present value of costs, the company should lease this particular asset.

Now we examine a more realistic example, one from the Anderson Company, which is conducting a lease analysis on some assembly line equipment that it will procure during the coming year (*FM12 Ch 20 Tool Kit.xls* at the textbook's Web site shows this analysis). The following data have been collected:

1. Anderson plans to acquire automated assembly line equipment with a 10-year life at a cost of $10 million, delivered and installed. However, Anderson plans to use the equipment for only 5 years and then discontinue the product line.
2. Anderson can borrow the required $10 million at a before-tax cost of 10%.
3. The equipment's estimated scrap value is $50,000 after 10 years of use, but its estimated salvage value after only 5 years of use is $2,000,000. Thus, if Anderson buys the equipment, it would expect to receive $2,000,000 before taxes when the equipment is sold in 5 years. Note that in leasing, the asset's value at the end of the lease is called its **residual value.**
4. Anderson can lease the equipment for 5 years for an annual rental charge of $2,600,000, payable at the beginning of each year, but the lessor will own the equipment upon the expiration of the lease. (The lease payment schedule is established by the potential lessor, as described in the next major section, and Anderson can accept it, reject it, or negotiate.)
5. The lease contract stipulates that the lessor will maintain the equipment at no additional charge to Anderson. However, if Anderson borrows and buys, it will have to bear the cost of maintenance, which will be done by the equipment manufacturer at a fixed contract rate of $500,000 per year, payable at the beginning of each year.
6. The equipment falls in the MACRS 5-year class, Anderson's marginal tax rate is 35%, and the lease qualifies as a guideline lease.

---

[8]If the lease had not met IRS guidelines, then ownership would effectively reside with the lessee, and TGC would depreciate the asset for tax purposes whether it was leased or purchased. However, only the implied interest portion of the lease payment would be tax deductible. Thus, the analysis for a nonguideline lease would consist of simply comparing the after-tax financing flows on the loan with the after-tax lease payment stream.

Table 20-2 shows the steps involved in the analysis. Part I of the table analyzes the costs of borrowing and buying. The company borrows $10 million and uses it to pay for the equipment, so these two items net out to zero and thus are not shown in Table 20-2. Then, the company makes the *after-tax* payments shown in Line 1. In Year 1, the after-tax interest charge is 0.10($10 million)(0.65) = $650,000, and other payments are calculated similarly. The $10 million loan is repaid at the end of Year 5. Line 2 shows the maintenance cost. Line 3 gives the maintenance tax savings. Line 4 contains the depreciation tax savings, which is the depreciation expense times the tax rate. The notes to Table 20-2 explain the depreciation calculation. Lines 5 and 6 contain the residual (or salvage) value cash flows. The tax is on the excess of the residual value over the asset's book value, not on the full residual value. Line 7 contains the net cash flows, and Line 8 shows the net present value of these flows, discounted at 6.5%.

Part II of Table 20-2 analyzes the lease. The lease payments, shown in Line 9, are $2,600,000 per year; this rate, which includes maintenance, was established by the prospective lessor and offered to Anderson Equipment. If Anderson accepts the lease, the full amount will be a deductible expense, so the tax savings, shown in Line 10, is 0.35(Lease payment) = 0.35($2,600,000) = $910,000. Thus, the after-tax cost of the lease payment is Lease payment − Tax savings = $2,600,000 − $910,000 = $1,690,000. This amount is shown in Line 11, Years 0 through 4.

The next step is to compare the net cost of owning with the net cost of leasing. However, we must first put the annual cash flows of leasing and borrowing on a common basis. This requires converting them to present values, which brings up the question of the proper rate at which to discount the costs. Because leasing is a substitute for debt, most analysts recommend that the company's cost of debt be used, and this rate seems reasonable in our example. Further, since the cash flows are after taxes, *the* **after-tax cost of debt,** *which is 10% (1 − T) = 10%(0.65) = 6.5%, should be used*. Accordingly, we discount the net cash flows in Lines 7 and 11 using a rate of 6.5%. The resulting present values are $7,534,000 for the cost of owning and $7,480,000 for the cost of leasing, as shown in Lines 8 and 12. The financing method that produces the smaller present value of costs is the one that should be selected. We define the **net advantage to leasing (NAL)** as follows (see Note e to Table 20-2):

$$\text{NAL} = \text{PV cost of owning} - \text{PV cost of leasing}$$
$$= \$7,534,000 - \$7,480,000$$
$$= \$54,000.$$

The PV cost of owning exceeds the PV cost of leasing, so the NAL is positive. Therefore, Anderson should lease the equipment.[9]

---

[9]The more complicated methods that exist for analyzing leasing generally focus on the issue of the discount rate that should be used to discount the cash flows. Conceptually, we could assign a separate discount rate to each individual cash flow component, then find the present values of each of the cash flow components, and finally sum these present values to determine the net advantage or disadvantage to leasing. This approach has been taken by Stewart C. Myers, David A. Dill, and Alberto J. Bautista (MDB) in "Valuation of Financial Lease Contracts," *Journal of Finance*, June 1976, pp. 799–819, among others. MDB correctly note that the use of a single discount rate is valid only if (1) leases and loans are viewed by investors as being equivalent and (2) all cash flows are equally risky, hence appropriately discounted at the same rate. The first assumption is probably valid for most financial leases, and even where it is not, no one knows how to adjust properly for any capital structure effects that leases might have. Regarding the second assumption, advocates of multiple discount rates often point out that the residual value is less certain than are the other cash flows, and they thus recommend discounting it at a higher rate. However, there is no way of knowing precisely how much to increase the after-tax cost of debt to account for the increased riskiness of the residual value cash flow. Further, in a market risk sense, all cash flows could be equally risky even though individual items such as the residual value might have more or less total variability than others. To complicate matters even more, the market risk of the residual value will usually be different than the firm's market risk. For more on residual value risk, see Schallheim, *op. cit.*, Chapter 8. For an application of option pricing techniques in the evaluation of the residual value, see Wayne Y. Lee, John D. Martin, and Andrew J. Senchack, "The Case for Using Options to Evaluate Salvage Values in Financial Leases," *Financial Management*, Autumn 1982, pp. 33–41.

Table 20-2

Anderson Company: Dollar Cost Analysis (Thousands of Dollars)

	Year 0	Year 1	Year 2	Year 3	Year 4	Year 5
I. Cost of Owning (Borrowing and Buying)						
1. After-tax loan payments		($ 650)	($ 650)	($ 650)	($ 650)	($10,650)
2. Maintenance cost	($ 500)	(500)	(500)	(500)	(500)	
3. Maintenance tax savings	175	175	175	175	175	
4. Depreciation tax savings		700	1,120	665	420	385
5. Residual value						2,000
6. Tax on residual value						(490)
7. Net cash flow (time line)	($ 325)	($ 275)	$ 145	($ 310)	($ 555)	($ 8,755)
8. PV cost of owning at 6.5% =	($7,534)					
II. Cost of Leasing						
9. Lease payment	($2,600)	($2,600)	($2,600)	($2,600)	($2,600)	
10. Payment tax savings	910	910	910	910	910	
11. Net cash flow (time line)	($1,690)	($1,690)	($1,690)	($1,690)	($1,690)	$ 0
12. PV cost of leasing at 6.5% =	($7,480)					

III. Cost Comparison

13. Net advantage to leasing (NAL) = | PV cost of owning | − | PV cost of leasing |
   = $7,534 − $7,480 = $54.

Notes:

[a]The after-tax loan payments consist of after-tax interest for Years 1–4 and after-tax interest plus the principal amount in Year 5.

[b]The net cash flows shown in Lines 7 and 11 are discounted at the lessee's after-tax cost of debt, 6.5%.

[c]The MACRS depreciation allowances are 0.20, 0.32, 0.19, 0.12, and 0.11 in Years 1 through 5, respectively. Thus, the depreciation expense is 0.20($10,000) = $2,000 in Year 1, and so on. The depreciation tax savings in each year is 0.35 × (Depreciation).

[d]The residual value is $2,000 while the book value is $600. Thus, Anderson would have to pay 0.35($2,000 − $600) = $490 in taxes, producing a net after-tax residual value of $2,000 − $490 = $1,510. These amounts are shown in Lines 5 and 6 in the cost-of-owning analysis.

[e]See **FM12 Ch 20 Tool Kit.xls** at the textbook's Web site for all calculations.

[f]In the NAL equation in Line 13, the PV costs are stated as absolute values. Therefore, a positive result means that leasing is beneficial, while a negative result means that leasing is not beneficial.

In this example, Anderson did not plan on using the equipment beyond Year 5. But if Anderson instead had planned on using the equipment after Year 5, the analysis would be modified. For example, suppose Anderson planned on using the equipment for 10 years and the lease allowed Anderson to purchase the equipment at the residual value. First, how do we modify the cash flows due to owning? Lines 5 and 6 (for residual value and tax on residual value) in Table 20-2 will be zero at Year 5, because Anderson will not sell the equipment then.[10] However, there will be the additional remaining year of depreciation tax savings in Line 4 for Year 6. There will be no entries for Years 6–10 for Line 1, the after-tax loan payments, because the loan is completely repaid at Year 5. Also, there will be no incremental maintenance costs and tax savings in Lines 2 and 3 for Years 6–10 because

---

[10]There might be a salvage value in Line 5 at Year 10 (and a corresponding tax adjustment in Line 6) if the equipment is not completely worn out or obsolete.

Anderson will have to do its own maintenance on the equipment in those years whether it initially purchases the equipment or whether it leases the equipment for 5 years and then purchases it. Either way, Anderson will own the equipment in Years 6–10 and must pay for its own maintenance. Second, how do we modify the cash flows if Anderson leases the equipment and then purchases it at Year 5? There will be a negative cash flow at Year 5 reflecting the purchase. Because the equipment was originally classified with a MACRS 5-year life, Anderson will be allowed to depreciate the purchased equipment (even though it is not new) with a MACRS 5-year life. Therefore, in Years 6–10, there will be after-tax savings due to depreciation.[11] Given the modified cash flows, we can calculate the NAL just as we did in Table 20-2.

In this section, we focused on the dollar cost of leasing versus borrowing and buying, which is analogous to the NPV method used in capital budgeting. A second method that lessees can use to evaluate leases focuses on the percentage cost of leasing and is analogous to the IRR method used in capital budgeting. The percentage approach is discussed in **Web Extension 20A** at the textbook's Web site.

SELF-TEST

Explain how the cash flows are structured in order to estimate the net advantage to leasing.

What discount rate should be used to evaluate a lease? Why?

Define the term "net advantage to leasing, NAL."

20.5 Evaluation by the Lessor

Thus far we have considered leasing only from the lessee's viewpoint. It is also useful to analyze the transaction as the lessor sees it: Is the lease a good investment for the party who must put up the money? The lessor will generally be a specialized leasing company, a bank or bank affiliate, an individual or group of individuals organized as a limited partnership or limited liability corporation, or a manufacturer such as IBM or GM that uses leasing as a sales tool. The specialized leasing companies are often owned by profitable companies such as General Electric, which owns General Electric Capital, the largest leasing company in the world. Investment banking houses such as Merrill Lynch also set up and/or work with specialized leasing companies, where brokerage clients' money is made available to leasing customers in deals that permit the investors to share in tax shelters provided by leases.

Any potential lessor needs to know the rate of return on the capital invested in the lease, and this information is also useful to the prospective lessee: Lease terms on large leases are generally negotiated, so the lessee should know what return the lessor is earning. The lessor's analysis involves (1) determining the net cash outlay, which is usually the invoice price of the leased equipment less any lease payments made in advance; (2) determining the periodic cash inflows, which consist of the lease payments minus both income taxes and any maintenance expense the lessor must bear; (3) estimating the after-tax residual value of the property when the lease expires; and (4) determining whether the rate of return on the lease exceeds the lessor's opportunity cost of capital or, equivalently, whether the NPV of the lease exceeds zero.

---

[11]There will also be an after-tax cash flow at Year 10 that depends on the salvage value of the equipment at that date.

Analysis by the Lessor

To illustrate the lessor's analysis, we assume the same facts as for the Anderson Company lease, plus the following: (1) The potential lessor is a wealthy individual whose current income is in the form of interest and whose marginal federal-plus-state income tax rate, T, is 40%. (2) The investor can buy 5-year bonds that have a 9% yield to maturity, providing an after-tax yield of $(9\%)(1 - T) = (9\%)(0.6) = 5.4\%$. This is the after-tax return that the investor can obtain on alternative investments of similar risk. (3) The before-tax residual value is $2,000,000. Because the asset will be depreciated to a book value of $600,000 at the end of the 5-year lease, $1,400,000 of this $2 million will be taxable at the 40% rate because of the recapture of depreciation rule, so the lessor can expect to receive $2,000,000 − 0.4($1,400,000) = $1,440,000 after taxes from the sale of the equipment after the lease expires.

The lessor's cash flows are developed in Table 20-3. Here we see that the lease as an investment has a net present value of $81,000. On a present value basis, the investor who invests in the lease rather than in the 9% bonds (5.4% after taxes) is better off by $81,000, indicating that he or she should be willing to write the lease. As we saw earlier, the lease is also advantageous to Anderson Company, so the transaction should be completed.

The investor can also calculate the lease investment's IRR based on the net cash flows shown in Line 9 of Table 20-3. The IRR of the lease, which is that discount rate that forces the NPV of the lease to zero, is 5.8%. Thus, the lease provides a 5.8% after-tax return to this 40% tax rate investor. This exceeds the 5.4% after-tax return on 9% bonds. So, using either the IRR or the NPV method, the lease would appear to be a satisfactory investment.[12]

e-resource

See **FM12 Ch 20 Tool Kit.xls** for details.

Setting the Lease Payment

In the preceding sections we evaluated the lease assuming that the lease payments had already been specified. However, in large leases the parties generally sit down and work out an agreement on the size of the lease payments, with these payments being set so as to provide the lessor with some specific rate of return. In situations in which the lease terms are not negotiated, which is often the case for small leases, the lessor must still go through the same type of analysis, setting terms that provide a target rate of return and then offering these terms to the potential lessee on a take-it-or-leave-it basis.

To illustrate all this, suppose the potential lessor described earlier, after examining other alternative investment opportunities, decides that the 5.4% after-tax bond return is too low to use to evaluate the lease and that the required after-tax return on the lease is 6.0%. What lease payment schedule would provide this return?

To answer this question, note again that Table 20-3 contains the lessor's cash flow analysis. If the basic analysis is computerized, it is easy to first change the discount rate to 6% and then change the lease payment—either by trial and error or by using the goal-seeking function—until the lease's NPV = $0 or, equivalently, its IRR = 6.0%. When we did this using **FM12 Ch 20 Tool Kit.xls**, we found that the lessor must set the lease payment at $2,621,232 to obtain an after-tax rate of

---

[12]Note that the lease investment is actually slightly more risky than the alternative bond investment because the residual value cash flow is less certain than a principal repayment. Thus, the lessor might require an expected return somewhat above the 5.4% promised on a bond investment.

Table 20-3

Lease Analysis from the Lessor's Viewpoint (Thousands of Dollars)

	Year 0	Year 1	Year 2	Year 3	Year 4	Year 5
1. Net purchase price	($10,000)					
2. Maintenance cost	(500)	($ 500)	($ 500)	($ 500)	($ 500)	
3. Maintenance tax savings	200	200	200	200	200	
4. Depreciation tax savings[a]		800	1,280	760	480	$ 440
5. Lease payment	2,600	2,600	2,600	2,600	2,600	
6. Tax on lease payment	(1,040)	(1,040)	(1,040)	(1,040)	(1,040)	
7. Residual value						2,000
8. Tax on residual value[b]						(560)
9. Net cash flow	($ 8,740)	$2,060	$2,540	$2,020	$1,740	$1,880

$$NPV = \sum_{t=0}^{5} \frac{NCF_t}{(1 + r)^t} = \$81 \text{ when } r = 5.4\%$$

$$IRR: NPV = 0 = \sum_{t=0}^{5} \frac{NCF_t}{(1 + IRR)^{t}}; \ IRR = 5.8\%$$

Notes:
[a]Depreciation times the lessor's tax rate.
[b](Residual value − Book value)T.

e-resource

See **FM12 Ch 20 Tool
Kit.xls** at the textbook's
Web site for all
calculations.

return of 6.0%. If this lease payment is not acceptable to the lessee, Anderson Company, then it may not be possible to strike a deal. Naturally, competition among leasing companies forces lessors to build market-related returns into their lease payment schedules.[13]

If the inputs to the lessee and the lessor are identical, then a positive NAL to the lessee implies an equal but negative NPV to the lessor. *However, conditions are often such that leasing can provide net benefits to both parties. This situation arises because of differentials in taxes, in borrowing rates, in estimated residual values, or in the ability to bear the residual value risk.* We will explore these issues in detail in a later section.

e-resource

Note that the lessor can, under certain conditions, increase the return on the lease by borrowing some of the funds used to purchase the leased asset. Such a lease is called a **leveraged lease.** Whether or not a lease is leveraged has no effect on the lessee's analysis, but it can have a significant effect on the cash flows to the lessor, hence on the lessor's expected rate of return. We discuss leveraged leases in more detail in **Web Extension 20C** at the textbook's Web site.

SELF-TEST

What discount rate is used in a lessor's NPV analysis?

What is the relationship between the lessor's IRR and the size of the lease payments?

---

[13]For a discussion of realized returns on lease contracts, see Ronald C. Lease, John J. McConnell, and James S. Schallheim, "Realized Returns and the Default and Prepayment Experience of Financial Leasing Contracts," *Financial Management*, Summer 1990, pp. 11–20.

20.6 Other Issues in Lease Analysis

The basic methods of analysis used by lessees and lessors were presented in the previous sections. However, some other issues warrant discussion.[14]

Estimated Residual Value

It is important to note that the lessor owns the property upon expiration of a lease; hence the lessor has claim to the asset's residual value. Superficially, it would appear that if residual values are expected to be large, owning would have an advantage over leasing. However, this apparent advantage does not hold up. If expected residual values are large—as they may be under inflation for certain types of equipment and also if real estate is involved—competition between leasing companies and other financing sources, as well as competition among leasing companies themselves, will force leasing rates down to the point where potential residual values are fully recognized in the lease contract. Thus, the existence of large residual values is not likely to result in materially higher costs for leasing.

Increased Credit Availability

As noted earlier, leasing is sometimes said to be advantageous for firms that are seeking the maximum degree of financial leverage. First, it is sometimes argued that firms can obtain more money, and for longer terms, under a lease arrangement than under a loan secured by a specific piece of equipment. Second, since some leases do not appear on the balance sheet, lease financing has been said to give the firm a stronger appearance in a *superficial* credit analysis and thus to permit the firm to use more leverage than would be possible if it did not lease.

There may be some truth to these claims for smaller firms, but since firms are required to capitalize financial leases and to report them on their balance sheets, this point is of questionable validity for any firm large enough to have audited financial statements. However, leasing can be a way to circumvent existing loan covenants. If restrictive covenants prohibit a firm from issuing more debt but fail to restrict lease payments, then the firm could effectively increase its leverage by leasing additional assets. Also, firms that are in very poor financial condition and facing possible bankruptcy may be able to obtain lease financing at a lower cost than comparable debt financing because (1) lessors often have a more favorable position than lenders should the lessee actually go bankrupt and (2) lessors that specialize in certain types of equipment may be in a better position to dispose of repossessed equipment than banks or other lenders.

Real Estate Leases

Most of our examples have focused on equipment leasing. However, leasing originated with real estate, and such leases still constitute a huge segment of total lease financing. (We distinguish between housing rentals and long-term business leases; our concern is with business leases.) Retailers lease many of their stores. In some situations, retailers have no choice but to lease—this is true of locations in malls and

---

[14]For a description of lease analysis in practice, as well as a comprehensive bibliography of the leasing literature, see Tarun K. Mukherjee, "A Survey of Corporate Leasing Analysis," *Financial Management*, Autumn 1991, pp. 96–107.

What You Don't Know *Can* Hurt You!

A leasing decision seems to be pretty straightforward, at least from a financial perspective: Calculate the NAL for the lease and undertake it if the NAL is positive. Right? But tracking down all the financial implications from lease contract provisions can be difficult, requiring the lessee to make assumptions about future costs that are not explicitly spelled out in the lease contract. For example, consider the purchase option embedded in the lease that Rojacks Food Stores undertook with GE Capital for restaurant equipment. The lease allowed Rojacks either to purchase the equipment at the current market value when the lease expired, or return the equipment. When the lease expired, GE set a purchase price that was much higher than Rojacks expected. Rojacks needed the equipment for its day-to-day operations so it couldn't just return the equipment without disrupting its business. Ultimately, Rojacks hired an independent appraiser for the equipment and negotiated a lower purchase price, but without the appraiser, Rojacks would have been stuck with the price GE decided to set for the equipment.

The Rojacks-GE situation isn't that unusual. Lessors often use high expected residual values or high expected penalties to offset low lease payments. In addition, some contracts may require that (1) all of the equipment covered under a lease must either be purchased or returned in its entirety, (2) equipment that is moved must be purchased, (3) large fees must be paid even for minor damage or missing parts, and/or (4) equipment must be returned in its original packaging. These conditions impose costs on the lessee when the lease is terminated and should be considered explicitly when making the leasing decision. The moral of the story for lessees is to read the fine print and request changes to objectionable terms before signing the lease. Here are some ways to reduce the likelihood of unanticipated costs: (1) specify residual value as a percentage of the initial cost of the equipment, (2) allow for portions of the equipment to be returned and portions to be purchased at the end of the lease, and (3) specify that disagreements will be adjudicated by arbitration.

Source: Linda Corman, "{Don't} Look Deep Into My Lease," *CFO,* July 2006, pp. 71–75.

certain office buildings. In other situations, they have a choice of building and owning versus leasing. Law firms and accounting firms, for example, can choose between buying their own facilities or leasing on a long-term basis (up to 20 or more years).

The type of lease-versus-purchase analysis we discussed in this chapter is just as applicable for real estate as for equipment—conceptually, there is no difference. Of course, such things as maintenance, who the other tenants will be, what alterations can be made, who will pay for alterations, and the like, become especially important with real property, but the analytical procedures upon which the lease-versus-buy decision is based are no different from any other lease analysis.

Vehicle Leases

Vehicle leasing is very popular today, both for large corporations and for individuals, especially professionals such as MBAs, doctors, lawyers, and accountants. For corporations, the key factor involved with transportation is often maintenance and disposal of used vehicles—the leasing companies are specialists here, and many businesses prefer to "outsource" services related to autos and trucks. For individuals, leasing is often more convenient, and it may be easier to justify tax deductions on leased than on owned vehicles. Also, most auto leasing to individuals is through dealers. These dealers (and manufacturers) use leasing as a sales tool, and they often make the terms quite attractive, especially when it comes to the down payment, which may be nonexistent in the case of a lease.

Vehicle leasing also permits many individuals to drive more expensive cars than would otherwise be possible. For example, the monthly payment on a new

Lease Securitization

Compared with many markets, the leasing market is fragmented and inefficient. There are millions of potential lessees, including all equipment users. Some are in high tax brackets, some in low brackets. Some are financially sophisticated, some are not. Some have excellent credit ratings, some have poor credit. On the other side of the market are millions of potential lessors, including equipment manufacturers, banks, and individual investors, with different tax brackets and risk tolerances. If each lessee had to negotiate a separate deal for each lease, information and search costs would be so high that few leases would be written.

Tax laws complicate the picture. For example, the alternative minimum tax often has the effect of limiting the amount of depreciation a firm can utilize. In addition, a firm can't take a full half-year's depreciation on purchases in the fourth quarter if those purchases comprise more than 40% of total annual purchases. Instead, it can take only a half-quarter's depreciation, which is the equivalent of one-eighth of a year's depreciation.

Lease brokers have for many years served as facilitators in this complicated and inefficient market. Working with many different equipment manufacturers and lenders, brokers are in a position to match lessees with appropriate lessors in such a way that the full benefit of tax laws can be utilized.

Lease securitization, a new procedure, is the ultimate method of matching lessees with appropriate lessors. The first step is to create a portfolio consisting of numerous leases. The second step is to divide the leasing cash flows into different streams of income, called *tranches*. For example, one tranche might contain only lease payments, which would appeal to an investor in a low tax bracket. A second tranche might consist of depreciation, which a high-tax-bracket investor could use to shelter income from other sources. A third might contain the residual cash flows, which will occur in the future when the leases end. This tranche would appeal to a high-tax-bracket investor who can take some risk. Tranches can also be allocated according to the credit rating of the lessees, allowing investors with different risk tolerances to take on their desired level of risk.

In addition, a company might obtain a lease in its fourth quarter, but if this is the third quarter of the lessor's fiscal year, the lessor can take a full half-year's depreciation.

Sound complicated? It is, but it's an efficient answer to an inefficient market.

Source: SMG Fairfax, Knoxville, Tennessee.

BMW might be $1,000 when financed with a 3-year loan, but the same car, if leased for 3 years, might cost only $499 a month. At first glance, it appears that leasing is less expensive than owning because the monthly payment is so much lower. However, such a simplistic analysis ignores the fact that payments end after the loan is paid off but continue indefinitely under leasing. By using the techniques described in this chapter, individuals can assess the true costs associated with auto leases and then rationally judge the merits of each type of auto financing.

Leasing and Tax Laws[15]

The ability to structure leases that are advantageous to both lessor and lessee depends in large part on tax laws. The four major tax factors that influence leasing are (1) investment tax credits, (2) depreciation rules, (3) tax rates, and (4) the alternative minimum tax. In this section, we briefly discuss each of these factors and how they influence leasing decisions.

The investment tax credit (ITC), when it is allowed, is a direct reduction of taxes that occurs when a firm purchases new capital equipment. Prior to 1987, firms could immediately deduct up to 10% of the cost of new capital investments from their corporate tax bills. Thus, a company that bought a $1,000,000 mainframe

---

[15]See Schallheim, *op. cit.*, Chapters 3 and 6, for an in-depth discussion of tax effects on leasing.

computer system would get a $100,000 reduction in current-year taxes. Because the ITC goes to the owner of the capital asset, low-tax-bracket companies that could not otherwise use the ITC could use leasing as a vehicle to pass immediate tax savings to high-tax-bracket lessors. The ITC is not currently in effect, but it could be reinstated in the future. If the ITC is put back into law, leasing will become especially attractive to low-tax-bracket firms.

Owners recover their investments in capital assets through depreciation, which is a tax-deductible expense. Because of the time value of money, the faster an asset can be depreciated, the greater the tax advantages of ownership. Recent tax law changes have tended to slow depreciation write-offs, thus reducing the value of ownership. This has also reduced the advantage to leasing by low-tax-bracket lessees from high-tax-bracket lessors. Any move to liberalize depreciation rules would tend to make leasing more desirable in many situations. The value of depreciation also depends on the firm's tax rate, because the depreciation tax saving equals the amount of depreciation multiplied by the tax rate. Thus, higher corporate tax rates mean greater ownership tax savings, hence more incentive for tax-driven leases.

Finally, the alternative minimum tax (AMT) also affects leasing activity. Corporations are permitted to use accelerated depreciation and other tax shelters on their tax books but then use straight-line depreciation for reporting results to shareholders. Thus, some firms report to the IRS that they are doing poorly and hence pay little or no taxes, but report high earnings to shareholders. The corporate AMT, which is roughly computed by applying a 20% tax rate to the profits reported to shareholders, is designed to force highly profitable companies to pay at least some taxes even if they have tax shelters that push their taxable income to zero. In effect, all firms (and individuals) must compute the "regular" tax and the AMT tax, and then pay the higher of the two.

Companies with large AMT liabilities look for ways to reduce their tax bills by lowering reported income. Leasing can be beneficial here—a relatively short-term lease with high annual payments will increase reported expenses and thus lower reported profits. Note that the lease does not have to qualify as a guideline lease and be deducted for regular tax purposes—all that is needed is to lower reported income as shown on the income statement.

We see that tax laws and differential tax rates between lessors and lessees can be a motivating force for leasing. However, as we discuss in the next section, there are some sound nontax economic reasons why firms lease plant and equipment.

SELF-TEST

Does leasing lead to increased credit availability?

How do tax laws affect leasing?

20.7 Other Reasons for Leasing

Up to this point, we have noted that tax rate or other differentials are generally necessary to make leasing attractive to both the lessee and lessor. If the lessee and lessor are facing different tax situations, including the alternative minimum tax, then it is often possible to structure a lease that is beneficial to both parties. However, there are other reasons firms might want to lease an asset rather than buy it.

More than half of all commercial aircraft are leased, and smaller airlines, especially in developing nations, lease an especially high percentage of their planes. One of the reasons for this lease usage is that airlines can reduce their risks by leasing. If an airline purchased all its aircraft, it would be hampered in its ability to respond to changing market conditions. Because they have become specialists at matching airlines with available aircraft, the aircraft lessors (which are multibillion-dollar concerns) are quite good at managing the changing demand for different types of aircraft. This permits them to offer attractive lease terms. In this situation, *leasing provides operating flexibility.* Leasing is not necessarily less expensive than buying, but the operating flexibility is quite valuable.

Leasing is also an attractive alternative for many high-technology items that are subject to rapid and unpredictable technological obsolescence. Say a small rural hospital wants to buy a magnetic resonance imaging (MRI) device. If it buys the MRI equipment, it is exposed to the risk of technological obsolescence. In a short time some new technology might lower the value of the current system and thus render the project unprofitable. Since it does not use much equipment of this nature, the hospital would bear a great deal of risk if it bought the MRI device. However, a lessor that specializes in state-of-the-art medical equipment would be exposed to significantly less risk. By purchasing and then leasing many different items, the lessor benefits from diversification. Of course, over time some items will probably lose more value than the lessor expected, but this will be offset by other items that retained more value than was expected. Also, because such a leasing company will be especially familiar with the market for used medical equipment, it can refurbish the equipment and then get a better price in the resale market than could a remote rural hospital. For these reasons, leasing can reduce the risk of technological obsolescence.

Leasing can also be attractive when a firm is uncertain about the demand for its products or services and thus about how long the equipment will be needed. Again, consider the hospital industry. Hospitals often offer services that are dependent on a single staff member—for example, a physician who does liver transplants. To support the physician's practice, the hospital might have to invest millions in equipment that can be used only for this particular procedure. The hospital will charge for the use of the equipment, and if things go as expected, the investment will be profitable. However, if the physician leaves the hospital, and if no replacement can be recruited, then the project is dead and the equipment becomes useless to the hospital. In this case, a lease with a cancellation clause would permit the hospital to simply return the equipment. The lessor would charge something for the cancellation clause, and this would lower the expected profitability of the project, but it would provide the hospital with an option to abandon the equipment, and the value of the option could easily exceed the incremental cost of the cancellation clause. The leasing company would be willing to write this option because it is in a better position to remarket the equipment, either by writing another lease or by selling it outright.

The leasing industry recently introduced a type of lease that even transfers some of a project's operating risk from the lessee to the lessor and also motivates the lessor to maintain the leased equipment in good working order. Instead of making a fixed rental payment, the lessee pays a fee each time the leased equipment is used. This type of lease originated with copy machines, where the lessee pays so much per month plus an additional amount per copy made. If the machine breaks down, no copies are made, and the lessor's rental income declines. This motivates the lessor to repair the machine quickly.

This type of lease is also used in the health care industry, where it is called a "per-procedure lease." For example, a hospital might lease an X-ray machine for a fixed fee per X-ray, say, $5. If demand for the machine's X-rays is less than expected by the hospital, revenues will be lower than expected, but so will the machine's capital costs. Conversely, high demand would lead to higher than expected lease costs, but these would be offset by higher than expected revenues. By using a per-procedure lease, the hospital is converting a fixed cost for the equipment into a variable cost, hence reducing the machine's operating leverage and break-even point. The net effect is to reduce the project's risk. Of course, the expected cost of a per-procedure lease might be more than the cost of a conventional lease, but the risk reduction benefit could be worth the cost. Note too that if the lessor writes a large number of per-procedure leases, much of the riskiness inherent in such leases could be eliminated by diversification, so the risk premiums that lessors build into per-procedure lease payments could be low enough to attract potential lessees.

Some companies also find leasing attractive because the lessor is able to provide servicing on favorable terms. For example, Virco Manufacturing, a company that makes school desks and other furniture, recently leased 25 truck tractors and 140 trailers that it uses to ship furniture from its plant. The lease agreement, with a large leasing company that specializes in purchasing, maintaining, and then reselling trucks, permitted the replacement of an aging fleet that Virco had built up over the years. "We are pretty good at manufacturing furniture, but we aren't very good at maintaining a truck fleet," said Virco's CFO.

There are other reasons that might cause a firm to lease an asset rather than buy it. Often, these reasons are difficult to quantify; hence they cannot be easily incorporated into an NPV or IRR analysis. Nevertheless, a sound lease decision must begin with a quantitative analysis, and then qualitative factors can be considered before making the final lease-or-buy decision.[16]

SELF-TEST

Describe some economic factors that might provide an advantage to leasing.

Summary

In the United States, more than 30% of all equipment is leased, as is a great deal of real estate. Consequently, leasing is an important financing vehicle. In this chapter, we discussed the leasing decision from the standpoints of both the lessee and lessor. The key concepts covered are listed below:

- The five most important types of lease agreement are (1) **operating lease,** (2) **financial,** or **capital, lease,** (3) **sale-and-leaseback,** (4) **combination lease,** and (5) **synthetic lease.**
- The IRS has specific guidelines that apply to lease arrangements. A lease that meets these guidelines is called a **guideline,** or **tax-oriented, lease,** because the IRS permits the lessor to deduct the asset's depreciation and allows the lessee to deduct the lease payments. A lease that does not meet the IRS guidelines is called a **non-tax-oriented lease,** in which case ownership for tax purposes resides with the lessee rather than the lessor.
- **FASB Statement 13** spells out the conditions under which a lease must be **capitalized** (shown directly on the balance sheet) as opposed to shown only in the notes to the financial statements. Generally, leases that run for a period equal to or greater than 75% of the asset's life must be capitalized.

---

[16]For more on leasing, see Thomas J. Finucane, "Some Empirical Evidence on the Use of Financial Leases," *The Journal of Financial Research,* Fall 1988, pp. 321–333; and Lawrence D. Schall, "The Evaluation of Lease Financing Opportunities," *Midland Corporate Finance Journal,* Spring 1985, pp. 48–65.

- The lessee's analysis consists basically of a comparison of the PV of costs associated with leasing versus the PV of costs associated with owning. The difference in these costs is called the **net advantage to leasing (NAL).**
- One of the key issues in the lessee's analysis is the appropriate discount rate. Because a lease is a substitute for debt, because the cash flows in a lease analysis are stated on an after-tax basis, and because they are known with relative certainty, the appropriate discount rate is the **lessee's after-tax cost of debt.** A higher discount rate may be used on the **residual value** if it is substantially riskier than the other flows.
- The lessor evaluates the lease as an **investment.** If the lease's NPV is greater than zero, or if its IRR is greater than the lessor's opportunity cost, then the lease should be written.
- Leasing is motivated by various differences between lessees and lessors. Three of the most important reasons for leasing are (1) **tax rate differentials,** (2) leases in which the lessor is better able to bear the **residual value risk** than the lessee, and (3) situations where the lessor can maintain the leased equipment more efficiently than the lessee.

Questions

(20-1) Define each of the following terms:
a. Lessee; lessor
b. Operating lease; financial lease; sale-and-leaseback; combination lease; synthetic lease; SPE
c. Off–balance sheet financing; capitalizing
d. FASB Statement 13
e. Guideline lease
f. Residual value
g. Lessee's analysis; lessor's analysis
h. Net advantage to leasing (NAL)
i. Alternative minimum tax (AMT)

(20-2) Distinguish between operating leases and financial leases. Would you be more likely to find an operating lease employed for a fleet of trucks or for a manufacturing plant?

(20-3) Would you be more likely to find that lessees are in high or low income tax brackets as compared with lessors?

(20-4) Commercial banks moved heavily into equipment leasing during the early 1970s, acting as lessors. One major reason for this invasion of the leasing industry was to gain the benefits of accelerated depreciation and the investment tax credit on leased equipment. During this same period, commercial banks were investing heavily in municipal securities, and they were also making loans to real estate investment trusts (REITs). In the mid-1970s, these REITs got into such serious difficulty that many banks suffered large losses on their REIT loans. Explain how its investments in municipal bonds and REITs could reduce a bank's willingness to act as a lessor.

(20-5) One alleged advantage of leasing voiced in the past is that it kept liabilities off the balance sheet, thus making it possible for a firm to obtain more leverage than it otherwise could have. This raised the question of whether or not both the lease obligation and the asset involved should be capitalized and shown on the balance sheet. Discuss the pros and cons of capitalizing leases and related assets.

(20-6) Suppose there were no IRS restrictions on what constituted a valid lease. Explain, in a manner that a legislator might understand, why some restrictions should be imposed. Illustrate your answer with numbers.

(20-7) Suppose Congress enacted new tax law changes that would (1) permit equipment to be depreciated over a shorter period, (2) lower corporate tax rates, and (3) reinstate the investment tax credit. Discuss how each of these potential changes would affect the relative volume of leasing versus conventional debt in the U.S. economy.

(20-8) In our Anderson Company example, we assumed that the lease could not be cancelled. What effect would a cancellation clause have on the lessee's analysis? On the lessor's analysis?

Self-Test Problem   Solution Appears in Appendix A

(ST-1)
Lease versus Buy

The Randolph Teweles Company (RTC) has decided to acquire a new truck. One alternative is to lease the truck on a 4-year guideline contract for a lease payment of $10,000 per year, with payments to be made at the *beginning* of each year. The lease would include maintenance. Alternatively, RTC could purchase the truck outright for $40,000, financing the purchase by a bank loan for the net purchase price and amortizing the loan over a 4-year period at an interest rate of 10% per year. Under the borrow-to-purchase arrangement, RTC would have to maintain the truck at a cost of $1,000 per year, payable at year end. The truck falls into the MACRS 3-year class. It has a residual value of $10,000, which is the expected market value after 4 years, when RTC plans to replace the truck irrespective of whether it leases or buys. RTC has a marginal federal-plus-state tax rate of 40%.
a. What is RTC's PV cost of leasing?
b. What is RTC's PV cost of owning? Should the truck be leased or purchased?
c. The appropriate discount rate for use in the analysis is the firm's after-tax cost of debt. Why?
d. The residual value is the least certain cash flow in the analysis. How might RTC incorporate differential riskness of this cash flow into the analysis?

Problems   Answers Appear in Appendix B

Easy Problems 1–2

(20-1)
Balance Sheet Effects

Reynolds Construction needs a piece of equipment that costs $200. Reynolds either can lease the equipment or borrow $200 from a local bank and buy the equipment. If the equipment is leased, the lease would *not* have to be capitalized. Reynolds's balance sheet prior to the acquisition of the equipment is as follows:

Current assets	$300	Debt	$400
Net fixed assets	500	Equity	400
Total assets	$800	Total claims	$800

a. (1) What is Reynolds's current debt ratio?
  (2) What would be the company's debt ratio if it purchased the equipment?
  (3) What would be the debt ratio if the equipment were leased?
b. Would the company's financial risk be different under the leasing and purchasing alternatives?

(20-2)
Lease versus Buy

Assume that Reynolds's tax rate is 40% and the equipment's depreciation would be $100 per year. If the company leased the asset on a 2-year lease, the payment would be $110 at the beginning of each year. If Reynolds borrowed and bought, the bank would charge 10% interest on the loan. In either case, the equipment is worth nothing after 2 years and will be discarded. Should Reynolds lease or buy the equipment?

Intermediate Problems 3–4

(20-3)
Balance Sheet Effects

Two companies, Energen and Hastings Corporation, began operations with identical balance sheets. A year later, both required additional manufacturing capacity at a cost of $50,000. Energen obtained a 5-year, $50,000 loan at an 8% interest rate from its bank. Hastings, on the other hand, decided to lease the required $50,000 capacity for 5 years, and an 8% return was built into the lease. The balance sheet for each company, before the asset increases, follows:

		Debt	$ 50,000
		Equity	100,000
Total assets	$150,000	Total claims	$150,000

a. Show the balance sheets for both firms after the asset increases and calculate each firm's new debt ratio. (Assume that the lease is not capitalized.)
b. Show how Hastings's balance sheet would look immediately after the financing if it capitalized the lease.
c. Would the rate of return (1) on assets and (2) on equity be affected by the choice of financing? How?

(20-4)
Lease versus Buy

Big Sky Mining Company must install $1.5 million of new machinery in its Nevada mine. It can obtain a bank loan for 100% of the purchase price, or it can lease the machinery. Assume that the following facts apply:
(1) The machinery falls into the MACRS 3-year class.
(2) Under either the lease or the purchase, Big Sky must pay for insurance, property taxes, and maintenance.
(3) The firm's tax rate is 40%.
(4) The loan would have an interest rate of 15%.
(5) The lease terms call for $400,000 payments at the end of each of the next 4 years.
(6) Assume that Big Sky Mining has no use for the machine beyond the expiration of the lease. The machine has an estimated residual value of $250,000 at the end of the 4th year.

What is the NAL of the lease?

Challenging Problem 5

(20-5)
Lease versus Buy

Sadik Industries must install $1 million of new machinery in its Texas plant. It can obtain a bank loan for 100% of the required amount. Alternatively, a Texas investment banking firm that represents a group of investors believes that it can arrange for a lease financing plan. Assume that these facts apply:

(1) The equipment falls in the MACRS 3-year class.
(2) Estimated maintenance expenses are $50,000 per year.
(3) The firm's tax rate is 34%.
(4) If the money is borrowed, the bank loan will be at a rate of 14%, amortized in 3 equal installments at the end of each year.
(5) The tentative lease terms call for payments of $320,000 at the end of each year for 3 years. The lease is a guideline lease.
(6) Under the proposed lease terms, the lessee must pay for insurance, property taxes, and maintenance.
(7) Sadik must use the equipment if it is to continue in business, so it will almost certainly want to acquire the property at the end of the lease. If it does, then under the lease terms it can purchase the machinery at its fair market value at that time. The best estimate of this market value is $200,000, but it could be much higher or lower under certain circumstances.

To assist management in making the proper lease-versus-buy decision, you are asked to answer the following questions:

a. Assuming that the lease can be arranged, should the firm lease or borrow and buy the equipment? Explain. (Hint: In this situation, the firm plans to use the asset beyond the term of the lease. Thus, the residual value becomes a *cost* to leasing in Year 3. The firm will depreciate the equipment it purchases under the purchase option starting in Year 3, using the MACRS 3-year class schedule. Depreciation will begin in the year in which the equipment is purchased, which is Year 3.)

b. Consider the $200,000 estimated residual value. Is it appropriate to discount it at the same rate as the other cash flows? What about the other cash flows—are they all equally risky? (Hint: Riskier cash flows are normally discounted at higher rates, but when the cash flows are *costs* rather than *inflows*, the normal procedure must be reversed.)

Spreadsheet Problem

(20-6)
Build a Model: Lessee's Analysis

e-resource

Start with the partial model in the file *FM12 Ch 20 P06 Build a Model.xls* at the textbook's Web site. As part of its overall plant modernization and cost reduction program, Western Fabrics' management has decided to install a new automated weaving loom. In the capital budgeting analysis of this equipment, the IRR of the project was found to be 20% versus the project's required return of 12%.

The loom has an invoice price of $250,000, including delivery and installation charges. The funds needed could be borrowed from the bank through a 4-year amortized loan at a 10% interest rate, with payments to be made at the end of each year. In the event the loom is purchased, the manufacturer will contract to maintain and service it for a fee of $20,000 per year paid at the end of each year. The loom falls in the MACRS 5-year class, and Western's marginal federal-plus-state tax rate is 40%.

Aubey Automation Inc., maker of the loom, has offered to lease the loom to Western for $70,000 upon delivery and installation (at t = 0) plus 4 additional annual lease payments of $70,000 to be made at the end of Years 1 to 4. (Note that there are 5 lease payments in total.) The lease agreement includes maintenance and servicing. Actually, the loom has an expected life of 8 years, at which time its expected salvage value is zero; however, after 4 years, its market value is expected to equal its book value of $42,500. Western plans to build an entirely new plant in 4 years, so it has no interest in either leasing or owning the proposed loom for more than that period.

a. Should the loom be leased or purchased?
b. The salvage value is clearly the most uncertain cash flow in the analysis. What effect would a salvage value risk adjustment have on the analysis? (Assume that the appropriate salvage value pre-tax discount rate is 15%.)
c. Assuming that the after-tax cost of debt should be used to discount all anticipated cash flows, at what lease payment would the firm be indifferent to either leasing or buying?

Cyberproblem

e-resource

Please go to the textbook's Web site to access any Cyberproblems.

Mini Case

Lewis Securities Inc. has decided to acquire a new market data and quotation system for its Richmond home office. The system receives current market prices and other information from several online data services and then either displays the information on a screen or stores it for later retrieval by the firm's brokers. The system also permits customers to call up current quotes on terminals in the lobby.

The equipment costs $1,000,000, and, if it were purchased, Lewis could obtain a term loan for the full purchase price at a 10% interest rate. Although the equipment has a 6-year useful life, it is classified as a special-purpose computer, so it falls into the MACRS 3-year class. If the system were purchased, a 4-year maintenance contract could be obtained at a cost of $20,000 per year, payable at the beginning of each year. The equipment would be sold after 4 years, and the best estimate of its residual value at that time is $200,000. However, since real-time display system technology is changing rapidly, the actual residual value is uncertain.

As an alternative to the borrow-and-buy plan, the equipment manufacturer informed Lewis that Consolidated Leasing would be willing to write a 4-year guideline lease on the equipment, including maintenance, for payments of $260,000 at the beginning of each year. Lewis's marginal federal-plus-state tax rate is 40%. You have been asked to analyze the lease-versus-purchase decision, and in the process to answer the following questions:

a. (1) Who are the two parties to a lease transaction?
    (2) What are the five primary types of leases, and what are their characteristics?
    (3) How are leases classified for tax purposes?
    (4) What effect does leasing have on a firm's balance sheet?
    (5) What effect does leasing have on a firm's capital structure?

b. (1) What is the present value cost of owning the equipment? (Hint: Set up a time line that shows the net cash flows over the period $t = 0$ to $t = 4$, and then find the PV of these net cash flows, or the PV cost of owning.)
    (2) Explain the rationale for the discount rate you used to find the PV.

c. What is Lewis's present value cost of leasing the equipment? (Hint: Again, construct a time line.)

d. What is the net advantage to leasing (NAL)? Does your analysis indicate that Lewis should buy or lease the equipment? Explain.

e. Now assume that the equipment's residual value could be as low as $0 or as high as $400,000, but that $200,000 is the expected value. Since the residual value is riskier than the other cash flows in the analysis, this differential risk should be incorporated into the analysis. Describe how this could be accomplished. (No calculations are necessary, but explain how you would modify the analysis if calculations were required.) What effect would increased uncertainty about the residual value have on Lewis's lease-versus-purchase decision?

f. The lessee compares the cost of owning the equipment with the cost of leasing it. Now put yourself in the lessor's shoes. In a few sentences, how should you analyze the decision to write or not write the lease?

g. (1) Assume that the lease payments were actually $280,000 per year, that Consolidated Leasing is also in the 40% tax bracket, and that it also forecasts a $200,000 residual value. Also, to furnish the maintenance support, Consolidated would have to purchase a maintenance contract from the manufacturer at the same $20,000 annual cost, again paid in advance. Consolidated Leasing can obtain an expected 10% pre-tax return on investments of similar risk. What would Consolidated's NPV and IRR of leasing be under these conditions?
    (2) What do you think the lessor's NPV would be if the lease payment were set at $260,000 per year? (Hint: The lessor's cash flows would be a "mirror image" of the lessee's cash flows.)

h. Lewis's management has been considering moving to a new downtown location, and they are concerned that these plans may come to fruition prior to the expiration of the lease. If the move occurs, Lewis would buy or lease an entirely new set of equipment, and hence management would like to include a cancellation clause in the lease contract. What effect would such a clause have on the riskiness of the lease from Lewis's standpoint? From the lessor's standpoint? If you were the lessor, would you insist on changing any of the lease terms if a cancellation clause were added? Should the cancellation clause contain any restrictive covenants and/or penalties of the type contained in bond indentures or provisions similar to call premiums?

Selected Additional Cases

The following cases from Textchoice, *Cengage Learning's online library, cover many of the concepts discussed in this chapter and are available at* **http://www.textchoice2.com.**

Klein-Brigham Series:
Case 25, "Environmental Sciences, Inc.," Case 49, "Agro Chemical Corporation," and Case 65, "Friendly Food Stores, Inc.," and Case 26, "Prudent Solutions, Inc.," all of which examine the lease decision from the perspectives of both the lessee and the lessor.

Brigham-Buzzard Series:
Case 12, "Powerline Network Corporation (Leasing)."

chapter 21

Hybrid Financing: Preferred Stock, Warrants, and Convertibles

The use of convertible securities—bonds or preferred stocks that can be exchanged for common stock of the issuing corporation—has soared during the last decade. Why do companies use convertibles so heavily? To answer this question, first recognize that convertibles virtually always have coupon rates that are lower than would be required on straight, nonconvertible bonds or preferred stocks. Therefore, if a company raises $100 million by issuing convertible bonds, its interest expense will be lower than if it financed with nonconvertible debt. But why would investors be willing to buy such a bond, given its lower interest payments? The answer lies in the conversion feature—if the price of the issuer's stock rises, the convertible bondholder can exchange it for stock and realize a capital gain.

A convertible bond's value is based partly on interest rates in the economy, partly on the issuing company's regular bond risk, and partly on the price of the stock into which it is convertible. In contrast, a nonconvertible bond's price is based entirely on interest rates and company risk. Therefore, convertibles' prices are much more volatile than regular bonds' prices, which make convertibles riskier than straight bonds. An article in *Forbes* reported that if a company's common stock increases in value, the returns on its convertibles also rise, but by only 70% of the stock's percentage increase. However, if the stock declines, the convertible will decline by only 50% of the stock's decline. Thus, while convertibles are more risky than straight bonds, they are less risky than common stocks.

To illustrate, consider Amazon.com, which in January 1999 issued $1.25 billion of convertible bonds, the largest such offering in history. Amazon's bonds had a par value of $1,000 and a 4.75% coupon rate. During 1999 Amazon's convertibles took their holders on a wild ride. Amazon's stock rose about 70% during the first four months, causing its convertibles to rise to $1,500. During the next four months, the stock lost more than 60% of its value, to a level 30% below where it had been trading when the convertibles were issued. This caused the convertibles' price to be cut in half, to $750. Three months later Amazon's stock rebounded, and its convertibles once again traded above $1,500. But they dropped once more, and by year-end 1999, the convertibles were back to their $1,000 issue price. Thus, someone holding the convertibles for the entire year would have ended up close to where he or she started, with a total return just shy of the 4.75% coupon rate, but probably also with a bad case of heartburn and a few gray hairs.

Source: John Gorham, "Chicken Little Stocks," *Forbes*, December 27, 1999, 200.

In previous chapters we examined common stocks and various types of long-term debt. In this chapter, we examine three other securities used to raise long-term capital: (1) *preferred stock*, which is a hybrid security that represents a cross between debt and common equity; (2) *warrants*, which are derivative securities issued by firms to facilitate the issuance of some other type of security; and (3) *convertibles*, which combine the features of debt (or preferred stock) and warrants.

e-resource

The textbook's Web site contains an *Excel* file that will guide you through the chapter's calculations. The file for this chapter is ***FM12 Ch 21 Tool Kit.xls,*** and we encourage you to open the file and follow along as you read the chapter.

21.1 Preferred Stock

Preferred stock is a hybrid—it is similar to bonds in some respects and to common stock in other ways. Accountants classify preferred stock as equity, hence show it on the balance sheet as an equity account. However, from a finance perspective preferred stock lies somewhere between debt and common equity—it imposes a fixed charge and thus increases the firm's financial leverage, yet omitting the preferred dividend does not force a company into bankruptcy. Also, unlike interest on debt, preferred dividends are not deductible by the issuing corporation, so preferred stock has a higher cost of capital than debt. We first describe the basic features of preferred, after which we discuss the types of preferred stock and the advantages and disadvantages of preferred stock.

Basic Features

Preferred stock has a par (or liquidating) value, often either $25 or $100. The dividend is stated as either a percentage of par, as so many dollars per share, or both ways. For example, several years ago Klondike Paper Company sold 150,000 shares of $100 par value perpetual preferred stock for a total of $15 million. This preferred had a stated annual dividend of $12 per share, so the preferred dividend yield was $12/$100 = 0.12, or 12%, at the time of issue. The dividend was set when the stock was issued; it will not be changed in the future. Therefore, if the required rate of return on preferred, r_p, changes from 12% after the issue date—as it did—then the market price of the preferred stock will go up or down. Currently, r_p for Klondike Paper's preferred is 9%, and the price of the preferred has risen from $100 to $12/0.09 = $133.33.

If the preferred dividend is not earned, the company does not have to pay it. However, most preferred issues are **cumulative,** meaning that the cumulative total of unpaid preferred dividends must be paid before dividends can be paid on the common stock. Unpaid preferred dividends are called **arrearages.** Dividends in arrears do not earn interest; thus, arrearages do not grow in a compound interest sense—they only grow from additional nonpayments of the preferred dividend. Also, many preferred stocks accrue arrearages for only a limited number of years, say, 3 years, meaning that the cumulative feature ceases after 3 years. However, the dividends in arrears continue in force until they are paid.

Preferred stock normally has no voting rights. However, most preferred issues stipulate that the preferred stockholders can elect a minority of the directors—say, three out of ten—if the preferred dividend is passed (omitted). Some preferreds even entitle their holders to elect a majority of the board.

Although nonpayment of preferred dividends will not bankrupt a company, corporations issue preferred with every intention of paying the dividend. Even if passing the dividend does not give the preferred stockholders control of the company, failure to pay a preferred dividend precludes payment of common dividends. In addition, passing the dividend makes it difficult to raise capital by selling

Where's the Dividend?

Suppose your company needs cash to finance a sure-winner expansion. However, its bond covenants forbid any additional borrowing, and these covenants also prohibit the payment of cash dividends, which rules out conventional preferred stock. To make matters worse, the company's stock price is trading near its 52-week low, so you don't want to issue new common stock. Is there any way you can raise the needed funds?

Two companies came up with innovative answers. Intermedia Communications Corp. issued $300 million of exchangeable preferred stock with a payment-in-kind (PIK) dividend. The 13.5% dividend is payable in additional shares of the preferred stock rather than in cash. Therefore, this instrument provided Intermedia with the cash it needed yet still complied with the bond covenants. In addition, the exchange feature allows

Intermedia to convert the preferred stock into debt when its financial situation improves to the point where the debt covenants are no longer binding.

Similarly, Nextel Communications issued $150 million of another first-time-ever security, zero coupon convertible preferred stock. The stock had a 15-year maturity, a $98 maturity value per share, and a $26 per share issue price, giving it a yield of 9.25% at the time of issue. Because it isn't debt and it doesn't pay coupons, the security avoided the restrictions in Nextel's debt covenants. The preferred stock can also be converted into common stock, and the preferred stockholders will exercise this option if Nextel's stock enjoys a sharp increase.

Sources: Ian Springsteel, "Take Your PIK," *CFO*, December 1997, p. 30; and Joseph McCafferty, "Less or More than Zero," *CFO*, March 1999, p. 20.

---

bonds, and virtually impossible to sell more preferred or common stock except at rock bottom prices. However, having preferred stock outstanding does give a firm the chance to overcome its difficulties—if bonds had been used instead of preferred stock, a company could be forced into bankruptcy before it could straighten out its problems. *Thus, from the viewpoint of the issuing corporation, preferred stock is less risky than bonds.*

However, for an investor preferred stock is riskier than bonds: (1) Preferred stockholders' claims are subordinated to those of bondholders in the event of liquidation, and (2) bondholders are more likely to continue receiving income during hard times than are preferred stockholders. Accordingly, investors require a higher after-tax rate of return on a given firm's preferred stock than on its bonds. However, since 70% of preferred dividends is exempt from corporate taxes, preferred stock is attractive to corporate investors. Indeed, high-grade preferred stock, on average, sells on a lower pre-tax yield basis than high-grade bonds. As an example, Du Pont's 3.5% dividend preferred stock in mid-2006 had a price of $67.52, for a market yield of about 5.18%. Du Pont's long-term bonds that mature in 2028 provided a yield of 5.54%, or 0.36 percentage points *more* than its preferred. The tax treatment accounted for this differential; the *after-tax yield* to corporate investors was greater on the preferred stock than on the bonds.[1]

About half of all preferred stock issued in recent years has been convertible into common stock. For example, on July 31, 2002, Corning Incorporated issued $500 million of mandatory convertible preferred stock with a 7% annual dividend rate. The issue is mandatorily convertible into between approximately 254 million and 313 million shares. Convertibles are discussed at length in Section 21.3.

For updates, go to **http://finance.yahoo.com** and get quotes for DD-PA, Du Pont's 3.5% preferred stock. For an updated bond yield, use the bond screener and search for Du Pont bonds.

---

[1]The after-tax yield on a 5.54% bond to a corporate investor in the 34% marginal tax rate bracket is 5.54%(1 − T) = 3.66%. The after-tax yield on a 5.18% preferred stock is 5.18%(1 − Effective T) = 5.18%[1 − (0.30)(0.34)] = 4.65%. Also, note that tax law prohibits firms from issuing debt and then using the proceeds to purchase another firm's preferred stock. If debt is used for stock purchases, then the 70% dividend exclusion is voided. This provision is designed to prevent a firm from engaging in "tax arbitrage," using tax-deductible debt to purchase largely tax-exempt preferred stock.

MIPS, QUIPS, TOPrS, and QUIDS: A Tale of Two Perspectives

Wall Street's "financial engineers" are constantly trying to develop new securities that appeal to issuers and investors. In the mid-1990s Goldman Sachs created a special type of preferred stock whose dividends are deductible for the issuing company, just like interest is deductible. These securities trade under a variety of colorful names, including MIPS (Modified Income Preferred Securities), QUIPS (Quarterly Income Preferred Securities), TOPrS (Trust Originated Preferred Stock), and QUIDS (Quarterly Income Debt Securities). The corporation that wants to raise capital (the "parent") establishes a trust, which issues fixed-dividend preferred stock. The parent then issues bonds (or debt of some type) to the trust, and the trust pays for the bonds with the cash raised from the sale of preferred. At that point, the parent has the cash it needs, the trust holds debt issued by the parent, and the investing public holds preferred stock issued by the trust. The parent then makes interest payments to the trust, and the trust uses that income to make the preferred dividend payments. Because the parent company has issued debt, its interest payments are tax deductible.

If the dividends could be excluded from taxable income by corporate investors, this preferred would really be a great deal—the issuer could deduct the interest, corporate investors could exclude most of the dividends, and the IRS would be the loser. The corporate parent does get to deduct the interest paid to the trust, but IRS regulations do not allow the dividends on these securities to be excluded.

Because there is only one deduction, why are these new securities attractive? The answer is as follows: (1) Because the parent company gets to take the deduction, its cost of funds from the preferred is $r_p(1 - T)$, just as it would be if it used debt. (2) The parent generates tax savings, and it can thus afford to pay a relatively high rate on trust-related preferred; that is, it can pass on some of its tax savings to investors to induce them to buy the new securities. (3) The primary purchasers of the preferred are low-tax-bracket individuals and tax-exempt institutions such as pension funds. For such purchasers, not being able to exclude the dividend from taxable income is unimportant. (4) Due to the differential tax rates, the arrangement results in net tax savings. Competition in capital markets results in a sharing of the savings between investors and corporations.

In the mid-1990s the Treasury attempted unsuccessfully to do away with the deductibility on these instruments, arguing that they were more like equity than debt. For example, in 1993 Enron issued MIPS through a subsidiary, deducted the interest, but described them as preferred stock when reporting to shareholders. Enron's stated intention was to use these securities to decrease its debt/equity ratio and improve its credit rating, apparently by issuing what amounted to equity, but still deducting the payments. But how does issuing these securities really affect the company's risk? The debt is still an obligation of the parent company and so may increase the parent's risk, not decrease it. In fact, the credit rating agencies determined that Enron's MIPS increased its risk, like debt would, and warned that these shenanigans would not improve its credit rating.

Sources: Kerry Capell, "High Yields, Low Cost, Funny Names," *BusinessWeek*, September 9, 1996, p. 122; Leslie Haggin, "SmartMoney Online MIPS, QUIDS, and QUIPS," *SmartMoney Interactive*, April 6, 1999; John D. McKinnon and Greg Hitt, "Double Play: How Treasury Lost in Battle to Quash a Dubious Security—Instrument Issued by Enron and Others Can Be Used as Both Debt and Equity—Win for Flotilla of Lobbyists," *The Wall Street Journal*, February 4, 2002, p. A1.

Some preferred stocks are similar to perpetual bonds in that they have no maturity date, but most new issues now have specified maturities. For example, many preferred shares have a sinking fund provision that calls for the retirement of 2% of the issue each year, meaning that the issue will "mature" in a maximum of 50 years. Also, many preferred issues are callable by the issuing corporation, which can also limit the life of the preferred.[2]

---

[2]Prior to the late 1970s, virtually all preferred stock was perpetual, and almost no issues had sinking funds or call provisions. Then, insurance company regulators, worried about the unrealized losses the companies had been incurring on preferred holdings as a result of rising interest rates, put into effect some regulatory changes that essentially mandated that insurance companies buy only limited life preferreds. From that time on, virtually no new preferred has been perpetual. This example illustrates the way securities change as a result of changes in the economic environment.

Nonconvertible preferred stock is virtually all owned by corporations, which can take advantage of the 70% dividend exclusion to obtain a higher after-tax yield on preferred stock than on bonds. Individuals should not own preferred stocks (except convertible preferreds)—they can get higher yields on safer bonds, so it is not logical for them to hold preferreds.[3] As a result of this ownership pattern, the volume of preferred stock financing is geared to the supply of money in the hands of corporate investors. When the supply of such money is plentiful, the prices of preferred stocks are bid up, their yields fall, and investment bankers suggest that companies that need financing consider issuing preferred stock.

For issuers, preferred stock has a tax *disadvantage* relative to debt—interest expense is deductible, but preferred dividends are not. Still, firms with low tax rates may have an incentive to issue preferred stock that can be bought by corporate investors with high tax rates, who can take advantage of the 70% dividend exclusion. If a firm has a lower tax rate than potential corporate buyers, the firm might be better off issuing preferred stock than debt. The key here is that the tax advantage to a high-tax-rate corporation is greater than the tax disadvantage to a low-tax-rate issuer. To illustrate, assume that risk differentials between debt and preferred would require an issuer to set the interest rate on new debt at 10% and the dividend yield on new preferred at 2% higher, or 12% in a no-tax world. However, when taxes are considered, a corporate buyer with a high tax rate, say, 40%, might be willing to buy the preferred stock if it has an 8% before-tax yield. This would produce an 8%(1 − Effective T) = 8%[1 − 0.30(0.40)] = 7.04% after-tax return on the preferred versus 10%(1 − 0.40) = 6.0% on the debt. If the issuer has a low tax rate, say, 10%, its after-tax costs would be 10%(1 − T) = 10%(0.90) = 9% on the bonds and 8% on the preferred. Thus, the security with lower risk to the issuer, preferred stock, also has a lower cost. Such situations can make preferred stock a logical financing choice.[4]

Other Types of Preferred Stock

In addition to the "plain vanilla" variety of preferred stocks, several variations are also used. Two of these, floating rate and market auction preferred, are discussed in the following sections.

Adjustable Rate Preferred Stock   Instead of paying fixed dividends, **adjustable rate preferred stocks (ARPs)** have their dividends tied to the rate on Treasury securities. ARPs are issued mainly by utilities and large commercial banks. When ARPs were first developed, they were touted as nearly perfect short-term corporate investments since (1) only 30% of the dividends are taxable to corporations, and (2) the floating rate feature was supposed to keep the issue trading at near par. The new security proved to be so popular as a short-term investment for firms with idle cash that mutual funds designed just to invest in them sprouted like weeds (shares of the funds, in turn, were purchased by corporations). However, the ARPs still had some price volatility due (1) to changes in the riskiness of the

---

[3]Some new preferreds are attractive to individual investors. See the box, "MIPS, QUIPS, TOPrS, and QUIDS: A Tale of Two Perspectives."

[4]For a more rigorous treatment of the tax hypothesis of preferred stock, see Iraj Fooladi and Gordon S. Roberts, "On Preferred Stock," *Journal of Financial Research*, Winter 1986, pp. 319–324. For an example of an empirical test of the hypothesis, see Arthur L. Houston, Jr. and Carol Olson Houston, "Financing with Preferred Stock," *Financial Management*, Autumn 1990, pp. 42–54. For more on preferred stock, see Michael J. Alderson, Keith C. Brown, and Scott L. Lummer, "Dutch Auction Rate Preferred Stock," *Financial Management*, Summer 1987, pp. 68–73; Michael J. Alderson and Donald R. Fraser, "Financial Innovations and Excesses Revisited: The Case of Auction Rate Preferred Stock," *Financial Management*, Summer 1993, pp. 61–75; and Bernard J. Winger et al., "Adjustable Rate Preferred Stock," *Financial Management*, Spring 1986, pp. 48–57.

issues (some big banks that had issued ARPs, such as Continental Illinois, ran into serious loan default problems) and (2) to the fact that Treasury yields fluctuated between dividend rate adjustments dates. Thus, the ARPs had too much price instability to be held in the liquid asset portfolios of many corporate investors.

Market Auction Preferred Stock   In 1984, investment bankers introduced **money market,** or **market auction, preferred.** Here the underwriter conducts an auction on the issue every seven weeks (to get the 70% exclusion from taxable income, buyers must hold the stock at least 46 days). Holders who want to sell their shares can put them up for auction at par value. Buyers then submit bids in the form of the yields they are willing to accept over the next 7-week period. The yield set on the issue for the coming period is the lowest yield sufficient to sell all the shares being offered at that auction. The buyers pay the sellers the par value; hence, holders are virtually assured that their shares can be sold at par. The issuer then must pay a dividend rate over the next 7-week period as determined by the auction. From the holder's standpoint, market auction preferred is a low-risk, largely tax-exempt, 7-week maturity security that can be sold between auction dates at close to par. However, if there are not enough buyers to match the sellers (in spite of the high yield), then the auction can fail, which has occurred on occasion.

Advantages and Disadvantages of Preferred Stock

There are both advantages and disadvantages to financing with preferred stock. Here are the major advantages from the issuer's standpoint:

1. In contrast to bonds, the obligation to pay preferred dividends is not firm, and passing a preferred dividend cannot force a firm into bankruptcy.
2. By issuing preferred stock, the firm avoids the dilution of common equity that occurs when common stock is sold.
3. Since preferred stock sometimes has no maturity, and since preferred sinking fund payments, if present, are typically spread over a long period, preferred issues reduce the cash flow drain from repayment of principal that occurs with debt issues.

There are two major disadvantages:

1. Preferred stock dividends are not normally deductible to the issuer; hence the after-tax cost of preferred is typically higher than the after-tax cost of debt. However, the tax advantage of preferreds to corporate purchasers lowers its pre-tax cost and thus its effective cost.
2. Although preferred dividends can be passed, investors expect them to be paid, and firms intend to pay the dividends if conditions permit. Thus, preferred dividends are considered to be a fixed cost. Therefore, their use, like that of debt, increases financial risk and thus the cost of common equity.

SELF-TEST

Should preferred stock be considered as equity or debt? Explain.

Who are the major purchasers of nonconvertible preferred stock? Why?

Briefly explain the mechanics of adjustable rate and market auction preferred stock.

What are the advantages and disadvantages of preferred stock to the issuer?

A company's preferred stock has a pre-tax dividend yield of 7%. The company's debt has a pre-tax yield of 8%. If an investor is in the 34% marginal tax bracket, what are the after-tax yields of the preferred stock and debt? (6.29%; 5.28%)

21.2 Warrants

A **warrant** is a certificate issued by a company that gives the holder the right to buy a stated number of shares of the company's stock at a specified price for some specified length of time. Generally, warrants are issued along with debt, and they are used to induce investors to buy long-term debt with a lower coupon rate than would otherwise be required. For example, when Infomatics Corporation, a rapidly growing high-tech company, wanted to sell $50 million of 20-year bonds in 2007, the company's investment bankers informed the financial vice president that the bonds would be difficult to sell, and that a coupon rate of 10% would be required. However, as an alternative the bankers suggested that investors might be willing to buy the bonds with a coupon rate of only 8% if the company would offer 20 warrants with each $1,000 bond, each warrant entitling the holder to buy one share of common stock at a strike price (also called an exercise price) of $22 per share. The stock was selling for $20 per share at the time, and the warrants would expire in the year 2017 if they had not been exercised previously.

Why would investors be willing to buy Infomatics' bonds at a yield of only 8% in a 10% market just because warrants were also offered as part of the package? It is because the warrants are long-term *call options* that have value since holders can buy the firm's common stock at the strike price regardless of how high the market price climbs. This option offsets the low interest rate on the bonds and makes the package of low-yield bonds plus warrants attractive to investors. (See Chapter 9 for a discussion of options.)

Initial Market Price of a Bond with Warrants

The Infomatics bonds, if they had been issued as straight debt, would have carried a 10% interest rate. However, with warrants attached, the bonds were sold to yield 8%. Someone buying the bonds at their $1,000 initial offering price would thus be receiving a package consisting of an 8%, 20-year bond plus 20 warrants. Because the going interest rate on bonds as risky as those of Infomatics was 10%, we can find the straight-debt value of the bonds, assuming an annual coupon for ease of illustration, as follows:

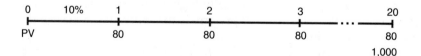

0	10%	1	2	3	20
PV		80	80	80	80
					1,000

Using a financial calculator, input N = 20, I/YR = 10, PMT = 80, and FV = 1000. Then, press the PV key to obtain the bond's value, $829.73, or approximately $830. Thus, a person buying the bonds in the initial underwriting would pay $1,000 and receive in exchange a straight bond worth about $830 plus 20 warrants presumably worth about $1,000 − $830 = $170:

$$\text{Price paid for bond with warrants} = \text{Straight-debt value of bond} + \text{Value of warrants} \quad \text{(21-1)}$$

$1,000 = $830 + $170.

Because investors receive 20 warrants with each bond, each warrant has an implied value of $170/20 = $8.50.

The key issue in setting the terms of a bond-with-warrants deal is valuing the warrants. The straight-debt value can be estimated quite accurately, as was done above. However, it is more difficult to estimate the value of the warrants. The Black-Scholes Option Pricing Model (OPM), which we discussed in Chapter 9, can be used to find the value of a call option. There is a temptation to use this model to find the value of a warrant, since call options are similar to warrants in many respects: Both give the investor the right to buy a share of stock at a fixed strike price on or before the expiration date. However, there are major differences between call options and warrants. When call options are exercised, the stock provided to the option holder comes from the secondary market, but when warrants are exercised, the stock provided to the warrant holders is either newly issued shares or treasury stock the company has previously purchased. This means that the exercise of warrants dilutes the value of the original equity, which could cause the value of the original warrant to differ from the value of a similar call option. Also, call options typically have a life of just a few months, while warrants often have lives of 10 years or more. Finally, the Black-Scholes model assumes that the underlying stock pays no dividend, which is not unreasonable over a short period but is unreasonable for 5 or 10 years. Therefore, investment bankers cannot use the Black-Scholes model to determine the value of warrants.

Even though the Black-Scholes model cannot be used to determine a precise value for a warrant, there are more sophisticated models that work reasonably well. In addition, investment bankers can simply contact portfolio managers of mutual funds, pension funds, and other organizations that would be interested in buying the securities and get an indication of how many they would buy at different prices. In effect, the bankers hold a presale auction and determine the set of terms that will just clear the market. If they do this job properly, they will, in effect, be letting the market determine the value of the warrants.

Use of Warrants in Financing

Warrants generally are used by small, rapidly growing firms as **sweeteners** when they sell debt or preferred stock. Such firms frequently are regarded by investors as being highly risky, so their bonds can be sold only at extremely high coupon rates and with very restrictive indenture provisions. To avoid such restrictions, firms such as Infomatics often offer warrants along with the bonds. However, some years ago, AT&T raised $1.57 billion by selling bonds with warrants. At the time, this was the largest financing of any type ever undertaken by a business firm, and it marked the first use ever of warrants by a large, strong corporation.[5]

Getting warrants along with bonds enables investors to share in the company's growth, assuming it does in fact grow and prosper. Therefore, investors are willing to accept a lower interest rate and less restrictive indenture provisions. A bond with

[5]It is interesting to note that before the AT&T issue, the New York Stock Exchange's stated policy was that warrants could not be listed because they were "speculative" instruments rather than "investment" securities. When AT&T issued warrants, however, the Exchange changed its policy, agreeing to list warrants that met certain requirements. Many other warrants have since been listed.

It is also interesting to note that, prior to the sale, AT&T's treasury staff, working with Morgan Stanley analysts, estimated the value of the warrants as a part of the underwriting decision. The package was supposed to sell for a total price in the neighborhood of $1,000. The bond value could be determined accurately, so the trick was to estimate the equilibrium value of the warrant under different possible exercise prices and years to expiration, and then to use an exercise price and life that would cause Bond value + Warrant value ≈ $1,000. Using a warrant pricing model, the AT&T/Morgan Stanley analysts set terms that caused the warrant to sell on the open market at a price that was only 35¢ off from the estimated price.

price of $22 per warrant. This will make the total value of Infomatics equal to $613.841 million (the $591.841 million existing value plus the $22 million raised by the exercise of the warrants). The total value remaining for stockholders is now $569.985 million ($613.841 million less the $43.856 million allocated to bondholders). There are now 11 million shares of stock (the original 10 million plus the new 1 million due to the exercise of the warrants), so the stock price will be $569.985/11 = $51.82 per share. Note that this is lower than the $54.80 price per share that Infomatics would have had if there had been no warrants. Thus, the warrants dilute the value of the stock.

A similar dilution occurs with earnings per share. After exercise, the asset base would increase from $591.841 million to $613.841 million, with the additional $22 million coming from the sale of 1 million shares of stock at $22 per share. If the new funds had the same basic earning power as the existing funds, then the new EBIT would be 0.135($613.841) = $82.869 million. Interest payments would still be $4 million, so earnings before taxes would be $82.869 − $4 = $78.869 million, and after-tax earnings would be $78.869(1 − 0.4) = $47.321 million. With 10 + 1 = 11 million shares now outstanding, EPS would be $47.321/11 = $4.30, down from $4.55. Therefore, exercising the warrants would dilute EPS.

Has this wealth transfer harmed the original shareholders? The answer is yes and no. Yes, because the original shareholders clearly are worse off than they would have been if there had been no warrants. However, if there had been no warrants attached to the bonds, then the bonds would have had a 10% coupon rate instead of the 8% coupon rate. Also, if the value of the company had not increased as expected, then it might not have been profitable for the warrant holders to exercise their warrants. In other words, the original shareholders were willing to trade off the potential dilution for the lower coupon rate. In this example, the original stockholders and the investors in the bonds with warrants would be getting what they expected. Therefore, the answer is no: The wealth transfer at the time of exercise did not harm the original shareholders, because they expected an eventual transfer and were fairly compensated by the lower interest payments.

Note, too, that investors would recognize the situation, so the actual wealth transfer would occur gradually over time, not in one fell swoop when the warrants were exercised. First, EPS would have been reported on a diluted basis over the years, and on that basis, there would be no decline in reported EPS. (We discuss this in a later section of this chapter.) Also, investors would know what was happening, so the stock price, over time, would reflect the likely future dilution. Therefore, it too would be stable when the warrants were exercised. Thus, the effects of the warrants would be reflected in EPS and the stock price on a gradual basis over time.

The Component Cost of Bonds with Warrants

When Infomatics issued its bonds with warrants, the firm received $1,000 for each bond. Simultaneously, the company assumed an obligation to pay $80 interest for 20 years plus $1,000 at the end of 20 years. The pre-tax cost of the money would have been 10% if no warrants had been attached, but each Infomatics bond had 20 warrants, each of which entitles its holder to buy one share of stock for $22. What is the percentage cost of the debt? As we shall see, the cost is well above the 8% coupon rate on the bonds.

As we demonstrated earlier, when the warrants expire 10 years from now and are exercised, the expected stock price is $51.82.[7] The company would then have to issue one share of stock worth $51.82 for each warrant exercised and, in return, Infomatics would receive the strike price, $22. Thus, a purchaser of the bonds, if he or she holds the complete package, would expect to realize a profit in Year 10 of $51.82 − $22 = $29.82 for each common share issued.[8] Since each bond has 20 warrants attached, and each warrant entitles the holder to buy one share of common stock, investors would have a cash flow of 20($29.82) = $596.40 per bond at the end of Year 10. Here is a time line of the expected cash flow stream to an investor:

0	1	9	10	11	20
−$1,000	+$80	+$80	+$ 80.00	+$80	+$ 80
			+ 596.40		+ 1,000
			+$676.40		+$1,080

The IRR of this stream is 10.7%, which is the investor's overall expected pre-tax rate of return on the issue. This return is 70 basis points higher than the 10% return on straight debt. The higher return reflects the fact that the issue is riskier to investors than a straight-debt issue because much of the return is expected to come in the form of stock price appreciation, and that part of the return is more risky than interest income.

The expected rate of return to investors is the same as the before-tax cost to the company—this is true of common stocks, straight bonds, and preferred stocks, and it is also true of bonds sold with warrants.[9]

SELF-TEST

What is a warrant?

Describe how a new bond issue with warrants is valued.

How are warrants used in corporate financing?

The use of warrants lowers the coupon rate on the corresponding debt issue. Does this mean that the component cost of a debt-plus-warrants package is less than the cost of straight debt? Explain.

Shanton Corporation could issue 15-year straight debt at a rate of 8%. Instead, Shanton issues 15-year debt with a coupon rate of 6%, but each bond has 25 warrants attached. The bonds can be issued at par ($1,000 per bond). Assuming annual interest payments, what is the implied value of each warrant? ($6.85)

---

[7]Given the expected growth rate in the value of the company, there is only a very small probability that value of the company will not increase sufficiently for the warrants to be exercised. Therefore, we assume a 100% probability that the warrants will be exercised.

[8]It is not strictly accurate to say that the expected profit from the warrant position is the expected stock price less the strike price: $29.82 = $51.82 − $22. This is because if the stock price drops below the strike price, in this case $22, then the warrant profit is $0, regardless of how low the stock price goes. Thus the expected payoff will be somewhat more than $29.82. Although this expectation can be calculated using options techniques similar to those in Chapter 9, it is beyond the scope of this chapter. However, if there is a very small probability that the stock price will drop below the exercise price, then $29.82 is very close to the true expected payoff.

[9]For more on warrant pricing, see Michael C. Ehrhardt and Ronald E. Shrieves, "The Impact of Warrants and Convertible Securities on the Systematic Risk of Common Equity," *Financial Review*, November 1995, pp. 843–856; Beni Lauterbach and Paul Schultz, "Pricing Warrants: An Empirical Study of the Black-Scholes Model and Its Alternatives," *Journal of Finance*, September 1990, pp. 1181–1209; David C. Leonard and Michael E. Solt, "On Using the Black-Scholes Model to Value Warrants," *Journal of Financial Research*, Summer 1990, pp. 81–92; and Katherine L. Phelps, William T. Moore, and Rodney L. Roenfeldt, "Equity Valuation Effects of Warrant-Debt Financing," *Journal of Financial Research*, Summer 1991, pp. 93–103.

21.3 Convertible Securities

Convertible securities are bonds or preferred stocks that, under specified terms and conditions, can be exchanged for (that is, converted into) common stock at the option of the holder. Unlike the exercise of warrants, which brings in additional funds to the firm, conversion does not provide new capital; debt (or preferred stock) is simply replaced on the balance sheet by common stock. Of course, reducing the debt or preferred stock will improve the firm's financial strength and make it easier to raise additional capital, but that requires a separate action.

Conversion Ratio and Conversion Price

e-resource

See **FM12 Ch 21 Tool Kit.xls** at the textbook's Web site for details.

One of the most important provisions of a convertible security is the **conversion ratio, CR,** defined as the number of shares of stock a bondholder will receive upon conversion. Related to the conversion ratio is the **conversion price, P_c,** which is the effective price investors pay for the common stock when conversion occurs. The relationship between the conversion ratio and the conversion price can be illustrated by Silicon Valley Software Company's convertible debentures issued at their $1,000 par value in July of 2007. At any time prior to maturity on July 15, 2027, a debenture holder can exchange a bond for 20 shares of common stock. Therefore, the conversion ratio, CR, is 20. The bond cost a purchaser $1,000, the par value, when it was issued. Dividing the $1,000 par value by the 20 shares received gives a conversion price of $50 a share:

$$\text{Conversion price} = P_c = \frac{\text{Par value of bond given up}}{\text{Shares received}} \quad \text{(21-2)}$$

$$= \frac{\$1,000}{\text{CR}} = \frac{\$1,000}{20} = \$50.$$

Conversely, by solving for CR, we obtain the conversion ratio:

$$\text{Conversion ratio} = \text{CR} = \frac{\$1,000}{P_c} \quad \text{(21-3)}$$

$$= \frac{\$1,000}{\$50} = 20 \text{ shares.}$$

Once CR is set, the value of P_c is established, and vice versa.

Like a warrant's exercise price, the conversion price is typically set some 20% to 30% above the prevailing market price of the common stock on the issue date. Generally, the conversion price and conversion ratio are fixed for the life of the bond, although sometimes a stepped-up conversion price is used. For example, the 2007 convertible debentures for Breedon Industries are convertible into 12.5 shares until 2016; into 11.76 shares from 2017 until 2027; and into 11.11 shares from 2027 until maturity in 2037. The conversion price thus starts at $80, rises to $85, and then goes to $90. Breedon's convertibles, like most, have a 10-year call-protection period.

Another factor that may cause a change in the conversion price and ratio is a standard feature of almost all convertibles—the clause protecting the convertible against dilution from stock splits, stock dividends, and the sale of common stock at prices below the conversion price. The typical provision states that if common stock is sold at a price below the conversion price, then the conversion price must be lowered (and the conversion ratio raised) to the price at which the new stock was issued. Also, if the stock is split, or if a stock dividend is declared, the conversion price must be lowered by the percentage amount of the stock dividend or split. For example, if Breedon Industries were to have a 2-for-1 stock split during the first 10 years of its convertible's life, the conversion ratio would automatically be adjusted from 12.5 to 25, and the conversion price lowered from $80 to $40. If this protection were not contained in the contract, a company could completely thwart conversion by the use of stock splits and stock dividends. Warrants are similarly protected against dilution.

The standard protection against dilution from selling new stock at prices below the conversion price can, however, get a company into trouble. For example, assume that Breedon's stock was selling for $65 per share at the time the convertible was issued. Further, suppose the market went sour, and Breedon's stock price dropped to $30 per share. If Breedon needed new equity to support operations, a new common stock sale would require the company to lower the conversion price on the convertible debentures from $80 to $30. That would raise the value of the convertibles and, in effect, transfer wealth from current shareholders to the convertible holders. This transfer would, de facto, amount to an additional flotation cost on the new common stock. Potential problems such as this must be kept in mind by firms considering the use of convertibles or bonds with warrants.

The Component Cost of Convertibles

In the spring of 2007, Silicon Valley Software was evaluating the use of the convertible bond issue described earlier. The issue would consist of 20-year convertible bonds that would sell at a price of $1,000 per bond; this $1,000 would also be the bond's par (and maturity) value. The bonds would pay a 10% annual coupon interest rate, or $100 per year. Each bond would be convertible into 20 shares of stock, so the conversion price would be $1,000/20 = $50. The stock was expected to pay a dividend of $2.80 during the coming year, and it sold at $35 per share. Further, the stock price was expected to grow at a constant rate of 8% per year. Therefore, $\hat{r}_s = D_1/P_0 + g = \$2.80/\$35 + 8\% = 8\% + 8\% = 16\%$. If the bonds were not made convertible, they would have to provide a yield of 13%, given their risk and the general level of interest rates. The convertible bonds would not be callable for 10 years, after which they could be called at a price of $1,050, with this price declining by $5 per year thereafter. If, after 10 years, the conversion value exceeds the call price by at least 20%, management will probably call the bonds.[10]

Figure 21-1 shows the expectations of both an average investor and the company.[11]

FM

e-resource

See *FM12 Ch 21 Tool Kit.xls* at the textbook's Web site for details.

---

[10]For a more detailed discussion of call strategies, see **Web Extension 21A** at the textbook's Web site.
[11]For a more complete discussion of how the terms of a convertible offering are determined, see M. Wayne Marr and G. Rodney Thompson, "The Pricing of New Convertible Bond Issues," *Financial Management*, Summer 1984, pp. 31–37.

Figure 21-1

Silicon Valley Software: Convertible Bond Model

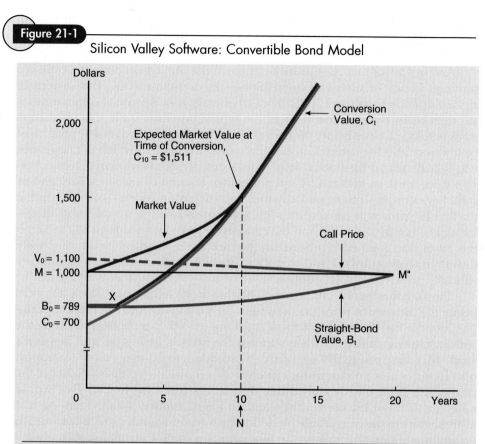

Year	Straight-Bond Value, B_t	Conversion Value, C_t	Maturity Value, M	Market Value	Floor Value	Premium
0	$ 789	$ 700	$1,000	$1,000	$ 789	$211
1	792	756	1,000	1,023	792	231
2	795	816	1,000	1,071	816	255
3	798	882	1,000	1,147	882	265
4	802	952	1,000	1,192	952	240
5	806	1,029	1,000	1,241	1,029	212
6	811	1,111	1,000	1,293	1,111	182
7	816	1,200	1,000	1,344	1,200	144
8	822	1,296	1,000	1,398	1,296	102
9	829	1,399	1,000	1,453	1,399	54
10	837	1,511	1,000	1,511	1,511	0
11	846	1,632	1,000	1,632	1,632	0
.	.	.	.	.	.	.
.	.	.	.	.	.	.
.	.	.	.	.	.	.
20	1,000	3,263	1,000	3,263	3,263	0

1. The horizontal line at M = $1,000 represents the par (and maturity) value. Also, $1,000 is the price at which the bond is initially offered to the public.
2. The bond is protected against a call for 10 years. It is initially callable at a price of $1,050, and the call price declines thereafter by $5 per year. Thus, the call price is represented by the solid section of the line V_0M''.
3. Since the convertible has a 10% coupon rate, and since the yield on a nonconvertible bond of similar risk is 13%, the expected "straight-bond" value of the convertible, B_t, must be less than par. At the time of issue, assuming an annual coupon, B_0 is $789:

$$\begin{matrix} \text{Pure-debt value} \\ \text{at time of issue} \end{matrix} = B_0 = \sum_{t=1}^{N} \frac{\text{Coupon interest}}{(1 + r_d)^t} + \frac{\text{Maturity value}}{(1 + r_d)^N} \qquad \textbf{(21-4)}$$

$$= \sum_{t=1}^{20} \frac{\$100}{(1.13)^t} + \frac{\$1,000}{(1.13)^{20}} = \$789.$$

Note, however, that the bond's straight-debt value must be $1,000 at maturity, so the straight-debt value rises over time. B_t follows the line B_0M'' in the graph.

4. The bond's initial **conversion value, C_t,** or the value of the stock an investor would receive if the bonds were converted at t = 0, is $P_0(CR) = \$35(20 \text{ shares}) = \$700$. Since the stock price is expected to grow at an 8% rate, the conversion value should rise over time. For example, in Year 5 it should be $P_5(CR) = \$35(1.08)^5(20) = \$1,029$. The conversion value given the expected stock price over time is given by the line C_t in Figure 21-1.

5. The actual market price of the bond can never fall below the higher of its straight-debt value or its conversion value. If the market price dropped below the straight-bond value, those who wanted bonds would recognize the bargain and buy the convertible as a bond. Similarly, if the market price dropped below the conversion value, people would buy the convertibles, exercise them to get stock, and then sell the stock at a profit. Therefore, the higher of the bond value and conversion value curves in the graph represents a *floor price* for the bond. In Figure 21-1, the floor price is represented by the thicker shaded line B_0XC_t.

6. The bond's market value will typically exceed its floor value. It will exceed the straight-bond value because the option to convert is worth something—a 10% bond with conversion possibilities is worth more than a 10% bond without this option. The convertible's price will also exceed its conversion value because holding the convertible is equivalent to holding a call option, and, prior to expiration, the option's true value is higher than its exercise (or conversion) value. We cannot say exactly where the market value line will lie, but as a rule it will be at or above the floor set by the straight-bond and conversion value lines.

7. At some point, the market value line will converge with the conversion value line. This convergence will occur for two reasons. First, the stock should pay higher and higher dividends as the years go by, but the interest payments on the convertible are fixed. For example, Silicon's convertibles would pay $100 in interest annually, while the dividends on the 20 shares received upon conversion would initially be 20($2.80) = $56. However, at an 8% growth rate, the

dividends after 10 years would be up to $120.90, but the interest would still be $100. Thus, rising dividends will push against the fixed interest payments, causing the premium to disappear and investors to convert voluntarily. Second, once the bond becomes callable, its market value cannot exceed the higher of the conversion value and the call price without exposing investors to the danger of a call. For example, suppose that 10 years after issue (when the bonds become callable), the market value of the bond is $1,600, the conversion value is $1,500, and the call price is $1,050. If the company called the bonds the day after you bought 10 bonds for $16,000, you would be forced to convert into stock worth only $15,000, so you would suffer a loss of $100 per bond, or $1,000, in one day. Recognizing this danger, you and other investors would simply not pay a premium over the higher of the call price or the conversion value after the bond becomes callable. Therefore, in Figure 21-1, we assume that the market value line hits the conversion value line in Year 10, when the bond becomes callable.

8. Let N represent the year when investors expect conversion to occur, either voluntarily because of rising dividends or because the company calls the convertibles to strengthen its balance sheet by substituting equity for debt. In our example, we assume that $N = 10$, the first call date.

9. Since $N = 10$, the expected market value at Year 10 is $\$35(1.08)^{10} \times (20) = \$1,511$. An investor can find the expected rate of return on the convertible bond, r_c, by finding the IRR of the following cash flow stream:

0	1		9	10
−$1,000	+$100	...	+$100	+$ 100
				+ 1,511
				+$1,611

The solution is $r_c = \text{IRR} = 12.8\%$.[12]

10. The return on a convertible is expected to come partly from interest income and partly from capital gains; in this case, the total expected return is 12.8%, with 10% representing interest income and 2.8% representing the expected capital gain. The interest component is relatively assured, while the capital gain component is more risky. Therefore, a convertible's expected return is more risky than that of a straight bond. This leads us to conclude that r_c should be larger than the cost of straight debt, r_d. Thus, it would seem that the expected rate of return on Silicon's convertibles, r_c, should lie between its cost of straight debt, $r_d = 13\%$, and its cost of common stock, $r_s = 16\%$.

11. Investment bankers use the type of model described here, plus a knowledge of the market, to set the terms on convertibles (the conversion ratio, coupon interest rate, and years of call protection) such that the security will just "clear

[12]As in the case with warrants, the expected conversion value is not precisely equal to the expected stock price multiplied by the conversion ratio. Here is the reason. If after 10 years the stock price happens to be low so that the conversion value is less than the call price, then the bondholders would not choose to convert—instead, they would surrender their bonds if the company called them. In this example, nonconversion occurs if the stock price after 10 years is less than $1,050/20 = $52.50. Since the company makes a call to force conversion, the company won't call the bonds if the stock price is less than $52.50. Therefore, when there is a low stock price, the bondholders will keep the bonds, whose value will depend primarily on interest rates at that time. Finding the expected value in this situation is a very difficult problem (and is beyond the scope of this text)! However, if the expected stock price is much greater than the conversion price when the bonds are called (in this case, $35[1.08]^{10} = $75.56 is much bigger than $52.50), the difference between the true expected conversion value and the conversion value that we calculated using the expected stock price will be very small. Therefore, we can estimate the component cost very accurately using the approach in the example.

the market" at its $1,000 offering price. In our example, the required conditions do not hold—the calculated rate of return on the convertible is only 12.8%, which is less than the 13% cost of straight debt. Therefore, the terms on the bond would have to be made more attractive to investors. Silicon Valley Software would have to increase the coupon interest rate on the convertible above 10%, raise the conversion ratio above 20 (and thereby lower the conversion price from $50 to a level closer to the current $35 market price of the stock), lengthen the call-protected period, or use a combination of these changes such that the resulting expected rate of return on the convertible is between 13% and 16%.[13]

Use of Convertibles in Financing

Convertibles have two important advantages from the issuer's standpoint: (1) Convertibles, like bonds with warrants, offer a company the chance to sell debt with a low interest rate in exchange for giving bondholders a chance to participate in the company's success if it does well. (2) In a sense, convertibles provide a way to sell common stock at prices higher than those currently prevailing. Some companies actually want to sell common stock, not debt, but feel that the price of their stock is temporarily depressed. Management may know, for example, that earnings are depressed because of start-up costs associated with a new project, but they expect earnings to rise sharply during the next year or so, pulling the price of the stock up with them. Thus, if the company sold stock now, it would be giving up more shares than necessary to raise a given amount of capital. However, if it set the conversion price 20% to 30% above the present market price of the stock, then 20% to 30% fewer shares would be given up when the bonds were converted than if stock were sold directly at the current time. Note, however, that management is counting on the stock's price to rise above the conversion price to make the bonds attractive in conversion. If earnings do not rise and pull the stock price up, hence conversion does not occur, then the company will be saddled with debt in the face of low earnings, which could be disastrous.

How can the company be sure that conversion will occur if the price of the stock rises above the conversion price? Typically, convertibles contain a call provision that enables the issuing firm to force holders to convert. Suppose the conversion price is $50, the conversion ratio is 20, the market price of the common stock has risen to $60, and the call price on a convertible bond is $1,050. If the company calls the bond, bondholders can either convert into common stock with a market value of 20($60) = $1,200 or allow the company to redeem the bond for $1,050. Naturally, bondholders prefer $1,200 to $1,050, so conversion would occur. The call provision thus gives the company a way to force conversion, provided the market price of the stock is greater than the conversion price. Note, however, that most convertibles have a fairly long period of call protection—10 years is typical. Therefore, if the company wants to be able to force conversion fairly early, then it will have to set a short call-protection period. This will, in turn, require that it set a higher coupon rate or a lower conversion price.

From the standpoint of the issuer, convertibles have three important disadvantages: (1) Although the use of a convertible bond may give the company the

---

[13]In this discussion, we ignore the tax advantages to investors associated with capital gains. In some situations, tax effects could result in r_c being less than r_d.

opportunity to sell stock at a price higher than the price at which it could be sold currently, if the stock greatly increases in price, the firm would have been better off if it had used straight debt in spite of its higher cost and then later sold common stock and refunded the debt. (2) Convertibles typically have a low coupon interest rate, and the advantage of this low-cost debt will be lost when conversion occurs. (3) If the company truly wants to raise equity capital, and if the price of the stock does not rise sufficiently after the bond is issued, then the company will be stuck with debt.

Convertibles and Agency Costs

A potential agency conflict between bondholders and stockholders is asset substitution, also known as "bait and switch." Suppose a company has been investing in low-risk projects, and because risk is low, bondholders charge a low interest rate. What happens if the company is considering a very risky but highly profitable venture, but potential lenders don't know about it? The company might decide to raise low-interest-rate debt without spelling out that the funds will be invested in the risky project. After the funds have been raised and the investment is made, the value of the debt should fall because its interest rate will be too low to compensate debtholders for the high risk they bear. This is a "heads I win, tails you lose" situation, and it results in a wealth transfer from bondholders to stockholders.

Let's use some numbers to illustrate this scenario. The value of a company, based on the present value of its future free cash flows, is $800 million. It has $300 million of debt, based on market value. Therefore, its equity is worth $800 − $300 = $500 million. The company now undertakes some very risky projects, with high but risky expected returns, and its expected NPV remains unchanged. In other words, the actual NPV will probably end up much higher or much lower than under the old situation, but the firm still has the same expected value. Even though its total value is still $800 million, the value of the debt falls because its risk has increased. Note that the debtholders don't benefit if the venture's value is higher than expected, because the most they can receive is the contracted coupon and the principal repayment. However, they will suffer if the value of the projects turns out to be lower than expected, since they might not receive the full value of their contracted payments. In other words, risk doesn't give them any upside potential, but it does expose them to downside losses, so the bondholders' expected value must decline.

With a constant total firm value, if the value of the debt falls from $300 to $200 million, then the value of equity must increase from $500 to $800 − $200 = $600 million. Thus, the bait-and-switch tactic causes a wealth transfer of $100 million from debtholders to stockholders.

If debtholders think that a company might employ the bait-and-switch tactic, they will charge a higher interest rate, and this higher interest rate is an agency cost. Debtholders will charge this higher rate even if the company has no intention of engaging in bait-and-switch behavior, since they don't know the company's true intentions. Therefore, they assume the worst and charge a higher interest rate.

Convertible securities are one way to mitigate this type of agency cost. Suppose the debt is convertible and the company does take on the high-risk project. If the value of the company turns out to be higher than expected, then bondholders can convert their debt to equity and benefit from the successful investment.

Therefore, bondholders are willing to charge a lower interest rate on convertibles, which serves to minimize the agency costs.

Note that if a company does not engage in bait-and-switch behavior by swapping low-risk projects for high-risk projects, the chance of hitting a home run is reduced. Because there is less chance of a home run, the convertible bond is less likely to be converted. In this situation the convertible bonds are actually similar to nonconvertible debt, except that they carry a lower interest rate.

Now consider a different agency cost, one due to asymmetric information between the managers and potential new stockholders. Suppose its managers know that a company's future prospects are not as good as the market believes, which means that the current stock price is too high. Acting in the interests of existing stockholders, managers can issue stock at the current high price. When the poor future prospects are eventually revealed, the stock price will fall, causing a transfer of wealth from the new shareholders to old shareholders.

To illustrate this, suppose the market estimates an $800 million present value of future free cash flows. For simplicity, assume that the firm has no nonoperating assets and no debt, so the total value of both the firm and the equity is $800 million. However, its managers know that the market has overestimated the future free cash flows, and the true value is only $700 million. When investors eventually discover this, the value of the company will drop to $700 million. But before this happens, suppose the company raises $200 million of new equity. The company uses this new cash to invest in projects with a present value of $200 million, which shouldn't be too hard, since these are projects with a zero NPV. Right after the new stock is sold, the company will have a market value of $800 + $200 = $1,000 million, based on the market's overly optimistic estimate of the company's future prospects. Note that the new shareholders own 20% of the company ($200/$1,000 = 0.20), and the original shareholders own 80%.

As time passes, the market will realize that the previously estimated value of $800 million for the company's original set of projects was too high, and that these projects are worth only $700 million. The new projects are still worth $200 million, so the total value of the company will fall to $700 + $200 = $900 million. The original shareholders' value is now 80% of $900 million, which is $720 million. Note that this is $20 million higher than it would have been if the company had issued no new stock. The new shareholders' value is now 0.20($900) = $180 million, which is $20 million less than their original investment. The net effect is a $20 million wealth transfer from the new shareholders to the original shareholders.

Because potential shareholders know this might occur, they interpret an issue of new stock as a signal of poor future prospects, which causes the stock price to fall. Note also that this will occur even for companies whose future prospects are actually quite good, because the market has no way of distinguishing between companies with good versus poor prospects.

A company with good future prospects might want to issue equity, but it knows the market will interpret this as a negative signal. One way to obtain equity and yet avoid this signaling effect is to issue convertible bonds. Because the company knows its true future prospects are better than the market anticipates, it knows that the bonds will likely end up being converted to equity. Thus, a company in this situation is issuing equity through the back door when it issues convertible debt.

In summary, convertibles are logical securities to use in at least two situations. First, if a company would like to finance with straight debt, but lenders are afraid the funds will be invested in a manner that increases the firm's risk profile, then convertibles are a good choice. Second, if a company wants to issue stock but thinks such a move would cause investors to interpret a stock offering as a signal of tough times ahead, then again convertibles would be a good choice.[14]

SELF-TEST

What is a conversion ratio? A conversion price? A straight-bond value?

What is meant by a convertible's floor value?

What are the advantages and disadvantages of convertibles to issuers? To investors?

How do convertibles reduce agency costs?

A convertible bond has a par value of $1,000 and a conversion price of $25. The stock currently trades for $22 a share. What are the bond's conversion ratio and conversion value at t = 0? (40; $880)

21.4 A Final Comparison of Warrants and Convertibles

Convertible debt can be thought of as straight debt with nondetachable warrants. Thus, at first blush, it might appear that debt with warrants and convertible debt are more or less interchangeable. However, a closer look reveals one major and several minor differences between these two securities.[15] First, as we discussed previously, the exercise of warrants brings in new equity capital, while the conversion of convertibles results only in an accounting transfer.

A second difference involves flexibility. Most convertibles contain a call provision that allows the issuer either to refund the debt or to force conversion, depending on the relationship between the conversion value and call price. However, most warrants are not callable, so firms must wait until maturity for the warrants to generate new equity capital. Generally, maturities also differ between warrants and convertibles. Warrants typically have much shorter maturities than convertibles, and warrants typically expire before their accompanying debt matures. Further, warrants provide for fewer future common shares than do convertibles, because with convertibles all of the debt is converted to stock whereas debt remains outstanding when warrants are exercised. Together, these facts suggest that debt-plus-warrant issuers are actually more interested in selling debt than in selling equity.

In general, firms that issue debt with warrants are smaller and riskier than those that issue convertibles. One possible rationale for the use of option securities, especially the use of debt with warrants by small firms, is the difficulty investors have in assessing the risk of small companies. If a start-up with a new, untested product seeks debt financing, it is very difficult for potential lenders to judge the riskiness of the venture; hence it is difficult to set a fair interest rate. Under these circumstances, many potential investors will be reluctant to invest,

---

[14]See Craig M. Lewis, Richard J. Rogalski, and James K. Seward, "Understanding the Design of Convertible Debt," *Journal of Applied Corporate Finance,* Vol. 11, no. 1 (Spring 1998), pp. 45–53. For more insights into convertible pricing and use, see Paul Asquith and David W. Mullins, Jr., "Convertible Debt: Corporate Call Policy and Voluntary Conversion," *Journal of Finance,* September 1991, pp. 1273–1289; Randall S. Billingsley and David M. Smith, "Why Do Firms Issue Convertible Debt?" *Financial Management,* Summer 1996, pp. 93–99; Douglas R. Emery, Mai E. Iskandor-Datta, and Jong-Chul Rhim, "Capital Structure Management as a Motivation for Calling Convertible Debt," *Journal of Financial Research,* Spring 1994, pp. 91–104; T. Harikumar, P. Kadapakkam, and Ronald F. Singer, "Convertible Debt and Investment Incentives," *Journal of Financial Research,* Spring 1994, pp. 15–29; Vahan Janjigian, "The Leverage Changing Consequences of Convertible Debt Financing," *Financial Management,* Autumn 1987, pp. 15–21; and V. Sivarama Krishnan and Ramesh P. Rao, "Financial Distress Costs and Delayed Calls of Convertible Bonds," *Financial Review,* November 1996, pp. 913–925.

[15]For a more detailed comparison of warrants and convertibles, see Michael S. Long and Stephen F. Sefcik, "Participation Financing: A Comparison of the Characteristics of Convertible Debt and Straight Bonds Issued in Conjunction with Warrants," *Financial Management,* Autumn 1990, pp. 23–34.

making it necessary to set a very high interest rate to attract debt capital. By issuing debt with warrants, investors obtain a package that offers upside potential to off-set the risks of loss.

Finally, there is a significant difference in issuance costs between debt with warrants and convertible debt. Bonds with warrants typically require issuance costs that are about 1.2 percentage points more than the flotation costs for convert-ibles. In general, bond-with-warrant financings have underwriting fees that approximate the weighted average of the fees associated with debt and equity issues, while underwriting costs for convertibles are more like those associated with straight debt.

SELF-TEST

What are some differences between debt-with-warrant financing and convertible debt? Explain how bonds with warrants might help small, risky firms sell debt securities.

21.5 Reporting Earnings When Warrants or Convertibles Are Outstanding

If warrants or convertibles are outstanding, a firm could theoretically report earn-ings per share in one of three ways:

1. *Basic EPS*, calculated as earnings available to common stockholders divided by the average number of shares actually outstanding during the period.
2. *Primary EPS*, calculated as earnings available divided by the average number of shares that would have been outstanding if warrants and convertibles "likely to be converted in the near future" had actually been exercised or con-verted. In calculating primary EPS, earnings are first adjusted by "backing out" the interest on the convertibles, after which the adjusted earnings are divided by the adjusted number of shares. Accountants have a formula that basically compares the conversion or strike (or exercise) price with the actual market value of the stock to determine the likelihood of conversion when deciding on the need to use this adjustment procedure.
3. *Diluted EPS*, which is similar to primary EPS except that *all* warrants and con-vertibles are assumed to be exercised or converted, regardless of the likeli-hood of exercise or conversion.

Under SEC rules, firms are required to report both basic and diluted EPS. For firms with large amounts of option securities outstanding, there can be a substan-tial difference between the basic and diluted EPS figures. For financial statement purposes, firms reported diluted EPS until 1997, when the Financial Accounting Standards Board (FASB) changed to basic EPS. According to FASB, the change was made to give investors a simpler picture of a company's underlying performance. Also, the change makes it easier for investors to compare the performance of U.S. firms with their foreign counterparts, which tend to use basic EPS.[16]

---

[16]As part of the FASB's short-term convergence project with the IASB to improve financial reporting in the United States while concurrently eliminating individual differences between U.S. GAAP and international financial reporting standards, the FASB is expected to issue a final statement making additional changes to FASB #128 (issued in February 1997), which is the basis for the discussion in this section.

SELF-TEST

What are the three possible methods for reporting EPS when warrants and convertibles are outstanding? Which methods are most used in practice?

Why should investors be concerned about a firm's outstanding warrants and convertibles?

Summary

While common stock and long-term debt provide most of the capital used by corporations, companies also use several forms of "hybrid securities." The hybrids include preferred stock, convertibles, and warrants, and they generally have some characteristics of debt and some of equity. We discussed the pros and cons of the hybrids from the standpoints of both issuers and investors, how to determine when to use them, and the factors that affect their values. The basic rationale for these securities, and the procedures used to evaluate them, are based on concepts developed in earlier chapters. The key concepts covered are listed below:

- **Preferred** stock is a hybrid—it is similar to bonds in some respects and to common stock in other ways.
- **Adjustable rate preferred stocks (ARPs)** are those whose dividends are tied to the rate on Treasury securities. **Market auction (money market) preferred** is a low-risk, largely tax-exempt, 7-week-maturity security that can be sold between auction dates at close to par.
- A **warrant** is a long-term call option issued along with a bond. Warrants are generally detachable from the bond, and they trade separately in the market. When warrants are exercised, the firm receives additional equity capital, and the original bonds remain outstanding.
- A **convertible** security is a bond or preferred stock that can be exchanged for common stock at the option of the holder. When a security is converted, debt or preferred stock is replaced with common stock, and no money changes hands.
- Warrant and convertible issues are generally structured so that the **strike (exercise) price** or **conversion price** is 20% to 30% above the stock's price at time of issue.
- Although both warrants and convertibles are option securities, there are several differences between the two, including **separability, impact when exercised, callability, maturity,** and **flotation costs.**
- Warrants and convertibles are **sweeteners** used to make the underlying debt or preferred stock issue more attractive to investors. Although the coupon rate or dividend yield is lower when options are part of the issue, the overall cost of the issue is higher than the cost of straight debt or preferred, because option-related securities are riskier.

Questions

(21-1) Define each of the following terms.
a. Preferred stock
b. Cumulative dividends; arrearages

    c. Warrant; detachable warrant
    d. Stepped-up price
    e. Convertible security
    f. Conversion ratio; conversion price; conversion value
    g. Sweetener

(21-2) Is preferred stock more like bonds or common stock? Explain.

(21-3) What effect does the trend in stock prices (subsequent to issue) have on a firm's ability to raise funds through (a) convertibles and (b) warrants?

(21-4) If a firm expects to have additional financial requirements in the future, would you recommend that it use convertibles or bonds with warrants? What factors would influence your decision?

(21-5) How does a firm's dividend policy affect each of the following?
    a. The value of its long-term warrants
    b. The likelihood that its convertible bonds will be converted
    c. The likelihood that its warrants will be exercised

(21-6) Evaluate the following statement: "Issuing convertible securities represents a means by which a firm can sell common stock at a price above the existing market."

(21-7) Why do corporations often sell convertibles on a rights basis?

(21-8) Suppose a company simultaneously issues $50 million of convertible bonds with a coupon rate of 10% and $50 million of straight bonds with a coupon rate of 14%. Both bonds have the same maturity. Does the fact that the convertible issue has the lower coupon rate suggest that it is less risky than the straight bond? Is the cost of capital lower on the convertible than on the straight bond? Explain.

Self-Test Problem   Solution Appears in Appendix A

(ST-1)
Warrants
    Connor Company recently issued two types of bonds. The first issue consisted of 10-year straight debt with a 6% annual coupon. The second issue consisted of 10-year bonds with a 4.5% annual coupon and attached warrants. Both issues sold at their $1,000 par values. What is the implied value of the warrants attached to each bond?

Problems   Answers Appear in Appendix B

**Easy
Problems 1–2**

(21-1)
Warrants
    Gregg Company recently issued two types of bonds. The first issue consisted of 20-year straight debt with an 8% annual coupon. The second issue consisted of 20-year bonds with a 6% annual coupon and attached warrants. Both issues sold

at their $1,000 par values. What is the implied value of the warrants attached to each bond?

(21-2)
Convertibles

Peterson Securities recently issued convertible bonds with a $1,000 par value. The bonds have a conversion price of $40 a share. What is the convertible issue's conversion ratio?

Intermediate
Problems 3–4

(21-3)
Warrants

Maese Industries Inc. has warrants outstanding that permit the holders to purchase 1 share of stock per warrant at a price of $25.

    a. Calculate the exercise value of the firm's warrants if the common sells at each of the following prices: (1) $20, (2) $25, (3) $30, (4) $100. (Hint: A warrant's exercise value is the difference between the stock price and the purchase price specified by the warrant if the warrant were to be exercised.)

    b. At what approximate price do you think the warrants would actually sell under each condition indicated above? What time value (price minus exercise value) is implied in your price? Your answer is a guess, but your prices and time values should bear reasonable relationships to one another.

    c. How would each of the following factors affect your estimates of the warrants' prices and time values in part b?

       (1) The life of the warrant

       (2) Expected variability (σ_p) in the stock's price

       (3) The expected growth rate in the stock's EPS

       (4) The company announces a change in dividend policy: whereas it formerly paid no dividends, henceforth it will pay out all earnings as dividends.

    d. Assume the firm's stock now sells for $20 per share. The company wants to sell some 20-year, annual interest, $1,000 par value bonds. Each bond will have attached 50 warrants, each exercisable into 1 share of stock at an exercise price of $25. The firm's straight bonds yield 12%. Regardless of your answer to part b, assume that each warrant will have a market value of $3 when the stock sells at $20. What coupon interest rate, and dollar coupon, must the company set on the bonds with warrants if they are to clear the market?

(21-4)
Convertible Premiums

The Tsetsekos Company was planning to finance an expansion. The principal executives of the company all agreed that an industrial company such as theirs should finance growth by means of common stock rather than by debt. However, they felt that the price of the company's common stock did not reflect its true worth, so they decided to sell a convertible security. They considered a convertible debenture but feared the burden of fixed interest charges if the common stock did not rise in price to make conversion attractive. They decided on an issue of convertible preferred stock, which would pay a dividend of $2.10 per share.

The common stock was selling for $42 a share at the time. Management projected earnings for 2006 at $3 a share and expected a future growth rate of 10%. It was agreed by the investment bankers and the management that the common stock would sell at 14 times earnings, the current price/earnings ratio.

    a. The conversion ratio will be 1.0; that is, each share of convertible preferred can be converted into 1 share of common. Therefore, the convertible's par value (and also the issue price) will be equal to the conversion price, which, in turn, will be determined as a premium (i.e., the percentage by which the conversion price exceeds the stock price) over the current market price of the common stock. What will the conversion price be if it is set at a 10% premium? What will the conversion price be if it is set at a 30% premium?

b. Should the preferred stock include a call provision? Why?

Challenging Problems 5–7

(21-5)
Convertible Bond Analysis

Fifteen years ago, Roop Industries sold $400 million of convertible bonds. The bonds had a 40-year maturity, a 5.75% coupon rate, and paid interest annually. They were sold at their $1,000 par value. The conversion price was set at $62.75; the common stock price was $55 per share. The bonds were subordinated debentures, and they were given an A rating; straight nonconvertible debentures of the same quality yielded about 8.75% at the time Roop's bonds were issued.

a. Calculate the premium on the bonds, that is, the percentage excess of the conversion price over the stock price at the time of issue.

b. What is Roop's annual before-tax interest savings on the convertible issue versus a straight-debt issue?

c. At the time the bonds were issued, what was the value per bond of the conversion feature?

d. Suppose the price of Roop's common stock fell from $55 on the day the bonds were issued to $32.75 now, 15 years after the issue date (also assume that the stock price never exceeded $62.75). Assume interest rates remained constant. What is the current price of the straight bond portion of the convertible bond? What is the current value if a bondholder converts a bond? Do you think it is likely that the bonds will be converted?

e. The bonds originally sold for $1,000. If interest rates on A-rated bonds had remained constant at 8.75% and the stock price had fallen to $32.75, what do you think would have happened to the price of the convertible bonds? (Assume no change in the standard deviation of stock returns.)

f. Now suppose the price of Roop's common stock had fallen from $55 on the day the bonds were issued to $32.75 at present, 15 years after the issue. Suppose also that the rate of interest had fallen from 8.75% to 5.75%. Under these conditions, what is the current price of the straight bond portion of the convertible bond? What is the current value if a bondholder converts a bond? What do you think would have happened to the price of the bonds?

(21-6)
Warrant/Convertible Decisions

The Howland Carpet Company has grown rapidly during the past 5 years. Recently, its commercial bank urged the company to consider increasing its permanent financing. Its bank loan under a line of credit has risen to $250,000, carrying an 8% interest rate. Howland has been 30 to 60 days late in paying trade creditors.

Discussions with an investment banker have resulted in the decision to raise $500,000 at this time. Investment bankers have assured the firm that the following alternatives are feasible (flotation costs will be ignored):

- *Alternative 1:* Sell common stock at $8.
- *Alternative 2:* Sell convertible bonds at an 8% coupon, convertible into 100 shares of common stock for each $1,000 bond (that is, the conversion price is $10 per share).
- *Alternative 3:* Sell debentures at an 8% coupon, each $1,000 bond carrying 100 warrants to buy common stock at $10.

John L. Howland, the president, owns 80% of the common stock and wishes to maintain control of the company. One hundred thousand shares are outstanding. The following are extracts of Howland's latest financial statements:

Balance Sheet

			Current liabilities	$400,000
			Common stock, par $1	100,000
			Retained earnings	50,000
Total assets		$550,000	Total claims	$550,000

Income Statement

Sales	$1,100,000
All costs except interest	990,000
EBIT	$ 110,000
Interest	20,000
EBT	$ 90,000
Taxes (40%)	36,000
Net income	$ 54,000
Shares outstanding	100,000
Earnings per share	$ 0.54
Price/earnings ratio	15.83×
Market price of stock	$ 8.55

a. Show the new balance sheet under each alternative. For Alternatives 2 and 3, show the balance sheet after conversion of the bonds or exercise of the warrants. Assume that half of the funds raised will be used to pay off the bank loan and half to increase total assets.

b. Show Mr. Howland's control position under each alternative, assuming that he does not purchase additional shares.

c. What is the effect on earnings per share of each alternative, if it is assumed that profits before interest and taxes will be 20% of total assets?

d. What will be the debt ratio (TL/TA) under each alternative?

e. Which of the three alternatives would you recommend to Howland, and why?

(21-7)
Convertible Bond
Analysis

Niendorf Incorporated needs to raise $25 million to construct production facilities for a new type of USB memory device. The firm's straight nonconvertible debentures currently yield 9%. Its stock sells for $23 per share and has an expected constant growth rate of 6%. Investment bankers have tentatively proposed that the firm raise the $25 million by issuing convertible debentures. These convertibles would have a $1,000 par value, carry a coupon rate of 8%, have a 20-year maturity, and be convertible into 35 shares of stock. Coupon payments would be made annually. The bonds would be noncallable for 5 years, after which they would be callable at a price of $1,075; this call price would decline by $5 per year in Year 6 and each year thereafter. For simplicity, assume that the bonds may be called or converted only at the end of a year, immediately after the coupon and dividend payments. Assume that management would call eligible bonds if the conversion value exceeded 20% of par value (not 20% of call price).

a. At what year do you expect the bonds will be forced into conversion with a call? What is the bond's value in conversion when it is converted at this time? What is the cash flow to the bondholder when it is converted at this time? (Hint: The cash flow includes the conversion value and the coupon payment, because the conversion is immediately after the coupon is paid.)

b. What is the expected rate of return (i.e., before-tax component cost) on the proposed convertible issue?

Spreadsheet Problem

(21-8)

Build a Model: Convertible Bond Analysis

e-resource

Start with the partial model in the file *FM12 Ch 21 P08 Build a Model.xls* from the textbook's Web site. Using the data from Problem 21-7, answer the following questions.

a. For each year, calculate (1) the anticipated stock price; (2) the anticipated conversion value; (3) the anticipated straight-bond price; and (4) the cash flow to the investor assuming conversion occurs. At what year do you expect the bonds will be forced into conversion with a call? What is the bond's value in conversion when it is converted at this time? What is the cash flow to the bondholder when it is converted at this time? (Hint: The cash flow includes the conversion value and the coupon payment, because the conversion is immediately after the coupon is paid.)

b. What is the expected rate of return (i.e., before-tax component cost) on the proposed convertible issue?

c. Assume that the convertible bondholders require a 12% rate of return. If the coupon rate is set at 8%, then what conversion ratio will give a bond price of $1,000? Given a conversion ratio of 35%, what coupon rate will give a bond price of $1,000?

Cyberproblem

e-resource

Please go to the textbook's Web site to access any Cyberproblems.

Mini Case

Paul Duncan, financial manager of EduSoft Inc., is facing a dilemma. The firm was founded 5 years ago to provide educational software for the rapidly expanding primary and secondary school markets. Although EduSoft has done well, the firm's founder believes that an industry shakeout is imminent. To survive, EduSoft must grab market share now, and this will require a large infusion of new capital.

Because he expects earnings to continue rising sharply and looks for the stock price to follow suit, Mr. Duncan does not think it would be wise to issue new common stock at this time. On the other hand, interest rates are currently high by historical standards, and with the firm's B rating, the interest payments on a new debt issue would be prohibitive. Thus, he has narrowed his choice of financing alternatives to two securities: (1) bonds with warrants or (2) convertible bonds. As Duncan's assistant, you have been asked to help in the decision process by answering the following questions:

a. How does preferred stock differ from both common equity and debt? Is preferred stock more risky than common stock? What is floating rate preferred stock?

b. How can a knowledge of call options help a financial manager to better understand warrants and convertibles?

c. One of the firm's alternatives is to issue a bond with warrants attached. EduSoft's current stock price is $20, and its investment banker estimates that the cost of a 20-year, annual coupon bond without warrants would be 10%. The bankers suggest attaching 45 warrants, each with an exercise price of $25, to each $1,000 bond. It is estimated that each warrant, when detached and traded separately, would have a value of $3.

   (1) What coupon rate should be set on the bond with warrants if the total package is to sell for $1,000?

   (2) Suppose the bonds were issued and the warrants immediately traded on the open market for $5 each. What would this imply about the terms of the issue? Did the company "win" or "lose"?

   (3) When would you expect the warrants to be exercised? Assume they have a 10-year life; that is, they expire 10 years after issue.

   (4) Will the warrants bring in additional capital when exercised? If so, how much, and what type of capital?

   (5) Because warrants lower the cost of the accompanying debt issue, shouldn't all debt be issued with warrants? What is the expected return to the holders of the bond with warrants (or the expected cost to the company) if the warrants are expected to be exercised in 10 years? EduSoft's stock price is currently $20 per share and is expected to grow at 8% per year. How would you expect the cost of the bond with warrants to compare with the cost of straight debt? With the cost of common stock?

d. As an alternative to the bond with warrants, Mr. Duncan is considering convertible bonds. The firm's investment bankers estimate that EduSoft could sell a 20-year, 8.5% annual coupon, callable convertible bond for its $1,000 par value, whereas a straight-debt issue would require a 10% coupon. The convertibles would be call protected for 5 years, the call price would be $1,100, and the company would probably call the bonds as soon as possible after their conversion value exceeds $1,200. Note, though, that the call must occur on an issue date anniversary. EduSoft's current stock price is $20, its last dividend was $1.00, and the dividend is expected to grow at a constant 8% rate. The convertible could be converted into 40 shares of EduSoft stock at the owner's option.

   (1) What conversion price is built into the bond?

   (2) What is the convertible's straight-debt value? What is the implied value of the convertibility feature?

   (3) What is the formula for the bond's expected conversion value in any year? What is its conversion value at Year 0? At Year 10?

   (4) What is meant by the "floor value" of a convertible? What is the convertible's expected floor value at Year 0? At Year 10?

   (5) Assume that EduSoft intends to force conversion by calling the bond as soon as possible after its conversion value exceeds 20% above its par value, or 1.2($1,000) = $1,200. When is the issue expected to be called?

(Hint: Recall that the call must be made on an anniversary date of the issue.)

(6) What is the expected cost of capital for the convertible to EduSoft? Does this cost appear to be consistent with the riskiness of the issue?

e. EduSoft's market value capital structure is as follows (in millions of dollars):

Debt	$ 50
Equity	50
	$100

If the company raises $20 million in additional capital by selling (1) convertibles or (2) bonds with warrants, what would its WACC be, and how would those figures compare with its current WACC? EduSoft's tax rate is 40%.

f. Mr. Duncan believes that the costs of both the bond with warrants and the convertible bond are close enough to one another to call them even, and also consistent with the risks involved. Thus, he will make his decision based on other factors. What are some of the factors that he should consider?

g. How do convertible bonds help reduce agency costs?

Selected Additional Cases

The following cases from Textchoice, Cengage *Learning's online library, cover many of the concepts discussed in this chapter and are available at **http://www.textchoice2.com.***

Klein-Brigham Series:
Case 27, "Virginia May Chocolate Company," which illustrates convertible bond valuation, and Case 98, "Levinger Organic Snack," which illustrates the use of convertibles warrants.

part 7

Special Topics

chapter 22

Working Capital Management

What do Qualcomm, Brightpoint, Quanex, Dell, 7 Eleven, and Best Buy have in common? Each of these companies led its industry in *CFO* magazine's latest annual survey of working capital management, which covered the 1,000 largest U.S. publicly traded firms. Each company is rated on the number of days tied up in working capital (DWC), defined as (Receivables + Inventory − Payables)/Daily sales.

The typical DWC ratio is about 55, but some companies have much lower ratios. For example, Dell, Apple Computer, and Anadarko Petroleum are among the relatively few companies that have negative DWC! This means that these companies have less in receivables and inventory than they do in payables. In other words, they get paid by their customers before they have to pay their suppliers, so their suppliers are in effect financing their operations.

How can a company drive its DWC down? Qualcomm focuses on continuous improvement in its working capital management. Due to a big improvement in the accuracy of its customer invoices and better training for its collections specialists, Qualcomm speeded up its collections and thus reduced its days sales outstanding from over 42 days to 35 days, a 19% improvement.

Brightpoint has taken a multi-pronged approach. With better processes to analyze its customers' credit risks, Brightpoint now has fewer slow-paying or uncollectable accounts. It has also installed supply-chain-management software that is used to pull its customers' sales data into its own system, which has helped lower its own inventory because it can now forecast its sales more accurately.

Nucor, one of the best in its industry at managing working capital, has tied bonuses to each business unit's return on assets. Lower working capital means a smaller asset base and a higher ROA, so Nucor's employees increase their take-home pay if they reduce working capital.

Keep these companies and their techniques in mind as you read this chapter.

Sources: Various issues of *CFO*, including an article by Randy Myers, "How Low Can It Go?" *CFO*, September 1, 2006. For an update on *CFO*'s survey, go to **http://www.cfo.com** and search for "working capital annual survey."

Working capital management involves two basic questions: (1) What is the appropriate amount of working capital, both in total and for each specific account, and (2) how should working capital be financed? Note that sound working capital management goes beyond finance. Indeed, the procedures for improving working capital management generally stem from other disciplines. For example, experts in logistics, operations management, and information technology often work with marketing people to develop better ways to deliver the firm's products. Also, engineers and production specialists develop ways to speed up the manufacturing process and thus reduce the goods-in-process inventory. Finance comes into play in evaluating how effective a firm's operating departments are in relation to others in its industry and in evaluating the profitability of alternative proposals made to improve working capital management. In addition, financial managers determine how much cash a company must keep on hand and how much short-term financing it should use.

e-resource

The textbook's Web site contains an *Excel* file that will guide you through the chapter's calculations. The file for this chapter is **FM12 Ch 22 Tool Kit.xls,** and we encourage you to open the file and follow along as you read the chapter.

Here are some basic definitions and concepts:

1. **Working capital,** sometimes called *gross working capital*, simply refers to current assets used in operations.
2. **Net working capital** is defined as current assets minus current liabilities.
3. **Net operating working capital (NOWC)** is defined as operating current assets minus operating current liabilities. Generally, NOWC is equal to cash, accounts receivable, and inventories, less accounts payable and accruals. Marketable securities and other short-term investments are generally not considered to be operating current assets, hence they are generally excluded when NOWC is calculated.

22.1 The Cash Conversion Cycle

Firms typically follow a cycle in which they purchase inventory, sell goods on credit, and then collect accounts receivable. This cycle is referred to as the *cash conversion cycle (CCC)*.

Calculating the CCC

Consider Real Time Computer Corporation (RTC), which in early 2007 introduced a new minicomputer that can perform 100 billion instructions per second and that

Corporate Valuation and Working Capital Management

Superior working capital management can dramatically reduce required investments in operations, which, in turn, can lead to larger free cash flows and greater firm value.

$$\text{Value} = \frac{\text{FCF}_1}{(1 + \text{WACC})^1} + \frac{\text{FCF}_2}{(1 + \text{WACC})^2} + \frac{\text{FCF}_3}{(1 + \text{WACC})^3} + \cdots + \frac{\text{FCF}_\infty}{(1 + \text{WACC})^\infty}$$

will sell for $250,000. RTC expects to sell 40 computers in its first year of production. The effects of this new product on RTC's working capital position were analyzed in terms of the following five steps:

1. RTC will order and then receive the materials it needs to produce the 40 computers it expects to sell. Because RTC and most other firms purchase materials on credit, this transaction will create an account payable. However, the purchase will have no immediate cash flow effect.
2. Labor will be used to convert the materials into finished computers. However, wages will not be fully paid at the time the work is done, so, like accounts payable, accrued wages will also build up.
3. The finished computers will be sold, but on credit. Therefore, sales will create receivables, not immediate cash inflows.
4. At some point before receivables are collected, RTC must pay off its accounts payable and accrued wages. This outflow must be financed.
5. The cycle will be completed when RTC's receivables have been collected. At that time, the company can pay off the credit that was used to finance production, and it can then repeat the cycle.

The **cash conversion cycle model,** which focuses on the length of time between when the company makes payments and when it receives cash inflows, formalizes the steps outlined above. The following terms are used in the model:

1. **Inventory conversion period,** which is the average time required to convert materials into finished goods and then to sell those goods. Note that the inventory conversion period is calculated by dividing inventory by sales per day. For example, if average inventories are $2 million and sales are $10 million, then the inventory conversion period is 73 days:

$$\text{Inventory conversion period} = \frac{\text{Inventory}}{\text{Sales per day}} \qquad (22\text{-}1)$$

$$= \frac{\$2,000,000}{\$10,000,000/365}$$

$$= 73 \text{ days.}$$

Thus, it takes an average of 73 days to convert materials into finished goods and then to sell those goods.[1]

2. **Receivables collection period,** which is the average length of time required to convert the firm's receivables into cash, that is, to collect cash following a sale. The receivables collection period is also called the *days sales outstanding (DSO),* and it is calculated by dividing accounts receivable by the average credit sales per day. If receivables are $657,534 and sales are $10 million, the receivables collection period is

---

[1]Some analysts define the inventory conversion period as inventory divided by daily cost of goods sold. However, most published sources use the formula we show in Equation 22-1. In addition, some analysts use a 360-day year; however, unless stated otherwise, we will base all our calculations on a 365-day year.

$$\text{Receivables collection period} = \text{DSO} = \frac{\text{Receivables}}{\text{Sales}/365} \qquad (22\text{-}2)$$

$$= \frac{\$657,534}{\$10,000,000/365}$$

$$= 24 \text{ days.}$$

Thus, it takes 24 days after a sale to convert the receivables into cash.

3. **Payables deferral period,** which is the average length of time between the purchase of materials and labor and the payment of cash for them. For example, if the firm on average has 30 days to pay for labor and materials, if its cost of goods sold is $8 million per year, and if its accounts payable average is $657,534, then its payables deferral period can be calculated as follows:

$$\text{Payables deferral period} = \frac{\text{Payables}}{\text{Purchases per day}}$$

$$= \frac{\text{Payables}}{\text{Cost of goods sold}/365} \qquad (22\text{-}3)$$

$$= \frac{\$657,534}{\$8,000,000/365}$$

$$= 30 \text{ days.}$$

The calculated figure is consistent with the stated 30-day payment period.[2]

4. **Cash conversion cycle,** which nets out the three periods just defined and therefore equals the length of time between the firm's actual cash expenditures to pay for productive resources (materials and labor) and its own cash receipts from the sale of products (that is, the length of time between paying for labor and materials and collecting on receivables). The cash conversion cycle thus equals the average length of time a dollar is tied up.

We can now use these definitions to analyze the cash conversion cycle. First, the concept is diagrammed in Figure 22-1. Each component is given a number, and the cash conversion cycle can be expressed by this equation:

$$
\begin{array}{ccccccc}
(1) & + & (2) & - & (3) & = & (4) \\
\text{Inventory} & & \text{Receivables} & & \text{Payables} & & \text{Cash} \\
\text{conversion} + & & \text{collection} & - & \text{deferral} & = & \text{conversion.} \\
\text{period} & & \text{period} & & \text{period} & & \text{cycle}
\end{array} \qquad (22\text{-}4)
$$

To illustrate, suppose it takes Real Time an average of 73 days to convert raw materials to computers and then to sell them, and another 24 days to collect on receivables. However, 30 days normally elapse between receipt of raw materials and payment for them. Therefore, the cash conversion cycle would be 67 days:

Days in cash conversion cycle = 73 days + 24 days − 30 days = 67 days.

---

[2]Some sources define the payables deferral period as payables divided by daily sales.

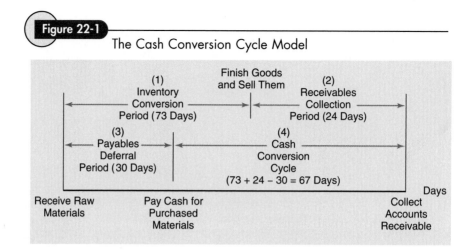

Figure 22-1

The Cash Conversion Cycle Model

To look at it another way,

$$\text{Cash inflow delay} - \text{Payment delay} = \text{Net delay}$$
$$(73 \text{ days} + 24 \text{ days}) - 30 \text{ days} = 67 \text{ days}.$$

Shortening the Cash Conversion Cycle

Given these data, RTC knows when it starts producing a computer that it will have to finance the manufacturing costs for a 67-day period. The firm's goal should be to shorten its cash conversion cycle as much as possible without hurting operations. This would increase RTC's value, because the shorter the cash conversion cycle, the lower the required net operating working capital and the higher the resulting free cash flow.

The cash conversion cycle can be shortened (1) by reducing the inventory conversion period by processing and selling goods more quickly, (2) by reducing the receivables collection period by speeding up collections, or (3) by lengthening the payables deferral period by slowing down the firm's own payments. To the extent that these actions can be taken *without increasing costs or depressing sales*, they should be carried out.

Benefits

We can illustrate the benefits of shortening the cash conversion cycle by looking again at Real Time Computer Corporation. As shown in Table 22-1, RTC currently has $2 million tied up in net operating working capital. Suppose RTC can improve its logistics and production processes so that its inventory conversion period drops to 65 days. The firm can also cut its receivable collection period to 23 days by billing customers daily rather than batching bills every other day as it now does. Finally, it can increase its payables deferral period by using remote disbursements, as discussed later in this chapter. Table 22-1 shows that the net effects of these improvements are a 10-day reduction in the cash conversion cycle and a $268,493 reduction in net operating capital.

Recall that free cash flow (FCF) is equal to NOPAT minus the net investments in operating capital. Therefore, if working capital decreases, FCF increases by that same amount. RTC's reduction in its cash conversion cycle would lead to a

Table 22-1

Benefits from Improving the Cash Conversion Cycle

	Original	Improved
Annual sales	$10,000,000	$10,000,000
Cost of goods sold (COGS)	8,000,000	8,000,000
Inventory conversion period (days)	73	65
Receivables collection period (days)	24	23
Payable deferral period (days)	(30)	(31)
Cash conversion cycle (days)	67	57
Inventory[a]	$ 2,000,000	$ 1,780,822
Receivables[b]	657,534	630,137
Payables[c]	(657,534)	(679,452)
Net operating working capital (NOWC)	$ 2,000,000	$ 1,731,507
Improvement in free cash flow = Original NOWC −		
Improved NOWC		$ 268,493

Notes:

[a]Inventory = (Inventory conversion period)(Sales/365)
[b]Receivables = (Receivables collection period)(Sales/365)
[c]Payables = (Payables deferral period)(COGS/365)

$268,493 increase in FCF. If sales stay at the same level, then the reduction in working capital would simply be a one-time cash inflow. However, suppose sales grow. When a company improves its working capital processes, they usually remain at their improved level. If the NOWC/Sales ratio remains at its new level, proportionately less working capital will be required to support the additional future sales, leading to an increase in projected FCF for each future year.

For example, if RTC's sales and costs increase next year by 10%, then its NOWC would also increase by 10%. Under the original working capital situation, the projected NOWC would be 1.10($2,000,000) = $2,200,000, which means RTC would have to make an investment of $2,200,000 − $2,000,000 = $200,000 in new working capital. Under the improved scenario, the projected NOWC would be 1.10($1,731,507) = $1,904,658. Its new projected investment is only $1,904,658 − $1,731,507 = $173,151, which is $26,849 less than was required under the original scenario ($2,000,000 − $1,731,507 = $268,493). As this example shows, not only does the improvement in working capital processes produce a one-time free cash flow of $268,493 at the time of the improvement, but it also leads to an improved FCF of $26,849 in the next year, with additional improvements in future years. Therefore, an improvement in working capital management is a gift that keeps on giving.

The combination of the one-time cash inflow and the long-term improvement in free cash flow can add substantial value to a company. Two professors, Hyun-Han Shin and Luc Soenen, studied more than 2,900 companies during a recent 20-year period and found a strong relationship between a company's cash conversion cycle and its performance.[3] In particular, their results show that for the average

---

[3]See Hyun-Han Shin and Luc Soenen, "Efficiency of Working Capital Management and Corporate Profitability," *Financial Practice and Education,* Fall/Winter 1998, pp. 37–45.

company a 10-day improvement in the cash conversion cycle was associated with an increase in pre-tax operating profit margin from 12.7% to 13.02%. They also demonstrated that companies with a cash conversion cycle 10 days shorter than average also had an annual stock return that was 1.7 percentage points higher than that of an average company, even after adjusting for differences in risk. Given results like these, it's no wonder firms now place so much emphasis on working capital management![4]

SELF-TEST

Define the following terms: inventory conversion period, receivables collection period, and payables deferral period. Give the equation for each term.

What is the cash conversion cycle? What is its equation?

What should a firm's goal be regarding the cash conversion cycle? Explain your answer.

What are some actions a firm can take to shorten its cash conversion cycle?

A company has $20 million in inventory, $5 million in receivables, and $4 million in payables. Its annual sales revenue is $80 million and its cost of goods sold is $60 million. What is its CCC? (89.73)

22.2 Alternative Net Operating Working Capital Policies

A **relaxed working capital policy** is one in which relatively large amounts of cash and inventories are carried, where sales are stimulated by the use of a credit policy that provides liberal financing to customers and a corresponding high level of receivables, and where a company doesn't take advantage of credit provided by accruals and accounts payable. Conversely, with a **restricted working capital policy,** the holdings of cash, inventories, and receivables are minimized, and accruals and payables are maximized. Under the restricted policy, NOWC is turned over more frequently, so each dollar of NOWC is forced to "work harder." A **moderate working capital policy** is between the two extremes.

Under conditions of certainty—when sales, costs, lead times, payment periods, and so on, are known for sure—all firms would hold only minimal levels of working capital. Any larger amounts would increase the need for external funding without a corresponding increase in profits, while any smaller holdings would involve late payments to suppliers along with lost sales due to inventory shortages and an overly restrictive credit policy.

However, the picture changes when uncertainty is introduced. Here the firm requires some minimum amount of cash and inventories based on expected payments, expected sales, expected order lead times, and so on, plus additional holdings, or *safety stocks*, which enable it to deal with departures from the expected values. Similarly, accounts receivable levels are determined by credit terms, and the tougher the credit terms, the lower the receivables for any given level of sales. With a restricted policy, the firm would hold minimal safety stocks of cash and inventories, and it would have a tight credit policy even though this meant running the risk of losing sales. A restricted, lean-and-mean working capital policy generally provides the highest expected return on this investment, but

---

[4]For more on the CCC, see James A. Gentry, R. Vaidyanathan, and Hei Wai Lee, "A Weighted Cash Conversion Cycle," *Financial Management*, Spring 1990, pp. 90–99.

it entails the greatest risk, while the reverse is true under a relaxed policy. The moderate policy falls in between the two extremes in terms of expected risk and return.

Recall that NOWC consists of cash, inventory, and accounts receivable, less accruals and accounts payable. Firms face a fundamental trade-off: Working capital is necessary to conduct business, and the greater the working capital, the smaller the danger of running short, hence the lower the firm's operating risk. However, holding working capital is costly—it reduces a firm's return on invested capital (ROIC), free cash flow, and value. The following sections discuss the individual components of NOWC.

SELF-TEST

Identify and explain three alternative working capital policies.

What are the principal components of net operating working capital?

What are the reasons for not wanting to hold too little working capital? For not wanting to hold too much?

22.3   Cash Management

Approximately 1.5% of the average industrial firm's assets are held in the form of cash, which is defined as demand deposits plus currency. Cash is often called a "nonearning asset." It is needed to pay for labor and raw materials, to buy fixed assets, to pay taxes, to service debt, to pay dividends, and so on. However, cash itself (and also most commercial checking accounts) earns no interest. Thus, the goal of the cash manager is to minimize the amount of cash the firm must hold for use in conducting its normal business activities, yet, at the same time, to have sufficient cash (1) to take trade discounts, (2) to maintain its credit rating, and (3) to meet unexpected cash needs. We begin our analysis with a discussion of the reasons for holding cash.

Reasons for Holding Cash

Firms hold cash for two primary reasons:

1. *Transactions.* Cash balances are necessary in business operations. Payments must be made in cash, and receipts are deposited in the cash account. Cash balances associated with routine payments and collections are known as **transactions balances.** Cash inflows and outflows are unpredictable, with the degree of predictability varying among firms and industries. Therefore, firms need to hold some cash in reserve for random, unforeseen fluctuations in inflows and outflows. These "safety stocks" are called **precautionary balances,** and the less predictable the firm's cash flows, the larger such balances should be.

2. *Compensation to banks for providing loans and services.* A bank makes money by lending out funds that have been deposited with it, so the larger its deposits, the better the bank's profit position. If a bank is providing services to a customer, it may require the customer to leave a minimum balance on deposit to help offset the costs of providing the services. Also, banks may require borrowers to hold deposits at the bank. Both types of deposits are called **compensating balances.** In a 1979 survey, 84.7% of responding companies reported that they were required to maintain compensating balances to help pay for

bank services.[5] Only 13.3% reported paying direct fees for banking services. By 1996 those findings were reversed: Only 28% paid for bank services with compensating balances, while 83% paid direct fees.[6] So, while the use of compensating balances to pay for services has declined, it is still a reason some companies hold so much cash.

In addition to holding cash for transactions, precautionary, and compensating balances, it is essential that the firm have sufficient cash to take **trade discounts.** Suppliers frequently offer customers discounts for early payment of bills. As we will see later in this chapter, the cost of not taking discounts is very high, so firms should have enough cash to permit payment of bills in time to take discounts.

Finally, firms often hold short-term investments in excess of the cash needed to support operations. We discuss short-term investments later in the chapter.

SELF-TEST

Why is cash management important?

What are the two primary motives for holding cash?

22.4 The Cash Budget

The **cash budget** shows the firm's projected cash inflows and outflows over some specified period. Generally, firms use a monthly cash budget forecasted over the next year, plus a more detailed daily or weekly cash budget for the coming month. The monthly cash budgets are used for planning purposes, and the daily or weekly budgets for actual cash control.

In Chapter 14, we saw that MicroDrive's projected sales were $3,300 million, resulting in a net cash flow from operations of $163 million. When all expenditures and financing flows were considered, its cash account was projected to increase by $1 million. Does this mean that it will not have to worry about cash shortages during the year? To answer this question, we must construct the cash budget.

To simplify the example, we will only consider the cash budget for the last half of the year. Further, we will not list every cash flow but rather focus on the operating cash flows. Sales peak in September, and all sales are made on terms of 2/10, net 40, meaning that a 2% discount is allowed if payment is made within 10 days, and, if the discount is not taken, the full amount is due in 40 days. However, like most companies, MicroDrive finds that some of its customers delay payment up to 90 days. Experience has shown that payment on 20% of dollar sales is made during the month in which the sale is made—these are the discount sales. On 70% of sales, payment is made during the month immediately following the month of sale, and on 10% of sales, payment is made in the second month following the month of sale.

Costs average 70% of the sales prices of the finished products. Raw material purchases are generally made one month before the firm expects to sell the finished products, but MicroDrive's terms with its suppliers allow it to delay payments for

[5]See Lawrence J. Gitman, E. A. Moses, and I. T. White, "An Assessment of Corporate Cash Management Practices," *Financial Management,* Spring 1979, pp. 32–41.
[6]See Charles E. Maxwell, Lawrence J. Gitman, and Stephanie A. M. Smith, "Working Capital Management and Financial-Service Consumption Preferences of US and Foreign Firms: A Comparison of 1979 and 1996 Preferences," *Financial Practice and Education,* Fall/Winter 1998, pp. 46–52.

30 days. Accordingly, if July sales are forecasted at $300 million, then purchases during June will amount to $210 million, and this amount will actually be paid in July.

Such other cash expenditures as wages and lease payments are also built into the cash budget, and MicroDrive must make estimated tax payments of $30 million on September 15 and $20 million on December 15. Also, a $100 million payment for a new plant must be made in October. Assuming that the **target cash balance** is $10 million, and that it projects $15 million to be on hand on July 1, what will MicroDrive's monthly cash surpluses or shortfalls be for the period from July to December?

The monthly cash flows are shown in Table 22-2. Section I of the table provides a worksheet for calculating both collections on sales and payments on purchases. Line 1 gives the sales forecast for the period from May through December. (May and June sales are necessary to determine collections for July and August.) Next, Lines 2 through 5 show cash collections. Line 2 shows that 20% of the sales during any given month are collected during that month. Customers who pay in the first month, however, take the discount, so the cash collected in the month of sale is reduced by 2%; for example, collections during July for the $300 million of sales in that month will be 20% times sales times 1.0 minus the 2% discount = (0.20)($300)(0.98) ≈ $59 million. Line 3 shows the collections on the previous month's sales, or 70% of sales in the preceding month; for example, in July, 70% of the $250 million June sales, or $175 million, will be collected. Line 4 gives collections from sales 2 months earlier, or 10% of sales in that month; for example, the July collections for May sales are (0.10)($200) = $20 million. The collections during each month are summed and shown on Line 5; thus, the July collections represent 20% of July sales (minus the discount) plus 70% of June sales plus 10% of May sales, or $254 million in total.

Next, payments for purchases of raw materials are shown. July sales are forecasted at $300 million, so MicroDrive will purchase $210 million of materials in June (Line 6) and pay for these purchases in July (Line 7). Similarly, MicroDrive will purchase $280 million of materials in July to meet August's forecasted sales of $400 million.

With Section I completed, Section II can be constructed. Cash from collections is shown on Line 8. Lines 9 through 14 list payments made during each month, and these payments are summed on Line 15. The difference between cash receipts and cash payments (Line 8 minus Line 15) is the net cash gain or loss during the month. For July there is a net cash loss of $11 million, as shown on Line 16.

In Section III, we first determine the cash balance MicroDrive would have at the start of each month, assuming no borrowing is done. This is shown on Line 17. MicroDrive would have $15 million on hand on July 1. The beginning cash balance (Line 17) is then added to the net cash gain or loss during the month (Line 16) to obtain the cumulative cash that would be on hand if no financing were done (Line 18). At the end of July, MicroDrive forecasts a cumulative cash balance of $4 million in the absence of borrowing.

The target cash balance, $10 million, is then subtracted from the cumulative cash balance to determine the firm's borrowing requirements (shown in parentheses) or its surplus cash. Because MicroDrive expects to have cumulative cash, as shown on Line 18, of only $4 million in July, it will have to borrow $6 million to bring the cash account up to the target balance of $10 million. Assuming that this amount is indeed borrowed, loans outstanding will total $6 million at the end of July. (MicroDrive did not have any loans outstanding on July 1.) The cash surplus or required loan balance is given on Line 20; a positive value indicates a cash

FM
e-resource

See **FM12 Ch 22 Tool Kit.xls** at the textbook's Web site for details.

Table 22-2

MicroDrive Inc.: Cash Budget (Millions of Dollars)

	May	Jun	Jul	Aug	Sep	Oct	Nov	Dec
I. COLLECTIONS AND PURCHASES WORKSHEET								
(1) Sales (gross)[a]	$200	$250	$300	$400	$500	$350	$250	$200
Collections								
(2) During month of sale:								
(0.2)(0.98)(month's sales)			59	78	98	69	49	39
(3) During first month after sale:								
0.7(previous month's sales)			175	210	280	350	245	175
(4) During second month after sale:								
0.1(sales 2 months ago)			20	25	30	40	50	35
(5) Total collections (2 + 3 + 4)			$254	$313	$408	$459	$344	$249
Purchases								
(6) 0.7(next month's sales)		$210	$280	$350	$245	$175	$140	
(7) Payments (prior month's purchases)			$210	$280	$350	$245	$175	$140
II. CASH GAIN OR LOSS FOR MONTH								
(8) Collections (from Section I)			$254	$313	$408	$459	$344	$249
(9) Payments for purchases (from Section I)			$210	$280	$350	$245	$175	$140
(10) Wages and salaries			30	40	50	40	30	30
(11) Lease payments			15	15	15	15	15	15
(12) Other expenses			10	15	20	15	10	10
(13) Taxes					30			20
(14) Payment for plant construction						100		
(15) Total payments			$265	$350	$465	$415	$230	$215
(16) Net cash gain (loss) during month (Line 8 − Line 15)			($ 11)	($ 37)	($ 57)	$ 44	$114	$ 34
III. LOAN REQUIREMENT OR CASH SURPLUS								
(17) Cash at start of month if no borrowing is done[b]			$15	$4	($33)	($90)	($46)	$68
(18) Cumulative cash: cash at start if no borrowing + gain or − loss (Line 16 + Line 17)			$4	($33)	($90)	($46)	$68	$102
(19) Target cash balance			10	10	10	10	10	10
(20) Cumulative surplus cash or loans outstanding to maintain $10 target cash balance (Line 18 − Line 19)[c]			($6)	($43)	($100)	($56)	$58	$92

Notes:

[a]Although the budget period is July through December, sales and purchases data for May and June are needed to determine collections and payments during July and August.

[b]The amount shown on Line 17 for July, the $15 balance (in millions), is on hand initially. The values shown for each of the following months on Line 17 are equal to the cumulative cash as shown on Line 18 for the preceding month; for example, the $4 shown on Line 17 for August is taken from Line 18 in the July column.

[c]When the target cash balance of $10 (Line 19) is deducted from the cumulative cash balance (Line 18), a resulting negative figure on Line 20 (shown in parentheses) represents a required loan, whereas a positive figure represents surplus cash. Loans are required from July through October, and surpluses are expected during November and December. Note also that firms can borrow or pay off loans on a daily basis, so the $6 borrowed during July would be done on a daily basis, as needed, and during October the $100 loan that existed at the beginning of the month would be reduced daily to the $56 ending balance, which, in turn, would be completely paid off during November.

The *CFO* Cash Management Scorecard

Each year *CFO* magazine publishes a cash management scorecard prepared by REL Consultancy Group based on the 1,000 largest publicly traded U.S. companies. REL defines the return on capital employed (ROCE) as EBIT/(ST debt + LT debt + equity). On the one hand, if a company holds more cash than needed to support its operations, its ROCE will be dragged down because cash earns a very low rate of return. On the other hand, if a company doesn't have enough cash, then it might experience financial distress if there is an unexpected downturn in business. How much cash is enough?

Although the optimum level of cash depends on a company's unique set of circumstances, REL defines an industry benchmark as the cash/sales ratio for the lowest quartile. The average benchmark cash/sales ratio is 5.5%. However, the average cash/sales ratio is 11.4%, which means that many firms have much more cash than indicated by the benchmark. REL estimates that if all firms could move to the benchmark, then the average ROCE would improve from 14.0% to 15.2%.

Potential improvements for some individual firms are even more pronounced. For example, Microsoft, with over $42 billion in excess cash, could improve its ROCE from 12.1% to 27.4% by moving to its industry benchmark. Motorola, with almost $7 billion in excess cash, could improve ROCE from 16.8% to 26.4%. Texas Instruments, with over $3 billion in excess cash, could improve ROCE from 16.4% to 21.6%.

It's one thing to talk about reducing cash, but how can a company do it? A great relationship with its banks is one key to keeping low cash levels. Jim Hopwood, treasurer of Wickes, says, "We have a credit revolver if we ever need it." The same is true at Haverty Furniture, where CFO Dennis Fink says, "You don't have to worry about predicting short-term fluctuations in cash flow," if you have solid bank commitments.

Sources: Randy Myers, "Stuck on Yellow," *CFO*, October 2005, 81–90; and S. L. Mintz, "Lean Green Machine," *CFO*, July 2000, pp. 76–94. For updates, go to **http://www.cfo.com** and search for "cash management."

surplus, whereas a negative value indicates a loan requirement. Note that the surplus cash or loan requirement shown on Line 20 is a *cumulative amount*. MicroDrive must borrow $6 million in July. Then, it has an additional cash shortfall during August of $37 million as reported on Line 16, so its total loan requirement at the end of August is $6 + $37 = $43 million, as reported on Line 20. MicroDrive's arrangement with the bank permits it to increase its outstanding loans on a daily basis, up to a prearranged maximum, just as you could increase the amount you owe on a credit card. MicroDrive will use any surplus funds it generates to pay off its loans, and because the loan can be paid down at any time, on a daily basis, the firm will never have both a cash surplus and an outstanding loan balance.

This same procedure is used in the following months. Sales will peak in September, accompanied by increased payments for purchases, wages, and other items. Receipts from sales will also go up, but the firm will still be left with a $57 million net cash outflow during the month. The total loan requirement at the end of September will hit a peak of $100 million, the cumulative cash plus the target cash balance. The $100 million can also be found as the $43 million needed at the end of August plus the $57 million cash deficit for September.

Sales, purchases, and payments for past purchases will fall sharply in October, but collections will be the highest of any month because they will reflect the high September sales. As a result, MicroDrive will enjoy a healthy $44 million net cash gain during October. This net gain can be used to pay off borrowings, so loans outstanding will decline by $44 million, to $56 million.

MicroDrive will have an even larger cash surplus in November, which will permit it to pay off all of its loans. In fact, the company is expected to have $58 million in surplus cash by the month's end, and another cash surplus in December will swell the excess cash to $92 million. With such a large amount of unneeded funds,

MicroDrive's treasurer will certainly want to invest in interest-bearing securities or to put the funds to use in some other way.

We intentionally kept this cash budget simple for illustrative purposes, but here are some potential refinements that you could easily incorporate: (1) Add dividend payments, stock issues, bond sales, interest income, and interest expenses. (2) Create a cash budget to determine weekly, or even daily, cash requirements. (3) Use simulation to estimate the probability distribution for the cash requirements. (4) Allow the target cash balance to vary over time, reflecting the seasonal nature of sales and operating activity.

SELF-TEST

What is the purpose of the cash budget?

What are the three major sections of a cash budget?

22.5 Cash Management Techniques

Most business is conducted by large firms, many of which operate regionally, nationally, or even globally. They collect cash from many sources and make payments from a number of different cities or even countries. For example, companies such as IBM, General Motors, and Hewlett-Packard have manufacturing plants all around the world, even more sales offices, and bank accounts in virtually every city where they do business. Their collection points follow sales patterns. Some disbursements are made from local offices, but most are made in the cities where manufacturing occurs, or else from the home office. Thus, a major corporation might have hundreds or even thousands of bank accounts, and since there is no reason to think that inflows and outflows will balance in each account, a system must be in place to transfer funds from where they come in to where they are needed, to arrange loans to cover net corporate shortfalls, and to invest net corporate surpluses without delay. We discuss the most commonly used techniques for accomplishing these tasks in the following sections.[7]

Synchronizing Cash Flow

If you as an individual were to receive income once a year, you would probably put it in the bank, draw down your account periodically, and have an average balance for the year equal to about half of your annual income. If instead you received income weekly and paid rent, tuition, and other charges on a weekly basis, and if you were confident of your forecasted inflows and outflows, then you could hold a small average cash balance.

Exactly the same situation holds for businesses—by improving their forecasts and by timing cash receipts to coincide with cash requirements, firms can hold their transactions balances to a minimum. Recognizing this, utility companies, oil companies, credit card companies, and so on, arrange to bill customers, and to pay their own bills, on regular "billing cycles" throughout the month. This **synchronization**

---

[7]For more information on cash management, see Bernell K. Stone and Tom W. Miller, "Daily Cash Forecasting with Multiplicative Models of Cash Flow Patterns," *Financial Management*, Winter 1987, pp. 45–54; Bruce J. Summers, "Clearing and Payment Systems: The Role of the Central Bank," *Federal Reserve Bulletin*, February 1991, pp. 81–91; John C. Wood and Dolores D. Smith, "Electronic Transfer of Government Benefits," *Federal Reserve Bulletin*, April 1991, pp. 204–207; and Keith C. Brown and Scott L. Lummer, "A Reexamination of the Covered Call Option Strategy for Corporate Cash Management," *Financial Management*, Summer 1986, pp. 13–17.

of cash flows provides cash when it is needed and thus enables firms to reduce the cash balances needed to support operations.

Speeding Up the Check-Clearing Process

When a customer writes and mails a check, the funds are not available to the receiving firm until the **check-clearing process** has been completed. First, the check must be delivered through the mail. Checks received from customers in distant cities are especially subject to mail delays.

When a customer's check is written upon one bank and a company deposits the check in its own bank, the company's bank must verify that the check is valid before the company can use those funds. Checks are generally cleared through the Federal Reserve System or through a clearinghouse set up by the banks in a particular city.[8] Before 2004, this process sometimes took 2 to 5 days. But with the passage of a bill in 2004 known as "Check 21," banks can exchange digital images of checks. This means that most checks now clear in a day.

Using Float

Float is defined as the difference between the balance shown in a firm's (or individual's) checkbook and the balance on the bank's records. Suppose a firm writes, on average, checks in the amount of $5,000 each day, and it takes 6 days for these checks to clear and be deducted from the firm's bank account. This will cause the firm's own checkbook to show a balance $30,000 smaller than the balance on the bank's records; this difference is called **disbursement float.** Now suppose the firm also receives checks in the amount of $5,000 daily, but it loses 4 days while they are being deposited and cleared. This will result in $20,000 of **collections float.** In total, the firm's **net float**—the difference between the $30,000 positive disbursement float and the $20,000 negative collections float—will be $10,000.

Delays that cause float arise because it takes time for checks (1) to travel through the mail (mail float), (2) to be processed by the receiving firm (processing float), and (3) to clear through the banking system (clearing, or availability, float). Basically, the size of a firm's net float is a function of its ability to speed up collections on checks it receives and to slow down collections on checks it writes. Efficient firms go to great lengths to speed up the processing of incoming checks, thus putting the funds to work faster, and they try to stretch their own payments out as long as possible, sometimes by disbursing checks from banks in remote locations.

Speeding Up Receipts

Two major techniques are now used both to speed collections and to get funds where they are needed: (1) lockbox plans and (2) payment by wire or automatic debit.

Lockboxes

A **lockbox plan** is one of the oldest cash management tools. In a lockbox system, incoming checks are sent to post office boxes rather than to corporate

---

[8]For example, suppose a check for $100 is written on Bank A and deposited at Bank B. Bank B will usually contact either the Federal Reserve System or a clearinghouse to which both banks belong. The Fed or the clearinghouse will then verify with Bank A that the check is valid and that the account has sufficient funds to cover the check. Bank A's account with the Fed or the clearinghouse is then reduced by $100, and Bank B's account is increased by $100. Of course, if the check is deposited in the same bank on which it was drawn, that bank merely transfers funds by bookkeeping entries from one depositor to another.

headquarters. For example, a firm headquartered in New York City might have its West Coast customers send their payments to a box in San Francisco, its customers in the Southwest send their checks to Dallas, and so on, rather than having all checks sent to New York City. Several times a day a local bank will collect the contents of the lockbox and deposit the checks into the company's local account. In fact, some banks even have their lockbox operation located in the same facility as the post office. The bank then provides the firm with a daily record of the receipts collected, usually via an electronic data transmission system in a format that permits online updating of the firm's accounts receivable records.

A lockbox system reduces the time required for a firm to receive incoming checks, to deposit them, and to get them cleared through the banking system so the funds are available for use. Lockbox services can accelerate the availability of funds by 2 to 5 days over the "regular" system.

Payment by Wire or Automatic Debit   Firms are increasingly demanding payments of larger bills by wire, or even by automatic electronic debits. Under an electronic debit system, funds are automatically deducted from one account and added to another. This is, of course, the ultimate in a speeded-up collection process, and computer technology is making such a process increasingly feasible and efficient, even for retail transactions.

SELF-TEST

What is float? How do firms use float to increase cash management efficiency?

What are some methods firms can use to accelerate receipts?

22.6 Inventory

Inventory management techniques are covered in depth in production management courses. Still, since financial managers have a responsibility both for raising the capital needed to carry inventory and for the firm's overall profitability, we need to cover the financial aspects of inventory management here.

The twin goals of inventory management are (1) to ensure that the inventories needed to sustain operations are available, but (2) to hold the costs of ordering and carrying inventories to the lowest possible level. While analyzing improvements in the cash conversion cycle, we identified some of the cash flows associated with a reduction in inventory. In addition to the points made earlier, lower inventory levels reduce costs due to storage and handling, insurance, property taxes, and spoilage or obsolescence.

Consider Trane Corporation, which makes air conditioners, and recently adopted just-in-time inventory procedures. In the past, Trane produced parts on a steady basis, stored them as inventory, and had them ready whenever the company received an order for a batch of air conditioners. However, the company reached the point where its inventory covered an area equal to three football fields, and it still sometimes took as long as 15 days to fill an order. To make matters worse, occasionally some of the necessary components simply could not be located, while in other instances the components were located but found to have been damaged from long storage.

Then Trane adopted a new inventory policy—it began producing components only after an order is received, and then sending the parts directly from the machines that make them to the final assembly line. The net effect: Inventories fell nearly 40% even as sales increased by 30%.

Such improvements in inventory management can free up considerable amounts of cash. For example, suppose a company has sales of $120 million and an inventory turnover ratio of 3. This means the company has an inventory level of

$$\text{Inventory} = \text{Sales}/(\text{Inventory turnover ratio})$$
$$= \$120/3 = \$40 \text{ million.}$$

If the company can improve its inventory turnover ratio to 4, then its inventory will fall to

$$\text{Inventory} = \$120/4 = \$30 \text{ million.}$$

This $10 million reduction in inventory boosts free cash flow by $10 million.

However, there are costs associated with holding too little inventory, and these costs can be severe. Generally, if a business carries small inventories, it must reorder frequently. This increases ordering costs. Even more important, firms can miss out on profitable sales and also suffer a loss of goodwill that can lead to lower future sales if they experience stockouts. So, it is important to have enough inventory on hand to meet customer demands.[9]

SELF-TEST

What are some costs associated with high inventories? With low inventories?

A company has $20 million in sales and an inventory turnover ratio of 2.0. If it can reduce its inventory and improve its inventory turnover ratio to 2.5 with no loss in sales, by how much will FCF increase? ($2 million)

22.7 Receivables Management

Firms would, in general, rather sell for cash than on credit, but competitive pressures force most firms to offer credit. Thus, goods are shipped, inventories are reduced, and an **account receivable** is created.[10] Eventually, the customer will pay the account, at which time (1) the firm will receive cash and (2) its receivables will decline. Carrying receivables has both direct and indirect costs, but it also has an important benefit—increased sales.

Receivables management begins with the credit policy, but a monitoring system is also important. Corrective action is often needed, and the only way to know whether the situation is getting out of hand is with a good receivables control system.[11]

---

[9]For additional insights into the problems of inventory management, see Richard A. Followill, Michael Schellenger, and Patrick H. Marchard, "Economic Order Quantities, Volume Discounts, and Wealth Maximization," *The Financial Review*, February 1990, pp. 143–152.

[10]Whenever goods are sold on credit, two accounts are created—an asset item entitled *accounts receivable* appears on the books of the selling firm, and a liability item called *accounts payable* appears on the books of the purchaser. At this point, we are analyzing the transaction from the viewpoint of the seller, so we are concentrating on the variables under its control, in this case, the receivables. We examine the transaction from the viewpoint of the purchaser later in this chapter, where we discuss accounts payable as a source of funds and consider their cost.

[11]For more on credit policy and receivables management, see George W. Gallinger and A. James Ifflander, "Monitoring Accounts Receivable Using Variance Analysis," *Financial Management*, Winter 1986, pp. 69–76; Shehzad L. Mian and Clifford W. Smith, "Extending Trade Credit and Financing Receivables," *Journal of Applied Corporate Finance*, Spring 1994, pp. 75–84; and Paul D. Adams, Steve B. Wyatt, and Yong H. Kim, "A Contingent Claims Analysis of Trade Credit," *Financial Management*, Autumn 1992, pp. 104–112.

Supply Chain Management

Herman Miller Inc. manufactures a wide variety of office furniture, and a typical order from a single customer might require work at five different plants. Each plant uses components from different suppliers, and each plant works on orders for many customers. Imagine all the coordination that is required. The sales force generates the order, the purchasing department orders components from suppliers, and the suppliers must order materials from their own suppliers. Then, the suppliers ship the components to Herman Miller, the factory builds the product, the different products are gathered together to complete the order, and then the order is shipped to the customer. If one part of that process malfunctions, then the order will be delayed, inventory will pile up, extra costs to expedite the order will be incurred, and the customer's goodwill will be damaged, which will hurt future sales growth.

To prevent such consequences, many companies are turning to a process called supply chain management (SCM). The key element in SCM is sharing information all the way from the point of sale at the product's retailer to the suppliers, and even back to the suppliers' suppliers. SCM requires special software, but even more important, it requires cooperation among the different companies and departments in the supply chain. This new culture of open communication is often difficult for many companies—they are reluctant to divulge operating information. For example, EMC Corp., a manufacturer of data storage systems, has become deeply involved in the design processes and financial controls of its key suppliers. Many of EMC's suppliers were initially wary of these new relationships. However, SCM has been a win-win situation, with increases in value for EMC and its suppliers.

The same is true at many other companies. After implementing SCM, Herman Miller was able to reduce its days of inventory on hand by a week and to cut two weeks off of delivery times to customers. Herman Miller was also able to operate its plants at a 20% higher volume without additional capital expenditures. As another example, Heineken USA can now get beer from its breweries to its customers' shelves in less than 6 weeks, compared with 10 to 12 weeks before implementing SCM. As these and other companies have found, SCM increases free cash flows, and that leads to higher stock prices.

Sources: Elaine L. Appleton, "Supply Chain Brain," *CFO,* July 1997, pp. 51–54; and Kris Frieswick, "Up Close and Virtual," *CFO,* April 1998, pp. 87–91.

Credit Policy

The success or failure of a business depends primarily on the demand for its products—as a rule, the higher its sales, the larger its profits and the higher its stock price. Sales, in turn, depend on a number of factors, some exogenous but others under the firm's control. The major controllable determinants of demand are sales prices, product quality, advertising, and the firm's **credit policy.** Credit policy, in turn, consists of these four variables:

1. *Credit period,* which is the length of time buyers are given to pay for their purchases. For example, credit terms of "2/10, net 30" indicate that buyers may take up to 30 days to pay.
2. *Discounts* given for early payment, including the discount percentage and how rapidly payment must be made to qualify for the discount. The credit terms "2/10, net 30" allow buyers to take a 2% discount if they pay within 10 days. Otherwise, they must pay the full amount within 30 days.
3. *Credit standards,* which refer to the required financial strength of acceptable credit customers. Lower credit standards boost sales, but also increase bad debts.
4. *Collection policy,* which is measured by its toughness or laxity in attempting to collect on slow-paying accounts. A tough policy may speed up collections, but it might also anger customers, causing them to take their business elsewhere.

The credit manager is responsible for administering the firm's credit policy. However, because of the pervasive importance of credit, the credit policy itself is normally established by the executive committee, which usually consists of the president plus the vice presidents of finance, marketing, and production.

The Accumulation of Receivables

The total amount of accounts receivable outstanding at any given time is determined by two factors: (1) the volume of credit sales and (2) the average length of time between sales and collections. For example, suppose Boston Lumber Company (BLC), a wholesale distributor of lumber products, opens a warehouse on January 1 and, starting the first day, makes sales of $1,000 each day. For simplicity, we assume that all sales are on credit, and customers are given 10 days to pay. At the end of the first day, accounts receivable will be $1,000; they will rise to $2,000 by the end of the second day; and by January 10, they will have risen to 10($1,000) = $10,000. On January 11, another $1,000 will be added to receivables, but payments for sales made on January 1 will reduce receivables by $1,000, so total accounts receivable will remain constant at $10,000. In general, once the firm's operations have stabilized, this situation will exist:

$$\frac{\text{Accounts}}{\text{receivable}} = \frac{\text{Credit sales}}{\text{per day}} \times \frac{\text{Length of}}{\text{collection period}} \qquad \text{(22-5)}$$

$$= \quad \$1,000 \quad \times \quad 10 \text{ days} \quad = \$10,000.$$

If either credit sales or the collection period changes, such changes will be reflected in accounts receivable.

Monitoring the Receivables Position

Investors—both stockholders and bank loan officers—should pay close attention to accounts receivable management, for, as we shall see, one can be misled by reported financial statements and later suffer serious losses on an investment.

When a credit sale is made, the following events occur: (1) Inventories are reduced by the cost of goods sold, (2) accounts receivable are increased by the sales price, and (3) the difference is profit, which is added to retained earnings. If the sale is for cash, then the cash from the sale has actually been received by the firm, but if the sale is on credit, the firm will not receive the cash from the sale unless and until the account is collected. Firms have been known to encourage "sales" to very weak customers in order to report high profits. This could boost the firm's stock price, at least until credit losses begin to lower earnings, at which time the stock price will fall. Analyses along the lines suggested in the following sections will detect any such questionable practice, as well as any unconscious deterioration in the quality of accounts receivable. Such early detection helps both investors and bankers avoid losses.

Days Sales Outstanding (DSO)   Suppose Super Sets Inc., a television manufacturer, sells 200,000 television sets a year at a price of $198 each. Further, assume that all sales are on credit with the following terms: If payment is made within 10 days, customers will receive a 2% discount; otherwise the full amount is due within

30 days. Finally, assume that 70% of the customers take discounts and pay on Day 10, while the other 30% pay on Day 30.

Super Sets's **days sales outstanding (DSO),** sometimes called the *average collection period (ACP),* is 16 days:

$$DSO = ACP = 0.7(10 \text{ days}) + 0.3(30 \text{ days}) = 16 \text{ days}.$$

Super Sets's *average daily sales (ADS)* is $108,493:

$$ADS = \frac{\text{Annual sales}}{365} = \frac{(\text{Units sold})(\text{Sales price})}{365} \qquad (22\text{-}6)$$

$$= \frac{200,000(\$198)}{365} = \frac{\$39,600,000}{365} = \$108,493.$$

Super Sets's accounts receivable, assuming a constant, uniform rate of sales throughout the year, will at any point in time be $1,735,888:

$$\text{Receivables} = (ADS)(DSO) \qquad (22\text{-}7)$$

$$= (\$108,493)(16) = \$1,735,888.$$

Note also that its DSO, or average collection period, is a measure of the average length of time it takes Super Sets's customers to pay off their credit purchases, and the DSO is often compared with an industry average DSO. For example, if all television manufacturers sell on the same credit terms, and if the industry average DSO is 25 days versus Super Sets's 16 days, then Super Sets either has a higher percentage of discount customers or else its credit department is exceptionally good at ensuring prompt payment.

Finally, note that if you know both the annual sales and the receivables balance, you can calculate DSO as follows:

$$DSO = \frac{\text{Receivables}}{\text{Sales per day}} = \frac{\$1,735,888}{\$108,493} = 16 \text{ days}.$$

The DSO can also be compared with the firm's own credit terms. For example, suppose Super Sets's DSO had been averaging 35 days. With a 35-day DSO, some customers would obviously be taking more than 30 days to pay their bills. In fact, if many customers were paying within 10 days to take advantage of the discount, the others must, on average, be taking much longer than 35 days. One way to check this possibility is to use an aging schedule as described in the next section.

Aging Schedules   An **aging schedule** breaks down a firm's receivables by age of account. Table 22-3 contains the December 31, 2006, aging schedules of two television manufacturers, Super Sets and Wonder Vision. Both firms offer the same credit terms, and both show the same total receivables. However, Super Sets's aging schedule indicates that all of its customers pay on time—70% pay on Day 10 while 30% pay on Day 30. On the other hand, Wonder Vision's schedule, which is more typical, shows that many of its customers are not abiding by its credit

Table 22-3

Aging Schedules

| Age of Account (Days) | Super Sets | | Wonder Vision | |
	Value of Account	Percentage of Total Value	Value of Account	Percentage of Total Value
0–10	$1,215,122	70%	$ 815,867	47%
11–30	520,766	30	451,331	26
31–45	0	0	260,383	15
46–60	0	0	173,589	10
Over 60	0	0	34,718	2
Total receivables	$1,735,888	100%	$1,735,888	100%

terms—some 27% of its receivables are more than 30 days old, even though Wonder Vision's credit terms call for full payment by Day 30.

Aging schedules cannot be constructed from the type of summary data reported in financial statements; they must be developed from the firm's accounts receivable ledger. However, well-run firms have computerized their accounts receivable records, so it is easy to determine the age of each invoice, to sort electronically by age categories, and thus to generate an aging schedule.

Management should constantly monitor both the DSO and the aging schedule to detect trends, to see how the firm's collection experience compares with its credit terms, and to see how effectively the credit department is operating in comparison with other firms in the industry. If the DSO starts to lengthen, or if the aging schedule begins to show an increasing percentage of past-due accounts, then the firm's credit policy may need to be tightened.

Although a change in the DSO or the aging schedule should signal the firm to investigate its credit policy, a deterioration in either of these measures does not necessarily indicate that the firm's credit policy has weakened. In fact, if a firm experiences sharp seasonal variations, or if it is growing rapidly, then both the aging schedule and the DSO may be distorted. To see this point, note that the DSO is calculated as follows:

$$DSO = \frac{\text{Accounts receivable}}{\text{Sales}/365}.$$

Since receivables at a given point in time reflect sales in the last month or so, but sales as shown in the denominator of the equation are for the last 12 months, a seasonal increase in sales will increase the numerator more than the denominator, hence will raise the DSO. This will occur even if customers are still paying exactly as before. Similar problems arise with the aging schedule if sales fluctuate widely. Therefore, a change in either the DSO or the aging schedule should be taken as a signal to investigate further, but not necessarily as a sign that the firm's credit policy has weakened.

SELF-TEST

Explain how a new firm's receivables balance is built up over time.

Define days sales outstanding (DSO). What can be learned from it? How is it affected by sales fluctuations?

What is an aging schedule? What can be learned from it? How is it affected by sales fluctuations?

A company has annual sales of $730 million dollars. If its DSO is 35, what is its average accounts receivables? ($70 million)

22.8 Accruals and Accounts Payable (Trade Credit)

Recall that net operating working capital is equal to operating current assets minus operating current liabilities. The previous sections discussed the management of operating current assets (cash, inventory, and accounts receivable), and the following sections discuss the two major types of operating current liabilities—accruals and accounts payable.[12]

Accruals

Firms generally pay employees on a weekly, biweekly, or monthly basis, so the balance sheet will typically show some accrued wages. Similarly, the firm's own estimated income taxes, Social Security and income taxes withheld from employee payrolls, and sales taxes collected are generally paid on a weekly, monthly, or quarterly basis; hence the balance sheet will typically show some accrued taxes along with accrued wages.

These **accruals** increase automatically, or spontaneously, as a firm's operations expand. However, a firm cannot ordinarily control its accruals: The timing of wage payments is set by economic forces and industry custom, while tax payment dates are established by law. Thus, firms use all the accruals they can, but they have little control over the levels of these accounts.

Accounts Payable (Trade Credit)

Firms generally make purchases from other firms on credit, recording the debt as an *account payable*. Accounts payable, or **trade credit,** is the largest single category of operating current liabilities, representing about 40% of the current liabilities of the average nonfinancial corporation. The percentage is somewhat larger for smaller firms: Because small companies often do not qualify for financing from other sources, they rely especially heavily on trade credit.

Trade credit is a "spontaneous" source of financing in the sense that it arises from ordinary business transactions. For example, suppose a firm makes average purchases of $2,000 a day on terms of net 30, meaning that it must pay for goods 30 days after the invoice date. On average, it will owe 30 times $2,000, or $60,000, to its suppliers. If its sales, and consequently its purchases, were to double, then its accounts payable would also double, to $120,000. So, simply by growing, the firm would spontaneously generate an additional $60,000 of financing. Similarly, if the terms under which it bought were extended from 30 to 40 days, its accounts payable would expand from $60,000 to $80,000. Thus, lengthening the credit period, as well as expanding sales and purchases, generates additional financing.

The Cost of Trade Credit

Firms that sell on credit have a *credit policy* that includes certain *terms of credit*. For example, Microchip Electronics sells on terms of 2/10, net 30, meaning that it gives its customers a 2% discount if they pay within 10 days of the invoice date, but the full invoice amount is due and payable within 30 days if the discount is not taken.

---

[12]For more on accounts payable management, see James A. Gentry and Jesus M. De La Garza, "Monitoring Accounts Payables," *Financial Review*, November 1990, pp. 559–576.

Note that the true price of Microchip's products is the net price, or 0.98 times the list price, because any customer can purchase an item at that price as long as the customer pays within 10 days. Now consider Personal Computer Company (PCC), which buys its memory chips from Microchip. One commonly used memory chip is listed at $100, so the "true" price to PCC is $98. Now if PCC wants an additional 20 days of credit beyond the 10-day discount period, it must incur a finance charge of $2 per chip for that credit. Thus, the $100 list price consists of two components:

$$\text{List price} = \$98 \text{ true price} + \$2 \text{ finance charge.}$$

The question PCC must ask before it turns down the discount to obtain the additional 20 days of credit from Microchip is this: Could we obtain credit under better terms from some other lender, say, a bank? In other words, could 20 days of credit be obtained for less than $2 per chip?

PCC buys an average of $11,923,333 of memory chips from Microchip each year at the net, or true, price. This amounts to $11,923,333/365 = $32,666.67 per day. For simplicity, assume that Microchip is PCC's only supplier. If PCC decides not to take the additional trade credit—that is, if it pays on the 10th day and takes the discount—its payables will average 10($32,666.67) = $326,667. Thus, PCC will be receiving $326,667 of credit from Microchip.

Now suppose PCC decides to take the additional 20 days credit and thus must pay the finance charge. Since PCC will now pay on the 30th day, its accounts payable will increase to 30($32,666.67) = $980,000.[13] Microchip will now be supplying PCC with an additional $980,000 − $326,667 = $653,333 of credit, which PCC could use to build up its cash account, to pay off debt, to expand inventories, or even to extend credit to its own customers, hence increasing its own accounts receivable.

The additional trade credit offered by Microchip has a cost—PCC must pay a finance charge equal to the 2% discount it is forgoing. PCC buys $11,923,333 of chips at the true price, and the added finance charges increase the total cost to $11,923,333/0.98 = $12,166,666. Therefore, the annual financing cost is $12,166,666 − $11,923,333 = $243,333. Dividing the $243,333 financing cost by the $653,333 of additional credit, we find the nominal annual cost rate of the additional trade credit to be 37.2%:

$$\text{Nominal annual costs} = \frac{\$243,333}{\$653,333} = 37.2\%.$$

If PCC can borrow from its bank (or from other sources) at an interest rate less than 37.2%, it should take discounts and forgo the additional trade credit.

The following equation can be used to calculate the nominal cost, on an annual basis, of not taking discounts, illustrated with terms of 2/10, net 30:

$$\begin{array}{c}\text{Nominal}\\\text{annual}\\\text{cost}\end{array} = \frac{\text{Discount percent}}{100 - \dfrac{\text{Discount}}{\text{percent}}} \times \frac{365}{\dfrac{\text{Days credit is}}{\text{outstanding}} - \dfrac{\text{Discount}}{\text{period}}} \qquad \text{(22-8)}$$

$$= \frac{2}{98} \times \frac{365}{20} = 2.04\% \times 18.25 = 37.2\%.$$

---

[13]A question arises here: Should accounts payable reflect gross purchases or purchases net of discounts? Generally accepted accounting principles permit either treatment if the difference is not material, but if the discount is material, then the transaction must be recorded net of discounts, or at "true" prices. Then, the higher payment that results from not taking discounts is reported as an additional expense called "discounts lost." Thus, we show accounts payable *net of discounts even if the company does not expect to take discounts.*

The numerator of the first term, Discount percent, is the cost per dollar of credit, while the denominator in this term, 100 − Discount percent, represents the funds made available by not taking the discount. Thus, the first term, 2.04%, is the cost per period for the trade credit. The denominator of the second term is the number of days of extra credit obtained by not taking the discount, so the entire second term shows how many times each year the cost is incurred, 18.25 times in this example.

The nominal annual cost formula does not take account of compounding, and in effective annual interest terms, the cost of trade credit is even higher. The discount amounts to interest, and with terms of 2/10, net 30, the firm gains use of the funds for 30 − 10 = 20 days, so there are 365/20 = 18.25 "interest periods" per year. Remember that the first term in Equation 22-8, (Discount percent)/(100 − Discount percent) = 0.02/0.98 = 0.0204, is the periodic interest rate. This rate is paid 18.25 times each year, so the effective annual cost of trade credit is

$$\text{Effective annual rate} = (1.0204)^{18.25} - 1.0 = 1.4459 - 1.0 = 44.6\%.$$

Thus, the 37.2% nominal cost calculated with Equation 22-8 understates the true cost.

Note, however, that the cost of trade credit can be reduced by paying late. Thus, if PCC could get away with paying in 60 days rather than in the specified 30 days, then the effective credit period would become 60 − 10 = 50 days, the number of times the discount would be lost would fall to 365/50 = 7.3, and the nominal cost would drop from 37.2% to 2.04% × 7.3 = 14.9%. The effective annual rate would drop from 44.6% to 15.9%:

$$\text{Effective annual rate} = (1.0204)^{7.3} - 1.0 = 1.1589 - 1.0 = 15.9\%.$$

In periods of excess capacity, firms may be able to get away with deliberately paying late, or **stretching accounts payable.** However, they will also suffer a variety of problems associated with being branded a "slow payer." These problems are discussed later in the chapter.

The costs of the additional trade credit from forgoing discounts under some other purchase terms are shown below:

Credit Terms	Cost of Additional Credit If the Cash Discount Is Not Taken	
	Nominal Cost	Effective Cost
1/10, net 20	36.9%	44.3%
1/10, net 30	18.4	20.1
2/10, net 20	74.5	109.0
3/15, net 45	37.6	44.9

As these figures show, the cost of not taking discounts can be substantial. Incidentally, throughout the chapter, we assume that payments are made either on the *last day* for taking discounts or on the *last day* of the credit period, unless otherwise noted. It would be foolish to pay, say, on the 5th day or on the 20th day if the credit terms were 2/10, net 30.[14]

---

[14]A financial calculator can also be used to determine the cost of trade credit. If the terms of credit are 2/10, net 30, this implies that for every $100 of goods purchased at the full list price, the customer has the choice of paying the full amount in 30 days or else paying $98 in 10 days. If a customer decides not to take the discount, then it is in effect borrowing $98, the amount it would otherwise have to pay, from Day 11 to Day 30, or for 20 days. It will then have to pay $100, which is the $98 loan plus a $2 financing charge, at the end of the 20-day loan period. To calculate the interest rate, enter N = 1, PV = 98, PMT = 0, FV = −100, and then press I to obtain 2.04%. This is the rate for 20 days. To calculate the effective annual interest rate on a 365-day basis, enter N = 20/365 = 0.05479, PV = 98, PMT = 0, FV = −100, and then press I/YR to obtain 44.6%. The 20/365 = 0.05479 is the fraction of a year the "loan" is outstanding, and the 44.6% is the annualized cost of not taking discounts.

On the basis of the preceding discussion, trade credit can be divided into two components: (1) **free trade credit,** which involves credit received during the discount period, and (2) **costly trade credit,** which involves credit in excess of the free trade credit and whose cost is an implicit one based on the forgone discounts. *Firms should always use the free component, but they should use the costly component only after analyzing the cost of this capital to make sure that it is less than the cost of funds that could be obtained from other sources.* Under the terms of trade found in most industries, the costly component is relatively expensive, so stronger firms will avoid using it.

SELF-TEST

What are accruals? How much control do managers have over accruals?

What is trade credit?

What is the difference between free trade credit and costly trade credit?

How does the cost of costly trade credit generally compare with the cost of short-term bank loans?

A company has credit terms of 2/12, net 28. What is the nominal annual cost of trade credit? The effective annual cost? (46.6%; 58.5%)

22.9 Alternative Short-Term Financing Policies

Up until this point we have focused on the management of net operating working capital. We now turn our attention to decisions involving short-term investments and short-term financing.

Most businesses experience seasonal and/or cyclical fluctuations. For example, construction firms have peaks in the spring and summer, retailers peak around Christmas, and the manufacturers who supply both construction companies and retailers follow similar patterns. Similarly, virtually all businesses must build up net operating working capital (NOWC) when the economy is strong, but they then sell off inventories and reduce receivables when the economy slacks off. Still, NOWC rarely drops to zero—companies have some **permanent NOWC,** which is the NOWC on hand at the low point of the cycle. Then, as sales increase during the upswing, NOWC must be increased, and the additional NOWC is defined as **temporary NOWC.** The manner in which the permanent and temporary NOWC are financed is called the firm's *short-term financing policy.*

Maturity Matching, or "Self-Liquidating," Approach

The **maturity matching,** or **"self-liquidating," approach** calls for matching asset and liability maturities as shown in Panel a of Figure 22-2. This strategy minimizes the risk that the firm will be unable to pay off its maturing obligations. To illustrate, suppose a company borrows on a 1-year basis and uses the funds obtained to build and equip a plant. Cash flows from the plant (profits plus depreciation) would not be sufficient to pay off the loan at the end of only 1 year, so the loan would have to be renewed. If for some reason the lender refused to renew the loan, then the company would have problems. Had the plant been financed with long-term debt, however, the required loan payments would have been better matched with cash flows from profits and depreciation, and the problem of renewal would not have arisen.

At the limit, a firm could attempt to match exactly the maturity structure of its assets and liabilities. Inventory expected to be sold in 30 days could be financed with a 30-day bank loan; a machine expected to last for 5 years could be financed

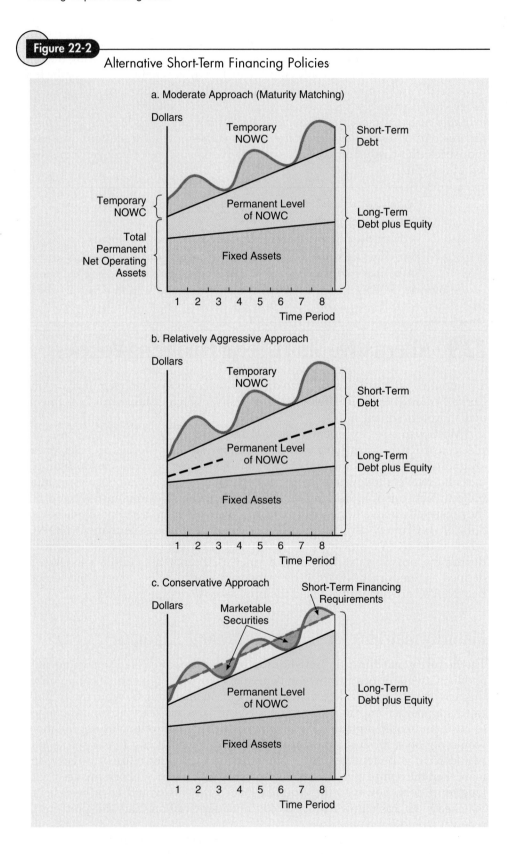

Figure 22-2

Alternative Short-Term Financing Policies

with a 5-year loan; a 20-year building could be financed with a 20-year mortgage bond; and so forth. In practice, firms don't actually finance each specific asset with a type of capital that has a maturity equal to the asset's life. However, academic studies do show that most firms tend to finance short-term assets from short-term sources and long-term assets from long-term sources.[15]

Aggressive Approach

Panel b of Figure 22-2 illustrates the situation for a relatively aggressive firm that finances all of its fixed assets with long-term capital and part of its permanent NOWC with short-term debt. Note that we used the term "relatively" in the title for Panel b because there can be different *degrees* of aggressiveness. For example, the dashed line in Panel b could have been drawn *below* the line designating fixed assets, indicating that all of the permanent NOWC and part of the fixed assets were financed with short-term credit; this would be a highly aggressive, extremely non-conservative position, and the firm would be very much subject to dangers from rising interest rates as well as to loan renewal problems. However, short-term debt is often cheaper than long-term debt, and some firms are willing to sacrifice safety for the chance of higher profits.

Conservative Approach

Panel c of Figure 22-2 has the dashed line *above* the line designating permanent NOWC, indicating that long-term sources are being used to finance all permanent operating asset requirements and also to meet some of the seasonal needs. In this situation, the firm uses a small amount of short-term debt to meet its peak requirements, but it also meets a part of its seasonal needs by "storing liquidity" in the form of marketable securities. The humps above the dashed line represent short-term financing, while the troughs below the dashed line represent short-term investing. Panel c represents a very safe, conservative current asset financing policy.

SELF-TEST

What is meant by the term "permanent NOWC"?

What is meant by the term "temporary NOWC"?

What are three alternative short-term financing policies? Is one best?

22.10 Short-Term Investments: Marketable Securities

For updates, see **http://finance.yahoo.com,** get a quote for DCX, and take a look at its balance sheets.

Realistically, the management of cash and marketable securities cannot be separated—management of one implies management of the other. In the first part of the chapter, we focused on cash management. Now, we turn to **marketable securities.**

Marketable securities typically provide much lower yields than operating assets. For example, recently DaimlerChrysler held approximately $5.8 billion in short-term marketable securities, in addition to the $9.1 billion it held in cash.

---

[15]For example, see William Beranek, Christopher Cornwell, and Sunho Choi, "External Financing, Liquidity, and Capital Expenditures," *Journal of Financial Research,* Summer 1995, pp. 207–222.

Why would a company such as DaimlerChrysler have such large holdings of low-yielding assets?

In many cases, companies hold marketable securities for the same reasons they hold cash. Although these securities are not the same as cash, in most cases they can be converted to cash on very short notice (often just a few minutes) with a single telephone call. Moreover, while cash and most commercial checking accounts yield nothing, marketable securities provide at least a modest return. For this reason, many firms hold at least some marketable securities in lieu of larger cash balances, liquidating part of the portfolio to increase the cash account when cash outflows exceed inflows. In such situations, the marketable securities could be used as a substitute for transactions balances or for precautionary balances. In most cases, the securities are held primarily for precautionary purposes—most firms prefer to rely on bank credit to make temporary transactions, but they may still hold some liquid assets to guard against a possible shortage of bank credit during difficult times.

There are both benefits and costs associated with holding marketable securities. The benefits are twofold: (1) the firm reduces risk and transactions costs because it won't have to issue securities or borrow as frequently to raise cash; and (2) it will have ready cash to take advantage of bargain purchases or growth opportunities. Funds held for the second reason are called **speculative balances.** The primary disadvantage is that the after-tax return on short-term securities is very low. Thus, firms face a trade-off between benefits and costs.

Recent research supports this trade-off hypothesis as an explanation for firms' cash holdings.[16] Firms with high growth opportunities suffer the most if they don't have ready cash to quickly take advantage of an opportunity, and the data show that these firms do hold relatively high levels of marketable securities. Firms with volatile cash flows are the ones most likely to run low on cash, so they tend to hold high levels of cash. In contrast, cash holdings are less important to large firms with high credit ratings, because they have quick and inexpensive access to capital markets. As expected, such firms hold relatively low levels of cash. Of course, there will always be outliers such as Microsoft, which is large, strong, and cash-rich, but volatile firms with good growth opportunities are still the ones with the most marketable securities, on average.

SELF-TEST Why might a company hold low-yielding marketable securities when it could earn a much higher return on operating assets?

22.11 Short-Term Financing

The three possible short-term financing policies described earlier were distinguished by the relative amounts of short-term debt used under each policy. The aggressive policy called for the greatest use of short-term debt, while the conservative policy called for the least. Maturity matching fell in between. Although short-term credit is generally riskier than long-term credit, using short-term funds does have some significant advantages. The pros and cons of short-term financing are considered in this section.

---

[16]See Tim Opler, Lee Pinkowitz, René Stulz, and Rohan Williamson, "The Determinants and Implications of Corporate Cash Holdings," *Journal of Financial Economics*, 1999, pp. 3–46. For additional insights into maturity choice, see Karlyn Mitchell, "The Debt Maturity Choice: An Empirical Investigation," *Journal of Financial Research*, Winter 1993, pp. 309–320.

Advantages of Short-Term Financing

First, a short-term loan can be obtained much faster than long-term credit. Lenders will insist on a more thorough financial examination before extending long-term credit, and the loan agreement will have to be spelled out in considerable detail because a lot can happen during the life of a 10- to 20-year loan. Therefore, if funds are needed in a hurry, the firm should look to the short-term markets.

Second, if its needs for funds are seasonal or cyclical, a firm may not want to commit itself to long-term debt: (1) Flotation costs are higher for long-term debt than for short-term credit. (2) Although long-term debt can be repaid early, provided the loan agreement includes a prepayment provision, prepayment penalties can be expensive. Accordingly, if a firm thinks its need for funds will diminish in the near future, it should choose short-term debt. (3) Long-term loan agreements always contain provisions, or covenants, which constrain the firm's future actions. Short-term credit agreements are generally less restrictive.

Third, the yield curve is normally upward sloping, indicating that interest rates are generally lower on short-term debt. Thus, under normal conditions, interest costs at the time the funds are obtained will be lower if the firm borrows on a short-term rather than a long-term basis.

Disadvantages of Short-Term Debt

Even though short-term rates are often lower than long-term rates, short-term credit is riskier for two reasons: (1) If a firm borrows on a long-term basis, its interest costs will be relatively stable over time, but if it uses short-term credit, its interest expense will fluctuate widely, at times going quite high. For example, the rate banks charged large corporations for short-term debt more than tripled over a two-year period in the 1980s, rising from 6.25 to 21%. Many firms that had borrowed heavily on a short-term basis simply could not meet their rising interest costs, and as a result, bankruptcies hit record levels during that period. (2) If a firm borrows heavily on a short-term basis, a temporary recession may render it unable to repay this debt. If the borrower is in a weak financial position, the lender may not extend the loan, which could force the firm into bankruptcy.

SELF-TEST   What are the advantages and disadvantages of short-term debt over long-term debt?

22.12   Short-Term Bank Loans

Loans from commercial banks generally appear on balance sheets as notes payable. A bank's influence is actually greater than it appears from the dollar amounts because banks provide *nonspontaneous* funds. As a firm's financing needs increase, it requests additional funds from its bank. If the request is denied, the firm may be forced to abandon attractive growth opportunities. The key features of bank loans are discussed in the following paragraphs.

Maturity

Although banks do make longer-term loans, *the bulk of their lending is on a short-term basis*—about two-thirds of all bank loans mature in a year or less. Bank loans to businesses are frequently written as 90-day notes, so the loan must be repaid or renewed at the end of 90 days. Of course, if a borrower's financial position has deteriorated, the bank may refuse to renew the loan. This can mean serious trouble for the borrower.

Promissory Notes

When a bank loan is approved, the agreement is executed by signing a **promissory note.** The note specifies (1) the amount borrowed; (2) the interest rate; (3) the repayment schedule, which can call for either a lump sum or a series of installments; (4) any collateral that might have to be put up as security for the loan; and (5) any other terms and conditions to which the bank and the borrower have agreed. When the note is signed, the bank credits the borrower's checking account with the funds, so on the borrower's balance sheet both cash and notes payable increase.

Compensating Balances

Banks sometimes require borrowers to maintain an average demand deposit (checking account) balance equal to from 10% to 20% of the face amount of the loan. This is called a **compensating balance,** and such balances raise the effective interest rate on the loans. For example, if a firm needs $80,000 to pay off outstanding obligations, but if it must maintain a 20% compensating balance, then it must borrow $100,000 to obtain a usable $80,000. If the stated annual interest rate is 8%, the effective cost is actually 10%: $8,000 interest divided by $80,000 of usable funds equals 10%.[17]

As we noted earlier in the chapter, recent surveys indicate that compensating balances are much less common now than 20 years ago. In fact, compensating balances are now illegal in many states. Despite this trend, some small banks in states where compensating balances are legal still require their customers to maintain compensating balances.

Informal Line of Credit

A **line of credit** is an informal agreement between a bank and a borrower indicating the maximum credit the bank will extend to the borrower. For example, on December 31, a bank loan officer might indicate to a financial manager that the bank regards the firm as being "good" for up to $80,000 during the forthcoming year, provided the borrower's financial condition does not deteriorate. If on January 10 the financial manager signs a promissory note for $15,000 for 90 days, this would be called "taking down" $15,000 of the total line of credit. This amount would be credited to the firm's checking account at the bank, and before repayment of the $15,000, the firm could borrow additional amounts up to a total of $80,000 outstanding at any one time.

Revolving Credit Agreement

A **revolving credit agreement** is a formal line of credit often used by large firms. To illustrate, in 2007 Texas Petroleum Company negotiated a revolving credit agreement for $100 million with a group of banks. The banks were formally committed for 4 years to lend the firm up to $100 million if the funds were needed. Texas Petroleum, in turn, paid an annual commitment fee of ¼ of 1% on the unused

---

[17]Note, however, that the compensating balance may be set as a minimum monthly *average*, and if the firm would maintain this average anyway, the compensating balance requirement would not raise the effective interest rate. Also, note that these *loan* compensating balances are added to any compensating balances that the firm's bank may require for *services performed*, such as clearing checks.

balance of the commitment to compensate the banks for making the commitment. Thus, if Texas Petroleum did not take down any of the $100 million commitment during a year, it would still be required to pay a $250,000 annual fee, normally in monthly installments of $20,833.33. If it borrowed $50 million on the first day of the agreement, the unused portion of the line of credit would fall to $50 million, and the annual fee would fall to $125,000. Of course, interest would also have to be paid on the money Texas Petroleum actually borrowed. As a general rule, the interest rate on "revolvers" is pegged to the prime rate, the T-bill rate, or some other market rate, so the cost of the loan varies over time as interest rates change. Texas Petroleum's rate was set at prime plus 0.5 percentage point.

Note that a revolving credit agreement is very similar to an informal line of credit, but with an important difference: The bank has a *legal obligation* to honor a revolving credit agreement, and it receives a commitment fee. Neither the legal obligation nor the fee exists under the informal line of credit.

Often a line of credit will have a **cleanup clause** that requires the borrower to reduce the loan balance to zero at least once a year. Keep in mind that a line of credit typically is designed to help finance negative operating cash flows that are incurred as a natural part of a company's business cycle, not as a source of permanent capital. For example, the total annual operating cash flow of Toys "R" Us is normally positive, even though its operating cash flow is negative during the fall as it builds up inventory for the Christmas season. However, Toys "R" Us has large positive cash flows in December through February, as it collects on Christmas sales. Their bankers would expect Toys "R" Us to use those positive cash flows to pay off balances that had been drawn against their credit lines. Otherwise, Toys "R" Us would be using its credit lines as a permanent source of financing.

SELF-TEST

Explain how a firm that expects to need funds during the coming year might make sure the needed funds will be available.

22.13 Commercial Paper

Commercial paper is a type of unsecured promissory note issued by large, strong firms and sold primarily to other business firms, to insurance companies, to pension funds, to money market mutual funds, and to banks. In mid-2006, there was approximately $1,793 billion of commercial paper outstanding, versus about $1,165 billion of commercial and industrial bank loans. Most commercial paper outstanding is issued by financial institutions.

For updates on the outstanding balances of commercial paper, go to **http://www.federalreserve .gov/releases** and check out the daily releases for Commercial Paper and the weekly releases for Assets and Liabilities of Commercial Banks in the United States.

Maturity and Cost

Maturities of commercial paper generally vary from 1 day to 9 months, with an average of about 5 months.[18] The interest rate on commercial paper fluctuates with supply and demand conditions—it is determined in the marketplace, varying daily as conditions change. Recently, commercial paper rates have ranged from 1½ to 3½ percentage points below the stated prime rate, and up to ½ of a percentage point above the T-bill rate. For example, in August 2006, the average rate on 3-month commercial paper was 5.21%, the stated prime rate was 8.25%, and the 3-month T-bill rate was 5.10%.

---

[18]The maximum maturity without SEC registration is 270 days. Also, commercial paper can only be sold to "sophisticated" investors; otherwise, SEC registration would be required even for maturities of 270 days or less.

Use of Commercial Paper

For current rates, see **http://www.federalreserve .gov/releases** and look at the Daily Releases for Selected Interest Rates.

The use of commercial paper is restricted to a comparatively small number of very large concerns that are exceptionally good credit risks. Dealers prefer to handle the paper of firms whose net worth is $100 million or more and whose annual borrowing exceeds $10 million. One potential problem with commercial paper is that a debtor who is in temporary financial difficulty may receive little help because commercial paper dealings are generally less personal than are bank relationships. Thus, banks are generally more able and willing to help a good customer weather a temporary storm than is a commercial paper dealer. On the other hand, using commercial paper permits a corporation to tap a wide range of credit sources, including financial institutions outside its own area and industrial corporations across the country, and this can reduce interest costs.

SELF-TEST

What is commercial paper?

What types of companies can use commercial paper to meet their short-term financing needs?

How does the cost of commercial paper compare with the cost of short-term bank loans? With the cost of Treasury bills?

22.14 Use of Security in Short-Term Financing

Thus far, we have not addressed the question of whether or not short-term loans should be secured. Commercial paper is never secured, but other types of loans can be secured if this is deemed necessary or desirable. Other things held constant, it is better to borrow on an unsecured basis, since the bookkeeping costs of **secured loans** are often high. However, firms often find that they can borrow only if they put up some type of collateral to protect the lender, or that by using security they can borrow at a much lower rate.

Several different kinds of collateral can be employed, including marketable stocks or bonds, land or buildings, equipment, inventory, and accounts receivable. Marketable securities make excellent collateral, but few firms that need loans also hold portfolios of stocks and bonds. Similarly, real property (land and buildings) and equipment are good forms of collateral, but they are generally used as security for long-term loans rather than for working capital loans. Therefore, most secured short-term business borrowing involves the use of accounts receivable and inventories as collateral.

To understand the use of security, consider the case of a Chicago hardware dealer who wanted to modernize and expand his store. He requested a $200,000 bank loan. After examining his business's financial statements, the bank indicated that it would lend him a maximum of $100,000 and that the effective interest rate would be 12.1%. The owner had a substantial personal portfolio of stocks, and he offered to put up $300,000 of high-quality stocks to support the $200,000 loan. The bank then granted the full $200,000 loan, and at the prime rate of 9.5%. The store owner might also have used his inventories or receivables as security for the loan, but processing costs would have been high.[19]

e-resource

For a more detailed discussion of secured financing, see *Web Extension 22A* at the textbook's Web site.

---

[19]The term "asset-based financing" is often used as a synonym for "secured financing." In recent years, accounts receivable have been used as security for long-term bonds, and this permits corporations to borrow from lenders such as pension funds rather than being restricted to banks and other traditional short-term lenders.

What is a secured loan?

What are some types of current assets that are pledged as security for short-term loans?

Summary

This chapter discussed working capital management and short-term financing. The key concepts covered are listed below.

- **Working capital** refers to current assets, and **net working capital** is defined as current assets minus current liabilities. **Net operating working capital** is defined as operating current assets minus operating current liabilities.
- The **cash conversion cycle model** focuses on the length of time between when the company makes payments and when it receives cash inflows.
- The **inventory conversion period** is the average time required to convert materials into finished goods and then to sell those goods.

$$\text{Inventory conversion period} = \text{Inventory/Sales per day}$$

- The **receivables collection period** is the average length of time required to convert the firm's receivables into cash, that is, to collect cash following a sale.

$$\text{Receivables collection period} = \text{DSO} = \text{Receivables/(Sales/365)}$$

- The **payables deferral period** is the average length of time between the purchase of materials and labor and the payment of cash for them.

$$\text{Payables deferral period} = \text{Payables/Purchases per day}$$

- The **cash conversion cycle** equals the length of time between the firm's actual cash expenditures to pay for productive resources (materials and labor) and its own cash receipts from the sale of products (that is, the length of time between paying for labor and materials and collecting on receivables).

$$\begin{array}{cccc}
\text{Cash} & \text{Inventory} & \text{Receivables} & \text{Payables} \\
\text{conversion} = \text{conversion} + & \text{collection} & - & \text{deferral} \\
\text{cycle} & \text{period} & \text{period} & \text{period}
\end{array}$$

- Under a **relaxed working capital policy,** a firm would hold relatively large amounts of each type of current asset. Under a **restricted working capital policy,** the firm would hold minimal amounts of these items.
- The **primary goal of cash management** is to reduce the amount of cash to the minimum necessary to conduct business.
- The **transactions balance** is the cash necessary to conduct day-to-day business, whereas the **precautionary balance** is a cash reserve held to meet random, unforeseen needs. A **compensating balance** is a minimum checking account balance that a bank requires as compensation either for services provided or as part of a loan agreement.
- A **cash budget** is a schedule showing projected cash inflows and outflows over some period. The cash budget is used to predict cash surpluses and deficits, and it is the primary cash management planning tool.

- The twin goals of **inventory management** are (1) to ensure that the inventories needed to sustain operations are available, but (2) to hold the costs of ordering and carrying inventories to the lowest possible level.
- **Inventory costs** can be divided into three types: carrying costs, ordering costs, and stock-out costs. In general, carrying costs increase as the level of inventory rises, but ordering costs and stock-out costs decline with larger inventory holdings.
- When a firm sells goods to a customer on credit, an **account receivable** is created.
- A firm can use an **aging schedule** and the **days sales outstanding (DSO)** to help keep track of its receivables position and to help avoid an increase in bad debts.
- A firm's **credit policy** consists of four elements: (1) credit period, (2) discounts given for early payment, (3) credit standards, and (4) collection policy.
- **Permanent net operating working capital** is the NOWC that the firm holds even during slack times, whereas **temporary NOWC** is the additional NOWC needed during seasonal or cyclical peaks. The methods used to finance permanent and temporary NOWC define the firm's **short-term financing policy.**
- A **moderate** approach to short-term financing involves matching, to the extent possible, the maturities of assets and liabilities, so that temporary NOWC is financed with short-term debt, and permanent NOWC and fixed assets are financed with long-term debt or equity. Under an **aggressive** approach, some permanent NOWC, and perhaps even some fixed assets, are financed with short-term debt. A **conservative** approach would be to use long-term sources to finance all permanent operating capital and some of the temporary NOWC.
- The advantages of short-term credit are (1) the **speed** with which short-term loans can be arranged, (2) increased **flexibility,** and (3) the fact that short-term **interest rates** are generally **lower** than long-term rates. The principal disadvantage of short-term credit is the **extra risk** the borrower must bear because (1) the lender can demand payment on short notice and (2) the cost of the loan will increase if interest rates rise.
- **Accounts payable,** or **trade credit,** arises spontaneously as a result of credit purchases. Firms should use all the **free trade credit** they can obtain, but they should use **costly trade credit** only if it is less expensive than other forms of short-term debt. Suppliers often offer discounts to customers who pay within a stated discount period. The following equation may be used to calculate the nominal cost, on an annual basis, of not taking discounts:

$$\text{Nominal annual cost} = \frac{\text{Discount percent}}{100 - \text{Discount percent}} \times \frac{365}{\text{Days credit is outstanding} - \text{Discount period}}.$$

- **Bank loans** are an important source of short-term credit. When a bank loan is approved, a **promissory note** is signed. It specifies: (1) the amount borrowed, (2) the percentage interest rate, (3) the repayment schedule, (4) the collateral, and (5) any other conditions to which the parties have agreed.
- Banks sometimes require borrowers to maintain **compensating balances,** which are deposit requirements set at between 10% and 20% of the loan amount. Compensating balances raise the effective interest rate on bank loans.
- A **line of credit** is an informal agreement between the bank and the borrower indicating the maximum amount of credit the bank will extend to the borrower.
- A **revolving credit agreement** is a formal line of credit often used by large firms; it involves a **commitment fee.**

- **Commercial paper** is unsecured short-term debt issued by large, financially strong corporations. Although the cost of commercial paper is lower than the cost of bank loans, it can be used only by large firms with exceptionally strong credit ratings.
- Sometimes a borrower will find that it is necessary to borrow on a **secured basis,** in which case the borrower pledges assets such as real estate, securities, equipment, inventories, or accounts receivable as collateral for the loan.

Questions

(22-1) Define each of the following terms:
a. Working capital; net working capital; net operating working capital
b. Inventory conversion period; receivables collection period; payables deferral period; cash conversion cycle
c. Relaxed NOWC policy; restricted NOWC policy; moderate NOWC policy
d. Transactions balance; compensating balance; precautionary balance
e. Cash budget; target cash balance
f. Trade discounts
g. Account receivable; days sales outstanding; aging schedule
h. Credit policy; credit period; credit standards; collection policy; cash discounts
i. Permanent NOWC; temporary NOWC
j. Moderate short-term financing policy; aggressive short-term financing policy; conservative short-term financing policy
k. Maturity matching, or "self-liquidating," approach
l. Accruals
m. Trade credit; stretching accounts payable; free trade credit; costly trade credit
n. Promissory note; line of credit; revolving credit agreement
o. Commercial paper; secured loan

(22-2) What are the two principal reasons for holding cash? Can a firm estimate its target cash balance by summing the cash held to satisfy each of the two reasons?

(22-3) Is it true that when one firm sells to another on credit, the seller records the transaction as an account receivable while the buyer records it as an account payable and that, disregarding discounts, the receivable typically exceeds the payable by the amount of profit on the sale?

(22-4) What are the four elements of a firm's credit policy? To what extent can firms set their own credit policies as opposed to having to accept policies that are dictated by "the competition"?

(22-5) What are the advantages of matching the maturities of assets and liabilities? What are the disadvantages?

(22-6) From the standpoint of the borrower, is long-term or short-term credit riskier? Explain. Would it ever make sense to borrow on a short-term basis if short-term rates were above long-term rates?

(22-7) "Firms can control their accruals within fairly wide limits." Discuss.

(22-8)   Is it true that most firms are able to obtain some free trade credit and that additional trade credit is often available, but at a cost? Explain.

(22-9)   What kinds of firms use commercial paper?

Self-Test Problems   Solutions Appear in Appendix A

(ST-1)
Working Capital Policy

The Calgary Company is attempting to establish a current assets policy. Fixed assets are $600,000, and the firm plans to maintain a 50% debt-to-assets ratio. Calgary has no operating current liabilities. The interest rate is 10% on all debt. Three alternative current asset policies are under consideration: 40%, 50%, and 60% of projected sales. The company expects to earn 15% before interest and taxes on sales of $3 million. Calgary's effective federal-plus-state tax rate is 40%. What is the expected return on equity under each alternative?

(ST-2)
Current Asset Financing

Vanderheiden Press Inc. and the Herrenhouse Publishing Company had the following balance sheets as of December 31, 2007 (thousands of dollars):

	Vanderheiden Press	Herrenhouse Publishing
Current assets	$100,000	$ 80,000
Fixed assets (net)	100,000	120,000
Total assets	$200,000	$200,000
Current liabilities	$ 20,000	$ 80,000
Long-term debt	80,000	20,000
Common stock	50,000	50,000
Retained earnings	50,000	50,000
Total liabilities and equity	$200,000	$200,000

Earnings before interest and taxes for both firms are $30 million, and the effective federal-plus-state tax rate is 40%.
a.   What is the return on equity for each firm if the interest rate on current liabilities is 10% and the rate on long-term debt is 13%?
b.   Assume that the short-term rate rises to 20%. While the rate on new long-term debt rises to 16%, the rate on existing long-term debt remains unchanged. What would be the return on equity for Vanderheiden Press and Herrenhouse Publishing under these conditions?
c.   Which company is in a riskier position? Why?

Problems   Answers Appear in Appendix B

**Easy
Problems 1–5**

(22-1)
Cash Management

Williams & Sons last year reported sales of $10 million and an inventory turnover ratio of 2. The company is now adopting a new inventory system. If the new system is able to reduce the firm's inventory level and increase the firm's inventory turnover ratio to 5 while maintaining the same level of sales, how much cash will be freed up?

(22-2)
Receivables Investment

Medwig Corporation has a DSO of 17 days. The company averages $3,500 in credit sales each day. What is the company's average accounts receivable?

(22-3)
Cost of Trade Credit

What is the nominal and effective cost of trade credit under the credit terms of 3/15, net 30?

(22-4)
Cost of Trade Credit

A large retailer obtains merchandise under the credit terms of 1/15, net 45, but routinely takes 60 days to pay its bills. Given that the retailer is an important customer, suppliers allow the firm to stretch its credit terms. What is the retailer's effective cost of trade credit?

(22-5)
Accounts Payable

A chain of appliance stores, APP Corporation, purchases inventory with a net price of $500,000 each day. The company purchases the inventory under the credit terms of 2/15, net 40. APP always takes the discount, but takes the full 15 days to pay its bills. What is the average accounts payable for APP?

**Intermediate
Problems 6–12**

(22-6)
Receivables Investment

McDowell Industries sells on terms of 3/10, net 30. Total sales for the year are $912,500. Forty percent of the customers pay on the 10th day and take discounts; the other 60% pay, on average, 40 days after their purchases.
a.   What is the days sales outstanding?
b.   What is the average amount of receivables?
c.   What would happen to average receivables if McDowell toughened up on its collection policy with the result that all nondiscount customers paid on the 30th day?

(22-7)
Cost of Trade Credit

Calculate the nominal annual cost of nonfree trade credit under each of the following terms. Assume payment is made either on the due date or on the discount date.
a.   1/15, net 20
b.   2/10, net 60
c.   3/10, net 45
d.   2/10, net 45
e.   2/15, net 40

(22-8)
Cost of Trade Credit

a.   If a firm buys under terms of 3/15, net 45, but actually pays on the 20th day and *still takes the discount*, what is the nominal cost of its nonfree trade credit?
b.   Does it receive more or less credit than it would if it paid within 15 days?

(22-9)
Cost of Trade Credit

Grunewald Industries sells on terms of 2/10, net 40. Gross sales last year were $4,562,500, and accounts receivable averaged $437,500. Half of Grunewald's customers paid on the 10th day and took discounts. What are the nominal and effective costs of trade credit to Grunewald's nondiscount customers? (Hint: Calculate sales/day based on a 365-day year; then get average receivables of discount customers; then find the DSO for the nondiscount customers.)

(22-10)
Effective Cost of Trade Credit

The D.J. Masson Corporation needs to raise $500,000 for 1 year to supply working capital to a new store. Masson buys from its suppliers on terms of 3/10, net 90, and it currently pays on the 10th day and takes discounts, but it could forgo discounts, pay on the 90th day, and get the needed $500,000 in the form of costly trade credit. What is the effective annual interest rate of the costly trade credit?

(22-11)
Cash Conversion Cycle

The Zocco Corporation has an inventory conversion period of 75 days, a receivables collection period of 38 days, and a payables deferral period of 30 days.
a.   What is the length of the firm's cash conversion cycle?
b.   If Zocco's annual sales are $3,421,875 and all sales are on credit, what is the firm's investment in accounts receivable?
c.   How many times per year does Zocco turn over its inventory?

(22-12)
Working Capital Cash Flow Cycle

The Christie Corporation is trying to determine the effect of its inventory turnover ratio and days sales outstanding (DSO) on its cash flow cycle. Christie's sales last year (all on credit) were $150,000, and it earned a net profit of 6%, or $9,000. It turned over its inventory 5 times during the year, and its DSO was 36.5 days. The firm had fixed assets totaling $35,000. Christie's payables deferral period is 40 days.
a.   Calculate Christie's cash conversion cycle.
b.   Assuming Christie holds negligible amounts of cash and marketable securities, calculate its total assets turnover and ROA.
c.   Suppose Christie's managers believe that the inventory turnover can be raised to 7.3 times. What would Christie's cash conversion cycle, total assets turnover, and ROA have been if the inventory turnover had been 7.3 for the year?

Challenging Problems 13–17

(22-13)
Working Capital Policy

The Rentz Corporation is attempting to determine the optimal level of current assets for the coming year. Management expects sales to increase to approximately $2 million as a result of an asset expansion presently being undertaken. Fixed assets total $1 million, and the firm wishes to maintain a 60% debt ratio. Rentz's interest cost is currently 8% on both short-term and longer-term debt (which the firm uses in its permanent structure). Three alternatives regarding the projected current asset level are available to the firm: (1) a tight policy requiring current assets of only 45% of projected sales, (2) a moderate policy of 50% of sales in current assets, and (3) a relaxed policy requiring current assets of 60% of sales. The firm expects to generate earnings before interest and taxes at a rate of 12% on total sales.
a.   What is the expected return on equity under each current asset level? (Assume a 40% effective federal-plus-state tax rate.)
b.   In this problem, we have assumed that the level of expected sales is independent of current asset policy. Is this a valid assumption?
c.   How would the overall riskiness of the firm vary under each policy?

(22-14)
Cash Budgeting

Dorothy Koehl recently leased space in the Southside Mall and opened a new business, Koehl's Doll Shop. Business has been good, but Koehl has frequently run out of cash. This has necessitated late payment on certain orders, which, in turn, is beginning to cause a problem with suppliers. Koehl plans to borrow from the bank to have cash ready as needed, but first she needs a forecast of just how much she must borrow. Accordingly, she has asked you to prepare a cash budget for the critical period around Christmas, when needs will be especially high.

Sales are made on a cash basis only. Koehl's purchases must be paid for during the following month. Koehl pays herself a salary of $4,800 per month, and the rent is $2,000 per month. In addition, she must make a tax payment of $12,000 in December. The current cash on hand (on December 1) is $400, but Koehl has agreed to maintain an average bank balance of $6,000—this is her target cash balance. (Disregard till cash, which is insignificant because Koehl keeps only a small amount on hand in order to lessen the chances of robbery.)

The estimated sales and purchases for December, January, and February are shown below. Purchases during November amounted to $140,000.

	Sales	Purchases
December	$160,000	$40,000
January	40,000	40,000
February	60,000	40,000

a. Prepare a cash budget for December, January, and February.
b. Now, suppose Koehl were to start selling on a credit basis on December 1, giving customers 30 days to pay. All customers accept these terms, and all other facts in the problem are unchanged. What would the company's loan requirements be at the end of December in this case? (Hint: The calculations required to answer this question are minimal.)

(22-15)
Cash Discounts

Suppose a firm makes purchases of $3.65 million per year under terms of 2/10, net 30, and takes discounts.
a. What is the average amount of accounts payable net of discounts? (Assume that the $3.65 million of purchases is net of discounts—that is, gross purchases are $3,724,489.80, discounts are $74,489.80, and net purchases are $3.65 million.)
b. Is there a cost of the trade credit the firm uses?
c. If the firm did not take discounts but it did pay on the due date, what would be its average payables and the cost of this nonfree trade credit?
d. What would its cost of not taking discounts be if it could stretch its payments to 40 days?

(22-16)
Trade Credit

The Thompson Corporation projects an increase in sales from $1.5 million to $2 million, but it needs an additional $300,000 of current assets to support this expansion. Thompson can finance the expansion by no longer taking discounts, thus increasing accounts payable. Thompson purchases under terms of 2/10, net 30, but it can delay payment for an additional 35 days—paying in 65 days and thus becoming 35 days past due—without a penalty because of its suppliers' current excess capacity problems. What is the effective, or equivalent, annual cost of the trade credit?

(22-17)
Bank Financing

The Raattama Corporation had sales of $3.5 million last year, and it earned a 5% return, after taxes, on sales. Recently, the company has fallen behind in its accounts payable. Although its terms of purchase are net 30 days, its accounts payable represent 60 days' purchases. The company's treasurer is seeking to increase bank borrowings in order to become current in meeting its trade obligations (that is, to have 30 days' payables outstanding). The company's balance sheet is as follows (thousands of dollars):

Cash	$ 100	Accounts payable	$ 600
Accounts receivable	300	Bank loans	700
Inventory	1,400	Accruals	200
Current assets	$1,800	Current liabilities	$1,500
Land and buildings	600	Mortgage on real estate	700
Equipment	600	Common stock, $0.10 par	300
		Retained earnings	500
Total assets	$3,000	Total liabilities and equity	$3,000

a. How much bank financing is needed to eliminate the past-due accounts payable?

b. Would you as a bank loan officer make the loan? Why or why not?

Spreadsheet Problem

e-resource

(22-18)

Build a Model: Cash Budgeting

Start with the partial model in the file *FM12 Ch 22 P18 Build a Model.xls* from the textbook's Web site. Helen Bowers, owner of Helen's Fashion Designs, is planning to request a line of credit from her bank. She has estimated the following sales forecasts for the firm for parts of 2008 and 2009:

	Sales	Labor and Raw Materials
May 2008	$180,000	$ 90,000
June	180,000	90,000
July	360,000	126,000
August	540,000	882,000
September	720,000	306,000
October	360,000	234,000
November	360,000	162,000
December	90,000	90,000
January 2009	180,000	NA

Collection estimates obtained from the credit and collection department are as follows: collections within the month of sale, 10%; collections the month following the sale, 75%; collections the second month following the sale, 15%. Payments for labor and raw materials are typically made during the month following the one in which these costs have been incurred. Total labor and raw materials costs are estimated for each month as shown above.

General and administrative salaries will amount to approximately $27,000 a month; lease payments under long-term lease contracts will be $9,000 a month; depreciation charges will be $36,000 a month; miscellaneous expenses will be $2,700 a month; income tax payments of $63,000 will be due in both September and December; and a progress payment of $180,000 on a new design studio must be paid in October. Cash on hand on July 1 will amount to $132,000, and a minimum cash balance of $90,000 will be maintained throughout the cash budget period.

a. Prepare a monthly cash budget for the last 6 months of 2008.

b. Prepare an estimate of the required financing (or excess funds)—that is, the amount of money Bowers will need to borrow (or will have available to invest)—for each month during that period.

c. Assume that receipts from sales come in uniformly during the month (that is, cash receipts come in at the rate of 1/30 each day), but all outflows are paid on the 5th of the month. Will this have an effect on the cash budget—in other words, would the cash budget you have prepared be valid under these assumptions? If not, what can be done to make a valid estimate of peak financing requirements? No calculations are required, although calculations can be used to illustrate the effects.

d. Bowers produces on a seasonal basis, just ahead of sales. Without making any calculations, discuss how the company's current ratio and debt ratio would vary during the year assuming all financial requirements were met by short-term bank loans. Could changes in these ratios affect the firm's ability to obtain bank credit?

e. If its customers began to pay late, this would slow down collections and thus increase the required loan amount. Also, if sales dropped off, this would have an effect on the required loan. Do a sensitivity analysis that shows the effects of these two factors on the maximum loan requirement.

---

e-resource

Cyberproblem

Please go to the textbook's Web site to access any Cyberproblems.

Mini Case

Dan Barnes, financial manager of Ski Equipment Inc. (SKI), is excited, but apprehensive. The company's founder recently sold his 51% controlling block of stock to Kent Koren, who is a big fan of EVA (Economic Value Added). EVA is found by taking the after-tax operating profit and then subtracting the dollar cost of all the capital the firm uses:

$$\text{EVA} = \text{NOPAT} - \text{Capital costs}$$
$$= \text{EBIT}(1 - \text{T}) - \text{WACC}(\text{Capital employed}).$$

If EVA is positive, then the firm is creating value. On the other hand, if EVA is negative, the firm is not covering its cost of capital, and stockholders' value is being eroded. Koren rewards managers handsomely if they create value, but those whose operations produce negative EVAs are soon looking for work. Koren frequently points out that if a company could generate its current level of sales with fewer assets, it would need less capital. That would, other things held constant, lower capital costs and increase its EVA.

Shortly after he took control of SKI, Kent Koren met with SKI's senior executives to tell them of his plans for the company. First, he presented some EVA data that convinced everyone that SKI had not been creating value in recent years. He then stated, in no uncertain terms, that this situation must change. He noted that

SKI's designs of skis, boots, and clothing are acclaimed throughout the industry, but something is seriously amiss elsewhere in the company. Costs are too high, prices are too low, or the company employs too much capital, and he wants SKI's managers to correct the problem or else.

Barnes has long felt that SKI's working capital situation should be studied—the company may have the optimal amounts of cash, securities, receivables, and inventories, but it may also have too much or too little of these items. In the past, the production manager resisted Barnes's efforts to question his holdings of raw materials inventories, the marketing manager resisted questions about finished goods, the sales staff resisted questions about credit policy (which affects accounts receivable), and the treasurer did not want to talk about her cash and securities balances. Koren's speech made it clear that such resistance would no longer be tolerated.

Barnes also knows that decisions about working capital cannot be made in a vacuum. For example, if inventories could be lowered without adversely affecting operations, then less capital would be required, the dollar cost of capital would decline, and EVA would increase. However, lower raw materials inventories might lead to production slowdowns and higher costs, while lower finished goods inventories might lead to the loss of profitable sales. So, before inventories are changed, it will be necessary to study operating as well as financial effects. The situation is the same with regard to cash and receivables. Barnes began collecting the ratios shown below.

	SKI	Industry
Current	1.75	2.25
Quick	0.83	1.20
Debt/assets	58.76%	50.00%
Turnover of cash and securities	16.67	22.22
Days sales outstanding (365-day basis)	45.63	32.00
Inventory turnover	4.82	7.00
Fixed assets turnover	11.35	12.00
Total assets turnover	2.08	3.00
Profit margin on sales	2.07%	3.50%
Return on equity (ROE)	10.45%	21.00%
Payables deferral period	30.00	33.00

	Nov	Dec	Jan	Feb	Mar	Apr
I. Collections and Purchases Worksheet						
(1) Sales (gross)	$71,218	$68,212	$65,213	$52,475	$42,909	$30,524
Collections						
(2) During month of sale (0.2)(0.98)(month's sales)			12,781.75	10,285.10		
(3) During first month after sale (0.7)(previous month's sales)			47,748.40	45,649.10		
(4) During second month after sale (0.1)(sales 2 months ago)			7,121.80	6,821.20		
(5) Total collections (Lines 2 + 3 + 4)			$67,651.95	$62,755.40		

	Nov	Dec	Jan	Feb	Mar	Apr
Purchases						
(6) (0.85)(forecasted sales 2 months from now)		$44,603.75	$36,472.65	$25,945.40		
(7) Payments (1-month lag)			44,603.75	36,472.65		
II. Cash Gain or Loss for Month						
(8) Collections (from Section I)			$67,651.95	$62,755.40		
(9) Payments for purchases (from Section I)			44,603.75	36,472.65		
(10) Wages and salaries			6,690.56	5,470.90		
(11) Rent			2,500.00	2,500.00		
(12) Taxes						
(13) Total payments			$53,794.31	$44,443.55		
(14) Net cash gain (loss) during month (Line 8 − Line 13)			$13,857.64	$18,311.85		
III. Cash Surplus or Loan Requirement						
(15) Cash at beginning of month if no borrowing is done			$ 3,000.00	$16,857.64		
(16) Cumulative cash (cash at start + gain or − loss = Line 14 + Line 15)			16,857.64	35,169.49		
(17) Target cash balance			1,500.00	1,500.00		
(18) Cumulative surplus cash or loans outstanding to maintain $1,500 target cash balance (Line 16 − Line 17)			$15,357.64	$33,669.49		

a. Barnes plans to use the preceding ratios as the starting point for discussions with SKI's operating executives. He wants everyone to think about the pros and cons of changing each type of current asset and how changes would interact to affect profits and EVA. Based on the data, does SKI seem to be following a relaxed, moderate, or restricted working capital policy?

b. How can one distinguish between a relaxed but rational working capital policy and a situation in which a firm simply has a lot of current assets because it is inefficient? Does SKI's working capital policy seem appropriate?

c. Calculate the firm's cash conversion cycle. Assume a 365-day year.

d. What might SKI do to reduce its cash without harming operations?

In an attempt to better understand SKI's cash position, Barnes developed a cash budget. Data for the first 2 months of the year are shown above. (Note that Barnes's preliminary cash budget does not account for interest income or interest expense.) He has the figures for the other months, but they are not shown.

e. Should depreciation expense be explicitly included in the cash budget? Why or why not?

f. In his preliminary cash budget, Barnes has assumed that all sales are collected and, thus, that SKI has no bad debts. Is this realistic? If not, how would bad debts be dealt with in a cash budgeting sense? (Hint: Bad debts will affect collections but not purchases.)

g. Barnes's cash budget for the entire year, although not given here, is based heavily on his forecast for monthly sales. Sales are expected to be extremely low between May and September but then increase dramatically in the fall and winter. November is typically the firm's best month, when SKI ships equipment to retailers for the holiday season. Interestingly, Barnes's forecasted cash budget indicates that the company's cash holdings will exceed the targeted cash balance every month except for October and November, when shipments will be high but collections will not be coming in until later. Based on the ratios shown earlier, does it appear that SKI's target cash balance is appropriate? In addition to possibly lowering the target cash balance, what actions might SKI take to better improve its cash management policies, and how might that affect its EVA?

h. What reasons might SKI have for maintaining a relatively high amount of cash?

i. What are the three categories of inventory costs? If the company takes steps to reduce its inventory, what effect would this have on the various costs of holding inventory?

j. Is there any reason to think that SKI may be holding too much inventory? If so, how would that affect EVA and ROE?

k. If the company reduces its inventory without adversely affecting sales, what effect should this have on the company's cash position (1) in the short run and (2) in the long run? Explain in terms of the cash budget and the balance sheet.

l. Barnes knows that SKI sells on the same credit terms as other firms in its industry. Use the ratios presented earlier to explain whether SKI's customers pay more or less promptly than those of its competitors. If there are differences, does that suggest that SKI should tighten or loosen its credit policy? What four variables make up a firm's credit policy, and in what direction should each be changed by SKI?

m. Does SKI face any risks if it tightens its credit policy?

n. If the company reduces its DSO without seriously affecting sales, what effect would this have on its cash position (1) in the short run and (2) in the long run? Answer in terms of the cash budget and the balance sheet. What effect should this have on EVA in the long run?

In addition to improving the management of its current assets, SKI is also reviewing the ways in which it finances its current assets. With this concern in mind, Dan is also trying to answer the following questions.

o. Is it likely that SKI could make significantly greater use of accruals?

p. Assume that SKI buys on terms of 1/10, net 30, but that it can get away with paying on the 40th day if it chooses not to take discounts. Also, assume that it purchases $506,985 of equipment per year, net of discounts. How much free trade credit can the company get, how much costly trade credit can it get, and what is the percentage cost of the costly credit? Should SKI take discounts?

q. SKI tries to match the maturity of its assets and liabilities. Describe how SKI could adopt either a more aggressive or more conservative financing policy.

r. What are the advantages and disadvantages of using short-term debt as a source of financing?

s. Would it be feasible for SKI to finance with commercial paper?

Selected Additional Cases

The following cases from Textchoice, *Cengage Learning's online case library, cover many of the concepts discussed in this chapter and are available at* **http://www.textchoice2.com.**

Klein-Brigham Series:
Case 29, "Office Mates, Inc.," which illustrates how changes in current asset policy affect expected profitability and risk; Case 32, "Alpine Wear, Inc.," which illustrates the mechanics of the cash budget and the rationale behind its use; Case 50, "Toy World, Inc.," and Case 66, "Sorenson Stove Company," which deal with cash budgeting; Case 33, "Upscale Toddlers, Inc.," which deals with credit policy changes; and Case 34, "Texas Rose Company," which focuses on receivables management.

Brigham-Buzzard Series:
Case 11, "Powerline Network Corporation (Working Capital Management)."

Derivatives and Risk Management

Bombardier Inc., a manufacturer of snowmobiles in Montreal, has always tried to control risks. However, its snowmobile division's profits depend on a risk that is notoriously hard to control: the weather. Early signs of a cold, snowy winter lead to a brisk sellout, whereas warmer temperatures force Bombardier to cut prices to shed excess inventory.

Bombardier can't change the weather, but it does its best to manage its weather-related risks. For example, one winter the company offered to pay a $1,000 rebate to snowmobile buyers in 16 Midwestern cities if the area snowfall that winter turned out to be less than one-half the average snowfall over the previous 3 years. Not surprisingly, the rebate led to higher sales. Bombardier then took an important step to limit its risks—it bought "snowfall options." For each snowmobile sold, Bombardier paid an option writer between $45 and $400, depending on the city in which the snowmobile was purchased. In return, the option writer fully reimbursed Bombardier each time it had to pay a customer the $1,000 rebate.

These snowfall options are just one example of "weather derivatives," a small but rapidly growing market. The Chicago Mercantile Exchange (CME) now trades a large number of weather-based futures and options contracts. Some of these contracts are based on the average monthly temperature, some on snowfall, and some on the number of frost days. Contracts are available for the weather in a variety of U.S. and international cities, from Des Moines to Berlin to Tokyo. Not surprisingly, many participants are electric and gas utilities whose earnings depend on weather.

Weather derivatives represent just one of many approaches companies can use to control risk. As you read this chapter, try to answer these questions: Why should a company try to manage its risks? What financial techniques can be used to manage risk? Can programs designed to limit risks actually increase them, and if so, what safeguards should companies put in place to prevent this unintended consequence?

Sources: Mark Golden and Ed Silliere, "Weather Derivatives Are Becoming a Popular Hedge," *The Wall Street Journal*, February 2, 1999, B9A; and the Chicago Mercantile Exchange, **http://www.cme.com**.

In this chapter, we discuss risk management, a topic of increasing importance to financial managers. The term *risk management* can mean many things, but in business it involves identifying events that could have adverse financial consequences and then taking actions to prevent and/or minimize the damage caused by these events. Years ago, corporate risk managers dealt primarily with insurance—they made sure the firm was adequately insured against fire, theft, and other casualties, and that it had adequate liability coverage. More recently, the scope of risk management has been broadened to include such things as controlling the costs of key inputs like petroleum by purchasing oil futures, or protecting against changes in interest rates or exchange rates through transactions in the interest rate or foreign exchange markets. In addition, risk managers try to ensure that actions intended to hedge against risk are not actually increasing risks.

e-resource

The textbook's Web site contains an *Excel* file that will guide you through the chapter's calculations. The file for this chapter is **FM12 Ch 23 Tool Kit.xls,** and we encourage you to open the file and follow along as you read the chapter.

Also, since the September 11, 2001, attacks on the World Trade Center and Pentagon, insurance against terrorist attacks has become a major issue. Unless possible terrorist targets—including large malls, office buildings, oil refineries, airlines, and ships—can be insured against attacks, lenders may refuse to provide mortgage financing, and that would crimp the economy. Private insurance companies are reluctant to insure these projects, at least without charging prohibitive premiums, so the federal government has been asked to step in and provide terrorist insurance. Normally, it is best to have private projects insured by private insurance, because then risk-reducing actions will be taken to hold down insurance costs.[1] However, losses due to terrorist attacks are potentially so large that they could bankrupt even strong insurance companies. How this new risk should be dealt with is currently being debated in Washington and around the world.

23.1 Reasons to Manage Risk

We know that investors dislike risk. We also know that most investors hold well-diversified portfolios, so at least in theory the only "relevant risk" is systematic risk. Therefore, if you asked corporate executives what type of risk worries them most, you might expect their answer to be "beta." However, this is almost certainly not the answer you would get. The most likely answer, if you asked a CEO to define risk, would be similar to this: "Risk is the possibility that our future earnings and free cash flows will be significantly lower than we expect." For example, consider Plastics Inc., which manufactures dashboards, interior door panels, and other plastic components used by auto companies. Petroleum is the key feedstock for plastic and thus makes up a large percentage of its costs. Plastics has a 3-year contract with an auto company to deliver 500,000 door panels each year, at a price of $20 each. When the company recently signed this contract, oil sold for $50 per barrel, and oil was expected to stay at that level for the next 3 years. If oil prices fell during this time, Plastics would have higher than expected profits and free cash flows, but if oil prices rose, profits would fall. Since Plastics' value depends on its profits and free cash flows, a change in the price of oil would cause stockholders to earn either more or less than they anticipated.

---

[1] Most insurance policies exclude claims that result from acts of war. Now claims based on terrorist attacks are also being excluded from new policies.

Corporate Valuation and Risk Management

Risk management can reduce firm risk, leading to a lower cost of capital. In some instances, derivatives such as swaps can actually reduce the effective interest rate paid by a corporation, again reducing its cost of capital.

$$\text{Value} = \frac{FCF_1}{(1 + WACC)^1} + \frac{FCF_2}{(1 + WACC)^2} + \frac{FCF_3}{(1 + WACC)^3} + \cdots + \frac{FCF_\infty}{(1 + WACC)^\infty}$$

Now suppose that shortly after signing the contract with its door panel supplier, Plastics announces that it plans to lock in a 3-year supply of oil at a guaranteed price of $50 per barrel, and the cost of getting the guarantee is zero. Would that cause its stock price to rise? At first glance, it seems that the answer should be yes, but maybe that's not correct. Recall that the value of a stock depends on the present value of its expected future free cash flows, discounted at the weighted average cost of capital (WACC). Locking in the cost of oil will cause an increase in Plastics' stock price if and only if (1) it causes the expected future free cash flows to increase or (2) it causes the WACC to decline.

Consider first the free cash flows. Before the announcement of guaranteed oil costs, investors had formed an estimate of the expected future free cash flows, based on an expected oil price of $50 per barrel. Therefore, while locking in the cost of oil at $50 per barrel will lower the riskiness of the expected future free cash flows, it might not change the expected *size* of these cash flows, because investors already expected a price of $50 per barrel. Note, though, that declining cash flows can disrupt a firm's operation, and that disruption can in turn adversely affect cash flows.

Now what about the WACC? It will change only if locking in the cost of oil causes a change in the cost of debt or equity, or the target capital structure. Assuming the foreseeable increases in the price of oil were not enough to raise the threat of bankruptcy, Plastics' cost of debt should not change, and neither should its target capital structure. Regarding the cost of equity, recall from Chapter 6 that most investors hold well-diversified portfolios, which means that the cost of equity should depend only on systematic risk. Moreover, even though an increase in oil prices would have a negative effect on Plastics' stock price, it would not have a negative effect on all stocks. Indeed, oil producers should have higher than expected returns and stock prices. Assuming that Plastics' investors hold well-diversified portfolios, including stocks of oil-producing companies, there would not appear to be much reason to expect its cost of equity to decrease. The bottom line is this: If Plastics' expected future cash flows and WACC will not change significantly due to an elimination of the risk of oil price increases, then neither should the value of its stock.

We discuss futures contracts and hedging in detail in the next section, but for now let's assume that Plastics has *not* locked in oil prices. Therefore, if oil prices increase, its stock price will fall. However, if its stockholders know this, they can build portfolios that contain oil futures whose values will rise or fall with oil prices and thus offset changes in the price of Plastics' stock. By choosing the correct amount of futures contracts, investors can thus "hedge" their portfolios and completely eliminate the risk due to changes in oil prices. There will be a cost to hedging, but that cost to large, sophisticated investors should be about the same as the cost to Plastics. Since stockholders can hedge away oil price risk themselves, why should they pay a higher price for Plastics' stock just because the company itself hedged away the risk?

The points raised above notwithstanding, companies clearly believe that active risk management is important. A 1998 survey reported that 83% of firms with market values greater than $1.2 billion engage in risk management, and that percentage is surely much higher today.[2] Here are several reasons companies manage risks:

1. *Debt capacity.* Risk management can reduce the volatility of cash flows, which decreases the probability of bankruptcy. As we discussed in Chapter 16, firms with lower operating risks can use more debt, and this can lead to higher stock prices due to the interest tax savings.

2. *Maintaining the optimal capital budget over time.* Recall from Chapter 16 that firms are reluctant to raise external equity due to high flotation costs and market pressure. This means that the capital budget must generally be financed with debt plus internally generated funds, mainly retained earnings and depreciation. In bad years, internal cash flows may be too low to support the optimal capital budget, causing firms to either slow investment below the optimal rate or else incur the high costs associated with external equity. By smoothing out the cash flows, risk management can alleviate this problem. This issue is most relevant for firms with large growth opportunities. A recent study by Professors Gerald Gay and Jouahn Nam found that such firms do in fact use derivatives more than low-growth firms.[3] Thus, maintaining an optimal capital budget is an important determinant of firms' risk management practices.

3. *Financial distress.* The stages of financial distress can range from stockholder concern, to higher interest rates on debt, to customer defections, to bankruptcy. Any serious level of financial distress causes a firm to have lower cash flows than expected. Risk management can reduce the likelihood of low cash flows, hence of financial distress.

4. *Comparative advantages in hedging.* Most investors cannot hedge as efficiently as a company. First, firms generally have lower transactions costs due to a larger volume of hedging activities. Second, there is the problem of asymmetric information—managers know more about the firm's risk exposure than outside investors; hence managers can create more effective hedges. And third, effective risk management requires specialized skills and knowledge that firms are more likely to have.

5. *Borrowing costs.* As discussed later in the chapter, firms can sometimes reduce input costs, especially the interest rate on debt, through the use of derivative instruments called "swaps." Any such cost reduction adds value to the firm.

6. *Tax effects.* The present value of taxes paid by companies with volatile earnings is higher than the present value of taxes paid by stable companies due to the treatment of tax credits and the rules governing corporate loss carryforwards and carrybacks. Moreover, if volatile earnings cause a company to declare

---

[2]See Gordon M. Bodnar, Gregory S. Hayt, and Richard C. Marston, "1998 Wharton Survey of Financial Risk Management by U.S. Non-Financial Firms," *Financial Management*, Winter 1998, pp. 70–91.
[3]See Gerald D. Gay and Jouahn Nam, "The Underinvestment Problem and Corporate Derivatives Use," *Financial Management*, Winter 1998, pp. 53–69.

bankruptcy, then the company usually completely loses its tax loss carryforwards. Therefore, using risk management to stabilize earnings can reduce the present value of a company's tax burden.[4]

7. *Compensation systems.* Many compensation systems establish "floors" and "ceilings" on bonuses, and also reward managers for meeting targets. To illustrate, suppose a firm's compensation system calls for a manager to receive no bonus if net income is below $1 million, a bonus of $10,000 if income is between $1 million and $2 million, and one of $20,000 if income is $2 million or more. Moreover, the manager will receive an additional $10,000 if actual income is at least 90% of the forecasted level, which is $1 million. Now consider the following two situations. First, if income is stable at $2 million each year, the manager gets a $30,000 bonus each year, for a 2-year total of $60,000. However, if income is zero the first year and $4 million the second, the manager gets no bonus the first year and $30,000 the second, for a 2-year total of $30,000. So, even though the company has the same total income ($4 million) over the 2 years, the manager's bonus is higher if earnings are stable. Therefore, even if hedging does not add much value for stockholders, it may still benefit managers.

Since perhaps the most important aspect of risk management involves derivative securities, the next section explains **derivatives,** which are securities whose values are determined by the market price of some other asset. Derivatives include *options,* which we discussed in Chapter 9, whose values depend on the price of some underlying asset; *interest rate and exchange rate futures and swaps,* whose values depend on interest rate and exchange rate levels; and *commodity futures,* whose values depend on commodity prices.

SELF-TEST

Explain why finance theory, combined with well-diversified investors and "homemade hedging," might suggest that risk management should not add much value to a company.

List and explain some reasons companies might actually employ risk management techniques.

23.2 Background on Derivatives

See the Chicago Board of Trade's Web site, **http:// www.cbot.com,** for a wealth of information on the operation and history of the exchange.

A historical perspective is useful for studying derivatives. One of the first formal markets for derivatives was the futures market for wheat. Farmers were concerned about the price they would receive for their wheat when they sold it in the fall, and millers were concerned about the price they would have to pay. Each party soon realized that the risks they faced could be reduced if they established a price earlier in the year. Accordingly, mill agents began going out to the Wheat Belt with contracts that called for the farmers to deliver grain at a predetermined price, and both parties benefited from the transaction in the sense that their risks were reduced. The farmers could concentrate on growing their crop without worrying about the price of grain, and the millers could concentrate on their milling operations. Thus, *hedging with futures* lowered aggregate risk in the economy.

These early futures dealings were between two parties who arranged transactions between themselves. Soon, though, intermediaries came into the picture,

---

[4]See Clifford W. Smith and René Stulz, "The Determinants of Firms' Hedging Policies," *The Journal of Financial and Quantitative Analysis,* December 1985, pp. 395–406.

and *trading* in futures was established. The Chicago Board of Trade, founded in 1848, was an early marketplace where *futures dealers* helped make a market in futures contracts. Thus, farmers could sell futures on the exchange, and millers could buy them there. This improved the efficiency and lowered the cost of hedging operations.

A third group—*speculators*—soon entered the scene. As we see in the next section, most derivatives, including futures, are highly leveraged, meaning that a small change in the value of the underlying asset will produce a large change in the price of the derivative. This leverage appealed to speculators. At first blush, one might think that the appearance of speculators would increase risk, but this is not true. Speculators add capital and players to the market, which tends to stabilize the market. Of course, derivatives markets are inherently volatile due to the leverage involved; hence risk to the speculators themselves is high. Still, the speculators bear much of the risk, which makes the derivatives markets more stable for hedgers.

Natural hedges, defined as situations in which aggregate risk can be reduced by derivatives transactions between two parties (called *counterparties*), exist for many commodities, for foreign currencies, for interest rates on securities with different maturities, and even for common stocks where investors want to "hedge their bets." Natural hedges occur when futures are traded between cotton farmers and cotton mills, copper mines and copper fabricators, importers and foreign manufacturers for currency exchange rates, electric utilities and coal mines, and oil producers and oil users. In all such situations, hedging reduces aggregate risk and thus benefits the economy.

Hedging can also be done in situations in which no natural hedge exists. Here one party wants to reduce some type of risk, and another party agrees to write a contract that protects the first party from that specific event or situation. Insurance is an obvious example of this type of hedge. Note, though, that with nonsymmetric hedges, risks are generally *transferred* rather than *eliminated*. Even here, though, insurance companies can reduce certain types of risk through diversification.

The derivatives markets have grown more rapidly than any other major market in recent years, for a number of reasons. First, analytical techniques such as the Black-Scholes Option Pricing Model, which was discussed in Chapter 9, have been developed to help establish "fair" prices, and having a good, transparent basis for pricing hedges makes the counterparties more comfortable with deals. Second, computers and electronic communications make it much easier for counterparties to deal with one another. Third, globalization has greatly increased the importance of currency markets and the need for reducing the exchange rate risks brought on by global trade. Recent trends and developments are sure to continue if not accelerate, so the use of derivatives for risk management is bound to grow.[5]

SELF-TEST

What is a "natural hedge"? Give some examples of natural hedges.

List three reasons the derivatives markets have grown more rapidly than any other major market in recent years.

---

[5]For more information on the derivatives markets, see Don M. Chance, *An Introduction to Derivatives and Risk Management* (Mason, OH: Thomson/South-Western, 2004); and Alger B. "Duke" Chapman, "Future of the Derivatives Markets: Products, Technology, and Participants," *Financial Practice and Education*, Fall/Winter 1994, pp. 124–128.

23.3 Derivatives in the News

Although derivatives are very important tools for corporate risk management, they also have a potential downside. These instruments are highly leveraged, so small miscalculations can lead to huge losses. They are also complicated and misunderstood by most people. This makes mistakes more likely than with less complex instruments and, importantly, it makes it harder for a firm's top management to understand and exercise proper control over derivatives transactions. This potential for miscalculation and misuse has led to some highly publicized losses for some large and well-respected companies in the past several years. Procter & Gamble (P&G), Gibson Greetings, Metallgesellschaft, Barings Bank, Long Term Capital Management (LTCM), Enron, and Orange County, California, all experienced losses that were either attributed to or associated with inappropriate use of derivatives. In the Barings Bank case, one relatively low-level 28-year-old employee operating in the Far East entered into transactions that led to the bankruptcy of Britain's oldest bank, the institution that held the accounts of the Queen of England. We give a more detailed explanation of the LTCM case and Enron Corporation's failure below.

Long Term Capital Management (LTCM)

The August 29, 1994, cover story of *BusinessWeek* described the formation of Long Term Capital Management LP (LTCM). The LP stands for **limited partnership,** and LTCM was a **hedge fund** set up as a limited partnership. A hedge fund is a money management organization that can invest in essentially any type of asset anywhere in the world, can (and does) sell securities short, can use as much leverage as banks and other lenders will permit, and is essentially unregulated. Originally, hedge funds truly hedged—they bought what they thought were undervalued securities and sold short what they thought were overvalued securities. Now, however, hedge funds also take positions in options and other complex derivatives. Because they are largely unregulated, hedge funds are open only to "sophisticated" investors, generally defined as individuals or institutions whose net worth is in the millions and whose income is in the hundreds of thousands.

LTCM's chairman, John Meriwether, was perhaps the best-known Wall Street trader. His team, described by *BusinessWeek* as the "Dream Team," included other renowned traders, the former vice chairman of the Federal Reserve Board (David Mullins), and two Nobel Prize winners (Myron Scholes, co-inventor of the Black-Scholes Option Pricing Model, and Robert Merton of the Massachusetts Institute of Technology). LTCM quickly attracted about $3 billion of equity capital from a "Who's Who" of financial leaders and institutions, including the chairmen of Merrill Lynch and Yale University, and it arranged to borrow more than $100 *billion* to leverage its positions.

The fund then made bets on securities all around the globe, and from 1994 through 1997, it earned huge annual returns—in the vicinity of 50% per year. Then, in 1998, the roof caved in. LTCM made a number of leveraged bets that didn't work out. Most importantly, it bet that there would be a "convergence" of interest rates between risk-free and riskier bonds, that is, that risk premiums would shrink. So, it sold Treasury bonds short and bought risky bonds to the tune of billions of dollars. It also established positions in stocks it thought were undervalued, in Russian securities, in European currencies, and so forth. But LTCM was wrong on almost all counts. Economies around the world began collapsing, leading to a "flight to quality." This meant that investors started selling risky securities and buying Treasury bonds, which widened bonds' risk premiums and led away from rather than toward the convergence LTCM was betting on.

With its 33-to-1 leverage, even a small miscalculation would have eroded LTCM's equity position, and the massive disruption in world markets led to losses of 50% *per month* during the summer of 1998. Worried bankers began to call in their loans, forcing LTCM to sell securities at a loss. Those distressed sales caused the securities' prices to fall further, which exacerbated the problem. It soon became clear that LTCM would have to default on some of its $100 billion of loans, putting the banks that made the loans at risk. At the same time, other hedge funds began to take hits, and the possibility of a worldwide financial collapse soon loomed. At that point, the Federal Reserve stepped in, twisted some bankers' arms, and induced the banks to provide $3.6 billion in new equity capital to LTCM and take control. As a result of the massive bailout, LTCM was able to liquidate its portfolio in an orderly fashion over the next 15 months, and it returned the entire $3.6 billion to the banks by the end of December 1999. However, LTCM's original investors lost about 90% of their investment.

Enron and Other Energy Traders

Most segments of the electric power industry were deregulated during the 1990s. Previously, all power users were required to buy from their local utility, but after deregulation large users, which account for about 65% of electricity usage, could buy from other suppliers. Independent power producers then built plants and began competing with the older utilities. Power users could either buy electricity on the "spot" market at prices that fluctuated depending on supply and demand, or else contract with independent producers to buy at a fixed price for delivery in the future. Thus, the electricity market was transformed from a regulated monopoly into a competitive market that was something akin to the wheat market, where farmers worked with grain merchants to deliver wheat to milling companies.

However, there is a major difference between wheat and electricity—wheat can be stored efficiently, and stored wheat mitigates the effects of supply and demand fluctuations on prices. Electricity cannot be stored, so supply and demand fluctuations result in wide price swings, which disrupt both users and producers. It did not take long for users and producers to realize that all parties would benefit by hedging with long-term supply contracts at fixed prices. Users would have an assured supply at a known price, and producers would have a guaranteed market for their power. Thus, hedging would help all parties, just as it helped wheat farmers and millers.

Enron Corporation was one of the first companies to get into the electricity trading business. Enron owned a few generating plants, but it operated primarily as a marketer, buying from merchant generators and reselling to large users. Enron would sign a multiyear contract to supply specific amounts of electricity at a fixed price to a customer such as General Motors. For example, it might agree to build a new plant, expecting to produce power at a cost of 3 cents per kilowatt-hour (kWh) and simultaneously contract to sell the plant's output at 3.1¢/kWh. The 0.1¢/kWh margin would cover administrative costs and provide a "normal" profit. Under those conditions, the PV of the expected revenues would be about equal to the PV of the expected costs, so the NPV of the new plant would be slightly above zero.[6]

Now suppose conditions changed so that the cost of producing power fell below 3.0¢/kWh, say to 2 cents, but the price remained at 3.1 cents. In that case, the expected cash flows from the new plant would rise, causing the contract's net present value to increase. Enron would report the increase in the contract's value as profit and add it to operating income. The higher profit would then boost the stock price and trigger executive bonuses.

Such a development would be legal, but Enron cheated. Its executives wanted to report higher profits in order to trigger bonuses and more stock options, so it inflated its profits by forecasting unreasonably high sales prices, unreasonably low purchase costs, and thus unreasonably high profits. It also downplayed the risk inherent in the contracts and discounted the overstated cash flows at unreasonably low discount rates. All of this should have been caught by its auditor, Arthur Andersen, but Andersen let Enron get away with it, resulting in reported profits that were far too high.

Note too that California environmentalists had for years prevented the construction of new plants. The growing demand for power caught up with a fixed supply in 2000, and a shortage resulted. This led to huge price spikes and enormous profits for generators and traders such as Enron. California then relaxed its restrictions on construction, and Enron's wonderful reported profits attracted other companies into considering construction of new plants and getting into the energy trading business. Some made careful forecasts and concluded that something was fishy because their forecasts did not produce results anywhere close to those reported by Enron. These companies wisely avoided the new market. However, others decided that if Enron could do it, so could they, and they charged ahead with new plant construction, financed primarily with debt.

When all the new capacity came online, it greatly exceeded demand. This led to huge price declines, and the builders of new plants found themselves in trouble. A new plant might have cost $100 million and shown an NPV of $10 million based on output prices when construction began. However, when the new plant came online the new low prices might have led to an actual NPV of *minus* $50 million. Similarly, a trading company that had contracted to buy power for a long period, at say 4¢/kWh, expecting to sell it in the spot market for 5 cents, might have found that it could only sell the power for 3 cents, and that too would have resulted in a *negative* NPV for the contract. Those results had to be reflected in the financial statements, so there were massive reported losses and huge write-downs, which lowered stockholder equity on the balance sheets. This, in turn, raised the companies' debt ratios, lowered their coverage ratios, and generally reduced their financial strength.

No one wants to sign a long-term contract with a party that might default if things go badly, so energy traders must have letters of credit that assure counterparties that they can make good on their contracts. They are required to maintain their financial ratios at specified levels, and if the covenants are violated, they must put up additional collateral. Many could not do so, and that led to bankruptcies.

Some old-line utilities built merchant plants and thus got into trouble. Examples include Duke Power and TECO Energy, both of which saw their stock

---

[6]Similarly, Enron might sign a long-term contract to buy electricity at 3¢/kWh, expecting to sell it on the spot market at 3.1 cents. The initial NPV of the contract would be close to zero. However, if demand for power rose sharply, then the spot price would rise above 3.1 cents, the expected cash flows would rise, and the contract's NPV would also rise.

prices decline by 50% or more in 2002. Southern Company, like several other utilities, put its merchant plants and trading business into a separate subsidiary (Mirant Corporation) and then spun it off to Southern's stockholders. That spin-off insulated Southern from the debacle, so its stock price dropped by only 12% during 2002, about the same as the general market. However, Mirant itself experienced a huge drop after the Enron troubles hit, falling from $47.20 to $1.90. If Southern had retained Mirant, it probably would have experienced a decline similar to that of TECO and Duke.

In spite of these problems, the U.S. electric market is not likely to return to a regulated monopoly status. Competition will continue and even increase, and that will lead power users and producers to hedge with forward contracts and other derivatives. Still, the recent problems have taught all participants that while hedging can lower risks, it can also increase risk, so it must be done with care. Also, the Enron problem demonstrates once more that if something looks too good to be true, it probably is. Our conclusion is that energy derivatives are useful and are here to stay, but future participants should be more careful than those in the recent past.[7]

Affairs such as those at LTCM and Enron make the headlines, causing some people to argue that derivatives should be regulated out of existence to "protect the public." However, derivatives are used far more often to hedge risks than in harmful speculation, and these beneficial transactions never make the headlines. So, while the horror stories point out the need for top managers to exercise control over the personnel who deal with derivatives, they certainly do not justify the elimination of derivatives.

In the balance of this chapter, we discuss how firms can manage risks and how derivatives are used in risk management.

23.4 Other Types of Derivatives

We discussed put and call options in Chapter 9. They represent an important class of derivative securities, but there are many other types of derivatives, including forward contracts, futures, swaps, structured notes, inverse floaters, and a host of other "exotic" contracts.

Forward Contracts versus Futures Contracts

Forward contracts are agreements in which one party agrees to buy a commodity at a specific price on a specific future date and the other party agrees to sell the product. *Goods are actually delivered under forward contracts.* Unless both parties are morally and financially strong, there is a danger that one party will default on the contract, especially if the price of the commodity changes markedly after the agreement is reached.

A **futures contract** is similar to a forward contract, but with three key differences: (1) Futures contracts are marked-to-market on a daily basis, meaning that

---

[7]The telecommunications industry experienced even worse problems. Companies such as WorldCom, Qwest, and Global Crossing reported tremendous growth and wonderful profits, and that prodded old-line companies such as AT&T to revise their business plans and move aggressively into apparently terrific new markets such as wireless and broadband communications. Most of the expansion was financed with debt, and the end result was massive overcapacity—according to reports, in early 2003 only about 20% of fiber-optic cable lines were being used. As a result, there have been huge price cuts, much fraud, and some major bankruptcies.

gains and losses are noted and money must be put up to cover losses. This greatly reduces the risk of default that exists with forward contracts. (2) With futures, physical delivery of the underlying asset is virtually never taken—the two parties simply settle up with cash for the difference between the contracted price and the actual price on the expiration date. (3) Futures contracts are generally standardized instruments that are traded on exchanges, whereas forward contracts are generally tailor-made, are negotiated between two parties, and are not traded after they have been signed.

Futures and forward contracts were originally used for commodities such as wheat, where farmers would sell forward contracts to millers, enabling both parties to lock in prices and thus reduce their risk exposure. Commodities contracts are still important, but today more trading is done in foreign exchange and interest rate futures. To illustrate how foreign exchange contracts are used, suppose GE arranges to buy electric motors from a European manufacturer on terms that call for GE to pay 1 million euros in 180 days. GE would not want to give up the free trade credit, but if the euro appreciated against the dollar during the next 6 months, the dollar cost of the million euros would rise. GE could hedge the transaction by buying a forward contract under which it agreed to buy the million euros in 180 days at a fixed dollar price, which would lock in the dollar cost of the motors. This transaction would probably be conducted through a money center bank, which would try to find a European company (a "counterparty") that needed dollars in six months. Alternatively, GE could buy a futures contract on an exchange.

Interest rate futures represent another huge and growing market. For example, suppose Simonset Corporation decides to build a new plant at a cost of $20 million. It plans to finance the project with 20-year bonds that would carry an 8% interest rate if they were issued today. However, the company will not need the money for about 6 months. Simonset could go ahead and sell 20-year bonds now, locking in the 8% rate, but it would have the money before it was needed, so it would have to invest in short-term securities that would yield less than 8%. However, if Simonset waits 6 months to sell the bond issue, interest rates might be higher than they are today, in which case the value of the plant would be reduced, perhaps to the point of making it unprofitable.

One solution to Simonset's dilemma involves *interest rate futures*, which are based on a hypothetical 20-year Treasury bond with a 6% semiannual coupon. If interest rates in the economy go up, the value of the hypothetical T-bond will go down, and vice versa. In our example, Simonset is worried about an increase in interest rates. Should rates rise, the hypothetical Treasury bond's value would decline. Therefore, Simonset could sell T-bond futures for delivery in 6 months to hedge its position. If interest rates rise, Simonset will have to pay a higher interest rate when it issues its own bonds. However, it will make a profit on its futures position because it will have presold the bonds at a higher price than it will have to pay to cover (repurchase) them. Of course, if interest rates decline, Simonset will lose on its futures position, but this will be offset by the fact that it will get to pay a lower interest rate when it issues its bonds.

Our examples show that forward contracts and futures can be used to hedge, or reduce, risks. It has been estimated that more than 95% of all such transactions are indeed designed as hedges, with banks and futures dealers serving as middlemen between hedging counterparties. Interest rate and exchange rate futures can, of course, be used for speculative as well as hedging purposes. One can buy a T-bond contract on $100,000 of bonds with only $900 down, in which case a small change in interest rates will result in a very large gain or loss. Still, the primary motivation behind the vast majority of these transactions is to hedge risks, not to create them.

Swaps

A **swap** is just what the name implies—two parties agree to swap something, generally obligations to make specified payment streams. Most swaps today involve either interest payments or currencies, but just about anything can be swapped, including equity swaps, credit spread swaps, and commodity swaps.[8] To illustrate an interest rate swap, suppose Company S has a 20-year, $100 million floating-rate bond outstanding, while Company F has a $100 million, 20-year, fixed-rate issue outstanding. Thus, each company has an obligation to make a stream of interest payments, but one payment stream is fixed while the other will vary as interest rates change in the future. This situation is shown in the top part of Figure 23-1.

Now suppose Company S has stable cash flows, and it wants to lock in its cost of debt. Company F has cash flows that fluctuate with the economy, rising when the economy is strong and falling when it is weak. Recognizing that interest rates also move up and down with the economy, Company F has concluded that it would be better off with variable-rate debt. If the companies swapped their payment obligations, an *interest rate swap* would occur. The bottom half of Figure 23-1 shows that the net cash flows for Company S are at a fixed rate, and those for Company F are based on a floating rate. Company S would now have to make fixed payments, which are consistent with its stable cash inflows, and Company F would have a floating obligation, which for it is less risky.

Our example illustrates how swaps can reduce risks by allowing each company to match the variability of its interest payments with that of its cash flows. However, there are also situations where swaps can reduce both the riskiness and the effective cost of debt. For example, Antron Corporation, which has a high credit rating, can issue either floating-rate debt at LIBOR + 1% or fixed-rate debt at 10%.[9] Bosworth Industries is less creditworthy, so its cost for floating-rate debt is LIBOR + 1.5%, and its fixed-rate cost is 10.4%. Due to the nature of its operations, Antron's CFO has decided that it will be better off with fixed-rate debt, while Bosworth's CFO prefers floating-rate debt. Paradoxically, both firms can benefit by issuing the type of debt they do not want, and then swapping their payment obligations.

First, each company will issue an identical amount of debt, which is called the **notional principal.** Even though Antron wants fixed-rate debt, it issues floating-rate debt at LIBOR + 1%, and Bosworth issues fixed-rate debt at 10.4%. Next, the two companies enter into an interest rate swap.[10] Assume that the debt maturities are 5 years; hence the length of this swap will also be 5 years. By convention, the floating-rate payments of most swaps are based on LIBOR, with the fixed rate adjusted upward or downward to reflect credit risk and the term structure. The riskier the company that will receive the floating-rate payments, the higher the fixed-rate payment it must make. In our example, Antron will be receiving floating-rate payments from Bosworth, and those payments will be set at LIBOR times the notional principal. Then, payments will be adjusted every 6 months to reflect changes in the LIBOR rate.

---

[8]In an equity swap, the cash flow based on an equity index is swapped for some other cash flow. In a commodity swap, the swapped cash flow is based on commodity prices. In a credit swap, the cash flow usually is based on the spread between a risky bond and a U.S. Treasury bond.
[9]LIBOR stands for the London Interbank Offer Rate, the rate charged on interbank dollar loans in the Eurodollar market.
[10]Actually, such transactions are generally arranged by large money center banks, and payments are made to the bank, which in turn pays the interest on the original loans. The bank assumes the credit risk and guarantees the payments should one of the parties default. For its services, the bank receives a percentage of the payments as its fee.

ensure that their own risks are hedged. For example, Citibank might arrange a swap with Company A. Company A would agree to make specified payments in euros to Citibank, while Citibank made dollar payments to Company A. Citibank would charge a fee for setting up the swap, and these charges would reflect the creditworthiness of Company A. To protect itself against exchange rate movements, the bank would hedge its position, either by lining up a European company that needed to make dollar payments or else by using currency futures.[11]

Structured Notes

The term **structured note** often means a debt obligation that is derived from some other debt obligation. For example, in the early 1980s, investment bankers began buying large blocks of 30-year, noncallable Treasury bonds and then *stripping* them to create a series of zero coupon bonds. The zero with the shortest maturity was backed by the first interest payment on the T-bond issue, the second shortest zero was backed by the next interest payment, and so forth, on out to a 30-year zero backed by the last interest payment plus the maturity value of the T-bond. Zeros formed by stripping T-bonds were one of the first types of structured notes.

Another important type of structured note is backed by the interest and principal payments on mortgages. In the 1970s, Wall Street firms began to buy large packages of mortgages backed by federal agencies, and they placed these packages, or "pools," with a trustee. Then bonds called *Collateralized Mortgage Obligations* (*CMOs*), backed by the mortgage pool held in trust, were sold to pension funds, individuals for their IRAs, and other investors who were willing to invest in CMOs but who would not have purchased individual mortgages. This *securitization* of mortgages made billions of dollars of new capital available to home buyers.

CMOs are more difficult to evaluate than straight bonds for several reasons. First, the underlying mortgages can be prepaid at any time, and when this occurs the prepayment proceeds are used to retire part of the CMO debt itself. Therefore, the holder of a CMO is never sure when his or her bond will be called. This situation is further complicated by the fact that when interest rates decline, bond prices normally rise. However, declining rates also lead to mortgage prepayments, which cause the CMOs to be called especially rapidly, and it is not good to have bonds called and have to reinvest funds at a lower rate. These opposing forces make it difficult to value CMOs.

It should also be noted that a variety of structured notes can be created, ranging from notes whose cash flows can be predicted with virtual certainty to other notes whose payment streams are highly uncertain. For example, investment bankers can (and do) create notes called *IOs* (for *Interest Only*), which provide cash flows from the interest component of the mortgage amortization payments, and *POs* (for *Principal Only*), which are paid from the principal repayment stream. In each case, the value of the note is found as the present value of an expected payment stream, but the length and size of the stream are uncertain. Suppose, for example, that you are offered an IO that you expect to provide payments of $100 for 10 years (you expect the mortgages to be refinanced after 10 years, at which time your payments will cease). Suppose further that you discount the expected

[11]For more information on swaps, see Keith C. Brown and Donald J. Smith, "Default Risk and Innovations in the Design of Interest Rate Swaps," *Financial Management*, Summer 1993, pp. 94–105; Robert Einzig and Bruce Lange, "Swaps at Transamerica: Applications and Analysis," *Journal of Applied Corporate Finance*, Winter 1990, pp. 48–58; John F. Marshall, Vipul K. Bansal, Anthony F. Herbst, and Alan L. Tucker, "Hedging Business Cycle Risk with Macro Swaps and Options," *Journal of Applied Corporate Finance*, Winter 1992, pp. 103–108; and Laurie S. Goodman, "The Uses of Interest Rate Swaps in Managing Corporate Liabilities," *Journal of Applied Corporate Finance*, Winter 1990, pp. 35–47.

payment stream at a rate of 10% and determine that the value is $614.46. You have $614.46 to invest, so you buy the IO, expecting to earn 10% on your money.

Now suppose interest rates decline. If rates fall, the discount rate would drop, and that would normally imply an increase in the IO's value. However, if rates decline sharply, this would lead to a rash of mortgage refinancings, in which case your payments, which come from interest only, would cease (or be greatly reduced), and the value of your IO would fall sharply. On the other hand, a sharp increase in interest rates would reduce refinancing, lengthen your expected payment stream, and probably increase the value of your IO.

Investment bankers can slice and dice a pool of mortgages into a bewildering array of structured notes, ranging from "plain vanilla" ones with highly predictable cash flows to "exotic" ones (sometimes called "toxic waste") whose risks are almost incalculable but are surely large.

Securitizing mortgages through CMOs serves a useful economic function—it provides an investment outlet for pension funds and others with money to invest, and it makes more money available to homeowners at a reasonable cost. Also, some investors want relatively safe investments, while others are willing to buy more speculative securities for the higher expected returns they provide. Structured notes permit a partitioning of risks to give investors what they want. There are dangers, though. In some cases the "toxic waste" is bought by naive officials managing money for local governments like Orange County, California, when they really ought to be holding only safe securities.

Inverse Floaters

A floating-rate note has an interest rate that rises and falls with some interest rate index. For example, if the prime rate were currently 8.5%, then the interest rate on a $100,000 note at prime plus 1% would be 9.5% and the note's rate would move up and down with the prime rate. Because both the cash flows associated with the note and the discount rate used to value it would rise and fall together, the market value of the note would be relatively stable.

With an **inverse floater,** the rate paid on the note moves counter to market rates. Thus, if interest rates in the economy rise, the interest rate paid on an inverse floater will fall, lowering its cash interest payments. At the same time, the discount rate used to value the inverse floater's cash flows will rise along with other rates. The combined effect of lower cash flows and a higher discount rate leads to a very large decline in the value of the inverse floater. Thus, inverse floaters are exceptionally vulnerable to increases in interest rates. Of course, if interest rates fall, the value of an inverse floater will soar.

Could an inverse floater be used for hedging purposes? The answer is "yes, perhaps quite effectively." These securities have a magnified effect, so not many are required to hedge a given position. However, because they are so volatile, they could make what is supposed to be a hedged position actually quite risky.

We have discussed the most important types of derivative securities, but certainly not all types. This discussion should, though, give you a good idea of how and why derivatives are created, and how they can be used and misused.

SELF-TEST

Briefly describe the following types of derivative securities: (1) futures and forward contracts; (2) swaps; (3) structured notes and CMOs; and (4) inverse floaters.

Messman Corporation issues fixed-rate debt at a rate of 9.00%. Messman agrees to an interest rate swap in which it pays LIBOR to Moore Inc. and Moore pays 8.75% to Messman. What is Messman's resulting net payment? (LIBOR + 0.25%)

23.5   Corporate Risk Management

As businesses become increasingly complex, it is becoming more and more difficult for CEOs and directors to know what problems might lie in wait. Therefore, companies need to have someone systematically look for potential problems and design safeguards to minimize potential damage. With this in mind, most large firms have a designated "risk manager" who reports to the chief financial officer, while the CFOs of smaller firms personally assume risk management responsibilities. In any event, **risk management** is becoming increasingly important, and it is something finance students should understand. Therefore, in the remainder of this chapter we discuss the basics of risk management, with particular emphasis on how derivatives can be used to hedge financial risks.[12]

Types of Risk

It is useful to begin our discussion of risk management by defining some commonly used terms that describe different risks. Some of these risks can be mitigated, or managed, and that is what risk management is all about.

1. *Pure risks* are risks that offer only the prospect of a loss. Examples include the risk that a plant will be destroyed by fire or that a product liability suit will result in a large judgment against the firm.
2. *Speculative risks* are situations that offer the chance of a gain but might result in a loss. Investments in new projects and marketable securities involve speculative risks.
3. *Demand risks* are associated with the demand for a firm's products or services. Because sales are essential to all businesses, demand risk is one of the most significant risks that firms face.
4. *Input risks* are risks associated with input costs, including both labor and materials. Thus, a company that uses copper as a raw material in its manufacturing process faces the risk that the cost of copper will increase and that it will not be able to pass this increase on to its customers.
5. *Financial risks* are risks that result from financial transactions. As we have seen, if a firm plans to issue new bonds, it faces the risk that interest rates will rise before the bonds can be brought to market. Similarly, if the firm enters into contracts with foreign customers or suppliers, it faces the risk that fluctuations in exchange rates will result in unanticipated losses.
6. *Property risks* are associated with destruction of productive assets. Thus, the threats of fire, floods, and riots impose property risks on a firm.
7. *Personnel risks* are risks that result from employees' actions. Examples include the risks associated with employee fraud or embezzlement, or suits based on charges of age or sex discrimination.
8. *Environmental risks* include risks associated with polluting the environment. Public awareness in recent years, coupled with the huge costs of environmental cleanup, has increased the importance of this risk.

---

[12]For an excellent overview of risk management, see Kenneth A. Froot, David S. Scharfstein, and Jeremy Stein, "A Framework for Risk Management," *Journal of Applied Corporate Finance*, 1994, pp. 22–32; Walter Dolde, "The Trajectory of Corporate Financial Risk Management," *Journal of Applied Corporate Finance*, Fall 1993, pp. 33–41; and Marshall Blake and Nelda Mahady, "How Mid-Sized Companies Manage Risk," *Journal of Applied Corporate Finance*, Spring 1991, pp. 59–65.

9. *Liability risks* are associated with product, service, or employee actions. Examples include the very large judgments assessed against asbestos manufacturers and some health care providers, as well as costs incurred as a result of improper actions of employees, such as driving corporate vehicles in a reckless manner.

10. *Insurable risks* are risks that can be covered by insurance. In general, property, personnel, environmental, and liability risks can be transferred to insurance companies. Note, though, that the *ability* to insure a risk does not necessarily mean that the risk *should be* insured. Indeed, a major function of risk management involves evaluating all alternatives for managing a particular risk, including self-insurance, and then choosing the optimal alternative. For a more detailed discussion of corporate insurance programs, see *Web Extension 23A* at the textbook's Web site.

e-resource

Note that the risk classifications we used are somewhat arbitrary, and different classifications are commonly used in different industries. However, the list does give an idea of the wide variety of risks to which a firm can be exposed.

An Approach to Risk Management

Firms often use the following process for managing risks:

1. *Identify the risks faced by the firm.* Here the risk manager identifies the potential risks faced by his or her firm. (See the box entitled, "Microsoft's Goal: Manage Every Risk!")

2. *Measure the potential effect of each risk.* Some risks are so small as to be immaterial, whereas others have the potential for dooming the company. It is useful to segregate risks by potential effect and then to focus on the most serious threats.

3. *Decide how each relevant risk should be handled.* In most situations, risk exposure can be reduced through one of the following techniques:

   a. *Transfer the risk to an insurance company.* Often, it is advantageous to insure against, hence transfer, a risk. However, insurability does not necessarily mean that a risk should be covered by insurance. In many instances, it might be better for the company to *self-insure*, which means bearing the risk directly rather than paying another party to bear it.

   b. *Transfer the function that produces the risk to a third party.* For example, suppose a furniture manufacturer is concerned about potential liabilities arising from its ownership of a fleet of trucks used to transfer products from its manufacturing plant to various points across the country. One way to eliminate this risk would be to contract with a trucking company to do the shipping, thus passing the risks to a third party.

   c. *Purchase derivative contracts to reduce risk.* As we indicated earlier, firms use derivatives to hedge risks. Commodity derivatives can be used to reduce input risks. For example, a cereal company may use corn or wheat futures to hedge against increases in grain prices. Similarly, financial derivatives can be used to reduce risks that arise from changes in interest rates and exchange rates.

   d. *Reduce the probability of occurrence of an adverse event.* The expected loss arising from any risk is a function of both the probability of occurrence and

Microsoft's Goal: Manage Every Risk!

Twenty years ago, risk management meant buying insurance against fire, theft, and liability losses. Today, though, due to globalization, volatile markets, and a host of lawyers looking for someone to sue, a multitude of risks can adversely affect companies. Microsoft addressed these risks by creating a virtual in-house consulting practice to help manage the risks faced by its sales, operations, and product groups, including these 12 major sources of risk:

1. *Business partners* (interdependency, confidentiality, cultural conflict, contractual risks).
2. *Competition* (market share, price wars, industrial espionage, antitrust allegations, etc.).
3. *Customers* (product liability, credit risk, poor market timing, inadequate customer support).
4. *Distribution systems* (transportation, service availability, cost, dependence on distributors).
5. *Financial* (foreign exchange, portfolio, cash, interest rate, stock market).
6. *Operations* (facilities, contractual risks, natural hazards, internal processes and control).
7. *People* (employees, independent contractors, training, staffing inadequacy).

8. *Political* (civil unrest, war, terrorism, enforcement of intellectual property rights, change in leadership, revised economic policies).
9. *Regulatory and legislative* (antitrust, export licensing, jurisdiction, reporting and compliance, environmental).
10. *Reputations* (corporate image, brands, reputations of key employees).
11. *Strategic* (mergers and acquisitions, joint ventures and alliances, resource allocation and planning, organizational agility).
12. *Technological* (complexity, obsolescence, the year 2000 problem, virus attacks, workforce skill-sets).

In many ways risk management mirrors the quality movement of the 1980s and 1990s. The goal of the quality movement was to take the responsibility for quality out of a separate Quality Control Department and to make all managers and employees responsible for quality. Microsoft has a similar goal—to have risk management permeate the thinking of all Microsoft managers and employees.

Source: Edward Teach, "Microsoft's Universe of Risk," CFO, March 1997, pp. 69–72.

---

the dollar loss if the adverse event occurs. In some instances, it is possible to reduce the probability that an adverse event will occur. For example, the probability that a fire will occur can be reduced by instituting a fire prevention program, by replacing old electrical wiring, and by using fire-resistant materials in areas with the greatest fire potential.

e. *Reduce the magnitude of the loss associated with an adverse event.* Continuing with the fire risk example, the dollar cost associated with a fire can be reduced by such actions as installing sprinkler systems, designing facilities with self-contained fire zones, and locating facilities close to a fire station.

f. *Totally avoid the activity that gives rise to the risk.* For example, a company might discontinue a product or service line because the risks outweigh the rewards, as with the decision by Dow-Corning to discontinue its manufacture of silicon breast implants.

Note that risk management decisions, like all corporate decisions, should be based on a cost/benefit analysis for each feasible alternative. For example, suppose it would cost $50,000 per year to conduct a comprehensive fire safety training program for all personnel in a high-risk plant. Presumably, this program would reduce the expected value of future fire losses. An alternative to the training program would be to place $50,000 annually in a reserve fund set aside to cover future fire losses. Both alternatives involve expected cash flows, and from an economic standpoint the choice should be made on the basis of the lowest present value of future costs. Thus, the same financial management techniques applied to other corporate decisions can also be applied to risk management decisions. Note, though, that if a fire occurs and a life is lost, the trade-off between fire prevention and expected losses may not sit well with a jury. The same thing holds true for product liability, as Firestone, Ford, GM, and others have learned.

SELF-TEST

Define the following terms: (1) pure risks, (2) speculative risks, (3) demand risks, (4) input risks, (5) financial risks, (6) property risks, (7) personnel risks, (8) environmental risks, (9) liability risks, (10) insurable risks, and (11) self-insurance.

Should a firm insure itself against all of the insurable risks it faces? Explain.

23.6   Using Derivatives to Reduce Risks

Firms are subject to numerous risks related to interest rate, stock price, and exchange rate fluctuations in the financial markets. For an investor, one of the most obvious ways to reduce financial risks is to hold a broadly diversified portfolio of stocks and debt securities, including international securities and debt of varying maturities. However, derivatives can also be used to reduce the risks associated with financial and commodity markets.[13]

For information about futures markets, including prices, see the CBOT's Web site, **http://www .cbot.com,** and the Web site of Ira Epstein & Company, **http://www .iepstein.com.**

Hedging with Futures

One of the most useful tools for reducing interest rate, exchange rate, and commodity risk is to hedge in the futures markets. Most financial and real asset transactions occur in what is known as the *spot*, or *cash, market*, where the asset is delivered immediately (or within a few days). *Futures*, or *futures contracts*, on the other hand, call for the purchase or sale of an asset at some future date, but at a price that is fixed today.

Today, futures contracts are available on hundreds of real and financial assets traded on dozens of U.S. and international exchanges, the largest of which are the Chicago Board of Trade (CBOT) and the Chicago Mercantile Exchange (CME). Futures contracts are divided into two classes, **commodity futures** and **financial futures.** Commodity futures, which cover oil, various grains, oilseeds, livestock, meats, fibers, metals, and wood, were first traded in the United States in the mid-1800s. Financial futures, which were first traded in 1975, include Treasury bills, notes, bonds, certificates of deposit, Eurodollar deposits, foreign currencies, and stock indexes.

To illustrate how futures contracts work, consider the CBOT's contract on Treasury bonds. The basic contract is for $100,000 of a hypothetical 6% coupon, semiannual payment Treasury bond with 20 years to maturity.[14] Table 23-2 shows Treasury bond futures data from the Chicago Board of Trade.

---

[13]In Chapter 26, we discuss both the risks involved with holding foreign currencies and procedures for reducing such risks.
[14]The coupon rate on the hypothetical bond was changed to 6% from 8% in March 2000. The CBOT contract doesn't actually specify a 20-year bond, but instead allows delivery of any noncallable bond with a remaining maturity greater than 15 years (or callable bond that is not callable for at least 15 years). Rather than simply deliver a bond, which might have an interest rate different than 6%, the actual bond price is adjusted by a conversion feature to make it equivalent to a 6% bond that is trading at par. Because the average maturity of bonds that are eligible for delivery is about 20 years, we use a 20-year maturity for the hypothetical bond in the futures contract.

Table 23-2

Futures Prices (Treasury Bonds: $100,000; Pts. 32nds of 100%)

Delivery Month (1)	Last (2)	Change (3)	Open (4)	High (5)	Low (6)	Estimated Volume (7)	Open Interest (8)
September 2006	109-08	+0-18	108-20	109-15	108-18	21,612	778,970
December 2006	109-17	+0-18	108-28	109-18	108-28	1,345	22,128
March 2007	109-11	+0-18	109-11	109-11	109-11	0	8
June 2007	109-09	+0-18	109-09	109-09	109-09	0	15

Source: The Wall Street Journal Online; **http://www.wsj.com,** August 5, 2006.

FM

e-resource

See **FM12 Ch 23 Tool Kit.xls** at the textbook's Web site for all calculations.

The first column of the table gives the delivery month, and the next two columns give the last price of the day and the change in price from the previous day. For example, the last price for the March 2007 contract, 109-11, means 109 plus $\frac{11}{32}$, or 109.34375% of par. This is often called the settlement price. The change was +0-18, which means the March 2007 contract's last price of the day was $\frac{18}{32}$ higher than the previous day's last trade, which must have been at 108-25. The next three columns show the opening, high, and low prices for that contract on that day. Column 7 shows the day's estimated trading volume. Notice that most of the trading occurs in the contract with the nearest delivery date. Finally, Column 8 shows the "open interest," which is the number of contracts outstanding.

To illustrate, we focus on the Treasury bonds for March delivery. The settlement price was 109.34375% of the $100,000 contract value. Thus, the price at which one could buy $100,000 face value of 6%, 20-year Treasury bonds to be delivered in March was 109.34375% of par, or (109.34375%)($100,000) = $109,343.75. The contract price increased by $\frac{18}{32}$ of 1% of $100,000 from the previous day, so if you had bought the contract yesterday, you would have made $562.50 = ($\frac{18}{32}$)($100,000). There were 8 contracts outstanding, representing a total value of about 8($109,343.75) = $874,750.

Note that the contract increased by $\frac{18}{32}$ of a percent on this particular day. Why would the value of the bond futures contract increase? Bond prices increase when interest rates fall, so interest rates must have fallen on that day. Moreover, we can calculate the implied rates inherent in the futures contracts. Recall that the contract relates to a hypothetical 20-year, semiannual payment, 6% coupon bond. The settlement price was 109.34375% of par. We can solve for r_d by using the following equation:

$$\sum_{t=1}^{40} \frac{\$30}{(1 + r_d/2)^t} + \frac{\$1,000}{(1 + r_d/2)^{40}} = \$1,093.4375.$$

Using a financial calculator, input N = 40, PV = −1,093.4375, PMT = 30, FV = 1,000 and solve for I/YR = 2.6202. This is the semiannual rate, which is equivalent to a nominal annual rate of 5.2404%, or approximately 5.24%. The previous day's last (settlement) price was 108 and $\frac{25}{32}$. Setting N = 40, PV = −1,087.8125,

PMT = 30, FV = 1,000 and solving for I/YR = 2.6418 implies an annual yield of 5.2836%, or approximately 5.28%. Therefore, interest rates fell by about four basis points from the previous day, but that was enough to increase the value of the contract by $562.50.

In August 2006, when the data in Table 23-2 were gathered, the yield on a 20-year T-bond was about 5.13%. But as we just calculated, the implied yield on the March 2007 futures contract was about 5.24%. The March yield reflects investors' beliefs as to what the interest rate level will be in March: The marginal trader in the futures market was predicting an 11-basis-point increase in yields between August and March. That prediction could, of course, turn out to be incorrect.

Now suppose that 3 months later, in November, implied yields in the futures market had fallen from the earlier levels, say, from 5.24% to 4.74%. Inputting N = 40, I/YR = 4.74/2 = 2.37, PMT = 30, FV = 1,000, and solving for PV = −1,161.6668 shows that the March contract would be worth about $116,166.68 in November if interest rates fell to 4.74%. Thus, the contract's value would have increased by $116,166.68 − $109,343.75 ≈ $6,823.

When futures contracts are purchased, the purchaser does not have to put up the full amount of the purchase price; rather, the purchaser is required to post an initial *margin*, which for CBOT Treasury bond contracts is $900 per $100,000 contract.[15] However, investors are required to maintain a certain value in the margin account, called a *maintenance margin*. If the value of the contract declines, then the owner may be required to add additional funds to the margin account, and the more the contract value falls, the more money must be added. The value of the contract is checked at the end of every working day, and margin account adjustments are made at that time. This is called "marking to market." If an investor purchased our illustrative contract and then sold it later for $116,166.68, he or she would have made a profit of $6,823 on a $900 investment, or a return of 658% in only 3 months. It is clear, therefore, that futures contracts offer a considerable amount of leverage. Of course, if interest rates had risen, then the value of the contract would have fallen, and the investor could easily have lost his or her $900, or more. Futures contracts are rarely settled by delivery of the securities involved. Rather, the transaction is completed by reversing the trade, which amounts to selling the contract back to the original seller.[16] The actual gains and losses on the contract are realized when the futures contract is closed.

For current margin requirements on hedging investments, see **http:// www.cbot.com/cbot/pub/ page /0,3181,2143,00 .html**.

Futures contracts and options are similar to one another—so similar that people often confuse the two. Therefore, it is useful to compare the two instruments. A *futures contract* is a definite agreement on the part of one party to buy something on a specific date and at a specific price, and the other party agrees to sell on the same terms. No matter how low or how high the price goes, the two parties must settle the contract at the agreed-upon price. An *option*, on the other hand, gives someone the right to buy (call) or sell (put) an asset, but the holder of the option does not have to complete the transaction. Note also that options exist both for individual stocks and for "bundles" of stocks such as those in the S&P and *Value Line* indexes, but generally not for commodities. Futures, on the other hand, are

---

[15]This is the margin requirement for hedgers. Speculators have a different margin requirement.
[16]The buyers and sellers of most financial futures contracts do not actually trade with one another—each trader's contractual obligation is with a futures exchange. This feature helps to guarantee the fiscal integrity of the trade.
Incidentally, commodities futures traded on the exchanges are settled in the same way as financial futures, but in the case of commodities much of the contracting is done off the exchange, between farmers and processors, as *forward contracts*, in which case actual deliveries occur.

Risk Management in the Cyber Economy

In the old bricks-and-mortar economy, most of a company's value was due to its tangible assets. Not so in the cyber economy, where value is due to intellectual property and networks that manage knowledge bases. Insurance companies are rapidly developing new types of insurance policies to protect these valuable cyber assets.

Intellectual property (IP) insurance now covers "all intellectual property—patents, trademarks, trade secrets, copyright—and includes defense, as well as enforcement, of intellectual property rights," according to Judith Pearson, director of Aon Corp.'s financial services group. These policies can cover losses in excess of $200 million, with premiums ranging from 1% to 5% of the coverage.

Insurers also provide coverage for breaches in network security. For example, companies can buy insurance to cover cases of cyberextortion, such as the recent demand for $100,000 by the hacker "Maxus" in exchange for not publicly releasing 300,000 credit card numbers stolen from CD Universe. Other policies cover content defamation, copyright and trademark infringement, denial-of-service attacks, viruses, theft of information, and destruction or alteration of data. Costs of insurance have fallen to between 1% and 3% of the policy's coverage, but most insurers subject applicants to a thorough review of their current security measures before granting coverage.

One thing is certain: As the cyber economy matures, look for even more sophisticated risk management techniques.

Sources: John P. Mello, Jr., "Blanketing Intellectual Risk," *CFO,* May 2000, p. 16; and Russ Banham, "Hacking It," *CFO,* August 2000, pp. 115–118.

used for commodities, debt securities, and stock indexes. These two types of instruments can be used for the same purposes. One is not necessarily better or worse than the other—they are simply different.[17]

Security Price Exposure

All investors are exposed to losses due to changes in security prices when securities are held in investment portfolios, and firms are also exposed during times when securities are being issued. In addition, firms are exposed to risk if they use floating-rate debt to finance an investment that produces a fixed income stream. Risks such as these can often be mitigated by using derivatives. As we discussed earlier, derivatives are securities whose value stems, or is derived, from the values of other assets. Thus, options and futures contracts are derivatives, because their values depend on the prices of some underlying asset. Now we will explore further the use of two types of derivatives, futures and swaps, to help manage certain types of risk.

Futures   Futures are used for both speculation and hedging. **Speculation** involves betting on future price movements, and futures are used because of the leverage inherent in the contract. **Hedging,** on the other hand, is done by a firm or individual to protect against a price change that would otherwise negatively affect profits. For example, rising interest rates and commodity (raw material) prices can hurt profits, as can adverse currency fluctuations. If two parties have mirror-image risks, then they can enter into a transaction that eliminates, as opposed to transfers, risks. This is a "natural hedge." Of course, one party to a

---

[17]For additional insights into the use of financial futures for hedging, see Stanley B. Block and Timothy J. Gallagher, "The Use of Interest Rate Futures and Options by Corporate Managers," *Financial Management,* Autumn 1986, pp. 73–78; and Mark G. Castelino, Jack C. Francis, and Avner Wolf, "Cross-Hedging: Basis Risk and Choice of the Optimal Hedging Vehicle," *Financial Review,* May 1991, pp. 179–210.

futures contract could be a speculator, the other a hedger. Thus, to the extent that speculators broaden the market and make hedging possible, they help decrease risk to those who seek to avoid it.

There are two basic types of hedges: (1) **long hedges,** in which futures contracts are *bought* in anticipation of (or to guard against) price increases, and (2) **short hedges,** where a firm or individual *sells* futures contracts to guard against price declines. Recall that rising interest rates lower bond prices and thus decrease the value of bond futures contracts. Therefore, if a firm or individual needs to guard against an *increase* in interest rates, a futures contract that makes money if rates rise should be used. That means selling, or going short, on a futures contract. To illustrate, assume that in August Carson Foods is considering a plan to issue $10,000,000 of 20-year bonds in March to finance a capital expenditure program. The interest rate would be 9% paid semiannually if the bonds were issued today, and at that rate the project would have a positive NPV. However, interest rates may rise, and when the issue is actually sold, the interest rate might be substantially above 9%, which would make the project a bad investment. Carson can protect itself against a rise in rates by hedging in the futures market.

In this situation, Carson would be hurt by an increase in interest rates, so it would use a short hedge. It would choose a futures contract on the security most similar to the one it plans to issue, long-term bonds, and so would probably hedge with March Treasury bond futures. We can see from Table 23-2 that each March contract has a value of 109-11, so the total value of one contract is $109,343.75. Because it plans to issue $10,000,000 of bonds, and because each contract is worth $109,343.75, Carson will sell $10,000,000/$109,343.75 = 91.45 ≈ 91 contracts for delivery in March. It will have to put up 91($900) = $81,900 in margin money and also pay brokerage commissions. The total value of the 91 contracts is 91($109,343.75) = $9,950,281, which is very close to the value of the bonds Carson wants to issue.

e-resource

See **FM12 Ch 23 Tool Kit.xls** at the textbook's Web site for all calculations.

Now suppose that in March when Carson issues its bonds renewed fears of inflation push interest rates up by 100 basis points. What would the bond proceeds be if Carson still tried to issue 9% coupon bonds when the market requires a 10% rate of return? We can find the total value of the offering with a financial calculator, inputting N = 40, I/YR = 5, PMT = −$450,000, FV = −10,000,000, and solving for PV = 9,142,046. Therefore, bonds with a 9% coupon, based upon its original plans, would bring proceeds of only $9,142,046, because investors now require a 10% return. Because Carson would have to issue $10 million worth of bonds at a 10% rate, Carson's cost would go up by $857,954 = $10,000,000 − $9,142,046 as a result of delaying the financing.

However, the increase in interest rates would also bring about a change in the value of Carson's short position in the futures market. Since interest rates have increased, the value of the futures contract would fall. If the interest rate on the futures contract also increased by the same full percentage point, from 5.24 to 6.24%, the new contract value can be found by inputting N = 40, I/YR = 6.24/2 = 3.12, PMT = −3,000, FV = −100,000 and solving for PV = $97,279.26 per contract. With 91 contracts, the total value of the position is $8,852,413 = 91($97,279.26). Carson would then close its position in the futures market by repurchasing for $8,852,413 the contracts that it earlier sold short for $9,950,281, giving it a profit of $1,097,868, less commissions.

Thus, Carson would, if we ignore commissions and the opportunity cost of the margin money, offset the loss on the bond issue. In fact, in our example Carson more than offsets the loss, pocketing an additional $239,914 = $1,097,868 − $857,954. Of course, if interest rates had fallen, Carson would have lost on its futures position, but this loss would have been offset by the fact that Carson could now sell its bonds with a lower coupon.

If futures contracts existed on Carson's own debt, and interest rates moved identically in the spot and futures markets, then the firm could construct a **perfect hedge,** in which gains on the futures contract would exactly offset losses on the bonds. In reality, it is virtually impossible to construct perfect hedges, because in most cases the underlying asset is not identical to the futures asset, and even when they are, prices (and interest rates) may not move exactly together in the spot and futures markets.[18]

Note too that if Carson had been planning an equity offering, and if its stock tended to move fairly closely with one of the stock indexes, the company could have hedged against falling stock prices by selling short the index future. Even better, if options on Carson's stock were traded in the options market, then it could use options rather than futures to hedge against falling stock prices.

The futures and options markets permit flexibility in the timing of financial transactions, because the firm can be protected, at least partially, against changes that occur between the time a decision is reached and the time when the transaction will be completed. However, this protection has a cost—the firm must pay commissions. Whether or not the protection is worth the cost is a matter of judgment. The decision to hedge also depends on management's risk aversion as well as the company's strength and ability to assume the risk in question. In theory, the reduction in risk resulting from a hedge transaction should have a value exactly equal to the cost of the hedge. Thus, a firm should be indifferent to hedging. However, many firms believe that hedging is worthwhile. Trammell Crow, a large Texas real estate developer, recently used T-bill futures to lock in interest costs on floating-rate construction loans, while Dart & Kraft used Eurodollar futures to protect its marketable securities portfolio. Merrill Lynch, Salomon Smith Barney, and the other investment banking houses hedge in the futures and options markets to protect themselves when they are engaged in major underwritings.

Swaps   A *swap* is another method for reducing financial risks. As we noted earlier, a swap is an exchange of cash payment obligations in which each party prefers the payment type or pattern of the other party.[19] Generally, one party has a fixed-rate obligation and the other a floating-rate obligation, or one has an obligation denominated in one currency and the other in another currency.

Major changes have occurred over time in the swaps market. First, standardized contracts have been developed for the most common types of swaps, which has had two effects: (1) Standardized contracts lower the time and effort involved in arranging swaps, and this lowers transactions costs. (2) The development of standardized contracts has led to a secondary market for swaps, which has increased the liquidity and efficiency of the swaps market. A number of international banks now make markets in swaps and offer quotes on several standard

---

[18]In this example, Carson hedged a 20-year bond with a T-bond futures contract. Rather than simply matching on maturity, it would be more accurate to match on duration (see **Web Extension 5C** at the textbook's Web site for a discussion of duration). A matching duration in the futures contracts could be accomplished by taking positions in the T-bond futures contract and in another financial futures contract, such as the 10-Year Treasury Note contract. Because Carson's bond had a 20-year maturity, matching on maturity instead of duration provided a good hedge. If Carson's bond had a different maturity, then it would be essential to match on duration.

[19]For more information on swaps, see Clifford W. Smith, Jr., Charles W. Smithson, and Lee Macdonald Wakeman, "The Evolving Market for Swaps," *Midland Corporate Finance Journal*, Winter 1986, pp. 20–32; and Mary E. Ruth and Steve R. Vinson, "Managing Interest Rate Uncertainty Amidst Change," *Public Utilities Fortnightly*, December 22, 1988, pp. 28–31.

types. Also, as noted above, the banks now take counterparty positions in swaps, so it is not necessary to find another firm with mirror-image needs before a swap transaction can be completed. The bank would generally find a final counterparty for the swap at a later date, so its positioning helps make the swap market more operationally efficient.[20]

To further illustrate a swap transaction, consider the following situation. An electric utility recently issued a 5-year floating-rate note tied to the prime rate. The prime rate could rise significantly over the period, so the note carries a high degree of interest rate risk. The utility could, however, enter into a swap with a counterparty, say, Citibank, wherein the utility would pay Citibank a fixed series of interest payments over the 5-year period, and Citibank would make the company's required floating-rate payments. As a result, the utility would have converted a floating-rate loan to a fixed-rate loan, and the risk of rising interest rates would have been passed from the utility to Citibank. Such a transaction can lower both parties' risks—because banks' revenues rise as interest rates rise, Citibank's risk would actually be lower if it had floating-rate obligations.

Longer-term swaps can also be made. Recently, Citibank entered into a 17-year swap in an electricity cogeneration project financing deal. The project's sponsors were unable to obtain fixed-rate financing on reasonable terms, and they were afraid that interest rates would increase and make the project unprofitable. The project's sponsors were, however, able to borrow from local banks on a floating-rate basis and then arrange a simultaneous swap with Citibank for a fixed-rate obligation.

Commodity Price Exposure

As we noted earlier, futures markets were established for many commodities long before they began to be used as financial instruments. We can use Porter Electronics, which uses large quantities of copper as well as several precious metals, to illustrate inventory hedging. Suppose that in May 2007, Porter foresaw a need for 100,000 pounds of copper in March 2008 for use in fulfilling a fixed price contract to supply solar power cells to the U.S. government. Porter's managers are concerned that a strike by Chilean copper miners will occur, which could raise the price of copper in world markets and possibly turn the expected profit into a loss.

Porter could, of course, go ahead and buy the copper that it will need to fulfill the contract, but if it does it will incur substantial carrying costs. As an alternative, the company could hedge against increasing copper prices in the futures market. The New York Commodity Exchange trades standard copper futures contracts of 25,000 pounds each. Thus, Porter could buy four contracts (go long) for delivery in March 2008. Assume that these contracts were trading in May for about $1.00 per pound and that the spot price at that date was about $1.02 per pound. If copper prices do rise appreciably over the next 10 months, the value of Porter's long position in copper futures would increase, thus offsetting some of

---

[20]The role of banks in the global swap market is worrisome to the Federal Reserve and other central banks. When banks take positions in swaps, they are themselves exposed to various risks, and if the counterparties cannot meet their obligations, a bank could suddenly become liable for making two sets of payments. Further, swaps are off-balance sheet transactions, so it is currently impossible to tell just how large the swap market is or who has what obligation. The fear is that if one large multinational bank gets into trouble, the entire worldwide swap market could collapse like a house of cards. See "Swap Fever: Big Money, Big Risks," *Fortune*, June 1, 1992.

the price increase in the commodity itself. Of course, if copper prices fall, Porter would lose money on its futures contracts, but the company would be buying the copper on the spot market at a cheaper price, so it would make a higher than anticipated profit on its sale of solar cells. Thus, hedging in the copper futures market locks in the cost of raw materials and removes some risk to which the firm would otherwise be exposed.

Many other companies, such as Alcoa with aluminum and Archer Daniels Midland with grains, routinely use the futures markets to reduce the risks associated with price volatility.

The Use and Misuse of Derivatives

Most of the news stories about derivatives are related to financial disasters. Much less is heard about the benefits of derivatives. However, because of these benefits, more than 83% of large U.S. companies use derivatives on a regular basis. In today's market, sophisticated investors and analysts are demanding that firms use derivatives to hedge certain risks. For example, Compaq Computer was sued by a shareholder group for failing to properly hedge its foreign exchange exposure. The shareholders lost the suit, but Compaq got the message and now uses currency futures to hedge its international operations. In another example, Prudential Securities reduced its earnings estimate for Cone Mills, a North Carolina textile company, because Cone did not sufficiently hedge its exposure to changing cotton prices. These examples lead to one conclusion: If a company can safely and inexpensively hedge its risks, it should do so.

There can, however, be a downside to the use of derivatives. Hedging is invariably cited by authorities as a "good" use of derivatives, whereas speculating with derivatives is often cited as a "bad" use. Some people and organizations can afford to bear the risks involved in speculating with derivatives, but others are either not sufficiently knowledgeable about the risks or else should not be taking those risks in the first place. Most would agree that the typical corporation should use derivatives only to hedge risks, not to speculate in an effort to increase profits. Hedging allows a manager to concentrate on running his or her core business without having to worry about interest rate, currency, and commodity price variability. However, big problems can arise if hedges are improperly constructed or if a corporate treasurer, eager to report relatively high returns, uses derivatives for speculative purposes.

One interesting example of a derivatives debacle involved Kashima Oil, a Japanese firm that imports oil. It pays with U.S. dollars but then sells oil in the Japanese market for yen. Kashima began by using currency futures to hedge, but it later started to speculate on dollar-yen price movements, hoping to increase profits. When the currency markets moved against Kashima's speculative position, lax accounting rules permitted it to avoid reporting the losses by simply rolling over the contract. By the time Kashima bit the bullet and closed its position, it had lost $1.5 billion. Other companies have experienced similar problems.

Our position is that derivatives can and should be used to hedge against certain risks, but that the leverage inherent in derivatives contracts makes them potentially dangerous. Also, CFOs, CEOs, and board members should be reasonably knowledgeable about the derivatives their firms use, should establish policies regarding when they can and cannot be used, and should establish audit procedures to ensure that the policies are carried out. Moreover, a firm's derivatives position should be reported to stockholders, because stockholders have a right to know when situations such as that involving Kashima might arise.

SELF-TEST

What is a futures contract?

Explain how a company can use the futures market to hedge against rising interest rates.

What is a swap? Describe the mechanics of a fixed-rate to floating-rate swap.

Explain how a company can use the futures market to hedge against rising raw materials prices.

How should derivatives be used in risk management? What problems can occur?

A Treasury bond futures contract is selling for 94-16. What is the implied annual yield? (6.5%)

Summary

Companies every day face a variety of risks, for it is hard to operate a successful business without taking some chances. Back in Chapter 6, we discussed the trade-off between risk and return. If some action can lower risk without lowering returns too much, then the action can enhance value. With this in mind, we described in this chapter the various types of risks that companies face, and we discussed the basic principles of corporate risk management. One important tool for managing risk is the derivatives market. Consequently, this chapter has also provided an introduction to derivative securities. The key concepts covered are listed below:

- There are several reasons **risk management** might increase the value of a firm. Risk management allows corporations (1) to increase their **use of debt**, (2) to maintain their **capital budget** over time, (3) to avoid costs associated with **financial distress**, (4) to utilize their **comparative advantages in hedging** relative to the hedging ability of individual investors, (5) to reduce both the risks and costs of borrowing by using **swaps**, and (6) to reduce the **higher taxes** that result from fluctuating earnings. Managers may also want to stabilize earnings in order to boost their own compensation.
- A **derivative** is a security whose value is determined by the market price or interest rate of some other security.
- A **hedge** is a transaction that lowers risk. A **natural hedge** is a transaction between two **counterparties** where the parties' risks are mirror images.
- A **futures contract** is a standardized contract that is traded on an exchange and is marked-to-market daily, but where physical delivery of the underlying asset usually does not occur.
- Under a **forward contract**, one party agrees to buy a commodity at a specific price and a specific future date and the other party agrees to make the sale. Delivery does occur.
- A **structured note** is a debt obligation derived from another debt obligation.
- A **swap** is an exchange of cash payment obligations. Swaps occur because the parties involved prefer the other's payment stream.
- In general, **risk management** involves the management of unpredictable events that have adverse consequences for the firm.

- The three key steps in risk management are as follows: (1) **identify** the risks faced by the company, (2) **measure** the potential impacts of these risks, and (3) **decide** how each relevant risk should be dealt with.
- In most situations, risk exposure can be dealt with by one or more of the following techniques: (1) **transfer the risk** to an insurance company, (2) **transfer the function** that produces the risk to a third party, (3) **purchase a derivative contract,** (4) **reduce the probability** of occurrence of an adverse event, (5) **reduce the magnitude** of the loss associated with an adverse event, and (6) totally **avoid** the activity that gives rise to the risk.
- **Financial futures** permit firms to create hedge positions to protect themselves against fluctuating interest rates, stock prices, and exchange rates.
- **Commodity futures** can be used to hedge against input price increases.
- **Long hedges** involve buying futures contracts to guard against price increases.
- **Short hedges** involve selling futures contracts to guard against price declines.
- A **perfect hedge** occurs when the gain or loss on the hedged transaction exactly offsets the loss or gain on the unhedged position.

Questions

(23-1)   Define each of the following terms:
a. Derivative
b. Corporate risk management
c. Financial futures; forward contract
d. Hedging; natural hedge; long hedge; short hedge; perfect hedge
e. Swap; structured note
f. Commodity futures

(23-2)   Give two reasons stockholders might be indifferent between owning the stock of a firm with volatile cash flows and that of a firm with stable cash flows.

(23-3)   List six reasons risk management might increase the value of a firm.

(23-4)   Discuss some of the techniques available to reduce risk exposures.

(23-5)   Explain how the futures markets can be used to reduce interest rate and input price risk.

(23-6)   How can swaps be used to reduce the risks associated with debt contracts?

Self-Test Problem   Solution Appears in Appendix A

(ST-1)   It is now March, and the current cost of debt for Wansley Construction is 12%.
Hedging   Wansley plans to issue $5 million in 20-year bonds (with coupons paid

semiannually) in September, but is afraid that rates will climb even higher before then. The following data are available:

Futures Prices: Treasury Bonds—$100,000; Pts. 32nds of 100%

Delivery Month (1)	Open (2)	High (3)	Low (4)	Settle (5)	Change (6)
Mar	96-28	97-13	97-22	98-05	+7
June	98-03	98-03	97-13	97-25	+8
Sept	97-03	97-17	97-03	97-13	+8

a. What is the implied interest rate on the September contract?
b. Construct a hedge for Wansley.
c. Assume all interest rates rise by 1 percentage point. What is the dollar value of Wansley's increased cost of issuing debt? What is Wansley's gain from the futures contract?

Problems Answers Appear in Appendix B

Easy Problems 1–2

(23-1)
Swaps

Zhao Automotive issues fixed-rate debt at a rate of 7.00%. Zhao agrees to an interest rate swap in which it pays LIBOR to Lee Financial, and Lee pays 6.8% to Zhao. What is Zhao's resulting net payment?

(23-2)
Futures

A Treasury bond futures contract has a settlement price of 89-8. What is the implied annual yield?

Intermediate Problems 3–4

(23-3)
Futures

What is the implied interest rate on a Treasury bond ($100,000) futures contract that settled at 100-16? If interest rates increased by 1%, what would be the contract's new value?

(23-4)
Swaps

Carter Enterprises can issue floating-rate debt at LIBOR + 2% or fixed-rate debt at 10.00%. Brence Manufacturing can issue floating-rate debt at LIBOR + 3.1% or fixed-rate debt at 11%. Suppose Carter issues floating-rate debt and Brence issues fixed-rate debt. They are considering a swap in which Carter will make a fixed-rate payment of 7.95% to Brence, and Brence will make a payment of LIBOR to Carter. What are the net payments of Carter and Brence if they engage in the swap? Will Carter be better off to issue fixed-rate debt or to issue floating-rate debt and engage in the swap? Will Brence be better off to issue floating-rate debt or to issue fixed-rate debt and engage in the swap?

Challenging Problem 5

(23-5)
Hedging

The Zinn Company plans to issue $10,000,000 of 20-year bonds in June to help finance a new research and development laboratory. The bonds will pay interest semiannually. It is now November, and the current cost of debt to the high-risk biotech company is 11%. However, the firm's financial manager is concerned that interest rates will climb even higher in coming months. The following data are available:

Futures Prices: Treasury Bonds—$100,000; Pts. 32nds of 100%

Delivery Month (1)	Open (2)	High (3)	Low (4)	Settle (5)	Change (6)	Open Interest (7)
Dec	94-28	95-13	94-22	95-05	+7	591,944
Mar	96-03	96-03	95-13	95-25	+8	120,353
June	95-03	95-17	95-03	95-17	+8	13,597

a. Use the given data to create a hedge against rising interest rates.
b. Assume that interest rates in general increase by 200 basis points. How well did your hedge perform?
c. What is a perfect hedge? Are most real-world hedges perfect? Explain.

Spreadsheet Problem

(23-6)
Build a Model: Hedging

e-resource

Start with the partial model in the file *FM12 Ch 23 P06 Build a Model.xls* from the textbook's Web site. Use the information and data from Problem 23-5.
  a. Create a hedge with the futures contract for Zinn Company's planned June debt offering of $10 million. What is the implied yield on the bond underlying the futures contract?
  b. Suppose interest rates fall by 300 basis points. What are the dollar savings from issuing the debt at the new interest rate? What is the dollar change in value of the futures position? What is the total dollar value change of the hedged position?
  c. Create a graph showing the effectiveness of the hedge if the change in interest rates, in basis points, is: −300, −200, −100, 0, 100, 200, or 300. Show the dollar cost (or savings) from issuing the debt at the new interest rates, the dollar change in value of the futures position, and the total dollar value change.

Cyberproblem

e-resource

Please go to the textbook's Web site to access any Cyberproblems.

Mini Case

Assume that you have just been hired as a financial analyst by Tennessee Sunshine Inc., a midsized Tennessee company that specializes in creating exotic sauces from imported fruits and vegetables. The firm's CEO, Bill Stooksbury, recently returned from an industry corporate executive conference in San Francisco, and one of the sessions he attended was on the pressing need for smaller companies to institute corporate risk management programs. Since no one at Tennessee Sunshine is familiar with the basics of derivatives and corporate risk management, Stooksbury has asked you to prepare a brief report that the firm's executives could use to gain at least a cursory understanding of the topics.

To begin, you gathered some outside materials on derivatives and corporate risk management and used these materials to draft a list of pertinent questions that need to be answered. In fact, one possible approach to the paper is to use a question-and-answer format. Now that the questions have been drafted, you have to develop the answers.

a. Why might stockholders be indifferent whether or not a firm reduces the volatility of its cash flows?

b. What are six reasons risk management might increase the value of a corporation?

c. What is corporate risk management? Why is it important to all firms?

d. Risks that firms face can be categorized in many ways. Define the following types of risk:
   (1) Speculative risks
   (2) Pure risks
   (3) Demand risks
   (4) Input risks
   (5) Financial risks
   (6) Property risks
   (7) Personnel risks
   (8) Environmental risks
   (9) Liability risks
   (10) Insurable risks

e. What are the three steps of corporate risk management?

f. What are some actions that companies can take to minimize or reduce risk exposures?

g. What is financial risk exposure? Describe the following concepts and techniques that can be used to reduce financial risks:
   (1) Derivatives
   (2) Futures markets
   (3) Hedging
   (4) Swaps

h. Describe how commodity futures markets can be used to reduce input price risk.

i. It is January and Tennessee Sunshine is considering issuing $5 million in bonds in June to raise capital for an expansion. Currently, TS can issue

20-year bonds with a 7% coupon (with interest paid semiannually), but interest rates are on the rise and Stooksbury is concerned that long-term interest rates might rise by as much as 1% before June. You looked online and found that June T-bond futures are trading at 111-25. What are the risks of not hedging and how might TS hedge this exposure? In your analysis, consider what would happen if interest rates all increased by 1%.

chapter 24

Bankruptcy, Reorganization, and Liquidation

In June 1993, Continental Airlines performed, for the second time, a feat few companies accomplish even once—it emerged from bankruptcy. When Continental Airlines Holdings Inc., along with 53 subsidiaries, filed for bankruptcy court protection in December 1990, it owed $3.96 billion. When it emerged from bankruptcy in 1993, the firm had only four subsidiaries, it had shaved its debt to $1.8 billion, and it had $635 million in cash. In addition, Continental instituted a new strategy that focused on transoceanic service to Europe and Asia while cutting back on short-haul flights.

While under court protection—which means that the Bankruptcy Court prevented Continental's creditors from seizing the assets securing its debt or even from collecting interest due on those debts—the company was able to take actions unavailable to its nonbankrupt competitors. In particular, it was able to abrogate its labor contracts and lower its wages. This action, along with not having to pay interest on its debt, permitted it to offer very low fares and still generate positive cash flows.

However, the operating and financing advantages provided by the bankruptcy were costly to some participants. The company's reorganization plan called for paying creditors only a fraction of what they were owed. Creditors were also required to take some stock in the "new" Continental. In addition, 55% of the equity went to Air Canada and to Air Partners, a Fort Worth investor group, which, between them, poured $450 million of new cash into the airline. As often happens, all of the equity went to creditors and new investors—the firm's original stockholders were totally wiped out.

Continental is one of the success stories of bankruptcy—the corporation itself has survived, its customers are receiving good service, its employees kept their jobs, its creditors got more than they would have received in a liquidation, and its new equity investors have made money. As we discuss in the chapter, though, other firms facing bankruptcy have not fared so well. The decisions that firms' managers, creditors, and other stakeholders make before and during bankruptcy proceedings determine the final results.

As you go through the chapter, think about the decisions that Continental's managers and creditors had to make regarding bankruptcy and reorganization, and the effects the firm's bankruptcy has had on all of its stakeholders as well as on competing airlines. It will be interesting to see whether the airlines in bankruptcy during 2006, including United, Delta, and Northwest, are able to emulate Continental and emerge as competitive companies.

e-resource

The textbook's Web site contains an *Excel* file that will guide you through the chapter's calculations. The file for this chapter is **FM12 Ch 24 Tool Kit.xls,** and we encourage you to open the file and follow along as you read the chapter.

Thus far, we have dealt with issues faced by growing, successful enterprises. However, many firms encounter financial difficulties, and some, including such big names as Refco, Calpine Corporation, Delta Air Lines, and Dana Corporation, are forced into bankruptcy. When a firm encounters financial distress, its managers must try to ward off a total collapse and thereby minimize losses. The ability to hang on during rough times often means the difference between forced liquidation versus rehabilitation and eventual success. An understanding of bankruptcy is also critical to the executives of healthy firms, because they must know the best actions to take when their customers or suppliers face the threat of bankruptcy.

24.1   Financial Distress and Its Consequences

We begin with some background on financial distress and its consequences.[1]

Causes of Business Failure

A Dun & Bradstreet study examined business failure causes, as shown in Table 24-1. Economic factors include industry weakness and poor location. Financial factors include too much debt and insufficient capital. The importance of the different factors varies over time, depending on such things as the state of the economy and the level of interest rates. Also, most business failures occur because a number of factors combine to make the business unsustainable. Further, case studies show that financial difficulties are usually the result of a series of errors, misjudgments, and interrelated weaknesses that can be attributed directly or indirectly to management. As you might guess, signs of potential financial distress are generally evident in a ratio analysis long before the firm actually fails, and researchers use ratio analysis to predict the probability that a given firm will go bankrupt.

The Business Failure Record

Although bankruptcy is more frequent among smaller firms, it is clear from Table 24-2 that large firms are not immune. However, some firms might be too

Table 24-1
Causes of Business Failure

Cause of Failure	Percentage of Total
Economic factors	37.1%
Financial factors	47.3
Neglect, disaster, and fraud	14.0
Other factors	1.6
	100.0%

Source: Dun & Bradstreet Inc., *Business Failure Record,* 1994.

[1]Much of the current academic work in the area of financial distress and bankruptcy is based on writings by Edward I. Altman. For a summary of his work and that of others, see Edward I. Altman, *Bankruptcy and Distressed Restructuring: Analytical Issues and Investment Opportunities* (Frederick, MD: Beard Group, 1999).

Table 24-2

The Ten Largest Bankruptcies since 1980 (Billions of Dollars)

Company	Business	Assets	Date
Worldcom, Inc.	Telecommunications	$103.9	July 21, 2002
Enron Corp.	Energy trading	63.4	December 2, 2001
Conseco, Inc.	Insurance, finance	61.4	December 18, 2002
Texaco, Inc.	Energy	35.9	April 12, 1987
Refco, Inc.	Finance	33.3	October 17, 2005
Global Crossing Ltd.	Telecommunications	30.2	January 28, 2002
Pacific Gas and Electric Co.	Energy	29.8	April 6, 2001
Calpine Corporation	Energy	27.2	December 20, 2005
UAL Corp.	Airline	25.2	December 9, 2002
Delta Air Lines, Inc.	Airline	21.8	September 14, 2005

Source: BankruptcyData.com, a division of New Generation Research, September 2006.

big or too important to be allowed to fail, and mergers or governmental intervention are often used as an alternative to outright failure and liquidation. The decision to give federal aid to Chrysler (now a part of DaimlerChrysler AG) in the 1980s is an excellent illustration. Also, in recent years federal regulators have arranged the absorption of many "problem" financial institutions by financially sound institutions. In addition, several U.S. government agencies, principally the Defense Department, were able to bail out Lockheed when it otherwise would have failed, and the "shotgun marriage" of Douglas Aircraft and McDonnell was designed to prevent Douglas's failure. Another example of intervention is that of Merrill Lynch taking over the brokerage firm Goodbody & Company, which would otherwise have gone bankrupt and would have frozen the accounts of its 225,000 customers while a bankruptcy settlement was being worked out. Goodbody's failure would have panicked investors across the country, so New York Stock Exchange member firms put up $30 million as an inducement to get Merrill Lynch to keep Goodbody from folding. Similar instances in other industries could also be cited.

Why do government and industry seek to avoid failure among larger firms? In the case of banks, the main reason is to prevent an erosion of confidence and a consequent run on the banks. With Lockheed and Douglas, the Defense Department wanted not only to maintain viable suppliers but also to avoid disrupting local communities. With Chrysler, the government wanted to preserve jobs as well as a competitor in the U.S. auto industry. Even when the public interest is not at stake, the fact that bankruptcy is a very expensive process gives private industry strong incentives to avoid outright bankruptcy. The costs and complexities of a formal bankruptcy are discussed in subsequent sections of this chapter, after we examine some less formal and less expensive procedures.

SELF-TEST
What are the major causes of business failure?
Do business failures occur evenly over time?
Which size of firm, large or small, is most prone to business failure? Why?

24.2   Issues Facing a Firm in Financial Distress

Financial distress begins when a firm is unable to meet scheduled payments or when cash flow projections indicate that it will soon be unable to do so. As the situation develops, these central issues arise:

1. Is the firm's inability to meet scheduled debt payments a temporary cash flow problem, or is it a permanent problem caused by asset values having fallen below debt obligations?
2. If the problem is a temporary one, then an agreement with creditors that gives the firm time to recover and to satisfy everyone may be worked out. However, if basic long-run asset values have truly declined, then economic losses have occurred. In this event, who should bear the losses, and who should get whatever value remains?
3. Is the company "worth more dead than alive?" That is, would the business be more valuable if it were maintained and continued in operation or if it were liquidated and sold off in pieces?
4. Should the firm file for protection under Chapter 11 of the Bankruptcy Act, or should it try to use informal procedures? (Both reorganization and liquidation can be accomplished either informally or under the direction of a bankruptcy court.)
5. Who should control the firm while it is being liquidated or rehabilitated? Should the existing management be left in charge, or should a trustee be placed in charge of operations?

In the remainder of the chapter, we discuss these issues.

SELF-TEST

What five major issues must be addressed when a firm faces financial distress?

24.3   Settlements without Going through Formal Bankruptcy

When a firm experiences financial distress, its managers and creditors must decide whether the problem is temporary and the firm is really financially viable, or whether a permanent problem exists that endangers the firm's life. Then, the parties must decide whether to try to solve the problem informally or under the direction of a bankruptcy court. Because of costs associated with formal bankruptcy—including the disruptions that occur when a firm's customers, suppliers, and employees learn that it has filed under the Bankruptcy Act—it is desirable, if possible, to reorganize (or liquidate) outside of formal bankruptcy. We first discuss informal settlement procedures, then procedures under a formal bankruptcy.

Informal Reorganization

In the case of an economically sound company whose financial difficulties appear to be temporary, creditors are generally willing to work with the company to help it recover and reestablish itself on a sound financial basis. Such voluntary plans, commonly called **workouts,** usually require a **restructuring** of the firm's debt, because current cash flows are insufficient to service the existing debt. Restructuring typically involves extension and/or composition. In an **extension,** creditors postpone the dates of required interest or principal payments, or both. In a **composition,** creditors voluntarily reduce their fixed claims on the debtor by accepting a lower principal amount, by reducing the interest rate on the debt, by taking equity in exchange for debt, or by some combination of these changes.

A debt restructuring begins with a meeting between the failing firm's managers and creditors. The creditors appoint a committee consisting of four or five of the largest creditors, plus one or two of the smaller ones. This meeting is often arranged and conducted by an **adjustment bureau** associated with and run by a local credit managers' association.[2] The first step is for management to draw up a list of creditors, with amounts of debt owed. There are typically different classes of debt, ranging from first-mortgage holders to unsecured creditors. Next, the company develops information showing the value of the firm under different scenarios. Typically, one scenario is going out of business, selling off the assets, and then distributing the proceeds to the various creditors in accordance with the priority of their claims, with any surplus going to the common stockholders. The company may hire an appraiser to get an appraisal of the value of the firm's property to use as a basis for this scenario. Other scenarios include continued operations, frequently with some improvements in capital equipment, marketing, and perhaps some management changes.

This information is then shared with the firm's bankers and other creditors. Frequently, it can be demonstrated that the firm's debts exceed its liquidating value, and it can also be shown that legal fees and other costs associated with a formal liquidation under federal bankruptcy procedures would materially lower the net proceeds available to creditors. Further, it generally takes at least a year, and often several years, to resolve matters in a formal proceeding, so the present value of the eventual proceeds will be lower still. This information, when presented in a credible manner, often convinces creditors that they would be better off accepting something less than the full amount of their claims rather than holding out for the full face amount. If management and the major creditors agree that the problems can probably be resolved, then a more formal plan is drafted and presented to all the creditors, along with the reasons creditors should be willing to compromise on their claims.

In developing the reorganization plan, creditors prefer an extension because it promises eventual payment in full. In some cases, creditors may agree not only to postpone the date of payment but also to subordinate existing claims to vendors who are willing to extend new credit during the workout period. Similarly, creditors may agree to accept a lower interest rate on loans during the extension, perhaps in exchange for a pledge of collateral. Because of the sacrifices involved, the creditors must have faith that the debtor firm will be able to solve its problems.

In a composition, creditors agree to reduce their claims. Typically, creditors receive cash and/or new securities that have a combined market value that is less than the amounts owed them. The cash and securities, which might have a value of only 10% of the original claim, are taken as full settlement of the original debt. Bargaining will take place between the debtor and the creditors over the savings

---

[2]There is a nationwide group called the National Association of Credit Management that consists of bankers and industrial companies' credit managers. This group sponsors research on credit policy and problems, conducts seminars on credit management, and operates local chapters in cities throughout the nation. These local chapters frequently operate adjustment bureaus.

that result from avoiding the costs of legal bankruptcy: administrative costs, legal fees, investigative costs, and so on. In addition to escaping such costs, the debtor gains because the stigma of bankruptcy may be avoided. As a result, the debtor may be induced to part with most of the savings from avoiding formal bankruptcy.

Often, the bargaining process will result in a restructuring that involves both extension and composition. For example, the settlement may provide for a cash payment of 25% of the debt immediately, plus a new note promising six future installments of 10% each, for a total payment of 85%.

Voluntary settlements are both informal and simple, and also relatively inexpensive because legal and administrative expenses are held to a minimum. Thus, voluntary procedures generally result in the largest return to creditors. Although creditors do not obtain immediate payment and may even have to accept less than is owed them, they generally recover more money, and sooner, than if the firm were to file for bankruptcy.

In recent years, one factor that has motivated some creditors, especially banks and insurance companies, to agree to voluntary restructurings is the fact that restructurings can sometimes help creditors avoid showing a loss. Thus, a bank that is "in trouble" with its regulators over weak capital ratios may agree to extend further loans that are used to pay the interest on earlier loans in order to keep the bank from having to write down the value of its earlier loans. This particular type of restructuring depends on (1) the willingness of the regulators to go along with the process, and (2) whether the bank is likely to recover more in the end by restructuring the debt than by forcing the borrower into bankruptcy immediately.

We should point out that informal voluntary settlements are not reserved for small firms. International Harvester (now Navistar International) avoided formal bankruptcy proceedings by getting its creditors to agree to restructure more than $3.5 billion of debt. Likewise, Chrysler's creditors accepted both an extension and a composition to help it through its bad years in the late 1970s before it merged with Daimler-Benz. The biggest problem with informal reorganizations is getting all the parties to agree to the voluntary plan. This problem, called the **holdout problem,** is discussed in a later section.

Informal Liquidation

When it is obvious that a firm is more valuable dead than alive, informal procedures can also be used to **liquidate** the firm. **Assignment** is an informal procedure for liquidating a firm, and it usually yields creditors a larger amount than they would get in a formal bankruptcy liquidation. However, assignments are feasible only if the firm is small and its affairs are not too complex. An assignment calls for title to the debtor's assets to be transferred to a third party, known as an **assignee** or **trustee.** The assignee is instructed to liquidate the assets through a private sale or public auction and then to distribute the proceeds among the creditors on a pro rata basis. The assignment does not automatically discharge the debtor's obligations. However, the debtor may have the assignee write on the check to each creditor the requisite legal language to make endorsement of the check acknowledgment of full settlement of the claim.

Assignment has some advantages over liquidation in federal bankruptcy courts in terms of time, legal formality, and expense. The assignee has more flexibility in disposing of property than does a federal bankruptcy trustee, so action can be taken sooner, before inventory becomes obsolete or machinery rusts. Also, because the assignee is often familiar with the debtor's business, better results may be achieved. However, an assignment does not automatically result in a full and legal discharge of all the debtor's liabilities, nor does it protect the creditors against fraud. Both of these problems can be reduced by formal liquidation in bankruptcy, which we discuss in a later section.

SELF-TEST

Define the following terms: (1) restructuring, (2) extension, (3) composition, (4) assignment, and (5) assignee (trustee).

What are the advantages of liquidation by assignment versus a formal bankruptcy liquidation?

24.4   Federal Bankruptcy Law

U.S. bankruptcy laws were first enacted in 1898. They were modified substantially in 1938, then they were changed substantially again in 1978, and some fine-tuning was done in 1986. In 2005, Congress further modified the bankruptcy code, speeding up bankruptcy proceedings for companies and making it more difficult for consumers to take advantage of provisions that can wipe out certain debts. The primary purpose of the bankruptcy law is to avoid having firms that are worth more as ongoing concerns be put out of business by individual creditors who could force liquidation without regard to the effects on other parties.

Currently, our bankruptcy law consists of eight odd-numbered chapters, plus one even-numbered chapter. (The old even-numbered chapters were deleted when the act was revised in 1978.) Chapters 1, 3, and 5 contain general provisions applicable to the other chapters. **Chapter 11,** which deals with business reorganization, is the most important section from a financial management viewpoint. **Chapter 7** details the procedures to be followed when liquidating a firm; generally, Chapter 7 does not come into play unless it has been determined that reorganization under Chapter 11 is not feasible. Chapter 9 deals with financially distressed municipalities; Chapter 12 covers special procedures for family-owned farms; Chapter 13 covers the adjustment of debts for "individuals with regular income;" and Chapter 15 sets up a system of trustees who help administer proceedings under the act.

A firm is officially bankrupt when it files for bankruptcy with a federal court. When you read that a company such as Southland (the owner of the 7-Eleven convenience store chain) has "filed for court protection under Chapter 11," this means that the company is attempting to reorganize under the supervision of a bankruptcy court. Formal bankruptcy proceedings are designed to protect both the firm and its creditors. On the one hand, if the problem is temporary insolvency, then the firm may use bankruptcy proceedings to gain time to solve its cash flow problems without asset seizure by its creditors. On the other hand, if the firm is truly bankrupt in the sense that liabilities exceed assets, the creditors can use bankruptcy procedures to stop the firm's managers from continuing to operate, lose more money, and thus deplete assets which should go to creditors.

Bankruptcy law is flexible in that it provides scope for negotiations between a company, its creditors, its labor force, and its stockholders. A case is opened by filing a petition with one of the 291 bankruptcy courts serving 90 judicial districts. The petition may be either **voluntary** or **involuntary;** that is, it may be filed either by the firm's management or by its creditors. After a filing, a committee of unsecured creditors is then appointed by the Office of the U.S. Trustee to negotiate with management for a reorganization, which may include the restructuring of debt. Under Chapter 11, a trustee will be appointed to take over the company if the court deems current management incompetent or if fraud is suspected. Normally, though, the existing management retains control. If no fair and feasible reorganization can be worked out, the bankruptcy judge will order that the firm be liquidated under procedures spelled out in Chapter 7 of the Bankruptcy Act, in which case a trustee will always be appointed.[3]

SELF-TEST

Define the following terms: (1) bankruptcy law, (2) Chapter 11, (3) Chapter 7, (4) trustee, (5) voluntary bankruptcy, and (6) involuntary bankruptcy.

How does a firm formally declare bankruptcy?

24.5   Reorganization in Bankruptcy

It might appear that most reorganizations should be handled informally because informal reorganizations are faster and less costly than formal bankruptcy. However, two problems often arise to stymie informal reorganizations and thus force debtors into Chapter 11 bankruptcy—the common pool problem and the holdout problem.[4]

To illustrate these problems, consider a firm that is having financial difficulties. It is worth $9 million as a going concern (this is the present value of its expected future operating cash flows) but only $7 million if it is liquidated. The firm's debt totals $10 million at face value—ten creditors with equal priority each have a $1 million claim. Now suppose the firm's liquidity deteriorates to the point where it defaults on one of its loans. The holder of that loan has the contractual right to *accelerate* the claim, which means the creditor can *foreclose* on the loan and demand payment of the entire balance. Further, since most debt agreements have *cross-default provisions*, defaulting on one loan effectively places all loans in default.

The firm's market value is less than the $10 million face value of debt, regardless of whether it remains in business or liquidates. Therefore, it would be impossible to pay off all of the creditors in full. However, the creditors in total would be better off if the firm is not shut down, because they could ultimately recover $9 million if the firm remains in business but only $7 million if it is liquidated. The problem here, which is called the **common pool problem,** is that, in the absence of protection under the Bankruptcy Act, individual creditors would have an incentive to foreclose on the firm even though it is worth more as an ongoing concern.

An individual creditor would have the incentive to foreclose because it could then force the firm to liquidate a portion of its assets to pay off that particular creditor's $1 million claim in full. The payment to that creditor would probably require the liquidation of vital assets, which might cause a shutdown of the firm and thus lead to a liquidation. Therefore, the value of the remaining creditors' claims would decline. Of course, all the creditors would recognize the gains to be had from this strategy, so they would storm the debtor with foreclosure notices. Even those creditors who understand the merits of keeping the firm alive would be forced to foreclose, because the foreclosures of the other creditors would reduce

---

[3]For a discussion of European bankruptcy laws, see Kevin M. J. Kaiser, "European Bankruptcy Laws: Implications for Corporations Facing Financial Distress," *Financial Management*, Autumn 1996, pp. 67–85.

[4]The issues discussed in this section are covered in more detail in Thomas H. Jackson, *The Logic and Limits of Bankruptcy Law* (Frederick, MD: Beard Group, 2001). Also, see Stuart C. Gilson, "Managing Default: Some Evidence on How Firms Choose between Workouts and Chapter 11," *Journal of Applied Corporate Finance*, Summer 1991, pp. 62–70; David T. Brown, "Claimholder Incentive Conflicts in Reorganization: The Role of Bankruptcy Law," *Review of Financial Studies*, 1989, pp. 109–123; and Yehning Chen, J. Fred Weston, and Edward I. Altman, "Financial Distress and Restructuring Models," *Financial Management*, Summer 1995, pp. 57–75.

the payoff to those who do not. In our hypothetical example, if seven creditors foreclosed and forced liquidation, they would be paid in full, and the remaining three creditors would receive nothing.

With many creditors, as soon as a firm defaults on one loan, there is the potential for a disruptive flood of foreclosures that would make the creditors collectively worse off. In our example, the creditors would lose $9 - $7 = $2 million in value if a flood of foreclosures were to force the firm to liquidate. If the firm had only one creditor, say, a single bank loan, the common pool problem would not exist. If a bank had loaned the company $10 million, it would not force liquidation to get $7 million when it could keep the firm alive and eventually realize $9 million.

Chapter 11 of the Bankruptcy Act provides a solution to the common pool problem through its **automatic stay** provision. *An automatic stay, which is forced on all creditors in a bankruptcy, limits the ability of creditors to foreclose to collect their individual claims.* However, the creditors can collectively foreclose on the debtor and force liquidation.

While bankruptcy gives the firm a chance to work out its problems without the threat of creditor foreclosure, management does not have a completely free reign over the firm's assets. First, bankruptcy law requires the debtor firm to request permission from the court to take many actions, and the law also gives creditors the right to petition the bankruptcy court to block almost any action the firm might take while in bankruptcy. Second, **fraudulent conveyance** statutes, which are part of debtor-creditor law, protect creditors from unjustified transfers of property by a firm in financial distress.

To illustrate fraudulent conveyance, suppose a holding company is contemplating bankruptcy protection for one of its subsidiaries. The holding company might be tempted to sell some or all of the subsidiary's assets to itself (the parent company) for less than the true market value. This transaction would reduce the value of the subsidiary by the difference between the true market value of its assets and the amount paid, and the loss would be borne primarily by the subsidiary's creditors. Such a transaction would be voided by the courts as a fraudulent conveyance. Note also that transactions that favor one creditor at the expense of another can be voided under the same law. For example, a transaction in which an asset is sold and the proceeds are used to pay one creditor in full at the expense of other creditors could be voided. Thus, fraudulent conveyance laws also protect creditors from each other.[5]

The second problem that the bankruptcy law mitigates is the holdout problem. To illustrate this problem, consider again our example with ten creditors owed $1 million each but with assets worth only $9 million. The goal of the firm is to avoid liquidation by remedying the default. In an informal workout, this would require a reorganization plan that is agreed to by each of the ten creditors. Suppose the firm offers each creditor new debt with a face value of $850,000 in exchange for the old $1,000,000 face value debt. If each of the creditors accepted the offer, the firm could be successfully reorganized. The reorganization would leave the equity holders with some value—the market value of the equity would be $9,000,000 - 10($850,000) = $500,000. Further, the creditors would have claims worth $8.5 million, much more than the $7 million value of their claims in liquidation.

Although such an exchange offer seems to benefit all parties, it might well not be accepted by the creditors. Here's why: Suppose seven of the ten creditors tender their bonds; thus, seven creditors each now have claims with a face value of

---

[5]The bankruptcy code requires that all transactions undertaken by the firm in the 6 months prior to a bankruptcy filing be reviewed by the court for fraudulent conveyance, and the review can go back as far as 3 years.

$850,000 each, or $5,950,000 in total, while the three creditors that did not tender their bonds each still have a claim with a face value of $1 million. The total face value of the debt at this point is $8,950,000, which is less than the $9 million value of the firm. In this situation, the three holdout creditors would receive the full face value of their debt. However, this probably would not happen, because (1) all of the creditors would be sophisticated enough to realize this could happen, and (2) each creditor would want to be one of the three holdouts that gets paid in full. Thus, it is likely that none of the creditors would accept the offer. The holdout problem makes it difficult to restructure the firm's debts. Again, if the firm had a single creditor, there would be no holdout problem.

The holdout problem is mitigated in bankruptcy proceedings by the bankruptcy court's ability to lump creditors into classes. Each class is considered to have accepted a reorganization plan if 2/3 of the amount of debt and 1/2 the number of claimants vote for the plan, and the plan will be approved by the court if it is deemed to be "fair and equitable" to the dissenting parties. This procedure, in which the court mandates a reorganization plan in spite of dissent, is called a **cramdown,** because the court crams the plan down the throats of the dissenters. The ability of the court to force acceptance of a reorganization plan greatly reduces the incentive for creditors to hold out. Thus, in our example, if the reorganization plan offered each creditor a new claim worth $850,000 in face value, along with information that each creditor would probably receive only $700,000 under the liquidation alternative, it would have a good chance of success.

It is easier for a firm with few creditors to informally reorganize than it is for a firm with many creditors. A 1990 study examined 169 publicly traded firms that experienced severe financial distress from 1978 to 1987.[6] About half of the firms reorganized without filing for bankruptcy, while the other half were forced to reorganize in bankruptcy. The firms that reorganized without filing for bankruptcy owed most of their debt to a few banks, and they had fewer creditors. Generally, bank debt can be reorganized outside of bankruptcy, but a publicly traded bond issue held by thousands of individual bondholders makes reorganization difficult.

Filing for bankruptcy under Chapter 11 has several other features that help the bankrupt firm:

1. Interest and principal payments, including interest on delayed payments, may be delayed without penalty until a reorganization plan is approved, and the plan itself may call for even further delays. This permits cash generated from operations to be used to sustain operations rather than be paid to creditors.
2. The firm is permitted to issue **debtor-in-possession (DIP) financing.** DIP financing enhances the ability of the firm to borrow funds for short-term liquidity purposes, because such loans are, under the law, senior to all previous unsecured debt.
3. The debtor firm's managers are given the exclusive right for 120 days after filing for bankruptcy protection to submit a reorganization plan, plus another 60 days to obtain agreement on the plan from the affected parties. The court may also extend these dates up to 18 months. After management's first right to submit a plan has expired, any party to the proceedings may propose its own reorganization plan.

---

[6]See Stuart Gilson, Kose John, and Larry Lang, "Troubled Debt Restructurings: An Empirical Study of Private Reorganization of Firms in Default," *Journal of Financial Economics,* October 1990, pp. 315–354.

Under the early bankruptcy laws, most formal reorganization plans were guided by the **absolute priority doctrine.**[7] This doctrine holds that creditors should be compensated for their claims in a rigid hierarchical order, and that senior claims must be paid in full before junior claims can receive even a dime. If there were any chance that a delay would lead to losses by senior creditors, then the firm would be shut down and liquidated. However, an alternative position, the **relative priority doctrine,** holds that more flexibility should be allowed in a reorganization, and that a balanced consideration should be given to all claimants. The current law represents a movement away from absolute priority toward relative priority.

The primary role of the bankruptcy court in a reorganization is to determine the **fairness** and the **feasibility** of the proposed plan of reorganization. The basic doctrine of fairness states that claims must be recognized in the order of their legal and contractual priority. Feasibility means that there is a reasonable chance that the reorganized company will be viable. Carrying out the concepts of fairness and feasibility in a reorganization involves the following steps:

1. Future sales must be estimated.
2. Operating conditions must be analyzed so that future earnings and cash flows can be predicted.
3. The appropriate capitalization rate must be determined.
4. This capitalization rate must then be applied to the estimated cash flows to obtain an estimate of the company's value.[8]
5. An appropriate capital structure for the company after it emerges from Chapter 11 must be determined.
6. The reorganized firm's securities must be allocated to the various claimants in a fair and equitable manner.

The primary test of feasibility in a reorganization is whether the fixed charges after reorganization will be adequately covered by earnings. Adequate coverage generally requires an improvement in earnings, a reduction of fixed charges, or both. Among the actions that must generally be taken are the following:

1. Debt maturities are usually lengthened, interest rates may be lowered, and some debt is usually converted into equity.
2. When the quality of management has been substandard, a new team must be given control of the company.
3. If inventories have become obsolete or depleted, they must be replaced.
4. Sometimes the plant and equipment must be modernized before the firm can operate and compete successfully.
5. Reorganization may also require an improvement in production, marketing, advertising, and/or other functions.

---

[7]For more on absolute priority, see Lawrence A. Weiss, "The Bankruptcy Code and Violations of Absolute Priority," *Journal of Applied Corporate Finance,* Summer 1991, pp. 71–78; William Beranek, Robert Boehmer, and Brooke Smith, "Much Ado about Nothing: Absolute Priority Deviations in Chapter 11," *Financial Management,* Autumn 1996, pp. 102–109; and Allan C. Eberhart, William T. Moore, and Rodney Roenfeldt, "Security Pricing and Deviations from the Absolute Priority Rule in Bankruptcy Proceedings," *Journal of Finance,* December 1990, pp. 1457–1469.

[8]Several different approaches can be used to estimate a company's value. Market-determined multiples such as the price/earnings ratio, which are obtained from an analysis of comparable firms, can be applied to some measure of the company's earnings or cash flow. Alternatively, discounted cash flow techniques may be used. The key point here is that fairness requires that the value of a company facing reorganization be estimated so that potential offers can be evaluated rationally by the bankruptcy court.

6. It is sometimes necessary to develop new products or markets to enable the firm to move from areas where economic trends are poor into areas with more potential for growth.

7. Labor unions must agree to accept lower wages and less restrictive work rules. This was a major issue for United Airlines in 2003 as it attempted to emerge from Chapter 11 bankruptcy protection. By threatening liquidation, UAL was able to squeeze a $6.6 billion reduction in payroll costs from its pilots over 6 years, and another $2.6 billion from its ground crew workers. This wasn't enough, though, and 3 years later UAL is still operating under bankruptcy protection.

These actions usually require at least some new money, so most reorganization plans include new investors who are willing to put up new capital.

It might appear that stockholders have very little to say in a bankruptcy situation in which the firm's assets are worth less than the face value of its debt. Under the absolute priority rule, stockholders in such a situation should get nothing of value under a reorganization plan. In fact, however, stockholders may be able to extract some of the firm's value. This occurs because (1) stockholders generally continue to control the firm during the bankruptcy proceedings, (2) stockholders have the first right to file a reorganization plan, and (3) for the creditors, developing a plan and taking it through the courts would be expensive and time consuming. Given this situation, creditors may support a plan under which they are not paid off in full and where the old stockholders will control the reorganized company just because the creditors want to get the problem behind them and to get some money in the near future.

Illustration of a Reorganization

Reorganization procedures may be illustrated with an example involving the Columbia Software Company, a regional firm that specializes in selling, installing, and servicing accounting software for small businesses.[9] Table 24-3 gives Columbia's balance sheet as of March 31, 2007. The company had been suffering losses running to $2.5 million a year, and, as will be made clear in the following discussion, the asset values in the balance sheet are overstated relative to their market values. The firm was **insolvent,** which means that the book values of its liabilities were greater than the market values of its assets, so it filed a petition with a federal court for reorganization under Chapter 11. Management filed a plan of reorganization with the court on June 13, 2007. The plan was subsequently submitted for review by the SEC.[10]

The plan concluded that the company could not be internally reorganized and that the only feasible solution would be to combine Columbia with a larger, nationwide software company. Accordingly, management solicited the interest of a number of software companies. Late in July 2007, Moreland Software showed an interest in Columbia. On August 3, 2007, Moreland made a formal proposal to take over Columbia's $6 million of $7\frac{1}{2}\%$ first-mortgage bonds, to pay the $250,000 in taxes owed by Columbia, and to provide 40,000 shares of Moreland common

---

[9]This example is based on an actual reorganization, although the company name has been changed and the numbers have been changed slightly to simplify the analysis.

[10]Reorganization plans must be submitted to the Securities and Exchange Commission (SEC) if (1) the securities of the debtor are publicly held and (2) total indebtedness exceeds $3 million. However, in recent years the only bankruptcy cases that the SEC has become involved in are those that are either precedent setting or that involve issues of national interest.

Table 24-3

Columbia Software Company: Balance Sheet
as of March 31, 2007 (Millions of Dollars)

Assets

Current assets	$ 3.50
Net fixed assets	12.50
Other assets	0.70
Total assets	$16.70

Liabilities and Equity

Accounts payable	$ 1.00
Accrued taxes	0.25
Notes payable	0.25
Other current liabilities	1.75
7½% first mortgage bonds, due 2015	6.00
9% subordinated debentures, due 2010[a]	7.00
Total liabilities	$16.25
Common stock ($1 par)	1.00
Paid-in capital	3.45
Retained earnings	(4.00)
Total liabilities and equity	$16.70

[a]The debentures are subordinated to the notes payable.

stock to satisfy the remaining creditor claims. Since the Moreland stock had a market price of $75 per share, the value of the stock was $3 million. Thus, Moreland was offering $3 million of stock plus assuming $6 million of loans and $250,000 of taxes—a total of $9.25 million for assets that had a book value of $16.7 million.

Moreland's plan is shown in Table 24-4. As in most Chapter 11 plans, the secured creditors' claims are paid in full (in this case, the mortgage bonds are taken over by Moreland Software). However, the total remaining unsecured claims equal $10 million against only $3 million of Moreland stock. Thus, each unsecured creditor would be entitled to receive 30% before the adjustment for subordination. Before this adjustment, holders of the notes payable would receive 30% of their $250,000 claim, or $75,000 in stock. However, the debentures are subordinated to the notes payable, so an additional $175,000 must be allocated to notes payable. (See footnote a in Table 24-4.) In Column 5, the dollar claims of each class of debt are restated in terms of the number of shares of Moreland common stock received by each class of unsecured creditors. Finally, Column 6 shows the percentage of the original claim each group received. Of course, both the taxes and the secured creditors were paid off in full, while the stockholders received nothing.[11]

The bankruptcy court first evaluated the proposal from the standpoint of fairness. The court began by considering the value of Columbia Software as estimated by the unsecured creditors' committee and by a subgroup of debenture

---

[11]We do not show it, but $365,000 of fees for Columbia's attorneys and $123,000 of fees for the creditors' committee lawyers were also deducted. The current assets shown in Table 24-3 were net of these fees. Creditors joke (often bitterly) about the "lawyers first" rule in payouts in bankruptcy cases. It is often said, with much truth, that the only winners in bankruptcy cases are the attorneys.

Table 24-4

Columbia Software Company: Reorganization Plan

Senior Claims

Taxes	$ 250,000	Paid off by Moreland
Mortgage bonds	$6,000,000	Assumed by Moreland

The reorganization plan for the remaining $10 million of liabilities, based on 40,000 shares at a price of $75 for a total market value of $3 million, or 30% of the remaining liabilities, is as follows:

Junior Claims (1)	Original Amount (2)	30% of Claim Amount (3)	Claim after Subordination (4)	Number of Shares of Common Stock (5)	Percentage of Original Claim Received (6)
Notes payable	$ 250,000	$ 75,000	$ 250,000[a]	3,333	100%
Unsecured creditors	2,750,000	825,000	825,000	11,000	30
Subordinated debentures	7,000,000	2,100,000	1,925,000[a]	25,667	28
	$10,000,000	$3,000,000	$3,000,000	40,000	30

[a]Because the debentures are subordinated to the notes payable, $250,000 − $75,000 = $175,000 must be redistributed from the debentures to the notes payable, leaving a claim of $2,100,000 − $175,000 = $1,925,000 for the debentures.

holders. After discussions with various experts, one group had arrived at estimated post-reorganization sales of $25 million per year. It further estimated that the profit margin on sales would equal 6%, thus producing estimated future annual earnings of $1.5 million.

This subgroup analyzed price/earnings ratios for comparable companies and arrived at 8 times future earnings for a capitalization factor. Multiplying 8 by $1.5 million gave an indicated equity value of the company of $12 million. This value was four times that of the 40,000 shares of Moreland stock offered for the remainder of the company. Thus, the subgroup concluded that the plan for reorganization did not meet the test of fairness. Note that under both Moreland's plan and the subgroup's plan, the holders of common stock were to receive nothing, which is one of the risks of ownership, while the holders of the first-mortgage bonds were to be assumed by Moreland, which amounts to being paid in full.

The bankruptcy judge examined management's plan for feasibility, observing that in the reorganization Moreland Software would take over Columbia's properties. The court judged that the direction and aid of Moreland would remedy the deficiencies that had troubled Columbia. Whereas the debt/assets ratio of Columbia Software had become unbalanced, Moreland had only a moderate amount of debt. After consolidation, Moreland would still have a relatively low 27% debt ratio.

Moreland's net income before interest and taxes had been running at a level of approximately $15 million. The interest on its long-term debt after the merger would be $1.5 million and, taking short-term borrowings into account, would total a maximum of $2 million per year. The $15 million in earnings before interest and taxes would therefore provide an interest charge coverage of 7.5 times, exceeding the norm of 5 times for the industry.

Note that the question of feasibility would have been irrelevant had Moreland offered $3 million in cash rather than in stock and had it offered to pay off the bonds rather than take them over. It is the court's responsibility to protect the interests of Columbia's creditors. Because the creditors are being forced to take common stock or bonds guaranteed by another firm, the law requires the court to look into the feasibility of the transaction. If Moreland had made a cash offer, however, the feasibility of its own operation after the transaction was completed would not have been a concern.

Moreland Software was told of the subgroup's analysis and concern over the fairness of the plan. Further, Moreland was asked to increase the number of shares it offered. Moreland refused, and no other company offered to acquire Columbia. Because no better offer could be obtained, and since the only alternative to the plan was liquidation (with an even lower realized value), Moreland's proposal was ultimately accepted by the creditors despite some disagreement with the valuation.

One interesting aspect of this case had to do with an agency conflict between Columbia's old stockholders and its management. Columbia's management knew, when it filed for bankruptcy, that the company was probably worth less than the amount of its debt, hence that stockholders would probably receive nothing. Indeed, that situation did materialize. If management has a primary responsibility to the stockholders, why would it file for bankruptcy knowing that the stockholders would receive nothing? First, management thought, but did not know for sure, that stockholders would receive nothing. What they were sure of was that if they did not file for bankruptcy protection, creditors would foreclose on the company's property and shut the company down, which would surely lead to liquidation and a total loss to stockholders. Also, if the company were liquidated, both management and the workforce would lose their jobs and the managers would get a very black mark on their records. Finally, Columbia's managers thought (correctly) that there was nothing they could do to protect the stockholders, so they might as well do what was best for the workforce, the creditors, and themselves, and that meant realizing the most value possible for the company's assets.

Some of the stockholders felt betrayed by management—they thought management should have taken more heroic steps to protect them, regardless of the cost to other parties. One stockholder suggested that management should have sold off assets, taken the cash to Las Vegas, and rolled the dice. Then, if they won, they should have paid off the debt and had something left for stockholders, but leave the debtholders holding the bag if they lost. Actually, management had done something a bit like this in the year preceding the bankruptcy. Management realized that the company was floundering and was likely to sink under its current operating plan and that only a "big winner" project would save the company. Therefore, they took on several very risky "bet the company" projects that had negative expected NPVs but at least some chance for high profits. Unfortunately, those projects did not work out.

Prepackaged Bankruptcies

In recent years, a new type of reorganization that combines the advantages of both the informal workout and formal Chapter 11 reorganization has become popular. This new hybrid is called a **prepackaged bankruptcy,** or **pre-pack.**[12]

---

[12]For more information on prepackaged bankruptcies, see John J. McConnell and Henri Servaes, "The Economics of Pre-Packaged Bankruptcy," *Journal of Applied Corporate Finance,* Summer 1991, pp. 93–97; Brian L. Betker, "An Empirical Examination of Prepackaged Bankruptcy," *Financial Management,* Spring 1995, pp. 3–18; Sris Chatterjee, Upinder S. Dhillon, and Gabriel G. Ramirez, "Resolution of Financial Distress: Debt Restructurings via Chapter 11, Prepackaged Bankruptcies, and Workouts," *Financial Management,* Spring 1996, pp. 5–18; and John J. McConnell, Ronald C. Lease, and Elizabeth Tashjian, "Prepacks as a Mechanism for Resolving Financial Distress," *Journal of Applied Corporate Finance,* Winter 1996, pp. 99–106.

In an informal workout, a debtor negotiates a restructuring with its creditors. Even though complex workouts typically involve corporate officers, lenders, lawyers, and investment bankers, workouts are still less expensive and less damaging to reputations than are Chapter 11 reorganizations. In a prepackaged bankruptcy, the debtor firm gets all, or most, of the creditors to agree to the reorganization plan *prior* to filing for bankruptcy. Then, a reorganization plan is filed along with, or shortly after, the bankruptcy petition. If enough creditors have signed on before the filing, a cramdown can be used to bring reluctant creditors along.

A logical question arises: Why would a firm that can arrange an informal reorganization want to file for bankruptcy? The three primary advantages of a prepackaged bankruptcy are (1) reduction of the holdout problem, (2) preserving creditors' claims, and (3) taxes. Perhaps the biggest benefit of a prepackaged bankruptcy is the reduction of the holdout problem, because a bankruptcy filing permits a cramdown that would otherwise be impossible. By eliminating holdouts, bankruptcy forces all creditors in each class to participate on a pro rata basis, which preserves the relative value of all claimants. Also, filing for formal bankruptcy can at times have positive tax implications. First, in an informal reorganization in which the debtholders trade debt for equity, if the original equity holders end up with less than 50% ownership, the company loses its accumulated tax losses. In formal bankruptcy, the firm may get to keep its loss carryforwards. Second, in a workout, when debt worth, say, $1,000, is exchanged for debt worth, say, $500, the reduction in debt of $500 is considered to be taxable income to the corporation. However, if this same situation occurs in a Chapter 11 reorganization, the difference is not treated as taxable income.[13]

All in all, prepackaged bankruptcies make sense in many situations. If sufficient agreement can be reached among creditors through informal negotiations, a subsequent filing can solve the holdout problem and result in favorable tax treatment. For these reasons, the number of prepackaged bankruptcies has grown dramatically in recent years.

Reorganization Time and Expense

The time, expense, and headaches involved in a reorganization are almost beyond comprehension. Even in $2 to $3 million bankruptcies, many people and groups are involved: lawyers representing the company, the U.S. Bankruptcy Trustee, each class of secured creditor, the general creditors as a group, tax authorities, and the stockholders if they are upset with management. There are time limits within which things are supposed to be done, but the process generally takes at least a year and probably much longer. The company must be given time to file its plan, and creditor groups must be given time to study and seek clarifications to it and then file counterplans to which the company must respond. Also, different creditor classes often disagree among themselves as to how much each class should receive, and hearings must be held to resolve such conflicts.

Management will want to remain in business, while some well-secured creditors may want the company liquidated as quickly as possible. Often, some party's plan will involve selling the business to another concern, as was the case with Columbia Software in our earlier example. Obviously, it can take months to seek out and negotiate with potential merger candidates.

---

[13]Note that in both tax situations—loss carryforwards and debt value reductions—favorable tax treatment can be available in workouts if the firm is deemed to be legally insolvent, that is, if the market value of its assets is demonstrated to be less than the face value of its liabilities.

The typical bankruptcy case takes about 2 years from the time the company files for protection under Chapter 11 until the final reorganization plan is approved or rejected. While all of this is going on, the company's business suffers. Sales certainly won't be helped, key employees may leave, and the remaining employees will be worrying about their jobs rather than concentrating on their work. Further, management will be spending much of its time on the bankruptcy rather than running the business, and it won't be able to take any significant action without court approval, which requires filing a formal petition with the court and giving all parties involved a chance to respond.

Even if its operations do not suffer, the company's assets will surely be reduced by its own legal fees and the required court and trustee costs. Good bankruptcy lawyers charge from $200 to $400 or more per hour, depending on the location, so those costs are not trivial. The creditors will also be incurring legal costs. Indeed, the sound of all of those meters ticking at $200 or so an hour in a slow-moving hearing can be deafening.

Note that creditors also lose the time value of their money. A creditor with a $100,000 claim and a 10% opportunity cost who ends up getting $50,000 after 2 years would have been better off settling for $41,500 initially. When the creditor's legal fees, executive time, and general aggravation are taken into account, it might make sense to settle for $20,000 or $25,000.

Both the troubled company and its creditors know the drawbacks of formal bankruptcy, or their lawyers will inform them. Armed with a knowledge of how bankruptcy works, management may be in a strong position to persuade creditors to accept a workout that on the surface appears to be unfair and unreasonable. Or, if a Chapter 11 case has already begun, creditors may at some point agree to settle just to stop the bleeding.

One final point should be made before closing this section. In most reorganization plans, creditors with claims of less than $1,000 are paid off in full. Paying off these "nuisance claims" does not cost much money, and it saves time and gets votes to support the plan.[14]

SELF-TEST

Define the following terms: (1) common pool problem, (2) holdout problem, (3) automatic stay, (4) cramdown, (5) fraudulent conveyance, (6) absolute priority doctrine, (7) relative priority doctrine, (8) fairness, (9) feasibility, (10) debtor-in-possession financing, and (11) prepackaged bankruptcy.

What are the advantages of a formal reorganization under Chapter 11?

What are some recent trends regarding absolute versus relative priority doctrines?

How do courts assess the fairness and feasibility of reorganization plans?

Why have prepackaged bankruptcies become so popular in recent years?

24.6   Liquidation in Bankruptcy

If a company is "too far gone" to be reorganized, then it must be liquidated. Liquidation should occur when the business is worth more dead than alive, or when the possibility of restoring it to financial health is remote and the creditors are exposed to a high risk of greater loss if operations are continued. Earlier we discussed assignment, which is an informal liquidation procedure. Now we

---

[14]For more information on bankruptcy costs, see Daryl M. Guffey and William T. Moore, "Direct Bankruptcy Costs: Evidence from the Trucking Industry," *Financial Review*, May 1991, pp. 223–235.

consider **liquidation in bankruptcy,** which is carried out under the jurisdiction of a federal bankruptcy court.

Chapter 7 of the Federal Bankruptcy Reform Act deals with liquidation. It (1) provides safeguards against fraud by the debtor, (2) provides for an equitable distribution of the debtor's assets among the creditors, and (3) allows insolvent debtors to discharge all their obligations and thus be able to start new businesses unhampered by the burdens of prior debt. However, formal liquidation is time-consuming and costly, and it extinguishes the business.

The distribution of assets in a liquidation under Chapter 7 is governed by the following priority of claims:

1. *Past-due property taxes.*
2. *Secured creditors, who are entitled to the proceeds of the sale of specific property pledged for a lien or a mortgage.* If the proceeds from the sale of the pledged property do not fully satisfy a secured creditor's claim, the remaining balance is treated as a general creditor claim (see Item 10 below).[15]
3. *Legal fees and other expenses to administer and operate the bankrupt firm.* These costs include legal fees incurred in trying to reorganize.
4. *Expenses incurred after an involuntary case has begun but before a trustee is appointed.*
5. *Wages due workers if earned within 3 months prior to the filing of the petition in bankruptcy.* The amount of wages is limited to $2,000 per employee.
6. *Claims for unpaid contributions to employee pension plans that should have been paid within 6 months prior to filing.* These claims, plus wages in Item 5, may not exceed the $2,000-per-wage-earner limit.
7. *Unsecured claims for customer deposits.* These claims are limited to a maximum of $900 per individual.
8. *Taxes due to federal, state, county, and other government agencies.*
9. *Unfunded pension plan liabilities.* These liabilities have a claim above that of the general creditors for an amount up to 30% of the common and preferred equity, and any remaining unfunded pension claims rank with the general creditors.[16]
10. *General, or unsecured, creditors.* Holders of trade credit, unsecured loans, the unsatisfied portion of secured loans, and debenture bonds are classified as general creditors. Holders of subordinated debt also fall into this category, but they must turn over required amounts to the senior debt.

---

[15]When a firm or individual who goes bankrupt has a bank loan, the bank will attach any deposit balances. The loan agreement may stipulate that the bank has a first-priority claim on any deposits. If this is the case, the deposits are used to offset all or part of the bank loan; this is called, in legal terms, "the right of offset." In this case, the bank will not have to share the deposits with other creditors. Loan contracts often designate compensating balances as security against a loan. Even if the bank has no explicit claim against deposits, the bank will attach the deposits and hold them for the general body of creditors, including the bank itself. Without an explicit statement in the loan agreement, the bank does not receive preferential treatment with regard to attached deposits.

[16]Pension plan liabilities have a significant bearing on bankruptcy settlements. As we discuss in **Web Chapter 29,** pension plans may be funded or unfunded. Under a funded plan, the firm makes cash payments to an insurance company or to a trustee (generally a bank), which then uses these funds (and interest earned on them) to pay retirees' pensions. Under an unfunded plan, the firm is obligated to make payments to retirees, but it does not provide cash in advance. Many plans are actually partially funded—some money has been paid in advance, but not enough to provide full pension benefits to all employees.

If a firm goes bankrupt, the funded part of the pension plan remains intact and is available for retirees. Prior to 1974, employees had no explicit claims for unfunded pension liabilities, but under the Employees' Retirement Income Security Act of 1974 (ERISA), an amount up to 30% of the equity (common and preferred) is earmarked for employees' pension plans and has a priority over the general creditors, with any remaining pension claims having status equal to that of the general creditors. This means, in effect, that the funded portion of a bankrupt firm's pension plan is completely secured, but that the unfunded portion ranks somewhat above the general creditors. Obviously, unfunded pension fund liabilities should be of great concern to a firm's unsecured creditors.

FM

e-resource

Table 24-5

Whitman Inc.: Balance Sheet at Liquidation (Millions of Dollars)

Current assets	$80.0	Accounts payable	$20.0
Net fixed assets	10.0	Notes payable (to banks)	10.0
		Accrued wages (1,400 @ $500)	0.7
		Federal taxes	1.0
		State and local taxes	0.3
		Current liabilities	$32.0
		First mortgage	6.0
		Second mortgage	1.0
		Subordinated debentures[a]	8.0
		Total long-term debt	$15.0
		Preferred stock	2.0
		Common stock	26.0
		Paid-in capital	4.0
		Retained earnings	11.0
		Total equity	$43.0
Total assets	$90.0	Total liabilities and equity	$90.0

[a]The debentures are subordinated to the notes payable.

11. *Preferred stockholders.* These stockholders can receive an amount up to the par value of their stock.
12. *Common stockholders.* These stockholders receive any remaining funds.[17]

To illustrate how this priority system works, consider the balance sheet of Whitman Inc., shown in Table 24-5. Assets have a book value of $90 million. The claims are shown on the right-hand side of the balance sheet. Note that the debentures are subordinated to the notes payable to banks. Whitman filed for bankruptcy under Chapter 11, but since no fair and feasible reorganization could be arranged, the trustee is liquidating the firm under Chapter 7.

The assets as reported in the balance sheet are greatly overstated; they are, in fact, worth less than half the $90 million at which they are carried. The following amounts are realized on liquidation:

From sale of current assets	$28,000,000
From sale of fixed assets	5,000,000
Total receipts	$33,000,000

The distribution of proceeds from the liquidation is shown in Table 24-6. The first-mortgage holders receive the $5 million in net proceeds from the sale of fixed property, leaving $28 million available to the remaining creditors, including a $1 million unsatisfied claim of the first-mortgage holders. Next are the fees and expenses of administering the bankruptcy, which are typically about 20% of gross proceeds (including the bankrupt firm's own legal fees); in this example, they are

---

[17]Note that if different classes of common stock have been issued, differential priorities may exist in stockholder claims.

Table 24-6

Whitman Inc.: Distribution of Liquidation Proceeds (Millions of Dollars)

Distribution to Priority Claimants

Proceeds from the sale of assets	$33.0
Less:	
1. First mortgage (paid from the sale of fixed assets)	5.0
2. Fees and expenses of bankruptcy	6.0
3. Wages due to workers within 3 months of bankruptcy	0.7
4. Taxes due to federal, state, and local governments	1.3
Funds available for distribution to general creditors	$20.0

Distribution to General Creditors

General Creditors' Claims (1)	Amount of Claim[a] (2)	Pro Rata Distribution[b] (3)	Distribution after Subordination Adjustment[c] (4)	Percentage of Original Claim Received[d] (5)
Unsatisfied portion of first mortgage	$ 1.0	$ 0.5	$ 0.5	92%
Second mortgage	1.0	0.5	0.5	50
Notes payable (to banks)	10.0	5.0	9.0	90
Accounts payable	20.0	10.0	10.0	50
Subordinated debentures	8.0	4.0	0.0	0
Total	$40.0	$20.0	$20.0	

[a]Column 2 is the claim of each class of general creditor. Total claims equal $40.0 million.
[b]From the top section of the table, we see that $20 million is available for distribution to general creditors. Since there are $40 million of general creditor claims, the pro rata distribution will be $20/$40 = 0.50, or 50 cents on the dollar.
[c]The debentures are subordinate to the notes payable, so up to $5 million could be reallocated from debentures to notes payable. However, only $4 million is available to the debentures, so this entire amount is reallocated.
[d]Column 5 shows the results of dividing the Column 4 final allocation by the original claim shown in Column 2, except for the first mortgage, where the $5 million received from the sale of fixed assets is included in the calculation.

assumed to be $6 million. Next in priority are wages due workers, which total $700,000, and taxes due, which amount to $1.3 million. Thus far, the total amount of claims paid from the $33 million received from the asset sale is $13 million, leaving $20 million for the general creditors. In this example, we assume that there are no claims for unpaid benefit plans or unfunded pension liabilities.

The claims of the general creditors total $40 million. Since $20 million is available, claimants will initially be allocated 50% of their claims, as shown in Column 3. However, the subordination adjustment requires that the subordinated debentures turn over to the notes payable all amounts received until the notes are satisfied. In this situation, the claim of the notes payable is $10 million, but only $5 million is available; the deficiency is therefore $5 million. After transfer of $4 million from the subordinated debentures, there remains a deficiency of $1 million on the notes; this amount will remain unsatisfied.

Note that 90% of the bank claim is satisfied, whereas a maximum of 50% of other unsecured claims will be satisfied. These figures illustrate the usefulness of the subordination provision to the security to which the subordination is made.

Because no other funds remain, the claims of the holders of preferred and common stocks, as well as the subordinated debentures, are completely wiped out. Studies of the proceeds in bankruptcy liquidations reveal that unsecured creditors receive, on the average, about 15 cents on the dollar, while common stockholders generally receive nothing.

SELF-TEST

Describe briefly the priority of claims in a formal liquidation.

What is the impact of subordination on the final allocation of proceeds from liquidation?

In general, how much do unsecured creditors receive from a liquidation? How much do stockholders receive?

24.7 Other Motivations for Bankruptcy

Normally, bankruptcy proceedings do not commence until a company has become so financially weak that it cannot meet its current obligations. However, bankruptcy law also permits a company to file for bankruptcy if its financial forecasts indicate that a continuation of current conditions would lead to insolvency. This provision was used by Continental Airlines in 1983 to break its union contract and hence lower its labor costs. Continental demonstrated to a bankruptcy court that operations under the then-current union contract would lead to insolvency in a matter of months. The company then filed a reorganization plan that included major changes in all its contracts, including its union contract. The court sided with Continental and allowed the company to abrogate its contract. Continental then reorganized as a nonunion carrier, and that reorganization turned the company from a money loser into a money maker.[18] Congress changed the law after the Continental affair to make it more difficult for companies to use bankruptcy to break union contracts, but this case did set the precedent for using bankruptcy to help head off financial problems as well as to help solve existing ones.

Bankruptcy law has also been used to hasten settlements in major product liability suits. The Manville asbestos and A. H. Robins Dalkon Shield cases are examples. In both situations, the companies were being bombarded by thousands of lawsuits, and the very existence of such huge contingent liabilities made normal operations impossible. Further, in both cases it was relatively easy to prove (1) that if the plaintiffs won, the companies would be unable to pay the full amount of the claims, (2) that a larger amount of funds would be available to the claimants if the companies continued to operate rather than liquidate, (3) that continued operations were possible only if the suits were brought to a conclusion, and (4) that a timely resolution of all the suits was impossible because of their vast number and variety. The bankruptcy statutes were used to consolidate all the suits and to reach settlements under which the plaintiffs obtained more money than they otherwise would have received, and the companies were able to stay in business. The stockholders did poorly under these plans, because most of the companies' future cash flows were assigned to the plaintiffs, but even so, the stockholders probably fared better than they would have if the suits had been concluded through the jury system.

SELF-TEST

What are some situations other than immediate financial distress that lead firms to file for bankruptcy?

---

[18]Continental's fortunes declined again in 1990 when it was unable to successfully integrate several acquisitions, including Eastern, and the company filed for bankruptcy a second time. It emerged successfully.

24.8 Some Criticisms of Bankruptcy Laws

Although bankruptcy laws, for the most part, exist to protect creditors, many critics claim that current laws are not doing what they were intended to do. Before 1978, most bankruptcies ended quickly in liquidation. Then Congress rewrote the laws, giving companies more opportunity to stay alive, on the grounds that this was best for managers, employees, creditors, and stockholders. Before the reform, 90% of Chapter 11 filers were liquidated, but now that percentage is less than 80%, and the average time between filing and liquidation has almost doubled. Indeed, large public corporations with the ability to hire high-priced legal help can avoid, or at least delay, liquidation, often at the expense of creditors and shareholders.

Critics believe that bankruptcy is great for businesses these days—especially for consultants, lawyers, and investment bankers, who reap hefty fees during bankruptcy proceedings, and for managers, who continue to collect their salaries and bonuses as long as the business is kept alive. The problem, according to critics, is that bankruptcy courts allow cases to drag on too long, depleting assets that could be sold to pay off creditors and shareholders. Too often, quick resolution is impossible because bankruptcy judges are required to deal with issues such as labor disputes, pension plan funding, and environmental liability—social questions that could be solved by legislative action rather than by bankruptcy courts.

For example, LTV Corporation was in bankruptcy from 1986 to 1993, mainly because of pension disputes between the company, its workers, retirees, and the federal government. During this time, the Dallas-based conglomerate spent $162 million in legal and consulting fees, but, under the final reorganization plan, creditors got only 4 to 53 cents on the dollar, and stockholders got nothing.

Critics contend that bankruptcy judges ought to realize that some sick companies should be allowed to die—and die quickly. Maintaining companies on life support does not serve the interests of the parties the bankruptcy laws were meant to protect. The 2005 changes to the bankruptcy code addressed this issue by limiting to 18 months the time management has to file a reorganization plan. Prior to the change, judges could extend the time management has to reorganize almost indefinitely. Now, after a maximum of 18 months, creditors may propose a plan if an acceptable plan hasn't been filed by management.

Other critics think the entire bankruptcy system of judicial protection and supervision needs to be scrapped. Some even have proposed a kind of auction procedure, where shareholders and creditors would have the opportunity to gain control of a bankrupt company by raising the cash needed to pay the bills. The rationale here is that the market is a better judge than a bankruptcy court as to whether a company is worth more dead or alive.

Finally, note that companies operating under the protection of Chapter 11 can damage and perhaps even bankrupt their otherwise healthy competitors. To illustrate, Eastern Airlines' cash costs were low during its bankruptcy because it did not have to service its debt, and it was also generating cash by selling off assets. Eastern used its cash to advertise heavily and to cut fares, both of which siphoned off traffic from other airlines. Obviously, this hurt the other airlines and indeed led to other airline bankruptcies. Had Eastern been put down in a timely fashion, the airline industry would be a lot healthier today.

SELF-TEST

According to critics, what are some problems with the bankruptcy system?

24.9 Other Topics in Bankruptcy

Some additional insights into the reorganization and liquidation process can be gained by reviewing case histories of bankruptcies. Therefore, in *Web Extension 24A* at the textbook's Web site, we discuss the Eastern Airlines and Revco bankruptcies. Also, financial analysts are constantly seeking ways to assess a firm's likelihood of going bankrupt. We discuss one method, multiple discriminant analysis (MDA), in *Web Extension 24B*.

FM

e-resource

Summary

This chapter discussed the main issues involved in bankruptcy and financial distress in general. The key concepts are listed below:

- The proportion of businesses that fail fluctuates with the economy, but the average liability per failure has tended to increase over time due to inflation and to an increase in the number of billion-dollar bankruptcies in recent years.
- The fundamental issue that must be addressed when a company encounters financial distress is whether it is "worth more dead than alive;" that is, would the business be more valuable if it continued in operation or if it were liquidated and sold off in pieces?
- In the case of a fundamentally sound company whose financial difficulties appear to be temporary, creditors will frequently work directly with the company, helping it to recover and reestablish itself on a sound financial basis. Such voluntary reorganization plans are called **workouts.**
- Reorganization plans usually require some type of **restructuring** of the firm's debts, involving either an **extension,** which postpones the date of required payment of past-due obligations, or a **composition,** by which the creditors voluntarily reduce their claims on the debtor or the interest rate on their claims.
- When it is obvious that a firm is worth more dead than alive, informal procedures can sometimes be used to **liquidate** the firm. **Assignment** is an informal procedure for liquidating a firm, and it usually yields creditors a larger amount than they would receive in a formal bankruptcy liquidation. However, assignments are feasible only if the firm is small and its affairs are not too complex.
- Current **bankruptcy law** consists of nine chapters, designated by Arabic numbers. For businesses, the most important chapters are **Chapter 7,** which details the procedures to be followed when liquidating a firm, and **Chapter 11,** which contains procedures for formal reorganizations.
- Since the first bankruptcy laws, most formal reorganization plans have been guided by the **absolute priority doctrine.** This doctrine holds that creditors should be compensated for their claims in a rigid hierarchical order, and that senior claims must be paid in full before junior claims can receive even a dime.
- Another position, the **relative priority doctrine,** holds that more flexibility should be allowed in a reorganization and that a balanced consideration should be given to all claimants. In recent years, there has been a shift away

from absolute priority toward relative priority. The primary effect of this shift has been to delay liquidations so as to give managements more time to rehabilitate companies in an effort to provide value to junior claimants.

- The primary role of the bankruptcy court in a reorganization is to determine the **fairness** and the **feasibility** of proposed plans of reorganization.
- Even if some creditors or stockholders dissent and do not accept a reorganization plan, the plan may still be approved by the court if the plan is deemed to be "fair and equitable" to all parties. This procedure, in which the court mandates a reorganization plan in spite of dissent, is called a **cramdown.**
- In the last few years, a new type of reorganization that combines the advantages of both the informal workout and formal Chapter 11 reorganization has become popular. This new hybrid is called a **prepackaged bankruptcy,** or **pre-pack.**
- The distribution of assets in a **liquidation** under Chapter 7 of the Bankruptcy Act is governed by a specific priority of claims.

Questions

(24-1)   Define each of the following terms:
   a.   Informal restructuring; reorganization in bankruptcy
   b.   Assignment; liquidation in bankruptcy; fairness; feasibility
   c.   Absolute priority doctrine; relative priority doctrine
   d.   Bankruptcy Reform Act of 1978; Chapter 11; Chapter 7
   e.   Priority of claims in liquidation
   f.   Extension; composition; workout; cramdown; prepackaged bankruptcy; holdout

(24-2)   Why do creditors usually accept a plan for financial rehabilitation rather than demand liquidation of the business?

(24-3)   Would it be a sound rule to liquidate whenever the liquidation value is above the value of the corporation as a going concern? Discuss.

(24-4)   Why do liquidations usually result in losses for the creditors or the owners, or both? Would partial liquidation or liquidation over a period limit their losses? Explain.

(24-5)   Are liquidations likely to be more common for public utility, railroad, or industrial corporations? Why?

Self-Test Problem   Solution Appears in Appendix A

(ST-1)
Liquidation
At the time it defaulted on its interest payments and filed for bankruptcy, Medford Fabricators Inc. had the following balance sheet (in millions of dollars). The court, after trying unsuccessfully to reorganize the firm, decided that the only recourse was liquidation under Chapter 7. Sale of the fixed assets, which were pledged as

collateral to the mortgage bondholders, brought in $750 million, while the current assets were sold for another $400 million. Thus, the total proceeds from the liquidation sale were $1,150 million. Trustee's costs amounted to $1 million; no single worker was due more than $2,000 in wages; and there were no unfunded pension plan liabilities.

Current assets	$ 800	Accounts payable	$ 100
		Accrued taxes	90
		Accrued wages	60
		Notes payable	300
		Total current liabilities	$ 550
Net fixed assets	1,100	First-mortgage bonds[a]	700
		Second-mortgage bonds[a]	400
		Debentures	500
		Subordinated debentures[b]	200
		Common stock	100
		Retained earnings	(550)
Total assets	$1,900	Total claims	$1,900

Notes:

[a]All fixed assets are pledged as collateral to the mortgage bonds.

[b]Subordinated to notes payable.

a. How much of the proceeds from the sale of assets remain to be distributed to general creditors after distribution to priority claimants?
b. After distribution to general creditors and subordination adjustments are made, how much of the proceeds are received by the second mortgage holders? By holders of the notes payable? By the subordinated debentures? By the common stockholders?

Problems Answers Appear in Appendix B

Easy Problem 1

(24-1)   Southwestern Wear Inc. has the following balance sheet:

Liquidation

Current assets	$1,875,000	Accounts payable	$ 375,000
Fixed assets	1,875,000	Notes payable	750,000
		Subordinated debentures	750,000
		Total debt	$1,875,000
		Common equity	1,875,000
Total assets	$3,750,000	Total liabilities and equity	$3,750,000

The trustee's costs total $281,250, and the firm has no accrued taxes or wages. The debentures are subordinated only to the notes payable. If the firm goes bankrupt and liquidates, how much will each class of investors receive if a total of $2.5 million is received from sale of the assets?

Intermediate
Problem 2

(24-2)
Reorganization

The Verbrugge Publishing Company's 2007 balance sheet and income statement
are as follows (in millions of dollars).

Balance Sheet

Current assets	$168	Current liabilities	$ 42
Net fixed assets	153	Advance payments	78
Goodwill	15	Reserves	6
		$6 preferred stock, $112.50 par value (1,200,000 shares)	135
		$10.50 preferred stock, no par, callable at $150 (60,000 shares)	9
		Common stock, $1.50 par value (6,000,000 shares)	9
		Retained earnings	57
Total assets	$336	Total claims	$336

Income Statement

Net sales	$540.0
Operating expense	516.0
Net operating income	$ 24.0
Other income	3.0
EBT	$ 27.0
Taxes (50%)	13.5
Net income	$ 13.5
Dividends on $6 preferred	7.2
Dividends on $10.50 preferred	0.6
Income available to common stockholders	$ 5.7

Verbrugge and its creditors have agreed upon a voluntary reorganization plan. In
this plan, each share of the $6 preferred will be exchanged for one share of $2.40
preferred with a par value of $37.50 plus one 8% subordinated income debenture
with a par value of $75. The $10.50 preferred issue will be retired with cash.
a. Construct the pro forma balance sheet assuming that reorganization takes
    place. Show the new preferred stock at its par value.
b. Construct the pro forma income statement. What is the income available to
    common shareholders in the proposed recapitalization?
c. *Required earnings* is defined as the amount that is just enough to meet fixed
    charges (debenture interest and/or preferred dividends). What are the
    required pre-tax earnings before and after the recapitalization?
d. How is the debt ratio affected by the reorganization? If you were a holder of
    Verbrugge's common stock, would you vote in favor of the reorganization?

Challenging
Problems 3–4

(24-3)
Liquidation

At the time it defaulted on its interest payments and filed for bankruptcy, the
McDaniel Mining Company had the following balance sheet (in thousands of

dollars). The court, after trying unsuccessfully to reorganize the firm, decided that the only recourse was liquidation under Chapter 7. Sale of the fixed assets, which were pledged as collateral to the mortgage bondholders, brought in $400,000, while the current assets were sold for another $200,000. Thus, the total proceeds from the liquidation sale were $600,000. Trustee's costs amounted to $50,000; no single worker was due more than $2,000 in wages; and there were no unfunded pension plan liabilities.

Current assets	$ 400	Accounts payable	$ 50
Net fixed assets	600	Accrued taxes	40
		Accrued wages	30
		Notes payable	180
		Total current liabilities	$ 300
		First-mortgage bonds[a]	300
		Second-mortgage bonds[a]	200
		Debentures	200
		Subordinated debentures[b]	100
		Common stock	50
		Retained earnings	(150)
Total assets	$1,000	Total claims	$1,000

Notes:

[a]All fixed assets are pledged as collateral to the mortgage bonds.

[b]Subordinated to notes payable only.

a. How much will McDaniel's shareholders receive from the liquidation?
b. How much will the mortgage bondholders receive?
c. Who are the other priority claimants in addition to the mortgage bondholders? How much will they receive from the liquidation?
d. Who are the remaining general creditors? How much will each receive from the distribution before subordination adjustment? What is the effect of adjusting for subordination?

(24-4)
Liquidation

The following balance sheet represents Boles Electronics Corporation's position at the time it filed for bankruptcy (in thousands of dollars):

Cash	$ 10	Accounts payable	$ 1,600
Receivables	100	Notes payable	500
Inventories	890	Wages payable	150
		Taxes payable	50
Total current assets	$ 1,000	Total current liabilities	$ 2,300
Net plant	4,000	Mortgage bonds	2,000
Net equipment	5,000	Subordinated debentures	2,500
		Preferred stock	1,500
		Common stock	1,700
Total assets	$10,000	Total claims	$10,000

The mortgage bonds are secured by the plant, but not by the equipment. The subordinated debentures are subordinated to notes payable. The firm was unable to reorganize under Chapter 11; therefore, it was liquidated under Chapter 7. The trustee, whose legal and administrative fees amounted to $200,000, sold off the assets and received the following proceeds (in thousands of dollars):

Asset	Proceeds
Plant	$1,600
Equipment	1,300
Receivables	50
Inventories	240
Total	$3,190

In addition, the firm had $10,000 in cash available for distribution. No single wage earner had over $2,000 in claims, and there were no unfunded pension plan liabilities.

a.   What is the total amount available for distribution to all claimants? What is the total of creditor and trustee claims? Will the preferred and common stockholders receive any distributions?

b.   Determine the dollar distribution to each creditor and to the trustee. What percentage of each claim is satisfied?

Spreadsheet Problem

(24-5)
Liquidation

e-resource

Start with the partial model in the file *FM12 Ch 24 P05 Build a Model.xls* at the textbook's Web site. Use the information and data from Problem 24-4, except assume that the fixed assets can be sold for $450,000 and that the current assets can be sold for $250,000. Determine the amounts available for distribution to each claimant.

Cyberproblem

e-resource

Please go to the textbook's Web site to access any Cyberproblems.

Mini Case

Kimberly MacKenzie, president of Kim's Clothes Inc., a medium-sized manufacturer of women's casual clothing, is worried. Her firm has been selling clothes to Russ Brothers Department Store for more than 10 years, and she has never experienced any problems in collecting payment for the merchandise sold. Currently, Russ Brothers owes Kim's Clothes $65,000 for spring sportswear that was delivered to the store just 2 weeks ago. Kim's concern was brought about by an article that appeared in yesterday's *Wall Street Journal* that indicated that Russ Brothers was having serious financial problems. Further, the article stated that Russ Brothers' management was considering filing for reorganization, or even liquidation, with a federal bankruptcy court.

Kim's immediate concern was whether or not her firm would collect its receivables if Russ Brothers went bankrupt. In pondering the situation, Kim also realized that she knew nothing about the process that firms go through when they encounter severe financial distress. To learn more about bankruptcy, reorganization, and liquidation, Kim asked Ron Mitchell, the firm's chief financial officer, to prepare a briefing on the subject for the entire board of directors. In turn, Ron asked you, a newly hired financial analyst, to do the groundwork for the briefing by answering the following questions.

a.   (1)   What are the major causes of business failure?
     (2)   Do business failures occur evenly over time?
     (3)   Which size of firm, large or small, is more prone to business failure? Why?

b.   What key issues must managers face in the financial distress process?

c.   What informal remedies are available to firms in financial distress? In answering this question, define the following terms:
     (1)   Workout
     (2)   Restructuring
     (3)   Extension
     (4)   Composition
     (5)   Assignment
     (6)   Assignee (trustee)

d.   Briefly describe U.S. bankruptcy law, including the following terms:
     (1)   Chapter 11
     (2)   Chapter 7
     (3)   Trustee
     (4)   Voluntary bankruptcy
     (5)   Involuntary bankruptcy

e.   What are the major differences between an informal reorganization and reorganization in bankruptcy? In answering this question, be sure to discuss the following items:
     (1)   Common pool problem
     (2)   Holdout problem
     (3)   Automatic stay
     (4)   Cramdown
     (5)   Fraudulent conveyance

f.   What is a prepackaged bankruptcy? Why have prepackaged bankruptcies become more popular in recent years?

g.   Briefly describe the priority of claims in a Chapter 7 liquidation.

h.   Assume that Russ Brothers did indeed fail, and that it had the following balance sheet when it was liquidated (in millions of dollars):

Current assets	$40.0	Accounts payable	$10.0
Net fixed assets	5.0	Notes payable (to banks)	5.0
		Accrued wages	0.3
		Federal taxes	0.5
		State and local taxes	0.2
		Current liabilities	$16.0
		First-mortgage bonds	3.0
		Second-mortgage bonds	0.5
		Subordinated debentures[a]	4.0
		Total long-term debt	$ 7.5
		Preferred stock	1.0
		Common stock	13.0
		Paid-in capital	2.0
		Retained earnings	5.5
		Total equity	$21.5
Total assets	$45.0	Total claims	$45.0

[a]The debentures are subordinated to the notes payable.

The liquidation sale resulted in the following proceeds:

From sale of current assets	$14,000,000
From sale of fixed assets	2,500,000
Total receipts	$16,500,000

For simplicity, assume that there were no trustee's fees or any other claims against the liquidation proceeds. Also, assume that the mortgage bonds are secured by the entire amount of fixed assets. What would each claimant receive from the liquidation distribution?

Selected Additional Cases

The following cases from Textchoice, Cengage Learning's online library, cover many of the concepts discussed in this chapter and are available at http://www.textchoice2.com.

Klein-Brigham Series:
Case 39, "Mark X Company (B)," which examines the allocation of proceeds under bankruptcy.

chapter 25

Mergers, LBOs, Divestitures, and Holding Companies

On January 28, 2005, Procter & Gamble (P&G) bid almost $55 billion to acquire Gillette in a friendly merger. When the deal was completed on October 1, 2005, it created the world's largest consumer goods company, making the merger the biggest of the year.

Combining Gillette and P&G has already produced several winners. When the deal was announced, Gillette's shareholders saw the value of their stock rise by more than 17%. One particular winner was Gillette's largest shareholder, Warren Buffett, who owned roughly 96 million shares. Other winners included Gillette's senior executives, who saw the value of their stock and stock options increase, and the investment banks that helped put the deal together.

Estimates suggest that Goldman Sachs, Merrill Lynch, and UBS each received $30 million from the transaction.

While many applauded the deal, others believe that P&G will have to work hard to justify the price it paid for Gillette. Moreover, as we point out in this chapter, the track record for acquiring firms in large deals has not always been good. As we write this in September 2006, P&G's stock is up 5.67% since the completion of the merger versus 6.33% for the S&P 500. Eleven months is too soon to evaluate the merger, so it remains to be seen whether the deal truly makes sense for P&G's shareholders. Nonetheless, keep the P&G-Gillette merger in mind as you read this chapter.

e-resource

The textbook's Web site contains an *Excel* file that will guide you through the chapter's calculations. The file for this chapter is ***FM12 Ch 25 Tool Kit.xls,*** and we encourage you to open the file and follow along as you read the chapter.

Most corporate growth occurs by *internal expansion*, which takes place when a firm's existing divisions grow through normal capital budgeting activities. However, the most dramatic examples of growth result from mergers, the first topic covered in this chapter. *Leveraged buyouts*, or *LBOs*, occur when a firm's stock is acquired by a small group of investors rather than by another operating company. Conditions change over time, causing firms to sell off, or divest, major divisions to other firms that can better utilize the divested assets. Divestitures are also discussed in the chapter. Finally, we discuss the *holding company* form of organization, wherein one corporation owns the stock of one or more other companies.

25.1 Rationale for Mergers

Many reasons have been proposed by financial managers and theorists to account for the high level of U.S. merger activity. The primary motives behind corporate **mergers** are presented in this section.[1]

Synergy

The primary motivation for most mergers is to increase the value of the combined enterprise. If Companies A and B merge to form Company C, and if C's value exceeds that of A and B taken separately, then **synergy** is said to exist, and such a merger should be beneficial to both A's and B's stockholders.[2] Synergistic effects can arise from five sources: (1) *operating economies*, which result from economies of scale in management, marketing, production, or distribution; (2) *financial economies*, including lower transaction costs and better coverage by security analysts; (3) *tax effects*, where the combined enterprise pays less in taxes than the separate firms would pay; (4) *differential efficiency*, which implies that the management of one firm is more efficient and that the weaker firm's assets will be more productive after the merger; and (5) *increased market power* due to reduced competition. Operating and financial economies are socially desirable, as are mergers that increase managerial efficiency, but mergers that reduce competition are socially undesirable and illegal.[3]

The 2001 merger of Wachovia and First Union, which created the nation's fourth largest bank at that time, illustrates the quest for synergies. The banks' operations overlapped in many parts of the Southeast, so closing neighboring branches could cut costs, and certain "backroom" operations could be consolidated to further reduce costs. Obviously, the best people and operations would be retained and those that performed subpar would be let go. Another synergistic

---

[1]As we use the term, *merger* means any combination that forms one economic unit from two or more previous ones. For legal purposes, there are distinctions among the various ways these combinations can occur, but our focus is on the fundamental economic and financial aspects of mergers.

[2]If synergy exists, then the whole is greater than the sum of the parts. Synergy is also called the "2 plus 2 equals 5 effect." The distribution of the synergistic gain between A's and B's stockholders is determined by negotiation. This point is discussed later in the chapter.

[3]In the 1880s and 1890s, many mergers occurred in the United States, and some of them were obviously directed toward gaining market power rather than increasing efficiency. As a result, Congress passed a series of acts designed to ensure that mergers are not used to reduce competition. The principal acts include the Sherman Act (1890), the Clayton Act (1914), and the Celler Act (1950). These acts make it illegal for firms to combine if the combination tends to lessen competition. The acts are enforced by the antitrust division of the Justice Department and by the Federal Trade Commission.

merger was the 1997 consolidation of Morgan Stanley with Dean Witter. Morgan Stanley was an elite investment bank that specialized in underwriting securities for large corporations, while Dean Witter was a nationwide brokerage house with thousands of sales representatives and 40 million retail customers. Dean Witter had been affiliated with Sears, Roebuck and had sold securities to Sears's customers, whereas Morgan Stanley's relatively few retail customers tended to be millionaires. So, the merger was said to be "uniting Wall Street with Main Street," and it meant that Dean Witter's brokers would have access to IPOs and other securities underwritten by Morgan Stanley and Morgan Stanley would have another channel for new offerings.[4]

Expected synergies are not always realized. For example, when AOL acquired Time Warner, it believed that Time Warner's extensive content library could be sold to AOL's Internet subscribers and that AOL subscribers could be shifted over to Time Warner's cable system. When the merger was announced, the new management estimated that such synergies would increase operating income by $1 billion per year. However, things didn't work out as expected, and the combined entity's market value has fallen sharply since the merger. Note, though, that the real losers were Time Warner's stockholders, while AOL's stockholders can count their blessings. The merger was announced in 2000, at the height of the Internet bubble, when AOL's stock was selling at an all-time record. At the same time, Time Warner was regarded as a stodgy, old-economy company. Therefore, AOL's stock had a much higher valuation, and its stockholders received the majority of the stock in the consolidated company. Since then, Internet stocks have crashed, but old-economy stocks have held up rather well. Without the merger, Time Warner stockholders would be much wealthier than they are, while AOL's would be much poorer.

Tax Considerations

Tax considerations have stimulated a number of mergers. For example, a profitable firm in the highest tax bracket could acquire a firm with large accumulated tax losses. These losses could then be turned into immediate tax savings rather than carried forward and used in the future.[5]

Also, mergers can serve as a way of minimizing taxes when disposing of excess cash. For example, if a firm has a shortage of internal investment opportunities compared with its free cash flow, it could (1) pay an extra dividend, (2) invest in marketable securities, (3) repurchase its own stock, or (4) purchase another firm. If it pays an extra dividend, its stockholders would have to pay immediate taxes on the distribution. Marketable securities often provide a good temporary parking place for money, but they generally earn a rate of return less than that required by stockholders. A stock repurchase might result in a capital gain for the selling stockholders. However, using surplus cash to acquire another firm would avoid all these problems, and this has motivated a number of mergers. Still, as we discuss later, the tax savings are often less than the premium paid in the acquisition. Thus, mergers motivated only by tax considerations often reduce the acquiring shareholders' wealth.

---

[4]Interestingly, First Union was much larger than Wachovia, and it was the acquiring company. However, Wachovia had a better reputation in the banking industry, so after the merger, the consolidated company took the Wachovia name. In the Morgan Stanley/Dean Witter case, both companies' names were used initially, but after a few years the Dean Witter part was dropped, and the company is now Morgan Stanley.
[5]Mergers undertaken only to use accumulated tax losses would probably be challenged by the IRS. In recent years Congress has made it increasingly difficult for firms to pass along tax savings after mergers.

Purchase of Assets below Their Replacement Cost

Sometimes a firm will be touted as an acquisition candidate because the cost of replacing its assets is considerably higher than its market value. For example, in the early 1980s oil companies could acquire reserves cheaper by buying other oil companies than by doing exploratory drilling. Thus, ChevronTexaco acquired Gulf Oil to augment its reserves. Similarly, in the 1980s several steel company executives stated that it was cheaper to buy an existing steel company than to construct a new mill. For example, in 1984 LTV (at the time the fourth largest steel company but now bankrupt and owned by Mittal Steel Co.) acquired Republic Steel (the sixth largest) to create the second largest firm in the industry.

Diversification

Managers often cite diversification as a reason for mergers. They contend that diversification helps stabilize a firm's earnings and thus benefits its owners. Stabilization of earnings is certainly beneficial to employees, suppliers, and customers, but its value to stockholders is less certain. Why should Firm A acquire Firm B to stabilize earnings when stockholders can simply buy the stocks of both firms? Indeed, research suggests that in most cases diversification does not increase the firm's value. In fact, many studies find that diversified firms are worth significantly less than the sum of their individual parts.[6]

Of course, if you were the owner-manager of a closely held firm, it might be nearly impossible to sell part of your stock to diversify. Also, selling your stock would probably lead to a large capital gains tax. So, a diversification merger might be the best way to achieve personal diversification for a privately held firm.

Managers' Personal Incentives

Financial economists like to think that business decisions are based only on economic considerations, especially maximization of firms' values. However, many business decisions are based more on managers' personal motivations than on economic analyses. Business leaders like power, and more power is attached to running a larger corporation than a smaller one. Most likely, no executive would admit that his or her ego was the primary reason behind a merger, but egos do play a prominent role in many mergers.[7]

It has also been observed that executive salaries are highly correlated with company size—the bigger the company, the higher the salaries of its top officers. This too could obviously cause unnecessary acquisitions.

Personal considerations deter as well as motivate mergers. After most takeovers, some managers of the acquired companies lose their jobs, or at least their autonomy. Therefore, managers who own less than 51% of their firms' stock look to devices that will lessen the chances of a takeover, and a merger can serve as such a device. For example, in 2005 MCI's board of directors, over the objection of large shareholders, turned down repeated acquisition offers from Qwest, at the time the nation's fourth largest local phone company, in favor of substantially smaller

[6]See, for example, Philip Berger and Eli Ofek, "Diversification's Effect on Firm Value," *Journal of Financial Economics*, 1995, pp. 37–65; and Larry Lang and René Stulz, "Tobin's Q, Corporate Diversification, and Firm Performance," *Journal of Political Economy*, 1994, pp. 1248–1280.
[7]See Randall Morck, Andrei Shleifer, and Robert W. Vishny, "Do Managerial Objectives Drive Bad Acquisitions?" *Journal of Finance*, March 1990, pp. 31–48.

offers from Verizon, the nation's largest phone company. MCI's management viewed Verizon as a stronger, more stable partner than Qwest even though Qwest's bid was at times 20% higher than Verizon's bid. In response to management's refusal to accept the higher bid, the holders of some 28% of MCI's stock withheld their votes to re-elect the board of directors in protest. Nonetheless, management proceeded with merger negotiations with Verizon and the two companies merged in June of 2006. In such cases management always argues that synergy, not a desire to protect their own jobs, is the motivation for the choice. However, it is difficult to rationalize rejecting a 20% larger bid for undocumented synergies, and some observers suspect that this and many mergers were ultimately designed to benefit managers rather than shareholders.

Breakup Value

Some takeover specialists estimate a company's **breakup value,** which is the value of the individual parts of the firm if they were sold off separately. If this value is higher than the firm's current market value, then a takeover specialist could acquire the firm at or even above its current market value, sell it off in pieces, and earn a profit.

SELF-TEST

Define *synergy*. Is synergy a valid rationale for mergers? Describe several situations that might produce synergistic gains.

Suppose your firm could purchase another firm for only half of its replacement value. Would that be a sufficient justification for the acquisition?

Discuss the pros and cons of diversification as a rationale for mergers.

What is breakup value?

25.2 Types of Mergers

Economists classify mergers into four types: (1) horizontal, (2) vertical, (3) congeneric, and (4) conglomerate. A **horizontal merger** occurs when one firm combines with another in its same line of business—the 2005 Sprint-Nextel merger is an example. An example of a **vertical merger** would be a steel producer's acquisition of one of its own suppliers, such as an iron or coal mining firm, or an oil producer's acquisition of a petrochemical firm that uses oil as a raw material. *Congeneric* means "allied in nature or action"; hence a **congeneric merger** involves related enterprises but not producers of the same product (horizontal) or firms in a producer-supplier relationship (vertical). The AOL and Time Warner merger is an example. A **conglomerate merger** occurs when unrelated enterprises combine.

Operating economies (and also anticompetitive effects) are at least partially dependent on the type of merger involved. Vertical and horizontal mergers generally provide the greatest synergistic operating benefits, but they are also the ones most likely to be attacked by the Department of Justice as anticompetitive.[8] In any event, it is useful to think of these economic classifications when analyzing prospective mergers.

SELF-TEST

What are the four economic types of mergers?

---

[8]For interesting insights into antitrust regulations and mergers, see B. Espen Eckbo, "Mergers and the Value of Antitrust Deterrence," *Journal of Finance*, July 1992, pp. 1005–1029.

25.3 Level of Merger Activity

Five major "merger waves" have occurred in the United States. The first was in the late 1800s, when consolidations occurred in the oil, steel, tobacco, and other basic industries. The second was in the 1920s, when the stock market boom helped financial promoters consolidate firms in a number of industries, including utilities, communications, and autos. The third was in the 1960s, when conglomerate mergers were the rage. The fourth occurred in the 1980s, when LBO firms and others began using junk bonds to finance all manner of acquisitions. The fifth, which involves strategic alliances designed to enable firms to compete better in the global economy, is in progress today.

As can be seen from Table 25-1, some huge mergers have occurred in recent years.[9] In general, recent mergers have been significantly different from those of the 1980s and 1990s. Most earlier mergers were financial transactions in which buyers sought companies that were selling at less than their true values as a result of incompetent or sluggish management. If a target company could be managed better, if redundant assets could be sold, and if operating and administrative costs could be cut, profits and stock prices would rise. In contrast, most recent mergers have been strategic in nature—companies are merging to gain economies of scale or scope and thus be better able to compete in the world economy. Indeed, many recent mergers have involved companies in the financial, defense, media, computer, telecommunications, and health care industries, all of which are experiencing structural changes and intense competition.

Table 25-1

The Ten Largest Completed Mergers Worldwide
through December 31, 2005

Buyer	Target	Completion Date	Value (Billions, U.S. $)
Vodafone AirTouch	Mannesmann	April 12, 2000	$161
Pfizer	Warner-Lambert	June 19, 2000	116
America Online	Time Warner	January 11, 2001	106
Exxon	Mobil	November 30, 1999	81
Glaxo Wellcome	SmithKline Beecham	December 27, 2000	74
Royal Dutch Petroleum	Shell Transport and Trading	Shareholder approved as of September 2005	74
SBC Communications	Ameritech	October 8, 1999	72
VodafoneGroup	AirTouch	June 30, 1999	69
Sanofi-Syntelabo SA	Aventis SA	July 30, 2004	60
Bell Atlantic	GTE	May 30, 2000	60

Sources: "A Look at the Top 10 Global Mergers," *Associated Press Newswires*, January 11, 2001; various issues of *The Wall Street Journal*'s "Year-End Review of Markets and Finance World-Wide Deals."

---

[9] For detailed reviews of the 1980s merger wave, see Andrei Shleifer and Robert W. Vishny, "The Takeover Wave of the 1980s," *Journal of Applied Corporate Finance*, Fall 1991, pp. 49–56.

Recent deals also differ in the way they are financed and how the target firms' stockholders are compensated. In the 1980s, cash was the preferred method of payment, because large cash payments could convince even the most reluctant shareholder to approve the deal. Moreover, the cash was generally obtained by borrowing, leaving the consolidated company with a heavy debt burden, which often led to difficulties. In recent years, stock has replaced borrowed cash as the merger currency for two reasons: (1) Many of the 1980s mergers were financed with junk bonds that later went into default. These defaults, along with the demise of Drexel Burnham, the leading junk bond dealer, have made it difficult to arrange debt-financed mergers. (2) Most recent mergers have been strategic—as between AT&T and MediaOne Group and between AOL and Time Warner— where the companies' managers realized that they needed one another. Most of these mergers have been friendly, and stock swaps are easier to arrange in friendly mergers than in hostile ones. Also, both sets of managers have been concerned about the post-merger financial strength of the consolidated company, and the surviving company will obviously be stronger if the deal is financed with stock rather than debt.

Although most recent large mergers have generally been stock-for-stock, many of the smaller mergers have been for cash. Even here, though, things have been different. In the 1980s, companies typically borrowed to get the money to finance cash acquisitions. In recent years, corporate cash flows have been very high, so companies have been able to pay for their smaller acquisitions out of cash flow.

There has also been an increase in cross-border mergers. Many of these mergers have been motivated by large shifts in the value of the world's leading currencies. For example, in the early 1990s, the dollar was weak relative to the yen and the mark. The decline in the dollar made it easier for Japanese and German acquirers to buy U.S. corporations. For example, in 1998 Daimler-Benz acquired Chrysler.

SELF-TEST ————————————————————————————
What five major "merger waves" have occurred in the United States?
What are some reasons for the current wave?

25.4 Hostile versus Friendly Takeovers

In the vast majority of merger situations, one firm (generally the larger of the two) simply decides to buy another company, negotiates a price with the management of the target firm, and then acquires the target company. Occasionally, the acquired firm will initiate the action, but it is much more common for a firm to seek companies to acquire than to seek to be acquired.[10] Following convention, we call a company that seeks to acquire another firm the **acquiring company** and the one that it seeks to acquire the **target company.**

Once an acquiring company has identified a possible target, it must (1) establish a suitable price, or range of prices, and (2) decide on the terms of payment—will it offer cash, its own common stock, bonds, or some combination? Next, the acquiring firm's managers must decide how to approach the target company's managers. If the acquiring firm has reason to believe that the target's management will approve

———————————
[10]However, if a firm is in financial difficulty, if its managers are elderly and do not think that suitable replacements are on hand, or if it needs the support (often the capital) of a larger company, then it may seek to be acquired. Thus, when a number of Texas, Ohio, and Maryland financial institutions were in trouble in the 1980s, they lobbied to get their state legislatures to pass laws that would make it easier for them to be acquired. Out-of-state banks then moved in to help salvage the situation and minimize depositor losses.

the merger, then one CEO will contact the other, propose a merger, and then try to work out suitable terms. If an agreement is reached, the two management groups will issue statements to their stockholders indicating that they approve the merger, and the target firm's management will recommend to its stockholders that they agree to the merger. Generally, the stockholders are asked to *tender* (or send in) their shares to a designated financial institution, along with a signed power of attorney that transfers ownership of the shares to the acquiring firm. The target firm's stockholders then receive the specified payment, either common stock of the acquiring company (in which case the target company's stockholders become stockholders of the acquiring company), cash, bonds, or some mix of cash and securities. This is a **friendly merger.** The P&G-Gillette merger is an example.

Often, however, the target company's management resists the merger. Perhaps they feel that the price offered is too low, or perhaps they simply want to keep their jobs. In either case, the acquiring firm's offer is said to be **hostile** rather than friendly, and the acquiring firm must make a direct appeal to the target firm's stockholders. In a hostile merger, the acquiring company will again make a **tender offer,** and again it will ask the stockholders of the target firm to tender their shares in exchange for the offered price. This time, though, the target firm's managers will urge stockholders not to tender their shares, generally stating that the price offered (cash, bonds, or stocks in the acquiring firm) is too low.

While most mergers are friendly, recently there have been a number of interesting cases in which high-profile firms have attempted hostile takeovers. For example, Wachovia defeated a hostile bid by Sun Trust and was acquired, instead, by First Union. Looking overseas, Olivetti successfully conducted a hostile takeover of Telecom Italia, and in another hostile telecommunications merger Britain's Vodafone AirTouch acquired its German rival, Mannesmann AG.

Perhaps not surprisingly, hostile bids often fail. However, an all-cash offer that is high enough will generally overcome any resistance by the target firm's management. This appears to be a trend in the current merger wave—strategic buyers often begin the hostile bidding process with a "preemptive" or "blowout" bid. The idea here is to offer such a high premium over the preannouncement price that no other bidders will be willing to jump into the fray, and the target company's board cannot simply reject the bid. If a hostile bid is eventually accepted by the target's board, the deal ends up as "friendly," regardless of the acrimony during the hostile phase.

SELF-TEST

What is the difference between a hostile and a friendly merger?

25.5 Merger Regulation

Prior to the mid-1960s, friendly acquisitions generally took place as simple exchange-of-stock mergers, and a proxy fight was the primary weapon used in hostile control battles. However, in the mid-1960s corporate raiders began to operate differently. First, it took a long time to mount a proxy fight—raiders had to first request a list of the target company's stockholders, be refused, and then get a court order forcing management to turn over the list. During that time, the target's management could think through and then implement a strategy to fend off the raider. As a result, management won most proxy fights.

Then raiders thought, "If we could bring the decision to a head quickly, before management can take countermeasures, that would greatly increase our probability of success." That led the raiders to turn from proxy fights to tender offers, which had a much shorter response time. For example, the stockholders of a company whose stock was selling for $20 might be offered $27 per share and be given 2 weeks to accept. The raider, meanwhile, would have accumulated a substantial block of the shares in open market purchases, and additional shares might have been purchased by institutional friends of the raider who promised to tender their shares in exchange for the tip that a raid was to occur.

Faced with a well-planned raid, managements were generally overwhelmed. The stock might actually be worth more than the offered price, but management simply did not have time to get this message across to stockholders or to find a competing bidder. This situation seemed unfair, so Congress passed the Williams Act in 1968. This law had two main objectives: (1) to regulate the way acquiring firms can structure takeover offers and (2) to force acquiring firms to disclose more information about their offers. Basically, Congress wanted to put target managements in a better position to defend against hostile offers. Additionally, Congress believed that shareholders needed easier access to information about tender offers—including information on any securities that might be offered in lieu of cash—in order to make rational tender-versus-don't-tender decisions.

The Williams Act placed the following four restrictions on acquiring firms: (1) Acquirers must disclose their current holdings and future intentions within 10 days of amassing at least 5% of a company's stock. (2) Acquirers must disclose the source of the funds to be used in the acquisition. (3) The target firm's shareholders must be allowed at least 20 days to tender their shares; that is, the offer must be "open" for at least 20 days. (4) If the acquiring firm increases the offer price during the 20-day open period, all shareholders who tendered prior to the new offer must receive the higher price. In total, these restrictions were intended to reduce the acquiring firm's ability to surprise management and to stampede target shareholders into accepting an inadequate offer. Prior to the Williams Act, offers were generally made on a first-come, first-served basis, and they were often accompanied by an implicit threat to lower the bid price after 50% of the shares were in hand. The legislation also gave the target more time to mount a defense, and it gave rival bidders and white knights a chance to enter the fray and thus help a target's stockholders obtain a better price.

Many states have also passed laws designed to protect firms in their states from hostile takeovers. At first, these laws focused on disclosure requirements, but by the late 1970s several states had enacted takeover statutes so restrictive that they virtually precluded hostile takeovers. In 1979, MITE Corporation, a Delaware firm, made a hostile tender offer for Chicago Rivet and Machine Co., a publicly held Illinois corporation. Chicago Rivet sought protection under the Illinois Business Takeover Act. The constitutionality of the Illinois act was contested, and the U.S. Supreme Court found the law unconstitutional. The court ruled that the market for securities is a national market, and even though the issuing firm was incorporated in Illinois, the state of Illinois could not regulate interstate securities transactions.

The Illinois decision effectively eliminated the first generation of state merger regulations. However, the states kept trying to protect their state-headquartered companies, and in 1987 the U.S. Supreme Court upheld an Indiana law that radically changed the rules of the takeover game. Specifically, the Indiana law first defined "control shares" as enough shares to give an investor 20% of the vote. It went on to state that when an investor buys control shares, those shares can be voted only after approval by a majority of "disinterested shareholders," defined as those who are neither officers nor inside directors of the company, nor associates of the raider. The law also gives the buyer of control shares the right to insist that a shareholders' meeting be called within 50 days to decide whether the shares may be voted. The Indiana law dealt a major blow to raiders, mainly because it slows down the action and thus gives the target firm time to mount a defense. Delaware (the state in which most large companies are incorporated) later passed a similar bill, as did New York and a number of other important states.

The new state laws also have some features that protect target stockholders from their own managers. Included are limits on the use of golden parachutes, onerous debt-financing plans, and some types of takeover defenses. Because these laws do not regulate tender offers per se, but rather govern the practices of firms in the state, they have withstood all legal challenges to date. But when companies such as IBM offer 100% premiums for companies such as Lotus, it is hard for any defense to hold them off.

SELF-TEST

Is there a need to regulate mergers? Explain.

Do the states play a role in merger regulation, or is it all done at the national level? Explain.

25.6 Overview of Merger Analysis

An acquiring firm must answer two questions. First, how much would the target be worth after being incorporated into the acquirer? Notice that this may be quite different from the target's current value, which does not reflect any post-merger synergies or tax benefits. Second, how much should the acquirer offer for the target? Obviously, a low price is better for the acquirer, but the target won't take the offer if it is too low. Also, a higher offer price might scare off potential rival bidders. Later sections discuss setting the offer's price and structure (cash versus stock), but for now we focus on estimating the post-merger value of the target.

There are two basic approaches used in merger valuation, discounted cash flow techniques (DCF) and market multiple analysis.[11] Survey evidence shows that 49.3% of firms use only discounted cash flow techniques, 33.3% use DCF and market multiples, and 12.0% use only market multiples. The market multiple approach assumes that a target is directly comparable to the average firm in its industry. Therefore, this procedure provides at best a ballpark estimate. Because it is less accurate and less frequently used than DCF approaches, we will focus on DCF methods.[12]

There are three widely used DCF methods: (1) the corporate valuation method, (2) the adjusted present value method, and (3) the equity residual method, which is also called the free cash flow to equity method. Chapter 15 explained the corporate valuation model, Section 25.7 explains the adjusted present value model, and Section 25.8 explains the equity residual model. Section 25.8 also provides a numerical illustration for a company with a constant capital structure and shows that all three models, when properly applied, produce identical valuations if the capital structure is held constant. However, in many situations, there will be

---

[11]See Chapter 8 for an explanation of market multiple analysis.
[12]For recent survey evidence on merger valuation methods, see Tarun K. Mukherjee, Halil Kiymaz, and H. Kent Baker, "Merger Motives and Target Valuation: A Survey of Evidence from CFOs," *Journal of Applied Finance*, Fall/Winter 2004, pp. 7–23. For evidence on the effectiveness of market multiples and DCF approaches, see S. N. Kaplan and R. S. Ruback, "The Market Pricing of Cash Flow Forecasts: Discounted Cash Flow vs. the Method of 'Comparables,'" *Journal of Applied Corporate Finance*, Winter 1996, pp. 45–60. Also see Samuel C. Weaver, Robert S. Harris, Daniel W. Bielinski, and Kenneth F. MacKenzie, "Merger and Acquisition Valuation," *Financial Management*, Summer 1991, pp. 85–96; and Nancy Mohan, M. Fall Ainina, Daniel Kaufman, and Bernard J. Winger, "Acquisition/Divestiture Valuation Practices in Major U.S. Firms," *Financial Practice and Education*, Spring 1991, pp. 73–81.

a nonconstant capital structure in years immediately following the merger. For example, this often occurs if an acquisition is financed with a temporarily high level of debt that will be reduced to a sustainable level as the merger is digested. In such situations it is extremely difficult to correctly apply the corporate valuation model or the equity residual model because the cost of equity and the cost of capital are changing as the capital structure changes. Fortunately, the adjusted present value model is ideally suited for such situations, as we show in the following section.

SELF-TEST

What are the two questions an acquirer must answer?

What are four methods for estimating a target's value?

25.7 The Adjusted Present Value (APV) Approach

Recall from Chapter 16 that interest payments are tax deductible. This means that the government receives less tax revenue from a levered firm than from an otherwise identical but unlevered firm, which leaves more money available for the levered firm's investors. More money for investors increases a firm's value, all else equal. In other words, the value of a levered firm is equal to the value of an unlevered firm plus an *adjustment* for tax savings. The **adjusted present value (APV) approach** explicitly employs this concept by expressing the value of operations as the sum of two components: (1) the unlevered value of the firm's operations (i.e., as though the firm had no debt), plus (2) the present value of the interest tax savings, also known as the **interest tax shield:**

$$V_{\text{Operations}} = V_{\text{Unlevered}} + V_{\text{Tax shield}}. \qquad (25\text{-}1)$$

The value of an unlevered firm's operations is the present value of the firm's free cash flows discounted at the unlevered cost of equity, and the value of the tax shield is the present value of all of the interest tax savings (TS), discounted at the unlevered cost of equity r_{sU}:[13]

$$V_{\text{Unlevered}} = \sum_{t=1}^{\infty} \frac{FCF_t}{(1 + r_{sU})^t} \qquad (25\text{-}2)$$

and

$$V_{\text{Tax shield}} = \sum_{t=1}^{\infty} \frac{TS_t}{(1 + r_{sU})^t}. \qquad (25\text{-}3)$$

To apply Equations 25-2 and 25-3, the FCF and TS must eventually stabilize at a constant growth rate. When they do so, we can use an approach similar to the ones we used for the nonconstant dividend model in Chapter 8 and the corporate

---

[13]Although some analysts discount the tax shield at the cost of debt or some other rate, we believe that the unlevered cost of equity is the appropriate discount rate for the interest tax savings. See Chapter 17 for a detailed explanation.

valuation model in Chapter 15. In those approaches, we explicitly projected the years with nonconstant growth rates, found the horizon value at the end of the nonconstant growth period, and then calculated the present value of the horizon value and the cash flows during the forecast period.

Here is a description of how to apply that approach in the APV model.

1. Calculate the target's unlevered cost of equity, r_{sU}, based upon its current capital structure at the time of the acquisition. In other words, you "unlever" the target's cost of equity. From Chapter 17, Equation 17-17 expresses a firm's levered cost of equity, r_{sL}, as a function of its unlevered cost of equity, its cost of debt (r_d), and the amount of debt (D) and equity (S) in its capital structure:

$$r_{sL} = r_{sU} + (r_{sU} - r_d)(D/S). \qquad (25\text{-}4)$$

Because the weights of debt and equity in a capital structure, w_d and w_s, are defined as D/(D + S) and S/(D + S), the ratio of D/S can be expressed as w_d/w_s. We make this substitution in Equation 25-4 and solve for the unlevered cost of equity:

$$r_{sU} = w_s r_{sL} + w_d r_d. \qquad (25\text{-}5)$$

Keep in mind that r_{sL}, r_d, w_d, and w_s are based upon the target's capital structure immediately before the acquisition.

2. Project the free cash flows, FCF_t, and the annual interest tax savings, TS_t. The tax savings are equal to the projected interest payments multiplied by the tax rate:[14]

$$\text{Tax savings} = (\text{Interest expense})(\text{Tax rate}). \qquad (25\text{-}6)$$

e-resource

See **Web Extension 25A** at the textbook's Web site.

You must project enough years so that the FCF and the tax savings are expected to grow at a constant rate (g) after the horizon, which is at Year N. This means that the capital structure must become constant at Year N − 1 to ensure that the projected interest payment at year N will grow at a constant rate after year N. See **Web Extension 25A** for a detailed explanation of how to project financial statements that reflect a constant capital structure. For the remainder of this chapter, we will assume that your trusty assistant has made such projections.

Notice that the APV approach does not require a constant capital structure in each and every year of the analysis, only that the capital structure must eventually become stable in the post-horizon period.

3. Calculate the horizon value of an unlevered firm at Year N ($HV_{U,N}$), which is the value of all free cash flows beyond the horizon discounted back to the horizon at the unlevered cost of equity. Also calculate the horizon value of

---

[14]The tax shield is based only on interest expense, not the net value of interest expense and interest income. This is because the impact of interest income is taken into account when the value of short-term investments is added later to the value of operations. Including the impact of interest income in the tax shield would be "double counting." In other words, there are no "side effects" due to owning a short-term investment: The value of the investment to the company is just the reported value. This is in contrast to debt, which does have a "side effect" in the sense that the cost to the company is less than the reported value due to the tax shield provided by the debt.

the tax shield at Year N ($HV_{TS,N}$), which is the value of all tax shields beyond the horizon discounted back to the horizon at the unlevered cost of equity. Because FCF and TS are growing at a constant rate of g in the post-horizon period, we can use the constant growth formula:

$$\text{Horizon value of unlevered firm } (HV_{U,N}) = \frac{FCF_{N+1}}{r_{sU} - g} = \frac{FCF_N(1 + g)}{r_{sU} - g} \qquad \text{(25-7)}$$

and

$$\text{Horizon value of tax shield } (HV_{TS,N}) = \frac{TS_{N+1}}{r_{sU} - g} = \frac{TS_N(1 + g)}{r_{sU} - g}. \qquad \text{(25-8)}$$

The unlevered horizon value is the horizon value of the company if it had no debt. The tax shield horizon value is the contribution the tax savings after year N make to the horizon value of the levered firm. Therefore the horizon value of the levered firm is the sum of the unlevered horizon value and the tax shield horizon value.

4. Calculate the present value of the free cash flows and their horizon value. This is the value of operations for the unlevered firm, that is, the value it would have if it had no debt. Also calculate the present value of the yearly tax savings during the forecast period and the horizon value of tax savings. This is the value that the interest tax shield contributes to the firm. The sum of the value of unlevered operation and the value of the tax shield is equal to the value of operations for the levered firm.

$$V_{\text{Unlevered}} = \sum_{t=1}^{N} \frac{FCF_t}{(1 + r_{sU})^t} + \frac{HV_{U,N}}{(1 + r_{sU})^N} \qquad \text{(25-9)}$$

$$V_{\text{Tax shield}} = \sum_{t=1}^{N} \frac{TS_t}{(1 + r_{sU})^t} + \frac{HV_{TS,N}}{(1 + r_{sU})^N} \qquad \text{(25-10)}$$

$$V_{\text{Operations}} = V_{\text{Unlevered}} + V_{\text{Tax shield}} \qquad \text{(25-11)}$$

5. To find the total value of the firm, add the value of operations to the value of any nonoperating assets, such as marketable securities. To find the value of equity, subtract the value of the debt before the merger from the total value of the firm.

> Unlevered value of operations
> +Value of tax shield
> _____
> Value of operations
> +Value of nonoperating assets
> _____
> Total value of firm
> −Value of debt
> _____
> Value of equity

To find the stock price per share, divide the value of equity by the number of shares.

The APV technique is especially useful in valuing acquisition targets. Many acquisitions are difficult to value using the corporate valuation model because (1) acquiring firms frequently assume the debt of the target firm, so old debt at different coupon rates is often part of the deal, and (2) the acquisition is usually financed partially by new debt that will be paid down rapidly, so the proportion of debt in the capital structure changes during the years immediately following the acquisition. Thus, the debt cost and capital structure associated with a merger are generally more complex than for a typical firm. The easiest way to handle these complexities is to specify each year's expected interest expense and use the APV method to find the value of the unlevered firm and the interest tax shields separately, and then sum those values.

SELF-TEST

Why is the adjusted present value approach appropriate for situations with a changing capital structure? Describe the steps required to apply the APV approach.

25.8 The Free Cash Flow to Equity (FCFE) Approach

Free cash flow is the cash flow available for distribution to *all* investors. In contrast, **free cash flow to equity (FCFE)** is the cash flow available for distribution to *common shareholders*. Because FCFE is available for distribution only to shareholders, it should be discounted at the cost of equity. Therefore, the **free cash flow to equity approach,** also called the **equity residual model,** discounts the projected FCFEs at the cost of equity to determine the value of the equity from operations.

Because FCFE is the cash flow available for distribution to shareholders, it may be used to pay common dividends, repurchase stock, purchase financial assets, or some combination of these methods. In other words, the uses of FCFE include all those of FCF except for distributions to debtholders. Therefore, one way to calculate FCFE is to start with FCF and reduce it by the net after-tax distributions to debtholders:

$$
\begin{aligned}
\text{FCFE} &= \begin{array}{c}\text{Free}\\\text{cash flow}\end{array} - \begin{array}{c}\text{After-tax}\\\text{interest expense}\end{array} - \begin{array}{c}\text{Principal}\\\text{payments}\end{array} + \begin{array}{c}\text{Newly issued}\\\text{debt}\end{array}\\[2mm]
&= \begin{array}{c}\text{Free}\\\text{cash flow}\end{array} - \begin{array}{c}\text{Interest}\\\text{expense}\end{array} + \begin{array}{c}\text{Interest}\\\text{tax savings}\end{array} + \begin{array}{c}\text{Net change}\\\text{in debt}\end{array}.
\end{aligned}
\tag{25-12}
$$

Alternatively, the FCFE can be calculated as

$$
\text{FCFE} = \text{Net income} - \begin{array}{c}\text{Net investment in}\\\text{operating capital}\end{array} + \begin{array}{c}\text{Net change}\\\text{in debt}\end{array}.
\tag{25-12a}
$$

Both calculations provide the same value for FCFE, but Equation 25-12 is used more often because analysts don't always estimate the net income for a target after it has been acquired.

Given projections of FCFE, the value of a firm's equity due to operations, V_{FCFE}, is

$$V_{FCFE} = \sum_{t=1}^{\infty} \frac{FCFE_t}{(1 + r_{sL})^t}.$$ (25-13)

Assuming constant growth beyond the horizon, the horizon value of the value of equity due to operations ($HV_{FCFE,N}$) is

$$\text{Horizon value of equity due to operations } (HV_{FCFE,N}) = \frac{FCFE_{N+1}}{r_{sL} - g} = \frac{FCFE_N(1 + g)}{r_{sL} - g}.$$ (25-14)

The value of equity due to operations is the present value of the horizon value and the FCFE during the forecast period:

$$V_{FCFE} = \sum_{t=1}^{N} \frac{FCFE_t}{(1 + r_{sL})^t} + \frac{HV_{FCFE,N}}{(1 + r_{sL})^N}.$$ (25-15)

Table 25-2

Summary of Cash Flow Approaches

	Approach		
	Corporate Valuation Model	Free Cash Flow to Equity Model	APV Model
Cash flow definition:	FCF=NOPAT − Net investment in operating capital	FCFE = FCF − Interest expense + Interest tax shield + Net change in debt	(1) FCF (2) Interest tax savings
Discount rate:	WACC	r_{sL} = Cost of equity	r_{sU} = Unlevered cost of equity
Result of present value calculation:	Value of operations	Value of equity due to operations	(1) Value of unlevered operations (2) Value of the tax shield. Together, these are the value of operations.
How to get equity value:	Value of operations + Value of nonoperating assets − Value of debt	Value of equity due to operations + Value of nonoperating assets	Value of operations + Value of nonoperating assets − Value of debt
Assumption about capital structure during forecast period:	Capital structure is constant.	Capital structure is constant.	None
Requirement for analyst to project interest expense:	No interest expense projections needed	Projected interest expense must be based on the assumed capital structure.	Interest expense projections are unconstrained.
Assumption at horizon:	FCF grows at constant rate g.	FCFE grows at constant rate g.	FCF and interest tax savings grow at constant rate g.

The total value of a company's equity, S, is the value of the equity from operations plus the value of any nonoperating assets:

$$S = V_{FCFE} + \text{Nonoperating assets.} \qquad \text{(25-16)}$$

To get a per share price, simply divide the total value of equity by the shares outstanding.[15] Like the corporate valuation model, the FCFE model can be applied only when the capital structure is constant.

Table 25-2 summarizes the three cash flow valuation methods and their assumptions.

SELF-TEST

What cash flows are discounted in the FCFE model and what is the discount rate?

How do the FCFE, corporate valuation, and APV models differ? How are they similar?

25.9 Illustration of the Three Valuation Approaches for a Constant Capital Structure

To illustrate the three valuation approaches, consider the analysis performed by Caldwell Inc., a large technology company, as it evaluates the potential acquisition of Tutwiler Controls. Tutwiler currently has a $62.5 million market value of equity and $27 million in debt, for a total market value of $89.5 million. Thus, Tutwiler's capital structure is comprised of $27/($62.5 + $27) = 30.17\% debt. Caldwell intends to finance the acquisition with this same proportion of debt and plans to maintain this constant capital structure throughout the projection period and thereafter. Tutwiler is a publicly traded company, and its market-determined pre-merger beta was 1.20. Given a risk-free rate of 7% and a 5% market risk premium, the Capital Asset Pricing Model produces a pre-merger required rate of return on equity, r_{sL}, of

$$r_{sL} = 7\% + 1.2(5\%) = 13\%.$$

Tutwiler's cost of debt is 9%. Its WACC is

$$\begin{aligned} WACC &= w_d(1 - T)r_d + w_s r_{sL} \\ &= 0.3017(0.60)(9\%) + 0.6983(13\%) \\ &= 10.707\%. \end{aligned}$$

How much would Tutwiler be worth to Caldwell after the merger? The following sections illustrate the application of the corporate valuation model, the APV model, and the FCFE model. All three models produce an identical value of equity, but keep in mind that this is only because the capital structure is constant. If the capital structure were to change throughout the projection period before

---

[15]The FCFE model is similar to the dividend growth model in that cash flows are discounted at the cost of equity. The cash flows in the FCFE model are those that are generated from operations, while the cash flows in the dividend growth model (i.e., the dividends) also contain cash flows due to interest earned on nonoperating assets.

becoming stable, then only the APV model could be used. Section 25.11 illustrates the APV in the case of a nonconstant capital structure.

Projecting Post-merger Cash Flows

The first order of business is to estimate the post-merger cash flows that Tutwiler will produce. This is by far the most important task in any merger analysis. In a **pure financial merger,** defined as one where no operating synergies are expected, the incremental post-merger cash flows are simply the target firm's expected cash flows. In an **operating merger,** where the two firms' operations are to be integrated, forecasting future cash flows is obviously more difficult, because potential synergies must be estimated. People from marketing, production, human resources, and accounting play leading roles here, with finance people focusing on financing the acquisition and doing an analysis designed to determine if the projected cash flows are worth the cost. In this chapter, we take the projections as given and concentrate on how they are analyzed. See **Web Extension 25A,** available at the textbook's Web site, for a discussion focusing on projecting financial statements in a merger analysis.

Table 25-3 shows Caldwell's post-merger projections for Tutwiler, taking into account all expected synergies and maintaining a constant capital structure. Both Caldwell and Tutwiler are in the 40% marginal federal-plus-state tax bracket. The cost of debt after the acquisition will remain at 9%. The projections assume that growth in the post-horizon period will be 6%.

Panel A of Table 25-3 shows selected items from the projected financial statements. Panel B shows the calculations for free cash flow, which is used in the corporate valuation model. Row 9 shows net operating profit after taxes (NOPAT), which is equal to EBIT$(1 - T)$. Row 10 shows the net investment in operating capital, which is the annual change in the total net operating capital in Row 8. Free cash flow, shown in Row 11, is equal to NOPAT less the net investment in operating capital. Panel C shows the cash flows that will be used in the APV model. In particular, Row 13 shows the annual tax saving, which is equal to the interest expense multiplied by the tax rate. Panel D provides the calculations for FCFE, based upon Equation 25-12.

Of course, the post-merger cash flows are extremely difficult to estimate, and in merger valuations, just as in capital budgeting analysis, sensitivity, scenario, and simulation analyses should be conducted.[16] Indeed, in a friendly merger the acquiring firm would send a team consisting of literally dozens of financial analysts, accountants, engineers, and so forth, to the target firm's headquarters. They would go over its books, estimate required maintenance expenditures, set values on assets such as real estate and petroleum reserves, and the like. Such an investigation, which is called **due diligence,** is an essential part of any merger analysis.

Following are valuations of Tutwiler using all three methods, beginning with the corporate valuation model.

Valuation Using the Corporate Valuation Model

Because Caldwell does not plan on changing Tutwiler's capital structure, the post-merger WACC will be equal to the premerger WACC of 10.707% that we previously calculated. Tutwiler's free cash flows are shown in Row 11 of Table 25-3.

e-resource

See **FM12 Ch 25 Tool Kit.xls** at the textbook's Web site for all calculations. Note that rounded intermediate values are shown in the text, but all calculations are performed in *Excel* using non-rounded values.

---

[16]We purposely kept the cash flows simple in order to focus on key analytical issues. In actual merger valuations, the cash flows would be much more complex, normally including such items as tax loss carryforwards, tax effects of plant and equipment valuation adjustments, and cash flows from the sale of some of the subsidiary's assets.

Table 25-3

Post-merger Projections for the Tutwiler Subsidiary (Millions of Dollars)

	1/1/08	12/31/08	12/31/09	12/31/10	12/31/11	12/31/12
Panel A: Selected Items from Projected Financial Statements[a]						
1. Net sales		$105.0	$126.0	$151.0	$174.0	$191.0
2. Cost of goods sold		80.0	94.0	113.0	129.3	142.0
3. Selling and administrative expenses		10.0	12.0	13.0	15.0	16.0
4. Depreciation		8.0	8.0	9.0	9.0	10.0
5. EBIT		$ 7.0	$ 12.0	$ 16.0	$ 20.7	$ 23.0
6. Interest expense[b]		3.0	3.2	3.5	3.7	3.9
7. Debt[c]	33.2	35.8	38.7	41.0	43.6	46.2
8. Total net operating capital	116.0	117.0	121.0	125.0	131.0	138.0
Panel B: Corporate Valuation Model Cash Flows						
9. NOPAT = EBIT(1 − T)		$ 4.2	$ 7.2	$ 9.6	$ 12.4	$ 13.8
10. Less net investment in operating capital		1.0	4.0	4.0	6.0	7.0
11. Free cash flow		$ 3.2	$ 3.2	$ 5.6	$ 6.4	$ 6.8
Panel C: APV Model Cash Flows						
12. Free cash flow		$ 3.2	$ 3.2	$ 5.6	$ 6.4	$ 6.8
13. Interest tax saving = Interest(T)		$ 1.2	$ 1.3	$ 1.4	$ 1.5	$ 1.6
Panel D: FCFE Model Cash Flows						
14. Free cash flow		$ 3.2	$ 3.2	$ 5.6	$ 6.4	$ 6.8
15. Less A-T interest = Interest(1 − T)		1.8	1.9	2.1	2.2	2.4
16. Plus change in debt[d]	6.2	2.6	2.9	2.5	2.5	2.6
17. FCFE	$ 6.2	$ 4.0	$ 4.1	$ 6.0	$ 6.7	$ 7.1

Notes:
[a]Rounded figures are presented here, but the full non-rounded values are used in all calculations. The tax rate is 40%.
[b]Interest payments are based on Tutwiler's existing debt, new debt to be issued to finance the acquisition, and additional debt required to finance annual growth.
[c]Debt is existing debt plus additional debt required to maintain a constant capital structure. Caldwell will increase Tutwiler's debt by $6.2 million from $27 million to $33.2 million at the time of the acquisition in order to keep the capital structure constant. This increase occurs because the post-merger synergies make Tutwiler more valuable to Caldwell than it was on a stand-alone basis. Therefore, it can support more dollars of debt and still maintain the constant debt ratio.
[d]The increase in debt at the time of acquisition is a source of free cash flow to equity.

The horizon value of Tutwiler's operations as of 2012 can be calculated with the constant growth formula that we used in Chapter 15:

$$HV_{\text{Operations,2012}} = \frac{FCF_{2013}}{(WACC - g)} = \frac{FCF_{2012}(1 + g)}{(WACC - g)}$$

$$= \frac{\$6.800(1.06)}{0.10707 - 0.006} = \$153.1 \text{ million.}$$

The value of operations as of 1/1/2008 is the present value of the cash flows in the forecast period and the horizon value:

$$V_{\text{Operations}} = \frac{\$3.2}{(1 + 0.10707)} + \frac{\$3.2}{(1 + 0.10707)^2} + \frac{\$5.6}{(1 + 0.10707)^3}$$

$$+ \frac{\$6.4}{(1 + 0.10707)^4} + \frac{\$6.8 + \$153.1}{(1 + 0.10707)^5}$$

$$= \$110.1.$$

There are no nonoperating assets, so the value of equity to Caldwell if Tutwiler is acquired is equal to the value of operations less the value of Tutwiler's debt:

$$\$110.1 - \$27 = \$83.1 \text{ million.}[17]$$

Valuation Using the APV Approach

The APV approach requires an estimate of Tutwiler's unlevered cost of equity. Inputting Tutwiler's capital structure, cost of equity, and cost of debt, Equation 25-5 can be used to estimate the unlevered cost of equity:

$$r_{sU} = w_s r_{sL} + w_d r_d \qquad (25\text{-}5a)$$

$$= 0.6983(13\%) + 0.3017(9\%)$$

$$= 11.793\%.$$

In other words, if Tutwiler had no debt, its cost of equity would be 11.793%.

The horizon value of Tutwiler's unlevered cash flows ($HV_{UL,2012}$) and tax shield ($HV_{TS,2012}$) can be calculated using the constant growth formula with the unlevered cost of equity as the discount rate as shown in Equations 25-7 and 25-8:[18]

$$HV_{U,2012} = \frac{FCF_{2013}}{(r_{sU} - g)} = \frac{FCF_{2012}(1 + g)}{(r_{sU} - g)} = \frac{\$6,800(1.06)}{0.11793 - 0.06} = \$124.4 \text{ million;}$$

$$HV_{TS,2012} = \frac{TS_{2013}}{(r_{sU} - g)} = \frac{TS_{2012}(1 + g)}{(r_{sU} - g)} = \frac{\$1.57(1.06)}{0.11793 - 0.06} = \$28.7 \text{ million.}$$

The sum of the two horizon values is the horizon value of operations, $153.1 million, which is the same as the horizon value calculation we reached with the corporate valuation model.

---

[17]Notice that we subtract the $27 million value of Tutwiler's debt, not the $33.2 million of debt supported *after* the merger, since this is the amount that must be paid off or assumed by Caldwell.
[18]Note that we report two decimal places for the 2012 tax shield even though Table 25-3 reports only one decimal place. All calculations are performed in *Excel*, which uses the full non-rounded values.

Row 11 in Table 25-3 shows the projected free cash flows. The unlevered value of operations is calculated as the present value of the free cash flows during the forecast period and the horizon value of the free cash flows:

$$V_{\text{Unlevered}} = \frac{\$3.2}{(1 + 0.11793)} + \frac{\$3.2}{(1 + 0.11793)^2} + \frac{\$5.6}{(1 + 0.11793)^3}$$
$$+ \frac{\$6.4}{(1 + 0.11793)^4} + \frac{\$6.8 + \$124.4}{(1 + 0.11793)^5}$$
$$= \$88.7 \text{ million.}$$

This shows that Tutwiler's operations would be worth $88.7 million if it had no debt.

Row 13 shows the yearly interest tax savings. The value of the tax shield is calculated as the present value of the yearly tax savings and the horizon value of the tax shield:

$$V_{\text{Tax shield}} = \frac{\$1.2}{(1 + 0.11793)} + \frac{\$1.3}{(1 + 0.11793)^2} + \frac{\$1.4}{(1 + 0.11793)^3}$$
$$+ \frac{\$1.5}{(1 + 0.11793)^4} + \frac{\$1.57 + \$28.7}{(1 + 0.11793)^5}$$
$$= \$21.4 \text{ million.}$$

Thus, Tutwiler's operations would be worth only $88.7 million if it had no debt, but its capital structure contributes $21.4 million in value due to the tax deductibility of its interest payments. Since Tutwiler has no nonoperating assets, the total value of the firm is the sum of the unlevered value of operations, $88.7 million, and the value of the tax shield, $21.4 million, for a total of $110.1 million. The value of the equity is this total value less Tutwiler's outstanding debt of $27 million: $110.1 − $27 = $83.1 million. This is also the value we obtained using the corporate valuation model.

Valuation Using the FCFE Model

The horizon value of Tutwiler's free cash flows to equity can be calculated using the constant growth formula of Equation 25-14:[19]

e-resource

See **FM12 Ch 25 Tool Kit.xls** at the textbook's Web site for all calculations. Note that rounded intermediate values are shown in the text, but all calculations are performed in *Excel* using non-rounded values.

$$HV_{\text{FCFE,2012}} = \frac{\text{FCF}_{2012}(1 + g)}{(r_{\text{sL}} - g)} = \frac{\$7.06(1.06)}{0.13 - 0.06} = \$106.9 \text{ million.}$$

Notice that this horizon value is different from the APV and corporate valuation horizon values. That is because the FCFE horizon value is only for equity while the other two horizon values are for the total value of operations. If the 2012 debt of $46.2 million shown in Row 7 of Table 25-3 is added to the $HV_{\text{FCFE,2012}}$, the result is the same $153.1 million horizon value of operations obtained with the corporate valuation model and APV model.

---

[19]Note that we report two decimal places for the 2012 FCFE even though Table 25-3 reports only one decimal place. All calculations are performed in *Excel*, which uses the full non-rounded valued.

Row 17 in Table 25-3 shows the yearly projections of FCFE. When discounted at the 13% cost of equity, the present value of these yearly FCFEs and the horizon value is the value of equity due to operations is:[20]

$$V_{FCFE} = \$6.2 + \frac{\$4.0}{(1 + 0.13)} + \frac{\$4.1}{(1 + 0.13)^2} + \frac{\$6.0}{(1 + 0.13)^3}$$

$$+ \frac{\$6.7}{(1 + 0.13)^4} + \frac{\$7.1 + \$106.9}{(1 + 0.13)^5}$$

$$= \$83.1 \text{ million.}$$

If Tutwiler had any nonoperating assets, we would add them to V_{FCFE} to determine the total value of equity. Since Tutwiler has no nonoperating assets, its total equity value is equal to the V_{FCFE} of $83.1 million. Notice that this is the same value given by the corporate valuation model and the APV approach.

All three models agree that estimated equity value is $83.1 million, which is more than the $62.5 million current market value of Tutwiler's equity, so Tutwiler is more valuable as a part of Caldwell than as a stand-alone corporation being run by its current managers.

SELF-TEST
Why is the adjusted present value approach appropriate for situations with a changing capital structure? Describe the steps required to apply the APV approach.

What are the differences among the FCFE, APV, and corporate valuation approaches?

25.10 Setting the Bid Price

Under the acquisition plan, Caldwell would assume Tutwiler's debt, and it would take on additional short-term debt as necessary to complete the purchase. The valuation models show that $83.1 million is the most it should pay for Tutwiler's stock. If it paid more, then Caldwell's own value would be diluted. On the other hand, if it could get Tutwiler for less than $83.1 million, Caldwell's stockholders would gain value. Therefore, Caldwell should bid something less than $83.1 million when it makes an offer for Tutwiler.

Now consider the target company. As stated earlier, Tutwiler's value of equity as an independent operating company is worth $62.5 million. If Tutwiler were acquired at a price greater than $62.5 million, its stockholders would gain value, while they would lose value at any lower price.

The difference between $62.5 million and $83.1 million, or $20.6 million, represents **synergistic benefits** expected from the merger. If there were no synergistic benefits, the maximum bid would be the current value of the target company. The greater the synergistic gains, the greater the gap between the target's current price and the maximum the acquiring company could pay.

The issue of how to divide the synergistic benefits is critically important. Obviously, both parties would want to get the best deal possible. In our example, if Tutwiler's management knew the maximum price that Caldwell could pay, it

---

[20]Row 16 in Table 25-3 shows that debt is forecast to increase from its pre-merger $27 million to $33.2 million at the acquisition date. This is because Tutwiler is more valuable after the merger, so it can support more dollars of debt while still maintaining 30% debt in its capital structure. The increase in debt of 33.2 − 27 = $6.2 million is a FCFE that is immediately available to Caldwell, and so is not discounted. See **FM12 Ch 25 Tool Kit.xls** for complete calculations and **Web Extension 25A** for a more detailed explanation.

would argue for a price close to $83.1 million. Caldwell, on the other hand, would try to get Tutwiler at a price as close to $62.5 million as possible.

Where, within the $62.5 to $83.1 million range, will the actual price be set? The answer depends on a number of factors, including whether Caldwell offers to pay with cash or securities, the negotiating skills of the two management teams, and, most important, the bargaining positions of the two parties as determined by fundamental economic conditions.

To illustrate the latter point, suppose there are many companies similar to Tutwiler that Caldwell could acquire, but no company other than Caldwell that could gain synergies by acquiring Tutwiler. In this case, Caldwell would probably make a relatively low, take-it-or-leave-it offer, and Tutwiler would probably take it because some gain is better than none. On the other hand, if Tutwiler has some unique technology or other asset that many companies want, then once Caldwell announces its offer, others would probably make competing bids, and the final price would probably be close to or even above $83.1 million. A price above $83.1 million presumably would be paid by some other company with a better synergistic fit or a management that is more optimistic about Tutwiler's cash flow potential.

Caldwell would, of course, want to keep its maximum bid secret, and it would plan its bidding strategy carefully. If it thought that other bidders would emerge or that Tutwiler's management might resist in order to preserve their jobs, it might make a high preemptive bid in hopes of scaring off competing bids and/or management resistance. On the other hand, it might make a lowball bid in hopes of "stealing" the company.[21]

SELF-TEST

Explain the issues involved in setting the bid price.

25.11 Analysis When There Is a Permanent Change in Capital Structure

Tutwiler currently has equity worth $62.5 million and debt of $27 million, giving it a capital structure financed with about 30% debt: $27.0/($62.5 + $27.0) = 0.302 = 30.2\%$. Suppose Caldwell has decided to increase Tutwiler's debt from 30% to 50% over the next 5 years and maintain the capital structure at that level from 2012 on. How would this affect Tutwiler's valuation? The free cash flows will not change, but the interest tax shield, the WACC, and the bid price will all change.[22] At a 30% debt level, the interest rate on Tutwiler's debt was 9%. However, at a 50% debt level, Tutwiler is more risky, and its interest rate would rise to 9.5% to reflect this additional risk. Because the capital structure is changing, we will only use the APV for this analysis.

The Effect on the Tax Shield

It is reasonable to assume that Caldwell will use more debt during the first 5 years of the acquisition if its long-run target capital structure is 50% debt. With more debt

---

[21]For an interesting discussion of the after-effects of losing a bidding contest, see Mark L. Mitchell and Kenneth Lehn, "Do Bad Bidders Become Good Targets?" *Journal of Applied Corporate Finance*, Summer 1990, pp. 60–69.

[22]We are assuming for simplicity that Tutwiler has no more expected bankruptcy costs at 50% debt than at 30% debt. If Tutwiler's risk of bankruptcy and hence its expected bankruptcy costs are larger at this higher level of debt, then its projected free cash flows should be reduced by these expected costs. In practice it is extremely difficult to estimate expected bankruptcy costs. However, these costs can be significant and should be considered when a high degree of leverage is being used.

and a higher interest rate, the interest payments will be higher than those shown in Table 25-3, thus increasing the tax savings shown in Line 15. The interest payments and tax savings with more debt and a higher interest rate are projected as follows:

	2008	2009	2010	2011	2012
Interest	$5.00	$6.00	$7.00	$7.50	$8.30
Interest tax savings	2.00	2.40	2.80	3.00	3.32

In these projections Tutwiler will reach its target capital structure of 50% debt and 50% equity by the start of 2012.[23]

The Effect on the Bid Price

The new capital structure would affect the maximum bid price by changing the value of Tutwiler to Caldwell. Based on the new tax shields, the unlevered and tax shield horizon values in 2012 are calculated as

$$HV_{U,2012} = \frac{FCF_{2013}}{(r_{sU} - g)} = \frac{FCF_{2012}(1 + g)}{(r_{sU} - g)} = \frac{\$6{,}800(1.06)}{0.11793 - 0.06} = \$124.4;$$

$$HV_{TS,2012} = \frac{TS_{2013}}{(r_{sU} - g)} = \frac{TS_{2012}(1 + g)}{(r_{sU} - g)} = \frac{\$3.32(1.06)}{0.11793 - 0.06} = \$60.7.$$

Based on the new interest payments and horizon values, the cash flows to be discounted at the unlevered cost of equity are as follows:

	2008	2009	2010	2011	2012
Free cash flow	$3.2	$3.2	$5.6	$6.4	$6.8
Unlevered horizon value					124.4
FCF plus horizon value	$3.2	$3.2	$5.6	$6.4	$131.2
Interest tax saving	2.0	2.4	2.8	3.0	3.3
Tax shield horizon value					$ 60.7
TS_t plus horizon value	$2.0	$2.4	$2.8	$3.0	$ 64.0

The present value of the free cash flows and their horizon value is $88.7 million, just as it was under the 30% debt policy; the unlevered value of operations is not impacted by the change in capital structure:

$$V_{Unlevered} = \frac{\$3.2}{(1 + 0.11793)} + \frac{\$3.2}{(1 + 0.11793)^2} + \frac{\$5.6}{(1 + 0.11793)^3}$$

$$+ \frac{\$6.4}{(1 + 0.11793)^4} + \frac{\$6.8 + \$124.4}{(1 + 0.11793)^5}$$

$$= \$88.7 \text{ million.}$$

---

[23]The last year's projected interest expense must be consistent with the assumed capital structure in order to use the relation $TS_{N+1} = TS_N(1 + g)$ in calculating the tax shield horizon value. For more information on projecting financial statements, see **Web Extension 25A** and **FM12 Ch 25 Tool Kit.xls.**

The present value of the tax shields and their horizon value is $44.3 million, which is $23.9 million more than the value of the tax shield under the 30% debt policy:

$$
\begin{aligned}
V_{\text{Tax shield}} = &\frac{\$2.0}{(1 + 0.11793)} + \frac{\$2.4}{(1 + 0.11793)^2} + \frac{\$2.8}{(1 + 0.11793)^3} \\
&+ \frac{\$3.0}{(1 + 0.11793)^4} + \frac{\$3.3 + \$60.7}{(1 + 0.11793)^5} \\
&= \$44.3 \text{ million.}
\end{aligned}
$$

Thus, Tutwiler is worth almost $24 million more to Caldwell if it is financed with 50% debt rather than 30% debt due to the added value of the tax shields.

The value of operations under the new 50% debt policy is the sum of the unlevered value of operations and the value of the tax shields, or $133.0 million. There are no nonoperating assets to add, and subtracting the value of the debt of $27 million leaves the value of Tutwiler's equity at $106.0 million. Because Tutwiler has 10 million shares outstanding, the maximum amount Caldwell should be willing to pay per share, given a post-merger target capital structure of 50% debt, is $10.60. This is more than the $8.31 maximum price if the capital structure had 30% debt. The difference, $2.29 per share, reflects the added value of the interest tax shields under the higher-debt plan.

SELF-TEST   How does a change in capital structure affect the valuation analysis?

25.12 Taxes and the Structure of the Takeover Bid

In a merger, the acquiring firm can either buy the target's assets or buy shares of stock directly from the target's shareholders. If the offer is for the target's assets, the target's board of directors will make a recommendation to the shareholders, who will vote either to accept or reject the offer. If they accept the offer, the payment goes directly to the target corporation, which pays off any debt not assumed by the acquiring firm, pays any corporate taxes that are due, and then distributes the remainder of the payment to the shareholders, often in the form of a liquidating dividend. In this situation, the target firm is usually dissolved and no longer continues to exist as a separate legal entity, although its assets and workforce may continue to function as a division or a wholly owned subsidiary of the acquiring firm. The acquisition of assets is a very common form of a takeover for small and medium-sized firms, especially those that are not publicly traded. A major advantage of this method relative to the acquisition of the target's stock is that the acquiring firm simply acquires assets and is not saddled with any hidden liabilities. In contrast, if the acquiring firm buys the target's stock, then it is responsible for any legal contingencies against the target, even for those that might have occurred prior to the takeover.

An offer for a target's stock rather than its assets can be made either directly to the shareholders, as is typical in a hostile takeover, or indirectly through the board of directors, which in a friendly deal, makes a recommendation to the shareholders to accept the offer. In a successful offer, the acquiring firm will end up

Tempest in a Teapot?

In 2001, amid a flurry of warnings and lobbying, the Financial Accounting Standards Board (FASB) in its Statement 141 eliminated the use of pooling for merger accounting, requiring that purchase accounting be used instead. Because the change would otherwise have required that all purchased goodwill be amortized, and reported earnings reduced, the FASB also issued Statement 142, which eliminated the regular amortization of purchased goodwill, replacing it with an "impairment test." The impairment test requires that companies evaluate annually their purchased goodwill and write it down if its value has declined. This impairment test resulted in Time Warner's unprecedented 2002 write-down of $54 billion of goodwill associated with the AOL merger.

So what exactly is the effect of the change? First and foremost, the change does *nothing* to the firm's actual cash flows. Purchased goodwill may still be amortized for federal income tax purposes, so the change does not affect the actual taxes a company pays, nor does it affect the company's operating cash flows. However, it does affect the earnings that companies report to their shareholders. Firms that used to have large goodwill charges from past acquisitions have seen their reported earnings increase, because they no longer have to amortize the remaining goodwill. Firms whose acquisitions have fared badly, such as Time Warner, must make large write-downs. Executives facing an earnings boost hope, while executives facing a write-down fear, that investors will not see through these accounting changes. However, evidence suggests that investors realize that a company's assets have deteriorated long before the write-down actually occurs, and they build this information into the price of the stock. For example, Time Warner's announcement of its $54 billion charge in January 2002 resulted in only a blip in its stock price at that time, even though the write-down totaled more than a third of its market value. The market recognized the decline in value months earlier, and by the time of the announcement Time Warner had already lost more than $100 billion in market value.

owning a controlling interest, or perhaps even all of the target's stock. Sometimes the target retains its identity as a separate legal entity and is operated as a subsidiary of the acquiring firm, and sometimes its corporate status is dissolved and it is operated as one of the acquiring firm's divisions.

The payment offered by the acquiring firm can be in the form of cash, stock of the acquiring firm, debt of the acquiring firm, or some combination. The structure of the bid affects (1) the capital structure of the post-merger firm, (2) the tax treatment of both the acquiring firm and the target's stockholders, (3) the ability of the target firm's stockholders to benefit from future merger-related gains, and (4) the types of federal and state regulations to which the acquiring firm will be subjected.

The tax consequences of the merger depend on whether it is classified as a *taxable offer* or a *nontaxable offer*.[24] In general, a nontaxable offer is one in which the form of payment is predominately stock, although the application of this simple principle is much more complicated in practice. The Internal Revenue Code views a mostly stock merger as an exchange rather than a sale, making it a nontaxable event. However, if the offer includes a significant amount of cash or bonds, then the IRS views it as a sale, and it is a taxable transaction, just like any other sale.

In a nontaxable deal, target shareholders who receive shares of the acquiring company's stock do not have to pay any taxes at the time of the merger. When they eventually sell their stock in the acquiring company, they must pay a tax on the gain. The amount of the gain is the sales price of their stock in the acquiring

[24]For more details, see J. Fred Weston, Mark L. Mitchell, and Harold Mulherin, *Takeovers, Restructuring, & Corporate Governance*, 4th edition (Upper Saddle River, NJ: Prentice-Hall, 2004), especially Chapter 4. Also see Kenneth E. Anderson, Thomas R. Pope, and John L. Kramer, eds., *Prentice Hall's Federal Taxation: Corporations, Partnerships, Estates, and Trusts*, 2006 edition (Upper Saddle River, NJ: Prentice-Hall, 2006), especially Chapter 7.

company minus the price at which they purchased their original stock in the target company.[25] In a taxable offer, the gain between the offer price and the original purchase price of the target stock is taxed in the year of the merger.[26]

All other things equal, stockholders prefer nontaxable offers, since they may then postpone taxes on their gains. Furthermore, if the target firm's stockholders receive stock, they will benefit from any synergistic gains produced by the merger. Most target shareholders are thus willing to give up their stock for a lower price in a nontaxable offer than in a taxable one. As a result, one might expect nontaxable bids to dominate. However, this is not the case—roughly half of all mergers have been taxable. The reason for this is explained in the following paragraphs.

The form of the payment also has tax consequences for the acquiring and target firms. To illustrate, consider the following situation. The target firm has assets with a book value of $100 million, but these assets have an appraised value of $150 million. The offer by the acquiring firm is worth $225 million. If it is a nontaxable offer, then after the merger the acquiring firm simply adds the $100 million book value of the target's assets to its own assets and continues to depreciate them according to their previous depreciation schedules. To keep the example simple, we assume the target has no debt.

The situation is more complicated for a taxable offer, and the treatment is different depending on whether the offer is for the target's assets or for its stock. If the acquiring firm offers $225 million for the target's assets, then the target firm must pay a tax on the gain of $225 − $100 = $125 million. Assuming a corporate tax rate of 40%, this tax is 0.40($125) = $50 million. This leaves the target with $225 − $50 = $175 million to distribute to its shareholders upon liquidation. Adding insult to injury, the target's shareholders must also pay individual taxes on any of their own gains.[27] This is truly a taxable transaction, with taxes assessed at both the corporate and individual levels! In contrast to the tax disadvantages for the target and its shareholders, the acquiring firm receives two major tax advantages. First, it records the acquired assets at their appraised value and depreciates them accordingly. Thus, it will depreciate $150 million of assets in this taxable transaction versus only $100 million in a nontaxable transaction. Second, it will create $75 million in a new asset account called **goodwill,** which is the difference between the purchase price of $225 million and the appraised value of $150 million. Tax laws that took effect in 1993 permit companies to amortize this goodwill over 15 years using the straight-line method and then to deduct the amortization from taxable income. The net effect is that the full purchase price of $225 million can be written off in a taxable merger versus only the original book value of $100 million in a nontaxable transaction.

Now suppose the acquiring firm offers $225 million for the target's stock, rather than just its assets as in the example above, in a taxable offer. After completing the merger, the acquiring firm must choose between two tax treatments. Under the first alternative, it will record the assets at their book value of $100 million and continue depreciating them using their current schedules. This treatment does not create any goodwill. Under the second alternative, it will record the assets at their appraised value of $150 million and create $75 million of goodwill. As described earlier for the asset purchase, this allows the acquiring firm to effectively depreciate the entire purchase price of $225 million for tax purposes.

---

[25]This is a capital gain if it has been at least 1 year since they purchased their original stock in the target.
[26]Even in nontaxable deals, taxes must be paid in the year of the merger by any stockholders who receive cash.
[27]Our example assumes that the target is a publicly owned firm, which means that it must be a "C corporation" for tax purposes. However, if it is privately held, it might be an "S corporation," in which case only the stockholders would be taxed. This helps smaller firms use mergers as an exit strategy.

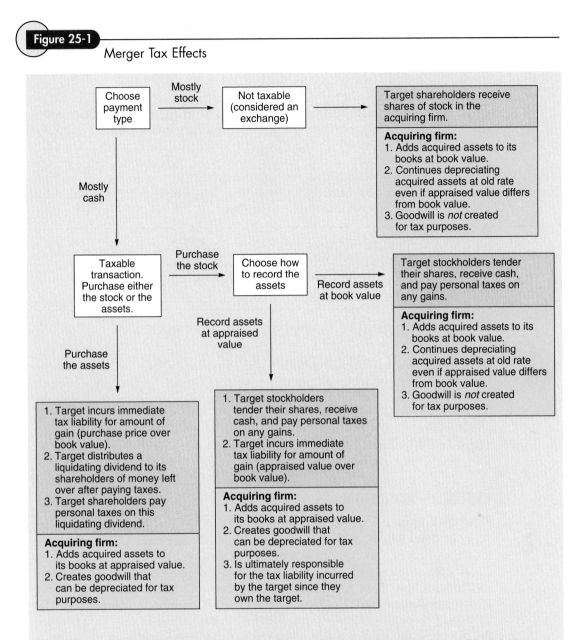

Figure 25-1

Merger Tax Effects

Note: These are actual cash tax effects. However, the tax effects reported to shareholders will be different since shareholder statements must conform to GAAP conventions, not federal Tax Code conventions. For example, purchased goodwill can no longer be deducted for shareholder reporting, even though it is still deductible for federal tax purposes. See the box "Tempest in a Teapot?" which deals with changes in the accounting treatment of mergers and goodwill.

However, there will also be an immediate tax liability on the $125 million gain, just as when the firm purchased assets.[28] Therefore, many companies choose not to mark up the assets. Figure 25-1 illustrates the tax implications for the various types of transactions.

---

[28]Technically speaking, it is the target firm that is responsible for this tax on the write-up. Keep in mind, however, that the acquiring firm previously purchased the stock in the target, so it must in reality bear the brunt of the tax.

If you think this is complicated, you are right! At this point you should know enough to talk with specialized accountants and lawyers, or be ready to delve into tax accounting texts, but merger taxation is too complex a subject to be covered thoroughly in a general finance textbook.

Securities laws also have an effect on the construction of the offer. The SEC has oversight over the issuance of new securities, including stock or debt issued in connection with a merger. Therefore, whenever a corporation bids for control of another firm through the exchange of equity or debt, the entire process must take place under the scrutiny of the Securities and Exchange Commission. The time required for such reviews allows target managements to implement defensive tactics and other firms to make competing offers, and as a result, nearly all hostile tender offers are for cash rather than securities.

SELF-TEST

What are some alternative ways of structuring takeover bids?

How do taxes influence the payment structure?

How do securities laws affect the payment structure?

25.13 Financial Reporting for Mergers

Although a detailed discussion of financial reporting is best left to accounting courses, the accounting implications of mergers cannot be ignored. Currently, mergers are handled using **purchase accounting**.[29] Keep in mind, however, that all larger companies are required to keep two sets of books. The first is for the IRS, and it reflects the tax treatment of mergers as described in the previous section. The second is for financial reporting, and it reflects the treatment described below. As you will see, the rules for financial reporting differ from those for the IRS.

Purchase Accounting

Table 25-4 illustrates purchase accounting. Here Firm A is assumed to have "bought" Firm B in much the same way it would buy any capital asset, paying for it with cash, debt, or stock of the acquiring company. If the price paid is exactly equal to the acquired firm's *net asset value*, which is defined as its total assets minus its liabilities, then the consolidated balance sheet will be the same as if the two statements were merged. Normally, though, there is an important difference. If the price paid exceeds the net asset value, then asset values will be increased to reflect the price actually paid, whereas if the price paid is less than the net asset value, then assets must be written down when preparing the consolidated balance sheet.

Note that Firm B's net asset value is $30, which is also its reported common equity value. This $30 book value could be equal to the market value (which is determined by investors based on the firm's earning power), but book value could also be more or less than the market value. Three situations are considered in Table 25-4. First, in Column 3 we assume that Firm A gives cash or stock worth $20 for Firm B. Thus, B's assets as reported on its balance sheet were overvalued, and A pays less than B's net asset value. The overvaluation could be in either fixed or current assets; an appraisal would be made, but we assume that it is fixed assets that are overvalued. Accordingly, we reduce B's fixed assets and also its common equity by $10 before constructing the consolidated balance sheet shown

---

[29]In 2001, the Financial Accounting Standards Board (FASB) issued Statement 141, which eliminated the use of pooling accounting.

Table 25-4

Accounting for Mergers: A Acquires B

	Firm A (1)	Firm B (2)	Post-merger: Firm A		
			$20 Paid[a] (3)	$30 Paid[a] (4)	$50 Paid[a] (5)
Current assets	$ 50	$25	$ 75	$ 75	$ 80[c]
Fixed assets	50	25	65[b]	75	80[c]
Goodwill[d]	0	0	0	0	10[d]
Total assets	$100	$50	$140	$150	$170
Liabilities	$ 40	$20	$ 60	$ 60	$ 60
Equity	60	30	80[e]	90	110[f]
Total claims	$100	$50	$140	$150	$170

Notes:
[a]The price paid is the *net asset value*, that is, total assets minus debt.
[b]Here we assume that Firm B's fixed assets are written down from $25 to $15 before constructing the consolidated balance sheet.
[c]Here we assume that Firm B's current and fixed assets are both increased to $30.
[d]*Goodwill* refers to the excess paid for a firm above the appraised value of the physical assets purchased. Goodwill represents payment both for intangibles such as patents and for "organization value" such as that associated with having an effective sales force. Beginning in 2001, purchased goodwill such as this could not be amortized for financial statement reporting purposes.
[e]Firm B's common equity is reduced by $10 prior to consolidation to reflect the fixed asset write-off.
[f]Firm B's equity is increased to $50 to reflect the above-book purchase price.

in Column 3. Next, in Column 4, we assume that A pays exactly the net asset value for B. In this case, the financial statements are simply combined.

Finally, in Column 5 we assume that A pays more than the net asset value for B: $50 is paid for $30 of net assets. This excess is assumed to be partly attributable to undervalued assets (land, buildings, machinery, and inventories), so to reflect this undervaluation, current and fixed assets are each increased by $5. In addition, we assume that $10 of the $20 excess of market value over book value is due to a superior sales organization, or some other intangible factor, and we post this excess as goodwill. B's common equity is increased by $20, the sum of the increases in current and fixed assets plus goodwill, and this markup is also reflected in A's post-merger equity account.[30]

Income Statement Effects

A merger can have a significant effect on reported profits. If asset values are increased, as they often are under a purchase, this must be reflected in higher depreciation charges (and also in a higher cost of goods sold if inventories are written up). This, in turn, will further reduce reported profits. Prior to 2001, goodwill was also amortized over its expected life. Now, however, goodwill is subject to an "annual impairment test." If the fair market value of the goodwill has declined

---

[30]This example assumes that additional debt was not issued to help finance the acquisition. If the acquisition were totally debt financed, the post-merger balance sheet would show increases in the liability account rather than increases in the equity account. If it were financed by a mix of debt and equity, both accounts would be changed.

Table 25-5

Income Statements Effects

	Pre-merger		Post-merger: Firm A
	Firm A (1)	Firm B (2)	Merged (3)
Sales	$100.0	$50.0	$150.0
Operating costs	72.0	36.0	109.0[a]
Operating income	$ 28.0	$14.0	$ 41.0[a]
Interest (10%)	4.0	2.0	6.0
Taxable income	$ 24.0	$12.0	$ 35.0
Taxes (40%)	9.6	4.8	14.0
Net income	$ 14.4	$ 7.2	$ 21.0
EPS[b]	$ 2.40	$ 2.40	$ 2.33

Notes:
[a]Operating costs are $1 higher than they otherwise would be to reflect the higher reported costs (depreciation and cost of goods sold) caused by the physical asset markup at the time of purchase.
[b]Firm A had 6 shares and Firm B had 3 shares before the merger. A gives 1 of its shares for each of B's, so A has 9 shares outstanding after the merger.

over the year, then the amount of the decline must be charged to earnings. If not, then there is no charge, but gains in goodwill cannot be added to earnings.

Table 25-5 illustrates the income statement effects of the write-up of current and fixed assets. We assume that A purchased B for $50, creating $10 of goodwill and $10 of higher physical asset value. As Column 3 indicates, the asset markups cause reported profits to be lower than the sum of the individual companies' reported profits.

The asset markup is also reflected in earnings per share. In our hypothetical merger, we assume that 9 shares exist in the consolidated firm. (Six of these shares went to A's stockholders, and 3 to B's.) The merged company's EPS is $2.33 while each of the individual companies' EPS is $2.40.

See **FM12 Ch 25 Tool Kit.xls** at the textbook's Web site for details.

SELF-TEST

What is purchase accounting for mergers?

What is goodwill? What impact does goodwill have on the firm's balance sheet? On its income statement?

25.14 Analysis for a "True Consolidation"

Most of our analysis in the preceding sections assumed that one firm plans to acquire another. However, in many situations it is hard to identify an "acquirer" and a "target"—the merger appears to be a true "merger of equals," as was the case with the Exxon/Mobil and First Union/Wachovia mergers. In such cases, how is the analysis handled?

The first step is to estimate the value of the combined enterprise, reflecting any synergies, tax effects, or capital structure changes. The second step is to decide how to allocate the new company's stock between the two sets of old stockholders. Normally, one would expect the consolidated value to exceed the sum of the pre-announcement values of the two companies because of synergy. For example,

Company A might have had a pre-merger equity value of $10 billion, found as (Number of shares)(Price per share), and Company B might have had a pre-merger value of $15 billion. If the post-merger value of new Company AB is estimated to be $30 billion, then that value must be allocated. Company A's stockholders will have to receive enough shares to cause them to have a projected value of at least $10 billion, and Company B's stockholders will have to receive at least $15 billion. But how will the remaining $5 billion of synergistic-induced value be divided?

This is a key issue, requiring intense negotiation between the two management groups. There is no rule or formula that can be applied, but one basis for the allocation is the relative pre-announcement values of the two companies. For example, in our hypothetical merger of A and B to form AB, the companies might agree to give $10/$25 = 40% of the new stock to A's stockholders and 60% to B's stockholders. Unless a case could be made for giving a higher percentage of the shares to one of the companies because it was responsible for more of the synergistic value, then the pre-merger value proportions would seem to be a "fair" solution. In any event, the pre-merger proportions will probably be given the greatest weight in reaching the final decision.

It should also be noted that control of the consolidated company is always an issue. Generally, the companies hold a press conference and announce that the CEO of one firm will be chairman of the new company, that the other CEO will be president, that the new board will consist of directors from both old boards, and that power will be shared. With huge mergers such as those we have been seeing lately, there is plenty of power to be shared.

SELF-TEST   How does merger analysis differ in the case of a large company acquiring a smaller one versus a "true merger of equals"?

Do you think the same guidelines for allocating synergistic gains would be used in both types of mergers?

25.15 The Role of Investment Bankers

Investment bankers are involved with mergers in a number of ways: (1) They help arrange mergers, (2) they help target companies develop and implement defensive tactics, (3) they help value target companies, (4) they help finance mergers, and (5) they invest in the stocks of potential merger candidates. These merger-related activities have been quite profitable. For example, the investment bankers and lawyers who arranged the Campeau-Federated merger earned fees of about $83 million—First Boston and Wasserstein Perella split $29 million from Campeau, and Goldman Sachs, Hellman & Friedman, and Shearson Lehman Hutton divided up $54 million for representing Federated. No wonder investment banking houses are able to make top offers to finance graduates!

Arranging Mergers

The major investment banking firms have merger and acquisition groups that operate within their corporate finance departments. (Corporate finance departments offer advice, as opposed to underwriting or brokerage services, to business firms.) Members of these groups identify firms with excess cash that might want to buy other firms, companies that might be willing to be bought, and firms that might, for a number of reasons, be attractive to others. Sometimes dissident stockholders of firms with poor track records work with investment bankers to oust management by helping to arrange a merger. Investment bankers are reported to have offered packages of financing to corporate raiders, where the package includes both designing the securities to be used in the tender offer, plus lining up people and firms who will buy the target firm's stock now and then tender it once the final offer is made.

Investment bankers have occasionally taken illegal actions in the merger arena. For example, they are reported to have *parked stock*—purchasing it for a raider under a guaranteed buy-back agreement—to help the raider de facto accumulate more than 5% of the target's stock without disclosing the position. People have gone to jail for this. Recently, the entire investment banking industry has come under scrutiny, and several of the largest firms have been hit with heavy fines. Regulators proved that supposedly objective analysts were providing glowing reports to retail customers about companies the analysts privately acknowledged were poor investments. This touting helped the investment banking side of the firm get underwriting business. Merrill Lynch was fined $100 million for one analyst's actions, and the larger firms collectively were forced to pay $1.5 billion to purchase and distribute independent research. Investors who claim they bought stock on the basis of the biased reports and then lost money are just now filing civil suits, and how much that will cost the industry is an open question.

Developing Defensive Tactics

Target firms that do not want to be acquired generally enlist the help of an investment banking firm, along with a law firm that specializes in mergers. Defenses include such tactics as (1) changing the bylaws so that only one-third of the directors are elected each year and/or so that a 75% approval (a *super majority*) versus a simple majority is required to approve a merger; (2) trying to convince the target firm's stockholders that the price being offered is too low; (3) raising antitrust issues in the hope that the Justice Department will intervene; (4) repurchasing stock in the open market in an effort to push the price above that being offered by the potential acquirer; (5) getting a **white knight** who is acceptable to the target firm's management to compete with the potential acquirer; (6) getting a **white squire** who is friendly to current management to buy enough of the target firm's shares to block the merger; and (7) taking a poison pill, as described next.

Poison pills—which occasionally really do amount to committing economic suicide to avoid a takeover—are such tactics as borrowing on terms that require immediate repayment of all loans if the firm is acquired, selling off at bargain prices the assets that originally made the firm a desirable target, granting such lucrative **golden parachutes** to their executives that the cash drain from these payments would render the merger infeasible, and planning defensive mergers that would leave the firm with new assets of questionable value and a huge debt load. Currently, the most popular poison pill is for a company to give its stockholders *stock purchase rights* that allow them to buy at half price the stock of an acquiring firm, should the firm be acquired. The blatant use of poison pills is constrained by directors' awareness that excessive use could trigger personal suits by stockholders against directors who voted for them, and, perhaps in the near future, bylaws that would further limit management's use of pills. Still, investment bankers and anti-takeover lawyers are busy thinking up new poison pill formulas, and others are just as busy trying to come up with antidotes.[31]

---

[31]It has become extremely difficult and expensive for companies to buy "directors' insurance," which protects the board from such contingencies as stockholders' suits, and even when insurance is available it often does not pay for losses if the directors have not exercised due caution and judgment. This exposure is making directors extremely leery of actions that might trigger stockholder suits.

Another takeover defense that is being used is the employee stock ownership plan (ESOP). ESOPs are designed to give lower-level employees an ownership stake in the firm, and current tax laws provide generous incentives for companies to establish such plans and fund them with the firm's common stock. Polaroid used an ESOP to help fend off Shamrock Holdings's hostile takeover attempt. Also, Procter & Gamble set up an ESOP that, along with an existing profit-sharing plan, eventually will give employees a 20% ownership stake in the company. Since the trustees of ESOPs generally support current management in any takeover attempt, and since up to 85% of the votes is often required to complete a merger, an ESOP can provide an effective defense against a hostile tender offer. Procter & Gamble stated that its ESOP was designed primarily to lower its costs by utilizing the plan's tax advantages and to improve employees' retirement security. However, the company also noted that the ESOP would strengthen its defenses against a takeover.

Establishing a Fair Value

If a friendly merger is being worked out between two firms' managements, it is important to document that the agreed-upon price is a fair one; otherwise, the stockholders of either company may sue to block the merger. Therefore, in most large mergers each side will hire an investment banking firm to evaluate the target company and to help establish the fair price. For example, General Electric employed Morgan Stanley to determine a fair price for Utah International, as did Royal Dutch to help establish the price it paid for Shell Oil. Even if the merger is not friendly, investment bankers may still be asked to help establish a price. If a surprise tender offer is to be made, the acquiring firm will want to know the lowest price at which it might be able to acquire the stock, while the target firm may seek help in "proving" that the price being offered is too low.[32]

Financing Mergers

Many mergers are financed with the acquiring company's excess cash. However, if the acquiring company has no excess cash, it will require a source of funds. Perhaps the single most important factor behind the 1980s merger wave was the development of junk bonds for use in financing acquisitions.

Drexel Burnham Lambert was the primary developer of junk bonds, defined as bonds rated below investment grade (BBB/Baa). Prior to Drexel's actions, it was almost impossible to sell low-grade bonds to raise new capital. Drexel then pioneered a procedure under which a target firm's situation would be appraised very closely, and a cash flow projection similar to that in Table 25-3 (but much more detailed) would be developed.

With the cash flows forecasted, Drexel's analysts would figure out a debt structure—amount of debt, maturity structure, and interest rate—that could be serviced by the cash flows. With this information, Drexel's junk bond people, operating out of Beverly Hills, would approach financial institutions (savings and

---

[32]Such investigations must obviously be done in secret, for if someone knew that Company A was thinking of offering, say, $50 per share for Company T, which was currently selling at $35 per share, then huge profits could be made. One of the biggest scandals to hit Wall Street was the disclosure that Ivan Boesky was buying information from Dennis Levine, a senior member of the investment banking house of Drexel Burnham Lambert, about target companies that Drexel was analyzing for others. Purchases based on such insider information would, of course, raise the prices of the stocks and thus force Drexel's clients to pay more than they otherwise would have had to pay. Levine and Boesky, among others, went to jail for their improper use of insider information.

loans, insurance companies, pension funds, and mutual funds) with a financing plan, and they would offer a rate of return several percentage points above the rate on more conservative investments. Drexel's early deals worked out well, and the institutions that bought the bonds were quite pleased. These results enabled Drexel to expand its network of investors, which increased its ability to finance larger and larger mergers. T. Boone Pickens, who went after Phillips, Texaco, and several other oil giants, was an early Drexel customer, as was Ted Turner.

To be successful in the mergers and acquisitions (M&A) business, an investment banker must be able to offer a financing package to clients, whether they are acquirers who need capital to take over companies or target companies trying to finance stock repurchase plans or other defenses against takeovers. Drexel was the leading player in the merger financing game during the 1980s, but since Drexel's bankruptcy Merrill Lynch, Morgan Stanley, Citigroup, and others are all vying for the title.

Arbitrage Operations

Arbitrage generally means simultaneously buying and selling the same commodity or security in two different markets at different prices and pocketing a risk-free return. However, the major brokerage houses, as well as some wealthy private investors, are engaged in a different type of arbitrage called *risk arbitrage*. The *arbitrageurs*, or "arbs," speculate in the stocks of companies that are likely takeover targets. Vast amounts of capital are required to speculate in a large number of securities and thus reduce risk, and also to make money on narrow spreads. However, the large investment bankers have the wherewithal to play the game. To be successful, arbs need to be able to sniff out likely targets, assess the probability of offers reaching fruition, and move in and out of the market quickly and with low transactions costs.

The risk arbitrage business has been rocked by insider trading scandals. Indeed, the most famous arb of all, Ivan Boesky, was caught buying inside information from executives of some leading investment banking houses and law firms. The Boesky affair slowed risk arbitrage activity for awhile, but it is now back.

SELF-TEST

What are some defensive tactics that firms can use to resist hostile takeovers?

What is the difference between pure arbitrage and risk arbitrage?

What role did junk bonds play in the merger wave of the 1980s?

25.16 Who Wins: The Empirical Evidence

All the recent merger activity has raised two questions: (1) Do corporate acquisitions create value, and, (2) if so, how is the value shared between the parties?

Most researchers agree that takeovers increase the wealth of the shareholders of target firms, for otherwise they would not agree to the offer. However, there is a debate as to whether mergers benefit the acquiring firm's shareholders. In particular, managements of acquiring firms may be motivated by factors other than shareholder wealth maximization. For example, they may want to merge merely to increase the size of the corporations they manage, because increased size usually brings larger salaries plus job security, perquisites, power, and prestige.

Merger Mistakes

Academics have long known that acquiring firms' shareholders rarely reap the benefits of mergers. However, this important information never seemed to make it up to the offices of corporate America's decision makers; the 1990s saw bad deal after bad deal, with no apparent learning on the part of acquisitive executives. *BusinessWeek* published an analysis of 302 large mergers from 1995 to 2001, and it found that 61% of them led to losses by the acquiring firms' shareholders. Indeed, those losing shareholders' returns during the first post-merger year averaged 25 percentage points less than the returns on other companies in their industry. The average returns for all the merging companies, both winners and losers, were 4.3% below industry averages and 9.2% below the S&P 500.

The article cited four common mistakes.

1. The acquiring firms often overpaid. Generally, the acquirers gave away all of the synergies from the mergers to the acquired firms' shareholders, and then some.

2. Management overestimated the synergies (cost savings and revenue gains) that would result from the merger.

3. Management took too long to integrate operations between the merged companies. This irritated customers and employees alike, and it postponed any gains from the integration.

4. Some companies cut costs too deeply, at the expense of maintaining sales and production infrastructures.

The worst performance came from companies that paid for their acquisitions with stock. The best performance, albeit a paltry 0.3% better than industry averages, came from companies that used cash for their acquisitions. On the bright side, the shareholders of the companies that were acquired fared quite well, earning on average 19.3% more than their industry peers, and all of those gains came in the 2 weeks surrounding the merger announcement.

Source: David Henry, "Mergers: Why Most Big Deals Don't Pay Off," *BusinessWeek*, October 14, 2002, pp. 60–70.

The question of who gains from corporate acquisitions can be tested by examining the stock price changes that occur around the time of a merger or takeover announcement. Changes in the stock prices of the acquiring and target firms represent market participants' beliefs about the value created by the merger and about how that value will be divided between the target and acquiring firms' shareholders. So, examining a large sample of stock price movements can shed light on the issue of who gains from mergers.

One cannot simply examine stock prices around merger announcement dates, because other factors influence stock prices. For example, if a merger was announced on a day when the entire market advanced, the fact that the target firm's price rose would not necessarily signify that the merger was expected to create value. Hence, studies examine *abnormal returns* associated with merger announcements, where abnormal returns are defined as that part of a stock price change caused by factors other than changes in the general stock market.

These "event studies" have examined both acquiring and target firms' stock price responses to mergers and tender offers.[33] Jointly, they have covered nearly every acquisition involving publicly traded firms from the early 1960s to the present, and they are remarkably consistent in their results: On average, the

---

[33]For more on the effects of mergers on value, see Bernard S. Black and Joseph A. Grundfest, "Shareholder Gains from Takeovers and Restructurings between 1981 and 1986: $162 Billion Is a Lot of Money," *Journal of Applied Corporate Finance*, Spring 1988, pp. 5–15; and James W. Wansley, William R. Lane, and Ho C. Yang, "Abnormal Returns to Acquired Firms by Type of Acquisition and Method of Payment," *Financial Management*, Autumn 1983, pp. 16–22.

stock prices of target firms increase by about 30% in hostile tender offers, while in friendly mergers the average increase is about 20%. However, for both hostile and friendly deals, the stock prices of acquiring firms, on average, remain constant. Thus, the event study evidence strongly indicates (1) that acquisitions do create value, but (2) that shareholders of target firms reap virtually all the benefits.

The event study evidence suggests that mergers benefit targets but not acquirers, hence that acquiring firms' stockholders should be skeptical of their managers' plans for acquisitions. This evidence cannot be dismissed out of hand, but neither is it entirely convincing. There are undoubtedly many good mergers, just as there are many poorly conceived ones. Like most of finance, merger decisions should be studied carefully, and it is best not to judge the outcome of a specific merger until the actual results start to come in.

SELF-TEST

Explain how researchers can study the effects of mergers on shareholder wealth.

Do mergers create value? If so, who profits from this value?

Do the research results discussed in this section seem logical? Explain.

25.17 Corporate Alliances

Mergers are one way for two companies to join forces, but many companies are striking cooperative deals, called **corporate,** or **strategic, alliances,** which stop far short of merging. Whereas mergers combine all of the assets of the firms involved, as well as their ownership and managerial expertise, alliances allow firms to create combinations that focus on specific business lines that offer the most potential synergies. These alliances take many forms, from simple marketing agreements to joint ownership of worldwide operations.

One form of corporate alliance is the **joint venture,** in which parts of companies are joined to achieve specific, limited objectives.[34] A joint venture is controlled by a management team consisting of representatives of the two (or more) parent companies. Joint ventures have been used often by U.S., Japanese, and European firms to share technology and/or marketing expertise. For example, Whirlpool announced a joint venture with the Dutch electronics giant Philips to produce appliances under Philips's brand names in five European countries. By joining with their foreign counterparts, U.S. firms are gaining a stronger foothold in Europe. Although alliances are new to some firms, they are established practices to others. For example, Corning Glass now obtains over half of its profits from 23 joint ventures, two-thirds of them with foreign companies representing almost all of Europe, as well as Japan, China, South Korea, and Australia.

A recent study of 345 corporate alliances found that the stock prices of both partners in an alliance tended to increase when the alliance was announced, with an average abnormal return of about 0.64% on the day of the announcement.[35] About 43% of the alliances were marketing agreements, 14% were R&D agreements, 11% were for licensing technology, 7% for technology transfers, and 25% were for some combination of the four basic reasons. Although most alliances

---

[34]Cross-licensing, consortia, joint bidding, and franchising are still other ways for firms to combine resources. For more information on joint ventures, see Sanford V. Berg, Jerome Duncan, and Phillip Friedman, *Joint Venture Strategies and Corporate Innovation* (Cambridge, MA: Oelgeschlager, Gunn and Hain, 1982).

[35]See Su Han Chan, John W. Kensinger, Arthur J. Keown, and John D. Martin, "When Do Strategic Alliances Create Shareholder Value?" *Journal of Applied Corporate Finance,* Winter 1999, pp. 82–87.

were for marketing agreements, the market reacted most favorably when the alliance was for technology sharing between two firms in the same industry. The study also found that the typical alliance lasted at least 5 years, and the allied firms had better operating performance than their industry peers during this period.

SELF-TEST
What is the difference between a merger and a corporate alliance?

What is a joint venture? Give some reasons why joint ventures may be advantageous to the parties involved.

25.18 Leveraged Buyouts

In a **leveraged buyout (LBO)** a small group of investors, usually including current management, acquires a firm in a transaction financed largely by debt. The debt is serviced with funds generated by the acquired company's operations and, often, by the sale of some of its assets. Generally, the acquiring group plans to run the acquired company for a number of years, boost its sales and profits, and then take it public again as a stronger company. In other instances, the LBO firm plans to sell off divisions to other firms that can gain synergies. In either case, the acquiring group expects to make a substantial profit from the LBO, but the inherent risks are great due to the heavy use of financial leverage. To illustrate the profit potential, Kohlberg Kravis Roberts & Company (KKR), a leading LBO specialist firm, averaged a spectacular 50% annual return on its LBO investments during the 1980s. However, high stock prices for target firms have dampened the returns on recent LBO investments, so current activity is slower than in its heyday of the 1980s.

An illustration of an LBO was KKR's buyout of RJR Nabisco. RJR, a leading producer of tobacco and food products with brands such as Winston, Camel, Planters, Ritz, Oreo, and Del Monte, was trading at about $55 a share in October 1988. Then, F. Ross Johnson, the company's chairman and CEO, announced a $75-a-share, or $17.6 billion, offer to outside stockholders in a plan to take the firm private. This deal, if completed, would have been the largest business transaction up to that time. After the announcement, RJR's stock price soared from $55 to $77.25, which indicated that investors thought the final price would be even higher than Johnson's bid. A few days later KKR offered $90 per share, or $20.6 billion. The battle between the two bidders raged until late November, when RJR's board accepted KKR's final bid of cash and securities worth about $106 a share, for a total value of about $25 billion. Of course, the investment bankers' fees reflected the record size of the deal—the bankers received almost $400 million, with Drexel Burnham Lambert alone getting over $200 million. Johnson lost his job, but he walked away with a multimillion-dollar golden parachute.

KKR wasted no time in restructuring the newly private RJR. In June 1989, RJR sold its five European businesses to France's BSN for $2.5 billion. Then, in September RJR sold the tropical fruit portion of its Del Monte foods unit to Polly Peck, a London-based food company, for $875 million. In the same month, RJR sold the Del Monte canned foods business to an LBO group led by Citicorp Venture Capital for $1.48 billion. Next, in October 1990 RJR sold its Baby Ruth, Butterfinger, and Pearson candy businesses to Nestlé, a Swiss company, for $370 million. In total, RJR sold off more than $5 billion worth of businesses in 1990 to help pay down the tremendous debt taken on in the LBO. In addition to asset sales, in 1991 RJR went public again by issuing more than $1 billion in new common stock, which placed about 25% of the firm's common stock in public hands. Also, as the firm's credit rating improved due to the retirement of some of its debt,

RJR issued about $1 billion of new debt at significantly lower rates and used the proceeds to retire even more of its high-cost debt.

The RJR Nabisco story is the classic LBO tale—a company is taken private in a highly leveraged deal, the private firm's high-cost junk debt is reduced through asset sales, and finally the company again goes public, which gives the original LBO dealmakers the opportunity to "cash out." This story, however, did not have a fairy-tale ending. When KKR finally sold the last of its RJR shares in early 1995, it made a profit of about $60 million on a $3.1 billion investment, hardly a stellar return. The best a KKR spokesman could say about the deal was that "it preserved investors' equity." The transaction was largely financed by outside investors, with KKR putting up only $126 million of the original investment. Even though the return on their investment was the same as that received by outside investors, KKR earned an additional $500 million in transactions, advisor, management, and directors' fees.

Regardless of the outcome of the RJR Nabisco deal, there have been some spectacularly successful LBOs. For example, in an early deal that helped fuel the LBO wave, William Simon and Raymond Chambers bought Gibson Greeting Cards in 1982 for $1 million in equity and $79 million in debt. Less than 18 months later, Simon's personal investment of $330,000 was worth $66 million in cash and stock. However, there have also been some spectacular failures. For example, in 1988 Revco became the first large LBO to file for Chapter 11 bankruptcy. It turned out that sales were nearly $1 billion short of the $3.4 billion forecasted at the time of the drugstore chain's buyout.[36]

SELF-TEST

What is an LBO?

Have LBOs been profitable in recent years?

What actions do companies typically take to meet the large debt burdens resulting from LBOs?

How do LBOs typically affect bondholders?

25.19 Divestitures

There are four types of **divestitures. Sale to another firm** generally involves the sale of an entire division or unit, usually for cash but sometimes for stock in the acquiring firm. In a **spin-off,** the firm's existing stockholders are given new stock representing separate ownership rights in the division that was divested. The division establishes its own board of directors and officers, and it becomes a separate company. The stockholders end up owning shares of two firms instead of one, but no cash has been transferred. In a **carve-out,** a minority interest in a corporate subsidiary is sold to new shareholders, so the parent gains new equity financing yet retains control. Finally, in a **liquidation** the assets of a division are sold off piecemeal, rather than as an operating entity. To illustrate the different types of divestitures, we now present some examples.

---

[36]See Karen H. Wruck, "What Really Went Wrong at Revco?" *Journal of Applied Corporate Finance*, Summer 1991, pp. 79–92. For a more detailed discussion of the impact of the RJR LBO on the firm's different classes of investors, see Nancy Mohan and Carl R. Chen, "A Review of the RJR-Nabisco Buyout," *Journal of Applied Corporate Finance*, Summer 1990, pp. 102–108. For interesting discussions of highly leveraged takeovers, see Martin S. Fridson, "What Went Wrong with the Highly Leveraged Deals? (Or, All Variety of Agency Costs)," *Journal of Applied Corporate Finance*, Fall 1991, pp. 47–57; and "The Economic Consequences of High Leverage and Stock Market Pressures on Corporate Management: A Round Table Discussion," *Journal of Applied Corporate Finance*, Summer 1990, pp. 6–57. Also see Jay R. Allen, "LBOs—The Evolution of Financial Strategies and Structures," *Journal of Applied Corporate Finance*, Winter 1996, pp. 18–29; George P. Baker, "Beatrice: A Study in the Creation and Destruction of Value," *Journal of Finance*, July 1992, pp. 1081–1119; George P. Baker and Karen H. Wruck, "Lessons from a Middle Market LBO: The Case of O. M. Scott," *Journal of Applied Corporate Finance*, Spring 1991, pp. 46–58.

PepsiCo spun off its fast-food business, which included Pizza Hut, Taco Bell, and Kentucky Fried Chicken. The spun-off businesses now operate under the name Yum! Brands. PepsiCo originally acquired the chains because it wanted to increase the distribution channels for its soft drinks. Over time, however, PepsiCo began to realize that the soft-drink and restaurant businesses were quite different, and synergies between them were less than anticipated. The spin-off was part of PepsiCo's attempt to once again focus on its core business. However, PepsiCo tried to maintain these distribution channels by signing long-term contracts that ensure that PepsiCo products will be sold exclusively in each of the three spun-off chains.

United Airlines sold its Hilton International Hotels subsidiary to Ladbroke Group PLC of Britain for $1.1 billion and also sold its Hertz rental car unit and its Westin hotel group. The sales culminated a disastrous strategic move by United to build a full-service travel empire. The failed strategy resulted in the firing of Richard J. Ferris, the company's chairman. The move into nonairline travel-related businesses had been viewed by many analysts as a mistake, because there were few synergies to be gained. Further, analysts feared that United's managers, preoccupied by running hotels and rental car companies, would not maintain the company's focus in the highly competitive airline industry. The funds raised by the divestitures were paid out to United's shareholders as a special dividend.

General Motors (GM) spun off its Electronic Data Systems (EDS) subsidiary. EDS, a computer services company founded in 1962 by Ross Perot, prospered as an independent company until it was acquired by GM in 1984. The rationale for the acquisition was that EDS's expertise would help GM both operate better in the information age and build cars that encompassed leading-edge computer technology. However, the spread of desktop computers and the movement of companies to downsize their internal computer staffs caused EDS's non-GM business to soar. Ownership by GM hampered EDS's ability to strike alliances and, in some cases, to enter into business agreements. The best way for EDS to compete in its industry was as an independent; hence it was spun off.

As these examples illustrate, the reasons for divestitures vary widely. Sometimes the market feels more comfortable when firms "stick to their knitting"; the PepsiCo and United Airlines divestitures are examples. Sometimes companies need cash either to finance expansion in their primary business lines or to reduce a large debt burden, and divestitures can be used to raise this cash. The divestitures also show that running a business is a dynamic process—conditions change, corporate strategies change in response, and as a result firms alter their asset portfolios by acquisitions and/or divestitures. Some divestitures are to unload losing assets that would otherwise drag the company down.

In general, the empirical evidence shows that the market reacts favorably to divestitures, with the divesting company typically having a small increase in stock price on the day of the announcement. The announcement-day returns are largest for companies that "undo" previous conglomerate mergers by divesting businesses in unrelated areas.[37] Studies also show that divestitures generally lead to superior operating performance for both the parent and the divested company.[38]

SELF-TEST   What are some types of divestitures?

What are some motives for divestitures?

---

[37]For details, see Jeffrey W. Allen, Scott L. Lummer, John J. McConnell, and Debra K. Reed, "Can Takeover Losses Explain Spin-Off Gains?" *Journal of Financial and Quantitative Analysis*, December 1995, pp. 465–485.
[38]See Shane A. Johnson, Daniel P. Klein, and Verne L. Thibodeaux, "The Effects of Spin-Offs on Corporate Investment and Performance," *Journal of Financial Research*, Summer 1996, pp. 293–307. Also see Steven Kaplan and Michael S. Weisbach, "The Success of Acquisitions: Evidence from Divestitures," *Journal of Finance*, March 1992, pp. 107–138.

25.20 Holding Companies

Holding companies date from 1889, when New Jersey became the first state to pass a law permitting corporations to be formed for the sole purpose of owning the stocks of other companies. Many of the advantages and disadvantages of holding companies are identical to those of any large-scale organization. Whether a company is organized on a divisional basis or with subsidiaries kept as separate companies does not affect the basic reasons for conducting a large-scale, multiproduct, multiplant operation. However, as we show next, the use of holding companies to control large-scale operations has some distinct advantages and disadvantages.

Advantages of Holding Companies

1. *Control with fractional ownership.* Through a holding company operation, a firm may buy 5%, 10%, or 50% of the stock of another corporation. Such fractional ownership may be sufficient to give the holding company effective working control over the operations of the company in which it has acquired stock ownership. Working control is often considered to entail more than 25% of the common stock, but it can be as low as 10% if the stock is widely distributed. One financier says that the attitude of management is more important than the number of shares owned: "If management thinks you can control the company, then you do." In addition, control on a very slim margin can be held through relationships with large stockholders outside the holding company group.

2. *Isolation of risks.* Because the various **operating companies** in a holding company system are separate legal entities, the obligations of any one unit are separate from those of the other units. Therefore, catastrophic losses incurred by one unit of the holding company system may not be translatable into claims on the assets of the other units. However, we should note that while this is a customary generalization, it is not always valid. First, the **parent company** may feel obligated to make good on the subsidiary's debts, even though it is not legally bound to do so, in order to keep its good name and to retain customers. An example of this was American Express's payment of more than $100 million in connection with a swindle that was the responsibility of one of its subsidiaries. Second, a parent company may feel obligated to supply capital to an affiliate in order to protect its initial investment; General Public Utilities' continued support of its subsidiary's Three Mile Island nuclear plant after the accident at that plant is an example. And, third, when lending to one of the units of a holding company system, an astute loan officer may require a guarantee by the parent holding company. To some degree, therefore, the assets in the various elements of a holding company are not really separate. Still, a catastrophic loss, as could occur if a drug company's subsidiary distributed a batch of toxic medicine, may be avoided.[39]

Disadvantages of Holding Companies

1. *Partial multiple taxation.* Provided the holding company owns at least 80% of a subsidiary's voting stock, the IRS permits the filing of consolidated returns, in

---

[39]Note, though, that the parent company would still be held accountable for such losses if it were deemed to exercise operating control over the subsidiary. Thus, Union Carbide was held responsible for its subsidiary's Bhopal, India, disaster.

which case dividends received by the parent are not taxed. However, if less than 80% of the stock is owned, then tax returns cannot be consolidated. Firms that own more than 20% but less than 80% of another corporation can deduct 80% of the dividends received, while firms that own less than 20% may deduct only 70% of the dividends received. This partial double taxation somewhat offsets the benefits of holding company control with limited ownership, but whether the tax penalty is sufficient to offset other possible advantages varies from case to case.

2. *Ease of enforced dissolution.* It is relatively easy to require dissolution by disposal of stock ownership of a holding company operation found guilty of antitrust violations. For instance, in the 1950s DuPont was required to dispose of its 23% stock interest in General Motors Corporation, acquired in the early 1920s. Because there was no fusion between the corporations, there were no difficulties from an operating standpoint in requiring the separation of the two companies. However, if complete amalgamation had taken place, it would have been much more difficult to break up the company after so many years, and the likelihood of forced divestiture would have been reduced.

Holding Companies as a Leveraging Device

The holding company vehicle has been used to obtain huge degrees of financial leverage. In the 1920s, several tiers of holding companies were established in the electric utility, railroad, and other industries. In those days, an operating company at the bottom of the pyramid might have $100 million of assets, financed by $50 million of debt and $50 million of equity. Then, a first-tier holding company might own the stock of the operating firm as its only asset and be financed with $25 million of debt and $25 million of equity. A second-tier holding company, which owned the stock of the first-tier company, might be financed with $12.5 million of debt and $12.5 million of equity. Such systems were extended to five or six levels. With six holding companies, $100 million of operating assets could be controlled at the top by only $0.78 million of equity, and the operating assets would have to provide enough cash income to support $99.22 million of debt. *Such a holding company system is highly leveraged—its consolidated debt ratio is 99.22%, even though each of the individual components shows only a 50% debt/assets ratio.* Because of this consolidated leverage, even a small decline in profits at the operating company level could bring the whole system down like a house of cards. This situation existed in the electric utility industry in the 1920s, and the Depression of the 1930s wreaked havoc with the holding companies and led to federal legislation that constrained holding companies in that industry.

SELF-TEST What is a holding company?

What are some of the advantages of holding companies? What are some of the disadvantages?

Summary

This chapter included discussions of mergers, divestitures, holding companies, and LBOs. The majority of the discussion in this chapter focused on mergers. We discussed the rationale for mergers, different types of mergers, the level of merger activity, merger regulation, and merger analysis. We also showed how to use the adjusted present value method to value target firms. In addition, we explained how the acquiring firm can structure its takeover bid, the different ways accountants treat mergers, and investment bankers' roles in arranging and financing mergers. Furthermore, we discussed two cooperative arrangements that fall short of mergers: corporate (or strategic) alliances and joint ventures. The key concepts covered are listed below:

- A **merger** occurs when two firms combine to form a single company. The primary motives for mergers are (1) synergy, (2) tax considerations, (3) purchase of assets below their replacement costs, (4) diversification, (5) gaining control over a larger enterprise, and (6) breakup value.
- Mergers can provide economic benefits through **economies of scale** and through putting assets in the hands of **more efficient managers.** However, mergers also have the potential for reducing competition, and for this reason they are carefully regulated by government agencies.
- In most mergers, one company (the **acquiring company**) initiates action to take over another (the **target company**).
- A **horizontal merger** occurs when two firms in the same line of business combine.
- A **vertical merger** combines a firm with one of its customers or suppliers.
- A **congeneric merger** involves firms in related industries, but where no customer-supplier relationship exists.
- A **conglomerate merger** occurs when firms in totally different industries combine.
- In a **friendly merger,** the managements of both firms approve the merger, whereas in a **hostile merger,** the target firm's management opposes it.
- An **operating merger** is one in which the operations of the two firms are combined. A **financial merger** is one in which the firms continue to operate separately; hence, no operating economies are expected.
- In a typical **merger analysis,** the key issues to be resolved are (1) the price to be paid for the target firm and (2) the employment/control situation. If the merger is a consolidation of two relatively equal firms, at issue is the percentage of ownership each merger partner's shareholders will receive.
- Four methods are commonly used to determine the **value of the target firm:** (1) **market multiple analysis,** (2) the **corporate valuation model,** (3) the **free cash flow to equity (FCFE) model,** and (4) the **adjusted present value (APV) model.** The three cash flow models give the same value if implemented correctly, but the APV model is the easiest to implement when the capital structure is changing.
- For accounting purposes, mergers are handled as a **purchase.**
- A **joint venture** is a **corporate alliance** in which two or more companies combine some of their resources to achieve a specific, limited objective.
- A **leveraged buyout (LBO)** is a transaction in which a firm's publicly owned stock is acquired in a mostly debt-financed tender offer, and a privately owned, highly leveraged firm results. Often, the firm's own management initiates the LBO.
- A **divestiture** is the sale of some of a company's operating assets. A divestiture may involve (1) selling an operating unit to another firm, (2) **spinning off** a unit as a separate company, (3) **carving out** a unit by selling a minority interest, and (4) the outright **liquidation** of a unit's assets.
- The **reasons for divestiture** include (1) to settle antitrust suits, (2) to clarify what a company actually does, (3) to enable management to concentrate on a particular type of activity, and (4) to raise the capital needed to strengthen the corporation's core business.

- A **holding company** is a corporation that owns sufficient stock in another firm to control it. The holding company is also known as the **parent company,** and the companies that it controls are called **subsidiaries,** or **operating companies.**
- Holding company operations are advantageous because (1) control can often be obtained for a smaller cash outlay, (2) risks may be segregated, and (3) regulated companies can operate separate subsidiaries for their regulated and unregulated businesses.
- Disadvantages to holding company operations include (1) tax penalties and (2) the fact that incomplete ownership, if it exists, can lead to control problems.

Questions

(25-1)   Define each of the following terms:
a.   Synergy; merger
b.   Horizontal merger; vertical merger; congeneric merger; conglomerate merger
c.   Friendly merger; hostile merger; defensive merger; tender offer; target company; breakup value; acquiring company
d.   Operating merger; financial merger
e.   Adjusted present value (APV) model
f.   Free cash flow to equity
g.   Purchase accounting
h.   White knight; poison pill; golden parachute; proxy fight
i.   Joint venture; corporate alliance
j.   Divestiture; spin-off; leveraged buyout (LBO)
k.   Holding company; operating company; parent company
l.   Arbitrage; risk arbitrage

(25-2)   Four economic classifications of mergers are (1) horizontal, (2) vertical, (3) conglomerate, and (4) congeneric. Explain the significance of these terms in merger analysis with regard to (a) the likelihood of governmental intervention and (b) possibilities for operating synergy.

(25-3)   Firm A wants to acquire Firm B. Firm B's management agrees that the merger is a good idea. Might a tender offer be used?

(25-4)   Distinguish between operating mergers and financial mergers.

(25-5)   Distinguish between the APV, FCFE, and corporate valuation models.

Self-Test Problem   Solution Appears in Appendix A

(ST-1)   Green Mountain Breweries is considering an acquisition of Ritta Markets. Ritta currently has a cost of equity of 10%; 25% of its financing is in the form of 6% debt, the rest in common equity. Its federal-plus-state tax rate is 40%. After the acquisition,

Green Mountain expects Ritta to have the following FCFs and interest payments for the next 3 years (in millions):

	Year 1	Year 2	Year 3
FCF	$10.00	$20.00	$25.00
Interest expense	28.00	24.00	20.28

After this, the free cash flows are expected to grow at a constant rate of 5%, and the capital structure will stabilize at 35% debt with an interest rate of 7%.

a.   What is Ritta's unlevered cost of equity? What are its levered cost of equity and cost of capital for the post-horizon period?

b.   Using the adjusted present value approach, what is Ritta's value of operations to Green Mountain?

Problems   Answers Appear in Appendix B

The following information is required to work Problems 25-1 through 25-4.

Hastings Corporation is interested in acquiring Vandell Corporation. Vandell has 1 million shares outstanding and a target capital structure consisting of 30% debt. Vandell's debt interest rate is 8%. Assume that the risk-free rate of interest is 5% and the market risk premium is 6%. Both Vandell and Hastings face a 40% tax rate.

Easy Problem 1

(25-1)
Valuation

Vandell's free cash flow (FCF_0) is $2 million per year and is expected to grow at a constant rate of 5% a year; its beta is 1.4. What is the value of Vandell's operations? If Vandell has $10.82 million in debt, what is the current value of Vandell's stock? (Hint: Use the corporate valuation model of Chapter 15.)

Intermediate Problems 2–3

(25-2)
Merger Valuation

Hastings estimates that if it acquires Vandell, interest payments will be $1,500,000 per year for 3 years, after which the current target capital structure of 30% debt will be maintained. Interest in the fourth year will be $1.472 million, after which interest and the tax shield will grow at 5%. Synergies will cause the free cash flows to be $2.5 million, $2.9 million, $3.4 million, and then $3.57 million, in Years 1 through 4, after which the free cash flows will grow at a 5% rate. What is the unlevered value of Vandell and what is the value of its tax shields? What is the per share value of Vandell to Hastings Corporation? Assume Vandell now has $10.82 million in debt.

(25-3)
Merger Bid

On the basis of your answers to Problems 25-1 and 25-2, if Hastings were to acquire Vandell, what would be the range of possible prices that it could bid for each share of Vandell common stock?

Challenging Problems 4–6

(25-4)
Merger Valuation with Change in Capital Structure

Assuming the same information as for Problem 25-2, suppose Hastings will increase Vandell's level of debt at the end of Year 3 to $30.6 million so that the target capital structure is now 45% debt. Assume that with this higher level of debt the interest rate would be 8.5% and that interest payments in Year 4 are based on the new debt level from the end of Year 3 and new interest rate. Again, free cash flows and tax shields are projected to grow at 5% after Year 4. What are the values of the unlevered firm and the tax shield, and what is the maximum price Hastings would bid for Vandell now?

(25-5)
Merger Analysis

Marston Marble Corporation is considering a merger with the Conroy Concrete Company. Conroy is a publicly traded company, and its beta is 1.30. Conroy has been barely profitable, so it has paid an average of only 20% in taxes during the last several years. In addition, it uses little debt, having a target ratio of just 25%, with the cost of debt 9%.

If the acquisition were made, Marston would operate Conroy as a separate, wholly owned subsidiary. Marston would pay taxes on a consolidated basis, and the tax rate would therefore increase to 35%. Marston also would increase the debt capitalization in the Conroy subsidiary to $w_d = 40\%$ for a total of $22.27 million in debt by the end of Year 4 and pay 9.5% on the debt. Marston's acquisition department estimates that Conroy, if acquired, would generate the following free cash flows and interest expenses (in millions of dollars) in Years 1–5:

Year	Free Cash Flows	Interest Expense
1	$1.30	$1.2
2	1.50	1.7
3	1.75	2.8
4	2.00	2.1
5	2.12	?

In Year 5 Conroy's interest expense would be based on its beginning-of-year (that is, the end-of-Year-4) debt, and in subsequent years both interest expense and free cash flows are projected to grow at a rate of 6%.

These cash flows include all acquisition effects. Marston's cost of equity is 10.5%, its beta is 1.0, and its cost of debt is 9.5%. The risk-free rate is 6%, and the market risk premium is 4.5%.

a. What is the value of Conroy's unlevered operations, and what is the value of Conroy's tax shields under the proposed merger and financing arrangements?

b. What is the dollar value of Conroy's operations? If Conroy has $10 million in debt outstanding, how much would Marston be willing to pay for Conroy?

(25-6)
Merger Valuation with
Change in Capital
Structure

VolWorld Communications Inc., a large telecommunications company, is evaluating the possible acquisition of Bulldog Cable Company (BCC), a regional cable company. VolWorld's analysts project the following post-merger data for BCC (in thousands of dollars, with a December 31 year-end):

	2007	2008	2009	2010	2011	2012
Net sales		$450	$518	$ 555	$ 600	$ 643
Selling and administrative expense		45	53	60	68	73
Interest		40	45	47	52	54
Total net operating capital	$800	850	930	1,005	1,075	1,150

Tax rate after merger: 35%

Cost of goods sold as a percent of sales: 65%

BCC's pre-merger beta: 1.40

Risk-free rate: 6%

Market risk premium: 4%

Terminal growth rate of free cash flows: 7%

If the acquisition is made, it will occur on January 1, 2008. All cash flows shown in the income statements are assumed to occur at the end of the year. BCC currently has a capital structure of 40% debt, which costs 10%, but over the next 4 years VolWorld would increase that to 50%, and the target capital structure would be reached by the start of 2012. BCC, if independent, would pay taxes at 20%, but its income would be taxed at 35% if it were consolidated. BCC's current market-determined beta is 1.40. The cost of goods sold is expected to be 65% of sales.

a.   What is the unlevered cost of equity for BCC?
b.   What are the free cash flows and interest tax shields for the first 5 years?
c.   What is BCC's horizon value of interest tax shields and unlevered horizon value?
d.   What is the value of BCC's equity to VolWorld's shareholders if BCC has $300,000 in debt outstanding now?

Spreadsheet Problem

(25-7)
Build a Model: Merger
Analysis

e-resource

Start with the partial model in the file *FM12 Ch 25 P07 Build a Model.xls* from the textbook's Web site. Wansley Portal Inc., a large Internet service provider, is evaluating the possible acquisition of Alabama Connections Company (ACC), a regional Internet service provider. Wansley's analysts project the following post-merger data for ACC (in thousands of dollars):

	2008	2009	2010	2011	2012
Net sales	$500	$600	$700	$760	$806
Selling and administrative expense	60	70	80	90	96
Interest	30	40	45	60	74

If the acquisition is made, it will occur on January 1, 2008. All cash flows shown in the income statements are assumed to occur at the end of the year. ACC currently has a capital structure of 30% debt, which costs 9%, but Wansley would increase that over time to 40%, costing 10%, if the acquisition were made. ACC, if independent, would pay taxes at 30%, but its income would be taxed at 35% if it were consolidated. ACC's current market-determined beta is 1.40. The cost of goods sold, which includes depreciation, is expected to be 65% of sales, but it could vary somewhat. Required gross investment in operating capital is approximately equal to the depreciation charged, so there will be no investment in net operating capital. The risk-free rate is 7%, and the market risk premium is 6.5%. Wansley currently has $400,000 in debt outstanding.

a.   What is the unlevered cost of equity?
b.   What is the horizon value of the tax shields and the unlevered operations? What is the value of ACC's operations and the value of ACC's equity to Wansley's shareholders?

Cyberproblem

e-resource

Please go to the textbook's Web site to access any Cyberproblems.

Mini Case

Hager's Home Repair Company, a regional hardware chain that specializes in "do-it-yourself" materials and equipment rentals, is cash rich because of several consecutive good years. One of the alternative uses for the excess funds is an acquisition. Doug Zona, Hager's treasurer and your boss, has been asked to place a value on a potential target, Lyons Lighting (LL), a chain that operates in several adjacent states, and he has enlisted your help.

The table below indicates Zona's estimates of LL's earnings potential if it came under Hager's management (in millions of dollars). The interest expense listed here includes the interest (1) on LL's existing debt, which is $55 million at a rate of 9%, and (2) on new debt expected to be issued over time to help finance expansion within the new "L division," the code name given to the target firm. If acquired, LL will face a 40% tax rate.

Security analysts estimate LL's beta to be 1.3. The acquisition would not change Lyons's capital structure, which is 20% debt. Zona realizes that Lyons Lighting's business plan also requires certain levels of operating capital and that the annual investment could be significant. The required levels of total net operating capital are listed below.

Zona estimates the risk-free rate to be 7% and the market risk premium to be 4%. He also estimates that free cash flows after 2012 will grow at a constant rate of 6%. Following are projections for sales and other items.

	2007	2008	2009	2010	2011	2012
Net sales		$ 60.00	$ 90.00	$112.50	$127.50	$139.70
Cost of goods sold (60%)		36.00	54.00	67.50	76.50	83.80
Selling/administrative expense		4.50	6.00	7.50	9.00	11.00
Interest expense		5.00	6.50	6.50	7.00	8.16
Total net operating capital	$150.00	150.00	157.50	163.50	168.00	173.00

Hager's management is new to the merger game, so Zona has been asked to answer some basic questions about mergers as well as to perform the merger analysis. To structure the task, Zona has developed the following questions, which you must answer and then defend to Hager's board.

a. Several reasons have been proposed to justify mergers. Among the more prominent are (1) tax considerations, (2) risk reduction, (3) control, (4) purchase of assets at below-replacement cost, (5) synergy, and (6) globalization. In general, which of the reasons are economically justifiable? Which are not? Which fit the situation at hand? Explain.

b. Briefly describe the differences between a hostile merger and a friendly merger.

c. What are the steps in valuing a merger?

d. Use the data developed in the table to construct the L division's free cash flows for 2008 through 2012. Why are we identifying interest expense separately since it is not normally included in calculating free cash flows or in a capital budgeting cash flow analysis? Why is investment in net operating capital included when calculating the free cash flow?

e. Conceptually, what is the appropriate discount rate to apply to the cash flows developed in part c? What is your actual estimate of this discount rate?

f.   What is the estimated horizon, or continuing, value of the acquisition; that is, what is the estimated value of the L division's cash flows beyond 2012? What is LL's value to Hager's shareholders? Suppose another firm were evaluating LL as an acquisition candidate. Would they obtain the same value? Explain.

g.   Assume that LL has 20 million shares outstanding. These shares are traded relatively infrequently, but the last trade, made several weeks ago, was at a price of $11 per share. Should Hager's make an offer for Lyons Lighting? If so, how much should it offer per share?

h.   How would the analysis be different if Hager's intended to recapitalize LL with 40% debt costing 10% at the end of 4 years? This amounts to $221.6 million in debt as of the end of 2011.

i.   There has been considerable research undertaken to determine whether mergers really create value and, if so, how this value is shared between the parties involved. What are the results of this research?

j.   What method is used to account for mergers?

k.   What merger-related activities are undertaken by investment bankers?

l.   What is a leveraged buyout (LBO)? What are some of the advantages and disadvantages of going private?

m.   What are the major types of divestitures? What motivates firms to divest assets?

n.   What are holding companies? What are their advantages and disadvantages?

Selected Additional Cases

*The following cases from Textchoice, Cengage Learning's online library, cover many of the concepts discussed in this chapter and are available at **http://www.textchoice2.com**.*

Klein-Brigham Series:
Case 40, "Nina's Fashions, Inc."; Case 53, "Nero's Pasta, Inc."; and Case 70, "Computer Concepts/CompuTech."

Multinational Financial Management*

From the end of World War II until the 1970s, the United States dominated the world economy. However, that situation no longer exists. Raw materials, finished goods, services, and money flow freely across most national boundaries, as do innovative ideas and new technologies. World-class U.S. companies are making breakthroughs in foreign labs, obtaining capital from foreign investors, and putting foreign employees on the fast track to the top. Dozens of top U.S. manufacturers, including Dow Chemical, Colgate-Palmolive, Hewlett-Packard, and Xerox, sell more of their products outside the United States than they do at home. Service firms are not far behind, as Citigroup, Disney, McDonald's, and Time Warner all receive more than 20% of their revenues from foreign sales.

Successful global companies must conduct business in different economies, and they must be sensitive to the many subtleties of different cultures and political systems. Accordingly, they find it useful to blend into the foreign landscape to win product acceptance and avoid political problems.

At the same time, foreign-based multinationals are arriving on American shores in ever greater numbers. Sweden's ABB, the Netherlands' Philips, France's Thomson, and Japan's Toyota and Honda are all waging campaigns to be identified as American companies that employ Americans, transfer technology to America, and help the U.S. trade balance. Few Americans know or care that Thomson owns the RCA and General Electric names in consumer electronics, or that Philips owns Magnavox.

The emergence of "world companies" raises a host of questions for governments. For example, should domestic firms be favored, or does it make no difference what a company's nationality is as long as it provides domestic jobs? Should a company make an effort to keep jobs in its home country, or should it produce goods and services where costs are lowest? What nation controls the technology developed by a multinational corporation, particularly if the technology can be used in military applications? Must a multinational company adhere to rules imposed in its home country with respect to its operations outside the home country? Keep these questions in mind as you read this chapter. When you finish it, you should have a better appreciation of both the problems facing governments and the difficult but profitable opportunities facing managers of multinational companies.

*This chapter benefited from the help of Professor Roy Crum of the University of Florida and Subu Venkataraman of Morgan Stanley.

e-resource

The textbook's Web site contains an *Excel* file that will guide you through the chapter's calculations. The file for this chapter is ***FM12 Ch 26 Tool Kit.xls,*** and we encourage you to open the file and follow along as you read the chapter.

Managers of multinational companies must deal with a wide range of issues that are not present when a company operates in a single country. In this chapter, we highlight the key differences between multinational and domestic corporations, and we discuss the effects these differences have on the financial management of multinational businesses.

26.1 Multinational, or Global, Corporations

The term **multinational,** or **global, corporation** is used to describe a firm that operates in an integrated fashion in a number of countries. During the past 20 years, a new and fundamentally different form of international commercial activity has developed, and this has greatly increased worldwide economic and political interdependence. Rather than merely buying resources from and selling goods to foreign nations, multinational firms now make direct investments in fully integrated operations, from extraction of raw materials, through the manufacturing process, to distribution to consumers throughout the world. Today, multinational corporate networks control a large and growing share of the world's technological, marketing, and productive resources.

Companies, both U.S. and foreign, "go global" for six primary reasons:

1. *To broaden their markets.* After a company has saturated its home market, growth opportunities are often better in foreign markets. Thus, such home-grown firms as Coca-Cola and McDonald's are aggressively expanding into overseas markets, and foreign firms such as Sony and Toshiba now dominate the U.S. consumer electronics market. Also, as products become more complex, and development becomes more expensive, it is necessary to sell more units to cover overhead costs, so larger markets are critical. Thus, movie companies have "gone global" to get the volume necessary to support pictures such as *Lord of the Rings*.

2. *To seek raw materials.* Many U.S. oil companies, such as ExxonMobil, have major subsidiaries around the world to ensure access to the basic resources needed to sustain the companies' primary business lines.

3. *To seek new technology.* No single nation holds a commanding advantage in all technologies, so companies are scouring the globe for leading scientific and design ideas. For example, Xerox has introduced more than 80 different office copiers in the United States that were engineered and built by its Japanese joint venture, Fuji Xerox. Similarly, versions of the superconcentrated detergent that Procter & Gamble first formulated in Japan in response to a rival's product are now being marketed in Europe and the United States.

4. *To seek production efficiency.* Companies in high-cost countries are shifting production to low-cost regions. For example, GE has production and assembly plants in Mexico, South Korea, and Singapore, and Japanese manufacturers are shifting some of their production to lower-cost countries in the Pacific Rim. BMW, in response to high production costs in Germany, has built assembly plants in the United States. The ability to shift production from country to country has important implications for labor costs in all countries. For example, when Xerox threatened to move its copier rebuilding work to Mexico, its union in Rochester agreed to work rule changes and productivity improvements that kept the operation in the United States. Some multinational companies make decisions almost daily on where to shift production. When Dow Chemical saw European demand for a certain solvent declining, the company scaled

back production at a German plant and shifted its production to another chemical that had previously been imported from the United States. Relying on complex computer models for making such decisions, Dow runs its plants at peak capacity and thus keeps capital costs down.

5. *To avoid political and regulatory hurdles.* The primary reason Japanese auto companies moved production to the United States was to get around U.S. import quotas. Now Honda, Nissan, Toyota, Mazda, and Mitsubishi are all assembling vehicles in the United States. One of the factors that prompted U.S. pharmaceutical maker SmithKline and Britain's Beecham to merge was that they wanted to avoid licensing and regulatory delays in their largest markets, Western Europe and the United States. Now SmithKline Beecham can identify itself as an inside player in both Europe and the United States. Similarly, when Germany's BASF launched biotechnology research at home, it confronted legal and political challenges from the environmentally conscious Green movement. In response, BASF shifted its cancer and immune system research to two laboratories in the Boston suburbs. This location is attractive not only because of its large number of engineers and scientists but also because the Boston area has resolved controversies involving safety, animal rights, and the environment. "We decided it would be better to have the laboratories located where we have fewer insecurities about what will happen in the future," said Rolf-Dieter Acker, BASF's director of biotechnology research.

6. *To diversify.* By establishing worldwide production facilities and markets, firms can cushion the impact of adverse economic trends in any single country. For example, General Motors softened the blow of poor sales in the United States during a recent recession with strong sales by its European subsidiaries. In general, geographic diversification works because the economic ups and downs of different countries are not perfectly correlated. Therefore, companies investing overseas benefit from diversification in the same way that individuals benefit from investing in a broad portfolio of stocks.

Interesting reports about the effect of trade on the U.S. economy can be found on the United States Trade Representative's home page at **http://www.ustr.gov.**

Over the past 10 to 15 years, there has been an increasing amount of investment in the United States by foreign corporations and in foreign nations by U.S. corporations. This trend is important because of its implications for eroding the traditional doctrine of independence and self-reliance that has been a hallmark of U.S. policy. Just as U.S. corporations with extensive overseas operations are said to use their economic power to exert substantial economic and political influence over host governments in many parts of the world, it is feared that foreign corporations are gaining similar sway over U.S. policy. These developments suggest an increasing degree of mutual influence and interdependence among business enterprises and nations, to which the United States is not immune.

SELF-TEST

What is a multinational corporation?

Why do companies "go global"?

26.2 Multinational versus Domestic Financial Management

In theory, the concepts and procedures discussed in earlier chapters are valid for both domestic and multinational operations. However, six major factors distinguish financial management in firms operating entirely within a single country from that of firms operating globally:

1. *Different currency denominations.* Cash flows in various parts of a multinational corporate system will be denominated in different currencies. Hence, an analysis of exchange rates must be included in all financial analyses.

2. *Economic and legal ramifications.* Each country has its own unique economic and legal systems, and these differences can cause significant problems when a corporation tries to coordinate and control its worldwide operations. For example, differences in tax laws among countries can cause a given economic transaction to have strikingly different after-tax consequences, depending on where the transaction occurs. Similarly, differences in legal systems of host nations, such as the Common Law of Great Britain versus the French Civil Law, complicate matters ranging from the simple recording of business transactions to the role played by the judiciary in resolving conflicts. Such differences can restrict multinational corporations' flexibility in deploying resources and can even make procedures that are required in one part of the company illegal in another part. These differences also make it difficult for executives trained in one country to move easily to another.

3. *Language differences.* The ability to communicate is critical in all business transactions, and here U.S. citizens are often at a disadvantage because we are generally fluent only in English, while European and Japanese businesspeople are usually fluent in several languages, including English. Thus, they can penetrate our markets more easily than we can penetrate theirs.

4. *Cultural differences.* Even within geographic regions that are considered relatively homogeneous, different countries have unique cultural heritages that shape values and influence the conduct of business. Multinational corporations find that matters such as defining the appropriate goals of the firm, attitudes toward risk, dealings with employees, and the ability to curtail unprofitable operations vary dramatically from one country to the next.

5. *Role of governments.* Most financial models assume the existence of a competitive marketplace in which the terms of trade are determined by the participants. The government, through its power to establish basic ground rules, is involved in the process, but its role is minimal. Thus, the market provides the primary barometer of success, and it gives the best clues about what must be done to remain competitive. This view of the process is reasonably correct for the United States and Western Europe, but it does not accurately describe the situation in most of the world. Frequently, the terms under which companies compete, the actions that must be taken or avoided, and the terms of trade on various transactions are determined not in the marketplace but by direct negotiation between host governments and multinational corporations. Such negotiation is essentially a political process, and it must be treated as such. Thus, our traditional financial models have to be recast to include political and other noneconomic aspects of the decision process.

6. *Political risk.* A nation is free to place constraints on the transfer of corporate resources and even to expropriate, without compensation, assets within its boundaries. This is political risk, and it tends to be largely a given rather than a variable that can be changed by negotiation. Political risk varies from country to country, and it must be addressed explicitly in any financial analysis. Another aspect of political risk is terrorism against U.S. firms or executives. For example, U.S. and Japanese executives have been kidnapped and held for ransom—with some killed to prove that the kidnappers were serious—in several South American countries.

These six factors complicate financial management, and they increase the risks faced by multinational firms. However, the prospects for high returns, diversification benefits, and other factors make it worthwhile for firms to accept these risks and learn how to manage them.

SELF-TEST Identify and briefly discuss six major factors that complicate financial management in multinational firms.

26.3 Exchange Rates

An **exchange rate** specifies the number of units of a given currency that can be purchased with one unit of another currency. Exchange rates appear daily in the financial sections of newspapers, such as *The Wall Street Journal*, and at financial Web sites, such as **http://www.bloomberg.com.** The values shown in Column 1 of Table 26-1 are the number of U.S. dollars required to purchase one unit of a foreign currency; this is called a **direct quotation.** Direct quotations have a dollar sign in their quotation and state the number of dollars per foreign currency unit, such as dollars per euro. Thus, the direct U.S. dollar quotation for the euro is $1.2841, because 1 euro could be bought for 1.2841 dollars.

The exchange rates given in Column 2 represent the number of units of a foreign currency that can be purchased for one U.S. dollar; these are called **indirect quotations.** Indirect quotations often begin with the foreign currency's equivalent to the dollar sign and express the foreign currency per dollar, such as euros per dollar. Thus, the indirect quotation for the euro is €0.7788. (The "€" stands for *euro*, and it is analogous to the symbol "$.")

Normal practice in currency trading centers is to use the indirect quotations (Column 2) for all currencies other than British pounds and euros, for which the direct quotations are given. Thus we speak of the pound as "selling at 1.9069 dollars, or at $1.9069," and the euro as "selling at $1.2841." For all other currencies,

---

Table 26-1

Selected Exchange Rates

	Direct Quotation: U.S. Dollars Required to Buy One Unit of Foreign Currency (1)	Indirect Quotation: Number of Units of Foreign Currency per U.S. Dollar (2)
Canadian dollar	0.8930	1.1198
Japanese yen	0.0087	115.1145
Mexican peso	0.0919	10.8778
Swiss franc	0.8157	1.2259
U.K. (British) pound	1.9069	0.5244
Euro	1.2841	0.7788

Note: The financial press usually quotes British pounds and euros as direct quotations, so Column 2 equals 1.0 divided by Column 1 for these currencies. The financial press usually quotes all other currencies as indirect quotations, so Column 1 equals 1.0 divided by Column 2 for these currencies.

Source: The Wall Street Journal, **http://online.wsj.com;** quotes for August 7, 2006.

The Bloomberg World Currency Values site provides up-to-the-minute foreign currency values versus the U.S. dollar, as well as a cross-currency table similar to that found in *The Wall Street Journal* for the world's major currencies. The site can be accessed at **http://www .bloomberg.com/ markets/currencies/ fxc.html.**

the normal convention is to use indirect quotations. For example, for the Japanese yen, we would quote the dollars as "being at ¥115.1145," where the "¥" stands for *yen* and is analogous to the symbol "$." This convention eliminates confusion when comparing quotations from one trading center—say, New York—with those from another—say, London or Zurich.

We can use the data in Table 26-1 to show how to work with exchange rates. Suppose a tourist flies from New York to London, then to Paris, and then on to Geneva. She then flies to Montreal, and finally back to New York. Her tour includes lodging, food, and transportation, but she must pay for any other expenses. When she arrives at London's Heathrow Airport, she goes to the bank to check the foreign exchange listings. The rate she observes for U.S. dollars is $1.9069; this means that £1 will cost $1.9069. Assume that she exchanges $3,000:

$$\$3,000 = \frac{\$3000}{\$1.9069 \text{ per pound}} = £1,573.23.$$

She then enjoys a week's vacation in London, ending with £1,000.

After taking a train under the Channel to France, she realizes that she needs to exchange her 1,000 remaining pounds for euros. However, what she sees on the board is the direct quotation for dollars per pound and the direct quotation for dollars per euro. The exchange rate between any two currencies other than dollars is called a **cross rate**. Cross rates are actually calculated on the basis of various currencies relative to the U.S. dollar. For example, the cross rate between British pounds and euros is computed as follows:

$$\text{Cross rate of euros per pound} = \frac{\$1.9069 \text{ per pound}}{\$1.2841 \text{ per euro}} = 1.4850 \text{ euros per pound.}$$

Therefore, for every British pound she would receive 1.4850 euros, so she would receive 1.4850(1,000) = 1,485.00 euros.

She has 800 euros remaining when she finishes touring in France and arrives in Geneva. She again needs to determine a cross rate, this time between euros and Swiss francs. The quotes she sees, as shown in Table 26-1, are a direct quote for euros ($1.2841 per euro) and an indirect quote for Swiss francs (SFr 1.2259 per dollar). To find the cross rate for Swiss francs per euro, she makes the following calculation:

$$\text{Cross rate of Swiss francs per euro} = \left(\frac{\text{Swiss francs}}{\text{Dollar}}\right)\left(\frac{\text{Dollars}}{\text{Euro}}\right)$$

$$= (\text{SFr } 1.2259 \text{ per dollar})(\$1.2841 \text{ per euro})$$

$$= 1.5742 \text{ Swiss francs per euro.}$$

For a nice currency calculator to determine the exchange rate between any two currencies, see **http://finance.yahoo.com/currency.**

Therefore, for every euro she would receive 1.5742 Swiss francs, so she would receive 1.5742(800) = 1,259.36 Swiss francs.

She has 500 Swiss francs remaining when she leaves Geneva and arrives in Montreal. She again needs to determine a cross rate, this time between Swiss francs and Canadian dollars. The quotes she sees, as shown in Table 26-1, are an indirect quote for Swiss francs (SFr 1.2259 per dollar) and an indirect quote for Canadian dollars (1.1198 Canadian dollars per U.S. dollar). To find the cross rate for Canadian dollars per Swiss franc, she makes the following calculation:

$$\text{Cross rate of Canadian dollars per Swiss franc} = \frac{\left(\dfrac{\text{Canadian dollars}}{\text{U.S. dollar}}\right)}{\left(\dfrac{\text{Swiss francs}}{\text{U.S. dollar}}\right)}$$

$$= \frac{(1.1198 \text{ Canadian dollars per U.S. dollar})}{(\text{SFr } 1.2259 \text{ per U.S. dollar})}$$

$$= 0.9135 \text{ Canadian dollars per Swiss franc.}$$

Therefore, she would receive 0.9135(500) = 456.75 Canadian dollars.

After leaving Montreal and arriving at New York, she has 100 Canadian dollars remaining. She sees the indirect quote for Canadian dollars and converts the 100 Canadian dollars to U.S. dollars as follows:

$$100 \text{ Canadian dollars} = \frac{100 \text{ Canadian dollars}}{1.1198 \text{ Canadian dollars per U.S. dollar}} = \$89.30.$$

In this example, we made three assumptions. First, we assumed that our traveler had to calculate all of the cross rates. For retail transactions, it is customary to display the cross rates directly instead of a series of dollar rates. Second, we assumed that exchange rates remain constant over time. Actually, exchange rates vary every day, often dramatically. We will have more to say about exchange rate fluctuations in the next section. Finally, we assumed that there were no transactions costs involved in exchanging currencies. In reality, small retail exchange transactions such as those in our example usually involve fixed and/or sliding scale fees that can easily consume 5% or more of the transaction amount. However, credit card purchases minimize these fees.

Major business publications, such as *The Wall Street Journal*, and Web sites, such as **http://www.bloomberg.com**, regularly report cross rates among key currencies. A set of cross rates is given in Table 26-2. When examining the table, note the following points:

1. Column 1 gives indirect quotes for dollars, that is, units of a foreign currency that can be bought with one U.S. dollar. Examples: $1 will buy 0.7788 euro or 1.2259 Swiss francs. Note the consistency with Table 26-1, Column 2.
2. Other columns show number of units of other currencies that can be bought with 1 pound, 1 Swiss franc, etc. For example, the euro column shows that 1 euro will buy 1.4379 Canadian dollars, 147.8185 Japanese yen, or 1.2841 U.S. dollars.
3. The rows show direct quotes, that is, number of units of the currency of the country listed in the left column required to buy one unit of the currency listed in the top row. The bottom row is particularly important for U.S. companies, as it shows the direct quotes for the U.S. dollar. This row is consistent with Column 1 of Table 26-1.
4. Note that the values on the bottom row of Table 26-2 are reciprocals of the corresponding values in the first column. For example, the U.K. row in the first

Table 26-2

Key Currency Cross Rates

	Dollar	Euro	Pound	SFranc	Peso	Yen	CdnDlr
Canada	1.1198	1.4379	2.1353	0.9135	0.1029	0.0097	—
Japan	115.1145	147.8185	219.5118	93.9020	10.5825	—	102.7992
Mexico	10.8778	13.9682	20.7429	8.8733	—	0.0945	9.7141
Switzerland	1.2259	1.5742	2.3377	—	0.1127	0.0106	1.0947
United Kingdom	0.5244	0.6734	—	0.4278	0.0482	0.0046	0.4683
Euro	0.7788	—	1.4850	0.6353	0.0716	0.0068	0.6954
United States	—	1.2841	1.9069	0.8157	0.0919	0.0087	0.8930

Source: Derived from Table 26-1; quotes for August 7, 2006.

column shows 0.5244 pound per dollar, and the pound column in the bottom row shows $1/0.5244 = 1.9069$ dollars per pound.

5. Now notice, by reading down the euro column, that 1 euro is worth 1.5742 Swiss francs. This is the same cross rate that we calculated for the U.S. tourist in our example.

The tie-in with the dollar ensures that all currencies are related to one another in a consistent manner—if this consistency did not exist, currency traders could profit by buying undervalued and selling overvalued currencies. This process, known as *arbitrage*, works to bring about an equilibrium wherein the same relationship described earlier exists. Currency traders are constantly operating in the market, seeking small inconsistencies from which they can profit. The traders' existence enables the rest of us to assume that currency markets are in equilibrium and that, at any point in time, cross rates are all internally consistent.[1]

SELF-TEST

What is an exchange rate?

Explain the difference between direct and indirect quotations.

What is a cross rate?

Assume that the indirect quote is for 10.0 Mexican pesos per U.S. dollar. What is the direct quote for dollars per peso? (0.10 dollar/peso)

Assume that the indirect quote is for 100 Japanese yen per U.S. dollar and that the direct quote is for 1.25 U.S. dollars per euro. What is the yen per euro exchange rate? (143.75 yen per euro)

26.4 Exchange Rates and International Trade

Just as the demand for consumer goods such as Tommy Hilfiger clothing and Nike shoes changes over time, so does the demand for currency. One factor affecting currency demand is the balance of trade between two countries. For example,

---

[1]For more discussion of exchange rates, see Jongmoo Jay Choi and Anita Mehra Prasad, "Exchange Risk Sensitivity and Its Determinants: A Firm and Industry Analysis of U.S. Multinationals," *Financial Management*, Autumn 1995, pp. 77–88; Jerry A. Hammer, "Hedging Performance and Hedging Objectives: Tests of New Performance Measures in the Foreign Currency Market," *Journal of Financial Research*, Winter 1990, pp. 307–323; and William C. Hunter and Stephen G. Timme, "A Stochastic Dominance Approach to Evaluating Foreign Exchange Hedging Strategies," *Financial Management*, Autumn 1992, pp. 104–112.

U.S. importers must buy yen to pay for Japanese goods, whereas Japanese importers must buy U.S. dollars to pay for U.S. goods. If U.S. imports from Japan were to exceed U.S. exports to Japan, then the U.S. would have a **trade deficit** with Japan, and there would be a greater demand for yen than for dollars. Capital movements also affect currency demand. For example, suppose interest rates in the United States were higher than those in Japan. To take advantage of high U.S. interest rates, Japanese banks, corporations, and sophisticated individuals would buy dollars with yen and then use those dollars to purchase high-yielding U.S. securities. This would create greater demand for dollars than for yen.

Without any government intervention, the relative prices of yen and dollars would fluctuate in response to changes in supply and demand in much the same way that prices of consumer goods fluctuate. For example, if U.S. consumers were to increase their demand for Japanese electronic products, then the accompanying increase in demand for the yen would cause its value to increase relative to the dollar. In this situation, the strong yen would be due to fundamental economic forces.

However, governments can and do intervene. A country's central bank can artificially prop up its currency by using its reserves of gold or foreign currencies to purchase its own currency in the open market. This creates artificial demand for its own currency, thus causing its value to be artificially high. A central bank can also keep its currency at an artificially low value by selling its own currency in the open markets. This increases the currency's supply, which reduces its price.

Why might an artificially low currency be a problem? After all, a cheap currency makes it less expensive for other nations to purchase the country's goods, which creates jobs in the exporting country. However, an artificially low currency value raises the cost of imports, which increases inflation. In addition, high import prices allow competing domestic manufacturers to raise their prices as well, further boosting inflation. The government intervention that causes the artificially low value also contributes to inflation: When a government creates currency to sell in the open markets, this increases the money supply, and, all else held constant, an increasing money supply leads to still more inflation. Thus, artificially holding down the value of a currency stimulates exports but at the expense of potentially overheating and inflating the economy. Also, other countries—whose economies are being weakened because their manufacturers cannot compete against the artificially low prices—may retaliate and impose tariffs or other restrictions on the country that is holding its currency value down.

For example, China had for many years artificially held down the value of the yuan (also called the rinminbi). This helped make China the world's largest exporter and greatly stimulated its economy. However, by 2004 the Chinese economy was growing at an unsustainably high rate, and inflation was rising rapidly. The United States and other nations began urging the Chinese government to allow the yuan to rise, which would help their economies by slowing Chinese exports and stimulating their own exports to China. On July 21, 2005, the Chinese government suddenly announced that it was changing the exchange rate to allow the yuan's value to rise by 2.1%.

A currency that is artificially high has the opposite effects: Inflation will be held down, and citizens can purchase imported goods at low domestic prices, but exporting industries are hurt, as are domestic industries that compete with the cheap imports. Because there is relatively little external demand for the currency, the government will have to create demand by purchasing its own currency, paying with either gold or foreign currencies held by its central bank. Over time, supporting an inflated currency can deplete the gold and foreign currency reserves, making it impossible to continue propping up the currency.

The following sections describe ways that governments handle changes in currency demands.

What is the effect on a country's economy caused by an artificially low exchange rate? By an artificially high exchange rate?

26.5 The International Monetary System and Exchange Rate Policies

The International Monetary Fund reports a full listing of exchange rate arrangements. See **http://www.imf.org/external/np/mfd/er/index.asp.** The IMF also publishes a more detailed listing in its *Annual Report on Exchange Arrangements and Exchange Restrictions.* For another listing of world currencies, see **http://fx.sauder.ubc.ca/currency_table.html.**

Every nation has a monetary system and a monetary authority. In the United States, the Federal Reserve is our monetary authority, and its task is to hold down inflation while promoting economic growth and raising our national standard of living. Moreover, if countries are to trade with one another, we must have some sort of system designed to facilitate payments between nations. The international monetary system is the framework within which exchange rates are determined. As we describe below, there are several different policies used by various countries to determine exchange rates.[2]

A Short History Lesson: The Bretton Woods Fixed Exchange Rate System

From the end of World War II until August 1971, most of the industrialized world operated under the Bretton Woods **fixed exchange rate system** administered by the International Monetary Fund (IMF). Under this system, the U.S. dollar was linked to gold (at $35 per ounce), and other currencies were then tied to the dollar. The United States took actions to keep the price of gold at $35 per ounce, and central banks acted to keep exchange rates between other currencies and the dollar within narrow limits. For example, when the demand for pounds was falling, the Bank of England would step in and buy pounds to push up their price, offering gold or foreign currencies in exchange for pounds. Conversely, when the demand for pounds was too high, the Bank of England would sell pounds for dollars or gold. The Federal Reserve in the United States performed the same functions, and central banks of other countries operated similarly. These actions artificially matched supply and demand, keeping exchange rates stable, but they didn't address the underlying imbalance. For example, if the high demand for pounds occurred because British productivity was rising and British goods were improving in quality, then the underlying demand for pounds would continue in spite of central bank intervention. In such a situation the Bank of England would find it necessary to continually sell pounds indefinitely. If the central bank stopped selling pounds, their value would rise; that is, the pound would strengthen and exceed the agreed-upon limits.

Many countries found it difficult and economically painful to maintain the fixed exchange rates required by Bretton Woods. This system began to crumble in August 1971, and it was abandoned completely by the end of 1973. The following sections describe several modern exchange rate systems.

---

[2]For a comprehensive history of the international monetary system and details of how it has evolved, consult one of the many economics books on the subject, including Robert Carbaugh, *International Economics* (Mason, OH: South-Western, 2004); Mordechai Kreinin, *International Economics: A Policy Approach*, 9th edition (Mason, OH: South-Western, 2002); Jeff Madura, *International Financial Management* (Eagan, MN: Thomson/South-Western, 2006); and Joseph P. Daniels and David D. Van Hoose, *International Monetary and Financial Economics*, 2nd edition (Mason, OH: South-Western, 2002).

Freely, or Independently, Floating Rates

In the early 1970s, the U.S. dollar was cut loose from the gold standard and, in effect, allowed to "float" in response to supply and demand caused by international trade and international investing activities. According to the International Monetary Fund, about 42 countries currently operate under a system of **floating exchange rates,** whereby currency prices are allowed to seek their own levels, with only modest central bank intervention to smooth out extreme exchange rate fluctuations. According to the International Monetary Fund, about 31 currencies have freely, or independently, floating exchange rates, including the dollar, euro, pound, and yen.

Currency Appreciation and Depreciation   Suppose the dollar cost of a pound is $1.9069 as shown in Table 26-1. If there were increased demand for pounds caused by a U.S. trade deficit with Great Britain, then the price of pounds might increase to $2. In this situation, the pound is said to be *appreciating*, because a pound would now buy more dollars. In other words, a pound would now be worth more than it was. This is called **currency appreciation.** Conversely, the dollar would be *depreciating*, because the dollar now buys fewer pounds (a dollar would previously buy $1/1.9069 = 0.5244$ pound, but afterward it would buy only $1/2 = 0.5$ pound). This is called **currency depreciation.** Notice that the more costly pound would make British imports more expensive to U.S. consumers, which would reduce imports—and, consequently, the demand for pounds—until the exchange rate reached equilibrium.

Exchange Rate Risk   Exchange rate fluctuations can have a profound effect on profits. For example, in 1985 it cost Honda Motors 2,380,000 yen to build a particular model in Japan and ship it to the United States. The model carried a U.S. sticker price of $12,000. Because the $12,000 sales price was the equivalent of (238 yen per dollar)($12,000) = 2,856,000 yen, which was 20% above the 2,380,000 yen cost, the automaker had built a 20% markup into the U.S. sales price. However, three years later the dollar had depreciated to 128 yen. Now if the car still sold for $12,000, the yen return to Honda would be only (128 yen per dollar)($12,000) = 1,536,000 yen, and the automaker would be losing about 35% on each auto sold. Therefore, the depreciation of the dollar against the yen turned a healthy profit into a huge loss. In fact, for Honda to maintain its 20% markup, the model would have had to sell in the United States for 2,856,000 yen/(128 yen per dollar) = $22,312.50. This situation, which grew even worse, led Honda to build its most popular model, the Accord, in Marysville, Ohio.

The inherent volatility of exchange rates under a floating system increases the uncertainty of the cash flows for a multinational corporation. Because its cash flows are generated in many parts of the world, they are denominated in many different currencies. When exchange rates change, the dollar-equivalent value of the company's consolidated cash flows also fluctuates. For example, Toyota estimates that each 1 yen drop in the dollar reduces the company's annual net income by about 10 billion yen. This is known as **exchange rate risk,** and it is a major factor differentiating a global company from a purely domestic one.

Managed Floating Rates

In a **managed floating rate** system, there is significant government intervention to manage the exchange rate by manipulating the currency's supply and demand. The government rarely reveals its target exchange rate levels if it uses a managed-float regime because this would make it too easy for currency speculators to profit. According to the IMF, about 53 countries have a managed floating rate system, including Colombia, India, Singapore, and Burundi.

Pegged Exchange Rates

In a **pegged exchange rates** system, a country locks, or "pegs," its currency's exchange rate to another currency or basket of currencies. It is common for a country with a pegged exchange rate to allow its currency to vary within specified limits or bands (often set at ±1% of the target rate) before the country intervenes to force the currency back within the limits. Examples in which a currency is pegged to another country's currency include Bhutan's ngultrum, which is pegged to the Indian rupee; the Falkland Islands' pound, which is pegged to the British pound; and Barbados's dollar, which is pegged to the U.S. dollar. An example of a currency being pegged to a basket is China, where the yuan is no longer just pegged to the U.S. dollar but rather to a basket of currencies. Interestingly, the Chinese government will not reveal the currencies that make up the basket, but the U.S. dollar is still likely an important component.

Currency Devaluation and Revaluation

As indicated earlier, countries with pegged exchange rates establish a fixed exchange rate with some other major currency or basket of currencies. When a government lowers the target fixed exchange rate, this is called **devaluation,** and when it increases the rate it is called **revaluation.** For example, from 1991 through early 2002, Argentina had a fixed exchange rate of 1 peso per U.S. dollar. Imports were high, exports were low, and the Argentinean government had to purchase huge amounts of pesos to maintain that artificially high exchange rate. The government borrowed heavily to finance these purchases, and eventually it was unable to continue supporting the peso. (Indeed, the government defaulted on some of its obligations.) As a result, the government had to devalue the peso to 1.4 pesos per dollar in early 2002. Notice that this made the peso weaker: Before the devaluation, 1 peso would buy 1 dollar, but afterward 1 peso would buy only 71 cents (1.4 pesos per dollar = 1/1.4 = 0.71 dollar per peso). The devaluation lowered the prices of Argentine goods on the world market, which helped its exporters, but prices rose for imported goods, including oil. The initial shock to the Argentine economy was severe, as employment fell in those industries that were not exporters. The problem was exacerbated because many Argentine companies and individuals had borrowed using debt denominated in dollars, which instantly cost much more to service. However, the economy gradually improved, with increased exports, tourism, and employment rates. Still, the initial pain caused by devaluation helps explain why many countries with fixed exchange rates tend to postpone needed measures until economic pressures build to explosive proportions.

Due to the expense of maintaining an artificially high exchange rate and the pain of large devaluations, many countries that once had pegged exchange rates now allow their currencies to float. For example, Mexico had a pegged exchange rate prior to 1994, but it depleted its foreign reserves trying to support the peso and was forced to devalue the peso in 1994. Mexico's currency now floats, as does that of Argentina.

Convertible versus Nonconvertible Securities

A pegged exchange rate per se isn't necessarily a deterrent to direct investment in the country by foreign corporations, as long as the local government's central bank supports the currency and devaluations are unlikely. This was generally the case in the Bretton Woods era, and so those currencies were considered to be **convertible** because the nation that issued them allowed them to be traded in the currency markets and was willing to redeem them at market rates. This is true today for all floating-rate currencies, which are also called **hard currencies** because of their convertibility. Some pegged currencies are also at least partially convertible, because their central banks will redeem them at market rates under specified conditions.

However, some countries set the exchange rate but do not allow their currencies to be traded on world markets. For example, the Chinese yuan is allowed to float in a very narrow band against a basket of securities. However, the yuan can be legally used and exchanged only within China. Furthermore, the Chinese government imposes restrictions on both residents and nonresidents from freely converting their holdings of yuans into another currency. Thus, the yuan is a **nonconvertible currency,** also called a **soft currency.** When official exchange rates differ from "market rates" or when there are restrictions on convertibility, a black market will often arise. For example, in mid-2005 Venezuela's official exchange rate was about 2,150 bolivars per dollar, but black market prices were estimated to be around 2,700.

A nonconvertible currency creates problems for foreign companies looking to make direct investments. Consider the situation faced by Pizza Hut when it wanted to open a chain of restaurants in the former Soviet Union. The Russian ruble was not convertible, so Pizza Hut could not take the profits from its restaurants out of the Soviet Union in the form of dollars. There was no mechanism to exchange the rubles it earned in Russia for dollars; therefore an investment in the Soviet Union was essentially worthless to a U.S. company. However, Pizza Hut arranged to use the ruble profit from the restaurants to buy Russian vodka, which it then shipped to the United States and sold for dollars. Pizza Hut managed to find a solution, but lack of convertibility significantly inhibits the ability of a country to attract foreign investment.

No Local Currency

A few countries don't have their own separate legal tender, but instead use the currency of another nation. For example, Ecuador has used the U.S. dollar since September 2000. Other countries belong to a monetary union, such as the 12 European Monetary Union nations whose currency is the euro, which is allowed to float. In contrast, member nations of the Eastern Caribbean Currency Union, the West African Economic and Monetary Union (WAEMU), and the Central African Economic and Monetary Community (CAEMC) use their respective union's currency, which is itself pegged to some other currency. For example, the Eastern Caribbean dollar is pegged to the U.S. dollar, and the CFA franc (used by both the WAEMU and CAEMC) is pegged to the euro.[3]

SELF-TEST   What is the difference between a fixed exchange rate system and a floating rate system?

What are pegged exchange rates?

What does it mean to say that the dollar is depreciating with respect to the euro?

What is a convertible currency?

---

[3]A few countries, such as Bosnia and Herzegovina, have currency board arrangements. Under this system, a country technically has its own currency but commits to exchange it for a specified foreign money unit at a fixed exchange rate. This requires it to impose domestic currency restrictions unless it has the foreign currency reserves to cover requested exchanges.

the foreign currency in the forward market. For example, the investor could simultaneously:

1. Convert $1,000 to 1,225.90 Swiss francs in the spot market: $1,000(1.2259 Swiss francs per dollar) = 1,225.90 Swiss francs.
2. Invest the Swiss francs in a 180-day Swiss bond that has a 4% annual return, or a 2% semiannual return. This investment will pay 1,225.90(1.02) = 1,250.42 Swiss francs in 180 days.
3. Agree today to exchange the Swiss francs in 180 days at the rate of 1.2029 Swiss francs per dollar, for a total of (1,250.42 Swiss francs)/(1.2029 Swiss francs per dollar) = $1,039.50.

This investment, therefore, has an expected 180-day return of $39.50/$1,000 = 3.950%, which translates into a nominal annual return of 2(3.950%) = 7.90%. In this case, 4% of the expected 7.90% is coming from the bond itself, and 3.90% arises because the market believes the Swiss franc will strengthen relative to the dollar. Note that by locking in the forward rate today, the investor has eliminated all exchange rate risk. And since the Swiss bond is assumed to be default-free, the investor is certain to earn a 7.90% annual dollar return.

Interest rate parity implies that an investment in the United States with the same risk as the Swiss bond should also have a return of 7.90%. We can express interest rate parity by the following equation:

$$\frac{\text{Forward exchange rate}}{\text{Spot exchange rate}} = \frac{(1 + r_h)}{(1 + r_f)}. \qquad (26\text{-}1)$$

Here r_h is the periodic interest rate in the home country, r_f is the periodic interest rate in the foreign country, and the forward and exchange rates are expressed as direct quotations (that is, dollars per foreign currency).

Using Table 26-3, the direct spot quotation is 0.81573 dollar per Swiss franc = (1/1.2259 Swiss francs per dollar), and the direct 180-day forward quotation is 0.83132 = (1/1.2029). Using Equation 26-1, we can solve for the equivalent home rate, r_h:

$$\frac{\text{Forward exchange rate}}{\text{Spot exchange rate}} = \frac{(1 + r_h)}{(1 + r_f)} = \frac{(1 + r_h)}{(1 + 0.02)} = \frac{0.83132}{0.81573}$$

$$(26\text{-}1a)$$

$$(1 + r_h) = \left(\frac{0.83132}{0.81573}\right)(1 + 0.02) = 1.03949395.$$

The periodic home interest rate is 3.9494%, and the annualized home interest rate is (3.949%)(2) = 7.90%, the same value we found above.

After accounting for exchange rates, interest rate parity states that bonds in the home country and the foreign country must have the same effective rate of return. In this example, the U.S. bond must yield 7.90% to provide the same return as the 4% Swiss bond. If one bond provides a higher return, investors will sell their low-return bond and flock to the high-return bond. This activity will cause the price of the low-return bond to fall (which pushes up its yield) and the price of the high-return bond to increase (driving down its yield). This will continue until the two bonds again have the same returns after accounting for exchange rates.

In other words, interest rate parity implies that an investment in the United States with the same risk as a Swiss bond should have a dollar value return of 7.90%. Solving for r_h in Equation 26-1, we indeed find that the predicted interest rate in the United States is 7.90%.

Interest rate parity shows why a particular currency might be at a forward premium or discount. Note that a currency is at a forward premium whenever domestic interest rates are higher than foreign interest rates. Discounts prevail if domestic interest rates are lower than foreign interest rates. If these conditions do not hold, then arbitrage will soon force interest rates and exchange rates back to parity.

SELF-TEST

What is interest rate parity?

Assume interest rate parity holds. When a currency trades at a forward premium, what does that imply about domestic rates relative to foreign interest rates? What about when a currency trades at a forward discount?

Assume that 90-day U.S. securities have a 4.5% annualized interest rate, whereas 90-day Swiss securities have a 5% annualized interest rate. In the spot market, 1 U.S. dollar can be exchanged for 1.2 Swiss francs. If interest rate parity holds, what is the 90-day forward rate exchange between U.S. and Swiss francs? (0.8323 $/SFr; 1.2015 SFr/$)

On the basis of your answer to the previous question, is the Swiss franc selling at a premium or discount on the forward rate? (Discount)

26.8 Purchasing Power Parity

We have discussed exchange rates in some detail, and we have considered the relationship between spot and forward exchange rates. However, we have not yet addressed the fundamental question: What determines the spot level of exchange rates in each country? While exchange rates are influenced by a multitude of factors that are difficult to predict, particularly on a day-to-day basis, over the long run market forces work to ensure that similar goods sell for similar prices in different countries after taking exchange rates into account. This relationship is known as "purchasing power parity."

Purchasing power parity (PPP), sometimes referred to as the *law of one price,* implies that the levels of exchange rates and prices adjust so as to cause identical goods to cost the same amount in different countries. For example, if a pair of tennis shoes costs $150 in the United States and 100 pounds in Britain, PPP implies that the exchange rate must be $1.50 per pound. Consumers could purchase the shoes in Britain for 100 pounds, or they could exchange their 100 pounds for $150 and then purchase the same shoes in the United States at the same effective cost, assuming no transaction or transportation costs. Here is the equation for purchasing power parity:

$$P_h = (P_f)(\text{Spot rate}) \tag{26-2}$$

or

$$\text{Spot rate} = \frac{P_h}{P_f}. \tag{26-3}$$

Here

P_h = the price of the good in the home country ($150, assuming the United States is the home country).

P_f = the price of the good in the foreign country (100 pounds).

Hungry for a Big Mac? Go to China!

Purchasing power parity (PPP) implies that the same product will sell for the same price in every country after adjusting for current exchange rates. One problem when testing to see if PPP holds is that it assumes that goods consumed in different countries are of the same quality. For example, if you find that a product is more expensive in Switzerland than it is in Canada, one explanation is that PPP fails to hold, but another explanation is that the product sold in Switzerland is of a higher quality and therefore deserves a higher price.

One way to test for PPP is to find goods that have the same quality worldwide. With this in mind, *The Economist* magazine occasionally compares the prices of a well-known good whose quality is the same in nearly 120 different countries: the McDonald's Big Mac hamburger.

The accompanying table provides information collected during May 2006. The first column shows the price of a Big Mac in local currency. For example, a Big Mac costs 48 rubles in Russia. The second column shows the cost in dollars (based on the actual exchange rate in the fourth column), which is the amount you would pay in that country if you exchanged dollars for local currency and then purchased a Big Mac at the local price. For example,

the exchange rate is 27.1 rubles per dollar, which means that a Big Mac in Russia costs $1.77 = (48 rubles)/(27.1 rubles per dollar).

The third column backs out the implied exchange rate that would hold under PPP. For example, the 48 ruble price of a Big Mac in Russia compared to the $3.10 price in the United States gives us the implied PPP exchange rate of (48 rubles per Big Mac)/($3.10 per Big Mac) = 15.5 rubles per dollar. The last column shows how much the local currency is over- or undervalued relative to the dollar. The ruble's implied PPP exchange rate of 15.5 rubles per dollar is 43% less than the actual exchange rate of 27.1 rubles per dollar, so the ruble is 43% undervalued relative to the dollar.

The evidence suggests that strict PPP does not hold, but the Big Mac test may shed some insights about where exchange rates are headed. Other than a few European countries, most currencies are undervalued against the dollar. The Big Mac 2006 test suggests that European currencies will fall over the next year or so, but that most others will rise.

One last benefit of the Big Mac test is that it tells us the cheapest places to find a Big Mac. According to the data, if you are looking for a Big Mac, head to China and avoid Switzerland.

Note that the spot market exchange rate is expressed as the number of units of home currency that can be exchanged for one unit of foreign currency ($1.50 per pound).

PPP assumes that market forces will eliminate situations in which the same product sells at a different price overseas. For example, if the shoes cost $140 in the United States, importers/exporters could purchase them in the United States for $140, sell them for 100 pounds in Britain, exchange the 100 pounds for $150 in the foreign exchange market, and earn a profit of $10 on every pair of shoes. Ultimately, this trading activity would increase the demand for shoes in the United States and thus raise P_h, increase the supply of shoes in Britain and thus reduce P_f, and increase the demand for dollars in the foreign exchange market and thus reduce the spot rate. Each of these actions works to restore PPP.

Note that PPP assumes that there are no transportation or transaction costs and no import restrictions, all of which limit the ability to ship goods between countries. In many cases, these assumptions are incorrect, which explains why PPP is often violated. An additional problem for empirical tests of the PPP theorem is that products in different countries are rarely identical. Frequently, there are real or perceived differences in quality, which can lead to price differences in different countries.

Still, the concepts of interest rate and purchasing power parity are critically important to those engaged in international activities. Companies and investors must anticipate changes in interest rates, inflation, and exchange rates, and they often try to hedge the risks of adverse movements in these factors. The parity relationships are extremely useful when anticipating future conditions.

	In Local Currency (1)	In Dollars (2)	Implied Exchange Rate Based on PPP[a] (3)	Actual $ Exchange Rate (4)	Local Currency Under(−)/ Over(+) Valuation(%) (5)
United States[b]	$3.10	3.10	—	—	—
Argentina	Peso 7	2.29	2.26	3.06	−26
Australia	A$3.25	2.44	1.05	1.33	−21
Brazil	Real 6.4	2.78	2.06	2.30	−10
Britain	£1.94	3.65	1.60[c]	1.88[c]	18
Canada	C$3.52	3.14	1.14	1.12	1
Chile	Peso 1,560	2.94	503	530	−5
China	Yuan 10.5	1.31	3.39	8.03	−58
Czech Republic	Koruna 59.05	2.67	19.0	22.1	−14
Denmark	DKr27.75	4.77	8.95	5.82	54
Egypt	Pound 9.5	1.65	3.06	5.77	−47
Euro areas	€2.94[d]	3.77	1.05[e]	1.28[e]	22
Hong Kong	HK$12	1.55	3.87	7.75	−50
Hungary	Forint 560	2.71	181	206	−12
Indonesia	Rupiah 14,600	1.57	4710	9325	−49
Japan	¥250	2.23	80.6	112.0	−28
Malaysia	Ringgit 5.5	1.52	1.77	3.63	−51
Mexico	Peso 29	2.57	9.35	11.30	−17
New Zealand	NZ$4.45	2.75	1.44	1.62	−11
Peru	New Sol 9.5	2.91	3.06	3.26	−6
Philippines	Peso 85	1.62	27.4	52.6	−48
Poland	Zloty 6.5	2.10	2.10	3.10	−32
Russia	Ruble 48	1.77	15.5	27.1	−43
Singapore	S$3.60	2.27	1.16	1.59	−27
South Africa	Rand 13.95	2.11	4.50	6.60	−32
South Korea	Won 2,500	2.62	806	952	−15
Sweden	SKr33.00	4.53	10.6	7.28	46
Switzerland	SFr6.30	5.21	2.03	1.21	68
Taiwan	NT$75.00	2.33	24.2	32.1	−25
Thailand	Baht 60	1.56	19.4	38.4	−50
Turkey	Lire 4.2	2.72	1.35	1.54	−12
Venezuela	Bolivar 5,701	2.17	1839	2630	−30

[a]Purchasing power parity: local price divided by price in United States
[b]Average of New York, Chicago, Atlanta, and San Francisco
[c]Dollars per pound
[d]Weighted average of prices in euro area
[e]Dollars per euro
Sources: McDonald's; and "McCurrencies," The Economist, May 27, 2006, p. 74.

26.9 Inflation, Interest Rates, and Exchange Rates

For current international interest rates, go to **http://www .bloomberg.com** and select Market Data. Then select Rates and Bonds.

Relative inflation rates, or the rates of inflation in foreign countries compared with that in the home country, have many implications for multinational financial decisions. Obviously, relative inflation rates will greatly influence future production costs at home and abroad. Equally important, inflation has a dominant influence on relative interest rates and exchange rates. Both of these factors influence decisions by multinational corporations for financing their foreign investments, and both have an important effect on the profitability of foreign investments.

The currencies of countries with higher inflation rates than that of the United States by definition *depreciate* over time against the dollar. Countries where this has occurred include Mexico and all the South American nations. On the other hand, the currencies of Switzerland and Japan, which have had less inflation than the United States, have generally *appreciate* against the dollar. *In fact, a foreign currency will, on average, depreciate or appreciate at a percentage rate approximately equal to the amount by which its inflation rate exceeds or is less than the U.S. rate.*

Relative inflation rates also affect interest rates. The interest rate in any country is largely determined by its inflation rate. Therefore, countries currently experiencing higher rates of inflation than the United States also tend to have higher interest rates. The reverse is true for countries with lower inflation rates.

It is tempting for a multinational corporation to borrow in countries with the lowest interest rates. However, this is not always a good strategy. Suppose, for example, that interest rates in Switzerland are lower than those in the United States because of Switzerland's lower inflation rate. A U.S. multinational firm could therefore save interest by borrowing in Switzerland. However, because of relative inflation rates, the Swiss franc will probably appreciate in the future, causing the dollar cost of annual interest and principal payments on Swiss debt to rise over time. Thus, *the lower interest rate could be more than offset by losses from currency appreciation.* Similarly, multinational corporations should not necessarily avoid borrowing in a country such as Brazil, where interest rates have been very high, because future depreciation of the Brazilian real could make such borrowing end up being relatively inexpensive.

26.10 International Money and Capital Markets

One way for U.S. citizens to invest in world markets is to buy the stocks of U.S. multinational corporations that invest directly in foreign countries. Another way is to purchase foreign securities—stocks, bonds, or money market instruments issued by foreign companies. Security investments are known as *portfolio investments*, and they are distinguished from *direct investments* in physical assets by U.S. corporations.

From World War II through the 1960s, the U.S. capital markets dominated world markets. Today, however, the value of U.S. securities represents less than one-fourth the value of all securities. Given this situation, it is important for both corporate managers and investors to have an understanding of international markets. Moreover, these markets often offer better opportunities for raising or investing capital than are available domestically.

Eurodollar Market

A **Eurodollar** is a U.S. dollar deposited in a bank outside the United States. (Although they are called Eurodollars because they originated in Europe, Eurodollars are really any dollars deposited in any part of the world other than the United States.) The bank in which the deposit is made may be a non-U.S. bank, such as Barclay's Bank in London; the foreign branch of a U.S. bank, such as Citibank's Paris branch; or even a foreign branch of a third-country bank, such as Barclay's Munich branch. Most Eurodollar deposits are for $500,000 or more, and they have maturities ranging from overnight to about one year.

The major difference between Eurodollar deposits and regular U.S. time deposits is their geographic locations. The two types of deposits do not involve different currencies—in both cases, dollars are on deposit. However, Eurodollars are outside the direct control of the U.S. monetary authorities, so U.S. banking regulations, including reserve requirements and FDIC insurance premiums, do not apply. The absence of these costs means that the interest rate paid on Eurodollar deposits can be higher than domestic U.S. rates on equivalent instruments.

Although the dollar is the leading international currency, British pounds, euros, Swiss francs, Japanese yen, and other currencies are also deposited outside their home countries; these *Eurocurrencies* are handled in exactly the same way as Eurodollars.

Eurodollars are borrowed by U.S. and foreign corporations for various purposes, but especially to pay for goods imported from the United States and to invest in U.S. security markets. Also, U.S. dollars are used as an international currency, or international medium of exchange, and many Eurodollars are used for this purpose. It is interesting to note that Eurodollars were actually "invented" by the Soviets in 1946. International merchants did not trust the Soviets or their rubles, so the Soviets bought some dollars (for gold), deposited them in a Paris bank, and then used these dollars to buy goods in the world markets. Others found it convenient to use dollars this same way, and soon the Eurodollar market was in full swing.

Eurodollars are usually held in interest-bearing accounts. The interest rate paid on these deposits depends (1) on the bank's lending rate, as the interest a bank earns on loans determines its willingness and ability to pay interest on deposits, and (2) on rates of return available on U.S. money market instruments.

If money market rates in the United States were above Eurodollar deposit rates, these dollars would be sent back and invested in the United States, whereas if Eurodollar deposit rates were significantly above U.S. rates, which is more often the case, more dollars would be sent out of the United States to become Eurodollars. Given the existence of the Eurodollar market and the electronic flow of dollars to and from the United States, it is easy to see why interest rates in the United States cannot be insulated from those in other parts of the world.

Interest rates on Eurodollar deposits (and loans) are tied to a standard rate known by the acronym **LIBOR,** which stands for **London Interbank Offer Rate.** LIBOR is the rate of interest offered by the largest and strongest London banks on dollar deposits of significant size. In August 2006, LIBOR rates were just a little above domestic U.S. bank rates on time deposits of the same maturity—5.36% for 3-month CDs versus 5.40% for LIBOR CDs. The Eurodollar market is essentially a short-term market; most loans and deposits are for less than 1 year.

International Bond Markets

Any bond sold outside the country of the borrower is called an *international bond*. However, there are two important types of international bonds: foreign bonds and Eurobonds. **Foreign bonds** are bonds sold by a foreign borrower but denominated in the currency of the country in which the issue is sold. For instance, Nortel Networks (a Canadian company) may need U.S. dollars to finance the operations of its subsidiaries in the United States. If it decides to raise the needed capital in the United States, the bond would be underwritten by a syndicate of U.S. investment bankers, denominated in U.S. dollars, and sold to U.S. investors in accordance with SEC and applicable state regulations. Except for the foreign origin of the borrower, this bond would be indistinguishable from those issued by equivalent U.S. corporations. Since Nortel is a foreign corporation, however, the bond would be a foreign bond. Furthermore, because it is denominated in dollars and sold in the United States under SEC regulations, it is also called a **Yankee bond.** In contrast, if Nortel issued bonds in Mexico denominated in pesos, it would be a foreign bond, but not a Yankee bond.

The term **Eurobond** is used to designate any bond issued in one country but denominated in the currency of some other country. Examples include a Ford Motor Company issue denominated in dollars and sold in Germany, or a British firm's sale of euro-denominated bonds in Switzerland. The institutional arrangements by which Eurobonds are marketed are different than those for most other bond issues, with the most important distinction being a far lower level of required disclosure than is usually found for bonds issued in domestic markets, particularly in the United States. Governments tend to be less strict when regulating securities denominated in foreign currencies, because the bonds' purchasers are generally more "sophisticated." The lower disclosure requirements result in lower total transaction costs for Eurobonds.

Eurobonds appeal to investors for several reasons. Generally, they are issued in bearer form rather than as registered bonds, so the names and nationalities of investors are not recorded. Individuals who desire anonymity, whether for privacy reasons or for tax avoidance, like Eurobonds. Similarly, most governments do not withhold taxes on interest payments associated with Eurobonds. If the investor requires an effective yield of 10%, a Eurobond that is exempt from tax withholding would need a coupon rate of 10%. Another type of bond—for instance, a domestic issue subject to a 30% withholding tax on interest paid to

Stock Market Indices around the World

In the United States the Dow Jones Industrial Average (^DJI) is the most well-known stock market index. Similar indices also exist for each major world financial center. As shown in the table below, India's market has had the strongest performance, while Japan's has had the weakest.

Hong Kong (^HSI)

In Hong Kong, the primary stock index is the Hang Seng. Created by HSI Services Limited, the Hang Seng index is composed of 33 large stocks.

Great Britain (^FTSE)

The FT-SE 100 Index (pronounced "footsie") is the most widely followed indicator of equity investments in Great Britain. It is a value-weighted index composed of the 100 largest companies on the London Stock Exchange.

Japan (^N225)

In Japan, the principal barometer of stock performance is the Nikkei 225 Index. The index consists of highly liquid equity issues thought to be representative of the Japanese economy.

Germany (^GDAXI)

The Deutscher Aktienindex, commonly called the DAX, is an index comprised of the 30 largest companies trading on the Frankfurt Stock Exchange.

India (^BSESN)

Of the 22 stock exchanges in India, the Bombay Stock Exchange (BSE) is the largest, with more than 6,000 listed stocks and approximately two-thirds of the country's total trading volume. Established in 1875, the exchange is also the oldest in Asia. Its yardstick is the BSE Sensex, an index of 30 publicly traded Indian stocks that account for one-fifth of the BSE's market capitalization.

Note: For easy access to world indices, see **http://finance.yahoo .com/m2** and use the ticker symbols shown in parentheses.

Relative Ten-Year Performance (Starting Values = 100)

	United States	Germany	Great Britain	Hong Kong	India	Japan
August 1996	100	100	100	100	100	100
August 2006	203	230	153	156	272	80

foreigners—would need a coupon rate of 14.3% to yield an after-withholding rate of 10%. Investors who desire secrecy would not want to file for a refund of the tax, so they would prefer to hold the Eurobond.

More than half of all Eurobonds are denominated in dollars. Bonds in Japanese yen, German marks, and Dutch guilders account for most of the rest. Although centered in Europe, Eurobonds are truly international. Their underwriting syndicates include investment bankers from all parts of the world, and the bonds are sold to investors not only in Europe but also in such faraway places as Bahrain and Singapore. Up to a few years ago, Eurobonds were issued solely by multinational firms, by international financial institutions, or by national governments. Today, however, the Eurobond market is also being tapped by purely domestic U.S. firms, because they often find that by borrowing overseas they can lower their debt costs.

International Stock Markets

New issues of stock are sold in international markets for a variety of reasons. For example, a non-U.S. firm might sell an equity issue in the United States because it can tap a much larger source of capital than in its home country. Also, a U.S. firm might tap a foreign market because it wants to create an equity market presence to accompany its operations in that country. Large multinational companies also occasionally issue new stock simultaneously in multiple countries. For example, Alcan Aluminum, a Canadian company, recently issued new stock in Canada, Europe, and the United States simultaneously, using different underwriting syndicates in each market.

In addition to new issues, outstanding stocks of large multinational companies are increasingly being listed on multiple international exchanges. For example, Coca-Cola's stock is traded on six stock exchanges in the United States, four stock exchanges in Switzerland, and the Frankfurt stock exchange in Germany. Some 500 foreign stocks are listed in the United States—an example here is Royal Dutch Petroleum, which is listed on the NYSE. U.S. investors can also invest in foreign companies through American Depository Receipts (ADRs), which are certificates representing ownership of foreign stock held in trust. About 1,700 ADRs are now available in the United States, with most of them traded on the over-the-counter (OTC) market. However, more and more ADRs are being listed on the New York Stock Exchange, including England's British Airways, Japan's Honda Motors, and Italy's Fiat Group.

SELF-TEST

Differentiate between foreign portfolio investments and direct foreign investments.

What are Eurodollars?

Has the development of the Eurodollar market made it easier or more difficult for the Federal Reserve to control U.S. interest rates?

Differentiate between foreign bonds and Eurobonds.

Why do Eurobonds appeal to investors?

26.11 Multinational Capital Budgeting

Up to now, we have discussed the general environment in which multinational firms operate. In the remainder of the chapter, we see how international factors affect key corporate decisions, beginning with capital budgeting. Although the same basic principles apply to capital budgeting for both foreign and domestic operations, there are some key differences, including types of risks the firm faces, cash flow estimation, and project analysis.[4]

Risk Exposure

Foreign projects may be more or less risky than equivalent domestic projects, and that can lead to differences in the cost of capital. Higher risk for foreign projects tends to result from two primary sources: (1) exchange rate risk and (2) political risk. However, international diversification might result in a lower risk.

Exchange rate risk relates to the value of the basic cash flows in the parent company's home currency. Foreign currency cash flows turned over to the parent must be converted into U.S. dollars, so projected cash flows must be translated to dollars

---

[4]Many domestic companies form joint ventures with foreign companies; see Insup Lee and Steve B. Wyatt, "The Effects of International Joint Ventures on Shareholder Wealth," *Financial Review*, November 1990, pp. 641–649. For a discussion of the Japanese cost of capital, see Jeffrey A. Frankel, "The Japanese Cost of Finance," *Financial Management*, Spring 1991, pp. 95–127. For a discussion of financial practices in the Pacific basin, see George W. Kester, Rosita P. Chang, and Kai-Chong Tsui, "Corporate Financial Policy in the Pacific Basin: Hong Kong and Singapore," *Financial Practice and Education*, Spring/Summer 1994, pp. 117–127.

at the expected future exchange rates. An analysis should be conducted to ascertain the effects of exchange rate variations on dollar cash flows, and, on the basis of this analysis, an exchange rate risk premium should be added to the domestic cost of capital. It is sometimes possible to hedge against exchange rate risk, but it may not be possible to hedge completely, especially on long-term projects. If hedging is used, the costs of doing so must be subtracted from the project's operating cash flows.

Political risk refers to potential actions by a host government that would reduce the value of a company's investment. It includes at one extreme expropriation of the subsidiary's assets without compensation, but it also includes less drastic actions that reduce the value of the parent firm's investment in the foreign subsidiary.[5] Included here are higher taxes, tighter repatriation or currency controls, and restrictions on prices charged. The risk of expropriation is small in traditionally friendly and stable countries such as Great Britain or Switzerland. However, in Latin America, Africa, the Far East, and Eastern Europe, the risk may be substantial. Past expropriations include those of ITT and Anaconda Copper in Chile, Gulf Oil in Bolivia, Occidental Petroleum in Libya, Enron Corporation in Peru, and the assets of many companies in Iraq, Iran, and Cuba.

Note that companies can take steps to reduce the potential loss from expropriation, including one or more of the following:

1. Finance the subsidiary with local capital.
2. Structure operations so that the subsidiary has value only as a part of the integrated corporate system.
3. Obtain insurance against economic losses from expropriation from a source such as the Overseas Private Investment Corporation (OPIC).

If OPIC insurance is purchased, the premiums paid must be added to the project's cost.

Several organizations rate countries according to different aspects of risk. For example, Transparency International (TI) ranks countries based on perceived corruption, which is an important part of political risk. Table 26-4 shows selected countries. TI rates Iceland as the most honest country, while Chad and Bangladesh are tied for the most dishonest. The United States is ranked seventeenth.

Cash Flow Estimation

Cash flow estimation is more complex for foreign than domestic investments. Most multinational firms set up separate subsidiaries in each foreign country in which they operate, and the relevant cash flows for the parent company are the dividends and royalties paid by the subsidiaries to the parent, translated into dollars. Dividends and royalties are normally taxed by both foreign and home country governments, although the home country may allow credits for some or all of the foreign taxes paid. Furthermore, a foreign government may restrict the amount of the cash that may be **repatriated** to the parent company. For example, some governments place a ceiling, stated as a percentage of the company's net worth, on the amount of cash dividends that a subsidiary can pay to its parent. Such restrictions are normally intended to force multinational firms to reinvest earnings in the foreign country, although restrictions are sometimes imposed to prevent large currency outflows, which might disrupt the exchange rate.

---

[5]For an interesting article on expropriation, see Arvind Mahajan, "Pricing Expropriation Risk," *Financial Management*, Winter 1990, pp. 77–86.

Table 26-4

The 2005 Transparency International Corruption Perceptions Index (CPI)

Top-Ranked Countries			Bottom-Ranked Countries		
Rank	Country	2005 CPI Score	Rank	Country	2005 CPI Score
1	Iceland	9.7	117 (tie)	Afghanistan	2.5
2 (tie)	Finland	9.6		Bolivia	2.5
	New Zealand	9.6		Ecuador	2.5
4	Denmark	9.5		Guatemala	2.5
5	Singapore	9.4		Guyana	2.5
6	Sweden	9.2	126 (tie)	Albania	2.4
7	Switzerland	9.1		Niger	2.4
8	Norway	8.9		Russia	2.4
9	Australia	8.8		Sierra Leone	2.4
10	Austria	8.7	155 (tie)	Haiti	1.8
11 (tie)	Netherlands	8.6		Myanmar	1.8
	United Kingdom	8.6		Turkmenistan	1.8
13	Luxembourg	8.5	158 (tie)	Bangladesh	1.7
14	Canada	8.4		Chad	1.7

Source: **http://www.transparency.org.**

Whatever the host country's motivation for blocking repatriation of profits, the result is that the parent corporation cannot use cash flows blocked in the foreign country to pay dividends to its shareholders or to invest elsewhere in the business. Hence, from the perspective of the parent organization, the cash flows relevant for foreign investment analysis are the cash flows that the subsidiary is actually expected to send back to the parent. Note, though, that if returns on investments in the foreign country are attractive, and if blockages are expected to be lifted in the future, then current blockages may not be bad, but dealing with this situation does complicate the cash flow estimation process.

Some companies attempt to circumvent repatriation restrictions (and also lower taxes paid) through the use of transfer pricing. For example, a foreign subsidiary might obtain raw materials or other input components from the parent. The price the subsidiary pays the parent is called a **transfer price.** If the transfer price is very high, then the foreign subsidiary's costs will be very high, leaving little or no profit to repatriate. However, the parent's profit will be higher because it sold to the subsidiary at an inflated transfer price. The net result is that the parent receives cash flows from the subsidiary via transfer pricing rather than as repatriated dividends. Transfer pricing can also be used to shift profits from high-tax to low-tax jurisdictions. Of course, governments are well aware of these possibilities, so governmental auditors are on guard to prevent abusive transfer pricing.

Project Analysis

First, consider a domestic project that requires foreign raw materials, or one where the finished product will be sold in a foreign market. Because the operation is based in the United States, any projected nondollar cash flows—costs in the first example and revenues in the second—should be converted into dollars. This conversion does not present much of a problem for cash flows to be paid or received in the short run, but there is a significant problem in estimating exchange rates for converting long-term foreign cash flows into dollars because forward exchange rates are usually not available for more than 180 days into the future. However, long-term expected forward exchange rates can be estimated using the interest rate parity relationship set forth in Equation 26-1. For example, if a foreign cash flow is expected to occur in 1 year, then the 1-year forward exchange rate can be estimated using domestic and foreign government bonds maturing in 1 year. Similarly, the 2-year exchange rate can be estimated using 2-year bonds. Thus, foreign cash flows can be converted into dollars and added to the project's other projected cash flows, and then the project's NPV can be calculated based on the project's cost of capital.

Now consider a project that will be based overseas, where most expected future cash flows will be denominated in a foreign currency. Two approaches can be used to estimate such a project's NPV. Both begin by forecasting the future cash flows denominated in the foreign currency and then determining the annual repatriations to the United States, denominated in the foreign currency. Under the first approach, we convert the expected future repatriations to dollars (as described earlier), and then find the NPV using the project's cost of capital. Under the second approach, we take the projected repatriations, denominated in the foreign currency, and discount them at the foreign cost of capital, which reflects foreign interest rates and relevant risk premiums. This produces an NPV denominated in the foreign currency, which can be converted into a dollar-denominated NPV using the spot exchange rate.

The following example illustrates the first approach. A U.S. company has the opportunity to lease a manufacturing facility in Great Britain for 3 years. The company must spend £20 million initially to refurbish the plant. The expected net cash flows from the plant for the next 3 years, in millions, are $CF_1 = £7$, $CF_2 = £9$, and $CF_3 = £11$. A similar project in the United States would have a risk-adjusted cost of capital of 10%. The first step is to estimate the expected exchange rates at the end of 1, 2, and 3 years using the multi-year interest rate parity equation:

$$\text{Expected t-year forward exchange rate} = \text{Spot exchange rate} \left(\frac{1 + r_h}{1 + r_f}\right)^t \quad \textbf{(26-1b)}$$

where the exchange rates are expressed in direct quotations. We are using the interest rate parity equation to calculate forward rates because market-based forward rates for maturities longer than a year are not generally available.

Suppose the spot exchange rate is 1.8000 dollars per pound. Interest rates on U.S. and U.K. government bonds are shown below, along with the expected forward rate implied by the interest rate parity relationship in Equation 26-1b:

Maturity (in Years)	r_h	r_f	Spot Rate ($/£)	Expected Forward Rate Based on Equation 26-1b ($/£)
1	2.0%	4.6%	1.8000	1.7553
2	2.8	5.0	1.8000	1.7254
3	3.5	5.2	1.8000	1.7141

Table 26-5

Net Present Value of International Investment (Cash Flows in Millions)

	Year			
	0	**1**	**2**	**3**
Cash flows in pounds	−£20	£7	£9	£11
Expected exchange rates	1.8000	1.7553	1.7254	1.7141
Cash flows in dollars	−$36.00	$12.29	$15.53	$18.86
Project cost of capital =	10%			
NPV =	$2.18			

The current dollar cost of the project is £20(1.8000 $/£) = $36 million. The Year 1 cash flow in dollars is £7(1.7553 $/£) = $12.29 million. Table 26-5 shows the complete time line and the net present value of $2.18 million.

SELF-TEST

List some key differences in capital budgeting as applied to foreign versus domestic operations.

What are the relevant cash flows for an international investment—the cash flow produced by the subsidiary in the country where it operates or the cash flows in dollars that it sends to its parent company?

Why might the cost of capital for a foreign project differ from that of an equivalent domestic project? Could it be lower?

What adjustments might be made to the domestic cost of capital for a foreign investment due to exchange rate risk and political risk?

26.12 International Capital Structures

Companies' capital structures vary among countries. For example, the Organization for Economic Cooperation and Development (OECD) recently reported that, on average, Japanese firms use 85% debt to total assets (in book value terms), German firms use 64%, and U.S. firms use 55%. One problem, however, when interpreting these numbers is that different countries often use very different accounting conventions with regard to (1) reporting assets on a historical- versus a replacement-cost basis, (2) the treatment of leased assets, (3) pension plan funding, and (4) capitalizing versus expensing R&D costs. These differences make it difficult to compare capital structures.

A study by Raghuram Rajan and Luigi Zingales of the University of Chicago attempted to account for differences in accounting practices. In their study, Rajan and Zingales used a database that covered fewer firms than the OECD but that provided a more complete breakdown of balance sheet data. They concluded that differences in accounting practices can explain much of the cross-country variation in capital structures.

Rajan and Zingales's results are summarized in Table 26-6. There are a number of different ways to measure capital structure. One measure is the average ratio of total liabilities to total assets—this is similar to the measure used by the OECD, and it is reported in Column 1. Based on this measure, German and Japanese firms appear to be more highly levered than U.S. firms. However, if you look at Column 2, where capital structure is measured by interest-bearing debt to total assets, it appears that German firms use less leverage than U.S. and Japanese firms. What explains this

Table 26-6

Median Capital Structures among Large Industrialized Countries
(Measured in Terms of Book Value)

Country	Total Liabilities to Total Assets (Unadjusted for Accounting Differences) (1)	Interest-Bearing Debt to Total Assets (Unadjusted for Accounting Differences) (2)	Total Liabilities to Total Assets (Adjusted for Accounting Differences) (3)	Debt to Total Assets (Adjusted for Accounting Differences) (4)	Times-Interest-Earned (TIE) Ratio (5)
Canada	56%	32%	48%	32%	1.55×
France	71	25	69	18	2.64
Germany	73	16	50	11	3.20
Italy	70	27	68	21	1.81
Japan	69	35	62	21	2.46
United Kingdom	54	18	47	10	4.79
United States	58	27	52	25	2.41
Mean	64%	26%	57%	20%	2.69×
Standard deviation	8%	7%	10%	8%	1.07×

Source: Raghuram Rajan and Luigi Zingales, "What Do We Know about Capital Structure? Some Evidence from International Data," *Journal of Finance,* December 1995, pp. 1421–1460. Published by Blackwell Publishing.

difference? Rajan and Zingales argue that much of this difference is explained by the way German firms account for pension liabilities. German firms generally include all pension liabilities (and their offsetting assets) on the balance sheet, whereas firms in other countries (including the United States) generally "net out" pension assets and liabilities on their balance sheets. To see the importance of this difference, consider a firm with $10 million in liabilities (not including pension liabilities) and $20 million in assets (not including pension assets). Assume that the firm has $10 million in pension liabilities that are fully funded by $10 million in pension assets. Therefore, net pension liabilities are zero. If this firm were in the United States, it would report a ratio of total liabilities to total assets equal to 50% ($10 million/$20 million). By contrast, if this firm operated in Germany, both its pension assets and liabilities would be reported on the balance sheet. The firm would have $20 million in liabilities and $30 million in assets—or a 67% ($20 million/$30 million) ratio of total liabilities to total assets. Total debt is the sum of short-term debt and long-term debt and excludes other liabilities including pension liabilities. Therefore, the measure of total debt to total assets provides a more comparable measure of leverage across different countries.

Rajan and Zingales also make a variety of adjustments that attempt to control for other differences in accounting practices. The effects of these adjustments are reported in Columns 3 and 4. Overall, the evidence suggests that companies in Germany and the United Kingdom tend to have less leverage, whereas firms in Canada appear to have more leverage, relative to firms in the United States, France, Italy, and Japan. This conclusion is supported by data in the final column, which shows the average times-interest-earned ratio for firms in a number of different

tied to the dollar. After August 1971, the world monetary system changed to a **floating system** under which major world currency rates float with market forces, largely unrestricted by governmental intervention. The central bank of each country does operate in the foreign exchange market, buying and selling currencies to smooth out exchange rate fluctuations, but only to a limited extent.

- The consolidation of the European market has had a profound impact on European exchange rates. The exchange rates for the currencies of each of the participating countries were fixed relative to the **euro.** Consequently, the cross rates between the various participating currencies were also fixed. However, the value of the euro continues to fluctuate.

- **Pegged exchange rates** occur when a country establishes a fixed exchange rate with a major currency. Consequently, the values of pegged currencies move together over time.

- A **convertible currency** is one that may be readily exchanged for other currencies.

- **Spot rates** are the rates paid for delivery of currency "on the spot," while the **forward exchange rate** is the rate paid for delivery at some agreed-upon future date, usually 30, 90, or 180 days from the day the transaction is negotiated. The forward rate can be at either a **premium** or a **discount** to the spot rate.

- **Interest rate parity** holds that investors should expect to earn the same risk-free return in all countries after adjusting for exchange rates.

- **Purchasing power parity,** sometimes referred to as the *law of one price*, implies that the level of exchange rates adjusts so that identical goods cost the same in different countries.

- Granting credit is more risky in an international context because, in addition to the normal risks of default, the multinational firm must worry about **exchange rate changes** between the time a sale is made and the time a receivable is collected.

- Credit policy is important for a multinational firm for two reasons: (1) Much trade is with less-developed nations, and in such situations granting credit is a necessary condition for doing business. (2) The governments of nations such as Japan, whose economic health depends on exports, often help their firms compete by granting credit to foreign customers.

- Foreign investments are similar to domestic investments, but political risk and exchange rate risk must be considered. **Political risk** is the risk that the foreign government will take some action that will decrease the value of the investment, while **exchange rate risk** is the risk of losses due to fluctuations in the value of the dollar relative to the values of foreign currencies.

- Investments in **international capital projects** expose firms to exchange rate risk and political risk. The relevant cash flows in international capital budgeting are the dollars that can be **repatriated** to the parent company.

- **Eurodollars** are U.S. dollars deposited in banks outside the United States. Interest rates on Eurodollars are tied to **LIBOR,** the **London Interbank Offer Rate.**

- U.S. firms often find that they can raise long-term capital at a lower cost outside the United States by selling bonds in the **international capital markets.** International bonds may be either **foreign bonds,** which are exactly like regular domestic bonds except that the issuer is a foreign company, or **Eurobonds,** which are bonds sold in a foreign country but denominated in the currency of the issuing company's home country.

Questions

(26-1) Define each of the following terms:
   a. Multinational corporation
   b. Exchange rate; fixed exchange rate system; floating exchange rates
   c. Trade deficit; devaluation; revaluation
   d. Exchange rate risk; convertible currency; pegged exchange rates
   e. Interest rate parity; purchasing power parity
   f. Spot rate; forward exchange rate; discount on forward rate; premium on forward rate
   g. Repatriation of earnings; political risk
   h. Eurodollar; Eurobond; international bond; foreign bond
   i. The euro

(26-2) Under the fixed exchange rate system, what was the currency against which all other currency values were defined? Why?

(26-3) Exchange rates fluctuate under both the fixed exchange rate and floating exchange rate systems. What, then, is the difference between the two systems?

(26-4) If the Swiss franc depreciates against the U.S. dollar, can a dollar buy more or fewer Swiss francs as a result?

(26-5) If the United States imports more goods from abroad than it exports, foreigners will tend to have a surplus of U.S. dollars. What will this do to the value of the dollar with respect to foreign currencies? What is the corresponding effect on foreign investments in the United States?

(26-6) Why do U.S. corporations build manufacturing plants abroad when they could build them at home?

(26-7) Should firms require higher rates of return on foreign projects than on identical projects located at home? Explain.

(26-8) What is a Eurodollar? If a French citizen deposits $10,000 in Chase Manhattan Bank in New York, have Eurodollars been created? What if the deposit is made in Barclay's Bank in London? Chase Manhattan's Paris branch? Does the existence of the Eurodollar market make the Federal Reserve's job of controlling U.S. interest rates easier or more difficult? Explain.

(26-9) Does interest rate parity imply that interest rates are the same in all countries?

(26-10) Why might purchasing power parity fail to hold?

Self-Test Problem   Solution Appears in Appendix A

(ST-1)
Cross Rates
Suppose the exchange rate between U.S. dollars and EMU euros is €0.98 = $1.00, and the exchange rate between the U.S. dollar and the Canadian dollar is $1.00 = C$1.50. What is the cross rate of euros to Canadian dollars?

Problems   Answers Appear in Appendix B

Easy
Problems 1–4

(26-1)
Cross Rates

A currency trader observes that in the spot exchange market, 1 U.S. dollar can be exchanged for 9 Mexican pesos or for 111.23 Japanese yen. What is the cross rate between the yen and the peso; that is, how many yen would you receive for every peso exchanged?

(26-2)
Interest Rate Parity

Six-month T-bills have a nominal rate of 7%, while default-free Japanese bonds that mature in 6 months have a nominal rate of 5.5%. In the spot exchange market, 1 yen equals $0.009. If interest rate parity holds, what is the 6-month forward exchange rate?

(26-3)
Purchasing Power Parity

A television set costs $500 in the United States. The same set costs 550 euros in France. If purchasing power parity holds, what is the spot exchange rate between the euro and the dollar?

(26-4)
Exchange Rate

If British pounds sell for $1.50 (U.S.) per pound, what should dollars sell for in pounds per dollar?

Intermediate
Problems 5–8

(26-5)
Currency Appreciation

Suppose that 1 Swiss franc could be purchased in the foreign exchange market for 60 U.S. cents today. If the franc appreciated 10% tomorrow against the dollar, how many francs would a dollar buy tomorrow?

(26-6)
Cross Rates

Suppose the exchange rate between U.S. dollars and the Swiss franc was SFr1.6 = $1, and the exchange rate between the dollar and the British pound was £1 = $1.50. What was the cross rate between francs and pounds?

(26-7)
Interest Rate Parity

Assume that interest rate parity holds. In both the spot market and the 90-day forward market 1 Japanese yen equals 0.0086 dollar. The 90-day risk-free securities yield 4.6% in Japan. What is the yield on 90-day risk-free securities in the United States?

(26-8)
Purchasing Power Parity

In the spot market 7.8 pesos can be exchanged for 1 U.S. dollar. A compact disk costs $15 in the United States. If purchasing power parity holds, what should be the price of the same disk in Mexico?

Challenging
Problems 9–14

(26-9)
Exchange Gains and Losses

You are the vice president of International InfoXchange, headquartered in Chicago, Illinois. All shareholders of the firm live in the United States. Earlier this month, you obtained a loan of 5 million Canadian dollars from a bank in Toronto to finance the construction of a new plant in Montreal. At the time the loan was received, the exchange rate was 75 U.S. cents to the Canadian dollar. By the end of the month, it has unexpectedly dropped to 70 cents. Has your company made a gain or loss as a result, and by how much?

(26-10)
Results of Exchange Rate Changes

Early in September 1983, it took 245 Japanese yen to equal $1. More than 20 years later that exchange rate had fallen to 108 yen to $1. Assume the price of a Japanese-manufactured automobile was $8,000 in September 1983 and that its price changes were in direct relation to exchange rates.

a. Has the price, in dollars, of the automobile increased or decreased during the 20-year period because of changes in the exchange rate?

b. What would the dollar price of the car be, assuming the car's price changes only with exchange rates?

(26-11)
Spot and Forward Rates

Boisjoly Watch Imports has agreed to purchase 15,000 Swiss watches for 1 million francs at today's spot rate. The firm's financial manager, James Desreumaux, has noted the following current spot and forward rates:

	U.S. Dollar/Franc	Franc/U.S. Dollar
Spot	1.6590	0.6028
30-day forward	1.6540	0.6046
90-day forward	1.6460	0.6075
180-day forward	1.6400	0.6098

On the same day, Desreumaux agrees to purchase 15,000 more watches in 3 months at the same price of 1 million francs.

a. What is the price of the watches, in U.S. dollars, if purchased at today's spot rate?

b. What is the cost, in dollars, of the second 15,000 batch if payment is made in 90 days and the spot rate at that time equals today's 90-day forward rate?

c. If the exchange rate for the Swiss franc is 0.50 to $1 in 90 days, how much will he have to pay for the watches (in dollars)?

(26-12)
Interesst Rate Parity

Assume that interest rate parity holds and that 90-day risk-free securities yield 5% in the United States and 5.3% in Germany. In the spot market, 1 euro equals $0.80 dollar.

a. Is the 90-day forward rate trading at a premium or discount relative to the spot rate?

b. What is the 90-day forward rate?

(26-13)
Foreign Investment Analysis

After all foreign and U.S. taxes, a U.S. corporation expects to receive 3 pounds of dividends per share from a British subsidiary this year. The exchange rate at the end of the year is expected to be $1.60 per pound, and the pound is expected to depreciate 5% against the dollar each year for an indefinite period. The dividend (in pounds) is expected to grow at 10% a year indefinitely. The parent U.S. corporation owns 10 million shares of the subsidiary. What is the present value in dollars of its equity ownership of the subsidiary? Assume a cost of equity capital of 15% for the subsidiary.

(26-14)
Foreign Capital Budgeting

Solitaire Machinery is a Swiss multinational manufacturing company. Currently, Solitaire's financial planners are considering undertaking a 1-year project in the United States. The project's expected dollar-denominated cash flows consist of an initial investment of $1,000 and a cash inflow the following year of $1,200. Solitaire estimates that its risk-adjusted cost of capital is 14%. Currently, 1 U.S. dollar will buy 1.62 Swiss francs. In addition, 1-year risk-free securities in the United States are yielding 7.25%, while similar securities in Switzerland are yielding 4.5%.

a. If this project were instead undertaken by a similar U.S.-based company with the same risk-adjusted cost of capital, what would be the net present value and rate of return generated by this project?
b. What is the expected forward exchange rate 1 year from now?
c. If Solitaire undertakes the project, what is the net present value and rate of return of the project for Solitaire?

Spreadsheet Problem

(26-15)
Build a Model:
Multinational Financial
Management

e-resource

Start with the partial model in the file *FM12 Ch 26 P15 Build a Model.xls* from the textbook's Web site. Yohe Telecommunications is a multinational corporation that produces and distributes telecommunications technology. Although its corporate headquarters are located in Maitland, Florida, Yohe usually must buy its raw materials in several different foreign countries using several different foreign currencies. The matter is further complicated because Yohe usually sells its products in other foreign countries. One product in particular, the SY-20 radio transmitter, draws its principal components, Component X, Component Y, and Component Z, from Germany, Mexico, and England, respectively. Specifically, Component X costs 84 euros, Component Y costs 650 Mexican pesos, and Component Z costs 105 British pounds. The largest market for the SY-20 is in Japan, where it sells for 38,000 Japanese yen. Naturally, Yohe is intimately concerned with economic conditions that could adversely affect dollar exchange rates. You will find Tables 26-1, 26-2, and 26-3 useful for this problem.

a. How much, in dollars, does it cost for Yohe to produce the SY-20? What is the dollar sale price of the SY-20?
b. What is the dollar profit that Yohe makes on the sale of the SY-20? What is the percentage profit?
c. If the U.S. dollar were to weaken by 10% against all foreign currencies, what would be the dollar profit for the SY-20?
d. If the U.S. dollar were to weaken by 10% only against the Japanese yen and remain constant relative to all other foreign currencies, what would be the dollar and percentage profits for the SY-20?
e. Using the forward exchange information from Table 26-3, calculate the return on 1-year securities in England, if the rate of return on 1-year securities in the United States is 4.9%.
f. Assuming that purchasing power parity (PPP) holds, what would be the sale price of the SY-20 if it were sold in England rather than in Japan?

Cyberproblem

e-resource

Please go to the textbook's Web site to access any Cyberproblems.

Mini Case

Citrus Products Inc. is a medium-sized producer of citrus juice drinks with groves in Indian River County, Florida. Until now, the company has confined its operations and sales to the United States, but its CEO, George Gaynor, wants to expand into Europe. The first step would be to set up sales subsidiaries in Spain and Sweden, then to set up a production plant in Spain, and, finally, to distribute the product throughout the European common market. The firm's financial manager, Ruth Schmidt, is enthusiastic about the plan, but she is worried about the implications of the foreign expansion on the firm's financial management process. She has asked you, the firm's most recently hired financial analyst, to develop a 1-hour tutorial package that explains the basics of multinational financial management. The tutorial will be presented at the next board of directors' meeting. To get you started, Schmidt has supplied you with the following list of questions.

a. What is a multinational corporation? Why do firms expand into other countries?

b. What are the six major factors that distinguish multinational financial management from financial management as practiced by a purely domestic firm?

c. Consider the following illustrative exchange rates.

	U.S. Dollars Required to Buy One Unit of Foreign Currency
Euro	0.8000
Swedish krona	0.1000

(1) Are these currency prices direct quotations or indirect quotations?

(2) Calculate the indirect quotations for euros and kronas.

(3) What is a cross rate? Calculate the two cross rates between euros and kronas.

(4) Assume Citrus Products can produce a liter of orange juice and ship it to Spain for $1.75. If the firm wants a 50% markup on the product, what should the orange juice sell for in Spain?

(5) Now, assume Citrus Products begins producing the same liter of orange juice in Spain. The product costs 2.0 euros to produce and ship to Sweden, where it can be sold for 20 kronas. What is the dollar profit on the sale?

(6) What is exchange rate risk?

d. Briefly describe the current international monetary system. How does the current system differ from the system that was in place prior to August 1971?

e. What is a convertible currency? What problems arise when a multinational company operates in a country whose currency is not convertible?

f. What is the difference between spot rates and forward rates? When is the forward rate at a premium to the spot rate? At a discount?

g. What is interest rate parity? Currently, you can exchange 1 euro for 0.8100 dollar in the 180-day forward market, and the risk-free rate on 180-day securities is 6% in the United States and 4% in Spain. Does interest rate parity hold? If not, which securities offer the highest expected return?

h. What is purchasing power parity? If grapefruit juice costs $2.00 a liter in the United States and purchasing power parity holds, what should be the price of grapefruit juice in Spain?

i. What effect does relative inflation have on interest rates and exchange rates?
j. Briefly discuss the international capital markets.
k. To what extent do average capital structures vary across different countries?
l. Briefly describe special problems that occur in multinational capital budgeting and describe the process for evaluating a foreign project. Now consider the following project: A U.S. company has the opportunity to lease a manufacturing facility in Japan for 2 years. The company must spend ¥1 billion initially to refurbish the plant. The expected net cash flows from the plant for the next 2 years, in millions, are CF_1 = ¥500 and CF_2 = ¥800. A similar project in the United States would have a risk-adjusted cost of capital of 10%. In the United States, a 1-year government bond pays 2% interest and a 2-year bond pays 2.8%. In Japan, a 1-year bond pays 0.05% and a 2-year bond pays 0.26%. What is the project's NPV?
m. Briefly discuss special factors associated with the following areas of multinational working capital management.
    (1) Cash management
    (2) Credit management
    (3) Inventory management

Selected Additional Case

The following case from Textchoice, Cengage Learning's online library, covers many of the concepts discussed in this chapter and is available at *http:// www.textchoice2.com.*

Klein-Brigham Series:
Case 18, "Alaska Oil Corporation."

appendix a

Solutions to Self-Test Problems

Chapter 2

(ST-1) a.

$1,000 is being compounded for 3 years, so your balance at Year 4 is $1,259.71:

$$FV_N = PV(1 + I)^N = \$1,000(1 + 0.08)^3 = \$1,259.71.$$

Alternatively, using a financial calculator, input $N = 3$, $I/YR = 8$, $PV = -1000$, $PMT = 0$, and $FV = ?$ Solve for $FV = \$1,259.71$.

b.

There are 12 compounding periods from Quarter 4 to Quarter 16.

$$FV_N = PV\left(1 + \frac{I_{NOM}}{M}\right)^{NM} = FV_{12} = \$1,000(1.02)^{12} = \$1,268.24.$$

Alternatively, using a financial calculator, input $N = 12$, $I/YR = 2$, $PV = -1000$, $PMT = 0$, and $FV = ?$ Solve for $FV = \$1,268.24$.

c.

$$FVA_4 = \$250\left[\frac{(1 + 0.08)^4}{0.08} - \frac{1}{0.08}\right] = \$1,126.53.$$

Using a financial calculator, input $N = 4$, $I/YR = 8$, $PV = 0$, $PMT = -250$, and $FV = ?$ Solve for $FV = \$1,126.53$.

d.

$$PMT\left[\frac{(1 + 0.08)^4}{0.08} - \frac{1}{0.08}\right] = \$1,259.71$$

$$PMT(4.5061) = \$1,259.71$$

$$PMT = \$279.56.$$

Using a financial calculator, input N = 4, I/YR = 8, PV = 0, FV = 1259.71, and PMT = ? Solve for PMT = −$279.56.

(ST-2) a. Set up a time line like the one in the preceding problem:

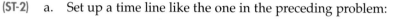

Note that your deposit will grow for 3 years at 8%. The deposit at Year 1 is the PV, and the FV is $1,000. Here is the solution:

N = 3; I/YR = 8; PMT = 0; FV = 1000; PV = ?; PV = $793.83.

Alternatively,

$$PV = \frac{FV_N}{(1 + I)^N} = \frac{\$1,000}{(1 + 0.08)^3} = \$793.83.$$

b. 0   8%   1   2   3   4
    ├────────────────┼────────────────┼────────────────┼────────────────┤
             ?   ?   ?   ?
                                                            FV = 1,000

Here we are dealing with a 4-year annuity whose first payment occurs 1 year from today and whose future value must equal $1,000. Here is the solution:

N = 4; I/YR = 8; PV = 0; FV = 1000; PMT = ?; PMT = $221.92.

Alternatively,

$$PMT\left[\frac{(1 + 0.08)^4}{0.08} - \frac{1}{0.08}\right] = \$1,000$$

$$PMT(4.5061) = \$1,000$$

$$PMT = \$221.92.$$

c. This problem can be approached in several ways. Perhaps the simplest is to ask this question: "If I received $750 1 year from now and deposited it to earn 8%, would I have the required $1,000 4 years from now?" The answer is no:

0   8%   1   2   3   4
├────────────────┼────────────────┼────────────────┼────────────────┤
          −750   FV = ?

$$FV_3 = \$750(1.08)(1.08)(1.08) = \$944.78.$$

This indicates that you should let your father make the payments rather than accept the lump sum of $750.
You could also compare the $750 with the PV of the payments:

0   8%   1   2   3   4
├────────────────┼────────────────┼────────────────┼────────────────┤
          221.92   221.92   221.92   221.92

N = 4; I/YR = 8; PMT = −221.92; FV = 0; PV = ?; PV = $735.03.

Alternatively,

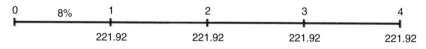

$$PVA_4 = \$221.92\left[\frac{1}{0.08} - \frac{1}{(0.08)(1 + 08)^4}\right] = \$735.03.$$

This is less than the $750 lump sum offer, so your initial reaction might be to accept the lump sum of $750. However, this would be a mistake. The problem is that when you found the $735.02 PV of the annuity, you were finding the value of the annuity *today*. You were comparing $735.02 today with the lump sum of $750 1 year from now. This is, of course, invalid. What you should have done was take the $735.02, recognize that this is the PV of an annuity as of today, multiply $735.02 by 1.08 to get $793.83, and compare $793.83 with the lump sum of $750. You would then take your father's offer to make the payments rather than take the lump sum 1 year from now.

d.

0	I = ?	1	2	3	4
		−750			1,000

$N = 3$; $PV = -750$; $PMT = 0$; $FV = 1000$; solve for $I/YR = 10.0642\%$.

e.

0	I = ?	1	2	3	4
		186.29	186.29	186.29	186.29 FV = 1,000

$N = 4$; $PV = 0$; $PMT = -186.29$; $FV = 1000$; solve for $I/YR = 19.9997\%$.

You might be able to find a borrower willing to offer you a 20% interest rate, but there would be some risk involved—he or she might not actually pay you your $1,000!

f.

0	8%	1	2	3	4
		400	?	?	? FV = 1,000

Find the future value of the original $400 deposit:

$$FV_6 = PV(1 + I)^6 = 400(1 + 0.04)^6 = \$400(1.2653) = \$506.12.$$

This means that at Year 4, you need an additional sum of $493.88:

$$\$1,000.00 - \$506.12 = \$493.88.$$

This will be accumulated by making 6 equal payments which earn 8% compounded semiannually, or 4% each 6 months:

$N = 6$; $I/YR = 4$; $PV = 0$; $FV = 493.88$; $PMT = ?$; $PMT = \$74.46$.

Alternatively,

$$PMT\left[\frac{(1 + 0.04)^6}{0.04} - \frac{1}{0.04}\right] = \$493.88$$

$$PMT(6.6330) = \$493.88$$

$$PMT = \$74.46.$$

g.

$$EFF\% = \left(1 + \frac{I_{NOM}}{M}\right)^M - 1.0$$

$$= \left(1 + \frac{0.08}{2}\right)^2 - 1.0$$

$$= 1.0816 - 1 = 0.0816 = 8.16\%.$$

(ST-3)   Bank A's effective annual rate is 8.24%:

$$\text{EFF\%} = \left(1 + \frac{0.08}{4}\right)^4 - 1.0$$

$$= 1.0824 - 1 = 0.0824 = 8.24\%.$$

Now Bank B must have the same effective annual rate:

$$\left(1 + \frac{I}{12}\right)^{12} - 1.0 = 0.0824$$

$$\left(1 + \frac{I}{12}\right)^{12} = 1.0824$$

$$\left(1 + \frac{I}{12}\right) = (1.0824)^{1/12}$$

$$\left(1 + \frac{I}{12}\right) = 1.00662$$

$$\frac{I}{12} = 0.00662$$

$$I = 0.07944 = 7.94\%.$$

Thus, the two banks have different quoted rates—Bank A's quoted rate is 8%, while Bank B's quoted rate is 7.94%; however, both banks have the same effective annual rate of 8.24%. The difference in their quoted rates is due to the difference in compounding frequency.

Chapter 3

(ST-1)   a.

EBIT	$5,000,000
Interest	1,000,000
EBT	$4,000,000
Taxes (40%)	1,600,000
Net income	$2,400,000

b.   NCF = NI + DEP and AMORT

   = $2,400,000 + $1,000,000 = $3,400,000.

c.   NOPAT = EBIT(1 − T)

   = $5,000,000(0.6)

   = $3,000,000.

d.   NOWC = Operating current assets

   − Operating current liabilities

   = $14,000,000 − $4,000,000

   = $10,000,000.

Total net operating capital = NOWC + operating long-term assets

   = $10,000,000 + $15,000,000

   = $25,000,000.

e.
$$\text{FCF} = \text{NOPAT} - \text{Net investment in operating capital}$$
$$= \$3,000,000 - (\$25,000,000 - \$24,000,000)$$
$$= \$2,000,000.$$

f.
$$\text{EVA} = \text{EBIT}(1 - T) - (\text{Total capital})(\text{After-tax cost of capital})$$
$$= \$5,000,000(0.6) - (\$25,000,000)(0.10)$$
$$= \$3,000,000 - \$2,500,000 = \$500,000.$$

Chapter 4

(ST-1) Argent paid $2 in dividends and retained $2 per share. Since total retained earnings rose by $12 million, there must be 6 million shares outstanding. With a book value of $40 per share, total common equity must be $40(6 million) = $240 million. Since Argent has $120 million of debt, its debt ratio must be 33.3%:

$$\frac{\text{Debt}}{\text{Assets}} = \frac{\text{Debt}}{\text{Debt} + \text{Equity}} = \frac{\$120 \text{ million}}{\$120 \text{ million} + \$240 \text{ million}}$$

$$= 0.333 = 33.3\%.$$

a. In answering questions such as this, always begin by writing down the relevant definitional equations, then start filling in numbers. Note that the extra zeros indicating millions have been deleted in the calculations below.

(1)
$$\text{DSO} = \frac{\text{Accounts receivable}}{\text{Sales}/365}$$

$$40.55 = \frac{\text{A/R}}{\text{Sales}/365}$$

$$\text{A/R} = 40.55(\$2.7397) = \$111.1 \text{ million}.$$

(2)
$$\text{Quick ratio} = \frac{\text{Current assets} - \text{Inventories}}{\text{Current liabilities}} = 2.0$$

$$= \frac{\text{Cash and marketable securities} + \text{A/R}}{\text{Current liabilities}} = 2.0$$

$$2.0 = \frac{\$100.0 + \$111.1}{\text{Current liabilities}}$$

$$\text{Current liabilities} = (\$100.0 + \$111.1)/2 = \$105.5 \text{ million}.$$

(3)
$$\text{Current ratio} = \frac{\text{Current assets}}{\text{Current liabilities}} = 3.0$$

$$= \frac{\text{Current assets}}{\$105.5} = 3.0$$

$$\text{Current assets} = 3.0(\$105.5) = \$316.50 \text{ million}.$$

(4)
$$\text{Total assets} = \text{Current assets} + \text{Fixed assets}$$
$$= \$316.5 + \$283.5 = \$600 \text{ million}.$$

(5)
$$\text{ROA} = \text{Profit margin} \times \text{Total assets turnover}$$

$$= \frac{\text{Net income}}{\text{Sales}} \times \frac{\text{Sales}}{\text{Total assets}}$$

$$= \frac{\$50}{\$1,000} \times \frac{\$1,000}{\$600}$$

$$= 0.05 \times 1.667 = 0.083333 = 8.3333\%.$$

(6)
$$\text{ROE} = \text{ROA} \times \frac{\text{Assets}}{\text{Equity}}$$

$$12.0\% = 8.3333\% \times \frac{\$600}{\text{Equity}}$$

$$\text{Equity} = \frac{(8.3333\%)(\$600)}{12.0\%}$$

$$= \$416.67 \text{ million.}$$

(7)
$$\text{Total assets} = \text{Total claims} = \$600 \text{ million.}$$

$$\text{Current liabilities} + \text{Long-term debt} + \text{Equity} = \$600 \text{ million}$$

$$\$105.5 + \text{Long-term debt} + \$416.67 = \$600 \text{ million}$$

$$\text{Long-term debt} = \$600 - \$105.5 - \$416.67 = \$77.83 \text{ million.}$$

Note: We could have found equity as follows:

$$\text{ROE} = \frac{\text{Net income}}{\text{Equity}}$$

$$12.0\% = \frac{\$50}{\text{Equity}}$$

$$\text{Equity} = \$50/0.12$$

$$= \$416.67 \text{ million.}$$

Then we could have gone on to find long-term debt.

b. Jacobus's average sales per day were $\$1,000/365 = \$2.7397$ million. Its DSO was 40.55, so $\text{A/R} = 40.55(\$2.7397) = \$111.1$ million. Its new DSO of 30.4 would cause $\text{A/R} = 30.4(\$2.7397) = \$83.3$ million. The reduction in receivables would be $\$111.1 - \$83.3 = \$27.8$ million, which would equal the amount of cash generated.

(1)
$$\text{New equity} = \text{Old equity} - \text{Stock bought back}$$

$$= \$416.7 - \$27.8$$

$$= \$388.9 \text{ million.}$$

Thus,

$$\text{New ROE} = \frac{\text{Net income}}{\text{New equity}}$$

$$= \frac{\$50}{\$388.9}$$

$$= 12.86\% \text{ (versus old ROE of } 12.0\%).$$

$$(2) \qquad \text{New ROA} = \frac{\text{Net income}}{\text{Total assets} - \text{Reduction in A/R}}$$

$$= \frac{\$50}{\$600 - \$27.8}$$

$$= 8.74\% \text{ (versus old ROA of } 8.33\%).$$

(3) The old debt is the same as the new debt:

$$\text{Debt} = \text{Total claims} - \text{Equity}$$

$$= \$600 - \$416.7 = \$183.3 \text{ million.}$$

$$\text{New total assets} = \text{Old total assets} - \text{Reduction in A/R}$$

$$= \$600 - \$27.8$$

$$= \$572.2 \text{ million.}$$

Therefore,

$$\frac{\text{Debt}}{\text{Old total assets}} = \frac{\$183.3}{\$600} = 30.6\%$$

while

$$\frac{\text{New debt}}{\text{New total assets}} = \frac{\$183.3}{\$572.2} = 32.0\%.$$

Chapter 5

(ST-1) a. Pennington's bonds were sold at par; therefore, the original YTM equaled the coupon rate of 12%.

b.
$$V_B = \sum_{t=1}^{50} \frac{\$120/2}{\left(1 + \dfrac{0.10}{2}\right)^t} + \frac{\$1,000}{\left(1 + \dfrac{1.10}{2}\right)^{50}}$$

$$= \$60\left[\frac{1}{0.05} - \frac{1}{0.05(1 + 0.05)^{50}}\right] + \frac{\$1,000}{(1 + 0.05)^{50}}$$

$$= \$1,182.56.$$

Alternatively, with a financial calculator, input the following: $N = 50, I/YR = 5,$ $PMT = 60, FV = 1000,$ and $PV = ?$ Solve for $PV = -\$1,182.56.$

c.
$$\text{Current yield} = \text{Annual coupon payment/Price}$$

$$= \$120/\$1,182.56$$

$$= 0.1015 = 10.15\%.$$

$$\text{Capital gains yield} = \text{Total yield} - \text{Current yield}$$

$$= 10\% - 10.15\% = -0.15\%.$$

d.
$$\$916.42 = \sum_{t=1}^{13} \frac{\$60}{(1 + r_d/2)^t} + \frac{\$1000}{(1 + r_d/2)^{13}}.$$

With a financial calculator, input the following: $N = 13$, $PV = -916.42$, $PMT = 60$, $FV = 1000$, and $r_d/2 = I/YR = ?$ Calculator solution $= r_d/2 = 7.00\%$; therefore, $r_d = 14.00\%$.

e.
$$\text{Current yield} = \$120/\$916.42 = 13.09\%;$$
$$\text{Capital gains yield} = 14\% - 13.09\% = 0.91\%.$$

f. The following time line illustrates the years to maturity of the bond:

1/1/07   7/01/07   12/31/07   7/1/08   12/31/08   12/31/11

3/1/07

Thus, on March 1, 2007, there were 13⅔ periods left before the bond matured. Bond traders actually use the following procedure to determine the price of the bond:

(1) Find the price of the bond on the next coupon date, July 1, 2007.

$$V_B = \$60\left[\frac{1}{0.0775} - \frac{1}{0.0775(1 + 0.0775)^{13}}\right] + \frac{\$1,000}{(1 + 0.0775)^{13}}$$

$$= \$859.76.$$

Using a financial calculator, input $N = 13$, $I/YR = 7.75$, $PMT = 60$, $FV = 1000$, and $PV = ?$ Solve for $PV = -\$859.76$.

(2) Add the coupon, $60, to the bond price to get the total value, TV, of the bond on the next interest payment date: $TV = \$859.76 + \$60.00 = \$919.76$.

(3) Discount this total value back to the purchase date:

$$\text{Value at purchase date (March 1, 2007)} = \frac{\$919.76}{(1 + 0.0775)^{(4/6)}}$$

$$= \$919.76(0.9515)$$

$$= \$875.11.$$

Using a financial calculator, input $N = 4/6$, $I/YR = 7.75$, $PMT = 0$, $FV = 919.76$, and $PV = ?$ Solve for $PV = \$875.11$.

(4) Therefore, you would have written a check for $875.11 to complete the transaction. Of this amount, $20 = (\frac{1}{3})(\$60)$ would represent accrued interest and $855.11 would represent the bond's basic value. This breakdown would affect both your taxes and those of the seller.

(5) This problem could be solved *very* easily using a spreadsheet or a financial calculator with a bond valuation function.

Chapter 6

(ST-1) a. The average rate of return for each stock is calculated simply by averaging the returns over the 5-year period. The average return for Stock A is

$$r_{\text{Avg A}} = (-18\% + 44\% - 22\% + 22\% + 34\%)/5$$
$$= 12\%.$$

The realized rate of return on a portfolio made up of Stock A and Stock B would be calculated by finding the average return in each year as

$$r_A(\% \text{ of Stock A}) + r_B(\% \text{ of Stock B})$$

and then averaging these annual returns:

Year	Portfolio AB's Return, r_{AB}
2003	(21%)
2004	34
2005	(13)
2006	15
2007	45
	r_{Avg} = 12%

b. The standard deviation of returns is estimated as follows:

$$\text{Estimated } \sigma = S = \sqrt{\frac{\sum\limits_{t=1}^{N} (\bar{r}_t - \bar{r}_{Avg})^2}{n-1}}.$$

For Stock A, the estimated σ is 30%:

$$\sigma_A = \sqrt{\frac{\begin{array}{c}(-18\% - 12\%)^2 + (44\% - 12\%)^2 + (-22\% - 12\%)^2 + \\ (22\% - 12\%)^2 + (34\% - 12\%)^2\end{array}}{5-1}}$$

$$= 30.265\% \approx 30\%.$$

The standard deviations of returns for Stock B and for the portfolio are similarly determined, and they are as follows:

	Stock A	Stock B	Portfolio AB
Standard deviation	30%	30%	29%

c. Because the risk reduction from diversification is small (σ_{AB} falls only from 30% to 29%), the most likely value of the correlation coefficient is 0.8. If the correlation coefficient were -0.8, the risk reduction would be much larger. In fact, the correlation coefficient between Stocks A and B is 0.8.

d. If more randomly selected stocks were added to a portfolio, σ_P would decline to somewhere in the vicinity of 20%; see Figure 6-7. σ_P would remain constant only if the correlation coefficient were $+1.0$, which is most unlikely. σ_P would decline to zero only if the correlation coefficient, ρ, were equal to zero and a large number of stocks were added to the portfolio, or if the proper proportions were held in a two-stock portfolio with $\rho = -1.0$.

(ST-2) a. $b = (0.6)(0.70) + (0.25)(0.90) + (0.1)(1.30) + (0.05)(1.50)$

$= 0.42 + 0.225 + 0.13 + 0.075 = 0.85.$

b. $r_{RF} = 6\%; RP_M = 5\%; b = 0.85.$

$r_p = 6\% + (5\%)(0.85)$

$= 10.25\%.$

c. $b_N = (0.5)(0.70) + (0.25)(0.90) + (0.1)(1.30) + (0.15)(1.50)$

$= 0.35 + 0.225 + 0.13 + 0.225$

$= 0.93.$

$r = 6\% + (5\%)(0.93)$

$= 10.65\%.$

$$\hat{r}_p = w_{RF}(r_{RF}) + (1 - w_{RF})(\hat{r}_M)$$

$$22 = w_{RF}(10) + (1 - w_{RF})(16.8)$$

$$= 10w_{RF} + 16.8 - 16.8w_{RF}$$

$$-6.8w_{RF} = 5.2$$

$$w_{RF} = -0.76 \text{ or } -76\%, \text{ which means that you borrow.}$$

$$1 - w_{RF} = 1.0 - (-0.76)$$

$$= +1.76 \text{ or } 176\% \text{ in the market portfolio.}$$

This investor, with $200,000 of net worth, thus buys stock with a value of $200,000(1.76) = $352,000 and borrows $152,000.

The risk of this leveraged portfolio is

$$\sigma_p = \sqrt{(-0.76)^2(0)^2 + (1.76)^2(8.5)^2 + 2(-0.76)(1.76)(0)(8.5)(0)}$$

$$= \sqrt{(1.76)^2(8.5)^2}$$

$$= (1.76)(8.5) = 15\%.$$

Your indifference curve suggests that you are not very risk averse. A risk-averse investor would have a steep indifference curve (visualize a set of steep curves that were tangent to CML to the left of Point C). This investor would hold some of A and B, combined to form portfolio M, and some of the riskless asset.

g. Given your assumed indifference curve, you would, when the riskless asset becomes available, change your portfolio from the one found in part e (with $\hat{r}_p = 18\%$, $\sigma_p = 13.5\%$) to one with $\hat{r}_p \approx 22.0\%$ and $\sigma_p \approx 15.00\%$.

h.

$$r_A = r_{RF} + (r_M - r_{RF})b_A$$

$$15 = 10 + (16.8 - 10)b_A$$

$$= 10 + (6.8)b_A$$

$$b_A = 0.74.$$

$$20 = 10 + (6.8)b_B$$

$$b_B = 1.47.$$

Note that the 16.8% value for r_M was approximated from the graph. Also, note that this solution *assumes* that you can borrow at $r_{RF} = 10\%$. This is a basic—but questionable—CAPM assumption. If the borrowing rate is *above* r_{RF}, then CML would turn down to the right of Point M.

Chapter 8

(ST-1)   The first step is to solve for g, the unknown variable, in the constant growth equation. Since D_1 is unknown but D_0 is known, substitute $D_0(1 + g)$ as follows:

$$\hat{P}_0 = P_0 = \frac{D_1}{r_s - g} = \frac{D_0(1 + g)}{r_s - g}$$

$$\$36 = \frac{\$2.40(1 + g)}{0.12 - g}.$$

Solving for g, we find the growth rate to be 5%:

$$\$4.32 - \$36g = \$2.40 + \$2.40g$$

$$\$38.4g = \$1.92$$
$$g = 0.05 = 5\%.$$

The next step is to use the growth rate to project the stock price 5 years hence:

$$\hat{P}_5 = \frac{D_0(1 + g)^6}{r_s - g}$$

$$= \frac{\$2.40(1.05)^6}{0.12 - 0.05}$$

$$= \$45.95.$$

(Alternatively, $\hat{P}_5 = \$36(1.05)^5 = \$45.95$.)

Therefore, Ewald Company's expected stock price 5 years from now, $\hat{P}_5$, is $\$45.95$.

(ST-2) a. (1) Calculate the PV of the dividends paid during the supernormal growth period:

$$D_1 = \$1.1500(1.15) = \$1.3225;$$
$$D_2 = \$1.3225(1.15) = \$1.5209;$$
$$D_3 = \$1.5209(1.13) = \$1.7186.$$

$$PVD = \$1.3225/(1.12) + \$1.5209/(1.12)^2 + \$1.7186/(1.12)^3$$
$$= \$3.6167 \approx \$3.62.$$

(2) Find the PV of Snyder's stock price at the end of Year 3:

$$\hat{P}_3 = \frac{D_4}{r_s - g} = \frac{D_3(1 + g)}{r_s - g}$$

$$= \frac{\$1.7186(1.06)}{0.12 - 0.06}$$

$$= \$30.36.$$

$$PV \; \hat{P}_3 = \$30.36/(1.12)^3 = \$21.61.$$

(3) Sum the two components to find the value of the stock today:

$$\hat{P}_0 = \$3.62 + \$21.61 = \$25.23.$$

Alternatively, the cash flows can be placed on a time line as follows:

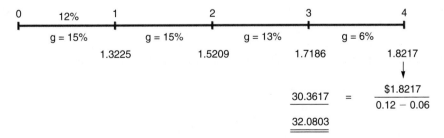

Enter the cash flows into the cash flow register ($CF_0 = 0$, $CF_1 = 1.3225$, $CF_2 = 1.5209$, $CF_3 = 32.0803$) and $I/YR = 12$, and press the NPV key to obtain $\hat{P}_0 = \$25.23$.

b. $\qquad \hat{P}_1 = \$1.5209/(1.12) + \$1.7186/(1.12)^2 + \$30.36/(1.12)^3$

$\qquad = \$26.9311 \approx \$26.93.$

(Calculator solution: $26.93.)

$\qquad \hat{P}_2 = \$1.7186/1.12 + \$30.36/(1.12)^2$

$\qquad = \$28.6429 \approx \$28.64.$

(Calculator solution: $28.64.)

c.

Year	Dividend Yield	+	Capital Gains Yield		=	Total Return
1	$\dfrac{\$1.3225}{\$25.23} \approx 5.24\%$	+	$\dfrac{\$26.93 - \$25.23}{\$25.23} \approx 6.74\%$		$\approx$	12%.
2	$\dfrac{\$1.5209}{\$26.93} \approx 5.65\%$	+	$\dfrac{\$28.64 - \$26.93}{\$26.93} \approx 6.35\%$		$\approx$	12%.
3	$\dfrac{\$1.7186}{\$28.64} \approx 6.00\%$	+	$\dfrac{\$30.36 - \$28.64}{\$28.64} \approx 6.00\%$		$\approx$	12%.

Chapter 9

(ST-1) The option will pay off $60 − $42 = $18 if the stock price is up. The option pays off zero if the stock price is down. Find the number of shares in the hedge portfolio:

$$N = \frac{C_u - C_d}{P_u - P_d} = \frac{\$18 - \$0}{\$60 - \$30} = 0.60.$$

With 0.6 shares, the stock's payoff will be either 0.6($60) = $36 or 0.6($30) = $18. The portfolio's payoff will be $36 − $18 = $18, or $18 − 0 = $18.

The present value of $18 at the daily compounded risk-free rate is PV = $18/[1 + (0.05/365)]^{365} = $17.12.

The option price is the current value of the stock in the portfolio minus the PV of the payoff:

$$V = 0.6(\$40) - \$17.12 = \$6.88.$$

(ST-2)

$$d_1 = \frac{\ln(P/X) + [r_{RF} + (\sigma^2/2)]t}{\sigma\sqrt{t}}$$

$$= \frac{\ln(\$22/\$20) + [0.05 + (0.49/2)](0.5)}{0.7\sqrt{0.5}}$$

$$= 0.4906.$$

$$d_2 = d_1 - \sigma(t)^{0.5} = 0.4906 - 0.7(0.5)^{0.5} = -0.0044.$$

$N(d_1) = 0.6881$ (from Excel NORMSDIST function).

$N(d_2) = 0.4982$ (from Excel NORMSDIST function).

$$V = P[N(d_1)] - Xe^{-r_{RF}t}[N(d_2)]$$

$$= \$22(0.6881) - \$20e^{(-0.05)(0.5)}(0.4982)$$

$$= \$5.42.$$

Chapter 10

(ST-1)   a.   Component costs are as follows:

Debt at $r_d = 9\%$:

$$r_d(1 - T) = 9\%(0.6) = 5.4\%.$$

Preferred with F = 5%:

$$r_{ps} = \frac{\text{Preferred dividend}}{P_{ps}(1 - F)} = \frac{\$9}{\$100(0.95)} = 9.5\%.$$

Common with DCF:

$$r_s = \frac{D_1}{P_0} + g = \frac{\$3.922}{\$60} + 6\% = 12.5\%.$$

Common with CAPM:

$$r_s = 6\% + 1.3(5\%) = 12.5\%.$$

b.
$$WACC = w_d r_d(1 - T) + w_{ps}r_{ps} + w_{ce}r_s$$
$$= 0.25(9\%)(1 - T) + 0.15(9.5\%) + 0.60(12.5\%)$$
$$= 10.275\%.$$

Chapter 11

(ST-1)   a.   **Payback:**

To determine the payback, construct the cumulative cash flows for each project:

	Cumulative Cash Flows	
Year	Project X	Project Y
0	($10,000)	($10,000)
1	(3,500)	(6,500)
2	(500)	(3,000)
3	2,500	500
4	3,500	4,000

$$Payback_X = 2 + \frac{\$500}{\$3,000} = 2.17 \text{ years}$$

$$Payback_Y = 2 + \frac{\$3,000}{\$3,500} = 2.86 \text{ years}$$

Net present value (NPV):

$$NPV_X = -\$10,000 + \frac{\$6,500}{(1.12)^1} + \frac{\$3,000}{(1.12)^2} + \frac{\$3,000}{(1.12)^3} + \frac{\$1,000}{(1.12)^4} = \$966.01.$$

$$NPV_Y = -\$10,000 + \frac{\$3,500}{(1.12)^1} + \frac{\$3,500}{(1.12)^2} + \frac{\$3,500}{(1.12)^3} + \frac{\$3,500}{(1.12)^4} = \$630.72.$$

Alternatively, using a financial calculator, input the cash flows into the cash flow register, enter I = 12, and then press the NPV key to obtain $NPV_X = \$966.01$ and $NPV_Y = \$630.72$.

Internal rate of return (IRR):

To solve for each project's IRR, find the discount rates that equate each NPV to zero:

$$IRR_X = 18.0\%;$$
$$IRR_Y = 15.0\%.$$

Modified internal rate of return (MIRR):

To obtain each project's MIRR, begin by finding each project's terminal value (TV) of cash inflows:

$$TV_X = \$6{,}500(1.12)^3 + \$3{,}000(1.12)^2 + \$3{,}000(1.12)^1 + \$1{,}000 = \$17{,}255.23;$$
$$TV_Y = \$3{,}500(1.12)^3 + \$3{,}500(1.12)^2 + \$3{,}500(1.12)^1 + \$3{,}500 = \$16{,}727.65.$$

Now, each project's MIRR is the discount rate that equates the PV of the TV to each project's cost, $10,000:

$$MIRR_X = 14.61\%;$$
$$MIRR_Y = 13.73\%.$$

b. The following table summarizes the project rankings by each method:

	Project That Ranks Higher
Payback	X
NPV	X
IRR	X
MIRR	X

Note that all methods rank Project X over Project Y. In addition, both projects are acceptable under the NPV, IRR, and MIRR criteria. Thus, both projects should be accepted if they are independent.

c. In this case, we would choose the project with the higher NPV at r = 12%, or Project X.

d. To determine the effects of changing the cost of capital, plot the NPV profiles of each project. The crossover rate occurs at about 6% to 7% (6.2%). See the graph on the next page.

If the firm's cost of capital is less than 6.2%, a conflict exists because $NPV_Y > NPV_X$, but $IRR_X > IRR_Y$. Therefore, if r were 5%, a conflict would exist. Note, however, that when r = 5.0%, $MIRR_X = 10.64\%$ and $MIRR_Y = 10.83\%$; hence, the modified IRR ranks the projects correctly, even if r is to the left of the crossover point.

NPV Profiles for Project X and Y

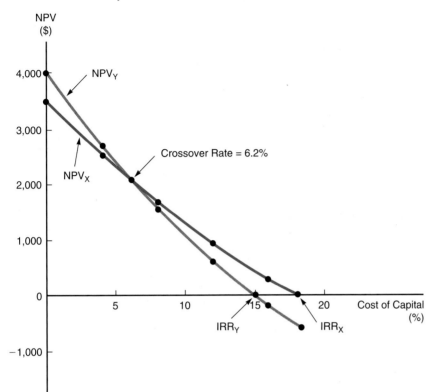

Cost of Capital	NPV$_X$	NPV$_Y$
0%	$3,500	4,000
4	2,545	2,705
12	1,707	1,592
16	966	631
18	307	(206)
18	5	(585)

e. The basic cause of the conflict is differing reinvestment rate assumptions between NPV and IRR. NPV assumes that cash flows can be reinvested at the cost of capital, while IRR assumes reinvestment at the (generally) higher IRR. The high reinvestment rate assumption under IRR makes early cash flows especially valuable, and hence short-term projects look better under IRR.

Chapter 12

(ST-1) a. **Estimated Investment Requirements:**

Price	($50,000)
Modification	(10,000)
Change in net working capital	(2,000)
Total investment	($62,000)

b. **Operating Cash Flows:**

	Year 1	Year 2	Year 3
1. After-tax cost savings[a]	$12,000	$12,000	$12,000
2. Depreciation[b]	19,800	27,000	9,000
3. Depreciation tax savings[c]	7,920	10,800	3,600
Operating cash flow (1+3)	$19,920	$22,800	$15,600

[a]$20,000(1 − T).

[b]Depreciable basis = $60,000; the MACRS percentage allowances are 0.33, 0.45, and 0.15 in Years 1, 2, and 3, respectively; hence, depreciation in Year 1 = 0.33($60,000) = $19,800, and so on. There will remain $4,200, or 7%, undepreciated after Year 3; it would normally be taken in Year 4.

[c]Depreciation tax savings = T(Depreciation) = 0.4($19,800) = $7,920 in Year 1, and so on.

c. **Termination Cash Flow:**

Salvage value	$20,000
Tax on salvage value[a]	(6,320)
Net working capital recovery	2,000
Termination cash flow	$15,680

[a]Calculation of tax on salvage value:
Book value = Depreciation basis − Accumulated depreciation
= $60,000 − $55,000 = $4,200

Sales price	$20,000
Less book value	4,200
Taxable income	$15,800
Tax at 40%	$ 6,320

d. **Project NPV:**

0	10%	1	2	3
Project Cash Flows −62,000		19,920	22,800	31,280

$$NPV = -\$62,000 + \frac{\$19,920}{(1.10)^1} + \frac{\$22,800}{(1.10)^2} + \frac{\$31,280}{(1.10)^3}$$

$$= -\$1,547.$$

Alternatively, using a financial calculator, input the cash flows into the cash flow register, enter I/YR = 10, and then press the NPV key to obtain NPV = −$1,547. Because the earthmover has a negative NPV, it should not be purchased.

(ST-2) a. First, find the expected cash flows:

Year		Expected Cash Flows			
0	0.2(−$100,000)	+0.6(−$100,000)	+0.2(−$100,000)	=	($100,000)
1	0.2($20,000)	+0.6($30,000)	+0.2($40,000)	=	$30,000
2					$30,000
3					$30,000
4					$30,000
5					$30,000
5*	0.2($0)	+0.6($20,000)	+0.2($30,000)	=	$18,000

```
0      10%    1           2           3           4           5
├──────────────┼───────────┼───────────┼───────────┼───────────┤
-$100,000    30,000      30,000      30,000      30,000      48,000
```

Next, determine the NPV based on the expected cash flows:

$$NPV = -\$100,000 + \frac{\$30,000}{(1.10)^1} + \frac{\$30,000}{(1.10)^2} + \frac{\$30,000}{(1.10)^3}$$

$$+ \frac{\$30,000}{(1.10)^4} + \frac{\$48,000}{(1.10)^5} = \$24,900.$$

Alternatively, using a financial calculator, input the cash flows in the cash flow register, enter I/YR = 10, and then press the NPV key to obtain NPV = $24,900.

b. For the worst case, the cash flow values from the cash flow column farthest on the left are used to calculate NPV:

```
0      10%    1           2           3           4           5
├──────────────┼───────────┼───────────┼───────────┼───────────┤
-$100,000    20,000      20,000      20,000      20,000      20,000
```

$$NPV = -\$100,000 + \frac{\$20,000}{(1.10)^1} + \frac{\$20,000}{(1.10)^2} + \frac{\$20,000}{(1.10)^3}$$

$$+ \frac{\$20,000}{(1.10)^4} + \frac{\$20,000}{(1.10)^5} = -\$24,184.$$

Similarly, for the best case, use the values from the column farthest on the right. Here the NPV is $70,259.

If the cash flows are perfectly dependent, then the low cash flow in the first year will mean a low cash flow in every year. Thus, the probability of the worst case occurring is the probability of getting the $20,000 net cash flow in Year 1, or 20%. If the cash flows are independent, the cash flow in each year can be low, high, or average, and the probability of getting all low cash flows will be

$$0.2(0.2)(0.2)(0.2)(0.2) = 0.2^5 = 0.00032 = 0.032\%.$$

c. The base-case NPV is found using the most likely cash flows and is equal to $26,142. This value differs from the expected NPV of $24,900 because the Year 5 cash flows are not symmetric. Under these conditions, the NPV distribution is as follows:

P	NPV
0.2	($24,184)
0.6	26,142
0.2	70,259

Thus, the expected NPV is $0.2(-\$24,184) + 0.6(\$26,142) + 0.2(\$70,259) = \$24,900$. As is always the case, the expected NPV is the same as the NPV of the expected cash flows found in part a. The standard deviation is $29,904:

$$\sigma_{NPV}^2 = 0.2(-\$24,184 - \$24,900)^2 + 0.6(-\$26,142 - \$24,900)^2$$
$$+ 0.2(-\$70,259 - \$24,900)^2$$
$$= \$894,261,126.$$
$$\sigma_{NPV} = \sqrt{\$894,261,126} = \$29,904.$$

The coefficient of variation, CV, is $\$29,904/\$24,900 = 1.20$.

Chapter 13

(ST-1)   a.   NPV of each demand scenario:

0	Probability	Year 1	Year 2	NPV This Scenario	Probability × NPV
			Future Cash Flows		
		$13	$13	$13.13	$3.28
	25%				
-$8	50%	$7	$7	$3.38	$1.69
	25%				
		$1	$1	-$6.37	-$1.59
				Expected NPV of future CFs =	$3.38

NPV high-demand scenario:

$$\text{NPV} = -\$8 + \frac{\$13}{(1 + 0.15)} + \frac{\$13}{(1 + 0.15)^2} = \$13.13.$$

NPV medium-demand scenario:

$$\text{NPV} = -\$8 + \frac{\$7}{(1 + 0.15)} + \frac{\$7}{(1 + 0.15)^2} = \$3.38.$$

NPV low-demand scenario:

$$\text{NPV} = -\$8 + \frac{\$1}{(1 + 0.15)} + \frac{\$1}{(1 + 0.15)^2} = -\$6.37.$$

Expected NPV = $0.25(\$13.13) + 0.50(\$3.38) + 0.25(-\$6.37) = \$3.38$ million.

b. NPV of operating cash flows if accept the additional project when optimal:

	Future Operating Cash Flows (Discount at WACC)				NPV This Scenario	Probability × NPV
Probability	Year 1	Year 2	Year 3	Year 4		
25%	$13	$13	$13	$13	$37.11	$9.28
50%	$7	$7	$7	$7	$19.98	$9.99
25%	$1	$1	$0	$0	$1.63	$0.41
				Expected NPV of future operating CFs =		$19.68

NPV of operating cash flows, high-demand scenario:

$$\text{NPV} = \frac{\$13}{(1 + 0.15)} + \frac{\$13}{(1 + 0.15)^2} + \frac{\$13}{(1 + 0.15)^3} + \frac{\$13}{(1 + 0.15)^4} = \$37.11.$$

NPV of operating cash flows, medium-demand scenario:

$$\text{NPV} = \frac{\$7}{(1 + 0.15)} + \frac{\$7}{(1 + 0.15)^2} + \frac{\$7}{(1 + 0.15)^3} + \frac{\$7}{(1 + 0.15)^4} = \$19.98.$$

NPV of operating cash flows, low-demand scenario:

$$\text{NPV} = \frac{\$1}{(1 + 0.15)} + \frac{\$1}{(1 + 0.15)^2} = \$1.63.$$

$$\text{Expected NPV of operating cash flows} = 0.25(\$37.11) + 0.50(\$19.98)$$
$$+ 0.25(\$1.63)$$
$$= \$19.68 \text{ million.}$$

Find NPV of costs, discounted at risk-free rate:

Cost of Implementing Project Now and Additional Project at Year 2 (Discount at Risk-Free Rate)

0	Probability	Year 1	Year 2	NPV This Scenario	Probability × NPV
	25%	$0	−$8	−$15.12	−$3.78
−$8	50%	$0	−$8	−$15.12	−$7.56
	25%	$0	$0	−$8.00	−$2.00
			Expected NPV of future operating CFs =		−$13.34

NPV of costs of high-demand scenario:

$$\text{NPV} = -\$8 + \frac{\$0}{(1 + 0.06)} + \frac{-\$8}{(1 + 0.06)^2} = -\$15.12.$$

will want to reduce its inventory holdings by not replacing inventories until the excess amounts have been used. We can account for this by setting up the revised AFN equation (using the new A^*/S_0 ratio), estimating the funds that will be needed next year if no excess inventories are currently on hand, and then subtracting out the excess inventories which are currently on hand:

Present Conditions:

$$\frac{\text{Sales}}{\text{Inventories}} = \frac{\$100}{\text{Inventories}} = 3,$$

so

$$\text{Inventories} = \$100/3 = \$33.3 \text{ million at present.}$$

New Conditions:

$$\frac{\text{Sales}}{\text{Inventories}} = \frac{\$100}{\text{Inventories}} = 4,$$

so

$$\text{New level of inventories} = \$100/4 = \$25 \text{ million.}$$

Therefore,

$$\text{Excess inventories} = \$33.3 - \$25 = \$8.3 \text{ million.}$$

Forecast of Funds Needed, First Year:

$$\text{DS in first year} = 0.2(\$100 \text{ million}) = \$20 \text{ million.}$$

$$\text{AFN} = 1.5167(\$20) - 0.4(\$20) - 0.1(0.55)(\$120) - \$8.3$$

$$= \$30.3 - \$8 - \$6.6 - \$8.3$$

$$= \$7.4 \text{ million.}$$

Forecast of Funds Needed, Second Year:

$$\Delta S \text{ in second year} = gS_1 = 0.2(\$120 \text{ million}) = \$24 \text{ million.}$$

$$\text{AFN} = 1.5137(\$24) - 0.4(\$24) - 0.1(0.55)(\$144)$$

$$= \$36.4 - \$9.6 - \$7.9$$

$$= \$18.9 \text{ million.}$$

(ST-3)   a.   Full capacity sales $= \dfrac{\text{Current sales}}{\text{Percentage of capacity at which FA were operated}}$

$$= \frac{\$36,000}{0.75} = \$48,000.$$

Percentage increase $= \dfrac{\text{New sales} - \text{Old sales}}{\text{Old sales}}$

$$= \frac{\$48,000 - \$36,000}{\$36,000} = 0.33$$

$$= 33\%.$$

Therefore, sales could expand by 33% before Van Auken Lumber would need to add fixed assets.

b. **Van Auken Lumber: Pro Forma Income Statement for December 31, 2008 (Thousands of Dollars)**

	2007	Forecast Basis	Pro Forma 2008
Sales	$36,000	$1.25(Sales_{07})$	$45,000
Operating costs	30,783	$85.508\%(Sales_{08})$	38,479
EBIT	$ 5,217		$ 6,521
Interest	717	$12\%(Debt_{07})$	1,017
EBT	$ 4,500		$ 5,504
Taxes (40%)	1,800		2,202
Net income	$ 2,700		$ 3,302
Dividends (60%)	$ 1,620		$ 1,981
Additions to RE	$ 1,080		$ 1,321

Van Auken Lumber: Pro Forma Balance Sheet for December 31, 2008 (Thousands of Dollars)

	2007	Percent of 2008 Sales	Additions	2008	AFN	2008 after AFN
Cash	$ 1,800	5.000%		$ 2,250		$ 2,250
Receivables	10,800	30.000		13,500		13,500
Inventories	12,600	35.000		15,750		15,750
Total current assets	$25,200			$31,500		$31,500
Net fixed assets	21,600			21,600[a]		21,600
Total assets	$46,800			$53,100		$53,100
Accounts payable	$ 7,200	20.000		$ 9,000		$ 9,000
Notes payable	3,472			3,472	+2,549	6,021
Accruals	2,520	7.000		3,150		3,150
Total current liabilities	$13,192			$15,622		$18,171
Mortgage bonds	5,000			5,000		5,000
Common stock	2,000			2,000		2,000
Retained earnings	26,608		1,321[b]	27,929		27,929
Total liabilities and equity	$46,800			$50,551		$53,100
AFN =				$ 2,549		

[a]From part a we know that sales can increase by 33% before additions to fixed assets are needed.

[b]See income statement.

Chapter 15

(ST-1) a.
$$V_{op} = \frac{FCF(1 + g)}{WACC - g} = \frac{\$100,000(1 + 0.07)}{0.11 - 0.07} = \$2,675,000.$$

b.   Total value = Value of operations + Value of nonoperating assets
$$= \$2,675,000 + \$325,000 = \$3,000,000.$$

c.   Value of equity = Total value − Value of debt
$$= \$3,000,000 - \$1,000,000 = \$2,000,000.$$

d.   Price per share = Value of equity/Number of shares
$$= \$2,000,000/50,000 = \$40.$$

Chapter 16

(ST-1)   a. $S = P_0 n = \$30(600,000) = \$18,000,000.$
                      $V = D + S = \$2,000,000 + \$18,000,000 = \$20,000,000.$

         b. $D/V = \$2,000,000/\$20,000,000 = 0.10.$
                     $S/V = \$18,000,000/\$20,000,000 = 0.90.$
                  $\text{WACC} = (D/V)r_d(1 - T) + (S/V)r_s$
                          $= (0.10)(10\%)(0.60) + (0.90)(15\%) = 14.1\%.$

         c. $\text{WACC} = (0.50)(12\%)(0.60) + (0.50)(18.5\%) = 12.85\%.$

         Since $g = 0$, FCF = NOPAT.
                  $V = \text{FCF}/\text{WACC} = \text{NOPAT}(1 - T)/0.1285 = \$4,700,000(0.60)/0.1285$
                  $= \$21,945,525.292.$
                  $D = w_d(V) = 0.50(\$21,945,525.292) = \$10,972,762.646.$

         Since it started with $2 million debt, it will issue
             $\$8,972,762.646 = \$10,972,762.646 - \$2,000,000.$
             $S = V - D = \$21,945,525.292 - \$10,972,762.646 = \$10,972,762.646.$
             $\text{New } P = (S + D - D_0)/n_0$
                  $= (\$10,972,762.646 + \$10,972,762.646 - \$2,000,000)/600,000$
                  $= \$33.243.$

         It used the proceeds of the new debt, $8,972,762.646, to repurchase X shares of stock at a price of $33.243 per share. The number of shares it will repurchase is $X = \$8,972,762.646/\$33.243 = 269,914.347 \approx 269,914$. Therefore, there are $600,000 - 269,914 = 330,086$. As a check the stock price should equal the market value of equity, S, divided by the number of shares: $P_0 = \$10,972,762.646/330,086 = \$33.242.$

(ST-2)   a.   LIC's current cost of equity is
                      $r_s = 6\% + 1.5(4\%) = 12\%.$

         b.   LIC's unlevered beta is
                      $b_U = 1.5/[1 + (1 - 0.40)(25\%/75\%)] = 1.5/1.2 = 1.25.$

         c.   LIC's levered beta at $D/S = 60\%/40\% = 1.5$ is
                      $b = 1.25[1 + (1 - 0.40)(60/40)] = 2.375.$

         LIC's new cost of capital will be
                      $r_s = 6\% + (2.375)(4\%) = 15.5\%.$

Chapter 17

(ST-1)   a.   Value of unleveraged firm, $V_U = \text{EBIT}(1 - T)/r_{sU}$:
                      $\$12 = \$2(1 - 0.4)r_{sU}$
                      $\$12 = \$1.2/r_{sU}$
                      $r_{sU} = \$1.2/\$12 = \$10.0\%.$

Therefore, $r_{sU} = WACC = 10.0\%$.

b. Value of leveraged firm according to MM mode with taxes:
$$V_L = V_U + TD.$$

As shown in the following table, value increases continuously with debt, and the optimal capital structure consists of 100% debt. Note: The table is not necessary to answer this question, but the data (in millions of dollars) are necessary for part c of this problem.

Debt, D	V_U	TD	$V_L = V_U + TD$
$ 0.0	$12.0	$0.0	$12.0
2.5	12.0	1.0	13.0
5.0	12.0	2.0	14.0
7.5	12.0	3.0	15.0
10.0	12.0	4.0	16.0
12.5	12.0	5.0	17.0
15.0	12.0	6.0	18.0
20.0	12.0	8.0	20.0

c. With financial distress costs included in the analysis, the value of the leveraged firm now is
$$V_L = V_U + TD - PC,$$

where

$V_U + TD$	=	value according to MM after-tax model.
P	=	probability of financial distress.
C	=	present value of distress costs.

D	$V_U + TD$	P	PC = (P)$8	$V_L = V_U + TD - PC$
$ 0.0	$12.0	0.0000	$0.00	$12.0
2.5	13.0	0.0000	0.00	13.0
5.0	14.0	0.0125	0.10	13.9
7.5	15.0	0.0250	0.20	14.8
10.0	16.0	0.0625	0.50	15.5
12.5	17.0	0.1250	1.00	16.0
15.0	18.0	0.3125	2.50	15.5
20.0	20.0	0.7500	6.00	14.0

Note: All dollar amounts are in millions.

Optimal debt level: D = $12.5 million.

Maximum value of firm: V = $16.0 million.

Optimal debt/value ratio: D/V = $12.5/$16 = 78%.

d. The value of the firm versus debt value with and without financial distress costs is plotted next (millions of dollars):

V_L = Value without financial distress costs.

V_B = Value with financial distress costs.

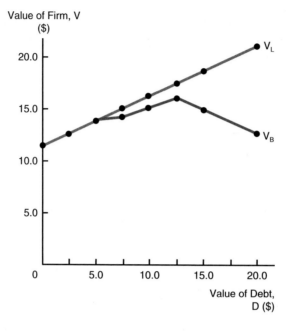

Chapter 18

(ST-1) a.

Projected net income	$2,000,000
Less projected capital investments	800,000
Available residual	$1,200,000
Shares outstanding	200,000

$$DPS = \$1,200,000/200,000 \text{ shares} = \$6 = D_1.$$

b. $EPS = \$2,000,000/200,000 \text{ shares} = \$10.$

Payout ratio = DPS/EPS = \$6/\$10 = 60\%, or

Total dividends/NI = \$1,200,000/\$2,000,000 = 60\%.

c. $$\text{Currently, } P_0 = \frac{D_1}{r_s - g} = \frac{\$6}{0.14 - 0.05} = \frac{\$6}{0.09} = \$66.67.$$

Under the former circumstances, D_1 would be based on a 20% payout on \$10 EPS, or \$2. With $r_s = 14\%$ and $g = 12\%$, we solve for P_0:

$$P_0 = \frac{D_1}{r_s - g} = \frac{\$2}{0.14 - 0.12} = \frac{\$2}{0.02} = \$100.$$

Although CMC has suffered a severe setback, its existing assets will continue to provide a good income stream. More of these earnings should now be passed on to the shareholders, as the slowed internal growth has reduced the need for funds. However, the net result is a 33% decrease in the value of the shares.

Chapter 19

(ST-1)   a.   Proceeds per share = $(1 - 0.07)(\$20) = \$18.60$.

Required proceeds after direct costs: $30 million + $800,000 = $30.8 million.
Number of shares = $30.8 million/$18.60 per share = 1.656 million shares.

b.   Amount left on table = (Closing price − offer price)(Number of shares)
= ($22 − $20)(1.656 million) = $3.312 million.

c.   Underwriting cost = $0.07($20)(1.656) = $2.318 million.
Total costs = $0.800 + $2.318 + $3.312 = $6.430 million.

Chapter 20

(ST-1)   a.   **Cost of Leasing:**

	Year 0	Year 1	Year 2	Year 3	Year 4
Lease payment	($10,000)	($10,000)	($10,000)	($10,000)	$0
Payment tax savings	4,000	4,000	4,000	4,000	0
Net cash flow	($ 6,000)	($ 6,000)	($ 6,000)	($ 6,000)	$0

PV cost of leasing @ 6% = ($22,038)

b.   **Cost of Owning:**

In our solution, we will consider the $40,000 cost as a Year 0 outflow rather than including all the financing cash flows. The net effect is the same since the PV of the financing flows, when discounted at the after-tax cost of debt, is the cost of the asset.

	Year 0	Year 1	Year 2	Year 3	Year 4
Net purchase price	($40,000)				
Maintenance cost		($1,000)	($1,000)	($1,000)	($1,000)
Maintenance tax savings		400	400	400	400
Depreciation tax savings		5,280	7,200	2,400	1,120
Residual value					10,000
Residual value tax					(4,000)
Net cash flow	($40,000)	$4,680	$6,600	$1,800	$6,520

PV cost of owning @ 6% = ($23,035)

Since the present value of the cost of leasing is less than the present value of the cost of owning, the truck should be leased. Specifically, the NAL is $23,035 − $22,038 = $997.

c.   Use the cost of debt because most cash flows are fixed by contract and consequently are relatively certain; thus lease cash flows have about the same risk as the firm's debt. Also, leasing is considered as a substitute for debt. Use an after-tax cost rate to account for interest tax deductibility.

d. The firm could increase the discount rate on the residual value cash flow. Note that since the firm plans to replace the truck after 4 years, the residual value is treated as an inflow in the cost of owning analysis. This makes it reasonable to raise the discount rate for analysis purposes. However, had the firm planned to continue using the truck, then we would have had to place the estimated residual value as an additional Year 4 outflow in the leasing section, but without a tax adjustment. Then, higher risk would have been reflected in a *lower* discount rate. This is all very ad hoc, which is why analysts often prefer to use one discount rate throughout the analysis.

Chapter 21

(ST-1)   First issue: 10-year straight bonds with a 6% coupon.

Second issue: 10-year bonds with 4.5% annual coupon with warrants. Both bonds issued at par $1,000. Value of warrants = ?

First issue: N = 10; PV = -1000, PMT = 60, FV = 1000, and solve for I/YR = r_d = 6%. (Since it sold for par, we should know that r_d = 6%.)

Second issue: $1,000 = Bond + Warrants. This bond should be evaluated at 6% (since we know the first issue sold at par) to determine its present value: N = 10; I/YR = r_d = 6; PMT = 45, FV = 1000, and solve for PV = $889.60.

The value of the warrants can be determined as the difference between $1,000 and the second bond's present value.

Value of warrants = $1,000 − $889.6 = $110.40.

Chapter 22

(ST-1)   **The Calgary Company: Alternative Balance Sheets**

	Restricted (40%)	Moderate (50%)	Relaxed (60%)
Current assets (% of sales)	$1,200,000	$1,500,000	$1,800,000
Fixed assets	600,000	600,000	600,000
Total assets	$1,800,000	$2,100,000	$2,400,000
Debt	$ 900,000	$1,050,000	$1,200,000
Equity	900,000	1,050,000	1,200,000
Total liabilities and equity	$1,800,000	$2,100,000	$2,400,000

The Calgary Company: Alternative Income Statements

	Restricted	Moderate	Relaxed
Sales	$3,000,000	$3,000,000	$3,000,000
EBIT	450,000	450,000	450,000
Interest (10%)	90,000	105,000	120,000
Earnings before taxes	$ 360,000	$ 345,000	$ 330,000
Taxes (40%)	144,000	138,000	132,000
Net income	$ 216,000	$ 207,000	$ 198,000
ROE	24.0%	19.7%	16.5%

(ST-2) a. and b.

Income Statements for Year Ended December 31, 2007 (Thousands of Dollars)

	Vanderheiden Press		Herrenhouse Publishing	
	a	b	a	b
EBIT	$ 30,000	$ 30,000	$ 30,000	$ 30,000
Interest	12,400	14,400	10,600	18,600
Taxable income	$ 17,600	$ 15,600	$ 19,400	$ 11,400
Taxes (40%)	7,040	6,240	7,760	4,560
Net income	$ 10,560	$ 9,360	$ 11,640	$ 6,840
Equity	$100,000	$100,000	$100,000	$100,000
Return on equity	10.56%	9.36%	11.64%	6.84%

The Vanderheiden Press has a higher ROE when short-term interest rates are high, whereas Herrenhouse Publishing does better when rates are lower.

c. Herrenhouse's position is riskier. First, its profits and return on equity are much more volatile than Vanderheiden's. Second, Herrenhouse must renew its large short-term loan every year, and if the renewal comes up at a time when money is very tight, when its business is depressed, or both, then Herrenhouse could be denied credit, which could put it out of business.

Chapter 23

(ST-1) a. The hypothetical bond in the futures contract has an annual coupon of 6% (paid semiannually) and a maturity of 20 years. At a price of 97-13 (this is the percent of par), a $1,000 par bond would have a price of $1,000(97 + 13/32)/100 = $974.0625. To find the yield, N = 40; PMT = 30; FV = 1000; PV = −974.0625; solve for I/YR = 3.1143% per 6 months. The nominal annual yield is 2(3.1143%) = 6.2286%.

b. In this situation, the firm would be hurt if interest rates were to rise by September, so it would use a short hedge or sell futures contracts. Because futures contracts are for $100,000 in Treasury bonds, the value of a futures contract is $97,406.25 and the firm must sell $5,000,000/$97,406.25 = 51.33 ≈ 51 contracts to cover the planned $5,000,000 September bond issue. Because futures maturing in June are selling for 97 ^{13}/32 of par, the value of Wansley's futures is about 51($97,406.25) = $4,967,718.75. Should interest rates rise by September, Wansley will be able to repurchase the futures contracts at a lower cost, which will help offset their loss from financing at the higher interest rate. Thus, the firm has hedged against rising interest rates.

c. The firm would now pay 13% on the bonds. With a 12% coupon rate, the PV of the new issue is only N = 40; I = 13/2 = 6.5; PMT = −0.12/2(5,000,000) = −300,000; FV = −5,000,000; and solve for PV = $4,646,361.83. Therefore, the new bond issue would bring in only $4,646,361.83, so the cost of the bond issue due to rising rates is $5,000,000 − $4,646,361.83 = $353,638.17.

However, the value of the short futures position began at $4,967,718.75. Now, if interest rates increased by 1 percentage point, the yield on the futures would go up to 7.2286% (7.2286 = 6.2286 + 1). The value of the futures contract is N = 40; I = 7.2286/2 = 3.6143 (from part a); PMT = 3000; FV = 100,000; and solve for PV = $87,111.04 per contract. With 51 contracts, the value of the futures position is $4,442,663.04. (Note: If you don't round in any previous calculations, the PV is $4,442,668.38.)

Because Wansley Company sold the futures contracts for $4,967,718.75, and will, in effect, buy them back at $4,442,668.04, the firm would make a profit of $4,967,718.75 − $4,442,668.04 = $525,050.71 on the transaction, ignoring transaction costs.

Thus, the firm gained $525,050.71 on its futures position, but lost $353,638.17 on its underlying bond issue. On net, it gained $525,050.71 − $353,638.17 = $171,412.54.

Chapter 24

(ST-1)   a.   Distribution to priority claimants (millions of dollars):

Total proceeds from the sale of assets	$1,150
Less:	
1. First mortgage (paid from sale of fixed assets)	700
2. Second mortgage (paid from sale of fixed assets after satisfying first mortgage: $750 − $700 = $50)	50
3. Fees and expenses of bankruptcy	1
4. Wages due to workers	60
5. Taxes due	90
Funds available for distribution to general creditors	$ 249

b.   Distribution to general creditors (millions of dollars):

General Creditor Claims	Amount of Claim	Pro Rata Distribution[a]	Distribution after Subordinate Adjustment[b]	% of Original Claim Received
Unsatisfied second mortgage	$ 350	$ 60	$ 60	28%[c]
Accounts payable	100	17	17	17
Notes payable	300	52	86	29
Debentures	500	86	86	17
Subordinated debentures	200	34	0	0
Total	$1,450	$249	$249	

Notes:
[a]Pro rata distribution: $249/$1,450 = 0.172 = 17.2%.
[b]Subordinated debentures are subordinated to notes payable. Unsatisfied portion of notes payable is greater than subordinated debenture distribution, so subordinated debentures receive $0.
[c]Includes $50 from sale of fixed assets received in priority distribution.

Total distribution to second mortgage holders: $50 + $60 = $110 million.

Total distribution to holders of notes payable: $86 million.

Total distribution to holders of subordinated debentures: $0 million.

Total distribution to common stockholders: $0 million.

Chapter 25

(ST-1) a. The unlevered cost of equity based on the pre-merger required rate of return and pre-merger capital structure is

$$r_{sU} = w_d r_d + w_s r_{sL}$$
$$= 0.25(6\%) + 0.75(10\%)$$
$$= 9\%.$$

The post-horizon levered cost of equity is

$$r_{sL} = r_{sU} + (r_{sU} - r_d)(D/S)$$
$$= 9\% + (9\% - 7\%)(0.35/0.65)$$
$$= 10.077\%.$$

$$WACC = w_d r_d(1 - T) + w_s r_s$$
$$= 0.35(7\%)(1 - 0.40) + 0.65(10.077\%)$$
$$= 8.02\%.$$

b. The horizon value of unlevered operations is

$$\text{Horizon value } U_3 = FCF_3(1 + g)/(r_{sU} - g)$$
$$= [\$25(1.05)]/(0.09 - 0.05)$$
$$= \$656.250 \text{ million.}$$

$$\text{Unlevered } V_{op} = \frac{\$10}{1.09} + \frac{\$20}{(1.09)^2} + \frac{\$25 + \$656.25}{(1.09)^3}$$

$$= \$552.058 \text{ million.}$$

Tax shields in Years 1 through 3 are

$$\text{Tax saving} = \text{Interest} \times T;$$
$$TS_1 = \$28.00(0.40) = \$11.200 \text{ million;}$$
$$TS_2 = \$24.00(0.40) = \$9.600 \text{ million;}$$
$$TS_3 = \$20.28(0.40) = \$8.112 \text{ million.}$$

$$HV_{TS,3} = TS_3(1 + g)/(r_{sU} - g)$$
$$= [\$8.112(1.05)]/(0.09 - 0.05)$$
$$= \$212.940 \text{ million.}$$

$$\text{Value of tax shield} = \frac{\$11.2}{1.09} + \frac{\$9.6}{(1.09)^2} + \frac{\$8.112 + \$212.940}{(1.09)^3}$$

$$= \$189.048 \text{ million.}$$

$$\text{Total value} = \text{Unlevered } V_{op} + \text{Value of tax shield}$$
$$= \$552.058 + \$189.048$$
$$= \$741.106.$$

Chapter 26

(ST-1)

$$\frac{\text{Euros}}{\text{C\$}} = \frac{\text{Euros}}{\text{US\$}} \times \frac{\text{US\$}}{\text{C\$}}$$

$$= \frac{0.98}{\$1} \times \frac{\$1}{1.5} = \frac{0.98}{1.5} = 0.6533 \text{ euro per Canadian dollar.}$$

appendix b

Answers to End-of-Chapter Problems

We present here some intermediate steps and final answers to selected end-of-chapter problems. Please note that your answer may differ slightly from ours due to rounding differences. Also, although we hope not, some of the problems may have more than one correct solution, depending on what assumptions are made in working the problem. Finally, many of the problems involve some verbal discussion as well as numerical calculations; this verbal material is not presented here.

(2-1) $FV_5 = \$16,105.10$.
(2-2) $PV = \$1,292.10$.
(2-3) $I/YR = 8.01\%$.
(2-4) $N = 11.01$ years.
(2-5) $N = 11$ years.
(2-6) $FVA_5 = \$1,725.22$;
$FVA_{5\,Due} = \$1,845.99$.
(2-7) $PV = \$923.98$; $FV = \$1,466.24$.
(2-8) $PMT = \$444.89$; $EAR = 12.6825\%$.
(2-9) a. \$530.
b. \$561.80.
c. \$471.70.
d. \$445.00.
(2-10) a. \$895.42.
b. \$1,552.92.
c. \$279.20.
d. \$160.99.
(2-11) a. $N = 10.24 \approx 10$ years.
b. $N = 7.27 \approx 7$ years.
c. $N = 4.19 \approx 4$ years.
d. $N = 1.00 \approx 1$ year.

(2-12) a. \$6,374.97.
b. \$1,105.13.
c. \$2,000.00.
d. (1) \$7,012.46.
(2) \$1,160.38.
(3) \$2,000.00.
(2-13) a. \$2,457.83.
b. \$865.90.
c. \$2,000.00.
d. (1) \$2,703.61.
(2) \$909.19.
(3) \$2,000.00.
(2-14) a. $PV_A = \$1,251.25$.
$PV_B = \$1,300.32$.
b. $PV_A = \$1,600$.
$PV_B = \$1,600$.
(2-15) a. 7%.
b. 7%.
c. 9%.
d. 15%.
(2-16) a. \$881.17.
b. \$895.42.
c. \$903.06.
d. \$908.35.
(2-17) a. \$279.20.
b. \$276.84.
c. \$443.72.
(2-18) a. \$5,272.32.
b. \$5,374.07.
(2-19) a. Universal, $EAR = 7\%$.
Regional, $EAR = 6.14\%$.
(2-20) a. $PMT = \$6,594.94$.
$Interest_1 = \$2,500$.
$Interest_2 = \$2,090.51$.
b. \$13,189.87.
c. \$8,137.27.
(2-21) a. $I = 14.87\% \approx 15\%$.

(2-22) I = 7.18%.

(2-23) I = 9%.

(2-24) a. $33,872.11.

      b. (1) $26,243.16.

         (2) $0.

(2-25) N = 14.77 ≈ 15 years.

(2-26) 6 years; $1,106.01.

(2-27) (1) $1,428.57.

      (2) $714.29.

(2-28) $893.26.

(2-29) $984.88.

(2-30) 57.18%.

(2-31) a. $1,432.02.

      b. $93.07.

(2-32) I_{NOM} = 15.19%.

(2-33) PMT = $36,949.61.

(2-34) First PMT = $9,736.96.

(3-1) 5.8%.

(3-2) 25%.

(3-3) $1,000,000.

(3-4) $2,500,000.

(3-5) $3,600,000.

(3-6) $20,000,000.

(3-7) Tax = $107,855; NI = $222,145; Marginal tax rate = 39%; Average tax rate = 33.8%.

(3-8) a. Tax = $3,575,000.

      b. Tax = $350,000.

      c. Tax = $105,000.

(3-9) AT&T preferred stock = 5.37%; Florida bond = 5%.

(3-10) NI = $450,000; NCF = $650,000.

(3-11) a. $2,400,000.

      b. NI = $0; NCF = $3,000,000.

      c. NI = $1,350,000; NCF = $2,100,000.

(3-12) a. NOPAT = $90,000,000.

      b. $NOWC_{06}$ = $210,000,000; $NOWC_{07}$ = $192,000,000.

      c. Operating capital$_{06}$ = $460,000,000; Operating capital$_{07}$ = $492,000,000.

      d. FCF = $58,000,000.

(3-13) Refund = $120,000. Future taxes = $0; $0; $40,000; $60,000; $60,000.

(4-1) AR = $400,000.

(4-2) D/A = 40%.

(4-3) M/B = 10.

(4-4) P/E = 16.0.

(4-5) ROE = 12%.

(4-6) S/TA = 5; TA/E = 1.5.

(4-7) CL = $2,000,000; Inv = $1,000,000.

(4-8) Net profit margin = 2%; D/A = 40%.

(4-9) $262,500; 1.19×.

(4-10) TIE = 3.86×.

(4-11) A/P = $90,000; Inv = $90,000; FA = $138,000.

(4-12) Sales = $2,592,000; DSO = 36.33 days.

(4-13) a. Current ratio = 1.98×; DSO = 76 days; Total assets turnover = 1.7×; Debt ratio = 61.9%.

(4-14) a. Quick ratio = 0.8×; DSO = 37 days; ROE = 13.1%; Debt ratio = 54.8%.

(5-1) $928.39.

(5-2) 12.48%.

(5-3) 8.55%.

(5-4) 7%; 7.33%.

(5-5) 2.5%.

(5-6) 0.3%.

(5-7) $1,085.80.

(5-8) YTM = 6.62%; YTC = 6.49%.

(5-9) a. 5%: V_L = $1,518.98; V_S = $1,047.62.

      8%: V_L = $1,171.19; V_S = $1,018.52.

      12%: V_L = $863.78; V_S = $982.14.

(5-10) a. YTM at $829 = 13.98%; YTM at $1,104 = 6.50%.

(5-11) 14.82%.

(5-12) a. 10.37%.

      b. 10.91%.

c. -0.54%.

d. 10.15%.

(5-13) 8.65%.

(5-14) 10.78%.

(5-15) YTC $= 6.47\%$.

(5-16) a. 10-year, 10% coupon $=$
6.75%;
10-year zero $= 9.75\%$;
5-year zero $= 4.76\%$;
30-year zero $= 32.19\%$;
$100 perpetuity $= 14.29\%$.

(5-17) $C_0 = \$1,012.79$; $Z_0 = \$693.04$;
$C_1 = \$1,010.02$; $Z_1 = \$759.57$;
$C_2 = \$1,006.98$; $Z_2 = \$832.49$;
$C_3 = \$1,003.65$; $Z_3 = \$912.41$;
$C_4 = \$1,000.00$; $Z_4 = \$1,000.00$.

(5-18) 5.8%.

(5-19) 1.5%.

(5-20) 6.0%.

(5-21) a. $\$1,251.22$.

b. $\$898.94$.

(5-22) a. 8.02%.

b. 7.59%.

(5-23) a. $r_1 = 9.20\%$; $r_5 = 7.20\%$.

(6-1) $b = 1.12$.

(6-2) $r = 10.90\%$.

(6-3) $\hat{r}_M = 11\%$; $r_s = 12.2\%$.

(6-4) $\hat{r} = 11.40\%$; $\sigma = 26.69\%$; CV
$= 2.34$.

(6-5) a. $\hat{r}_M = 13.5\%$; $\hat{r}_j = 11.6\%$.

b. $\sigma_M = 3.85\%$; $\sigma_j = 6.22\%$.

c. $CV_M = 0.29$; $CV_j = 0.54$.

(6-6) a. $b_A = 1.40$.

b. $r_A = 15\%$.

(6-7) a. $r_i = 15.5\%$.

b. (1) $r_M = 15\%$; $r_i = 16.5\%$.
(2) $r_M = 13\%$; $r_i = 14.5\%$.

c. (1) $r_i = 18.1\%$.
(2) $r_i = 14.2\%$.

(6-8) $b_N = 1.16$.

(6-9) $b_p = 0.7625$; $r_P = 12.1\%$.

(6-10) $b_N = 1.1250$.

(6-11) 4.5%.

(6-12) a. $\bar{r}_A = 11.30\%$; $\bar{r}_B = 11.30\%$.

b. $\bar{r}_p = 11.30\%$.

c. $\sigma_A = 20.8\%$; $\sigma_B = 20.8\%$;
$\sigma_P = 20.1\%$.

d. $CV_A = 1.84$; $CV_B = 1.84$;
$CV_P = 1.78$.

(6-13) a. $b_X = 1.3471$; $b_Y = 0.6508$.

b. $r_X = 12.7355\%$; $r_Y =$
9.254%.

c. $r_p = 12.04\%$.

(7-1) 1.4.

(7-2) 12%.

(7-3) 15.96%.

(7-4) 45.9%.

(7-5) a. $r_i = r_{RF} + (r_M - r_{RF})\dfrac{\rho_{iM}\sigma_i}{\sigma_M}$.

(7-6) a. 14.15%.

b. 16.45%.

(7-7) a. $b = 0.56$.

b. X: 10.6%; 13.1%.
M: 12.1%; 22.6%.

c. 8.6%.

(7-8) a. $b = 0.62$.

(8-1) $D_1 = \$1.5750$; $D_3 = \$1.7364$;
$D_5 = \$2.1011$.

(8-2) $\hat{P}_0 = \$18.75$.

(8-3) $\hat{P}_1 = \$22.00$; $\hat{r}_s = 15.50\%$.

(8-4) $r_{ps} = 10\%$.

(8-5) $\$50.50$.

(8-6) $g = 9\%$.

(8-7) $\hat{P}_3 = \$27.32$.

(8-8) a. 13.3%.

b. 10%.

c. 8%.

d. 5.7%.

(8-9) $\$25.26$.

(8-10) a. $r_C = 10.6\%$; $r_D = 7\%$.

(8-11) $\$25.03$.

(8-12) $\hat{P}_0 = \$19.89$.

(8-13) a. $\$125$.

b. $\$83.33$.

(8-14) a. 7%.

b. 5%.

c. 12%.

(8-15) a. (1) $\$9.50$.
(2) $\$13.33$.

b. (1) Undefined.

(8-16) a. $\hat{P}_0 = \$21.43$.

b. $\hat{P}_0 = \$26.47$.

c. $\hat{P}_0 = \$32.14$.

d. $\hat{P}_0 = \$40.54$.

(8-17) b. PV = $5.29.
d. $30.01.

(8-18) a. D_5 = $3.52.
b. $\hat{P}_0$ = $39.42.
c. Dividend yield t = 0,
5.10%; t = 5, 7.00%.

(8-19) $\hat{P}_0$ = $54.11.

(9-1) $5; $2.

(9-2) $27.00; $37.00.

(9-3) $1.67.

(9-4) $3.70.

(9-5) $1.90.

(9-6) $2.39.

(9-7) $1.91.

(10-1) a. 13%.
b. 10.4%.
c. 8.45%.

(10-2) 5.2%.

(10-3) 9%.

(10-4) 5.41%.

(10-5) 13.33%.

(10-6) 10.4%.

(10-7) 9.17%.

(10-8) 13%.

(10-9) 7.2%.

(10-10) a. 16.3%.
b. 15.4%.
c. 16%.

(10-11) a. 8%.
b. $2.81.
c. 15.81%.

(10-12) a. g = 3%.
b. EPS_1 = $5.562.

(10-13) 16.1%.

(10-14) $(1 - T)r_d$ = 5.57%.

(10-15) a. $15,000,000.
b. 8.4%.

(10-16) Short-term debt = 11.14%;
Long-term debt = 22.03%;
Common equity = 66.83%.

(10-17) $w_{d(Short)}$ = 0%; $w_{d(Long)}$ = 20%;
w_{ps} = 4%; w_{ce} = 76%;
r_d(After-tax) = 7.2%;
r_{ps} = 11.6%; $r_s \approx$ 17.5%.

(11-1) NPV = $7,486.68.

(11-2) IRR = 16%.

(11-3) MIRR = 13.89%.

(11-4) PI = 1.14.

(11-5) 4.34 years.

(11-6) DPP = 6.51 years.

(11-7) 5%: NPV_A = $16,108,952;
NPV_B = $18,300,939.
10%: NPV_A = $12,836,213;
NPV_B = $15,954,170.
15%: NPV_A = $10,059,587;
NPV_B = $13,897,838.

(11-8) NPV_T = $409; IRR_T = 15%;
$MIRR_T$ = 14.54%; Accept.
NPV_P = $3,318; IRR_P = 20%;
$MIRR_P$ = 17.19%; Accept.

(11-9) NPV_E = $3,861; IRR_E = 18%;
NPV_G = $3,057; IRR_G = 18%;
Purchase electric-powered
forklift; it has a higher NPV.

(11-10) NPV_S = $814.33; NPV_L =
$1,675.34; IRR_S = 15.24%;
IRR_L = 14.67%;
$MIRR_S$ = 13.77%; $MIRR_L$ =
13.46%; PI_S = 1.081; PI_L =
1.067.

(11-11) $MIRR_X$ = 13.59%; $MIRR_Y$ =
13.10%.

(11-12) a. NPV = $136,578; IRR =
19.22%.

(11-13) b. IRR_A = 18.1%; IRR_B =
24.0%.
c. 10%: NPV_A = $283.34;
NPV_B = $178.60.
17%: NPV_A = $31.05;
NPV_B = $75.95.
d. (1) $MIRR_A$ = 14.07%;
$MIRR_B$ = 15.89%.
(2) $MIRR_A$ = 17.57%;
$MIRR_B$ = 19.91%.

(11-14) a. $0; -$10,250,000;
$1,750,000.
b. 16.07%.

(11-15) a. NPV_A = $18,108,510; NPV_B
= $13,946,117; IRR_A =
15.03%; IRR_B = 22.26%.
b. NPV_Δ = $4,162,393; IRR_Δ
= 11.71%.

(11-16) Extended NPV_A = $12.76
million; NPV_B = $9.26 million.

EAA_A = \$2.26 million; EAA_B
= \$1.64 million.

(11-17) Machine A; Extended NPV_A
= \$4.51 million.
EAA_A = \$0.85 million; EAA_B
= \$0.69 million.

(11-18) NPV of 360-6 = \$22,256.
Extended NPV of 190-3 =
\$20,070.
EAA of 360-6 = \$5,723.30;
EAA of 190-3 = \$5,161.02.

(11-19) d. 7.61%; 15.58%.

(11-20) a. Undefined.
b. NPV_C = −\$911,067;
NPV_F = −\$838,834.

(11-21) a. A = 2.67 years; B = 1.5
years.
b. A = 3.07 years; B = 1.825
years.
c. NPV_A = \$12,739,908;
choose both.
d. NPV_A = \$18,243,813;
choose A.
e. NPV_B = \$8,643,390; choose
B.
f. 13.53%.
g. $MIRR_A$ = 21.93%; $MIRR_B$
= 20.96%.

(11-22) a. 3 years.
b. No.

(12-1) \$12,000,000.

(12-2) \$2,600,000.

(12-3) \$4,600,000.

(12-4) a. −\$126,000.
b. \$42,518; \$47,579; \$34,926.
c. \$50,702.
d. NPV = \$10,841; Purchase.

(12-5) a. (\$89,000).
b. \$26,220; \$30,300; \$20,100.
c. \$24,380.
d. NPV = −\$6,704; Don't
purchase.

(12-6) a. NPV = \$106,537.

(12-7) E(NPV) = \$3 million; σ_{NPV} =
\$23.622 million; CV_{NPV} =
7.874.

(12-8) a. Expected CF_A = \$6,750;
Expected CF_B = \$7,650;

CV_A = 0.0703.
b. NPV_A = \$10,036; NPV_B =
\$11,624.

(12-9) a. E(IRR) ≅ 15.3%.
b. \$38,589.

(12-10) a. \$117,779.
b. σ_{NPV} = \$445,060; CV_{NPV} =
3.78.

(13-1) a. \$1.074 million.
b. \$2.96 million.

(13-2) a. \$4.6795 million.
b. \$3.208 million.

(13-3) a. −\$19 million.
b. \$9.0981 million.

(13-4) a. −\$2.113 million.
b. \$1.973 million.
c. −\$70,222.
d. \$565,090.
e. \$1.116 million.

(13-5) a. \$2,562.
b. ENPV = \$9,786; Value of
growth option = \$7,224.

(13-6) P = \$18.646 million; X = \$20
million; t = 1; r_{RF} = 0.08; σ^2
= 0.0687;
V = \$2.028 million.

(13-7) P = \$10.479 million; X = \$9
million; t = 2; r_{RF} = 0.06; σ^2
= 0.0111;
V = \$2.514 million.

(13-8) P = \$18,646; X = \$20,000; t =
2; V = \$5,009.

(14-1) AFN = \$410,000.

(14-2) AFN = \$610,000.

(14-3) AFN = \$200,000.

(14-4) ΔS = \$68,965.52.

(14-5) a. \$480,000.
b. \$18,750.

(14-6) AFN = \$360.

(14-7) a. \$13.44 million.
b. Notes payable = \$31.44
million.

(14-8) a. Total assets = \$33,534;
AFN = \$2,128.
b. Notes payable = \$4,228.

(14-9) a. AFN = \$128,783.
b. Notes payable = \$284,783.

(15-1) FCF = \$37.0.

(15-2) $V_{op} = \$6,000,000$.

(15-3) V_{op} at 2009 = $15,000.

(15-4) $V_{op} = \$160,000,000$.
MVA = −$40,000,000.

(15-5) $259,375,000.

(15-6) a. $HV_2 = \$2,700,000$.
b. $2,303,571.43.

(15-7) a. $713.33.
b. $527.89.
c. $43.79.

(15-8) $416 million.

(15-9) $46.90.

(15-10) a. $34.96 million.
b. $741.152 million.
c. $699.20 million.
d. $749.10 million.
e. $50.34.

(16-1) 20,000.

(16-2) 1.0.

(16-3) 3.6%.

(16-4) $300 million.

(16-5) $30.

(16-6) 40 million.

(16-7) a. ΔProfit = $850,000; Return
= 21.25% > r_s = 15%.
b. $Q_{BE,Old}$ = 40; $Q_{BE,New}$ =
45.45.

(16-8) a. ROE_C = 15%; σ_C = 11%.

(16-9) a. V = $3,348,214.
b. $16.74.
c. $1.84.
d. 10%.

(16-10) 30% debt: WACC = 11.14%;
V = $101.023 million.
50% debt: WACC = 11.25%;
V = $100 million.
70% debt: WACC = 11.94%;
V = $94.255 million.

(16-11) a. 0.870.
b. b = 1.218; r_s = 10.872%.
c. WACC = 8.683%; V =
$103.188 million.

(16-12) 11.45%.

(17-1) $500 million.

(17-2) $821 million.

(17-3) $620.68 million.

(17-4) a. b_U = 1.13.
b. r_{sU} = 15.625%; 5.625%.

c. 16.62%; 18.04%; 20.23%.
d. 20.23%.

(17-5) a. $V_U = V_L$ = $20 million.
b. r_{sU} = 10%; r_{sL} = 15%.
c. S_L = $10 million.
d. $WACC_U$ = 10%; $WACC_L$ =
10%.

(17-6) a. V_U = $12 million; V_L =
$16 million.
b. r_{sU} = 10%; r_{sL} = 15%.
c. S_L = $6 million.
d. $WACC_U$ = 10%; $WACC_L$ =
7.5%.

(17-7) a. V_U = $12 million.
b. V_L = $15.33 million.
c. $3.33 million versus $4
million.
d. V_L = $20 million; $0.
e. V_L = $16 million; $4
million.
f. V_L = $16 million; $4
million.

(17-8) a. V_U = $12.5 million.
b. V_L = $16 million; r_{sL} =
15.7%.
c. V_L = $14.5 million; r_{sL} =
14.9%.

(17-9) a. $V_U = V_L$ = $14,545,455.
b. At D = $6 million: r_{sL} =
14.51%; WACC = 11.0%.
c. V_U = $8,727,273; V_L =
$11,127,273.
d. At D = $6 million: r_{sL} =
14.51%; WACC = 8.63%.
e. D = V = $14,545,455.

(17-10) a. V = $3.29 million.
b. D = $1.71 million; yield =
8.1%.
c. V = $3.23 million; D =
$1.77 million; yield =
6.3%.

(18-1) Payout = 55%.

(18-2) Payout = 20%.

(18-3) Payout = 52%.

(18-4) V_{op} = $175 million; n = 8.75
million.

(18-5) P_0 = $60.

(18-6) $3,250,000.

(18-7) n = 4,000; EPS = $5.00; DPS = $1.50; P = $40.00.

(18-8) D_0 = $3.44.

(18-9) Payout = 31.39%.

(18-10) a. (1) $3,960,000.
          (2) $4,800,000.
          (3) $9,360,000.
          (4) Regular = $3,960,000; Extra = $5,400,000.

(18-11) a. $6,000,000.
          b. DPS = $2.00; Payout = 25%.
          c. $5,000,000.
          d. No.
          e. 50%.
          f. $1,000,000.
          g. $8,333,333.

(19-1) a. $700,000.
          b. $3,700,000.
          c. −$2,300,000.

(19-2) $964,115.

(19-3) a. 2007: $12,000; $6,000; $90,000.
          b. Edelman: g_{EPS} = 8.0%; g_{DPS} = 7.4%.
          e. 2007: $3.00; $1.50; $22.50.
          f. Kennedy: 15.00%; Strasburg: 13.64%.
          g. 2007: Kennedy: 50%; Strasburg: 50%.
          h. Kennedy: 43%; Strasburg: 37%.
          i. Kennedy: 8×; Strasburg: 8.67×.

(19-4) a. A–T call cost = $2,640,000.
          b. Flotation cost = $1,600,000.
          c. $1,920,000; $768,000.
          d. $3,472,000.
          e. New tax savings = $16,000.
             Lost tax savings = $19,200.
          f. $360,000.
          g. PV = $9,109,413.
          h. $5,637,413.

(19-5) a. NPV = $2,717,128.

(20-1) a. (1) 50%.
          (2) 60%.
          (3) 50%.

(20-2) Cost of owning = −$127; cost of leasing = −$128.

(20-3) a. Energen: Debt/TA = 50%. Hastings: Debt/TA = 33%.
          b. TA = $200.

(20-4) a. NAL = $108,048.

(20-5) a. Cost of leasing = $637,692. Cost of owning = $713,242.

(21-1) $196.36.

(21-2) 25 shares.

(21-3) a. (1) −$5, or $0.
          (2) $0.
          (3) $5.
          (4) $75.
          d. 10%; $100.

(21-4) Premium = 10%: $46; Premium = 30%: $55.

(21-5) a. 14.1%.
          b. $12 million before tax.
          c. $331.89.
          d. Value as a straight bond = $699.25; value in conversion = $521.91.
          f. Value as a straight bond = $1,000.00; value in conversion = $521.91.

(21-6) b. Plan 1: 49%; Plan 2: 53%; Plan 3: 53%.
          c. Plan 1: $0.59; Plan 2: $0.64; Plan 3: $0.88.
          d. Plan 1: 19%; Plan 2: 19%; Plan 3: 50%.

(21-7) a. Year = 7; CV_7 = $1,210.422; CF_7 = $1,290.422.
          b. 10.20%.

(22-1) $3,000,000.

(22-2) A/R = $59,500.

(22-3) r_{NOM} = 75.26%; EAR = 109.84%.

(22-4) EAR = 8.49%.

(22-5) $7,500,000.

(22-6) a. DSO = 28 days.
b. A/R = $70,000.
c. A/R = $55,000.

(22-7) a. 73.74%.
b. 14.90%.
c. 32.25%.
d. 21.28%.
e. 29.80%.

(22-8) a. 45.15%.

(22-9) Nominal cost = 14.90%;
Effective cost = 15.89%.

(22-10) 14.91%.

(22-11) a. 83 days.
b. $356,250.
c. 4.87×.

(22-12) a. 69.5 days.
b. (1) 1.875×.
(2) 11.25%.
c. (1) 46.5 days.
(2) 2.1262×.
(3) 12.76%.

(22-13) a. ROE_T = 11.75%; ROE_M = 10.80%;
ROE_R = 9.16%.

(22-14) a. Feb. surplus = $2,000.
b. $164,000.

(22-15) a. $100,000.
c. (1) $300,000.
(2) Nominal cost = 37.24%;
Effective cost = 44.59%.
d. Nominal cost = 24.83%;
Effective cost = 27.86%.

(22-16) a. 14.35%.

(22-17) a. $300,000.

(23-1) Net payment = LIBOR + 0.2%.

(23-2) r_d = 7.01%.

(23-3) r_d = 5.96%.

(23-4) Net to Carter = 9.95% fixed.
Net to Brence = LIBOR + 3.05% floating.

(23-5) a. Sell 105 contracts.

b. Bond = −$1,414,552.69;
Futures = +$1,951,497.45;
Net = $536,944.76.

(24-1) AP = $375,000; NP = $750,000; SD = $750,000;
Stockholders = $343,750.

(24-2) a. Total assets: $327 million.
b. Income: $7 million.
c. Before: $15.6 million.
After: $13.0 million.
d. Before: 35.7%.
After: 64.2%.

(24-3) a. $0.
b. First mortgage holders: $300,000.
Second mortgage holders: $100,000 plus $12,700 as a general claimant.
c. Trustee's expenses: $50,000.
Wages due: $30,000.
Taxes due: $40,000.
d. *Before subordination:*
Accounts payable = $6,350.
Notes payable = $22,860.
Second mortgage = $12,700 + $100,000.
Debentures = $25,400.
Sub. debentures = $12,700.
After subordination:
Notes payable = $35,560.
Sub. debentures = $0.

(24-4) a. $0 for stockholders.
b. AP = 24%; NP = 100%;
WP = 100%;
TP = 100%; Mortgage = 85%.
Subordinated debentures = 9%;
Trustee = 100%.

(25-1) P_0 = $25.26.

(25-2) P_0 = $41.54.

(25-3) $25.26 to $41.54.

(25-4) Value of equity = $43.60 million.

(25-5) a. $V_{op\ Unlevered}$ = $32.02 million; $V_{Tax\ shields}$ = $11.50 million.

b. V_{op} = $43.52 million; max = $33.52 million.

(25-6) a. 10.96%.

b. (All in millions) FCF_1 = $23.12, TS_1 = $14.00; FCF_3 = $12.26, TS_3 = $16.45; FCF_5 = $23.83, TS_5 = $18.90.

c. HV_{TS} = $510.68 million; HV_{UL} = $643.89 million.

d. Value of equity = $508.57 million.

(26-1) 12.358 yen per peso.

(26-2) f_t = $0.00907.

(26-3) 1 euro = $0.9091 or $1 = 1.1 euro.

(26-4) 0.6667 pound per dollar.

(26-5) 1.5152 SFr.

(26-6) 2.4 Swiss francs per pound.

(26-7) $r_{NOM-U.S.}$ = 4.6%.

(26-8) 117 pesos.

(26-9) +$250,000.

(26-10) b. $18,148.00.

(26-11) a. $1,659,000.

b. $1,646,000.

c. $2,000,000.

(26-12) b. f_t = $0.7994.

(26-13) $468,837,209.

(26-14) a. $52.63; 20%.

b. 1.5785 SF per U.S.$.

c. 41.54 Swiss francs; 16.92%.

appendix C

Selected Equations and Data

Chapter 1

$$\text{Value} = \frac{\text{FCF}_1}{(1 + \text{WACC})^1} + \frac{\text{FCF}_2}{(1 + \text{WACC})^2} + \frac{\text{FCF}_3}{(1 + \text{WACC})^3} + \cdots + \frac{\text{FCF}_\infty}{(1 + \text{WACC})^\infty}.$$

Chapter 2

$$\text{FV}_N = \text{PV}(1 + I)^N.$$

$$\text{PV} = \frac{\text{FV}_N}{(1 + I)^N}.$$

$$\text{FVA}_N = \text{PMT}\left[\frac{(1 + I)^N}{I} - \frac{1}{I}\right] = \text{PMT}\left[\frac{(1 + I)^N - 1}{I}\right].$$

$$\text{FVA}_{\text{due}} = \text{FVA}_{\text{ordinary}}(1 + I).$$

$$\text{PVA}_N = \text{PMT}\left[\frac{1}{I} - \frac{1}{I(1 + I)^N}\right] = \text{PMT}\left[\frac{1 - \dfrac{1}{(1 + I)^N}}{I}\right].$$

$$\text{PVA}_{N\,\text{due}} = \text{PVA}_{\text{ordinary}}(1 + I).$$

$$\text{PV of a perpetuity} = \frac{\text{PMT}}{I}.$$

$$\text{PV}_{\text{Uneven stream}} = \sum_{t=1}^{N} \frac{\text{CF}_t}{(1 + I)^t}.$$

$$\text{FV}_{\text{Uneven stream}} = \sum_{t=1}^{N} \text{CF}_t(1 + I)^{N-t}.$$

$$I_{\text{PER}} = \frac{I_{\text{NOM}}}{M}.$$

$$\text{APR} = (I_{\text{PER}})M.$$

Number of periods = NM.

$$FV_N = PV(1 + I_{PER})^{\text{Number of periods}} = PV\left(1 + \frac{I_{NOM}}{M}\right)^{MN}.$$

$$EFF\% = \left(1 + \frac{I_{NOM}}{M}\right)^{M} - 1.0.$$

Chapter 3

EBIT = Earnings before interest and taxes = Sales revenues − Operating costs.

EBITDA = Earnings before interest, taxes, depreciation, and amortization
= EBIT + Depreciation + Amortization.

Net cash flow = Net income + Depreciation and amortization.

NOWC = Net operating working capital
= Operating current assets − Operating current liabilities
= (Cash + Accounts receivable + Inventories)
− (Accounts payable + Accruals).

Total net operating capital = Net operating working capital
+ Operating long−term assets.

NOPAT = Net operating profit after taxes = EBIT(1 − Tax rate).

Free cash flow (FCF) = NOPAT − Net investment in operating capital
= NOPAT − (Current year's total net operating capital
− Previous year's total net operating capital).

Operating cash flow = NOPAT + Depreciation and amortization.

$$\frac{\text{Gross investment in}}{\text{operating capital}} = \frac{\text{Net investment}}{\text{in operating capital}} + \text{Depreciation.}$$

FCF = Operating cash flow − Gross investment in operating capital.

$$\text{Return on invested capital (ROIC)} = \frac{\text{NOPAT}}{\text{Total net operating capital}}.$$

MVA = Market value of stock − Equity capital supplied by shareholders
= (Shares outstanding)(Stock price) − Total common equity.

MVA = Total market value − Total investor-supplied capital

= (Market value of stock + Market value of debt)
      − Total investor-supplied capital.

EVA = Net operating profit after taxes (NOPAT)
         − After–tax dollar cost of capital used to support operations

= EBIT(1 − Tax rate) − (Total net operating capital)(WACC).

EVA = (Total net operating capital)(ROIC − WACC).

Chapter 4

$$\text{Current ratio} = \frac{\text{Current assets}}{\text{Current liabilities}}.$$

$$\text{Quick, or acid test, ratio} = \frac{\text{Current assets} - \text{Inventories}}{\text{Current liabilities}}.$$

$$\text{Inventory turnover ratio} = \frac{\text{Sales}}{\text{Inventories}}.$$

$$\text{DSO} = \text{Days sales outstanding} = \frac{\text{Receivables}}{\text{Average sales per day}} = \frac{\text{Receivables}}{\text{Annual sales}/365}.$$

$$\text{Fixed assets turnover ratio} = \frac{\text{Sales}}{\text{Net fixed assets}}.$$

$$\text{Total assets turnover ratio} = \frac{\text{Sales}}{\text{Total assets}}.$$

$$\text{Debt ratio} = \frac{\text{Total liabilities}}{\text{Total assets}}.$$

$$\text{D/E} = \frac{\text{D/A}}{1 - \text{D/A}}, \text{ and } \text{D/A} = \frac{\text{D/E}}{1 + \text{D/E}}.$$

$$\text{Equity multiplier} = \frac{\text{Total assets}}{\text{Common equity}} = \frac{\text{A}}{\text{E}}.$$

$$\text{Debt ratio} = 1 - \frac{1}{\text{Equity multiplier}}.$$

$$\text{Times-interest-earned (TIE) ratio} = \frac{\text{EBIT}}{\text{Interest charges}}.$$

$$\text{EBITDA coverage ratio} = \frac{\text{EBITDA} + \text{Lease payments}}{\text{Interest} + \text{Principal payments} + \text{Lease payments}}.$$

$$\text{Profit margin on sales} = \frac{\text{Net income available to common stockholders}}{\text{Sales}}.$$

$$\text{Return on total assets (ROA)} = \frac{\text{Net income available to common stockholders}}{\text{Total assets}}.$$

$$\text{Basic earning power (BEP) ratio} = \frac{\text{EBIT}}{\text{Total assets}}.$$

$$\text{ROA} = \text{Profit margin} \times \text{Total assets turnover}.$$

$$\text{ROA} = \frac{\text{Net income}}{\text{Sales}} \times \frac{\text{Sales}}{\text{Total assets}}.$$

$$\text{Return on common equity (ROE)} = \frac{\text{Net income available to common stockholders}}{\text{Common equity}}.$$

$$\text{ROE} = \text{ROA} \times \text{Equity multiplier}$$
$$= \text{Profit margin} \times \text{Total assets turnover} \times \text{Equity multiplier}$$
$$= \frac{\text{Net income}}{\text{Sales}} \times \frac{\text{Sales}}{\text{Total assets}} \times \frac{\text{Total assets}}{\text{Common equity}}.$$

$$\text{Price/earnings (P/E) ratio} = \frac{\text{Price per share}}{\text{Earnings per share}}.$$

$$\text{Price/cash flow ratio} = \frac{\text{Price per share}}{\text{Cash flow per share}}.$$

$$\text{Book value per share} = \frac{\text{Common equity}}{\text{Shares outstanding}}.$$

$$\text{Market/book (M/B) ratio} = \frac{\text{Market price per share}}{\text{Book value per share}}.$$

Chapter 5

$$V_B = \sum_{t=1}^{N} \frac{\text{INT}}{(1 + r_d)^t} + \frac{M}{(1 + r_d)^N}.$$

$$\text{Price of callable bond} = \sum_{t=1}^{N} \frac{\text{INT}}{(1 + r_d)^t} + \frac{\text{Call price}}{(1 + r_d)^N}.$$

$$\text{Current yield} = \frac{\text{Annual interest}}{\text{Bond's current price}}.$$

$$V_B = \sum_{t=1}^{2N} \frac{\text{INT}/2}{(1 + r_d/2)^t} + \frac{M}{(1 + r_d/2)^{2N}}.$$

$$r_d = r^* + IP + DRP + LP + MRP.$$

$$r_{RF} = r^* + IP.$$

$$r_d = r_{RF} + DRP + LP + MRP.$$

$$IP_N = \frac{I_1 + I_2 + \cdots + I_N}{N}.$$

Chapter 6

$$\text{Expected rate of return} = \hat{r} = \sum_{i=1}^{n} P_i r_i.$$

$$\text{Historical average, } \bar{r}_{Avg} = \frac{\sum_{t=1}^{n} \bar{r}_t}{n}.$$

$$\text{Variance} = \sigma^2 = \sum_{i=1}^{n} (r_i - \hat{r})^2 P_i.$$

$$\text{Standard deviation} = \sigma = \sqrt{\sum_{i=1}^{n} (r_i - \hat{r})^2 P_i}.$$

$$\text{Historical estimated } \sigma = S = \sqrt{\frac{\sum_{t=1}^{n} (\bar{r}_t - \bar{r}_{Avg})^2}{n - 1}}.$$

$$CV = \frac{\sigma}{\hat{r}}.$$

$$\hat{r}_p = \sum_{i=1}^{n} w_i \hat{r}_i.$$

$$\sigma_p = \sqrt{\sum_{i=1}^{n} (r_{pi} - \hat{r}_p)^2 P_i}.$$

$$\text{Estimated } \rho = R = \frac{\sum_{t=1}^{n} (\bar{r}_{i,t} - \bar{r}_{i,Avg})(\bar{r}_{j,t} - \bar{r}_{j,Avg})}{\sqrt{\sum_{t=1}^{n} (\bar{r}_{i,t} - \bar{r}_{i,Avg})^2 \sum_{t=1}^{n} (\bar{r}_{j,t} - \bar{r}_{j,Avg})^2}}.$$

$$COV_{iM} = \rho_{iM}\sigma_i\sigma_M.$$

$$b_i = \left(\frac{\sigma_i}{\sigma_M}\right)\rho_{iM} = \frac{COV_{iM}}{\sigma_M^2}.$$

$$b_p = \sum_{i=1}^{n} w_i b_i.$$

Required return on stock market $= r_M$.

Market risk premium $= RP_M = r_M - r_{RF}$.

$$RP_i = (r_M - r_{RF})b_i = (RP_M)b_i.$$

$$SML = r_i = r_{RF} + (r_M - r_{RF})b_i = r_{RF} + RP_M b_i.$$

Chapter 7

$$\hat{r}_p = w_A\hat{r}_A + (1 - w_A)\hat{r}_B.$$

$$\text{Portfolio SD} = \sigma_p = \sqrt{w_A^2\sigma_A^2 + (1 - w_A)^2\sigma_B^2 + 2w_A(1 - w_A)\rho_{AB}\sigma_A\sigma_B}.$$

$$\text{Minimum} = \text{risk portfolio: } w_A = \frac{\sigma_B(\sigma_B - \rho_{AB}\sigma_A)}{\sigma_A^2 + \sigma_B^2 - 2\rho_{AB}\sigma_A\sigma_B}.$$

$$\hat{r}_p = \sum_{i=1}^{N} (w_i\hat{r}_i).$$

$$\sigma_p^2 = \sum_{i=1}^{N} \sum_{j=1}^{N} (w_i w_j \sigma_i \sigma_j \rho_{ij}).$$

$$\sigma_p^2 = \sum_{i=1}^{N} w_i\sigma_i^2 + \sum_{i=1}^{N} \sum_{\substack{j=1 \\ j\neq i}}^{N} 2w_i\sigma_i w_j\sigma_j\rho_{ij}.$$

$$\sigma_p = \sqrt{(1 - w_{RF})^2\sigma_M^2} = (1 - w_{RF})\sigma_M.$$

$$\text{CML: } \hat{r}_p = r_{RF} + \left(\frac{\hat{r}_M - r_{RF}}{\sigma_M}\right)\sigma_p.$$

$$r_i = r_{RF} + \frac{(r_M - r_{RF})}{\sigma_M}\left(\frac{Cov(r_i, r_M)}{\sigma_M}\right) = r_{RF} + (r_M - r_{RF})\left(\frac{Cov(r_i, r_M)}{\sigma_M^2}\right).$$

$$b_i = \frac{\text{Covariance between Stock i and the market}}{\text{Variance of market returns}}$$

$$= \frac{Cov(r_i, r_M)}{\sigma_M^2} = \frac{\rho_{iM}\sigma_i\sigma_M}{\sigma_M^2} = \rho_{iM}\left(\frac{\sigma_i}{\sigma_M}\right).$$

$$\text{SML} = r_i = r_{RF} + (r_M - r_{RF})b_i = r_{RF} + (RP_M)b_i.$$

$$\sigma_i^2 = b_i^2 \sigma_M^2 + \sigma_{e_i}^2.$$

$$r_i = r_{RF} + (r_1 - r_{RF})b_{i1} + \cdots + (r_j - r_{RF})b_{ij}.$$

$$r_i = r_{RF} + a_i + b_i(r_M - r_{RF}) + c_i(r_{SMB}) + d_i(r_{HML}).$$

Chapter 8

$$\hat{P}_0 = \text{PV of expected future dividends} = \sum_{t=1}^{\infty} \frac{D_t}{(1 + r_s)^t}.$$

$$\hat{P}_0 = \frac{D_0(1 + g)}{r_s - g} = \frac{D_1}{r_s - g}.$$

$$\hat{r}_s = \frac{D_1}{P_0} + g.$$

$$\text{Capital gains yield} = \frac{\hat{P}_1 - P_0}{P_0}.$$

$$\text{Dividend yield} = \frac{D_1}{P_0}.$$

$$\text{For a zero growth stock, } \hat{P}_0 = \frac{D}{r_s}.$$

$$\text{Horizon value} = \hat{P}_N = \frac{D_{N+1}}{r_s - g}.$$

$$V_p = \frac{D_p}{r_p}.$$

$$\hat{r}_p = \frac{D_p}{V_p}.$$

$$\bar{r}_s = \text{Actual dividend yield} + \text{Actual capital gains yield}.$$

Chapter 9

$$\text{Exercise value} = \text{Current price of stock} - \text{Strike price}.$$

$$\text{Number of stock shares in hedged portfolio} = N = \frac{C_u - C_d}{P_u - P_d}.$$

$$V = P[N(d_1)] - Xe^{-r_{RF}t}[N(d_2)].$$

$$d_1 = \frac{\ln(P/X) + [r_{RF} + (\sigma^2/2)]t}{\sigma\sqrt{t}}.$$

$$d_2 = d_1 - \sigma\sqrt{t}.$$

Chapter 10

After-tax component cost of debt $= r_d(1 - T)$.

$$M(1 - F) = \sum_{t=1}^{N} \frac{INT(1 - T)}{[1 + r_d(1 - T)]^t} + \frac{M}{[1 + r_d(1 - T)]^N}.$$

$$r_{ps} = \frac{D_{ps}}{P_{ps}(1 - F)}.$$

Market equilibrium: Expected rate of return $= \hat{r}_M = \dfrac{D_1}{P_0} + g = r_{RF} + RP_M$

$$= r_M = \text{Required rate of return}.$$

CAPM: $r_s = r_{RF} + b_i(RP_M)$.

DCF: $r_s = \hat{r}_s = \dfrac{D_1}{P_0} + \text{Expected g}$.

Bond-yield-plus risk-premium: $r_s = $ Bond yield + Bond risk premium.

$g = $ (Retention rate)(ROE) $= (1.0 - $ Payout rate)(ROE).

$$r_e = \hat{r}_e = \frac{D_1}{P_0(1 - F)} + g.$$

$WACC = w_d\, r_d(1 - T) + w_{ps}\, r_{ps} + w_{ce}r_s.$

Chapter 11

$$NPV = CF_0 + \frac{CF_1}{(1 + r)^1} + \frac{CF_2}{(1 + r)^2} + \cdots + \frac{CF_N}{(1 + r)^N}$$

$$= \sum_{t=0}^{N} \frac{CF_t}{(1 + r)^t}.$$

$$IRR: CF_0 + \frac{CF_1}{(1 + IRR)^1} + \frac{CF_2}{(1 + IRR)^2} + \cdots + \frac{CF_N}{(1 + IRR)^N} = 0.$$

$$NPV = \sum_{t=0}^{n} \frac{CF_t}{(1 + IRR)^t} = 0.$$

MIRR: PV of costs = PV of terminal value.

$$\sum_{t=0}^{N} \frac{COF_t}{(1 + r)^t} = \frac{\displaystyle\sum_{t=0}^{N} CIF_t(1 + r)^{N-t}}{(1 + MIRR)^N}.$$

$$PV \text{ of costs} = \frac{\text{Terminal value}}{(1 + MIRR)^N}.$$

$$PI = \frac{PV \text{ of future cash flows}}{\text{Initial cost}} = \frac{\displaystyle\sum_{t=1}^{N} \frac{CF_t}{(1 + r)^t}}{CF_0}.$$

$$Payback = \begin{array}{c}\text{Number of}\\\text{years prior to}\\\text{full recovery}\end{array} + \frac{\begin{array}{c}\text{Unrecovered cost}\\\text{at start of year}\end{array}}{\begin{array}{c}\text{Cash flow during}\\\text{full recovery year}\end{array}}.$$

Chapter 12

$$FCF = \begin{array}{c}\text{Investment outlay}\\\text{cash flow}\end{array} + \begin{array}{c}\text{Operating}\\\text{cash flow}\end{array} + \begin{array}{c}\text{NOWC}\\\text{cash flow}\end{array} + \begin{array}{c}\text{Salvage}\\\text{cash flow}\end{array}.$$

$$NPV = \sum_{t=0}^{N} \frac{NCF_t}{(1 + r_{NOM})^t} = \sum_{t=0}^{N} \frac{RCF_t(1 + i)^t}{(1 + r_r)^t(1 + i)^t} = \sum_{t=0}^{N} \frac{RCF_t}{(1 + r_r)^t}.$$

$$\text{Expected NPV} = \sum_{i=1}^{n} P_i(NPV_i).$$

$$\sigma_{NPV} = \sqrt{\sum_{i=1}^{n} P_i(NPV_i - \text{Expected NPV})^2}.$$

$$CV_{NPV} = \frac{\sigma_{NPV}}{E(NPV)}.$$

Chapter 13

$$CV = \frac{\sigma(PV \text{ of future CF})}{E(PV \text{ of future CF})}.$$

$$\text{Variance of project's rate of return: } \sigma^2 = \frac{\ln(CV^2 + 1)}{t}.$$

Chapter 14

$$
\begin{array}{ccccc}
\text{Additional} & & \text{Required} & \text{Spontaneous} & \text{Increase in} \\
\text{funds} & = & \text{asset} & - \quad \text{liability} & - \quad \text{retained} \\
\text{needed} & & \text{increase} & \text{increase} & \text{earnings}
\end{array}
$$

$$ \text{AFN} = (A^*/S_0)\Delta S - (L^*/S_0)\Delta S - MS_1(RR). $$

$$
\begin{array}{c}
\text{Full} \\
\text{capacity} \\
\text{sales}
\end{array}
=
\dfrac{\text{Actual sales}}{\begin{array}{c}\text{Percentage of capacity}\\ \text{at which fixed assets}\\ \text{were operated}\end{array}}.
$$

$$ \frac{\text{Target fixed assets}}{\text{Sales}} = \frac{\text{Actual fixed assets}}{\text{Full capacity sales}}. $$

$$ \text{Required level of fixed assets} = (\text{Target fixed assets/Sales})(\text{Projected sales}). $$

Chapter 15

V_{op} = Value of operations

= PV of expected future free cash flows

$$ = \sum_{t=1}^{\infty} \frac{FCF_1}{(1 + WACC)^t}. $$

$$ \text{Horizon value: } V_{op(\text{at time N})} = \frac{FCF_{N+1}}{WACC - g} = \frac{FCF_N(1 + g)}{WACC - g}. $$

Total value = V_{op} + Value of nonoperating assets.

Value of equity = Total value − Preferred stock − Debt.

Operating profitability (OP) = NOPAT/Sales.

Capital requirements (CR) = Operating capital/Sales.

$EROIC_t$ = Expected return on invested capital

$$ = NOPAT_{t+1}/Capital_t $$

$$ = NOPAT_t(1 + g)/Capital_t. $$

For constant growth:

$$V_{op(at\ time\ N)} = Capital_N + \left[\frac{Sales_N(1 + g)}{WACC - g}\right]\left[OP - WACC\left(\frac{CR}{1 + g}\right)\right]$$

$$= Capital_N + \frac{Capital_N(EROIC_N - WACC)}{WACC - g}.$$

Chapter 16

$$V_{op} = \sum_{t=1}^{\infty}\frac{FCF_t}{(1 + WACC)^t}.$$

$$WACC = w_d(1 - T)r_d + w_{ce}r_s.$$

$$ROIC = \frac{NOPAT}{Capital} = \frac{EBIT(1 - T)}{Capital}.$$

$$EBIT = PQ - VQ - F.$$

$$Q_{BE} = \frac{F}{P - V}.$$

$$V_L = D + S.$$

MM, no taxes: $V_L = V_U$.

MM, corporate taxes: $V_L = V_U + TD$.

Miller, corporate and personal taxes: $V_L = V_U - \left[1 - \frac{(1 - T_c)(1 - T_s)}{(1 - T_d)}\right]D$.

$$b = b_U[1 + (1 - T)(D/S)].$$

$$b_U = b/[1 + (1 - T)(D/S)].$$

$$r_s = r_{RF} + RP_M(b).$$

$$r_s = r_{RF} + Premium\ for\ business\ risk + Premium\ for\ financial\ risk.$$

If $g = 0$: $V_{op} = \dfrac{FCF}{WACC} = \dfrac{EBIT(1 - T)}{WACC}$.

Total corporate value = V_{op} + Value of short-term investments.

S = Total corporate value − Value of all debt.

$$D = w_d V_{op}.$$

$$S = (1 - w_d)V_{op}.$$

Cash raised by issuing debt $= D - D_0.$

$$P_{Prior} = S_{Prior}/n_0.$$

$$P = P_{Prior}.$$

$$N - n_0 = (D - D_0)/P.$$

$$n = n_0 - (D - D_0)/P.$$

$$P = [S + (D - D_0)]/n_0.$$

$$NI = (EBIT - r_dD)(1 - T).$$

$$EPS = NI/n.$$

Chapter 17

MM, no taxes:

$$V_L = V_U = \frac{EBIT}{WACC} = \frac{EBIT}{r_{sU}}.$$

$$r_{sL} = r_{sU} + \text{Risk premium} = r_{sU} + (r_{sU} - r_d)(D/S).$$

MM, corporate taxes:

$$V_L = V_U + TD.$$

$$V_U = S = \frac{EBIT(1 - T)}{r_{sU}}.$$

$$r_{sL} = r_{sU} + (r_{sU} - r_d)(1 - T)(D/S).$$

Miller, personal taxes:

$$V_U = \frac{EBIT(1 - T_c)}{r_{sU}} = \frac{EBIT(1 - T_c)(1 - T_s)}{r_{sU}(1 - T_s)}.$$

$$CF_L = (EBIT - I)(1 - T_c)(1 - T_s) + I(1 - T_d).$$

$$V_L = V_U + \left[1 - \frac{(1 - T_c)(1 - T_s)}{(1 - T_d)}\right]D.$$

Ehrhardt & Daves, impact of growth:

$$V_U = \frac{FCF}{r_{sU} - g}.$$

General case:

$$V_L = V_U + V_{\text{Tax shield}}.$$

$$V_{\text{Tax shield}} = \frac{r_d TD}{r_{TS} - g}.$$

$$V_L = V_U + \left(\frac{r_d}{r_{TS} - g}\right)TD.$$

Case for $r_{TS} = r_{sU}$:

$$V_L = V_U + \left(\frac{r_d TD}{r_{sU} - g}\right).$$

$$r_{sL} = r_{sU} + (r_{sU} - r_d)\frac{D}{S}.$$

$$b = b_U + (b_U - b_D)\frac{D}{S}.$$

Chapter 18

Dividends = Net income − [(Target equity ratio)(Total capital budget)].

Chapter 19

Amount left on table = (Closing price − Offer price)(Number of shares).

Chapter 20

NAL = PV cost of owning − PV cost of leasing.

Chapter 21

$$\frac{\text{Price paid for}}{\text{bond with warrants}} = \frac{\text{Straight-debt}}{\text{value of bond}} + \frac{\text{Value of}}{\text{warrants}}.$$

$$\text{Conversion price} = P_c = \frac{\text{Par value of bond given up}}{\text{Shares received}}.$$

$$= \frac{\text{Par value of bond given up}}{\text{CR}}.$$

$$\text{Conversion ratio} = CR = \frac{\text{Par value of bond given up}}{P_c}.$$

Chapter 22

$$\text{Inventory conversion period} = \frac{\text{Inventory}}{\text{Sales}/365}.$$

$$\text{Receivables collection period} = \text{DSO} = \frac{\text{Receivables}}{\text{Sales}/365}.$$

$$\text{Payables deferral period} = \frac{\text{Payables}}{\text{Cost of goods sold}/365}.$$

$$\begin{array}{c} \text{Inventory} \\ \text{conversion} \\ \text{period} \end{array} + \begin{array}{c} \text{Average} \\ \text{collection} \\ \text{period} \end{array} - \begin{array}{c} \text{Payables} \\ \text{deferral} \\ \text{period} \end{array} = \begin{array}{c} \text{Cash} \\ \text{conversion} \\ \text{cycle} \end{array}.$$

$$\begin{array}{c} \text{Accounts} \\ \text{receivable} \end{array} = \begin{array}{c} \text{Credit sales} \\ \text{per day} \end{array} \times \begin{array}{c} \text{Length of} \\ \text{collection period} \end{array}.$$

$$\text{ADS} = \frac{(\text{Units sold})(\text{Sales price})}{365} = \frac{\text{Annual sales}}{365}.$$

$$\text{Receivables} = (\text{ADS})(\text{DSO}).$$

$$\begin{array}{c} \text{Nominal annual cost} \\ \text{of trade credit} \end{array} = \frac{\text{Discount}\%}{100 - \text{Discount}\%} \times \frac{365}{\begin{array}{c} \text{Days credit is} \\ \text{outstanding} \end{array} - \begin{array}{c} \text{Discount} \\ \text{period} \end{array}}.$$

Chapter 25

$$r_{sL} = r_{sU} + (r_{sU} - r_d)(D/S).$$

$$r_{sU} = w_s r_{sL} + w_d r_d.$$

$$\text{Tax savings} = (\text{Interest expense})(\text{Tax rate}).$$

$$\text{Horizon value of unlevered firm } (HV_{U,N}) = \frac{FCF_{N+1}}{r_{sU} - g} = \frac{FCF_N(1 + g)}{r_{sU} - g}.$$

$$\begin{array}{c} \text{Horizon value of} \\ \text{tax shield } (HV_{TS,N}) \end{array} = \frac{TS_{N+1}}{r_{sU} - g} = \frac{TS_N(1 + g)}{r_{sU} - g}.$$

$$V_{\text{Unlevered}} = \sum_{t=1}^{N} \frac{FCF_t}{(1 + r_{sU})^t} + \frac{HV_{U,N}}{(1 + r_{sU})^N}.$$

$$V_{\text{Tax shield}} = \sum_{t=1}^{N} \frac{TS_t}{(1 + r_{sU})^t} + \frac{HV_{TS,N}}{(1 + r_{sU})^N}.$$

$$V_{Operations} = V_{Unlevered} + V_{Tax\ shield}.$$

$$FCFE = \begin{matrix} Free \\ cash\ flow \end{matrix} - \begin{matrix} After\text{-}tax \\ interest\ expense \end{matrix} - \begin{matrix} Principal \\ payments \end{matrix} + \begin{matrix} Newly\ issued \\ debt \end{matrix}$$

$$= \begin{matrix} Free \\ cash\ flow \end{matrix} - \begin{matrix} Interest \\ expense \end{matrix} + \begin{matrix} Interest \\ tax\ shield \end{matrix} + \begin{matrix} Net\ change \\ in\ debt \end{matrix}.$$

$$HV_{FCFE,N} = \frac{FCFE_{N+1}}{r_{sL} - g} = \frac{FCFE_N(1 + g)}{r_{sL} - g}.$$

$$V_{FCFE} = \sum_{t=1}^{N} \frac{FCFE_t}{(1 + r_{sL})^t} + \frac{HV_{FCFE,N}}{(1 + r_{sL})^N}.$$

$$S = V_{FCFE} + Nonoperating\ assets.$$

Chapter 26

$$\frac{Forward\ exchange\ rate}{Spot\ exchange\ rate} = \frac{(1 + r_h)}{(1 + r_f)}.$$

$$P_h = (P_f)(Spot\ rate).$$

$$Spot\ rate = \frac{P_h}{P_f}.$$

appendix d

Values of the Areas under the Standard Normal Distribution Function

Values of the Areas under the Standard Normal Distribution Function

z	0.00	0.01	0.02	0.03	0.04	0.05	0.06	0.07	0.08	0.09
0.0	.0000	.0040	.0080	.0120	.0160	.0199	.0239	.0279	.0319	.0359
0.1	.0398	.0438	.0478	.0517	.0557	.0596	.0636	.0675	.0714	.0753
0.2	.0793	.0832	.0871	.0910	.0948	.0987	.1026	.1064	.1103	.1141
0.3	.1179	.1217	.1255	.1293	.1331	.1368	.1406	.1443	.1480	.1517
0.4	.1554	.1591	.1628	.1664	.1700	.1736	.1772	.1808	.1844	.1879
0.5	.1915	.1950	.1985	.2019	.2054	.2088	.2123	.2157	.2190	.2224
0.6	.2257	.2291	.2324	.2357	.2389	.2422	.2454	.2486	.2517	.2549
0.7	.2580	.2611	.2642	.2673	.2704	.2734	.2764	.2794	.2823	.2852
0.8	.2881	.2910	.2939	.2967	.2995	.3023	.3051	.3078	.3106	.3133
0.9	.3159	.3186	.3212	.3238	.3264	.3289	.3315	.3340	.3365	.3389
1.0	.3413	.3438	.3461	.3485	.3508	.3531	.3554	.3577	.3599	.3621
1.1	.3643	.3665	.3686	.3708	.3729	.3749	.3770	.3790	.3810	.3830
1.2	.3849	.3869	.3888	.3907	.3925	.3944	.3962	.3980	.3997	.4015
1.3	.4032	.4049	.4066	.4082	.4099	.4115	.4131	.4147	.4162	.4177
1.4	.4192	.4207	.4222	.4236	.4251	.4265	.4279	.4292	.4306	.4319
1.5	.4332	.4345	.4357	.4370	.4382	.4394	.4406	.4418	.4429	.4441
1.6	.4452	.4463	.4474	.4484	.4495	.4505	.4515	.4525	.4535	.4545
1.7	.4554	.4564	.4573	.4582	.4591	.4599	.4608	.4616	.4625	.4633
1.8	.4641	.4649	.4656	.4664	.4671	.4678	.4686	.4693	.4699	.4706
1.9	.4713	.4719	.4726	.4732	.4738	.4744	.4750	.4756	.4761	.4767
2.0	.4773	.4778	.4783	.4788	.4793	.4798	.4803	.4808	.4812	.4817
2.1	.4821	.4826	.4830	.4834	.4838	.4842	.4846	.4850	.4854	.4857
2.2	.4861	.4864	.4868	.4871	.4875	.4878	.4881	.4884	.4887	.4890
2.3	.4893	.4896	.4898	.4901	.4904	.4906	.4909	.4911	.4913	.4916
2.4	.4918	.4920	.4922	.4925	.4927	.4929	.4931	.4932	.4934	.4936
2.5	.4938	.4940	.4941	.4943	.4945	.4946	.4948	.4949	.4951	.4952
2.6	.4953	.4955	.4956	.4957	.4959	.4960	.4961	.4962	.4963	.4964
2.7	.4965	.4966	.4967	.4968	.4969	.4970	.4971	.4972	.4973	.4974
2.8	.4974	.4975	.4976	.4977	.4977	.4978	.4979	.4979	.4980	.4981
2.9	.4981	.4982	.4982	.4982	.4984	.4984	.4985	.4985	.4986	.4986
3.0	.4987	.4987	.4987	.4988	.4988	.4989	.4989	.4989	.4990	.4990

absolute priority doctrine States that claims must be paid in strict accordance with the priority of each claim, regardless of the consequence to other claimants.

account receivable Created when a good is shipped or a service is performed, and payment for that good is not made on a cash basis, but on a credit basis.

accounting income Income as defined by Generally Accepted Accounting Principles (GAAP).

accounting profit A firm's net income as reported on its income statement.

acquiring company A company that seeks to acquire another firm.

actual, or realized, rate of return, $\bar{r}_s$ The rate of return that was actually realized at the end of some holding period.

additional funds needed (AFN) Those funds required from external sources to increase the firm's assets to support a sales increase. A sales increase will normally require an increase in assets. However, some of this increase is usually offset by a spontaneous increase in liabilities as well as by earnings retained in the firm. Those funds that are required but not generated internally must be obtained from external sources.

aggressive short-term financing policy Refers to a policy in which a firm finances all of its fixed assets with long-term capital but part of its permanent current assets with short-term, nonspontaneous credit.

aging schedule Breaks down accounts receivable according to how long they have been outstanding. This gives the firm a more complete picture of the structure of accounts receivable than that provided by days sales outstanding.

alternative minimum tax (AMT) A provision of the tax code that requires profitable firms to pay at least some taxes if such taxes are greater than the amount due under standard tax accounting. The AMT has provided a stimulus to leasing for those firms paying the AMT because leasing lowers profits reported to stockholders; figured at about 20% of the profits reported to stockholders.

amortization A noncash charge against intangible assets, such as goodwill.

amortization schedule An amortization schedule is a table that breaks down the periodic fixed payment of an installment loan into its principal and interest components.

amortized loan An amortized loan is one that is repaid in equal periodic amounts (or "killed off" over time).

annual report A report issued annually by a corporation to its stockholders. It contains basic financial statements, as well as management's opinion of the past year's operations and the firm's future prospects.

annuity An annuity is a series of payments of a fixed amount for a specified number of periods.

annuity due An annuity due is an annuity with payments occurring at the beginning of each period.

APR The nominal annual interest rate is also called the annual percentage rate, or APR.

arbitrage The simultaneous buying and selling of the same commodity or security in two different markets at different prices, thus pocketing a risk-free return.

Arbitrage Pricing Theory (APT) An approach to measuring the equilibrium risk/return relationship for a given stock as a function of multiple factors, rather than the single factor (the market return) used by the Capital Asset Pricing Model. The APT is based on complex mathematical and statistical theory, but can account for several factors (such as GNP and the level of inflation) in determining the required return for a particular stock.

arrearages Preferred dividends that have not been paid, and hence are "in arrears."

asset management ratios A set of ratios that measure how effectively a firm is managing its assets.

assets-in-place Refers to the land, buildings, machines, and inventory that the firm uses in its operations to produce its products and services. Also known as operating assets.

assignment An informal procedure for liquidating debts which transfers title to a debtor's assets to a third person, known as an assignee or trustee.

average stock's beta, $b_A = b_M$ The beta coefficient (b) is a measure of a stock's market risk. It measures the stock's volatility relative to an average stock, which has a beta of 1.0.

average tax rate Calculated by taking the total amount of tax paid divided by taxable income.

balance sheet A statement of the firm's financial position at a specific point in time. It specifically lists the firm's assets on the left-hand side of the balance sheet, while the right-hand side shows its liabilities and equity, or the claims against these assets.

Bankruptcy Reform Act of 1978 Enacted to speed up and streamline bankruptcy proceedings. This law represents a shift to a relative priority doctrine of creditors' claims.

basic earning power (BEP) ratio Calculated by dividing earnings before interest and taxes by total assets. This ratio shows the raw earning power of the firm's assets, before the influence of taxes and leverage.

behavioral finance A field of study that analyzes investor behavior as a result of psychological traits. It does not assume that investors necessarily behave rationally.

benchmarking When a firm compares its ratios to other leading companies in the same industry.

best efforts arrangement A type of contract with an investment banker when issuing stock. In a best efforts sale, the investment banker is only committed to making every effort to sell the stock at the offering price. In this case, the issuing firm bears the risk that the new issue will not be fully subscribed.

beta coefficient, b A measure of a stock's market risk, or the extent to which the returns on a given stock move with the stock market.

bird-in-the-hand theory Assumes that investors value a dollar of dividends more highly than a dollar of expected capital gains because the dividend yield component, D_1/P_0 is less risky than the g component in the total expected return equation $\hat{r}_s = D_1/P_0 + g$.

Black-Scholes Option Pricing Model A model to estimate the value of a call option. It is widely used by option traders.

bond A promissory note issued by a business or a governmental unit.

book value per share Common equity divided by the number of shares outstanding.

break-even point The level of unit sales at which costs equal revenues. Break-even analysis may be performed with or without the inclusion of financial costs. If financial costs are not included, breakeven occurs when earnings before interest and taxes equals zero. If financial costs are included, breakeven occurs when earnings before taxes equals zero.

breakup value A firm's value if its assets are sold off in pieces.

business risk The risk inherent in the operations of the firm, prior to the financing decision. Thus, business risk is the uncertainty inherent in a total risk sense, future operating income, or earnings before interest and taxes. Business risk is caused by many factors. Two of the most important are sales variability and operating leverage.

call option An option that allows the holder to buy the asset at some predetermined price within a specified period of time.

call provision Gives the issuing corporation the right to call the bonds for redemption. The call provision generally states that if the bonds are called, the company must pay the bondholders an amount greater than the par value, a call premium. Most bonds contain a call provision.

capacity option Allows a company to change the capacity of its output in response to changing market conditions. This includes the option to contract or expand production. It also includes the option to abandon a project if market conditions deteriorate too much.

Capital Asset Pricing Model (CAPM) A model based on the proposition that any stock's required rate of return is equal to the risk-free rate of return plus a risk premium reflecting only the risk remaining after diversification. The CAPM equation is $r_i = r_{RF} + b_i(r_M - r_{RF})$.

capital budget Outlines the planned expenditures on fixed assets.

capital budgeting The whole process of analyzing projects and deciding whether they should be included in the capital budget.

capital gain (loss) The profit (loss) from the sale of a capital asset for more (less) than its purchase price.

capital gains yield Results from changing prices and is calculated as $(P_1 - P_0)/P_0$, where P_0 is the beginning-of-period price and P_1 is the end-of-period price.

capital intensity ratio The dollar amount of assets required to produce a dollar of sales. The capital intensity ratio is the reciprocal of the total assets turnover ratio.

capital market Capital markets are the financial markets for long-term debt and corporate stocks. The New York Stock Exchange is an example of a capital market.

capital rationing Occurs when management places a constraint on the size of the firm's capital budget during a particular period.

capital structure The manner in which a firm's assets are financed; that is, the right side of the balance sheet. Capital structure is normally expressed as the percentage of each type of capital used by the firm such as debt, preferred stock, and common equity.

capitalizing Incorporating the lease provisions into the balance sheet by reporting the leased asset under fixed assets and reporting the present value of future lease payments as debt.

cash budget A schedule showing cash flows (receipts, disbursements, and cash balances) for a firm over a specified period.

cash conversion cycle The length of time between the firm's actual cash expenditures on productive resources (materials and labor) and its own cash receipts from the sale of products (that is, the length of time between paying for labor and materials and collecting on receivables). Thus, the cash conversion cycle equals the length of time the firm has funds tied up in current assets.

cash discounts The amount by which a seller is willing to reduce the invoice price in order to be paid immediately, rather than in the future. A cash discount might be 2/10, net 30, which means a 2% discount if the bill is paid within 10 days, otherwise the entire amount is due within 30 days.

Chapter 11 The business reorganization chapter of the Bankruptcy Reform Act. The chapter provides for the reorganization, rather than the liquidation, of a business.

Chapter 7 The chapter of the Bankruptcy Reform Act that provides for the liquidation of a firm to repay creditors.

characteristic line Obtained by regressing the historical returns on a particular stock against the historical returns on the general stock market. The slope of the characteristic line is the stock's beta, which measures the amount by which the stock's expected return increases for a given increase in the expected return on the market.

classified stock Sometimes created by a firm to meet special needs and circumstances. Generally, when special classifications of stock are used, one type is designated "Class A", another as "Class B", and so on. For example, Class A might be entitled to receive dividends before dividends can be paid on Class B stock. Class B might have the exclusive right to vote.

clientele effect The attraction of companies with specific dividend policies to those investors whose needs are best served by those policies. Thus, companies with high dividends will have a clientele of investors with low marginal tax rates and strong desires for current income. Similarly, companies with low dividends will attract a clientele with little need for current income and who often have high marginal tax rates.

closely held corporation Refers to companies that are so small that their common stocks are not actively traded; they are owned by only a few people, usually the companies' managers.

coefficient of variation, CV Equal to the standard deviation divided by the expected return; it is a standardized risk measure that allows comparisons between investments having different expected returns and standard deviations.

collection policy The procedure for collecting accounts receivable. A change in collection policy will affect sales, days sales outstanding, bad debt losses, and the percentage of customers taking discounts.

combination lease Combines some aspects of both operating and financial leases. For example, a financial lease which contains a cancellation clause—normally associated with operating leases—is a combination lease.

commercial paper Unsecured, short-term promissory notes of large firms, usually issued in denominations of $100,000 or more and having an interest rate of somewhat below the prime rate.

commodity futures Futures contracts which involve the sale or purchase of various commodities, including grains, oilseeds, livestock, meats, fiber, metals, and wood.

common stockholders' equity (net worth) The capital supplied by common stockholders—capital stock, paid-in capital, retained earnings, and, occasionally, certain reserves. Paid-in capital is the difference between the stock's par value and what stockholders paid when they bought newly issued shares.

comparative ratio analysis Compares a firms own ratios to other leading companies in the same industry. This technique is also known as benchmarking.

compensating balance (CB) A minimum checking account balance that a firm must maintain with a bank to compensate the bank for services rendered or for making the loan, generally equal to 10% to 20% of the loans outstanding.

composition Creditors voluntarily reduce their fixed claims on the debtor by accepting a lower principal amount, reducing the interest rate on the debt, accepting equity in place of debt, or some combination of these changes.

compounding The process of finding the future value of a single payment or series of payments.

computer/telephone network A computer/telephone network, such as Nasdaq, consists of all the facilities that provide for security transactions not conducted at a physical location exchange. These facilities are, basically, the communications networks that link buyers and sellers.

congeneric merger Involves firms that are interrelated but do not have identical lines of business. One example is Prudential's acquisition of Bache & Company.

conglomerate merger Occurs when unrelated enterprises combine, such as Mobil Oil and Montgomery Ward.

conservative short-term financing policy Refers to using permanent capital to finance all permanent asset requirements, as well as to meet some or all of the seasonal demands.

consol Another term for perpetuity. Consols were originally bonds issued by England in 1815 to consolidate past debt.

continuous probability distribution Contains an infinite number of outcomes and is graphed from $-\infty$ and $+\infty$.

conversion price The effective price per share of stock if conversion occurs; the par value of the convertible security divided by the conversion ratio.

conversion ratio The number of shares of common stock received upon conversion of one convertible security.

conversion value The value of the stock that the investor would receive if conversion occurred; the market price per share times the conversion ratio.

convertible bond Security that is convertible into shares of common stock, at a fixed price, at the option of the bondholder.

convertible currency A currency that can be traded in the currency markets and can be redeemed at current market rates.

convertible security Bonds or preferred stocks that can be exchanged for (converted into) common stock, under specific terms, at the option of the holder. Unlike the exercise of warrants, conversion of a convertible security does not provide additional capital to the issuer.

corporate alliance A cooperative deal that stops short of a merger; also called a strategic alliance.

corporate bond Debt issued by corporations and exposed to default risk. Different corporate bonds have different levels of default risk, depending on the issu-

ing company's characteristics and on the terms of the specific bond.

corporate risk management Relates to the management of unpredictable events that have adverse consequences for the firm. This effort involves reducing the consequences of risk to the point where there would be no significant adverse impact on the firm's financial position.

corporate valuation model Defines the total value of a company as the value of operations plus the value of nonoperating assets plus the value of growth options.

corporation A corporation is a legal entity created by a state. The corporation is separate and distinct from its owners and managers.

correlation The tendency of two variables to move together.

correlation coefficient, ρ (rho) A standardized measure of how two random variables covary. A correlation coefficient (ρ) of $+1.0$ means that the two variables move up and down in perfect synchronization, while a coefficient of -1.0 means the variables always move in opposite directions. A correlation coefficient of zero suggests that the two variables are not related to one another; that is, they are independent.

cost of common stock, r_s The return required by the firm's common stockholders. It is usually calculated using Capital Asset Pricing Model or the dividend growth model.

cost of new external common equity, r_e Project's financed with external equity must earn a higher rate of return, because the project must cover the flotation costs. Thus, the cost of new common equity is higher than that of common equity raised internally by reinvesting earnings.

cost of preferred stock, r_{ps} The return required by the firm's preferred stockholders. The cost of preferred stock, r_{ps}, is the cost to the firm of issuing new preferred stock. For perpetual preferred, it is the preferred dividend, D_{ps}, divided by the net issuing price, P_n.

costly trade credit Credit taken in excess of free trade credit whose cost is equal to the discount lost.

coupon interest rate Stated rate of interest on a bond, defined as the coupon payment divided by the par value.

coupon payment Dollar amount of interest paid to each bondholder on the interest payment dates.

coverage ratio Similar to the times-interest-earned ratio, but it recognizes that many firms lease assets and also must make sinking fund payments. It is found by adding earnings before interest, taxes, depreciation, and amortization and lease payments, then dividing this total by interest charges, lease payments, and sinking fund payments over 1 minus the tax rate.

cramdown Bankruptcy court–mandated reorganization plans which are binding on all parties.

credit policy The firm's policy on granting and collecting credit. There are four elements of credit policy, or credit policy variables: credit period, credit standards, collection policy, and discounts.

crossover rate The cost of capital at which the NPV profiles for two projects intersect.

cumulative preferred dividends A protective feature on preferred stock that requires all past preferred dividends to be paid before any common dividends can be paid.

current ratio Indicates the extent to which current liabilities are covered by those assets expected to be converted to cash in the near future; it is found by dividing current assets by current liabilities.

current yield (on a bond) The annual coupon payment divided by the current market price.

days sales outstanding (DSO) Used to appraise accounts receivable and indicates the length of time the firm must wait after making a sale before receiving cash. It is found by dividing receivables by average sales per day.

DCF (discounted cash flow) techniques The net present value (NPV) and internal rate of return (IRR) techniques are discounted cash flow (DCF) evaluation techniques. These are called DCF methods because they explicitly recognize the time value of money.

dealer market In a dealer market, a dealer holds an inventory of the security and makes a market by offering to buy or sell. Others who wish to buy or sell can see the offers made by the dealers and can contact the dealer of their choice to arrange a transaction.

debenture An unsecured bond, and as such, it provides no lien against specific property as security for the obligation. Debenture holders are, therefore, general creditors whose claims are protected by property not otherwise pledged.

debt ratio The ratio of total liabilities to total assets, it measures the percentage of funds provided by creditors.

decision trees A form of scenario analysis in which different actions are taken in different scenarios.

declaration date The date on which a firm's directors issue a statement declaring a dividend.

default risk The risk that a borrower will not pay the interest and/or principal on a loan as it becomes due. If the issuer defaults, investors receive less than the promised return on the bond. Default risk is influenced by both the financial strength of the issuer and the terms of the bond contract, especially whether collateral has been pledged to secure the bond. The greater the default risk, the higher the bond's yield to maturity.

default risk premium (DRP) The risk that a borrower will not pay the interest and/or principal on a loan as they become due. Thus, a default risk premium (DRP) is added to the real risk-free rate to compensate investors for bearing default risk.

defensive merger Occurs when one company acquires another to help ward off a hostile merger attempt.

depreciation A noncash charge against tangible assets, such as buildings or machines. It is taken for the purpose of showing an asset's estimated dollar cost of the capital equipment used up in the production process.

derivative Claims whose value depends on what happens to the value of some other asset. Futures and options are two important types of derivatives, and their values depend on what happens to the prices of other assets. Therefore, the value of a derivative security is derived from the value of an underlying real asset or other security.

detachable warrant A warrant that can be detached and traded separately from the underlying security. Most warrants are detachable.

devaluation The lowering, by governmental action, of the price of its currency relative to another currency. For example, in 1967 the British pound was devalued from $2.80 per pound to $2.50 per pound.

development bond A tax-exempt bond sold by state and local governments whose proceeds are made available to corporations for specific uses deemed (by Congress) to be in the public interest.

discount bond Bond prices and interest rates are inversely related; that is, they tend to move in the opposite direction from one another. A fixed-rate bond will sell at par when its coupon interest rate is equal to the going rate of interest, r_d. When the going rate of interest is above the coupon rate, a fixed-rate bond will sell at a "discount" below its par value. If current interest rates are below the coupon rate, a fixed-rate bond will sell at a "premium" above its par value.

discount on forward rate Occurs when the forward exchange rate differs from the spot rate. When the forward rate is below the spot rate, the forward rate is said to be at a discount.

discounted cash flow (DCF) method A method of valuing a business that involves the application of capital budgeting procedures to an entire firm rather than to a single project.

discounted payback period The number of years it takes a firm to recover its project investment based on discounted cash flows.

discounting The process of finding the present value of a single payment or series of payments.

distribution policy The policy that sets the level of distributions and the form of the distributions (dividends and stock repurchases).

diversifiable risk Refers to that part of a security's total risk associated with random events not affecting the market as a whole. This risk can be eliminated by proper diversification. Also known as company-specific risk.

divestiture The opposite of an acquisition. That is, a company sells a portion of its assets, often a whole division, to another firm or individual.

dividend irrelevance theory Holds that dividend policy has no effect on either the price of a firm's stock or its cost of capital.

dividend reinvestment plan (DRIP) Allows stockholders to automatically purchase shares of common stock of the paying corporation in lieu of receiving cash dividends. There are two types of plans—one involves only stock that is already outstanding, while the other involves newly issued stock. In the first type, the dividends of all participants are pooled and the stock is purchased on the open market. Participants benefit from lower transaction costs. In the second type, the company issues new shares to the participants. Thus, the company issues stock in lieu of the cash dividend.

dividend yield Defined as either the end-of-period dividend divided by the beginning-of-period price, or the ratio of the current dividend to the current price. Valuation formulas use the former definition.

Du Pont chart A chart designed to show the relationships among return on investment, asset turnover, the profit margin, and leverage.

Du Pont equation A formula which shows that the rate of return on equity can be found as the product of the profit margin times the total assets turnover times the equity multiplier.

EBITDA Earnings before interest, taxes, depreciation, and amortization.

ECN In an ECN (electronic communications network), orders from potential buyers and sellers are automatically matched, and the transaction is automatically completed.

economic life The number of years a project should be operated to maximize its net present value; often less than the maximum potential life.

Economic Value Added (EVA) A method used to measure a firm's true profitability. EVA is found by taking the firm's after-tax operating profit and subtracting the annual cost of all the capital a firm uses. If the firm generates a positive EVA, its management has created value for its shareholders. If the EVA is negative, management has destroyed shareholder value.

effective (or equivalent) annual rate (EAR or EFF) The effective annual rate is the rate that, under annual compounding, would have produced the same future value at the end of 1 year as was produced by more frequent compounding, say quarterly. If the compounding occurs annually, the effective annual rate and the nominal rate are the same. If compounding occurs more frequently, the effective annual rate is greater than the nominal rate.

efficient frontier The set of efficient portfolios out of the full set of potential portfolios. On a graph, the efficient frontier constitutes the boundary line of the set of potential portfolios.

Efficient Markets Hypothesis (EMH) States (1) that stocks are always in equilibrium and (2) that it is impossible for an investor to consistently "beat the market." The EMH assumes that all important information regarding a stock is reflected in the price of that stock.

efficient portfolio Provides the highest expected return for any degree of risk. The efficient portfolio is that which provides the lowest degree of risk for any expected return.

embedded options Options that are a part of another project. Also called real options, managerial options, and strategic options.

entrenchment Occurs when a company has such a weak board of directors and has such strong anti-takeover provisions in its corporate charter that senior managers feel there is very little chance that they will be removed.

equilibrium The condition under which the intrinsic value of a security is equal to its price; also, its expected return is equal to its required return.

ESOP (employee stock ownership plan) A type of retirement plan in which employees own stock in the company.

euro The currency used by the nations in the European Monetary Union.

Eurobond Any bond sold in some country other than the one in whose currency the bond is denominated. Thus, a U.S. firm selling dollar bonds in Switzerland is selling Eurobonds.

Eurodollar A U.S. dollar on deposit in a foreign bank or in a foreign branch of a U.S. bank. Eurodollars are used to conduct transactions throughout Europe and the rest of the world.

exchange rate Specifies the number of units of a given currency that can be purchased for one unit of another currency.

exchange rate risk Refers to the fluctuation in exchange rates between currencies over time.

ex-dividend date The date when the right to the dividend leaves the stock. This date was established by stockbrokers to avoid confusion and is four business days prior to the holder-of-record date. If the stock sale is made prior to the ex-dividend date, the dividend is paid to the buyer. If the stock is bought on or after the ex-dividend date, the dividend is paid to the seller.

exercise price The price stated in the option contract at which the security can be bought (or sold). Also called the strike price.

exercise value Equal to the current price of the stock (underlying the option) less the strike price of the option.

expectations theory States that the slope of the yield curve depends on expectations about future inflation rates and interest rates. Thus, if the annual rate of inflation and future interest rates are expected to increase, the yield curve will be upward sloping; the curve will be downward sloping if the annual rates are expected to decrease.

expected rate of return, $\hat{r}_s$ The rate of return expected on a stock given its current price and expected future cash flows. If the stock is in equilibrium, the required rate of return will equal the expected rate of return.

extension A form of debt restructuring where creditors postpone the dates of required interest or principal payments, or both.

extra dividend A dividend paid, in addition to the regular dividend, when earnings permit. Firms with volatile earnings may have a low regular dividend that can be maintained even in low-profit (or high-capital-investment) years, and then supplement it with an extra dividend when excess funds are available.

fairness The standard of fairness states that claims must be recognized in the order of their legal and contractual priority. In simpler terms, the reorganization must be fair to all parties.

Fama-French three-factor model Includes one factor for the excess market return (the market return minus the risk-free rate), a second factor for size (defined as the return on a portfolio of small firms minus the return on a portfolio of big firms), and a third factor for the book-to-market effect (defined as the return on a portfolio of firms with a high book-to-market ratio minus the return on a portfolio of firms with a low book-to-market ratio).

FASB Statement 13 The Financial Accounting Standards Board statement (November 1976) that spells out in detail the conditions under which a lease must be capitalized and the specific procedures to follow.

feasibility The standard of feasibility states that there must be a reasonably high probability of successful rehabilitation and profitable future operations.

feasible set Represents all portfolios that can be constructed from a given set of stocks; also known as the attainable set.

financial futures Provide for the purchase or sale of a financial asset at some time in the future, but at a price established today. Financial futures exist for Treasury bills, Treasury notes and bonds, certificates of deposit, Eurodollar deposits, foreign currencies, and stock indexes.

financial intermediary An intermediary that buys securities with funds that it obtains by issuing its own securities. An example is a common stock mutual fund that buys common stocks with funds obtained by issuing shares in the mutual fund.

financial lease Covers the entire expected life of the equipment; does not provide for maintenance service, is not cancellable, and is fully amortized.

financial leverage The extent to which fixed-income securities (debt and preferred stock) are used in a firm's capital structure. If a high percentage of a firm's capital structure is in the form of debt and preferred stock, then the firm is said to have a high degree of financial leverage.

financial merger A merger in which the companies will not be operated as a single unit and no operating economies are expected.

financial risk The risk added by the use of debt financing. Debt financing increases the variability of earnings before taxes (but after interest); thus, along with business risk, it contributes to the uncertainty of net income and earnings per share. Business risk plus financial risk equals total corporate risk.

financial service corporation A corporation that offers a wide range of financial services such as brokerage operations, insurance, and commercial banking.

fixed assets turnover ratio Measures how effectively the firm uses its plant and equipment. It is the ratio of sales to net fixed assets.

fixed exchange rate system The system in effect from the end of World War II until August 1971. Under the system, the U.S. dollar was linked to gold at the rate of $35 per ounce, and other currencies were then tied to the dollar.

floating exchange rate system System currently in effect where the forces of supply and demand are allowed to determine currency prices with little government intervention.

floating-rate bond A bond whose coupon payment may vary over time. The coupon rate is usually linked to the rate on some other security, such as a Treasury security, or to some other rate, such as the prime rate or LIBOR.

flotation cost, F Those costs occurring when a company issues a new security, including fees to an investment banker and legal fees.

foreign bond A bond sold by a foreign borrower but denominated in the currency of the country in which the issue is sold. Thus, a U.S. firm selling bonds denominated in Swiss francs in Switzerland is selling foreign bonds.

foreign trade deficit A deficit that occurs when businesses and individuals in the U.S. import more goods from foreign countries than are exported.

forward contract A contract to buy or sell some item at some time in the future at a price established when the contract is entered into.

forward exchange rate The prevailing exchange rate for exchange (delivery) at some agreed-upon future date, usually 30, 90, or 180 days from the day the transaction is negotiated.

founders' shares Stock owned by the firm's founders that have sole voting rights but restricted dividends for a specified number of years.

free cash flow (FCF) The cash flow actually available for distribution to all investors after the company has made all investments in fixed assets and working capital necessary to sustain ongoing operations.

free trade credit Credit received during the discount period.

friendly merger Occurs when the target company's management agrees to the merger and recommends that shareholders approve the deal.

FVA_N The ending value of a stream of equal payments, where N is the number of payments of the annuity.

$FVIFA_{I,N}$ The future value interest factor for an ordinary annuity of N periodic payments paying I percent interest per period.

$FVIF_{I,N}$ The future value interest factor for a lump sum left in an account for N periods paying I percent interest per period.

FV_N (future value) The ending amount in an account, where N is the number of periods the money is left in the account.

going public The act of selling stock to the public at large by a closely held corporation or its principal stockholders.

golden parachute A payment made to executives that are forced out when a merger takes place.

greenmail Targeted share repurchases that occur when a company buys back stock from a potential acquirer at a higher than fair-market price. In return, the potential acquirer agrees not to attempt to take over the company.

growth option Occurs if an investment creates the opportunity to make other potentially profitable investments that would not otherwise be possible, including options to expand output, options to enter a new geographical market, and options to introduce complementary products or successive generations of products.

guideline lease Meets all of the Internal Revenue Service (IRS) requirements for a genuine lease. If a lease meets the IRS guidelines, the IRS allows the lessor to deduct the asset's depreciation and allows the lessee to deduct the lease payments. Also called a tax-oriented lease.

hedging A transaction which lowers a firm's risk of damage due to fluctuating commodity prices, interest rates, and exchange rates.

holder-of-record date If a company lists the stockholder as an owner on the holder-of-record date, then the stockholder receives the dividend.

holding company A corporation formed for the sole purpose of owning stocks in other companies. A holding company differs from a stock mutual fund in that holding companies own sufficient stock in their operating companies to exercise effective working control.

holdout A problematic characteristic of informal reorganizations where all of the involved parties do not agree to the voluntary plan. Holdouts are usually made by creditors in an effort to receive full payment on claims.

horizon value The value of operations at the end of the explicit forecast period. It is equal to the present value of all free cash flows beyond the forecast period, discounted back to the end of the forecast period at the weighted average cost of capital.

horizontal merger A merger between two companies in the same line of business.

hostile merger Occurs when the management of the target company resists the offer.

hurdle rate The project cost of capital, or discount rate. It is both the rate used in discounting future cash flows in the net present value method and the rate that is compared to the internal rate of return.

improper accumulation The retention of earnings by a business for the purpose of enabling stockholders to avoid personal income taxes on dividends.

income bond Pays interest only if the interest is earned. These securities cannot bankrupt a company, but from an investor's standpoint, they are riskier than "regular" bonds.

income statement Summarizes the firm's revenues and expenses over an accounting period. Net sales are shown at the top of each statement, after which various costs, including income taxes, are subtracted to obtain the net income available to common stockholders. The bottom of the statement reports earnings and dividends per share.

incremental cash flow Those cash flows that arise solely from the asset that is being evaluated.

indentures A legal document that spells out the rights of both bondholders and the issuing corporation.

independent projects Projects that can be accepted or rejected individually.

indexed, or purchasing power, bond The interest rate of such a bond is based on an inflation index such as the consumer price index (CPI), so the interest paid rises automatically when the inflation rate rises, thus protecting the bondholders against inflation.

indifference curve The risk/return trade-off function for a particular investor; reflects that investor's attitude toward risk. An investor would be indifferent between any pair of assets on the same indifference curve. In risk/return space, the greater the slope of the indifference curve, the greater is the investor's risk aversion.

inflation premium (IP) The premium added to the real risk-free rate of interest to compensate for the expected loss of purchasing power. The inflation premium is the average rate of inflation expected over the life of the security.

informal debt restructuring An agreement between the creditors and troubled firm to change the existing debt terms. An extension postpones the required payment date, while a composition is a reduction in creditor claims.

information content, or signaling, hypothesis A theory that holds that investors regard dividend changes as "signals" of management forecasts. Thus, when dividends are raised, this is viewed by investors as recognition by management of future earnings increases. Therefore, if a firm's stock price increases with a dividend increase, the reason may not be investor preference for dividends but expectations of higher future earnings. Conversely, a dividend reduction may signal that management is forecasting poor earnings in the future.

initial public offering (IPO) Occurs when a closely held corporation or its principal stockholders sell stock to the public at large.

initial public offering (IPO) market Going public is the act of selling stock to the public at large by a closely held corporation or its principal stockholders, and this market is often termed the initial public offering market.

I_{NOM} The nominal, or quoted, interest rate.

insiders The officers, directors, and major stockholders of a firm.

interest rate parity Holds that investors should expect to earn the same return in all countries after adjusting for risk.

interest rate risk Arises from the fact that bond prices decline when interest rates rise. Under these circumstances, selling a bond prior to maturity will result in a capital loss; the longer the term to maturity, the larger the loss.

internal rate of return (IRR) method The discount rate that equates the present value of the expected future cash inflows and outflows. IRR measures the rate of return on a project, but it assumes that all cash flows can be reinvested at the IRR rate.

international bond Any bond sold outside of the country of the borrower. There are two types of international bonds: Eurobonds and foreign bonds.

intrinsic (fundamental) value, $\hat{P}_0$ The present value of a firm's expected future free cash flows.

inventory conversion period The average length of time to convert materials into finished goods and then to sell them; calculated by dividing total inventory by sales per day.

inventory turnover ratio Sales divided by inventories.

inverted (abnormal) yield curve A downward-sloping yield curve.

investment banker A middleman between businesses and investors. Investment banking houses assist in the design of corporate securities and then sell them to investors in the primary markets.

investment timing option Gives companies the option to delay a project rather than implement it immediately. This option to wait allows a company to reduce the uncertainty of market conditions before it decides to implement the project.

investment grade bond Securities with ratings of Baa/BBB or above.

joint venture Involves the joining together of parts of companies to accomplish specific, limited objectives. Joint ventures are controlled by the combined management of the two (or more) parent companies.

junk bond High-risk, high-yield bond issued to finance leveraged buyouts, mergers, or troubled companies.

lessee The party leasing the property.

lessee's analysis Involves determining whether leasing an asset is less costly than buying the asset. The lessee will compare the present value cost of leasing the asset with the present value cost of purchasing the asset (assuming the funds to purchase the asset are obtained through a loan). If the present value cost of the lease is less than the present value cost of purchasing, the asset should be leased. The lessee can also analyze the lease using the IRR approach or the equivalent loan method.

lessor The party receiving the payments from the lease (that is, the owner of the property).

lessor's analysis Involves determining the rate of return on the proposed lease. If the internal rate of return of the lease cash flows exceeds the lessor's opportunity cost of capital, the lease is a good investment. This is equivalent to analyzing whether the net present value of the lease is positive.

leveraged buyout (LBO) A transaction in which a firm's publicly owned stock is acquired in a mostly debt-financed tender offer, and a privately owned, highly leveraged firm results. Often, the firm's own management initiates the LBO.

leveraged lease The lessor borrows a portion of the funds needed to buy the equipment to be leased.

limited liability partnership A limited liability partnership (LLP), sometimes called a limited liability company (LLC), combines the limited liability advantage of a corporation with the tax advantages of a partnership.

limited partnership A partnership in which limited partners' liabilities, investment returns, and control are limited, while general partners have unlimited liability and control.

line of credit An arrangement in which a bank agrees to lend up to a specified maximum amount of funds during a designated period.

liquidation in bankruptcy The sale of the assets of a firm and the distribution of the proceeds to the creditors and owners in a specific priority.

liquidity Liquidity refers to a firm's cash and marketable securities position and to its ability to meet maturing obligations. A liquid asset is any asset that can be quickly sold and converted to cash at its "fair" value. Active markets provide liquidity.

liquidity premium (LP) A liquidity premium is added to the real risk-free rate of interest, in addition to other premiums, if a security is not liquid.

liquidity ratio A ratio that shows the relationship of a firm's cash and other current assets to its current liabilities.

long hedges Occur when futures contracts are bought in anticipation of (or to guard against) price increases.

lumpy assets Those assets that cannot be acquired smoothly, but require large, discrete additions. For example, an electric utility that is operating at full capacity cannot add a small amount of generating capacity, at least not economically.

managerial options Options that give opportunities to managers to respond to changing market conditions. Also called real options.

margin requirement The margin is the percentage of a stock's price that an investor has borrowed in order to purchase the stock. The Securities and Exchange Commission sets margin requirements, which are the maximum percentage of debt that can be used to purchase a stock.

marginal tax rate The tax rate on the last unit of income.

market multiple method Applies a market-determined multiple to net income, earnings per share, sales, book value, or number of subscribers, and is a less precise method than discounted cash flow.

market portfolio A portfolio consisting of all stocks.

market risk That part of a security's total risk that cannot be eliminated by diversification; measured by the beta coefficient.

market risk premium, RP_M The difference between the expected return on the market and the risk-free rate.

Market Value Added (MVA) The difference between the market value of the firm (that is, the sum of the market value of common equity, the market value of debt, and the market value of preferred stock) and the book value of the firm's common equity, debt, and preferred stock. If the book values of debt and preferred stock are equal to their market values, then MVA is also equal to the difference between the market value of equity and the amount of equity capital that investors supplied.

market value ratios Relate the firm's stock price to its earnings and book value per share.

maturity date The date when the bond's par value is repaid to the bondholder. Maturity dates generally range from 10 to 40 years from the time of issue.

maturity matching Refers to matching the maturities of debt used to finance assets with the lives of the assets themselves. The debt would be amortized such that the outstanding amount declined as the asset lost value due to depreciation.

maturity risk premium (MRP) The premium that must be added to the real risk-free rate of interest to compensate for interest rate risk, which depends on a bond's maturity. Interest rate risk arises from the fact that bond prices decline when interest rates rise. Under these circumstances, selling a bond prior to maturity will result in a capital loss; the longer the term to maturity, the larger the loss.

merger The joining of two firms to form a single firm.

moderate net operating working capital policy A policy that matches asset and liability maturities. It is also referred to as the maturity matching, or self-liquidating approach.

modified internal rate of return (MIRR) method Assumes that cash flows from all projects are reinvested at the cost of capital as opposed to the project's own IRR. This makes the modified internal rate of return a better indicator of a project's true profitability.

money market A financial market for debt securities with maturities of less than 1 year (short-term). The New York money market is the world's largest.

money market fund Mutual funds that invest in short-term debt instruments and offer their investors check-writing privileges; thus, they are essentially interest-bearing checking accounts.

Monte Carlo simulation analysis A risk analysis technique in which a computer is used to simulate probable future events and thus to estimate the profitability and risk of a project.

mortgage bond A bond for which the corporation pledges certain assets as security. All such bonds are written subject to an indenture.

multinational (global) corporation A corporation that operates in two or more countries.

municipal bond Issued by state and local governments. The interest earned on most municipal bonds is exempt from federal taxes, and also from state taxes if the holder is a resident of the issuing state.

municipal bond insurance An insurance company guarantees to pay the coupon and principal payments should the issuer of the bond (the municipality) default. This reduces the risk to investors who are willing to accept a lower coupon rate for an insured bond issue compared to an uninsured issue.

mutual fund A corporation that sells shares in the fund and uses the proceeds to buy stocks, long-term bonds, or short-term debt instruments. The resulting dividends, interest, and capital gains are distributed to the fund's shareholders after the deduction of operating expenses. Some funds specialize in certain types of securities, such as growth stocks, international stocks, or municipal bonds.

mutually exclusive projects Projects that cannot be performed at the same time. A company could choose either Project 1 or Project 2, or it can reject both, but it cannot accept both projects.

National Association of Securities Dealers (NASD) An industry group primarily concerned with the operation of the over-the-counter (OTC) market.

natural hedge A transaction between two counterparties where both parties' risks are reduced.

net advantage to leasing (NAL) The dollar value of the lease to the lessee. It is, in a sense, the net present value of leasing versus owning.

net cash flow The sum of net income plus noncash adjustments.

net operating working capital (NOWC) Operating current assets minus operating current liabilities. Operating current assets are the current assets used to support operations, such as cash, accounts receivable, and inventory. They do not include short-term investments. Operating current liabilities are the current liabilities that are a natural consequence of the firm's operations, such as accounts payable and accruals. They do not include notes payable or any other short-term debt that charges interest.

net present value (NPV) method The present value of the project's expected future cash flows, discounted at the appropriate cost of capital. NPV is a direct measure of the value of the project to shareholders.

net working capital Current assets minus current liabilities.

new issue market The market for stock of companies that go public.

preferred stock A hybrid that is similar to bonds in some respects and to common stock in others. Preferred dividends are similar to interest payments on bonds in that they are fixed in amount and generally must be paid before common stock dividends can be paid. If the preferred dividend is not earned, the directors can omit it without throwing the company into bankruptcy.

premium bond Bond prices and interest rates are inversely related; that is, they tend to move in the opposite direction from one another. A fixed-rate bond will sell at par when its coupon interest rate is equal to the going rate of interest, r_d. When the going rate of interest is above the coupon rate, a fixed-rate bond will sell at a "discount" below its par value. If current interest rates are below the coupon rate, a fixed-rate bond will sell at a "premium" above its par value.

premium on forward rate Occurs when the forward exchange rate differs from the spot rate. When the forward rate is above the spot rate, it is said to be at a premium.

prepackaged bankruptcy (pre-pack) A type of reorganization which combines the advantages of informal workouts and formal Chapter 11 reorganization.

price/cash flow ratio Calculated by dividing price per share by cash flow per share. This shows how much investors are willing to pay per dollar of cash flow.

price/earnings (P/E) ratio Calculated by dividing price per share by earnings per share. This shows how much investors are willing to pay per dollar of reported profits.

primary markets Markets in which newly issued securities are sold for the first time.

priority of claims in liquidation Established in Chapter 7 of the Bankruptcy Act. It specifies the order in which the debtor's assets are distributed among the creditors.

private markets Markets in which transactions are worked out directly between two parties and structured in any manner that appeals to them. Bank loans and private placements of debt with insurance companies are examples of private market transactions.

private placement The sale of stock to only one or a few investors, usually institutional investors. The advantages of private placements are lower flotation costs and greater speed, since the shares issued are not subject to Securities and Exchange Commission registration.

pro forma (projected) financial statement Shows how an actual statement would look if certain assumptions are realized.

probability distribution A listing, chart, or graph of all possible outcomes, such as expected rates of return, with a probability assigned to each outcome.

professional corporation (PC) Has most of the benefits of incorporation but the participants are not relieved of professional (malpractice) liability. Known in some states as a professional association (PA).

profit margin on sales Calculated by dividing net income by sales; gives the profit per dollar of sales.

profitability index Found by dividing the project's present value of future cash flows by its initial cost. A profitability index greater than 1 is equivalent to a positive net present value project.

profitability ratios A group of ratios which show the combined effects of liquidity, asset management, and debt on operations.

progressive tax Tax system in which the higher one's income, the larger the percentage paid in taxes.

project cost of capital The risk-adjusted discount rate for that project.

project financing Arrangements used to finance mainly large capital projects such as energy explorations, oil tankers, refineries, utility power plants, and so on. Usually, one or more firms (sponsors) will provide the equity capital required by the project, while the rest of the project's capital is supplied by lenders and lessors. The most important aspect of project financing is that the lenders and lessors do not have recourse against the sponsors; they must be repaid from the project's cash flows and the equity cushion provided by the sponsors.

promissory note A document specifying the terms and conditions of a loan, including the amount, interest rate, and repayment schedule.

prospectus Summarizes information about a new security issue and the issuing company.

proxy A document giving one person the authority to act for another, typically the power to vote shares of common stock.

proxy fight An attempt to take over a company in which an outside group solicits existing shareholders' proxies, which are authorizations to vote shares in a shareholders' meeting, in an effort to overthrow management and take control of the business.

public markets Markets in which standardized contracts are traded on organized exchanges. Securities that are issued in public markets, such as common stock and corporate bonds, are ultimately held by a large number of individuals.

public offering An offer of new common stock to the general public.

publicly owned corporation Corporation in which the stock is owned by a large number of investors, most of whom are not active in management.

purchase accounting A method of accounting for a merger in which the merger is handled as a purchase. In this method, the acquiring firm is assumed to have "bought" the acquired company in much the same way it would buy any capital asset.

purchasing power parity Implies that the level of exchange rates adjusts so that identical goods cost the same in different countries. Sometimes referred to as the "law of one price."

put option Allows the holder to sell the asset at some predetermined price within a specified period of time.

PV (present value) The value today of a future payment, or stream of payments, discounted at the appropriate rate of interest. PV is also the beginning amount that will grow to some future value.

PVA$_N$ The value today of a future stream of equal payments (an annuity).

PVIF$_{I,N}$ The present value interest factor for a lump sum received N periods in the future discounted at I percent per period.

PVIFA$_{I,N}$ The present value interest factor for an ordinary annuity of N periodic payments discounted at I percent interest per period.

quick, or acid test, ratio Found by taking current assets less inventories and then dividing by current liabilities.

real options Occur when managers can influence the size and risk of a project's cash flows by taking different actions during the project's life. They are referred to as real options because they deal with real as opposed to financial assets. They are also called managerial options because they give opportunities to managers to respond to changing market conditions. Sometimes they are called strategic options because they often deal with strategic issues. Finally, they are also called embedded options because they are a part of another project.

real rate of return, r$_r$ Contains no adjustment for expected inflation. If net cash flows from a project do not include inflation adjustments, then the cash flows should be discounted at the real cost of capital. In a similar manner, the internal rate of return resulting from real net cash flows should be compared with the real cost of capital.

real risk-free rate of interest, r* That interest rate which equalizes the aggregate supply of, and demand for, riskless securities in an economy with zero inflation. The real risk-free rate could also be called the pure rate of interest since it is the rate of interest that would exist on very short-term, default-free U.S. Treasury securities if the expected rate of inflation were zero.

realized rate of return, r̄ The actual return an investor receives on his or her investment. It can be quite different than the expected return.

receivables collection period The average length of time required to convert a firm's receivables into cash. It is calculated by dividing accounts receivable by sales per day.

red herring (preliminary) prospectus A preliminary prospectus that may be distributed to potential buyers prior to approval of the registration statement by the Securities and Exchange Commission. After the registration has become effective, the securities, accompanied by the prospectus, may be offered for sale.

redeemable bond Gives investors the right to sell the bonds back to the corporation at a price that is usually close to the par value. If interest rates rise, investors can redeem the bonds and reinvest at the higher rates.

refunding Occurs when a company issues debt at current low rates and uses the proceeds to repurchase one of its existing high coupon rate debt issues. Often these are callable issues, which means the company can purchase the debt at a lower than market price.

registration statement Required of companies by the Securities and Exchange Commission before the securities can be offered to the public. This statement is used to summarize various financial and legal information about the company.

reinvestment rate risk Occurs when a short-term debt security must be "rolled over." If interest rates have fallen, the reinvestment of principal will be at a lower rate, with correspondingly lower interest payments and ending value.

relative priority doctrine More flexible than absolute priority. Gives a more balanced consideration to all claimants in a bankruptcy reorganization than does the absolute priority doctrine.

relaxed net operating working capital policy A policy under which relatively large amounts of cash, marketable securities, and inventories are carried and under which sales are stimulated by a liberal credit policy, resulting in a high level of receivables.

reorganization in bankruptcy A court-approved attempt to keep a company alive by changing its capital structure in lieu of liquidation. A reorganization must adhere to the standards of fairness and feasibility.

repatriation of earnings The cash flow, usually in the form of dividends or royalties, from the foreign branch or subsidiary to the parent company. These cash flows must be converted to the currency of the parent, and thus are subject to future exchange rate changes. A foreign government may restrict the amount of cash that may be repatriated.

replacement chain (common life) approach A method of comparing mutually exclusive projects that have unequal lives. Each project is replicated such that they will both terminate in a common year. If projects with lives of 3 years and 5 years are being evaluated, the 3-year project would be replicated 5 times and the 5-year project replicated 3 times; thus, both projects would terminate in 15 years.

required rate of return, r_s The minimum acceptable rate of return considering both its risk and the returns available on other investments.

reserve borrowing capacity Exists when a firm uses less debt under "normal" conditions than called for by the trade-off theory. This allows the firm some flexibility to use debt in the future when additional capital is needed.

residual distribution model States that firms should pay dividends only when more earnings are available than needed to support the optimal capital budget.

residual value The market value of the leased property at the expiration of the lease. The estimate of the residual value is one of the key elements in lease analysis.

restricted net operating working capital policy A policy under which holdings of cash, securities, inventories, and receivables are minimized.

restricted voting rights A provision that automatically deprives a shareholder of voting rights if the shareholder owns more than a specified amount of stock.

retained earnings The portion of the firm's earnings that have been saved rather than paid out as dividends.

return on common equity (ROE) Found by dividing net income by common equity.

return on invested capital (ROIC) Net operating profit after taxes divided by the operating capital.

return on total assets (ROA) The ratio of net income to total assets.

revaluation Occurs when the relative price of a currency is increased. It is the opposite of devaluation.

revolving credit agreement A formal, committed line of credit extended by a bank or other lending institution.

rights offering Occurs when a corporation sells a new issue of common stock to its existing stockholders. Each stockholder receives a certificate called a stock purchase right giving the stockholder the option to purchase a specified number of the new shares. The rights are issued in proportion to the amount of stock that each shareholder currently owns.

risk arbitrage Refers to the practice of purchasing stock in companies (in the context of mergers) that may become takeover targets.

risk aversion A risk-averse investor dislikes risk and requires a higher rate of return as an inducement to buy riskier securities.

risk premium for Stock i, RP_i The extra return that an investor requires to hold risky Stock i instead of a risk-free asset.

risk-adjusted discount rate Incorporates the riskiness of the project's cash flows. The cost of capital to the firm reflects the average risk of the firm's existing projects. Thus, new projects that are riskier than existing projects should have a higher risk-adjusted discount rate. Conversely, projects with less risk should have a lower risk-adjusted discount rate.

roadshow Before an IPO, the senior management team and the investment banker make presentations to potential investors. They make presentations in 10 to 20 cities, with three to five presentations per day, over a 2-week period.

S corporation A small corporation that, under Subchapter S of the Internal Revenue Code, elects to be taxed as a proprietorship or a partnership yet retains limited liability and other benefits of the corporate form of organization.

sale-and-leaseback A type of financial lease in which the firm owning the property sells it to another firm, often a financial institution, while simultaneously entering into an agreement to lease the property back from the firm.

salvage value The market value of an asset after its useful life.

scenario analysis A shorter version of simulation analysis that uses only a few outcomes. Often the outcomes are for three scenarios: optimistic, pessimistic, and most likely.

seasonal effects on ratios Seasonal factors can distort ratio analysis. At certain times of the year a firm may have excessive inventories in preparation of a "season" of high demand. Therefore, an inventory turnover ratio taken at this time as opposed to after the season will be radically distorted.

secondary market Markets in which securities are resold after initial issue in the primary market. The New York Stock Exchange is an example.

secured loan A loan backed by collateral, often for inventories or receivables.

Securities and Exchange Commission (SEC) A government agency which regulates the sales of new securities and the operations of securities exchanges. The SEC, along with other government agencies and self-regulation, helps ensure stable markets, sound brokerage firms, and the absence of stock manipulation.

securitization The process whereby financial instruments that were previously thinly traded are converted to a form that creates greater liquidity. Securitization also applies to the situation where specific assets are pledged as collateral for securities, and hence asset-backed securities are created. One example of the former is junk bonds; an example of the latter is mortgage-backed securities.

Security Market Line (SML) Represents, in a graphical form, the relationship between the risk of an asset as measured by its beta and the required rates of return for individual securities. The SML equation is essentially the Capital Asset Pricing model, $r_i = r_{RF} + b_i(r_M - r_{RF})$.

semistrong form of market efficiency States that current market prices reflect all publicly available information. Therefore, the only way to gain abnormal returns on a stock is to possess inside information about the company's stock.

sensitivity analysis Indicates exactly how much net present value will change in response to a given change in an input variable, other things held constant. Sensitivity analysis is sometimes called "what if" analysis because it answers this type of question.

shelf registration Frequently, companies will file a master registration statement and then update it with a short-form statement just before an offering. This procedure is termed shelf registration because companies put new securities "on the shelf" and then later sell them when the market is right.

short hedges Occur when futures contracts are sold to guard against price declines.

sinking fund Facilitates the orderly retirement of a bond issue. This can be achieved in one of two ways: (1) the company can call in for redemption (at par value) a certain percentage of bonds each year or (2) the company may buy the required amount of bonds on the open market.

sole proprietorship A business owned by one individual.

spin-off Occurs when a holding company distributes the stock of one of the operating companies to its shareholders, thus, passing control from the holding company to the shareholders directly.

spontaneously generated funds Funds generated if a liability account increases spontaneously (automatically) as sales increase. An increase in a liability account is a source of funds, thus funds have been generated. Two examples of spontaneous liability accounts are accounts payable and accrued wages. Note that notes payable, although a current liability account, is not a spontaneous source of funds since an increase in notes payable requires a specific action between the firm and a creditor.

spot rate The exchange rate which applies to "on the spot" trades, or, more precisely, exchanges that occur two days following the day of trade (in other words, current exchanges).

spread The difference between the price at which an underwriter sells the stock in an initial public offering and the proceeds that the underwriter passes on to the issuing firm; the fee collected by the underwriter. It is often about 7% of the offering price.

stand-alone risk The risk an investor takes by holding only one asset.

standard deviation, σ A statistical measure of the variability of a set of observations. It is the square root of the variance.

statement of cash flows Reports the impact of a firm's operating, investing, and financing activities on cash flows over an accounting period.

statement of retained earnings Shows how much of the firm's earnings were retained in the business rather than paid out in dividends. Note that retained earnings represents a claim against assets, not assets per se. Firms retain earnings primarily to expand the business, not to accumulate cash in a bank account.

stepped-up exercise price A provision in a warrant that increases the strike price over time. This provision is included to prod owners into exercising their warrants.

stock dividend Increases the number of shares outstanding, but at a slower rate than splits. Current shareholders receive additional shares on some proportional basis. Thus, a holder of 100 shares would receive 5 additional shares at no cost if a 5% stock dividend were declared.

stock option Allows its owner to purchase a share of stock at a fixed price, called the exercise price, no matter what the actual price of the stock is. Stock options always have an expiration date, after which they cannot be exercised.

stock repurchase Occurs when a firm repurchases its own stock. These shares of stock are then referred to as treasury stock.

stock split Current shareholders are given some number (or fraction) of shares for each stock share owned. Thus, in a three-for-one split, each shareholder would receive three new shares in exchange for each old share, thereby tripling the number of shares outstanding. Stock splits usually occur when the stock price is outside of the optimal trading range.

strategic options Options that often deal with strategic issues. Also called real options, managerial options, or embedded options.

stretching accounts payable The practice of deliberately paying accounts late.

strike price The price stated in the option contract at which the security can be bought (or sold). For example, if the underlying stock sells for $50 and the strike price is $20, the exercise value of the option would be $30. Also called the exercise price.

strong form of market efficiency Assumes that all information pertaining to a stock, whether public or inside information, is reflected in current market prices. Thus, no investors would be able to earn abnormal returns in the stock market.

structured note A debt obligation derived from another debt obligation. Permits a partitioning of risks to give investors what they want.

subordinated debenture Debentures that have claims on assets, in the event of bankruptcy, only after senior debt as named in the subordinated debt's indenture has been paid off. Subordinated debentures may be subordinated to designated notes payable or to all other debt.

sunk cost A cost that has already occurred and is not affected by the capital project decision. Sunk costs are not relevant to capital budgeting decisions.

swap An exchange of cash payment obligations. Usually occurs because the parties involved prefer someone else's payment pattern or type.

sweetener A feature that makes a security more attractive to some investors, thereby inducing them to accept a lower current yield. Convertible features and warrants are examples of sweeteners.

synergy Occurs when the whole is greater than the sum of its parts. When applied to mergers, a synergistic merger occurs when the postmerger earnings exceed the sum of the separate companies' premerger earnings.

takeover An action whereby a person or group succeeds in ousting a firm's management and taking control of the company.

target capital structure The relative amount of debt, preferred stock, and common equity that the firm desires. The weighted average cost of capital should be based on these target weights.

target cash balance The desired cash balance that a firm plans to maintain in order to conduct business.

target company A firm that another company seeks to acquire.

tax loss carryback and carryforward Ordinary corporate operating losses can be carried backward for 2 years or forward for 20 years to offset taxable income in a given year.

tax preference theory Proposes that investors prefer capital gains over dividends, because capital gains taxes can be deferred into the future but taxes on dividends must be paid as the dividends are received.

taxable income Gross income less a set of exemptions and deductions that are spelled out in the instructions to the tax forms individuals must file.

temporary net operating working capital The NOWC required above the permanent level when the economy is strong and/or seasonal sales are high.

tender offer The offer of one firm to buy the stock of another by going directly to the stockholders, frequently over the opposition of the target company's management.

term structure of interest rates The relationship between yield to maturity and term to maturity for bonds of a single risk class.

time line A graphical representation used to show the timing of cash flows.

times-interest-earned (TIE) ratio Determined by dividing earnings before interest and taxes by the interest charges. This ratio measures the extent to which operating income can decline before the firm is unable to meet its annual interest costs.

total assets turnover ratio Measures the turnover of all the firm's assets; it is calculated by dividing sales by total assets.

trade credit Debt arising from credit sales and recorded as an account receivable by the seller and as an account payable by the buyer.

trade deficit Occurs when a country imports more goods from abroad than it exports.

trade discounts Price reductions that suppliers offer customers for early payment of bills.

transactions balance The cash balance associated with payments and collections; the balance necessary for day-to-day operations.

Treasury bond Bonds issued by the Federal government that are not exposed to default risk. Sometimes referred to as government bonds.

trend analysis An analysis of a firm's financial ratios over time. It is used to estimate the likelihood of improvement or deterioration in its financial situation.

underwritten arrangement A type of contract with an investment banker when issuing stock. An investment banker agrees to buy the entire issue at a set price and then resells the stock at the offering price. Thus, the risk of selling the issue rests with the investment banker.

value drivers The four value drivers are the growth rate in sales (g), operating profitability (OP = NOPAT/Sales), capital requirements (CR = Capital/Sales), and the weighted average cost of capital (WACC).

value-based management Managing a firm with shareholder value in mind. It typically involves use of a model of shareholder value, like the corporate value model.

value of operations The present value of all the future free cash flows that are expected from current assets-in-place and the expected growth of assets-in-place when discounted at the weighted average cost of capital.

variance, σ^2 A measure of the distribution's variability. It is the sum of the squared deviations about the expected value.

venture capitalist The manager of a venture capital fund. The fund raises most of its capital from institutional investors and invests in start-up companies in exchange for equity.

vertical merger Occurs when a company acquires another firm that is "upstream" or "downstream"; for example, an automobile manufacturer acquires a steel producer.

warrant A call option issued by a company allowing the holder to buy a stated number of shares of stock from a company at a specified price. Warrants are generally distributed with debt, or preferred stock, to induce investors to buy those securities at lower cost.

weak form of market efficiency Assumes that all information contained in past price movements is fully reflected in current market prices. Thus, information about recent trends in a stock's price is of no use in selecting a stock.

weighted average cost of capital (WACC) The weighted average of the after-tax component costs of capital—debt, preferred stock, and common equity. Each weighting factor is the proportion of that type of capital in the optimal, or target, capital structure.

white knight A friendly competing bidder which a target management likes better than the company making a hostile offer; the target solicits a merger with the white knight as a preferable alternative.

window dressing A technique employed by firms to make their financial statements look better than they really are.

working capital A firm's investment in short-term assets—cash, marketable securities, inventory, and accounts receivable.

workout Voluntary reorganization plans arranged between creditors and generally sound companies experiencing temporary financial difficulties. Workouts typically require some restructuring of the firm's debt.

yield curve The curve that results when yield to maturity is plotted on the Y axis with term to maturity on the X axis.

yield to call (YTC) The rate of interest earned on a bond if it is called. If current interest rates are well below an outstanding callable bond's coupon rate, the YTC may be a more relevant estimate of expected return than the YTM, since the bond is likely to be called.

yield to maturity (YTM) The rate of interest earned on a bond if it is held to maturity.

zero coupon bond Pays no coupons at all, but is offered at a substantial discount below its par value and hence provides capital appreciation rather than interest income.

name index

subject index